The
Illustrated Biographical
Encyclopedia of Artists
of the American West

The Illustrated Biographical Encyclopedia of Artists of the American West

Peggy and Harold Samuels

DOUBLEDAY & COMPANY, INC.
GARDEN CITY, NEW YORK
1976

Library of Congress Cataloging in Publication Data

Samuels, Peggy.

The illustrated biographical encyclopedia of artists of the American West.

1. The West in art. 2. Indians of North America—Pictorial works. 3. Artists—Biography. 4. Artists—United States—Biography. I. Samuels, Harold, joint author. II. Title.

N8214.5.U6S25   709'.2'2 [B]

ISBN 0-385-01730-8

Library of Congress Catalog Card Number 76-2816

ACKNOWLEDGMENTS

Nicki Thiras, Registrar, Addison Gallery of American Art; Norman S Rice, Director, Albany Institute of History and Art; Priscilla Ward, Scientific Assistant, The American Museum of Natural History; Douglas A Bakken, Archivist, Anheuser-Busch, Inc; Mrs J Hammond, Archives of American Art; Marge Patterson, Secretary, *Arizona Highways;* Ken Smith-Brunet, Acting Director, University Art Collections, Arizona State University; Steven Smith and Kitty Dixon, The Art Institute of Chicago; Joe W Back; Suzanne H Gallup, Reference Librarian, The Bancroft Library; Joe Beeler; Noah Berry, Jr; Bill Bender; David Boles; Nancy H Carter, Secretary-Registrar, Brandywine River Museum; Mrs Ann Datta, The Library, Zoological Dept, British Museum (Natural History); Steven Wunderlich, Iconography Dept, Buffalo and Erie County Historical Society; Ruth Willet, History Dept, Buffalo and Erie County Public Library; Catherine Hoover, Assistant Curator, California Historical Society; Fenton Kastner, Achenbach Foundation for Graphic Arts, California Palace of the Legion of Honor; Muriel Cassese; Floyd C Chandler; Ethel Taggart Christensen; Earl E Olson, Church Archivist, The Church of Jesus Christ of Latter-Day Saints; José Cisneros; Joyce Dayton, Librarian, Cokeville Branch, Lincoln County Library; Milo M Naeve, Director, Colorado Springs Fine Arts Center; William J Mahoney, Chairman of Department of Art and Education, Teachers College; members of Cowboy Artists of America; Barney Delabano, Associate Curator, Dallas Museum of Fine Arts; Carol Rawlings, Assistant, Publications Department, The Denver Art Museum; Eleanor M Gehres, Head, and Mrs Opal Harber, Acting Head, and Sandra Turner, Research, Western History Department, Denver Public Library; Larry Curry, Curator of American Art, The Detroit Institute of Arts; Lester Dworetsky; Jeff Dykes; Martin E Petersen, Curator of Painting, Fine Arts Gallery of San Diego; Nicholas S Firfires; Bert Freed; Joyce Zogott, Free Library of Philadelphia; Carolyn Tannehill, Curator of Art, and Mrs Jeanne O Snodgrass, Registrar, Thomas Gilcrease Institute of American History & Art; Dennis Flynn; W D Harmsen, Harmsen's Western Americana; Elsie S Heaton; Ionne Ladd, Historical Museum of Arizona; Paul Hogarth; Mrs Valerie Franco, Assistant Curator, Huntington Library; Mark Isaacson; Anne Rhodes, Editor, Art Directories, The Jaques Cattell Press; Roy Kerswill; Phyllis Kihn; John H Kittelson; Mrs Dana Young, Koehler Cultural Centre; Ruth Koerner Oliver; Tom K Enman, Director, Laguna Beach Museum of Art; Stuart Leech; Renata V Shaw, Bibliographic Specialist, and Ronald S Wilkinson, Specialist American Cultural History, The Library of Congress; Locust Valley Library; Samuel L Lowe, Jr; Eugenia Calvert Holland, Assistant Curator, Maryland Historical Society; Barbara and David McCoy; Donna Christian, and Margaret Lawson, Departmental Secretary, and Marcy Philips, Assistant, The Metropolitan Museum of Art; Ms Terry Pink Alexander, Assistant Director, Mills College Art Gallery; Gail R Guidry, Curator, Pictorial, Missouri Historical Society; Sam Gilluly, Director, and Mrs Harriett C

Meloy, Librarian, Montana Historical Society; Frederick J Dockstader, Director, and Mary Williams, Museum of the American Indian; Mrs Edna C Robertson, Curator, Fine Arts Collections, Museum of New Mexico; Barton A Wright, Museum Curator, Museum of Northern Arizona; Alice Armstrong, Chief, Reproductions and Rights, and Helen Clark, Head, Photograph Sales, The National Gallery of Canada; Chang-su Houchins, Museum Specialist, National Anthropological Archives, National Museum of Natural History; Mrs Fearn C Thurlow, Curator of Painting & Sculpture, The Newark Museum; T E Waterbury, Executive Director, Newport Historical Society; Roberta W Wong, Prints Division, New York Public Library; Sina Fosdick, Nicholas Roerich Museum; Anne Nostrand; Mrs Marjorie Arkelian, Art Department Historian, The Oakland Museum; Mrs Grace Winder, Oakland Public Library; Roger Ohler, Bernie Rosenberg, Olana Gallery; James K Reeve, Curator, Philbrook Art Center; Raymond W Hillman, Curator of History, Pioneer Museum & Haggin Galleries; Liam Purdon; Mrs D Ferris, Secretary, Office of Postmaster, Phoenix; Ed Pollock; Walt Reed; W Tjark Reiss; Fred and Ginger Renner; Constance-Anne Parker, Assistant Librarian, The Royal Academy of Arts, Piccadilly; Ms Janet Holmes, Research Assistant, Royal Ontario Museum; Bob Ruben; Ann B Abid, Librarian, The St Louis Art Museum; Roger Bailey, Director, Salt Lake Art Center; Dorothy Buckley Casey, Executive Secretary, San Antonio Art League; Jack R McGregor, Director, San Antonio Museum Association; Miss Mary Ashe, Art and Music Department, San Francisco Public Library; Carol Jensen, registrar assistant, Santa Barbara Museum of Art; Anne S Hobler, Assistant to the President, Sarah Lawrence College; Stan Schirmacher; Jessie Scott; Mrs Elizabeth de Fato, Librarian, Seattle Art Museum; Virginia Reich, Head, Art Department, Seattle Public Library; Doris Serroen; Peggy Parris, Director, Sioux City Art Center; Irene Lichens, Librarian, The Society of California Pioneers; Bob and Tino Stango; Alice L Sharp, Reference Librarian, The State Historical Society of Colorado; Guy St Clair, Librarian and Curator, The Union League Club; J C Kenefick, President, Union Pacific Railroad Company; Cleta H Downey, Curator, University Art Museum, The University of New Mexico; Elizabeth Roberts, Research Associate, University Art Museum, The University of Texas at Austin; Wilburn C West, Director, Utah State Institute of Fine Arts; A P Burton, Assistant Keeper of the Library, Victoria and Albert Museum; Mrs Gwen Lerner, Registrar, Walker Art Center; Bonnie L Ross, Reference Librarian, The Roswell P Flower Memorial Library, Watertown; Edward Morris, Keeper of Foreign Art, Walker Art Gallery, Liverpool; Larry Weitz; Mrs Susanna S Hennum, Registrar, The Wichita Art Museum; Timothy A Riggs, Assistant Curator, Worcester Art Museum; Beth Urdang, Zabriskie Gallery.

INTRODUCTION

An introduction to a reference book is never read. Yet, it must be written. Explanations are called for and appreciations are due.

This book began as an accumulation of data for our own use. Like life, it is a work in progress. It is finished for publication because it contributes as it is. It is as complete as we can make it now.

The primary intent is toward practicality. When and where did the artist live? What was his specialty? What were his honors and memberships? What collections contain his work? What references are there to him in the general biographical dictionaries we find most valuable? Which Western source books we use provide evaluations? What is the most his paintings have sold for at a recent public auction? What did his signature look like? What was his art schooling and body of work? What was his Western experience?

An additional aim is to provide the feel of the artist as a person, generally from sparse and second-hand data, and to gauge his importance. As an economic indicator, actual auction prices are given for specific works, where available from our own records or from published sources, primarily Sotheby Parke Bernet. When the auction price given is for a non-Western painting, and the artist is primarily a Western artist, the values tend to be less than they would be for a Western painting. Where no actual auction price was available, we used the auction house estimate for a specific work. Failing these, we at times offered our own estimate of a fictitious painting of a Western subject at the height of the art-

ist's powers. Obviously, any estimate is a weaker guide than fact.

Note that we provide auction prices, not retail prices. Auction prices are relatively factual and they are published. Generally speaking, auction prices represent sales to dealers and are in effect the dealer's cost on which his retail prices are based. A retail price is in practice a multiple of the auction price.

Another basis for weighing the artist's importance is the number and quality of references and sources. "The Dictionary of American Biography" is a major reference for the timely dead. A string of sources is an indication. It is wrong, though, to equate listings with price. A painting is not necessarily worth more because the artist is listed in Fielding's "Dictionary of American Painters."

Comparing the references and sources frequently produced conflicts concerning dates and facts. The discrepancies were resolved by selecting the data that is more likely to have come from the artist, or, often both facts are given.

The abbreviations used are standard, as can be noted in the table of abbreviations. The three-letter symbols for the references and sources are intended to suggest the full name, eg, BEN for "Benezit" and DAB for "Dictionary of American Biography," ALA for "Art and Life in America" and ANT for *Antiques*. There are only a few symbols that appear often, and these are the simplest, eg, FIE for "Fielding" and MAL for "Mallett." For convenience, we have continued the reference "American Art Annual" beyond A33 to A34 etc for "Who's Who in American Art." It is the same series and avoids confusion with "Who's Who in America."

There is no reference book that is without fault. The books that are most critical of other books have equal errors, some data springing from the same cockeyed fount. There is just so much that has to be accepted on faith in a reference book of any size that errors are built in. Here, the sources and references are listed, out in the open. If a fact is critical to an evaluation, check the original materials.

Fortunately, the staffs of hundreds of museums, societies, libraries, associations, railroads, companies, publishers, etc all over the world and many artists and the families of artists have been amazingly forthcoming with time, advice, and photostats, as you will note from the credits.

When we began, an early question was style. What should be in a Western biography? E Welker Marchand who has over 5,000,000 published words to his credit led us to the informal track we followed. A New York based writer born in Florida in 1932, he rewrote our first sample biography and created a style manual.

In September 1973 we were into the B's when we met Mrs Nancy G Wynne, the Librarian of the Amon Carter Museum of Western Art in Fort Worth since 1967. A native of Fort Worth, married, with a degree in history from the University of Texas and a master's degree from Texas Woman's University, she describes herself as a happy museum librarian who loves her work. To us, she remained a constant encouragement and she reviewed the original manuscript.

At just about the same time Mrs Laura M Hayes, the Curator of the Wyoming State Art Gallery in Cheyenne, also involved herself in the project. A native of Alabama married to a retired US Air Force officer, she is trained in art, conservation, museology, and is a professional photographer. Her job is to work with Wyoming artists, and she says, "I need not tell you that I love it." Mrs Hayes reviewed the original manuscript and undertook to ascertain data more current than has been published.

By December 1973 it became apparent to us that the Cowboy Artists of America were key Western artists. E D McGwire of Albuquerque who was then Business Manager of the CAA read the manuscript and secured photographs for illustrations. A native of New Jersey, Mac was an executive of New York Life Insurance until he retired in 1970 to write, lecture, and manage. His comments on living artists gave biographies a personalized view.

Similarly, advice on the illustrators proved essential. Except for landmark research by Robert Taft for the years 1850–1900 and by Walt Reed for 1900–1960, no published information is available for the hundreds of painters who produced the artwork for Western books and magazines. These are highly desirable storytelling drawings and paintings, signed with names and pseudonyms not always listed in art reference books. Carl J Pugliese, a native New York City expert on US military history and on American illustrators, suggested specific painters and examples of their work in addition to reading the original manuscript.

Our historian was George Schriever, Curator of The Anschutz Collection with about 20 years' experience in Western art, mostly with Kennedy Galleries in NYC. George is certainly a most knowledgeable man on major Western paintings that have come on the market since 1950 and on sources of information for any Western painter back to Weiditz in the 16th century. George, too, read the manuscript, providing the fifth in what was surely a most august and learned group of readers.

The approach in selecting the artists for the book was to be generous. The guide was to include an artist if he could have been working by 1950 and if one might find a professional work on the

American West with his name on it. Many painters are listed who do not appear in any general reference. They belong here, names taken from Western paintings of quality or culled from regional collections like pioneer Utah or Texas artists. This list is intended only as an aid in determining the collectibility of a work of art. Copyists and primitive artists are generally excluded, even when shown in dealers' trade catalogs.

In defining West, the limit became a state of mind: the frontier as it moved from the early Eastern seaboard to the Pacific shores, an Indian any place, California at one time, a landscape that could have been the backdrop for an Indian or cowboy. The test was the subject matter, not the geographical location of the artist. We compiled a master list of more than 3,000 artists, then cut back to about 1,700 we could authenticate as Western. Eastern artists who retired to California were not automatically included, nor were other artists living in the West who could not be shown to have developed Western subjects.

In defining American, artists from Canada and the United States were considered one group. We also recognized that the West "has got a-holt of" so many of us that it did so even oceans away. Listed are foreign artists who painted Western scenes. An example would be Rosa Bonheur who painted Buffalo Bill's portrait in France.

The illustrations in the book are for a range of artists, the most familiar and the less. Similarly, the works shown are the famous examples alongside others not previously published. The intent was to use not only works in museum collections but also work that could be in private hands—a Fraser medal rather than a monument, a drawing rather than a mural.

A look at the artists allows division into simplistic categories:

First, the explorer artists, the Seymour who came to the headwaters of the Platte in 1820. Catlin entering the trans-Mississippi wilderness in the 1830s. Bodmer and Miller. Paul Kane. The Indian portraits and dignified genre scenes.

Second, the railway survey artists in the 1850s. Stanley and Sohon. Straightforward reportage, topography and people.

Third, the correspondents on horseback after the Civil War. The lithographic artist Mathews. A R Waud sent to make sketches. Western people doing things. "Bohemian" Tavernier and chic Frenzeny.

Fourth, the onslaught of the panoramic landscapists. The Rocky Mountain School. Bierstadt's 1859 tour in the Rockies. Thomas Hill in 1861. Samuel Colman in 1870. Thomas Moran in 1871. Some painters unwilling to paint the West as it really was because no one back East would believe.

Fifth, the pioneer artists. Ottinger in Utah in the 1860s, painting 223 pictures that sold for an average of $15 each. Gentilz in Texas.

Sixth, the myth makers. The magazine illustrators. Remington and Russell in the 1880s. Farny.

Seventh, the Taos sophisticates. Sharp in Paris in 1897 selling the Southwest to Blumenschein and Phillips. Rolshoven and art deco Indians.

Eighth, the cowboy artists. Nostalgia painters. Olaf Wieghorst, Burt Procter. The CAA.

Ninth, the modernists moving in. Tom Thomson in northern Ontario. Robert Henri to Santa Fe in 1916. John Sloan in 1920. The Group of Seven. Edward Hopper in 1925. John Marin in 1929. Georgia O'Keeffe buys an adobe house near the village of Abiquiu NM in 1940.

Goodbye, Old Paint.

The West that was Wild is gone, except for the nostalgia painters. It certainly was wild, once, in the sense of primitive and far from civilization. Wild in terms of dangerous it was, too, particularly because of weather and terrain. The vision of the murderous Indian, though, is questionable for the artists.

The number of painters who wandered through the early West on foot and on their own seems incredible when contrasted with the image of the wild Indian. Yet, we have only two artists killed by Indians. These are the Kern brothers, both of whom were serving in the employ of the uniformed military. Benjamin Kern was killed by Utes who had been mangled by US troops a few days earlier.

Richard Kern was ambushed by Paiutes while with Capt Gunnison and a military escort. As a comparison, more Western artists died from paint fumes in their studios than from Indians.

So, we offer you what is known of these artists of the American West. Be careful. They may get a-holt of you, just like they did us. That is why, to answer a usual question, we wrote this book.

ABBREVIATIONS

AA—Art Association

AAAL—American Academy of Arts and Letters

AAU—American Art-Union

AC—Art Center

Acad—Academy

ACM—Amon Carter Museum of Western Art

AFA—American Federation of Arts

AG—Art Gallery

AI—Art Institute

AIC—Art Institute of Chicago

Ala—Alabama

Alta—Alberta (Canada)

AM—Art Museum

Am—America(n)

Amer—America(n)

Amer AA—American Art Academy

Amer Philos Soc—American Philosophical Society in Philadelphia

Am Inst FA—American Institute of Fine Arts

AMNH—American Museum of Natural History, New York City

ANA—Associate of the National Academy (of Design), New York

ARA—Associate of the Royal Academy (England)

ARCA—Associate of the Royal Canadian Academy of Arts

Arch—Architecture

Ariz—Arizona

Ariz St Fed—Arizona State Federation

Ark—Arkansas

AS—Art School

ASL—Art Students League (New York)

ASPCA—American Society for the Prevention of Cruelty to Animals

Assn—Association

Assoc—Associate

AWCS—American Watercolor Society

BC—British Columbia

Bibliot Nat—Bibliothèque Nationale (Paris)

Bklyn—Brooklyn

Bklyn Mus Mem Colln—Brooklyn Museum Memorial Collection

Bklyn Poly Inst—Brooklyn Polytechnical Institute

Bldg(s)—Building(s)

BM—Brooklyn Museum

BMFA—Boston Museum of Fine Arts

Brit Mus—British Museum

Buffalo FAA—Buffalo Fine Arts Association

Bur Ind—Bureau of Indian Affairs

BYU—Brigham Young University

CAA—Cowboy Artists of America

Cal—California

Cal IFA—California Institute of Fine Arts

Cal SFA—California Society of Fine Arts

Can—Canada

Canadian Natl Exh—Canadian National Exhibition

Can Pac Ry—Canadian Pacific Railway

Cap—Capitol

CD—City Directory

CGP—The Canadian Group of Painters

Chicago AFA—Chicago Academy of Fine Arts

Cin—Cincinnati

Cnty—County

Col—College

Col City of NY—College of the City of New York

Colln—Collection

Colo—Colorado

Colo Spr—Colorado Springs

Columb Expos—World's Columbian Exposition

Comn—Commission

Conn—Connecticut

COR—Corcoran Gallery
CR—Center right
CSFAC—Colorado Springs Fine Arts Center
Ct—Court
Cthse—Courthouse
DAM—Denver Art Museum
Del—Delaware
Des—Design
DIA—Detroit Institute of Arts
DPL—Denver Public Library
Educ—Educational
Eng—England
Expos—Exposition
FA—Fine Arts
FAA—Fine Arts Association
FAC—Fine Arts Center
FAG—Fine Arts Gallery
Fed—Federation
Fndn—Foundation
FWA—Federal Works Administration
Ga—Georgia
Gall—Gallery
Gen—General
Gen Fed Women's Club—General Federation of Women's Clubs
Govt—Government
Hist—Historical
IA—Institute of Art
IFA—Institute of Fine Arts
Ill—Illinois
ILN—Illustrated London News
Ind—Indiana
Indep SA—Independent Society of Artists
Ins Co of N Am—Insurance Company of North America
Inst—Institute, Institution
Int—International
Ire—Ireland
Journ—Journal
Kan—Kansas
Ky—Kentucky
LA—Los Angeles
LAAA—Los Angeles Art Association
LACMA—Los Angeles County Museum of Art
LA Cnty MNH—Los Angeles County Museum of Natural History
LA Comcl Club—Los Angeles Commercial Club

LA County AI—Los Angeles County Art Institute
LA County AM—Los Angeles County Art Museum
LA County MS—Los Angeles County Museum of Science
LAMA—Los Angeles County Museum of Art
LASA—Los Angeles School of Art
LC—Lower center
LDS—Latter-Day Saints
LI—Long Island
Lib—Library
Lib Cong—Library of Congress
LL—Lower left
LR—Lower right
MA—Museum of Art
MAI—Museum of the American Indian
Mass—Massachusetts
MCA—Mills College Art Gallery
Md—Maryland
Mem—Memorial
MFA—Museum of Fine Arts
Mich—Michigan
MIL—National Gallery, Milburn
Minn—Minnesota
MIT—Massachusetts Institute of Technology
MMA—Metropolitan Museum of Art
MNH—Museum of Natural History
MNM—Museum of New Mexico
Mo—Missouri
MOMA—Museum of Modern Art
Mont—Montana
Mo Pac RR—Missouri Pacific Railroad
Mtn(s)—Mountain(s)
Munic AG—Municipal Art Gallery
Mus—Museum
Mus No Amer Ind—Museum of the North American Indian
NA—National Academy
NAD—National Academy of Design
Nat—National
Nat Geog Mag—National Geographic Magazine
Nat Port Gall—National Portrait Gallery
NA Women PS—National Association of Women Painters and Sculptors
NB—New Brunswick
NC—North Carolina
ND—North Dakota

Neb—Nebraska
N Eng—New England
Nev—Nevada
NGA—National Gallery of Art
NGC—National Gallery of Canada
NH—New Hampshire
NIAL—National Institute of Arts and Letters
NJ—New Jersey
NM—New Mexico
Nn Pac RR—Northern Pacific Railroad
No—North
NSS—National Sculpture Society
N Tex Agri Col—North Texas Agricultural College
NW—Northwestern
NY(C)—New York (City)
NYHS—New York Historical Society
NYPL—New York Public Library
NZ—New Zealand
Okla—Oklahoma
Ont—Ontario
Ore—Oregon
Pa—Pennsylvania
Pac—Pacific
PAFA—Pennsylvania Academy of Fine Arts
Pan-Amer Expos—Pan-American Exposition
Pan-Pac Int Expos—Panama-Pacific International Exposition
PB—Parke Bernet
Penn—Pennsylvania
Phila—Philadelphia
Phila Art All—Philadelphia Art Alliance
pl—plate
PL—Public Library
PO—Post Office
PQ—Province of Quebec
Pres—President
Ptrs—Painters
Pub—Public
Pub Archives—Public Archives (Ottawa)
Pub Lib—Public Library
PWA—Public Works of Art Project
QMC—Quartermasters Corps
RA—Royal Academy
RAFA—Royal Academy of Fine Arts
RCA—Royal Canadian Academy of Arts

RI—Rhode Island
RI Sch of Des—Rhode Island School of Design
ROM—The Royal Ontario Museum, Toronto
Roy Soc Brit Artists—Royal Society of British Artists
RR—Railroad
RSA—Royal Society of Artists
Ry—Railway
SA—Society of Artists
SAA—Society of American Artists
SAE—Society of American Etchers
SAGA—Society of American Graphic Artists
SAM—Seattle Art Museum
San Fran—San Francisco
Sat Eve Post—The Saturday Evening Post
SC—South Carolina
Sch—School
Sch Indl Art—School of Industrial Arts
Sci—Science
SD—South Dakota
SE—Southeast
SE Mus No Am Indians—Southeast Museum of North American Indians
SFA—Society of Fine Arts
SF Maritime Mus—San Francisco Maritime Museum
S Fr CD—San Francisco City Directory
SI—Society of Illustrators
SIA—Society of Independent Artists
Soc—Society
So Dak St Col—South Dakota State College
SPB—Sotheby Parke Bernet
St—State
St Cap—State Capitol
St Col—State College
SW—Southwest
Tenn—Tennessee
Tex—Texas
Tol Mus—Toledo Museum (Ohio)
Tucson Fed S & L Assn—Tucson Federal Savings and Loan Association
U—University
UBC—University of British Columbia
UCLA—University of California in Los Angeles
UR—Upper right

US—United States
USAF—United States Air Force
USIA—United States Information Agency
USN Acad—United States Naval Academy
Va—Virginia
Va Mil Inst—Virginia Military Institute
Vict and Albert Mus—Victoria and Albert Museum
VMI—Virginia Military Institute
Vt—Vermont
Wash—Washington
Wash Terr—Washington Territory
Wis—Wisconsin
WMAA—Whitney Museum of American Art

Wm Penn Mem Mus—William Penn Memorial Museum
Wn—Western
Wn Reserve Hist Soc—Western Reserve Historical Society
Wom—Women
WPA—Works Progress Administration, Art Program
WWI—World War I
WWII—World War II
Wyom—Wyoming
Yale U AG—Yale University Art Gallery
Yuk—Yukon

SOURCES AND
SOURCE ABBREVIATIONS

AAC   Anonymous. "Advertising Arts & Crafts. Eastern Edition." NY: Lee & Kirby Inc, Jan 1924.

AAR   *American Art Review*. LA: Kellaway Publishing Company, beginning 1974.

AAT   Anonymous. "American Art Today." NY: National Art Society, 1939.

AAW   Anonymous. "Advertising Arts & Crafts. Western Edition." Chicago: Lee & Kirby Inc, 1924.

ABA   Mugridge, Donald H. "An Album of American Battle Art 1755–1918." Washington: Government Printing Office, 1947.

ABC   *American Book Collector*. Chicago: W B Thorsen.

ABE   Abert, Lt James W. "Through the Country of the Comanche Indians in the Fall of the Year 1845." San Francisco: John Howell, 1970.

ABF   Harris, Joel Chandler. "A Book of Drawings by A B Frost." NY: P F Collier & Son, 1904.

ACM   Anonymous. "Catalogue of the Collection 1972." Fort Worth: Amon Carter Museum of Western Art, 1972.

ACO   Anonymous. "Western Art in Arizona Collections." Tucson: Tucson Art Center, 1973.

ADD   Anonymous. "Addison Gallery of American Art Handbook." Andover: Phillips Academy, 1939.

ADM   Dick, Ruth W. "Kenneth M Adams, NA." Santa Fe: University of New Mexico Art Museum, 1972.

AHI   *Arizona Highways*. Phoenix: Arizona Department of Transportation.

AIA   *Art in America*. NY: Art in America Company, Inc.

AIC   Rich, Daniel Catton. "A Century of Progress Exhibition of Paintings and Sculpture." Chicago: The Art Institute, 1933.

AIM   Rummell, John. "Aims and Ideals of Representative American Painters." Buffalo: E M Berlin, 1901.

AIP   Snodgrass, Jeanne O. "American Indian Painters." NY: Museum of the American Indian, Heye Foundation, 1968.

AIW   Taft, Robert. "Artists and Illustrators of the Old West 1850–1900." NY: Charles Scribner's Sons, 1953.

ALA   Larkin, Oliver W. "Art and Life in America." NY: Rinehart & Company, Inc, 1949.

AMA   Jackman, Rilla Evelyn. "American Arts." NY: Rand McNally & Company, 1928.

AMP   King, Pauline. "American Mural Painting." Boston: Noyes, Platt & Company, 1901.

AMR	Anonymous. "American Artists and Their Works." Boston: Estes & Lauriat, 1889.
ANA	*American Artist*. NY: Billboard Publications, Inc.
ANS	Schriever, George. "American Masters in the West." Denver: The Anschutz Collection, 1974.
ANT	*ANTIQUES, The Magazine*. NY: Straight Enterprises, Inc.
AOA	Kouwenhoven, John A. "Adventures of America 1857–1900." NY: Harper & Brothers, 1938.
AOH	Hogarth, Paul "Artists on Horseback." NY: Watson-Guptill Publications, 1972.
AOS	Peters, Harry T. "America on Stone." Garden City: Doubleday, Doran & Co, Inc, 1931.
AOW	Ewers, John C. "Artists of the Old West." Garden City: Doubleday & Company, Inc, 1965.
APT	Pousette-Dart, Nathaniel. "American Painting Today." NY: Hastings House, 1956.
ARC	Shepard, Lewis A. "American Painters of the Arctic." Amherst: Mead Art Gallery, 1975.
ARI	Kloster, Paula R. "The Arizona State College Collection of American Art." Tempe: Arizona State College, 1954.
ARM	Anonymous. "1913 Armory Show 50th Anniversary Exhibition 1963." NY: Henry Street Settlement, 1963.
ARS	Arthurs, Stanley. "The American Historical Scene." NY: Carlton House, 1936.
ART	*Art News*. NY: Newsweek, Inc.
ASD	Petersen, Martin E. "Contemporary Artists of San Diego." *The Journal of San Diego History,* Fall 1970.
ASF	Thiel, Yvonne Greer. "Artists and People" (of San Francisco). NY: Philosophical Library Inc, 1959.
ATH	Swan, Mabel Munson. "The Athenaeum Gallery." Boston: The Boston Athenaeum, 1940.
AUD	Rourke, Constance. "Audubon." NY: Harcourt, Brace and Company, 1936.
AWM	DeVoto, Bernard. "Across the Wide Missouri." NY: Houghton Mifflin Company, 1957.
BAL	Ewing, Robert A. "Henry C Balink." Santa Fe: Museum of New Mexico, 1966.
BAR	Barker, Virgil. "American Painting." NY: The Macmillan Company, 1950
BAW	Monaghan, Jay. "The Book of the American West." NY: Bonanza Books, 1963.
BDW	Dawdy, Doris Ostrander. "Artists of the American West." Chicago: The Swallow Press Incorporated, 1974.
BEN	Benton, Thomas Hart. "An Artist in America." NY: Robert M McBride & Company, 1937.
BER	Berea, T B. "Handbook of 17th, 18th and 19th Century American Painters." Chattanooga: Dalewood Enterprises, 1971.
BEY	Richardson, Albert D. "Beyond the Mississippi." NY: Bliss & Company, 1867.
BIE/ACM	Hendricks, Gordon. "A Bierstadt." Fort Worth: Amon Carter Museum, 1972.

BIE/KNO	Hendricks, Gordon. "Albert Bierstadt." NY: M Knoedler & Co, Inc, 1972.
BOA	Tuckerman, Henry T. "Book of the Artists." NY: James F Carr, 1967.
BOL	Bolton, Theodore. "Early American Portrait Draughtsmen in Crayons." Charleston: Garnier & Company, 1969.
BOR	Davidson, Harold G. "Edward Borein Cowboy Artist." Garden City: Doubleday & Company, Inc, 1974.
BRO	Broder, Patricia Janis. "Bronzes of the American West." NY: Harry N Abrams, Inc, 1975.
BRY	Williamson, George C. "Bryan's Dictionary of Painters and Engravers." NY: The Macmillan Company, 1903.
BUC	Ludeke, H. "Frank Buchsers amerikanische Sendung 1866–1871." Basel: Holbein, 1941.
BWB	Lewis, Oscar. "Bay Window Bohemia." Garden City: Doubleday & Company, Inc, 1956.
CAA	Cummings, Paul. "Dictionary of Contemporary American Artists." NY: St Martin's Press, 1966.
CAE	Harper, J Russell. "Early Painters and Engravers in Canada." Toronto: University of Toronto Press, 1970.
CAH	Reid, Dennis. "A Concise History of Canadian Painting." Toronto: Oxford University Press, 1973.
CAN	Colgate, William. "Canadian Art 1820–1940." Toronto: The Ryerson Press, 1943.
CAP	Meigs, John. "The Cowboy in American Prints." Chicago: The Swallow Press, 1972.
CAR	Hubbard, Robert H. "An Anthology of Canadian Art." Toronto: Oxford University Press, 1960.
CAT	McCracken, Harold. "George Catlin and the Old Frontier." NY: Bonanza Books, 1959.
CHA	Walker, John. "John Gadsby Chapman." Washington: National Gallery of Art, 1962.
C&I	Peters, Harry T. "Currier & Ives." Garden City: Doubleday, Doran & Co, Inc, 1943.
CIN	Anonymous. "Cincinnati Museum. Catalogue of the Permanent Collection of Paintings." Cincinnati: Cincinnati Museum Association, 1919.
CIV	Williams, Hermann Warner, Jr. "Civil War Drawings." Washington: The International Exhibitions Foundation, 1974.
CMW	Morgan, Henry James. "The Canadian Men and Women of the Time." Toronto: William Briggs, 1912.
CON	Pagano, Grace. "Contemporary American Painting." NY: Duell, Sloan and Pearce, 1945.
COO	Cook, Clarence. "Art and Artists of Our Time." NY: Selmar Hess, 1888.
COR	Anonymous. "Illustrated Handbook of Paintings, Sculpture and Other Art Objects." Washington: The Corcoran Gallery of Art, 1939.
COS	Peters, Harry T. "California on Stone." NY: Doubleday, Doran & Co, Inc, 1935.
COW	Ainsworth, Ed. "The Cowboy in Art." NY: The World Publishing Company, 1968.
CRR	Shadbolt, Doris. "Emily Carr." Vancouver: The Vancouver Art Gallery, 1971.
CRS	Roberts, Warren. "Paintings from the C R Smith Collection." Austin: The University of Texas at Austin, 1970.

C30   Hill, Charles C. "Canadian Painting in the Thirties." Ottawa: The National Gallery of Canada, 1975.

C71   Muno, Richard. "Cowboy Artists of America Sixth Annual Exhibition 1971." Flagstaff: Northland Press, 1971.

C72   McCrea, Joel. "Cowboy Artists of America Seventh Annual Exhibition 1972." Flagstaff: Northland Press, 1972.

C73   Speed, U Grant. "Cowboy Artists of America 1973." Flagstaff: Northland Press, 1973.

C74   Boren, James. "Cowboy Artists of America 1974." Flagstaff: Northland Press, 1974.

CUR   Simkin, Colin. "Currier and Ives' America." NY: Crown Publishers, Inc, 1952.

CUS   Russell, Don. "Custer's Last." Fort Worth: Amon Carter Museum of Western Art, 1968.

CWW   Anonymous. "Constance Whitney Warren 1888–1948." Memorial Exhibition, NY, 1953.

DAA   Bach, Cile M and Trenton, Patricia. "American Art The Denver Art Museum Collection." Denver: The Denver Art Museum, 1969.

DBW   Hassrick, Royal B. "Building the West." Denver: Denver Art Museum, 1955.

DCA   MacDonald, Colin S. "A Dictionary of Canadian Artists." Ottawa: Canadian Paperbacks, vol one A to F, 1967, vol two G to Jackson, 1968, vol three (part one) Jacobi to Lismer, 1971, vol four Little to Myles, 1974.

DCC   Bach, Cile M and Chambers, Marlene. "Colorado Collects Historic Western Art." Denver: Denver Art Museum, 1973.

DCP   Fairman, Charles E. "Art and Artists of the Capitol of the United States of America." Washington: Government Printing Office, 1927.

DEL   Dellenbaugh, Frederick S. "The Romance of the Colorado River." NY: G P Putnam's Sons, 1902.

DEP   Brown, Milton W. "American Painting from the Armory Show to the Depression." Princeton: Princeton University Press, 1955.

DIC   Byrnes, Gene. "A Complete Guide to Drawing Illustration Cartooning and Painting." NY: Simon and Schuster, 1948.

DIG   *The Art Digest*. NY: The Art Digest, Inc.

DIN   Stoutenburgh, John, Jr. "Dictionary of the American Indian." NY: Philosophical Library, 1960.

DOB   Dobie, J Frank. "The Longhorns." Boston: Little, Brown and Company, 1941.

DPL   Card files of the Western History Department, Denver Public Library.

DUS   Vigtel, Gudmund. "The Düsseldorf Academy and the Americans." Atlanta: The High Museum of Art, 1972.

DWF   Hassrick, Royal B. "The Western Frontier." Denver: Denver Art Museum, summer 1966.

EAK   Goodrich, Lloyd. "Thomas Eakins." NY: Whitney Museum of American Art, 1970.

EAS   Hills, Patricia. "Eastman Johnson." NY: Clarkson N Potter, Inc, 1972.

EDJ   Edouard-Joseph. "Dictionnaire Biographique des Artistes Contemporains 1910–1930." Paris: Art & Edition, 1931.

EDW   Sutro, Theodore. "Thirteen Historical Marine Paintings of Edward Moran." NY: Theodore Sutro, 1905.

EIT   Eiteljorg, Harrison. "West America, the Eiteljorg Collection." Evansville Museum of Arts & Science, 1972.

EST   Bushnell, David I. "Seth Eastman." Washington: Smithsonian Institution, 1932.

50G   Dykes, Jeff. "Fifty Great Western Illustrators." Flagstaff: Northland Press, 1975.

500   Simon, Howard. "500 Years of Art in Illustration." Garden City: Garden City Publishing Co, Inc, 1949.

FOR   Stenzel, Franz. "Anton Schonborn Western Forts." Fort Worth: Amon Carter Museum of Western Art, 1972.

FRO   Fairbanks, Jonathan L. "Frontier America: The Far West." Boston: Museum of Fine Arts, Boston, 1975.

FUC   Fuchs, Emil. "With Pencil, Brush and Chisel." NY: 1925.

GAN   Garnier, John H. "Auction Prices of American Antique Paintings 1968 through 1972." Charleston: Garnier & Company, 1973.

GAR   Garbisch, Edgar William and Bernice Chrysler. "101 Masterpieces of American Primitive Painting." NY: The American Federation of Arts, 1961.

GAW   Garbisch, Edgar William and Bernice Chrysler. "101 American Primitive Water Colors and Pastels." Washington: National Gallery of Art, 1966.

GIF   Cikovsky, Nicolai, Jr. "Sanford Robinson Gifford." Austin: The University of Texas Art Museum, 1970.

GIL   Rossi, Paul A & Hunt, David C. "The Art of the Old West." NY: Alfred A Knopf, 1973.

GOD   Sprague, Marshall. "A Gallery of Dudes." Boston: Little, Brown and Company, 1966.

GRT   Harman, Fred. "The Great West in Paintings." New Jersey: Castle Books, 1969.

GWP   Carlson, Raymond. "Gallery of Western Paintings." NY: McGraw-Hill Book Company, Inc, 1951.

HAA   Hartmann, Sadakichi. "A History of American Art." Boston: L C Page & Company, 1902.

HAD   Hardman, Sammy J. "Hardman's Dictionary of Artists & Estimates." Atlanta: Sammy J Hardman, 1974.

HAR   Harmsen, Dorothy. "Harmsen's Western Americana." Flagstaff: Northland Press, 1971.

HAW   Anonymous. "The Permanent Collection of the Harwood Foundation." Taos: The Harwood Foundation, 1970.

HMA   Harrington, Dennis. "Days on the Range." Houston: The Museum of Fine Arts, 1972.

HOE   Hoeber, Arthur. "Painters of Western Life," *The Mentor* (June 15, 1915), pp 1–12.

HON   Baird, Joseph Armstrong, Jr. "Catalogue of Original Paintings, Drawings and Watercolors in the Robert B Honeyman, Jr Collection." Berkeley: The Friends of the Bancroft Library, 1968.

HOP   Barr, Alfred H, Jr. "Edward Hopper." NY: The Museum of Modern Art, 1933.

HOR   Horgan, Paul. "The Centuries of Santa Fe." NY: E P Dutton & Company, Inc, 1956.

HUD	Howat, John K. "The Hudson River and Its Painters." NY: The Viking Press, 1972.
HUT	Waters, Clara Erskine Clement, and Hutton, Laurence. "Artists of the Nineteenth Century and Their Works." Boston: Houghton, Mifflin and Company, 1894.
H72	Hayden, F V. "Sixth Annual Report of the United States Geological Survey of the Territories 1872." Washington: Government Printing Office, 1873.
H73	Hayden, F V. "Annual Report of the US Geological and Geographical Survey of the Territories 1873." Washington: Government Printing Office, 1874.
H77	Hayden, F V. "Eleventh Annual Report of the US Geological and Geographical Survey of the Territories 1877." Washington: Government Printing Office, 1879.
150	Anonymous. "150 Years in Western Art." Cheyenne: Cheyenne Centennial Committee, 1967.
190	Rose, Barbara. "American Art since 1900." NY: Frederick A Praeger, 1967.
ILA	Reed, Walt. "The Illustrator in America 1900–1960's." NY: Reinhold Publishing Corporation, 1966.
ILG	Calkins, Earnest Elmo. "Artists Guild Annual." NY: The Artists Guild, Inc, 1939.
IL 94	Anonymous. "The Quarterly Illustrator for 1894." NY: Harry C Jones, 1894.
IL 95	Anonymous. "The Monthly Illustrator for the Second Quarter of 1895." NY: Harry C Jones, 1895.
IL 36	Anonymous. "Fifteenth Annual of Advertising Art." NY: Art Directors Club, 1936.
IL 42	Anonymous. "Art Directors 21st Annual." NY: Watson-Guptill Publications, Inc, 1942.
IL 59	Hawkins, Arthur. "Illustrators '59." NY: Hastings House, 1959.
IL 60	Munce, Howard. "Illustrators '60." NY: Hastings House, 1960.
IL 61	Fawcett, Robert. "Illustrators '61." NY: Hastings House, 1961.
IL 62	Briggs, Austin. "Illustrators '62." NY: Hastings House, 1962.
IL 63	Carter, Harry. "Illustrators '63." NY: Hastings House, 1963.
ILN	*Illustrated London News.*
ILP	Latimer, Louise P. "Illustrators, a Finding List." Boston: The F W Faxon Company, 1929.
IMP	Domit, Moussa M. "American Impressionist Painting." Washington: National Gallery of Art, 1973.
IND	Glaser, Nosta. "Indians." Philadelphia: Nosta Glaser, no date.
INS	*The International Studio.*
ISH	Isham, Samuel. "The History of American Painting." NY: The Macmillan Company, 1936 (new edition).
JAC	Getlein, Frank. "Harry Jackson." NY: Kennedy Galleries Inc, 1969.
JAK	Jacobsen, Anita. "Jacobsen's Painting Price Guide." Staten Island: Manor Publishing Company, 1973.
JCA	James, George Wharton. "California Romantic & Beautiful." Boston: The Page Company, 1914.
JGC	James, George Wharton. "In and Around the Grand Canyon." Boston: Little, Brown, and Company, 1893.

JNB   Anonymous. "Catalogue of American Paintings and Sculpture, Historical —Western." NY: J N Bartfield Art Galleries, number 120.

JNM   James, George Wharton. "New Mexico the Land of the Delight Makers." Boston: The Page Company, 1920.

JUT   James, George Wharton. "Utah the Land of Blossoming Valleys." Boston: The Page Company, 1922.

KAH   Arkelian, Marjorie. "The Kahn Collection of Nineteenth Century Paintings by Artists in California." Oakland: The Oakland Museum, Art Dept, 1975.

KAR   Anonymous. "M and M Karolik Collection of American Paintings 1815 to 1865." Boston: The Museum of Fine Arts, 1949.

KEN   *The Kennedy Quarterly.*

KER   Paladin, Vivian A. "W H D Koerner and Montana." Helena: The Montana Historical Society, 1971.

KOE   Hutchinson, W H. "W H D Koerner Illustrating the Western Myth." Fort Worth: Amon Carter Museum of Western Art, 1969.

KUH   Bartlett, Fred S. "Walt Kuhn an Imaginary History of the West." Fort Worth: Amon Carter Museum of Western Art, 1964.

KW1, 2   Rossiter, Henry P. "M & M Karolik Collection of American Water Colors & Drawings." Boston: Museum of Fine Arts, 1962.

LAA   Elliott, James H. "Artists of Los Angeles." LA: Los Angeles County Museum, 1957.

LAF   LaFarge, Oliver. "A Pictorial History of the American Indian." NY: Crown Publishers, 1956.

LET   Bassford, Amy O and Fryxell, Fritiof. "Letters of Thomas Moran to Mary Nimmo Moran." East Hampton: East Hampton Free Library, 1967.

LOS   Robertson, Edna C. "Los Cinco Pintores." NM: University of New Mexico, 1975.

MAC   Storz, Frank. "The Western Paintings of Frank C McCarthy." NY: Ballantine Books, 1974.

MAP   Boswell, Peyton, Jr. "Modern American Painting." NY: Dodd, Mead & Company, 1940.

MAR   Marriott, Alice. "Maria: The Potter of San Ildefonso." Norman: University of Oklahoma Press, 1948.

MAY   Mayer, E. "International Auction Records." France: E Mayer, volumes for each year 1966–75.

MCA   Ross, Elizabeth E. "Selections from the Drawing and Watercolor Collection." Oakland: Mills College Art Gallery, 1972.

MEC   Bach, Otto Karl. "Frank Mechau Retrospective 1904–1946." Denver: The Denver Art Museum, 1972.

MEI   Anonymous. "Meisterwerke der Holzschneidekunst." Leipzig: Verlagsbuchhandlung von J J Weber, 1882.

MEL   Carpenter, James M and others. "Landscape in Maine." Waterville: Colby College, 1970.

M15   Gardner, Albert Ten Eyck and Feld, Stuart P. "American Paintings. Painters born by 1815." NY: The Metropolitan Museum of Art, 1965.

M19   Howat, John K. "19th-Century American Paintings and Sculpture." NY: The Metropolitan Museum of Art, 1970.

M31   Burroughs, Bryson. "Catalogue of Paintings." NY: The Metropolitan Museum of Art, 1931.

M50	Hale, Robert Beverly. "American Painting Today." NY: The Metropolitan Museum of Art, 1950.
M57	Gardner, Albert Ten Eyck. "A Concise Catalogue of the American Paintings." NY: The Metropolitan Museum of Art, 1957.
MIL	Anonymous. "Catalogue British School." London: National Gallery Millbank, 1924.
MIS	Rathbone, Perry T. "Mississippi Panorama." St Louis: City Art Museum of St Louis, 1950.
MNM	Robertson, Edna C. "Handbook of the Collections." Santa Fe: Museum of New Mexico, 1974.
MON	Burk, Dale A. "New Interpretations." Missoula: Western Life Publications, Inc, 1969.
MOR	Gatling E I. "The Moran Family." Huntington: Heckscher Museum, 1965.
MSL	Earle, Helen L. "Biographical Sketches of American Artists." Lansing: Michigan State Library, 1915.
MWS	*Montana, the magazine of Western History.* Helena: Montana Historical Society.
M/H	Mitchell, William J. "99 Drawings by Marsden Hartley." Lewiston: Bates College Art Department, 1970.
NA 74	Poor, Alfred Easton. "149th Annual Exhibition." NY: National Academy of Design, 1974.
NCB	Anonymous. "The National Cyclopaedia of American Biography."
NCW	Allen, Douglas and Allen, Douglas, Jr. "N C Wyeth." NY: Crown Publishers, Inc, 1972.
NEU	Robbins, Daniel. "The Neuberger Collection." Providence: Rhode Island School of Design, 1968.
NEW	Sprague, Marshall. "Newport in the Rockies." Chicago: The Swallow Press, 1971.
NGA	Campbell, William P. "American Paintings and Sculpture." Washington: National Gallery of Art, 1970.
NHE	*Nation's Heritage.* NY: Heritage Magazine Incorporated.
NJA	Gerdts, William H. "Early New Jersey Artists." Newark: The Newark Museum, 1957.
NMX	*New Mexico.* Santa Fe: New Mexico Department of Development.
NSS 23	MacNeil, Hermon A. "Exhibition of American Sculpture Catalogue." NY: The National Sculpture Society, 1923.
NSS 29	Weinman, A A. "Contemporary American Sculpture." San Francisco: The National Sculpture Society, 1929.
NWA	Gunther, Erna. "Art in the Life of the Northwest Coast Indians." Portland: The Portland Art Museum, 1966.
NYG	Anonymous. "Fine Art Reproductions." Greenwich: New York Graphic Society Ltd, 1968.
OCA	White, Stewart Edward. "Old California." Garden City: Doubleday, Doran & Company, Inc, 1937.
OKE/ACM	Wilder, Mitchell A. "Georgia O'Keeffe." Fort Worth: Amon Carter Museum, 1963.
OKE/AIC	Rich, Daniel Catton. "Georgia O'Keeffe." Chicago: The Art Institute of Chicago, 1943.
OKE/BMC	Wofford, Harris. "The M Carey Thomas Awards 1971." Bryn Mawr: Bryn Mawr College, 1971.

OSR Hedgpeth, Don. "OS Ranch Steer Roping & Art Exhibit." Post: OS Ranch Committee, 1972.

PAF Rutledge, Anna Wells. "The Pennsylvania Academy of the Fine Arts 1807–1870." Philadelphia: The American Philosophical Society, 1955.

PAW Hinshaw, Merton E. "Painters of the West." Santa Ana: Charles W Bowers Memorial Museum, 1972.

PAX Stenzel, Franz R. "E S Paxson—Montana Artist." Helena: Montana Historical Society, ⚡14.

PB Anonymous. Auction Catalogs. NY and LA: Sotheby Parke Bernet Inc.

PCN Smith, Prof Walter. "The Masterpieces of the Centennial Exhibition." Philadelphia: Gebbie & Barrie, 1876.

PER *Persimmon Hill.* Oklahoma City: Western Art Fund, Inc for the National Cowboy Hall of Fame.

PET Ott, Wendall. "Gerald P Peters Collection." Roswell, NM: Roswell Museum, 1975.

PIC Bryant, William Cullen. "Picturesque America." NY: D Appleton and Company, 1872.

PIT Trenton, Pat. "Picturesque Images from Taos and Santa Fe." Denver: Denver Art Museum, 1974.

PNW Stenzel, Dr Franz R. "an art perspective of the historic pacific northwest." Portland: Montana Historical Society, 1963.

POI Pitz, Henry C. "The Practice of Illustration." NY: Watson-Guptill Publications, Inc, 1947.

POR Lee, Cuthbert. "Contemporary American Portrait Painters." NY: W W Norton & Company, Inc, 1929.

POW McCracken, Harold. "Portrait of the Old West." NY: McGraw-Hill Book Company, Inc, 1952.

PPE Neuhaus, Eugen. "The Art of the Exposition." San Francisco: Paul Elder and Company, 1915.

PTG Harman, Fred. "The Great West in Paintings." NJ: Castle Books, 1969.

PUA Heaton, Elsie S. "Pioneers of Utah Art." Logan: Kaysville Art Club, 1968.

PWA Anonymous. "The 1974 Gold Medal Portfolio of Western Art." Franklin Center: The Franklin Mint Gallery, 1974.

PWA 3/75 *The Franklin Mint Almanac,* March 1975.

PYL Morse, Willard S and Brinckle, Gertrude. "Howard Pyle." Wilmington: The Wilmington Society of Fine Arts, 1921.

RAN Grubar, Francis S. "William Ranney Painter of the Early West." NY: Clarkson N Potter, Inc, 1962.

REM/COE Anonymous. "Frederic Remington." NY: Coe Kerr Gallery, Inc, 1974.

REM/ILL Jackson, Marta. "The Illustrations of Frederic Remington." NY: Bounty Books, 1970.

REM/SKE Remington, Frederic. "Remington's Frontier Sketches." Chicago: The Werner Company, 1898.

REM/WAR Allen, Douglas. "Frederic Remington and the Spanish-American War." NY: Crown Publishers, 1971.

REM/WES Remington, Frederic. "Frederic Remington's Own West." NY: Promontory Press, 1960.

REN Renner, Frederic G. "Charles M Russell." Austin: University of Texas Press, 1966.

ROC   Buechner, Thomas S and Prideaux, Tom. "Norman Rockwell." NY: Harry N Abrams Inc, 1970.

ROO   Roosevelt, Theodore. "Hunting Trips of a Ranchman." NY: G P Putnam's Sons, 1902.

RUS   Adams, Ramon F and Britzman, Homer E. "Charles M Russell The Cowboy Artist." Pasadena: Trail's End Publishing Co, Inc, 1948.

RUS/MED   Russell, Charles M. "Good Medicine." Garden City: Garden City Publishing Company, Inc, 1929.

RYD   Goodrich, Lloyd. "Albert P Ryder," NY: George Braziller, Inc, 1959.

SCA   Moure, Nancy Dustin Wall. "Dictionary of Art and Artists in Southern California before 1930." Los Angeles: Privately printed, 1975.

SCH   Innes, Mary. "Schools of Painting." NY: G P Putnam's Sons, 1911.

SHO   Shalkop, Robert L. "A Show of Color." Colorado Springs: Colorado Fine Arts Center, 1971.

SHU   Boileau, Thornton I and Margo. "Three Decades of Plains Indians by Joe Scheuerle." Reprinted from MWS, Autumn 1971.

SLO   Sloane, Eric. "Return to Taos." NY: Wilfred Funk, Inc, 1960.

SNI   Snidow, Gordon. "Chronicler of the Contemporary West." Flagstaff: Northland Press, 1973.

SOA   Collins, Alan C. "The Story of America in Pictures." NY: Doubleday, Doran & Company, Inc, 1941.

SOU   King, Edward. "The Great South." Hartford: American Publishing Company, 1875.

SPR   McClurg, Gilbert. "Brush and Pencil in Early Colorado Springs." *Colorado Springs Gazette and Telegraph,* 1924.

SPT   Anonymous. "The Crossroads of Sport, Inc." NY: 1967–68.

SSF   Altrocchi, Julia Cooley. "The Spectacular San Franciscans." NY: E P Dutton and Company, Inc, 1949.

STI   Gerdts, William H and Burke, Russell. "American Still-Life Painting." NY: Praeger Publishers, 1971.

STU   Walker, John. "Gilbert Stuart." Washington: National Gallery of Art, 1967.

SUG   *Sugar and Spice.* Wheatridge, Colo: the Jolly Rancher.

SUR   Wallace, Edward S. "The Great Reconnaissance." Boston: Little, Brown and Company, 1955.

SWA   Anonymous. "Third Annual Exhibition of the Society of Western Artists." Chicago: The Art Institute of Chicago, 1899.

TAL   Luhan, Mable Dodge. "Taos and Its Artists." NY: Duell, Sloan and Pearce, 1947.

TAW   Curry, Larry. "The American West." NY: The Viking Press, 1972.

TEI   Teichert, Minerva Kohlhepp. "Selected Sketches of the Mormon March." No data.

TEP   Pinckney, Pauline A. "Painting in Texas." Austin: The University of Texas Press, 1967.

TEW   Hendricks, Patricia D. "20th Century Women in Texas Art." Austin: Laguna Gloria Art Museum, 1974.

TOB   Forrester-O'Brien, Esse. "Art and Artists of Texas." Dallas: Tardy Publishing Company, 1935.

TRA   Anonymous. "Catalogue." London: National Gallery Trafalgar Square, 86th edition.

TSF	Coke, Van Deren. "Taos and Santa Fe." Albuquerque: University of New Mexico Press, 1963.
T20	Remy, Caroline. "Selected 20th Century Texas Artists." University of Texas, 1966, manuscript.
TWR	Baird, Joseph A, Jr. "The West Remembered." San Francisco: California Historical Society, 1973.
TXF	Fisk, Francis Battaille. "A History of Texas Artists and Sculptors." Abilene: Fisk Publishing Company, 1928.
USM	Carroll, John M. "Illustrators of the American West." West Point: United States Military Academy, 1973.
VON	Anonymous. "Harold Von Schmidt Draws and Paints the Old West." Flagstaff: Northland Press catalog sheet for Walt Reed book.
WAA	Collins, J L. "Women Artists in America." Chattanooga: J L Collins, 1973.
WAC	Anderson, Antony. "Elmer Wachtel." LA: Antony Anderson, 1930.
WAI 71	Rossi, Paul A. "The West artists and illustrators." Tucson: The Tucson Art Center, 1971.
WAI 72	Hedgpeth, Don. "The West artists and illustrators." Tucson: The Tucson Art Center, 1972.
WAN	Wills, Olive. "Artists of Wyoming." *Annals of Wyoming,* October 1932.
WBB	McCracken, Harold. "The West of Buffalo Bill." NY: Harry N Abrams, Inc, 1974.
WBD	Neilson, William Allan. "Webster's Biographical Dictionary." Springfield: G & C Merriam Co, 1951.
WCA	Hitchcock, Ripley. "The Art of the World in the World's Columbian Exposition." NY: D Appleton and Company, 1894.
WCE	Kurtz, Charles M. "Illustrations from the Art Gallery of the World's Columbian Exposition." Philadelphia: George Barrie, 1893.
WES	Rathbone, Perry T. "Westward the Way." St. Louis: City Art Museum of St Louis, 1954.
WHI	Hills, Patricia. "The American Frontier." NY: Whitney Museum of American Art, 1973.
WHJ	Jackson, William H. "Picture Maker of the Old West." NY: Chas Scribner's Sons, 1947.
WIL	Donnelly, Joseph P. "Wilderness Kingdom." NY: Holt, Rinehart and Winston, 1967.
WIM	Rathbone, Perry T. "Charles Wimar." St Louis: City Art Museum of Saint Louis, 1946.
WNW	Appleton, Marion Brymner. "Who's Who in Northwest Art." Seattle: Frank McCaffrey, 1941.
WOL	Palmer, A H. "The Life of Joseph Wolf, Animal Painter." London: Longmans, Green & Co, 1895.
WOM	Leonard, John William. "Woman's Who's Who of America." NY: The American Commonwealth Company, 1914.
WOM 64	Anonymous. "Who's Who of American Women." Chicago: The A N Marquis Company, 1963.
WYA	Smith, J B and Brown, W R. "Wyoming Artists." Laramie: Wyoming Art Association, 1946.
WYG	Exhibition catalogs, The Wyoming State Art Gallery, Cheyenne.
WYW	*Wyoming Wildlife.*

| Y/H | Young-Hunter, John. "Reviewing the Years." NY: Crown Publishers, 1963. |
| YUP | Haseltine, James L. "100 Years of Utah Painting." Salt Lake City: Salt Lake City Art Center, 1965. |

REFERENCES AND REFERENCE ABBREVIATIONS

A98 to A33	Levy, Florence N. "American Art Annual." NY: The Macmillan Company, 1899. Beginning 1913, Washington: The American Federation of Arts, 1913 to 1933.
A34 to A76	McGlauflin, Alice Coe. "Who's Who in American Art." Washington: The American Federation of Arts, 1935 continuing to NY: Jaques Cattell Press, 1976.
BEN	Benezit, E. "Dictionnaire des Peintres, Sculpteurs, Dessinateurs, et Graveurs." Paris: Librairie Grund, 1966.
CHA	Champlin, John Denison, Jr. "Cyclopedia of Painters and Painting." NY: Charles Scribner's Sons, 1913.
DAB	Johnson, Allen. "Dictionary of American Biography." NY: Charles Scribner's Sons, 1928.
DABS	Supplements 1 and 2 to above.
ENB	Garvin, J L. "The Encyclopaedia Britannica" 14th edition. NY: Encyclopaedia Britannica, Inc, 1929.
FIE	Fielding, Mantle. "Dictionary of American Painters, Sculptors and Engravers." NY: James F Carr, 1965.
G&W	Groce, George C and Wallace, David H. "The New-York Historical Society's Dictionary of Artists in America 1564–1860." New Haven: Yale University Press, 1957.
MAL	Mallett, Daniel Trowbridge. "Mallett's Index of Artists." NY: Peter Smith, 1948.
MAS	Mallett, Daniel Trowbridge. "Supplement to Mallett's Index of Artists." NY: Peter Smith, 1948.
SMI	Smith, Ralph Clifton. "A Biographical Index of American Artists." Baltimore: The Williams & Wilkins Company, 1930.

The Illustrated Biographical Encyclopedia of Artists of the American West

ABDY, Mrs Rowena Meeks. Born Vienna, Austria 1887, died probably San Francisco, Cal 1945. California landscape painter, illustrator, decorator. Work in Mills Col AG, Seattle AM, Vanderpoel colln (Chicago), Cal Palace Legion of Honor, etc. References A47 (obit)-BEN-FIE-MAL-SMI. Sources INS 6/25 (article)-WAA. No auction record. Signature example p 191 INS 6/25.

Born abroad of American parents of Puritan descent, Mrs. Abdy studied at the Mark Hopkins AI and was the pupil of Arthur F Mathews. She sketched in Europe but after 1913 concentrated on California's scenery under varying weather conditions and on views of historical California. Typical titles were *Waterside Lane, San Francisco Bay, A Main Street of Early Spanish California Days,* and *The Casa of the Commandante.* Other subjects were the old missions and gold mining camps.

To travel the state, Mrs Abdy remodeled her big car into a studio so that "from the privacy of locked doors she sketches in comfort—secure from wind and dust and noisy, over-interested spectators." INS.

ABERT, Lt James William. Born Mt Holly, NJ 1820, died probably Columbia, Mo 1871. Landscape painter, topographical artist in Colo 1845 and 1846–47, teacher, writer. Work in ABE, Congressional documents, family collns. Reference G&W. Sources ABE-FRO-SHO-SUR. No current auction record. Painting examples ABE, FRO.

Son of the head of the Army's Topographical Bureau, Abert graduated from West Point in 1842, the pupil of R W Weir in drawing. He served with his father's corps, illustrating with watercolors the reports of Western expeditions. One of these expeditions was with Frémont, following the controversial Stephen Watts Kearny. In 1845 Abert accompanied Frémont on the expedition to South Pass, making Abert perhaps the third artist in Colorado, following Seymour and Titian Peale. Frémont assigned Abert to lead the survey of the prairie region southward and eastward along the Canadian River to the Arkansas and St Louis. Abert was uniquely equipped for the task, a young man who read books on the natural sciences until dinner, history after dinner, and finished off with poetry. His diary is a joy: "While one of our sentinels was walking his post, from some cause his gun went off. Startled by the report, he thought the Indians had fired on him, but on examining his rifle he began to think that at least he had not been seriously wounded." In the winter of 1846–47, Abert was back at Bent's Fort, returning to St Louis via the usual Santa Fe trail.

Abert returned to West Point from 1848 to 1850, as assistant to Weir who had been named professor. In the fifties he was working on engineering analyses of various Western rivers. He served in the Union Forces during the Civil War, until a serious wound forced his retirement in 1864 with the rank of colonel. He then became professor of math and drawing at the U of Missouri.

ABEYTA, Narciso Platero. Born Canoncito, NM 1918, living Gallup, NM 1967. Navaho painter, illustrator. Work in Ariz St Mus (Tucson), MAI, MNM, U Okla MA, Philbrook AC. No reference. Source AIP. No current auction record or signature example.

Abeyta, Navaho names Ha So Deh (Ascending) and Hoskiel (Forceful), graduated Santa Fe Indian School in 1939. After having been chosen to demonstrate painting at the San Francisco World's Fair in 1939–40, he studied at Somerset Art School near Williamsburg, Pa in the summer of 1940. The offer of a scholarship to Stanford was lost due to army induction. He served four years in WWII, participating in Okinawa and Iwo Jima invasions. He suffered shellshock that continued after the war to diminish the quantity of his paintings. In 1961 his work, called "excellent" and "unique," was published in *Art in America*.

ACHEY, Mary E (Mrs Phillip Achey). Active 1860–80 in Central City, Colo. Self-taught artist, muralist. Work *Nevadaville* in St Hist Soc of Colo. No reference. Sources DCC-*Central City Register* 10/23, 10/28, 11/28/1868. No auction record or signature example.

In 1868 Mrs Achey exhibited a landscape painting of Mt Lincoln and specialized in portraits painted from photographs. Her studio according to her ad in the newspaper NOTICE column was opened "just above the bridge" where "she would be happy to receive visitors." When she advertised "Achey's Oil Painting Carnival," it featured a sale of tickets for a drawing of her paintings including *Pike's Peak with Buffalo Chase* price $150, *Douglas Mountain* $100, one *Canada View* $45, one *View of the Plains* $15, and one *View in the South Park* $5. Six portraits were $240 the lot, with "those drawing the portraits expected to furnish a likeness" and "frames not furnished." After 1880 Mrs Achey moved near Aberdeen, Wash to execute a commission for murals.

ACOSTA, Manuel Gregorio. Born Villa Aldama, Chihuahua, Mex 1921, living El Paso, Tex 1976. Contemporary painter, illustrator, muralist, and sculptor of Western and Mexican subjects. Work in MNM, El Paso Mus, W Tex Mus, *Time* colln; murals in Western banks. Reference A76. Source HAR. No current auction record. Signature example p 9 HAR.

Acosta grew up in El Paso. He studied at the U of Texas at El Paso, at U of California, at Chouinard AI in Los Angeles, and with Urbici Soler, sculptor. Peter Hurd, to whom Acosta was apprenticed in 1952, has said, Acosta's "work is so immediate in its warm appeal that to enter a room hung with his paintings is to become at once a part of the world that surrounds his doorstep."

ADAM, William. Born Tweedmouth, Eng 1846, living Pacific Grove, Cal 1931. California landscape painter, teacher. Work in Del Monte Gall (Cal). References A31-BEN-FIE-MAL-SMI. Source BDW. No auction record or signature example.

Adam studied with Delecluse in Paris and with Greenlees and Brydall in Glasgow. He was a member of the Boston Art Club before coming to California by 1915 when his *Sundry Old California Gardens* was listed for the Del Monte Gallery.

ADAMS, Cassily. Born Zanesville, Ohio 1843, died Trader's Point, Ind 1921. Western genre and historical painter of *Custer's Last Fight* reproduced p 56 MWS W/74, illustrator. Work in Dentzel colln, Harmsen colln. No reference. Sources AIW-ANT 12/69-DCC-KW1-POW-WHI. Oil 9½ ×13¾" still-life *Old Weapon and Water Pipe* estimated for sale 3/4/72 at $80 to $100 for auction in LA. Signature example p 847 ANT 12/69. (See illustration 1.)

The son of a lawyer and amateur artist, descendant of John Adams, he studied at Boston Academy of Arts. Adams then served as an ensign on the USS *Osage* and was wounded at the battle of

Vicksburg in the Civil War. In 1870 he studied under Thomas S Noble at Cincinnati Art School. His studio was opened at 5th and Olive in St Louis where he worked as artist and engraver from 1878 to 1885.

About 1884 Adams started *Custer's Last Fight,* the 9½ ×16½′ painting that took more than a year to complete. The figures were posed by Sioux Indians in their war paint and by cavalrymen in costume. There were two end panels, the first with Custer as a boy and the other with Custer dead in the setting sun. The painting was exhibited about the country, sometimes accompanied by Adams, and was then sold to a St Louis saloon. The brewer Anheuser-Busch acquired the painting as a creditor, had it lithographed in color and printed in 1896. This lithograph is one of America's most familiar pictures, with over a million copies printed.

The three original panels were given by Busch to the 7th cavalry in 1895, lost, then found in 1925 in bad condition, found again in 1934 and restored by the WPA in Boston. They were hung at Fort Bliss, Tex until destroyed by fire in 1946. Adams was overshadowed by the lithograph of his major painting, but he painted many others including Indians hunting buffalo and he illustrated "Conquering the Wilderness."

ADAMS, Charles Partridge. Born Franklin, Mass 1858, died Pasadena, Cal 1942. Colo landscape painter, teacher. Work in Kan City AA, DAM, Adams colln, Denver clubs. References A47 (obit)-BEN-FIE. Sources DAA-DPL-HAR-TWR-WHO 40. Two oils 12×18″, 10×15″ *Sunset, Landscape* sold 1/26/72 for $450 the pair at auction. Signature example p 55 DAA. (See illustration 2.)

For reasons of health Adams moved to Denver in 1876, finding work as an engraver for a book store. He was briefly the pupil of Mrs James Albert Chaim (or Chain), an Inness student who ran an art school in Denver. By the time he was 25 his landscapes were artistic and financial successes. His business card offered his services in "landscapes and crayon portraits." Summers were spent at his studio "The Sketch Box" in Estes Park, Colo. Subjects ranged from Mt Long to Spanish Peaks, the Tetons, Yellowstone Park, and the New Mexico desert. He was a charter member of the Denver Artists Club in 1893.

Adams made his tour of the European galleries in 1914. When he retired to Laguna Beach, Cal in 1920, he specialized in marine subjects. At his death Adams had completed 800 paintings plus a large number of sketches. One Denver collector alone had 200 of Adams' works.

ADAMS, Kenneth Miller. Born Topeka, Kan 1897, died Albuquerque, NM 1966. Taos realist figure and landscape painter, muralist, lithographer, teacher. Taos Soc Artists 1927, ANA 1938, NA 1961. Work in WMAA, U NM, Colo Springs FAC, LAMA, Dallas MFA, DAM, etc. References A66-BEN. Sources AAT-COW-HAR-NA 74-PET-PIT-TAL-TSF-TWR-WHO 60. No current auction record but M50 listed oil *Harvest* at the artist's price of $3,000. Signature example p 9 *Adams Retrospective Catalog* 1972 U NM. (See illustration 3.)

At 16 Adams studied with G M Stone in Topeka, then entered the AIC in 1916. After serving in the Army as a private in World War I, he studied at the ASL beginning 1919, the pupil of K H Miller, Bridgman, Sterne, and Speicher. Summers were with Dasburg in Woodstock. From 1921 to 1923 Adams studied in France and Italy, painting landscapes he exhibited in Topeka.

In 1924 Adams followed Dasburg's advice, settling in Taos with an introduction to Ufer. He became the youngest and last member of the Taos Society of Artists, but he was more than a duplicate of the original members' emphasis on the romantic Indian. Adams was a contemporary realist, influenced by Dasburg and working in the tradition of Rivera and Orozco. Technically conservative, Adams was nevertheless concerned with the daily lives of his agrarian neighbors. In 1929 Adams began teaching at the U of New Mexico in Taos. The dominant subjects in his work became the Spanish Americans and landscapes. In 1938 he moved to Albuquerque, NM, where his work by 1950 was devoted to nudes, portraits, and still life, while his summer subjects in Taos were flowers, the Indians, and the rural Spanish Americans.

ADAMS, Willis A (distinguish Willis Seaver Adams, Mass still-life painter). Born Goshen, Ind 1854, died Salt Lake City, Utah 1932. Utah landscape and still-life painter. Work in Utah State colln. No reference. Source PUA-YUP. No auction record. Signature p 17 YUP. Photograph p 41 PUA.

Kin of the Massachusetts Adams family, W A Adams was raised on a frontier farm. Artistic in nature, he moved to Goshen to try the farm implement business and then photography where his talent was in retouching. After brief training at the AIC, he and his brother settled in Utah. Adams ran a prosperous studio in Park City, Utah, in the midst of a booming mining camp. He remained there for 50 years.

When Adams married, he devoted his time to painting, as a self-trained artist influenced by John Hafen. During the spring, summer, and fall, he turned out a large volume of landscapes of the canyons and mountains. In one Salt Lake City private colln, there are about 350 works. The harsh winters, however, are not recorded in any Adams painting. He also painted muted still lifes, but he is not the Willis Adams referred to in STI.

ADNEY, Edwin Tappan. Born Athens, Ohio 1868, died Woodstock, New Brunswick, Can 1950. Field artist covering the Klondike for *Harper's,* illustrator and writer on outdoor subjects, painter, lecturer ASPCA, Can military expert. Work in Explorers Club. References A13-BEN-FIE-MAL-SMI. Sources ARC-DCA-WHO 40. No current auction record. Signature example ✕50 ARC.

Son of a military officer-professor, Tappan Adney was educated at the U of North Carolina where he sketched birds. He then studied at the ASL for three years. In 1897–98 he was special artist for *Harper's Weekly* and the *London Chronical* in the Klondike during the gold rush. A book of his experiences was published in 1899. In 1900 he was special artist for *Collier's Weekly* at Cape Nome. He was best known as author and illustrator of outdoor subjects, eg, *Harper's* "Outdoor Book for Boys" in 1908 and as illustrator for "Birds of Eastern North America." Adney served as lieutenant in the Canadian Engineers in WWI. After the war he was in charge of model making for the Canadian military.

Adney became a British subject in 1917. In New Brunswick he lived with the Indians to learn language, customs, and his specialty, canoe making. During the rest of his life, he made about 90 specimens of bark canoes. His other interest was heraldry. A Canadian flag he created was used in French Canada, and he designed armorials and shields for Canadian libraries, railways, colleges, and hotels. He exhibited, and on a 1931 information form for the NGC mentioned that the early illustrations for his books had been sold to friends in and around NYC.

AGATE, Alfred T. Born Sparta, NY 1812, died Washington, DC 1846. Artist with the Wilkes exploring expedition, illustrator, miniaturist. Work published in Wilkes's report. ANA 1832, honorary NA 1840. References BEN-DAB-FIE-G&W-MAL-SMI. Sources KW1-PNW. No current auction record. Wash drawing p 4 PNW.

The pupil of his older brother Frederick Styles Agate, he was also the pupil of T S Cummings and was trained as a miniaturist. His studio was in NYC where he exhibited beginning 1831. Agate and Joseph Drayton became artists for the Wilkes exploring expedition that from 1838 to 1842 surveyed the Antarctic, the Pacific islands, and for the first time the American northwest coast. Agate settled in Washington in 1846, working until his death on the preparation of his sketches for the Wilkes report that was published in sections from 1844 to 1874. Many Agate illustrations of animals and plants are included, along with important views along the coast. PNW reproduced an 1840 wash drawing of a Wilkes party following an Indian trail overland from Fort Vancouver south into California.

AKIN, Louis B. Born Portland, Ore 1868, died Flagstaff, Ariz 1913. Western painter of Hopi Indian life beginning 1903 and of Southwestern landscapes. Work in AMNH, Mus Northern Ariz. References A14 (obit)-BEN-FIE-MAL-SMI. Sources "The Westerners Brand Book, LA Corral" 1956 book 6-*Amer Mus Journ* vol xiii no 3 1913. No current auction record. Signature example p 114 *Amer Mus Journ* above.

Akin's grandparents followed the Oregon Trail west from Iowa in 1852. In Portland, Akin worked as a sign painter. About 1886 he built a hut in the Cascades to observe Rocky Mtn goats. With his savings he went to NYC to study with Chase and DuMond. In 1901 *Harper's Weekly* published Akin's nostalgic doggerel and illustrations, "a-hittin' up the trail, instead o' sittin'." In 1903 Akin traveled to Oraibi, Ariz, where for 75¢ a week he rented a room in a Hopi pueblo. Late that year he wrote he was "getting at" his painting in earnest, the subject being "the best stuff in America and scarcely touched." *Journ.* Given the name "Mapli," he was initiated into a Hopi secret society. By 1904 he had completed a series of Hopi paintings, one of which *The Oraibi Plaza* was sold to W H Jackson and reproduced for sale at curio stands in Santa Fe RR stations. The painting *Storm Over Grand Canyon* was also reproduced and sold, while the RR bought *El Tovar* for reproduction on travel posters.

Akin settled in the desert country, sleeping on the floor of his studio in Babbit Bros store building in Flagstaff, except for trips such as one to the Fraser River in British Columbia in 1909. In 1911 the AMNH commissioned Akin to decorate its new Southwest Indian room. He had completed 20 oil sketches for exhibition—"the Indians in their dancing garb, Indian spinners and weavers, scenes in the pueblos, and one or two of the desert," *Journ*—when he died from pneumonia. Akin's masterpiece was considered to have been his painting of the Grand Canyon he could not sell and so did not sign. In 1929 it was hanging in Verkamp's Curio Store at Bright Angel on the rim of the Canyon.

ALBRIGHT, Floyd Thron (or Lloyd Lhron). Born Cleburne, Tex 1897, living Dalhart, Tex 1948. Painter of West Texas and Taos subjects, muralist, craftsman. Work in Dalhart banks, theater, and public buildings. References A41-MAS. Source TOB. No current auction record or signature example.

Albright studied at the Chicago AFA,

with Emil Bisttram in Taos, with Dunton, and in Denver, Colo. "His best subjects" are "the aspens, pines, blue mountains, thin air, the Indian pueblos, Mexican adobes, old Mission churches." TOB. Albright also worked as an architect and as a carver of furniture, both French-style garlands and miniatures and primitive American and Mexican designs. His Dalhart studio had adobe walls and grilled doors, furnished with his own carvings.

ALBRIGHT, Hermann Oliver. Born Mannheim, Germany 1876, died probably San Francisco, Cal 1944. California landscape painter, photographer. References A41-BEN-FIE-MAL. Source BDW. No auction record or signature example.

A photographer, Albright was the pupil of Gertrude Partington who became his wife. He began earning awards by 1920, painting the mountains and camps as well as the San Francisco area. Mrs Albright had studied with her father, worked as a newspaper artist, and specialized in painting the Bay area.

ALDEN, James Madison (distinguish his uncle James Alden). Born Boxboro, Mass 1834, died Orlando, Fla 1922. Coastal survey and Rocky Mtn watercolorist, Civil War artist. Work in BMFA. Reference G&W. Sources HON-KW1, 2-TAW. No auction record. Signature p 59 KW2.

From 1854 to 1857 James M Alden was topographer on the US Pacific Coast Survey, employed by his uncle James Alden. From 1857 to 1861 he was official artist for the US-Canada Boundary Survey in the Rockies, completing a large number of watercolor landscapes from Fort Roberts to the summit of the

Rockies. In the Civil War he served in the Union Navy beginning 1863, with Rear Admiral D D Porter. Continuing with Porter in various capacities after the war, he worked in Washington, DC until 1891. The period during which he painted was at least 40 years.

His uncle James Alden was born Portland, Me 1810 and died San Francisco, Cal 1877. A naval officer and amateur watercolorist, he signed as James Alden, it is said, while his nephew signed James M Alden. "California Pictorial" by Van Nostrand, 1948, U Cal Press.

ALLEN, John D. Born Italy Hill, NY 1851, died Mandan, ND 1947. Pioneer North Dakota painter of Sioux Indians, taxidermist. No reference. Sources BDW-KEN 6/68. Oil 22×30" *Scouting the Herd* estimated for sale 10/28/74 at $1,500 to $2,500 for auction in Los Angeles and sold for $1,300. Signature example lot 113 above.

J D Allen moved to Mandan as a taxidermist in 1881. He also painted in oil, recording the genre of the Sioux Indians.

ALLEN, Thomas. Born St Louis, Mo 1849, died Worcester, Mass 1924. Massachusetts landscape and animal painter in the Rockies 1869 and in Tex 1878–79; businessman. Member SAA 1880, ANA 1884. Work in BMFA, City AM (St Louis), Berkshire Athenaeum, San Antonio Pub Lib. References A24 (obit)-BEN-CHA-FIE-MAL-SMI. Sources AIW-ANT 6/48-NA 74-NCB-TEP-WHO 24. No current auction record. Signature example p 458 ANT 6/48 *Evening, Market Plaza,* San Antonio (1879).

Son of a Congressman-RR president-editor, Thomas Allen was educated at

Washington U in St Louis. While a student in 1869, he sketched in the Rockies west of Denver with his teacher. The results were encouraging enough in 1871 to take Allen to Düsseldorf where he graduated from the RA in 1877, having studied with A Achenbach, Carl Müller, and Eugen Ducker.

After a vacation in Texas the winter of 1878–79, he moved to Écouen near Paris. His first painting in the Paris Salon was in 1882, *Evening at the Market Place, San Antonio*. In Texas, he had also painted *Mexican Women Washing at San Pedro Spring* and *The Portal of San Jose Mission*. Probably from this time are *The Covered Wagon* and *Toilers of the Plains*. Allen returned to a Boston studio in 1880. New England pastoral subjects were then his specialty. He was also president of business enterprises and an official of many fine arts groups.

ALLISON, William Merle. Born Kansas 1880, living NYC 1934. Illustrator, specializing in Western and historical subjects. Member SI. References A33-MAL. Source AAC. No auction record or signature example.

Allison studied in Chicago at the John Herron Art Inst and the AIC. He shows as working in NYC from the early 1920s on. Books he illustrated are "Heroes of Liberty" and "Women in American History."

AMES, Ezra. Born Framingham, Mass 1768, died Albany, NY 1836. NY portrait painter, miniaturist. Work in MMA, NYHS, Albany Inst. References BEN-DAB-FIE-G&W-MAL-SMI. Sources ANT 12/53, 11/55, 5/61, 11/64, 6/65, 3/66-M31-PAF-STI. No current auction record. Painting examples p 418 ANT 3/66 (portraits).

Son of a farmer who moved the family to Staatsburg, NY, Ames returned to Massachusetts by 1790. A carriage and furniture painter, Ames was also a miniaturist. When he settled in Albany in 1795, he gilded frames, lettered clock faces, decorated flags, and engraved, as well as painting oil portraits. The 1794 portrait price was four pounds sterling. By 1812 his greatest fame was achieved through a full-length painting of Gov Clinton. About 500 works have been recorded. Some political portraits were reproduced as engravings.

Ames painted few portraits of Indians. The best known was of Joseph Brant, the Mohawk chief who fought with the Tories in the Revolution. Brant in Mohawk regalia was also painted earlier by Romney while Brant was in England before the war.

AMICK, Robert Wesley. Born Canon City, Colo 1879, died probably Old Greenwich, Conn about 1970. Illustrator of Western subjects, painter, printmaker, commercial artist, teacher. Member SI 1913. Work in GIL; murals in Canon City AM, schools, pub bldgs. References A62-BEN-FIE-MAL-SMI. Sources NYG (*The Overland Mail* and *The Indian Scout* reproduced as color lithographs)— data from Mrs R W Amick. No current auction record. Signature example p 490 NYG. (See illustration 4.)

Born in a log cabin, Amick grew up in the Colorado cattle country during the 1880s when the scene around him included the cowboy, the prospector, Ute and Sioux Indians, the homesteader—all of the characters on the Westerner's stage. Amick was educated in Canon City public schools and at Yale where he earned a law degree while also taking art courses. After practicing law in Ohio for two years, he gave up law for art study with private teachers and at the ASL.

Although successful as an illustrator

with commissions from *Harper's, Scribner's, The American,* and other publications, Amick felt that his most rewarding paintings would be of the West he knew, the mountains, the brilliant sun and vivid desert colors, the movement of riders and horses. This was proved true when 12 of his Western paintings were reproduced as art prints for use in schools. His painting subjects also included marines, animals, landscapes, and portraits.

ANDERSON, Clarence William. Born Wahoo, Neb 1891, living Mason, NH 1972. Illustrator specializing in horses, etcher, lithographer, writer. Member SAE, SAGA. References A62-MAL. Source CAP, with signature example p 85 *Rodeo Sketches.*

A pupil of the AIC, C W Anderson won an honorable mention from the SAE in 1932. He was living in NYC in 1935. Specializing in horses, he wrote and illustrated a series of books from "Thoroughbreds" in 1942 to "Bred to Run" in 1960 and "Lonesome Little Pony" in 1961.

ANDRES, Charles John. Born Hastings-on-Hudson, NY 1913, living North Berwick, Me 1976. Eastern illustrator of paperback Westerns beginning 1946 and of dust jackets for Zane Grey novels; muralist, teacher. No reference. Source, March 1975 data from C J Andres. No auction record or signature example. (See illustration 5.)

Andres attended the US Naval Academy 1932–35 but failed mechanics. He studied at the ASL 1935 to 1938, the pupil of Charles S Chapman and George Bridgman. His most important influence was Harvey Dunn when he studied at the Grand Central Art School 1936 to 1940.

He also studied with Thomas Fogarty and Frank Reilly.

After service in the Navy in WWII, Andres was one of the first illustrators to work for Bantam Books, including Western subjects. He also illustrated for most of the major book publishers. A juvenile "Moby Dick" for example called for 96 paintings in two months with Ahab required to resemble Gregory Peck. Zane Grey illustrations were "The Man in the Forest," "Thunder Mountain," "Light of the Western Stars," "Code of the West," and "Mysterious Rider." Andres also did film strips and textbook art. In 1950 Andres married and moved to Maine. He continued to free-lance as an illustrator while teaching art at Berwick Academy and painting murals.

ANDREWS, George Henry. Born Lambeth, London, Eng 1816, died Hammersmith, London, Eng 1898. English Special Artist-illustrator, marine watercolorist. Work in Cardiff Museum, Royal Ontario Museum. References BEN-MAL. Source AOH. Oil *Signing the Marriage Register* sold 11/28/72 for $3,600 at Sotheby auction. No signature example.

Andrews was trained as an engineer but preferred art. From 1840 to 1850 he exhibited at the Old Water Color Society, and beginning with 1850, at the Royal Academy. At that time the *Illustrated London News* was in the course of becoming the most successful weekly of the century. In the spring of 1860 the publisher Herbert Ingram decided to visit the US, bringing Andrews as the paper's first Special Artist in North America, to cover the state visit of the Prince of Wales. Ingram lost his life in an excursion steamer collision on Lake Michigan in September, but Andrews accompanied the Prince on the Canadian portion of his royal tour.

The Canadian views by Andrews in *Illustrated London News* in 1860 showed frontier life in Ontario along the Grand Trunk Railway. A second series was published in 1862 as "Sketches of Canada."

APPLEGATE, Frank G. Born Atlanta, Ill 1882, died Santa Fe, NM 1934 (or 1931). New Mexico painter after 1921, sculptor, ceramist. Work in MNM; illustrations in "Native Tales of N Mex." References A31 (obit)-BEN-FIE-MAL-SMI. Sources LOS-TSF-WHO 30. No auction record or signature example.

He was the pupil of F F Frederick at the U of Illinois where he was educated in 1906. He studied two years at the PAFA under Grafly and at the Julien Academy in Paris under Verlet. He then taught sculpture, modeling, and ceramics at the Trenton (NJ) Industrial AS, 1908–20.

In 1921 Applegate came to Santa Fe, devoting himself to painting. His house was on Camino del Monte Sol, in line with the adobe huts built by Los Cinto Pintores, Mruk, Bakos, Nash, Ellis, and Shuster. He was "their close friend and sometimes financial helper." LOS. He became a member of the New Mexico Painters society in 1923, exhibiting extensively. He wrote "Indian Stories from the Pueblos" in 1929.

ARMIN, Emil. Born Radautz, Romania 1883, living Chicago, Ill 1953. Painter, illustrator, sculptor in the Southwest by 1929. References A41-MAL. Source AIC. No current auction record or signature example.

Armin listed his birthplace with AIC as both Romania and Austria. He studied evenings at the AIC from 1908–11 and days from 1916–20 with A Sterba, J W Reynolds, Geo Bellows, Randall Davey, and Herman Sachs. He exhibited woodcarvings at the AIC in 1922 and paintings in 1923. New Mexico painting subjects included *In Santa Fe and Far Away, Buena Vista, Santa Fe,* and *The Storm* in 1929, *Taos* in 1930, *Canyon* in 1931, *Mountain Street* 1932, *Corn Dance* 1934, *In the Valley* 1935, and *Green Corn Dance* 1940. Armin was the art instructor at the Jewish Peoples Inst in Chicago from 1930 to 1932. He exhibited at the AIC as late as 1953.

ARMSTRONG, M K. Active as illustrator for *Harper's Weekly* in 1865. No reference. Source AOA. No current auction record. Drawing example p 163 AOA.

Main Street of Vermilion, Dakota Territory is the sketch reproduced in *Harper's* with Armstrong probably on the spot because he was not a staff artist. The subject is the US Land Office, a small and undistinguished structure from which there had been assigned to settlers more than 100,000 acres in the three years following the Homestead Act.

ARMSTRONG, William W. Born Dublin, Ireland 1822, died probably Canada 1914. Topographical artist, landscape painter, in the Can Northwest in 1870. Work in ACM, ANS, Can institutions, NGC, Can Nat Rys, J Ross Robertson colln (Toronto). No reference. Sources CAH-CAN-CMW. No current auction record. Painting examples p 73 CAH. (See illustration 6.)

Armstrong worked for the first Grand Trunk Ry beginning 1851 when he emigrated to Toronto. His paintings were illustrations of current events in Toronto and portraits of Indians. As chief engineer for the Wolseley expedition to the Northwest in 1870 following Canadian confederacy, Armstrong made topographical sketches. In the early 1940s, it is said, his original studies were still available for purchase in Canadian bookshops and at auctions. CAN. "Painting for him was a serious hobby" producing "modest works of art" by this "earnest craftsman with a documentary aim." CAH.

ARPA Y PEREA (or Arpa), José. Born Carmona near Seville, Spain 1868 (or 1858, or 1859, or 1862), living San Antonio, Tex 1941. "The Colorist Painter," etcher, illustrator, muralist, teacher. Work in Art Acad (Seville), Witte Mus (San Antonio), World's Columbian Expos (1893). References A36-BEN-FIE-MAL. Sources TOB-T20-TXF. No current auction record. Painting example opp p 32 TXF.

Arpa was the pupil of Eduardo Cano de la Peña at the AFA in Seville. He then studied for six years in Rome before traveling through Africa and Europe. About 1894 he was brought to Mexico on a warship to become head of the AFA in Mexico City. Instead, he visited a friend in Puebla, Mexico where he remained, painting as "The Sunshine Man." About 1903 Arpa came to San Antonio as guardian of his friend's children. Although successful as a Texas painter, he returned to Spain to be a special correspondent covering the Moroccan war.

After 20 years traveling to Spain, South America, Mexico, and Texas, Arpa settled in San Antonio in 1923. His oil *Grand Canyon* was widely exhibited, as were *Cactus Flower* and *Picking Cotton*. One San Antonio collector had 75 of his canvases, while another had 66. Arpa's nephew and assistant was Xavier Gonzáles (see entry).

ARRIOLA (or Ariola), Fortunato. Born Cosala, State of Sinaloa, Mexico

1827, died on ship en route to Cal 1872. San Fran landscape and portrait painter, teacher. Work in Cal Hist Soc. Reference G&W. Sources AAR 11,12/74 with signature example p 81-BAR-KAH-POW. No auction record.

Arriola emigrated to San Francisco in 1857. Though trained as a portraitist, he also painted luminist California landscapes. "San Francisco's Golden Era" by Beebe and Clegg, 1960 Howell-North, reproduced Arriola's night scene of Howard Street in a fog surrounding a brightly lit horsecar about 1865. Most of his landscapes were remembered views of Mexico and of the Central American tropics. "While his figures were faulty, the landscapes were filled with luminous sunlight or moonlight, and with tropical birds and other exotic accents." KAH. When Arriola traveled to NYC in 1871, the two paintings he exhibited at the NAD in 1872 were landscapes of Mexico, a popular subject in the East at the time. Arriola's death resulted from a fire aboard the ship returning him to San Francisco.

ARTHURS, Stanley Massey. Born Kenton, Del 1877, died probably Wilmington, Del 1950. Illustrator of historical subjects including Indians and the West, muralist, writer. Member SI 1905, Soc of Mural Painters. Work in Rochester Athenaeum (NY-*Pontiac's Indian Raid*); murals in St Capitol (St Paul, Minn and Dover, Del), U of Del, etc. References A41-BEN-FIE-MAL-SMI. Sources ILA-WHO 50. No current auction record. Signature examples "The American Historical Scene."

Arthurs studied at Drexel Institute in Philadelphia and at the Howard Pyle School of Art. His first illustration purchased was by *Harper's* in 1900. Pyle remained Arthurs' central influence, to the extent that Arthurs moved into Pyle's studio after Pyle died. Arthurs dedicated himself to an authentic portrayal of American historical subjects. Half his time was spent in research in depth so that each detail of an illustration would be accurate. His work was selected for James Truslow Adams' "History of the US" and for Gabriel's "Pageant of America" in addition to illustrations and articles for *Scribner's*.

A unique tribute to Arthurs was the 1936 publication of "The American Historical Scene," reproducing 50 Arthurs illustrations from *George Washington* to *The Modern Crusaders* of WWI. Each illustration was accompanied by descriptive text prepared by 50 eminent writers. The paintings included *Landing of the Swedes* with Indians on the shore, *LaSalle at an Indian Lead Mine, The Rising of Pontiac, Tecumseh and Wm Henry Harrison, The Siege of Boonesboro,* and *Osceola's Defiance.*

ASAH, Spencer. Born near Carnegie, Okla about 1907, died Norman, Okla 1954. Kiowa painter, one of the "Five Kiowas"; farmer. Work in Denver AM, GIL, MAI, MNM, U of Okla MA. Reference MAL. Sources AIP-COW. No current auction record or signature example.

Asah's Kiowa name was Lallo, Little Boy. The son of a Buffalo medicine man, he was educated in Indian schools and St Patrick's Mission School. The government field matron who organized a fine arts club for the young Kiowas considered the resulting drawings important enough to bring them to an art dealer in 1926. Encouraged, she took Asah to Dr O B Jacobson, a painter and professor of art at the neighboring U of Oklahoma. Jacobson arranged for support and instruction at the U for Asah, Hokeah, Mopope, and Tsatoke. A fifth Kiowa, Lois Smoky, was added in 1927.

The Five Kiowas exhibited throughout the country and at the First International Art Expos in Prague in 1928. Their paintings were reproduced in major art magazines. During the 1930s they decorated many public buildings with Kiowa murals. Two books were written about them. "Asah grew up in an atmosphere of tribal legends and rituals, the influence of which is evident in his paintings." He earned funds while at the university by dancing—"rhythmic, methodical, ritualistic." AIP.

ASMAR, Alice. Born Flint, Mich 1929, living Hollywood, Cal 1976. Cal painter of Indian life and animals, muralist. Work in Huntington Hartford colln. (NYC), Roswell Mus & AC (NM), banks, stores, and in SW Indian Arts exhibition in Belgium 1973; murals in Cal stores and banks. Reference A76. Source AHI 6/73. The published estimate is $4,000 to $5,000 (no supporting auction record). Signature example AHI 6/73.

Ms Asmar was educated at Lewis & Clark Col. She studied at the U of Washington with Edward Melcarth and Archipenko, as well as on scholarship at the École Nat Supérieure des Beaux-Arts in Paris and with M Souverbie. She was aided by awards for Paris 1958–59, for Italy 1959, the MacDowell Colony 1959–60, and the Hartford Fndn 1960, 1961, and 1964. After having worked as an aircraft draftsman 1952–54, she taught art at Lewis & Clark Col 1955–58 and at Lennox Adult Educ 1963–65. Ms Asmar paints in casein, indelible india inks, acrylics, and oil. Her paintings are reproduced as color prints.

ATENCIO, Gilbert Benjamin. Born Greeley, Colo 1930, living Santa Fe, NM 1968. San Ildefonso Indian painter, illustrator. Work in GIL, MAI, MNM, Philbrook AC. No reference. Sources

AHI 8/52-AIP-COW. No current auction record. Signature example p 20 AHI 8/52 *Agapito* dated 1944 of the "last of the San Ildefonso Kossa" and two women Kossa, one with a toe-hole in her moccasin. Atencio was 14 when he painted *Agapito*.

Gilbert Atencio's Indian name is Wah Peen, Mountain of the Sacred Wind. Educated in San Ildefonso, he served in the Marines and graduated from Santa Fe in 1947. His style of painting is traditional and flat. He has a "strong sense of tribal responsibility" and seldom leaves his native pueblo. AIP. In 1966 he was pueblo governor.

ATWOOD, Robert. Born Orange, NJ 1892, living Bartonsville, Vt 1953. Painter who was artist in residence Ariz St Col 1938–41, designer, teacher. References A53-MAL. Source BDW. No auction record or signature.

Atwood studied at the Faucett School of Art and the PAFA. During WWII he was an industrial designer.

AUCHIAH, James. Born near Medicine Park, Okla 1906, living Carnegie, Okla 1967. One of the "Five Kiowas," replacing Lois Smoky; painter, muralist. Work in GIL, MAI, McNay AI (San Antonio), Philbrook AC. References A41-MAL. Source AIP. No current auction record or signature example.

Auchiah is the grandson of Chief Satanta who committed suicide in prison after leading the Wagon Train Massacre and the Battle of Adobe Walls. Auchiah joined the "Five Kiowas" at Oklahoma U in the fall of 1927 as Lois Smoky dropped out. He was in time to benefit from the supporting contributions of Lew Wentz and from the worldwide acclaim for the art of the Kiowas. The First International Art Exposition was held in Prague in 1928, including Kiowa paintings. "Kiowa Indian Art," a book resulting from the Expos, was published in France in 1929. In the 1930s, the Kiowas painted murals in public buildings. Auchiah served in the Coast Guard in WWII. He has worked as a civilian employee in the Fort Sill paint shop.

AUDUBON, John James (LaForest). Born Les Cayes, Haiti 1785, died NYC 1851. Honorary NA 1833. Important bird and quadruped painter, naturalist. Work in "Birds of Amer," "Quadrupeds of N Amer," ARI, MMA, DAM, BMFA, U of Liverpool, NYHS, NGA, etc. References BEN - CHA - DAB - ENB - FIE - G&W - MAL - SMI. Sources AIW - ANT 6/46, 11/47, 11/51; 1, 2, 3, 11/54; 6/55, 4/57, 11/58, 10/62, 4/65, 3/71, 1/73; 4, 7/74; 2/75-ARI-AWM-BAR-BOA-DAA-DBW-GIL-HUD-KW1-MIS-M19-M57-NGA-POW-STI-TEP-WES. Watercolor/pencil 12½×17½″ *Robin* sold 6/24/71 for $16,300 at auction. Signature examples ※33 M19 *Hawk Pouncing on Quail;* p 76 KW1 (portrait).

Audubon's father was a ship captain successful as merchant, planter, and slave dealer in Haiti while his wife remained in France. Audubon's mother was a Creole slave. Brought to France at four, Audubon was legitimatized and educated among the well-to-do. At 15 he was drawing French birds, and at 17 studied drawing with David in Paris. In 1803 Audubon was sent to Pennsylvania to manage his father's estate, a sportsman in pumps, beginning his ventures into ornithology. From 1807 to 1819 he engaged in a series of failing businesses on the Kentucky frontier. When he was jailed for debt, bankruptcy left him only his clothes, his gun, and his drawings of birds. After a short stay as taxidermist at the Cincinnati museum 1819–20, he set his goals on publishing his bird drawings.

While Mrs Audubon supported the family, he traveled the Ohio and Mississippi rivers and the Great Lakes, exploring for birds. Unable to find a publisher in Phila in 1824, Audubon went to Liverpool, Edinburgh, and London 1826–27 where William Lizars and Robert Havell Jr were his engravers. The original drawings of more than 1,000 birds were in mixed media, watercolor, pencil, pen, and pastel to accomplish the various effects desired, but when he paid his way with copies of the drawings, the copies were in oil. Audubon returned to the US in 1831 as its foremost naturalist.

In 1837 Audubon was granted a naval cutter to explore the coastline from New Orleans to Galveston where he spent three weeks. In Houston, he met with Gen Houston at the time of the celebration of Texas independence, but found no new bird species. In 1843 Audubon went up the Missouri to Fort Union and made an overland trip along the Yellowstone, seeing birds where Catlin had seen Indians. He returned in Indian hunting dress with live deer, badgers, and foxes in addition to his portfolios and collected artifacts. His later years were spent at his Hudson River estate.

AUDUBON, John Woodhouse. Born Henderson, Ky 1812, died NYC 1862. Painter of wildlife, of the 49ers on the overland route, and of portraits. ANA 1847. Work in SW Mus (LA). References BEN-FIE (under Victor)-G&W-MAL-SMI. Sources COS-DBW-DWF-HUD-NA 74-TEP-*Cal Centennials Exhib of Art* LA Cnty MA 1949. Oil 22×27″ *Harris' Antelope Ground Squirrel* sold 1970 for $5,000 at auction. Monogram example "The Drawings of J W Audubon" 1957 Book Club of Cal.

Younger son of the legendary ornithologist J J Audubon, John Audubon was fonder of sports than studies when he was raised in the South. With his brother Victor, he was the pupil of his father in collecting specimens and sketching. In 1833 he accompanied his father on a field trip to Labrador and in 1834 the family went to Europe where John sketched. In 1837 Pres Jackson granted J J Audubon and John a Navy cutter to explore the Texas coast for birdlife. From 1839 on, John's residence was NYC. John returned to Texas in 1845 on a collecting trip for his father's "Quadrupeds of North America." He talked to Sam Houston and to the captain of the Texas Rangers about the cougar and the safest way to find one. The resulting painting of a cougar was regarded by J J Audubon as particularly fine. In 1846 John was again in Europe.

J J Audubon never reached the Rockies or the Far West, but when John was offered the post of commissary for Webb's California Company in 1849, he joined the party traveling from NYC to New Orleans by boat and then overland through Texas and Mexico to San Diego. En route, Audubon was given command of the company. He sketched on the trail but the way was rigorous so that paper was used for gun wadding and paints were abandoned in the desert. In California, Audubon toured the southern mines, making hundreds of sketches of sites like Wood's Diggings and Hawkins' bar. One batch of sketches was sent back to NYC and there disappeared. The remainder went with a friend who drowned at sea. The Southwest Museum has 34 pencil drawings and watercolors. In addition, Audubon later finished some sketches to illustrate his journal that was privately printed. In NYC, Audubon completed his father's work painting half of the illustrations for "Quadrupeds of North America."

AULT, George C. Born Cleveland, Ohio 1891, died Woodstock, NY 1948. Eastern realistic landscape and marine painter. Member SIA. Work in MMA, MOMA, WMAA, PAFA, BM, etc. References A53 (obit)-FIE-MAL. Sources ANT 7/73-CAA-DEP-DIG 2/49-190-NEU. Oil 14×18″ *Le Cap Gris Nez* 1911 sold 4/30/69 for $400 at auction. Oil 28×14″ *Desert Landscape* 1941 sold 5/16/73 for $275 at auction as part of Halpert colln. Signature example Ault 1969 catalog Zabriskie Gall. Painting examples p 124 DEP, p 26 NEU, p 107 190.

Ault was raised in London where his father introduced American printing ink to Europe by opening the Ault & Wiborg Printing Ink Co in 1899. He was educated at University College School and studied at Slade School, the department of art at London U, tutored by H Tonks and Wilson Steer, and St John's Wood Art School, the pupil of Orchardson and Clausen. While living in London, Ault spent his summers in France. In 1911 Ault returned to NYC and New Jersey, with summers in Provincetown, Mass. During the Depression he worked on WPA projects. Poor health in 1937 led Ault to Woodstock where he died in a flooded river. His painting *Universal Symphony* was hung during the funeral service.

In the work of Ault we had a "picture of the world reduced to blocks and cylinders," a simplified Cubist-realism. DEP. Other painters of the period with related styles would have been Sheeler, Lozowick, and Niles Spencer, interpreting native American subjects as abstract design. 190.

AUSTIN, Amanda Petronella (Mrs R Lee Allen). Born Carrollton, Mo 1856, died NYC 1917. Painter of landscapes, still-lifes, and portraits, sculptor. Work in Honeyman colln. References A15-BEN. Source HON. No current auction record or signature example.

Daughter of a doctor, Miss Austin was briefly a pupil of George Bingham in Missouri. In California she was the pupil of Bush and W F Jackson, then spent three years at the San Francisco School of Design, the pupil of Virgil Williams. She had her studio in California in 1884 where she painted a watercolor of Sutter's Fort in ruins. Her signatures were variously A P Austin, Amanda P Austin, and (early) A Austin.

She studied and exhibited painting and sculpture in Paris for four years, about 1911 to 1915. She was the pupil there of E Renard and Delecluse before marrying a doctor in 1917, the year of her death. When she died, she was sculpting for the city of Sacramento.

AUSTIN, Charles Percy. Born Denver, Colo 1883, died Santa Monica, Cal 1948. California poster designer, painter, illustrator, decorator. Work in Cal churches as decorations. References A53-FIE-MAL. Source BDW. Oil *After the Hunt* sold 3/6/71 for $100 at auction. No signature example.

Austin studied with Henry Read, at the Denver School of Art, at the ASL, with Twachtman, and with Castelucho in Paris. In 1930 Austin was the illustrator for the book "Capistrano Nights." His paintings include *Summer Morning Surf* and *Late Afternoon, Capistrano*.

AWA TSIREH (Alfonso Roybal). Born San Ildefonso Pueblo, NM about 1895, died there 1955. Important early Pueblo painter. Work in AMNH, BM, COR, Denver AM, MAI, MOMA, MNM, Philbrook AC, Smithsonian Inst. Reference MAL. Sources AHI 2/50,8/52-AIP. No auction record but the estimated price of a watercolor 16×20″ *Koshares as Clowns* would be about $1,000 to

$1,200 at auction in 1976. Signature example AHI 8/52.

Awa Tsireh (Cattail Bird) was educated in the primary grades at the Pueblo school. He was the nephew of Crescencio Martínez. By 1917 he was receiving commissions for paintings. Self-taught, he painted at the School of American Research along with Fred Kabotie and Velino Shije Herrera. John Sloan's influence entered Awa Tsireh's painting at the Society of Independent Artists in NYC in 1918. *The New York Times* called his drawings "as precise and sophisticated as a Persian miniature."

Awa Tsireh was the leader of the San Ildefonso artists. One of his styles was naïvely realistic, with perspective from a roof top as a Pueblo Indian would see dancers below. A second style combined realism with symbolism, as with realistic dancers climbing a rainbow. The third style is completely nonrealistic. It is this variety that led John Sloan to comment that Awa Tsireh "remembers not only the way a deer looks when leaping but feels himself leaping in the dance." AIP.

AYRES, Thomas A. Born New Jersey about 1820, died at sea near San Francisco 1858. Landscape and panorama painter of the Yosemite, illustrator. Work in HON, Yosemite Mus (drawings acquired from James Alden's family), NY Pub Lib. Reference G&W. Sources AOW-COW-HON. No auction record. Signature example pl 74 COS *The Mammoth Tree Grove.*

Ayres shipped to San Francisco via the *Panama* in 1849. After a year in the mines, he traveled widely in interior California as an artist sketching scenes of miners and Indians as well as views of the San Francisco area. Some of the work was for the publisher James Mason Hutchings who planned a new illustrated magazine. Hutchings was intrigued by stories of a thousand-foot waterfall that followed the 1851 discovery of Yosemite Valley by a volunteer battalion pursuing Indians. He organized an 1855 expedition with Ayres as artist. Using Indian guides, they followed an old Waiwona trail into the valley where they remained for five days. Ayres's black chalk on sandpaper drawing of the vista from Inspiration Point was the first depiction of the Yosemite. The drawing was made into a lithograph and was published in the initial issue of Hutchings' *California Illustrated* along with another three of the eight or ten made. Ayres's drawings were also the subject of a panorama *Yosemite Valley and Fall* with which the painter Thomas A Smith was associated. The panorama was successfully exhibited in Sacramento.

In 1856 Ayres made a second series of drawings of the Yosemite. These he took to NYC in 1857 for exhibition at the American Art-Union. The exhibition led to a commission from *Harper's* to illustrate articles on California. Ayres returned to Southern California where he completed a sketching trip at San Pedro in 1858. En route to San Francisco, he drowned when his ship sank in a storm.

BABCOCK, Dean. Born Canton, Ill 1888, living Longs Peak, Colo 1939 (died 1969 per BDW). Illustrator of Western subjects, painter, printmaker. Work (bookplates) in NY St Lib, Newark Pub Lib, DAM, U Denver Lib. References A38-BEN-FIE-MAL-SMI. Source BDW. No auction record but the published estimate is $200 to $300. No signature example.

Babcock was the pupil of John Vanderpoel, Robert Henri, and Helen Hyde. He illustrated "Songs of the Rockies" and "Westering." In 1938 he was research associate in the print department of DAM.

BABCOCK, Ida Dobson. Born Darlington, Wis 1870, living Redlands, Cal 1941. California landscape painter. Work in U of Neb Gall (Lincoln). References A41-MAL. Source BDW. No auction record or signature.

Ms Babcock was the pupil of William Lippincott, George de Forest Brush, and C F Browne. Her listed work was *The Desert Verbena in Winter*.

BACHMANN, Max. Born Brunswick, Germany 1862, active NYC by 1899, died NYC 1921. Sculptor of allegorical figures including typical Indian heads. Work, figures of the continents designed for Pulitzer Bldg in NYC. References A21 (obit)-FIE-MAL-SMI. Source BRO. Bronze, dark green patina, 21" high *Bust of Indian Warrior* dated 1902 estimated for sale 10/28/74 at $800 to $1,000 at auction in LA and sold for $700. A bronze figure of an Indian Chief, height 7½" inscribed Copyright 1908 by Theodore Starr Max Bachmann SC, sold at auction 10/10/75 for $2,000.

BACK, Joe W. Born Ohio 1899, living Dubois, Wyom, 1973. Wyom sculptor, painter, writer, specializing in horses with cowboy figures and in game animals. Honorary member CAA. No reference. Source WYA. No auction record. Signature example "Horses, Hitches and Rocky Trails" by Joe Back, 1959, Swallow Press. Sculpture examples p 18 *Jackson Hole Guide* 11/8/73.

Joe Back served in the Navy in WWI, then homesteaded in Wyoming in 1919 and worked as ranch hand on the Fiddleback Ranch, and as freighter, packer, and guide in the northwest mountains of Wyoming. He studied at the AIC 1925–27 and 1930–31, with St John, Poole, Philbrick, and Obertauffer. After returning to the cowboy role he calls an "old-time roughneck of the high Wyoming mountains," he began to sculpt during the winter of 1940. His materials are clay, plastic resin, plaster, fiberglass, and bronze. Listed sculpture titles include *Stop! My Hat's Gone* and *Git Over, Sunnybitch*. Back has also written and illustrated three lighthearted books, the first in 1959 detailing methods of packing into the mountains, with 52 drawings. Back's wife Mary attended the AIC with Back. She paints.

BACON, Frank. Reported as an English painter who traveled through the West. No direct reference or other source.

BWB and SSF mention a Frank Bacon raised on his father's sheep ranch near Marysville, Cal who was a photographer in Napa, Cal before winning fame with the play "Lightnin'."

MAL lists Frederick Bacon, an engraver, painter, and illustrator born London 1803 and died in California 1887. BEN and BRY state that Bacon retired to California in 1882.

BACON, Irving R. Born Fitchburg, Mass 1875, died El Cajon, Cal 1962. Detroit genre painter, illustrator, sculptor. Work in Art Assn (Louisville), Buffalo Bill Historical Center, Book Tower Club (Detroit), Hotel Irma (Cody), Edison Inst, Ford Mus. References A62-BEN-FIE-MAL-SMI. Sources BDW-WBB. No auction record but the published estimate is $200 to $300. This would not apply to Western work. No signature example.

Bacon studied at Gies Art School in Detroit, Chase School of Art, and the Royal Art Academy in Munich with von Zügel and von Marr. Bacon was the artist who designed the greyhound and quail radiator ornaments for Ford automobiles in the early 1930s and made museum reproductions of early Ford inventions. He also painted a series of portraits of notables: Henry Ford, Mark Twain, Geo Washington Carver, etc. One of his best-known paintings was *The Conquest of the Prairie*. The Buffalo Bill Historical Center, Cody, Wyoming, has a collection of Bacon's early historical paintings featuring Buffalo Bill Cody. These were painted from 1902 to 1911 while Cody was still living.

BAGG, Henry Howard. Born Wauconda, Ill 1852, died Lincoln, Neb 1928. Painter of Western life, teacher at Neb Wesleyan U and Cotner Col. References A28 (obit)-MAL. Source BDW. No auction record or signature example.

BAGLEY, James M. Born Maine 1837, died probably Denver, Colo 1910. Pioneer Colorado landscape painter, engraver. Work in DPL. No reference. Source DPL. No auction record or signature example.

A NYC wood engraver, Bagley worked in Denver beginning 1872. By 1880 he was painting Colorado scenes. Examples of his work are in the Denver Public Library.

BAKER, George Holbrook. Born East Medway, Mass 1827, died San Fran, Cal 1906. Cal artist, lithographer, publisher. Reference G&W. Sources ACM-COS. No recent auction record. Lithograph example p 276 ACM.

Baker was born in the home of his maternal grandfather, an organ builder and the first bell caster in America. His mother was a music teacher and singer. When he was 17 he was apprenticed to a commercial artist in NYC. He became a prize-winning art student at the NA because he grew bored drawing maps. In 1849 he joined a party of 12 bound for the gold fields traveling via Mexico "in preference to a long dreary voyage" around the Cape, surviving a battle with guerrillas in which "pistols were used on both sides." COS.

In San Francisco, Baker preferred the business of peddling Eastern goods to mining. He organized Baker's Express to bring the mail to the mines, sketching as he went. His close friend was George Henry Goddard, another artist. From 1852 to 1862 Baker was up river in Sacramento, engaged in various mercantile and publishing ventures including the firm of Barber & Baker turning out woodcut views of California. After the 1862 flood in Sacramento, Baker set up his lithographing business in San Francisco. In 1873 he made a sketching trip to Yosemite to provide views as a part of a Pacific Coast series of lithographs. Baker died in 1906, just before the great earthquake and fire. His diaries were preserved and published in the *Quarterly of the Society of California Pioneers*.

BAKER, H Ray. Born Thomas, Okla 1911, living Taos, NM 1971. Contemporary Western painter, commercial artist, author. Work in U of Wyom. No reference. Source HAR. No current auction record. Signature example p 15 HAR.

Baker's father was a cotton farmer and cattle rancher. After Baker graduated from high school in 1929, he worked as an itinerant sign painter throughout the West. In the 1930s he lived in Steamboat Springs, Colo, then moved to Denver as a commercial artist. From 1949 to 1969 Baker was editor and art director of the *Denver Post Sunday Empire Magazine*. His Western illustrations and manuscripts are in the H Ray Baker collection at the U of Wyoming.

BAKER, William Henry. Born Dallas, Tex 1899, living Ft Worth, Tex 1948. Painter, illustrator, muralist, teacher. Work in Ft Worth school; murals in post office. References A41-MAS. Sources TOB-TXF. No current auction record or signature example.

After graduating from high school in Dallas 1918, Baker worked in engineering while studying with Frank Reaugh. He moved to Chicago in 1924, studying at the AIC at night until 1928. Son of parents who were artists, Baker married a fellow student at the AIC, Ora Baker, while he was working as a commercial artist. The couple moved to Texas where Ora Baker became director of a Dallas gallery while William Baker was the commercial artist for the Fort Worth *Star Telegram*.

BAKOS, Jozef G (listed as Joseph up to 1941). Born Buffalo, NY 1891, living Sante Fe, NM 1976. Santa Fe painter, sculptor, teacher. Member, Los Cinco Pintores. Work in Hereford Assn (Kan

City—40 paintings), Ford Fndn, WMAA, BM, MNM, DAM, Roerich Mus (NY). References A59-BEN-FIE-MAL-SMI. Sources AIW-LOS-PET-TSF. No current auction record. Signature example p 83 TSF. (See illustration 7.)

Of Polish descent, Bakos studied at the Albright AS in Buffalo, in Toronto, and in Denver with John E Thompson. He was the first art instructor at the U of Colorado in Boulder. When he moved to Santa Fe in 1921, he built a studio on the Camino del Monte Sol near the others of Los Cinco Pintores. Bakos taught at the U of Denver 1931–33 and in the Santa Fe high school beginning 1940. His brightly colored painting style changed with the subject, from openness "conveying the largeness of the land" to "unexpectedly detailed" objects. TSF. His wife Teresa is also an artist.

"A sociable, ebullient person, an emotional and dramatic painter," Bakos was called one of "the five little nuts in five adobe huts." LOS. The Pintores—Bakos, Ellis, Mruk, Nash, and Shuster—in the early 1920s were the serious avant-garde artists in Santa Fe, although they were at first unable to earn a living through art. Bakos also worked as a carpenter and furniture maker. Their leisure hours were dedicated to fun, with frequent parties and homemade beer. By 1926 the Pintores were no longer exhibiting as a group.

BALDRIDGE, Cyrus Leroy. Born Alton, NY 1889, living Santa Fe, NM 1962. Illustrator, painter, printmaker, teacher. Member Artists Guild. Work in Fisk U (Nashville), BMFA, NY Pub Lib, MNM, NGA. References A62-BEN-FIE-MAL-SMI. Sources ILG-WHO 62. No current auction record but the published appraisal is $50 to $75 for prints. Signature example p 4 ILG.

Baldridge was graduated from the U of Chicago in 1911, becoming the pupil of

Frank Holme in Chicago. He was a WWI newspaper correspondent in 1914, enlisting with the French 1917 and the AEF 1918–19 when he became an artist for *Stars and Stripes*. Baldridge illustrated more than 40 books, specializing in African and Chinese subjects.

BALDWIN, Clifford Park. Born Cincinnati, Ohio 1889, living Oceanside, Cal 1962. Staff artist Southwest Mus (Los Angeles) 1933–41, illustrator, painter, photographer. Member Southwestern Archeological Soc. Work in Southwest Mus. References A62-MAL. Source BDW. No auction record or signature example.

Baldwin was the pupil of Jean Mannheim, Paul Lauritz, and George Otis. Books he illustrated included "Gypsum Cave" and "Navaho Weaving."

BALINK, Henry C (or Hendricus Cornelius). Born Amsterdam, Holland 1882, died Santa Fe, NM 1963. Santa Fe painter of Pueblo Indians, printmaker, teacher. Work in Henry B Balink colln, Harmsen colln, MNM. References A21-FIE. Sources COW-DCC-HAR-PIT-TSF-1917 letter Balink to MNM-Balink retrospective catalog 1966 MNM. No current auction record. Signature example p 14 PIT. (See illustration 8.)

After leaving home at 11, Balink studied from 1909 to 1914 at the Royal Academy in Amsterdam, the pupil of C L Dake, van der Waay, and Derkinderen. In 1914 he went to NYC "to do some copying" in the MMA on assignment from the Archaeological Museum in Berlin and the Louvre in Paris. "I moved to Chicago where I had portrait commissions and sold 18 paintings. I made a large mural but they wanted to cut the price for others. I was not satisfied so I wanted to go more West and I landed in Taos where I am now 6 weeks, and all ready I sold 5 pieces." 1917 Balink letter. It is said that Balink chose Taos and the West because of a railway poster he saw in a terminal. After returning from a visit to Holland and Germany in 1922, Balink settled in Santa Fe in 1923. His home and studio were on Old Pecos Road. By 1925 he was exhibiting Indian portraits and in 1927 he received the commission to paint portraits of Oklahoma Indian chiefs for the Marland Museum to be built in Ponca City.

Balink had had a classical master's art education. His graduation piece alone involved almost 300 studies, in the Barbizon tight brushwork and gray-brown palette. In New Mexico his brushwork loosened and his colors brightened into red and pink and purple. He carved his own frames to be integral with his many paintings of Indians and Southwestern landscapes.

BALLOU, Bertha. Born Hornby, NY 1891, living Spokane, Wash 1962. Washington painter, sculptor, teacher. Work in Eastern Wash Hist Mus, Spokane Pub Lib, Spokane Cnty Cthse, Wash St Col. References A62-MAL. Sources BDW-WAA. No auction record or signature example.

Ms Ballou was educated at Randolph-Macon Woman's College. She studied at the ASL, COR school, and BMFA school, the pupil of DuMond, Tarbell, Grafly, Blumenschein, etc. Beginning 1955 she was an instructor at Holy Names College in Washington State. Her painting in the Spokane Public Library is *Chief Joseph*.

BANCROFT, Albert Stokes. Born Denver, Colo 1890, died Bailey, Colo 1972.

Colo landscape painter, teacher, lawyer. Work in DAM, Lindbergh Mus (St Louis). References A62-MAL. Sources DPL-*Denver Post* 3/2/72 (obit). No auction record or signature example.

Albert S Bancroft, the son of a pioneer Denver family, was educated as a lawyer at Cornell, graduating in 1910. He practiced law in Denver until 1914 when he moved to Bailey. Self-taught as a painter, he exhibited nationally.

Lindbergh Peak was a high point of his career. It was commissioned by contributions from Colorado school children in 1929 as a gift to the aviator and hung in the Brown Palace Hotel where Lindbergh stayed. By 1930 Bancroft was accepting about 50 painting commissions a year, although he reduced his workload to 20 paintings a year when he was older.

BANCROFT, William Henry. Born Derby, Eng 1860, died Colo Springs, Colo 1932. Early Colo painter of landscapes. Work in Myron Stratton Home (Colo). No reference. Sources SHO-SPR. No current auction record but the estimated price of an oil 30×20" *The Miner's Wall* would be about $900 to $1,100 at auction in 1976. Signature example p 23 SHO *The Miner's Last Dollar.*

Son of a farmer, Bancroft was educated in Derby schools. He won a drafting scholarship to the RA and briefly studied drawing at the U of Manchester. At 15 he ran away, shipping to Nova Scotia, making his way to Santa Fe where he joined Gen Crook's scouts to fight the Apaches for two years. In 1878 he studied for a few months at the St Louis AS, but left for Leadville to decorate bars and paint signs. When Thomas Moran came to Leadville on a sketching trip, Bancroft carried Moran's paint box.

To become a landscape painter, Bancroft settled in Colorado Springs in 1881, after sketching with Joe Hitchens near Pueblo and with W H M Coxe. His first subjects were *Black Cañon, Bear Creek Cañon,* and *Morning on the Prairies,* exhibited in 1884. When "he found himself in hard luck, without a dollar, and in debt," a NYC merchant made a series of purchases that provided financial stability. Bancroft even tried to buy back a key still-life, offering 10 times the original price. He exhibited nationally and was commissioned by the Santa Fe RR to paint the Grand Canyon. With technique influenced by Harvey Young toward brighter colors and more dashing brushstrokes, a Bancroft landscape could be painted on location in one day.

BANVARD, John. Born NYC 1815, died Watertown, SD 1891. Panorama, landscape, and portrait painter, writer of fiction and travel books, poet. Work in Minn Hist Soc, Mus City NY. References BEN - DAB - FIE - G&W - MAL - SMI. Sources ALA-ANT 8/49,11/61-BAR-MIS-TEP. No current auction records. Signature example p 109 ANT 8/49. Painting example p 436 ANT 11/61, pp 53–54 MIS.

Banvard was the son of an architect who drew sketches for him of NYC buildings as they had been in Colonial times. In a happy boyhood while educated in NYC schools, "I remember gathering wild greens, for my mother to cook, in the open lots and fields in the vicinity of Canal Street and Broadway, before the creek was arched over and made into a subterranean canal." ANT 11/61. At 15, Banvard went to Louisville, Ky when his father died. Fired as a drugstore clerk, he turned to itinerant portrait painting, passing the 1830s traveling the Ohio and Mississippi Rivers from Cincinnati to New Orleans.

In 1840 he spent several months making 400 sketches of the Mississippi River below St Louis, then used a makeshift studio in Louisville to begin painting his panorama. In 1841 the panorama was displayed while it was in process. On its completion in 1846, it unrolled scenes of the Mississippi from the Missouri to New Orleans. Banvard took this "largest painting in the world" on a triumphal tour of the US. When exhibited in Boston in 1846 the "three-mile painting" inspired Whittier's poem "The Panorama." The greatest success was overseas, particularly in England through the blessing of Queen Victoria, but in its travels the panorama was first preserved only in a few sections, then lost entirely. On his return to the US, Banvard moved to the fabulous castle Glenada in Cold Spring Harbor on Long Island, NY. He traveled widely in Europe, Africa, and Asia, painting scenes in Palestine and making a panorama of the Nile. In 1861 the first chromo in the US was made from his painting *The Orison.* Then in 1880 he settled with his children in Watertown, SD, a rough Western town where Banvard began writing about and drawing the old NYC buildings he had known as a child.

BARCHUS, Eliza R (Mrs John H Barchus). Born Salt Lake City, Utah 1857, died Portland, Ore 1959. Landscape painter specializing in mountains. Work in Portland church (22 oil paintings) and in collns of Woodrow Wilson, Theodore Roosevelt, and William Jennings Bryan. No reference. Sources ANT 7/61 p 2-WNW. Oil on board 10×12" *Sunset at Mt Hood* with signature example and stamped J H Barchus sold 11/16/73 for $400 at auction. Oil 20× 30" *Sunrise on the Hills* signed Eliza R Barchus estimated at $400–$500 for sale 3/4/74 at auction in LA and sold for $175. (See illustration 9.)

Mrs Barchus was the pupil of Will S Parrott in Portland. She was exhibiting in Portland by 1888 and at the NAD in NYC by 1900. ANT 7/61 p 2 offers for

$135 what appears similar to *Sunset at Mt Hood* above, dating it about 1875 and calling it *Mt Shasta.*

BARKER, Charles F. Born London, Eng 1875, living Victoria, BC 1941. Canadian landscape painter. No reference. Source WNW. No auction record or signature example.

Barker studied with John Innes after Innes moved to Vancouver in 1913, and with J Radford. He worked in oils and watercolor showing his work in Victoria, Vancouver, and Toronto. Two of his works, *Mt Burgess* and *Cathedral Peak,* are in the Douglas & Co collection in Vancouver.

BARKER, George. Born Omaha, Neb 1882, died Pacific Palisades, Cal 1965. California painter, lecturer. Work in Olympic Lib (LA), Joslyn AM (Omaha). References A62-MAL. Sources BDW-SCA. No auction record or signature example.

Barker studied with J Laurie Wallace and Edwin Scott before going to Grande Chaumière in Paris, the pupil of André Lhote. He lectured on "French Painting" and "Explorations in Color." His wife was Olive R Barker who also painted.

BARKER, Olive Ruth (Mrs George Barker). Born Chicago, Ill 1885, living Pacific Palisades, Cal 1962. California painter. Work in schools and hospital. References A62-MAL. Sources BDW-SCA-WAA. No auction record or signature example.

Mrs Barker studied at the NY School of Fine and Applied Art (Paris branch)

and at the Oberlin Conservatory, the pupil of J Laurie Wallace, Paul Sample, Millard Sheets.

BARNES, Matthew Rackham. Born Scotland 1880, died San Francisco, Cal 1951. San Francisco painter. References A41-MAS. Sources AAT-BDW. No auction record. Signature example p 54 AAT.

Barnes was winning prizes in San Francisco by 1926.

BARNETT, Isa. Born Carbondale, Pa 1924, living probably Philadelphia, Pa 1966. Magazine illustrator, teacher. Work in "Illustrators 59." No reference. Sources ILA-IL 59. No current auction record. Signature example ⚡89 IL 59.

Barnett studied at the Philadelphia Mus SA and the Barnes Fndn, the pupil of Henry Pitz, Robert Riggs, and Robert Fawcett. After serving as a paratrooper in WWII he sold his first illustration to *Argosy*. IL 59 shows a painting for *American Weekly*. Other commissions have come from *Life, The Saturday Evening Post, Cosmopolitan, Outdoor Life,* etc. Barnett has taught at the Philadelphia Mus SA, Moore Inst, and the Philadelphia College of Art.

BARNOUW, Dr. Adriaan Jacob. Born Amsterdam, Holland 1877, living NYC 1953. Historian, lecturer, Taos painter. Work in HAW. Reference A53. Sources TAL-WHO 50. No current auction record. Painting example *Taos Indian Man* TAL.

Dr Barnouw received his PhD from U of Leyden in Holland in 1902. He taught Dutch Language and Literature at The Hague 1902–19, English at U of Leyden 1907–13. He was correspondent and editor 1913–21, and thereafter Professor of Dutch Language and Literature at Columbia U in NYC. His specialty was the art history of the Low Countries.

It was said that Dr Barnouw was "definitely a Taos painter" in his "interpretation of Taos Valley and the Indian life," even though he was a visitor rather than resident. TAL. His paintings in the Harwood Fndn colln are *Taos Landscape* and *Portrait of Andrew Dasburg*.

BARR, Paul E. Born Goldsmith (Tipton Cnty), Ind 1892, died Grand Forks, ND 1953. North Dakota landscape painter, teacher. Member NIAL. Work in IBM colln, Capitol Bldg (Bismarck), U North Dakota, other colleges and schools. References A53-MAL. Source BDW. No auction record or signature example.

Barr was educated at the U Chicago, U Indiana, Sorbonne, U Paris, and U North Dakota. He became the head of the art department at the U North Dakota in 1928. His paintings were exhibited nationally beginning 1936. Barr's landscapes include views of the Badlands.

BARR, William. Born Glasgow, Scotland 1867, died San Francisco, Cal 1933. Landscape and portrait painter, illustrator. Work in City Hall and Union League Club (San Francisco), town of Paisley colln. References A33 (obit)-BEN-FIE-MAL-SMI. Source BDW. No current auction record or signature example.

Barr studied at the Glasgow School of Art, at South Kensington school in London, and at the Julien Academy in Paris. He settled in San Francisco in 1915 and devoted himself to "portraying the beauty of California, and its historic associations both in landscape and in portraiture." A33 (obit).

BARRETT, Lawrence Lorus. Born Guthrie, Okla 1897, died Colo Springs, Colo 1973. Colo painter, illustrator, printmaker, sculptor, teacher, writer. Work in MMA, Colo Spr FAC, BM, Carnegie Inst, Lib Cong. References A53-MAS. Sources AAT-BRO-CAP-SHO. No recent auction record but the published estimate for prints is $100 to $150. Signature example p 53 SHO.

Barrett was raised in Hutchinson, Kan. He studied at the Broadmoor AA beginning 1920, the pupil of Robert Reid, Randall Davey, Ernest Lawson, J F Carlson, and Boardman Robinson. From 1937 to 1952 he was instructor in lithography at Broadmoor and Colo Spr FAC. A Guggenheim Fellow in 1940, he and Rudolph Dehn wrote the 1946 text on lithography. Barrett wrote the lithography article in the ENB. CAP reproduced *Horse Wrangler,* while *Bucking Horse* was Barrett's 1966 prize-winning bronze.

BARSE, George Randolph, Jr. Born Detroit, Mich 1861, died probably Katonah, NY 1938. Decorative figure and portrait painter in Tex about 1886, engineer. Member SAA 1889, ANA 1898, NA 1900. Work Lib Cong, Carnegie Inst, Syracuse MFA, Kan City AI, Minneapolis IA. References A41 (obit)-BEN-FIE-MAL-SMI. Sources KEN 6/71-NA 74-WHO 30. Pastel 30×18″ *Two Muses* sold 1969 for $25 at auction; this is no index of value for a Barse Western painting. Signature example KEN 6/71.

Barse had a public school education in Kansas City, Mo. From 1878–85 he studied in Paris at the École des Beaux-Arts and Julien Academy, with Cabanel, Boulanger, and Lefebvre. Before settling down in Katonah, NY as a decorative portraitist, he visited Texas. KEN 6/71 reproduced an 1886 painting of two cowboys on the LX Ranch in the Panhandle at a time when the ranch was owned by foreign investors while the cattle business was at the height of its early development.

Barse went on to win the first Hallgarten prize at NAD in 1895, the Shaw fund purchase in 1898 for *The Night and the End of the Day,* and the silver medal at the Pan-Am Exposition in Buffalo in 1901. He had married Rose Ferrara of Rome in 1891.

BARTHOLOMEW, William Newton. Born Boston, Mass 1822, died Newton Centre, Mass 1898 (or, living there 1905. A05). Boston landscape and portrait painter in Cal 1850–52, teacher, writer. References A05-G&W-MAL (necrology indicates this to be properly W H Bartholomew as in A19-BEN-SMI, the Brooklyn pioneer in color engraving). Source BDW. No auction record or signature example.

Bartholomew was trained as a cabinetmaker but quit for painting. In 1850 he went to California with J Wesley Jones, the daguerreotypist. He then taught drawing in Boston high schools 1852–71 and wrote drawing books.

BARTLETT, Dana. Born Ionia, Mich 1878, died Los Angeles, Cal 1957. California landscape painter, illustrator, etcher, teacher. Work in Sacramento St Lib, LAMA, SW Mus, Huntington colln, LA Pub Lib, schools. References A59 (obit)-BEN-FIE-MAL-SMI. Source BDW. No current auction record but the published estimate is $150 to $200. No signature example.

Bartlett studied at the ASL and was the pupil of Wm M Chase and Coussens in Paris. Typical painting titles were *California Landscape, High Sierras, The Blue Hill.*

BARTLETT, Gray. Born Rochester, Minn 1885, died Los Angeles, Cal 1951. Western genre painter of nostalgic cowboys and Indians. Work in Ariz St U, Santa Fe RR colln. No reference. Sources ACO-COW-GWP-PAW. No auction record. Signature example p 27 GWP (brand following signature not used in early painting).

Bartlett's family moved to Colorado about 1890. He became a working cowboy when he was 16, making untutored paintings of Western scenes. He then studied art at the Greeley (Colo) Art School and at AIC on scholarship. When his mother died, he returned to Colorado to help support the family as a commercial artist for photoengravers. With $1,800 that he borrowed, he bought an interest in an engraving firm, retiring in 1937 after business successes.

In California when he was 52, he began painting again, traveling to Arizona, New Mexico, Texas, Colorado, and Utah. He had studios in California and Utah, a cattle ranch in Utah, and he visited among the Indians. "While out on these trips I make numerous pencil sketches of anything which might be useful in the makeup of a painting. I also take many photographs of people and scenery. Much of the material I get is retained in my memory and when the time comes for the painting to be put on canvas, I do this in my studio." GWP.

Soc in 1831, and drew two views of Dighton Rock inscriptions for the Society. Bartlett moved to NYC as an importer of foreign books, was elected Secretary of the NYHS, and wrote well-known texts such as "Dictionary of Americanisms."

When he retired from business at 45, Bartlett was appointed by Pres Taylor as US Commissioner during 1850–53 for the US-Mexico boundary survey. Although a bookish man, Bartlett sought the political post because of his study of Indian languages. To find Indians for word testing, Bartlett wandered far from the border he was surveying, charging the unauthorized expenses to the survey appropriation. Bartlett as an amateur artist also worked with the official artist for the survey, H C Pratt, who made hundreds of sketches of the botany and zoology, the towns and terrain, as well as oil portraits of Indians. In the final report titled "Personal Narrative of Explorations and Incidents in Texas, New Mexico, California, Sonora, and Chihuahua, Connected with the US and Mexico Boundary Commission," Bartlett used some of his own sketches rather than those of Pratt, to the artistic detriment of the report according to AIW and KW1. When Bartlett returned to Rhode Island, he was elected Secretary of State each term for 17 years. In 1882 he published an indispensable bibliography on early Americana.

BARTLETT, John Russell. Born Providence, RI 1805, died there in 1886. Amateur artist, historian, ethnologist, bibliographer. References DAB-G&W. Sources AIW-KW1-PAF-SUR-TEP. No auction record or signature example. *Portrait of J R Bartlett* by H C Pratt ✳155 ACM.

Educated in Canadian schools, Bartlett returned to Providence in 1824 as a bank cashier. He was elected to the RI Hist

BARTLETT, Paul Wayland. Born New Haven, Conn 1865, died Paris, France 1925. Expatriate classical sculptor. ANA 1916, NA 1917, NSS, NIAL, Commander Legion of Honor 1924. Work in BM, AIC, MMA, Luxembourg Mus (Paris), PAFA, Lib Cong, statues, doors, pediments, etc. References A25 (obit)-BEN-DAB-ENB-FIE-MAL-SMI. Sources ALA-AMA-ANT 7/73-COR-MSL-M19-NA 74-SCU-WHO 24. No auction record. Sculpture example p 91

SCU *Bohemian Bear Tamer.* (See illustration 10.)

Paul Bartlett was the son of a Boston sculptor-teacher who carried out his vow never to have a son get his art education in the US. Raised in Paris, Bartlett entered the École des Beaux-Arts at 15, the pupil of Cavelier and Frémiet. His first sculpture was of animals. By 1887 he was winning awards at the Paris Salon and by 1895 the French Government had awarded him its ribbon of honor. He made frequent trips to the US to accept commissions such as statues for the Rotunda of the Lib of Cong, marble figures for the NY Pub Lib, the pediment for the House of Representatives, and the bronze equestrian statue of Lafayette in the Louvre.

A favorite bronze at MMA is the *Bohemian Bear Tamer* shown at the Paris Salon in 1887. As an American artist, Bartlett chose an American Indian boy and a pair of cubs to represent the Bohemian and his animals. PAFA describes *Ghost Dancer* exhibited at the World's Columbian Expos in 1893 as "a lithe savage performing a tribal rite." DAB. *Preparedness,* a bronze statuette of an eagle, was modeled the day after the sinking of the *Lusitania* in 1916. As a mature man, Bartlett's step was springy. He wore a Van Dyke beard below a strong aquiline nose, and had brilliant blue eyes and a broad brow.

BARTOLI, J (or F). 18th-century portrait painter. Work in NYHS. References BEN-G&W-MAL-SMI. Source, 1796 portrait of the Seneca Indian chief Ki-on-twog-ky, Cornplanter. No current auction record. Painting example NYHS 1974 brochure.

Bartoli exhibited at the Royal Academy in London up to 1783. He was working in NYC before 1796, having also painted a portrait of George Washington at about that time.

BARTON, Loren Roberta (Mrs Perez Rogers Babcock, Mrs Jervis R Miller). Born Oxford, Mass 1893, living Pomona, Cal 1975. Modern Cal painter, illustrator, etcher, teacher. Fellow RSA (London). Work in AIC, Cal St Lib, NGA, BM, San Diego FAG, MMA, etc. References A59-BEN-FIE-MAL-SMI. Sources CON-WAA-W64-WHO 70. No current auction record but the published estimate for prints is $80 to $100. Signature example plate 1 CON.

Born in the home of her great-aunt Clara, the founder of the American Red Cross, Loren Barton was raised in California and educated at the U of Southern California. She began the study of painting at an early age. As an artist, she believed in "beauty and high ideals of strong, healthy lovers of life who face a world courageously and defiantly." CON. She was known for her studies of the historic Spanish types in California. Among the many books she illustrated were "Spanish Alta California" and "California" in 1938.

BASSETT, Reveau Mott. Born Dallas, Tex 1897, living there 1973. Tex painter of birds and landscapes, etcher, teacher. NA 1925. Work in Dallas Hall of State, Dallas MFA. References A53-FIE-MAL. Sources COW-TOB-TXF. No current auction record. Painting example opp p 96 TXF *Marsh Twilight.*

Son of a Texas engineer and railroad builder, Reveau Bassett studied briefly at the ASL, the pupil of Pennell for etching, Leigh, and Boardman Robinson, as well as at the NAD with Curran. Considered mainly self-taught, Bassett also sketched with Frank Reaugh in New Mexico, West Texas, and the Dallas area. He visited Taos with Alexandre Hogue, SW Texas with Charles E Cusack, and East Texas with John Douglass. Typical Bassett painting titles are *The Old Church in Arroya Secco, Texas Stubblefield, Duck*

Time. Bassett has been an artist for the Dallas MNH and instructor in etching at Dallas AI. His first national recognition was at the 100th annual NAD exhibition in 1925. Frank Reaugh said then that "to have one's work" so "hung might be truly said to put one in the frame." TXF.

BATTESE, Stanley. Born Fort Defiance, Ariz 1936, living Gallup, NM 1968. Navaho painter. No reference. Sources AHI 7/56,8/68-AIP-COW. No auction record. Signature example, cover AHI 8/68.

Battese's Navaho name is Kehdoyah, Follower. He graduated from St Michael's Catholic High School in Arizona in 1956 and received his degree from Arizona State College at Tempe in 1961. He has since then been a teacher and a blue collar worker.

After grammar school, Battese had studied art under Martha Kenney in Gallup, showing promise as a pianist as well as a watercolorist. He is said to have made remarkable progress as a painter while in school but to have lost interest after graduating.

BAUMANN, Gustave. Born Magdeburg, Germany 1881, died Santa Fe, NM 1971. Santa Fe painter of Indian figures and landscapes, woodblock printmaker, woodcarver, writer. Work in MMA, NYPL, AIC, MNM, BMFA, NGA, NGC, etc. References A62-BEN-FIE-MAL-SMI. Sources AAT-AIW-PIT-TSF-WHO 54. No current auction record for paintings but woodcut 12×10¾″ printed in five colors *Aspen Thicket* was estimated for sale 10/27/74 at $400 to $600 at auction. Signature example p 17 PIT. (See illustration 11.)

Baumann was brought to Chicago with his family in 1891. He studied drawing and printmaking at the Kunstgewerbe Schule in Munich and then at the AIC. Moving to Indiana, he designed, cut, and printed woodblocks illustrative of Indiana authors. Exhibiting nationally and in Paris, by 1915 he won the printmaking award at the San Francisco Expos.

After a few years of pampering his "wanderlust," he settled in Santa Fe in 1918, one of the colony's founders along with John Sloan, Randall Davey, and Fremont Ellis. Continuing as a rare worker in woodblocks, he also painted in bright colors. His paintings were sometimes for fun, a *Deer Dance* showing the dancers as the animals and *Pasa Tiempo* as a kachina ceremony with dolls dancing. After 1931 he worked with the Marionette Theater, carving his own "little people." PIT. Baumann wrote and illustrated "Frijoles Canyon Pictographs" selected as one of 50 books of the year 1940. His woodcuts were his own version of the sacred Indian pictographs of northern New Mexico. Baumann also carved church figures, saying, "If a man had to harp on one string, he'd go flat." PIT.

BAUMHOFER, Walter Martin. Born Brooklyn, NY 1904, living Northport, NY 1976. Magazine illustrator including Western subjects, painter. Member SI. Work in Custer Mus (Monroe, Mich), Dept of Agri (DC), Riveredge Fndn (Calgary), Northport bank and school. References A76-MAS. Sources data from Walter Baumhofer-ILA. No auction record. Signature example p 171 ILA. (See illustration 12.)

Baumhofer studied at Pratt Institute in Brooklyn in 1923 and was the pupil of Dean Cornwell. He began doing black and white headings for *Adventure* and sold his first pulp cover in 1926, developing "a bold, dramatic approach" that "has characterized his work ever since."

ILA. By 1933 Baumhofer received a contract from Street & Smith to do 50 covers a year. He also painted the original covers for *Doc Savage* magazine.

In 1936 Baumhofer painted 84 illustrations for Street & Smith, *Popular,* and *Liberty,* a total he now considers "incredible." His calendar subjects were historical, hunting dogs, horses, and fishing. His work appeared in *Argosy, Outdoor Life, Sports Afield,* and *American* as well as *Woman's Day* and *Ladies' Home Journal.* All of the books that have been written on the pulp magazines mention Walter Baumhofer's illustrations, and one of the books reproduces Baumhofer's paintings on its dust jacket.

BAUR, Theodore. Born Württemberg, Germany 1835, living NYC 1894, active Germany 1902. Sculptor, including Indian bronzes, decorator. Member Fellowcraft Club in NY, 1894. Work in DAM, Eiteljorg colln. No reference. Sources BRO-*Century* mag, vol 20, p 97-DAA-DCC-KEN 5/65-NYPL. No current auction record but the estimated price of a bronze sculpture 25" *Indian Chief* would be about $5,000 to $6,000 at auction in 1976. Sculpture example p 31 DAA. Signature example *Century* mag above.

Baur "came to America at the age of 15. In Ottawa he designed much of the rich and tasteful sculptured ornament in the Parliament Houses, and in New York, he has adorned the mansions of our millionaires. A bronze head of an Indian, modelled upon the suggestion of the head of Sitting Bull, though not as a portrait, is Mr Baur's most recent and striking work." NYPL. An 1885 lost wax bronze *Head of Indian Chief* was cast by The Henry Bonnard Bronze Co, NY and was signed Th Baur. This appears to have been the first work of Baur's "given to the public under his own name." DAA.

BEAMENT, Thomas Harold. Born Ottawa, Ont, Can 1898, living Montreal, PQ 1976. Realistic Can landscape and figure painter in the Arctic 1947. Assoc RCA 1935, RCA 1946. Work in NGC, Archives Can, Montreal MFA, Quebec Provincial Mus, AG Hamilton. References A76-MAL. Sources DCA-NGC catalog p 7 with painting example. No current auction record. (See illustration 13.)

Harold Beament grew up in Ottawa and was in the Naval Reserve in WWI. He studied law in Toronto and also painting with J W Beatty in 1922. Admitted to the bar as a lawyer in 1923, he joined the Navy in 1924 and served as a command officer in WWII. Beament continued to paint and exhibit and was a Naval War Artist 1943–47.

After retirement in 1947, Beament studied the Eskimos at Baffin Island and traveled the ten Canadian provinces as well as Europe and the US. Called a "landscape, figure, and marine painter of decorative realistic style," he has taught in Montreal and in Nova Scotia.

BEARD, Daniel Carter. Born Cincinnati, Ohio 1850, died Suffern, NY 1941. Illustrator of the outdoors and wildlife including Western animals, painter, cartoonist of historical Americana, teacher, writer. Member SI. Work in Lib Cong, magazines, newspapers, books. References A47 (obit)-BEN-FIE-MAL-SMI. Sources NCB-POW-WHO 40. No current auction record; the published estimate of $300 to $400 would be insufficient for a Western subject in 1976. Signature example and portrait NCB.

The fourth son of the painter James H Beard, Dan Beard was educated in the Cincinnati public schools and in Worrall's Academy in Covington, Ky. Good in math but poor in language, he failed the Naval Academy exam and was employed by a NYC mapmaker as a surveyor. Said to have visited "every town on the east side of the Mississippi river between the gulf and the lakes," he made drawings of fish, which were seen and published. As a result, "Mr Beard dropped the tripod" to pick up the brush. NCB. At the ASL, Beard was the pupil of Sartain and Beckwith.

As illustrator and writer, Beard's specialty was the outdoor life including Western animals. He was the author in 1882 of "American Boys' Handy Book." He drew for *Cosmopolitan, Harper's, Century, Scribner's, Life, Puck, Judge,* etc. He edited for the *Ladies' Home Journal, Woman's Home Companion, American Boy, NY Herald,* etc. He illustrated the works of Mark Twain. As a teacher, he held the first class in animal drawing 1893–1900 at the Woman's School of Applied Design. In 1910 Dan Beard became a household name as the founder of the Boy Scouts in the US. Mt Beard near Mt McKinley was named for him.

BEARD, George. Born Stone Heads, Cheshire, Eng 1855, died Coalville, Utah 1944. Pioneer Utah landscape painter. Work in Utah St Inst FA. No reference. Sources PUA-YUP. No auction record. Painting example p 14 PUA *Tetons, Wyo, Lee Creek Divide.*

George Beard was born in Robin Hood and druid country and went to work at 11. His mother died at sea during their 52-day voyage to the US when he was 13. The company of Mormons he was with went by rail to Benton City, west of Omaha, and then to Utah by ox train. As a Mormon, Beard settled in Coalville where he worked on a farm, hauled coal, and in 1870 began working for the co-op. He also served as doctor, nurse, and politician.

Sketching and painting were his hobbies. They reflected his love of the high mountain country though which he trav-

eled, "climbing every old mountain worth while in this section of the West." PUA. He specialized in scenes of the Uinta Mtns, painted in a large atmospheric treatment based on Bierstadt and Thomas Moran. YUP.

BEARD, James Carter. Born Cincinnati, Ohio 1837, died New Orleans, La 1913. Illustrator of nature and animal life said to have been in the West about 1880, painter, writer. Work in ACM, Stenzel colln. References A14 (obit)-BEN-DAB-G&W-MAL-SMI. Sources ACM-AIW-PNW-POW-WHO 12. No current auction record; the published estimate of $300 to $400 is not applicable to a Western scene in 1976. Signature example ⚹14 ACM *Three Buffaloes and a Calf.*

The oldest son of the painter J H Beard, J Carter Beard was privately educated in Cincinnati. He read law with Rutherford B Hayes (later President of US) and was admitted to the bar 1861. After he won his first case, he handed his diploma to his father, saying, "I did this for you. I am now going into art for myself." DAB. In the Civil War, he served with the Hundred Days' volunteers.

Until 1910 Beard lived in Brooklyn. He drew and wrote for *Harper's, St Nicholas, Century, Outing, Country Life,* etc, specializing in animals, and was an editor for D Appleton & Co. In 1886, he was chosen to illustrate Theodore Roosevelt's "Hunting Trips of a Ranchman" with seven animal heads and two habitat drawings (*The Bighorn at Home* opp p 230 is easily the most elaborate). Beard is one of the small group of Western artists whose careers preceded 1885, so that their firsthand experiences occurred within the "old days." POW. On the other hand, Roosevelt in his introduction notes that the illustrations for his book were mainly from photographs and from stuffed heads.

BEARD, James Henry. Born Buffalo, NY 1812, died Flushing, LI, NY 1893. Painter of the South and Southwest genre, portraits, and domestic animals. Honorary NA 1848, NA 1872. References BEN-CHA-DAB-FIE-MAL-SMI. Sources ANT 1/46,12/57,6/66,1/70;2, 4/74-BAR-BOA-COO-HUT-POW-STI-TEP. Oil 19¾×23¾″ *The Ohio Land Speculator* sold 10/27/71 for $3,750 at auction. Signature example p 379 ANT 2/74 *Good-Bye, Ole Virginia* dated 1872.

James H Beard was raised in the northern Ohio wilderness in Painesville. When Beard was 12, his father died. Beard became a portrait painter after four lessons for $2 from the itinerant Hanks. At 14 he left home for Pittsburgh and the river cities to paint, charging $5 for a head portrait and $15 for a bust including the hand holding a book. Beard settled in Cincinnati in 1834, a successful painter of children and of prominent politicians—John Quincy Adams, Henry Clay, Presidents Taylor and Harrison.

In 1846 Beard moved his studio to NYC. His painting *North Carolina Emigrants* (p 42 ANT 7/65) exhibited at the NA was sold for $750, the highest price then paid to an American artist. The subject of the westward movement was popular for Beard. During the Civil War, Beard served as a staff captain with Gen Lew Wallace. He exhibited from 1871 to 1884. Known as the "Landseer of America," he devoted himself in his later years to painting domestic animals acting as humans. His brother William Holbrook Beard was equally famous as an animal painter, his four sons became artists of note, and his daughters were illustrators.

BEARD, Thomas Francis (known as "Frank"). Born Cincinnati, Ohio 1842, died Chicago, Ill 1905. Social and moral illustrator, war correspondent, cartoonist. Work reproduced in periodicals. References A05 (obit)-BEN-FIE-MAL-SMI. Sources BEY-KW2-PAF-WHO 05. No current auction record. Signature example p 101 BEY.

Part of the Beard family of artists, Frank Beard was educated in Cincinnati and Painesville. At 12 he was sending sketches for publication. At 18 he served in the Civil War and at the same time was special artist for *Leslie's* and *Harper's Weekly*. After the war, Beard originated "chalk talks," lectures illustrated with quick drawings.

Beard was one of the former Civil War correspondents engaged to illustrate Richardson's "Beyond the Mississippi" in 1867. The eight drawings show Kansas, Indian Territory, Santa Fe, and Denver. AIW notes that the "Beyond" sketches were probably redrawn from earlier depictions. Beard became a Chautauqua lecturer for 17 years, professor of painting at Syracuse U, editor of *Judge,* writer of short stories, and cartoonist for religious causes. "His cartoons against the evils of the liquor traffic were often extremely effective." A05.

BEARD, William Holbrook. Born Painesville, Ohio 1824, died NYC 1900. Eastern animal, landscape, portrait painter in the Rockies 1866. NA 1862. Work in AIC, NYHS, Buffalo FAG. References A00 (obit)-BEN-CHA-DAB-ENB-FIE-G&W-MAL-SMI. Sources AIW-ANT 7/65,4/67,5/72;1,9/74-BAR-BOA-COO-HUT-ISH-PAF-POW-STI-TEP-WHO 00. Oil 18×24″ *An Indian Idyll* sold 10/22/69 for $3,000. Signature example p 10 ANT 1/74 *Indian Girl* 1876. Portrait drawing CHA.

W H Beard grew up in a wilderness town with more interest in nature and sports than schooling. The pupil of his older brother John Henry Beard, he set off as an itinerant portrait painter, as had his brother before him. In 1845 he joined his brother in NYC, then in 1850 established a studio in Buffalo, a former family home. By 1856 he was successful enough to undertake the traditional two-year tour of Europe. In a summer at Düsseldorf and sketching in Switzerland, France, and Rome, he associated with important American artists like S R Gifford and Whittredge. Beard moved back to NYC in 1860. He was "so successful with humorous story-pictures of animals that he was condemned to paint animals acting like human beings all the rest of his life." DAB.

One break in Beard's routine came in 1866. He joined the writer Bayard Taylor in a trip across the plains to Colorado, traveling by overland stage from Kansas to Denver. He wrote, "Safe at Denver at last! From the stories of Indians I did not feel I should ever reach here. I only saw a few Buffalo on the plains but enough to study them, and ascertain they are not very available for pictures." After two weeks touring in Colo, he added, "The fact is I am disappointed in the Rocky Mts somewhat." AIW. The trip at least qualified Beard as a buffalo judge, a position to which the painter W J Hays had nominated Beard in resolving a question of the placement of the hump on a buffalo.

BEARDSLEY, Jefferson. Genre painter active in Ithaca, NY and NYC in 1859. Painter of *The Prairie Fire* signed J Beardsley dated 1857 and illustrated p 12 in DWF. Reference G&W. Source DWF. No current auction record but the estimated price of a major Western genre oil would be about $2,000 to $2,500 at auction in 1976.

Jefferson Beardsley exhibited at the NA in NYC in 1859.

30

BEATIEN YAZZ (Jimmy Toddy). Born near Wide Ruins, Ariz 1928, living Chambers, Ariz 1967. Navaho painter in casein, illustrator, commercial artist. Work in Bern Mus (Switzerland), GIL, MAI, MNM, Philbrook AC, Southeast Mus (Fla), Southwest Mus (LA). Sources AHI 7/56,12/58,7/59,8/68-AIP-COW. No auction record. Signature example back cover AHI 8/68.

Bea Etin Yazz, Little No Shirt in Navaho, known as Jimmy, was recognized as an artist while drawing with crayons at 8. He was educated at Santa Fe Indian Art School. During WWII, he served as a combat communications specialist with the Navaho Signal Corps of the US Marines when the Navaho language was used as an "unbreakable" code.

He became famous as Little No Shirt in Alberta Hannum's 1945 book "Spin a Silver Dollar" about his early struggles and successes. He worked in the Navaho Police Department and as an art teacher before becoming a full-time artist. He received a scholarship to Mills in 1949, studying under Kuniyoshi. Alberta Hannum's second book, "Paint the Wind," was published in 1958. Beatien Yazz paintings emphasize animals and people, not landscapes, and evidence color, action, imagery, and feeling for the beautiful.

BEATTY, John William. Born Toronto, Ont, Can 1869, died there in 1941. Landscape painter of the Ontario Northland and the Rockies, teacher. Assoc RCA 1903, RCA 1913. Work in NGC, Ontario Col of Art, AG of Toronto. Reference MAL. Sources CAH-CAN-DCA. No current auction record. Signature example p 79 CAN.

Beatty quit school early, became a house painter, and then volunteered for military service in the Riel Rebellion in 1885. A member of the Toronto Fire Brigade from 1889 to 1900, he studied painting as the pupil of William Cruikshank and F M Bell-Smith. His savings took him to Paris in 1901, the pupil of Laurens and Constant. In 1906 he returned to Europe, the pupil of Burroughs in London, studied in Paris, and traveled until 1909. Beginning 1912 Beatty taught painting at the Ontario College of Art until he died.

His landscapes developed from the traditional rich and dark European styles to something of the bright Canadian nationalistic lyricism of his friend Tom Thomson and the Group of Seven. Beatty was one of the first of the painters into the Ontario Northland after the turn of the century. Before 1910 the Canadian Northern Ry commissioned A Y Jackson and Beatty to paint scenes of the laying of tracks through the Rockies. Other members of the Group went into the Northwest later, but outstripped Beatty in their development as painters. "Though he went on many sketching trips to Algonquin Park and to the Rockies, his chief interest remained in the cultivated countryside, his placid pictures at variance with his forceful personality." CAN.

BEAUGUREAU, Francis Henry. Born Chicago, Ill 1920, living Scottsdale, Ariz 1972. Painter, illustrator, teacher. Work in Phoenix AM, Depts Air Force and Army, Frye Mus (Seattle). Reference A59. Source AHI 3/66. No current auction record. Signature example p 11 AHI 3/66.

Francis Beaugureau studied at Mizen Academy and AIC. He painted illustrations for the USAF in 1951–52, working as consultant in the formulation of an art program and the USAF museum.

BEAULAURIER, Leo James. Born Great Falls, Mont 1912, living there 1974. Traditional Western painter, illustrator, muralist. Murals in post offices. References A53-MAS. Sources MON-WNW. No current auction record. Signature example p 183 MON.

Beaulaurier studied for three years at the U of Notre Dame, then worked at odd jobs until 1936 when he studied at the Los Angeles Art Center until WWII. After the war he entered his family's construction business.

In 1963 he began painting full time. Occasionally he models figures in clay or wax to work out the action for a painting of Western history. His specialty is the painting of portraits of famous Indians, particularly on black velvet. The velvet absorbs paint so Beaulaurier believes his pictures will be longer lasting because they are practically solid paint. He feels that interpretations of history should be made now because, "A hundred years from now you won't be able to look at this country as we see it now. Someday there won't be a full-blooded Indian left." MON.

BEAUREGARD, Donald. Born Fillmore, Utah 1884, died there 1914. Utah painter, muralist, illustrator, writer. Work in MNM, Fillmore Mus (Utah), Springville AG, The Louvre. References A15 (obit)-BEN-MAL-SMI. Sources PUA-YUP. No current auction record. Painting examples p 26 YUP. Portrait photo p 117 PUA. (See illustration 14.)

Beauregard went to grade school in Fillmore, later describing the period as "spent in a desert town in southern Utah, living on a ranch, and in the saddle until I was 16, never seeing a railroad until then." YUP. After a year tramping he studied at Brigham Young U 1901–3 and at U of Utah 1903–6, the pupil of Edwin Evans. During 1906–8 Beauregard studied in Paris at the Julien Academy, the pupil of Laurens, supporting himself with newspaper articles and cartoons.

When Beauregard returned to Utah, he became director of art for Ogden schools during 1909–10. Summers were with the U of Utah archaeological expeditions to Arizona and New Mexico, evaluating relics of the Indians and the Franciscan monks and reporting for *Deseret News* and *Western Monthly Magazine*. At Rito de Los Frijoles in 1910, Beauregard met Frank Springer who became his patron. Beauregard was enabled to paint landscapes in Europe and in Utah and New Mexico—*Cliffs near St George* and *Over the Mesa*. Springer commissioned Beauregard to paint six murals for MNM on the life of St Francis of Assisi, but Beauregard, barely thirty, died before the work was completed. His sketches and plans were followed by Carlos Vierra and Kenneth M Chapman so that the murals could be installed in the museum along with a large collection of Beauregard paintings and sketches including Indian and desert subjects. Beauregard's was a "muscular art," called "tragic in that a career so full of promise should be so early ended." YUP.

BEAVER, Fred. Born Eufaula, Okla 1911, living Ardmore, Okla 1976. Creek painter, muralist. Outstanding Indian artist, 1963. Work in GIL, MAI, Philbrook AC. Reference A76. Source AIP. No current auction record or signature example.

Beaver's Creek name is Eka La Nee, Brown Head. His grandfather led his people from Alabama to Oklahoma. Beaver graduated Eufaula High School in 1931 and Haskell Business College in 1935. He entered BIA Field Service in 1935 as clerk and interpreter, working until 1942 when he was inducted into the US Air Corps for the European Theater. While in Italy during the war, he had private instruction in art and voice.

His work was published in *Newsweek* in 1950. As of 1967 he had had 103 exhibitions, 19 one-man shows, and had won 32 awards.

BECHER, Arthur E. Born Freiberg, Germany 1877, living Ardsley, NY 1941. Illustrator specializing in horses including Westerns, painter. Member SI 1910, Artist Guild. Work in *Leslie's,* etc. References A41-BEN-FIE-MAL. Signature example drawings for "When the Breach Was Closed" by Litsey in *Leslie's.*

Becher was the pupil of Otto Strutzel in Munich and of Louis Mayer and Howard Pyle in the US. He worked as an illustrator for both books and magazines.

BECKER, August H. Born Cologne, Germany 1840, died probably St Louis, Mo 1903. Painter of Indian genre, portraits, murals. Work in St Louis courthouse, Mo Hist Soc, Harmsen colln. Reference G&W. Sources DCC-WIM. Oil *War Party Attacking Pioneers* sold 2/28/71 for $2,200 at auction. No signature example. *Portrait of August H Becker* by Wimar p 70 WIM.

Son of an innkeeper, Becker was raised in St Louis where "real Indians pitched their tents and lit their fires at his doorstep." WIM. He was influenced by the accomplishment of his 12 years older half-brother Charles Wimar to become a painter and to specialize in Indian scenes. Like Wimar, his first teacher was Léon Pomarede, a muralist called "a beautifully embodied personification of Parisian art" full of "careless folly and vanity." WIM. While Wimar was studying at Düsseldorf, he kept in touch with Becker by correspondence.

When Wimar received his first important public commission in 1861, murals for the rotunda of the St Louis courthouse, he named Becker as his partner although Becker was only 21. The work designed by Wimar and painted by the partners included *The Indian Attack on St Louis* and buffaloes grazing in a canyon of the Rockies. Unfortunately Wimar died of consumption the following year. *Buffaloes Drinking at the Yellowstone* by Becker is in the Harmsen colln. *The Founding of St Louis* by Becker is in the Mo Hist Soc.

BECKER, F Otto. Born Dresden, Germany 1854, died Milwaukee, Wis 1945. Wis painter, lithographic artist of *Custer's Last Stand*. Reference MAL (O Becker active St Louis 1896). Sources AIW-BAW-CUS-POW-11/14/73 letter from Douglas A Bakken, Archivist, Anheuser-Busch Inc. No auction record. Lithograph *Custer's Last Fight* reproduced as ※54 AIW. (See illustration 15.)

Becker studied at the Royal Academy of Arts in Dresden. He emigrated to NYC in 1873, working as artist and lithographer in NYC, Boston, Philadelphia, and St Louis. In 1880 he began his 35-year association with Milwaukee Lithographic and Engraving Company, painting in oil and watercolor and supervising stone preparation. In 1894 Anheuser-Busch owned the Cassily Adams painting *Custer's Last Fight* and ordered it lithographed in color. Becker received sketches to work from, and consulted with available authorities and data. He wrote, "I painted *Custer's Last Stand* in 1895. The original painting (of mine) is still in my possession, but unfortunately, I was forced to cut it into pieces so that a number of artists could work on it at the same time, making the color plates." Letter 11/14/73. In 1936 the sections were mounted on Masonite and Becker repainted the seams. Anheuser-Busch purchased the painting in 1939.

Becker's widely distributed reproduction varies in details from the Adams original. The battlefield topography is more realistic, the background shows the river valley rather than a hill, and Custer is preparing a saber blow rather than lunging forward. The lithograph has gone through many editions. One edition omitted reference to Anheuser-Busch after the print was physically attacked in 1904 by a disciple of Carrie Nation, the Prohibitionist, because it was distributed by a brewer. Later in his career, Becker actively painted in oils as a fine artist, doing Westerns "after Remington" as well as city, marine, religious, and interior views.

BECKER, Frederick W. Born Vermillion, SD 1888, living Palm Springs, Cal 1953. Western landscape painter, muralist. Work in U Oklahoma, Okla City Art League; mural *War Chief Posay* in Okla Hist Bldg. References A53-BEN-FIE-MAL-SMI. Source BDW. No current auction record but the published estimate of prints is $125 to $150. No signature example.

Becker studied at the Los Angeles School of Art & Design, Mackey School of Art, PAFA, and the ASL of LA, the pupil of Hugh Breckenridge, Daniel Garber, Robert Reid, and Emil Carlsen. He was listed as living in Oklahoma (A33) and Texas (A41). Typical titles would be *Gray Day* and *Cliffs at Laguna*.

BECKER, Joseph. Born Pottsville, Pa 1841, died Brooklyn, NY 1910. *Leslie's* illustrator, painter, art director, crossed the Rockies in 1869. Work in GIL, MMA. References A10-BEN-MAL-SMI. Sources AIW-BAR-GIL. No auction record. Monogram example ※40 AIW, *Station Scene* on the Union Pac Ry.

Becker joined *Frank Leslie's Illus-*

trated Newspaper as an errand boy in 1859. The staff artists taught him to sketch, and Frank Leslie took an interest in the budding artist. By 1863 the demand for Civil War artists caused Becker to be sent to sketch the Army of the Potomac. Becker's Western experience was confined to 1869 when he was on the first special cross-Rockies Pullman train leaving Omaha Oct 19 and arriving in San Francisco in 81 hours. The pictorial record of the trip began in *Leslie's* with the Omaha departure and totaled about 40 published illustrations not signed by Becker but assumed to be his. In California for six weeks, Becker made studies of the Chinese who had been imported as laborers. He returned by train via Salt Lake City to do sketches of the Mormons and drew landscapes from the rear coach's platform, saying in 1905, "I furnished designs for" the observation car "to Mr Pullman, which afterwards were utilized." A painting by Becker from one of his sketches was exhibited MMA in 1939.

Leslie's regular circulation was less than *Harper's* 100,000, but after the Chicago fire in 1871 where many of the illustrations were sketched by Becker, the circulation jumped to 470,000 for one issue. From 1875 to 1900 Becker was head of the *Leslie* art department, supervising other important illustrators like Yeager, Ogden, and Berghaus. He also illustrated at least one book, "Beyond the Mississippi," in 1867, but probably from photos.

BECKMANN, Max. Born Leipzig 1884, died NYC 1950. Important modern painter and engraver of the German Expressionist school. Work in AIC, MOMA, MMA, etc. References A70 (under Pat Adams)-BEN-MAL. Sources, texts on modern painting-CAH-190. Complete series of 127 pen and ink drawings for Goethe's "Faust II" sold 12/1/71 for $180,000 at auction.

Beckmann studied at Weimar under F Smith, then in Florence and Paris. He exhibited in 1929 at the Exposition of Contemporary German Painters. In 1934 he was professor of art in Berlin. By 1947 he was exhibiting at MOMA, and in 1949 a resident in the US, he won first prize at the Carnegie International Exhibition.

At the MMA 1950 exhibition "American Painting Today," Beckmann's self-portrait 1950 was for sale at $2,500. His self-portrait 1908 was sold 6/8/72 for $41,600. The reference to Beckmann with a Western subject is casual, for example, sideshow Indians in the triptych *Acrobats*. This is the rare instance where a painter's Western work may be of less value than his other subjects.

BECKWITH, Arthur. Born London, Eng 1860, died probably San Francisco, Cal 1930. San Francisco landscape painter. Work in San Fran's Golden Gate Park Mus and Sequoia Club. References A30 (obit)-BEN-FIE-MAL-SMI. Source BDW. No current auction record or signature example.

Beckwith studied at the South Kensington Schools in London. Listed titles were *Foggy Morning on the Coast* and *Sunlight and Shadow*.

BEELER, Joe. Born Joplin, Mo 1931, living Sedona, Ariz 1976. Traditional Western painter, sculptor. Member CAA. Work in GIL, Mont Hist Soc, Nat Cowboy Hall of Fame. Reference A76. Sources ACO-AHI-AIP-CAP-COW-C71 to 74-HAR-OSR-TWR-WAI 71,72-"Joe Beeler Shows at the C M Russell Gallery" 1970-"Joe Beeler Shows at the Spiva Art Center," 1973. No current auction record. Signature example CAP. (See illustration 16.)

Part Cherokee Indian, Beeler graduated from Joplin high school. "I wardanced in feathered costume and have then gone to the creeks to bathe as the other Indian youths did." Shows at CMR above. He attended U of Tulsa to study with Alexandre Hogue until service in the Korean War for two years during which he did artwork for *Stars and Stripes*. After graduating from Kansas State, Beeler worked in "Fats" Jones's Hollywood stables decorating Western movie props and studied at the Los Angeles Art Center School. In 1958, with his wife and first child, Beeler moved into a cabin on Indian land in northeast Oklahoma to work in fine arts with Western subjects, although he knew only George Phippen and Olaf Wieghorst to be financially secure in Western art at the time.

Beeler survived by painting bull and cow portraits and with book illustrations until his one-man show in 1960. Additional shows followed including the National Cowboy Hall of Fame and his paintings were reproduced as widely distributed prints. "Soon rabbit and quail gave way to beefsteak at our dinner table." Shows at CMR. By 1965, paintings were on commission only. The same year, Beeler began sculpting in bronze. He was a founder of the CAA, along with Charlie Dye, George Phippen, and John Hampton.

BEERY, Noah. See Berry, Noah, Jr.

BEGAY, Apie ("Son of Milk"). Born probably New Mexico date unknown, died "many years before 1936." Navaho crayon artist. Work in MNM. No refer-

ence. Sources AHI 2/50-AIP. No auction record or signature example.

In 1902 Kenneth Chapman found Apie Begay seated on the floor of his hogan making crude sketches of sandpainting figures with black and red pencils. Chapman gave Begay a box of crayons, permitting "a little more life to his drawings than tradition allowed in the picture made of sand. Streamers are flying in the air; so too are sash ends. Even the beads about the necks of the dancers are represented in motion. Decorative art, curbed by techniques and materials, plus a religious art curbed and conventionalized by tradition, gave Apie Begay no model of unrestrained realism which he could copy." AHI 2/50.

In working with colors, Apie Begay was returning to the forgotten innovations of the Navaho artist Choh in 1886. Within 10 years, however, the use of watercolors became more general among the Indians of the Southwest, opening the way for the professional Indian artists.

BEGAY, Harrison (Haskay Yah Ne Yah, Warrior Who Walked Up to His Enemy). Born White Cone, Ariz 1917, living Greasewood Trading Post, Ganado, Ariz 1968. Navaho painter, illustrator, printmaker, muralist. Work in DAM, GIL, MAI, MNM, Okla U MA, Philbrook AC. No reference. Sources AHI 2/50,12/58-AIP-COW-LAF. No current auction record. Signature examples pp 18, 20, 23 AHI 2/50. Portrait photo p 27 AHI 2/50.

Harrison Begay attended Fort Wingate Indian School in New Mexcio in 1927, Fort Defiance and Tohatchi in New Mexico, and graduated from Santa Fe Indian School in 1939. He attended Black Mtn in North Carolina and Phoenix Jr Col before WWII in which he served for three years in the Army. It is said that his internationally known paintings have been more influential with Navaho artists than any other. AIP. His work is characterized as "quiet and peaceful." AHI. Extreme delicacy is achieved in lighter colors, as by softening brilliant colors with Chinese white.

Begay has been able to work as a full-time artist and has had his paintings reproduced in quantity as silk screens. He exhibited beginning 1946. His painting p 131 LAF *Navaho Women Weaving and Spinning* is a genre work that also records costume and personal styles.

BEIL (or Biel), Charles A. Traditional Western sculptor active 1920s–60s, living Red Deer, Alberta, Canada 1975. Work in English Royal colln. No reference. Sources BRO-WAI 71,72-RUS. No auction record or signature example.

Beil became a friend of Charles Russell when Beil was a working Montana cowboy who wanted to sculpt. Beil established a studio in Great Falls where Russell visited. RUS lists "Biel" as an artist friend like Schreyvogel, Borein, and "Krieghoff." Two days before Russell died, Russell took the local newspaperman to Charlie Beil's little studio to get publicity for "Biel," calling "Biel" the "best feller I ever seen modeling hosses an' cowpunchers." RUS. At Russell's funeral in 1926 Beil led the procession with Russell's empty-saddled horse. In 1930 Beil went to Canada, settling in Banff.

BELL, Thomas Sloan. Active 1894–98 in Denver, Colo as landscape and marine painter. Reference BEN. Sources DPL letter 11/6/73-article *Rocky Mtn News* 3/3/18. No current auction record, but in the fourth annual exhibition of the Denver Artists Club in 1897, Bell exhibited *Geranium* with an asking price of $15 and *Pipe* (*Berlin, Germany*) $10. No signature example.

T Sloan Bell (sometimes Thomas S Bell) is listed BEN as painting in Colorado in the 19th and 20th centuries. His name was in the Denver City Directory for 1894, living in Arvada and maintaining a Denver studio in the Kittredge Bldg. At the November 1895 exhibition, "The largest picture in the display is a Southern California coast scene, faithfully depicting the massive breakers as they relentlessly dash over the rocks. Thomas S Bell is the artist, having just returned from California, whither he went especially for the study of marine subjects." Unidentified newspaper clipping.

BELL, William Abraham. Born probably Ireland 1841, died Bletchingly, Surrey, Eng 1921. English doctor who was *Harper's* illustrator 1867, Kansas-Pacific survey sketch artist and photographer of the Indian War, early resident and press agent for Colo Springs, writer. No reference. Sources AIW-GOD-NEW-11/11/73 letter from J C Kenefick, President, Union Pacific Railroad company. No auction record or signature example.

Dr Bell was in St Louis at an international medical convention in 1867 when he heard about the Kansas-Pacific rail survey from Salina to San Francisco. Bell took the job of survey photographer, "an art with which I was then quite unacquainted," and spent three days learning photography. Near Pikes Peak, he met the cavalry hero Gen Will Palmer who was the survey leader. The survey party spent nine months fighting Indians, low rations, desert heat, snow storms in the mountains, and wrong directions before getting back to Denver.

Dr Bell returned to England where he wrote and illustrated "New Tracks in North America" published in London in 1869. The book describes "physical geography, the aboriginal tribes, and the expedition." Illustrations were drawn from photographs. The text is a delight: "What curious freaks of nature these North American buffalo are! The small hind-quarters look out of all proportion to the massive strength of the shoulders and chest; smooth, and apparently shaven, like the back of a French poodle, they do not seem to belong to the same animal. The huge head hangs low; it is completely covered with long shaggy hair matted together, which hides the features. The little corkscrew tail ends in a tuft." By September 1869 Dr Willie Bell was back at Pikes Peak to plan a southbound railroad with his friend Will Palmer.

BELLOWS, George Wesley. Born Columbus, Ohio 1882, died NYC 1925. Important painter of NY realist school. ANA 1909, NA 1913. Work in major museums: MMA, PAFA, AIC, etc. References A25 (obit)-BEN-DAB-ENB-FIE-MAL-SMI. Sources AIC-ANT 10/55, 3/65, 5/66, 6/68, 5/70, 10/71; 4, 6/74-ARI-ARM-CON-COR-DEP-HMA-190-MAP-M19-M31-MSL-TSF-WHO 24. Oil 38×30″ *Portrait of Margaret Budd* inscribed George Bellows and painted 1914 was estimated at $20,000 to $25,000 for sale 5/23/74 at auction but did not sell. Signature example ⚹49 SPB 12/13/73 *The Last Ounce*. (See illustration 17.)

Bellows left Ohio State U in his senior year, 1904, to study art in NYC. His paintings were seen by Robert Henri who accepted Bellows as pupil and friend. By 1906 Bellows had his own NYC studio. His "realistic pictures of drunks, prize fighters, and lovers in the park" shocked the public. MAP. In 1907 he sold his first major painting *Forty-Two Kids* and painted *Stag at Sharkey's,* which made him famous. In 1908 he won a landscape prize at the NA, and PAFA bought *North River.* In 1909 he was elected

ANA, and MMA bought *Up the Hudson.* By 1913 he was NA, an exhibitor at the Armory Show, and he taught at the ASL.

Bellows became "the most popular artist of his time, the most 'American' painter of his generation," according to his biographer Peyton Boswell Jr. Bellows never left the US and, indeed, seldom left NYC except for annual summer excursions. When Robert Henri moved to Santa Fe in 1916, Bellows joined him for the summer of 1917. HMA fig 19 reproduces *Chimayo.* The West had no impact on Bellows, and Bellows had none on the West.

BELL-SMITH, Frederic Marlett. Born London, Eng 1846, died in Toronto, Can 1923. Canadian painter including Rocky Mountain scenes, illustrator, teacher. ARCA 1880, RCA 1886. Work in Simpson Company colln (Toronto). No reference. Sources CAH-CAN-CAR-DCA. No current auction record. Signature example ⚹72 CAR. (See illustration 18.)

Son of John Bell-Smith, an English painter who emigrated to Montreal in 1867 to become founder-president of the Society of Canadian Artists, F M Bell-Smith had studied at the South Kensington Art Schools in London. He lived in Montreal from 1867 to 1871, in Hamilton until 1874, in Toronto until 1879, and again in Hamilton until 1881.

Bell-Smith was one of the 20 Canadian and American artists who collaborated on the illustrations for "Picturesque Canada" published in 1882. These drawings, reproduced as wood engravings, were important in awakening Canadians to "the natural beauties of their own country." CAN. Bell-Smith was in the Canadian West around this time. He began teaching in 1881 in London, Toronto, and St Thomas, Ontario, continuing until 1910. In England in 1895 to paint a series on the death of the Canadian prime minister, he went on to Paris in 1896 where he studied at the Colarossi Academy. The result of his French study was apparent, when earlier paintings "based on simple observation are compared to his Rocky Mountain pictures with their elaborate atmospheric effects." CAR.

BEMIS, William Otis. Born Spencer, Mass 1819, died there 1883. Mass landscape painter specializing in cattle scenes. Work in Worcester AM (three N Eng landscapes painted about 1850). References BEN-FIE-G&W. Source, "Historical Sketches relating to Spencer, Mass" from Worcester AM. No auction record. Painting example p 188 ANT 8/73 reproducing 47×63" view of Denver, Colo with cattle in foreground about 1860.

Bemis was put to work on the family farm when small. He learned boot bottoming to earn money to study art in Philadelphia. On his return he studied with George Loring Brown, a Worcester landscape painter, and Francis Alexander, a Boston portrait painter. From 1847 to 1850 he had his own studio in Worcester "with good success." He settled on the family homestead when he married in 1850, occasionally traveling for "new and unique landscape views as a setting for his cattle pieces." It may be that one of his travels was to Denver, or that he used a published view of Denver as a backdrop.

Bemis was the first man in Spencer to introduce Jersey cattle and make giltedge butter. It is said that when his brother Amasa found a hay wain painting to "have got a curious mix-up of cattle attached to your cart, an ox and a cow yoked up together is a little extraordinary," Bemis replied, "Sure enough, but my mind is on cows so much that I think cow, dream cow, and it seems paint cow without realizing what I am about." Hist Sketches.

BENDA, Wladyslaw Theodor. Born Poznań, Poland 1873, died probably NYC 1948. Eastern illustrator, painter, muralist, designer, specializing in masks. Member SI 1907, Arch L 1916. References A53(obit)-BEN-ENB (masks)-FIE-MAL-SMI. Sources AAC-CAP-DIC-WHO 48. No current auction record but the estimated price of a watercolor 10×14" Branding the Calf would be about $400 to $600 at auction in 1976. Signature example plate IV vol 15 ENB 14th ed Modern Dramatic Masks.

The son of a Polish pianist and composer, Benda was a pupil of the Acad FA in Kraków and also studied in Vienna, San Francisco, and NYC. He came to the US in 1899 and was naturalized in 1911. Benda won the silver medal at the Pan-Pac Exp in San Francisco in 1915, was a decorative painter, and illustrated books and magazines such as Century, Scribner's, Cosmopolitan which often included Western subjects. An example of Benda's technique in charcoal illustration is given pp 248–49 DIC: He first blocks in his subject, then determines his areas for primary tones, and completes his conventional pretty-girl drawing while balancing light and shadow.

Benda is remembered as the creator of Benda stage masks and as the writer and illustrator of encyclopedia articles on modern masks. In contrast, CAP reproduces his quite traditional Western illustration Seventy Odd Head of Our Cattle Were Driven Away by Three Men for "Cowboy Life on the Western Plains," 1910.

BENDER, Bill. Born El Segundo, Cal 1920, living Oro Grande, Cal 1976. Traditional Western painter, illustrator. Work in USAF Acad (Colo Springs), USN (Pensacola), Pentagon, White House, Palm Springs Mus. Reference A76. Sources COW-10/30/73 letter from Bill Bender. No auction record. Signature example centerfold COW *Two of Fifty-Five.*

Bender was a working cowboy. When ranching allowed, he moonlighted as a movie stuntman to try for his $16 a day. On holidays would come rodeo riding: "I just rode for the hell of it on Fourth of July, Labor Day, or some other blow out. The money ain't big but it gave us a chance to head for town, whoop it up, and swap lies with old friends." "Busted up" while riding, he turned to writing and illustrating stories during his recuperation. When he was well enough to accompany James Swinnerton on painting trips, Swinnerton's advice was, "Learn the subtle colors of the desert first" as a landscape painter, "and then go back to painting horses later." Through years of struggling with color in desert landscapes, Bender developed his own style. Only then did he return to the subjects he knew best: horses, cattle, and ranch scenes.

One of the myths of "in" cowboy painter lore is that Bill Bender was close to Will James and privy to James's secret origins in Canada: "How this got started is a mystery to me, but I never met Will James in my whole life." In addition to his cowboying, Bender felt that "the doggonest thing to happen since painting is my first airplane ride." This was as a civilian artist for the Air Force about 1963, and it was followed by painting for the Navy in 1966.

BENJAMIN, Mrs Lucile Joullin. See Joullin.

BENRIMO, Thomas Duncan. Born San Francisco, Cal 1887, died probably Taos, NM 1958. Contemporary Taos painter, illustrator, commercial artist, teacher. Work in DAM, MNM, HAR,

Fort Worth AM. Reference MAL. Sources APT-DAA-IL 36,39-TAL-TSF. No current auction record but the estimated price of an oil 20×30″ of a New Mexico landscape would be about $1,000 to $1,200 at auction in 1976. Signature example p 61 DAA *Taos Valley 1948.*

Tom Benrimo's family lost its possessions in the San Francisco earthquake and fire of 1906. They began anew in NYC. Tom Benrimo studied briefly at the ASL but was largely self-taught. His brother, an actor and playwright, started him on Broadway as art director and designer for plays. He also worked as an illustrator for major magazines and in commercial art for advertising companies. Benrimo became instructor of design at Pratt Institute in 1935.

In 1939 Benrimo moved to Taos with his wife who had also taught at Pratt. He painted as a Western surrealist, superimposing, for example, unrelated structures on a New Mexico landscape. Other Taos paintings are more traditional modern landscapes. In contrast, his painting *Reflections* reproduced in APT (1956) was abstract. In the catalog of the 1965 Benrimo retrospective exhibition at the Fort Worth AM, Benrimo is quoted, "The artist powerfully contracts certain spaces and expands others into submission intuitively—instinctively."

BENSELL, George Frederick. Born Philadelphia, Pa 1837, died probably there 1879. Portrait, genre, and historical painter, poet. Work in Hist Soc of Pa. References BEN-FIE-G&W-MAL-SMI. Sources AAR 11/75-ANT 2/44-BOL-PAF. No auction record. Signature and painting example *Indians Camping at Riverside,* oil 48×69¾″ dated 1867, AAR 11/75 p 11.

Bensell was born and seems to have spent his entire life in Philadelphia. A student of John Lambdin, he worked in both oils and crayons. Between the years 1856 and 1868 he exhibited his paintings at the Pennsylvania Academy. Collaborating with Samuel Diffield, a fellow Philadelphian, he wrote a 22-page poem, "The Artist's Dream," which is in the Hist Soc of Pa.

Bensell's Indians are of the Eastern frontier, and are probably imaginary rather than real.

BENTON, Colonel James Gilchrist. Born Lebanon, NH 1820, died Springfield, Mass 1881 (not 1861). Regular Army ordnance specialist, topographical artist for *The Texas and California Panorama* 1852. References DAB-MAS. Source TEP. No current auction record or signature example.

Son of a wool merchant, Benton graduated from West Point in 1842. He studied topographical and figure drawing under Robert W Weir. Benton was assigned to the Ordnance Corps, on duty up to 1857 in Washington and in various arsenals. He taught ordnance at West Point until 1861, was assistant to the chief in Washington until 1863, and then commander of the Washington Arsenal and the Springfield Armory. Benton invented rifle improvements, testing devices, loading methods, etc, but never took out a patent because "the government that educated him was entitled to his time." DAB.

While Benton was in command of the San Antonio Ordnance Depot as a lieutenant in 1849–52, he made drawings for Sala and Stearn, civilian promoters of a moving panorama. The locale was along the Brazos River, from Washington-on-the-Brazos to San Felipe. Included were the incidents of the Texas Revolution and the missions. Benton's sketches were taken to the New Orleans studio of Charles Smith to be refined into a painting nine feet high equaling "10,000 sf." A section of the panorama that still exists is

reproduced in TEP, and shown to be quite painterly rather than just scenery depiction like other panorama "newsreels."

BENTON, Thomas Hart. Born Neosho, Mo 1889, died Kansas City, Mo 1975. Important realist painter of the regional school, muralist, printmaker, teacher, writer. NA 1956. Work in MMA, MOMA, BM, PAFA, WMAA, etc. References A73-BEN-ENB-FIE-MAL-SMI. Sources AAT-AIC-ALA-CAA-CAP-CON-COW-DAA-DEP-HMA-190-MAP-M57-STI-TSF-WHO 70. Tempera on canvas 20½×29¼" *The Boy* 1950 sold 12/13/73 for $21,000 at auction. Signature example p 91 CAP *The Corral*.

A member of the famous Missouri political family, Tom Benton grew up near the Ozarks. He left at 17 to study at the AIC 1906–7 and in Paris at the Julien Academy 1908–11. Back in NYC he was a professional painter beginning 1912, but unable to sell his paintings based on European modernism. In WWI, Benton was an architectural draftsman for the Navy, forced into realism. At his first postwar exhibition, some of his new paintings sold. He taught at the ASL 1926–35. During this period, Benton traveled all over the US, sketching in the industrial centers, the South, the Far West, Texas, and New Mexico. His painting *New Mexico* dated 1926 and reproduced fig 26 HMA and p 63 DAA was from a sketch made near Raton.

After 20 years in NYC, Benton left what he termed an intellectually diseased lot of painters to return to Missouri as director of painting at Kansas City AI. He had become famous when he painted the *Contemporary America* mural called "tabloid art" for the New School in NYC. When he painted the 45,000 sq ft mural for the Mo St Capitol in 1935–36, he rejected customary heroic figures for Boss Pendergast, Jesse James, and

Frankie and Johnny. With Grant Wood and John Steuart Curry, Benton realistically portrayed the essence of an American region.

BERGHAUS, Albert (or Alfred). Active 1869–80 in NYC as a *Leslie's* lithographic artist, engraver, illustrator. Work in ACM. No reference. Sources ACM-AIW-CUS. No auction record. Signature example ⚹1845 ACM, woodcut inscribed Bghs, *1877/Streeter and Small's/Cheyenne and Black Hills/Fast Freight and Slow Passenger Line.*

After the Civil War, Berghaus was listed among *Leslie's* NYC illustrators. In 1869 he redrew on wood for engraving some of the Joseph Becker sketches made during the first trans-Rockies train trip. In 1871 some of Worrall's (which see) Kansas sketches were redrawn by Berghaus and signed Bghs. At that time *Leslie's* listed its NYC art staff as Joseph Becker, James E Taylor, T de Thulstrup, Walter Yeager, and Berghaus. In 1879 Berghaus redrew Edward Jump's illustrations of Leadville.

In addition to his work for *Leslie's,* Berghaus teamed with Remington to illustrate "Tenting on the Plains" by Mrs Custer. He also painted a *Custer's Last Stand* for "Custer's Last Shot; or, The Boy Trailer of the Little Big Horn" in the "Pluck and Luck" series.

BERKE, Ernest. Born probably NYC 1921, living Santa Fe, NM 1975. Traditional Western painter, illustrator, sculptor, writer, specializing in Indians. No reference. Sources ACO-*Amer Artist* 7/72-EIT-WAI 71,72-1/9/74 letter from Ernest Berke. Bronze, dark brown patina 4 7/8″ high *Cow Skull and Vulture* numbered 24, signed and dated 1966 was estimated at $300 to $400 for sale 10/28/74 at auction in LA. Signature example p 45 *Amer Artist* 7/72 oil painting *Reduced to Coarse Fur.* (See illustration 19.)

Son of a metal worker, Berke left high school without graduating. After serving in the Air Force in WWII, he worked as a commercial artist making slide films for three years, then doing product drawings for Sears newspaper ads. As a hobby, Berke began handicrafting Indian articles using Indian methods. When he started painting Indians he utilized advice from the famous illustrator Harold Von Schmidt to improve his technique. By 1960 his paintings and sculpture were selling. In 1963 he was commissioned to write and illustrate a children's book on Indians.

In the 1960s Berke lived on Long Island, NY, spending several months a year in the West, in the mountains and deserts and on the reservations, making color notes and taking photographs. Then he returned East, to the libraries and museums. For sculpture, he generally starts with clay, then wax, then a rubber mold to provide wax duplicates for the bronze castings made in the "lost wax" process. In painting, he limits himself to one work at a time, a matter of five or six months including research. To recall details, he projects his slides. He starts an egg tempera painting with 30 or more thumbnail sketches he composes into a larger drawing for projection onto his canvas. A complete ink cartoon is drawn on the canvas, gray is drybrushed in for pattern, the underpainting is washed in with large brushes, and the painting is completed with watercolor brushes.

BERKELEY, Stanley. Active in London 1878–1902, died probably London 1909. English Special Artist-illustrator, military and animal painter. Reference BEN. Source AOH. No auction record. Signature example facing p 296 "Woodstock;

or The Cavalier" by Sir Walter Scott, 1899 London.

There is no reason to believe Berkeley ever visited the US, but beginning 1882 he signed Western scenes in the *Illustrated London News*. Berkeley also drew Western illustrations for the boys' paper *Chums,* one example being *Twixt Life and Death* where a buffalo pushes a horseman off a cliff.

Berkeley from 1878 to 1902 exhibited paintings at the Royal Academy, at the Royal Institute of Painters in Water Colours, and at the Royal Society of British Artists.

BERNINGHAUS, Julius Charles. Born St Louis, Mo 1905, living Taos, NM 1971. Western landscape painter, muralist. Work in State Teachers Col (Maryville, Mo), Raton Lib (NM), Ute Park (NM). References A53-MAL. Sources HAR-TAL. No current auction record. Signature example p 19 HAR oil *Taos Pueblo River.*

Charles Berninghaus, son of the Taos pioneer artist Edmund Berninghaus, studied at the St Louis School FA, AIC, and ASL. His family had moved to Taos when he was in his late teens. He worked with his father on the murals for the Missouri St Capitol and for commercial clients.

BERNINGHAUS, Oscar Edmund. Born St Louis, Mo 1874, died Taos, NM 1952. Important Taos painter, illustrator, muralist, specializing in the genre of the Pueblo Indians. Member, Taos SA 1912, ANA 1926. Work ACM, ANS, MNM, Philbrook AC, City AM St Louis, GIL, HAR, Eiteljorg colln; murals Mo St Cap (5 lunettes), USPO Phoenix; series of historical paintings on the opening of the West. References A53 (obit)-BEN-FIE-MAL-SMI. Sources AAT-ACM-ANT 9/53-COW-CRS-DBW-DCC-EIT-GIL-HAR-HMA-PAW-POW-TAL-TSF-T20-TWR-WHO 50. Oil on canvasboard 12×16″ *Stream in the Desert* signed and dated 1951 estimated for sale 3/4/74 at $9,000 to $11,000 for auction in LA but did not sell. In same sale oil 25×30 *The Water Hole,* est at $8,000 to $10,000 sold for $14,000. Signature example p 19 PIT *Dance at the Pueblo.* (See illustration 20.)

Son of a lithograph salesman, O E Berninghaus was educated in St Louis grammar schools. Even then he sold spot news sketches to the local newspapers. In the tradition of an earlier era of painters he began work in lithography in 1889 and as a printing apprentice in 1893 while he attended night classes at St Louis SFA for three terms. Established first as an illustrator and then as a largely self-taught fine artist, he was in the course of getting his first one-man show in St Louis in 1899.

That year he was the guest of the Denver and Rio Grande RR on a junket to Colorado. Intrigued by tales of Taos he made a brief side trip 25 miles by wagon to the still-untouched village. Thereafter, although St Louis was his base, he returned to Taos each summer, remaining for longer periods until he settled permanently in 1925. His paintings were of the Pueblo Indians, the Spanish Americans, the adobes, the mountains, generally with at least one horse. With his practice as lithographic artist and illustrator, his approach was direct and objective, showing the Indians as they were rather than posed or nostalgic stereotypes. His technique was to work out of doors, painting on the scene. After he moved to Taos, his style became more modern. His compositions were more complex, his colors richer, and frequently he painted from memory at his easel within his studio. His time was spent in Taos or St Louis, except for a 1932 trip to Mexico. His son J Charles Berninghaus is a landscape painter.

BERRY (or Beery), Noah, Jr. Born NYC 1916, living Keene, Cal 1975. Sculptor in bronze of Western subjects, actor. No reference. Sources ACO-COW-WAI 71-note Nov '73 from Noah Berry. No auction record. Sculpture example *Geronimo* p 175 COW.

Berry is the nephew of the famous actor Wallace Beery and is himself an actor in Western films. His sculpting inspiration came from Charles Russell. ACO listed *Custer,* a bronze 19" high. WAI 71 listed *The Ghost Stage,* a sculpture 9" high and 26" long, in an edition of 1.

BEST, Arthur W. Born Mt Pleasant near Peterboro, Ont, Can about 1865, active in San Francisco, Cal up to 1919. Cal landscape painter, teacher. Work in Mark Hopkins IA (San Fran), Oakland AM, ANS. References p 243 A19-BEN. Sources WAI 72-*Out West* Jan 1914. No current auction record or signature example. (See illustration 21.)

In 1887 Best played clarinet and his brother Harry Cassie Best the violin in a Peterboro band that traveled west before breaking up in Portland, Ore. Harry became a landscape painter as well as a musician. When Harry sold a painting for $100 about 1895, the brothers moved to San Francisco. There they organized a sketch club in 1897 that became Arthur's "Best Art School" which he conducted with his wife Alice M Best. In 1917 he and his wife (both as Alice M and as Mrs A W) were listed as painters at the school's address 1625 California Street. Best was known as a painter of the Grand Canyon.

BEST, Harry Cassie. Born Mt Pleasant near Peterboro, Ont, Can 1863, died San Francisco, Cal 1936. Cal landscape painter known as "the artist of the Yosemite Valley and the Cal Mountains." Work in Carnegie Inst, Cosmos Club (DC), Jonathon Club (LA), Yosemite Nat Park. References A38 (obit)-BEN-MAL. Sources *Out West* Jan 1914–11/15/73 letter Mary Ashe, SF Pub Lib. Oil 28½ ×18½" *California Redwoods* with signature example sold 11/28/73 for $250 at auction in LA. (See illustration 22.)

In 1887 Best and his brother Arthur played violin and clarinet in a Peterboro band that traveled west. The band dispersed in Portland, Ore where Best played the violin while his passion became painting. For four years Best studied the changing colors of the 14,000-foot mountains in the passing hours and seasons. He also began submitting cartoons to the San Francisco papers. In 1891 his band played in Silverton, Ore where Best did scene painting and met Homer Davenport the cartoonist. When Best was in funds, he took art lessons from Rodríguez in San Francisco. About 1895 Best sold a painting of Mt Hood for $100, quit the band, and left for San Francisco with his brother. During his five years with the *San Francisco Post,* he was an organizer of the sketch club that became his brother's Best Art School.

About 1900 the painter Thad Welch took Best on a sketching trip to the Yosemite. Best married Anne Rippey at the foot of Bridal Veil Falls 1901, and in 1902 they erected the Best studio as a Yosemite concession. By 1907 when Pres Theodore Roosevelt bought *Evening at Mt Shasta,* Best was able to spend three months each in Italy and Paris. Winters were in Santa Barbara, then San Diego. As he became more worldly, Best's *The Yosemite Valley from Artist's Point* and *The Two Domes, Yosemite Valley* were succeeded by the semi-nude *Innocence* and *Ramona Going Through the Wild Mustard to Meet Father Salviaderra.* Best advertised in the *San Diego Union* for the models made into a composite for "Ramona when she walks through the mustard." He leased the painting to the "Ramona's Marriage Place" exhibit, and then sold it for $2,500 to a Texan.

BETTS, Edwin C. Born Hillsdale, Mich 1856, died Denver, Colo 1917. Colo landscape and portrait painter, muralist, interior decorator. References A17 (obit)-BEN-FIE-MAL. Source *Denver Times* 4/20/17 obit-10/31/73 letter from Alice Sharp, St Hist Soc of Colo. No auction record or signature example. Portrait photo *Denver Times*.

Betts was educated in Hillsdale. While a boy, he successfully assisted an interior decorator doing fresco and touch work. This led him to four years' study at the Metropolitan AS in NYC. He moved to Pueblo, Colo in 1888, then three months later settled in Denver where he worked as a journeyman painter during the building of the Metropole Hotel. He became a master painter and a prominent member of the union. The 1915 Denver CD listed Betts as "Edwin S, painter rear 1822 Broadway rms Crest Hotel."

His last painting was his best known, *The Valley of the Housatonic*. It depicted Pittsfield, Mass looking toward Mt Greylock. "Other landscapes and portraits of prominent Denver people have occupied his time in 'spare' moments." *Denver Times*.

BETTS, Harold Harrington. Born NYC 1881, living Chicago 1929 (or, died 1915). Chicago painter of the Grand Canyon and Pueblo Indians, illustrator. Work in ANS. References A17-BEN-MAL. Oil 56×38″ *Grand Canyon from Hermit Road* with signature example H Betts and dated 1913 was estimated for sale 10/28/74 at $1,500 to $2,000 at auction in LA. The oil 30×20″ *Taos Scene* sold 1/24/73 for $1,100.

H Harrington Betts was the son and pupil of Edwin Daniel Betts, Sr who died in Chicago 1915. Three of the other sons and one daughter also painted professionally. The most famous was Louis Betts.

ANS also listed *Grand Canyon* 1929 and *Grand Canyon from Pima Point*.

BIDDLE, George. Born Philadelphia, Pa 1885, died Croton-on-Hudson, NY 1973. Important modern painter, graphic artist, muralist, sculptor, teacher, author. Member, Nat Soc Mural Painters. Work in Berlin, Mexico City, Tokyo, Rio de Janeiro, Tel Aviv, Venice, Canadian mus; MMA, MNM, MOMA, WMAA, etc. References A73-BEN-FIE-MAL-SMI. Sources AAT, AHI 3/66-AIC-ALA-CAA-CON-DEP-190-MAP-M50-M57-SHO-WHO 70. Oil 16¼×20″ *Negro Spirituals* signed Biddle and dated 1937 sold 10/14/70 for $750 at auction. M50 lists an oil *Job and His Comforters* offered for sale at MMA in 1950 for $2,000. Signature example CON.

Biddle went to Groton School for his preparatory education 1898–1904. He knew F D Roosevelt there. He graduated Harvard with honors in 1908 and Harvard Law School in 1911, all to please his socially prominent family. Instead of practicing as a lawyer, however, he studied at the Julien Academy in Paris in 1911 and became an artist. He enlisted in the U S Army in 1917, serving on the General Staff in France. After the war he experimented in graphics and sculpture in Tahiti and France before returning to America. During the Depression his correspondence with President Roosevelt resulted in the creation of the Federal Arts Project of the WPA in 1933. Biddle participated in the Artists' Congress in 1936, hoping "that one of the effects of the Depression would be a socially conscious art." ALA. His murals were to show that "the sweatshop and tenement of yesterday can be the life planned with justice of tomorrow." CON. He had more than 100 one-man exhibitions on four continents, serving in numerous governmental advisory posts.

Biddle taught in various schools including Colorado Springs FAC 1936–37. He painted in the West at the time, including *Buffalo Dance* dated 1937.

BIEL. See Beil.

BIERHALS, Otto. Born Nürnberg, Bavaria, Germany 1879, living Tenafly, NJ 1948. Painter, illustrator for pulp magazines including Westerns, teacher. Work in Street & Smith magazines. References A41-BEN-MAS. Sources AAC-NJA. No current auction record or signature example. (See illustration 23.)

Bierhals' parents were American. He studied at Cooper Union, the NAD, the PAFA, in Munich where he was the pupil of Herman Groeber, in Paris, and in Italy. As a pulp illustrator he worked for Street & Smith and for McFadden Publications. His summer studio was in Woodstock, NY.

BIERSTADT, Albert. Born Solingen near Düsseldorf, Germany 1830, died NYC 1902. Very important painter of the Rocky Mtn School, "America's greatest painter of the 1870s." NA 1860, Legion of Honor 1867. Work in ACM, ANS, MMA, COR, Montreal Mus, Capitol (DC), Hermitage (Russia), etc. References A02 (obit)-BEN-CHA-DAB-ENB-FIE-G&W-MAL-SMI. Sources AIW-ALA-AMA-ANT 1/49, 6/50; 2, 10/51; 11/53,2/56,1/58; 8,10/60; 9, 10, 11/62; 11/64, 8/65, 9/67; 5, 10/68; 1, 2, 4/69; 10/70; 9, 11/72; 1, 3, 10, 11, 12/73; 2, 4, 9, 11/74; 1, 2/75-BAR-BOA-CAH-COR-CRS-DBW-DCC-DEP-DWF-EIT-GIL-GOD-HAR-HMA-HON-HUD-HUT-150-ISH-JNB-KAR-KW1-M19-M31-MSL-PAF-PAW-POW-PNW-SSF-STI-TAW-TEP-WAI 71, 72-WES-WHI-WHO 02. Oil 34¾ × 52½" *Farallon Island* with signature example painted about 1887 sold 4/11/73 for $110,000 at auction. (See illustration 24.)

Brought to New Bedford, Mass when he was 2, Bierstadt was exhibiting crayon landscapes and teaching at 20. In 1854, he returned to Düsseldorf to study landscape painting with A Achenbach and Lessing. An average student, he improved his technique on field trips along the Rhine, in the Alps, and in Italy with Whittredge, S R Gifford, and Haseltine. When he came back to New Bedford in 1857, he painted in his familiar White Mtns as a step in his desire to portray the least-known American landscape. In 1859 his lifetime's opportunity came, to join Gen Lander's expedition to survey a wagon route to the Pacific. The party was in South Fork by June. Bierstadt spent the summer sketching in the Wind River range and the Shoshone Indian country. When Lander's party was west of the Rockies in the Wasatch range, Bierstadt left for Fort Laramie in the company of only two other men.

In 1860 Bierstadt exhibited the first of his panoramic paintings from the Rocky Mtn sketches. It brought his immediate and overwhelming popularity, so that by 1865 Bierstadt was surpassing F E Church as America's most popular painter. His second trip West had been in 1863, when he reached the Pacific. In 1872 and 1873 he lived on the Pacific coast. By 1882 his fortunes began their decline. The American Committee for the 1889 Paris Expos rejected *Last of the Buffalo* as not in keeping with current American painting. In 1893 his *Landing of Columbus* was refused for the World's Columbian Expos. A handsome, polished man, formal and persuasive, Bierstadt had lost out to the more imaginative landscapists. In recent years appreciation of Bierstadt has significantly revived, not only for the melodramatic canvases of heroic proportion but also for the smaller oil studies that witness the accuracy of his perception.

BIG BOW, Woodrow Wilson. Born Carnegie, Okla 1914, living probably Okla 1967. Kiowa painter. Work in GIL, MAI, Philbrook AC, Southwest Mus. No reference. Sources AIP-ANT 8/66. No current auction record. Signature example p 144 ANT 8/66. (See illustration 25.)

Woody Big Bow's Kiowa name is Tse Ko Yate. His grandfather was Chief Big Bow, active in raids with the war chief Satanta in the 1870s and a pictographic artist. Big Bow, who was educated in Oklahoma in 1939, designed the red and yellow thunderbird insignia of the Oklahoma 45th Inf Div in WWII. After the war, he was a set painter for Western movies.

BINGHAM, George Caleb. Born on a plantation in Augusta Cnty, Va 1811, died Kansas City, Mo 1879. Very important frontier genre and portrait painter, "the greatest painter the Mississippi produced," teacher. Work in MMA, City AM St Louis, BMFA, Houston MFA, DAM, etc. References BEN-DAB-FIE-G&W-MAL-SMI. Sources ACM-AIW-ALA-ANT 11/47,12/49; 3,12/51; 3/55, 5/61, 10/62, 10/67, 3/68, 9/69, 11/72, 12/73; 4, 9/74-BAR-BOA-DAA-DBW-HMA-KAR-KW1-M15-M19-MIS-PAF-POW-SHO-TAW-TEP-WES-WHI. No recent auction sale but the engraving of his painting *Canvassing for a Vote* sold 10/27/71 for $1,000 at auction. Signature example p 102 TAW. (See illustration 26.)

Bingham's family moved to frontier Missouri at Boon's Lick in 1819. After his father died in 1827, he was apprenticed to a cabinetmaker but resolved to become an artist. He followed the advice of the painter Chester Harding to teach himself to paint by copying engravings with homemade pigments. By 1835 he was recognized as an able native frontier painter, charging $20 per portrait in St Louis. In 1836 he moved to Natchez where he charged $40. His portraits had become standard decorations in prosperous Missouri homes. He was able to afford three months at the PAFA in 1837, observing genre as well as portrait painting. From 1838 to 1840 he sent paintings for exhibition in NYC. In 1841 he went to Washington, DC to paint portraits of leading politicians.

In St Louis in 1845 he finished *The Jolly Flatboatmen* that was immediately popular in the form of an American Art-Union engraving. This was followed by *Fur Traders Descending the Missouri, Raftmen Playing Cards,* and *Lighter Relieving a Steamboat Aground*. Bingham entered politics in 1848, an interest that provided *Stump Speaking* and *The Verdict of the People*. A series of government jobs and European travel left less time for painting, but in 1872 he visited Colorado and thereafter painted the *View of Pikes Peak* that is in the ACM colln. TAW records a Colorado trip as 1878. Bingham was described as small and delicate but dynamic, an excellent conversationalist married three times, and always wigged to cover baldness from measles at 19.

BIRCHIM, Dorcas. Born Danville, Ind 1923, living Owens Valley, Cal in 1968. Traditional Western painter. No reference. Source COW. No recorded auction sale. Signature example and photograph p 107 COW.

Mrs Birchim was educated at UCLA, then served for two years in the Marines in WWII. Her familiarity with her subject comes from the ranch life at her home near Mt Whitney. She has been president of the Sierra-Desert Art Association. Her paintings "breathe action, dust, sweat, movement, and all the virility of outdoor Western life." COW.

BISBING, Henry Singlewood. Born Philadelphia, Pa 1849, died Ledyard, Conn 1933. Expatriate Eastern animal painter who had illustrated the 1872 and 1873 reports of the Hayden survey. Chevalier, Legion of Honor 1902. Work in PAFA, Mulhouse Mus, Berlin Nat Gall, Mus of Nantes (France), World's Columb Expos 1893. References A33 (obit)-BEN-FIE-MAL-SMI. Sources H72,73-MSL-WCE-WHO 18. Oil 20×29″ *The Siesta* sold in 1972 for $550 at auction. Signature example p 144 WCE.

Bisbing began as a wood engraver, then studied at the PAFA. In 1872 he worked for Appleton's *Art Journal.* In 1876 he studied at the Munich Academy, the pupil of Barth and Loefftz. In 1879 he was in Brussels, the pupil of J H L de Haas, the famous animal painter who later acclaimed Bisbing as among the greatest animal painters. In 1884 Bisbing was in Paris, the pupil of du Vuillefroy. He settled in Paris, painting rural scenes in France and in Holland. His cow paintings in the World's Columbian Expos were *Afternoon in the Meadows* and *On the River Bank.*

In H72, fig 5 is a fold-out illustration drawn by Bisbing from W H Jackson 1871 photographs of the hot springs and geysers of the Yellowstone and Madison. Acknowledged by Hayden as a "fine" drawing, it first appeared in the *Illustrated Christian Weekly.* Fig 5 in H73 is smaller but equally fine. Bisbing is not listed as a member of Hayden's party. There is no record of his having been West.

BISCHOFF, Eugene Henry. Born Pforzheim, Germany 1880, died probably North Bennington, Vt 1954. Painter, teacher. Work in Bennington Mus. References A41-MAS. Source, painting of Taos Pueblo. No current auction record but the estimated price of a Taos oil would be $1,000 to $1,200 at auction in 1976. No signature example. (See illustration 27.)

E H Bischoff studied at the ASL, the pupil of George Bridgman, at Pratt Inst, and at the Cal SFA. In 1941 he was the art director of Vermont Gravure. In the early 1940s he began to summer in Taos, painting colorful landscapes.

BISTTRAM, Emil James. Born Hungary 1895, died Taos, NM 1976. Modern Taos painter, muralist, teacher. Member Transcendental Painting Group 1938 (Santa Fe). Work in ANS, Albright AG, Roerich Mus, U of NM; murals in Taos courthouse, Dept Justice (DC), USPO Ranger (Tex). References A62-FIE. Sources AAT-CAA-CAH-PIT-TAL-TSF. Pastel and crayon 12½×16¼″ *Taos Mtn Landscape* sold 9/13/72 for $125 at auction. Oil 42×27″ *Penetration* sold 3/21/74 for $550 at auction. Signature example p 26 PIT. (See illustration 28.)

Emil Bisttram studied in NYC at the NAD, Cooper Union, and NY School of Fine & Applied Art, the pupil of Howard Giles, Ivan Olinsky, and Leon Kroll. He also studied composition with Jay Hambidge before becoming an instructor at the NY School. In 1930 he visited Taos for the first time but found he was blocked from painting by the "grandeur of the scenery and the limitless space."

TSF. He went on to Mexico to study fresco painting with Rivera, becoming influenced by the strong realism and sculptured surfaces.

In 1931 Bisttram returned to establish the Taos SA. His work at the time remained realistic. For his 1932 portrait *Indian Girl with Basket* he constructed elements of the composition in wood and clay for more perfect details. In the mid-1930s he painted under the WPA. By 1938 he was a founder of the Transcendental movement in New Mexico as he turned toward non-objectivity, where paintings were composed of universal rather than physical forms. Bisttram did not limit himself to a non-objective style, however. He also painted realistic subjects. In 1974 Bisttram was "still a vigorous artist." PIT.

BJORKLUND, Lorence F. Born Minnesota before 1915, living Croton Falls, NY 1976. One of the "50 Great Western Illustrators," writer. Work in John Carroll colln. No reference. Sources CUS-50G-USM-letter L F Bjorklund 2/76. No current auction record. Signature example USM.

As a child, Larry Bjorklund lived near Ft Snelling (now St Paul) and became familiar with horses and the military. He also traveled 1,826 miles of the Mississippi with a boyhood friend in a homemade flat-bottomed skiff. A scholarship to Pratt Institute in Brooklyn brought Bjorklund East in the early 1930s and he combined school with illustrating for the pulp Western magazines. Through 1972 he had also illustrated more than 300 adult and juvenile books including "Indian Wars and Warriors West." In 1967 Bjorklund wrote and illustrated "Faces of the Frontier." His second book "The Bison: The Great American Buffalo" was published in 1970. An additional specialty is the Plains Indian. His illustrations for John Carroll included water-

colors on Custer and drawings for "The Black Military Experience in the American West."

"I am primarily a book illustrator, so most of my work is in black and white—ie, pencil, charcoal, dry brush, pen and ink, wash—etc—'most any medium which would reproduce well for illustration of books." Letter 2/76.

BJURMAN, Andrew. Born Sweden 1876, died probably Los Angeles, Cal 1943. Portrait sculptor including Indian subjects, craftsman, teacher. Work in John Morton Mem Mus (Philadelphia). References A47 (obit)-BEN-FIE-MAL-SMI. Sources SCA-p 28 NSS 29 illustrating *Spirit of the Southwest* in wood. No auction record.

A self-taught sculptor and craftsman, Bjurman taught at Franklin high school in the 1920s.

BLACK, Laverne Nelson. Born Viola, Kickapoo Valley, Wis 1887, died Chicago, Ill 1938. Painter of Southwest Indian genre, illustrator, sculptor. Work in ANS, HAR, Adams colln, Valley Nat Bank; murals USPO Phoenix, Treas Dept (DC). References A41-MAL. Sources COW-HAR-PAW-PIT-TWR-WAI 72. Gouache 22×29" *On the Trail* sold 10/27/71 for $1,600 at auction. Signature example p 29 PIT. (See illustration 29.)

Son of an innkeeper, Black drew with natural materials as a child in Wisconsin. When his family moved to Chicago he studied at the Academy from 1906 to 1908. Summers were spent in the West when he worked as an illustrator in Minneapolis and as a newspaper artist in Chicago and NYC. Some paintings were on commission and his sculpted bronzes of Indians were sold at Tiffany's. When his health failed he moved to Taos about 1925. He painted the Southwest Indian genre but with only limited recognition, although *Before the Fiesta and Buffalo Dance* were bought by the Santa Fe Ry.

About 1937 Black moved to Phoenix. The Depression years had been difficult for Black except for Santa Fe commissions. In 1937, however, Black and Berninghaus were selected to paint murals for the USPO in Phoenix. Black's designs depicted the movement of Arizona from the covered wagon pioneers through the pony express days to the cattle and mining industries of the '30s. Black's death was thought to have been from paint poisoning. His memorial exhibition was sponsored in Phoenix by the Arizona Soc of Painters and Sculptors.

BLACKOWL, Archie. Born Custer Cnty, Okla 1911, living Clinton, Okla 1967. Cheyenne painter, muralist. Work in GIL, MAI, Mus Northern Ariz, Okla Hist Soc Mus, Philbrook AC; murals in public buildings. No reference. Source AIP. No auction record. No signature example. (See illustration 30.)

Blackowl's Cheyenne name is Mis Ta Moo To Va, Flying Hawk. He is a descendant of Roman Nose, the celebrated war chief of the Cheyennes whose village was destroyed by Gen Custer in 1867 while T R Davis was on the scene as special artist for *Harper's*. The defeat of Roman Nose in 1868 was an illustration by Zogbaum for *Harper's*.

He was educated at Haskell and studied painting under muralist Olaf Nordmark. He began to paint professionally in the early 1930s, encouraged by Woody Crumbo (which see).

BLAIR, John. Active late 19th century in the Canadian West. Work in NGC with signature example p 21 NGC catalog. Reference perhaps BEN. Sources CAE-NGC catalog. No auction record. (See illustration 31.)

Blair painted Winnipeg prairie scenes in oil. It is suggested he may be the John Blair listed BEN as active in Scotland the second half of the 19th century and exhibiting watercolors 1885 to 1888 in London. NGC.

BLAKE, William Phipps. Born NYC 1825, died probably Tucson, Ariz 1910. Railway survey sketch artist, geologist, mining engineer. References DAB-G&W. Source AIW. No current auction record but the estimated price of a landscape view would be about $300 to $500 at auction in 1976. No signature example.

Blake was educated as a mineralogist and chemist. He was the geologist and Charles Koppel the official artist of Lt Williamson's 1853 survey of the two possible rail routes in Southern California. Blake's "Report of a Geological Reconnaissance in California" included scientific sketches of the land formations of the California deserts and the Sierra Nevada Mountains and also some views of general significance, eg, *San Diego from the Bay*.

Blake became professor of mineralogy and geology in the U of California and the director of the School of Mines of the U of Arizona.

BLAKELOCK, Ralph Albert. Born NYC 1847, died Adirondacks, NY 1919. Important Eastern painter of landscapes with Indians, in the Southwest and Far West about 1869–72. ANA 1913, NA 1916. Work in ANS, BM, COR, MMA, NGA, etc. References A19 (obit)-BEN-CHA-DAB-ENB-FIE-MAL-SMI. Sources ACO-AIC-ALA-AMA-ANT

5/62,1/64,4/67,7/68,2/69,8/70,12/72, 1/73-ARI-BAR-COR-DBW-DEP-HAR-HMA-150-ISH-KW1-M19-M31-MSL-NJA-PAW-POW-PNW-STI-TWR-WAI 72-WES-WHO 18. Oil 28×36″ *Indian Encampment* signed but not dated was estimated for sale 10/25/73 at $15,000 to $20,000 at auction, but not sold. Signature example p 152 POW. (See illustration 32.)

Blakelock, the son of a NYC doctor, entered the Free Academy of the City of NY in 1864, turning to music and fine arts after one year. He left college in 1866 to paint landscapes, considering himself to have been self-taught. By 1867 he was exhibiting realistic paintings in the NA resulting from his Eastern travels, and by 1869 he declined European studies to travel West. There is no exact record of Blakelock's movements, but he actually lived among the Indians, working his way to California and through Mexico to Panama and the West Indies. In the West from 1869 to at least 1872, he made hundreds of sketches.

He returned to NYC about 1876. His painting style had evolved to the impressionist, so radically different from his contemporaries that he could not sell his work at all. One group of 33 paintings was bought by a NYC dealer from the artist for $100. Blakelock lived in absolute poverty with his wife and nine children, peddling his paintings from door to door, generally without success. Throughout his ordeal, Blakelock maintained his style of pure romanticism, studying cracks in the walls as designs, resorting to music to capture a painting mood.

In 1899 he succumbed to the constant economic strain, became violent, and was removed to an asylum near Middletown, NY where he painted paper landscapes that simulated money in his delusion of immense wealth. After Blakelock was unable to paint seriously, his romantic work came into vogue, and by 1916 the Toledo AM paid $20,000 at auction for his *Brook by Moonlight,* a painting that Blakelock had sold for less than the cost

of the auction catalog. A16 frontispiece. This acceptance did not benefit the artist in the asylum or his family who had all lived in a one-room shack at the bottom of a Catskill ravine. When Blakelock's oldest daughter Marian discovered that she could paint as her father had, she sold similar paintings to a dealer who changed her signature to her father's, driving her into an asylum in 1915. The Blakelock story may be the bitterest tragedy in American art, while his major paintings may be the purest, the image of an Indian encampment beneath silhouetted trees before the blue-white moon.

BLUE EAGLE, Acee (Alex C McIntosh). Born on the Wichita Reservation north of Anadarko, Okla 1907, died Okla 1959. Painter, lecturer, writer, teacher. Work in DAM, GIL, MNM, Philbrook AC; murals in public buildings and in the USS *Oklahoma.* References A41 (lists birth as 1910)-MAL. Source AIP. No auction record or signature example.

Blue Eagle was Che Bon Ah Bu La, Laughing Boy, a Creek-Pawnee. He graduated Chilocco Indian School (Oklahoma) in 1928 and represented Oklahoma Boy Scouts on a European trip 1929. He visited museums in North America and Europe to research the various Indian tribes. In 1934 he painted Oklahoma murals for the WPA. In 1935 he was invited to lecture on Indian art at Oxford U in England. He continued touring the US and Europe, lecturing on the life and character of the American Indian. This was after the establishment of the popularity of the "Five Kiowas" (see Spencer Asah).

Blue Eagle founded the art department at Bacone College and acted as head 1935–38. Twelve of his paintings were owned by the King of Spain. His work was reproduced by the silk screen process. In 1937 *American Magazine* named him "foremost living Indian artist." He divorced his Cherokee wife, then married and divorced a Javanese about 1946. He became a television critic and personality. By 1958, he was named "outstanding Indian in the US." A memorial biography was issued. Oklahoma honored him posthumously for service to the state.

BLUM, Jerome S. Born Chicago 1884, living NYC 1934. Painter. References BEN-MAL. No source. Oil 32×39½" *The Grand Canyon* sold 3/25/31 for $50 at auction listed A31.

Blum was a pupil of the Smith Art Academy, AIC, and École des Beaux-Arts in Paris. He exhibited portraits and landscapes at the Salon d'Automne in 1909–10.

BLUMENSCHEIN, Ernest Leonard. Born Pittsburgh, Pa 1874, died Taos, NM 1960. Member SI 1901, ANA 1910, Taos SA 1912, NA 1927. Important Southwestern Indian painter, illustrator, muralist, teacher. Work in ANS, MMA, BM, MOMA, NGA, Eiteljorg colln, MNM, HAW, etc. References A62 (obit)-BEN-FIE-MAL-SMI. Sources AAR 3/74-AAT-AIC-AIW-AMA-ARI-COW-CUS-DCC-GIL-HAR-HMA-ILA-MSL-M57-PAW-PET-PIT-POW-TAL-TSF-TWR-WAI 71,72-WHO 60. Oil on canvas mounted on board, 20×44½" *Indians in the Mountains* with signature example and inscribed Taos sold 4/11/73 for $29,000 at auction. (See illustration 33.)

Son of a prominent musician, E L Blumenschein graduated from Dayton, Ohio high school. He attended Cincinnati College of Music on a scholarship in 1891 and also studied at the Cincinnati Art Academy. When he went on to the ASL, he worked as a symphonic violinist. He also studied in Paris at the Julien Academy with Constant, Laurens, and Collin. While in Paris in 1895 Joseph Sharp praised Taos, NM as a novel painting subject for Blumenschein and his friend Bert Phillips. When they returned to NYC the same year, Blumenschein and Phillips shared a studio. Blumenschein worked as an illustrator. In the winter of 1897–98 *McClure's Magazine* commissioned a Southwestern sketching trip for Blumenschein that sent him into New Mexico for the first time. In 1898 *McClure's* also published Blumenschein's *We Circled All Around Him* that became a book illustration as *The Last of Custer*.

In the summer of 1898 Blumenschein and Phillips established the art colony of Taos as the result of a broken wheel on their wagon that ended a sketching trip from Denver. They were followed by Sharp, Couse, Berninghaus, and Blumenschein's pupil, Dunton. Blumenschein continued to divide his time among NYC where he worked as an illustrator and taught at the ASL, Paris where he studied again 1902–8 and where he married the established artist Mary Shepard Greene, and Taos. His summer sketching trips were to Taos where his Indian paintings were stylized but still influenced by the realistic illustrations he did for books of Jack London and Booth Tarkington as well as *Harper's, Century, Scribner's,* etc. In 1919 Blumenschein moved to Taos with his family. He gave up illustrating for painting. Aware of the modernists like Dasburg and Marin, he began paying more attention to complex compositions and free colors.

BLUMENSCHEIN, Helen Greene. Born NYC 1909, living Santa Fe, NM 1975. Southwestern landscape painter, illustrator, lithographer. Work in NY Pub Lib, MNM, Lib Cong, Carnegie Inst,

Newark (NJ) Pub Lib, Cincinnati AM. References A62-BEN-MAL. Sources TAL-TSF-WAA. No current auction record. Painting example ✕10 TAL.

Helen Blumenschein moved to Taos in 1919 with her parents, Ernest Blumenschein, the pioneer Taos painter, and Mary Shepard Greene, the illustrator. She was the pupil of Harry Sternberg in graphic arts at the ASL and of André Lhote in Paris, exhibiting at the Paris Salon in 1930–31. The Taos calendar that was silk-screened in the 1940s was her design.

BLUMENSCHEIN, Mary Shepard Greene (Mrs E L). Born NYC 1869 (or 1868), died Taos, NM 1958. Painter in Taos, book illustrator, teacher, silver craftsman, sculptor. ANA 1913, SI. Work in Bklyn Mus AI, Pratt Inst, Lovelace Clinic (Albuquerque). References A59 (obit)-BEN-FIE-MAL-SMI. Sources AAT-AMA-HAW-MSL-NA 74-PIT-TAL-TSF-WAA-WHO 50-WOM. No current auction record but the estimated price of a Taos oil would be about $1,500 to $1,700 at auction in 1976. Signature example p 41 PIT.

Mrs Blumenschein was educated in Adelphi Academy and studied at Pratt Institute in Brooklyn, the pupil of Herbert Adams. She then studied in Paris, the pupil of Raphaël Collin. Exhibiting in the Paris Salon beginning 1900, she became the first American woman to receive a second-class medal. Successful as a painter, she married the younger Ernest Blumenschein in Paris in 1905, working with him as an illustrator to support his continued studies. When they returned to NYC in 1909, she taught at Pratt.

Blumenschein had been a founder of the Taos art colony along with Bert Phillips in 1898. He went back for summer sketching trips, taking the family in 1913, but not settling in Taos until 1919 when Mrs Blumenschein's inheritance made the move possible. They bought an adobe building on Ledoux Street with studios for each and for daughter Helen. Mrs Blumenschein continued to work as a book illustrator in a decorative style emphasizing flat designs. In the late 1920s she again studied at Pratt, finding satisfaction in silver work. As a painter she exhibited at the NAD from 1906 to 1946.

BODFISH, William P. Active from 1865 to 1894. Cartoonist, illustrator. No reference. Sources IL 94-POW. No auction record but the estimated price of a cartoon 10✕7″ showing a trapper trapped would be about $200 to $300 at auction in 1976. Signature example p 74 IL 94 *Three of a Difference*.

Bodfish is listed as among "the few able cartoonists" who went West after the Civil War. POW. He is quoted as deriving satisfaction from genre scenes with domestic animals and children. P250 IL 94.

BODMER, Karl. Born Riesbach, Switzerland 1809, died Barbizon, France 1893. Very important Swiss explorer-painter, etcher. Legion of Honor 1876. Work in GIL, Joslyn AM, Bern, Luxembourg, etc. References BEN-CHA-FIE-G&W-MAL. Sources AIW-ALA-ANT 9/43,5/44,4/62-AOW-AWM-BAR-COW-DBW-GIL-GOD-HMA-HON-HUT-150-LAF-MIS-NJA-PAW-TEP-WAI 71,72-WES. Ink and pencil drawing 9½✕16½″ *Buffalo Hunt* with stamp signature but not dated sold 4/20/72 for $10,000 at auction. Signature example ✕21 PB 5/26/71. (See illustration 34.)

Bodmer, the tall and handsome student of his uncle Johann Jakob Meyer and of Cornu in Paris, was already at 23

quite experienced in drawing for reproduction, having had German valley views
engraved. He was engaged by the stocky
middle-aged Prussian prince Maximilian
in 1832 as artist for an exploratory expedition to the American West. During
their preparations, which took nine
months, the royal scholar Maximilian
and the top-hatted Bodmer talked to Titian Peale in Philadelphia, examining the
Peale and Seymour paintings from the
Long Expedition in 1819. They bought
Rindisbacher watercolors from the 1820s,
and they viewed Catlin's paintings of
1830, thus learning from the only major
artists to precede them. After side trips
into the Alleghenys and to New Orleans,
they wintered in New Harmony, Ind, the
home of the artist-naturalist Thomas Say.

They reached St Louis in March 1833,
taking passage on the Fur Company's
steamboat *Yellowstone* for 1,500 miles in
seven weeks to move trade goods to Fort
Pierre, SD. Bodmer sketched Indian subjects at every stop, taking a whole day
for a single watercolor portrait, doing a
detailed pencil drawing of the person and
the entire costume. The journey upriver
continued on the steamboat *Assiniboin*
to Fort Union, another 500 miles on the
Missouri River through North Dakota,
and then by keelboat *Flora* following the
Lewis and Clark route of 1805 to Fort
McKenzie, a lonely new outpost in Montana within 100 miles of the backbone of
the Rockies. They remained for five
weeks, in the midst of 20,000 Blackfeet,
beyond where Catlin had gone, Bodmer
painting portraits and the party surviving
an attack on the fort by a large force of
Assiniboin and Cree. Bodmer's painting
of the attack is a major product of the
entire trip. Rather than continue into the
hostile Rockies, the party returned to
Fort Clark, ND for the winter, with
Bodmer the last white artist to record the
Mandan tribe before the 1837 smallpox
epidemic. Bodmer's wildlife watercolors
included a panorama of a great herd of
buffalo descending to the river. He continued to make sketches of Indian ceremonies and life-styles that are superb
ethnological documentation, even though
his frozen colors had to be heated in
water. In May 1834 the party reached St
Louis where they again saw Catlin paintings. Via stage, canalboat, and steamer,
they went back to NYC and Europe.

Bodmer became a resident of Barbizon
in the Fontainebleau forest near Paris.
He made 81 finished paintings to illustrate the journal of the trip, then himself
completed many of the etching plates.
The 1839 full-color edition of the prints
is the finest depiction of the Indians of
the Missouri frontier. They certainly
served as the fieldwork for Indian
painters who never left their studios, for
example, some Currier & Ives lithographic artists. The other major original
artist was Catlin, but there was surpris-
ingly little duplication in exact subject
matter and none in style between eager
Catlin and disciplined Bodmer.

The Western trip was but a short portion of the career of this important Barbizon painter who worked with Millet
and Théodore Rousseau but never again
visited America. Bodmer began exhibiting in the Paris Salon in 1836. He illustrated books and magazines and was
known for forest landscapes and depictions of birds and mammals. By the time
of his death, Bodmer's Indian engravings
were entirely forgotten.

BOFILL, Antoine. Born Barcelona,
Spain in the 19th century, active Paris
1921. French-school sculptor. Work in
Harmsen colln. Reference BEN. Source
DCC. Bronze 17¼″ high *Le Dernier
d'une Race* sold 6/11/69 for $200 at
auction.

Bofill studied at the Barcelona Academy of Beaux-Arts. He won an honorable mention at the Salon d'Artistes
Français in 1902 and exhibited in 1921.

BOGDANOVICH, Borislav. Born 1900, died 1970. Painter. Work in Valley Nat Bank colln. No reference. Source ACO. Oil 36×50″ *Still Life with Fruit* sold 5/24/68 for $150 at auction. No signature example.

BOISSEAU, Alfred. Born Paris, France 1823, living Cleveland, Ohio 1859. Portrait and genre painter, daguerreotypist. References BEN-G&W. Source MIS. Oil 36¼×52¼″ *Flood on the Mississippi* sold 10/22/69 for $1,000 at auction. Signature example p 68 MIS.

Boisseau was the pupil of P Delaroche in Paris. He exhibited at the Paris Salon in 1842. He was in New Orleans in 1845–46, then exhibited *Louisiana Indians Walking Along a Bayou* dated 1847 at the Paris Salon in 1847. He exhibited in NYC at the NA in 1849 and at the American Art-Union in 1852, moving to Cleveland in 1852.

"The squaws went by, walking one behind the other, with their hair growing low on the forehead, loose, or tied back of the head. These squaws carried large Indian baskets on their backs, and shuffled along, barefooted, while their lords paced before them." MIS.

BOLES, David. Born Artesia, Cal 1947, living Cornville, Ariz 1974. Southwestern trompe l'oeil painter in chalk. Work in Valley Nat Bank. No reference. Sources pp 46–47 AHI 1/73 *Portrait of Alchise* with signature example-p 39, AHI 5/72 *Jerome*-11/16/73 letter from David Boles. No auction record.

Boles has lived in Arizona since he was 10. He attended Northern Arizona U but dropped out because of the "generally avant-garde atmosphere." The trompe l'oeil compositions include Western objects—a framed photo of an Apache scout, a warp-weave Indian blanket, a Hopi bowl, a kachina, and a Navaho necklace.

BOLTON, Hale William. Born Honey Grove, Tex 1885, died Dallas, Tex 1920 (or 1919). Painter specializing in Western landscapes in oil and pastel. References A20(obit)-BEN-MAL-SMI. Sources TOB-TXF. No current auction record or signature example.

Bolton was the pupil of Frank Reaugh. He studied at the St Louis SFA and in Holland and France where he lived for years. "Western subjects were his choice. *Snowstorm in Dallas* is one of his best known canvases." TOB. He also "painted with much success on the Pacific Slope." TXF.

BONHEUR, Marie Rosa. Born Bordeaux, France 1822, died Thomery, France 1899. French animal painter and sculptor. Legion of Honor 1865. Work in most major museums. References BEN-CHA-ENB-MAL. Sources COR-COW-DEP-M31-PAF-TEP-WBB. Oil 32¾×51¼″ *Return from the Pasture* sold 12/5/75 for $23,000 at auction. Signature example BEN.

Rosa Bonheur was the pupil of her father Raymond, a painter. As a young girl, she dressed as a man to visit the slaughterhouses to learn animal anatomy, and Georges Sand was the decisive influence on her life. Her first two paintings were exhibited at Bordeaux in 1841, her first sculpture in 1842, and worldwide fame followed by 1855. During the Franco-Prussian War, her studio and residence were protected by order of the German royalty. She was also a close friend of Queen Victoria.

In 1892 Rosa Bonheur was caught up in the spirit of the Wild West when

Buffalo Bill and his show came to Paris. She painted a full-length portrait of Buffalo Bill, and this is the painting that led Robert Lindneux (which see) to Denver.

BONNER, Mary Anita. Born Bastrop, La 1885, died San Antonio, Tex 1935. Painter of Texas scenes, illustrator, etcher. Works in Luxembourg Mus, French Govt colln, Brit Mus, NY Pub Lib. References A36 (obit)-BEN-MAL. Sources TOB-T20-TXF. No current auction record or signature example.

Mary Bonner was born on a northern Louisiana plantation and raised in Texas. She was the pupil of Richard Miller, Bolton Brown, and Édouard Léon in Paris where she was well known for her watercolors and etchings of Texas scenes. She spent her summers in Paris and was decorated by the French Government which bought her works for permanent display. She was equally popular in Texas where in 1927 "she sold etchings to the amount of $300 in one afternoon" in Corpus Christi. TXF.

BONWELL, E. Illustrator active 1867–73 with four sketches included in BEY. No birth or death date. No reference. Sources BEY-H72, with signature example opp p 51 H72. No auction record.

"Beyond the Mississippi" by Albert D Richardson was published in 1867 "with more than 200 illustrations, from photographs and original sketches, of the prairies, deserts, mountains, rivers, mines, cities, Indians, trappers, pioneers, and great natural curiosities. 1857–1867." Each of the illustrations is credited to the artist, generally a Civil War field artist. Four illustrations are by E Bonwell. They are finely drawn, complete scenes rather than cartoons, from Kansas to Or-egon. The first is the residences of Brigham Young in Salt Lake City. The second is a topographic view of Virginia City in Nevada. The last two are street scenes in Portland and Leavenworth. None of the illustrations is signed.

H72 opp p 51 includes fig 10, *Yellowstone Lake* (*East Side*), an accomplished full-page view signed "Bonwell del." Fig 29 p 119 is a vignette *Second Cañon of Yellowstone River* signed "Bonwill del." Fig 35 p 132 is a vignette *Upper Falls of Yellowstone River, 140 feet* signed "Bonwill del." This would appear to be the same E Bonwell as in BEY, with the variant to Bonwill the caprice of the engraver. In H72, the name Bonwell does not appear in the initial listing of the personnel of the Hayden expedition.

BOREIN, John Edward. Born San Leandro, Cal 1872, died Santa Barbara, Cal 1945. Important Western genre painter. "The cowpuncher artist," illustrator, etcher, writer. Work in GIL, NYPL, Cowboy Hall of Fame, Glenbow-Alberta Inst. References A41-BEN-FIE-MAL-SMI. Sources ACO-ANT 8/72-BOR-CAP-COW-GIL-HAR-HON-KEN 6/71-PAW-POW-TWR-WAI 71,72. Oil 22×30″ *Buffalo Hunt* with signature example, dated 1913, sold 10/27/71 for $20,000 at auction.

Son of a county politician, Ed Borein was educated in Oakland schools. A poor student, he left at 17 for a job with a saddler where he learned about gear and he braided riatas. After working at odd jobs on a local ranch, he attended the San Francisco AA Art School for one month in 1891, meeting Swinnerton and Maynard Dixon there. When he hired on at a cattle ranch, the first sketches he sold in 1896 were printed in the Los Angeles *The Land of Sunshine* as "illustrated by Ed Borein, a vaquero on the Jesus Maria Rancho, Santa Barbara Co."

Borein's reference when he left the ranch that year recommended him as "of sober and industrious habits, and a competent Vacquero." He continued to sketch at his next job in Malibu where the owner financed a trip to Mexico for 1897–99. Some of the Mexican drawings have double lines and double signatures—pencil on the spot by day and ink at night. He returned to Oakland via New Mexico and Arizona, becoming staff artist on the San Francisco *Call* at $8 per week. In 1901, he teamed with Maynard Dixon on a sketching trip north through the Sierras, Carson City, Oregon, and Idaho. Mexico drew him again in 1903, and there he began painting watercolors on the backs of photographic prints. Returning, he sketched his way through Pueblo Indian country.

In 1904 Borein rented an Oakland studio, specializing in illustrations of Mexico and in advertising display cards. He turned out dozens of oils of uneven quality. A few pieces of sculpture were also attempted. By 1907 Oakland palled. Borein went to NYC where his studio in the theatrical district was a gathering point for Swinnerton, Russell, Leo Carrillo, Will Rogers, Dixon, Will James, Olaf Seltzer, Carl Oscar Borg, etc. In January 1909 he went back to a studio in Oakland, sketching in Oregon in August, and was in NYC again by September. This time he was a successful illustrator for *Harper's, Collier's, Sunset, Century,* and *Western World* as well as for advertising. About 1911 Borein began etching, with advice from Hassam and Roth. Russell found work for Borein in Canada in 1912 and 1913. In NYC in 1914 and 1915, Borein studied etching with Preissig at the ASL. This was a time of prosperity. In 1919 he was back in Oakland, via Russell in Great Falls. He married in 1921, moved to Santa Barbara, and kept his base there, this gray-eyed man with glasses, 5'7", who weighed about 160 lbs, and wore cowboy gear, boots, string tie, and Stetson.

BOREN, James. Born Waxahatchie, Tex 1921, living near Clifton, Tex 1976. Traditional Western painter specializing in watercolors, illustrator, teacher, art director. Member CAA. Reference A76. Sources ACO-AHI-C 71 to 74-COW-HAR-OSR-WAI 71,72. No current auction record. Signature example C 71. (See illustration 35.)

Boren grew up in the ranch country of West Texas where he lived in Snyder, Big Spring, Lamesa, and Sweetwater, graduating from Temple high school in 1939. He served for four years in WWII, then earned a fine arts degree in 1949 and a master's in 1951 at Kansas City AI. After two years of teaching at St Mary College in Kansas, he traveled in the West and Northwest before moving to Denver. Boren worked as a commercial illustrator.

In 1965 Boren became the first art director of the National Cowboy Hall of Fame. Dean Krakel, director of the museum, was Boren's biographer in 1968, writing "James Boren: A Study in Discipline." In order to be able to give full time to painting, Boren resigned from the museum in 1969. A native Westerner, he feels that the cowboy was the star role in the drama of the West, the most beautiful country anywhere, and that painting the West is what he does best. COW. His watercolor paintings have won awards at the annual CAA exhibition each year since 1968.

BORG, Carl Oscar. Born Grinstad, Sweden 1879, died Santa Barbara, Cal 1947. Western genre painter specializing in desert and Indian subjects, illustrator, teacher. Work in U of Cal (series on Southwest Indian ceremonies), Hearst Free Lib, LAMA, Montclair AM, Bibliothèque Nationale (Paris), Seattle AM, Lib Cong, Göteborg Mus (Sweden). ANA 1938. References A47 (obit)-BEN-FIE-MAL-SMI. Sources ANT

10/61-COW-HAR-JNB-PNW-TWR-WAI 71-WHO 46. Oil 38×40″ *Sons of the Desert* sold 4/20/72 for $5,500 at auction. Signature example p 50 COW. (See illustration 36.)

Apprentice housepainter Borg left Sweden by freighter in 1899. Although he considered himself self-taught as a painter, he did study in London where he worked as a scene painter. Borg emigrated to NYC in 1902 but moved to Canada before settling in California in 1904. Employed as a scene painter for the movies, he had his first exhibition in 1905. Introduced to the West as a subject, he sketched throughout California and the Southwest until he was sponsored by the mother of William Randolph Hearst for five years of European study. He received awards in France in 1913–14 and 1920 as well as in the US beginning 1915 at the Pan-Pac Expos. Borg lived in Santa Barbara, California from 1914 to 1930, a friend of Ed Borein, painting Indian ceremonials and cowboy genre subjects and teaching art. He also painted in Central and South America, Spain, Morocco, the Valley of the Nile, and Italy.

Borg, Millard Sheets, and Dr Eugene Bolton of the U of California wrote and illustrated a 1936 book on the history of California, "Cross, Sword, and Gold Pan." The same year, he published a book of etchings, "The Great South West." His own biography was published in Sweden.

BORGLUM, James Lincoln de la Mothe. Born Stamford, Conn 1912, living Harlingen, Tex 1976. Western monument sculptor, photographer, writer. Work on Mt Rushmore Nat Memorial. Reference A76. Sources COW-WHO 70. No auction record or signature example.

Lincoln Borglum, the son of Gutzon Borglum, was educated in Texas and Wyoming. He was the pupil of his father for 12 years and studied in Europe in 1929 and 1931. In charge of measurements and of enlarging models, he worked at the Mt Rushmore Memorial beginning 1932. After the death of his father in 1941 he was appointed official sculptor to complete the memorial. Thereafter he was superintendent.

His color photographs have been exhibited and used as illustrations in *This Week* and *The Saturday Evening Post*. His sculpture has included a 300′ statue of Christ and a colossal bust of President Johnson in South Dakota and a religious statue in Texas.

BORGLUM, John Gutzon de la Mothe. Born near Bear Lake, Idaho 1867, died Chicago, Ill 1941. Monumental Western sculptor, painter. Member RSBA, Société Nationale des Beaux-Arts. Work includes the Mt Rushmore (SD) Nat Memorial, *Mares of Diomedes* (MMA), *Lincoln* (Capitol Rotunda, Washington and in Newark), Trail Drivers' Assoc (San Antonio), *A Nation Moving Westward* (Marietta, Ohio). References A47 (obit)-BEN-ENB-FIE-MAL-SMI. Sources ALA-AMA-BWB-COR-COW-DEP-190-MSL-PAW-SCU-TOB-TXF-WHO 40. No auction record for sculpture; painting 29¾×42″ *Riderless Horse by a Campfire at Night* with signature example, dated 1903, estimated for sale 10/28/74 at $1,000 to $1,200 at auction in LA.

Gutzon Borglum, the son of an immigrant Danish woodcarver who became a doctor, was born at a place not exactly named because it was on the plains before settlements. He began carving in public school in Nebraska and at St Mary College in Kansas, then was apprenticed to a Los Angeles lithographer and worked for a fresco painter in the early 1880s. About 1885 he studied painting with Virgil Williams and William Keith at the San Francisco AA. He returned to Los Angeles to paint Western subjects later given to California benefactors who sent him to Paris about 1888. Borglum studied at Julien Academy, École des Beaux-Arts, and with the sculptor Stephan Sinding. He exhibited in Paris in 1891, then toured Spain before returning to California 1893–94. From 1895 to 1901 he had his first important exhibitions in London and Paris where he was considered to be a disciple of Rodin.

Borglum opened his NY studio in 1902, teaching at the ASL in 1906–7. Early sculpture subjects were *Indian Scouts, Death of a Chief,* and *Apaches Pursued by US Troops.* The huge scale of his later conceptions is unique, described as "sculpture with dynamite" by the artist who blasted stone within a few inches of the desired contour.

Borglum felt only the colossal matched the spirit of the US. On Mt Rushmore, Washington's nose measures 20 feet from brow to tip. Borglum was also an independent politician, identified with the agrarian revolt in the Northwest and serving as exposé-investigator for President Wilson.

BORGLUM, Solon Hannibal. Born Ogden, Utah 1868, died Stamford, Conn 1922. Traditional Western sculptor. ANA 1911. Work in Prescott (Ariz), MMA, Detroit Mus, Cincinnati AM. References A22 (obit)-BEN-ENB-FIE-MAL-SMI. Sources ALA-AMA-ARM-COW-MSL-POW-SCU-WAI 71-WHO 40. Bronze 30″ *Cowboys Lassoing Horses* sold 4/20/72 for $9,000 at auction. Signature example p 163 COW. (See illustration 37.)

Solon Borglum was the younger brother of Gutzon Borglum. In Nebraska and in California, Solon was a working cowboy until 1894, riding and roping, learning about horses and Indians. Gutzon took Solon as his pupil based on untutored animal sketches, the brothers living in Sierra Madre and Santa Ana, close to the Indians and outlaws in the Saddleback Mountains in California. When he went to study with Rebisso in the Cincinnati Art School, 1895–97, Solon dissected horses and attended human surgical clinics to learn anatomical details. Then he studied with Frémiet and Puech in Paris, winning Salon awards with Western sculpture: *Lassoing Wild Horses, Stampede of Wild Horses,* and *The Lame Horse.*

In 1899 Solon returned briefly to the West, studying the Indians. He opened his studio in NYC in 1900, and in a few years moved to "Rocky Ranch" in Silvermine, Conn. He exhibited seven sculptures at the landmark 1913 Armory Show in NYC. In 1918 he became YMCA secretary with the French Army, was cited for bravery and won the Croix de Guerre. He was in charge of the department of sculpture in the AEF educational system. After the war he founded the School of American Sculpture before dying from war disabilities. Solon Borglum was described as "a breezy, whole-souled western American" whose "stampedes and bucking broncos were furious small bronzes." ALA.

BORTHWICK, John David. Born Edinburgh, Scotland 1825, died probably England about 1900. English Special Artist-illustrator, genre and portrait painter, author, the first artist-correspondent in the West for an English paper. References BEN-G&W. Sources AOH-COS-11/13/73 letter from the Royal Academy. No current auction record or signature example.

Borthwick was an English artist who went to NYC during the 1840s, then on to California in 1851 as gold prospector and artist. He remained in California until 1854 when he left for Nicaragua and Australia. His experiences were the subject of his book "Three Years in California," containing eight illustrations lithographed in London. Borthwick exhibited genre paintings in London from 1860 to 1870, including the RA in 1863 and 1865. Some of these paintings may have been of California.

He was the first British artist-correspondent to report the West for a British paper. ILN in 1852 states that *Miners Working the Bed of the American River* "has been sketched by Mr John Borthwick, a clever watercolour painter who first visited the locality as a gold-seeker, but is now settled in the neighborhood, and is actively engaged in his profession, by taking portraits of successful adventurers."

BOSIN, Francis Blackbear. Born Cement (Anadarko), Okla 1921, living Wichita, Kan 1976. Kiowa-Comanche painter of the Plains Indians, illustrator, muralist. Work in Bur Ind Affairs, Denver AM, GIL, Heard Mus, Philbrook AC, Whitney Gall Wn Art, Wichita AA and AM; mural in Wichita bank. Reference A76. Sources AIP-COW-LAF. No auction record. Painting example *And They Moved Without Him* p 164 LAF.

Blackbear Bosin is of Kiowa-Comanche descent (Indian name "Tsate Kongia"), the oldest of four children. He graduated from high school in Cyril, Okla in 1940. Bosin attended Oklahoma U and studied with J Havard MacPherson and Spencer Asah but had little formal training because family obligations prevented acceptance of two scholarships. He worked as color separator and platemaker for Western Lithograph and as illustrator for Boeing. Bosin has owned Great Plains Studio and Gallery since 1960.

He was the only American Indian artist represented in the 1965 White House Festival of the Arts. His work has appeared in *National Geographic Magazine, Life International,* and *Oklahoma Today.* A sculpture design for Wichita was commissioned in 1969.

BOSS, Homer. Born Blandford, Mass 1882, died Santa Cruz, NM 1956. Realist painter, teacher. Work in MNM, HAR. References A53-BEN-FIE-MAL. Sources ARM-DEP-MNM-SUG-TSF. No current auction record but the estimated price of an oil 30×25″ showing a medicine man would be about $1,000 to $1,500 at auction in 1976. Painting example p 44 MNM *Pueblo Indian.*

Boss studied with Anschutz at the PAFA. He also studied with Henri at Chase's school about 1905 when he was a member of the Fifteen Group in NYC 1905–10. This was composed of 15 Henri students including Hopper, Bellows, Kent, and Coleman who organized to exhibit together. Boss also exhibited two paintings in the 1913 Armory Show. He taught anatomy at the ASL during winters from 1922 to 1941, following Henri.

Boss came to Santa Fe for his summers beginning in 1925. He moved permanently to Santa Cruz, NM in 1933 when he was 51. Boss's major Western work was a series of portraits of Indians. He also rode into the neighboring desert to sketch landscapes for elaboration in his studio. He died at 73 from emphysema.

BOTKE, Cornelius. Born Leeuwarden, Holland 1887, died Santa Paula, Cal 1954. Cal landscape painter, etcher. Work in libraries Santa Monica, US Congress, Cal State, NY, LA; AIC, Lincoln AA (Neb). References A53-BEN-FIE-MAL-SMI. Sources AAT-BDW. No current auction record but the published estimate is $500 to $600. No signature example.

Botke studied at the School of Applied Art in Haarlem, Holland, at the AIC, and was the pupil of Chris Le Beau. He was winning prizes in Chicago by 1916 and in California by 1931. He had been etching in Europe in the mid-1920s. Typical titles were *Desert Evening, California Pastoral, Lifting Clouds.* His wife was Jessie Arms Botke, also an artist.

BOTKE, Jessie Arms (Mrs Cornelius Botke). Born Chicago, Ill 1883, died Santa Paula, Cal 1971. Cal painter, muralist. Work in AIC, Munic Gallery (Chicago), Neb AA, San Fran art colln, San Diego FAG, etc. References A66-BEN-FIE-MAL-SMI. Sources SCA-WAA-WHO 50. No current auction record but the published estimate is $300 to $400. No signature example.

Mrs Botke attended Chicago high school and studied at the AIC with John Johanson and Charles Woodbury. She won prizes in Chicago by 1917 and in California by 1928. Typical titles were *Geese, Nest in the Jimson-Weeds.*

BOUNDEY, Burton Shepard. Born Oconomowoc, Wis 1879, died Monterey, Cal 1962. Cal landscape painter, muralist, teacher. Work in Old Custom House Mus (Monterey), schools, libraries. References A62-MAL. Source BDW. No current auction record or signature example.

Boundey studied at the AIC, at Smith Art School in Chicago, and with Robert Henri. Typical titles were *Lumber Industry, Golden Hills, Monterey Coast, Old Monterey.* He taught at the Carmel AI.

BOUTELLE, De Witt Clinton. Born Troy, NY 1820, died Bethlehem Pa 1884. NY and Pa landscape and portrait painter including Indian figures. ANA 1851. Work in Karolik colln, Moravian Archives (Bethlehem). References BEN-FIE-G&W-MAL-SMI. Sources AAR 5/74-ANT 5/47,4/71,7/74-HUT-KAR-NA 74-NJA-PAF. Oil 20×30″ *Landscape with Houses and Trestle Bridge* signed and dated 1867 sold 5/22/73 for $4,500 at auction in Los Angeles. Signature example lot 5 catalog above.

Self-taught, Boutelle was influenced by Cole and Durand. His first painting was sold for $5 in 1839 and repurchased 40 years later for $50. He painted in NYC in 1846 when he began exhibiting at the NA, in Philadelphia 1855, and in Bethlehem, Pa beginning 1858. His works included a number of views of Niagara as well as the Hudson, Catskills, and the Susquehanna.

KAR p 139 shows *Indian Surveying a Landscape* dated 1855. This is the warrior looking down on his now civilized lands. The Indian is identified as of a Western tribe despite no evidence that Boutelle was "west of the eastern seaboard." KAR.

BOVEE, I A. Active 1883–86. Painter of the Yosemite Valley. Source KEN. No other data available.

BOYLE, Ferdinand Thomas Lee. Born Ringwood, Eng 1820, died Brooklyn, NY 1906. Portrait, genre, miniature painter, teacher. ANA 1849. Work in DAM, Union League Club. References A07-BEN-CHA-FIE-G&W. Sources DAA-POW. Oil portrait of Gen W S Hancock sold 1/27/38 for $280 at auction. Signature example F Boyle p 35 DAA.

Boyle came to the US when young. He was a pupil of Henry Inman, an important Eastern portraitist. He lived in New Rochelle, NY in 1843, with a studio in NYC from 1844 to 1855. Boyle settled in St Louis in 1855, where he organized the Western Academy of Art. After serving in the Union Army throughout the Civil War, Boyle returned to NYC in 1866, painting portraits of celebrities such as Dickens, Poe, and General Grant. He was for many years professor, Brooklyn Institute of Art, and head of the Art Department of Adelphi.

BOYLE, John J. Born NYC 1851 (or 1852), died there 1917. Eastern sculptor specializing in Indian subjects. ANA 1910, NSS 1893. Work in Lincoln Park (Chicago), Fairmount Park (Philadelphia), Lib Cong, etc. References A17 (obit)-BEN-DAB-ENB-FIE-MAL-SMI. Sources ALA-AMA-MSL-WHO 16. Bronze, brown patina 31½″ high *The Struggle* with signature example J J Boyle and dated '05, incised Roman Bronze Works, NY, N. 5, sold 9/28/73 for $2,000 at auction.

Boyle, son of a stonecutter, was raised in Philadelphia. When his father died, Boyle left public school to work as an iron-molder, stonecutter, and stone-carver. At the same time, he studied drawing at Franklin Inst and sculpture with Eakins at PAFA. With his savings, he studied at the École des Beaux-Arts in Paris from 1877 to 1880, the pupil of Dumont and also Thomas and E Millet. To support himself he did decorative work in London and portraits in Paris.

In 1880 Boyle received the commission for *An Indian Family* bronze group for Lincoln Park in Chicago. "Before beginning this work, he spent two months among the Indians to be commemorated." DAB. From his studio in Philadelphia, his career was then established, "particularly successful in the portrayal of Indians." ENB. In 1902 Boyle moved to NYC where he was sculptor-member of the Art Commission of NYC. In 1906 Boyle received a $50,000 commission from Congress for a bronze figure of Commodore John Barry that was unveiled by President Wilson.

BOYNTON, Ray Scepter. Born Whitten, Iowa 1883, died New Mexico 1951. Muralist, Cal genre painter, illustrator, teacher. Member, Nat Soc Mural Painters. Work in MNM; murals in Spokane, Berkeley, San Francisco, Washington, DC, etc. References A41-MAL. Sources ASF-WHO 40. No current auction record or signature example.

Son of a farmer-schoolteacher, Boynton was graduated in 1901 from Strawberry Point, Iowa high school near the Mississippi River. After surviving the 1903 Chicago theater fire, he studied at the AIC 1904–7. Boynton moved to Spokane where he painted and taught. In 1914 he went to San Francisco to assist in the 1915 Exposition. He began teaching at the California School of Fine Arts in 1919. One course given was in fresco he had learned from Rivera and Orozco in Mexico. He also started teaching at the U of California in 1923.

Boynton spent 1931 sketching life underground in the mines in the Mother Lode country. The portfolio of drawings recorded Downieville, California and the Empire Mine and North Star Mine in Grass Valley. Some of these drawings were made into paintings. During the Federal Arts Project, Boynton supervised the mural work of 25 painters and helpers. He also did ceiling decorations and the organ screen in Mills College, a hotel lunette, a building panel, and a post office decoration. His studio was high in the Berkeley hills, decorated in Mexican motif.

BRAMLETT, James E. Born southeast Oklahoma 1932, living Wine Glass Ranch, Prescott, Ariz 1968. Traditional Western painter, illustrator. Source COW. No current auction record. Signature example p 158 COW.

Bramlett has worked as a commercial artist and has illustrated Western magazines. He was raised on a ranch and believes that a Western artist has to "live what he paints" in order to achieve the "authenticity, excitement and honesty of a day's work on a cow outfit." COW.

BRANDRIFF, George Kennedy. Born Millville, NJ 1890, died Laguna Beach, Cal 1936. Cal landscape and marine painter, muralist. Work in Phoenix Munic colln, LAMA, U So Cal; murals in Cal schools. References A38 (obit)-MAL. Source TWR. No auction record or signature example.

George K Brandriff, a dentist, was considered mainly self-taught, although he was listed as the pupil of Carl Oscar Borg and Jack Wilkinson Smith. He won prizes at Laguna Beach beginning 1927. The Adams colln includes *A New Outfit,* an undated oil of two Indians unloading their wagons at a hogan.

BRANDT, Carl Ludwig. Born Hamburg (Holstein), Germany 1831, died Savannah, Ga 1905. Eastern and Southern landscape, historical, and portrait painter in the West about 1862, teacher. NA 1872. Work in Telfair Acad (Savannah, Ga—bequeathed most of his paintings and art effects), NYHS. References A05 (obit)-BEN-FIE-G&W-MAL-SMI. Sources ANT 1/49,4/71,12/73,3/74-HUT-NA 74-PAF-WHO 03. Oil 16×20" *Sheep* sold for $250 at auction in 1972. Painting examples p 590 ANT 4/71 *The South West,* p 1010 ANT 12/73 *Ariz Landscape.*

Brandt studied in Copenhagen and Hamburg as well as at other principal European galleries. He moved to NYC in 1852, after serving in the 1848–50 war between Germany and Denmark. Brandt exhibited at the NAD and PAFA beginning 1855, with Western landscapes painted in 1862. After returning to Europe 1865–69, he settled in Hastings-on-Hudson, NY in a house that had been built by Adm Farragut. His winters were spent in Savannah after 1883 when he became director of Telfair Academy of Arts & Sciences.

BRANSOM, John Paul. Born Washington, DC 1885, living NYC 1976. Wildlife illustrator, painter, teacher. Work reproduced in magazines and in over 40 books. References A76-BEN-FIE-MAL-SMI. Sources DIC-ILA-ILP. No current auction record. Signature example p 223 DIC.

Paul Bransom left school at 13 to become an apprentice for mechanical drawings for patent applications. In his spare time he taught himself to draw wild animals by sketching at the zoo. When he came to NYC he did the comic strip "The Latest News from Bugville" for the *NY Evening Journal,* and he was allowed to sketch at the lion house in the Bronx Zoo. *The Saturday Evening Post* bought four paintings for covers, starting Bransom on his career of wildlife illustration. In 1966 he was teaching in the summer at Jackson Hole, Wyom.

DIC describes Bransom's procedure. He starts with rough sketches in charcoal to determine the composition. He enlarges the selected sketch by dividing it and the enlargement into squares, again in charcoal. "I use plenty of charcoal, rubbing on the tones with the fingers."

DIC. He then applies a shellac fixitive. If color is required, Bransom paints in watercolor over the fixitive or uses pastels.

BRAUN, Maurice. Born Nagy Bittse, Hungary 1877, died Point Loma, Cal 1941. Western landscape painter, lecturer, teacher. Work in San Diego Mus, Wichita AA, Waco AG, LA Mus, Phoenix Munic colln. References A47 (obit)-BEN-FIE-MAL-SMI. Sources ASD-WHO 43-11/30/73 letter from Martin E Petersen, Fine Arts Gall of San Diego. Oil 30×36″ *Mountain Landscape* sold 2/28/72 for $500 at auction. Painting example ASD.

Braun was brought to NYC by his parents in 1881. He grew up in the city. Apprenticed to a jeweler at 14, he rebelled. After five years at the NAD with E M Ward and F C Jones, he studied for one year at the Chase SA and one year in Europe. Braun had preferred painting portraits, but when he moved to San Diego in 1910 he turned to landscapes. In his work, "the light and airy style and the technique of the French Impressionists and Chase left their influence on Braun." ASD. California appealed to Braun in its "bigness, its richness, and its optimism." It was said that Braun landscapes put San Diego into the national art scene. Braun taught adult education at San Diego high school.

BRENEISER, Stanley Grotevent. Born Reading, Pa 1890, living Santa Fe, NM 1953. Cal and NM painter, etcher, writer, teacher. Work in Santa Maria (Cal) clubs. References A53-MAL. Source BDW. No current auction record or signature example.

Breneiser studied at the Philadelphia Museum School of Industrial Art, the PAFA, the ASL, the NY School of Fine & Applied Art, and also in Europe. In 1928 he was a delegate to the 6th Int Congress of Art in Prague. He was head of the art dept in Santa Maria (Cal) high school (A33) and director of the Hill & Canyon School of Art in Santa Fe (A47).

BRENNER, Carl Christian (or Charles C). Born Lauterecken, Bavaria 1838, died Louisville, Ky 1888. Kentucky landscape painter, etcher. Work in Addison Gall (Andover, Mass), J B Speed AM and Liberty Nat Bank (both Louisville). References MAL-SMI. Sources p 84 ANT 2/49-*The American-German Review* 4/51 (article)-1/74 letter from Nicki Thiras, Addison Gall. Oil 26¼×46¼″ *The Railroad* with signature example Carl C Brenner dated 1887 sold 1/26/74 for $1,500 at auction. (See illustration 38.)

Carl C Brenner's only art instruction was the study of drawing as part of his public schooling in Bavaria. Granted a scholarship to the Royal Academy in Munich, Brenner was instead brought to Louisville by his parents in 1854. He worked with his father as a glazier. In 1861 he was a house painter, listed as Charles C Brenner. In 1864 he was a sign and ornamental painter. At the age of 40, a family man with six children, he changed his name to Carl C Brenner and his occupation to landscape painter. A cautious man, he had already painted and sold major paintings as Charles—eg, *Race on the Mississippi* which is in the Addison Gallery. He had exhibited at the Philadelphia Centennial, too.

Beginning 1878 he exhibited at the NAD and the PAFA. He made a trip to the Rocky Mtns in 1884. "Scenes from Colorado are among his pictures; a Rocky Mountain scene is still in the possession of his family." *Review.* Brenner's prices were up to $400 in 1877, $1,000 in 1879, and $1,500 in 1886, but even though he was called "Kentucky's greatest artist," he did not receive financial support from museums or collectors. Each year, he held a Christmas sale in his studio, and the prices he obtained were modest. His specialty was painting the beech trees near his house. When he was not in his studio, he was out walking in the woods, a "vigorous, burly man, topped with his large felt hat and carrying a walking stick." *Review*. His career as a landscape painter was a brief ten years.

BRETT, Dorothy Eugenie. Born London, Eng 1883, probably living Taos, NM 1976. Modern Taos painter, writer. Work in Earl C Adams colln, ANS, MNM, Mus of Science (Buffalo). References A62-MAL. Sources M50-PIT-TAL-TSF-TWR-WAA. No recent auction record but M50 lists a price of $500 for *The Blessing of the Mares* in 1950. Signature example *Women's Dance* p 44 PIT. (See illustration 39.)

The Honorable Dorothy Brett was educated privately and took dancing lessons with Queen Victoria's grandchildren. Beginning in her mid-20s, she studied four years at the Slade School of Art in London and at University College. An aristocrat, she painted portraits of the English celebrities of the time including the novelist D H Lawrence. When the Lawrences and Lady Brett visited Taos in 1924, she remained, becoming a citizen in 1938. She is remembered as with her "fabulous brass ear-trumpet named Tobey, a long contraption with a round half-open slot at the end." TAL.

Her paintings are consciously "primitive" in style, aiming at "combining the real and spiritual worlds." Also, "her Indians are subtle, wild and sweet, with the slant-eyed look of fauns." Her women are "intensely feminine." She makes it "glamorous and always stylish." She wrote "Lawrence and Brett" and contributed to *The New Yorker* magazine. Like other Europeans of her generation, her preoccupation with the American Indian came from seeing the touring Wild West Show of Buffalo Bill: "I fell in love with" one of the Indians who "rode wildly around the arena, naked, painted lemon yellow, wearing a great war bonnet with its feathers cascading down to his horse's feet." PIT. To paint the Indian ceremonials, she draws from memory, setting down her personal interpretations rather than reporting.

BREUER, Henry Joseph. Born Philadelphia, Pa 1860, died San Francisco, Cal 1932. Cal landscape painter, illustrator. Work in Seattle Expos 1909, San Francisco 1915. References A21-BEN-FIE-MAL-SMI. Sources MSL-SCA. No current auction record but the estimated price of a Sierra mountainscape would be about $1,000 to $1,200 at auction in 1976. No signature example. (See illustration 40.)

Breuer studied in Buffalo before working as a Rookwood pottery decorator in Cincinnati 1880–82 and a lithographic designer 1882–84. He moved to NYC as a mural decorator 1884–88. From 1890–92, he was an artist for the San Francisco *Chronicle* and art editor of a California magazine 1892–93.

Breuer studied in Paris and after 1893 concentrated on landscape painting. He was influenced by Corot and the Barbizons although his style was more realistic. Typical titles are *Yosemite Valley, A California Sunset,* and *Mt Brewer in the Sierras.* He was commissioned to paint views of the San Gabriel Valley for the St Louis Exposition in 1904.

BREWER, Nicholas Richard. Born High Forest (Olmsted Cnty), Minn 1857, died probably St Paul, Minn 1949. Landscape and portrait painter, writer. Work in NGA (colln of governors' portraits), AIC, Witte Mus, St Capitols, etc. References A41-BEN-FIE-MAL-SMI. Source WHO 44. No current auction record but the published estimate is $400 to $600. No signature example.

Brewer was educated in the district public school until he was 15. He began his art studies after his marriage in 1879, as the pupil of D W Tryon and Chas Noel Flagg. By 1885 he was exhibiting at the NAD. He wrote "Trails of a Paintbrush." Painting titles include *Aliso Canon* (Decatur, Ill AI), *San Gabriel Range* (Progress Club), *Fading Glories* (Woman's Club, Birmingham), *Old Baldy* (So Shore CC), *The Cotton Harvest* (Witte Mus).

BREWERTON, George Douglas. Born probably Eastern seaboard 1827 (or 1820), died probably same 1901. Western landscape painter in oil and pastel, writer, army officer. Work in Oakland Mus. Reference G&W. Sources BRE-DWF-WHI. Oil 20×29" *Landscape* signed and n/d but about 1858, sold 10/27/71 for $1,900 at auction. Drawing inscribed Brewerton p 66 BRE.

In May 1848, Lt G D Brewerton was part of the US Army in California. He was ordered to accompany Kit Carson's party with dispatches for Independence, Mo and then report for further duty in Mississippi. On muleback, they crossed the Rockies and the desert, eluding Indians along the Old Spanish Trail to reach Taos where Carson's wife lived. In 1853 Brewerton wrote and illustrated his recollections of the journey for *Harper's*. The portion of the article that dealt with Taos and Santa Fe was reprinted as BRE. Brewerton as a Yankee Protestant reflected the anti-Mexican attitudes prevalent after the 1846 Mexican War. About Taos, he noted "its inhabitants exhibit all the indolent, lounging characteristics of the lower order of Mexicans, the utter want both of moral and mental culture." BRE. After an attack of influenza, Brewerton followed the Santa Fe Wagon Road toward Independence.

Brewerton's later paintings were based on this Western experience. His *Mohave Desert* was described as "surreal with its scorched yellow terrain, conjured up images of exhaustion and death." WHI. He was in Brooklyn in 1854 and exhibited Western views at the NA in 1854–55. In 1859 he gave his address as Newport, RI when he exhibited at the PAFA *Night Scene in the Upper Arkansas—Burning Prairie* and *Sunset House, Rocky Mtn Scenery*.

BRINLEY, Daniel Putnam. Born Newport, RI 1879, died probably New Canaan, Conn 1963. Illustrator of Western Canada, muralist, landscape painter. ANA 1930, Nat Soc Mur Painters. Murals in bank, churches, post office; stained glass in churches; terrestrial globe in *Daily News* Bldg (NYC). References A66 (obit)-BEN-FIE-MAL-SMI. Sources AAT-ANT 10/72-ARM-190-INS 6/25-WHO 62. No current auction record. Painting example p 43 AAT.

"Put" Brinley was educated at King's School in Stamford and Dwight School in NYC. He studied at the ASL and in Paris and Florence. Beginning as an academic landscape painter, he was by 1911 a charter member of the Association of American Painters and Sculptors that put on the radical 1913 Armory Show. In WWI he served with the YMCA in France. After 1919 Brinley specialized in mural painting.

Brinley's watercolors and crayon drawings were used as 100 illustrations in Canadian travel books by Gordon Brinley. This included "Away to the Canadian Rockies and British Columbia" in 1938.

BROMLEY, Valentine Walter. Born London, Eng 1848, died there 1877. Important English Special Artist-illustrator, genre and mythological painter. Works in Dept of External Affairs, Ottawa. Assoc, Soc Brit Artists and Inst of Painters in Water Colors. References BEN-MAL. Sources AIW-ANT 7/74-AOH-GOD-HUT. No auction record but the estimated price for an oil 20×30" showing Indian games would be about $8,000 to $10,000 at auction in 1976.

Bromley was the pupil of his father, an engraver who was a member of the Society of British Artists. His grandfather and great-grandfather were also recognized engravers. He exhibited at the Royal Academy and at the New Water-Colour Society beginning 1865 when he was 17. A tall and dashing figure with flowing handlebar mustaches, he was a Home Artist (ie, domestic and a Special Artist (traveling) for the *Illustrated London News*.

In 1874 the Earl of Dunraven retained Bromley as artist to portray the hunting adventures on his third trip to the American West where Dunraven already had traveled with Buffalo Bill and where he owned a 4,000-acre Colorado ranch. The exploration was of the Upper Yellowstone in Montana. Dunraven and Bromley did not get along because the artist avoided hunting to concentrate on Indian genre scenes, recording one of the most significant studies of Indian hide trading, women's tasks, burials, games, war, and courtship. Some of the drawings appeared in *Illustrated London News* from 1875 to 1877. Bromley also depicted the hunting trip through the Yellowstone, across what is now Dunraven Pass, near Mount Dunraven. He then returned to England to complete the 17 paintings illustrating the Earl's book published in 1876. He died from smallpox in 1877 at 29, while the Indian paintings were being exhibited in London. Dunraven in his book never acknowledged that Bromley made the American trip. GOD suggests he did not.

BROMWELL, Elizabeth Henrietta. Born Charleston, Ill no date, living Denver, Colo 1929. Colo landscape painter, teacher, writer, sculptor. References A29-FIE. Sources DAM-DPL-WAA-WOM. No current auction record or signature example.

Daughter of a Congressman, Henrietta Bromwell was educated privately and traveled widely in the US, northern Mexico, and Canada. She studied art in Denver and in Europe. An active suffragette, she was also a charter member of the Denver AC in 1893, serving as Secretary in 1895 when she exhibited two landscape views at the Camera Club on Sixteenth Street. By 1914 she was exhibiting nationally. In 1910 Ms Bromwell had written "The Bromwell Genealogy."

BROOKES, Samuel Marsdon. Born Newington Green (Middlesex), Eng 1816, died San Francisco, Cal 1892. Cal still-life, landscape, and portrait painter specializing in fish subjects. Work in De Young Mus, Cal Hist Soc, Lyman Allyn Mus (New London, Conn), Crocker AG (Sacramento). References G&W-MAL. Sources BAR-STI. No current auction record. Signature example p 130 STI.

Brookes emigrated to Michigan with his parents in 1833. By 1841 he was painting miniatures and was able to pay $30 to itinerant portrait painters for lessons. In 1842 and 1846–58 he painted portraits and historical scenes including Indian studies in Milwaukee. His landscapes were called topographical. In 1845 he had sold paintings by lottery to finance further study in England that refined his style.

In 1862 Brookes moved to San Francisco, becoming the leading West Coast still-life painter of the 19th century. Reviews were in verse, "Prolific Brookes! / By thy great art, / The salmon from / Thy canvas start /." Western fish were favorite subjects, *String of Salmon, California Smelts.* The finish of Brookes's paintings was microscopically detailed, almost equivalent to trompe l'oeil with the accurately recorded colors and shadows. His financial rewards were "second to no other California artist" of the time. STI. In 1872 he sold two paintings for $1,000. In 1880 he sold *Peacock* for $1,000 and received a gratuity of another $1,000. Brookes was a founder of the San Francisco Art Assn and the Bohemian Club. He went on landscape sketching trips throughout California, along with fellow still-life painter Edwin Deakin.

BROOME, B C. Illustrator of *A Man and His Partner* in *Field and Stream* for June 1900, showing a cowboy leading his horse across the desert. No reference or other source. No auction record. Signature example on illustration above.

BROWERE, Albertis del Orient. Born Tarrytown, NY 1814, died Catskill, NY 1887. Important California gold-mining painter, Hudson River painter, genre, and still-life painter. Work in Albany Inst, NY St Hist Assoc, Carnegie Mus A, Oakland Mus. References BEN-FIE-G&W-MAL-SMI. Sources AIW-ALA-ANT 8/45,1/54,11/65,1/69,9/72-BAR-DBW-HON-HUD-M19-STI-WHI. No current auction record but the estimated price of an oil 20×30″ showing miners panning gold would be about $2,500 to $3,000 at auction in 1976. Painting example ✳71 M19.

A D O Browere was the assistant to his father, John Henri Isaac Browere, a sculptor who made life masks of Jefferson and Gilbert Stuart. He studied paint-ing at the NA, exhibited at the NA from 1831 to 1846 and at the AAU, the American Academy, and the Apollo Association from 1833 to 1838. Browere moved to Catskill in 1834 after his father died of cholera and lived there for the rest of his life except for his California trips. He spent considerable time painting with Thomas Cole. His subjects included illustrations of Rip Van Winkle, Indian history, river landscapes, and genre scenes.

The Gold Rush compelled artists as it did miners, and in 1852 Browere sailed for California via Cape Horn, a four-month voyage. He returned to Catskill in 1856, then in 1858 set out again for California, this time by mule over Panama. He remained in San Francisco until 1861. The art historians vary widely in appreciation: "Even landscapes have an anecdotal element" ANT; "knowingly differentiates species of trees and captures the textures of rocks and water" HUD; "a personally picturesque figure but secondary in every branch of work" BAR; and, "Hogarthian anecdote solidly if soberly painted without dynamics or humor" ALA.

BROWN, Benjamin Chambers. Born Marion, Ark 1865, died Pasadena, Cal 1942. Cal landscape painter, etcher. Work in MNM, Munic collns of Oakland (Cal), LA, and Phoenix (Ariz); libraries Cal State, Pasadena, Boise, Helena (Ark), Lib Cong, etc. References A33-BEN-FIE-MAL-SMI. Sources SCA-WHO 34. Oil 25×30″ *Mountainous Landscape, California* estimated for sale 3/4/74 at $800 to $1,000 for auction in LA and sold for $225. No signature example.

Brown was educated at the U of Tennessee and Washington U. He studied at the St Louis SFA under Paul Harney and John Fry before becoming the pupil of

Laurens and Constant at the Julien Academy in Paris. By 1905, Brown was winning medals in national exhibitions. See Howell Chambers Brown.

BROWN, Don. Born Taylor, Tex 1899, living Cleveland, Ohio 1948. Painter specialized in East Texas landscapes such as cypress trees, graphic artist, teacher. Work in museums in Paris, Copenhagen, Warsaw, Dallas MFA. References A41-MAS. Sources AAT-TOB-TXF. No current auction record. Signature example p 48 AAT.

Brown, an athlete at Centenary College, was reporter-illustrator on the *Shreveport Journal* before enlisting in the AEF for WWI. He studied briefly at the AIC, then four years at the ASL under Boardman Robinson, Benton, Miller, and Sloan. Up to 1926 he was the pupil of André Lhote in Paris, returning to paint "Texas landscapes and Texas people. I may not be a great American, but it's certain I can't be a great Frenchman." TXF. By 1928 he was living and painting on the banks of the Cypress Bayou in East Texas, above Caddo Lake. "In the red hills of East Texas, in the negroes, and in the vast plains of West Texas, he finds his material." TXF. In 1935 he was director of the School of Art in Marshall and head of the art department at Centenary College in Shreveport, La.

BROWN, Mrs Dorothy Woodhead. Born Houston, Tex 1899, living Malibu, Cal 1966. Cal painter, etcher, teacher. Work in U Cal at LA colln, Long Beach MA, La Jolla A Center, Santa Barbara MA. References A66-MAS. Sources BDW-WAA-W64. No recent auction record or signature example.

Mrs Brown was educated at Stanford and at U of California at LA. She studied with Henry Lee McFee and was associate professor of art at UCLA beginning 1945. She received the 1956 award "Woman of the Year in Art."

BROWN, Grafton Tyler. Born Harrisburg, Pa 1841, died St Peter, Minn 1918. Landscape, lithographic, and survey artist. Work in Evansville Mus (Ind), State Capitol Mus (Wash), Kahn colln. References G&W-MAS. Sources CAE-COS-KAH-letter Del McBride, State Capitol Mus, Wash. No current auction record. Signature example p 16 KAH. (See illustration 41.)

As free Negroes, Brown's family had moved from Maryland in 1837. His father was a laborer. By about 1860, Brown was in San Francisco employed as a lithographic artist for C C Kuchel and later for Kuchel & Dresel. He drew views for reproduction in California and Nevada including Santa Rosa, Fort Churchill, and Virginia City. By 1864 he was advertising as a traveling artist in Nevada. He formed G T Brown & Co as lithographers in San Francisco in 1867, selling out in 1872.

By 1882 Brown had moved to British Columbia. He joined the geological survey party led by Amos Bowman to explore the east side of the Cascade Mtns. Brown painted watercolor sketches of the Smith and Thompson rivers, Lake Okanagan, and Mt Baker. From 1883 to 1885 he maintained a studio in Victoria, exhibiting landscapes. Brown was listed in Portland, Ore from 1886 to 1889, and also in Tacoma, Wash, although one 1886 oil is of the Grand Canyon. His painting of the Lower Falls of the Yellowstone was dated 1891. From 1892 to 1897 he worked as a civil engineer in St Paul. Brown's death certificate recorded his race as White. His younger brother Cassius was a newspaper editor.

BROWN, H Harris. Born Eng 1864, died probably Chelsea, Eng 1948. French and English-school portrait painter. References BEN-MAL. Sources EDJ-KEN. No current auction record but the estimated price of an oil 30×20″ portrait of Plains Indian would be about $900 to $1,100 at auction in 1976. Signature example KEN 6/70.

Brown was the student of Bouguereau and T Robert-Fleury in Paris. He exhibited beginning 1889 at the RA in London and in Paris at the Salon de la Nationale. He is listed as a portraitist, at Northampton, and as living in Chelsea in 1934. He painted Montana Indian portraits about 1925.

BROWN, Henry Box (or Harry, or Harrison B). Born Portland, Me 1831, died London, Eng 1915. Maine landscape and marine painter in San Francisco 1852. Work in City AM (St Louis). References A15 (obit)-BEN-FIE-G&W-MAL-SMI. Sources ANT 2/72-BDW-HUT-"Landscape in Maine" Colby Col 1970-PAF-SUR (under Bartlett). No current auction record but the published estimate for Henry B is $200 to $300, for Harrison B $400 to $500. Painting example p 31 "Landscape in Maine."

"Harrison B" Brown was apprenticed at 15 to Portland house, sign, and ship painters. In 1851 he set up in Portland as an independent banner and ornamental painter. In March 1852, "Henry" Brown was in San Francisco, retained by Mexican Boundary Commissioner John Bartlett to redraw Bartlett's own sketches of California's Napa Valley, geysers, redwoods, and quicksilver mines for use in the published report of the Commission. Bartlett also had Henry Brown paint portraits of the Indian chiefs and studies of Indian genre.

"Harrison" Brown was in Portland in the 1850s, metamorphosing from sign painting into landscapes. By the 1860s he was painting in the White Mountains with Champney, Hart, and Casilear. By 1892 when he moved to London, Harrison Brown was Maine's best-known native painter, famous for studies of Casco Bay. Are Harrison Brown and Henry Brown the same painter? G&W says yes, and BDW places Henry in San Francisco.

BROWN, Howell Chambers. Born Little Rock, Ark 1880, died Pasadena, Cal 1954. Painter of the desert Indians, etcher. Work in Mus Hist Sci and Art (LA), Cal St Lib, Lib Cong, Smithsonian Inst. References A41-BEN-FIE-MAL-SMI. Sources BDW-SCA. No current auction record but the published estimate is $300 to $400. No signature example.

Howell C Brown was best known as an etcher. His specialty was "Western scenes of the Indian country" such as *Edge of the Desert*. FIE. Note Benjamin Chambers Brown.

BROWN, Paul. Born Mapleton, Minn 1893, died Mineola, NY 1958. Illustrator, specialty horses in action, writer. References A41-MAL. Sources AAC-DIC-ILA-interview Sallie Brown 1/76. No auction record. Signature example ILA p 121.

Born in Minneapolis, Paul Brown was brought to NYC at the age of seven. His only formal education was several years at the High School of Commerce in NYC. In 1915 his family moved to Long Island and his "school" became the polo fields, steeplechase courses, and horse show grounds. After serving in the infantry in WWI, Brown devoted himself to drawing horses, action sports, and Western subjects—the cowboy, Indian, and cavalry.

Paul Brown did most of his drawings on ordinary typing paper with BBBBBB pencil. He never took photographs or worked from models. He said of himself that he couldn't draw a female unless she had four legs. He wrote and illustrated 33 books, mainly for children, and his work was published in *Cosmopolitan, Collier's, Spur, Polo* and *Blue Book.* His Western work included "War Paint" written and illustrated by him, and "Army Mule" and "Seventh Cavalry Staghound" by Fairfax Downey. He illustrated over 100 books.

BROWN (or BROWNE), William Garl, Jr. Born Leicester, Eng 1823, died Buffalo, NY 1894. Eastern portrait painter. Work in COR, VMI, Va Hist Soc, U of NC. Reference G&W. Sources BAR-KEN. No current auction record but the estimated price for a 20×16″ portrait of General Taylor would be about $900 to $1,000 at auction in 1976. Signature example KEN 6/71.

Brown and his father, an English landscape painter, came to the US in 1837. He began exhibiting at the NA in 1840. In 1846 he was established as a portrait painter in Richmond, Va when he was commissioned to go to Monterey, Mexico to make a bust portrait of Gen Zachary Taylor. The result was a group scene of Taylor with his staff and his horse at mail call in camp—"an Historical Picture, true to life, for every officer placed himself in position." Later writers call Brown "a reasonably competent technician with a prosaic mind who thought it was a portraitist's business to gloss over any signs of character in the ladies, though he might not find them out of place in a man." BAR. Brown lived in NYC and Richmond. He died on a visit to Buffalo to his sister Mary Ann Brown who was also an artist.

BROWNE, Belmore. Born Tompkinsville, SI, NY 1880, died probably Ross, Marin Cnty, Cal 1954. Mountain landscape and animal painter, illustrator, sculptor, teacher. ANA 1928. Work in NGA, AMNH (diorama), Albright AG, Santa Barbara Mus Nat Hist, Cal Acad Sciences. References A53-FIE-MAL. Source WHO 54. No current auction record or signature example.

Educated in private schools, Browne studied with Chase, Carroll Beckwith, and in Paris at the Julien Academy. He worked as an illustrator 1902–12, then married and began easel painting in 1913 when he wrote and illustrated "The Conquest of Mt McKinley," part of a series of Alaskan adventure and travel books. Browne served in aviation in WWI. In WWII he was an Air Force consultant particularly on the Arctic and on training manuals. Browne became director of the Santa Barbara School of Arts in 1930 when he spent winters in California, summers in Alberta.

BROWNE, Charles Francis. Born Natick, Mass 1859, died Waltham, Mass 1920. Eastern landscapist, teacher. ANA 1913. References A20 (obit)-BEN-FIE-MAL-SMI. Source WHO 20. Oil 16×24″ *The Pueblo of Zuni, New Mexico, 1895* sold 11/14/72 for $900 at auction. In NYC in 1944, *Rocky River, 1916,* sold for $125 at auction. No signature example.

Browne was a student of the MFA in Boston 1882–84, of Eakins at PAFA 1885–87, and of Gérôme and Schenck in Paris 1887–90. He was an instructor at the AIC, living in Chicago in 1917, and had been superintendent of the US section of FA at the Pan-Pac Expos in San Francisco in 1915 where he also won a painting award. In 1909 Browne had married the sister of the sculptor Lorado Taft.

BROWNE, John Ross. Born Dublin, Ireland 1821, died Oakland, Cal 1875. Illustrator of his own travel articles including Cal and the Apache country, *Harper's* field artist-correspondent. Reference DAB. Source AIW. No auction record or signature example.

Browne was brought to Louisville, Ky by his parents about 1832. At 18 he studied shorthand. In 1841–42 he worked as reporter for the US Senate. The next 25 years were spent in travel and in writing and illustrating books on his trips: whaling in 1846, the Near East in 1853, "Adventures in California and Washoe" 1864, Germany 1866, "The Land of Thor" 1867, and "Adventures in the Apache Country: A Tour through Arizona and Sonora" in 1869. Many of his sketches were published in *Harper's Magazine*.

In 1870 Browne settled in Oakland and became interested in San Francisco real estate. He was said to have had a good sense of humor and to have been modest and good-natured, but his appointment as minister to China in 1868 lasted only long enough for him to express his opinions on arrival there.

BRUFF, Joseph Goldsborough. Born Washington, DC 1804, died there 1889. Amateur Western illustrator, writer, draftsman. Work in Huntington Lib (San Marino, Cal). Reference G&W. Sources AIW-ANT 10/51. No auction record. Signature example "Gold Rush" below.

Bruff was one of 10 children of a doctor who died in 1816, apparently poisoned in connection with the theft of an invention to forge lead bullets. His mother died in 1821 after Bruff had resigned from West Point. Bruff had taken "umbrage at a trifling insult, fought a duel," and was "rusticated." Without a home, Bruff became a cabin boy on a merchant ship, roving the world until 1827 when he was hired as a draftsman at the Norfolk (Va) Navy Yard at $1.37½ per day. After nine years he was hired as a draftsman for Fortress Monroe at $2 per day with quarters and nine cords of wood. His own résumé of his activities for the period beginning 1838 reads, "11 years, The Draughtsman to the Bur of Topographical Engineers—comes up to Spring of 1849, Organiz'd and Commanded an overland expedition to Cal, via the South pass of the Rocky Mts: which, with engagements of drawing for the Tehantepec Survey, and working up Genl Stevens overland surveys, &c would make a labor of 2½ yrs."

What Bruff organized was the Washington City and California Mining Assn to take the overland trail to California to join the 1849 Gold Rush. He kept a journal of the trip, illustrated with his own pen sketches. On his return he exhibited at the Washington Art Assn in 1859, and from 1876 was in the Office of the Supervising Architect, Treasury Dept. His sketches are said to be a most important record of the overland trail. The drawings of people are crude but with his cadet's training the drawings pay meticulous attention to detail and are topographically correct. They remain among the few original pictorial records of the emigration. Bruff's journal was published in 1944 by Columbia University Press as "Gold Rush. The Journals, Drawings, and Other Papers of J Goldsborough Bruff. Captain, Washington City and California Mining Association. April 2, 1849 –July 20, 1851."

BRUSH, George de Forest. Born Shelbyville, Tenn 1855, died Hanover, NH 1941. "The poet of the Indian painters," figure painter. ANA 1888, NA 1908. Work in MMA, COR, Carnegie Inst,

BMFA, NGA, PAFA, BM. References A47 (obit)-BEN-CHA-FIE-MAL-SMI. Sources AIC-AIW-ALA-AMA-COR-DEP-DCC-HAR-INS 4/08-ISH-MSL-M31-POW-TSF-WHO 40. Oil 9½ × 7½" *Indian Carrying Home the Kill* sold 4/30/69 for $350 at auction. Oil 12 × 11" *Portrait of a Young Girl* sold 1970 for $1,200 at auction. Signature example INS 4/08 (article).

Brush attended the NA from 1871 to 1874, then along with Abbott Thayer studied with Gérôme in Paris until 1880. On his return he went West and into Canada, a contemporary of Remington and Russell. From 1882 to 1886 he lived in Crow, Sioux, and Mandan villages. He became a serious participant in the Indian crafts and traditions. The West was just changing: "In 1880, thousands of buffalo darkened the rolling plains. In the fall of 1883, there was hardly a buffalo remaining on the range" in Montana. Brush wrote, "Every one who goes far West sees Indians as dark-skinned tramps, their old people blind and dirty." He painted "the world of the Indian before the white man came," an idealized Indian that never was.

The paintings brought wide acclaim but did not sell. "Among the Indians of the northland, Brush may have found braves who would stop to gather water lilies on their way home from the hunt but the manner would seem better suited for the portrayal of Greeks in their period of highest culture." AMA. Brush went back to Europe in 1890 and "from the Florentine learned how to paint his American madonnas," ALA, using his wife and children as subjects. These paintings had a ready market. Brush taught at the ASL, and developed the concept of camouflaging warships in an 1898 suggestion to the Navy. Like Inness or Thayer he was regarded as the epitome of the art of the turn of the century, less exciting than Matisse just as a "lady" is less exciting than a "vitriol-throwing suffragette." DEP.

BRUTON, Margaret. Born Brooklyn, NY 1894, living Alameda, Cal 1948. Cal painter in NM 1929, muralist. Work (mural) in Golden Gate Expos 1939. References A41-MAS. Source BDW. No auction record or signature example.

Margaret Bruton studied at the California School of Fine Art and at the ASL. In 1929 she painted in New Mexico, including Indian portraits and street scenes of Taos and Santa Fe. In 1933 she painted views of Nevada mining towns. Her sisters Esther and Helen were fashion and mural artists.

BRYAN, William Edward. Born Iredell, Tex 1876, living probably Dublin, Tex 1935. Painter of central Texas landscapes, portrait and figure painter, illustrator, teacher. Work in Carnegie Lib (Fort Worth). References A27-MAL. Sources TOB-TXF. No current auction record or signature example.

Bryan was raised on a ranch near Dublin, Tex. He studied art at Baylor U, then in 1901 attended the Cincinnati AA, the pupil of Duveneck until 1905 when he went to Paris. The pupil of Laurens, he studied at the Julien Academy and in 1906 at the Colarossi. After touring Europe he taught at the Cincinnati AA from 1907 to 1909 when a long illness forced him back to a studio at his father's ranch in Dublin. "While almost a recluse for several years, this gentle and refined soul" sketched Texas and Florida landscapes. By 1928 he was "besieged with orders." He believed that the "real artist has love for the old masters Titian, Rembrandt, Velásquez, Inness, and Duveneck." TXF.

BRYANT, Harold Edward. Born Pickrell, Neb 1894, died Grand Junction, Colo 1950. Painter of Southwestern ranch life, illustrator. No reference.

1. Cassilly Adams. *Custer's Last Fight*, oil on canvas 15 x 25 feet (various sizes given), painted 1878–86 as a commercial exhibition piece and later used as model for 150,000 lithographic prints. CREDIT, ANHEUSER-BUSCH, INC, ST LOUIS.

2. Charles Partridge Adams. *Mt Edlus between Durango and Silverton, Colo and Las Animas Canyon,* oil on canvas 30 x 44″ signed LL and dated 1885. A major work by a minor master of the Rocky Mountain School. CREDIT, THE AUTHORS.

3. Kenneth Miller Adams. *The Mission Church,* oil on canvas 20 x 25″ painted about 1924 by the youngest and last member elected to the Taos Society of Artists. CREDIT, THE ANSCHUTZ COLLECTION.

4. Robert Wesley Amick. *Still as It Was*, oil on canvasboard 8 x 15″ signed LR. A Westerner who went East as an illustrator of Western scenes. CREDIT, THE AUTHORS.

5. Charles Andres. *The Man of the Forest,* oil on canvas 28 x 32″ signed LR, painted about 1950 as the dust-jacket illustration in color for a juvenile edition of Zane Grey. CREDIT, THE AUTHORS.

6. William Armstrong. *Buck Board, Macleod*, watercolor over pen and ink 8⅛ x 10⅞″ signed (LR) W Armstrong 1902. Canadian railroad engineer who painted "as a serious hobby." CREDIT, ROYAL ONTARIO MUSEUM, TORONTO.

7. Jozef G Bakos. *Upper Palace Avenue, Santa Fe,* oil on canvas 30 x 40″ signed LR. A member of Los Cinco Pintores. CREDIT, THE ANSCHUTZ COLLECTION.

8. Henry C. Balink. *Marie and Julian of the Pueblo of Sa[n] Ildefonso,* oil on canvas 16 x 20″ signed LR and inscribe[d] Santa Fe, NM. A double portrait of the potter and the painter[.] CREDIT, THE ANSCHUTZ COLLECTION.

9. Eliza Barchus. *Yosemite Falls, Yellowstone,* oil on board 8 x 4″ signed (LL) barchus. A mountain landscape painter who lived an artist's years—102. CREDIT, THE AUTHORS.

10. Paul Wayland Bartlett. *Preparedness,* bronze statuette of an eagle 12½″ high signed P W Bartlett and dated 1916. The expatriate sculptor who still thought of Indian and eagle. CREDIT, THE METROPOLITAN MUSEUM OF ART, GIFT OF THOMAS HENRY RUSSELL AND FREDERICK NEWLIN PRICE, 1925.

12. Walter M Baumhofer. *Boomer Bride*, oil on canvas 23 x 34″ signed LL and painted as an illustration for *The American Magazine* for Sept 1953. A most popular pulp painter. CREDIT, THE AUTHORS.

. Gustave Baumann. *Pasa Tiempo*, gesso and mixed dia on board 31 x 35″ signed UR and titled UL. Santa Fe ist who posed and painted Indian figurines and dolls. EDIT, THE ANSCHUTZ COLLECTION.

. Harold Beament. *The Mountain*, oil on canvas 36¼ x ⅝″ signed LL and dated 1925. An early painting by an icer in the Canadian Navy. CREDIT, THE NATIONAL LLERY OF CANADA, OTTAWA.

14. Donald Beauregard. *Portrait of the Artist*, oil on canvas 32 x 20″ signed LR. Never saw a railroad until 16 and died before 30. CREDIT, COLLECTIONS IN THE MUSEUM OF NEW MEXICO.

15. Otto Becker. *Custer's Last Fight*, oil on canvas 24 x 40" signed (LR) O Becker and painted 1895. The adaptation of the Cassilly Adams showpiece for lithographic reproduction. CREDIT, ANHEUSER BUSCH, INC, ST LOUIS.

16. Joe Beeler. *The Comancheros*, oil on panel 30 x signed LL and painted 1974. CAA member whose li work is painting the West. CREDIT, THE ARTIST.

17. George Bellows. *Chimayo,* oil on canvas 30 x 44" signed (LC) Geo Bellows and painted 1917. The "most popular artist of his time" briefly in the West. CREDIT, MUSEUM OF NEW MEXICO.

18. F M Bell-Smith. *Mists and Glaciers of the Selkirks,* on canvas 33¼ x 49½" signed LR and dated 1911. In his la style emphasizing atmospheric effects. CREDIT, THE N TIONAL GALLERY OF CANADA, OTTAWA.

19. Ernest Berke. *January, the Hard Month*, bronze statuette 18" high with marble base. CREDIT, KENNEDY GALLERIES INC NYC.

20. Oscar Berninghaus. *Dance at the Pueblo*, oil on ca 30 x 40" signed (LL) O E Berninghaus and painted 191(Taos by 1899, he was an original member of the Taos Soc of Artists. CREDIT, THE ANSCHUTZ COLLECTION.

21. Arthur Best. *Grand Canyon,* oil on canvas 40 x 50" signed (LL) A
V Best. The brother of Harry Cassie Best, he operated the Best Art
chool. CREDIT, THE ANSCHUTZ COLLECTION.

22. Harry Cassie Best. *California Mountain Pass*, oil
on canvas 36 x 22" signed (LR) H C Best. "The artist of
the Yosemite Valley" who even married at the foot of
Bridal Veil Falls. CREDIT, THE AUTHORS.

. Otto Bierhals. *Cowboy*, woodcut 7 x 5" signed (LR) O
erhals. An illustrator for the pulp Western Magazines.
EDIT, THE AUTHORS.

24. Albert Bierstadt. *Elk Feeding at First Light*, oil on canvas 14 x 19" signed (LR) A Bierstadt. The principal
panoramist of the Rocky Mountain School now appreciated
for smaller studies. CREDIT, THE AUTHORS.

26. George Caleb Bingham. *Fur Traders Descending th*
Missouri, oil on canvas 29 x 36½". The "greatest painter o
the Mississippi." CREDIT, THE METROPOLITAN MUSEUM
OF ART, MORRIS K JESUP FUND, 1933.

25. Woody Big Bow. *Shooting Star*, tempera on panel
signed LR and dated 4/27/69. A Kiowa who has also been a
set painter for Western movies. CREDIT, THE ANSCHUTZ
COLLECTION.

27. E H Bischoff. *Governor's House, Taos*, oil on canvas 32
x 42" signed LR and painted about 1941. A summer visitor
from Vermont. CREDIT, THE AUTHORS.

28. Emil Bisttram. *Hopi Snake Dance*, oil on canvas 36 x 2
signed (LR) Bisttram. A founder of the Transcendental Pain
ing Group in Santa Fe in 1938. CREDIT, THE ANSCHUT
COLLECTION.

29. La Verne Nelson Black. *Buffalo Dance*, oil on canvas 40 x 49″ signed LL and painted before 1931. Indian painter who worked in poverty until the year before he died. CREDIT, THE ANSCHUTZ COLLECTION.

30. Archie Blackowl. *Hoop Dancer—Cheyenne*, tempera on board 18 x 10″ signed (LR) A Blackowl. Cheyenne painter encouraged by Woody Crombo. CREDIT, THE AUTHORS.

31. John Blair. *Winnipeg—Buffalo on the Prairie*, oil on canvas 27⅝ x 47¾″ signed (LR) Jno Blair. Late 19th-century painter of prairie scenes near Winnipeg. CREDIT, THE NATIONAL GALLERY OF CANADA, OTTAWA.

32. Ralph Albert Blakelock. *Pipe Dance*, oil on canvas 48¼ x 72½″ signed LR. Important Indian painter with the most tragic life in American art. CREDIT, THE METROPOLITAN MUSEUM OF ART, GIFT OF GEORGE A HEARN, 1909.

33. Ernest L Blumenschein. *Taos Valley*, oil on canvas 25 x 35″ signed (LL) E L Blumenschein. Original member and best known of Taos Society of Artists. CREDIT, THE METROPOLITAN MUSEUM OF ART, GEORGE A HEARN FUND, 1934.

34. Karl Bodmer. *Sauk and Fox Indians*, ink wash and watercolor on paper 6 x 9″ drawn in the wilderness 1833–34 by the formal young Swiss picture maker for Prince Maximilian. CREDIT, THE ANSCHUTZ COLLECTION.

35. James Boren. *Beneath the Cliffs of Acoma*, watercolor 24 x 38″ signed LL and dated 1971. Gives the cowboy the star role in the drama of the West. CREDIT, THE ARTIST.

36. Carl Oscar Borg. *Canyon de Chelly*, oil on canvas 42 x 52″ signed LL. Highly trained painter of Indian genre who began as a housepainter in Sweden. CREDIT, THE ANSCHUTZ COLLECTION.

38. Carl C Brenner. *Artist in the Woods*, pencil drawing 6 x 10″ signed LL and dated 1877 when Brenner was changing his given name to suit his position as Kentucky's leading painter. CREDIT, THE AUTHORS.

Solon Borglum. *On the Border of the White Man's Land*, nze statuette 19″ high signed and dated 1906. "Breezy, ole-souled Western American." CREDIT, THE MET-POLITAN MUSEUM OF ART, ROGERS FUND, 1907.

orothy Brett. *The Indian Madonna*, oil 39¼ x 25¼″ d by Taos' resident English aristocrat who saw her women as glamorous and stylish. CREDIT, MUSEUM W MEXICO.

40. H J Breuer. *Mt Whitney*, oil on canvas 30 x 20″ signed LL. Typically realistic view by a California landscape painter popular at the turn of the century. CREDIT, THE AUTHORS.

41. Grafton Tyler Brown. *The Grand Canyon from Lookout Point, Yellowstone National Park*, oil on canvas 30½ x 18″ signed (LR) G T Brown and dated 1886. An early California artist who later went to Canada as a survey artist. CREDIT, EVANSVILLE MUSEUM OF ARTS & SCIENCE.

42. Charles Livingston Bull. *Ruffed Grouse*, pen and ink on paper 11½ x 7½″ signed LR. A taxidermist before he became an illustrator of wildlife, particularly birds. CREDIT, THE AUTHORS.

43. Ferdinand Burgdorff. *Golden Morning, Grand Canyon National Park*, oil on canvas 50 x 60″ signed LR by this trained painter in the Southwest about 1927. CREDIT, THE ANSCHUTZ COLLECTION.

44. Howard Russell Butler. *Yankee Point, Monterey*, oil on canvas 40 x 40″ signed (LL) H R Butler. Known for his paintings of eclipses. CREDIT, THE METROPOLITAN MUSEUM OF ART, GEORGE A HEARN FUND, 1926.

46. William Cary. *The High Toss*, wash drawing 16 x 20″ signed (LR) Wm de la Montaigne Cary. With two other NYC youths he made a sketching trip across the prairies and Rockies in 1861. CREDIT, THE AUTHORS.

45. Emily Carr. *The Beaver Totem*, oil on canvas 36⅜ x 21⅜″ signed (LL) M Emily Carr and painted probably 1920s. The "little old lady on the edge of nowhere" who became a most important Canadian painter. CREDIT, THE NATIONAL GALLERY OF CANADA, OTTAWA, GIFT OF MR AND MRS CHARLES S BAND, TORONTO.

48. Gerald Cassidy. *Navajos on the Way to Laguna Fiesta*, oil on canvas 72 x 96″ signed LL including sun symbol and painted 1916. Settled in Santa Fe 1912 with a modern palette. CREDIT, THE ANSCHUTZ COLLECTION.

47. (Left) J W Casilear. *In the Rockies*, oil on canvas 16 x 14″ signed (LR) JWC. Both his life and his paintings were as "harmonious as a poem." CREDIT, THE AUTHORS.

49. George Catlin. *Indians and Grizzlies*, oil on canvas 18⅝ x 26³/₁₆″. Began in 1830 to apply his life to recording "the looks and customs of the vanishing races." CREDIT, ROYAL ONTARIO MUSEUM, TORONTO.

50. Charles S Chapman. *Grand Canyon*, oil on Masonite 21½ x 27½ signed LR and painted after 1926. Eastern illustrator and with Harvey Dunn a teacher of illustrators. CREDIT, THE AUTHORS.

51. Frederick T Chapman. *Swords and Arrows*, pen and ink drawing 6½ x 7″ signed (LR) F T Chapman. Eastern Illustrator and military historian. CREDIT, THE AUTHORS.

52. Robert Chee. *Navaho See-Saw*, tempera on paper 9 x 11″ signed LR. Navaho pupil of Allan Houser. CREDIT, THE AUTHORS.

53. Ernest Chiriacka. *Apache*, oil on board 24 x 30″ signed LL. Contemporary Easterner painting the West that was. CREDIT, KENNEDY GALLERIES INC NYC.

54. C C A Christensen. *Handcart Pioneers*. Painted from experience with a handcart company on foot from Illinois to Utah in 1857. CREDIT, CORPORATION OF THE PRESIDENT OF THE CHURCH OF JESUS CHRIST OF LATTER-DAY SAINTS, 1975.

55. Matt Clark. *Bitter Creek*, watercolor 8 x 13″ signed (CR) MC. Illustration from *The Saturday Evening Post* 11/5/38. CREDIT, THE AUTHORS.

56. John Clymer. *The Trader*, oil 24 x 40″ signed LR and painted 1971. Retired as an illustrator in 1964 to paint the history of the West. CREDIT, THE ARTIST.

57. Vincent V Colby. *Pikes Peak, Colorado, on the Santa Fe*, oil 36 x 50″ dated 1912. One of the many landscapes commissioned by the Santa Fe Railway. CREDIT, THE ANSCHUTZ COLLECTION.

58. A P Coleman. *Hudson Bay Post, Lac Ste Anne, Alberta*, watercolor over pencil 4⅞ x 6⅞″ painted 1907 by an important Canadian geologist. CREDIT, ROYAL ONTARIO MUSEUM, TORONTO.

60. Howard Cook. *"Koshare"-Santo Domingo Corn Dance*, oil on canvas mounted on Masonite 30 x 40″ signed LR and painted 1948. Illustrator turned Taos modernist. CREDIT, THE ANSCHUTZ COLLECTION.

59. Samuel Colman. *Colorado Cañon*, gouache 14¾ x 15¾″ signed (LR) Saml Colman and dated 1888. Hudson River School painter who went West by train. CREDIT, THE AUTHORS.

61. Emma Lampert Cooper. *Adobe House*, oil on board 10½ x 8½″ signed (LC) E Lampert Cooper. Pupil of Chase and wife of Colin Campbell Cooper. CREDIT, THE AUTHORS.

62. Dean Cornwell. *Sketch for Frontier Operation*, ink and wash on yellow paper 3½ x 5½″. Important Eastern illustrator a regular in the studios of Western painters. CREDIT, THE AUTHORS.

64. Eanger Irving Couse. *The Peace Pipe*, oil on canvas 26 x 32″ signed (LR) E I Couse. "Taos is pronounced tah′-ose and rhymes with Couse." CREDIT, THE METROPOLITAN MUSEUM OF ART, GIFT OF MRS ADOLPHE OBRIG IN MEMORY OF HER HUSBAND, 1917.

63. Kate Cory. *Prescott, Arizona*, oil on canvas 40 x 30″ signed (LL) Kate T Cory. Eastern painter settled in Oraibi by 1905, living in a pueblo. CREDIT, THE AUTHORS.

. Russell Cowles. *Summer Shower, New Mexico*, oil on nvas 28 x 40″ signed (LR) Cowles. International painter 10 resolved his style in New Mexico. CREDIT, THE SCHUTZ COLLECTION.

66. Charles Craig. *Indian Warrior*, oil 10½ x 8″ signed (LR) Chas Craig. One of the first trained artists resident in Colorado. CREDIT, DENVER PUBLIC LIBRARY, WESTERN HISTORY DEPARTMENT.

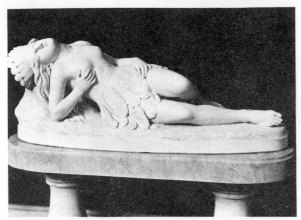

67. Thomas Crawford. *Mexican Princess* (or, *The Dying Indian Girl*), marble 20½ x 52½″ signed Crawford fecit and dated Rome 1848. Typical Victorian "fancy piece." CREDIT, THE METROPOLITAN MUSEUM OF ART, GIFT OF MRS ANNETTE W W HICKS-LORD, 1897.

68. Will Crawford. *Sketch of the Sun Dance*, pencil on board 15 x 20″ addressed to Jim Cagney, signed Bill Crawford, and dated 8/19/43. Crawford was in the West early enough to have seen the Sun Dance. CREDIT, THE AUTHORS.

69. Henry H Cross. *The Days of the Buffalo*, oil on canvas 20 x 31″ signed (LL) H H Cross. Painter of circus wagons known for his Indian portraits. CREDIT, THE ANSCHUTZ COLLECTION.

70. John J Dalton. *Indian Buffalo Hunters in the Foothills the Rocky Mountains*, watercolor 27 x 40″ signed (LR) John Dalton, DTS. Dominion Topographical Surveyor on the Canadian plains 1882. CREDIT, ROYAL ONTARIO MUSEUM, TORONTO.

71. Andrew Dasburg. *Cottonwoods*, oil 20 x 24″ signed by the painter who transported Cézanne and Cubism to New Mexico. CREDIT, MUSEUM OF NEW MEXICO.

72. James Daugherty. *Illustration from "Leaves of Grass"*, watercolor over print 8 x 14″ signed LR. Eastern illustrator American History. CREDIT, THE AUTHORS.

Sources AAW-BDW-Grand Central Galleries Catalog 11/9/44. No auction record or signature example.

Bryant studied at the AIC before service in WWI. He returned to the family ranch in Colorado and made a sketching trip to the Navaho and Hopi in northern Arizona. In 1919 he worked as a commercial artist in Chicago, with another Southwestern sketching trip in 1921. In the late 1920s Bryant was a NYC illustrator before he was able to succeed as a painter of Western ranch life.

BRYANT, Will. Illustrator of magazines, including Western subjects before 1950. No reference. Source, perusal of magazines. No auction record or signature example.

Note MAS listing of William Bryant living Bradford, Mass in 1948, with work in Andover colln. Will Bryant wrote and illustrated "Kit Carson and the Mountain Men" in 1960, as well as a book on gun history and articles on hunting and camping.

BUCHSER, Frank. Born Feldbrunnen near Solothurn, Switzerland 1828, died there 1890. Painter of portraits, genre, and landscapes, engraver. Founder, Assoc of Swiss Artists. Work in Basle Mus, Nat Portrait Gall. References BEN-CHA-MAS. Sources ANT 3/62, 11/66-BUC-DBW-WES. Oil 31×24⅜″ *Misericordia* sold 6/16/72 for $6,500 in Swiss francs at auction. Signature example, cover BUC.

Franz Buchser was apprenticed to an organ maker, then traveled to Paris and Italy before deciding in 1847 to become a painter. He served briefly in the papal guards, studying in Rome about 1848. He continued his studies in Paris and Antwerp, going to Spain in 1850, painting genre subjects in England 1851–54

before returning to Solothurn 1855–56. In 1857 he became battle painter in the suite of Spanish Gen O'Donnell in the Moroccan campaign, working until 1860 when he went to England until 1863.

In 1866 he began his American travels. He experienced considerable success, going from one side of the country to the other making oil sketches used later for celebrated paintings. Buchser changed his given name to Frank while in Virginia painting portraits of political figures including Gens Lee and Sherman and of Negroes. The summer of 1866 he traveled the West as the companion of Gen Sherman: "We had a Swiss artist, M Buchser, sent over by his government to make a grand painting illustrating our late war. Having a month or two, he was making a run to the Plains and the Rocky Mountains. Now he was hurrying on to join Gen Sherman at Julesburg on a tour to Fort Laramie, Buford, Denver, and then east again via the Arkansas. He sketched constantly en route, making sketches of the Platte valley from the top of the stagecoach." WES. The summer of 1868 he went to the Great Lakes region. Buchser returned to Europe in 1871 and continued his travels in Greece, Corfu, Dalmatia, and Montenegro.

BUFF, Conrad. Born Speicher, Switzerland 1886, living Laguna Hills, Cal 1976. Modern Cal painter, illustrator, lithographer, muralist. Murals in California buildings, lithographs in MMA, BMFA, DIA, NGA, Brit Mus. References A76-MAL. Sources AAT-CON-WHO 70. No current auction record. Signature example pp 14–15 CON.

Buff, the son of an Alpine farmer, studied lace designing, attending the School of Arts and Crafts in St Gallen, Switzerland 1900–3. At 18 he attended art school in Munich. At 19 he emigrated to a Dakota ranch, working as a sheep herder while painting in his spare time.

By 1923 he was listed as a professional artist: "a very personal and descriptive kind of painting—an awareness of architectural values and a command of color able to cope with spectacular if remote grandeur." CON. In 1937 he illustrated his wife's book for children, "Dancing Cloud, the Navaho Boy," continuing as co-author and illustrator until the 1968 "The Colorado: River of Mystery."

museum than could have been purchased." Bugbee also illustrated national magazines such as *Field and Stream* and painted commissioned portraits of pioneer cow-men. A "strapping" six-footer, Bugbee was not "besmocked" but rather dressed in "true cowboy style." TXF. Like his boyhood hero Charles Russell, Bugbee drew letterheads for his own correspondence showing "bucking broncs, fleeing buffalo, or savage Indians." TXF.

BUGBEE, Harold Dow. Born Lexington, Mass 1900, died probably Clarendon, Tex 1963. Traditional Western illustrator, painter of ranch scenes, portraitist, muralist, curator. Murals in Panhandle Plains Hist Soc, Dallas Hall of State, Amarillo Army Air Field. References A62-MAL. Sources COW-TOB-T20-TSF. No current auction record but the estimated price for a sketch $10 \times 8''$ of a trail herder would be about $500 to $700 at auction in 1976. Signature example p 40 COW.

Bugbee was brought to the Texas Panhandle in 1912 when some of the larger ranches were breaking up and the old-time ranch style was passing. Rather than becoming a stockman like his father, he wanted to record this phase of Texas life as an artist. After studying at Clarendon College and Texas A&M, on the advice of Bert Phillips he attended Cummings School of Art in Des Moines for three years. His art education was completed in NYC and in Taos with Herbert Dunton. In 1926 he exhibited paintings featuring the buffalo, the "savage" Indian, the horse wrangler, the cowboy, and New Mexico landscapes. TXF.

By 1950, Bugbee was recognized as a "modern master of Texas cattle scenes," COW, exhibiting *The Chuckwagon, The Trail Herd, Branding*. When he became a curator, the museum considered itself "extremely fortunate, for each year Bugbee has prepared far more art for the

BUHLER, F. "An oldtime California engraver" (self-description on reverse of paintings) active as sketch artist around Berkeley about 1871–81. Work in Honeyman colln. No reference. Source HON. No auction record or signature example.

One of the paintings in the collection is a genre oil sketch of gold mining.

BULL, Charles Livingston. Born near Rochester, NY 1874, died Oradell, NJ 1932. Eastern illustrator of wild animals, particularly the American eagle; painter, muralist, writer, taxidermist, naturalist. Member SI, Artists Guild. Work in conservation posters as well as books and magazines. References A32 (obit)-BEN-FIE-MAL-SMI. Sources AAC-ILA-ILP-WHO 32. No current auction record but the estimated price of a wildlife painting would be about $1,000 to $1,500 at auction in 1976. Signature example p 49 ILA. (See illustration 42.)

At 16 Bull worked in taxidermy for Ward's Museum in Rochester and later for the National Museum in Washington where he mounted groups on display including some from the collection of Theodore Roosevelt. He left taxidermy to study at the Philadelphia Art School, the pupil of Harvey Ellis and M Louise

Stowell. "His skill as taxidermist so familiarized him with animal anatomy that his drawings and paintings were unusually accurate," and his drawings of eagles came into demand. A32. He illustrated many magazine articles and books such as "Kindred of the Wild" in 1902. Bull was associated with an expedition into Mexico, Central and South America, writing "Under the Roof of the Jungle" in 1911. During WWI, eagles were featured on Bull's patriotic posters. When Bull lived in NYC, it was near the Bronx Zoo. As a conservationist he was interested in the preservation of the American eagle.

BUNNELL, Charles Ragland. Born Kansas City, Mo 1897, died Colorado Springs, Colo 1968. Impressionist Western landscape painter, teacher. Reference MAS. Source SHO. No current auction record but the estimated price of an oil 20×30″ of a mountain range would be about $500 to $700 at auction in 1976. Signature example p 54 SHO.

Bunnell moved to Colorado Springs about 1915. He studied at Broadmoor AA in 1922–23 and with Ernest Lawson. In 1927–28 Bunnell's broken-color impressionism was shown at Carnegie Institute. He exhibited widely in the West, taught at Broadmoor and at Kansas City AI. In the 1940s Bunnell turned to abstraction.

BURBANK, Elbridge Ayer. Born Harvard, Ill 1858, died San Francisco, Cal 1949. Indian portrait painter. Work in Newberry Lib (Chicago), Smithsonian Inst. References A23-BEN-FIE-MAL-SMI. Sources ACO-AIW-ANT 12/54,9/58-DCC-HAR-JNB-PAW-PNW-WHO 36. Oil on canvasboard 13½×10¾″ *Chief Geronimo, Apache* with signature

example sold 10/27/71 for $4,000 at auction.

E A Burbank graduated from the Chicago Art Academy. In his first job for *Northwest Magazine,* he traveled along the territory of the Northern Pac Ry, across the Rockies to the Pacific coast. His assignment was to paint scenes that would sell the area to homesteaders. In 1886 Burbank left Chicago for Munich, Germany to study with Paul Nauen and Frederick Fehr. His fellow students included Leigh, Sharp, and Rosenthal. When he returned to Chicago in 1892, he specialized in painting Negro subjects, particularly children. His work was exhibited in Chicago, Atlanta, and Paris.

In 1895 Burbank's uncle Edward Ayer, a museum president, commissioned a series of portraits of Western Indians, setting a course for Burbank that proved to be his life's work. Burbank started at Fort Sill, painting the first portrait of Geronimo. He continued through the tribes of the Southwest, the West, and the Pacific coast, recording the likenesses of such famous Indians as Chiefs Joseph, Sitting Bull, Rain-in-the-Face, Curley, and Red Cloud. His initial exhibition of Indian portraits was in Philadelphia in 1897. Given the Indian name Many Brushes, Burbank depicted the leaders of about 125 tribes in more than 1,200 works. The two principal collections are the Newberry Library and the Smithsonian Institution. Similar to a number of other Western painters such as Groll, Reiss, and Kihn, Burbank was expert in the use of crayons as well as oil and watercolor. His autobiography was "Burbank among the Indians." Burbank's work is regarded as historically important because his portraits are in some instances the only pictures of the Indian subjects.

BURGDORFF, Ferdinand. Born Cleveland, Ohio 1881 (or 1883), living Pebble Beach, Cal 1962. Painter, print-maker, craftsman. Work in San Francisco MA, Cleveland MA, and hospitals in Ariz and Cal including 36 paintings given to six USAF hospitals in the Arctic. References A62-FIE-MAL. Source, *Grand Canyon* in Cleveland MA. Oil 14×18″ on board *Corral in Moonlight, Arizona Desert* signed but not dated, estimated for sale 10/28/74 at $400 to $500 for auction in Los Angeles and sold for $250. Signature example lot 98 catalog above. (See illustration 43.)

Burgdorff studied at the Cleveland School of Art and was the pupil of Menard in Paris. He painted in the Southwest about 1927.

BURGESS, George Henry. Born London, Eng 1831 (or 1830), died Berkeley, Cal 1905. Landscape and portrait painter in San Francisco beginning 1849, engraver, lithographer. Work in ACM, Honeyman colln. Reference G&W. Source HON. No auction record or signature example.

Son of a surgeon, his older brother was an artist and teacher who also emigrated to San Francisco. His younger brother remained in England as an engraver. Burgess studied at Somerset House School of Design in London before emigrating to San Francisco in 1849. He engraved a view in San Francisco in 1854. ACM. Active in Berkeley and Sacramento as well, Burgess traveled to the British Columbia gold rush in 1858. A founder of the San Francisco Art Institute, he exhibited watercolor landscapes in San Francisco in 1858–59 and portraits in the 1870s.

Burgess visited England, Wales, and probably Hawaii beginning 1871. In 1891 Burgess painted a view of *San Francisco in 1849,* exhibiting another view in 1894. The earlier view was lithographed by Crocker in the 1890s. Burgess painted until 1903.

BURLIN, Harry Paul. Born NYC 1886, died there 1969. Early Santa Fe school international painter. Work in WMAA, MOMA, BM, Newark MA, LAMA, DAM, US State Dept. References A70 (obit)-BEN-FIE-MAL. Sources AAT-ALA-APT-ARM-CAA-COW-DEP-190-M50-SHO-TSF-WYA-WHO 68. Ink and wash drawing 7×11½″ allegorical battle scene sold 5/26/71 for $60 at auction. M50 offered Burlin's *Look! No Fish* for sale at $1,800 in 1950. Signature example p 43 SHO.

Paul Burlin was educated at the NAD in NYC and in England. He became an internationally celebrated landscape, mural, and figure painter, living in NYC in 1919, Paris in 1931, NYC in 1941, exhibiting widely. He was lecturer on painting at Washington U in St Louis 1949–54, and visiting professor at Union College NY 1954–55. Burlin married Natalie (an ethnologist specializing in Indian music) in 1917, Margot in 1925, Helen in 1937, and Margaret in 1947. There were retrospective exhibitions of his art at Ford Fndn in 1960, WMAA in 1962, and Boston U in 1964.

Burlin was an early member of the Santa Fe school of Western painting, beginning with his visit in 1913. He spent much time in the Southwest up to 1920, the first visitor who had exhibited in the 1913 Armory Show. His Santa Fe Indian portraits and landscapes applied his personal approaches to color and distortion. His early style was semiabstract, then increasingly expressionistic, and not at all understood by his peers in the West. He was also a visiting artist at the U of Wyoming, and instructor at Colorado Springs FAC in the summer of 1936.

BURR, George Elbert. Born Monroe Falls (near Cleveland), Ohio 1859, died Phoenix, Ariz 1939. Western etcher, painter. Etchings in MMA, NY Pub Lib, AIC, BMFA, London, Paris, Berlin.

References A41(obit)-BEN-FIE-MAL-SMI. Sources ACO-HAR-WHO 38. No current auction record but the estimated price of a watercolor 16×20″ of desert sky would be about $600 to $900 at auction in 1976. Signature example p 41 HAR.

Burr studied at the AIC. In 1890 he was an illustrator for *Harper's* and *Leslie's*. He then secured the commission to make 1,000 ink drawings to illustrate a MMA catalog of a bronze and jade collection. After four years at this task Burr was enabled to study for five years in France and Italy.

When Burr's health failed about 1906, he moved to Denver where he created a set of 16 etchings called *Mountain Moods*. He spent his winters in the deserts of Arizona, New Mexico, and Southern California. From this came his well-known set of 35 desert etchings. Burr is said to have painted about 1,000 watercolors and to have drawn 25,000 etchings, generally small in size and showing "the miniaturist's precise delicacy."

BURT, Marie Haines. See Haines.

BUSH, Norton. Born Rochester, NY 1834, died San Francisco, Cal 1894. Cal landscape and portrait painter. References BEN-CHA-FIE-G&W-MAL-SMI. Sources BAR-HUT. Oil 36×20″ *Landscape* (1881) sold 1/7/70 for $400 at auction. Oil 16×13″ *Tropical Landscape* sold 8/7/73 for $800 at auction. Signature example ⚹53 PB 5/22/73.

Bush was a pupil of James Harris in Rochester and J F Cropsey beginning 1852 in NYC. He exhibited at the NA in 1852 and 1871 while his studio was in NYC. His specialty was the subtropical landscape. Bush traveled to South and Central America in 1853, at the same time as F E Church, and again in 1868 and 1875, painting *The Andes of Peru, Bay of Panama, Nicaragua Lake*.

In 1874 Bush became a member of the San Francisco AA, painting *Summit of the Sierras* and *Lake Tahoe*. "His services in connection with the local Art Association were of greater historical consequence than his landscapes, for these lack the pictorial clarity of Browere." BAR.

BUSH-BROWN, Henry Kirke. Born Ogdensburg, NY 1857, died Washington, DC 1935. Sculptor of *The Buffalo Hunt*, equestrian statues, arch, fountain, memorials, and portrait busts. Member NSS 1893. Work in MNM, Gettysburg, Valley Forge, Charleston (WVa), NYC, MMA. References A36 (obit)-BEN-DAB-FIE-MAL-SMI. Sources COR-HAA-NSS-WHO 34. No current auction record or signature example.

The pupil and adopted son of his uncle Henry Kirke Brown, Bush assumed his hyphenated name at the death of his uncle in 1886. He had been educated at the Siglar School in Newburgh and studied at the NAD, the pupil of his uncle. From 1886 to 1889 he studied in Paris and Florence, the pupil of A Mercié at Julien Academy.

When he returned to the Brown farm near Newburgh in 1889, he began on a large Indian group called *The Buffalo Hunt*. For models he brought to Newburgh a buffalo, an Indian pony, and a young Blackfoot named Lone Wolf. This colossal work was completed for exhibition in 1893 at the World's Columbian Exposition, but it remained unsold. The day before Bush-Brown died, a committee of the House of Representatives recommended the purchase of a bronze replica of *The Buffalo Hunt* for Potomac Park in Washington but no funds were allocated. "Invariably optimistic and friendly, Bush-Brown always had in mind some measure for the betterment of mankind." DAB. He was survived by his wife Margaret Lesley Bush-Brown, a portrait painter, and by his daughter Lydia Bush-Brown Head, who did silk murals. A38.

BUTLER, Howard Russell. Born NYC 1856, died Princeton, NJ 1934. Eastern landscape, marine, and portrait painter noted for depictions of eclipses, lawyer. ANA 1898, NA 1902, NIAL. Work in AMNH, MMA, Lotus Club. References A36 (obit)-BEN-FIE-MAL-SMI. Sources ANT 2/71 with signature example p 181 *Mexican Street Scene*-M31-NJA-WHO 34. Oil 14×19″ *California Landscape* sold 10/1/69 for $500 at auction. (See illustration 44.)

Butler graduated from Princeton in 1876, received a law degree from Columbia in 1882, and practiced law in NYC until 1884. By 1886 he was a painter receiving honorable mention at the Paris Salon. He had studied with F E Church in Mexico, at the ASL, and in Paris. In 1918 he accompanied the US Naval Observatory Expedition to Baker, Ore to paint the June 8 solar eclipse. He also painted the 1923 solar eclipse at Lampoc, Cal and the 1925 eclipse at Middletown, Conn. These paintings were in the AMNH where Butler became supervisor of astronomy exhibits.

BUTMAN, Frederick A. Born Gardiner, Me 1820, died there 1871. Active 1857–71 as San Francisco landscape painter. Reference G&W. Sources ANT 6/67-HON-PAF. Oil 21×32″ *Cattle in the Grassy Hills* (San Fran 1858) sold 11/13/72 for $375 at auction. Painting example p 672 ANT 6/67 *Cabin in the High Sierras.*

Butman owned a drugstore in Gar-

diner until 1857 when he moved to San Francisco as a landscape and figure painter. From 1860 to 1865 he explored a thousand miles up the Columbia River. Called a "showy" painter, he is said to have sold landscapes in California for as much as $8,000 in gold. HON. He exhibited at the NA in 1867, showed *On Bear River* at the PAFA giving his address as NYC in 1868, and sketched in Europe in the summer of 1869.

BYWATERS, Jerry (or Gerald). Born Paris, Tex 1906, living Dallas, Tex 1976. Modern Texas painter, illustrator, teacher, writer, museum director. Work in ACM, Dallas MFA, Texas colleges; murals in Texas post offices. References A76-MAL. Sources AAT-ACM-ALA-CAP-M50-T20-TOB-TXF-WHO 70. Painting *Houses in West Texas* offered for sale for $500 in 1950 (M50) but no current auction record. Signature example p 48 AAT.

Bywaters graduated from Southern Methodist U in 1927, then went to Europe, studying at the Tate, Louvre, and Prado museums. In 1928 he studied the frescoes of Orozco and Rivera in Mexico and attended the ASL in NYC. After 1929 he maintained a studio in Dallas with sketching trips to Mexico and New Mexico, painting *West Texas Town, Taos Mountains, Mexican Woman.* His subjects are landscape, portrait, and still life. "Perhaps Orozco suggested to Jerry Bywaters how the shapes of cactus could be made to writhe against Texas cliffs." ALA. He has illustrated magazines and books.

Bywaters is a lecturer, a contributor to *Art in America,* the author of monographs on his contemporaries Dozier, Spruce, and Dasburg. He was art critic from 1933 to 1939, professor of art beginning 1936, museum director from 1943 to 1964, and director of fine arts center after 1966.

CABOT, Hugh. Born Boston, Mass 1930, living Nogales, Ariz 1973. Southwestern painter, illustrator, sculptor, writer. Member, Assoc Am A. Work in USN Mus; murals in industrial buildings. Reference A73. Source AHI 12/72. No current auction record. Signature example p 17 AHI 12/72.

Cabot studied at the Vesper George Sch A, BMFA Sch A, Mexico City Col, Oxford U in England. He was Official Navy Combat Artist in the Korean War and has contributed newspaper and magazine illustrations. His subjects include Southwestern Americana and the Mexican frontier.

CADENASSO, Giuseppe. Born Genoa, Italy 1858, died San Francisco, Cal 1918. San Francisco landscape painter, teacher. Work in Golden Gate Park Mus, Alaska-Yuk-Pac Expos 1909. References A18 (obit)-MAL. Sources BDW-JCA. No auction record or signature example.

Cadenasso worked on a California ranch and in a San Francisco restaurant to earn funds for study at the Mark Hopkins Institute, the pupil of Arthur F Mathews. From 1903 on, he taught at Mills College. A typical painting title is *Evening*. Favorite subjects were the eucalyptus tree and sunlight on the marshes.

CAHILL, Arthur James (or JA). Born San Francisco, Cal 1878, living there 1970. San Fran illustrator, art editor, portrait painter. Work (oil portraits) widely held in Cal. References A25-BEN -FIE-MAL-SMI. Sources AOA-BWB-SCA-WHO 70. No current auction record. Signature example ✳247 AOA as J A Cahill.

Cahill was educated in the public schools of Eureka and in the Jesuit Bros school in San Jose, Cal. He studied in the California Art School and in Paris. From 1892 to 1906 Cahill was artist for San Francisco newspapers and the NY *World*. His 1898 drawing of flower-decorated soldiers off for the Philippines was printed in *Harper's* with Cahill's initials reversed in the engraving.

Briefly a NYC magazine illustrator, Cahill returned to San Francisco 1910–15 as art editor for *Sunset Magazine* and the Southern Pac RR. After 1915 he was a portrait painter. Sitters included Pres Hoover, Gen Pershing, scientist Millikan, and banker Giannini.

CALHOUN, Major A R. Active 1867. Railway survey artist, photographer, special artist-correspondent for *Harper's Weekly* and *The Phila Press*. No reference. Sources AIW-12/12/73 letter from Joyce Zogett, Free Lib of Phila. No auction record. Sketch examples p 468 *Harper's Weekly* 7/27/1867.

Calhoun was a member of the Union Pacific surveying party associated with Gen Wright and Dr William Bell in New Mexico, Arizona, and Colorado. He described for *Harper's* the Indian War battle near Fort Wallace 6/26/1867 in which "Corporal Harris placed the muzzle of the Spencer rifle he carried in his right hand at the breast of the savage Roman Nose and fired." The illustration of the battle and a view of Fort Wallace "are from sketches by Calhoun and Bell." Calhoun also contributed to Bell's book "New Tracks in North America."

In *The Philadelphia Press* for 7/13/1867, Calhoun reported the same event, including, "On a mule in the advance rode Gen Wright, a good healthy look on his bronzed face, and an expression of anything but scare at the Indians playing around his mouth." The report published 7/24/1867 describes the humdrum of life in the desert with the survey party, where following the government map made them err 42 miles in 75 miles.

CALKINS, Frank W. Active 1896. Illustrator. No reference. Source AIW. No auction record or signature example.

Hemmed In With the Chief by Calkins appeared in *St Nicholas* in Jan 1896.

CALYO, Nicolino Vicompte. Born Naples, Italy 1799, died NYC 1884. NYC landscape, genre, and portrait painter, panoramist of Texas. Work in BMFA, NY Hist Soc, Mus City NY. References BEN-FIE-G&W-MAL-SMI. Sources ANT 12/44,5/49,12/52,4/53; 1,3,8/54; 3/56,1/57,11/59,5/67,3/73, 12/74-BAR-KW1. Oil *View of NY Fire on Dec 17, 1835* sold 4/8/71 for $850 at auction. Signature example p 500 ANT 12/52.

Calyo fled Italy in 1821 as a political refugee. He studied and traveled in Europe, settling in Malta in 1829 and then Spain. He emigrated to Baltimore following the Spanish civil war in 1833, moving to NYC in 1835. His most famous paintings were of the NYC fire of Dec 1835 that raged for two days, destroying 19 blocks and 674 buildings. W J Bennett aquatints were taken from Calyo's fire paintings. His watercolor series *Cries of NY* was also reproduced about 1840. Calyo painted gouache views of NYC, Baltimore, and Philadelphia.

From 1847 to 1852 Calyo's scenes from the Mexican war were exhibited in NYC, Philadelphia, Boston, and New Orleans, along with his 40-foot panorama *The Connecticut River*. The listed sources do not indicate that Calyo went to Texas. His sons John A and Hannibal also painted.

CAMERER, Eugene. Born probably Germany 1823, died probably Stuttgart, Germany 1898. Active in Cal late 1850s as landscape and genre painter, printmaker. Reference G&W. Sources ACM-COS-WHI (as Eugen Camere)-12/13/73 letter from Raymond W Hillman, Pioneer Mus & Haggin Galls. No auction record or signature example.

Before 1849 Eugene Camerer had emigrated from Germany to work in the Middle West as an artist. He came to NYC in 1849 to board the vessel on which he would sail steerage to California. Ill on arrival, he worked on the family farm where he was Onkel Eugen, the inept putterer who lived on the largesse of his brother-in-law. When he went off to seek gold, he returned because all the locations to mine were taken.

Camerer moved with the family to Stockton. After an unsuccessful turn as a sign painter, he held himself out as a portrait painter. In 1858 he visited the Calaveras grove of big trees and the Yosemite, only three years after Ayres. His sketches were the basis of Kuchel & Dresel lithographs, as were sketches of Stockton in 1858 and San Francisco in 1859. He returned to Germany in 1859 because of an unhappy love affair, according to his nephew. The Pioneer Museum in Stockton has the painting *Mike Schuler's Freighting Outfit* where the signature is enclosed in a painted box so small that the name is shortened to Eugen Camere. WHI calls this painting an amusing genre scene of the ordeal involved in reaching the mining camps. Camerer was in Stuttgart in 1872, painting, printmaking, and teaching.

CAMES, Vina. Born Oakland, Cal about 1908, living in Laramie, Wyom in 1948. Wyom painter. Work in U of Wyom, DAM, IBM at Denver. References A41-MAL. Source WYA. No auction record.

Cames studied at U of Wyoming,

Colorado Springs FA Center, Broadmoor Academy FA, the pupil of H V Poor, Frank Mechau, Boardman Robinson, and Lawrence Barrett, and exhibited in Colorado and Wyoming.

CAMFFERMAN, Margaret Gove (Mrs Peter Camfferman). Born Rochester, Minn about 1895, living Langley, Wash 1962. Northwest landscape painter. Work in SAM. References A62-MAL. Sources WAA-WNW. No current auction record or signature example.

Mrs Camfferman was educated at the U of Minnesota. She studied at the Minneapolis School of Art, the NY School of Applied Design, the Henri School of Art, and in Paris at André Lhote's atelier. Typical painting titles were *Orchard on Sound* and *View from Old Homestead Ranch.*

CAMFFERMAN, Peter Marienus. Born The Hague, Holland 1890, died Langley, Wash 1957. Northwest landscape painter, etcher, teacher. Work in U of Washington, SAM, Golden Gate Int Expos 1939. References A59 (obit)-FIE-MAL. Source WNW. No current auction record or signature example.

Camfferman studied at the Minneapolis School of Art and in Paris at André Lhote's atelier. He taught in Seattle at Helen Bush School and at Camfferman Art School. Typical painting titles are *The Passing of the Virgin Forest, Granite Falls, The Last of the Giants.* His wife was the painter Margaret Gove Camfferman.

CAMPARET. See Compara.

CAMPBELL, Albert H. Born Charleston, WVa 1826, died Ravenswood, WVa 1899. Railway survey artist, engineer and surveyor. Reference G&W. Sources ACM -AIW. No auction record or signature example.

Campbell was an 1847 graduate of Brown U as a civil engineer. Beginning 1853 he was engineer and surveyor for the exploration of railway routes across the Rockies to the Pacific, and is considered to have been one of the 11 important survey artists. He was with Lt Whipple's 35th parallel expedition from Arkansas westward through Oklahoma, New Mexico, and Arizona to California. Mollhausen was the official artist but some of the important illustrations such as the crossing of the Colorado River are by Campbell. "All views show the Mojaves in various activities and it can be seen that evidently men and women alike wore little more for the evening's festivities than they did the day they were born." AIW. In the fall of 1854 Campbell joined the 32nd parallel expedition, working from San Jose, Cal to San Diego to Arizona and New Mexico, and the eight full-page illustrations are all credited to Campbell.

From 1857 to 1860 Campbell was in Washington as Superintendent of Pacific Wagon Roads. In the Civil War, Campbell was mapmaker for the Confederate Army, and thereafter was chief engineer of railroads based in West Virginia.

CAMPBELL, Orson D. Born Fillmore, Utah 1876, died Provo, Utah 1933. Utah painter. Reference MAL. Source YUP. No current auction record. Signature example p 24 YUP.

Campbell studied at BYU and at the ASL in 1908-9 under Bridgman, Taylor, DuMond, and Cox. He also studied at the California School of FA in 1920, the AIC in 1922. He taught at BYU from 1903 to 1915, at Ricks College 1915-18, and at Dixie College 1918–20. He is said to be "a less important second generation Utah painter" with greatest interest in the works of his ASL period. YUP.

CAPLES, Robert Cole. Painter active Reno, Nev 1939–48. Work in IBM colln. References A41-MAL. Source AAT. No auction record. Signature example p 63 AAT.

Caples exhibited the pastel *Cloud Woman* at the NY World's Fair in 1939.

CARPENTER, Earl. Born Long Beach, Cal 1931, living Sodona, Ariz 1976. Traditional Western genre painter specializing in Indians. Reference A76. Sources AHI 7/73-WAI 71,72-WYG. No current auction record. Signature example p 24 AHI 7/73.

Carpenter studied at Chouinard AI and at the Art Center School in Los Angeles. His approach is toward spontaneity. Sketches and watercolors precede major oils, and in technique, the watercolor and oil palettes are related to promote the transfer from sketch to finished painting. WYG also refers to less traditional treatments where "he abstracts a form from nature and paints it directly out of context." Listed painting titles are *The Dineh* and *Dance at Hotevilla*.

CARPENTER, Ellen Maria. Born Killingly, Conn 1836 (or 1830, or 1831), died Boston, Mass probably 1909. Boston landscape and portrait painter, teacher. References BEN-FIE-G&W-MAL-SMI. Sources HUT-WAA-WHO 12. No current auction record but the published estimate is $200 to $300. No signature example.

Miss Carpenter was educated at Milford high school. She studied with Thomas Edwards, the Boston portrait and miniature painter, and at Lowell Institute in Boston where she lived beginning 1858. In 1867 and 1873 she studied and sketched in Europe, the pupil of Fleury and Lefebvre in Paris. She was a well-known painter and teacher in Boston where her address was the Hoffman House. Her paintings included landscapes of Italy, the Alps, New England, and *A View from Mariposa Trail of the Yosemite Valley*.

CARR, M Emily. Born Victoria, BC, Can 1871, died there 1945. Painter of Can West Coast Indian villages and landscape, book illustrator, teacher, craftsman, writer. Work in Vancouver Art Gallery. References BEN-MAS. Sources CAH-CAN-CAR-DCA. Oil on canvas 27×40" *Near Langford, British Columbia* sold 10/21/74 for $30,000 at auction in Canada. Signature example p 98 CAR. (See illustration 45.)

Emily Carr studied at the San Francisco SA from 1889 to about 1895, returning to the Canadian West Coast to teach and to visit the Indian villages beginning 1897. She studied at the Westminster SA in London from about 1899 to 1904, again going back to the West Coast where she began painting totem poles in landscapes. In France 1910–11 to study at Colarossi and on a visit to Sweden, she was influenced to begin painting the Indian villages in a Fauve manner. This style was so rejected she lost her teaching jobs. After 1913 she made Indian-design pottery and carpets, took in roomers, and raised 350 Old English Bobtail Sheepdogs.

About 1922–25 Emily Carr was influenced to some extent by her American contemporary Mark Tobey as she began again to paint. In 1927 she had her first exhibition in Eastern Canada. Exposed to the "Group of Seven" and particularly to Lawren Harris' enthusiastic nationalism, the older Emily Carr in her 60s provided "the revelation of one of the most passionate personalities in modern painting." CAR. She began painting large and powerful oils of the primitive totem poles and of the surging rain forests. This is regarded as her characteristic and "ardently Canadian" expression, although the traditional critics of the time called her later period "an eccentricity of design and a cloudiness of colour hard to explain unless it be failing vision." CAN. In 1928 she illustrated the Marius Barbeau Indian book, along with Jackson and Kihn. Her own first book "Klee Wyck" on her life among the West Coast Indians won the Canadian nonfiction award for 1941. "The Book of Small" followed in 1942.

CARTER, Charles Milton. Born North Brookfield, Mass 1853, died Los Angeles, Cal 1929. Painter, teacher, writer. References A30 (obit)-BEN-FIE-MAL-SMI. Sources DPL-WHO 16. No current auction record but the published estimate is $200 to $300. No signature example.

Carter was the pupil of the Massachusetts Normal Art School in Boston where he later taught in 1923. He also studied in European schools. He served as state supervisor of drawing in Massachusetts and as director of art for the Denver Public Schools. He was a charter member of the Denver AC in 1893. In 1900 he was honorary president of the US section of the Paris International Congress for Teaching of Drawing. In 1908 he was Dept of Interior delegate to the London Art Congress.

CARVALHO, Solomon Nunes. Born Charleston, SC 1815, died NYC 1894. Expedition artist, portrait and Western landscape painter, the first official photographer on a Western expedition. Work in Md Hist Soc, Rose AM (Brandeis). Reference G&W. Sources AIW-ANT 2/57,2/75-KW1-PAF-SUR-12/11/73 letter from Eugenia Calvert Holland, Md Hist Soc. No auction record. Painting example p 231 ANT 2/75 *Portrait of Lincoln*.

The Carvalho family moved to Baltimore in 1828 and to Philadelphia in 1835. S N Carvalho worked as an artist in Philadelphia from 1838 to 1850, with trips to Charleston and Washington. In 1849 he exhibited at the PAFA, and from 1850 to 1860 he lived in Baltimore, exhibiting at the Maryland Historical Society and owning a daguerreotype studio.

During 1853–54 the "tenderfoot" Carvalho served as artist-photographer with Frémont's expedition to demonstrate for political reasons that the Central Pacific railway route could be followed in winter. Egloffstein, who was one of the 11 important railway survey artists, served as topographical engineer on this expedition. Ten Delaware Indians completed the party of 22 which began crossing the ranges in the dead of winter. Food gave out and horses were eaten while Frémont threatened to shoot to prevent cannibalism. One man died from exhaustion and when the party reached southern Utah, Frémont wrote, "The Delawares all came in sound but the whites were all exhausted and broken up and more or less frost bitten." AIW. All of Carvalho's plates and prints were destroyed in a fire.

Carvalho refused further survey employment, becoming a popular portrait painter in Salt Lake City and California. He returned to Baltimore where he wrote "Incidents of Travel and Adventure in the Far West," published in NYC in 1859. He also painted Western scenes, including the then-famous *Grand Canyon of the Colorado*. In 1860 he moved to NYC where he was listed as artist and photographer until 1880 and thereafter as president of the Carvalho Heating and Super-heating Co.

CARY, William de la Montagne. Born Rockland (Lake Tappan), NY 1840, died Boston (Brookline), Mass 1922. Important Western genre painter, illustrator. Work in ACM, GIL. References G&W-MAS. Sources ACM-AIW-ANT 1/56 - BAR - BRO - CAP - COW - DBW - DCC-GIL-HAR-IND-JNB-TWR-WHI. No current auction record but the estimated price of an oil 20×30″ *Indian Encampment* would be about $5,000 to $10,000 at auction in 1976. Signature example p 95 GIL. (See illustration 46.)

An established illustrator for *Harper's* and *Leslie's* when he was 20, Cary with two other youths left NYC in 1860 to start a storybook trip west with no particular destination in mind. They took the river boat *Spread Eagle* from St Louis in May 1861, transferring to the *Chippewa* at Fort Union in mid-June to see the upper Missouri. On the way to Fort Benton the boat caught fire and the entire party returned on a handmade flatboat. The young New Yorkers remained at Fort Union for six weeks, exploring with the neighboring Indians. In August they joined a wagon train for Fort Benton that was captured by Crow Indians, then freed because of the presence of an official of the fur company. From Benton in September the three youths started west again with only a guide and a cook, until by chance after 300 miles on their own, they met with a railway survey team that took them toward Portland, Ore. Cary left for home via San Francisco and the Isthmus, arriving at the outbreak of the Civil War and loaded with sketches of the forts along the upper Missouri just before the forts were abandoned.

Cary then spent the rest of his life painting the West from his sketches and his memory, beginning about 1866 and continuing for at least 30 years. His illustrations appeared in *Leslie's Weekly, Harper's Weekly, Scribner's,* etc. He also illustrated the account of his 1860 trip written in 1895 by one of his companions. He made at least one other trip west, in the summer of 1874 when he was invited to accompany the US Government's survey of the Northern Boundary.

CASILEAR, John William. Born NYC 1811, died Saratoga, NY 1893. Hudson River landscape painter, engraver. ANA 1835, NA 1851. References BEN-CHA-DAB-FIE-G&W-MAL-SMI. Sources ALA-ANT 11/65,1/72-BAR-BOA-COR-DCC-HUD-HUT-ISH-KW1-M15-PAF. Work in MMA, COR, NYHS, Peabody Inst. Oil 38×60″ *Lake George* signed with monogram sold 1/21/71 for $4,750 at auction. Monogram example p 95 KW1. (See illustration 47.)

As the sole support of his widowed mother and his brothers and sisters, Casilear was apprenticed to the engraver Peter Maverick in 1827. He was one of a number of artists in the first half of the 19th century who trained by producing the graceful portraits and pictorial embellishments used on bank notes. His work was considered equal to the old-master engravers and made him rich. Casilear's love was landscapes. He had advice from Thomas Cole and took the traditional tour of Europe in 1840 with Durand, Kensett, and Rossiter. After 1854, when he ceased engraving, his studio was at 51 West 10th Street in NYC. His summers were spent in the hills of Vermont "in one of which he lately found a congenial life-companion" (BOA), the Genesee Valley in NY, and the Adirondacks, particularly Lake George. The landscapes reflected the even tenor of Casilear's life, "as harmonious as a poem" with sunny skies, silvery clouds, quiet reaches. His works were highly regarded in his time and were bought by leading collectors. He sold *Lake Lucerne* in 1876 for $1,000.

CHA lists *View of the Rocky Mountains* as dated in 1881. KEN has illustrated two landscapes with Indians, one near Greeley, Colo and the other described as near the Rockies. The listed sources do not provide an exact date for a Casilear trip west, although he was presumed to have gone as far as the Rockies by 1879–80. His friend Kensett went in 1857, Whittredge in 1866, and S R Gifford in 1870.

CASNELLI, Victor. No birth or death date. No reference. No other source. Watercolor 12¼×20″ *Indian Encampment* with signature example V Casnelli but not dated was estimated 11/28/73 at $400 to $800 for auction at LA and sold for $550.

CASSIDY, Ira Diamond Gerald. Born Covington, Ky 1879, died Santa Fe, NM 1934. Santa Fe painter, illustrator, printmaker, muralist. Work in San Diego Mus, Freer colln, MNM, Southwest Mus, MFA Houston, NYPL, Paris, Berlin, Bombay, Vienna mus. References A36 (obit)-BEN-FIE-MAL-SMI. Sources COW-DCC-HAR-PIT-SCA-TSF-TWR-WHO 32-12/73 data from Edna Robertson, MNM. No auction record. Signature example p 47 PIT *Navajos on the Way to Leguna Fiesta*. (See illustration 48.)

Son of a builder, Cassidy grew up in Cincinnati. He was the pupil of Duveneck at the Institute of Mechanical Arts when he was 12. By the time he was 20, he was art director of a NYC lithographer. Stricken by pneumonia in 1899, he entered a sanitarium in Albuquerque where he first painted the Southwest, changing his signature from Ira Diamond Cassidy to Gerald Cassidy. When he recovered sufficiently, he moved to Denver as a commercial artist and lithographer specializing in theatrical subjects. After returning briefly to NYC where he studied at the NAD and the ASL, he married Ina Sizer Davis and settled in Santa Fe in 1912, following Carlos Vierra (1904) and Kenneth Chapman (1909). He was also active in Los Angeles, California 1913 to 1921.

Intending to devote his talent to recording Indian life in the context of New Mexican light and color, his first Indian drawings reproduced on post cards were sophisticated and art nouveau rather than the typical Victorian. Recognition came by 1915 with his mural *The Cliff Dwellers of the Southwest*. In the 1920s his small on-the-spot landscapes were most prized, as Cassidy's style resisted the influence of the New Mexico modernists. He traveled abroad in 1926, visiting Europe and North Africa. While in France, he utilized 1925 sketches of Navaho subjects to paint two oils, one commissioned by the Santa Fe Ry and the other for the French Government. Cassidy died of poisoning while working on a mural for the Santa Fe Federal Building.

CASTAIGNE, J André. Born Angoulême, France about 1860, died Paris, France 1930. French portrait painter, illustrator. Awarded Legion of Honor, 1899. References A00 (in the directory of illustrators, not as a painter)-BEN-MAL. Sources EDJ-*The Century Magazine* Jan 1893. Oil 25×17¾″ *The Youthful Napoleon* dated 1893 sold 2/20/69 for $125 at auction. This is not relevant to the estimated price of an oil depicting, for example, the tribal customs of the Omahas. Signature example p 445 *Century* 1/93.

André Castaigne was a pupil of Gérôme in Paris. He exhibited portraits in Paris between 1885 and 1896, as a member of the Society of French Artists beginning 1888.

There is no mention of Castaigne in Western sources, but *Century* uses eight of his highly professional 1892 paintings of Omaha Indian dance rites for engravings to illustrate Alice C Fletcher's article "Personal Studies of Indian Life." The paintings are handled with an ethnologist's attention to detail. In 1900 Castaigne's address was care of Century Co in NYC.

CATHERWOOD, Frederick. Born London, Eng 1799, lost at sea 1854. English panorama and historical painter in Cal 1851–54, illustrator, archaeologist, architect. Hon NA 1837 as architect. References BEN-G&W. Sources ALA-BAR-NA 74-TEP. No current auction record or signature example.

Catherwood was an apprentice architect in London 1815–20. He exhibited paintings at the RA 1821–25, then traveled in Europe and the Near East. In 1837 he built a permanent rotunda in NYC for exhibiting the first American panorama, painted from his own sketches of *Jerusalem*. In Central America 1839–40 and 1841–42 he sketched the Yucatán Indian relics for his 1844 *Views of Ancient Monuments in Central America*. He was in California 1851–53. In 1854 he was on the SS *Arctic* when it sank at sea en route to NYC.

CATLIN, George. Born Wilkes Barre, Pa 1796, died Jersey City, NJ 1872. Very important Indian painter, portrait painter, author, anthropologist. NA 1826, as a miniaturist. Work in GIL, US National Museum. References BEN-CHA-DAB-ENB-FIE-G&W-MAL-SMI. Sources ACM-AIW-ALA-ANT 3,6/48; 10/56; 7/58; 10/68; 11/71; 10/72; 3,4/73; 2/75-AOW-AWM-BAR-BOA-CAH-COW-DAA-DBW-DCC-DWF-GIL-GOD-HMA-150-KW1-LAF-M19-MIS-NGA-NJA-PAF-PAW-POW-SUR-TAW-TEP-TSF-TWR-WAI 71,72-WES-WHI. Watercolor on parchment 15¼×12″

Group of North American Indians sold 10/27/71 for $10,000 at auction. Watercolor similarly described estimated at $18,000 to $22,000 for sale at auction 10/28/74 in LA but did not sell. (See illustration 49.)

Catlin's mother at the age of 8 had been captured by the Indians (AOW), so his early life was influenced by family legend and frontier guests. He was educated at home, was outdoors oriented, and collected Indian relics. In 1817 he began studying law in Litchfield, Conn and at the same time teaching himself to paint portraits. He practiced law in Luzerne, Pa until 1823 when he moved to Philadelphia to devote himself to portrait painting, as a friend of Rembrandt Peale, Thomas Sully, and John Neagle. His portraits up to 1829 included New York and Washington politicians. His *Constitutional Convention* painting in 1829 contained 115 figures.

In 1824 Catlin had seen a "delegation of dignified Indians from the wilds of the West, tinted and tasseled off exactly for the painter's palette." POW. This and his background resolved him "to use my art and so much of the labor of my future life as might be required in rescuing from oblivion the looks and customs of the vanishing races of native man in America." DAB. He began in 1830 in St Louis as the first artist of real stature to paint the tribes on the lower Missouri. In 1831 he traveled up the Platte River, and in 1832 headed up the Missouri to Fort Union. From 1834 to 1836 he painted among the Indians in the summers and in the winters he would return East to earn funds for the coming summer. From 1829 to 1838 he painted his collection of about 600 Indian portraits and sketches of the Indian civilization including exactly how they lived. The collection was offered for sale to the Congress but was not accepted. It was exhibited in the US and in Europe between 1837 and 1852, was taken as security for a loan, and eventually donated to the National Museum.

After 1852 Catlin made his "cartoon collection" of 603 paintings copying his earlier paintings, working from sketches and from memory, and adding new paintings of South American Indians. In 1861 Catlin wrote "The Breath of Life" in which he advocated keeping one's mouth closed, particularly during sleep. KW1. Catlin was lean and agile, about 5'8", with blue eyes, black hair. He walked with the straight, measured pace of an Indian. KW1.

CAYLOR, Harvey Wallace (or Henry W). Born near Noblesville, Ind 1867, died Big Spring, Tex 1932. Texas painter of the longhorn, "The Great Painter of Western Life." No reference. Sources AIW-TXF. No current auction record. Painting examples plate 87 AIW *The Trail Herd Headed for Abilene* and opp p 144 TXF *Stampede*.

Ninth of 12 children born in a log cabin and son of a shoemaker, Caylor received drawing lessons as a child. At 14 he left home for odd jobs that included herding cattle in Kansas. With his savings Caylor studied painting as the pupil of Jacob Cox in Indianapolis. Following Remington's advice to go to nature, he headed west, working as needed to pay his way through ranches and cities toward the Pacific, then into Arizona to observe the Indians in the early 1880s. Caylor returned to Indiana when he married in 1886. After sketching in the Rockies he settled in Big Spring, Tex in 1890, outfitting his ranch with the vanishing Texas longhorns as models.

Caylor continued to travel western Texas, sketching ranch life, the old forts, cattle, and painting portraits. He spent the rest of his life as a cowboy artist, following cattle drives and roundups. The cattlemen were his patrons. His first exhibition was not until 1927: *Prayer for Rain, The Drift Fence, The Rim Rock.*

His second exhibition the same fall had *The Chuck Wagon, Cowboy Sanctuary, Romance at the Mail Box*. Caylor's *The Passing of the Old West* has been reproduced. The indicia of "the passing" were in Caylor's studio in 1928, paintings of buffaloes, pioneers, cowboys, longhorns, wildlife, the West Texas landscape, and "the men of the plains, manly, yet gentle with hearts of gold." TXF. Caylor was a contemporary of Frank Reaugh who became more famous.

CE-KOMO-PYN (Naranjo, José Dolores). Living 1967 Santa Clara Pueblo, Espanola, NM. Pueblo painter. No reference. Source AIP. No auction record or signature example.

Ce-Komo-Pyn's work was in the "Contemporary American Indian Paintings" exhibition at the National Gallery of Art, Washington, DC in 1953.

CHAIN (or Chaim), Mrs James Albert. Born 1852, died 1892. Active Denver in the 1870s. Colo painter, teacher. Reference BEN (under Charles Partridge Adams). Source DPL. No current auction record or signature example.

Mrs J Chain was a student of Inness who ran an art school in Denver in the 1870s.

CHALEE. See Pop Chalee.

CHAMBERLAIN, Norman Stiles. Born Grand Rapids, Mich 1887, died Orange Cnty, Cal 1961. Painter who spent summers in Taos, muralist. Work in LA

Mus of Hist, Sci, and Art; murals in US post offices. References A41-MAL. Source BDW. No current auction record or signature example.

Chamberlain was the pupil of Mathias Alten in Grand Rapids and Alson Clark in California. A listed work is *Adobe Flores*.

CHAMPNEY, James Wells. Born Boston, Mass 1843, died NYC 1903. International genre painter, illustrator, correspondent, teacher. ANA 1882. Work in BMFA (large colln of drawings), Deerfield Acad. References A03 (obit)-BEN-CHA-DAB-FIE-MAL-SMI. Sources AIW (as T Willis Champney)-ANT 10/62,11/64,4,6,11/65-HUT-KW1-MSL-WHO 02. Oil 18×36″ *Harbingers of Spring* sold 1970 for $375 at auction; the estimated price for a watercolor 10×14″ of an Indian shelling beans would be about $1,000 to $1,200 at auction in 1976. Signature example p 632 ANT 6/65.

After having studied drawing at Lowell Institute, "Champ" was apprenticed to a wood engraver until the Civil War, in which he served at Gettysburg. After the war he taught drawing in Lexington, Mass. In 1866 he studied in Paris, and in 1867 with the genre painter Édouard Frère. In 1868 he was the pupil of Van Lerius in Antwerp. He exhibited in the 1869 Paris Salon, returned to Boston in 1870 and was back in Paris in 1871 for the excitement of the Commune. In 1872 he made a sketching tour of Germany.

In 1873 *Scribner's Monthly* engaged "Champ" to illustrate Edward King's articles "The Great South." Some of the sketches are of the trans-Mississippi West, "in the wilderness and in Indian territory." KW1. He made more than 500 sketches during the 20,000 miles of travel. The Western sketches are only a small part. He went on to make illustrations at the camp of Don Carlos in Spain in 1875 and in South America in 1878. He taught at Smith College and at the Hartford Society of Decorative Art. In 1885 he began to paint pastel portraits ranked with Whistler and he made pastel copies of European masterpieces. As a painter he was among the first of the American impressionists. Tall and sociable with reddish hair and blue eyes, he loved the stage. He was the subject of special interest in 1964–65 when ANT publicized the Deerfield Academy study of his life and works in connection with the acquisition of 50 paintings from a Deerfield resident.

CHANDLER, Floyd C (F Copeland Chandler). Born San Diego, Cal 1920, living there 1974. Realistic Western landscape painter, commercial artist, teacher. Work in Jerome Hist Soc (Ariz). No reference. Sources AHI 5/72,10/72, with signature examples-1/8/74 data from Floyd Chandler. No auction record.

Chandler began studying art at the San Diego AFA at the age of seven and in 1939 studied at Otis AI in LA. After WWII service in the Coast Guard he studied at the ASL 1946–50, the pupil of DuMond, and remained in NYC until 1954 as a commercial illustrator. In 1955 Chandler began teaching in the adult division of San Diego schools, earning his own BA in art in 1964 and his MA in 1969.

In 1970 Chandler completed nine paintings of the copper mining ghost town Jerome, Ariz. Six of these were published in AHI 5/72. In 1971, 12 paintings were completed on Miami and Globe, Ariz for AHI 10/73. In 1972, 12 oils were painted of the Padre Kino Missions in Sonora, Mexico, also for AHI. In 1973 Chandler painted 16 oils of the gold mining area, Julian, Cal.

CHANLER, Robert Winthrop (improperly listed as Chandler). Born NYC 1872, died Woodstock, NY 1930. Member Nat Soc Mural Ptrs. NYC decorative painter, muralist, designer. Work in MMA, Luxembourg (Paris). References A30 (obit)-BEN-FIE-MAL-SMI. Sources ALA-ARM-ISH. No current auction record or signature example.

Descended from Colonial politicians, Chanler turned from politics to art. He studied at the École des Beaux-Arts in Paris. His most famous work was *Giraffes* completed in 1905 and purchased by the French Government in 1923.

Chanler exhibited decorated screens at the 1913 Armory Show. By using Chanler as a safe bridge to the Fauves, "Everything possible had been done to ease the shock: in the entrance corridor stood delightfully whimsical screens by Robert Chanler with swans and leopards in blue, white, and silver on black." ALA. There were also ✕1023, Screen, *Hopi Snake Dance,* 1913 and ✕1027, Screen, *Indian*. In the Coe House, Brookville, LI, NY there is a ceiling fresco with buffaloes.

CHAPIN, John R. Born Providence, RI 1823, died Buffalo, NY 1904. Eastern illustrator, painter, editor, designer. Work in ACM. References A05-BEN-G&W-MAL-SMI. Sources AIW-AOS-CAP (as R Chapin)-12/18/73 letter Ruth Willet, Buffalo Pub Lib. No auction record but the estimated price of a sketch 8✕10″ *Ranch by the Rails* would be about $400 to $500 at auction in 1976. Signature examples CAP, ACM.

Descended from the Pilgrims, Chapin grew up in NYC, studying law and art. In 1843 Chapin was hired as artist-correspondent for *Gleason's Pictorial,* touring the South to write about and illustrate sites of general interest. When *Gleason's* failed in 1845, Chapin worked as a NYC commercial illustrator until 1850 when he moved to Washington, DC to make drawings for the Patent Office. In 1860 *Harper's* hired Chapin to establish an art department, with F O C Darley as his assistant, but Chapin left to become an important field artist in the Civil War.

In 1865 Chapin received government commissions to design coins and bank notes, using historical scenes such as the explorers meeting Indians. At the same time he started his own wood-engraving firm, specializing in business catalogs in NYC, Buffalo, and Chicago. Chapin also made book illustrations in NYC, such as Western scenes for "Beyond the Mississippi" in 1867. He returned to illustrating in 1875 in NYC and 1880–90 in Boston where he drew for "Ten Years a Cowboy" in 1888. He was in Buffalo 1890–92 and remained there after he retired. Chapin loved Civil War subjects which he continued to paint in watercolors and to draw in India ink until the day he died from apoplexy. It is not known whether Chapin visited the West.

CHAPMAN, Charles Shepard. Born Morristown, NJ 1879, died Leonia, NJ 1962. Eastern landscape painter, illustrator, muralist. ANA 1919, NA 1926. Work in MMA, Montclair AM, Remington Mem Mus, Amer MNH, Cleveland MA, Amherst, NGA. References A66 (obit)-BEN-FIE-MAL-SMI. Sources AAT-COW-ILA-M31-WHO 50-WYA. Oil 18✕24″ *Landscape* sold 1969 for $400 at auction. Signature example p 50 ILA *The Loon Call*. (See illustration 50.)

Chapman was educated at Pratt Inst High School from 1896 to 1898 and at Chase's Art School in NYC in 1899, the pupil of William Chase and W Appleton Clark. Chapman became an instructor at the ASL and a book illustrator. With Harvey Dunn he established a school of illustration in Leonia, NJ. Chapman specialized in landscapes including scenes of

Wyoming and the Grand Canyon. He painted murals for the American Museum of Natural History and for a West Virginia post office.

CHAPMAN, Frederic A. Born Connecticut 1818, died probably Brooklyn, NY 1891. Civil War painter; portrait, historical, and landscape painter; illustrator; craftsman. Reference G&W. Source BEY. No current auction record or signature example.

Chapman was in Boston in 1850, painting historical scenes and exhibiting at the American Art-Union in NYC. He settled in Brooklyn about 1850, the first president of the Brooklyn Art Association. In the 1860s he was known for a series of oils depicting Civil War scenes. Chapman was also a designer of stained glass.

The list of illustrators for "Beyond the Mississippi" published in 1867 "reads like a roll call of the field artists of the Civil War." AIW. Two of the illustrations are credited to F A Chapman— *Down the Shaft* and *Lead Miners under Ground* which are careful depictions of the genre of mining in Missouri at the time. Although it is assumed that the "Beyond" illustrations were redrawn from existing material, the author claims some original sketches, and it may well be that the Chapman drawings were made on the spot.

CHAPMAN, Frederick Trench. Born Windsor, Cal 1887, living Mahwah, NJ 1966. Illustrator specializing in historical figures in action including Indian and military subjects. Member SI. Work in Smithsonian Inst, dioramas of battle scenes in West Point Mil Acad Mus. References A62-MAL. Sources ILA-ILG-POI. No auction record. Monogram example p 124 ILA. (See illustration 51.)

Chapman studied at the ASL, the pupil of George Bridgman, and worked with Vojtech Preissig, the printmaker. Through the 1930s Chapman illustrated historical action subjects for magazines such as *Liberty* (example p 75 POI). Beginning in 1942 he turned to book illustrations, particularly military history subjects including "Custer's Last Stand" by Quentin Reynolds in 1951. He was also known for textbook illustrations, especially "History of Virginia" in 1957. Founder of "The Company of Military Collectors and Historians," Chapman drew plates for its *Quarterly*.

CHAPMAN, John Gadsby. Born Alexandria, Va 1808, died Brooklyn, NY 1889 (or 1890). International landscape, historical, and portrait painter, illustrator, etcher, writer. NA 1836. Work in Rotunda of Capitol, Boston Athenaeum, NY Hist Soc, NAD, Valentine Mus (Richmond, Va), BMFA. References BEN-CHA-DAB-FIE-G&W-MAL-SMI. Sources ALA-ANT 6/58 (p 506 a reappraisal), 11/58,11/59,7/66,9/72, 1/73-BAR-BOA-HUT-ISH-JNB-NAD. See *John Gadsby Chapman* 1962 NGA. Oil 10×14″ *Fra Placido Astride His Burro* sold in 1971 for $950 at auction. Signature p 21 NGA.

Chapman, the son of a business man, was educated at the Academy in Alexandria. In art he was the pupil of George Cooke and C B King. At 18 Chapman began painting in Winchester, Va. For training as a historical painter he studied with Peter Ancora at the PAFA, then went to Italy where his painting in 1830 was the first by an American to be engraved for reproduction in Italy. Returning to NYC in 1831, Chapman held extensive exhibitions, received many portrait commissions, and was the first popular book illustrator in America. For Harper's "Bible" alone he made 1,400 wood engravings. His "American Drawing-Book"

90

was published and republished between 1847 and 1877. Despite his success Chapman was impoverished, though "he was a genial fellow of quiet humor, 5 feet 5 inches tall with a short fringe beard, who loved his little jokes and enjoyed life immensely." In 1848 he sailed for Europe, living in Rome from 1850 to 1884. Even in Europe he was destitute, forced to sell the copyright of his books. The profits from his work went to his publishers, not to him. BOA.

His best work had been accomplished before 1850. The portrait of Col David Crockett was painted about 1835. *The Baptism of Pocahontas* in the Rotunda had taken from 1837 to 1840. The *Landing at Jamestown* in 1841 shows Indians on the shore. Nowhere in the literature, though, is there a mention of a trip West. At the end of his life, he was dependent on his sons, Conrad Wise Chapman and John Linton Chapman. Both were painters, and as poverty-stricken as he.

CHAPMAN, Kenneth Milton. Born Ligonier, Ind 1875, died probably Santa Fe, NM 1968. Santa Fe painter, muralist, authority on Indian art, teacher. Murals in MNM. References A62-BEN-FIE-MAL-SMI. Sources AHI 2/50-COW-HOR-TSF-WHO 66-7/16/65 clipping *The New Mexican*. No current auction price or signature example.

Chapman, a graduate of the AIC and the ASL, was a member of the first field school conducted by the Museum and School of American Research in New Mexico, at a site that became Bandelier National Monument and Puye. He considered himself to have been resident in New Mexico by 1899. As a painter he was the second artist in Santa Fe when he settled in 1909, preceded only by Carlos Vierra. As a scientist he was curator of Indian art at the MNM 1909–29, one of the leading authorities. About 1917

Chapman was the discoverer of the pictographs cut into the Indian caves and painted in Frijoles Canyon. He taught Southwest Indian art at the U of New Mexico beginning 1926, and worked with the Laboratory of Anthropology beginning 1929. Chapman wrote "Pueblo Indian Pottery" in 1933, "The Pottery of Santo Domingo Pueblo" in 1936, and also wrote on the pottery of San Ildefonso.

Chapman is said to have helped start contemporary Indian art in 1902 when he gave the Navaho painter Apie Begay a box of colored crayons. Apie Begay then enlivened traditional sandpicture styles with color and with accentuations of motion in pictures on paper. Chapman is also included among the scientists who studied lost Indian handicrafts so that the techniques could be re-established in the pueblos. HOR.

CHAPPEL, Alonzo. Born NYC 1828 (not France 1820), died Middle Island, LI, NY 1887 (not 1885). Historical painter with Indians in scenes; portrait, naval, and landscape painter, illustrator. Work in NYHS, BMFA, Chicago Hist Soc. References G&W-MAL. Sources ANT 3/72 p 445 (*Indians Meeting Henry Hudson*)-BAR-DIG 2/45 p 21-KW2-PAF. Oil 10×13″ *Battle of Long Island* sold 1969 for $3,300 at auction. Painting example p 62 KW2.

Chappel began painting portraits for $10 when he was 12. He may have studied at the NA as early as 1844 when he had exhibited twice and was listed in the NYC directory. After moving to Brooklyn in 1845, he was listed there as an artist from 1848 until 1868 when he moved to Long Island to illustrate historical books. Chappel's most popular work was the series of paintings for the "National Portrait Gallery" published as a set of books in 1862. The depictions were not from life but rather from available material. In showing Gen Meade, "Chappel moved him from chair to campstool, and the general trustingly relaxes on air." BAR.

CHAPPELL, Bill. Born Van Zandt Cnty, Tex 1919, living South Fork, Colo 1974. Traditional Western painter, sculptor, craftsman in leather. Leatherwork portrait of Will Rogers in Nat Cowboy Hall of Fame. No reference. Sources COW-*People* 6/73 with signature example-4/16/74 letter from Bill Chappell. No auction record.

Chappell's parents made bridles and belts by hand, working the leather with homemade tools of wood and nails. Since he started at 10, Chappell has crafted more than 500 saddles plus thousands of other leather goods including carved boots. After service in the Navy in WWII, Chappell started a saddle business in Seymour, Tex, then moved to a ranch near Alamosa where he began to paint about 1955. His specialty became paintings of hunting deer and elk in the mountains of Colorado, New Mexico, and Texas.

Chappell's schedule calls for about one painting a week and two bronzes a year in series of 30. Typical painting subjects are an old cabin, old houses dimly lit, wildlife, windmills, rivers, and mountains. A 1973 bronze showed a stagecoach five feet long under Indian attack. Chappell has also painted illustrations for magazine covers, *Western Horseman, Paint Horse Journal, Craftsman.* "This art thing is sure working good for me and it's much better at this age to paint cowboy history than to make it. Those cowboy years are good to draw dope from now but at the time it sure did take a lot of sweat and hard knocks to make $30 to $40 a month."

CHARLTON, John. Born Bamborough, Northumberland, Eng 1849, died probably England about 1910. English illustrator of the West, painter of hunting and battle scenes. Work in Blackburn, Nottingham, Sydney museums. References BEN-MAL. Source AOH. Oil 33×43" *Young Boy on a Shetland Pony* dated 1872–73 sold 11/28/72 for $2,280 at Sotheby auction. Signature example p 14 AOH.

Charlton was a pupil of W Bell Scott in Newcastle, influenced by Bewick, and also studied at RA schools. He showed regularly beginning 1870 at the RA. After 1882 he specialized in battle scenes of the Egyptian campaign.

In 1891 and 1892 Charlton painted Western scenes for *Graphic* including settlers crossing the plains and sport in California. He reported the second London visit of Buffalo Bill's Wild West Show in 1892. This report is Charlton's only recorded contact with the American West which he probably never saw.

CHEE, Robert. Born St Michaels, Ariz 1938, living there 1967. Navaho painter. Work in Ariz St Mus, MAI, Mus Northern Ariz, MNM, Philbrook AC. Source AIP. No auction record. No signature example. (See illustration 52.)

Chee attended school in Bellemont, Ariz and at Intermountain Indian School under Allan Houser at Brigham City, Utah. He is one of the few Indians able to work full time as an artist. The first reproduction of his work appeared in *New Mexico* magazine 12/60. Multiples of Chee paintings have been released as silkscreens.

CHENEY, Russell. Born So Manchester, Conn 1881, died Kittery, Me 1945. Eastern landscape painter who lived in Colorado Springs, Colo. Work in Morgan Mem Mus (Hartford), San Francisco MA, Newark Mus Assn, BMFA, Sweat Mem AM (Portland, Me), MNM. References A47 (obit)-BEN-FIE-MAL. Sources AIC-ALA-SCA-WHO 44. Oil *Inland Waterways* sold 1/29/70 for $60 at auction. No signature example.

Cheney graduated Hartford high school in 1899 and Yale in 1904. He studied at the ASL 1904–7, the pupil of Kenyon Cox, Chase, and Woodbury, and in Paris at the Julien Academy 1907–9, the pupil of Laurens. Listed paintings include *Ute Pass* and *Garden of the Gods*. In the modernizing of American painting after the Armory show in 1913, Cheney's self-criticism was that his painting "looks as if it was done at too low a temperature." ALA. Cheney also painted and exhibited in Los Angeles 1926–27.

CHERRY, Mrs Emma Richardson. Born Aurora, Ill 1859, living Houston, Tex 1941. Texas landscape, portrait, still-life painter, teacher. Work in Texas AA, San Antonio A League, Houston MFA, DAM, Carnegie Pub Lib (Houston). References A41-BEN-FIE-MAL-SMI. Sources DPL-TOB-TXF-WAA-WOM. No current auction record. Painting example opp p 40 TXF.

Mrs Cherry studied in Chicago, at the ASL in NYC with Chase and Cox, with André Lhote at the Julien Academy in Paris, with Zanetti-Zilla in Venice. She was a charter member of the Denver Art Club in 1893, exhibiting in 1894–95: "Mrs Cherry of Texas contributes an artistic galaxy of three water colors and three oils, a fine painting of a basket of lilies being among the number. She also has an excellent painting in oil of a corner of a studio, showing the various bric-a-brac promiscuously strewn

around." DPL. Mrs Cherry moved to Houston in 1899. She was a prolific painter and helped organize the Houston MFA.

CHIRIACKA, Ernest. Born in US 1920, living NY State 1975. Painter, illustrator. No reference. Source Kennedy Gallery 10/25/75. No auction record or signature example. (See illustration 53.)

Chiriacka studied at ASL, NA, and the Grand Central School of Art in NYC. He began as an illustrator and his work was published in *The Saturday Evening Post, Esquire,* and *Cosmopolitan.* For research material he traveled and sketched in the West, where he also was commissioned to paint the portraits of film stars. In recent years he has concentrated on painting Indian and Western life as it was in the past. His impressionistic style is different from the hard realism of some of his contemporaries.

CHITTENDEN, Larry. Contemporary painter of Western scenes, living in Fort Worth, Tex in 1968. Source COW.

CHOH (bird). Born about 1864, active 1886 near Fort Wingate, NM. Early Navaho sketch artist in colored crayons. No reference. Sources AHI 2/50-AIP-Annual Smithsonian Report (Shufeldt) 1886. No auction record. Drawing example, plate 111, Report.

Choh was a nephew of the chief. His face was severely disfigured by fire when he was a baby. At about 22 he drew with red and blue pencils upon wrapping paper. Subjects included a mounted chief, "flaming red frogs with blue stripes," figures of Indians, and a locomotive with its tender and baggage cars —"truly a wonderful piece of work for any of these people." Report. The reproduced drawing contains a representation of a bird upper left, perhaps Choh's signature.

The secondary source on Choh is "Contemporary Indian Art" by Clara Lee Tanner. In 1950 she noted that watercolor is the art trend of the Southwest Indians. She mentioned Choh as making in 1886 colored drawings of Indians, wildlife, and a "gaudily dressed chief riding at full tilt upon his Indian steed." She regarded as "noteworthy" that Choh drew costume features in such detail, and called Choh the first known Southwest Indian artist "to make drawings on paper independent of traditional craft or ceremonial attachment."

CHORIS, Louis (or Login) Andrevitch. Born Iekaterinoslav, Russia 1795, died Vera Cruz, Mexico 1828. Russian artist, illustrator, lithographer, author, explorer. References BEN-G&W-MAS. Sources COS-HON-IND. No auction record, but lithographs printed in Paris in 1822 depicting California Indians were listed in a recent catalog at $95 each.

Choris studied in Moscow and made drawings of botanical specimens for the naturalist F A Marschall von Bieberstein in the Russian Caucasus. From 1815 to 1818 he was official artist for the South Seas expedition of Capt Otto de Kotzebue. In 1816 Choris made watercolors of the Presidio at San Francisco and of the native Indians. These sketches were reproduced in his 1822 book "Voyage Pittoresque Autour du Monde."

Choris returned to Paris and studied with Gérard and Regnault. In 1827 he left for South America and in 1828 was killed in Mexico.

CHRISTADORO, Charles. Active 1920s as sculptor. Heroic statue of the cowboy actor William S Hart and his horse Paint at the Valley of the Yellowstone for Billings, Mont in 1927. No reference. Source MWS winter/74. No current auction record. No signature example.

A 38″ sculpted portrait of the actor drawing his sidearms was modeled on commission for Hart.

CHRISTENSEN, Carl Christian Anton. Born Copenhagen, Denmark 1831, died Ephraim, Utah 1912. Important pioneer Utah genre painter. Panorama in BYU; decorations in LDS temples in Utah. Sources PAU-YUP-1/24/74 letter from Ethel T Christensen. No current auction record, but the estimated price of an oil 20×30″ of a Salt Lake theater opening would be about $4,000 to $6,000 at auction in 1976. Signature example p 10 YUP. (See illustration 54.)

CCA's parents were former innkeepers totally impoverished. At 11 he went to a Danish state school for the worthy poor to learn to make paper toys. At 15 he was apprenticed to a carpenter. At 17 he was apprenticed to the painter C Rosent and also was baptized into the LDS Church. At 22 he was titled "artist-painter" but instead served as a missionary in his own country for four years. In 1857 he joined a company of Saints emigrating to the US, pushing a handcart from Illinois across the deserts and mountains to the valley of the Great Salt Lake, painting the scenes and happenings as he traveled. In Utah he laid brick, painted theater scenery and murals until 1865 when he served another mission to Scandinavia during which he also studied painting with Philip Barlag.

CCA's time for painting was severely limited by the requirements of his Church and his family. His finest achievement was the panorama scroll begun in 1869. It consisted of 26 paintings each 8×10′ that illustrated the history of the Church from the vision of Joseph Smith in the Sacred Grove to the arrival of the Saints in Utah. CCA traveled Utah, Colorado, Arizona, and Idaho in a covered wagon, rolling open each picture as he related the history of the Church. *American Heritage* used these pictures in February 1963 to tell the story of Mormonism, "as solid and appealing as any American work of this period. Touching in its praise of old-fashioned virtues, it is a gentle masterpiece."

CHRISTY, Howard Chandler. Born Morgan Cnty, Ohio 1873, died NYC 1952. Illustrator of "the Christy girl," portrait painter, teacher, writer. Member SI 1915. Work in Capitol, White House, State Dept, House of Reps, Italy, England, etc. References A53 (obit)-BEN-FIE-MAL-SMI. Sources AAC-ALA-ANT 8/70,5/72,11/73,3/75-COW-ILA-MSL-SPR-WHO 52. Watercolor 24×34″ *The Cavalier and the Cowboy* 1901 sold 7/2/68 for $350 at auction in London. Oil 30×25″ *Nude on a Sofa* 1933 sold 1/29/70 for $2,100 at auction. Signature example p 758 ANT 5/72.

Christy was educated at Duncan Falls, Ohio before going to NYC in 1893 to study at the NAD, the ASL, and the Chase school. He began working for illustrated periodicals, making his reputation with the 2nd US regulars and the Rough Riders in Cuba in the form of *Scribner's* and *Leslie's* illustrations. The Christy girl started with *The Soldier's Dream* in *Scribner's*. "From then on he did beautiful girl pictures, for *McClure's* and other magazines, almost entirely." ILA. One of "those minor Gibsons, charming but on the softer side." ALA. When called for by the text, the beauty was a Christy cowgirl. In the 1920s Christy came into favor as a portrait painter for the celebrities of the world

and for historical personages such as in the re-creation of *Signing the Constitution* in the Capitol.

CISNEROS, José. Born Ocampo, Durango, Mexico 1910, living El Paso, Tex 1974. Southwestern illustrator specializing in Spanish-American horsemen since 1570. No reference. Sources AHI 3/72-USM-3/73 catalog of Mexico City exhibition-Amer Book Collector summer/67-Guynes Printing Company biography Christmas 1972-12/29/73 letter from José Cisneros with clippings *El Paso Times*. No auction record. Signature examples p 19 Collector *The El Paso Salt War;* p 2 USM.

Cisneros grew up in Dorado, Chihuahua. At 15 his family moved to Juárez and Cisneros was educated in Lydia Patterson Institute in El Paso until 1928. Although he had no other art study, his illustrations were accepted in Mexico by 1934. The painter Tom Lea saw Cisneros' drawings in 1937 and introduced him to Carl Herzog then beginning as a publisher and since called "the Southwest's finest designer-printer." Cisneros illustrated dozens of books for Herzog including decorated and lettered maps. By 1972 he had also illustrated more than 40 books for other publishers.

Cisneros' major work is drawing the different horsemen of the Mexican border country since 1570. The leading authority on the subject, Cisneros has amassed all of the data in his personal library, with detail concerning costumes, weapons, trappings. To enable him to work on his drawings, he received a fellowship in 1969. A series of exhibitions of the drawings in process have been given and 30 were published as "Riders of the Border." Eventually Cisneros will select 100 of his drawings as the final collection, choosing among *Conquistador, Texas Ranger, Mexican Dragoon, Texas Cowboy, Scouting Brave, Vaquero,*

Charro, etc. Cisneros was also an illustrator for "Buffalo Soldiers West" and "The Black Military Experience in the American West."

CLARK, Allan. Born Missoula, Mont 1898 (or 1896), died Grand Junction, Colo 1950. Sculptor of Indian subjects. Member NSS, NIAL. Work in Seattle AM, Honolulu AA, U of Wash Lib (Seattle), House of Navaho Religion (Santa Fe), MNM, MMA. References A53 (obit)-FIE-MAL-SMI. Sources AAT-NSS-SCU-WHO 50-WNW. No current auction record. Sculpture example p 185 AAT.

Clark was educated at Puget Sound College in Tacoma. He was the pupil of Polasek at the AIC and Aitken at the ASL. He began as a sculptor in 1917 in NYC, working in stone and terra cotta while teaching at the Beaux-Arts Institute of Design. From 1924 to 1927 Clark traveled in Japan, Korea, and China, studying under Eastern masters. He is said to have adopted Oriental techniques in woodcarving. Clark was a member of the second Fogg Museum expedition to the Chinese cave chapels near Turkestan. His 20 resulting drawings in color were exhibited in 1930.

Also in 1930 Clark moved his studio to Santa Fe, exhibiting 10 Indian heads in NYC. His sculpture included *Maria of Cochiti* and *Klah—Navaho Medicine Man.*

CLARK, Alson Skinner. Born Chicago, Ill 1876, died probably Pasadena, Cal 1949. Cal landscape and genre painter, illustrator, muralist, printmaker, teacher. Work in AIC, Cal St Lib, Albert and Victoria Mus (London), San Diego FAG; murals in public buildings. References A53 (obit)-BEN-FIE-MAL-SMI.

Source WHO 48. Oil 32×26" *The Church of San Geronimo, 1923* sold in 1972 for $80 at auction, but the published estimate is $1,000 to $1,500. No signature example.

Clark studied at the AIC in 1898, at the Chase Art School in NYC 1898–99, in Paris at the Whistler and Mucha schools 1900–1, and was the pupil of Simon, Cottet, and Merson. He received Exposition medals by 1904 and taught landscape classes at Occidental College in Eagle Rock, Cal. Principal works were *The Coffee House, The Bridge Builders,* and *The Song of the Nightingale.* He illustrated "Manley's Death Valley in '49."

CLARK, Benton Henderson. Born Coshocton, Ohio 1895 (or 1900), died there 1964. Eastern illustrator of the West, painter. Member SI 1932. Murals in Chicago and Columbus. References A62-MAL. Sources HAR-ILA. No current auction record but the estimated price of an oil 20×30" of a parley in the woods would be about $800 to $1,000 at auction in 1976. Signature example p 126 ILA.

After taking drawing lessons from Arthur Woelfle, Benton Clark went to NYC in 1913 to study at the NAD. About 1915 he studied at the AIC in Chicago, selling some illustrations while still a student. His influences were Harvey Dunn, Frank Hoffman, and Remington. After beginning work in the MGM art dept in Culver City, Cal he moved to Chicago to work for advertising art studios. By 1925 Clark was illustrating for *Liberty.*

Clark returned to NYC in 1932, shared a studio with his brother Matt Clark, and painted illustrations for the leading magazines, *The Saturday Evening Post, McCall's, Cosmopolitan, Good Housekeeping.* It was said that Clark made brief trips to the South and West for background material. HAR.

CLARK, Eliot Candee. Born NYC 1883, living Charlottesville, Va 1976. Landscape painter in Ariz Painted Desert in 1926, 1935; teacher, writer. NA 1944. Work in MMA, NAD, Baltimore MA, San Antonio AM. References A76-BEN-FIE-MAL-SMI. Sources M57-WHO 70. Oil 20×27″ *Cold Spring Harbor, Long Island* with signature example but not dated, estimated for sale 3/5/74 at $1,000 to $1,500 for auction in LA and sold for $2,000.

Son of the landscape painter Walter Clark, he was educated in NYC public schools. Said to be self-taught in art, he was exhibiting at the NYWC Club at 9 and at the NA at 13. He acutally studied at the ASL, the pupil of Twachtman, and also in Europe from 1904–6. The winner of national painting awards by 1912, he was writing books on American artists by 1916 and on the history of the NA, in addition to working as a NY art critic. Clark has also taught painting at the ASL and elsewhere and has lectured on art. A political painter, he has a long list of memberships and offices such as president of the NAD 1956–59.

Clark made sketching trips to the Painted Desert of Arizona in 1926 and 1935. During 1937–38 he made a painting trip to the Himalayas, studying art in India.

CLARK, James Lippitt. Born Providence, RI 1883, living NY 1957. Animal sculptor, explorer. Member NSS 1933, Bison Society. Work in Nairobi, Amer Mus Nat Hist, Ohio State U, U of Neb, Nat Mus, RI School of Design, Brookgreen Gardens. References A47-FIE-MAL. Source WHO 58. No current auction record but the estimated price of a terra-cotta 8″ Bison Bust would be about $800 to $900 at auction in 1976.

Clark was the pupil of the RI School of Design. While working as a designer for Gorham, he was asked to mount specimens in the American Museum of Natural History. He became director of preparation and installation there until his retirement in 1949. He was a taxidermist, big game hunter, and creator of habitat groups for the museum, maintaining his office at the museum and at his own Industrial Exhibits company.

He visited the West in 1906, Europe and Africa in 1908. He was the co-leader of the McConnell-Clark Wyoming expedition in 1937 in addition to Asiatic and African expeditions from 1926 to 1948. Clark was an author and lecturer on animals including "Exploring and Studying Wild Game in America."

CLARK, Matt. Born Coshocton, Ohio 1903, living probably NYC 1966. Eastern illustrator of the West. Member SI. References A47-MAL. Sources DIC-ILA-IL 42-ILG. No current auction record. Signature example p 262 DIC. (See illustration 55.)

Matt Clark, younger brother of Benton Clark, attended the NAD in NYC. His first illustration was for *College Humor* in 1929 with work in the 1930s for *American, Cosmopolitan, Good Housekeeping*. His expertise in portraying the Old West extended to details of equipment.

Matt Clark's style involved an underlying black-ink drawing with dry brush combined with watercolor. DIC p 262 used a Western illustration from *The Saturday Evening Post* to demonstrate Clark's method, from compositional pencil sketch to the work finished for two-color magazine reproduction.

CLARKE, John Louis (or Man Who Speaks Not). Born Highwood, Mont 1881, died Cut Bank, Mont 1970. Blackfoot woodcarver, painter in oil and watercolor. Listed "Indians of Today."

Work in AIC, Mont Hist Soc, Mus of Plains Indians (Browning). References FIE-MAL. Sources AIP-MON-WNW. No current auction record. Sculpture examples MON.

Grandson of Malcolm Clarke, an entrepreneurial pioneer murdered by the Piegans, and son of Horace Clarke who lived on the Blackfoot lands, Clarke became deaf as a child. He attended Indian school, then schools for the deaf beginning 1894. About 1900 he worked in a Milwaukee factory carving altars.

In 1913 Clarke established his studio in East Glacier. His exhibition in Helena in 1916 resulted in recognition in the East, with Clarke "generally considered the best portrayer of Western wildlife in the world." WNW. His favorite material was cottonwood for his principal subjects, bears and mountain goats. "In whatever he did, John Clarke's intensity belied the odds that faced him throughout his life." MON.

CLAVEAU, Antoine. Landscape, portrait, and panorama painter active in San Francisco 1857–59 (or 1854–72). His panorama of Yosemite Valley was first exhibited in 1857 in San Francisco. Reference G&W. Source BDW. No auction record or signature example.

CLAWSON, John Willard. Born Beehive House, Salt Lake City, Utah 1858, died Salt Lake City 1936. Western portrait painter. No reference. Sources PUA-YUP-1/22/74 letter from Earl E Olson, Church Archivist. No auction record but the estimated price of an oil 30×20″ portrait of a Saint would be about $400 to $500 at auction in 1976.

John W Clawson, a grandson of Brigham Young, was a pupil of George Ot-

tinger, the Utah pioneer painter. From 1880 to 1883 he studied at the NAD in NYC. He then established a Salt Lake City studio until 1891 when he went to Paris to attend the Julien Academy, initiating five years in Europe that included extensive exposure to the Impressionists. On his return, he was a founder of the Society of Utah Artists, then moved to San Francisco until the earthquake and fire of 1906 destroyed his studio and 20 paintings valued at $80,000. He moved to Los Angeles, New York, then back to Salt Lake City.

Clawson was a successful Impressionist portraitist "who made more money than" the other second-generation Utah artists. He painted entertainment personalities as well as religious and business leaders and was referred to as "The Sargent of the West." PUA.

CLEENEWERCK (or Cleanwork), Henry. Born Waton, Belgium date unknown, active 19th century as painter of the French School. Landscape painter in the West by 1854. Reference BEN. Source ANT 4/60,12/61. No auction record but in 1923, Cleenewerck's *Site in Cuba* sold for 100 fr at auction. Painting examples oil 41×72″ *Yosemite Valley* signed Henry Cleenewerck and dated 1882 shown p 339 ANT 4/60, oil 36×54″ *Indians Hunting Deer* signed Henry Cleanwork and dated 1854 shown p 529 ANT 12/61.

Born of French parents, Cleenewerck debuted at the Paris Salon in 1869.

CLUNIE, Robert. Born Eaglesham, Scotland 1895 (or 1885), living Bishop, Cal 1962. Cal painter. Work in Cal, Idaho, Utah schools. References A62-

MAS. Source BDW. No auction record or signature example.

Clunie studied in Scotland. He came to NY in 1911, and moved to Hollywood seven years later to work as a scenic artist. He painted landscapes which were exhibited locally. He began winning awards in California in 1936.

CLYMER, John. Born Ellenburg, Wash 1907, living Teton Village, Wyom 1976. Traditional Western painter, important Eastern illustrator. Member CAA, Nat Acad of Western Art. Work in Glenbow Fndn (Calgary), Whitney Gall (Cody), Montana Hist Soc. References A76-MAL. Sources Casper *Star-Tribune*-ACO-AHI 11/71-CA 71 to 74-CAN-ILA-ILG-PER vol III, ✕3-WAI 71,72. No auction record. Signature example CA 71 *The Trader*. (See illustration 56.)

Clymer studied in the Vancouver (BC) School of Art, Ontario College of Art, Wilmington Academy of Art, and Grand Central Art School, with George Southwell, H Varley, J W Beatty, Frank Schoonover, N C Wyeth, and Harvey Dunn. The latter two were his inspiration. Dunn told him, "Son, you'll never make a painter—you look too skinny and frail for this work." His first illustrations were for Canadian magazines, followed by contributions to the major American magazines such as *The Saturday Evening Post* and *Field and Stream* featuring animal subjects. Clymer also made advertising illustrations for the largest American corporations.

After 40 years of illustration with more than 80 *Post* covers alone, Clymer "retired" in 1964 to paint the history of the West, using extensive museum research and retracing the steps of Lewis and Clark and following the Oregon Trail. His technique involves preparation with both sketch and photograph: "The sketch gives the feel but photos give you

facts." Next is a small oil on canvas for mood. Then comes the finished painting to emphasize the "beautiful and wonderful and leave everything else out." A quiet, gentle man, Clymer has achieved more fame in a few years with his historical paintings of the Northwest than in his whole career as an important illustrator.

COAST, Oscar Regan. Born Salem, Ore 1851, died Santa Barbara, Cal 1931. Cal landscape painter specializing in desert scenes. Work in World's Columb Expos 1893. References A31 (obit)-BEN-FIE-MAL. Source BDW. No current auction record or signature example.

Salem, Ore in 1851 was recovering from the Gold Rush depletions and had just been named capital. Coast studied in the US, Paris, and Rome, the pupil of Yewell, Thomas Hicks, and Faller. While claiming Iowa City as legal residence, Coast established his studio in NYC until 1896 when his health declined. In California his health improved and he was able to continue painting out-of-door subjects. He specialized in desert landscapes.

COE, Ethel Louise. Born Chicago, Ill about 1880, died probably there 1938. Chicago painter, illustrator including Western subjects, teacher. Work in Sioux City AM, Vanderpoel AA (Chicago), Chicago Munic art colln, Kohler Gall (Wis). References A41 (obit)-BEN-FIE-MAL-SMI. Sources WAA-WOM-1/17/74 letter from Anne Hobler, Sarah Lawrence Col. No current auction record or signature example.

E L Coe graduated from the AIC and was a pupil of Hawthorne and in Madrid of Sorolla. She became a lecturer at AIC and director of the art department at Sarah Lawrence College from 1931 to 1938.

COLBY, Vincent V. Birthplace unknown 1879, active Southwest 1912. Western landscape painter, printmaker. Work in ANS-MNM. No reference. Source MNM. No auction record or signature example. (See illustration 57.)

Colby's mezzotint *The Old Mission at Jemez Springs, NM* is in the MNM collection. *Pikes Peak* painted 1912 is in the ANS collection.

COLE, Joseph Foxcroft. Born Jay, Me 1837, died Winchester, Mass 1892. Eastern landscape painter in California about 1880. Work in Winchester Lib, Honeyman colln, Boston clubs, Phila Centennial Exhibition. References BEN-DAB-FIE-G&W-MAL-SMI. Sources BOA-HON-HUT-ISH-PAF. No current auction record or signature example.

After a public school education in Boston, J Foxcroft Cole became an apprentice lithographer along with Winslow Homer. By 1860 he had saved enough for study in Europe. He chose Lambient in Paris, becoming the first Bostonian after Hunt to pick France. Selling his European paintings in Boston permitted continued French studies until Charles Jacque in 1865 employed him to paint Jacque landscapes from sketches. After a stay in Boston, Cole was again in Paris from 1873 to 1877. Then he built a studio in Winchester. "Here he painted his serious, low-toned landscapes and advocated collections of French art." DAB. In 1882 he sold his retained paintings, "realizing for them about $20,000 in Boston." HUT. Cole remained in Winchester "except for brief trips to Europe and to California." DAB. The

Honeyman collection includes an undated watercolor *Twilight, Mission San Jaun Capistrano*.

COLE, Thomas. Born Bolton-le-Moor, Lancashire, Eng 1801, died Catskill, NY 1848. Important Hudson River school landscape, portrait, and allegorical painter, writer. A founder, NA 1826. Work in MMA, COR, DIA, Wadsworth Atheneum, NYHS, etc. References BEN-CHA-DAB-ENB-FIE-G&W-MAL-SMI. Sources AAR 9/73;5,11/74-ALA-AMA-ANT 10,11/48,4/51; 11/52; 4/53; 1,7, 11/64;4/65;10/68;4/69;3/70;2,7/71;1, 5/72;3,10,11/73;5/74-BAR-BOA-BOL-COR-DAA-HUD-HUT-ISH-KAR-KW1-M15-M19-NA 74-NEU-NGA-PAF-STI-TEP-WHI. Oil 14×20″ *Landscape with Indian* 1843 sold 3/19/69 for $3,500. Oil 41×62″ *Italian Landscape* 1832 sold 12/10/72 for $21,000 at auction. Signature example ☒49 M19.

Son of a woolen manufacturer, Cole was educated in Chester and worked as an engraver for calico designs. When his family emigrated to Steubenville, Ohio, Cole worked as a wood engraver in Philadelphia, sketched in 1820 in the West Indies, and then walked from Philadelphia to Ohio. Until 1822 Cole worked as an engraver for his father on what was then the American frontier, playing his flute on trips in the wilderness. A failure as an itinerant portraitist, he painted and wrote fiction in Philadelphia in 1823. He came to NYC in 1824 and painted landscapes along the Hudson that were sold to the established painters Trumbull, Durand, and Dunlap and to the poet Bryant. "His fame spread like wildfire." DAB quoting Durand. Cole visited England 1829–31 and Paris and Italy 1831–32. He is best known for the series *The Course of Empire* and *The Voyage of Life*. F E Church, the leading American painter of the 1860s, was his only pupil, carrying on the tradition of the panoramic bird's-eye landscape.

Familiar with the American frontier of the time, Cole frequently populated his landscapes with Indians. *The Last of the Mohicans*, for example, was painted in several versions; see fig 13 WHI and ANT 11/52 p 353. In his *American Lake Scene,* "the small accessory figure of an Indian locates the scene in the New World." WHI.

COLEMAN, Arthur Philemon. Born Lachute, Quebec, Can 1852, died probably Toronto, Ont 1939. Can geologist, teacher, alpinist, watercolorist. Member Can Inst. Work in ROM. No reference. Source CMW. No auction record. (See illustration 58.)

Son of a Methodist minister, Coleman graduated from Cobourg College Inst, Victoria U in 1876 with his master's degree awarded 1880. He received his doctorate from U of Breslau in 1882 where he "required some months geologizing in the Giant Mtns on the border of Lower Silesia." CMW. He taught in Canadian colleges beginning 1881 and was also geologist for the Ontario Bureau of Mines beginning 1893.

President of the Alpine Club of Canada and the author of many scientific papers, Coleman was an amateur watercolorist frequently in the Candadian West. ROM has *Hudson Bay Post, Lac Ste Anne, Alberta,* a 1907 watercolor.

COLEMAN, Edmund (or Edward) Thomas. Born England 1823, died London, Eng 1892. English illustrator in Western Canada 1863–77, painter, mountain climber. Work in Stenzel colln. Reference BEN. Source PNW. No current auction record. Signature example p 7 PNW.

Coleman exhibited at the Royal Academy 1849–54, becoming an illustrator for the *Illustrated London News*. He wrote and illustrated a book on his mountain-climbing experiences in the Alps.

In 1863 Coleman established his studio in Victoria, BC. He traveled and sketched all over Vancouver Island, the coast of Washington, and Oregon. After climbing the mountain peaks of the Northwest, he lectured and wrote about his experiences. Coleman returned to England in 1877. "There were few recorders of the early Northwest scene with Coleman's competence." PNW.

COLEMAN, Mary Darter (or Mary Sue Darter). Born Fort Worth, Tex 1894, living Los Angeles, Cal 1935. Landscape painter of Texas, Oklahoma, and California; portrait painter, teacher. Reference MAL. Sources TOB-TXF. No auction record or signature example.

Mrs Coleman studied at Texas Christian U, the pupil of Mrs E R Cockrell until 1915. She studied at the ASL 1915–16, the pupil of Bridgman and Mora, then returned to Texas as art instructor at Midland College. In summers she was the pupil of John F Carlson at Woodstock, NY. In 1919–20 she taught at Phillips U in Oklahoma and 1924–25 at Texas Christian U. In 1925 she married Harvey B Coleman, another landscape painter, and moved to Los Angeles where she studied with Edgar Payne among others.

COLLINGS, Charles John. Born Devonshire, Eng 1848, died probably Salmon Arms, BC, Can 1931. Watercolor painter of the Canadian West. Work in NGC. References BEN-MAL. Sources CAN-DCA. Watercolor heightened with body color 6¼×10¼″ *A Coast Scene* sold 5/1/73 for $225 at auction in London. No signature example.

Collings was a recognized painter of the English school early in his career. He exhibited at the RA 1893–95 and again in London 1898. When he emigrated to the Canadian West in 1910, he was considered to be "in some respects the finest colorist who ever worked in Canada." CAN. The market for his paintings continued to be in England where he exhibited in 1912. His studio was in Shuswap Lake, BC, where he painted landscapes of the Rockies with an "oriental-like approach." DCA.

COLMAN (or Coleman), Samuel. Born Portland, Me 1832, died NYC 1920. Hudson River School painter in the West about 1870, collector of Oriental art, writer. ANA 1855, NA 1862. Work in MMA, NGA, AIC, BMFA, NYPL, RI Sch of Des, Union League Club, etc. References A20 (obit)-BEN-DAB-ENB-FIE-G&W-MAL-SMI. Sources ANT 10/62,4/65-BAR-BOA-DCC-HON-HUD-ISH-KW1-M19-M31-PAF-TAW-WES-WHI-WHO 20. Oil 30×40″ *Ausable River, Adirondacks* sold 9/13/72 for $4,600 at auction. Signature examples p 156 TAW, p 122 KW1. Portrait photo opp p 264 A20. (See illustration 59.)

Son of a well-to-do bookseller, Colman grew up in NYC familiar with authors and artists. The pupil of A B Durand, he exhibited at the NA by 1850. A disciple of the Hudson River school, he painted the river, the White Mtns, and Lake George, his favorite subjects. From 1860 to 1862 he traveled and studied in Paris, Spain, and Morocco. When he returned to a NYC studio and the honor of election as NA, he "strove for more exotic subjects." HUD. In 1870, a year after the completion of the transcontinental railroad, Colman began painting a series of Western subjects, starting with Medicine Bow and Yosemite Valley. In 1871 there appeared *The Green River, Wyoming,* followed by numerous Western subjects the rest of Colman's career. *Sycamore Canyon* was inscribed as painted Feb 20, 1868 and was signed and dated 1877. KW1.

From 1871 to 1875 Colman was again in Europe, visiting Holland, Normandy, Brittany, Switzerland, and England. On his return, he lived in Irvington-on-Hudson in an opulent "gem of a house, the most beautiful and artistic in its interior decoration, and the designs are all his own." KW1. His studio in NYC was "richly decorated with rare tapestries, Chinese pottery, and Japanese armor." DAB. In 1895 Colman exhibited Mexican paintings. Colman made another visit to the Pacific coast, perhaps including Alaska, about 1899. He wrote "Nature's Harmonic Unity" in 1912 and "Proportional Form" in 1920. Colman is credited with making the "American public mindful of the natural wonders becoming ever more accessible." TAW.

COLTON, Mary Russell Ferrell (Mrs Harold S Colton). Born Louisville, Ky 1889, living Flagstaff, Ariz 1966. Arizona painter, sculptor, museum curator, writer. References A66-FIE-MAL. Sources WAA-W64. No auction record or signature example.

Mrs Colton studied at Moore Institute and at the Philadelphia School of Design for Women 1904–9, the pupil of Elliott Daingerfield and Henry Snell. She married a zoology instructor in 1912 and moved with him to Arizona for research in 1924. When he became director of the Museum of Northern Arizona in 1928, she was named curator of art. Mrs Colton has written on Indian art and folklore, Hopi dyes, has edited "Truth of a Hopi," and has contributed to the Museum periodical.

COLTON, Walter. Born Rutland Cnty, Vt 1797, died Philadelphia, Pa 1851. Amateur sketch artist, chaplain, writer. References DAB-G&W. Source, biography of George Heilge. No auction record or signature example.

Son of a weaver, Colton was raised near Lake Champlain. After apprenticeship to a cabinetmaker, Colton was educated in the Hartford, Conn grammar school 1816–17 and graduated Yale as valedictorian in 1822. He then entered Andover Theological Seminary, becoming a chaplain-professor in Middletown, Conn in 1825. Sent to Washington in 1830 to edit a paper to aid the Indians in Georgia, Colton was appointed naval chaplain when his health and mission both failed. His three-year cruise to the Mediterranean was the subject of two travel books.

In 1845 he went to California on the Pacific Squadron flagship. He was appointed alcalde of Monterey in 1846. His announcement of the discovery of gold was the first published word to the East. Two more travel books followed, on the cruise to California and on the residence there. When Colton returned to Philadelphia in 1849, George Heilge used Colton's sketches for the *Panorama of the Route to California.*

COLYER, Vincent (also Collyer, Collier). Born Bloomingdale, NY 1825, died Contentment Island, Darien, Conn 1888. Painter of Western landscapes relating to Indians, Eastern crayon portraitist. ANA 1851. Work in GIL, NAD. References BEN - CHA - FIE - G&W - MAL - SMI. Sources AIW-BAW-BOA-GIL-HON-HUT-KW1-PAF-TWR-WES. No current auction record. Signature example ✻52 AIW.

Colyer began work in a NY drugstore until 1844 when he became the pupil of John R Smith and of the NAD for four years. His crayon portraits were successful in NYC from 1848 to 1860, bringing $150 each. During the Civil War he was a member of the Christian Commission, serving as a medical corpsman, caring for the sick and wounded. In 1866 he settled in Darien to resume his painting, naming his studio after his friend Kensett.

Beginning in 1869 Colyer served as a special US Indian Commissioner, visiting tribes all over the US and Alaska by 1871. As secretary of the Board of Indian Commissioners, he tried unsuccessfully in 1871 to make peace after the Camp Grant massacre. During his travels he made hundreds of Western sketches, drawings, and watercolors in Indian locales. On his return to Darien he enlarged these into paintings for exhibition at the NA and the Philadelphia Centennial. Examples were *Passing Shower, Columbia River* and *The Home of the Yackamas, Oregon.* Some of the Alaskan sketches were reproduced in Congressional reports and in *Harper's Weekly.* Several hundred original sketches were acquired by one NYC dealer in 1952.

COMPERA, Alexis (Alexis Comparet, Alexander Compara). Born South Bend, Ind 1856, died Coronado Beach, Cal 1906. Pioneer Colorado landscape painter. Work in Colo St Mus. References A05-BEN-MAL-SMI. Source SHO. No current auction record but the estimated price of an oil 20✕30″ of a Colorado landscape would be about $800 to $1,000 at auction in 1976. Signature example p 21 SHO.

Compera settled in Colorado City about 1868, painting murals in bars in this oldest town in the Pikes Peak area. He studied in Paris in the early 1870s with Harvey Young, W H M Cox, and Benjamin Constant, then established his studio in Denver.

He is said to have changed his name

from Comparet to Compera because of the constant mispronunciation. He taught at the Academy of FA Association of Colorado in 1882 and became successful in Denver with the help of his friend Sarah Bernhardt. He maintained his studio in Denver at 1184 South Penn Avenue until a few months before he died in California.

COMSTOCK, Enos Benjamin. Born Milwaukee, Wis 1879, died Leonia, NJ 1945. Painter, illustrator, writer. Work: decorations in Leonia schools. References A47 (obit)-BEN-FIE-MAL-SMI. Source, an oil 19×31″ *Crossing the Great Desert* sold 5/22/72 for $200 at auction in LA. No signature example.

Enos B Comstock was the pupil of John H Vanderpoel and Frederick W Freer at the AIC. He was an illustrator for Boy Scout publications, school books, and also wrote "Tuck-Me-In Stories" and "When Mother Lets Us Tell Stories."

CONSTANTINE (Constantine Cherkas). Born Moscow, Russia 1919, living California 1968. Impressionist Western painter, restorer. No reference. Source COW. No current auction record. Signature example p 216 COW.

Constantine studied at the Moscow Academy of Arts until his wife and he were placed in Nazi forced-labor camps in WWII. He emigrated to the US in 1950, settling in California after living in NYC and Philadelphia. "Man gains in meaning and depth in the American West. To show this on canvas will be a lifetime task."

To avoid confusion, he paints as "Constantine" and he does restorations of the paintings of others under his family name "Cherkas."

COOK, Harold. Traditional Texas painter, living Fort Worth 1968. No reference. Source COW: "To this day, despite the passing of the longhorn era, Texas has continued to exert its spell upon artists."

COOK, Howard Norton. Born Springfield, Mass 1901, living Ranchos de Taos, NM 1976. Contemporary Taos painter, etcher, muralist, teacher. NA 1949, SAE. Prints in MMA, Fogg, NYPL, WMAA, AIC, BM, Paris, Berlin, London; paintings in ANS, DAM, MNM, Philadelphia MA; murals in hotels and public buildings. References A76-MAL. Sources AAT-APT-CAA-DAA-M50-PIT-TAL-TSF-WHO 70. No current auction record but in M50 his painting *Towers* had a sales price of $1,000 in 1950. Signature example p 51 PIT. (See illustration 60.)

Howard Cook studied at the ASL 1919–21 with Dasburg and in Europe. He began work as a commercial artist. From 1922 to 1927 he was an illustrator for *Century, Scribner's,* and *Harper's,* traveling on sketching assignments to Europe, Africa, Asia, and South America. In 1926 *Forum* sent Cook to Taos for woodcuts to illustrate "Death Comes for the Archbishop." Cook remained in Taos for a year and a half, specializing in graphics. By 1931 he had been represented in "50 Prints of the Year" four times. Next Cook turned to murals. On fellowships 1932–33 and 1934–35 he studied fresco in Mexico and sketched scenes of poverty in the American South for murals in Pittsburgh and San Antonio.

Cook settled in Taos in 1935 with his wife, the artist Barbara Latham. Most of his work was in painting and murals. During WWII, Cook was an artist for the US Navy. He became a teacher in NM universities and a guest professor. By the end of the 1940s his landscapes were moving toward the abstract. His scenes of

Indian dances went beyond the reality of earlier painters, into a personal view of the essence of the movement. His palette was generally confined to earth colors. In the 1950s Cook exhibited collages.

COOKE (or Cook), George. Born St Mary's Cnty, Md 1793, died New Orleans, La 1849. Portrait, landscape, and historical painter. ANA (not listed NA 74). Work in Valentine Mus (Richmond, Va), BM, Chicago Hist Soc, Va Hist Soc, U of Ga. References FIE-G&W-SMI. Sources ANT 3/53,9/72(article), 1/73-BAR-IND-KW1-PAF. No current auction record but the estimated price of an oil 30×25″ of an Indian brave would be about $5,000 to $7,000 at auction in 1976.

Cooke was the son of a country lawyer who elected not to pay Rembrandt Peale's fee of $2,000 for tutelage to Cooke at 14. Instead, Cooke became a merchant at 17, failed at 25, "and went west." In 1819 Cooke took free instruction from Charles Bird King. In 1820 he set himself up as a portrait painter in Richmond. By September 1825 Cooke in a period of 28 months had painted 130 portraits on commission and 20 "fancy pieces." From 1826 to 1831 he studied in Italy and France. During the 1830s Cooke worked in NYC, Washington, and their environs. His landscapes were reproduced as Bennett aquatints.

While Cooke failed to obtain a commission from Congress to decorate the Capitol, he did obtain employment by the War Department to paint portraits of six Indian chiefs in Washington in 1837. Five of these portraits were reproduced as color lithographs in Vol II of McKenny and Hall's "History of the Indian Tribes of North America." His rendering of Kish-ke-kosh has been deprecated as "woebegone," but the print now sells at a premium over other prints in the series. The original paintings were de-stroyed in the Smithsonian fire of 1865. Toward the end of his life Cooke had a gallery and studio built for him by a benefactor in New Orleans.

COOPER, Astley David Montague. Born St Louis, Mo 1856, died San Jose, Cal 1924. Cal Indian and figure painter, *Leslie's* illustrator. Work in Stanford U Mus, Harmsen colln. No reference. Sources ANT 11/72-BWB-DCC-HAR-HMA-JNB-PAW-STI. The estimated price of an oil 34×60″ *Buffalo Inquest* with signature example and dated 1907 was $4,000 to $6,000 for sale 10/28/74 at auction in LA and sold for $3,000.

Descendant of Maj O'Fallon who was Catlin's friend and of George Rogers Clark the explorer, Cooper studied art at Washington U in St Louis. His first success was a series of portraits of Indian chiefs, completed before he was 21. In 1883 he moved to San Jose, Cal where he "achieved what is perhaps the ultimate expression in the age of vulgar wealth that followed the agriculturally rich mid-century, in his painting of Mrs Leland Stanford's jewelry collection." STI.

From California, Cooper maintained contacts with Eastern art dealers, so that his Western wildlife series of paintings was popular both in this country and in Europe. He became an authority on the history of the American West, although his San Jose studio was decorated in an Egyptian motif. Not generally recorded in Cooper's biography as a Western painter is that in the 1890s, he was the most widely known of the local painters of the large barroom oils of plump nudes realistically depicted. BWB.

COOPER, Colin Campbell. Born Philadelphia, Pa 1856, died Santa Barbara,

Cal 1937. International painter of buildings and street scenes. ANA 1908, NA 1912. Work in PAFA, FAG (San Diego), MMA, City AM (St Louis), etc. References A41 (obit)-BEN-FIE-MAL-SMI. Sources AMA-ANT 3/72-INS 4/08-MSL-M57-NA 74-WHO 36. Oil 29×36″ *5th Ave at 42nd St* sold 4/15/70 for $2,300 at auction. Signature example p 159 INS 4/08.

Son of a doctor and brother of a lawyer, Cooper studied at the PAFA before going to Paris to study at the Julien and Delecluse academies. He married the painter Emma Lampert in 1897. Cooper spent much time in Europe developing his specialty of architectural subjects. In 1902 he began a series of oils depicting the skyscraper in NYC. About 1913 he visited the Far East to paint architectural works with "such charm as to make them dreams of beauty." MSL. Cooper also painted watercolors "on canvas so cleverly that they can scarcely be distinguished from oils." MSL.

The Mentor magazine in a 1920s article on Taos indicates that Cooper was there before J H Sharp, that is, before 1883. This would make Cooper one of the earliest artists at the Pueblos, along with Remington, Charles Craig, and Thomas Moran. In 1927 Cooper remarried. He moved to Santa Barbara and painted California landscapes.

COOPER, Emma Lampert (Mrs Colin Campbell Cooper). Born Nunda, NY about 1865, died Pittsfield (Monroe Cnty), NY 1920. Painter specializing in genre and street scenes, teacher. Work in World's Columbian Expos (1893). References A20 (obit)-BEN-FIE-MAL-SMI. Sources AMA-ANT 4/68-MSL-WHO 20. No current auction record. Painting example ANT 4/68. (See illustration 61.)

Mrs Cooper was a graduate of Wells College in Aurora, NY. She began the study of art at Cooper Union and the ASL before becoming the pupil of W M Chase and of Agnes D Abbatt in watercolors. She also studied with Harry Thompson in Paris and J Kever in Holland. On her return, she was in charge of the art department of Foster School in Clifton Springs, NY 1891–93 and of Mechanics' Institute in Rochester, NY 1893–97 when she married the artist Colin Campbell Cooper. Her visit to the West occurred after this date.

COOPER, George Victor. Born Hanover, NJ 1810, died NYC 1878. Genre, landscape, portrait painter, illustrator, lithographer, cameo cutter, sculptor. References G&W-MAL. Sources ACM-COS-NJA-OCA. No auction record. Inscription example ⚒1036 ACM.

Cooper was painting in NYC from 1835–49, exhibiting portraits at the Apollo Assn and NA in 1839. From 1849–52 Cooper toured the California mining territory, making the drawings for all of the numerous plates for J M Letts's "Pictorial View of California: including a Description of the Panama and Nicaragua Routes, with Information and Advice Interesting to All, Particularly Those Who Intend to Visit the Golden Region. By a Returned Californian." Cooper's sketches are a "record of the long trip, of the young cities, of the mission-founding padres, and of the actual life of the Forty-Niners, with its flavor of roughing it, humor, hope, and all the luring magic of the yellow streak." OCA.

The rest of Cooper's life was spent in NYC. The highlight was a portrait he painted of Abraham Lincoln in 1865.

COOPER, James Graham. Born NYC 1830, died Hayward, Cal 1902. Railway survey artist, naturalist, medical doctor. References DAB-G&W. Source AIW. No auction record or signature example.

Cooper's father was a founder of the Lyceum of Natural History of New York and a friend of Audubon and Nuttall (ornithologists), and Torrey (botanist). Cooper graduated as a physician in 1851 and interned until 1853 when he contracted with Gov Stevens to act as a doctor for the Pacific Railroad Survey Expedition for a northern route. Two of the published sketches are credited to Cooper: *Mt Rainier Viewed from near Steilacoom* and *Puget Sound and Mt Rainier from Whitby's Island*.

Cooper became familiar with the zoologic features of the Pacific coast in the railway survey, in private collecting expeditions, and as zoologist for the Geological Survey of California. His work was called "by far the most valuable contribution to the biography of American birds since Audubon." "A pioneer collector and writer on the natural history of California and Washington, Cooper left an impress for all time on the records of these Western states." DAB. Cooper settled in Santa Cruz, Cal in 1866 as a medical doctor.

COOPER, J (perhaps John). Wood engraver in 19th-century London. Reference BEN. Source GOD. No current auction record. Signature example p 77 GOD.

GOD lists sketches by J Cooper, R P Leitch, and T W Wilson as illustrations for "The North West Passage by Land" by Milton and Cheadle published about 1864. The book describes an overland exploration across the Canadian Rockies. It is specified that Cooper's sketch of the authors with an Assiniboine Indian family was from a photo.

COPE, Gordon Nicholson. Born Salt Lake City, Utah 1906, living San Francisco, Cal 1973. 20th century Utah portrait painter, teacher. Work in Salt Lake City library. References BEN-MAS. Source YUP. No auction record or signature example.

Cope studied with LeConte Stewart and A B Wright 1916–23 in Utah and with Lawrence Squires 1923–24 in Arizona. In keeping with the Utah practice for promising artists at and after the turn of the century, Cope went to the Julien Academy in Paris in 1928, after having studied the old masters at European galleries beginning 1924. He exhibited at the 1928 spring Salon in Paris.

On his return to Utah, Cope was head of the art department at LDS U 1930–31 and held other Utah teaching positions until 1941. He painted portraits of Utah notables.

CORDERO (or Cardero), José (or Josef). Spanish painter active in California 1792 with the Galiano-Valdés expedition. Work (sketch of the Mission of San Carlos at Carmel) in Museo Naval (Madrid), wash drawing *Vista del Presidio de Monte Rey* in Honeyman colln. Reference G&W. Sources ANT 11/53-HON. No current auction record. Unsigned drawing example by either Cordero or Tomas Suria p 371 ANT 11/53.

CORNWELL, Dean. Born Louisville, Ky 1892, died NYC 1960. Eastern illustrator, mural painter, teacher. Member SI, NA 1940, Nat Soc Mural Painters, fellow RSA. Work: illustrations in major magazines; murals in libraries, government buildings, hotels, industrial buildings, shrines, etc in US and Europe. References A62 (obit)-FIE-MAL-SMI. Sources AAC-COW-DIC-DIG 2/49-ILA-ILG-INS 4/24-WHO 60. No current auction record. Signature example p 82 ILA. (See illustration 62.)

A left-handed painter, Cornwell studied at the AIC and then in NYC with Harvey Dunn and Charles S Chapman. An important illustrator, Cornwell was president of the SI by 1922. He worked for many national periodicals and advertisers and taught illustration at the ASL. He later studied mural painting with the English artist Frank Brangwyn and in 1954 was president of the National Mural Painters Society.

A celebrity himself and a friend of Charles Russell, Ed Borein, Frank Tenney Johnson, and Clyde Forsythe, Cornwell was a regular in the studios of the Western artists. He painted Western scenes when called for by the text. His series *Pioneers of American Medicine* included *The Dawn of Abdominal Surgery* performed in the Kentucky of 1809 that was the frontier of the time. All of Cornwell's research, studies, and renderings of this "backwoods operation" are documented in detail in DIC, a worthwhile reference for analysis of Cornwell's procedures. He traveled to the site and to a museum, with detail drawings for each element. Then, he sketched his first visualization in ink and wash on yellow paper about 3×5". Preliminary figure studies followed with a model. Next, there were as many as four oil sketches, sometimes made on top of photostats of an acceptable drawing. For the finished painting, a print of the final sketch was traced onto the canvas with black pencil. Tones were washed in with a varnish medium before the figures were modeled.

CORWIN, Charles Abel. Born Newburgh, NY 1857, died Chicago, Ill 1938. Indian genre painter, muralist, lithographic artist. Work in Piedmont Gall (Berkeley, Cal), Field Mus (Chicago). References A41 (obit)-BEN-FIE-MAL-SMI. Sources BAW-CUS-TWR. Oil 12×18" *American Indians* sold 1/27/71

for $450 at auction. Signature example p 22 BAW, *Indians Chasing Wild Horses*.

Corwin began his art studies in NYC, then went to Munich, Germany where he was the pupil of Duveneck. In 1883 Corwin became an instructor at the AIC. He was part of the staff under E Pierpont that painted the *Cyclorama of Custer's Last Fight* for the Boston Cyclorama Company in 1888. Corwin's responsibility was the foreground figures for the exhibition piece, now lost.

Corwin specialized in museum murals. In 1903 he was hired by the Field MNH in Chicago as habitat preparator. About 80 of the museum habitats have background paintings by Corwin.

CORY, Kate T. Born Waukegan, Ill 1861, living Prescott, Ariz 1957. Ariz Indian genre and landscape painter, muralist, sculptor. Work in Smithsonian Inst, Pub Mus Prescott, U of Ariz Tucson, Tuzigoot Mus (Clarkdale, Ariz). References A47-FIE-MAL. Sources ARM-WAA-1/23/74 data from Ionne Ladd, Hist Mus of Ariz. No current auction record but the estimated price for an oil 30×20" of a Prescott landscape would be about $800 to $1,000 at auction in 1976. No signature example. Portrait photo *Prescott Evening Courier* 2/8/57. (See illustration 63.)

Daughter of a newspaper publisher, Kate Cory grew up in Waukegan. About 1879 she moved to NYC where she studied at Cooper Union. She also attended the ASL, the pupil of Cox and Weir, and associated with the painters interested in the outdoor life, Seton and Dan Beard. When she met Louis Akin, he had just returned from Arizona and was seeking to establish an art colony among the Hopis. Ms Cory took the train to Canyon Diablo in 1905, rented an Indian house at Oraibi overlooking the Painted Desert, and began her lifelong task to understand and paint the Hopi people. Until 1912 she lived at Oraibi and Walpi, attending Kiva ceremonials, taking photographs, and painting.

In 1912 Ms Cory moved to Prescott where she remained, except during WWI when she was a pioneer in camouflage. In 1913 her painting *Arizona Desert* was part of the Armory Show. After she returned to her Prescott studio, it was as an expert on Indian life. She also painted Arizona landscapes including the Grand Canyon. The government announcement of the intent to build Boulder Dam led her to hire a prospector as her cook so she could sketch the area in order to leave a painted record. Typical of this "petite painter" was her refusal of the Hopi invitation to join the tribe, simply because she did not want to "cramp their style."

COTTON, John Wesley. Born Toronto, Ont, Can 1868, died there 1931. Can painter who lived in Cal and was also known for NM views, etcher. Work (etchings) in NGC, Toronto AM, Lib Cong, NY Pub Lib, AIC, Cal St Lib. References A32 (obit)-BEN-FIE-MAL-SMI. Source CAN. No current auction record but the published estimate is $300 to $400. No signature example.

Cotton was an early member of the Toronto ASL founded in 1886. He was the pupil of E Marsden Wilson in London and a student of the AIC. His drawing *The Trapper* was reproduced in the 1898 calendar of the Toronto Art League. Referred to in CAN as a leading etcher of the 1880s–90s, Cotton became a resident of California for many years. He won awards at the Pan-Pac Expos 1915 and the Pac SW Expos 1928, specializing in views of NM.

COUSE, Eanger Irving. Born Saginaw, Mich 1866, died Albuquerque, NM

1936. Important Taos Indian painter. ANA 1902, NA 1911, Taos SA 1912. Work in ANS, NGA, BM, MNM, Dallas MFA, Detroit IA, GIL, MMA. References A38 (obit)-BEN-FIE-MAL-SMI. Sources ACO-ACM-AMA-ANT 5/73-COW-CRS-DCC-EIT-HAR-HMA-ISH-M31-MSL-NJA-PAW-PET-PIT-POW-PNW-TAL-TSF-TWR-WAI 71,72-WHO 36. Oil 30×36″ *Moonlight Scene* signed n/d estimated for sale 3/4/74 at $12,000 to $15,000 at auction in LA and sold for $17,000. In 1933, *Indian Campfire* had sold for $160 at auction. Signature example p 24 ANS Moki Snake Dance. (See illustration 64.)

E Irving Couse painted houses in Saginaw to earn tuition for the AIC in 1884. He then studied at the NAD and from 1887 to 1890 at the Julien Academy in Paris under Robert Fleury and Bouguereau. He met in Paris and in 1889 married an Oregon girl. They moved to Oregon where Couse painted Northwest coast Indians but the paintings did not sell. Couse complained that the Indians were not red and that the weather was gray. He spent the next 10 years on the coast of Normandy, painting marketable pastorals and marines, then returned to a studio in NYC.

On the recommendation of Joseph Sharp and also of Blumenschein, Couse made his first visit to Taos in June 1902. "Taos is pronounced *tah'-ose,* almost in one syllable and rhymes with Couse." AMA. He spent his winters in NYC and each summer in Taos where the Indians called him "Green Mountain" because he was rather "large and round, and often wears a green sweater." In 1927 Couse gave up his NYC studio and settled permanently in Taos, bringing recognition to "the community and its Indian heritage. Each of his compositions gives a true picture of some phase of Indian life, and each Indian is true to the type. He has come as close to the spirit of the Indian as the white man ever can." It was said in 1927 that Couse "has become practically ineligible as a competitor in annual art contests because he has already been awarded most of the important prizes." AMA. A good merchandiser of his own paintings, Couse produced about 1,500 in his lifetime.

COUTTS, Alice. Active early 20th century. Cal painter of Indians, particularly children. Reference A17. Source 4/30/74 data from Grace Winder, Oakland PL. Oil 7×8½" *Song of the Sea* depicting Navaho child with seashell to his ear did not sell 5/26/71 at auction.

Alice Coutts is listed in 1917 as resident at Pacific Avenue, Piedmont, Cal, the same as Gordon Coutts who painted Indian portraits about that time. She is said in *Cal Hist Soc Quarterly* for March 1958 to have been "roughly contemporary" with Grace Hudson (1865–1937) on whose work she modeled herself, and that her paintings are confused with those of Grace Hudson because of the similarity in style and subjects.

COUTTS, Gordon. Born Aberdeen, Scotland 1868 (or 1880), died Palm Springs, Cal 1937. Landscape, portrait, and figure painter, illustrator, teacher, writer. Work in NA Gall, Adelaide Nat Gall, Melbourne Art Gall (all Australia); Cleveland MA. References A38 (obit)-BEN-FIE-MAL. Source ANT 1/69. Oil *Indian Chief* sold July 1974 for $500 at auction. Signature example p 41 ANT 1/69.

Coutts was the pupil of Carl Rossi, Lefebvre, Fleury, and Deschenot at the Julien Academy in Paris. He exhibited in the RA in London and served for 10 years as government instructor of art in New South Wales, Australia. Coutts won

medals from the Alaska-Yukon Pac Expos in 1909 and the Sacramento Expos in 1930. His wife was the painter Alice Coutts.

COWLES, Russell. Born Algona, Iowa 1887, living NYC 1976. Modern Eastern painter living in Santa Fe about 1930. Work in Andover, Britannica, Dartmouth, DAM, MNM, ANS, LA Cnty MA, PAFA, etc. References A76-FIE-MAL. Sources CAA-CON with signature example p 24. No current auction record. (See illustration 65.)

Cowles graduated from Dartmouth College in 1909 and studied at the ASL and the NAD in NYC. In 1915 he won the Prix de Rome providing five years at the American Academy in Rome. When he returned to Chicago, dissatisfaction with the classical tradition he had learned caused him to destroy every existing painting: "I had been infected by the germs of the old Armory Show, even though the germs had lain dormant so long." CON.

After a year traveling in Asia and Europe, Cowles settled in Santa Fe. Painting there in the company of Lockwood, Adams, and Bisttram led him to the contemporary style that produced 40 one-man shows by 1948.

COX, Charles Brinton. Born Philadelphia, Pa 1864, died there 1905. Philadelphia painter, sculptor. References A05-BEN-FIE-MAL. Sources DBW-KEN 6/71. No current auction record. Signature example p 21 DBW *Pony Express*.

Cox was the pupil of Thomas Eakins at PAFA. He also studied at the ASL. As a sculptor of animals, it was said that he showed "beauty and power." Like his contemporary Edward Borein, Cox painted the Mexican vaquero "in his distinctive costume," some features of which were adapted by the American cowboy. KEN. He also did historical paintings of Western subjects such as the Pony Express.

COX, Charles Hudson. Born Liverpool, Eng 1829, died Boulder, Colo (or Waco, Tex) 1901. Painter of Texas landscapes, watercolorist, illustrator, teacher, cotton broker. Work in Norwich Mus (Eng), Waco Art League, Waco high school, World's Columbian Expos (1893). References A03 (obit)-BEN-G&W-MAL-SMI. Source TOB. No current auction record or signature example.

Cox studied at the Kensington School of Art in London where he later taught. In addition he was an illustrator and a cotton broker. He emigrated to Norfolk, Va, then settled in Waco in 1891. While continuing as a cotton exporter, he interpreted "Texas life and landscape as though he had roamed the plains during childhood." Favorite subjects were "old prairie schooners, heat on the plains, and especially the bluebonnets." TOB. He organized the Waco Art League in 1900 and was an instructor at the summer Chautauqua at Boulder, Colo. Cox is regarded as having preserved for Texas many depictions of landscapes of historical interest.

COX, Clark. Texas landscape watercolorist active about 1905 to 1920, theatrical scene painter. No reference. Source TXF. No auction record or signature example.

Cox appears to have been born about 1850. He is said to have worked almost 60 years as a scene painter. After assisting in the decoration of the French Opera House in New Orleans in 1903, he settled in Dallas but did not begin easel painting until about 1920.

A realist, Cox specialized in watercolors of the Davis Mountain region, saying, "I shall never more be happy on the studio scaffold. I am impelled to go direct to nature to paint in the open air." TXF.

COX, Jacob. Born Philadelphia, Pa 1812, died Indianapolis, Ind 1892. Portrait and landscape painter on the frontier of the time, panoramist, teacher. References BEN-G&W-MAL-SMI. Sources ALA-BAR-KW1. Oil 26×36" *The Rendez-Vous* sold 3/16/67 for $600. No signature example.

Cox was a tinsmith who moved from Western Pennsylvania to Indianapolis when it was the edge of the wilderness in 1833. Self-taught, he began painting portraits about 1840. "He was able to quit his trade of tinsmith in the 1850s and even to sell some landscapes." BAR. Through his paintings, "Fall Creek" was made "classic to the lovers of Indianapolis." ALA. Although he was successful in the end, the community newspapers initially had to exhort their readers to buy Cox's paintings. Unknown in the East, he exhibited and painted in Cincinnati where he may have had some training.

A 30-scene temperance panorama was painted with the assistance of Henry Waugh in 1853–54. Cox had many Indiana pupils, among them Lew Wallace who ground Cox's colors and painted a portrait of Black Hawk before becoming general and author.

COX (or Coxe), W H M. Active Colorado 1870–80s. Colo portrait and landscape painter. Work in Harmsen colln. No reference. Sources DCC-SPR. No current auction record or signature example.

Probably the first Colorado Springs portrait painter, Cox exhibited in Denver in 1883 at the Mining and Exposition Bldg. One of his landscape sketching companions at that time was William H Bancroft (see entry). He painted portraits of public figures in Colorado, the "successful pioneers" of Leadville, Colorado Springs, and Denver. SPR. Cox moved to Texas in 1886 where he continued painting.

COZE (Coze-Dabija), Paul. Born Beirut, Lebanon (or Beyrouth, Liberia) 1903, died probably Phoenix, Ariz 1975. Painter, decorator, writer. Chevalier, Legion of Honor. Work in Victoria Mus (Ottawa), Southwest Mus (LA), Heard Mus (Phoenix); murals in Southwest buildings. References A73-BEN-MAL. Source AHI 3/63 with mural example. No current auction record.

Coze had dual citizenship, French and American. He studied at Lycée Janson Sailly, at the École Nationale des Arts Décoratifs in Paris, and with J F Gonin. In 1922 he began exhibiting in Paris. National commissioner of the Scouts of France, he taught private classes in quick sketching beginning 1935. The writer of "Moeurs et histoire des Peaux Rouges," Coze worked as technical director for the movies, as the head of a French ethnological expedition into Northern Canada, as a teacher in Pasadena beginning 1942, as a teacher in Phoenix beginning 1953, and as French consul for Arizona.

The 75×16' mural *Phoenix Bird* was dedicated for Phoenix Sky Harbor in 1962. The Phoenix is a three-dimensional rendering with 365 feathers in relief, one for each day of the year, and 52 materials, one for each week.

CRAIG, Charles. Born Morgan Cnty, Ohio 1846, died Colorado Springs, Colo 1931. Important Indian genre painter, Western landscapist, illustrator. Work in DAM, DPL, Harmsen colln. References A23-BEN-FIE-MAL-SMI. Sources AAR 1/74-ACO-ANT 12/67,3/70,7/73-DCC -HAR-MSL-NEW-PNW-POW-SHO-SPR-TSF-WHO 30. Oil 20×30" *Pueblo Village* 1884 sold 10/27/71 for $3,500 at auction. Signature example p 345 ANT 3/70. (See illustration 66.)

Charles Craig was born on a farm. Self-taught as an artist, he made his first Western trip up the Missouri River in 1865, spending four years with various tribes of Indians and getting as far as Fort Benton, Mont. He then opened his studio in Zanesville, Ohio to earn his tuition for art training by painting portraits from life or photo at $75 each. He was a student at PAFA in 1872–73 and also studied with Peter Moran, the younger brother of Thomas Moran. When he returned to Zanesville, he painted *Custer's Last Charge* using descriptions and implements from the battlefield.

On his way to Colorado Springs at the urging of the painter Jack Howland, he was in 1881 the first major Western artist to paint in Taos. In 1883 he came back to sketch in Taos and Santa Fe. Craig settled in Colorado Springs where he made his home for 50 years. His first studio was in Howbert's Opera House building. His paintings of this period are noted for the accuracy of ethnological detail resulting from his many trips to the Ute reservation in southwestern Colorado. The 1893 trip was with Frank Sauerwein. His style at the time was hard-edged and literal. A large number of paintings of this period were lost in 1895 due to a fire in the old Antlers Hotel where Craig maintained a studio at that time. As one of the first trained Western artists in the area, he took an active part in the art life of Colorado, and his later painting style demonstrated the Barbizon influence. Called "Pink-Face Charlie," he was always sunny and optimistic and so were his paintings. SPR.

CRAM, Allan Gilbert. Born Washington, DC 1886, died Ojai, Cal 1947. Painter, illustrator, etcher. Work in Court House (Santa Barbara, Cal), Hazard Memorial (RI), US Govt. References A41-BEN-FIE-MAL-SMI. Sources SCA-TWR. No current auction record or signature example.

Cram was the pupil of William M Chase, Charles H Woodbury, and Shurtleff. His illustrations were for Dodd, Mead books. He was living in Marblehead, Mass in 1926 and in Santa Barbara by 1934. Cram is called "little known." TWR.

CRANE, G W (or W T). American illustrator active 1857–65 who is credited in "Beyond the Mississippi" with the drawing of *The Fontaine Qui Bouille* at Colorado City, Colo. The initials shown in the printed drawing would appear to have been interpreted as GWC by the engraver. No reference. No other source. No auction record. Monogram p 277 BEY.

Many of the BEY illustrators were Civil War field artists. AIW lists W T Crane as a *Leslie's* illustrator. In highlighting the BEY illustrators as "a roll call of the field artists," however, AIW does not mention a Crane by either initials. G&W quotes AIW and introduces William T Crane.

CRAWFORD, Thomas. Born NYC (or Ireland) 1813 (or 1811, or 1814), died London, Eng 1857. Classic international sculptor of the *Armed Liberty* on the Capitol dome. Honorary NA 1838. Sculpture in Senate (pediment and doors), BMFA, MMA, NYHS, etc. References BEN-DAB-ENB-FIE-G&W-MAL-SMI. Sources ALA-AMA-ANT 1/54,11/72-BOA-HUT-KW1-M19-NA 74-SCU. A white marble bust of George

Washington 32" high, signed with monogram TC, sold at auction 12/12/75 for $2,250. Sculpture example p 11 SCU. (See illustration 67.)

At 14 Crawford worked for a woodcarver in NYC. At 19 he was apprenticed to the leading monument maker, studying art evenings at the NAD. At 22 he went to Rome to study with the major sculptor Thorwaldsen. When he opened his own studio in Rome, commissions were coming in by 1837, and he was prosperous by 1839. There was a suite of studios by 1842, with workmen to carve for him. Friendships and marriage provided the needed political connections to get commissions. "Tall, handsome, brighteyed, he lived his ardent life unassailed by doubts." DAB. Later critics said of the famous sculpture on the Capitol dome, "She was not the last of her kind, but perhaps the worst, a pregnant squaw 300 feet in the air." ALA.

Crawford frequently modeled classical Indians, *Dying Indian Maiden* (1848) and *Indian Woman*. "No American subject has been treated in marble with such profound significance as the *Indian Chief*. This statue should be cast in bronze and set up in one of the squares of the Eternal City." HUT. Crawford's early death was from a brain tumor.

CRAWFORD, Will. Born Washington, DC 1869, died Scotch Plains, NJ 1944. Important pen and ink illustrator of Americana, the frontier, and the West. Pen sketches in ACM, "Some Incidents of Western Life" by C M Russell. References A47 (obit)-MAL. Sources ACM-COW-ILA-RUS-letter from Mrs Joseph Tomasetti-interview of Free Acres residents arranged by Joe Romano. No auction record but the estimated price of a drawing of a cowboy would be $800 to $1,000 at auction in 1976. Signature examples "Some Incidents" above, p 19 ILA. (See illustration 68.)

Born in Washington where his father worked for the US Treasury, Crawford was brought to Irvington, NJ when he was one year old. While in his teens, he became staff artist for the Newark *Daily Advertiser* and worked for the *Sunday Call*. Although self-taught, by his early 20s he was hired as illustrator for the *New York World*. At the turn of the century, Crawford was established with John N Marquand and Albert Levering in a large Union Square studio that served as barroom, junk shop, and forum. He was a successful free-lance illustrator for the leading magazines of the day, *Life, Munsey's, Puck, Cosmopolitan, Collier's,* etc. The usually told story about Crawford is that in 1902 Marquand and he took a vacation in Montana. They met Russell, persuading him to go East in 1903 to sell illustrations to NYC publishers. Russell did not make immediate sales and was forced to share Crawford's studio to ease the financial burden. The trained Crawford lent a new fluidity to Russell's drawing.

By 1918 when the bachelor Crawford had been a leading illustrator for 20 years, he tired of deadlines. He settled in Free Acres, NJ, a single-tax community where he built a two-room log cabin with the help of a Sioux Indian named Matt and the actor Jimmy Cagney. Crawford became MacKinlay Kantor's "My Most Unforgettable Character," an "elderly, dwarfish Robin Hood" with a "bow over one shoulder and a quiver of arrows over the other." Town forester and head of the archery guild, Crawford collected antique firearms, engaged in carving of whimsical street signs, and did complete-issue illustration for *Adventure* magazine. In 1940 Crawford worked in Hollywood as an expert on Indian costumes and as a sculptor of wax likenesses for a museum.

CREUTZFELDT, Benjamin (or J). Birth place and date unknown, died near Sevier Lake, Utah, 1853. Railway survey botanist and topographical artist. Scenic views of Colorado published in survey report. No reference. Sources AIW-SHO-SUR. No auction record or signature example.

SHO states that "with Frémont came Benjamin Creutzfeldt and Richard and Edward Kern, artists who produced scenic views for publication as lithographs to illustrate written reports" depicting Colorado. AIW lists all three Kern brothers as on Frémont's unsuccessful fourth expedition to cross the Colorado Rockies in the winter of 1848–49. This is the expedition on which Benjamin Kern was killed, but AIW does not mention Creutzfeldt here.

According to AIW, Creutzfeldt (listed as "J") was botanist on Capt Gunnison's 1853 survey of the central railway route. Richard Kern was the artist. After traveling from St Louis in June to central Utah in October, an exploring party of Gunnison, Kern, and Creutzfeldt was ambushed by Paiute Indians and killed along with their military escort. The expedition continued under Lt Beckwith and met up with elements of a later Frémont party. Despite all of the activity in Indian homelands at that time, artists led a charmed life, so that Indian attacks as on the Kerns were quite rare.

CREWS, Seth Floyd. Born Mt Vernon, Ill about 1885, living El Paso, Tex 1948. Painter of desert and Mexican border scenes, lithographer, theatrical artist. Reference MAS. Source TOB. No current auction record or signature example.

Raised in Chicago, Crews studied at the AIC and then ran a commercial art studio. The specialty was theatrical posters for Midwest lithographers. In 1916 he moved to NYC where his client was J J Shubert. Crews's wife died in 1918.

Crews went to New Mexico where he "began painting the heat, the desolation and the brilliant desert color." TOB. In

1925 he settled in El Paso where he painted both the desert and Western scenes and also crossed to Mexico where the subjects were "more theatrical in appearance." A typical picture would be *When the Evening Sun Is Low.* A colorist, he added pastels even as a lithographer.

CRITCHER, Catherine Carter. Born Westmoreland Cnty, Va 1879 (or 1868), living Washington, DC 1947. DC painter, teacher. Member Taos SA. Work in NAD, Boston AC, COR, New Mus (Santa Fe), Witte Mus (San Antonio). References A41-BEN-FIE-MAL-SMI. Sources COR-TSF-WAA-WHO 44-WOM-2/15/74 letter from Mrs Dana Young, San Antonio Art League. No current auction record or signature example.

Catherine Critcher was a pupil of Cooper Union in NYC, the Corcoran SA in Washington, and Richard Miller and Charles Hoffbauer in Paris. She remained in Paris until 1910, the founder of Cours Critcher painting school, and exhibiting in 1911 at the Salon des Artistes Français. From 1911 to 1917 she was an instructor at the Corcoran SA. In 1923 she became director of the Critcher School of Painting and Applied Arts in Washington.

She came to Taos, NM in the summer of 1920. In 1923 she was named the first and only woman member of the Taos SA. She is remembered as a lively and attractive person who kept a Taos painting in the school window and who returned from Taos to Washington in the fall with a wrinkled, deeply suntanned skin in the 1920s when that was not fashionable.

CROSS, Frederick George. Born Exeter, Devonshire, Eng 1881, died Lethbridge, Alberta, Can 1941. Painter of the Canadian prairies specializing in watercolors, sculptor. Reference MAS. Sources CAN with signature example p 182-DCA. No current auction record.

Cross studied civil engineering, painting in his leisure time. In 1906 he emigrated to the Canadian West as a railway survey and land development artist. Living in Brooks, Alberta as Irrigation Superintendent for the Railway, he sketched prairie scenes of livestock and drought although he did not exhibit until three temperas were shown by the Canadian Pacific Ry in 1921.

"Not great pageantry, his art is a series of vignettes on aspects of life on the range." CAN. An artist of the outdoors, he was known for his treatment of the sky which may occupy two-thirds of his picture, in keeping with his concept that the clouds are the mountains of the prairie. Typical titles are *The Open Range, Drought, The Horse Barn,* and *Head of the Herd.* By 1932 Cross's work "appeared at all important exhibitions in Canada" and two were shown in Scotland. CAN.

CROSS, Henry H. Born Flemingville, Tioga Cnty, NY 1837, died Chicago, Ill 1918. Painter of Indian portraits and genre and of racehorses. Work in Chicago Hist Soc, GIL, ANS, HAR. References A18 (obit)-BEN-G&W-MAL-SMI. Sources AIW-ANT 8/72,12/73-COW-DCC-GIL-HAR-PAW. The estimated price of an oil 71½ ×108" *Tables Turned* was $6,500 to $7,500 for an auction in 1971. Oil 30½ ×25½" *Old Chief American Horse* dated 1873 was sold 10/27/73 for $4,500 at auction. (See illustration 69.)

Cross twice ran away from home to join the circus before he was 15. He studied animal painting with Rosa Bonheur in Paris when he was 16. On his return to the US, he again traveled with a circus headed West, painting animals on the wagon sides. In 1860 he opened his studio in Chicago, but in 1862 he left for southwestern Minnesota during the Sioux uprising there. He painted all of the Sioux sentenced to death by President Lincoln because of their massacre of white settlers. Afterward he traveled with P T Barnum's circus, again as a wagon and sign painter. He also made trips into the Indian country on his own, sketching and painting Indian and animal life as well as cavalrymen and scouts.

After 1900 he returned to Chicago, executing commissioned paintings, particularly Indian portraits. His noted sitters included King Edward VII, President Grant, and King Kalakana of Hawaii. A plump, bespectacled man with a walrus mustache, he spoke Sioux fluently and painted his Indians "in a stern-faced pose with their backs to a stormy sky." PAW. Buffalo Bill Cody called Cross the "greatest painter of Indian portraiture of all times." HAR. Cross's portrait of the Sioux chief Red Cloud was best known. His painting *Camp of Sitting Bull in the Big Horn Mtns* 1873 was the cover illustration for the Vestal biography of Sitting Bull.

CRUMBO, Woodrow Wilson. Born Lexington, Okla 1912, living Colorado 1971. Creek-Potawatomi painter, teacher, dancer, musician. Work in GIL, MAI, Mus No Ariz, U of Okla library, Philbrook AC. References A41-MAS. Sources AIP-COW-GIL. No current auction record. Signature example p 58 GIL.

When he was nine, Woody Crumbo's formal education was interrupted for eight years. His art education, however, was begun during this time when he was encouraged by Mrs Susie Peters in Anadarko to paint along with Spencer Asah and the "Five Kiowas": "Some of us were so small that we sat on gallon

buckets and used the backs of chairs for easels." AIW. Crumbo, a Creek-Potawatomi, returned to school at 17. He studied murals with Olaf Nordmark, watercolor with Clayton Henri Staples, and painting with O B Jacobson who had sponsored the "Five Kiowas."

Crumbo conducted a dance group in 1933 and won a national dance contest in 1935. He was silversmith instructor at U of Oklahoma 1936–37, director of art at Bacone College 1938–41 and 1943–45, aircraft designer 1941–42, artist in residence at GIL 1945–48, and assistant director at El Paso Museum of Art. In 1952 Crumbo said, "Half of my life passed in striving to complete the pictorial record of Indian history, religion, rituals, customs, way of life, and philosophy." AIR.

CUE, Harold James. Born place unknown 1887, died 1961. Illustrator of children's Western and historical books. No reference. Source 50G. No auction record. Signature example p 70 50G.

Very little can be found on the life of Cue, except that all of his work was published in Boston. He illustrated the book by James Willard Schultz "The Great Apache Forest," H H Knibbs's "The Iroquois Scout" and "The Boast of the Seminole," and Eleanor Porter's "Pollyanna" series.

CULMER, Henry (or Harry) Lavender Adolphus. Born Darington, Kent, Eng 1854, died Salt Lake City, Utah 1914. Early Utah landscape painter, writer, businessman. Work in Utah St Capitol Bldg, Utah Hist Soc, BYU Art Center. References A14 (obit)-BEN-MAL-SMI. Sources ANT 6/74-JUT-PUA-YUP-

WHO 12. Oil 42×60″ *Natural Bridge* sold 5/27/73 for $1,350 at auction. Signature example opp p 288 JUT *Monument Park in Southeastern Utah.*

Henry Culmer emigrated to Utah with his parents in 1868. He worked as an accountant and as a newspaper editor. A weekend painter, he found time to study with Utah artist Alfred Lambourne and California artist Julian Rix. He met Thomas Moran who influenced Culmer's style, emphasizing the grandiose in rock-country landscapes of southern Utah. His paintings of the natural bridges were published in the *National Geographic* in 1907.

Near the end of his career, he was undoubtedly the most popular artist in Utah. Geologists claimed they could identify the age of rocks in his pictures. *The Mystery of the Desert* considered to be his masterpiece was completed in 1906 and appraised at $25,000. His fame was near legendary despite the few formal lessons. "When asked to name his teacher, Culmer would reply, 'N A Ture.'" PUA. His favorite subjects were the Red Rock country, the Vermillion Cliffs, the Monument Park region, and the Colossal Bridges in watercolor, the Uinta and Wasatch ranges, the Tetons, the cypresses of Monterey in oil. Called "Utah's finest painter," Culmer did not paint full time until four years before his death.

CUMMING, Charles Atherton. Born Knox Cnty, Ill 1858, died probably San Diego, Cal 1932. Portrait, landscape, and mural painter, teacher. Work in (landscapes) Des Moines and Cedar Rapids Galls; (portraits) St Hist Gall (Ia) and St U of Iowa; murals Polk Cnty Cthse. References A31-BEN-FIE-MAL-SMI. Source WHO 30. No current auction record but the published estimate is $300 to $400. No signature example.

Cumming studied at the AIC and in Paris at the Julien Academy with Boulanger, Lefebvre, and Constant. He founded the Cumming School of Art in Des Moines in 1895. The title of his Iowa mural was *Departure of the Indians from Fort Des Moines.* Cumming's book was "The White Man's Art Defined." His wife was the painter S Alice McKee.

CUNEO, Cyrus Cincinnati. Born San Francisco, Cal 1878, died London, Eng 1916. Expatriate Special Artist-illustrator of the West, portrait painter. Work in Liverpool Gall (Eng), Nat Gall of Art (Sydney). Reference A16 (obit)-BEN-MAL. Source AOH. No current auction record. Signature example p 31 AOH *Gigantic Rabbit Drive.*

Of Italian descent, Cuneo financed his art training with Whistler in Paris by boxing professionally. He settled in London, becoming "an Englishman by preference and adoption." He was a member of the Royal Institute of Oil Painters and exhibited at the RA from 1905 to 1912.

In 1908 Cuneo made an extended trip through California and Western Canada as the last of the Special Artists for *Illustrated London News* and the guest of the Canadian Pacific. In 1910 the ILN printed *Raiding a Chinese Lottery Den in San Francisco, A Gigantic Jack Rabbit Drive,* and *Cornered! Bear Hunting in the Rockies,* in 1911 *Betrayed by Their Blowholes in the Snow,* in 1912 *The Difficulties of an American Sleeper* and *Bruin as a "Turn."* The original paintings of the railway series were destroyed in Liverpool during WWI.

CUNEO, Rinaldo. Born San Francisco, Cal 1877, probably died there 1939. Cal landscape and marine painter, in Ariz

1928. Work in De Young Mem Gall, San Fran MA; murals Coit Tower. Reference A41 (obit)-FIE-MAL. Source BDW. No current auction record or signature example.

Cuneo painted marines early in his career, while working on harbor boats. Many of his paintings were oil on paper and small. He also painted California landscapes including the High Sierras and in 1928 painted in the Arizona desert: *The Alabama Range, Hoodlum Peak, Rainy Season in the Desert, The Ancient Sea Bed.*

CUPRIEN, Frank W. Born Bklyn, NY 1871, died Laguna Beach, Cal 1948. Cal painter. Work in del Vecchio Gall (Leipzig), school in Laguna Beach. References A53 (obit)-BEN-FIE-MAL-SMI. Source BDW-SCA. No current auction record but the published estimate would be $600 to $700. No signature example.

Raised in Brooklyn, Cuprien attended night classes at the Cooper Union Institute and ASL.

Cuprien was the pupil of Carl Weber in Philadelphia. He also studied in Munich, Dresden, Leipzig, Paris, and in Italy. He settled in Laguna Beach in 1913 in his studio which he called "The Viking." He was known as the painter of the ocean.

CURRIER, Edward Wilson. Born Marietta, Ohio 1857, died San Francisco, Cal 1918. Cal painter in watercolor and oil. Work in Alask-Yuk-Pac Expos (Seattle) in 1909. References A19 (obit)-BEN-MAL-SMI. Source BDW. No current auction record or signature example.

E W Currier studied at the Chicago Academy of Fine Arts and was the pupil of George Clough in New York.

CURRIER, Walter Barron. Born Springfield, Mass 1879, died Santa Monica, Cal 1934. Cal landscape painter, illustrator, printmaker, teacher. Work in LA schools, Expos Park Galls, library, and institution. Reference A36 (obit)-BEN-FIE-MAL-SMI. Source A33 listing *Dalton Canyon, Sunset Glow from Bigbear, Sunrise in San Leandro Hills.* No current auction record but the published estimate is $300 to $400. No signature example.

Currier was educated at Brown and Cornell U. He was the pupil of Arthur Wesley Dow, Kenyon Cox, and Eben Comins. After moving to California in 1902, he taught at U of California at Berkeley. In 1926 he founded the Currier Creative Art School in Santa Monica where he wrote and lectured on art, exhibiting widely.

CURRY, John Steuart. Born Dunavent, Kans 1897, died Madison, Wisc 1946. Important Midwestern regional painter of the 1930s, muralist, illustrator. ANA 1937, NA 1943. Work in AIC, MMA, City AM (St Louis), WMAA, Wichita AM. References A47 (obit)-BEN-MAL. Sources AAT-AIC-ANT 11/66-ALA-CAA-CON-COW-DEP-190-MAP-M57-STI-TSF-WHO 46. Oil 30×24¾" *Self-Portrait* dated 1935 sold 12/10/70 for $4,000 at auction. Oil on paper 26×20" *Baby Ruth* with signature example and dated 1932 sold 5/23/74 for $7,500 at auction.

Curry's childhood consisted of farm chores first and studies later. His father said, "With his powerful shoulders, John was an outstanding athlete, a mediocre student, and a devoted artist." COW. After earning his tuition working as a railroad section hand, Curry studied at the Kansas City AI 1916, the AIC 1916–18, and Geneva College 1918–19 where he played football. For the next five years Curry earned a marginal living as an illustrator of pulp Western magazines. The first break came when an art patron paid for study in the Russian Studio of B Schoukhaieff in Paris in 1926–27. Convinced of his ability as a painter but discouraged, Curry staked his future on *Baptism in Kansas,* painted from memory in Westport, Conn in 1928. The painting was purchased for the WMAA with Curry subsidized for two years and on his way to success as a painter of rural genre. He became best known for paintings of the struggle of man with nature—"line storms, floods, and tornadoes." ALA. Curry taught at the ASL from 1932 to 1936, becoming artist in residence at the U of Wisconsin, the youngest of the regionalists Benton-Wood-Curry.

As a Western artist, Curry used southern Utah as a locale, showing for example "cattle heading into a canyon with a cowboy in the foreground." COW. *Line Storm* painted in 1934 in Westport was praised as "one of his finest Western landscapes." Reproduced p 72 MAP.

CURTIS, Leland. Born Denver, Colo 1897, living Carson City, Nev 1972. Western landscape painter known for Antarctic subjects. Work in City of LA Col, Dept of Interior (Washington), LA clubs, school. References A62-MAL. Source A41 listings *High Sierras, Sierra Dawn, The Everlasting Mountains.* No current auction record or signature example.

Curtis was winning California awards with his paintings of the Sierras by 1924. From 1939 to 1941 he was official artist for the US Antarctic Expedition, and in 1957 he was with US Navy Operation Deepfreeze III in the Antarctic.

CURTIS, Philip Campbell. Born Jackson, Mich 1907, living Scottsdale, Ariz 1976. Western painter of surrealism, mus director. Member RSA. Work in Phoenix AM, Ariz St U, Des Moines AC. References A76-MAS. Sources AHI 10/71-WAI 71,72-WHO 70. No current auction record or signature example.

Phil Curtis was educated at Albion College (1930) and U Michigan Law School. He studied at Yale Sch FA. His work has been reproduced in AHI. Curtis founded the Phoenix AC, served as director 1936–39. After WWII, Curtis returned to Arizona to paint. His work has been called "magic realism," a combination of whimsy and surrealism with grim subjects and strong color. WAI 72. Named by some as Arizona's greatest painter, Curtis' paintings evoke apprehensiveness and disquietude. WAI 71. Listed painting titles are *The Fight, House of Ill Repute, The Dummer* (1957), and *The Meeting* (1960).

CUSHING, Howard Gardner. Born Boston, Mass 1869, died NYC 1916. Painter of women's portraits, muralist. ANA 1906. Work in MMA. References A16 (obit)-BEN-FIE-MAL-SMI. Sources ISH-M31-WHO 14. Oil 40×30″ *Yosemite* listed in A23 as sold for $220 at auction. Oil *Oriental Scene* sold 10/17/69 for $210 at auction. No signature example.

After graduating from Groton School 1887, Cushing studied at Harvard until 1891, then spent five years at the Julien Academy in Paris, the pupil of Laurens, Constant, and Doucet. He exhibited at the Nationale in Paris, with paintings "delicately and elegantly ingenious." ISH. His listed works were *A Woman in White, Woman in a Silver Dress,* and *Sunlight.*

DA, Popovi (Tony Martínez). Born New Mexico about 1920, died Santa Fe, NM 1971. Painter of the San Ildefonso movement, ceramic artist. Black-on-black ware bowl in ACM. No reference. Sources AHI 2/50-AIP. No auction record or signature example. Bowl photo ✕687 ACM.

Da was the son of Julián and María Martínez, the "potter of San Ildefonso." Da legally changed his name from Tony Martínez. Like Julián Martínez, Da's outstanding paintings are symbolic designs and geometric figures. After 1943 Da designed and decorated his mother's pottery, using motifs similar to those of his father. He also owned an arts and crafts shop in the pueblo. Da served six terms as governor of San Ildefonso Pueblo and developed the Sienna ware used in 1964. Da's son Anthony is also an artist.

DABICH, George. Born California 1922, living Cody, Wyom 1974. Traditional Western painter and sculptor. Work in Whitney Gall of Western Art (Cody), Baker Collector Gall (Lubbock, Tex). Source Wyom St Art Gall. No auction record or signature example.

Dabich joined the Navy in 1939. After the war he moved to Wyoming and for more than 20 years worked as trapper, guide, and hunter in the "high" country. His favorite subject is historical Wyoming: the mountain man in *Jim Bridger's Lie,* the Indian in *Summer Indian Camp,* and life in the Old West in *Fort Laramie, 1843.*

DAHLGREN, Carl Christian. Born Skelsior, Denmark 1841, died probably Oakland, Cal 1920. Painter of landscapes and genre, illustrator. Work in Kahn colln, Oakland, Cal. No reference.

Sources BDW-KAH. No auction record. Signature example KAH p 19.

Carl Dahlgren's training in Denmark had been delayed by his service in the Danish Army during the Franco-Prussian War so he was 26 when he enrolled in the Copenhagen Academy of Arts. He later became a pupil of Carsten Henreksen, a landscape and animal painter. After coming to the US in 1872 with his younger brother Marius, Dahlgren first settled in Utah working as a draftsman and artist-explorer for the Surveyor General's Office. In 1875 he started an art school in Salt Lake City. In 1878 he moved to San Francisco, opened a studio and married.

Dahlgren was known as the "sunshine painter" (KAH) because he painted a shaft of sunlight in most of his works. He was the chief illustrator for the *Californian* magazine and he painted many scenes showing the destruction of the 1906 earthquake. In 1916 he was chosen by the naturalist Luther Burbank to paint his botany specimens and the views on Burbank Creek.

DAHLGREN, Marius. Born Skelsior, Denmark 1844, died Tucson, Ariz 1920. Landscape painter, illustrator, and muralist. Work in Kahn colln, Oakland, Cal. No reference. Sources BDW-KAH. No auction record. Signature example KAH p 19.

The younger brother of Carl Christian Dahlgren, Marius came to the US with his brother in 1872 and settled in California. Marius' earliest American painting was dated 1873 and he was listed as an artist in the 1874, 1875 San Jose Directory.

In 1878 he moved to Oakland, Cal, keeping a studio in San Francisco where he exhibited his work. In 1905 he settled in Tucson, Ariz, remaining there the rest of his life. His earlier work included local San Francisco and Oakland scenes,

Alameda County Courthouse, East Oakland, and *View from Goat Island, San Francisco Bay.* In Tucson he painted the frescoes in St Augustine's Cathedral.

Two Braves $210, Gilbert Gaul's *Tempering the Arrow* $270, Frank Tenney Johnson's *A Rider of the Range* $85, and Remington's *A Plainsman* $970.

DAINGERFIELD, Elliott. Born Harper's Ferry, W Va 1859, died NYC 1932. Visionary landscape painter of NC and NY, later of Grand Canyon; illustrator, art critic, teacher. ANA 1902, NA 1906. Work in MMA, NGA, City AM (St Louis), LA Mus; murals in NYC church. References A32 (obit)-BEN-ENB-FIE-MAL-SMI. Sources ANT 9/68,12/70,4/71 (article)-DEP-ISH-M31-MSL-NA 74-POW-WHO 32. Oil 12×10″ *The Dancers* signed but not dated sold 4/19/72 for $1,000 at auction. Signature example p 336 ANT 9/68.

Daingerfield was educated in schools and by private tutor in Fayetteville, NC where he began painting. At 21 he moved to a NYC studio, studying at the ASL and with his neighbor George Inness. Exhibiting immediately at the NA, he emphasized his NC childhood in his early paintings. In 1897 he studied in Europe. He also painted religious subjects including NYC church murals in 1902. By 1906 he was depending upon color in mystical landscapes.

In his later years he painted Western landscapes, particularly of the Grand Canyon. Daingerfield wrote books on Inness, Blakelock, and Ryder. As an art critic he sided with the academicians in calling the modernists of 1913 "not only revolutionary but even anti-God" in mouthing the "chatter of anarchistic monkeys." DEP. His important paintings included *Christ Stilling the Tempest, Slumbering Fog, An Arcadian Huntress.* At auction in 1917 *The Drama of the Mountain Tops* sold for $500, *Mountain Showers* for $575, and the 8×10″ *The Canyon Rim* for $70. This was a year when Bierstadt's *Scene in the Rocky Mountains* sold for $130, Couse's *The*

DALE, John B. Born place and date unknown, died place unknown 1848. Naval expedition artist 1838–42. Work in report of Wilkes's US Exploring Expedition. Reference G&W. Source BDW. No auction record or signature example.

Dale was a midshipman in 1829, lieutenant 1845.

DALLIN, Cyrus Edwin. Born Springville, Utah 1861, died Arlington Heights, Mass 1943. Important international and Western sculptor. ANA 1912, NA 1931, NSS, RSA (London), Fellow Am Acad A & Sciences. Principal works *Pioneer Monument* (Salt Lake City), *Medicine Man* (Fairmount Park, Phila), *Appeal to the Great Spirit* (MFA), *Indian Hunter* (Arlington, Mass), *The Scout* (Kansas City), *Statue of Massasoit* (Plymouth, Mass). References A47 (obit)-BEN-DAB-ENB-FIE-MAL-SMI. Sources ALA-AMA-ANT 4/70,10/73-MSL-POW-PUA-WHO 42. Bronze, brown patina 21½″ *Appeal to the Great Spirit* signed and dated 1913 sold 5/22/73 for $8,000 at auction; a bronze, green patina 111″ *The Passing of the Buffalo* signed, sold 10/31/75 for $150,000. Signature example ✕129 PB 9/28/73.

Cyrus Dallin, son of a covered-wagon pioneer, was born on a log-cabin farm. He was sent to Boston to learn to sculpt in 1884, financed by contributions from friends. He studied under Truman Howe Bartlett, immediately receiving a commission from Boston for a park statue. He won a gold medal by 1888, the year he went to the usual art school for Utahans, Julien Academy in Paris. There he executed a statue of Lafayette, presented to the city of Paris as a token from the people of America. In WWI, Gen Pershing said to the statue, "Lafayette, we are here"; in WWII, Gen Eisenhower said, "Lafayette, we have come."

Dallin was most successful in representing the character of the Indian. While he was in Paris, Buffalo Bill arrived with his Wild West Show. Dallin and Rosa Bonheur worked side by side at the Show's Indian Encampment. There are four major equestrian statues of Indians by Dallin in the US. Dallin became an instructor at Drexel Inst, Philadelphia, then moved to Boston as an instructor at Massachusetts State Normal Art School. He maintained his studio in Arlington but made frequent trips West: "I have received medals galore, Master of Arts, Doctor of Arts, but my greatest honor of all is that I came from Utah."

DALTON, John Joseph. Born Toronto, Ont, Can 1856, died probably Canada 1935. Dominion Topographical Surveyor, watercolorist. Work in ROM. No reference. Source ROM catalog of collection. No auction record or signature example. (See illustration 70.)

Son of a doctor, Dalton was commissioned Dominion Land Surveyor 1879 and Dominion Topographical Surveyor 1881. He worked during the summer of 1882 near Carlyle, Saskatchewan.

DAMROW, Charles. Born Sheboygan, Wis 1916, living Apache Junction, Ariz 1975. Cherokee painter of Western subjects. Work in Ariz and Wis banks and restaurants. No reference. Source AIP. Oil 36×48″ *Hopi Home Dance* with signature example sold for $2,700 3/4/74 at auction in LA.

Damrow is self-taught as an artist,

after working as cowboy, forester, and sign painter. He has been visiting Wisconsin Dells since 1950, decorating taverns and restaurants with Western scenes. Subjects are nostalgic scenes of cowboys, Indians, and buffalo.

DANN, Frode N. Born Jelstrup, Havbro, Denmark 1892, living Pasadena, Cal 1966. Painter, teacher, critic. References A66-MAS. Source, oil 20×24″ *Landscape, New Mexico* signed but undated, estimated 3/5/74 at $350 to $450 for auction in LA and sold for $125.

Dann studied at Danish Technical Trade School and the University and Royal Academy in Copenhagen. He was exhibiting at PAFA in 1938 and in California in 1944. Dann taught at Pasadena SFA and was art critic for a Pasadena newspaper.

DARGE, Fred. Born Hamburg, Germany 1900, living Dallas, Tex 1948. Painter of Western scenes. Work in Chicago schools. References A41-BEN-MAS. Source, *Prairie's Edge* in school colln. Traditional Western oil 24×32″ *Visiting My Neighbors* signed but not dated, estimated for sale 10/28/74 at $600 to $800 for auction in Los Angeles but did not sell. Signature example lot 23 catalog above.

Darge studied at the AIC. He won Chicago purchase prizes in 1928–29.

DARLEY, Felix Octavius Carr. Born Philadelphia, Pa 1822, died Claymont, Del 1888. Important early illustrator, lithographic artist, painter. NA 1852 (graphics). Work in NAD, Harmsen colln. References BEN-CHA-DAB-FIE-

G&W-MAL-SMI. Sources ACM-AIW-ALA-ANT 11/44,11/68 (article-AWM-BAR-BAW-BOA-COW-DCC-HUT-ILP-KW1-PAF-PNW-POW. Oil, *Touchstone and Audrey, As You Like It* 27×22″ signed and dated 1856 sold 1/15/76 for $600 at auction. The estimated value of an oil on board 8×10″ of Indians hunting bears would be about $3,000 to $4,000 at auction in 1976. Signature example p 270 ANT 11/44 *Puritans Barricading Their House Against Indians*.

The son of an English comic actor, F O C Darley entered business in Philadelphia immediately after leaving school. Without art training, he made woodcuts for a magazine as a hobby. The amount of payment he received convinced Darley he was an artist. In 1842 he took a sketching trip across the Mississippi that resulted in an 1843 book of drawings portraying the life of an Indian chief. Edgar Allan Poe wrote, "Every American should purchase this tribute to the aborigines." Darley became a successful Philadelphia illustrator and painter, exhibiting at the NA in 1845. Moving to NYC in 1848, Darley was the leading American book and magazine illustrator and a designer of bank note vignettes featuring Indian scenes and buffalo hunts. The best possible wood engravers translated his energetic sketches. He also painted Western scenes that were engraved or lithographed for framing. "He was an affable man, one who enjoyed his profession, and who seems to have been destined to it from the start." ANT.

Beginning with 1850 Darley gained prominence as a clever and original draftsman by virtue of his engravings of Irving's works for the American Art-Union. He also illustrated the finest editions of Cooper, Dickens, and Hawthorne. His work was mainly in black and white. Darley did not visit Europe "until the maturity of his life and career" in 1866, so he did not change "his romantic handling of landscapes or exaggerated figure drawings." BOA. It was said that "his characters always act their parts. His figures are solidly placed, seen in the round." ANT. His brother E H Darley and his sister-in-law Jane Cooper Darley were portraitists.

DASBURG, Andrew Michael. Born Paris, France 1887, living Ranchos de Taos, NM 1976. Important contemporary Taos school painter, teacher. Work in MMA, Dallas MFA, LAMA, Denver AM, WMAA, etc. References A76-BEN-FIE-MAL. Sources AAT-ALA-ARM-ART 8/47-CAA-DAA-DEP-HAR-ISH-190-M57-PET-PIT-SHO-TAL-TSF. Oil *Still Life of Tulips* sold 10/43 for $150 at auction. No current auction record. Signature example SHO p 44. (See illustration 71.)

Raised in Germany, Dasburg came to the US with his mother in 1892. He studied at the ASL with Kenyon Cox and DuMond, privately in Woodstock with Birge Harrison and at the NYSA with Henri. He studied in Paris in 1908, the same year as Benton, returning in 1911. "Young Andrew Dasburg abandoned the tepid manners he had learned from Kenyon Cox and soon painted a vase of tulips with the rugged force of Cézanne and reduced American trees and roof tops to their underlying shapes and colors." ALA. He exhibited three oils and a sculpture at the epochal 1913 Armory Show, acting as the butt of the critic Thomas Craven's dated denunciation, "What fine old American families were represented! Bouche, Dasburg, Halpert, Kuniyoshi, Stella, Zorach—scions of our colonial aristocracy!" In 1923 Dasburg was one of the leading proponents of Cubism. From there, he progressed toward "pure" art, but later returned to a modified version of Cubism, finding "in the landscape of the Southwest an apt vehicle for his Cubist vision." DEP.

Dasburg had visited New Mexico in 1917 at the urging of Maurice Sterne, and finally settled in Taos in 1930. Applying Cézanne and Cubism to New Mexico produced both powerful Western landscapes and a shock wave for New Mexico artists. His new European ideas affected even the older Taos group, Higgins, Berninghaus, and Blumenschein. As an influence for pioneering modernism, for re-evaluating the same subjects originally painted by Couse and Ufer, Dasburg was of the greatest importance in New Mexico. In turn, Dasburg became less abstract.

DATUS, Jay. Born Jackson, Mich 1914, died probably Phoenix, Ariz 1974. Painter, muralist, teacher, writer. Fellow, RSA. Work in U Wis, Beloit Col, Ariz St Capitol Bldg; murals in Arizona banks and public buildings. References A73-BEN-MAS. Source AHI 3/64. No auction record. Signature example p 43 AHI 3/64.

Datus studied at the Worcester Museum School and the Yale U School FA. He wrote a newspaper art column and was the founder of the Kachina SA in 1948 in Phoenix. His mural *The Builder* illustrated in AHI 3/64 is 10×40 feet, the largest of a series of his murals in the First National Bank of Arizona in Phoenix.

DAUGHERTY, James Henry. Born Asheville, NC 1889, died probably Weston, Conn 1974. Illustrator of historical subjects including Indians; painter, muralist, writer. Work in MOMA, WMAA, Yale MFA, NY Pub Lib, Wilmington Pub Lib, Achenbach Fndn, etc. References A73-BEN-FIE-MAL-SMI. Sources 500-Il 59-POI-WHO 70. No auction record. Illustrations pp 420,421 in 500. (See illustration 72.)

Daugherty studied at COR, PAFA,

and in London with Frank Brangwyn. As an illustrator he specialized in American historical subjects. After the "stilted and quaint" lithographs of Currier and Ives, Daugherty's vitality and naturalness were a "happy change." 500. In 1939 he received the Newberry Medal for distinguished contribution to children's literature.

DAVEY, Randall. Born East Orange, NJ 1887, died California 1964. Contemporary Santa Fe school painter specializing in horses, muralist. Taos SA 1922, ANA 1937, NA 1938. Work in AIC, COR, WMAA, Montclair AM, Kansas City AI, Cleveland MA, Detroit IA, Will Rogers' Shrine (Colo Springs). References A66 (obit)-BEN-FIE-MAL-SMI. Sources AAT-AIW-ARM-CAA-CON-COW-HAR-HOR-M50-NEW-PIT-SHO-TSF-WHO 62. In M50, *Jockey's Girl* was offered for sale at $1,500 in 1950. Watercolor 16½×11¾" *After the Race* sold 1/13/71 for $150 at auction. Photo of Davey painting a 1937 mural *The Shrine of the Sun* p 302 NEW. (See illustration 73.)

Davey, educated in architecture at Cornell 1905–7, began his art studies with Robert Henri, first in NYC in 1909 and then in Europe in 1910. Together they analyzed the old masters. Both Henri and Davey exhibited at the important 1913 Armory Show.

Davey was one of the early members of the Santa Fe art colony in 1919, persuading John Sloan to motor to Santa Fe in Davey's 1912 Simplex open touring car. Davey immediately bought an old mill in a nearby canyon, establishing himself as the rare Western artist who preferred nudes to Indians. "Not opposed to Indians as subjects for others, he has failed to find in their color and customs any pictorial stimulation." TSF. He taught at the AIC 1920, Kansas City AI 1921–24, Broadmoor AA (Colo

Springs) 1924–31, U of NM 1945–46. At Broadmoor his salary in 1924 was twice the usual rate because he "was also a first-class polo player." When polo declined as a Broadmoor sport, Davey left. NEW. "Horse racing subjects, with all the magnificent pageantry, are among his most noted canvases, painted in a clean, direct way. He puts them down with spirit." A sophisticated and extroverted man, he died in an auto accident. HAR.

DAVIES, Arthur Bowen. Born Utica, NY 1862, died Florence, Italy 1928. Romantic Eastern painter in Mexico 1880, in Cal 1905; illustrator, printmaker, sculptor, designer. Work in MMA, AIC, Minneapolis IA, Bklyn Inst Mus, San Fran AI, RI School of Des, etc. References A29 (obit)-BEN-DAB-ENB-FIE-MAL-SMI. Sources AAR 1,3/74-AIC-ALA-AMA-ANT 2/58,10/62,4/65,10/69,5/72,3/74-ARI-ARM-CIV-CON-COR-DEP-190-ISH-M31-MSL-NGA-NEU-SCU-WHO 24. Oil 35×66″ *Dawn* dated 1926 sold 5/21/70 for $5,000 at auction. Oil *A Lake in the Sierras* sold for $1,525 at auction in 1917. P 351 A17. Signature example p 112 ANT 2/58.

Son of a Welsh tailor, Davies at 15 was the pupil of Dwight Williams. When the family moved to Chicago in 1878, Davies was the pupil of Charles Corwin at the AIC. From 1880 to 1882 he worked as a civil engineer on an expedition in Mexico which gave him a taste of Western life. After additional study in Chicago he moved to NYC in 1887, a pupil of the ASL, friend of Robert Henri and George Luks. From 1888 to 1891 he was a successful illustrator for *St Nicholas* but quit for fine art. By 1894 Davies had patrons to give him a NYC studio and a European trip. His small idyllic pastorals were the beginnings of a cult. About 1900, larger canvases featured nude abstract figures.

In 1905 Davies visited California, painting in the Sierras which also had an influence in enlarging his work, although he had told Wood Gaylor "never to paint anything you can't carry under your arm because that's where the painting is most of the artist's life." AIA. A recluse, his only public undertaking was the presidency of the Society of Independent Artists and the arrangement for the epochal 1913 Armory Show. Slight and alert, Davies never spoke first, "but if you addressed him, he responded charmingly and with tact." DAB. Late in his life, Davies believed that Greek art depended upon the act of inhaling, with the model and the artist both inhaling as the painting stroke was made. Davies sculpted in wood, ivory, marble, and wax, designed in enamel, glass, tapestry, and rugs.

DAVIS, Mrs Cornelia Cassady. Born Cleves, Ohio 1870, died Cincinnati, Ohio 1920. Ohio painter. Work in Westminster Central Hall (London). References A21 (obit)-FIE. Source, *The Hopi Indian Snake Ceremony* in El Tovar Gall (Grand Canyon, Ariz). No auction record or signature example.

Mrs Davis studied at the Cincinnati Art Academy, the pupil of Lutz, Noble, and Duveneck. She received an award for her 1912 Ohio suffrage poster.

DAVIS, Floyd Macmillan. Born place unknown 1896, died probably NYC 1966. Magazine illustrator of 1930s specializing in Southern rural and frontier types. Member SI. Work in Pentagon; *American* and *Woman's Home Companion* magazines. References A47-MAL. Sources AAW-ILA-IL 42,59-POI. No auction record. Signature examples p 25 IL 42, ✳14 IL 59, p 133 ILA. (See illustration 74.)

Floyd Davis was listed AAW as an illustrator resident in Chicago in 1924. His illustrations of the period were advertisements of class products. In the 1930s he began to specialize in rural and frontier types as illustrations for magazine stories by William Faulkner and MacKinlay Kantor. Davis' special touch was the unrelated detail hidden for the viewer to find, for example, the salamander on the tree trunk p 132 ILA. In WWII, Davis was an artist correspondent for the War Department. Many of these paintings were reproduced in *Life*.

In creating his illustrations Davis did not use models, preferring to rely on his memory. His approach was to overdraw the folksy, thus maintaining country humor. Gladys Rockmore Davis the painter was his wife, credited for the critical view that made him "one of the great figures of American illustration." ILA.

DAVIS, Georgina A. Born NYC about 1850, living NYC 1900. Illustrator in the West in 1877 as part of the much publicized Leslie train trip. Reference A00. Source AIW. No auction record. Signature example p 74 IL 94 with self portrait p 454 taken from the back of her head.

Miss Davis as a friend of Mrs Leslie traveled with the Frank Leslie party on its railway tour from NYC in 1877 to the West Coast. Events were illustrated in *Leslie's* with almost 200 sketches, most attributed to Ogden and Yeager who were also on the trip. None of the sketches is noted as by Miss Davis who did not become well known as an illustrator until later. She was, however, an artist, and certainly one of the first woman artists exposed to the Plains, Cheyenne, Colorado Springs, Salt Lake City, the Indians, Chinese laborers, tramps, and the California landscape including Yosemite.

DAVIS, Jessie Freemont Snow. Born near Georgetown, Williamson Cnty, Tex 1887, living Dallas, Tex 1962. Texas painter, teacher. Work in Dallas MFA, Oak Cliff Gall, school and library. References A62-BEN-MAL. Source TOB. No auction record or signature example.

Daughter of a painter, Jessie Davis studied in Dallas with Frank Reaugh, Martha Simkins, and John Knott before going to the ASL where she was the pupil of George Bridgman and Dmitri Romanovsky. Beginning 1929 she was instructor at the Dallas Public Evening School. Her listed painting was *Feeding Time*.

DAVIS, Leonard Moore. Born Winchendon, Mass 1864, died probably Tarzana, Cal 1938. Landscape painter of Alaska and Canadian Rockies, illustrator, muralist, lecturer. Work in Washington St AM (Seattle), Munic AG (Seattle), MNM, St James's Palace (London), Mus Pub Archives of Canada, Hayden Planetarium of AMNH, Yukon RR Office. References A41 (obit)-FIE-MAL-SMI. Sources ANT 2/75-WHO 38. No current auction record for Western landscapes but an oil 12×18" *Peaches* signed and dated 1891 sold 1/26/72 for $300 at auction against an estimate of $50. Signature example p 294 ANT 2/75. (See illustration 75.)

Davis was educated at the college of the City of NY. He began work as a woodfinisher, printer, and lithographic artist up to 1884. He studied at the ASL 1884–89 and at the Julien Academy in Paris under Laurens, Lefebvre, and Constant 1889–90 and 1894–95, as well as École des Beaux-Arts in Paris. Davis became a portrait painter, an art teacher, a gold miner in Alaska, a landscape painter, and a lecturer for nine years on art and on Alaska.

His specialty after 1898 was scenes of Alaska (127 at the 1915 San Francisco Exposition alone), of the Canadian Rockies (over 600), of the Duke of Windsor's Canadian ranch (over 27), and of US National Parks (over 100). He also painted 27 views of the aurora borealis for the AMNH planetariums. His mural *Dreamland* was for the children's ward of the LA Cnty Hospital.

DAVIS, Lew E. Born Jerome, Ariz 1910, living Scottsdale, Ariz 1976. Semiabstract Ariz landscape and still-life painter. Work in Newark MA, Mus Northern Ariz, Pasadena AI, Santa Barbara MA; murals in public buildings in Cal, Okla, Ariz. References A76-BEN-MAL. Sources AAT-AHI 10/71-ARI. No current auction record. Signature example p 65 AAT *Copper Camp—Spring.*

Davis studied at the NAD, the pupil of Leon Kroll. He was director of the Arizona Art Foundation in Scottsdale and teacher at Arizona State College. Before WWII he painted realistically, specializing in the Arizona mining area. His *Market* (1952) reproduced p 54 ARI is called "semiabstract," that is, a realistic subject matter abstracted in form. Davis' wife was Mathilde Schaefer, a sculptor.

DAVIS, Richard. Born NYC 1904, living there 1953. Eastern sculptor, lecturer. Member NSS, Sculptors Guild. Work in USPO (Springfield, Ky), exhibited NY World's Fair 1939. References A53-BEN-MAS. Source AAT. No auction record. Sculpture example *Bison* in black granite p 187 AAT.

Davis studied with Bourdelle, José de Creeft, Ahron Ben-Shemuel, and John Flanagan.

DAVIS, Stuart. Born Philadelphia, Pa 1894, died NYC 1964. Very important Eastern abstract painter, muralist, illustrator. Work in ACM, MOMA, WMAA, PAFA, Cranbrook AA, Newark AM. References A66 (obit)-BEN-FIE-MAL. Sources AAR 9/73,3/74-AAT-ACM-ALA-APT-ARI-ARM-ART 2/45-CAA-CON-DEP-HMA-190-M57-NEU-PIT-STI-TSF-WHO 62. Oil 36×45" *Hot Still-Scape for 6 Colors,* signed and dated New York, Aug 1940 sold 3/14/73 for $175,-000 at auction as a part of the Edith G Halpert colln. Oil 15¼×27¼" *New Mexican Landscape* 1923 sold 12/13/73 for $12,000 at auction. Signature example ⚒120 PB 5/16/73.

Davis' father was art director of the *Philadelphia Press,* supervising Sloan, Luks, Shinn, and Glackens. Davis graduated from high school in 1910 and studied at the Henri School of Art in NYC between 1910 and 1913. He became a cartoonist for *Harper's Weekly* in 1913. Thereafter he specialized in easel paintings in New York, Gloucester, and Paris. "In all of my work, there is no intention to make a replica of the optical appearance of the place. Instead, its elements of form, color and space are changed to meet the requirements of a sense of dimensional unity, which develops and becomes complete as I study them. The result is a permanent record of an emotional experience expressed in terms of coherent color-space dimensions." CON.

"This most daring and powerful of American moderns" (CON) spent the summer of 1923 in Santa Fe, following John Sloan, Marsden Hartley, and Robert Henri, the contemporary Westerns. HMA illustrates these in "Days on the Range," with Davis painting as a realist in shorthand: "I did not do much work. There's the great dead population. It's a place for an ethnologist, not an artist. Not sufficient intellectual stimulation. Forms made to order, to imitate." When Davis left the "too picturesque" scenes of

New Mexico that had so inhibited him, he was able to get back into his development of abstract forms. TSF.

DAVIS, Theodore Russell. Born Boston, Mass 1840, died Asbury Park, NJ 1894. Important Western illustrator, Special Artist-correspondent for *Harper's Weekly,* watercolorist. Reference G&W. Sources AIW-AOA-AOW-COW-CUS-KW1,2-POW. No current auction record but the estimated value of a sketch 8×10″ of a cavalry skirmish with Sioux Indians would be about $1,000 to $1,200 at auction in 1976. Signature example p 203 AOW.

Educated at Rittenhouse Academy in DC, T R Davis moved to Brooklyn when he was about 15. He had some instruction in drawing and wood engraving, perhaps from James Walker, and exhibited a crayon drawing when he was 16. He joined the staff of *Harper's* in 1861 as a traveling correspondent. His first trip through the South before the war he considered the most dangerous he ever made. A most prolific Civil War artist, he witnessed the battle between the *Monitor* and the *Merrimac,* Shiloh, Antietam, the Atlanta campaign, and the Grand March to the sea. He was wounded twice, holding off at gunpoint surgeons who wanted to amputate his leg.

Davis was the earliest of the Special Artists to cross the plains after the Civil War, sent to picture the mining camps and boom towns of Colorado. He left Atchison Nov 17, 1865 by Butterfield Overland Despatch. The fifth day out, the modest Davis reported he "saw a band of Indians charging on the coach, less than 60 yards distant. Mr D, the moment that he gave the alarm, picked up his rifle and sent its contents at the most gaudily gotten up Indian, who not liking the dose ran off. One of the Indians had charged on the stock herder, driving arrows at him meanwhile, when Mr

Davis sent the interior arrangements of his Ballard rifle into Mr Indian's back, causing a series of very curious gyrations on the part of the Indian who was tied to his horse, so saved his scalp." This incident became the prototype of all the classic Indian attacks on the overland stage, reenacted by Buffalo Bill and in the movies. The coach arrived in Denver after 15 days, Davis writing, "Cooper might have *his* Indians; we did not care for their company." AOW. Davis made Denver his headquarters until Feb 1866. "Possessed of a buoyant and sunny disposition, he made friends wherever he went." AIW. By October he was sketching in Texas. By April 1867 he was in Kansas, invited by Gen Hancock to accompany the Indian expedition. He was with Gen Custer in Nebraska and Colorado, leaving in August when the campaign appeared to be a failure. He had been four months in the saddle, covering 3,000 miles, recording the best eyewitness pictures of the realities of the Plains Indian Wars. Davis did not return to the West, although he continued to do Western illustrations.

DAVIS, Wayne Lambert. Born Oak Park, Ill 1904, living Putnam, Conn 1976. Eastern landscape painter, illustrator, engraver, photographer. Work in NY Pub Lib, Bur of Aeronautics, Smithsonian Inst. References A76-BEN-MAL. Source AHI. No current auction record.

Davis attended Columbia and NYU. He was the pupil of Ronald Norman McLeod and Jos Pennell at the ASL. An illustrator for business and popular magazines such as *Fortune* and *Liberty,* Davis' specialties have been aviation and skiing subjects along with tempera paintings of the Western landscape. He was art director of Grumman Aircraft 1941–53 and a high school art instructor 1953–63.

DAWSON-WATSON, Dawson (or Watson, Dawson). Born London, Eng 1864, died probably San Antonio, Tex 1939. Texas landscape painter, engraver, woodcarver, designer, teacher. Work in City AM (St Louis), Witte Mus (San Antonio), U of Texas. References A41 (obit)-BEN-FIE-MAL-SMI. Sources TOB-TXF-WHO 38. Oil 30×24″ *Grand Canyon* with signature example was estimated for sale 10/28/74 at $350 to $400 for auction in LA and sold for $300. (See illustration 76.)

Son of a fashionable English illustrator, Dawson-Watson was the pupil of Mark Fisher until he volunteered to serve with the Royal Welsh Fusileers in 1882. A brewer sponsored his study in Paris with Duran and Morot until 1885, when he discontinued funds after D-W's marriage to an American girl touring France with the Texas painter Mrs E R Cherry. After five years in Giverny, D-W was recommended to the US by Carroll Beckwith. He painted in New England 1893–97, was briefly back in England, then Canada for three years, then the Woodstock (NY) art colony, and the St Louis SFA 1904–15.

In 1926 he was in Boston when he heard about the $5,000 Wild Flower Painting Contest in San Antonio. He sold a painting and left Boston in 36 hours for San Antonio where in six months he made 70 cactus paintings as studies. Then he painted the prize-winning oil from memory in 3½ hours—*The Glory of the Morning*. After he established his studio in San Antonio, it was said that his work "stands out quite by itself in the history of Texas art." TXF.

DAY, Benjamin Henry, Jr. Born NYC 1838, died Summit, NJ 1916. *Leslie's* and *Harper's* staff artist, illustrator of Western scenes for "Beyond the Mississippi," inventor of process for shading the drawings to be printed, painter. Work in periodicals. References A16 (obit)-G&W-MAL. Sources AOA-BEY. No auction record. Signature example p 72 BEY.

Son of the founder of the "penny press" *New York Sun,* Day was educated in NYC and studied art in Paris. He worked as a designer for the illustrated weekly his father started after the *Sun* was sold, until the Civil War caused a paper shortage. Day then worked for many years as a staff artist for *Leslie's* and *Harper's Weekly.* About 1879 he invented the process that bears his name, the Ben Day that mechanically adds tints to line engravings, avoiding hand-drawn tints that were irregular and costly. Like Morse and his code, Ben Day is an artist whose name survives through invention.

Along with a number of Civil War field artists, Day was an illustrator for "Beyond the Mississippi." His five drawings would have placed him in Kansas, Nevada, and California between 1857 and 1867 if they had been drawn on the spot, but it is likely that they were redrawn from existing materials. By 1885 Day was exhibiting at the NA.

DEAKIN, Edwin. Born Sheffield, Eng 1838, died Berkeley, Cal 1923. Spanish Mission painter, landscapist, still-life. Work in Cal Hist Soc, M H De Young Mus. References FIE-MAL-SMI. Sources ANT 5/68-MSL-STI-WHI. No current auction record but the estimated price of an oil 20×30″ of an Indian camp in Idaho would be about $2,000 to $2,500 at auction in 1976. Signature examples STI.

Deakin received his art education in England and established himself as an architectural painter in England and France. He emigrated to Chicago in 1869, painting memorial portraits of Civil War heroes. In 1870 he opened a studio in San Francisco as a landscape and portrait painter. He became a member of the Bohemian Club along with his close friend Samuel Marsden Brookes, the still-life painter.

His specialty was the series of paintings of old Franciscan missions. From 1870 to 1899 he painted scenes of 21 of the missions begun by Father Junipero Serra in 1769. Even a still life of Salt Lake grapes used a background of a mission window. In 1874 he painted his friend Brookes at work in Brookes's dilapidated studio painting a still life of fish. There are also California and Idaho landscapes dated 1877. Deakin is said to have been active as late as 1920. He was the author of "A Gallery of California Mission Paintings" published posthumously in 1966. STI.

DEAS, Charles. Born Philadelphia, Pa 1818, died in an asylum probably in St Louis 1867. Important early painter of Indians and frontier life on the Great Plains. ANA 1839. Work in BM, MFA, Shelburne Mus. References BEN-FIE-G&W-MAL-SMI. Sources AAR 11/74-ALA-ANT 11/60, 10/62-AWM-BOA-COW-DWF-HUT-KAP-KW1-MIS-PAF-POW-TEP-WES-WHI. No current auction record but the estimated price of an oil 20×30" showing an Indian wounded on the prairie would be about $15,000 to $20,000 at auction in 1976. Signature example p 106 POW.

Deas, grandson of the Revolutionary War leader Ralph Izard, was exposed to art as a visitor at the PAFA and in Sully's studio while receiving his general education from John Sanderson. He failed to gain appointment to West Point in 1836 when the Hudson River outdoor life attracted him more than life as a cadet. He then spent two years at the NA in NYC, exhibiting beginning 1838 "a variety of cabinet pictures drawn chiefly from familiar life." BOA. During a visit to Philadelphia in 1838 he was enthralled by an exhibition of Catlin's Indian paintings: "To visit the scenes of Nature's own children, to share the repast of the hunter, and taste the wild excitement of frontier life." BOA.

In 1840 Deas left the East to visit his brother at Fort Crawford, Prairie du Chien, Wis, only 10 years after Seth Eastman, at the same time as Stanley, and 10 to 20 years before the better known Western artists. He collected sketches of Indians and frontier scenery. "In passing from lodge to lodge, the most extraordinary incidents presented themselves, and in the stillness of the moonlit nights, the echoes of the Indian lover's flute blent with the battle-chant or the maiden's shrill song." BOA. In the winter of 1841 he visited Fort Winnebago. The summer of 1842 he made a tour to Fort Snelling, St Anthony's Falls, and the Sioux. He had a permanent studio in St Louis as his headquarters. In 1844, when he traveled to the Pawnees, he was nicknamed "Rocky Mountain" because he dressed "like a fur hunter" and "he could go where he pleased. Mr Deas seemed to possess the whole secret of winning the good graces of the Indians. Whenever he entered a lodge it was with a grand flourish so that the whole lodge would burst out into a roar of laughter." POW. Eighteen of Deas's frontier works were exhibited at the NA in NYC. Others were shown at the American Art-Union. He returned to NYC in 1847, only to suffer a mental breakdown that affected his painting. Despite his huge successes that started from the time he was 20, only a very few canvases have survived.

DE BATZ (or Batz, or de Bat), Alexander. Born Montaterre, Picardy, France about 1685, died probably Louisiana after 1737. Work in Smithsonian colln, Natl Archives (Paris). Engineer with French military forces in Louisiana, sketch artist. Reference G&W. Source "Drawings by A De Batz in Louisiana

1732–1735." 1927. Smithsonian Institution with signature example. No current auction record.

De Batz arrived from France soon after the settlement of New Orleans. His drawings are of Indians as untouched by whites as those depicted earlier by Jacques LeMoyne in Florida and by John White in Virginia. The De Batz drawings show the Acolapissa chief and his family alongside their cabin in 1732; Buffalo Tamer the chief of the Tunica with wife and child; Illinois, Fox, and Atakapa Indians near New Orleans in 1735; Choctaw warriors, etc.

The drawings are meaningful ethnologically in terms of religion, wood carvings, political successions, obligations to widows and orphaned children, pets, games, costumes, etc. For example, one sketch indicates domesticated whooping crane "as tame and familiar as dung-hill fowls."

DE BEAUMONT, Charles Édouard. Born Lannion, France 1821, died Paris, France 1888. French landscape and genre painter, lithographer, illustrator. Work in French museums. References BEN - CHA - MAL. Sources COS-HUT - PAF. Oil 17½ × 23¼" *Shipboard Walk* sold 10/24/69 in Switzerland for $1,100 at auction. No signature example.

De Beaumont was the son of the sculptor Jean Baptiste Beaumont and the pupil of the painter Boissellier. He began exhibiting in the Paris Salon in 1838 with landscapes of Cernay. Genre paintings followed a trip to Italy in 1847, and paintings in the style of the 18th century were exhibited beginning 1853. A founder of the society, his greatest fame in France came from watercolors, from illustrations for magazines and books, and from lithographs.

The standard references do not place de Beaumont in the US, although G&W does record an unrelated John P Beaumont of Boston who exhibited in 1834 a portrait of Black Hawk. COS, however, lists six lithographs from de Beaumont with California subjects, all printed by Chez Aubert in Paris.

DECAMP, Ralph Earll. Born Attica, NY 1858, died Chicago, Ill 1936. Montana landscape painter, muralist, illustrator, photographer. Work in Montana Hist Soc, Montana Club, law library of State Capitol Bldg, Helena, Mont. No reference. Sources BDW-WNW-Britzman, Linderman, Renner books on Charles Russell-*Montana Post* 2/76 (Mont Hist Soc newsletter). No auction record or signature example. Photo of DeCamp, p 1 newsletter.

DeCamp spent his childhood near Milwaukee where he studied art with W A Sydaten. In 1871 the family moved to Moorhead, Minn in the Red River Valley. DeCamp operated a threshing business while painting and teaching. When his wife died, he spent 1881 studying at the Penn School of Art. In 1885 DeCamp was commissioned by the Northern Pacific RR to paint in Yellowstone Park. The next 50 years he lived in Helena, working as a draftsman and painting in his spare time. With Charles Russell he founded the Helena Sketch Club about 1890. In 1912 and 1927 he was commissioned to paint landscape murals for the Montana Capitol.

The ACM catalog on its Russell collection mentions that Russell, Paxson, and DeCamp met at the Schatzlein home in Butte. This brought together "Montana's triumvirate of outstanding artists." Newsletter. Linderman in his "Recollections of Charles Russell" (U of Okla Press, Norman 1963) quotes Russell on DeCamp's landscape in the Montana Club as "that old boy can sure paint the wettest water. You can hear his rivers ripple." Russell then painted out DeCamp's doe and added his own. After Russell died, DeCamp worked on Russell's painting *Finding the Trail*.

DE CORA, Angel (or Hinook Mahiwi Kalinaka, Fleecy Clouds Wafting into Place, or Mrs William H Dietz). Born Dakota Cnty, Neb 1871, died Northampton, Mass 1919. Winnebago painter, illustrator, muralist, teacher. Work (murals) in Carlisle Indian School. No reference. Sources AIP-BDW. No auction record or signature example.

Miss De Cora was educated at Hampton Institute in Hampton, Va and studied art in Boston. An instructor at Carlisle, she had work published in "The Middle Five; Indian Boys at School" by Francis LaFlesche in 1900. "Old Indian Legends" published in 1901 contained 14 of her Dakota illustrations. She exhibited in Paris in 1910.

DE FOREST, Henry J. Born Rothesay, NB Can 1860, died Calgary, Alberta, Can 1924. Canadian landscape painter of the Western mountains. No reference. Source CAN. No current auction record or signature example.

De Forest studied at the South Kensington SA in London, the Julien Academy in Paris, and in Edinburgh. After a long sketching trip, he settled in Vancouver in 1898. "Ardently Victorian, he was inclined at first to rather literal interpretation, but later affected more vigorous and broader brush work." CAN. He made many paintings of the mountains near Banff.

DE FOREST, Lockwood. Born NYC 1850, died Santa Barbara, Cal 1932. Cal landscape painter, architect, writer. ANA 1891, NA 1898. Work in Smith Col, Herron AI (Indianapolis), Cleveland MA. References A32 (obit)-FIE-MAL-SMI. Source WHO 32. No current auction record but the published estimate is $300 to $400. No signature example.

De Forest was educated in NYC and in Europe. He studied with Herman Corrode in Rome in 1869 and in NYC in 1870 with F E Church and James Hart. After extensive travel in Egypt, Syria, and Greece 1875–78, he spent 1881–82 in India where he founded workshops for the revival of woodcarving. He collected specimens of Indian and Tibetan handicrafts for museums in the US, England, and India. "Indian Domestic Architecture" was published in 1885 and "Illustrations of Design" in 1912. Painting titles were *The Rameseum Thebes* and *Mission Canyon, Santa Barbara.*

DE GRANDMAISON (Grandmaison), Nicolas (Nicola de). Born Moscow, Russia 1892 (or 1895), living Banff, Alberta, Can 1970. Canadian painter of Indian portraits in pastel. Assoc member RCA. Work in Woolaroc MFA (Bartlesville), Nat Mus of Canada (Ottawa), Glenbow Fnd of Calgary (Alberta), portraits in Manitoba Law Soc. Reference A70. Source PAW. No current auction record or signature example.

De Grandmaison was captured by the Germans while serving as an officer in the Russian Army during WWI. He then studied in Paris and at St. John's Wood SA in London before emigrating to Canada in 1923. His specialty became pastel portraits of Indians who according to his practice signed their portraits. "One of his works was a portrait of *High Eagle* the last survivor of the Custer massacre." PAW. Another was a pastel portrait 20×14″ of *John Hunter*. De Grandmaison began exhibiting at the RCA in 1943 and in California in 1959.

DE GRAZIA, Ettore (Ted). Born Morenci, Ariz 1909, living Tucson, Ariz 1976. Impressionist Western painter, illustrator, muralist, lithographer. Work *Way of the Cross,* Kino colln. Reference A76. Sources ACO-AHI 3/49-WAI 72-WHO 70. No current auction record. Signature example AHI 3/49.

Ted De Grazia, son of a copper miner, graduated from high school at 23, delayed because of four years spent in Italy with his family beginning 1920. The Depression closed the mines so he went to the University to learn to paint. After dropping out of the University for a brief business career, he went to Mexico about 1942, studying fresco techniques with Rivera and Orozco. De Grazia returned to Tucson, building his own adobe studio: "I am intimately acquainted with every adobe in my studio. I put them up." When a visitor commented, "My, what attractive ruins," De Grazia replied, "Yes! All in a lifetime." Illustrations for greeting cards brought him attention. In 1944–45 he was awarded his delayed BA degrees in both music and art at U of Arizona. His MA thesis was "Relation of Color and Sound."

Rivera said in 1942, "His paintings greatly interest me because of his brilliant artistic gift," while Orozco wrote, "He is able to go from simple and graceful movement to deep understanding of human misery." He is also the author of "De Grazia Paints the Yaqui Easter" and "De Grazia and His Mountain."

DE HAAN, Chuck. Referred to in COW as a painter from Fort Worth, Tex.

DE HAVEN, Franklin. Born Bluffton, Ind 1856, died NYC 1934. Colorist landscape painter. ANA 1902, NA 1920. Work in NGA, BM, Butler AI (Youngstown, Ohio). References A36 (obit)-BEN-FIE-MAL-SMI. Sources MSL-

SCH-WHO 32. Oil *Beach Scene* sold 1/28/70 for $400 at auction. No signature example.

Frank De Haven—known to his fellow artists as "Pop"—bought his first paints with his earnings at 16. It was not until 1886 that he became the pupil of George H Smille in NYC. His painting *Indian Camp Near Custer* is in the Brooklyn Museum. *Castle Creek Canyon, S Dak* is in the National Gallery. "His subjects are simple and poetical. His chief interest is to manipulate his color so as to make his canvas the means of imparting an emotion that he himself has experienced." MSL. He was also a musician and a maker of violins.

DEHN, Adolf Arthur. Born Waterville, Minn 1895, died NYC 1968. Painter of social satire, landscape watercolorist, illustrator, lithographer. NA 1961 (graphics). Work in MMA, MOMA, WMAA, BM, AIC. References A70 (obit)-BEN-MAL. Sources AAT-ALA-APT-ARI-CAA-CON-DEP-SHO-WHO 68. No current auction record but the estimated price of a watercolor 18×24″ of a Colorado landscape would be $1,000 to $1,200 at auction in 1976. Signature example CON.

Adolf Dehn, the great-grandson of pioneers, was the pupil of the Minneapolis AI 1914–17 and of Boardman Robinson at the ASL 1917–18. About 1921 he traveled in Germany, France, and England, then remained in Vienna until 1929. After 1930 his studio was in NYC. He worked in black and white drawings and in lithography entirely until 1937, afterward almost entirely in watercolor.

Dehn taught at Colorado Springs FA Center in the summers of 1941 and 1942. He painted landscapes in Colorado both before and later, giving "the Southwest a more muscular treatment" in lithographs and watercolors. ALA.

DELANO, Gerard Curtis. Born Marion, Mass 1890, living Denver, Colo 1968. Traditional Western painter of the Navaho. Member CAA. Reference MAL. Sources ACO-AHI 8/68-COW-EIT-GWP-HAR-WAI 71,72. No current auction record. Signature example GWP. (See illustration 77.)

Delano, descendant of a 1621 Pilgrim, began his art studies in New Bedford, Mass. In 1910 he became the pupil of George Bridgman at the ASL and of Dean Cornwell, Harvey Dunn, and N C Wyeth at the Grand Central School of Art. He was a successful commercial artist and illustrator in NYC until WWI. He first visited the West in 1919, working as a hand on a Colorado ranch. In 1920 he homesteaded at Cataract Creek in Colorado, building his own dirt-roof studio. He commuted to NYC for commercial art assignments. In 1933 during the Depression, he moved West permanently. In 1937 he sold *Western Story Magazine* a series of illustrated articles on the development of the West.

After 1940 Delano was enabled to paint full time. In 1943 he visited the Navaho Reservation: "Arizona's picturesque settings provide to my mind the greatest possible opportunity for pictorial beauty. The People are themselves naturally artistic. I feel a great sympathy for them. They have survived a life of hardship, yet have done so with heads held proudly high." AHI. Delano worked in oil and watercolor. His "art is exceptional for the strong sense of design, the color, and the simplicity of composition." GWP.

DELESSARD (or Dellessard), Auguste Joseph. Born Paris 1827, died probably Paris after 1891. French portrait, landscape, interior painter, engraver. References BEN-G&W-MAL. Source, oil *Landscape of the Rocky Mountains* sold 1909 in London for $50 at auction. Oil

$25\frac{1}{2} \times 22''$ *Landscape* sold 10/18/73 for $992 at auction in Switzerland. Signature example p 368 ANT 3/75.

He exhibited at the Salon de Paris from 1844 to 1882. He was working in NYC and exhibiting at the NA in 1851 and 1858–60s. He exhibited at the American Art-Union 1849–52.

DELLENBAUGH, Frederick Samuel. Born McConnelsville, Ohio 1853, died NYC 1935. Artist-explorer known for Colorado River subjects, topographer, author. Work in MAI. References A36 (obit)-BEN-DABS-FIE. Sources ANT 1/62-KEN 6/70-POW. No current auction record. Signature example p 163 DEL. (See illustration 78.)

Son of a doctor, Dellenbaugh attended Buffalo, NY public schools and studied art in NYC, Munich, and Paris, the pupil of Carolus Duran and at the Julien Academy. At 17 he was chosen as artist for Major Powell's second Colorado River expedition 1871–73. Dellenbaugh sketched for the geologists on the three-year survey, helped with the mapping, and carried the first Grand Canyon maps on horseback to Salt Lake City. In 1871 the party started by boat down the Green and Colorado to Kaibab Plateau. In 1872 the journey was on horseback to the bottom of the Grand Canyon and back to Kaibab Plateau. In 1873 Dellenbaugh made his ride to Salt Lake City. In 1875 he was back in the Canyon, and in 1876 in the vicinity of Mt Dellenbaugh. In 1885 he went by rail to New Mexico, Arizona, and California, with sidetrips to mountain summits and passes and canyons. In 1899 Dellenbaugh was again in the Green River area.

This adventure of his youth set the pattern of Dellenbaugh's life, in his continuing involvement with Indians, the Grand Canyon, and adventure. He was one of the artists on the 1899 Harriman Alaska Expedition, with paintings reproduced in the reports. His first book was "The North Americans of Yesterday" in 1901, and his "Romance of the Colorado River" was written in 1902 with illustrations by Dellenbaugh, Thomas Moran, Holmes, and Mollhausen and photos by Jackson. Other voyages and additional books carried on the scientific record. A charming man, he married a famous actress Harriet Rogers Otis.

DEL MUE, Maurice August. Born Paris, France 1875, died probably Marin Cnty, Cal 1955. Cal landscape painter, muralist, teacher. Work in Comparative MA, Golden Gate Park Mus, Walters colln (all San Francisco); murals in schools and Hamilton Field Air Base. References A41-BEN-FIE-MAL. Source BDW. No auction record or signature example.

Listed paintings include *Late Afternoon in the Sierras, West Winds,* and *Forest Knolls.* He was a supervisor for the Federal Art Project.

DEL PINO, José Moya. Born Priego, Córdoba, Spain 1891, living San Francisco, Cal 1959. Cal portrait and landscape painter, illustrator, muralist, teacher. Member Nat Soc Mural Ptrs. Work in Art Circle (Barcelona), BM, Cal Pal of Legion of Honor, San Fran MA; murals in public and trade buildings. References A41-BEN-MAS. Source ASF. No current auction record or signature example. (See illustration 79.)

Son of a soapmaker, del Pino was raised in Alcalá la Real, Spain. At 10 he ran away as apprentice to an itinerant religious painter. At 11 he was apprenticed to a commercial painter in Granada, attending a night school of arts and crafts. From 1908 to 1911 he studied at the Academy FA in Madrid. A national scholarship sent him to Italy and Paris where he met Diego Rivera and Picasso. Forced back to Spain by WWI, he painted both travel illustrations and the King's portrait. From 1921 to 1925 he painted copies of Velásquez masterpieces for the Spanish Government, then brought the copies to the US for exhibition. Funds from Spain ran out in San Francisco where del Pino was stranded. He painted portraits, married, and settled.

His murals include one painted in 1937 on the Spanish conquest of California, and another showing a three-part history of California: the Spanish Colonial period, the 1849 gold rush, and the contemporary view. A listed painting is a view of Downieville. A teacher at the California School FA, del Pino was praised for his "sense of humor, his kindness and courtesy to all." ASF.

DEMING, Edwin Willard. Born Ashland, Ohio 1860, died NYC 1942. Painter of Indian and animal subjects in the West beginning 1887, sculptor, muralist, illustrator, writer. Member Bison Soc. Work in ACM, MMA, AMNH, Nat Mus, BM, MAI, WMAA. References A47 (obit)-BEN-FIE-MAL-SMI. Sources ACM-AIW-ANT 11/67,10/71, 2/72,10/73-CUS-HMA-ILP-IL 2/95-INS 4/08-MSL-PAW-POW-SCU-TWR-WHO 42. Gouache 14¼×20" *Attacked by Bears* sold 4/20/72 for $1,900 at auction; a bronze 12¾" *Bighorn Sheep* inscribed Copyright 1905 by E W Deming Roman Bronze Works NY sold 10/8/75 for $900 at auction. Signature example p 471 ANT 10/71. (See illustrations 80, 81.)

Deming grew up with Indian playmates in western Illinois. He studied at the ASL until 1884, then in Paris for a year with Boulanger and Lefebvre. From 1885 to 1887 he painted cycloramas. His first Western trip was in 1887 when he visited the Apaches and the Pueblo Indians in the Southwest and the Umatillas in Oregon. During 1889–90 he painted Indian portraits. His Indian paintings which were first exhibited in 1891 included *The Grand Charge That Ended the Fight* against Custer. In 1893 he teamed with fellow artist DeCost Smith traveling West to write and illustrate "Sketching Among the Sioux" and "Sketching Among the Crow Indians" for the magazine *Outing*. The last article written by the two artists, "With Gun and Palette Among the Red Skins," was illustrated by a third artist, Frederic Remington, who shared other illustrating assignments with Deming.

Deming's 1916 murals of Indian life are in the AMNH and in the MAI. His paintings *Mourning Brave* and *Buffalo Hunt* are in the National Museum. As a sculptor he modeled only a few small bronze studies between 1905 and 1910. The bronzes *The Fight* and *Mutual Surprise* are in the MMA. Deming illustrated his wife's books on Indian life. His historical painting *Landfall of Jean Nicholet* was selected for a commemorative US stamp. During WWI he served as a captain in the US Army's camouflage dept at Camp Benning, Ga.

DENNY, J G (or J C, or G J, or Gideon Jacques). Born probably Baltimore, Md 1830, died San Francisco, Cal 1886. Cal marine painter active in 1860s–70s. Reference BEN (as J C)-MAS (same). Sources ANT 12/70 (As G J),5/71 (as Gideon Jacques)-PNW (as J G). No current auction record. Oil *The Abandonment* sold in 1906 for $100 at auction. No signature example.

"California painters active" in the 1870s included "Thomas Hill, William Keith, James Hamilton, J G Denny, Arthur Nahl, Charles D Robbins," and J E Stuart. Denny "was an exhibitor at the California Art Union in 1865." ANT.

DE RYKE, Emma. Illustrator of Western scenes in "Beyond the Mississippi," Albert D Richardson's 1867 book of travel "from the great river to the great ocean. In exhaustlessness, no other country equals ours." No reference. No other source. No auction record or signature example.

Three drawings are credited to Miss De Ryke, one of Kansas, the second of New Mexico, and the third of California noted as "from a photograph." It is assumed that the three drawings were redrawn rather than made on the spot.

DE SMET, Father Pierre-Jean, SJ (Blackrobe). Born Termonde, Belgium 1801, died St Louis, Mo 1873. Sketch artist of Western and Indian subjects, Jesuit missionary, writer. References DAB-G&W. Sources AWM-WIL. No auction record or signature example.

Educated in the seminary at Malines, the young de Smet was called "Samson" for his strength at 200 lbs and 5′6″ height. He emigrated to Baltimore in 1821, entering the Jesuit novitiate there. He was chosen in 1823 for St Louis where he became a priest in 1827. His vocation as missionary to the Indians began in 1838 at Council Bluffs among the Potawatomi. In 1840 he went to Oregon. De Smet founded St Mary's Mission among the Flatheads in 1841 with Father Point, among the Kalispels, and among the Coeur d'Alenes.

Beginning 1851 Blackrobe also served as mediator between the races, even risking his life in an appeal to Sitting Bull in 1868. De Smet liked Indians, accepting their old supernatural beliefs and asking only that they grant his religion to be a more potent medicine than their own. All the people he met were willing to be his friends. DAB. De Smet wrote several books on his 180,000 miles of travels, with illustrations from his own and from Father Point's (see entry) sketches.

DE THULSTRUP, Thure (Bror Thure Thulstrup). Born Stockholm, Sweden 1848, died NYC 1930. Painter of military history, illustrator. Member SI. References A30 (obit)-BEN-DAB-FIE-MAL-SMI. Sources AIW-BAW-ILA-IND-WHO 30. No current auction record but the estimated price of a drawing 8×10″ showing subduing hostile Indians would be about $800 to $1,000 at auction in 1976. Signature example p 218 BAW.

Thulstrup, son of the Swedish secretary of naval defense, was educated as a soldier in Stockholm. In 1871 he became a captain in the French Foreign Legion, serving in Algeria and in the war with Germany. He studied topographical engineering in Paris, emigrating to Canada about 1875. He moved to Boston and NYC, where he attended the ASL, although he claimed to be self-taught. He changed his name to Thure de Thulstrup and was staff artist on *Harper's Weekly* for 20 years, covering the inaugurations of four Presidents and the visit of the Kaiser to the Tsar in 1888. During this period he produced some of the best-known paintings of American Colonial life.

There is no record of de Thulstrup having been in the American West, but his drawing *Indian Warfare—the Attack on the Village* for *Harper's Weekly* in 1885 has been reproduced for framing and is an illustration in BAW.

DE TROBRIAND, Régis Denis de Keredern. Born near Tours, France 1816, died Bayport, LI, NY 1897. Amateur painter of Western landscapes and Indian genre, US Army general, writer. Work in Post colln (NYC). Reference DAB. Source BDW. No auction record or signature example.

A French nobleman, de Trobriand graduated from the College of Tours in 1834 and received a law degree from Poitiers in 1837. Duelist, poet, and novelist, he toured the US in 1841 and returned to NYC in 1847 with his American wife. During the Civil War he became an American citizen and a general of volunteers. In 1867 he was assigned to Dakota, in 1869 to Montana, and in 1871 to Utah and Wyoming as a Regular Army colonel. An amateur painter, he recorded Indian portraits and genre, landscapes, and Western buildings.

DE VAUDRICOURT, A. Active 1835–51. Boundary survey artist. Reference G&W. Sources AIW-ANT 6/48-SUR-TEP. No auction record but the estimated price of a drawing 8×10″ of El Paso peons would be about $400 to $600 at auction in 1976. Graphics examples pp 162,4 TEP.

A lithographer, topographical draftsman, and teacher of drawing and piano, de Vaudricourt was working in New Orleans in 1835. He did lithographic work in Boston in 1844 and in NYC 1845–46.

In 1850 he worked under Emory on the US-Mexico boundary survey, along with the more widely represented artist Arthur Schott and John E Weyss. He was head of the topographic party to proceed from Indianola, Tex to El Paso, an "accomplished and gentlemanly draftsman and interpreter who has made a number of beautiful sketches of the most striking parts of our country." TEP. The only known works are *The Plaza and Church of El Paso,* a colored lithograph after his sketch, and *Rio San Pedro-Above Second Crossing,* an engraving.

DE VERE, J. Active in California 1851. Lithographic artist. Reference G&W.

Sources COS-OCA. No auction record but the estimated price of a sketch 8×10″ showing a view of the San Francisco fire in 1851 would be about $400 to $500 at auction in 1976. No signature example.

DE WOLF, Wallace Leroy. Born Chicago, Ill 1854, died Pasadena, Cal 1930. Western landscape painter, etcher, lawyer, real estate broker. Work in Union League Club, AIC, Vanderpoel colln (all Chicago), Glacier Park Comn, Springfield AA. References A31 (obit)-BEN-FIE-MAL-SMI. Source WHO 30. No current auction record but the published estimate is $300 to $400. No signature example.

De Wolf graduated Union College of Law in Chicago and practiced as a lawyer beginning 1876. He operated a real estate firm beginning 1894, and was a collector of Zorn etchings, which he gave to the AIC in 1913. He was a self-taught painter, his subject being the West. Listed titles were *Lake Louise, Hermit Range, Mojave Desert, Among the Redwoods,* and illustrations of New Mexico.

DE YONG, Joe. Born Webster Grove, Mo 1894, died Los Angeles, Cal 1975. Traditional Western painter, sculptor. Honorary member, CAA. Work in Free Public Library, Santa Barbara, Cal; mural *Up the Trail* Texas PO. References A41-MAS. Sources COW-WAI 71-WNW. No current auction record but the estimated price of an oil 20×30″ showing cowboys' evening chow would be about $1,000 to $1,500 at auction in 1976. Signature example centerfold COW. (See illustration 82.)

De Yong as a boy saw Charles Russell's paintings at the St Louis World's Fair. He was brought up in the Indian Territory, a friend of Will Rogers who taught him fancy roping. At 14 he began "riding for wages." At 17 he was in charge of cattle for Tom Mix in making a movie, continuing with Mix in Arizona as a cowboy bit player.

An attack of spinal meningitis caused deafness. During his convalescence, he wrote to Russell for advice on sculpting. The illustrated reply drew De Yong to Montana where he worked in Russell's studio from 1916 to 1926 when Russell died. De Yong became an important Western artist in his own right, a friend of other Western artists including Borein, Dixon, Frank Tenney Johnson, and Clyde Forsythe. De Yong's deafness led him to Indian sign language and to an interest in all things Indian so that he became a technical adviser on Indians for the movie industry.

DE YOUNG, Harry Anthony. Born Chicago, Ill 1893, died probably San Antonio, Tex 1956. Texas landscape painter, muralist, teacher. Work in Ill, Ind, Wis, Tex schools and Witte Mus (San Antonio). References A41-FIE-MAL. Sources TOB-WHO 42. No current auction record.

De Young studied at the AIC in 1917 and the U of Illinois, the pupil of John W Norton and Edward Lake. After service as a sergeant in the QMC in WWI, he began painting in 1919 and teaching in 1922. Beginning in 1928 his studio was in San Antonio, where he taught and in summers conducted teaching camps. His mural in the Witte Museum is *Early Basket Weaver Indians of West Texas*.

DIAZ, Cristóbal. Spanish painter and naval chaplain in Monterey, Cal late 18th century accompanying the visit of a Spanish ship. Work, a painting of the

Mission San Carlos Borromeo, was in the Soc of Cal Pioneers until it was destroyed by fire in 1906. Reference G&W. No other source, auction record, or signature example.

DIBBLE, George Smith. Born Laie, Oahu, Hawaii 1904, living Salt Lake City, Utah 1974. Watercolor landscape painter, teacher, art critic. Work in Col of Southern Utah, Utah St U. No reference. Sources YUP-3/74 data from G S Dibble. No auction record or signature example.

George Dibble studied at the ASL 1929–30, receiving from Columbia U his BS in 1938 and his MA in 1940. He taught at the U of Utah beginning 1943 and has been visiting professor at Utah, California, and Washington colleges. Dibble has "chosen watercolor as primary means of expression. His work has at times a direct, raw-boned quality based on cubism." YUP. A newspaper art critic, Dibble has also written a textbook on watercolor materials and techniques.

DICK, George. Born Manitowoc, Wis 1916, living Albuquerque, NM 1973. Traditional Western painter of cowboys, wildlife, horses. Work in C R Smith colln. No reference. Sources COW-CRS-WAI 71,72-biographical data from George Dick. No current auction record. Signature example p 5 CRS. (See illustration 83.)

Dick was educated at the U of Michigan where he earned a BS in Forestry, becoming a biologist and game manager of the US Fish and Wildlife Service. He also traveled in Alaska as a ranger. In 1947, with no previous art training, he went to the U of New Mexico under the GI Bill, receiving his MA in art in 1951.

His teachers were Kenneth Adams and Randall Davey.

Until 1953 Dick painted mainly nonobjective subjects. Then, his game management training led him back to traditional depiction of waterfowl and mustangs: "I've only done a few landscapes. I like to have something animated in my pictures, or otherwise I get bored." WAI 71. Brown is a favorite color, and a year's painting in Jalisco, Mexico influenced experiments in mosaics and religious subjects. In 1974 Dick turned to winter scenes of cowboys and cowponies as well as Western wildlife, with a switch from predominant dark brown and golden tones into the white of winter. He has also specialized in scenes of racing quarter horses.

DICKESON, Dr Montroville Wilson. Born Philadelphia, Pa 1810, died probably there 1882. Sketch artist for the Egan *Panorama of the Monumental Grandeur of the Mississippi Valley* 1850, archaeologist, medical doctor. Panorama in University Mus (Philadelphia). Reference G&W. Sources ANT 12/49-BAR-MIS. No auction record or signature example.

Dickeson was educated in Woodbury, NJ, evidencing an interest in animals, taxidermy, and fossils. He began studying medicine in 1828. His practice was in Philadelphia. Between 1837 and 1844 he was in the Ohio and Mississippi River valleys, sketching more than a thousand Indian mounds he claimed to have opened and collecting 40,000 Indian artifacts. "Wishing to publicize his work" (BAR), Dickeson engaged the painter John J Egan to translate his sketches into a moving panorama that was tempera on muslin sheeting 7½×348'. Instead of limiting the views to landscape, Dickeson's scenes emphasized Indian genre and archaeology. The panorama opened with the Indian mounds at Marietta, Ohio, continuing down the Ohio River to the Mississippi and south. As "journalism in paint," the scenes also included news in the tornado of 1844, humor in a squatter pursued by wolves, history in the burial of De Soto, and features in a view of the distant Rockies.

The only Mississippi panorama still surviving, it was exhibited by Dr Dickeson along with his artifacts on a tour of the country in 1852. The charge was 25¢, children under 12 at 12½¢. The handbill said, "Dr Dickeson will lecture on the Antiquities and Customs of the Unhistoried Indian Tribes and also on the mounds, tumuli, fossas, &c." MIS.

DICKINSON, Darol. Born Fort Worth, Tex 1942, living near Calhan, Colo 1973. Traditional Western painter, horse portraitist. Member CCA. No reference. Sources C71 to 73-COW. No current auction record. Signature example p 25 C72 *Horse Tank Armada*.

When Dickinson was 13 his family moved to Colorado. He studied art at Colorado College, Colorado Springs. Dickinson in 1971 was the youngest member of the CAA. His specialties are horse portraits, cowhands, and genre scenes of ranch life, painted in oil. On his own ranch, he raises quarter horses and cattle.

DICKMAN, Charles John. Born Demmin, Germany 1863, died probably San Francisco, Cal 1943. Cal marine and landscape painter, muralist, lithographer. Work (murals) in commercial buildings. References A47 (obit)-FIE-MAL. Source BDW. No auction record or signature example.

Dickman studied in Europe 1896–1901, the pupil of Laurens and Constant in Paris. He had emigrated to California

as a lithographer about 1893. His specialty was marine painting but he also painted landscapes of Shasta, Lake Tahoe, Death Valley, and Tonopah, Nev. Called the "painter of California sunlight," he moved from Monterey to San Francisco about 1915.

DIEDERICH, Wilhelm Hunt. Born Hungary 1884, died NYC 1953. Sculptor specializing in animals and in figures for monuments. Member NSS. Work in MMA, Seattle AM, WMAA, Newark AM, Cleveland MA. References A41-BEN-FIE-MAL-SMI. Sources ALA-AMA-NSS-SCU. No current auction record but the estimated price of a bronze 10″ high showing a cowboy mounting his horse would be about $1,200 to $1,500 at auction in 1976. Sculpture example p 50 NSS *Cats*.

Diederich was educated in Switzerland. At 16 he went to Boston to stay with his grandfather, the painter William Morris Hunt. He attended Milton Academy until he was 18, then went West to live as a cowboy for two years in Wyoming, New Mexico, and Arizona. When he was 20 he returned East to become the pupil of the sculptor Paul Manship at the PAFA, although he listed himself in A41 as the pupil of his grandfather. Diederich also studied in Rome and Paris. From 1911 to 1924 he exhibited busts, dogs, and decorations at the Salon of French Artists and at the Salon of Autumn: "When Diederich reduced a jockey and his prancing horse to a few bronze planes and nervous curves, it was in the interest of a decorative silhouette." ALA.

DIXON, Lafayette Maynard. Born Fresno, Cal 1875, died Tucson, Ariz 1946. Important traditional painter interpreting Western life, muralist, illustrator. Work in ACM, San Diego FA Gall, Pasadena AI, De Young Mus, BM, SW Mus; murals in ships, schools, hotels, libraries, museums. References A47 (obit)-FIE-MAL-SMI. Sources AHI 10/72-ANT 8/66,6/68-AIW-ALABOR-BWB-CAP-CON-COW-CRS-GWP-HAR-HON-PAW-PNW-POW-TSF-TWR-WAI 71,72-WHO 46. Oil *The Golden Range* sold 3/8/71 for $3,500 at auction in San Fran; oil *Ledges of Sunland* 25×30¼" signed and dated sold 12/12/75 for $8,500. Signature example p 36 CON.

Maynard Dixon was descended from Virginia aristocracy who had moved to the sandy flats of the San Joaquin Valley. Frail as a youth, he taught himself to draw. At 16 he sent sketches to Remington, receiving encouraging comment. He was led to attend the School of Design in San Francisco in 1891, but found the approach too formal. He became a cowpuncher, wandering over Arizona, New Mexico, and southeast California. His first job in art was in 1895 as a newspaper illustrator in San Francisco, sketching on the spot for crime and feature stories. He also became a key figure in the bohemian life. As his draftsmanship and sense of design improved, he did illustrations for magazines and books. When he was 23, his drawings were published in the Los Angeles magazine *Land of Sunshine*. He made his first trip to NM in 1900. In 1901 he and Borein headed Northwest on horseback. His sketches were sold to *Harper's*.

After the San Francisco earthquake of 1906 destroyed Dixon's accumulated work, he moved to NYC as an illustrator. In 1909 he was again in the Northwest, sketching Indians in Idaho and Nevada. When he returned to San Francisco, his studio was a central point for the Western art world. More of his time was devoted to easel painting, and by 1920 he was able to minimize illustration work. He was considered the leading desert painter, the most successful of the Westerners painting the Southwest. As a colorist he was said to have been influenced by Maxfield Parrish in the blue of the lava ridges, but it is probably truer to say that Dixon painted the earth and sky colors he saw simplified as his style grew increasingly modern. In the 1930s Dixon devoted his time to murals. He died of asthma after completing a mural of the Grand Canyon.

DODGE, Aydee (or Adee). Navaho painter. Work in Ariz St U. No reference. Sources AHI 12/58,7/59,8/65-AIP-COW. No auction record. Signature example p 5 AHI 12/58 *The Emergence*.

DODGE, William De Leftwich. Born Liberty, Va 1867, died NYC 1935. Muralist, illustrator. Member Soc of Mural Painters. Work in Lib Cong, NY State Cap (Albany). References A36 (obit)-BEN-DABS-FIE-MAL-SMI. Sources AAC-ALA-AMP-HOE-ISH-MSL-WHO 34. Oil 45×36" *My Pergola* sold at auction in 1972 for $700. Signature example *Century* magazine vol 20, p 261.

Dodge was brought to Munich at the age of 14 by his mother to start his art studies. Later he became a pupil of Gérôme in Paris. Then, although only 25, he was chosen to paint the mural for the largest dome at the Columbian Expos. He "led a most confined existence being obliged to climb up some 300 feet of ladders and scaffolding every morning, and sometimes not descending to earth again until past midnight." AMP.

In all official listings Dodge did not mention his work as an illustrator. However his work appeared in *Century* illustrating a series of Western articles, sharing the commission with Remington and Gilbert Gaul. He is also listed by Hoeber as starting his career by showing *Death of Minnehaha* and *Burial of a Brave* in the Paris Salon.

DONAHUE, Vic. Born Nebraska 1917, living Tucson, Ariz 1968. Traditional Western painter, illustrator. No reference. Source COW. No auction record. Signature example p 199 COW.

Donahue had previously maintained studios in Vermont and in Omaha, Neb. His specialty is illustrations of Western subjects for magazines, books, and calendars.

DONSHEA, Clement. National advertising illustrator active in NYC in 1924 who painted some cowboy subjects. Donshea listed his specialties in AAC as women's figures and pretty girl heads for national advertising. No reference. Source AAC. No auction record or signature example.

DOUGAL, William H. Born New Haven, Conn 1822, died Washington, DC 1895. Eastern sketch artist in San Francisco 1849–50, engraver, draftsman. References FIE-G&W. Sources AIW-TEP-1/30/74 data from Catherine Hoover, Cal Hist Soc. Oil 29½×39½" *A View of Georgetown* sold 12/05/70 for $2,750 at auction. Signature example *View of San Fran from Yerba Buena Island* p 248 "Letters of an Artist in the Gold Rush" Cal Hist Soc Quarterly 22, 1943. Portrait photo p 234 ibid.

Dougal grew up in New Haven and was apprenticed at 15 to the NYC map engravers Sherman & Smith. About 1845 he established his own engraving studio in Washington, DC. His assign-

ments were government publications and bank notes. He made engravings for the reports on the Wilkes Expedition and Marcy's Expedition to the Red River. When the 1849 gold bug bit, he and his associates bought a ship to convey goods and passengers for the seven-month voyage. In San Francisco by Nov 1849, he set up a livery and grocery store. He then sold out July 1850, when he decided to return to Washington, DC. He visited the mines only as a tourist and went back to the East in November 1850 via Panama.

Dougal sketched San Francisco as he saw it, the mission and homes and a panoramic drawing of San Francisco from Nob's Hill. The sketches were found in Dougal's portfolio after he died. Dougal married in Washington, DC in 1851, continuing to work as an engraver, including work done with James D Smillie on some of the Emory report plates on the Mexican boundary survey where the artists were Schott, Weyss, and de Vaudricourt.

DOUGHERTY, Paul. Born Brooklyn, NY 1877, died probably Carmel, Cal 1947. Eastern marine and Western landscape painter. ANA 1906, NA 1907, NIAL. Work in MMA, NGA, COR, AIC, NGC, Luxembourg (Paris), etc. References A47-BEN-ENB-FIE-MAL-SMI. Sources AIC-AMA-ANT 12/73-COR-DEP-M31-MSL-NA 74-WHO 46. Oil 40×50" *Landscape of Finistère* sold 1969 for $1,200 at auction. Signature example ✳27 *Shadowed Mesa* "Painting-Sculpture by Living Americans" MOMA 1930.

Son of a NYC lawyer, Dougherty graduated Bklyn Poly Inst in 1896 and NY Law School 1898 but abandoned legal practice for art. Dougherty studied with Henri in NYC, then studied perspective and form with Constantin Hertzberg, leaving for Europe in 1900 for five years in the galleries of Paris, London, Florence, Venice, and Munich. He exhibited in Paris as early as 1901, experimenting with sculpture but specializing in marine paintings. "It is the ocean itself that interests him." AMA. He conveys "a profound impression of its depth, latent cruelty, and rhythmic power of wave." MSL.

In addition to marine subjects, he painted cloud, mountain, and plain. By 1930 he was living in California. Listed Western titles include *Lake Louise* and *Cañon After Rain*.

DOW, Arthur Wesley. Born Ipswich, Mass 1857, died NYC 1922. Eastern landscape painter, etcher, teacher, writer. Member Soc Western Artists. Work in Teachers Col (Columbia U), Ipswich Pub Lib. References A22 (obit)-BEN-FIE-MAL-SMI. Sources AMA-ALA-DEP-190-WHO 22-1/31/74 data from W J Mahoney, Teachers Col. Oil *Landscape in Brittany* sold 4/15/70 for $175 at auction. In comparison, A24 lists "Paintings, drawings, prints by Prof Arthur Wesley Dow and his collection of Japanese prints, together with objects and books. Sold for $18,688. ₩397 *Enchanted Mesa* 14×20″ $80. ₩412 *The Wall of the Grand Canyon* 12×18″ $70. ₩419 *Yellowstone Park* 18×24″ $550." No signature example.

After a classical education privately and in public schools, Dow did not begin to study painting until 1880 in Boston, modeling his work after the French Barbizon landscapes. This carried over to his years in Paris, 1884–89, when he was the pupil of Boulanger, Lefebvre, Doucet, and Delance. His influence was Puvis de Chavannes and Whistler, not the Impressionists whose life style was opposed to Dow's strict Puritan background. He became curator of Japanese prints at the BMFA, an intimate of Fenellosa and a developer of a personal system of teaching art. When he became director of the FA department of Teachers College in 1904, he taught the future teachers so his impact on the country's educational system was important. His concept was that painting involved selection of forms without regard to nature and that the artist must begin with the whole object rather than its components.

Dow visited the West—Grand Canyon, Yosemite, Crater Lake—as a mature landscape painter. His Grand Canyon oils were exhibited in 1913 as the Armory Show closed, providing confrontation between Dow's 19th-century values and those of the new era. In contrast, Dow's importance as a teacher of painters was that he prepared his students to be accepting of modern ideas, thus helping talents like Max Weber and Georgia O'Keeffe.

DOZIER, Otis. Born Forney, Tex 1904, living Dallas, Tex 1976. Contemporary Texas painter of landscapes and genre, lithographer, muralist. Work in MMA, WMAA, Dallas MFA, Denver AM, Newark AM; murals in Texas post offices. References A76-MAL. Sources AAT-APT-CAP-M50-T20-TOB-SHO. No current auction record but the oil *Fishermen* illustrated in M50 was offered for sale at $600 in 1950. Signature example plate 32 M50.

Dozier studied at the Aunspaugh Art School in Dallas. He has lived and worked in Texas most of his life, exhibiting nationally beginning 1932, with one-man exhibitions beginning 1948. He taught at the Colorado Springs FAC from 1939 to 1945, then began as instructor at the Dallas MFA in 1945. He also studied with Boardman Robinson 1945–49. His subjects are figure, landscape, and still life, mostly in oil. His work is characterized as strong and bold.

143

DRAYTON, Joseph. Active 1819 to after 1842. One of the two artists with the Wilkes exploring expedition, illustrator, portrait painter, engraver. References BEN-DAB (under Agate)-FIE-G&W. Source NJA. No auction record or signature example.

Drayton was in Philadelphia from 1819 to about 1838, an engraver in aquatint of Scotch landscapes, a line engraver for book illustrations, and a print colorist. In 1838 Alfred T Agate and Drayton joined the Wilkes expedition as artists, sketching the coast of Antarctica, 280 Pacific islands, and the American northwest coast. Surveyed were 800 miles of streams and coastline in the Oregon country, as well as overland Indian trails. At the conclusion of the voyage in 1842, Wilkes wrote, "To Messrs Drayton and Agate, the Artists of the Expedition, I feel it due to make known how constantly and faithfully they have performed their duties. The illustrations of these volumes will bear ample testimony to the amount of their labors, and the accuracy with which they have been executed." DAB.

To illustrate the Wilkes report Drayton was "employed for some years in Washington." FIE. The first volume was issued in 1844, and Wilkes was involved in publishing the reports until the outbreak of the Civil War. The last scientific report did not appear until 1874.

DRESEL, Emil. Active 1853 to 1859 in San Francisco, Cal. Lithographic artist, lithographer. Work in ACM. Reference G&W. Sources ACM-COS-OCA. No auction record but the estimated price of a watercolor sketch 8×10" of a Scott's Bar store would be about $800 to $1,000 at auction in 1976. Signature example OCA.

Dresel during the 1850s worked on the West Coast. He traveled in Oregon to sketch views there. After 1855 he was a partner in Kuchel & Dresel, lithographers in San Francisco.

DUBÉ, Louis Theodore. Born Quebec, Can 1861, living France 1929. Genre painter and miniaturist. References BEN-MAL. Source DWF. No current auction record but the estimated price of an oil 20×30" showing Indians hunting buffalo would be about $1,500 to $2,000 at auction in 1976. Signature DWF as J Dietz.

Dubé was a pupil of Gérôme. Credited to the French School, he exhibited at the Society of the Salon of French Artists ending 1929. His work *The Buffalo Chase* ascribed in 1966 to "J. Dietz" was called closer "to the more elegant manner of the Düsseldorf painters. Certainly, the artist has been subjected to the lure of the West, the buffalo herds and the Indians." DWF.

DUDLEY, Jack. Active 1972. California painter of Latin American and Mexican genre scenes including Indians. Source p 1 AHI 10/72 with signature example. No auction record.

Dudley has exhibited widely in California. His work is based on extensive travels.

DUER, Douglas. Born Baltimore Cnty, Md 1887, died Huntingdon Valley, Pa 1964. Illustrator of fiction and national advertising. Member SI. References A27-FIE-MAS. Sources AAC-letter from Leslie Duer. No auction record although it is estimated that the price of a genre Western painting would be about $900 to $1,100 at auction in 1976. No signature example. (See illustration 84.)

Duer was educated at Marston's School for Boys in Baltimore. During 1908–9 he was a student of Chase at the Academy FA in Philadelphia. When he became a Pyle student, his studio was in Wilmington, Del 1909–17. In WWI he served overseas as a camouflage specialist. From about 1920 his studio was at 51 W 10 Street in NYC. After 1929 he moved to Philadelphia, finally locating in Huntingdon Valley in 1940.

Duer worked mainly in oil and tempera, always from costumed models rather than photographs.

DUFAULT, Joseph. See James, Will.

DUMAS, Jack. Born Seattle, Wash 1916, living Bainbridge Island, Wash 1966. Illustrator specializing in wildlife. No reference. Source ILA. No auction record. Signature example *Argosy* 9/59 *Trouble at Crazy Woman Creek*.

Dumas studied at the Cornish School of Allied Arts and the Seattle Acad of Arts, the pupil of Ernest Norling. He became an artist for the *Los Angeles Examiner* and then a commercial artist before serving in the Army 1941–46 in an engineering battalion. After the war he worked as an illustrator in San Francisco alongside Stan Galli and Fred Ludekins. Dumas returned to Washington, illustrating for Western advertisers and Eastern magazines and paperback books.

DUMOND, Frederick Melville. Born Rochester, NY 1867, died Monrovia, Cal 1927. Animal painter known in Europe for interpretations of the Southwestern desert. References A27 (obit)-BEN-MAL-SMI. Source BDW-SCA. Oil

25½ ×19½" *The Smoker Louis XIII* dated 1888 sold 12/7/73 for $294 at auction in Paris. Oil 24×36" *The Petrified Forest* sold 5/18/65 for $140 at auction. No signature example.

Of French parents, DuMond studied in Paris, the pupil of Lefebvre, Constant, Cormon, and Laurens. He exhibited at the Salon in Paris in 1893. The brother of the more famous artist Frank Vincent DuMond, Frederick lived and painted in the Southwest from 1909 to 1912. In 1913 he homesteaded in the Mojave Desert.

DUMOND (du Mond, Dumond), Frank Vincent. Born Rochester, NY 1865, died NYC 1951. Painter, muralist, illustrator, teacher. Member NA 1906, NIAL, Soc Mural Painters. References A53 (obit)-BEN (as Frank T)-FIE-MAL-SMI-WHO 44. Sources ALA-AMA-COW-HOE-ISH-NA 74-WCE. No auction record. Signature example WCE, p 188.

In 1888 DuMond studied in Paris under Boulanger, Lefebvre, and Constant. He contributed *Monastic Life,* a painting, to the Columbian Expos and worked on murals for the San Francisco Expos. His greatest influence in the world of art was as a teacher. He taught life classes briefly at Pratt Inst, Brooklyn, and then for 49 years at the ASL.

He illustrated for *Harper's Weekly* and *Century* including Western subjects. Hoeber in his "Painters of Western Life" lists DuMond as a Western painter and resident of the Southwest. Hoeber may have confused Frank with his brother Frederick.

DUNCANSON, Robert S. Born NY State about 1817, died Detroit, Mich 1872. Cincinnati portrait, landscape, and genre painter. Work in Taft Mus (Cincinnati), Detroit IA, City AM (St Louis), COR. References G&W-MAL. Sources ANT 1/46,7/64,8/67,4/68; 4,6/74-BAR-CAH-STI. Oil *The Ohio River* sold 11/16/68 for $5,250 at auction. Signature example p 67 ANT 7/64.

After spending his youth with his Scotch-Canadian father in Montreal, Canada, Duncanson joined his black mother near Cincinnati in 1841. He had studied art in Canada and had been sent to Scotland for further study by the Cincinnati branch of the Anti-Slavery League before 1840. He began exhibiting in Cincinnati in 1842, maintaining his home there except for two more visits to Europe and extended travel in the US. Duncanson's first major commission about 1850 was for Belmont, the Cincinnati Longworth home that is now the Taft Museum. He was said to have been teaching in Montreal in 1861.

His work is typical of the Hudson River School, eg Whittredge and Wyant whose paintings he had seen in Cincinnati. It is said that his work followed scenes in 19th-century literature and that he continued in the romantic tradition after it had gone out of fashion. His painting *Waiting for a Shot* dated 1869 depicts a hunter using a prairie fire to drive buffalo toward him.

DUNN, Harvey T. Born Manchester, SD 1884, died Tenafly, NJ 1952. Important magazine illustrator of the prairie. NA 1945, SI 1913. Work in Harmsen colln, Smithsonian Inst, So Dak St Col (Brookings). References A53 (obit)-MAL. Sources AAC-COW-DCC-DIC-HAR-ILA-ILG-ILP-TWR-WHO 52. No current auction record but the estimated price of an oil 20×30″ showing wagons moving West would be about $5,000 to $7,000 at auction in 1976. Signature example p 53 ILA.

Dunn was born in a sod house in the Red Stone Valley, Dakota Territory.

Large and powerful, he earned his art tuition by "sod-busting" for neighboring homesteaders. After rural school he studied art in 1901 at State College, Brookings, the pupil of Ada Caldwell, before attending the AIC 1902–4. On invitation from Howard Pyle, he studied at Chadds Ford 1904–6, becoming deeply influenced by Pyle's philosophy. Dunn opened his own studio in Leonia, NJ in 1906, an immediate success as an illustrator. In WWI, Dunn was an official artist with the AEF.

Dunn was a prolific magazine illustrator specializing in Western subjects. He also taught at Grand Central School of Art. His pupils included Burt Procter, Von Schmidt, Delano, Dye, Shope, Clymer, Hal Stone, Tepper, Edmund F Ward, Frank Street, Jack Roberts, Robert Wagoner, Dean Cornwell. In 1950 Dunn gave to South Dakota State College a collection of his paintings on prairie subjects. The gift is commemorated on a roadside marker near Dunn's boyhood home. A memorial art center was dedicated at the college to house "The Harvey Dunn Colln and Archives." The more popular paintings like *The Prairie Is My Garden* were reproduced for sale as prints. Dunn's favorite subjects were the sod-busting pioneers, not the shoot-em-ups of Remington and Russell. He called the purpose of an illustration the setting of the stage for the reader to imagine the story. His intent was to select an incident not described in detail in the text so the illustration could control the mood. In painting, Dunn first established the darker tones of the design to provide the basic pattern for color values and contrasts. He taught that figure drawing started with the head, which had to be kept most interesting.

DUNNELL, John Henry. Born Millbury, Mass 1813, died NY 1904. Businessman painting in Cal 1849–51, 1857–60. References A05 (obit)-G&W-MAL-SMI. Source HON. No current auction record but the published estimate is $400 to $600. No signature example.

Dunnell was a NY businessman and soldier who painted for recreation. NY and NJ views were exhibited at the NA 1847–48. In Coloma, Cal on business in 1849 Dunnell made three views of Sutter's Mill while also serving as justice of the peace. When he returned to California in 1857 for the Singer Mfg Co, he exhibited at the Mechanics Fair.

DUNTON, William Herbert ("Buck"). Born Augusta, Me 1878, died Albuquerque, NM 1936. Important Western illustrator, painter, muralist, lithographer. Member Taos SA 1912. Work in ACM, ANS, Witte Mem Mus, MNM, the White House; murals in Mo St Capitol. References A38 (obit)-BEN-FIE-MAL-SMI. Sources AIW-AMA-ANS-COW-CUS-HAR-HMA-ILA-PIT-POW-TAL-TSF-WHO 36. Oil 26×39″ *Open Range* sold 5/23/73 for $9,500 at auction. Signature example p 76 PIT *The Shower*. (See illustration 85.)

W Herbert Dunton worked as a ranch hand in his youth. He studied at Cowles Art School in Boston, Mass and briefly at the ASL in 1912, the pupil of Joseph De Camp and E L Blumenschein who told Dunton about Taos. In 1912 Dunton opened his summer studio in Taos. He was invited to join Blumenschein, Sharp, Couse, Phillips, and Berninghaus in the formation of the Taos SA. Dunton worked as an illustrator on Western life for the popular magazines, sketching the West in the summer and composing his illustrations to order in the winter. He settled permanently in Taos in 1921 to avoid the pressure of illustration deadlines. A picturesque character familiarly known as Buck, he was one of the most popular of the Taos painters. He wrote "Painters of Taos" for *American Maga-*

zine of Art in 1922, emphasizing the advantages of light, color, and Indian life.

In Taos, Dunton was a successful illustrator for *Harper's* and *Scribner's,* his subject matter usually Western or outdoors like that of his good friend Philip R Goodwin. He also created book jackets for Western classics. In addition to his illustrations, he painted and exhibited widely, keeping his paintings simple and nostalgic: "The West has passed— more's the pity. In another 25 years, the old-time westerner will have gone with the buffalo and the antelope. I'm going to hand down to posterity a bit of the unadulterated real thing." PIT.

DURKIN, John. Born probably in the West 1868, died NYC 1903. Illustrator for *Harper's Weekly* in the 1880s, specializing in lumber operations in the West. References A03 (obit)-MAL-SMI. Source AIW. No auction record or signature example.

In 1886 a party of *Harper's Weekly* illustrators including Durkin, Horace Bradley, and Charles Graham made a lengthy tour of the South. The trip was described in "The House of Harper" published in 1912. Durkin moved to NYC from the West about 1891.

DU TANT, Charles. Born Eschiti, Okla 1908, living Taos, NM 1947. Modern Taos landscape painter. No reference. Source TAL. No auction record. Signature example ✕20 TAL.

DYCK, Paul. Born Chicago 1917, living Rimrock, Ariz 1976. Western painter, illustrator, author. Work in Phoenix Mus, Mus Northern Ariz, Harmsen colln. Reference A76. Sources AHI 10/71-COW-WAI 71,72. No auction record. Signature example p 44 AHI 10/71.

Dyck's parents were pioneers in Calgary near the Blackfoot reservation. He grew up among Alberta's Cheyenne, Crow, and Blackfoot Indians. Following "family tradition," he studied at Munich Academy with Johann von Skramlik as well as in Prague, Florence, Rome, and Paris. Dyck paints in egg tempera with the "old master" oil glazes. Given the Sioux name of Rainbow Hand and initiated into the peyote ritual, he lectures on American Indian culture. The painter of *The Indians of the Overland Trail* series, he wrote "Brule: The Sioux People of the Rosebud." Dyck has been a rancher in Northern Ariz since about 1950.

DYE, Charlie. Born Canon City, Colo 1906, died probably Sedona, Ariz 1972. Traditional Western painter, illustrator. Member CAA. Work in Nat Cowboy Hall of Fame. Sources AHI 11/71-C 71, 72-COW-HAR-OSR-WAI 71,72. Oil 27×24" *Seated Indian* was estimated 3/10/75 at $200 to $300 for auction in LA and sold for $1,000. Signature example p 31 AHI 11/71.

Dye was born in a cow town and rode for ranches in Colorado, Arizona, and California until he was 21. "I cannot recall a time when I was not at home on horseback, or that I didn't portray the life I led with pen and pencil." C71. During convalescence from a riding accident, he was influenced by Russell reproductions to become a commercial artist. He painted at night at the AIC and the American Academy. In 1936 he moved to NYC to become a magazine illustrator, studying at night with Harvey Dunn. He painted covers and illustrations for many of the major American publications.

His first Western easel paintings were successful. In 1960 he moved to Sedona, Ariz. In 1964 Dye, Joe Beeler, and John Hampton while on a roundup conceived the idea of the Cowboy Artists of America, an association of professional artists who paint cowboys and who are capable of working as cowboys. Dye was the second president of the CAA: "I have always tried to paint what I can remember of a life I led before I became dishonest and studied art. My old man could have forgiven me if I had turned out playing piano in a whore house, but artists rated one step below pimps in his book." OSR.

EAKINS, Thomas. Born Philadelphia, Pa 1844, died there 1916. Very important Eastern portrait, genre, and sports painter, sculptor, teacher, in the ND Badlands 1887. ANA 1902, NA same. Work in BM, AIC, GIL, COR, Jefferson Med Col, BMFA, MMA, NGA, Philadelphia MA. References A16 (obit)-BEN-CHA-DAB-ENB-FIE-MAL-SMI. Sources AAR 3/74-AIW-ALA-AMA-ANT 6/44,7/52,11/64,11/67; 5,10/70; 7,11/73; 4,11/74-ARI-ART 4/64-BAR-CAH-CAN-DAA-DBW-DEP-EAK-GIL-HMA-HUD-HUT-190-ISH-MAP-M19-MSL-SCU-STI-TSF-WHO 16. Oil 32½×45½″ *Cowboy in the Badlands* with signature example, dated 1888 sold 12/10/70 for $210,000 at auction. *Portrait statuette of Eakins* by Samuel Murray p 105 SCU.

Eakins, son of a writing master, enrolled at PAFA after high school graduation. In 1866 he went to Paris to attend the École des Beaux-Arts, becoming a favorite pupil of Gérôme. Ill health caused him to go to Spain in 1869, where he was influenced by works of the realist Velásquez. After he returned to Philadelphia in 1870, he studied anatomy at Jefferson Medical College. In 1873 he was engaged as an instructor at PAFA where he became dean of the faculty. His masterpiece *Clinic of Dr Gross* was completed in 1875. His achievement in art was as a proponent of naturalism, along with Winslow Homer. As a teacher, his importance was in the classroom study of the nude and of anatomy.

Eakins was vigorous and determined, a methodical painter who was an ardent sportsman. He rode his "bronco at a mad pace" in the Pennsylvania mountains. When he spent the summer of 1887 on a ranch in the Badlands of North Dakota, Eakins rode all the first day without distress. *Cowboy in the Badlands* is a product of this trip. In 1895 Eakins painted a full-length portrait of the ethnologist Cushing dressed as a Zuni priest, but this was staged in the Philadelphia studio made into a replica of a Zuni room. The object of widespread hostility in his youth and of neglect in his middle years, he was recognized after 1900 for what he had become, one of the most important painters of the reality of American life.

EARLE, Eyvind. Born NYC 1916, living Solvang, Cal 1974. Western landscape painter, designer, illustrator, commercial artist. Work in MMA; mural for US Navy (Jacksonville). References A62-MAS. Sources AHI 12/72-*Amer Artist* 5/72-IL 42-3/8/74 data from Joan Earle. No current auction record. Signature example p 76 IL 42. Portrait photo p 28 *Amer Artist* 5/72.

Earle's father Ferdinand Earle was a painter and movie art director and his mother was a concert pianist, the fourth of Earle's father's five wives. As the pupil of his father, Earle began painting at 10, in Mexico City, France, England, and Belgium. He exhibited at 14, the year he ran away to live with his mother in Hollywood at the start of the Depression. His first sponsor gave him $25 a month for the year 1936 to permit him to paint in Mexico. In 1937 he toured the US by bicycle and sold out his first NYC one-man show at $25 per painting. Service in WWII was as a conscientious objector.

After the war Earle worked for Disney for seven years. In 1961 he established his own animation motion picture company. In 1946 he had designed best-selling greeting cards which have utilized more than 500 paintings. Throughout the years, Earle continued to paint landscapes, in acrylics before 1971 and oil thereafter. Self-taught in the sense that he had little formal study, Earle describes his style as "designed realism," a sparse and abstracted view that reflects his belief that Van Gogh and Georgia O'Keeffe were the most original artists. His most famous paintings are of California mountains and valleys and of Western Canada.

EARLE, Lawrence C. Born NYC 1845, died Grand Rapids, Mich 1921. Portrait, landscape, genre painter; muralist. Member ANA 1897. Work in AIC, Chicago Nat Bank. References A21 (obit)-BEN-FIE-SMI. Sources ANT 4/74-HOE-ISH-NA 74-NJA-WHO 20. Pastel 25×18" *Cardplayer* sold in 1971 for $100. No signature example.

Earle was trained in Munich, Florence, and Rome. He was one of the artists chosen to do the murals for the Columbian Exposition. He also did murals for the Chicago National Bank showing Western pioneer scenes. HOE.

EAST, Mrs Pattie Richardson. Born Hardesty, Okla 1894, living Ft Worth, Tex 1962. Texas landscape painter, muralist, etcher, teacher. Mural in Ft Worth country club. References A62-MAL. Sources TOB-WAA. No auction record or signature example.

Mrs East studied at the AIC and Broadmoor Art Academy, the pupil of Birger Sandzen, José Arpa, H A De Young and Joseph Fleck. In the 1930s she sketched in Texas' Big Ben country where a farmer asked her whether she painted outdoors so the work would "dry faster." TOB.

EASTMAN, Harrison. Born New Hampshire about 1823, died San Francisco, Cal about 1886. Pioneer Cal landscape and marine painter, illustrator, lithographer, engraver. Reference G&W. Sources BDW-HON. No auction record or signature example.

Eastman sailed from Boston to San Francisco in 1849 on a packet brig. While he was working for San Francisco lithographers in 1852, Mexican Boundary Commissioner John Bartlett commissioned him to redraw Bartlett's own sketches of the surrounding area. Eastman also made watercolors of San Francisco and Sutter's Fort, exhibiting at the 1857 Mechanics Fair. He was a friend of the artist C C Nahl.

About 1859 Eastman established the firm of wood engravers Eastman & Loomis. The important painter William Keith worked for Eastman's firm in 1862. Eastman also illustrated *Annals of San Francisco* and *Hutchings Illustrated California Magazine*. By 1860 Eastman was successful enough to own $9,000 in real estate and $1,200 in personal property.

EASTMAN, Seth. Born Brunswick, Me 1808, died Washington, DC 1875. Indian painter, illustrator, Army officer. Honorary NA (amateur) 1838. Work in ACM, COR, St Louis AM, Joslyn AM, the Capitol. References BEN-FIE-G&W-MAL-SMI. Sources AIW-ALA-ANT 11/44,6/48,10/62,10/69,11/71,11/72-AWM-BAR-COR-COW-DAM-DBW-DWF-EAS-FRO-HMA-150-KAR-KW1-M19-MIS-POW-SUR-TAW-TEP-TSF-WES-WHI. No current auction record but the estimated price of a watercolor 4×7" of Fort Crawford would be about $6,000 to $8,000 at auction in 1976. *Fort Snelling* sold at auction for $165 in 1932 and $475 in 1944. Signature example p 881 ANT 11/72.

Eastman was graduated from West Point in 1829 after having studied drawing under Thomas Gimbrede. He was assigned to Fort Crawford on the Mississippi in what is now Wisconsin. In 1829, before Catlin arrived, Eastman began making pencil sketches as documentaries in this meeting place for the surrounding Indian tribes. Eastman was moved to Fort Snelling (now Minneapolis) in 1830. This was the principal military stronghold to keep peace. In 1831 Eastman was selected for topographical reconnaissance, beginning a series of sketches of the frontier forts. He returned to West Point as assistant teacher of drawing 1833–40, studying privately with C R Leslie and Robert W Weir and exhibiting at the NAD and the Apollo Gallery.

Eastman went back to Fort Snelling as a captain 1841–48. He began seriously to sketch the Indian country, often working from daguerreotypes. After a march through Texas in 1849 he was ordered to Washington. His wife wrote and he illustrated a successful Indian chronicle "Dakotah" published in 1849. This book was the prototype of Longellow's poem "Hiawatha." In 1851 he began his five-year task of illustrating the six volumes authorized by Congress to record all the Indian tribes of the US. His wife and he also wrote and illustrated "The Romance of Indian Life" in 1853 and "Chicora" in 1854. The Indian drawings were offered to any college that would give free tuition to Eastman's children, apparently with no taker. He was on duty in Texas in 1855 and in Utah in 1858. Eastman served in the Civil War, retiring as a general until he was commissioned by Congress in 1867 to paint Indian and fort scenes to hang in the Capitol.

EASTMOND, Elbert Hindley. Born American Fork, Utah 1876, died Provo, Utah 1936. Second-generation Utah painter, graphic artist, teacher. Source YUP. No auction record or signature example.

Eastmond studied at the AIC 1901, Pratt Inst (NYC) 1902, Stanford U under John Lemos 1903–4. He then traveled extensively throughout Europe before returning to Utah where he staged and designed costumes for Mormon pageants. He also exhibited paintings and prints in major cities of the US. It is said that he was especially effective in graphics. Eastmond was head of the Art Department at Brigham Young U 1921–36.

EATON, Charles Henry (C Harry). Born Akron, Ohio 1850, died Leonia, NJ 1901. NY landscape painter, illustrator. ANA 1893. Work in Detroit IA. References A03 (obit)-BEN-CHA-FIE-MAL-SMI. Sources NJA-POW-WHO 01. Watercolor 17×23″ *Rural Landscape with Fisherman* sold 1971 for $170 at auction. In 1902 *The Banks of the Pond* sold for $150 at auction. No signature example.

C Harry Eaton began painting as a self-taught amateur. After his father died, Eaton lost his inheritance and so moved to NYC where he painted for a living. POW states that Eaton did Western landscapes including *The Three Tetons* as an illustration for Theodore Roosevelt's "Hunting Trips of a Ranchman," but Eaton does not appear on the list of these distinguished illustrators in all editions. Eaton had three paintings at the Pan-American Expo in 1901, winning a bronze medal after his death.

EBER, Elk (or Wilhelm Emil). Born Haardt, Germany 1892, died probably Germany 1944. Painter of *Custer's Last Stand* at the Custer Battlefield, illustrator. Work in Karl May Mus (Dresden, Germany). No reference. Sources CUS-MWS winter/74 with painting example. No current auction record.

Custer's Last Stand by Elk Eber dated 1926 was considered to be an evidence of the postwar disillusionment that produced symbols like de-emphasizing Custer. Eber was thought to have painted the Indian view, as the son of a Sioux woman who witnessed the battle and married a German professor while touring with Buffalo Bill. As an Indian painting of the battle, it featured a giant Indian chief. The painting was also praised by Army experts because of its pictorial accuracy in showing short-haired pistol-firing Custer and a soldier with a jammed carbine.

From the 1940s through 1969, Eber's painting was an illustration in the National Park Service booklet on the battlefield. It was then discovered that Elk Eber was Wilhelm Emil Eber, a German who posed as an Indian in 1926 but then returned to Germany to design posters for Hitler as a Nazi party member and propagandist. The painting was said to be appropriate for the Karl May Museum, which was named for the German writer of Western stories featuring ostrich hunts on Nebraska plains. CUS.

Daughter of a judge, Miss Eckford was educated in Dallas schools. She studied at the Aunspaugh Art School and with Hale Bolton and Frank Reaugh in Dallas, with Felicie Waldo Howell in Massachusetts, and with E Roscoe Shrader in LA. She was winning Dallas medals by 1916, typical paintings being *The Head of the Concho River* and *Prickly Pear*. In 1934 Miss Eckford began exhibiting woodblocks.

ECHOHAWK, Brummett. Born Pawnee, Okla about 1920, living Tulsa, Okla 1968. Pawnee illustrator, commercial and comic strip artist. Work in GIL. No reference. Source AIP-COW-CUS. No auction record. No signature example.

Echohawk, grandson of a US cavalry scout under Major Frank North in the Indian Wars, was inspired by Winslow Homer, George Catlin, Charles Russell, and Frederic Remington. He studied at the AIC and the Detroit AI. An authority on the American Indian and the West, his painting in the GIL is *Trail of Tears* depicting the Cherokees being driven out of their homes. Echohawk worked with Thomas Hart Benton on the Western mural for the Truman Library. He has created Christmas cards depicting the Indian spirit. His comic strip *Little Chief* has appeared Sundays in the *Tulsa World*.

ECKFORD, Jessiejo. Born Dallas, Tex 1895, living there 1941. Texas landscape painter, woodblock artist. Work in Elisabet Ney Mus (Austin), Witte Mus (San Antonio), and N Tex Agri Col. References A41-BEN-FIE-MAL. Sources TOB-TXF. No auction record or signature example.

EDOUART, Alexander. Born London, Eng 1818, died Los Angeles, Cal 1892. San Francisco landscape, portrait, and genre painter, photographer. Reference G&W. Sources ANT 1/36,1/54-BOA-HON. No auction record but the estimated price of an oil 20×30″ showing a feast day at the mines would be about $3,000 to $3,500 at auction in 1976. Wash drawing example p 63 ANT 1/54.

Edouart was the son of Auguste Edouart, a successful silhouettist who came to the US from England in 1839 and worked from Boston to New Orleans for 10 years, completing 50,000 silhouettes. Alexander Edouart had been educated in Edinburgh, Scotland and had studied art in Italy. In 1848–50 he was working in NYC, exhibiting at the NAD and the American Art-Union.

About 1852 Edouart moved to San Francisco, probably as A Edwart on the clipper *Queen of the East*. After trying prospecting he made a brief trip to Europe before settling down in 1859. BOA refers to him as a painter of genre. ANT 1/36 shows his 1860 painting of a religious ceremony to bless a quicksilver mine in California. Edouart was better known at the time as a photographer. He moved to Los Angeles about 1889 with his son. In 1951, Edouart paintings were said to have been still in the possession of his grandson.

EDWARDS, Harry C. Born Philadelphia, Pa 1868, died Brooklyn, NY 1922. Eastern illustrator, painter specializing in adventure and Western subjects. References A23 (obit)-FIE-MAL-SMI. Source IL 93. Oil 36×24" *Danger on the Trail* with signature example and dated 1917 sold 4/11/73 for $1,200 at auction. (See illustration 86.)

Edwards studied at Adelphi College in Brooklyn, the pupil of J B Whittaker, and at the ASL with Mowbray. He lived in Brooklyn and spent summers in Gananoque, Ont, Can. Books he illustrated included "The Gun Brand" and "Blackwater Bayou."

EDWARDS, Lonnie Joe. Active Lubbock, Tex 1972 as sculptor of Western subjects. Work in W Tex Mus. No reference. Sources AHI 3/72-Baker Collector Gall catalog Hubbard-Edwards with signature example and portrait photo-BRO. No auction record.

A native of West Texas, Edwards was educated at Texas Tech. He has specialized in Western and animal subjects. Listed titles are *Indian Hunter, Owl, Dove, Water Bird.*

EGAN, John J (or I J). Active 1850–51 in Philadelphia. Painter of moving panoramas, landscape painter. Work in Univ Mus (Philadelphia). Reference G&W. Sources ANT 12/49-BAR-MIS-PAF-TEP. No auction record or signature example.

Egan was the painter of a panorama of Ireland exhibited in Philadelphia in 1850 when he also exhibited two landscapes of Ireland and England in the PAFA. Egan was commissioned by Dr Montroville Wilson Dickeson to paint the *Panorama of the Monumental Grandeur of the Mississippi Valley* from Dickeson's sketches made on the spot between 1837 and 1844. The moving panorama that resulted was tempera on muslin sheeting 7½×348', shown by Dr Dickeson in a national tour that began December 1851 in Philadelphia. The scenes emphasized Dr Dickeson's expertise in Indian culture rather than landscape.

The moving panorama was theatrical entertainment, not art. The performance lasted about 35 minutes for a charge of 25 cents, children under 12 at 12½ cents. The painting was unwound from one roller to another so that one scene at a time was visible. Footlights and sound effects were employed with a musical background. In the panorama, Egan had "all the forms simplified for quick appeal to hasty eyes: journalism in paint." BAR.

EGGENHOFER, Nick. Born Gauting, southern Bavaria, Germany 1897, living Cody, Wyom 1976. Traditional Western painter, illustrator, sculptor. Work in Nat Cowboy Hall of Fame. Member CAA, Nat Acad of Western Art. No reference. Sources ACO-AHI 3/72-C71,72-COW-CRS-CUS-HAR-ILA-ILG-PER vol III, ⅏3-USM-WAI 71,72-WYG. Oil 29× 20" with signature example, dated 1923 *Making Friends* sold 4/11/73 for $8,000 at auction (painting reproduced as cover *Western Story Magazine* 1923). (See illustration 87.)

Eggenhofer grew up in Germany familiar with horses and playing "Cowboys and Indians" at the same age as children in America, due to a European craze inspired by Buffalo Bill's continental tours with his Wild West Show. He also saw Western movies and Remington and Russell works reproduced in German pulp magazines. He came to NYC in 1913 and starting 1916 managed four years of study at night at Cooper Union, subordinated to a variety of jobs including apprenticeship at the American Lithography Company. Eggenhofer decided to become a Western artist, preparing by making scale models of wagons, stagecoaches, and other props for his paintings. His first illustration was sold in 1920 to *Western Story Magazine* of Street & Smith, the pulp publishers.

In 1925 Eggenhofer married and visited Santa Fe in a model T. Even then he saw a ten-horse trader, and mail delivered by buckboard. From the log cabin home he built in West Milford, NJ, Eggenhofer illustrated many Western books and magazines. In 1961 he wrote and illustrated his own book, "Wagons, Mules and Men." In the early 1960s Eggenhofer moved to Cody, saying, "The West got hold of me at a very early age and hasn't turned loose yet." He is in "the forefront of those who portray the wagon-train era of America" (COW) and has won top prize at the Cowboy Hall of Fame. In Cody he completed a series of bronzes of his scale-model Western vehicles. In 1971 it was said that Eggenhofer had made 30,000 Western illustrations. C71.

EILSHEMIUS, Louis Michel. Born Arlington (near Newark), NJ 1864, died NYC 1941. Eastern painter of studied primitives, author, composer. Work in Phillips Mem Gall (Washington), MMA, MNM, MOMA, WMA, DIA, Cleveland AM, BMFA, NEU. References A47 (obit)-BEN-MAL. Sources ALA-ANT 11/68; 3,4/69; 8/71-ARI-ART 2/45-DEP-NEU-NJA-WHO 40. Oil 30×40″ *Fillettes a la Rivière* dated 1915 sold 10/14/70 for $2,300 at auction. Signature example p 195 ANT 8/71.

Of Dutch descent and wealthy, Eilshemius was educated in Geneva and Dresden, returning to the US in 1881. He attended Cornell for bookkeeping and agricultural studies 1882–84. He then studied art at the ASL until 1886, the pupil of Kenyon Cox, and was the pupil of Bouguereau at the Julien Academy in Paris until 1889. His early paintings were accepted for exhibition at the NAD. For 20 years he traveled to Europe, Africa, the South Seas, and around the US. In 1908 he established his studio in NYC where he called himself the "Grand Parnassian and Transcendental Eagle of the Arts." He "brought to Romantic painting an almost inexhaustible fantasy. The influence of Corot seems strongest." He was "most authentically a primitive in his visions of nude creatures bathing or dancing." And "when he stopped painting in 1921 he had explored a wider range of Romantic iconography than perhaps any other American painter—scenes from literature, moonlit nudes, melancholy landscapes, Oriental subjects, stormy sea pieces, scenes of passion and disaster." See "Romantic Painting in America," MOMA, 1943.

In the large Neuberger Collection of Eilshemius' works, there are Western subjects: ╳124 *Mission House, Cal* 1888 (p 140), ╳175 *Indian Belle by the Brook in Moonlight* 1910 (p 199), ╳243 *El Capitan* n/d (p 162), ╳249 *Mtn Landscape Yosemite* n/d (p 162), ╳253 *Peak-Yosemite* n/d (p 161). Although a prolific painter, Eilshemius did not have his first one-man exhibition until 1920. In spite of his self-advertising, he was little known until the 1930s.

EISENLOHR, Edward G. Born Cincinnati, Ohio 1872, died Dallas, Tex 1961. Modern Texas landscape painter, printmaker, author. NA. Work in Santa Fe Mus (NM), Dallas MFA, Elisabet Ney Mus (Austin), MNM, Witte Mus, New Orleans MA. References A62 (obit)-FIE-MAL-SMI. Sources AAT-COW-TOB-T20-TXF. No current auction record. Painting example *November* opp p 64 TXF.

Eisenlohr's parents moved to Dallas when he was two. He worked in a bank until he was 35. In 1907 he was a late-blooming student with Frank Reaugh and R J Onderdonk whom he acknowledged as his most profound influences. He then studied in NYC and Woodstock with Birge Harrison, going on to seven years in Europe which included the class of Gustave Schoenleber in Karlsruhe, Germany. He exhibited watercolors on his return in 1915. One-man shows of oils began in Dallas in 1926, and he was represented at a MOMA exhibit in 1933. The books he has written are on art appreciation.

Eisenlohr was a frequent visitor to the art colonies at Santa Fe and Taos. His oils were boldly worked with broad brush strokes or with palette knife. "A man of virile physique, his face is that of a profound thinker with the eyes of a poet. His mind seems to be a sensitive plate." TXF. Listed titles are *Where the Prairie Begins, Mist in the Mtns, The Sentinels of Box Canyon.*

ELDER, John Adams. Born Fredericksburg, Va 1833, died there 1895. Southern portrait, genre, landscape, and military painter including *Battle of the Little Big Horn.* Work in COR, St of NY colln, Westmoreland Club (Richmond). References FIE-G&W-MAL-SMI. Sources ANT 8/65-BAR-COR-CUS-MWS winter/74. No current auction record. Signature example p 50 CUS.

Elder began as a cameo carver. At 17 he went to NYC to study with Daniel Huntington. The next year he studied with Emanuel Leutze in Düsseldorf, remaining in Europe until 1855. After working in NYC, Elder returned to Fredericksburg about 1860. He fought in the Confederate Army after a Union shell "set his bed afire" during the Civil War. He painted portraits of Gens Lee and Jackson. CUS. His *"Battle of the Crater* is the most adequate Southern counterpart" to Northern paintings. BAR.

At work in the South in 1884 Elder was one of the more competent artists to paint an early version of Custer's battle. He portrayed a "last charge" rather than a "last stand," following the German military technique, an erroneous "eyewitness report" carried in the 1876 newspapers, and the 1876 print by Feodor Fuchs.

ELKINS, Henry Arthur. Born Vershire, Vt 1847, died Georgetown, Colo 1884. Early Western landscape painter. Work in ANS, Dentzel colln. References FIE-MAL-SMI. Sources AIW-DBW-POW. Oil 35½×60″ *Western Landscape* dated 1877 sold 9/13/72 for $1,300 at auction. Painting example p 27 DBW *Long's Peak.* (See illustration 88.)

Elkins lived in Chicago from 1856 to 1873, working after about 1864 as a self-taught artist. In 1866 he formed a party of eight along with the established Chicago artists Gookins and Ford to tour Colorado by wagon. In the West at the same time were Whittredge and W H Beard. Gookins' sketches of the trip including unpopular views of Denver were published in *Harper's Weekly* with his commentary. Bayard Taylor reported having met the party which "had made the entire trip from the Missouri in their wagon and were on their way to the Parks for the summer." AIW. In 1867, Western paintings by the three artists were on exhibit in Chicago.

Elkins moved to Kansas City in 1873, having become known in the Midwest for his landscape oils of Colorado and California. His paintings were reviewed in the Chicago newspapers as they were exhibited, with reprints in the Denver papers, covering such grandiose works as *Elk Park, Colorado, The Thirty-Eighth Star,* and *The Crown of the Continent.* Elkins' obituary was printed in Chicago, Kansas City, and Colorado, indicating the breadth of his acceptance as an artist.

ELLIOTT (or Elliot), Henry Wood. Born Cleveland, Ohio 1846, living Lakewood, Ohio 1940 (per WHO; or, died 1930. FRO). Geological survey artist, writer on seals, naturalist. No reference. Sources "Anton Schonborn, Western Forts" ACM 1972; WHO 1912, 1940. No auction record. Signature example ⩔94 FRO.

Elliott was private secretary to Joseph Henry, secretary of the Smithsonian, from 1862 to 1878. During this period, he was assigned as official artist for the US Geological Survey 1869-71. The 1871 expedition was Dr F V Hayden's fifth annual Western survey, with Elliott as official artist and W H Jackson as official photographer of the Yellowstone basin. The guest artist was Thomas Moran, the center of all artistic attention on his first Western trip. While the official artist drew the required scientific studies, the guest artist sketched where he wanted. The resulting oils by Moran led to legislation establishing Yellowstone Park and the largest oil sold for $10,000.

From 1872 to 1874 Elliott was commissioner to investigate Alaska's Seal Islands. Three Elliott monographs resulted, along with many papers. In 1872 he also met and married Alexandra Melovidov of St Paul's Island, Alaska. In 1905 Elliott prepared the fur-seal treaty with Canada, Japan, and Russia for the protection of Alaska's seal herd.

ELLIS, Fremont F. Born Virginia City, Mont 1897, living Santa Fe, NM 1976. Santa Fe painter, printmaker, teacher, a founder of Los Cinco Pintores. Work in Springville AM (Utah), MNM, El Paso MA; mural on SS *America*. References A76-BEN-FIE-MAL. Sources AIW-ANA 7/75-LOS-PIT-TOB (as Treemont F Ellis)-TSF. No auction record. Signature example p 19 ANA 7/75. (See illustration 89.)

Ellis' father, an itinerant dentist in Montana mining towns, became a carnival performer and theater operator. Ellis grew up without a formal education but began painting at 13. He was self-taught except for three months at the ASL when he was 18. To learn a trade he went to optometry school in Los Angeles. A shop he set up in El Paso failed and at 20 he became a full-time painter. In 1919 he visited and married in Santa Fe. Unable to sell his paintings he moved back to California where he lived on Freedom Hill in the San Fernando Valley.

Ellis soon returned to Santa Fe, finding work as sign painter and photographer. In 1921 he with Bakos, Mruck, Nash, and Shuster formed Los Cinco Pintores; Ellis as an impressionist was most conservative of the group. Building their own studios on the Camino del Monte Sol, they created an artists' colony. They exhibited together as a matter of convenience, adding a five-pointed mark to their signatures. Ellis' landscape *When Evening Comes* won a national prize in 1924. Although the Pintores separated in 1926, Ellis remained in Santa Fe. He uses a camera while he is sketching and also while he is painting, to try different tones by adjusting the color setting on the camera. On the back of each painting, he specifies whether the work is oil or acrylic.

ELLSWORTH, Clarence Arthur. Born Holdrege, Neb 1885, died Los Angeles, Cal 1961. Traditional Western painter, illustrator. Work in Southwest Mus. References A62 (obit)-MAL. Sources COW-PAW. Oil on board 12×10" *Portrait of Lone Wolf, a Sioux* with signature example sold 5/22/73 for $1,000 at auction.

Clarence Ellsworth was a premature frontier baby, born in the back room of his father's drug store, rubbed with whiskey and warmed in the oven. He grew up witnessing the end of the "horse-drawn Westward migration." PAW. Self-taught as a painter, he was a newspaper artist for 10 years in Denver. He made 25¢ portraits for tourists at the Garden of the Gods in Colorado Springs. While in Denver he received commissions from Eastern magazines for covers and illustrations on Western subjects. He also worked on sports illustrations.

About 1924 he moved to Hollywood, Cal where he worked as a title artist for motion pictures for seven years. He illustrated Western books including two on North American Indians by the curator of the Southwest Museum. By 1941 he was being given one-man exhibitions at the Southwest Museum. His specialties were Indians and horses.

ELWELL (or Ellwell), Robert Farrington. Born near Boston, Mass 1874, died Phoenix, Ariz 1962. Traditional Western painter, illustrator, sculptor. No reference. Sources AHI 10/59-ANT 12/73, 1/74-COW-HAR. Oil 30×15″ *Hunter* with signature example and inscribed Rampart Ridge, Wyom was estimated for sale 10/28/74 at $1,500 to $2,000 for auction in LA but did not sell.

Bob Elwell was sketching the cowboys and Indians at Buffalo Bill's Wild West Show as a newspaper artist in Boston about 1890 when Colonel Cody happened by. Elwell was invited to spend the summers at Cody's Wyoming ranch. In 1896 Elwell became ranch manager, a job he held for 25 years of increasing management of Cody's affairs. Through Cody, Elwell knew the celebrities of the day such as Teddy Roosevelt and Diamond Jim Brady. Annie Oakley taught Elwell's daughter how to shoot.

Elwell was self-taught as an artist. His approach for the horse, for example, was to practice drawing each part in as many action positions as he could. After two summers with Cody, his 1,000 sketches secured him commissions for Western illustrations. He worked in black and white for 10 years, adding color only when requested by his publisher. Elwell painted Western illustrations for the magazines of the 1930s including *Harper's, Century,* and *American.* His subjects remained vigorous and youthful, and he painted bucking horses and stagecoaches after he was 85. Elwell left the East as a teenager, but he retained his Boston accent and demeanor his entire life.

EMEREE, Berla Ione (Mrs William Henry Emery). Born Wichita, Kan 1899, living El Paso, Tex 1962. Texas painter, teacher. Work in Texas high school, officer's club. References A62-BEN-MAL. Sources TOB-WAA. No current auction record or signature example.

Having painted since the age of seven, Miss Emeree at 17 studied with Frank Linton in Philadelphia. Her later Texas teachers were José Arpa, Rolla Taylor, and Xavier González. In 1928 she studied in Europe, after having founded in 1924 her Berla Ione Emeree School of Painting in El Paso. Two of her paintings were *On the River San Antonio* and *Bluebonnets.*

EMERSON, Robert E. Born Peoria Ill about 1920, living Columbia Falls, Mont 1969. Montana landscape painter. No reference. Source MON. No auction record or signature example.

Raised in Gary, Ind, Emerson moved to northwestern Montana in the late 1940s as a construction worker on the Hungry Horse Dam. A mountaineer, he was the first to climb several of the peaks in Glacier National Park. These are the mountains he specializes in painting, along with the flowers, lakes, and waterfalls. His painting procedure is to rough in the work on location and then take a photograph of the light conditions so he can accurately finish the painting back in his studio.

ENDERTON, S B. Field artist for *Harper's Weekly* which in 1866 printed his sketch *Mounted Messengers Attacked by Indians on the Plains*. No reference. Source BAW. No auction record or signature example.

ENSOR, Arthur John. Born Cardiff, Wales 1905, living in Toronto, Can about 1970. Painter in Western Canada 1939, industrial designer, muralist, illustrator. Work in NGC; murals in Science Mus (London, Eng) and Empire Marketing Board. No reference. Source NGC catalog with painting example. No auction record. (See illustration 90.)

John Ensor studied at the Royal College of Art in London and in Florence and Stockholm. He traveled in Africa, painting murals for the Empire Marketing Board, and painted a mural in the Science Museum in London. In addition he illustrated books.

When Ensor came to Canada, he settled in Victoria, British Columbia.

ERNESTI, Richard. Born Chemnitz, Germany 1856, living Seattle, Wash 1941. Painter of the Colo Rockies, teacher, educator. No reference. Source WNW. No auction record or signature example.

Ernesti studied at the Real Gymnasium in Chemnitz and the Chicago Acad of Design, the pupil of Fedor Flinzer and of

Dr Knorr in Munich. He was director of art education for Colorado schools and taught at Colorado State Teachers College, Pennsylvania State College, and Drake U (Des Moines).

He exhibited widely in the US. WNW. It is said that when he lived in Colorado Springs, colored photos of his paintings of the Rockies were sold to tourists. His wife was the painter Ethel H Ernesti.

ERTZ, Edward Frederick. Born Canfield, Tazewell Cnty, Ill 1862, living Pulborough, Sussex, Eng 1941. Watercolorist, illustrator, etcher, teacher. Member Roy Soc Brit Artists. Work in Alexander Palace Mus (London), Public Gall (Liverpool), Lib Cong, Cal St Lib, BMFA, Amer Consulate (London), etc. References A41-BEN-FIE-MAL-SMI. Source WHO 32. No recent auction record but the published estimate of prints is $80 to $100. No signature example.

Ertz studied in Paris, the pupil of Lefebvre, Constant, and Delance. He was made professor of watercolor at the Delecluse Academy in Paris 1893–97. Later he taught at a school in King's Langley, Herts, Eng. His first wife Ethel Margaret Horsfall was a miniaturist and watercolorist. Included in his body of work are a number of paintings of Western American subjects. Listed painting titles included *The Gardener, Spanish Water Carrier, Amberley Bridge,* and *Sunset, Grand Canyon.*

EVANS, Edwin. Born Lehi, Utah 1860, died in California 1946. Second-generation Utah landscape painter, muralist, teacher. Work in Brigham Young U, U of Utah. References A29-BEN-FIE-MAL. Sources PUA-YUP. No current auction record but the estimated price of an oil 20×30″ showing chickens on the mountain would be about $900 to $1,100 at auction in 1976. Signature example p 20 YUP.

Evans' father had been sent by Brigham Young to colonize the area surrounding the ranch where Evans was raised. He worked as a telegrapher, painting as a hobby. When he was 30 he was influenced to attend the U of Utah to study under the "Fathers of Utah Art," Ottinger and Weggeland. Brigham Young selected Evans to go to Paris to the Julien Academy under Laurens and Constant. In return, when he came back from Paris in 1893, Evans painted murals in Utah temples along with John Hafen. Unlike Hafen who painted in poverty, Evans prospered, and became the first president of the Society of Utah Artists in 1895. He was chairman of the art department U of Utah (1898–1920) and president, Utah Art Institute 1904–16. Evans returned to Paris in 1916 and again 1920–22 after spending 1917–18 in NYC studying at the Beaux-Arts.

Evans' mature works offer "sternness and an intellectual rigor found in no other Utah painter. The most significant body of work in Utah paintings would probably be the late watercolors." YUP. It is said that Evans insisted on completely finishing one of his watercolors before retiring to his deathbed.

EVANS, Mrs Jessie Benton. Born Akron (or Uniontown), Ohio 1866, living Scottsdale (or Jakake), Ariz 1941. Chicago and Arizona landscape painter, etcher, teacher. Work in Vanderpoel colln (Chicago), AI (Akron), Ariz St Fed, schools in Ill and Ariz, etc. References A41-BEN-FIE-MAL. Source WHO 48. No current auction record or signature example.

Mrs Evans was educated at Oberlin College in 1882 and was married in 1886. She graduated from the AIC in 1904, was the pupil of Wm Chase in Chicago, and studied with Zanetti-Zilla in Venice, exhibiting at the Paris Salon 1911–12. A31 indicates residence in Chicago with winters in Scottsdale. In 1934 she translated and illustrated "Giulietta and Romeo" by Luigi da Porto. Typical painting titles were *On the Verde River, On the Way to McDowel,* and *Gray Day.*

EVANS, Richard. Born Chicago 1923, living Laramie, Wyom 1976. Contemporary Wyom painter, printmaker, teacher. Work in San Fran FA colln, U of Wyom, Col of Southern Utah. Reference A76. Source Cheyenne-Wyom *State Tribune.* No auction record or signature example.

Evans graduated from Otis AI in LA. He studied at California College Arts & Crafts, with Geo Miller in NYC, at U of Wyoming, and received fellowships: Stacey in 1947, Tiffany in 1948 and 1950, U of Wyoming in 1964, and Ford Fndn in 1964 and 1966. He taught at California College of Arts and Crafts and at Miami U (Ohio) before becoming professor of art at U of Wyoming in 1957. He has had widespread one-man shows and has been in international exhibitions.

His work is described as "strongly realistic, with an element of surrealism. The 'Icon Series' employs many contemporary devices such as multiple perspectives."

EVERETT, Joseph Alma Freestone. Born Salt Lake City, Utah 1883 (or 1884), died there 1945. Utah watercolorist, muralist, teacher. Work in Springville Art Gall (Utah), U of Utah, Utah St Capitol, Utah AI. References

A47 (obit)-BEN-MAL. Sources PUA-YUP. No current auction record but the estimated price of a watercolor 18×24" showing a rainy day in the canyon would be about $400 to $600 at auction in 1976. No signature example.

Everett's parents were English converts to the LDS Church. His artistic talent was recognized as early as the first grade. He studied in Utah with Harwood and Hafen, then while on a Church mission to England 1906–8 studied at South Kensington School of Art with the watercolorist E A Smith. He traveled extensively through Europe visiting art centers. In NYC he studied with muralist Kenyon Cox.

He was a prolific painter, although he was for a time employed as an engineer-draftsman. In addition to the landscape watercolors painted for sale, he continually sketched genre scenes—hospital patients receiving treatments and the razing of the Salt Lake Theatre.

EVERETT, Raymond. Born Englishtown, NJ 1885, living Austin, Tex 1941. Texas landscape painter, sculptor, bookplate designer, teacher. Work in Detroit Pub Lib, Ney Mus (Austin), U of Colo Mus. References A41-BEN-FIE-MAL. Sources TOB-TXF. No current auction record or signature example.

Son of a socially prominent minister, Everett graduated from Drexel Inst in 1906 and from Harvard in 1909, receiving a teaching fellowship. He had been the pupil of Howard Pyle, Joseph Lindon Smith, and Denman Ross. After studying in Paris at the Julien Academy and in Rome, he taught at the U of Pennsylvania and the U of Michigan.

In 1917 Everett settled in Austin as professor of drawing and painting, U of Texas. His series of bluebonnet paintings included *Texas Bluebonnets, A March Morning,* and *Golden Evening.*

EYTEL (or Eytell), Carl. Born Stuttgart, Germany 1862, died Palm Springs, Cal 1925. Western desert and animal painter. Reference MAL. Sources COW-KEN-SCA. No current auction record but the estimated price of an oil 20×30" showing moving the steers would be about $3,000 to $3,500 at auction in 1976. Signature example p 124 COW.

After Eytel worked his way to the US, he managed to obtain a job as a ranch hand in the San Joaquin Valley, Cal. His spare time was spent in painting scenes of the cattle on the ranch. Eytel became a desert painter, working the area that has been developed as Palm Springs. A shy and sensitive man, he was often without funds, depending upon friends for canvas and paints. In 1906 he illustrated James's "The Wonders of the Colorado Desert."

EYTH, Louis (or E). Born place unknown 1838, died probably San Antonio, Tex about 1889. Texas historical and portrait painter, illustrator. Work in State Capitol (Austin). No reference. Sources TOB (as E)-TEP. No current auction record but the estimated price of a historical painting would be about $4,000 to $5,000 at auction in 1976. Signature example p 189 TEP.

"Eyth migrated to Galveston at 14." TEP. He worked for the leading daguerreotypists Blessing and Company. In 1873 he petitioned the governor, "I am desirous to secure commissions for the exercise of historical portraiture—that being the highest attainable degree of any art." He was given the task of copying the early portrait of Stephen F Austin, which he did, for the State Capitol.

Eyth moved to San Antonio about 1878 where he painted illustrations for the historical books of James DeShields. The subjects included *The Speech of Travis to His Men at the Alamo, Surrender of Geronimo* (painted 1885), *Death* of Bowie: *A Command from the Mexicans that He Be Killed,* and *Battle of Plum Creek*. The paintings of this period have been lost, with only photographic reproductions remaining. "Eyth had a knack of representing the historic scene with spirit and, at the same time, accuracy." TEP.

EYTINGE, Solomon, Jr. Born probably NYC 1833, died Bayonne, NJ 1905. *Harper's Weekly* staff artist, illustrator, genre painter. Work in magazines, books. References A05 (obit) - BEN - G&W - MAL-SMI. Sources AIW-AOA-BEY-NJA. No current auction record. Drawing example ※74 AOA.

Son of an actor, Eytinge was a staff artist for *Harper's Weekly* and a friend of Charles Dickens. His 1862 drawing of Gen Phil Sheridan's ride inspired Read's poem "Up from the South at break of day." "His pictures of the Southern negro published during the Civil War gained him a wide reputation." A05. In AOA the "humorous Blackville series" was shown as appearing in *Harper's* in the 1880s.

In 1867 Eytinge appeared with a host of Civil War field artists as an illustrator for BEY. His one drawing *A Scene Like This* depicted the bucolic Kansas legislature about 1858. It was undoubtedly redrawn from existing material, as his *Young Bucks on the Warpath* and *Young Bucks Returning with Spoils* appearing in *Harper's Weekly* in 1873 were redrawings of T R Davis.

FAIRBANKS, Avard Tennyson. Born Provo, Utah 1897, living Salt Lake City, Utah 1976. Western sculptor. Member NSS. Work includes Old Oregon Trail marker, Pony Express (Utah Centennial), series of portrait busts for Western Hall of Fame, Pioneer Mother Memorial (Vancouver, Wash), statue of Esther Morris (Cheyenne). References A76-FIE-MAL. Sources AAT-MSL-NEW-PUA-WHO 62-WNW. No current auction record. Signature example PUA. Sculpture examples p 190 AAT, p 299 NEW. (See illustration 91.)

When he was 8, his father who was an intermittent painter moved to a homestead in Western Canada. At 10 Fairbanks was back in Utah, assisting his father at his art ventures in copying old masters. At 12 he won a gold medal at the Utah State Fair for a sculpted rabbit. He became known as the Mormon Michelangelo, accompanying his father to NYC, studying at the ASL under James E Fraser. When he was 14, they returned to Utah, Fairbanks helping his father in his art gallery which was profitable enough to send father and son to Paris in 1913 to study under Injalbert at the Beaux-Arts until WWI.

Fairbanks had further instruction from A Phimister Procter and Charles R Knight, beginning his professional career in 1918. He was assistant professor of art at U of Oregon 1920–27, associate professor of sculpture at U of Michigan 1927–47, and professor of sculpture at U of Utah beginning 1947. He had received a Guggenheim fellowship to do creative sculpture in Europe 1927–28. He built a retirement studio in Utah for his father John B Fairbanks, as a token for his father's "Christlike character."

in Brigham Young U, Utah AI; murals in LDS temples. References A47 (obit)-BEN-FIE-MAL. Sources PUA-YUP. No current auction record but the estimated price of an oil 20×30″ of a barn in the valley would be about $500 to $600 at auction in 1976. Painting example p 24 YUP.

John B Fairbanks' father was a bishop, farmer, storekeeper, and Indian agent. Fairbanks began painting by copying chromos for sale. He was offered lessons by John Hafen who then recommended Fairbanks as a mural painter for the new Temple. In preparation, he was in 1890 sent to the Julien Academy in Paris where he was influenced by Riglot toward Corot-school landscapes. On his return in 1892 he painted the huge French-style temple decorations coming into vogue at the time, then taught at BYU Academy. To supplement his income for his 12 children including painter John Leo and sculptor Avard Tennyson, he also established a photographic studio in Provo. In 1902 he was director of art and photography for an archaeological trip to Mexico, Central and South America. In 1905 he became a homesteader in Alberta, Canada, until he "dreamed he must return to his art."

Back in Utah he copied and sold "old masters." In 1909 he launched a NYC venture where his patrons paid $50 a month as an installment toward $130 for a copied old master. When this business failed, he returned to Salt Lake City to open an art gallery that proved profitable enough to pay for a year in France with his son Avard. The start of WWI forced them home with 15¢ in their pockets when he was 60. His first wife having died, he remarried, fathering 5 more children.

FAIRBANKS, John Boylston. Born Payson, Utah 1855, died Salt Lake City, Utah 1940. Second-generation Utah painter, copyist, muralist, teacher. Work

FAIRBANKS, John Leo. Born Payson, Utah 1878, died Corvallis, Ore 1946. Utah painter, sculptor, teacher. Frieze

162

and murals in LDS temples, colleges, libraries, memorials. References A47 (obit)-BEN-FIE-MAL. Sources WHO 44-WNW-YUP. No current auction record or signature example.

Fairbanks was the pupil of his father John Boylston Fairbanks. He worked as an artist to help support the family before 1890, and was the primary source of family funds in 1902 when his father was off on an archaeological expedition. He studied in Paris for two years at the usual Utahan resource, Julien Academy, with Laurens, Simon, and the sculptors Bohn and Verlet. On his return, he became art supervisor of the Salt Lake City public schools from 1904 to 1923, and was again called on to support his father's family after their Canadian homesteading. He also taught at LDS U and studied at Columbia and Chicago U.

J Leo Fairbanks illustrated The Book of Mormon. He was the head of the art department at Oregon State College 1923–46. In contrast to his father, he held two jobs for 42 years, and it was said that his painting was crisp and bright rather than like Corot.

FAIRCHILD, Hurlstone. Born Danville, Ill 1893, died probably Tucson, Ariz 1966. Painter of the Southwest, illustrator, writer. Fellow, RSA (England). Work in DAM, Grand Canyon Nat Park colln, Brazil. Reference A66. Source, oil unframed 26×30″ *Santa Catalinas, Arizona* signed and dated '31, estimated for sale 3/27/74 at $500 to $600 for auction in Los Angeles. Signature example, same oil illustrated as lot 100 estimated for sale 10/28/74 at $400 to $600 for auction in Los Angeles but did not sell.

Fairchild was educated at the U of Illinois, U of Michigan, and Missouri School of Mines in Rollo. He wrote and illustrated "An Artist's Notebook" in 1950 and "Grand Canyon Sketches & Verse."

FALTER, John Philip. Born Plattsmouth, Neb 1910, living Philadelphia, Pa 1976. Illustrator. Member SI. References A76-MAS. Sources ILA-ILG-IL 62-POI. No current auction record. Signature example ✗36 IL 62.

Raised in Falls City, Neb, Falter studied at the Kansas City AI, the ASL, and the Grand Central SA in NYC. His teachers included Mahonri Young, George Wright, and Monte Crews. Beginning as an illustrator for the Western pulp magazines, Falter sold his first "slick magazine" illustration when he was only 20. Covers for *The Saturday Evening Post* were his best-known works. Some of these depicted his own Nebraska experiences. Another series of illustrations showed American street scenes.

FANSHAW, Hubert (or Herbert) Valentine. Born Sheffield, Eng 1878, died Winnipeg, Manitoba, Can 1940. Landscape painter and woodblock printer of Canadian Western subjects. Work in NGC. Reference MAL. Sources CAN-DCA. No current auction record or signature example.

H Valentine Fanshaw studied at the Sheffield Technical School of Art, the Royal College of Art (London), and the Antwerp Academy. He emigrated to Canada 1912, teaching in the Winnipeg high school 1913–40. His watercolor in the NGC is *A Threat to Harvest*. In 1923–24 he painted in Southern California.

FARNHAM, Sally James. Born Ogdensburg, NY 1876, died NYC 1943. Monument and portrait sculptor. Work includes Will Rogers on his pony, cowboy group *Pay Day,* cowboy statuette (Remington Memorial). References A29-FIE-MAL-SMI. Sources AMA-COR-COW-

NSS-WAA-WHO 42. Bronze *Will Rogers* 21¾″ high signed and dated 1938 and inscribed Roman Bronze Works was estimated for sale 10/31/75 at $1,400 to $1,800 and sold that day for $13,000. No signature example.

After she had married and had a child, Mrs Farnham while hospitalized played with wax as a pastime. She soon opened her own studio, an absolutely untrained sculptor immediately successful. She did have the criticism of Henry M Schrady, Augustus Lukeman, and Frederick Roth. Her hometown friend Frederic Remington told her that some of her work was "ugly as the devil but it's full of ginger. Keep it up, Sally." Her most famous monument was the equestrian statue of Simón Bolívar unveiled in Central Park, NYC in 1921 after she won the commission in competition with 20 other sculptors.

FARNY, Henry F. Born Ribeauville, Alsace, France 1847, died Cincinnati, Ohio 1916. Very important painter of Indians and Western life, illustrator. Work in ACM, ANS, Cincinnati AM, C R Smith colln, U of Texas at Austin, Taft Mus (Cincinnati). References A17 (obit)-BEN-CHA-FIE-MAL-SMI. Sources AIW-ANT 4/43,6/56,4/69,9/72,10/72, 12/72,1/74-BAR-BAW-COW-CRS-DAA-DBW-DCC-DWF-GIL-HON-IND-MSL-POW-TAW-WHI-WHO 16. Gouache 16×10″ *Over the Divide* sold 10/27/71 for $34,000 at auction. Gouache 15¼×8¾″ *Lone Brave* sold 10/19/72 for $31,000 at auction. Signature example p 163 TAW. (See illustration 92.)

Farny's family fled France as political refugees. His lifelong interest in Indians came from experiences with the Senecas near his boyhood home in the pine forests of western Pennsylvania 1853–59. When the family moved to Cincinnati by

raft down the rivers, he was apprenticed as a lithographer. By 1865 *Harper's Weekly* published a two-page spread of his Cincinnati views. Between 1867 and 1870 he studied art in Düsseldorf, Vienna, and Italy, at the studio of Thomas Buchanan Read and with Munkacsy, supporting himself with odd jobs. When he returned to Cincinnati, which was becoming an active art center, he worked as an illustrator. In 1873 he shared his studio with Frank Duveneck and Frank Dengler, spending 1875–76 in Munich with them and Twachtman. He continued as an illustrator, including works for "McGuffey Readers." In 1878 he made a 1,000-mile canoe trip down the Missouri.

In 1881 Farny began his much reproduced Indian sketches with Sitting Bull and the forbidden Ghost Dance at the Sioux Agency. His Indian genre paintings avoided sensationalism in favor of a literal rendering of tribal life. Assignments came from both *Harper's* and *Century*. In the decade he had about 30 illustrations in *Harper's Weekly* alone. In 1883 Farny covered the completion of the Northern Pacific railroad for *Harper's,* including Sioux and Crow drawings. In Bismarck he introduced Sitting Bull to General Grant. In 1884 he visited the Piegan lodges on the Missouri. By 1890 he was concentrating on easel paintings that told stories of the West, particularly the contrast between the civilizations. In 1894 he visited the Fort Sill reservation in Oklahoma where he saw Geronimo and the remnants of the Apache nation. He made many visits to Indian encampments, filling his studio with sketches, photographs, Indian attire, and gear: "He draws Indians, he paints Indians, he sleeps with an Indian tomahawk near him, he lays the greatest store by his necklaces and Indian pipe, he talks Indian and he dreams of Indian warfare." AIW. A huge man, a friend of many celebrities, he was certainly one of the most important 19th-century American painters, although relatively unrecognized before 1950.

FAULKNER, Barry. Born Keene, NH 1881, died there (or NYC) 1966. Muralist, painter. ANA 1926, NA 1931. Murals and decorations in public buildings, schools, commercial buildings. References A70 (obit)-BEN-FIE-MAL-SMI. Sources AMA-ISH-WHO 66. No current auction record. Signature example p 296 AMA.

Faulkner was educated at Phillips Exeter Academy and Harvard. He studied art at the ASL, the American Academy in Rome, and with George de Forest Brush, Abbott H Thayer. His specialty was building decorations in the form of picture maps: One of *Lange Eylandt* shows the Indian villages there, while another is *The Path of the Fur Trade.*

FAUSETT, Lynn. Born Price, Utah 1894, living Salt Lake City, Utah 1976. Utah genre muralist, painter. Murals in City Hall of Price, U of Wyom, LDS chapels. References A76-MAS. Sources WYA-YUP. No auction record. Painting example p 30 YUP.

Fausett studied at Brigham Young U 1910–12, U of Utah 1914–16, ASL 1922–27, and in France at Fontainebleau 1933–36. From 1943–46 he was art director, Special Services Div, 9th Service Command, US Army. His murals in Utah include *First Marriage* in Price, a Mormon ceremony in the open fields with pigs and a dog, while *First Meeting of Primary Association* in the LDS chapel is the tens of children, the teachers, and the parents caught in motion. It is said that "later easel paintings by Fausett became harder, drier and more sharply focused." YUP.

Fausett is the older brother of Dean Fausett, a muralist-painter who left Utah in the early 1930s and was resident in Vermont in 1970.

FECHIN, Nicolai Ivanovich. Born Kazan, Russia 1881, died Santa Monica, Cal 1955. Taos painter of Indian portraits, sculptor. Member Imperial Academy FA, Russia. Work in Imperial Acad FA (Petrograd), Kuingi Galleries (Petrograd), Mus of Kazan, Albright A Gall, AIC, MNM, Colorado Springs FA Center, National Cowboy Hall of Fame, Harrison Eiteljorg colln. References A41-BEN-FIE-MAL. Sources ACO-AIC-AHI 2/52-COW-DCC-HAR-PAW-PER vol 5 ✗3-PIT-TAL-TSF-TWR-WAI 71,72. Oil 20✕16″ *Young Indian Girl* sold 2/19/72 for $2,394 at Christie auction. Signature example p 83 PIT *Old Indian.*

Nicolai Fechin's father was a destitute craftsman in wood and metal in Russia. When Fechin was four, he became seriously ill and was given up for dead but restored by the touch of the Ikon of Tischinskoya. His boyhood was spent in the dark Volga forest with its wild Tartar tribes. When he was 13 he received a scholarship to the Art School of Kazan founded by his grandfather. At 19 he began his studies at the Imperial Academy of Art in St Petersburg, the pupil of Ilya Repin who had introduced contemporary Russian art to the West in 1893. Fechin graduated in 1909 and was awarded a traveling scholarship through Europe. He was called "the Tartar painter" and was an instant success in European and American exhibitions with his palette-knife technique. When the Bolshevik Revolution followed WWI, Fechin left Russia for America after six years of privation. He was immediately popular in NYC with portrait commissions from celebrities and a first prize for portraits from the National Academy in 1924.

In 1927 he moved permanently to Taos, beginning at once on his stream of portraits of Southwestern types, painting by day and sculpting at night. Fechin was of medium build, quick and direct, as sparse in speech as in art, painting only from life, a master of color. Fechin never lacked technical deftness but he did limit depicted emotions to "rugged and sober" for Indians and "exuberant and pleasing" for his other sitters. TSF. About 1936 he traveled through Mexico, making drawings. In 1938 he moved to Bali but was forced back to the US by WWII. He settled in Santa Monica, again painting people of the Southwest.

FELL, Olive. Born on Big Timber Creek at the foot of the Crazy Mtns in Mont about 1900, living Four Bear Ranch near Cody, Wyom 1949. Wyom painter, etcher, muralist, sculptor, caster of life masks. Work in Buffalo Bill Mus (Cody), "100 Best Prints of the Year." Reference MAL. Sources WYA-*The Cody Enterprise* 4/27/49. No auction record or signature example.

Miss Fell's mother was the proprietress of the Cody Flower Shop and her father freighted supplies to mining camps and isolated trading posts. She grew up in wilderness areas and was educated in Cody high school and Wyoming U. Her art studies were at the AIC and the ASL.

As an artist, her specialty was animals. Her creations of "Little Cub Bear" on cards and novelties were sold to tourists in national parks and resorts. In the Buffalo Bill Museum in Cody, there was an Olive Fell Room in which her work was hung. Her subjects were Western scenes and wildlife, *Fenced Sagebrush, The Lone Rider, Wading Moose.*

FELLOWS, Fred. Born Ponca City, Okla 1935, living Big Fork, Mont 1976. Traditional Western painter, sculptor. Member CAA. Reference A76. Sources AHI 11/71,3/72-C71 to 74-COW-MON-OSR-1/74 data from Fred Fellows. No current auction record. Signature exam-

ple p 83 MON *Attack on the Stage*. (See illustration 93.)

Fellows grew up in California where he worked as a cowboy and was apprenticed for four years to a saddlemaker. He also roped calves and steers on the rodeo circuit. Without formal art training, he spent 10 years as a commercial artist and as an art director. In 1964 he moved his family to Big Fork, Mont to devote himself to painting. His studio contains a serious collection of early Western guns, Plains Indian artifacts, cowboy gear, and a research library as a part of his study of Western history. Fellows also has a firsthand knowledge of modern ranch life, spending his spare time roping on the big Montana cow outfits. He specializes in cowboys, Indians, and the West. He is said to consider color and draftsmanship the keys to painting.

"Certainly the development of technique and style of painting is most important to me, but I find that I paint to please myself." MON. Painting titles include *The Home Seekers, When Cold Winds Warm the Heart, Back to Camp, The Best Things in Life.*

FENN, Harry. Born Richmond, Eng 1838, died Montclair, NJ 1911. Eastern illustrator in the West in 1870, painter, wood engraver. Work in AIC, BMFA, Kahn colln. References A11 (obit)-BEN-FIE-MAL-SMI. Sources AIW-ALA-ANT 7/74-AOA-HON-HUD-KAH-KW1-MSL-NJA-POW-WHO 10. No current auction record but the estimated price of a watercolor 10×14" of a mountain view would be about $1,000 to $1,200 at auction in 1976. Signature example ⚒15 HUD.

Educated in England, Fenn was trained as a wood engraver before he began painting. He came to the US in 1857 to see Niagara Falls and remained to marry in Brooklyn in 1862. In 1863 he went to Italy for further study, returning to the US in 1864. He illustrated Whittier's "Ballads of New England" about 1870 and "Snow-Bound" in 1881, gift books that were among the first with pictures in the US.

In 1870 Fenn traveled through the West, making sketches for "Picturesque America" along with Alfred Waud, Swain Gifford, James Smillie, Thomas Moran, Darley, Whittredge. He also illustrated "Picturesque Europe" in 1873, "Picturesque Palestine," "Picturesque California," and many other books. Fenn was an important illustrator of the 1880s "with his clever black and white renderings of landscape" and his sensitive stylish people. ALA. After 1881 he maintained his studio in NYC.

FERRAN, Augusto. Born Palma, Majorca 1813, died Havana, Cuba 1879. Spanish sculptor active as painter in California in 1849. Bust of a Spanish queen in Mus of Madrid. References BEN-G&W. Sources ACM-HON. No current auction record. Signature example ✳️52 ACM.

Ferran studied at the Academy of San Fernando in Madrid as well as in Paris and Havana. He exhibited sculpture regularly in Madrid. While in California in 1849–50, he collaborated with a young Cuban artist José Baturone on a series of 12 sketches of Gold Rush miners that was lithographed and printed in Havana about 1849 as "Album Californiano." HON also has a signed Ferran oil not dated showing vaqueros lassoing a steer.

FERRIS, Jean Leon Gerome. Born Philadelphia, Pa 1863, died there 1930. Historical painter, illustrator, etcher. Work in Congress Hall (Philadelphia). References A30 (obit)-BEN-DAB-FIE-MAL-SMI. Sources NJA-WHO 30. Watercolor

12×18″ *The Harem Favorite* 1890 sold 1972 for $45 at auction. Oil *That Which I Have Allowed Behind Me* sold for $145 at auction in 1909. No signature example.

Ferris was the pupil of his father, the portrait painter Stephen James Ferris, a devotee of Gérôme and Fortuny. His mother's brother was Thomas Moran so the adolescent atmosphere was fine art. He studied in Spain in 1881, and under Bouguereau at the Julien Academy in Paris in 1884 where he received the impetus to concentrate on historical painting. Until 1900 he prepared himself by traveling and sketching in England, France, Spain, Morocco, and Belgium, specializing in historical analyses of architecture, customs, and dress as they might apply to the US. He also investigated early American vehicles and boats, constructing accurate miniatures he gave to the NY Historical Society and to the National Museum. Toward the end of his life, in 1927, he was able to donate to the National Museum the most important print collection the museum had had, 3,000 pieces of graphics of the 16th through the 19th centuries.

About 1900 Ferris began the 70 historical paintings intended to depict consecutively the story of the American people from 1492 to 1865. The paintings cover early settlements through the nation's development, up to Abraham Lincoln. Indian and Western subjects were included. Two later additions were made, with scenes of 1902 and 1917. The collection was hung in Philadelphia's Congress Hall in 1930 in a gallery built for the purpose. It is said that Ferris was droll, genial, and witty, and that he lived a fruitful and happy life.

FERY, John. Born Hungary about 1865, died Everett, Wash 1934. Western landscape painter. No reference. Sources JNB-YUP. No current auction record but the estimated price of an oil 20×30″ showing a cabin on the mountain would be about $700 to $900 at auction in 1976. Signature example ⚡31 JNB.

Fery studied in Europe. He conducted European nobility on hunting expeditions to the Northwest before moving permanently to the US in 1886. He exhibited at the Columbian Exposition in Chicago in 1893.

About 1900 Fery worked in Utah, painting "many large oils of the natural wonders of the West." YUP. He also lived in Minnesota, Arizona, Washington, Oregon, and California. He worked for the railroads and for the *Oregon Journal*.

FIELD, Laurence B. Born place unknown about 1905, living Colorado Springs, Colo 1948. Colorado landscape painter exhibiting beginning 1935. Work Cleveland MA, Colo Spr FAC. References A41-MAS. Source AAT. No auction record. Watercolor example *Petrified Forest* p 74 AAT.

FIRFIRES, Nicholas S. Born Waunakee Ranch near Santa Barbara, Cal 1917, living Montecito, Cal 1976. Traditional Western painter, illustrator specializing in the West of the 1920s and '30s. Member CCA. Reference A76. Sources AHI 3/72-C71 to 74-COW-HAR-OSR-WAI 71-*Cal Living* 6/24/73 (article)-11/- 30/73 letter from Mrs Nicholas Firfires. No auction record. Signature example C71 *Time Out*.

Firfires is a descendant of the California vaqueros depicted by James Walker in the 1870s, living on the big ranches back of Santa Barbara in San Luis Obispo County. He worked with horses until he was 24, alongside the old vaqueros, then attended the Art Center

School and the Otis AI in Los Angeles. During WWII he served with the Army Engineers as an artist.

In 1945 Firfires turned to illustrations for Western magazines, and beginning in 1957 devoted himself to easel paintings. He remains a member of the Rancheros Visitadores, the annual celebration by hundreds of men moving from rancho to rancho as a re-creation of the colorful Spanish era of California history. In 1969 Firfires won the silver medal at the Cowboy Hall of Fame exhibition. In 1970 he married the daughter of the cowboy actor Buck Jones whose comic strip Firfires drew in the 1950s. "Someone asked me once," he said, "why my cowboys always are moving toward the right of my paintings. It's because a cowboy has his rope on the right side of his horse, so I paint him in a way that it shows." *Cal Liv*. By 1973 his drawings and paintings were priced from $500 to $3,000, averaging $2,500. Firfires' studio has a mirror at his back while he paints because the use of the mirror is the quickest way for him to locate any compositional defect.

FIRKS, Henry. Active San Francisco 1849. California painter, lithographic artist. Work in ACM. Reference G&W. Sources COS-OCA-1/20/73 letter from Marcy Philips, MMA-1/29/74 letter from T E Waterbury, Newport Hist Soc. No auction record. Painting example ⚡142 "Paintings of Life in America" 1939 MMA.

Firks was the artist for one of the best-known views of San Francisco, the shoreline in 1849, published in NYC and San Francisco the same year. The painting shows the harbor and identifies 42 ships, the Customhouse, Parker's Hotel, the island Yerba Buena, and the Golden Gate. The second issue of the resulting lithograph by G & W Endicott of NY is considered the correct view of the five issues recorded. There is no other biographical data available on Firks nor is the lithograph signed.

FISCHER, Anton Otto. Born Munich, Bavaria, Germany 1882, died probably Woodstock, NY 1962. Eastern illustrator specializing in *Sat Eve Post* sea stories and Western books, serials. Member SI. Work in Coast Guard Acad (New London). References A62-BEN-FIE-MAL-SMI. Sources AAC-ANT 6/74-COW-50G-ILA-IL 42-WHO 50. No current auction record. Signature example p 39 IL 42.

Fischer was educated at the Archiepiscopal Seminary, Scheyern, Bavaria. Orphaned, he ran away at 16, working as a sailor until he came to NYC in 1903. To earn money for art, he worked as model and handyman for the illustrator A B Frost, taught seamanship, and crewed for racing yachts. He studied at the Julien Academy in Paris 1906–8, the pupil of Laurens, and with Howard Pyle in Wilmington where his fellow students were W H D Koerner, N C Wyeth, Harvey Dunn, and Frank Schoonover.

Harper's Weekly bought Fischer's first illustration, and he started on Jack London stories for *Everybody's*. In 1910 he began his long association with *The Saturday Evening Post* for "Tugboat Annie" and Kenneth Roberts' stories. Books illustrated included "Black Hawk," "Law of the Gun," "Good Indian," "Flying U Last Stand," etc. In WWII, Fischer was Artist Laureate for the Coast Guard. He illustrated his autobiography "Fo'cs'le Days" in 1947.

FISH, C B. Artist active in Colorado in 1860s. No reference (G&W lists Charles Fish, a young engraver in NYC in 1850). Source DBW. No auction record. Painting example p 19 DBW.

Painter of *Young Hiram and Winchip* in DAM exemplifying the men "who really struck it rich" in the "Pikes Peak or bust" gold rush, "who built brown stone mansions, bedecked their wives with maribou, owned high-stepping trotters." DBW.

FISHER, Alvan (or Alvin). Born Needham, Mass 1792, died Dedham, Mass 1863. Important early 19th-century Eastern painter. Honorary NA 1827. Work in Amherst Col colln, Royal Ontario Mus, Munson-Williams-Proctor Inst. References BEN-DAB-FIE-G&W-MAL-SMI. Sources AAR 3/74-ACM-ALA-ANT 4/48,6/50,8/55,4,8/56,11/58,4/62,8,9/65; 4,6/68,5,7/70,9/72-BAR-BOA-ISH-KAR-KW1-PAF-STI-WHI. Oil 30¼ × 25¼" *Dogs and Game* dated 1840 sold 9/13/72 for $3,600 at auction. Signature example p 162 KW1.

When he was 18, Fisher left his country-store job to study with the ornamental painter John Penniman. He remained two years. Fisher began painting in 1812, offering inexpensive portraits. He was more successful in 1815 when he turned to rural genre scenes and barnyard animals. By 1819 he again concentrated on his lifelong specialty, portraiture, painting in cities such as Charleston, SC and Hartford, Conn. He made the European tour in 1825, then established his studio in Boston. He was said to be the first professional Boston artist who painted landscapes. The feature of incidents in his landscapes made them unique. He rarely painted from nature, depending upon sketches, and was also the first American artist to paint race horses.

Fisher made painting pay. At the age of 43 he lost his entire savings but was able to accumulate wealth again. His own favorites among his paintings included *The Savages*. Indians were incidental to many of his paintings, such as *Niagara Falls—Canadian Side*. He also painted scenes such as *Wagon Train in the Rockies* dated 1837 but he is not recorded as having traveled West. His painting *The Buffalo Hunt* was reproduced as an etching.

FISHER, Hugo (or Hugh) Antoine. Born probably Brooklyn, NY about 1850 (or 1867), died Alameda, Cal 1916. NY and Cal landscape painter. References A17 (obit as Hugh)-DAB (under Harrison Fisher)-FIE (Hugh corrected to Hugo)-MAL-SMI. Sources ANT 5/71-ILA (under Harrison). No current auction record. Signature example p 742 ANT 5/71 *The Coming of the Iron Horse.*

Son of a "painter of distinction" (DAB), Hugo A Fisher's birth date is given as 1867, but his sons were born 1875 and 1876. He was a landscape painter and an etcher who moved to San Francisco about 1890. Fisher's son Harrison born in 1875 was an important illustrator whose specialty was the "Harrison Fisher girl." Son Hugo Melville Fisher born in Brooklyn 1876 (or 1878) studied in Paris and lived in NYC. BEN, FIE.

FISHER, Philip D. Active 1867. Illustrator of Plains Indian War for *Harper's Weekly.* No reference. Source AIW. No auction record or signature example.

Fisher was an Ohio resident who served in the Civil War. After the war he worked as a civil engineer for the eastern division of the Union Pacific railroad operating through Kansas. Four views sketched by Fisher along the UP right-of-way were published in *Harper's.*

Fisher was on the scene of the Indian War in Kansas before *Harper's* special artist T R Davis arrived. At that time the railroad had been constructed only about a third of the way across Kansas. Fisher was already at Fort Harker for the railroad while the famous Davis was snowbound in a stagecoach. Three of Fisher's drawings pertaining to the war were published by *Harper's* in 1867 including a sketch of the Hancock expedition camped at Fort Harker. Davis went into the field with Hancock to cover all of the subsequent parleys and skirmishes.

FISK, Harry T. Active NYC 1921–48. NYC illustrator including Western subjects. Member, Guild of Free Lance Artists of the Authors League of America. Work in *This Week.* References A27-MAS. Sources AAC-ILG. Oil 36×27" *Indian Prayer* signed and dated 1926 sold 10/27/71 for $750 at auction. Signature example opp p 32 ILG.

Fisk is dated as "early 20th century," living in NYC 1921–27. He was a member of the Guild that had been founded in 1920.

FISK, W. Active 1857–67. Illustrator. No reference (BEN lists William Fisk and his son William Henry Fisk, English painters). Source BEY. No auction record. Drawing example p 220 BEY.

Fisk drew *A Counter-irritant* for BEY, depicting the "physicians" of the Indian Territory who "are firm believers in the counter-irritant principle, and for every internal inflammation press a burning brand against the body." BEY.

BEY notes its illustrations are both "from photographs and original sketches," generally leaving the reader to determine which is which.

FITZGERALD, Lionel LeMoine. Born Winnipeg, Manitoba, Can 1890, died there 1956. Canadian landscape painter in the West in the 1940s, teacher. Member of the "Group of Seven" 1932–33, Can Group Ptrs. Work in NGC, U of Toronto, Winnipeg AG. References A53-MAS. Sources CAH-CAN-CAR-DCA. Watercolor 23½×7¾" *Weathervane* dated 1942 sold 5/14/73 for $700 at auction in Canada. Signature example ⚹97 CAR. (See illustration 94.)

Born and raised in Winnipeg, L LeMoine Fitzgerald studied about 1910 at A S Keszthelyi's School of Art in Winnipeg. He worked at a publishing house and as a decorator. In 1921 he studied at the ASL in NYC, the pupil of Kenneth Hayes Miller and Boardman Robinson. He taught in the Winnipeg SA beginning 1924 and was principal 1929–49. Originally a realist landscape painter, he softened his style in the 1930s. In 1932–33 Fitzgerald became a member of the Canadian nationalistic modern painters, the Group of Seven. The broadened group was renamed the Canadian Group of Painters and further expanded.

Fitzgerald "visited the West Coast several times between 1942 and 1949 and Mexico in 1951." CAR. In the 1940s he painted "in softly modulated tones of gray, an atmospheric and poetic quality. There is a certain sketchiness, but a fine simplicity." CAN. "He painted little, and that little with precise care." DCA. His periods have included impressionist, abstract, and pointillist, but his subjects showed him to be a regionalist.

FITZGERALD, Pitt Loofbourrow. Born Washington Court House, Ohio 1893, living Columbus, Ohio 1941. Illustrator and writer specializing in historical views of Indians and settlers. References A41-BEN-FIE-MAL. Source, illustrations in "Trail of the Ragged Fox" and "Young Men in Leather." No auction record. Initials p 70 "The Black Spearman," a story

of the builders of the great mounds, published by Books, Inc. 1934.

Pitt L Fitzgerald studied at the PAFA and was the pupil of N C Wyeth, living in Chadds Ford in 1926.

FLECK, Joseph Amadeus. Born Vienna, Austria 1893, living Taos, NM 1963. Taos painter 1924–43, lithographer, muralist. Work in Witte Mem Mus, War Dept Mus, Fort Worth AM, Houston MFA, MNM, HAR, Carnegie MFA. References A62-BEN-MAL. Sources AAT-TAL-TSF. Oil 25×30" *Geraniums* with signature example estimated for sale 3/4/74 at $2,000 to $2,500 at auction in LA and sold for $2,250. (See illustration 95.)

Fleck studied at the Royal Academy FA and the School Graphic Indust Art, Vienna. He was winning awards at the Kansas City AI by 1923, with a one-man show in Houston in 1930 and in both Paris and Chicago in 1931. In the Depression he painted government-sponsored murals. Fleck lectured on Spanish art and was Artist in Residence as well as Dean FA at the U of Kansas City, 1943–46.

Fleck arrived in Taos in 1924, after seeing New Mexico paintings exhibited by the Taos SA in Kansas City. He was then a representational painter, working in a straightforward style. By the 1940s he became impressionist, particularly after exposure to Benton during his tenure at the U of Kansas City.

FLEMING, John. Born Kirkcaldy, Fifeshire, Scotland 1836, died Toronto, Can 1876. Survey artist of Canadian Northwest territories. Work in J Ross Robertson Historical colln (Toronto), Public Archives (Ottawa). No reference. Sources CAE-CAN. No current auction record or signature example.

Fleming came to Canada as a young man, and in 1857–58 joined Henry Youle Hind on his expeditions to Red River, Assiniboine, and Saskatchewan. He worked up in watercolor the many sketches he made on these expeditions.

FLETCHER, Calvin. Born Provo, Utah 1882, died Logan, Utah 1963. 20th-century Utah landscape painter, teacher. Work in LDS temples, Vanderpoel colln. References A62-BEN-FIE-MAL. Sources PUA-YUP. No auction record but the estimated price of an oil 20×30″ showing a mountain road would be $400 to $600 at auction in 1976. Painting example p 34 YUP.

Fletcher was the pupil of J B Fairbanks, learning by copying. In 1905, on graduation from Brigham Young U, he was appointed assistant supervisor of art in Provo. He studied in NYC in 1906–7 including a night class under Robert Henri. His paintings of this period emphasized design. Fletcher started teaching at Utah State Agricultural College in 1907 where he continued until he became Professor Emeritus in 1952.

In 1928 he began the practice of bringing visiting artists to the Logan campus, to provide summer classes that reflected progressive experimentation. This made for a controversial art department. It also affected Fletcher's painting which was influenced by the visitors to the point that he became "a man without a developed style." YUP. The paintings of his third wife Irene Thompson Fletcher are close to his in feeling.

FLETCHER, Clara Irene Thompson. Born Hooper, Utah 1900, living Logan, Utah 1965. Utah landscape painter. Works in Utah St Fair, Inst FA (USU); murals in Logan library and LDS Tem-

ple. Reference MAS. Sources PUA-YUP. No current auction record. Painting example p 34 YUP.

Irene Thompson was Calvin Fletcher's pupil in 1926. When they married that year, he had had two previous wives. His home at that time had eight children, the oldest 19. Thereafter, she confined her art studies to summer classes with visiting artists—Cornaby, Hansen, Nordfeldt, Oldfield, Pearson, Randolph, Sandzen. She exhibited nationally. Mrs Fletcher's paintings "are close in feeling to those of her husband and teacher." YUP.

FLETCHER, Sydney E (or Sidney). Illustrator specializing in Western subjects and horses, active 1924–39 at 126 Lexington Ave, NYC, working for national advertisers. No reference. Sources AAC-IL 36-ILG. No auction record. Illustration examples *The Power of 75,000,-000 Horses* p 48 IL 36, *Mountain Men* p 35 ILG.

FLEURY, Albert François. Born Le Havre, France 1848, living Chicago, Ill 1925. Chicago landscape painter, muralist, teacher. Work in ANS colln. References A25-BEN-FIE-MAL. Source *Panorama of Grand Canyon from El Tovar* in ANS. No auction record or signature example. (See illustration 96.)

Albert Fleury was the student of École des Beaux-Arts in Paris, the pupil of Lehmann and Renouf. He worked as officer of public instruction in France, debuting at the Paris Salon in 1880. After emigrating to Chicago in 1888, he painted murals and taught.

FOOTE, Mary Hallock. Born Milton, NY 1847, died Boston, Mass 1938. The

73. Randall Davey. *Buffalo Dancer*, oil on canvas 32 x 26″ signed LR. Unusual subject for a polo player who preferred nudes. CREDIT, THE ANSCHUTZ COLLECTION.

74. Floyd Davis. *Coyote on My Shoulder*, dry brush 11 x 10″. Not signed but related to examples in IL 42. CREDIT, THE AUTHORS.

75. Leonard M Davis. *Alaskan Shore*, oil on canvas 18 x 24″ signed LL and dated 1911. The painter of Alaska, the Canadian Rockies, and the aurora borealis. CREDIT, THE AUTHORS.

76. Dawson Dawson-Watson. *Grand Canyon*, oil 120 x 144″. An Englishman who hurried to Texas in 1926 to win the Wild Flower Painting contest. CREDIT, THE ANSCHUTZ COLLECTION.

78. F S Dellenbaugh. *Indian Women Grinding Corn*, oil 18 x 24″ painted about 1875. A life of continuing involvement with adventure. CREDIT, MUSEUM OF NEW MEXICO.

77. Gerard Curtis Delano. *Sunlight and Shadow*, oil 18 x 20″ signed (LR) Delano and painted about 1960. Eastern commercial artist homesteading at Cataract Creek in 1920. CREDIT, DENVER PUBLIC LIBRARY, WESTERN HISTORY DEPARTMENT.

79. Moya del Pina. *Spanish-American Dancer*, pastel 10 x 7″ signed (LR) Moya and (UR) Moya del Pina. His touring funds ran out in San Francisco. CREDIT, THE AUTHORS.

80. E W Deming. *The Fight*, bronze statuette of a grizzly bear attacked by a panther, height 7¾″ signed and modeled about 198 . Deming sculpture subjects are few. CREDIT, THE METROPOLITAN MUSEUM OF ART, ROGERS FUND, 1907.

81. E W Deming. *Madalena SA Indian*, sepia over pencil 4 x 5″ signed LR. Deming grew up with Indian playmates and became a specialist in Indian subjects. CREDIT, THE AUTHORS.

82. Joe De Yong. *Sime* — Old Texas Trail Boss, Gunmaster, pencil on board 20 x 16″ signed LR. He talked to Russell in Indian signs. CREDIT, THE AUTHORS.

George Dick. *On the Slopes*. Wildlife painting by a ~~er~~ game manager and ranger. CREDIT, THE ARTIST.

84. Douglas Duer. *The Section Hand's Daughter*, oil on canvas 30 x 22″ signed LL and dated 1919. An illustrator who was the pupil of both Chase and Pyle. CREDIT, THE AUTHORS.

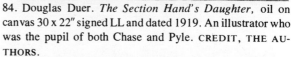

85. W Herbert Dunton. *The Buffalo Hunter*, watercolor on paper 8 x 8″ signed LL. Taos illustrator of the "unadulterated real" old-time Westerner. CREDIT, THE AUTHORS.

86. H C Edwards. *The Prospectors*, oil on canvas 1(signed LR and dated 1909. Brooklyn illustrator speci in adventure subjects. CREDIT, THE AUTHORS.

87. Nick Eggenhofer. *Wagon Trains West*, wash drawing 11 x 17″. The man "the West got hold of" as a child in Germany. CREDIT, THE AUTHORS.

88. H A Elkins. *Elk Park, Colorado*, oil on canvas 3(dated 1878. He made a wagon tour of Colorado when 19. CREDIT, THE ANSCHUTZ COLLECTION.

9. Fremont F Ellis. *Springtime in New Mexico*; oil on canvas 36 x 30″ signed LR. A founder of Los Cinco Pintores Santa Fe. CREDIT, THE ANSCHUTZ COLLECTION.

90. John Ensor. *Summer's Stores*, watercolor 11¼ x 15¼″ signed LR and dated 1941, inscribed (LL) Peace River/Sexsmith Grain Elevators, 8 out of 21. A resident of British Columbia. CREDIT, THE NATIONAL GALLERY OF CANADA, OTTAWA.

92. Henry Farny. *Crow Warrior*, gouache on paper 11 x 17″ signed (LR) H F Farny and dated 1897. "He draws Indians, he talks Indian and he dreams of Indian warfare." CREDIT, THE ANSCHUTZ COLLECTION.

91. (Left) Avard Fairbanks. *Esther Morris Statue* in Cheyenne. The Utah prodigy who was called the "Mormon Michelangelo." CREDIT, WYOMING STATE ARCHIVES AND HISTORICAL DEPARTMENT.

93. Fred Fellows. *The Relic of the Past*, oil 20 x 30″ signed (LR) Fellows. CAA member who was a cowboy and a rodeo roper. CREDIT, THE ARTIST.

94. Lionel LeMoine Fitzgerald. *Red Barn*, oil on canvas 1... 13⅞″. ''He painted little, and that little with precise care... CREDIT, THE NATIONAL GALLERY OF CANADA, OTT... WA, GIFT FROM THE DOUGLAS M DUNCAN COLLECTIO... 1970.

95. Joseph Fleck. *The Guitarist*, oil 35⅛ x 32″ signed UL. Influenced by a Taos Society of Artists exhibition in Kansas City. CREDIT, MUSEUM OF NEW MEXICO.

96. Albert Fleury. *Panorama of Grand Canyon fro... Tovar*, oil on canvas 31 x 56″. Contrasts the canyon wit... tourist conveniences. CREDIT, THE ANSCHUTZ COL... TION.

97. J Bond Francisco. *Grand Canyon of Arizona—Morning*, oil on canvas 28 x 44″ signed LR. A "major painter" of his time in southern California. CREDIT, THE AUTHORS.

98. J A Fraser. *The Rogers Pass*, oil on canvas 22 x 30″ signed LL with JAF in monogram. He took a free ride to the Canadian Rockies in 1886. CREDIT, THE NATIONAL GALLERY OF CANADA, OTTAWA.

99. James Earle Fraser. *Pony Express/New Frontiers*, bronze medal 3″ diameter signed and dated 1952. By the sculptor who gave us the buffalo nickel. CREDIT, THE AUTHORS.

100. Feodor Fuchs. *Mountain Torrent*, oil on board 13¾ x 19¾″ signed (LL) F Fuchs. The designer of the lithograph *Custer's Last Charge/Custer's Todes-Ritt*. CREDIT, THE AUTHORS.

101. Charles Wellington Furlong. *The Peace Pipe*, pen, ink and crayon on paper 6 x 4½″ signed (LR) C Wellington Furlong and dated 1938. A drawing on the fly leaf of his book ''Let Er Buck.'' CREDIT, THE AUTHORS.

102. George W Gage. *He Found Himself Part of a Caravan*, oil grisaille on canvas 30 x 20″ signed (LL) G W Gage. Book illustrator who turned easel painter. CREDIT, THE AUTHORS.

103. John Gannam. *The Next Move*, wash over ink highlighted with white and brown 10 x 17″ separated for two pages. Illustrator known for blankets and babies. CREDIT THE AUTHORS.

104. Gilbert Gaul. *Mustangs on the Mesa*, oil on canvas 40 x 31″ signed LR. He said Indians were "like the white man— some were very good fellows and some were bad." CREDIT, THE ANSCHUTZ COLLECTION.

105. Sanford Robinson Gifford. *Mountain Landscape*, oil on canvas 25 x 36″. Hudson River School luminist in the Rockies 1870. CREDIT, SEATTLE ART MUSEUM, EUGENE FULLER MEMORIAL COLLECTION.

106. R F Gilder. *Yucca Plants/Cloudy Day near Tucson, Ariz*, oil on board 5 x 7″ signed LR. Nebraska newspaperman and archaeologist. CREDIT, THE AUTHORS.

7. Karl Gillessen. *Galveston*, oil on canvas mounted on ard 8 x 12½″ signed LL and painted about 1865. German ilitary painter in the Southwest as a medic. CREDIT, THE UTHORS.

108. Bill Gollings, *Warfare on e Plains*, oil on canvas 28 x 39″ signed (LR) Gollings. As a boy he was in Idaho when it was "full of Indians" with "no settlers at all." CREDIT, THE ANSCHUTZ COLLECTION.

109. Charles Graham. *Log Dwelling in the Forest*, watercolor 9 x 10″ signed (LL) C Graham and painted about 1870. Early work by the prolific *Harper's* illustrator. CREDIT, DENVER PUBLIC LIBRARY, WESTERN HISTORY DEPARTMENT.

110. H H Green. *The Long Trek*, oil on canvas 36 x 72″ signed LR. Buffalo illustrator of bird's-eye views. CREDIT, THE ANSCHUTZ COLLECTION.

111. Albert Lorey Groll. *Cliff Dwellers, Arizona*, crayon drawing 16 x 12″ textured on paper signed (LR) Groll and dated 1948. A landscape painter due to lack of money for models. CREDIT, THE AUTHORS.

112. William Grotz. *Looking for Trouble*, gouache 8 x 7″ signed LR. Illustrator for *Western Stories* in the 1920s. CREDIT, THE AUTHORS.

113. John Hafen. *The Harvest*, signed LR. A modest man whose life-style was poverty. CREDIT, CORPORATION OF THE PRESIDENT OF THE CHURCH OF JESUS CHRIST OF LATTER-DAY SAINTS, 1975.

114. Cyrenius Hall. *Scott's Bluffs*, small early watercolor signed (LL) C Hall and dated 1853. Hall's best-known work was a portrait of Chief Joseph. CREDIT, WYOMING STATE ARCHIVES AND HISTORICAL DEPARTMENT.

115. Arthur J Hammond. *Desperation Pass*, oil on canvas 32 x 40″ signed (LR) A J Hammond. Impressionist painter in New Mexico in the 1930s. CREDIT, THE AUTHORS.

116. John Hammond. *British Columbia Landscape*, oil on canvas 20 x 30″ signed LR. Member of Canadian railway survey party in the West 1870. CREDIT, THE NATIONAL GALLERY OF CANADA, OTTAWA.

117. John Hampton. *Roping*, oil signed (LL) J W Hampton with J W H as monogram and dated 1970. CAA member "the stork dropped on the wrong range." CREDIT, THE ARTIST.

118. T K Hanna. *View of a Western Fort*, oil on canvas 8 x 10″ signed (LL) Hanna and dated 1896. Early work by an illustrator. CREDIT, THE AUTHORS.

119. H W Hansen. *The Empty Saddle*, watercolor 20 x 30″ signed LR. By 1906, Tucson hadn't the "pictorial value of a copper cent." CREDIT, THE ANSCHUTZ COLLECTION.

120. Fred Harman. *Naughty Cowboys*, oil 28 x 38″ signed LR. The cartoonist of "Red Ryder" and CAA member. CREDIT, THE ARTIST.

121. Charles H Harmon. *Gunnison River Cañon,* oil 19½ x 15½″ signed LR and dated 1894. Landscape painter active in California and Colorado. CREDIT, DENVER PUBLIC LIBRARY, WESTERN HISTORY DEPARTMENT.

122. Lawren Harris, *North Shore, Baffin Island*, oil on board 11⅞ x 14¾″ dated 1930. Important theoretician of the Canadian Group of Seven. CREDIT, THE NATIONAL GALLERY OF CANADA, OTTAWA.

123. R G Harris. *Cover for Double Action Western*, oil on canvas 21 x 22″ signed LL and painted in 1934. From the pulps 1930s to slicks 1940s and portrait commissions 1960s. CREDIT, THE AUTHORS.

124. Marsden Hartley. *El Santo*, oil on canvas 26 x 32″ painted 1919. In Germany in 1922, he still painted images of New Mexico. CREDIT, MUSEUM OF NEW MEXICO.

125. J T Harwood. *Mountain in Spring*, signed LR. The first Utah painter to study in Paris. CREDIT, CORPORATION OF THE PRESIDENT OF THE CHURCH OF JESUS CHRIST OF LATTER-DAY SAINTS, 1975.

126. Childe Hassam. *Golden Afternoon, Oregon*, oil on canvas 30 x 40″ signed LL and dated 1908. Important painter of realistic impressions. CREDIT, THE METROPOLITAN MUSEUM OF ART, ROGERS FUND, 1911.

127. Earle Heikka. *Pack String*, bronze 15 x 41″. Montana taxidermist, painter of dioramas, wildlife painter, and sculptor. CREDIT, THE ANSCHUTZ COLLECTION.

128. Arthur Heming. *Pressing the Question*, wash drawing heightened with white 14 x 18″ signed LL and dated 1901. Color blind, he painted only in black, white, and yellow. CREDIT, THE AUTHORS.

129. William Penhallow Henderson. *In Old Mormontown, Santa Cruz, NM*, pastel on dark paper 7½ x 10″ signed LR and also with monogram. Studies of dances and landscapes were in pastel. CREDIT, THE AUTHORS.

131. E Martin Hennings. *Old Taos Plaza (The Hitching Post)*, oil on canvas 34 x 40″ painted 1921 and also called *Taos Plaza, Winter*. Pleasant decorative style. CREDIT, THE ANSCHUTZ COLLECTION.

). Albin Henning. *Smashing Western*, oil on canvas 30 x ′ signed LL and dated 1936. Harvey Dunn pupil best own for military illustration. CREDIT, THE AUTHORS.

Robert Henri. *Miguel of Tesuque*, oil on canvas 24 x ainted 1917. The "ashcan school" was urban, not ı. CREDIT, THE ANSCHUTZ COLLECTION.

133. Hermann Herzog. *Indian Hogans in the California Sierras*, oil on canvas 36 x 48″ signed (LR) H Herzog. German-American painter of mountain landscapes. CREDIT, THE ANSCHUTZ COLLECTION.

135. Eugene Higgins. *Southwest Town*, pencil on paper 8 x 10″ signed LR. Realist "who paints beggars because he is one." CREDIT, THE AUTHORS.

134. Bobby Hicks, *Girl Picking Corn*, gouache 10 x 8″ signed LR. Navaho painter and teacher. CREDIT, THE AUTHORS.

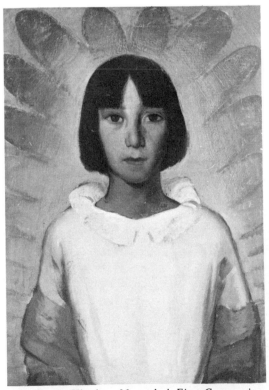

136. Victor Higgins. *Mercedes' First Communion*, oil 28 x 16″ signed LL. Eighth member of the Taos Society of Artists whose style moved from romantic to modern. CREDIT, MUSEUM OF NEW MEXICO.

137. Thomas Hill. *Mountain Cascade*, oil on canvas 23 signed T Hill and dated 1881 on reverse. He painted *Yo Valley* while in Boston. CREDIT, THE AUTHORS.

only woman who was an important early Western illustrator, engraver, painter, author. Work in AIC, Worcester AM. References A31 (as Mary Foote living NYC)-BEN-FIE-MAL-SMI. Sources AIW-ARM-HUT-POW-WAA-WHO 31-WOM. No current auction record but the estimated price for a sketch 10×14″ of a view looking toward the mine would be about $1,000 to $1,200 at auction in 1976. Illustration examples plates 63, 64 AIW.

Mrs Foote studied with Dr William Rimmer at Cooper Inst in NYC during the Civil War. She was also the pupil of William J Linton, the wood engraver, and Frost Johnson, the still-life and genre painter who was professor of art at Fordham in the 1870s. Her first illustrations in 1867 included Western subjects although she did not visit the West until after her 1876 marriage to Arthur De Wint Foote, a mining engineer. Beginning with 1877 she wrote and illustrated articles for *Scribner's Monthly* on life in a California mining camp. She was immediately popular. At Leadville, Colo in 1879 she was sought by Helen Hunt Jackson, the proponent of justice for Indians, and by the more famous *Harper's* illustrator W A Rogers. In Colorado she illustrated for *Scribner's* and wrote romantic novels with Colorado backgrounds. Next, the Foote family went to Mexico, with articles in *The Century Magazine* 1881–82. From 1883 to 1893 Mr Foote was engineer on an Idaho irrigation project. Mrs Foote wrote stories with an Idaho background and painted her most successful illustrations, 11 of which were published in *Century* in 1888–89. She spent the last 30 years of her life at North Star Mine in Grass Valley, Cal but her oil portrait *Old Lady* was exhibited at the revolutionary 1913 Armory Show along with the French Fauves and the Impressionists.

Mrs Foote's reputation as a writer has diminished with time. In 1922 she said of her first novel, "What a silly sort of heroine she would seem today." AIW. Her importance as a Western illustrator will grow although her original sketches have disappeared. In the beginning she drew directly on the wood engraving blocks which were destroyed in printing. Her teacher called her "the best of our designers on the wood."

FORBES, Edwin. Born NYC 1839, died Brooklyn, NY 1895. Important Civil War illustrator, historical painter, etcher. Work in War Dept, Washington. References BEN-CHA-DAB-FIE-G&W-MAL-SMI. Sources AIW-ANT 7/68-AOA-BOA-CIV-HUT-KW1-MSL-NJA. No current auction record. Signature example p 2 ANT 7/68.

Forbes began studying art in 1857, becoming the pupil of Arthur F Tait in 1859. He was initially an animal painter, then broadened his subjects to include genre and landscape. In 1861 he was a Civil War illustrator for *Frank Leslie's Illustrated Newspaper*. A leading special artist, Forbes sketched camp life and battles with the Army of the Potomac, remaining in the South. He returned to New York in 1865, spending the rest of his life elaborating on these war sketches. The most famous painting that resulted was *Lull in the Fight*, painted in 1865 from a drawing of the Battle of the Wilderness.

In 1867 Forbes was one of the illustrators for A D Richardson's "Beyond the Mississippi," turning to Western subjects along with other great correspondents of the war. In 1876, 92 of his war sketches were republished as "Life Studies of the Great Army." In 1884 Congress considered buying for the nation the "Forbes Historical Collection" including the war sketches but the appropriation bill was defeated. When his right side was paralyzed late in his career, Forbes learned to paint with his left hand.

FORBES, Helen Katherine. Born San Francisco, Cal 1891, living there (summers Palo Alto, Cal) 1941. Cal landscape and mural painter, etcher. Member, Mural Ptrs. Work in San Diego FAG, MCA; murals Zoo Mother House (San Francisco), PO (Merced). References A41-BEN-FIE-MAL. Sources BDW-WAA. No auction record of signature example.

Miss Forbes studied at the San Francisco IA and was the pupil of A Hansen, Van Sloun, Graeber, and Ernest Leyden. She also studied in Paris with Lhote. Her landscapes were painted at Mono Lake area in the late 1920s, Death Valley in the early 1930s, and Virginia City, Nev.

FORD, Henry Chapman. Born Livonia, NY 1828, died Santa Barbara, Cal 1894. Early Western landscape painter, illustrator. Reference G&W. Sources AIW-HON-POW. No current auction record or signature example.

Ford studied in Europe 1857–60, in Paris and Florence. He enlisted in the Civil War, receiving a disability discharge in 1862. His war sketches were published in the illustrated papers of the day. In 1863 he opened a studio as the first professional landscape painter in Chicago.

In 1866 Ford, his wife and child, along with fellow Chicago painters J F Gookins and H A Elkins, formed a wagon party of 8 to tour the West at the same time that T R Davis, Alfred Mathews, A R Waud, W H Beard, and Whittredge were sketching in the West. Ford's party joined an immigrant train from Omaha. A *Storm on the Plains* was recorded by Gookins' sketch in *Harper's Weekly*. The party returned to Chicago after the summer, with the three painters exhibiting their work in 1867. Ford went back to the West in 1869. Little is known of his Western work, particularly in view of the destruction of his studio in the fire of 1871. He was the president of the Chicago Academy of Design in 1873,

moved to Santa Barbara for reasons of health in 1875, and is remembered for his 1883 series of 24 etchings on the Franciscan missions of California.

FORSYTHE, Victor Clyde. Born Orange, Cal 1885, died California 1962. Important Western desert painter, sculptor, illustrator, cartoonist. Member, Painters of the West. Work in Munic AG (Phoenix), HAR, Earl C Adams colln. References A41-BEN-FIE-MAL. Sources COW-HAR-TWR-WAI 71. No current auction record but the estimated price of an oil 30×25″ showing a bronc rider would be about $5,000 to $6,000 at auction in 1976. Signature example p 81 HAR. Photo p 130 BOR.

Forsythe's family came from Tombstone where his father had witnessed the fight at the OK Corral. In Los Angeles, Forsythe studied with Louisa MacLeod at the School of Art and Design. At 19 he went East to study at the ASL where he was the pupil of DuMond. The next year, he became a staff artist for the *New York World,* covering news events with his drawings. He also did cartoons and comic strips such as "Way Out West." During WWI he painted propaganda posters. By the time he was 35 he was immensely successful. He owned a yacht, played golf with Damon Runyon, started Norman Rockwell at *The Saturday Evening Post,* knew illustrators Charles Dana Gibson and Howard Chandler Christy.

At this point Forsythe elected to return to California, to paint as a Westerner and to associate with California celebrities like Walt Disney, Will Rogers, and Gary Cooper. He shared a big studio with Frank Tenney Johnson, complete with cowboy gear and Indian artifacts. He produced a large volume of paintings of the desert remembered, the mining camps as they had been, the prospectors, and the ghost towns. His subjects and colors became a stereotype of the desert sky and the prospector's burro.

FOSTER, Benjamin. Born North Anson, Me 1852, died NYC 1926. Conn landscape painter, member Society of Men Who Paint the Far West, writer. ANA 1901, NA 1904, NIAL. Work in COR, NGA, PAFA, MMA, AIC, etc. References A26 (obit)-BEN-DAB-FIE-MAL-SMI. Sources AMA-COR-M31-MSL-NA 74-WHO 24. OIL 42×48" *New England Landscape* signed but not dated sold 5/22/72 for $300 at auction. Painting example opp p 181 AMA.

Son of a politician, Ben Foster was raised in Richmond, Me. He went to NYC at 18, working in the mercantile trade. In 1882 he turned to art, studying with Abbott Thayer and at the ASL. He spent 1886 in Paris, the pupil of Merson and Morot. Thereafter, he settled at his Cornwall Hollow, Conn farm, painting atmospheric landscapes. His paintings were begun on location but finished from memory in the studio to permit reality to reach the "sublimation of the ideal." DAB. His winter home was in NYC. Success started with the World's Columbian Expos in 1893.

With Elliott Daingerfield and DeWitt Parshall, Foster was an official of the Society of Men Who Paint the Far West.

FOX, Charles Lewis. Born Portland, Me 1854, died there 1927. Painter of Indians. References A27 (obit)-MAL. No other source, auction record, or signature example.

Fox studied architecture at MIT and was the painting pupil of Bonnat and Cabanel in Paris for six years. He was known as a socialist and a philanthropist.

FOX, R Atkinson. Born Toronto, Can 1860, living Philadelphia, Pa 1900. Illustrator specializing in the Can Northwest, painter. Reference A00. No other source.

No auction record or signature example. Photo of Fox p 455 A98.

Fox was the pupil of J W Bridgeman at the Ontario Society of Artists in Toronto. A member of the Art Club of Philadelphia, he exhibited in 1898 ※124 *Cattle* and ※158 *A Bull*. Two collections of Western works have come to light.

FRANCISCO, John Bond. Born Cincinnati. Ohio 1863, died Los Angeles, Cal 1931. Cal painter of figures and mountain landscapes, teacher, violinist. References A31-BEN-FIE-MAL-SMI. Sources AAR 11/74-BDW-JCA-WHO 30. No current auction record. Signature example p 130 AAR 11/74. (See illustration 97).

Francisco was educated at Ohio State U. In painting he was the pupil of Fechner in Berlin and Nauen in Munich. In Paris he studied at Julien and Colarossi academies, with Bouguereau, Robert-Fleury, and Courtois. While in Europe he sketched in Switzerland, the Tyrol, Germany, and France, and studied the violin in Berlin and Paris.

In 1887 he settled in Los Angeles, specializing in paintings of California mountains and trees. His view of the Grand Canyon was reproduced for a travel ad. Francisco also painted the "gorgeous glowing" of the Southwestern desert, occasionally including a prospector and his burro. JCA. He and Judson were called the "major painters in the first decade of the 20th century in LA." AAR.

FRASER, James Earle. Born Winona, Minn 1876, died Westport, Conn 1953. Important sculptor. NSS, ANA 1912, NA 1917. Work, *The End of the Trail,* in Brookgreen Gardens, Detroit IA, City AM (St Louis), Cowboy Hall of Fame, also statues, coins, medals, decorations.

References A53-BEN-ENB-FIE-MAL-SMI. Sources ACM-ALA-AMA-ANT 1/75-ARM-COW-DEP-ISH-JNB-MSL-PER vol 5 ✕2-SCU-WHO 52. Bronze, green patina, 12″ high, *The End of the Trail* with signature example, marked Roman Bronze Works sold 10/27/71 for $3,250 at auction. Bronze, brown patina *44″ The End of the Trail,* signed and dated, marked Gorham & Co sold 10/31/75 for $42,500. (See illustrations 99a & b.)

In public school in Minneapolis, Fraser carved blackboard chalk when that was the only available medium. His father was a railroad engineer in charge of laying track across the Western plains. Their home was a railway car, and Fraser was in the Dakotas as a boy, familiar with Indians and buffalo bones. At 18 Fraser went to the AIC for drawing classes and was the pupil of Richard Bock for sculpture. At 20, he entered the École des Beaux-Arts in Paris under Falguière, the Julien Academy, and Colarossi. At 22 he became assistant to the major sculptor Augustus Saint-Gaudens, remaining until 1902 when Fraser opened his own studio in NYC. His first important commission was a bust of Theodore Roosevelt now in the Capitol. In 1913 Fraser married his former student, Laura Gardin, who was an accomplished sculptor in her own right.

Fraser designed the five-cent "buffalo nickel" that was issued in 1913. He used three different Indians to obtain the portrait. One was the Sioux chief Iron-Tail. The bison on the reverse was modeled after Black Diamond in the NY Zoo, slaughtered in 1915 and mounted. Fraser made the figure full, intending no inscription, so there was no room for "In God We Trust." His statue *The End of the Trail* was the most popular work at the Panama-Pacific Exposition at San Francisco in 1915. There were more requests for purchase of this design than any other work. It was also issued in various usual bronze sizes, and has been reissued by Modern Art foundry.

In 1968 the Cowboy Hall of Fame acquired and restored the original 16′ plaster of *The End of the Trail.*

FRASER, John Arthur. Born London, Eng 1838 (or 1839), died NYC 1898. Can landscape painter in the Rockies 1886; photograph tinter. A founder, Royal Can Acad 1879. Work in NGC. References A98 (necrol)-BEN-MAL-SMI. Sources CAH-CAN-CAR-DCA. No auction record. Signature example ✕57 CAR. (See illustration 98.)

Fraser studied at the RA Schools in London with F W Topham and R Redgrave, earning his way by painting portraits. He emigrated to Canada with his family in 1856. When William Notman hired Fraser to tint photographs in Montreal, Fraser proved so skillful "it was difficult for even artists to detect the photographic base." CAN. Notman made Fraser a partner in charge of the new Toronto branch in 1868. Fraser had been a founding member of the Society of Canadian Artists in 1867 and became a charter member of the Royal Canadian Artists. In 1883 he went to the US where Notman opened offices.

In 1886 the Canadian Pacific Ry offered free transportation to the Rockies for artists, enabling Fraser to paint the landscapes of the Rockies for which he was best known: "He saw clearly the beauty as well as the grandeur of mountain scenery." DCA. *In the Rockies* had "wonderfully luminous colour" and a "profound sweep of the Canadian sky." CAH.

FRASER, Thomas Douglass. Born Vallejo, Cal 1883 (or 1885), died probably there 1955. Cal landscape painter, muralist. Work in White House (Washington), schools, ships, clubs; mural panels in Bohemian Club (San Francisco). References A47-BEN-MAL. Source, A41 listings *Our Camp, Bohemian Grove, Donner Lake, Cliff Shadows, Monterey Cypress Trees*. No auction record or signature example.

Douglass Fraser studied at Mark Hopkins IA with Arthur Mathews, at the California School of Design, at the ASL, and was the pupil of DuMond and Hawthorne.

FRAZER, Mabel Pearl. Born West Jordan, Utah 1887, living Salt Lake City, Utah 1965. Utah painter of realism, teacher. Work in State of Utah colln; murals in LDS Temple, schools. References A62-MAL. Source YUP. No current auction record. Painting example p 28 YUP.

Miss Frazer was the pupil of Edwin Evans at the U of Utah in 1914, after teaching at Beaver, Utah 1910–11. She taught at Jr High School in Ogden 1914–16, then studied with DuMond at the ASL in NYC 1916–17. She taught at the Col of Southern Utah 1918–19, then studied at the Beaux-Arts in NYC 1919–20. She was professor of art at the U of Utah 1920 until her retirement in 1953, with time for study in Europe 1930–32 and for Latin American research 1949–52.

She is regarded as continuing the Evans approach toward painting realism in life. "Though not prolific, she has produced works of exceptional strength." YUP.

FRAZIER, Esther Yates. Active in Colorado as a self-taught painter in the 1860s. Mrs. Frazier's address was Highland, Denver, Colo Territory. Work in State Hist Soc of Colo. No reference.

Sources DBW (oil 40×36″ *Arapahoe Encampment* not dated)-DCC (oil 19×32″ *Arapahoe and Cheyenne Encampment* dated 1861). No auction record or signature example.

FREDERIKSEN, Mary Monrad (Mrs Walter Ufer). Born Copenhagen, Denmark 1869, living Taos, NM 1941. Taos painter, lecturer, teacher. Member SIA. References A41-MAL. Source BDW. No auction record or signature example.

Miss Frederiksen studied in France and was the pupil of Constant, Laurens, Hofmann, Merson, and Whistler. She married Walter Ufer in Chicago in 1905, the year he began with the advertising department of Armour & Co. The Ufers arrived in Taos in 1914. Walter Ufer died in Albuquerque in 1936.

FREE, John D. Born Osage Cnty, Okla 1929, living on a ranch near Bigheart, Okla 1976. Traditional Western sculptor, painter, specializing in works showing cowboys in action. Member CAA, Nat Acad of Western Art. Work in GIL, Nat Cowboy Hall of Fame. Reference A76. Sources C73,74-COW-OSR. No current auction record. Signature example C74 *A Doubtful Dally*.

Free, grandson of an Osage Indian, was brought up on a ranch as a working hand. He attended college for veterinary studies. In Western art he feels an advantage because it is a subject known to him. Free wants to document the cowboy and ranch work in bronze and on canvas. His original models for sculpture are in wax. Typical titles for bronzes are *Layin' Him Down, Signal to String 'Em, Nothin' Like a Chaw*. Paintings include *One Found, Three Homeward Bound, Tough Money, Headin' for the Pay Window*.

FREEMAN, W E (Bill). Born Greensboro, NC 1927, living Scottsdale, Ariz 1975. Traditional Western painter, illustrator, sculptor. No reference. Sources BRO-COW-WAI 71. No current auction record. Signature example p 122 COW.

Freeman's father was a portrait painter who died in 1930. To support the family, his mother continued as a painter and as a teacher. Freeman grew up in El Paso. He was a working cowboy before devoting himself full time to painting in 1957. Freeman has hunted lions and has painted big game animals and illustrated a book on javelina. "When I paint horses," the tall cowboy says, "I try to make them appear either at work, as pack animals, or at play." WAI 71.

FRENZENY, Paul. Born in France about 1840, died probably London 1902. Active in US 1868–89. Important special artist, illustrator for *Harper's Weekly* in the West. Work in GIL, DPL, BMFA. No reference. Sources AIW-ANT 10/62-AOA-CAP-DCC-GIL-HON-IND-KW1-POW-WES. Oil 12¼ ×21" *Indians on Horseback Attacking* dated 1898 sold 10/16/69 for $5,280 at auction in London. Signature examples p 125 WES, p 165 KW1.

Frenzeny had served in the French cavalry in Mexico about 1865. By 1868 he was an illustrator for *Harper's Weekly* with 20 published sketches of Mexico, NYC, and Pennsylvania. In 1873 he was commissioned with another French artist Jules Tavernier to sketch westward across the country. It is thought that they worked directly on the wood engraving block, Frenzeny probably doing the foreground detail because he was more skilled with the pencil. We can assume they were chosen for the trip because, although they were foreign, excitable, and eccentric, the West was unusual to them even in its commonplace features so they would record it all. They began with the Western emigrants in NYC and followed them by train to Pittsburgh. The pair then went by train to the end of the line in Texas, north to Wichita, west again by train and stage to Denver where they wintered. In 1874 they visited Wyoming, Nebraska, and Utah before proceeding by train to San Francisco. The resulting illustrations provide "pictorial records of the West—towns, living conditions, transportation, industries of plain and mountain, emigrant life, Indian troubles and affairs, and minor but revealing incidents of Western life—that are nowhere else available. The illustrations are authentic and made from direct observation of the scenes depicted." AIW.

Frenzeny became a member of the Bohemian Club in San Francisco in 1874. *Harper's Weekly* published his California and Nevada sketches until 1878. In 1879 he was responsible for views of Central America. From 1882 to 1887 his illustrations appear in *Leslie's Weekly*. In 1889 he illustrated a book on Western life, "Fifty Years on the Trail." This is the last date generally given for him, except for the auction record above.

FRIBERG, Arnold. Born Winnetka, Ill 1913, living Salt Lake City, Utah 1976. Traditional Western painter, illustrator. Member RSA (London). Reference A76. Source AHI 8/73. No current auction record. Signature example p 9 AHI 8/73.

Friberg's parents were Mormons who moved to Arizona when he was three. When he was 10 he had a correspondence course in cartooning and advice from Fred Smith, cartoonist for *The Arizona Republican*. When he was 17 he went to Chicago to study. By 1937 he was a commercial artist in Chicago when he received a continuing commission for a series on the Northwest Mounted

Police used as calendar art. He also illustrated The Book of Mormon and received an Academy Award nomination for his paintings and designs for the movie *The Ten Commandments*. In 1969 he began a commissioned series of historical paintings of the American West.

Friberg became a Western painter in 1971, regarding painting as an extension of illustrating: "Most of the best American painters did at least some illustrative work. Edwin Abbey, Winslow Homer, John Sloan, Frederic Remington, for example. They developed into painters but their training was in the illustrative world that makes you observe. For myself, I have no purpose but to tell a story." AHI.

FRIEND, Washington F. Born Washington, DC about 1820, died probably England after 1881. Landscape watercolorist in the West in 1870, panoramist, topographic artist, musician. Work in Honeyman and Karolik collns. Reference BEN. Sources ANT 9/68 (offering watercolors at $500 each, p 272)-HON-KW1,2. Watercolor 15×22″ *Genesee River* sold 4/10/68 for $540 at auction in London. Signature example p 272 ANT 9/68.

Friend's Boston music school failed in 1847 after one year when he suffered financial losses in a theater fire. His Wabash River "Floating Museum" failed in 1848 through navigational difficulties. In 1849 he began his three-year and 5,000-mile sketching tour of east and central United States and Canada for a panorama he painted back in NYC. The canvas was made on a special loom in England. The panorama was exhibited first in Quebec, then Montreal, NYC, Boston, Philadelphia, etc. When it was shown in London in 1864, it lasted two hours and cost one shilling. Friend sang songs appropriate to the views—"Massa's in the Cold, Cold Ground" to accompany

Poughkeepsie by Sunset. He offered a 32-page pamphlet with engravings and sold his original sketches. The Queen bought one.

"In 1950 several New York dealers had watercolors of the American West by Friend." KW2. Subjects listed in collections include *In the Rocky Mountains, Garden of the Gods, Yosemite Falls* (dated 1870), and *Placer Mining.* Of English descent, Friend had until 1962 been classified as English.

FRIPP, Charles Edwin. Born Hampstead, London, Eng 1854, died Montreal, Can 1906. English Special Artist-illustrator, war correspondent, Western landscape painter, author. Work in McCord Mus (Montreal), Centennial Mus (Vancouver). References BEN-MAL. Source AOH. No recent auction record but the estimated price for an ink and wash drawing heightened with white 14×10″ of a Northwest Indian would be about $800 to $1,000 at auction in 1976. Signature example p 238 AOH.

Fripp's father was a major landscape watercolorist. Fripp was educated at London and Nürnberg and at the Royal Academy in Munich. When he was 24 he began as Special Artist for *Graphic,* covering the Kaffir War in 1878, the Zulu War in 1879, the Boer War in 1881, a world trip by yacht 1881–84, in Sudan 1885, then Western Canada while going to and from the Far East 1889–90, the Sino-Japanese War 1894–95, in Africa for the Matabele War 1896–97, in Canada and Alaska for the Klondike gold rush in 1898 before covering the Philippines Campaign of the Spanish-American War, and finally the South African War in 1900.

Fripp had settled in British Columbia in 1893 with his brother Thomas. It was from there that he left for the Klondike in answer to the *Graphic*'s cable. His report was in the form of 18 letters with 50 drawings in the *Daily* and another 22 drawings in the weekly. Fripp's views showed the official route to the Klondike to have been practically impassable, the trip from Victoria to Dawson consuming three months of misery from ice, cold, terrain, mud, rustling, mosquitoes. In Dawson the gold was illusory, the diggings having been already claimed. In a month the Klondike story dwindled in importance and Fripp's editors called him to the Philippines.

FRIPP, Thomas William. Born London, Eng 1864, died Vancouver, BC, Can 1931. Watercolorist of the Canadian Western landscape. Work in NGC, Govt House (Ontario and BC), Vancouver AG. Reference MAL. Sources AOH-CAN-WNW. Watercolor 7⅜×10¼" *A Hilly Landscape* sold 5/15/73 for $340 at auction in Toronto.

Son and grandson of English watercolorists, Fripp studied at the Royal Academy School and was the pupil of his father. He also studied in Italy. His older brother Charles Edwin Fripp, a special artist for the London *Graphic,* had been in the Canadian West in 1889. A third brother, Robert MacKay Fripp, was an architect in Vancouver.

In 1893, poor opportunities in England led Fripp, his bride, and his brother Charles to emigrate to the pioneer life on a homestead near Hatzic, BC where they established a ranch. Charles left for the Yukon in 1898 as a "special" for the *Graphic.* Fripp was forced back to painting in 1901 when an injured hand precluded farming. "Said to have been the best watercolor painter of the West Coast," Fripp for 30 years produced "many pictures of the Rocky Mountains and the Pacific Coast." CAN. At his death a life-size bust was paid for by popular subscription for exhibition at the Vancouver AG.

FROMENT (or Froment-Delormel), Jacques Victor Eugène. Born Paris, France 1820, died there 1900. French history, genre, and landscape painter. Chevalier, Legion of Honor 1863. Work in French museums Autun, Bourges, Dieppe, Lyon. References BEN-CHA-MAS. Source, listed paintings, *Indians Surprising Camp of Hostile Tribe* (1849), *Pawnee Children on the Platte River* (1853). No current auction record but *Amours* sold 1/23/03 for $250 at auction. No signature example.

Froment was the pupil of Jollivet, P Lecompte, and Amaury-Duval. He exhibited in the Paris Salon from 1842 to 1880.

FROST, Arthur Burdett. Born Philadelphia, Pa 1851, died Pasadena, Cal 1928. Humorous illustrator of rural and sporting subjects, painter. Member SI 1905. Work in World's Columb Expos (1893), Kahn colln. References A28 (obit)-BEN-DAB-FIE-MAL-SMI. Sources AIW-ALA-ANT 6/41,7/64; 3, 7/68; 3,11/69; 1/70,3/72,5/73-AOA-CAN-ILA-ILP-190-KAH-MSL-NJA-WHO 28. Watercolor en grisaille 18¾ × 21¼" *The Yellow-Green Paper off a Block of Chocolate* signed and used as a Scribner's 1916 illustration, sold 5/11/74 for $1,900 at auction. In 1947 his watercolor *Breaking the Ice* sold for $1,550 at auction. Signature example "A Book of Drawings" by A B Frost, P F Collier & Son, NY 1904.

Son of a textbook editor who died when Frost was eight, Frost worked for a wood engraver and then a lithographer while sketching in the evenings. He studied briefly with Eakins at the PAFA. His long career as an illustrator began with drawing on wood for "Hurly Burly" in 1874. By 1876 Frost was on the staff of *Harper's,* on his way to becoming one of the major Eastern illustrators of the turn of the century along with Pyle and

Abbey. His specialty was folk humor such as *Uncle Remus* and *The Tar-Baby*. In London in 1877–78, he went to Paris 1908–16, to enable his two sons to study there. His residence was in New Jersey and Pennsylvania 1883–1907.

In the course of his book and magazine illustrations, Frost made Western drawings as commissioned. The most notable were for Theodore Roosevelt's "Hunting Trips of a Ranchman" (1885): *Sage-Fowl Shooting, Cutting Off Band of Prong-Horn, Shot at a Mountain Ram,* the Frostian *Tête-à-Tête* of the buffalo at the top of a cliff meeting the dude hunter concluding his climb to the top, and *Close Quarters with Old Ephraim*. Frost also illustrated "Stories of a Western Town" (1893). He died at the home of his son John Frost the California landscapist.

FROST, John (Jack). Born Philadelphia, Pa 1890, died Pasadena, Cal 1937. Pa and Cal landscape painter, illustrator. References A41-BEN-FIE-MAL-SMI. Sources SCA-WHO 36. No current auction record or signature example.

Frost was the son and pupil of the illustrator A B Frost. He worked in California in the 1920s, winning a landscape prize at the Southwest Museum in 1922.

FUCHS, Feodor (or Theodore). Active 1856–76. Lithographic artist, landscape painter. Work in DPL, Lib Cong. Reference G&W. Sources CUS-DBW. Colored lithographic print 21×26½" *Custer's Last Charge/Custer's Todes-Ritt* signed in the stone only and dated 1876 sold 10/27/71 for $900 at auction. Signature example p 23 CUS. (See illustration 100.)

The only reference to Feodor Fuchs is as a lithographer at 17 Minor Street in Philadelphia in 1856. Fuchs illustrated the "Horticulturist and Journal of Rural Art and Rural Taste" and painted portraits of Civil War personalities. He is not listed as of sufficient importance to have exhibited at the PAFA.

The print *Custer's Last Charge* was "designed by Feodor Fuchs" who signed the work. It was entered by Seifert Gugler & Co which was a lithographic firm in Milwaukee and published by the Milwaukee Litho & Engr Co which also published the most popular 1896 lithograph by Otto Becker of *Custer's Last Fight*.

FURLONG, Charles Wellington. Born Cambridge, Mass 1874, living Scituate, Mass 1962. Painter, ethnologist, writer, explorer. Life drawings of Indians in Smithsonian Inst, Dartmouth Col. References A62-BEN-FIE-MAL-SMI. Sources WHO 68-preface by G P Putnam to Furlong's "let 'Er Buck!" No auction record. Drawing example p xxi "let 'Er Buck!" (See illustration 101.)

Son of a musician-painter, Furlong attended Boston public schools, graduated from Mass Normal Art School in 1895, and went to Cornell and Harvard. He taught at Cornell beginning 1896 and studied in Paris at École des Beaux-Arts and Julien Academy 1901–2 with Bouguereau and Laurens. In his roving adventure-filled life, Furlong stayed in the skin tents of the Patagonians, fought in the Sahara, rode with both Moroccan tribesmen and Venezuelan vaqueros, served as military aide to Pres Wilson, wrote six successful books, exhibited paintings in leading art museums, and drew illustrations for national magazines.

Furlong lived in the Western range country and knew the life, particularly the early rodeo and the Pendleton Round-Up. In "let 'Er Buck!" Furlong is pictured participating in the bucking bull rough-riding.

GAGE, George William. Born Lawrence, Mass 1887, living NYC 1962. Illustrator for books and magazines including Western subjects, painter, teacher. Member Artists Guild. Work in colleges, libraries, hospitals, schools, companies, NAD. References A62-FIE-MAL. Source AAC. No auction record but the estimated price of a Western illustration in oil would be about $600 to $800 at auction in 1976. No signature example. (See illustration 102.)

G W Gage studied at the BMFA School with Philip Hale and Frank W Benson and then the PAFA with William Chase and Howard Pyle. In AAC (1924) and A33, Gage was listed as an illustrator, living at 61 Poplar Street in Brooklyn and designing covers for "leading" magazines and illustrating "numerous" books as well as teaching book illustration at the NY Evening School of Industrial Art. In A62 he was listed as a painter with studios in NYC and exhibiting throughout the East with works in public collections. As a book illustrator Gage was more simplified and sketchy than his mentor Pyle.

GALLI, Stanley W. Born probably California 1912, living probably Kentfield, Cal 1966. Illustrator for magazine and advertising commissions. Work in *McCall's, True,* book covers. No reference. Sources ILA-IL 59, 63. No current auction record. Signature example ✳217 IL 63.

Galli graduated from high school about 1930. For seven years he worked at physical jobs, roustabout, ranch hand, longshoreman. With his savings he studied at California SFA in San Francisco and worked for a San Francisco art service until after WWII. When he became a free-lance illustrator, his editorial and advertising assignments included Western subjects that were made easier by his experience as a cowboy in Nevada. IL 63

shows a Galli cover for a paperback Western book.

GALPIN, Cromwell. Active 1895. Western illustrator for *St Nicholas* magazine, NYC. No reference. Source AIW. No auction record or signature example.

The only listed illustration by Galpin is *The Bronco's Best Race* published in 1895.

GAMBEE, Martin. Born Newark, NJ 1905, living San Miguel de Allende, Mexico 1962. Illustrator specializing in Southwestern genre including Navaho, painter, printmaker, teacher. Member Artists Guild. Work in MNM, Albany Inst Hist & Art, Phila Art All. References A62-MAL. Source ILG. No auction record. Signature example p 37 ILG.

Gambee studied with Howard Giles, Gustave Cimiotti, James Pinto, Eliot O'Hara, with André Lhote in Paris, and at Pratt Institute Art School in Brooklyn. Gambee spent three summers with the Navaho.

In the 1930s Gambee lived in Pawling, NY, a member of the Artists Guild as an illustrator. The Guild Annual for 1939 shows two Western illustrations. In 1947 Gambee lived in Carmel, Cal, listed as a painter. In 1962 Gambee was instructor in painting at the Instituto Allende, San Miguel, Mexico.

GANNAM, John. Born in Lebanon 1907, died Danbury, Conn 1965. Illustrator, watercolorist. ANA, member SI. References A66 (obit)-MAL. Sources DIC-ILA-ILG-IL 42,63. No current auction record but the estimated price of a watercolor detailed with opaque 10×14" showing a Western barroom confrontation would be about $600 to $800 at auction in 1976. Signature example p 183 ILA. (See illustration 103.)

Gannam was raised in Chicago. He left school at 14 when his father died. Gannam was hired as a messenger boy for an engraving house, eventually teaching himself to become an artist for engravers, working in Chicago and Detroit. He established his studio in NYC by 1935, doing magazine and advertising illustrations. He painted mainly in watercolor, exhibiting easel paintings at the AWCS, and teaching at the Danbury, Conn AA.

It is not known whether Gannam visited the West, but, like other major illustrators of the period, he did receive commissions for Western paintings. One is illustrated in ILA. His technique in developing compositions is shown in detail in DIC, involving progression from a chalk sketch to a tempera sketch to the finished watercolor.

GAREL, Leo. Born NYC, NY 1917, living Mt Tremper, NY 1962. Painter, illustrator, cartoonist, teacher. Reference A62. Source TAL. No auction record. Painting example ✗24 TAL.

Garel studied at the Parsons School Fine & Applied Art and at the ASL, the pupil of George Grosz and Vaclav Vytlacil. In 1947 he was a resident of Taos, "a big, robust fellow and his work is all of a piece with him." TAL. He illustrated "how to" and quiz books and contributed cartoons to major magazines.

GASPARD, Leon. Born Vitebsk, Russia 1882, died Taos, NM 1964. Important Taos painter. Work in MNM, AIC, ANS, HAR, Harrison Eiteljorg colln, Earl C Adams colln. References A41-FIE-MAL-SMI. Sources AAR 3/74-ANT 11/66,7/67,4/74-COW-DCC-HAR-PAW-PET-PIT-TAL-TSF-TWR-WAI 71,72-WHO 46. No current auction record but the estimated price of an oil 20×30″ showing Taos on Christmas would be about $10,000 to $15,000 at auction in 1976. Signature example p 88 PIT.

Gaspard was the son of a retired Russian army officer who took him along as a boy on fur trading trips to Siberia. In Vitebsk he became the pupil of Julius Penn, along with Marc Chagall, a most important Post-Impressionist artist. Gaspard also studied in Odessa and Moscow before going to Paris at 17 for study at the Julien Academy with Édouard Toudouze and Bouguereau, "the supreme academician." His first one-man show while still a student resulted in the purchase of 35 Paris sketches by a NY collector. Gaspard took his American wife on a two-year horseback honeymoon in Siberia in 1908. The resulting paintings were a Paris success. He was seriously wounded as a French aviator shot down in WWI and moved to NYC in 1916.

When his doctors recommended a warmer climate, he settled in Taos in 1918. Although the established Taos artists received him coldly, except for Dunton, Gaspard found in the Indians and the terrain the basis for commercial success with his "bright palette and freely drawn, loosely painted scenes." TWR. His paintings show "a love of exciting color and highly developed pattern. The intricate fabric of his methods of design are to an extent concealed by the accomplished way in which he preserves the casual immediacy of a sketch, even in large-scale studio work." TSF. Gaspard continued to travel extensively and to paint productively until his death.

GAUL, William Gilbert. Born Jersey City, NJ 1855, died NYC 1919. Important military and Western painter, illustrator. ANA 1879, NA 1882. Work in Toledo MA, Peabody Inst (Baltimore), Democratic Club NYC, GIL, ANS, KAH, C R Smith colln. References A19 (obit)-BEN-CHA-DAB-ENB-FIE-MAL-SMI. Sources AIW-ANS-ANT 4/57,12/61, 12/66,12/67,4/69,5/72,3/73-COW-CRS-DCC-GIL-ILA-ISH-KAH-MSL-PAW-POW-WHO 18. Oil 40×30″ *Indian Camp* signed not dated sold 4/11/73 for $13,000 at auction. Signature example p 451 ANT 4/69. (See illustration 104.)

Gilbert Gaul was educated at Claverack Military Academy. He was the pupil of L E Wilmarth at the NAD 1872–76 and privately under J G Brown. His early subjects emulated his teachers' popular and sentimental genre works. This was revised by his commission from *Century* magazine to illustrate the historical "Battles and Leaders of the Civil War" published in 1887. He became known as a foremost American painter of battle scenes: "Uniforms and arms of many kinds were to be seen in his studio. The historic accuracy of each detail was studiously sought, and the models who posed as soldiers were fit types. All of these canvases were remarkable for energy of action and, above all, their spirit of belligerency." DAB.

Gaul spent much time in the West at army posts and on Indian reservations in the 1880s. He was one of the five special agents who took the census of 1890 among the Indians, illustrating the "Report on Indians Taxed and Indians Not Taxed" with a strong portrait of Sitting Bull painted from life. Gaul visited the Cheyenne River and Standing Rock agencies then, with later trips to the northwest coast. Some years after, Gaul commented that Indians were "very picturesque" and that "they were a good deal like the white men—some were very good fellows and some were very bad." AIW.

GENTILZ, Jean Louis Théodore. Born Paris, France 1819, died San Antonio, Tex 1906. Important Texas pioneer genre and portrait painter, teacher. Work in Daughters of the Repub of Tex Lib, St Mary's U, Dallas MFA, Witte Mus, the Alamo (all in Tex). Reference G&W. Sources ANT 6/48-TEP-TOB. No current auction record but the estimated price of an oil 9×12″ showing Comanches fishing would be about $3,000 to $4,000 at auction in 1976. Signature example p 100 TEP.

Théodore Gentilz, the small and industrious son of a wealthy coachmaker, was trained as an artist in France. He attended the National School of Math and Drawing, the pupil of Viollet-le-Duc. When he was 24, he emigrated to Texas with Count Castro as a settler. After three years he visited France, returning to San Antonio as a painter and as clerk-surveyor for Castro. In 1849 he went again to Paris, bringing a bride back to Texas. While surveying, Gentilz carried his sketchbook in his saddlebag. He drew Indian genre scenes and portraits that were later completed into his small oils. His focus was on the Indian and the details of Indian life, subordinating landscape. He painted the Comanche, Lipan Apache, and Kiowa. In 1879 he settled down as teacher.

In 1882 he worked as a surveyor in northern Mexico, making drawings for his sympathetic paintings of life in the Mexican towns. He also painted a series of views of Spanish missions. In 1888 Gentilz listed his paintings, indicating he made copies of his more successful works. He charged more for the copies (eg, $150) than for originals because the original paintings were in the typical early dark tones while the later copies were good quality paint from New Orleans permitting bright colors and greater contrast. At his death 100 paintings were in his studio. Many others had been left with relatives in France.

GIBBERD, Eric Waters. Born London, Eng 1897, died probably Taos, NM 1972. Taos painter, teacher. Work in MNM, Pasadena AM, English schools, Balearic Is. Reference A73 (obit). Sources A59 listed membership Taos AA-HAW.

Gibberd was the pupil of Oscar Van Young, Ejnar Hansen, and studied in Barcelona, Spain. He exhibited widely in the US and Europe, with one-man shows in Los Angeles 1951, Pasadena, Santa Fe, Denver, Texas, Paris, London, Barcelona, Amsterdam, etc.

GIBBS, George. Born Sunswick near Astoria, LI, NY 1815, died New Haven, Conn 1873. Pacific Northwestern US sketch artist, ethnologist, lawyer, writer. Work in Smithsonian Inst. References DAB-G&W. Sources LAF-"Drawings by George Gibbs in the Far Northwest, 1849–51," Smithsonian Misc collns, 1938. No auction record. Signature example p 186 LAF.

Educated at Round Hill School in Northampton, Mass, Gibbs spent 1832–34 in Europe. He graduated from Harvard Law School in 1838 and practiced law in NYC where he was NY Historical Society librarian 1842–48. He wrote legal and historical books.

In 1849 Gibbs accompanied the Mounted Rifles overland from St Louis to Oregon. He was appointed collector of the port of Astoria, Ore, then settled on a ranch near Fort Steilacoom, Wash. In 1851 he participated in the McKee exploration of northwestern California and later was geologist for the Northwest boundary survey, filing his own lengthy report. During his 12-year stay, he studied the language and customs of the Northwest Indians. From 1862 to 1867, while living in Washington, DC, he wrote on Indian languages. His drawings and ethnological materials are in the Smithsonian colln.

GIBSON, George. Born in England about 1810, died probably Cincinnati, Ohio after 1860. Engraver and lithographer perhaps in San Francisco via Panama during the Gold Rush. Reference G&W. Sources CIV-HON. No current auction record or signature example.

George Gibson with his wife and five children emigrated to the US about 1848. He established the firm of Gibson & Co, engravers and lithographers, in Cincinnati about 1851, joined by three of his sons the oldest 17 and by a relative.

The Honeyman colln has seven pencil, ink, and watercolor drawings that are ascribed to George Gibson. They show California in 1849, Valparaiso in 1849, Panama in 1850, and California again in 1851. These are "seemingly made on trip via Panama and South America to California." HON. See also CIV listing George Gibson as drawing *Scenes in the Wilderness* during the Civil War.

GIDEON, Samuel Edward. Born Louisville, Ky 1875, living Austin, Tex 1941. Texas landscape and historical painter, architect, teacher, writer. Work in U Texas, Bethany Col (Kansas); paintings reproduced in magazines. References A41-FIE-MAL. Sources TOB-TXF. No current auction record. Signature example opp p 40 TXF.

Gideon, a trained architect, was educated at MIT and Harvard. He also studied at L'École des Beaux-Arts in Paris and in Fontainebleau, the pupil of Ross Turner, Despradelle, Gorguet, Duquesne, and Carlu. In 1913 Gideon came to Austin, Tex as Professor of Architectural Design and Architectural History. He wrote and illustrated "Historic and Picturesque Austin."

Gideon specialized in painting architectural subjects including the old Spanish missions in California. *The Alamo* was such a historical subject. His wife

Sadie Cavitt Gideon painted landscapes and portraits in addition to working as a painting restorer.

GIFFORD, Charles B. Born Mass 1830, active San Francisco 1860–72. Lithographic landscape artist, publisher. Reference G&W. Sources ACM-COS. No auction record. Signature example COS.

Gifford was active as a landscape artist in San Francisco in 1860. His wife was from Nicaragua and two of his children were born in California. Gifford worked with various publishers: G T Brown & Company, Nahl Brothers, Nagel's, Thomas Hackett in 1864, as well as his own firm Gray & Gifford in 1868, 1869, and 1872. Gifford's views were finely drawn in comparison with other artists resident in San Francisco at the time.

GIFFORD, Robert Swain. Born on the island of Naushon (or Nonamesset), Mass 1840, died NYC 1905. Eastern landscape and marine painter, illustrator, etcher, teacher. ANA 1867, NA 1878. Work in ACM, COR, MMA, Pittsburgh, and London. References A05 (obit)-BEN-CHA-DAB-ENB-FIE-G&W-MAL-SMI. Sources AAR 3/74,5/74-AIW-AMA-ANT 7/41, 6/74-BAR-BOA-GOD-HUT-ISH-KW1-MSL-PAF-POW-WHO 05. Oil 18×30″ *Scene in Boston Harbor* dated 1866 sold 4/30/69 for $2,200 at auction. Signature example p 51, photo p 63 AAR 5/74; sculpted portrait p 33 SCU.

Gifford's father, a sailor, named him for the owner of a yacht the father captained. Gifford was raised near New Bedford where he received drawing instruction from William Bradford and Bradford's mentor, Albert van Beest, in return for catboat sailing trips. Gifford was then given studio painting space by Walton

Ricketson, a sculptor. When Gifford's parents offered carpentry as his vocation, Gifford asked for a test painting period, and the test paintings sold. In 1864 Gifford moved to Boston as a painter, a professional and financial success from the outset. He went to NYC in 1866, becoming a 30-year fixture as a teacher at Cooper Union, an important "Grand Scenery" marine painter breaking away from the tighter style of the Hudson River School.

In 1869 he was engaged as an illustrator for the two volumes of "Picturesque America" edited by William Cullen Bryant. Other artists on the project were Alfred Waud, Harry Fenn, James Smillie, Thomas Moran, Darley, and Whittredge. Gifford made the journey to the Pacific Coast, sketching in California, Oregon, and Washington, gathering material for later landscapes. In 1870 he toured Europe and Northern Africa. He married a student, Fannie Eliot, in 1873, and in 1874 made a similar European trip. In 1885 both Gifford and his wife (who signed "Fannie E. Gifford") made illustrations for Theodore Roosevelt's "Hunting Trips of a Ranchman." Gifford also had Western sketches in *Harper's* and *Century* that year. In 1899 Gifford was the artist on a scientific expedition to Alaska that resulted in scenes of the coast up to the Bering Strait.

GIFFORD, Sanford Robinson. Born Greenfield near Saratoga, NY 1824, died NYC 1880. Important Eastern "Hudson River School" landscape painter. ANA 1851, NA 1854. Work in ACM, NGA, AIC, MMA, COR, NY Hist Soc. References BEN-CHA-DAB-FIE-G&W-MAL-SMI. Sources AAR 9/73,1/74-AIW-ALA-ANT 1/49,5/58,12/61,10/62,7/64,11/65,10/66,5/67,1/69; 5,12/70; 2/71; 6,11/72; 1,3,11/73-BAR-BAW-BOA-FRO-GIF-HUD-HUT-ISH-KW1-M19-PAF-POW-STI-TAW-WHI. Oil

7¾×18½″ *Along the Beach* sold 10/22/69 for $4,250 at auction. Signature example p 69, photo p 2 GIF. (See illustration 105.)

Gifford, the son of a wealthy manufacturer, was raised across the Hudson from Catskill, NY where Thomas Cole and his pupil Frederick E Church were painting. In 1844 Gifford quit Brown U as a sophomore to go to NYC to study with John Rubens Smith to become a landscape painter like Cole. In 1846 Gifford made a sketching tour of the Catskills and Berkshires. By 1847 he exhibited at the NAD and sold to the American Art-Union. From 1855 to 1857 he made his first European trip, meeting Whittredge and Bierstadt abroad. On his return he took #19 in the new Studio Building on West Tenth Street in NYC, a building designed for artists. In the Civil War, Gifford was one of the few professional artists to bear arms.

In 1870 Gifford joined the experienced Whittredge and Kensett on a sketching trip to the Rockies. He took advantage of the opportunity to join Col F V Hayden's surveying expedition on horseback through the Indian country of Colorado and Wyoming. In 1874 he made his second Western trip, sketching on the Pacific Coast in California, Oregon, British Columbia, and Alaska where his paintings were appropriately larger in size than his Eastern work. Gifford's existing paintings of the Western landscape are extremely rare although his addition of luminist effects to Hudson River forms made his Western views most successful.

GILDER, Robert Fletcher. Born Flushing, NY 1856, died Omaha, Neb 1940. Western landscape painter, newspaperman, archaeologist. Work in Neb schools, libraries, and clubs, St Paul Inst, Amherst Col. References A41-FIE-MAL-SMI. Source WHO 38. No current auction record but the estimated price of an oil 8×10″ showing Tucson on a windy day would be about $700 to $800 at auction in 1976. No signature example. (See illustration 106.)

Gilder, the son of a minister, was educated in Newark, NJ public schools and The Gunnery School in Washington, Conn. He studied art in NYC, the pupil of August Will, and in Omaha. He was archaeologist of the U of Nebraska Museum for 12 years, the discoverer of (1) prehistoric flint quarries in Wyoming in 1904, (2) the Nebraska Loess man, the oldest American man found till then, (3) a prehistoric culture in Nebraska, and (4) 47 pueblo ruins in the southern Arizona desert. Gilder was with the *Omaha World-Herald* for 27 years. His paintings are mainly Nebraska landscapes and scenes of the Arizona desert.

GILLEN, Denver L. Born Vancouver, BC, Can 1914, living probably Chicago, Ill 1966. Illustrator for magazine and commercial commissions, watercolor painter of the Western outdoors, muralist. Member SI. Murals for Mo Pac RR. Reference MAS. Source ILA. No current auction record. Signature example p 220 ILA.

Son of a ship captain, Gillen studied drawing when he was ill at 17. He became the pupil of Frederick Horsman Varley, one of the important Canadian nationalistic "Group of Seven," at the Vancouver SA. Supporting himself by working in the art department of the Hudson's Bay Company, he also went on outdoor painting trips. In 1948 he was listed as living in Toronto. When he moved to Chicago he made catalog drawings for a mail order house before becoming a free-lance illustrator. Gillen has also continued with his easel paintings which he exhibits.

GILLESSEN, Karl. Born Aachen, Germany 1842, died probably Germany after 1880. German painter of military and Indian scenes. References BEN-CHA-von Boetticher-Thieme und Becker. Source p 372 ANT 9/73 *Indian Encampment* with signature example and dated 1880. No current auction record. (See illustration 107.)

Gillessen studied at the Antwerp Academy in 1860 with N de Keyser who influenced Gillessen to paint military scenes. Gillessen also studied with W Huenten in Düsseldorf. To observe the military in action, Gillessen volunteered with a Belgian aid corps in the Mexican War of 1864. When he was himself wounded in 1866, he returned to Europe and established his residence in Düsseldorf. Based on sketches made during this Mexican experience, Gillessen painted Indian and Mexican scenes and landscapes including Galveston, the works dated up to 1880.

In 1870 Gillessen served as a medic in the Franco-Prussian War, enabling him to make sketches of combat scenes. These sketches were expanded into paintings exhibited in Berlin in 1872 and in Dresden and Düsseldorf from 1874 to 1880.

GISSING, Roland. Born England 1895, living Cochrane, Alberta, Can 1948. Western Can painter of mountains and Alberta foothills. Work in Edmonton MA, U of Alberta, Vancouver AG, the Royal Eng collns. Reference MAS. Sources CAN-DCA. No current auction record or signature example.

Son of an author, Gissing studied at George Watson's College in Edinburgh. Influenced by American cowboy movies, Gissing emigrated to Canada in 1913. For 10 years he worked as a ranch hand in Alberta, Montana, Nebraska, and Arizona. Encouraged by the painter C W

Jefferys in Calgary, he settled near Cochrane at the fork of the Ghost and Bow rivers, painting without instruction but influenced by the work of Leonard Richmond and A C Leighton. His first one-man show in 1929 was successful. When his studio burned in 1944 Gissing's accumulated oils were destroyed. He turned to watercolors "of the traditional English school. His pictures are clear and soft in their tones and lit by a calm, subdued radiance." CAN.

Gissing's favorite subjects were mountains and rivers in sunlight. His field trips into the mountains were for weeks at a time, sometimes by backpack, with oil sketches on $12\times16''$ canvases. The paintings were popular for calendars and Christmas cards. Gissing's hobby was an elaborate outdoors model railroad.

GLOVER, Edwin S., Born Michigan 1845, died Tacoma, Wash 1919. Active in California at the time of the Gold Rush as topographical artist and publisher of lithographed views. No reference. Sources ACM-ANT 1/54 pp 40, 63,64-SCA. No auction record. Lithograph examples ACM.

Glover is said to have worked in California, Colorado, Washington, and Oregon. ANT reproduced his illustrated Gold Rush stationery showing *Big Bar-Middle Fork* and also his *Bird's Eye View of Santa Barbara, California, 1877.*

GODDARD, George Henry. Born Bristol, Eng 1817, died Berkeley, Cal 1906. Lithographic artist, landscape and flower painter, civil engineer. Work in ACM. Reference G&W. Sources COS, OCA. No auction record. Lithograph example ⚹1131 ACM.

Goddard was educated at Oxford and exhibited flower paintings in London between 1837 and 1844. He emigrated to California in 1850, settling in Sacramento as a civil engineer and government-appointed surveyor. He produced many sketches and paintings of the area. Some of the drawings were for California lithographers such as Britton & Rey from 1852–68.

Goddard moved to San Francisco in 1862 and planned to publish a series of several hundred California views. His collection of Californiana was entirely destroyed in the fire of 1906, and the artist died soon after. One of the high Sierra peaks was named for him "in honor of a Civil Engineer who has done much to advance our knowledge of the geography of California." OCA.

GOLLINGS, Elling William (Bill). Born Pierce City, Idaho 1878, died Sheridan, Wyom 1932. Important Wyom genre painter. Work in Casper Col, ANS, Wyom St Capitol. Reference A05. Sources AIW-ANT 5/68-COW-HAR-MWS Spr/65-PNW-WAI 71,72-WAN-WYA-WYG. Oil 14×10" *Winter Evening on the Reservation* sold 3/20/69 for $1,300 at auction. Signature examples pp 18, 19 PB 9/13/72. (See illustration 108.)

Bill Gollings was raised on farms in Michigan and New York by his grandmother. When his father remarried in 1886, Gollings was sent by five-day Northern Pacific train and stern-wheeler steamboat up the Snake River to Lewiston, Idaho near his father's mine. The family moved to Chicago in 1889 but Gollings ran away in 1896 and "hoboed" through Nebraska and South Dakota, calling "Belle Fourche the most typical cow town in the north, working as sheep herder and cowboy. I realized the cowboy days were about over and I longed to be a part of at least the last of it.

"In the spring of 1903 I sent to Montgomery Ward & Company for some oil colors to paint with. My brother had taken the first attempts to Sheridan, Wyom, and Mr W E Freeman in a furniture store became interested. I was working with a horse outfit said to be the largest in the world. In July 1904 a letter came to me from Mr Freeman with a check for $50 enclosed and the advice that I had better make some more pictures. I did not feel I could devote all my time to that, so I broke some horses for my brother and rode line on the Cheyenne Reservation fence and painted. Now my brother sent pictures to the editor of the Chicago Fine Arts Journal who said I should come east. In Chicago I made a couple of pictures I sold for $200 that were reproduced at the Portland Exhibition. The Chicago Academy of Fine Arts was the school I attended for two months, at the end of which I won a scholarship in composition. The following winter I took two months of study on my scholarship. Finances were always short so school soon let out for me. I came back to Sheridan, painted hard until the old fever came back and again I found myself on the Cheyenne Reservation running the beef-issue job. This ended my riding for wages for I determined to paint steadily. I never did get settled until February 1909, when I built a shack and called it a studio.

"I have met and talked with a few painters: J H Sharp, Howard Russell Butler, William P Henderson, C M Russell, Frederic Remington. They have all had a good influence on my work." WAN.

GÓMEZ, Marco Antonio (Tony). Born Durango, Mexico 1910, died Manhattan Beach, Cal 1972. Traditional Western painter. Source COW-WYG. No current auction record but the estimated price for an oil 20×30" depicting a stampede would be about $1,500 to $2,000 at auction in 1976. Signature example p 201 COW.

Tony Gómez was the pupil of his father, a famous Mexican portrait painter who moved to northern Arizona in 1918. This was still unsettled country and "I used to ride a lot with Indian kids." He studied at Chouinard's, the Art Center in Los Angeles, and later with Martin Syverston. During WWII he was official artist for the 433rd Fighter Squadron.

Gómez painted the Old West exclusively, dedicated to the nostalgic portrayals of the cowboy, the Indian, and the land: "Russell and Remington didn't do it all, and what they did do is mostly in museums." COW.

GONZALES, Boyer. Born Houston, 1878, died Galveston, Tex (not Woodstock, NY) 1934. Texas marine painter. Work in Galveston Art League, Delgado Mus (New Orleans), Witte Mus (San Antonio), Vanderpoel AA (Chicago). References A36 (obit)-BEN (as Gonzalez)-FIE-MAL-SMI. Sources TOB-T20-TXF. No current auction record or signature example.

Son of the president of the Galveston Cotton Exchange, Gonzales studied in NYC with Wm J Whittemore, at the ASL the pupil of the landscape painter Birge Harrison, and in Boston with the marine painter Walter F Lansil. He then studied in Paris, in Holland, and with Giuliani in Florence before spending four summers painting at Prout's Neck with Winslow Homer. Later, summers were spent at his Woodstock, NY studio and winters in San Antonio while he also maintained his home in Galveston. Gonzales' marines included scenes of the sandy shores of the Gulf of Mexico and the movement in the busy gulf port: *A Texas Bayou, Dawn of Texas, Norther,* and *Wind Swept Beach* (Galveston). His landscapes

were painted in Arizona as well as Texas. His son was also a painter named Boyer Gonzales (see A76).

GONZÁLEZ (or Gonzáles), Xavier. Born Almería (or Madrid), Spain 1898, living NYC 1976. Modern painter and sculptor in Texas 1920s–'30s, muralist, teacher, writer. NA 1955, Nat Assn Mur Ptrs. Work in WMAA, MMA, New Orleans MA, Witte Mus (San Antonio), Seattle MFA, etc. References A76-MAL (as Gonzáles). Sources APT-*Art Digest* 2/49-CAA-M50-NA 74-TOB-T20-TXF. In M50, *City* was offered for $1,500. Oil on paper 21½×29½" *Composition* sold 2/16/67 for $325 at auction. Bronze, black patina 18" long *Agony* sold 10/14/70 for $225 at auction. Signature example p 21 DIG 2/49.

From a family of artists, González studied in Spain. He emigrated to San Antonio as the nephew and student of José Arpa whose style he followed as a painter of landscapes and figures. TXF. He studied in the San Carlos Academy of Mexico City, in Paris, in the Orient, and at the AIC 1921–23. González taught in Texas artists' camps, art schools, and colleges: "His methods are more than unorthodox. Classes are kept continually alert." TOB. In the 1940s González won grants and fellowships that moved him north and east as well as into the mainstream of modern art.

GOODWIN, Philip Russell. Born Norwich, Conn 1882, died Mamaroneck, NY 1935. Eastern illustrator of the outdoors, painter. References A21-FIE-MAS. Sources ANT 10/73-COW-ILA. No current auction record but the estimated price of an oil 20×30" showing hunting the mountain sheep would be $4,000 to

$5,000 at auction in 1976. Signature example p 23 ILA.

Philip R Goodwin was a student of the RI School of Design, the Howard Pyle School, and the ASL. His specialty was the outdoors, particularly hunting and fishing. He is also listed among the artists who successfully depicted the ranch life of the cowboy.

Persimmon Hill magazine has reproduced on its cover Goodwin's 1910 *When Things Are Quiet,* noting that Goodwin's cowboy paintings were influenced by Charles Russell. Goodwin, one of the few New Yorkers Russell liked, visited Russell at the Lazy KY ranch and at Bull Head Lodge. During the Depression, Goodwin's savings bank failed, causing serious financial distress. The only important work he had was gun ads and calendar art. His friends felt his worries caused his early death. A few months after his death, Goodwin was rediscovered as an artist. In his estate, however, there were only a few landscapes and the small "comp" sketches prepared for commissions sought, his illustrations having been to order and held by the customers.

GOODWIN, Richard La Barre. Born Albany, NY 1840, died Orange, NJ 1910. Painter of hanging game and cabin door still-lifes, portrait and landscape painter. Work in Stanford U Mus, Smithsonian Inst. References G&W-SMI. Sources ALA-ANT 2,11/56; 1/60; 5/71; 9/72; 7,11/73; 3,6/74-NJA-STI. Oil 50×31″ *A Trophy of the Hunt* sold 4/7/71 for $17,000 at auction. Oil 27×22″ *A Brace of Hanging Woodcocks* dated 1888 sold 5/10/74 for $3,300 at auction. Signature example p 149 STI.

Goodwin was the son of Edwin Weyburn Goodwin, a western NY portrait and miniature painter. After studying with his father and in NYC, Goodwin following the Civil War was an itinerant portrait painter upstate NY, living in Syracuse, NY in the 1880s. He then turned to still-lifes, his "earliest known cabin-door picture dated 1889" and based on Harnett's *After the Hunt.* STI. Like Harnett, he used devices such as a floating feather and the appearance of an incised signature.

Of the still-life painters such as Harnett, Peto, and Chalfant, Goodwin "was indeed the most peripatetic." STI. He was in Washington, DC by 1892, in Chicago 1893–1900, in the Rockies at Colorado Springs 1900–2, in Los Angeles and San Francisco 1902–6, and in Portland, Ore 1906–8. The most famous Goodwin work was *Theodore Roosevelt's Cabin Door* painted for the Lewis and Clark Centennial in Portland in 1905. The painting incorporated a view of the door of a Dakota hunting cabin that was exhibited at the Centennial. The price of the painting was $2,500 but the Roosevelt admirers could not raise sufficient funds to buy it.

GOOKINS, James Farrington. Born Terre Haute, Ind 1840, died NYC 1904 (FIE lists as James Cookins born 1825, active Cincinnati 1861). Midwestern landscape and portrait painter, illustrator. References FIE-G&W-MAL-SMI. Sources AIW-POW. No current auction record or signature example.

Gookins was active in Terre Haute until 1865. He was a Civil War illustrator for *Harper's Weekly* in 1861–62, a member of the staff of Lew Wallace, the general who successfully defended Washington, DC and later wrote "Ben-Hur." Gookins moved to Chicago in 1865. In the summer of 1866 he formed a party of eight including the artists H C Ford and H A Elkins to join an emigrant wagon train for Denver. Eight Gookins sketches of the trip were published in *Harper's* in the fall of 1866: "Fort Wicked, Colorado, is noted as a ranche where a brave man and wife named Godfrey held over 200 Indians at bay for two days during the troubles last year—killing many and wounding others, and finally driving them off." AIW. Another view was of Denver. *The Daily Rocky Mountain News* commented, "His picture of Denver is a most miserable caricature." The party spent the summer at "the Parks," exhibiting their paintings in Chicago in the spring of 1867.

Gookins studied in Munich in 1870–73. He painted in Indianapolis 1873–80 and 1887–89, in Terre Haute 1880–83, and in Chicago 1883–87, 1889–1904. He is considered to have been an Indiana artist.

GORDON-CUMMINGS (or Cummings), Constance Frederica. Born Altyre, Morayshire, Scotland 1837, died Crieff, Scotland 1924. Scotch world-traveler and sketch artist in Yosemite 1878. Work in Kahn colln. No reference. Sources BDW-KAH. No auction record. Signature example p 23 KAH.

Miss Gordon-Cummings was a member of the Scotch nobility where it was usual to write about one's world travels. She spent three months in Yosemite the summer of 1878, en route from Tahiti. After completing 50 watercolors and 25 drawings, she left Yosemite for the other natural wonders of the world. She climbed Mt Fujiyama in Japan and Adam's Peak in Ceylon. Her book "Granite Crags of California" was published in 1886.

GOTZSCHE, Kai G. Born Copenhagen, Denmark 1886, living Elmhurst, LI, NY 1934. Taos painter. Member Mural Ptrs. Work in BM. References A33-BEN-MAL. Source BDW. No auction record or signature example.

Gotzsche studied at the Royal Academy in Copenhagen. His listed work is *Deer and Cactus*.

GRAHAM, Charles. Born Rock Island, Ill 1852, died NYC 1911. A prolific Western illustrator of the 1880s, painter, railway survey topographer. Work in ACM, DAM, DPL, Honeyman colln, Kahn colln. No reference. Sources AIW-ANT 1/67-AOA-DAA-DBW-DCC-HON-IND-KAH-POW. No current auction record but the estimated price of a watercolor 10×14" showing Indians crossing the river would be about $3,000 to $4,000 at auction in 1976. Signature example p 39 DAA. (See illustration 109.)

Graham was self-taught as an artist. In 1873 he worked as topographer for a Northern Pacific survey in Montana and Idaho, as "a young man, very short of stature and inclined to corpulency, who waddled along making maps." AIW. Beginning 1874 he was scenic artist for Chicago and NYC theaters. From 1877 to 1892 he was an artist for *Harper's Weekly,* working in pencil and in watercolor. His friend at this time was the senior Western illustrator W A Rogers who referred to "little Charley Graham." In 1893 Graham was an official artist for the Columbian Exposition in Chicago. From 1893 to 1896 he was in California, a member of San Francisco's Bohemian Club and illustrator for the San Francisco Midwinter Fair of 1894. After 1896 he was in NYC. He worked as an illustrator and as a lithographic artist so his works have been widely reproduced.

Graham was also a special correspondent in the West. He covered the completion of the Northern Pacific railroad in 1883, made a winter trip to the Yellowstone in 1887, and toured from the Dakotas to New Mexico in 1890, all as recorded weekly in *Harper's*. After 1900 Graham began painting in oil, with European scenes. His favorite subject, as an illustrator, was city views showing the development of the West, as opposed to, for example, Gookins' views of marauding Indians.

GRANDEE, Joe Ruiz. Born Dallas, Tex 1929, living Arlington, Tex 1976. Western painter of history, military, portraits; illustrator. Work in the White House, Nat Cowboy Hall of Fame (Okla City), US Marine headquarters (DC), Custer Battlefield Nat Mon. Reference A76. Sources AHI 3/72-COW-HAR-PWA-USM. No current auction record. Signature examples p 87 HAR, USM. Portrait photo PWA.

Grandee is third-generation Texan. He studied at Aunspaugh Art School in Dallas about 1947. He has been cited for historically accurate works of art depicting the Dragoons and Cavalrymen of the US Army. Authenticity of detail is aided by his large collection of Western artifacts in the "Joe Grandee Gallery and Museum of the Old West" in Arlington. He was one of the illustrators of "The Black Military Experience in the American West." In 1974 Grandee was the first living Western artist to have a one-man retrospective in the US Capitol.

GRANT, Blanche Chloe. Born Leavenworth, Kan 1874, died Taos, NM 1948. Taos landscape and Indian painter, illustrator, author. Work in HAW. References A41-MAL. Sources TSF-WOM. No current auction record or signature example.

Blanche Grant was educated at Indianapolis High School and was a graduate of Vassar College. She was a leader of working girls' clubs, living at College Settlement in Philadelphia for two winters and also heading a Brooklyn club. In art, she studied at the Boston Museum SFA, the PAFA, and the ASL, the pupil of Paxton, Hale, McCarter, and Johansen. By 1914 she was established as a magazine illustrator and landscape painter.

In 1920 she came to Taos. She was the author and editor of books on the history of Taos and on Western personalities such as Kit Carson.

GRAY, U (or Una). Painter active in California in 1930. Reference MAL. Source, oil on board 13×16″ *Mount Shasta, California* estimated for sale 10/28/74 at $300 to $400 for auction in Los Angeles. No signature example.

GRAYSON, J H Lee. Born England about 1885, living probably Saskatchewan, Can 1940. Landscape painter of the Canadian West. No reference. Source CAN. No current auction record or signature example.

Grayson studied in England, France, and Holland before emigrating to Canada in 1906. He continued to paint despite the loss of an eye in WWI, specializing in Saskatchewan landscapes.

GREATOREX, Mrs Eliza Pratt. Born Manor Hamilton, Ireland 1820, died Paris, France 1897. Landscape and cityscape painter, etcher, illustrator. ANA for graphics 1869. Work in MMA, Phila Centennial (1876); etchings published in books. References BEN-CHA-FIE-G&W-MAL-SMI. Sources BOA-HUT-MSL-NA 74-PAF-SHO-SPR-STI-WAA. Oil 8×11″ *Long Island Landscape* 1865 sold 4/20/72 for $500 at auction. No signature example.

She emigrated to NYC with her parents in 1840, marrying the organist Henry W Greatorex in 1849. When he died in 1858, Mrs Greatorex studied landscape painting in NYC with William W Wotherspoon and the Harts. She then studied for a year with Lambinet in Paris in 1861 and at the Pinakothek in Munich. When she returned, she became best known for her drawings and etchings of NYC. Along with the portrait painter Mrs James Bogardus, she was the first woman elected to the NA. Mrs Greatorex was the teacher of her daughters Kate and Eleanor who also exhibited at the NA beginning 1875. All three spent much time in Paris after 1878.

Mrs Greatorex was in Colorado the summer of 1873. She made pen and ink sketches published as "Summer Etchings in Colorado." She was one of the earliest professional artists in Colorado. Her hostess' introduction to the book emphasized the civilizing of Colorado Springs that had taken place, "When the Italian Bravura Waked the Echos of the Cañons supplanting warhoops of the savages and the Boston Dip and New York Glide had followed the scalp dance." SPR.

GREEN, Hiram Harold. Born Paris, Oneida Cnty, NY 1865, died Buffalo, NY 1930. Painter of Western landscapes and Indian genre, illustrator, specializing in pictorial maps, etcher. Member AFA. Work in ANS. References A31 (obit)-FIE-MAL. Source, *The Long Trek* in ANS colln. No auction record or signature example. (See illustration 110.)

H H Green was educated in Utica and Troy. While still young, he moved to Buffalo to study art, then continued his studies at the ASL, the pupil of Mowbray, Cox, and Bridgman. He traveled extensively. The first listed award was from Albright Art Academy in 1898. Green created patriotic posters in WWI.

Green painted *The Apache Trail* for the Southern Pac Ry and *The Grand Canyon* for the Santa Fe Ry. He settled in Fort Erie, Ont, Can about 1905, illustrating for Buffalo newspapers and commercial firms. His specialty was bird's-eye views of the Niagara frontier. His frequent trips between his home and Buffalo made him an early advocate of the bridge between Fort Erie and Buffalo.

GREENE, Hamilton. Birth place unknown 1904, living probably NY 1966. Illustrator specializing in children's books including Westerns. No reference. Source ILA. No auction record. Painting examples in "Walt Disney's Tonka" published by Golden Press 1959.

Greene began as an illustrator for the pulp magazines, then in the men's slick magazines like *Argosy, True,* and *Cavalier* and in paperback book covers. The subjects were action and Westerns. In WWII he was an artist-correspondent in Germany, wounded during an attack. In 1951 he was a correspondent for the Korean War.

Since 1951 Greene had specialized in illustrations for children's textbooks and fiction.

GREENE, LeRoy E. Born Dover, NJ 1893, living Billings, Mont 1969. Montana landscape and portrait painter, etcher, craftsman. Work in IBM colln, Mont St Hist Soc, Montana library and school. References A62-MAS. Sources MON-WNW. No current auction record. Signature example, centerfold MON.

Son of a painter, Green was raised in Dover. He went to Florida in 1911, then to eastern Montana where he worked in construction. Operating his own business in sculptured jewelry in Billings provided him with funds to study art with Roscoe Shrader and Edouart Vysekal in Los Angeles, with the portrait painter Wayman Adams, and with George Elmer Browne.

Greene built his first studio in Billings. He has painted "landscapes from Mexico to Massachusetts and Banff in Canada to

New Mexico." MON. From 1933 to 1943 he taught art in Billings. By 1946 he was able to build a mountain studio in the Beartooth Range at East Rosebud Lake in Montana. His procedure is to paint in the field to record the impression of what he sees, adding the detail in his studio. A painting can take him a few hours or a few days depending upon its complexity.

GREER, James E. Living Bristol, RI 1948. Painter. Reference MAS. Source ANS. No current auction record or signature example.

The Anschutz collection lists a Western landscape done by James E Greer. See Jefferson E Greer entry.

GREER, Jefferson E. Born Chicago, Ill 1905, living Bristol, RI in 1948. Muralist, painter, sculptor. References A41-MAS. Source TOB. No current auction prices or signature example.

Jefferson Greer was educated in Chicago and at U of Wisconsin before studying at the Chicago AFA and the Loyton AI in Milwaukee. After settling on a Texas ranch in 1925, he assisted in fresco murals in the El Paso School of Mines and in 1934 assisted Gutzon Borglum at Mount Rushmore. He also made Post Office decorations for the FWA in Prairie du Chien. See James E Greer entry.

GREMKE, Henry Dietrich (or Dick). Born San Francisco, Cal 1860, died Oakland, Cal 1933. California mountain landscape painter, railway muralist, illustrator, photographer. Work in Kahn colln. No reference. Sources BDW-KAH.

No auction record. Signature example p 25 KAH.

The Jewish Gremke was the son of German pioneers who sailed around the Horn in the 1850s. His father was a ship's chandler for the clippers and also mined gold. Gremke became the pupil of R D Yelland at the California School of Design and exhibited in San Francisco and Oakland.

Gremke specialized in oils and watercolors of the Sierra Nevada mtns, based on summer pack trips. He illustrated his sister's "To Tehipite Through Silver Canyon" in *Sunset* magazine for March 1901. The Southern Pacific and the Santa Fe railroads commissioned Gremke murals for their stations. These paintings were destroyed over the years.

GRENET, Edward Louis. Born San Antonio, Tex 1856 (or 1857, or 1859), died probably Paris, France 1922. Texas portrait and genre painter, illustrator, teacher. Work in private collns. References A09-BEN-MAL. Sources TEP-TOB. No current auction record but the estimated price of a Texas genre painting would be about $2,000 to $2,500 at auction in 1976. Signature example p 175 TEP.

Son of a well-to-do French merchant who rented the Alamo to store his goods, Grenet studied briefly in NYC and then in Paris, the pupil of Robert-Fleury and Bouguereau. He returned to San Antonio in 1878, establishing a studio in the Dauenhauer Building and marrying the daughter of a French-Texas-Mexican frontier family.

Grenet's portraits of the affluent Texans were his most successful. His genre paintings included *Mexican Candy Seller, Mexican Hut,* and *Child Peeping Through the Fence.* "By inheritance and temperament Grenet was attracted to France, to which he returned" about 1884. TEP. He continued to exhibit in European cities until his death.

GRIFFITH, Louis Oscar. Born Green-castle, Ind 1875, died probably Nashville, Ind 1956. Texas and Indiana landscape painter, cityscape etcher. Work in Delgado MA (New Orleans), Oakland AG, Vanderpoel colln, NGA, Witte Mus (San Antonio). References A59 (obit)-BEN-MAL-SMI. Sources TOB-TXF. No current auction record or signature example.

When Griffith was a bellhop in the old Windsor Hotel in Dallas in 1896, his first teacher was Frank Reaugh. He went on to study at the St Louis SFA, the AIC, and the NA. After Griffith had become established as an etcher and landscape painter in Indiana, he returned to Dallas in 1926 to sketch the Dallas skyline and landmarks in preparation for a series of prints. Again, in 1928, Griffith came back to Texas to sketch the Big Bend district of West Texas and the vicinity of Dallas.

GRIGWARE, Edward T. Born Caseville, Mich 1889, died Cody, Wyom 1960. Western painter of realism illustrator, teacher. Murals in LDS temples, Chicago City Hall. References A41-BEN-FIE. Sources AAW-WYA-WYO. No current auction record but the estimated price of an oil 20×30″ showing a pack outfit would be about $1,500 to $2,500 at auction in 1976. Signature example p 16 WYO 8–9/57.

Grigware was raised in Spokane, Wash where he played minor league baseball until he was about 20. Later, as an art student at Chicago AFA, he decided that "those would-be artists who were short on talent were the ones who turned to modern art as an escape from discipline." WYO. He began as a commercial artist: "I've done advertising work and it has never hurt me a lick." In the 1930s he was a successful Chicago illustrator. He visited Wyoming in 1936, locating his home so that the backyard overlooked the canyon of the Shoshone River winding toward a cleft in the mountains. In WWII he was a War Record painter for the Navy, working from the carrier *Enterprise* in the midst of the Pacific campaigns, a series published by *Life* magazine.

After the war, Grigware began doing murals. He insisted that "every element in the composition hold up its end in telling the story." Grigware's views on modern art were constant: "Trivial stuff, and, worse, conceived in such a way that the beholder cannot understand it," with "a similarity between modern art and communism." As "old faces that have lived, Wyoming and Grigware have deserved each other." WYO.

GRIMM, Paul. American landscape painter of the Western desert and mountains. Dates unknown. No reference. Source, two paintings reproduced—*Desert Domain* and *Pleasant Retreat*—in NYG. No current auction record. Signature example p 488 NYG.

GRISET, Ernest Henry. Born France 1844, died England 1907. European animal painter in watercolors, illustrator. Work in Smithsonian Inst, Victoria & Albert Mus. References BEN-MAL. Source POW. No current auction record but an autumn 1973 English catalog offered a Griset watercolor 12×18″ for $70. No signature example.

Griset worked in London drawing for *Punch* and *Fun* and illustrating books for Dalziel Bros. His animal paintings were exhibited in London in 1871. He illustrated "The Plains of the Great West" by Col R I Dodge published in 1877. Thirty of his watercolors of Western Indian life are in the Smithsonian Institution.

GRISWOLD, Casimir Clayton. Born Delaware, Ohio 1834, died Poughkeepsie, NY 1918. International painter specializing in landscapes and coastal scenes. ANA 1866, NA 1867. References A18 (obit)-BEN-CHA-FIE-G&W-MAL-SMI. Sources BOA-HON-HUT-NA 74-PAF-WHO 18. No current auction record or signature example.

Son of an early Ohio newspaperman, he studied with his older brother Victor Moreau Griswold. When he went to Cincinnati to learn wood-engraving, his employer took him to NYC in 1850. Without further instruction, C C Griswold became a painter, exhibiting at the NAD in 1857. His works were regarded as "simple, truthful, and tender in feeling." BOA. While living in Rome 1872–86, he continued to exhibit in the US with scenes of Italy.

The Honeyman colln included a wash drawing of *San Francisco from Alcatraz* that is signed with the initials CCG. Not dated, it is considered "late 19th-century."

GROB, Trautman. Active 1856–61 on the Pacific Coast. Artist, teacher of drawing. Reference G&W. Source COS. No auction record or signature example.

Grob was the artist for such lithographs as *Execution of James P. Casey & Charles Cora* in 1856 and *Puget Mills Co's Mills, Teekalet, WT.*

GROLL, Albert Lorey. Born NYC 1866, died there 1952. Eastern landscape painter specializing in Western scenes, etcher. ANA 1906, NA 1910. Work in COR, BM, NGA, Montclair AM, MNM, MMA, BMFA, City AM (St Louis). References A53-BEN-FIE-MAL-SMI. Sources AMA-ANT 5,6/65; 9/70-COR-JNB-M57-MSL-POW-TSF-WHO 50. Oil

36×50″ *Arizona Landscape* signed but not dated sold 12/10/70 for $1,600 at auction. In 1903, *Landscape* sold for $110 at auction. Signature example p 313 ANT 9/70. (See illustration 111.)

Groll studied with the few Americans who attended the Royal Academy in Antwerp. He became a landscape painter on his return in 1895, it is said, because he was then too poor to pay for models. In 1899 he studied at the Royal Academy in Munich under N Gysis and Loefftz as well as in London.

Groll painted landscapes in the vicinity of New York until about 1904. He then went west with Professor Stuart Culin of the Brooklyn Museum, a famous ethnologist who wrote a treatise on Indian games. Groll sketched desert and mountain scenes in Arizona and New Mexico. The resulting painting *Arizona* won a gold medal at the PAFA in 1906 and was reviewed by "a critic familiar with the desert who said it glows like a gem with the indescribable color of the Colorado desert." AMA. Groll was the rare painter in northern New Mexico before WWI, choosing "bare mesas and towering cloud formations" rather than mountains. Laguna Pueblo was a favorite area, as it was for Thomas Moran. There are also many crayon paintings by Groll, particularly of the Taos area, as complete landscapes in crayon mixed with oil, the paper surface scuffed for texture.

GROPPER, William. Born NYC 1897, living Great Neck Estates, LI, NY 1976. Painter of social comment, muralist, lithographer, author. Member NIAL. Work in MMA, MNM, MOMA, Mus of Western Art (Moscow), AIC, WMAA, etc. References A76-BEN-FIE-MAL. Sources AAR 1,5/74-AAC-AAT-ALA-ARI-CAA-CON-DEP-DIC-500-190-MAP-M51-NEU-WHO 70. Oil 14×18″ *The Trip* sold 5/16/73 for $1,800 at auction. Signature example p 30 ARI.

At 14 Gropper was working in a NYC "sweatshop," six days a week for $6 a week for four years. He studied at night, the Ferrer School 1912–13, NAD 1913–14, NY School of Fine and Applied Art 1915–18 with Howard Giles and Jay Hambidge, and later with Henri and Bellows. In 1919 he became a staff artist for the *New York Tribune* and listed himself as an illustrator for character studies, contributing "to magazines that ranged from *Spur* to *The New Masses*." CON. Gropper was also painting fine arts but he did not exhibit until 1936.

Gropper's interest in the West as a subject has been constant. His cowboy illustrations are shown in 500. ARI reproduces a painting of the 1930s showing the effects of the dust bowl. It also lists as its lithograph *Davy Crockett*. DIC describes his technique as a cartoonist: crayon on a rough-surfaced board varied with "spatters" of ink.

GROSE, D C. Active 1860s–80s as painter in the Rockies. Work in Quebec Mus. No reference. Source, CAE-oil 8×12" *Indian Encampment* with signature example and dated 1867 as illustrated p 30 *Newtown Bee* 9/6/74. Oil *Landscape with a Church* sold 6/19/70 for $50 at auction.

Grose is variously said to have been an English army officer who painted during his travels around the world, including India, and, "a noted Canadian-born artist who also worked in Maine and the Hudson Valley. His work is represented in all major Canadian museums." BEE. He also did romantic landscapes of the Quebec and Montreal districts.

GROTH, John August. Born Chicago, Ill 1908, living NYC 1976. International illustrator, field artist, painter, teacher, author. Member SI, ANA 1958 as aquarellist. Work in MOMA, MMA, BM, AIC, etc. References A76-MAS. Sources AAT-DIC-EIT-ILA-IL 59, 63-NA 74-NEU-WHO 70. Watercolor 13× 10½" *Jockeys* 1966 sold 2/16/67 for $225. Signature example p 156 DIC.

John Groth studied at the AIC 1926–27. "Advised by an artist to make 100 drawings a day, John took the suggestion literally and kept up the practice for years." ILA. He was the first art director of *Esquire* magazine 1933–36 when he traveled and sketched in Mexico and Europe. After studying at the ASL 1937–38, he was WWII artist-correspondent for the *Chicago Sun*. As a friend of Ernest Hemingway, Groth illustrated "Men Without Women." He also illustrated many major magazines and books including Westerns. DIC contains a demonstration of the cartoon technique he practices and teaches: (1) a rough sketch of the idea including shading; (2) pencil outline drawing; (3) drawing over the pencil in ink; and (4) adding shading to complete the cartoon.

GROTZ, William. Active 1920s in NYC offering "illustrations for every advertising need." Work in *Western Stories*. No reference. Source AAC. No current auction record. Signature example p 67 AAC. (See illustration 112.)

Grotz was an illustrator for magazines including the pulps, specializing in Westerns. He also did "pretty girl" heads, with commissions from *Today's Housewife*.

GROVER, Oliver Dennett. Born Earlville, Ill 1861, died Chicago, Ill 1927. Chicago mural and landscape painter. ANA 1913. Murals in libraries; work in

Union League Club (Chicago), AIC, City AM (St Louis), Detroit AI. References A27 (obit)-BEN-FIE-MAL-SMI. Sources AIC-ANT 3/74-MSL-WHO 26. Oil on panel 11¼×17″ *Tuscan Hills* with signature example O D Grover and dated 1912 sold 5/27/74 for $700 at auction.

Grover was educated at the U of Chicago 1877–79 and studied at the Royal Academy in Munich 1879–80, at the Duveneck School in Florence, Italy 1880–84, and in Paris with Boulanger, Lefebvre, and Laurens 1884–86. He then married Louise Rolshoven. Winning prizes by 1892, his paintings were often of Italian subjects. Grover also traveled to the Pacific Northwest, painting Banff landscapes.

GUILLAUME, Louis Mathieu Didier. Born Nantes, France 1816, died Washington, DC 1892. Portrait, landscape, historical painter in the South. Work in U of Michigan, Valentine Mus (Richmond), U of Texas (Austin), Norton AG (Shreveport). References BEN-G&W-MAL. Sources ANT 1/73-BAR-TEP. No current auction record. Signature example p 144 TEP.

Guillaume, the pupil of Paul Delaroche and Pierre Lacour in Paris, exhibited beginning 1837. He emigrated to NYC about 1855, exhibiting at the NAD. In Richmond by 1857 he "confers upon all the ladies soft hair and rose-petal complexions and regular features—without making them unrecognizable." BAR. Guillame witnessed the surrender of Lee, sketching "the participants and articles in the room" for his painting. TEP.

While in Washington in 1892, he painted *Battle of San Jacinto* which showed Houston's 1836 victory over the Mexican army. This appears to have been done from materials existing in Washington and was his last work.

HAAG, Herman H. Born Stuttgart, Germany 1871, died Salt Lake City, Utah 1895. Utah artist, teacher. No reference. Source YUP. No auction record or signature example.

Haag emigrated to Salt Lake City at age 11, as a LDS convert. He became a pupil of Harwood and also studied in Paris in 1889. Haag was a special instructor at the U of Utah and the first secretary of the Society of Utah Artists the year of his death. The 1895 constitution of the Society of Utah Artists excluded women from membership.

HADDOCK, Arthur E. Birth place unknown 1895, living Santa Fe, NM 1975. Watercolor painter of Southwestern landscapes and deserts. Reference MAS. No other source, auction record, or signature example.

Haddock was the pupil of Maynard Dixon. He has painted in California, Utah, Arizona, Nevada, and New Mexico for more than 50 years, according to James Parsons of Santa Fe.

HADRA, Ida Weisselberg. Born Castroville, Tex 1861, died San Antonio, Tex 1885. Texas landscape and portrait painter. Work in private collns. No reference. Source TEP. No current auction record. Signature example p 180 TEP.

Ida Weisselberg was the daughter of a German doctor who fled the revolution of 1848 just after Castroville was founded by Count Castro and Gentilz. She became the pupil of the portrait painter Ella Moss Duval about 1880 in Austin where her father had been appointed to the staff of the State Hospital for the Insane. She was also the pupil of the landscape painter Hermann Lungkwitz at the Texas Female Institute. After marrying a doctor in 1882, she moved to San Antonio.

Mrs Hadra's subjects include *View of the Military Academy from East Austin, Tenth Street, Austin, Looking West,* views of old homes and of the San Antonio River, and *The Hunter's Quest,* a still life.

HAFEN, John. Born Scherzingen, Switzerland 1856, died Brown Cnty, Ind 1910. Important Utah landscape painter. Work in LDS Church colln, Springville AG. References A10 (obit)-BEN-MAL-SMI. Sources PUA-YUP. No current auction record but the estimated price of an oil 20×30″ showing cows in pasture would be about $1,000 to $1,200 at auction in 1976. Signature example frontispiece YUP. (See illustration 113.)

Hafen's parents were converts to the LDS Church. They emigrated to Utah in 1862, traveling the Plains in a covered wagon and then forced out of their first home by Indians. Hafen was educated in Provo, having dedicated himself to art when he was 8. He was self-taught until he met John B Fairbanks and Lorus Pratt. For a living, he sold corn shellers and he opened a photography gallery but did not prosper. He peddled paintings for food.

In 1890 the church sent Hafen on a mission to the Julien Academy for special training: "Today I commenced to work from life. None of the Utah artists knows how to draw the big toe." PUA. He called Paris a city of terrible sins. In 1891 he painted English landscapes, evidencing the influence of Corot. In 1892 he returned to Utah en route to the Monterey coastline in California, where he painted landscapes until 1901. Then the church sent him to paint in the East at $100 a month. In 1902 his studio was in Springville, Utah. He was a modest, retiring man whose life-style was poverty: "Too chaste, too delicate to suit a western audience whose inclination ran to bright colors and photographic likeness." PUA. As he wrote to his wife in 1905: "I have been busy every day trying to get men to buy my paintings with nothing but discouraging results. I had no dinner and no money to get one and only a 10-cent meal this morning." YUP. In 1907 Hafen moved to Indiana for a wealthy patron but soon contracted pneumonia.

ited at the San Francisco Art Association, including a still life, and at the Graphics Sketching Club, with his paintings also offered for sale at retail stores. Hahn was rediscovered in 1939 when MMA included his work in its *Life in America* exhibition. Data on Hahn's life has been surfacing since then, so that chronology given in 1950 publications may not now be reliable.

HAHN, William. Born Ebersbach, Saxony, Germany 1829, died Dresden, Germany 1887. Important California genre painter of 1870s and 1880s. Work in Yonkers Mus Science & Art, Dresden Mus, Oakland AM, W H De Young Mem Mus, Cal Palace Legion of Honor, Kahn colln. References BEN-MAS. Sources AAR 9/73-ANT 4/56,11/56, 11/58, 1/62, 11/65, 3/73, 2/74 - FRO - JNB-KAH-STI-TAW-WHI. Oil 26×42" *California Immigrants* signed and dated San Francisco 1879 sold 5/22/73 for $17,000 at auction. Signature example p 150 TAW.

At 14 Hahn was the pupil of Julius Huebner, at the academy in Dresden. He also attended art school in Düsseldorf, and studied in Paris and Naples, winning an award in Dresden in 1851 and exhibiting in 1869–70. Before 1871 he came to NYC, studying with Huebner, and exhibiting at the NAD. In 1872 he worked briefly with William Keith in Boston, then took a studio in the Mercantile Library Building in San Francisco, a part of the group that included Virgil Williams, Thomas Hill, and Keith.

Beginning in the 1870s Hahn made sketching trips to Yosemite, Napa Valley, San Gabriel, Placerville, Russian River, and the Sierras. In 1873 a large oil of the San Francisco market was sold for $2,500. In 1874 he painted a scene of the Sacramento railway depot. He exhib-

HAINES, Marie Bruner (or Marie Haines Burt). Born Cincinnati, Ohio 1885, living Bennington, Vt 1962. Texas and Taos painter, portrait and mural painter, block printer, writer. Work in Tex A&M Col, Vermont public buildings. References A62 (as Burt)-BEN-FIE-MAL. Sources TOB-TXF-WAA. No current auction record or signature example.

Miss Haines first studied at the Cincinnati Art Academy, then the Pa School of Industrial Art in Philadelphia, the AIC with the portraitist Louis Wilson, the NAD with portraitists Francis Jones and Douglas Volk, and two years at the ASL with DuMond and Romanovsky. After a stay in St Augustine, Fla, she settled with her married sister at College Station, Tex in 1921. Miss Haines painted Texas landscapes but achieved most interest with her gesso lunettes on which the designs were in bas-relief overpainted in gold with black and red.

About 1926 she spent her summer in New Mexico, painting *Old Church at Ranchos de Taos* and *Mountains at Taos*. Gesso panels also "show the stolid, strong forms of Indians": *Indian Family, Mountains, Mesa, and Sheep, Pueblo Family in Black, Gold, and Ivory*. TOB. In 1935 she was working on a series of gesso panels concerning the lowlands along the Brazos River. After 1958 she specialized in designing workshops for Vermont churches.

HALL, Cyrenius. Born 1830, living 1878. Active in the West 1852–78. Work in Nat Port Gall (Smithsonian Inst), 40 small watercolors and drawings 1852–53 in Wyom State AG. No reference. Source ANT 11/68 p 728-CAE. No auction record but the estimated price of an oil 30×25″ portrait of Indian chief would be about $4,000 to $4,500 at auction in 1976. No signature example. (See illustration 114.)

Hall is said to have studied in Europe and painted in South America and Canada as well as in the West. The Chief Joseph portrait in the National Gallery is dated 1878. This is the year (see DAB) after Joseph exhibited his military genius in leading his band of 800 Nez Percé Indians including 600 women and children in a retreat of 1,000 miles from Oregon toward escape into Canada, while fighting four Army generals. Chief Joseph was taken first to Fort Leavenworth, Kan, then to Indian Territory July 1878, and finally to the Colville reservation in the state of Washington. The portrait, which could have been painted at any of these Western locations, shows a proud, somber, handsome man.

HALL, Sydney Prior. Born Newmarket, Cambridgeshire, Eng 1842, died London, Eng 1922. English Special Artist-illustrator, genre and portrait painter. Work in Dublin Mus, Public Archives of Canada, GIL. References BEN-CHA-MAL. Sources AOH-HUT. No current auction record but the estimated price of an oil 20×30″ showing a wounded buffalo would be about $3,000 to $4,000 at auction in 1976. Signature example p 166 AOH.

Sydney Hall was the pupil of his father, Harry Hall, painter of sporting scenes, and also studied in London at Heatherley's, at the RA, and with Arthur Hughes. He then relinquished art in favor of the church, taking his MA at Oxford. A chance acceptance of boating sketches by the new *Graphic* in 1869, however, led Hall to a job as a staff artist specializing in reporting the affairs of royalty. This included the marriage of the Marquis of Lorne in 1871, the Prince of Wales's tour of India in 1876, and a trip to Ottawa in 1878 when Disraeli appointed Lorne as Governor-General of Canada.

In 1881, as part of a campaign to attract settlers to Western Canada, Lorne invited a corps of correspondents including Hall on a three-month 6,000-mile tour as guests of the Canadian Pacific. The trip proceeded from Toronto by train and boat and portage and cavalcade to the Rockies, then by stern-wheeler north to Battleford and by wagon to Blackfoot Crossing to the great powwow between Lorne and Chief Crowfoot. The Indians were tame and the buffalo were gone. The party continued west to Calgary, then south to Montana and east on the Union Pacific. The *Graphic* published 100 of Hall's sketches, weekly from August 1881 to February 1882. In 1883, 70,000 settlers entered Western Canada. "Sketches," Hall said, "always set a person to thinking, and they prompt people to become better acquainted with the country." AOH. Hall remained with the *Graphic* for 40 years. He reported Buffalo Bill's Wild West Show when it visited London for the first time in 1887. He returned to Canada for a third visit in 1901 accompanying the Duke and Duchess of York on a world tour. Hall remained a close friend of Lorne's and a distinguished Victorian artist.

HALL, William (Bill). Born Louis Center, Ohio 1914, living Las Vegas, Nev 1975. Painter specializing in Indians and

Western scenes. No reference. Sources COW-Letter Wm Hall 9/23/75. No auction record or signature example.

Bill Hall went to Nevada in 1947. From Las Vegas he travels throughout the West taking photographs for his reference file. He paints in vivid colors, taking about one month to complete an oil. In technique he is influenced by the old artists who "tried to make everything live in a painting. They had third dimension." Letter. For many years he has participated in the Death Valley Invitational.

HAMBIDGE, Edward John (or Jay). Born Simcoe, Ont, Can 1867, died NYC 1924. Eastern illustrator, painter, inventor of "dynamic symmetry." References A24 (obit) - BEN - DAB - FIE - MAL. Sources AAC-ALA-AMA-CAH-DEP-190-ISH-TSF-WHO 22. Gouache 17¼ × 7¾" *Cavalry Scout with Rifle* signed but not dated, estimated 3/4/74 at $800 to $1,000 for sale at auction in Los Angeles and sold for $725. Signature example in illustration of above.

The oldest of nine children, Hambidge ran away from home at 15 to see the West. He became a surveyor's helper in Council Bluffs, Iowa. From 1885 to 1895 he worked for the *Kansas City Star* as a reporter. When he moved to the *New York Herald,* he studied at the ASL, the pupil of Chase. Sent by *Century* in 1900 to draw Greek ruins, he developed the theory that the Greeks knew and used a mathematical formula of proportion rather than an instinct for design. After years of study and controversy, his theory of dynamic symmetry gained acceptance at Harvard and Yale in addition to usage by important artists like Henri, Bellows, and Kroll. In the 1920s some art teachers accepted Hambidge as gospel while others called the theory "pseudoscience." DEP.

HAMILTON, James. Born near Belfast, Ireland 1819, died San Francisco, Cal 1878. Marine and landscape painter, illustrator. Work in MMA, BMFA, BM, Oakland AM (Cal). References BEN-CHA - FIE - G&W - MAL - SMI. Sources ANT 4/65,5/66,5/67,5/68,3/72,2/75-ARC-BAR-BOA-HUT-KAH-KW1-M31-PAF-PNW-STI. Oil 36×32" *Egyptian Ruins—Sunset* dated 1875 sold 9/13/73 for $2,000 at auction. Signature example p 173 KW1.

Hamilton emigrated to Philadelphia with his parents at 15. Through the engraver John Sartain, he was by 1840 exhibiting landscapes and teaching drawing. His pupils included Thomas Moran. He visited London 1854–55. On his return to Philadelphia he redrew the on-the-spot sketches for "Arctic Explorations" for the Grinnell Expedition of 1850–51 and then redrew the Carvalho sketches and daguerreotypes of Frémont's 1855–56 Western expedition for "Memoirs." In 1861 he illustrated selections from James Fenimore Cooper.

After Hamilton's wife died in 1871, he remarried, sold 109 paintings at auction in Philadelphia in 1875, and set off around the world at 56. On his arrival in the West the San Francisco press hailed his *Shipping on the Golden Gate.*

HAMMOCK, Earl G. Active 1948–60 in the West as still-life painter of Pueblo and Navaho Indian art and culture, living Phoenix, Ariz 1971. Work in DAM. Reference MAS. Source AHI 7/60. No current auction record. Signature example AHI 7/60.

Hammock is listed as living in Delta, Colo in 1948 and Phoenix, Ariz in 1960 and 1971. He is said to have been a mature and successful artist who has done much research into Indian symbols and designs.

HAMMOND, Arthur J. Born Vernon, Conn 1875, died probably Rockport, Mass 1947. Eastern Impressionist landscape and genre painter in NM 1930s. Member AFA. Work in Lynn Pub Lib (Mass), Woman's Club (Roswell, NM). References A41-BEN-FIE-MAL. Source ANT 10/68, with signature example p 503 *The Fishing-Racing Schooner "Gertrude L Thebault."* (See illustration 115.)

HAMMOND, John. Born Montreal, Can 1843, died Sackville, NB, Can 1939. Eastern landscape and marine painter who was an early interpreter of Western Canada, teacher. Member RCA 1893. Work in NGC, Winnipeg AG. References BEN-MAL. Sources CAH-CAN-DCA. No current auction record or signature example. (See illustration 116.)

Hammond at 23 joined the "Ladies Pets" regiment of the Army, then spent 2½ years as a gold prospector in New Zealand. When he came back to Canada in 1870, he joined the Transcontinental Railway Survey party that reached Yellowhead Pass. In 1871 he started as a painter over photographs for the studio of William Notman in Montreal, as did Henry Sandham and J A Fraser. He became part of the European-dominated Quebec group of artists who were members of the RCA. Most of his mature life was spent in New Brunswick where he painted landscapes like the Tantramar Marshes and marine scenes. His work was characterized by "low-toned harmonies of colour, soft quiet charm, and tranquility." CAN. In 1880 he was in Saint John specializing in portraits, and in 1885 he went to Europe to study with Whistler.

As an early painter of Western Canada, he was thus one of those Eastern artists who toured the West beginning 1870, like L R O'Brien and F M Bell-Smith. He was later commissioned by the Canadian Pacific Ry to do large murals and paintings of the railroad's part in opening the West. In 1885 Hammond became principal of the Owens Art Inst in Saint John, running the school there and in Sackville until he retired in 1919. He traveled in America, Europe, and the Orient.

HAMP, Mrs Francis. Pioneer watercolor landscapist active in Colorado Springs, Colo beginning 1877. No reference. Source SPR. No auction record or signature example.

Mrs Hamp studied at Kensington in London. With her four children, she moved to Weber Street when the town of Colorado Springs had been settled for only five years. On trips back to England, she also studied with Sir James Lincoln. In Colorado Springs, "her watercolors commanded good prices, receipts devoted to her charities." SPR. Her favorite view around Pikes Peak was Cheyenne Mountain. She also painted *Cypresses at Monterey.* Her son Sidford Hamp wrote boys' books with a Colorado background.

HAMPTON, Bill. Born Simi Valley, Cal 1925, living Apple Valley, Cal 1976. Traditional Western painter, illustrator, sculptor. Reference A76. Source COW. No current auction record. Signature example p 120 COW.

Hampton served in the Navy Air Corps in WWII. He then worked in the Walt Disney Studio until he could become a professional painter. Horses including cowboys and vaqueros in ranch scenes are favorite subjects. He also specializes in the flesh tones of Indian children. His illustrations have been for magazines.

HAMPTON, John W. Born NYC 1918, living Scottsdale, Ariz 1976. Traditional Western painter of nostalgic ranch scenes, illustrator, gallery owner. A founder, CAA. Work in Nat Cowboy Hall of Fame. Reference A76. Sources ACO-AHI 7/63-C71 to 74-COW-HAR-OSR-WAI 71,72. No current auction record. Signature example p 147 COW. Portrait photo C71. (See illustration 117.)

Hampton dreamed of the West as a child: "The stork dropped me on the wrong range." When he won a newspaper sketching contest in 1935, it was with a rodeo scene. He obtained his first car and "drifted West t'stir up my own dust, make my own tracks, an' travel some of those same ol' trails" as the old-timers. "If I couldn't help win the West, mebbe I could help keep the romance of it alive, picture what it was like. Mebbe that's why hombres like me were born." C71. To learn ranch life, he lived in a bunkhouse.

After service in the South Pacific in WWII, Hampton bought a small ranch near Gila, NM. He drew for the pulp magazines and made layouts for Western comic strips. His paintings were horses in action and the kind of cowboys who rode in the early 1900s, tall crown hats, high-topped boots, and fork saddles. He has also illustrated books on Western history which he considers the real Americana.

HANNA, Thomas King, Jr. Born Kansas City, Mo 1872, died probably Chester, Conn 1951. Eastern illustrator of national magazines, painter. Work in Nat Art Gall (Australia). References A53 (obit) - BEN - FIE - MAL - SMI. Sources AAC-ILA. No current auction record but the published estimate for paintings is $600–800. Signature examples p 169 *Harper's Monthly* vol XCVII (1898), p 27 ILA (1914). (See illustration 118.)

Hanna was educated at Yale U. He studied at the ASL with Kenyon Cox, Douglas Volk, Irving Wiles, C S Reinhart, and John Carlson, with a sketching trip West in 1896. His illustrations appeared in *Harper's* by 1898 and in *Scribner's, Life, The Saturday Evening Post, American,* etc. By 1935 he was exhibiting as a painter.

HANSEN, Armin Carl. Born San Francisco, Cal 1886, died probably Monterey, Cal 1957. Cal marine, coastal, and figure painter, etcher, teacher. ANA 1926, NA 1948. Work in Memorial Mus (SF), LA Mus Hist, Sci, and Art, Palace FA (SF), NAD. References A59 (obit)-BEN-FIE-MAL-SMI. Sources AAT-NA 74-PAW-WHO 54. No current auction record or signature example.

Son of the well-known Western painter H W Hansen, Armin Hansen studied with Mathews at Mark Hopkins IA in San Francisco 1903–6, at the Royal Academy in Stuttgart, Germany with Carlos Grethe 1906–8, and in Paris and Holland. He continued to exhibit in Europe as well as in the US, specializing primarily in etchings.

PAW included an oil *Bronco Buster,* stating "his works are known for their great impressionistic manner."

HANSEN, Herman (or Henry) Wendelborg. Born Dithmarschen, Germany 1854, died Oakland, Cal 1924. Important California watercolorist of the traditional Western genre, etcher. Work in DAM, Eastman Mem Fndn (Miss), ANS, Harmsen colln. No reference. Sources AIW-ANT 11/58, 11/59, 3/61, 10/62, 12/67, 11/68, 10/71-COW-DBW-HAR-PAW-POW. Oil 36½ × 50" *Attack on the Stagecoach* signed H W Hansen but not dated sold 10/27/71 for $25,000 at auction. Watercolor on paper mounted on board 20×16" *Indian on Horseback* signed H W Hansen but not dated sold 4/11/73 for $15,000 at auction. A31 lists a watercolor *Cowboys and Cattle* as sold in 1931 for $180 at auction, the highest price of three. Signature example ✳51 PB 4/11/73. (See illustration 119.)

Hansen's father, a draftsman, sent him to Hamburg, Germany when he was 16 to study under Simmonsen, a painter of battle scenes. In 1876 he studied in England for a year, then emigrated to NYC. He worked as a commercial artist there and in Chicago where the railroad in 1879 commissioned three paintings, one of a locomotive in the Dakotas. This was Hansen's first Western experience. In 1882, after further study at AIC, he went to California, making San Francisco his permanent home.

Hansen made frequent summer sketching trips in Texas, New Mexico, Arizona, and Mexico, accumulating the data for his historically accurate and realistic portrayals. His most famous painting *The Pony Express* was completed in 1900 and was widely reproduced. In 1903 he spent the summer at the Crow Agency in Montana. From 1906 on, Hansen's paintings were all sold each year, mainly in the East and in Europe. Unlike his contemporary Remington, he was not an illustrator, although he did concentrate on genre relating to the horse and rider, professionally depicting a story or an incident. By 1908 the living West had passed him by, as "Tucson is killed from my point of view. They have shut down all the gambling houses tight, and not a gun in sight. Why the place hasn't the pictorial value of a copper cent any longer." AIW.

HANSEN, Oscar J W. Born Norway 1892, living Charlottesville, Va 1962. International sculptor, writer, in the Southwest 1935–39. Work in Smithsonian Inst, Boulder Dam, Hoover Dam, York-town Monument, etc. Reference MAL. Sources COW-WHO 62. No auction record. Signature example and portrait photo p 176 COW.

Hansen went to sea as a cabin boy, traveling around the world five times. After coming to the US in 1910, he was educated at Port Arthur College (Tex), Evanston Academy (Ill), and 1914–15 at Northwestern U. His bronze, marble, and wood figures are in many permanent collections in the US and abroad. In 1935 he was awarded the commission for sculpture including colossal figures and 36 other works for Boulder Dam in Arizona, California, and Nevada. The sculptures were completed and installed in 1938. Hansen is mentioned as touring the Arizona desert with writer Ainsworth and painter John Hilton in 1939.

HAPPEL, Carl (or Karl). Born Heidelberg, Germany 1819, living Munich, Germany 1876. German genre and portrait painter. Work in Heidelberg and Munich museums. Reference BEN. Source, oil 40×30¼" *Seminole Indian Chief* signed and dated 1860 sold 9/13/72 for $3,200 at auction. No signature example.

Happel was the pupil of Gozenberger in Mannheim from 1847 to 1850 and of Gleyre in Paris from 1852 to 1857. He then traveled to America, returning to Munich where he continued his studies in 1867. He exhibited in Vienna and in Munich from 1873 to 1876.

HARDING, Chester. Born Conway, Mass 1792, died Boston, Mass 1866. Portrait painter on the frontier until 1821. Hon NA 1828. Work in MMA, BMFA, AIC, NGA, COR. References BEN-CHA-DAB-ENB-FIE-G&W-MAL-SMI. Sources AIC-ALA-AMA-ANT 5/47,2/50,5/73,4/74-BAR-BOA-COR-

206

HUT-ISH-KAR-KW1-M15-M19-MSL-NA 74-NGA-PAF-TEP. Oils 35×30″ *Portraits of Benj R Gilbert and Wife* sold 3/16/67 for $850 at auction. Portrait example p 281 KAR.

Son of a poor inventor, Harding went to work at 12. After serving as a drummer in the War of 1812, he was a NY frontier cabinetmaker arrested as a debtor on his wedding day. He fled on a raft to Pittsburgh where he became a successful sign painter in 1817 and a self-taught portrait painter in Pittsburgh and Paris, Ky. After two months' study at the PAFA, he painted profitably in St Louis until 1821. In Boston in 1822 in homage to Gilbert Stuart, this "large-framed muscular man" started the "Harding fever" through which he "painted 80 portraits in six months," earning enough for two years' study and work in England where he was a social and artistic success. DAB. On his return, "there was hardly a great man of the day who did not sit for him." KAR.

As an indication of Harding's Western experience, while in St Louis in 1820, James Otto Lewis "had watched Chester Harding paint savage chiefs." ANT 5/47. In June of the same year, Harding made a long journey to Daniel Boone's cabin in Tennessee, painting Boone's portrait "on a fragment of tablecloth in place of a canvas." TEP. Back in St Louis, Harding had Lewis engrave the portrait on copper for reproduction.

HARMAN, Fred, Jr. Born Ohio (or St Joseph Mo) 1902, living Pagosa Springs, Colo 1974. Traditional Western painter of genre, illustrator, cartoonist. Member CAA. Work in Missouri Bar Assn, Harmsen colln. Reference A70. Sources C71 to 74-COW-GRT. No current auction record. Signature example GRT. (See illustration 120.)

Harman, son of a Colorado lawyer in Pagosa Springs, was brought up in Indian country. In 1916 the family moved to Kansas City but Harman soon returned to Colorado to work on a ranch as he did intermittently from then on. About 1921 Harman did animated cartooning in Kansas City, along with Walt Disney. In 1927 Harman was a catalog illustrator in St Joseph, Mo. After a number of ventures, in 1933 he built a cabin in Pagosa Springs.

An exhibition in Los Angeles in 1934 was unproductive but Harman then started his cartoon strip "The Bronc Peeler and Red Ryder." In 1935 Harman suddenly had all the book-illustration commissions he could handle. He then won a 10-year contract with the Scripps-Howard newspapers for his Red Ryder-Little Beaver cartoon strip that ran in 750 newspapers with 40,000,000 readers, a radio show, 38 movies, and 40 products. In 1960 Harman canceled "Red Ryder" in order to have time to paint. His first series of paintings sold out, including even the preliminary sketches. His book "The Great West Remembered" reproduces 89 Harman paintings: "With my hair showing many winters, each morning before sun-up finds me hurriedly returning to my easel." GRT.

HARMER, Alexander F. Born Newark, NJ 1856, died Santa Barbara, Cal 1925. Painter of Indians and "Old California," *Harper's* illustrator. Work in LA County MA, CRS. References A25 (obit)-MAL-SMI. Sources AIW-CRS-NJA-PNW. No current auction record but the estimated price of an oil 20×30″ showing the Snake Dance would be about $3,000 to $4,000 at auction in 1976. Signature example pl 16 CRS.

Harmer left Newark for Lincoln, Neb when he was 13. At 16 he decided to study painting in the East but when he had worked his way as far as Cincinnati, he joined the U S Army. After two years of service in California, he studied art at the PAFA, the pupil of Eakins and Anshutz about 1874. Then, in order to get to the West to paint Indians, he re-enlisted in the Army about 1881. He was assigned cavalry duty in Arizona, participating in expeditions against Geronimo and his Apaches. His illustrations for *Harper's Weekly* on the Apaches appeared in the summer of 1883 and in 1886. He also painted 31 color plates for "The Snake-Dance of the Moquis of Arizona" by Capt J G Bourke, his former commanding officer.

Harmer returned to the PAFA with his field sketches and notes, producing a series of oil paintings and watercolors of the Apaches. He was also a commercial illustrator. After 1890 he moved to Santa Barbara, marrying into one of the "old families" and devoting his painting to genre scenes of early California life, to the California missions and the Mission Indians, and to local landscapes.

HARMON, Charles H. Landscape painter active 19th and 20th century in Cal and Colo. No reference. Sources BDW-DPL. Oil 40×60″ *Evening at Santa Barbara Mission* illustrated and estimated at $1,500 to $2,000 for sale 10/28/74 at auction in LA but did not sell. (See illustration 121.)

Harmon lived in San Jose, Cal in the 1880s, painting landscapes of mountains and redwoods as well as coastal scenes. He also painted Colorado landscapes. It is said that some of his paintings were done with a palette knife.

HARRINGTON, Joseph. Born 1841, died 1900. Active San Francisco 1875. Painter of California mining scenes. Work in FA Museum of San Francisco. No reference. Source WHI. No current

auction record but the estimated price of an oil 20×30″ showing miners panning gold would be about $2,000 to $2,500 at auction in 1976. No signature example.

Harrington's *Discovery of the Comstock Lode* painted in 1875 re-created the establishment of the claim.

HARRIS, Lawren Stewart. Born Brantford, Ont, Can 1885, died probably Vancouver, BC, Can 1970. Important modern landscape and genre painter, illustrator, teacher. Founder, Group of Seven, 1920; Can Group Ptrs, Fed of Can Artists 1942. Work in MNM, NGC, AA Montreal, AG Toronto, Detroit IA, Williams AG (Ontario). References A70-(BEN is Lawren Harris' son)-MAL. Sources AAT-CAH-CAN-CAR-DCA-MNM-TSF. Oil *Sun and Fog and Ice, Smith Sound* sold 10/14/71 for $27,000 at auction in Montreal. Painting examples p 149 CAH. (See illustration 122.)

Lawren Harris was educated at the U of Toronto in 1903, then studied art in Munich and Berlin 1905–7. After traveling in Europe, he was a *Harper's Monthly* illustrator in Palestine in 1909 and in Minnesota lumber camps. When he returned to Toronto in 1910, he was a central figure in the emergence of a progressive movement in Canadian art. Harris "began to paint the shabbier streets of Toronto." CAR. He sketched in northern Ontario with J E H MacDonald in 1912 and in 1913 was influenced by an exhibition of paintings in the Scandinavian version of Fauvism. WWI delayed the movement, but in 1920 it became the Group of Seven with Harris writing the text for the initial exhibition: "Do you read books you already know? If not, you should hardly want to see pictures that show you what you can see for yourselves." CAR.

Harris painted all over Canada, Nova Scotia in 1921, the Rockies in 1924 and after, the Arctic in 1930, the Gaspé in

1932, and New Mexico in 1940 where he joined the Transcendental Painting Group. He moved to Vancouver in 1942, teaching at the School of Art. Harris' style became increasingly simplified and abstracted.

HARRIS, Robert George. Born Kansas City, Mo 1911, living Carefree, Ariz 1976. Woman's magazine illustrator who began in pulp Westerns, portrait painter. Member SI. Work in Phoenix Jr Col. References A76-MAS. Sources ILA-POI. No current auction record. Signature example p 186 ILA. (See illustration 123.)

Raised in Kansas City, R G Harris studied at the Art Institute there, the pupil of Monte Crews. He traveled to NYC on a motorcycle to attend Grand Central School of Art, the pupil of Harvey Dunn, and the ASL, the pupil of George Bridgman. He was selling illustrations when he was 23 in NYC, beginning with pulp Western magazines like *Double Action Western.* By 1939 he was receiving commissions from *McCall's* and *The Saturday Evening Post,* by 1940 *Good Housekeeping* and *Ladies' Home Journal,* associations that continued until 1961. He was best known for "sympathetic renderings of children and young love." ILA. By 1962 he had a one-man show of portraits at the Phoenix Art Museum. He moved to Arizona and concentrated on portrait commissions.

HARRISON, Lovell (or Lowell) Birge. Born Philadelphia, Pa 1854, died Woodstock, NY 1929. Eastern landscape painter in New Mexico in 1883 and in California. ANA 1902, NA 1910, NIAL. Work in PAFA, DIA, COR, AIC, France, etc. References A29 (obit)-BEN-CHA-DAB-FIE-SMI. Sources

ALA-AMA-MSL-NA 74-WHO 28. Oil 30×40″ *Winter Landscape* signed but not dated sold 5/26/71 for $750 at auction. Signature example opp p 185 AMA.

Birge Harrison, brother of artists Alexander and Butler, studied at the PAFA. Sargent's advice in 1875 led him to Paris to the École des Beaux-Arts where he studied with Carolus-Duran and Cabanel. By 1882 the French Government bought the figure piece *November.* Poor health prompted Harrison to travel the world: India, Australia, Ceylon, South Africa, Egypt, the Mediterranean countries, and Quebec. When he returned to the US, he specialized in winter landscapes and in cityscapes. He was immediately successful, taught landscape painting at the ASL, and founded the Woodstock art colony. "Our business is to transmit the impressions direct from nature," he wrote.

During his travels in 1883, Harrison painted in New Mexico. Following the chronology in TSF, Sharp was in New Mexico the same year as Harrison, with Thomas Moran only one year earlier. Harrison also painted for several seasons in California: *Moonrise off Santa Barbara, Road near Santa Barbara.*

HART, Alfred. Born Norwich, Conn 1816, active Hartford, Conn 1879, and perhaps California until 1900. Early Cal painter of landscapes and portraits, panoramist. References FIE-G&W-MAS. No other source. No current auction record or signature example.

Hart studied in Norwich and in NYC. He moved to Hartford, Conn in 1848, painting there a panorama of Bunyan's "Pilgrim's Progress." In 1852 his panorama of the New Testament and the Holy Land was exhibited in NYC. About 1861 Hart moved to California where he painted until at least 1878. He was also an inventor.

HARTLEY, Marsden. Born Lewiston, Me 1877, died Ellsworth, Me 1943. Pioneer international modernist painter. Work in ACM, ANS, MMA, MOMA, Phillips Mem Gall (Washington), WMAA, Barnes Fndn (Philadelphia), MNM, AIC. References A47 (obit) BEN - FIE - MAL - SMI. Sources AAR 9/73, 3/74 - AAT - ALA - ANT 4/61, 11/64, 3/68, 5/73, 6/74 - ARI - ARM - CAA-DAA-DEP-DIG 1/44,2/49-HMA-190-NEU-PIT-STI-TAL-TSF. Oil on masonite 40×30″ *Young Sea Dog with Friend Billy* signed with initials and dated '42 sold 3/14/73 for $14,000 at auction of Halpert colln. Immediately after his death *Window on the Sea* had sold for $1,500. Signature example PB 3/14/73 above. (See illustration 124.)

Hartley studied in 1892 at the Cleveland IA with Cullen Yates and Nina Waldeck and privately with John Semon, in 1898–99 at the Chase School in NYC with Mora, DuMond, and Chase, at the NAD in 1900 with Blashfield among others, and at the ASL. In his early style about 1907–8, Hartley was an impressionist with a bright palette. By 1909 the palette was more somber as he exhibited at the gallery "291," a part of the Stieglitz group of Weber, Marin, Dove, and Walkowitz. When he went to Europe in 1912, he was influenced first by French Cubism and then more permanently by the German expressionists. He remained in Europe until 1915.

By 1918 when Hartley went to Taos on a grant from a NY art dealer, he turned to softer pastel landscapes. In 1919 in Santa Fe, he painted a series of still-life oils featuring santos and dramatic landscapes with rudimentary forms. After 1920 Hartley did not paint in the Southwest again, but when he returned to Germany in 1922–23, what he painted was canvas after canvas of his recollections of New Mexico. The palette is gray relieved with green, the forms are simplified, and remembered New England shapes are combined with those of New Mexico. This is not an instance of an Eastern artist casually visiting and painting the West but an example of an artist whose Western experience was a recognized stage in his development.

HARTUNG, F. Painter active 19th century. No reference. Source, oil 23×28″ *Sentinels* sold 10/28/74 for $650 at auction in Los Angeles. The same titled, described, and sized oil had been reported sold 9/28/73 for $500 in NYC after having been estimated at $800 to $1,000 for the auction. No other source. No signature record.

HARVEY, Eli. Born Odgen, Ohio 1860, died Alhambra, Cal 1957. Animal sculptor, painter. Member NSS 1902. Work (sculpture) in MMA, NY Zoo, medals, Victory Arch (NY), BPOE, Amer Mus Nat Hist, etc. References A37-BEN-FIE-MAL-SMI. Sources AMA-NSS-WHO 50. No auction record but the published estimate for a painting is $1,200 to $1,500. Signature example p 94 NSS.

Harvey studied at the AFA in Cincinnati, the pupil of Leutz, Noble, and Rebisso. In 1889 he entered the Julien Academy in Paris, studying drawing and painting under Constant, Lefebvre, and Doucet and animal sculpture under Frémiet at the Jardin des Plantes. He also studied at the Delecluse Academy, the pupil of Delance and Callot.

By 1894 he was exhibiting painting and sculpture at the Paris Salon. Honors came by 1900, and major commissions by 1901—the sculpture for the Lion House at the NY Zoo. His work included American bald eagles for MMA and the NY Victory Arch and an American elk for the BPOE.

HARVEY, George (his nephew was a painter with the same name). Born Tottenham, Eng 1800–1, died probably London, Eng 1878. Landscape painter, miniaturist. ANA 1828. Work in BMFA, NYHS. References FIE-G&W-MAL-SMI. Sources AAR 5/74-ALA-ANT 6/44, 9/45, 11/47, 5/48, 12/62, 4/68, 8/71, 10/74-BAR-KAR-KW1-NYHS-STI. Pair of oils 10×12" *Early Views of Illinois* sold in 1970 for $800 the pair at auction. Signature example p 299 KAR.

Probably trained in England, where he may have exhibited, Harvey wrote in his journal that in 1820 "he found himself in the remote wilds of the New World, hunting and trapping, scribbling poetry and prose, drawing and sketching . . . thus two years passed in the far West." It is assumed that he was in Ohio, Michigan, and Canada, able to have seen the prairies. Back in NYC and then Boston, his miniatures were popular. From about 1831 to 1833 he was in London for further study and for exhibitions. After he returned to Boston his failing health led him in 1835 to buy country land along the Hudson where he recorded in watercolor the special atmospheric effects of the American climate. Among the 40 views were *Western Prairie* and *Road Opening of the Primitive Forest* from his 1820 experiences. Harvey was unable to get these views published as a set because the estimated reproduction cost was $100,000. He was "as proficient in still life as he was in his landscapes" and "may have been the first American floral specialist." STI.

In 1848 Harvey returned to London. "His original watercolors were the basis of huge paintings to illustrate his London lectures on the primitive wonders of the frontier." ALA. His catalog "Harvey's Royal Gallery of Illustration" published in 1850 was used with his nightly talks in the London theatrical district.

HARVEY, Gerald (Gerald Harvey Jones). Born San Antonio, Tex 1933, living Austin, Tex 1974. Traditional Western painter of frontier scenes. No reference. Source COW. No current auction record. Signature example p 215 COW.

Harvey is third-generation Texas rancher, "telling with the brush the story of the days of my grandfather and men like him." COW. He has worked as supervisor of arts and crafts at the U of Texas. His commissions included 12 landscapes for the LBJ Ranch and one painting for Texas' former Gov Connally.

Harvey's field trips are into the Texas Panhandle where he joins the ranch hands. Oil sketches and photographs record the scenes. Back in his studio, he composes in charcoal on the canvas, then develops with oils, working on as many as six paintings at a time. Each painting is framed and hung in Harvey's home before final touches. Harvey paintings are now being reproduced as limited edition prints.

HARWOOD, Burt S. Born Iowa 1897, died Taos, NM 1924 (or 1922, 1923). Painter of Taos Indians and their genre. Work in Harwood Fndn (Taos). References A15-BEN-FIE-MAL. Sources BDW-Harwood Fndn catalog-JNM-TSF. No auction record or signature example.

Harwood studied in Paris, the pupil of Laurens, Collin, and Benjamin-Constant. To avoid WWI he returned to the US, settling in Taos where his specialty was painting of the Indians. The Foundation lists *Comanche Dance—Taos Pueblo*. The Foundation contains a Harwood Room with paintings by both Harwood and his wife Lucy Case Harwood who established the Foundation in 1923 as a semiprivate gallery. In 1936 Mrs Harwood donated the property to the U of New Mexico.

HARWOOD, James Taylor. Born Lehi, Utah 1860, died Salt Lake City, Utah 1940. Utah landscape painter and teacher, muralist, etcher. Work in state colln Utah, U of Utah, BYU, Springville (Utah) AM. References A41-BEN-MAL. Sources PUA-YUP. No current auction record but the estimated price of an oil 20×30″ showing an old Harwood barn would be $300 to $400 at auction in 1976. Signature example p 4 YUP. (See illustration 125.)

Harwood worked in his father's harness shop to pay for art studies with Weggeland and Lambourne in Salt Lake City. In 1885 he studied under Virgil Williams at the Academy of Design in San Francisco. In 1886 he opened his studio in Salt Lake City. In 1888 he became the first Utah artist to study in Paris, the pupil of Laurens, Lefebvre, and Constant at the Julien Academy. He traveled between Paris and Salt Lake City frequently, with the exception of two years' residence in California 1920–22.

As a painter he followed the "neo-classic manner and taught this." From the 1920s on, he adopted a "mechanical kind of impressionism." It was said of Harwood that he "missed the point of pointillism," yet his students prospered. YUP. Late in life he specialized in colored etchings.

HASKELL, Ernest. Born Woodstock, Conn 1876, died near Bath, Me 1925. Eastern printmaker, painter including a set of 50 Cal watercolors, illustrator, writer. References A28 (necrol)-BEN-DAB-FIE-MAL-SMI. Source AMA. No current auction record but the published estimate is $600 to $800. No signature example.

Haskell worked in the *New York American* art dept before spending 1897–98 in Paris, studying and making pastel monotypes. After two years of caricature and theatrical posters, he was back in Paris during 1900–2 to study Rembrandt, Dürer, and Leonardo. When he moved to Phippsburg, Me, he painted a series of watercolor landscapes of woods and country towns. A trip to California produced a series of etchings and drypoints and a set of 50 watercolors. Haskell was described as an "eager experimenter" with "rare taste, delicacy of feeling, and appreciation." DAB.

HASSAM, Frederick Childe. Born Dorchester near Boston, Mass 1859, died East Hampton, LI, NY 1935. Important Eastern Impressionist "plein-air" painter and etcher. Member The Ten American Painters 1898, ANA 1902, NA 1906, NIAL. Work in World's Columb Expos (1893), ARM, NGA, AIC, MMA, BM, DIA, PAFA, COR, etc. References A36 (obit)-BEN-DABS-ENB-FIE-MAL-SMI. Sources AAR 1/74-AIC-ALA-AMA-ANT 1/36,12/54,9/55; 1,10/60; 7,9,12/61; 4/62,10/64; 1,4,5,6/65; 3,8, 11/67; 3,7/68; 2,6,12/69; 4,5,9,12/70; 2/71; 2,4,11/72; 7,12/73; 10,11/74-ARI-ARM-CON-DEP-IMP-INS 4/31-ISH-M19-MSL-NA 74-NGA. Oil 24×36″ *The Water Garden* signed and dated 1909 with monogram on reverse, estimated for sale 5/23/74 at $50,000 to $60,000, and sold that day for $140,000 at auction. Signature example p 305 ALA. (See illustration 126.)

Son of a merchant, the athletic Childe Hassam was educated in Dorchester high school. Without graduating, he went to work for a commercial wood engraver in 1876, also free-lancing as an illustrator for *Harper's, Scribner's,* and *Century.* About 1878 he attended evening life classes at the Boston Art Club. His signature then was F Childe Hassam. About 1879 he studied painting with I M

Gaugengigl in Boston. In 1883 he painted in Europe. From 1886 to 1889 he lived in Paris, studying at the Julien Academy with Boulanger, Lefebvre, and Doucet but in his independent painting adopting the techniques of Monet and the Impressionists. Hassam settled in NYC with his studio at Fifth Avenue and 17th Street where he was soon acclaimed a leading exponent of the American Impressionists. He painted the rich textures, sunlight, and atmosphere he saw, in vivid colors, out of doors, and as a realistic "impression." A founding member of The Ten, Hassam left all the paintings in his estate to the American Academy of Arts and Letters.

In 1908 Hassam painted in the Pacific Northwest including views of Mt Hood. MMA has *Golden Afternoon, Oregon* in its collection. P 591 ANT 10/74 shows the watercolor 6×9" *North Bend, Neb.*

HAUGHEY, James M. Born Courtland, Kan about 1915, living Billings, Mont 1969. Montana landscape painter in watercolor, lawyer. Work in AWCS and USIA exhibitions, Mont Inst of the Arts. No reference. Source MON. No current auction record. Signature example p 174 MON.

After studying art at the U of Kansas, Haughey worked for a year in Texas before transferring to law school in the mid-30s. When he moved his legal practice to Montana in 1943, he began weekend painting with LeRoy Greene. In the field he sketches and takes 35 mm color slides so he can complete the work back in his studio.

Haughey prefers watercolor because it is "spontaneous," it is a "chancy thing," and "you have to do it right the first time." MON. He feels that "in Montana, the country dictates realism. In New York I might become an abstract painter." MON.

HAUSER, John. Born Cincinnati, Ohio 1858 (or 1859), died Clifton, Ohio 1913. Important painter of Western Indians. Work in Smithsonian Inst, GIL, ANS, HAR. References A14 (obit)-MAL-SMI. Sources AAR 11/74-ANT 7/58,6/59-HAR. Gouache 15½×23¾" *Indians on the Trail* signed and dated 1902 sold 10/27/71 for $4,500 at auction. Signature example p 93 HAR.

Hauser studied at the Ohio Mechanic's Institute and at the Cincinnati AA before he was 15. By 1873 he was the pupil of Thomas A Noble at the McMicken AS in Cincinnati. In 1880 he became the pupil of Nicholas Gysis at the RAFA in Munich, with further studies up to 1891 in Düsseldorf and Paris. He taught drawing in Cincinnati public schools.

Hauser traveled in New Mexico and Arizona in 1891, adopting as his specialty the American Indian. He made yearly visits to the reservations, painting portraits of documentary accuracy and genre scenes of Indians in canoes and on horseback. He was adopted into the Sioux nation as "Straight White Shield" in 1901, with his wife Minnie called "Bring Us Sweets."

HAWTHORNE, Edith G. Born Copenhagen, Denmark 1874, living San Francisco, Cal 1933. Painter, sculptor, craftsman, teacher, writer. Reference A31. Source, oil on board *Pink Hills of Nevada*. No auction record or signature example.

Ms Hawthorne was a pupil of Chase.

HAYS, William Jacob (erroneously Hayes). Born NYC 1830, died there 1875. Important early painter of Western fauna and landscape. ANA 1852. Work in COR, ACM, DAM, GIL, City AM (St Louis), AMNH, NY Pub Lib, Washington Univ. References BEN-CHA-DAB-FIE-G&W-MAL-SMI. Sources AIW-ANT 10/56, 3/65-BOA-DAA-DCC-DWF-GIL-HUT-150-ISH-MIS-PAF-PNW-POW-STI-WES. No current auction record of a Western painting but an oil *Terrier with a Rabbit* sold 1/29/70 for $450 at auction. Signature example p 263 ANT 3/65.

Hays, grandson of a NY high constable, studied drawing under John Rubens Smith. *Dogs in a Field* in 1850 was his first NAD exhibit. He also painted deer, race horses, game birds, fish, fruit, and flowers, traveling to Nova Scotia and the Adirondacks. His name was not well known as a painter; he resigned from the NA in 1857 and he ceased exhibiting toward the end of his short career.

He spent most of his life in NYC, yet is important today chiefly because of the paintings resulting from one trip up the Missouri in the summer of 1860. This is the same territory visited years before by Bodmer, Catlin, Audubon, Stanley, and Wimar. Hays left St Louis on May 3 on the steamboat *Spread Eagle,* arriving Fort Union on June 15, having come 1,800 miles to the mouth of the Yellowstone. Here Hays began his field sketches which were said to have been in two sizes, on drawing paper about 10×14″ and in a book 2×4″. The subjects are the forts on the river, buffalo, elk, and a Crow war chief portrait. Some of the forts are pictured only in these sketches, and field sketches of buffalo are few. It appears that Hays went no farther than Fort Stewart despite source references to the Rockies. By the fall of 1860 Hays was back in NYC, starting on his buffalo paintings *The Herd on the Move,* then *The Stampede* and *The Wounded Bison.* Some of Hays's Western paintings have been reproduced as lithographs. He was a naturalist, publishing papers in professional journals and priding himself on the accuracy of his Western plants that were part of the painted backgrounds. Hays's son, William Jacob Hays, Jr, was also a painter. PNW classifies him as a Western painter with his subjects including the Rockies.

HEANEY, Charles Edward. Born Oconto Falls, Wis 1897, living Portland, Ore 1950. Northwestern printmaker, landscape painter. Work in Seattle AM, Bucknell U, Western Wash Col (Bellingham), NY World's Fair (1939). References A41-MAS. Sources AAT-M50-WNW. No current auction record but the published estimate is $40 to $60 for prints. M50 listed *Ancestor* as for sale for $500 at MMA in 1950. Wood engraving example *Village, Eastern Oregon* p 276 AAT.

Heaney studied at Museum Art School (Portland), U of Oregon Ext, and with H Heinie in Milwaukee. Listed titles are *Harney County Store* and *Library Corner*.

HEAP, Gwinn Harris. Born Chester, Pa 1817, died Constantinople, Turkey 1887. Railway survey artist 1853, Govt camel expert 1855–57, writer, diplomat. Work in "Central Route to the Pacific from the Valley of the Mississippi to California" by Heap, Philadelphia 1854. Reference G&W. Source SUR (indexed under E F Beale). No auction record. Lithographic example opp p 139 SUR, *Wrestling Camel from Asia Minor.*

Gwinn Heap accompanied Naval Lt Edward F Beale on the pioneering railway survey along the 38th parallel from Westport, Mo to Los Angeles starting May 10, 1853. With 10 men they took the old Santa Fe trail until it turned south, then crossed southern Colorado, southern Utah, the Mohave Desert, and Cajon Pass through the Sierras. The trip was 100 days, even after Heap had a

350-mile detour to Taos to replenish supplies lost to the Colorado River and the absence of trade goods had caused a tense confrontation with Utes. Heap's cheerful account was published with 13 lithographs from his sketches.

In 1855 Sec of War Jefferson Davis initiated an experimental allotment of $30,000 for the purchase of camels for military purposes. Maj Henry Wayne, in charge of the project, consulted camel authorities in Europe before meeting Gwinn Heap in Tunis where Heap's father had been US Consul for 30 years. Heap knew camels, Arabs, the language, and as an artist provided 15 camel sketches for the official report. Heap bought good camels in Smyrna in January 1856. The 33 camels were taken on board the Navy's *Supply* in February for the three-month voyage to Indianola, Tex, with a net gain of one camel through calving. Heap returned to Asia Minor where he bought and brought back another 41 camels in February 1857, ending Heap's camel venture. He became US Consul to Tunis 1867–78 and Consul General at Constantinople 1878–87. The camels were trained by Major Wayne at Camp Verde, Tex, then successfully employed on a trial trip from Texas to California in 1857 under Lt Beale and Heap's son David Porter Heap. Unfortunately the Civil War ended the camel experiment.

HEATH, Frank L. Born 1857, died probably California 1921. American landscape painter active at least 1887–1900 in California. No reference. Source, oil 36×26″ *By the Foaming Merced,* Yosemite Valley, signed, titled, and dated 1900 sold 11/13/72 for $400 at auction. In the same sale *Ocean Beach,* the seaside resort of San Diego, signed, inscribed, and dated 1887, sold for $1,800.

HEGER, Joseph. Born Hesse, Germany 1835, living Goodlettsville, Tenn 1897. Sketch artist in the West 1858–60, illustrator, lithographer. Work in Coe colln (Yale), W J Halliday colln (Ariz Pioneers Hist Soc). Reference G&W. Sources AIW-FRO-MWS W/74. No auction record. Drawing example p 21 MWS W/74 *Fort Union, NM.* Signature example p 69 FRO *Camp Floyd, Cedar Valley, Utah* July 1858.

A lithographer, Heger emigrated to the US as a youth. He enlisted in the US Army, serving 1855–60. While in the Army, Heger sketched towns, military installations, and landscapes in Utah 1858–60 and along the return march to New Mexico. Sixteen of his Utah sketches were reproduced in "Campaigns in the West 1856–61." It is said that he was later denied a disability pension because his military service had been in the West.

HEIKKA, Earle Erik. Born Belt, Mont 1910, died Great Falls, Mont 1941. Western sculptor, painter, taxidermist. Work in ANS, Hearst colln. No reference. Sources COW-DCC-JNB-WAI 71-WNW. No current auction record but the estimated price of an oil 20×30″ showing buffalo crossing a river would be about $3,000 to $4,000 at auction in 1976. Appraisals of Heikka sculpture would be higher. Signature example ⚹35 JNB. (See illustration 127.)

Heikka was raised in Great Falls where he watched Russell painting and sculpting, although Heikka is considered to have been self-taught. By 1928 he was sculpting major works. In 1929 he sculpted cowboys at the Gary Cooper ranch. An exhibition in Los Angeles was most successful.

He had worked as a taxidermist and as a painter of dioramas. He received advice from the staff of the Field Museum of Natural History in Chicago and also from Gutzon Borglum, Lorado Taft, and Frederick Hibbard in Chicago. After exhibiting at the World's Fair in Chicago in 1932, he was offered a studio there but elected to return to Montana. He was regarded as a leading painter of Western genre in addition to his sculpting in clay, stone, and bronze.

HEILGE, George. Active NYC and Philadelphia 1838–55. Landscape and theatrical scene painter of the 1849 *Panorama of the Route to California*. Reference G&W. Source PAF. No auction record or signature example.

Heilge, probably a native New Yorker, may have visited Europe before decorating a NYC theater 1838–39. In 1840 he was in Philadelphia, exhibiting *Dutch Drawbridge* at the PAFA and giving his address as the American Theatre. Between 1844 and 1855 Heilge painted panoramas listed in G&W as views of Jerusalem, of the Antediluvian World, of Kane's Arctic explorations, of the siege of Sebastopol, and of California. These were all apparently based on materials available in Philadelphia.

For the California panorama, Heilge used the sketches of the amateur artist Walter Colton, a fellow Philadelphian who traveled to California in 1845, served as alcade of Monterey, and returned in 1849.

HEINRICH, Roy Frederic. Born Goshen, Ind 1881, died probably NYC 1943. Illustrator of historical subjects including Indians. Member SI, Art Dirs Club. Work in advertising, books. References A41-MAS. Sources ILA-IL 42. No current auction record. Monogram example p 60 IL 42.

Raised in NY state, Heinrich studied at the Conn League of Art Students, the pupil of C N Flagg, R B Brandegree. After beginning newspaper work, he became an early illustrator for the automobile industry, moving to Detroit in 1910. Accounts included Packard and Graham-Paige.

Heinrich was best known for his 100 litho-crayon illustrations of the history of Vermont for National Life Insurance Co. ILA shows *French and Indians Prepare to Sack Deerfield, Mass, 1704*. These drawings were exhibited in galleries and at the 1939 NY World's Fair as well as published in book form by the advertiser for distribution to schools.

HEINZE, Adolph. Born Chicago, Ill 1887, living Downers Grove, Ill 1941. Chicago landscape painter in the Rockies in the 1920s. Work in Illinois and Utah high schools. References A41-BEN-MAL. Source, *Mt Wilbur,* in American Forks high school, Utah. No signature example.

Heinze was the pupil of Buehr, Grant, Chase, Snell.

HELBIG, Bud. Born Butte, Mont about 1915, living Kalispell City, Mont 1974. Traditional Western painter of contemporary Montana genre. Member CAA. No reference. Source C73,74-OSR. No auction record. Signature example p 38 C73 *Tools of the Trade*.

Helbig was raised on a small cow and horse ranch in the foothills of Bitterroot Valley of Montana. He attended art school in Minnesota, then after WWII became the pupil of William Mosby at the American AA in Chicago. He worked as an illustrator for a Chicago advertising agency for many years, until he returned to Montana to paint. Helbig "concentrates on the contemporary scene, and can be found poking around at small rodeos, looking for a subject for his next work." C73.

HEMING, Arthur Henry Howard. Born Paris, Ont, Can 1870, died Hamilton, Ont, Can 1940. Illustrator of animals and wildlife, painter, author. Member SI, assoc RCA, member RSA. Work in Canada House (Eng), NGC, Royal Ont Mus. References A41-BEN-FIE-MAL-SMI. Sources CAN-DCA-ILP-POW-WHO 22. Pair of watercolors with gouache 9×14" *Hunting Scenes* dated 1899 sold 10/16/69 for $1,344 the pair at auction in London. No signature example. (See illustration 128.)

Son of a cavalry captain, Arthur Heming was educated in Hamilton. An athlete of note although weighing only 128 lbs, he began wilderness trips at 16. He studied at Hamilton AS, then taught there 1887–90. Starting about 1890, Heming was a free-lance illustrator and worked until 1899 for Canadian publications such as *Canadian Magazine* and *Massey's,* an interpreter of Western Canada for modern Canadian illustration. *Harper's* accepted a series on Iroquois Indians. In 1899 he went to the US to study with DuMond at the ASL and in 1904 went to London with Frank Brangwyn. Told he was color blind, he painted just in black, white, and yellow until he was 60, when it was discovered that he could distinguish colors. His paintings were thus in color for only 10 years, and that at the end of his life.

Heming became an illustrator for the leading American magazines such as *The Saturday Evening Post* and *Harper's* as well as books and periodicals in Canada, England, France, and Germany. He studied life in the Canadian wilderness at first hand, drawing the illustrations for his own books, "Spirit Lake" in 1907, "Drama of the Forests" in 1921, and "The Living Forest" in 1925. In A23 he listed his residence as Toronto with summers in Old Lyme, Conn. His travel record included patroling by pack train into the Rockies, 550 miles by raft, 1,100 miles by dog team, 1,700 miles on snowshoes, and 3,300 miles by canoe.

HENCKEL, Carl (Charles). Born Berlin, Germany 1862, living Munich, Germany 1891. German painter, illustrator. Work in Roscoe E Hazard Mus (San Diego, Cal). Reference BEN. Source COW. No current auction record but the estimated price of a drawing 12×10" showing an Indian on horseback dated Munich 1891 would be about $600 to $800 at auction in 1976. Signature example p 34 COW.

Henckel worked in Dresden, Munich, and Stuttgart in Germany. There is no indication that he visited the US, but as Charles Henckel he made what he called drawings from life as illustrations for "Buffalo Bill and His Wild West" dated Munich, 1891.

HENDERSON, James. Born Glasgow, Scotland 1871, died Regina, Saskatchewan, Can 1951. Western Canada painter of landscape, genre, and portraits, including Indian subjects. Work in NGC, Regina Col, Pub Lib Calgary, Edmonton AG, etc. Reference MAL. Sources CAH-CAN-DCA. No current auction record or signature example.

Son of a sea captain, Henderson studied evenings in Glasgow and London, painting in the traditional British school, while he worked as a commercial artist. He emigrated to Winnipeg in 1909, working as a lithographic artist there and in Regina. In 1915 Henderson settled in Fort Qu'Appelle, becoming one of the early painters of Western Canada. His specialty was Indian subjects and the painting of a "vivid landscape with incidents of rude frontier life." CAN. Near his home were Crees, Sioux, Salteaux, and Assiniboines, and Henderson's Indian portraits provide "a record of the Indian appearance and character which has an important place in Western history." DCA. The portraits were immediately successful for collectors and exhibitions.

HENDERSON, John R. Active Denver, Colo 1893–98 as sculptor, painter, printmaker. Charter member of the Artists Club. Work in DPL (sketches and woodblocks). Reference MAS lists John E Henderson as carver living in Denver, no date given, connected with DAM. Source DPL. No auction record or signature example.

In 1898 Henderson exhibited a head modeled in relief and was reported to have served in the Colorado Cavalry in Jacksonville (probably in Florida, in the Spanish-American War).

HENDERSON, William Penhallow. Born Medford, Mass 1877, died Santa Fe, NM 1943. New Mexico painter in oil and pastel, muralist, architect, craftsman, teacher. Work in AIC, ANS, Denver AA, MNM; architect of Mus Navaho Ceremonial Arts (Santa Fe). References A47 (obit)-BEN-FIE-MAL-SMI. Sources AIC-ANS-COW-PAW-PIT-TSF-WHO 42. No current auction record but the estimated price of an oil 20×30″ depicting Pueblo dancers would be $5,000 to $6,000 at auction in 1976. Signature example p 99 PIT. (See illustration 129.)

Henderson's father was a Texas rancher and a Kansas banker before returning to Massachusetts in 1891. After graduation from high school, Henderson studied at the Massachusetts Normal Art School and was the pupil of Tarbell at the BMFA School where he won a traveling scholarship. After two years in Europe 1901–3, Henderson taught at the Chicago AFA and painted murals in Chicago schools in 1907. In 1911 Henderson and his wife the poet Alice Corbin collaborated on children's books. In 1915 he designed theatrical scenery and costumes.

In 1916 Henderson settled in Santa Fe, having previously been a summer visitor. In the West he was influenced by the modernists toward a flat decorative style. Henderson had a one-man exhibition in Chicago at the AIC which owns his work *The Green Cloak,* a series of Indian dances in pastel. These dance pastels were drawn from memory with no attention to ethnological detail but rather a capturing of the movement and emotion.

HENDRICKS, Mrs Emma Stockman. Born Solano Cnty, Cal 1869, living San Antonio, Tex 1941. Texas landscape and portrait painter in Taos in 1930s. Member Soc Ind Artists. Work in schools, Canyon (Tex) Hist Soc. References A41-MAL. Sources TOB-TXF. No current auction record or signature example.

Mrs Hendricks studied with Gerald Cassidy, José Arpa, Ernest Lawson, at the NAD, at Santa Fe School of Art, and Broadmoor Acad (Colo Spr). She settled in Texas in 1894, organizing the Amarillo Art Assn in 1921. Painting subjects include *Palo Duro Canyon* and *Taos Pueblo.* She lectured on "Art of the South West."

HENNING, Albin. Born Oberdorla, Germany (or St Paul, Minn) 1886, died probably Woodstock, Conn 1943. Illustrator of the 1920s specializing in adventure including Westerns and military subjects. Reference MAL. Source ILA. No current auction record but the estimated price of a Western illustration would be about $1,000 to $1,200 at auction in 1976. Signature example p 91 ILA. (See illustration 130.)

Raised in St Paul, Henning studied at the AIC and then in NYC at the Grand Central School of Art, the pupil of Harvey Dunn. In addition to his illustrations for the slick magazines like *The Saturday Evening Post,* he also painted for boys' magazines as well as covers for pulp Westerns, for example, *Powder Smoke* for *Smashing Western* magazine in July 1936. He was best known for his illustrations of stories about WWI.

HENNINGS, Ernest Martin. Born Pennsgrove, NJ 1886, died Taos, NM 1956. Early Taos painter of Indian genre subjects and Western landscapes. Member Taos SA 1921. Works in ANS, PAFA, Houston MFA, HAR, LA Cnty MA, GIL, Adams colln. References A41-BEN-FIE-MAL-SMI. Sources ACO-ANS-COW-DCC-HAR-PIT-TAL-TSF-TWR-WAI 71,72-WHO 56. Oil 25×30" *Indian Children at Taos Pueblo* with signature example, estimated for sale 3/10/75 at $10,000 to $12,000 for auction in LA. (See illustration 131.)

Hennings studied briefly at PAFA, then five years at AIC in Chicago where he had been brought up. In 1914 he went to Germany, the pupil of Walter Thor at the Munich Academy and of Angelo Junk at the RA in Munich, where he learned the style of academic realism. At the outbreak of WWI he returned to Chicago as a commercial artist and muralist. In 1917 he visited Taos, becoming a resident in 1921. After his first one-man exhibition in Chicago, he married and painted for a year in Europe and Northern Africa. He traveled frequently, maintaining his base in Taos.

The usual description of Hennings' work is pleasant with a definite decorative pattern. The paintings are bright and technically sophisticated but obvious in composition and subject-matter. Just before his death, Hennings completed a series of paintings for the Santa Fe Ry.

HENRI, Robert. Born Cincinnati, Ohio 1865, died NYC 1929. Very important international teacher of the "Ashcan School," painter. ANA 1904, NA 1906, Taos SA. Work in Luxembourg Gall (Paris), AIC, ANS, MNM, Carnegie Inst, BM, PAFA, MMA, COR, City AM (St Louis). References A29 (obit)-BEN-DAB-ENB-FIE-MAL-SMI. Sources AAR 9/73,11/74-AIC-ALA-AMA-ARI-ARM-ANT 2/58,6/61;1,11/62; 11/64,4/65,1/67,12/73,7/74-CON-COR-DCC-DEP-EIT-HAR-HMA-ISH-190-M19-M57-MSL-NGA-PIT-STI-TSF-TWR-WAI 71,72-WHO 28. Oil 24×20" *The Young Sport* signed Robert Henri but not dated sold 12/10/70 for $13,500 at auction. An oil *Betalo Rubiro, a dancer* sold for $850 at auction in 1935. Signature example p 68 HMA. (See illustration 132.)

Henri's origins are not clear. The FIE addendum alleges Henri's father was John Jackson Cozad, forced to flee Nebraska and renamed Richard H Lee, calling Henri "Son of the Gamblin' Man." The standard biography, as DAB, places Henri native to Ohio, the son of John Henri, educated in Cincinnati, Denver, and NY schools. He was the pupil of Eakins and Hovenden (DAB says Anshutz) at PAFA 1886–88. From 1888 to 1891 he was the pupil of Bouguereau and Robert-Fleury at the Julien Academy in Paris. He also sought independent development through travel in Europe. In 1891 he returned to Philadelphia as instructor at the Women's School of Design, becoming the center of the realist group including Sloan, Glackens, Luks, and Shinn. From 1896 to 1900 he was back in Paris, teaching a class and selling a painting to the French museum. He then established his studio in NYC, teaching at the Valtin school, the Chase school, the Henri school, the Ferrar school, and the ASL. As a teacher, he emphasized visual honesty, the quality of being true to one's self. As a painter in 1929 he was regarded as one of the three most important living American artists, with portraits "under three headings, graceful young women, frolicking children, and foreign types." AMA. His life-span was from the end of the Civil War to the end of Hoover's prosperity.

None of the standard references mentions the Western experience. Henri visited San Diego in 1914, painting Indian portraits. He spent the summer of 1916 in Santa Fe, painting a total of about 30 portraits then, in 1917, and in 1922: "I was not interested in these people to mourn that we have destroyed the Indian. I am only seeking to capture what I have discovered in a few of the people." TSF. Henri's value to the West was mainly in his prestige that caused his friends and students to follow him to New Mexico. The "Ashcan School" was urban, not Indian, and pueblo poverty was not personal to the painters.

HERBST, Frank C. Illustrator living Newark NJ 1920s. Member SI. Work *The Outlaw* in ANS colln. Reference A31. No other source, auction record, or signature example.

HERMAN, Mr, of St Paul, Minn. Active about 1863, he sketched for *Harper's Weekly* the hanging of 38 Sioux Indians from a single gallows at Mankato, Minn.

No reference. Source AOA. No auction record or signature example.

Mr Herman sketched the scene on the spot, to be redrawn by the *Harper's* staff artist. The hanging followed Indian raids on white settlements, precipitated by nonpayment of annuities for Indian lands. Western oils signed "Herman" have also been reported.

HERRERA, Joe Hilario. Born Cochiti Pueblo, NM 1923, living Santa Fe, NM 1967. Pueblo painter. Work in Denver AM, MAI, Mus Northern Ariz, Colorado Springs FAC. References AHI 2/50-AIP. No auction record. Signature example p 20 AHI 2/50.

J H (or Joe H) Herrera received his BA from New Mexico U in 1953, was an instructor in Albuquerque high school 1953–56, and was Assistant Director of Indian Education (NM) beginning 1956. He received his MA in education in 1962 and studied painting under Raymond Jonson. Listed in "Indians of Today," he was the subject of an educational movie "Joe Herrera—Pueblo Artist." In painting he is considered a master of dance figures, posed in restrained action and with refined detail.

He has served as executive secretary, All-Pueblo Council, and as Chairman, Annual Governors Inter-State Indian Council. He conducted a Santa Fe radio program as information center for the Pueblos.

HERRERA, Velino Shije (Ma Pe Wi). Born Zia Pueblo, NM 1902, died probably Santa Fe, NM 1973. Pueblo painter. Work in ACM, AMNH, COR, Denver AM, GIL, MAI, MNM, Philbrook AC. Reference MAS. Sources ACM-AHI 2/50-AIP-LAF. No auction record but the estimated price of a watercolor

20×16″ showing a buffalo dance festival would be about $1,000 to $1,200 at auction in 1976. Signature example and portrait photo p 256 LAF.

Velino Herrera went to school in Santa Fe and was started in art by Dr Edgar L Hewett. He began painting about 1917, had a successful studio in Santa Fe in 1932, and was painting instructor at the Albuquerque Indian School in 1936. He was a part of the "San Ildefonso movement" in the Rio Grande area that established the trends in art for the pueblos. His *Buffalo Dancer* is a much copied work.

Herrera's Zia name is Ma Pe Wi, a name that has a double meaning, oriole (red bird) and bad egg. This is the name by which he signed paintings. Herrera was accused of betraying his tribe when he was said to have given the sun symbol to the state of New Mexico for use as the official insignia. He ceased painting in 1950 following a disabling auto accident.

HERRICK, Henry W (distinguish miniaturist with same name in Nashville, Tenn in 1843). Born Hopkinton, NH 1824, died Manchester, NH 1906. NYC illustrator of books including BEY, wood engraver, watercolor painter of NH views, teacher. Work in books, Manchester Hist Assn, Currier Gall of Art. References FIE (see addenda)-G&W-MAL (wrong Herrick)-SMI. Sources AIW-ANT 8/68,12/69 (article)-BEY-KW2. No current auction record. Monogram example p 480 BEY.

Herrick worked as a wood engraver in Concord and Manchester, NH. In 1844, he moved to NYC to do wood engraving for book publishers and bank-note printers while studying painting at the NAD. He was best known for his engravings of the illustrations of F O C Darley, the leading American genre painter of the day, and particularly "The Sketchbook of Geoffrey Crayon" by Washington Irving. Herrick returned to Manchester in 1865, an important wood engraver at a time when the engraver signed the plate as prominently as the artist. In 1875 Herrick began his career as a NH watercolorist with a series of paintings on famous men and distinctive buildings.

While in NYC, Herrick also worked as an illustrator. For BEY he drew a major scene of *The Hurdy-Gurdy House, Virginia, Montana* showing gold miners and dancehall girls in 1867. It is assumed that the drawing was made from materials available in NYC rather than on the spot in Montana.

HERZOG, Hermann. Born Bremen, Germany 1832, died West Philadelphia, Pa 1932. Eastern painter of mountain landscapes in Cal in the 1870s. Work in NY Pub Lib, Reading Mus, Cincinnati Mus, Gotha, Hanover, and Mulhouse Mus (Europe). References A32 (obit)-BEN-CHA-MAL-SMI-von Boettischer-Thieme und Becker. Sources AAR 3/74-ANT 5/71,10/73,2/74-HON-PAF-SCA. Oil 22×30″ *Mountainous Landscape with Two Bears at the Edge of a Lake* with signature example but not dated, estimated for sale 3/5/74 at $1,200 to $1,500 at auction in LA but did not sell. (See illustration 133.)

Herzog entered the Düsseldorf Academy in 1849, the pupil of J W Schirmer, Lessing, A Achenbach, and H Gude. He traveled to Norway, Switzerland, Italy, and the Pyrénées for the mountain landscapes he favored in his early paintings. He also painted some genre works, eg, *The Flag Swinging Festival in Switzerland*. His patrons included Queen Victoria and Grand Duke Alexander of Russia. In PAF he listed his address as Düsseldorf 1863–66 and 1869, Berlin 1867–68.

In 1869 Herzog emigrated to Philadelphia, at the time his free Hanseatic

State of Bremen was absorbed by Germany. He painted landscapes in Pennsylvania and along the Hudson River. He sketched in California's Yosemite Valley and Sierra Nevada in 1874–75. The painting of *El Capitan, Yosemite* was called his masterpiece. A few months before his death in 1932, he held a joint NYC exhibition with his son Lewis Herzog.

HESS, Sara M. Born Troy Grove, Ill 1880, living San Diego, Cal 1962. Cal landscape painter. Work in Oshkosh MA (Wis), Vanderpoel colln (Chicago); murals in public buildings. References A62-MAL. No current auction record. No signature example.

Sara Hess was the pupil of Richard Miller and Ossip Linde at the AIC. She also studied at the Julien Academy in Paris and with Henry Hubbel. She is listed as living in Hillsdale, NJ in 1921 and in San Diego in 1953.

HESSELIUS, Gustavus. Born Folkära, Dalarna, Sweden 1682, died Philadelphia, Pa 1755. Colonial painter of portraits including Delaware Indians, "the earliest important painter in America." Work in MMA, Penn Hist Soc. References BEN-DAB-FIE-G&W-MAL-SMI. Sources ALA-ANT 5/58,7/71,11/72-BAR-BOA-M31. No current auction record but the estimated price of an oil 30×25″ portrait of a Delaware would be about $15,000 to $25,000 at auction in 1976. Painting example p 95 BAR *Tishcohan*.

Hesselius emigrated to Wilmington (then Christina), Del in 1711. He lived in Philadelphia until about 1714, then probably in Wilmington until about 1718, in Prince Georges County (Md) until about 1733, and finally in Philadelphia again. The first commission for public art in America was from St Barnabas' Church in Maryland in 1721 for an altarpiece *The Last Supper,* painted by Hesselius for £17. Only about 40 paintings in all are attributed to Hesselius. Very few signed paintings are known. Late in his life, Hesselius worked at building organs, being paid for example £25, 9s for an organ for a Moravian church. At this time, Hesselius referred portrait commissions to his son John who was the most prolific Colonial painter.

Two of the Hesselius portraits in the Historical Society of Penn are of Delaware Indian chiefs Tishcohan and Lapowinsa, painted in 1735 for the son of William Penn. These portraits are called "peculiarly modeled" and "somber," perhaps because the chiefs are "foreseeing the shameful trick played on them two years later in the acquisition of their tribe's valuable land holdings." BAR. It is truer today to say these portraits "anticipated the documentary thoroughness of Catlin's Indians a century later." ALA.

HICKS, Bobby. Born Arizona 1934, living Window Rock, Ariz 1967. Navaho painter. Work in Riverside Mus, NYC. No reference. Source AIP. No auction record. No signature example. (See illustration 134.)

Hicks received his education on a scholarship to Arizona. He has been an art instructor in Fort Defiance, Ariz schools.

HICKS, Edward. Born Langhorne (then Attleboro), Bucks Cnty, Pa 1780, died Bucks Cnty 1849. Best-known American primitive painter. Work in Newark AM, NGA, DAM, Cleveland AM, Garbisch colln. References G&W-MAL. Sources AAR 3/74-ALA-ANT 1/36; 7,12/43; 11/45, 7/46, 10/47, 3/51; 5,6/57;

9/60; 3,9/72; 7,9/73; 1,4/74; 2/75-BAR-DAA-GAR-NGA. Oil 16¾×20" *The Peaceable Kingdom* not signed or dated sold 11/14/73 for $65,000 at auction as part of the Halpert Folk Art colln. Signature example pl 75 GAR.

At the end of the Revolutionary War, Hicks's family who had been royalist gentry were destitute. Hicks grew up on a prosperous Quaker farm he had visited with a servant. From ages 13 to 20 he was apprenticed to a coachmaker. He then advertised as a sign painter, turning to easel painting relatively late in life after he had become a leading Quaker. When he urged the value of art in life, however, he was criticized by his fellow Quakers.

Hicks became widely known only after 1932 when one of his *The Peaceable Kingdom* paintings toured nationally. About 100 versions of this subject survive, all different. Generally, they include little figures of Indians depicting "When the great PENN his famous treaty made/ with indian chiefs beneath the elm tree's shade."

HIGGINS, Eugene. Born Kansas City, Mo 1874, died NYC 1958. Painter of poverty and sadness, etcher. NA 1928. Work in MMA, WMAA, LAMA, BM, Bibliothèque Nat (Paris), Brit Mus. References A59 (obit)-BEN-FIE-MAL-SMI. Sources AAT-AMA-ANT 6/68-ARM-DEP-INS 6/25-190-MSL-WHO 58. Oil 24×16" *Woman with a Sack* sold 1/29/70 for $1,400 at auction. Signature example p 89 AAT. (See illustration 135.)

The son of a stonecutter, Higgins was inspired to paint when he was 12 by reading about Millet, the French peasant painter. Educated in St Louis, Mo, then for seven years at L'École des Beaux-Arts and Julien Academy in Paris, he was the "poor beggar in a garret who paints beggars because he is one." DEP.

He returned to NYC in 1904 as an independent realist, to seek the "lower depths" where "the slums are hell—nothing less." He painted people who had suffered because he too had known extreme poverty. He never used a model but painted from memory, eliminating all detail: "When I paint people it is really to use them as symbols." AMA.

Higgins was a painter of Western scenes who did not belong to the Taos or any other group. He saw himself as an artistic outcast who could not expect official recognition, although as early as 1904 a French satirical journal devoted an entire issue to him and he certainly was an important parallel to the Ashcan School, exhibiting with them in 1908 and participating in the 1913 Armory Show.

HIGGINS, William Victor. Born Shelbyville, Ind 1884, died Taos, NM 1949. Early Taos painter of Indians and New Mexico genre. ANA 1921, NA 1935, Taos SA 1914. Work in AIC, ANS, PAFA, LA Cnty MA, GIL, MNM, COR. References A53 (obit)-BEN-FIE-MAL-SMI. Sources AMA-COW-DCC-HAR-HMA-ISH-PAW-PET-PIT-TAL-TSF-WHO 48. Oil 27×30" *Taos Landscape* with signature example, estimated for sale 10/28/74 at $10,000 to $12,000 for auction in LA but did not sell. (See illustration 136.)

The son of a farmer, Victor Higgins began painting at nine. At 15 he took his savings and went to Chicago to study at the AIC and the Academy FA. A patron sponsored four years in Europe, at the Académie de la Grande Chaumière in Paris with René Ménard and Lucien Simon, and under Haas von Hyeck in Munich. Back in Chicago, he taught at the Academy FA. In 1914 his patron, a former Chicago mayor, sent him to Taos to paint landscapes on commission. He was admitted to the exclusive Taos SA, making the membership eight. His early style was impressionist and romantic and successful. In 1923 he had a one-man traveling exhibition with 23 canvases of Taos Indian genre subjects.

In the mid-Twenties, first Berninghaus and Blumenschein, then Higgins, left the popular painting formulas. Higgins was influenced by Dasburg and Marin toward varying perspectives and planes, in restructuring nature in the manner of Cézanne with cubistic devices added. The result for Higgins was a greater approval than he had had as an academic painter, even in Chicago which continued to consider Higgins as its own artist despite his roots in Taos.

HIGHAM, Sydney. Active 1890–1905. English Special Artist-illustrator, writer. No reference. Sources AOH-12/6/73 letter from A P Burton, Victoria and Albert Mus. No current auction record. Signature example in the Supplement to the *Graphic* 7/22/05.

Higham visited Canada in 1904 as Special Artist for the *Graphic* to report on immigration to the western provinces, as "An Artist's Tour Through Canada." Included were *Among the Selkirks: Viewing the Rockies from the Back of a Pullman Car* ("A curious experience it is, to view the landscape from the back of the car, the apparently receding objects having an effect both weird and unreal."), *Cowboy Sports at Calgary* ("The difficult feat of steer-riding is a great feature of these rough, manly exercises."), *Hotel Life at Banff: on the Terrace Overlooking Bow Valley* ("Twentieth-century civilisation has made a home here."). *Graphic*.

HILL, Abby Williams (or Abby Rhoda Hill, Mrs Frank Riley Hill). Born Grinnell, Iowa 1861, living Tacoma, Wash (and San Diego, Cal) 1941. Western landscape painter specializing in National Park scenery, Indians. Work in Alaska-Yuk-Pac (1909) and World's Columb Expos (1893), Grinnell Col, Ames Col (Iowa), Wash schools. Reference A41. Source WNW. No current auction record or signature example.

Mrs Hill studied with H F Spread at AIC, William Chase at ASL, and Herman Hesse in Munich. She exhibited Indian subjects in 1909. Listed paintings are *Yellowstone Falls* and *Forest Scene —Hood Canal, Wash*. She painted outdoor views in the "hope of arousing interest in the preservation of our scenery." WNW.

HILL, Alice Stewart. Born probably Beaver Dam, Wis about 1850, active 1875–80 in Colorado, died about 1921. Painter of Colorado flowers, illustrator. Work in Pioneers' Mus (Colorado). No reference. Sources SHO-SPR. No current auction record but the estimated price of a watercolor 10×8″ showing a bouquet of wildflowers would be about $150 to $250 at auction in 1976. Signature example p 16 SHO.

Daughter of a pioneer Colorado judge, A Stewart Hill studied drawing in Wisconsin and worked in black and white at Cooper Inst and the NAD in NYC. After moving to Colorado Springs with her family, she studied flower painting in Chicago in order to specialize in the flora of Colorado. She picked her models from canyon, mountain, and plains, transported by her pony "Gypsy." Back in her studio, she arranged the cuttings for composition. Her work was engraved by Thomas Parrish for Susan Coolidge's "Her Garden." She illustrated Helen Hunt's "Procession of Flowers in Colorado" and Virginia McClurg's books.

Married to an officer of the Humane Society, Mrs Hill was remembered as gentle and graceful in her dedication to recording previously unclassified and unpainted flora.

HILL, Edward Rufus. Born 1852, died probably California 1908. Western landscape painter, active at least 1888–89. No reference. Source, oil 7½×5″ *Sunset, Lake Tahoe* signed but not dated sold 11/14/72 for $130 at auction in Los Angeles. Oil 26×36″ *Eagle Rock, Platt Canyon, Colorado* signed Edward Hill and dated 1889 was offered at auction 1/27/71 but not sold. No signature example.

HILL, Evelyn Corthell. Born Laramie, Wyom 1886, living there 1948. Wyoming landscape painter, teacher. Member Rocky Mtn Artists. References A41-MAS. Sources WAN-WYA-WYG. No auction record or signature example.

Mrs Hill was educated privately, then at U of Wyoming and Wellesley College. She studied at PAFA with Daniel Garber, at the AIC, at the ASL with John Sloan, at Broadmoor Academy with Boardman Robinson, and was the pupil of Thomas Benton. She was an important Wyoming painter of "beautiful scenes." WAN. She exhibited mountain views in Chicago in 1928. In connection with her teaching at the U of Wyoming, she collected the works of other Wyoming artists for exhibition in Laramie.

HILL, John Henry. Born West Nyack, NY 1839, died place unknown 1922. Eastern landscape and still-life painter, etcher. Prints in NY Pub Lib. References FIE-G&W-SMI. Sources ANT 4/68-FRO-KN1-NJA-PAF-STI. No current auction record but the estimated price of a watercolor 14×20″ of the Yosemite Valley would be about $750 to $900 at aucton in 1976. Signature example p 114 STI.

Hill was the grandson of John Hill, a landscape engraver who emigrated from London in 1816, and the son of John William Hill, a landscape painter who was the leading American "Pre-Raphaelite" spirit. John Henry Hill, the pupil of his father, was best known for his undated "Sketches from Nature" etchings, mostly landscapes. In the 1860s he was regarded as a major still-life artist, included in an 1864 survey of "true works of art." In 1888 he brought out "An Artist's Memorial" to honor his father with his own etchings of his father's paintings.

ANT illustrates an 1871 watercolor of Yosemite Valley by Hill that is different from prints of the valley, indicating a trip West. That makes Hill an early visitor to Yosemite, probably with "Clarence King's survey of the Fortieth Parallel" in 1868. FRO.

HILL, Robert Jerome. Born Austin, Tex 1878, living Dallas, Tex 1941. Texas landscape and miniature painter, illustrator, craftsman, teacher. Work in Texas schools, Confederate Mus (Austin). References A41-FIE-MAL. Sources TOB-TXF. No current auction record or signature example.

R Jerome Hill was educated at Texas U. He studied with Janet Downie in Texas and at the ASL, the pupil of Twachtman, W A Clark, Bridgman, Blum, and Christy. When he returned to Texas, he studied for two years in Dallas with the visiting Kunz-Meyer. After beginning work as a newspaper staff artist and as a teacher, he opened a studio in NYC. Before 1927 Hill was back in

Texas, painting landscapes and miniatures while working as curator of the Dallas Public AG.

HILL, Thomas. Born Birmingham, Eng 1829, died Raymond, Cal 1908. Important as the "Artist of Yosemite," a painter of the Rocky Mtn School. Work in DAM, Cal St Capitol, LA Cnty MA, Worcester MA, U of Kan MA, ANS, Oakland Mus. References A09 (obit)-BEN-CHA-DAB-FIE-G&W-MAL-SMI. Sources AAR 11/74-AIW-ALA-ANT 3/56, 9/57, 2/58, 11/61; 6,10,11/62; 11/64,6/67,10/68;1,5,7/72;1,3,9/73; 7/74,2/75-BAR-BOA-BWB-DCC-HAR-HON-HUT-JCA-POW-SSF-STI-TAW-WHI-WHO 08. Oil 59×35¼" *The Yosemite Valley* listed as dated 1863 sold 3/20/73 for $4,500 at auction in London. Oil 35½×28¾" *Portrait of Abraham Lincoln* signed Thomas Hill and dated 1865 was estimated at $4,000 to $6,000 for sale 3/5/74 at auction and sold for $4,250. ANT 6/62 illustrated *The Yosemite Valley* signed and dated and offered for sale at $300. Signature example p 27 PB 10/27/71. (See illustration 137.)

Hill, educated in public school in Massachusetts, was apprenticed to a coach painter until he was 15. He worked in Boston as an ornamental painter, then studied at the PAFA with Rothermel while working in Philadelphia. By 1853 his allegorical painting won a Baltimore prize. In 1861 Hill's health caused him to move to San Francisco. He specialized in painting portraits until 1866 when he went to Paris as the pupil of Paul Meyerheim. Hill was advised to paint landscapes, which he did, in Boston from 1867 to 1871. While in Boston he also painted the immense *Yosemite Valley* that he sold for $5,000. It was reproduced both as a Prang chromo and engraved as a book frontispiece in 1870.

In 1871 Hill returned to San Francisco, again for his health. He spent his summers sketching in Yosemite until 1888 when he built his studio there. From 1887 to 1891 Hill worked from photographs to paint the 98×138" *The Driving of the Last Spike* joining the transcontinental rails. About 400 figures were included, 70 as then-familiar portraits. The painting is now owned by the State of California. Until the last few years, it was fashionable to evaluate Hill as "in wait for the moneyed tourists, his supply of Yosemites as inexhaustible as their demand." ALA.

HILTON, John William. Born Carrington, ND 1904, living Twentynine Palms, Cal 1976. Painter of the Western desert, muralist, illustrator, author. Work in US Air Force, US National Parks, Tokyo City Hall, San Diego Mus Nat Hist, MNM, Ariz Botanical Gardens (Phoenix). Reference A76. Sources AHI 3/60, 11/62-COW. No current auction record. Signature example p 17 AHI 3/60.

Hilton was raised traveling with parents who were missionaries. He was educated in California, then worked as a jewelry designer in Los Angeles. In the Depression of the 1930s, he started a curio business in the California desert and began painting. He worked with Fechin, Dixon, Swinnerton, and Forsythe. Following his first one-man show in Palm Springs in 1935, he has had more than 100 shows nationally. Hilton has illustrated his own books beginning with "Sonora Sketch Book" in 1947, "This Is My Desert" in 1960, and "Hilton Paints the Desert" in 1964. "My desert paintings are usually unpeopled because I am trying to present the feel of the country rather than what man is trying to do with it. The land of little rain and plenty of

time will be waiting to bring peace."
AHI.

Hilton has also painted the Hawaiian cowboys, their horses and cattle.

HINCKLEY, Thomas Hewes. Born Milton, Mass 1813, died same 1896. Eastern animal painter in Cal 1870. Work in BMFA, MMA. References BEN-CHA-FIE-G&W-MAL-SMI. Sources ANT 5/41,10/55,10/68-BOA-HAR-HUT-KAR-M57-PAF. Oil 19¾×23¾" *Pastoral Scene* 1849 estimated 1/30/75 for sale at $3,000 to $4,000 at auction and sold for $3,400. Signature example p 524 ANT 10/68.

Son of a captain, Hinckley was apprenticed at 15 to a Philadelphia merchant. He studied at evening art classes with William Mason, his only instruction. At 18 he went to Boston. When his father died in 1833, Hinckley returned to Milton as a sign and fancy painter. In 1843 he successfully painted dogs, thereafter devoting himself to specializing in animal paintings in his Milton studio. He became one of the earliest American cattle painters, visiting Europe in 1851 to study Landseer and the Flemish masters. In late years Hinckley painted landscapes, but he rarely exhibited.

In 1870 Hinckley visited California, sketching the elk. Some of his paintings were engraved, but his competitor A F Tait monopolized Currier & Ives.

HIND, Prof Henry Youle. Born probably Nottingham, Eng 1823, died probably Canada after 1861. Topographic and ethnologic survey artist, watercolorist, professor of geography, author. No reference. Sources CAH-CAN. No recent auction record or signature example.

Hind emigrated to Canada in 1846, becoming professor of chemistry and geography when Trinity U opened in Toronto. In 1857 he was geographer on the first Red River expedition. He wrote two books that year, one on the prevention of wheat rust and the other the Red River report. In 1858 he led the Assiniboine and Saskatchewan explorations. In 1861 he was in charge of the exploration of Labrador, with his brother William G R Hind as artist. He also made surveys of New Brunswick, of gold in Nova Scotia, and of minerals in Newfoundland.

A large collection of drawings and watercolors resulted, both topographic as *Red River from the Stone Fort* and ethnologic as *Typical Group of Ojibway Indians at Fort Frances, 1857.*

HIND, William George Richardson. Born Nottingham, Eng 1833, died Sussex, NB, Can 1888 (or 1889). Canadian landscape painter in the West and Far West, survey artist, teacher. Work in ACM, Toronto Pub Lib, The Public Archives, John Ross Robertson colln, survey reports, etc. No reference. Sources CAH-CAN-DCA. No current auction record. Self-portrait p 75 CAH.

Hind studied in London and in Europe, emigrating to Toronto in 1852. He taught drawing before returning to England in 1854. When his brother was placed in charge of the government expedition to Labrador in 1861, Hind came back to Canada as expedition artist to sketch topography and Indian genre. Many of these Indian drawings are in the John Ross Robertson colln of early Canadiana.

In 1863–64 and in the 1870s, Hind sketched in Manitoba and British Columbia. Sketch subjects from 1861 in Labrador include *Seal Hunting in the Gulf of St. Lawrence, A Montagnais Indian Taking His Squaw to Burial,* and

Scene from Top of the Ridge Portage. Buffalo Herd on the Western Prairies and *British Columbia Miner* are watercolors from 1864. His later years were as a painter in New Brunswick. It was said of his work that it "is valuable from the historic, if not the aesthetic point of view." CAN. Hind had "drifted into obscurity" until a six-gallery retrospective of 62 works in 1967. DCA.

studying the methods of the old masters. Success came only in the 1920s, when he had already reached maturity as a painter. Hinkle taught in the Chouinard School and the Santa Barbara School.

His only interest painting, Hinkle as an impressionist aimed at the emotional reactions of the viewer rather than the literal. He "lays on his pigments lavishly in hillocks," giving a "third-dimensional feeling." CON.

HINE, Henry George. Born Brighton, Eng 1811, died Hampstead, Eng 1895. Active in the Can West in 1847. Work in ROM, Brighton, Cardiff, Victoria and Albert, and Sydney museums. References BEN-MAL. Sources CAE-HUT. No recent auction record or signature example. (See illustration 138.)

Hine was an engraver self-taught as a painter. Beginning as a marine painter, his first exhibition in London was not until 1856. He later "devoted himself to landscapes to which really it is extremely difficult to impart any lasting interest." HUT.

In the 1840s Hine was on the staff of *Punch* and contributed illustrations to *Illustrated London News*. A landscape *Buffalo Hunt on the Prairies,* 1847 indicates he may have been in America.

HITCHENS, Joseph. Born England 1838, died probably Pueblo, Colo 1893. Colorado landscape and genre painter. Work in Colo St Mus, MNM. No reference. Sources BDW-DPL-SPR. No auction record or signature example.

Hitchens' *Admission of Colorado* as a state was painted before the event took place in 1876. He moved to Pueblo in the 1880s, painting landscapes in the San Luis and Arkansas River valleys, and was "Pueblos's best-known artist." SPR.

HINKLE, Clarence K. Born Auburn, Cal 1880, died Santa Barbara, Cal 1960. Cal painter, teacher. Work in San Diego FA Soc, LAMA, Santa Barbara MA, de Young Mem Mus, Crocker AG, etc. References A62 (obit)-MAL. Source CON. Oil 30×30" *The Blue Basin, Trinidad* sold 12/1/67 for $175 at auction. Signature example ✕54 CON, *La Cumbre Peak.*

Hinkle studied at the PAFA and was the pupil of William Chase, Anshutz, and Laurens. He traveled widely in Europe,

HITTELL, Charles J (Carlos, Karl). Born San Francisco, Cal 1861, died Pacific Grove, Cal 1938. Painter of Western American figures and landscapes. Work in HON, AMNH, Mus of Vertebrate Zoology (Berkeley, Cal). References A17-BEN-FIE-MAL-SMI. Sources HON-POW-WHO 22. No current auction record or signature example.

Hittell was the son of an author, member of a pioneer San Francisco family. The San Francisco Public Library collection includes his drawings from age 12 on. Hittell was educated in San Francisco schools 1865–79 and attended U of California 1879–81. He studied at the San Francisco School of Design 1881–83, at the RAFA in Munich 1884–88 and again 1889–92, then the Julien Academy in Paris 1892–93.

In 1893 Hittell established his studio in San Francisco. He painted Western American figures, landscapes, and a series on California adobes. Among the landscapes were seven large backgrounds for AMNH. HON holds about 75 pencil drawings including a series on Yosemite in 1880. The drawings indicate a variety of signatures.

HOCKADAY, Hugh. Born Little Rock, Ark 1892, died Lakeside, Mont 1968. Montana landscape and Indian portrait painter, commercial artist, watercolorist. Work in Hist Soc of Mont (Helena). Reference A70 (obit). Source MON. No current auction record. Signature example p 105 MON.

Hockaday graduated in 1924 from the St Louis SFA, the pupil of Oscar Berninghaus, Goetsch, Carpenter, and Wuerple, and studied at Commercial Art in St Louis, the pupil of D C Nicholson. For 26 years he worked as decorator for Scruggs, Vandervoort & Barney, a St Louis department store. In 1946 he moved to Montana to manage his father's fruit ranch on Flathead Lake where he continued his work in commercial art, creating theatrical posters and animated displays.

In the late 1950s Hockaday began fulltime at painting landscapes and portraits in watercolor. He sketched on location, with color slides as reference. Snow scenes were favored for commissions. "A quiet, unassuming and gentlemanly demeanor characterized Hockaday's approach to his work and every-day life." MON.

HOEFFLER (Höffler), Adolf Johann. Born Frankfurt, Germany 1826, died probably there 1898. German landscape and portrait painter active in the West 1852. Work in Frankfurt Mus. References BEN-G&W. Sources KEN-PAF. Oil 22×37¾" *Midday Rest in the Fields* sold 6/7/72 for $704 at auction in Germany. Signature example p 22 KEN 6/70.

Hoeffler was the pupil of his father, a Frankfurt religious painter, as well as a student of the Frankfurt City Institute and the Munich and Düsseldorf academies. In 1848 he left for Canada. In December 1848 he came to New Orleans, painting and sketching along the lower Mississippi in 1849, along the Ohio and in the East in 1850, then south from NYC to Cuba in 1851.

In 1852 he painted and sketched in Minnesota and the upper Mississippi. At Fort Snelling he painted a watercolor portrait of a seated Sioux chief garbed partly in manufactured clothes and facially as German as he was Indian. This was of course early days for a painter in Fort Snelling—Seth Eastman left only in 1848, William Hays did not arrive until 1860, and Cary 1861.

HOFFMAN, Frank B. Born Chicago, Ill 1888, died Taos, NM 1958. Traditional Western illustrator, painter, sculptor. Work in Adams colln, HAR. References A53-MAL. Sources AAW-COW-HAR-ILA-PAW-TAL-TSF-TWR. No current auction record but the estimated price of an oil 20×30" showing bloodhounds on the range would be $7,000 to $8,000 at auction in 1976. Signature example p 95 ILA.

Hoffman grew up around his father's New Orleans racing stables. Through a family friend he was hired to make sketches for the *Chicago American,* later becoming head of the art department. While working for the paper, he had five years of formal art training in private lessons from J Wellington Reynolds, a portrait painter. In 1916 Hoffman went West to paint, living with the Indian tribes and the cowboys. He worked as public relations director for Glacier National Park where he met John Singer Sargent.

In 1920 he joined the art colony in Taos. He studied with Leon Gaspard, gaining effective freedom in use of color. He painted for corporate advertising campaigns and made illustrations on Western subjects for the leading national magazines in the 1920s. Successful as the best-known New Mexico illustrator, he bought his own Hobby Horse Rancho where he raised quarter horses and kept as live models his longhorns, dogs, eagles, burros, and a bear. In the 1930s he sculpted animal models. Beginning with 1940 he was under exclusive contract to Brown and Bigelow for calendar art, producing more than 150 Western paintings.

betterment, and Woman of the Year 1957. She was the author of "Heads and Tales," a 1936 autobiography, and "Sculpture Inside and Out" in 1939.

"Heads and Tales" concentrates on the 101 life-size bronze figures and heads for the Hall of Man at the Field Museum in Chicago. Miss Hoffman saved the American Indian for last, traveling to the West, starting with New Mexico and providing 40 pages of art and ethnology: "One of the most primitive Zuni masks is known as 'mud head,' a spherical hollow of hard earth with two round knobs for ears, a top knot, and three openings for eyes and mouth. I found I could make my Indian models laugh when they asked me what I was doing with clay and tools. 'I am making mud heads,' I would answer, and as my initials were M H, I adopted 'mud head' as my Indian nickname."

HOFFMAN, Malvina Cornell (Mrs Samuel B Grimson). Born NYC 1887, died there 1966. International sculptor, writer, painter. Member NA 1931, NSS. Work in NAD, Rome Acad, Stockholm AM, Bush House (London), League (Paris), Glenbow Fndn (Canada), etc. References A70 (obit)-BEN-ENB-FIE-MAL-SMI. Sources AAT-ALA-AMA-ANT 12/74-NAD-NSS-SCU-WAA-WHO 62-WOM 64. Bronze brown patina 24½″ high *Blackfoot Indian* signed and dated 1933 sold 4/20/72 for $2,400 at auction. Signature example p 97 PB 4/20/72. (See illustrations 139 a & b.)

Malvina Hoffman was educated at the Brearley School in NYC. She studied painting with John Alexander in NYC and sculpture with Herbert Adams and Gutzon Borglum in NYC, then with Auguste Rodin in Paris. She won a first prize for *Russian Dancers* in Paris as early as 1911. She was selected Woman of Achievement in 1935, one of 12 women contributing most toward human

HOGAN, Thomas. Born probably Ireland about 1839, died probably NYC after 1900. Illustrator for *Harper's Weekly* and BEY, lithographer. Work in periodicals, books. Reference A09 (obit for Francis H Schell)-G&W. Sources AAR 11/74-AOA (under Schell)-BEY. No current auction record. Signature example p 453 BEY.

Hogan was referred to as a 21-year-old Irish lithographer in NYC in 1860. He contributed 11 illustrations to "Beyond the Mississippi," a book of travel "from the great river to the great ocean" from 1857 to 1867. Hogan's drawings depict scenes from 1857 to 1865, from Kansas to Mexico to Colorado to Utah to California, showing subjects from topography to *A Mexican Fandango*. The text applicable to *California Fruits and Vegetables* refers to a photograph rather than the drawing, so it can be assumed that all of Hogan's drawings for BEY were done in NYC, not on the spot in the West.

After the Civil War, F H Schell left *Leslie's* art department that he had headed. "Later he formed a partnership with Thomas Hogan and for 30 years these two artists worked together as illustrators." A09. The 1876 and 1884 *Harper's* illustrations reproduced in AOA are both NYC subjects.

HOGNER, Nils. Born Whiteville, Mass 1893, living NYC 1962. Illustrator of Western and Indian books, mural and portrait painter, printmaker, teacher. Member Nat Soc Mural Ptrs. Work in Okla school, Mo library; murals in public buildings, banks. References A62-MAS. Source, books illustrated, "Navajo Winter Nights," "Pedro the Potter," "The Navajo Flute Player," "Santa Fe Caravans," "Education of a Burro." No auction record or signature example.

Hogner studied at the Boston School of Painting, the BMFA School, Rhodes Academy in Copenhagen (Denmark), and was the pupil of Leon Gaspard and Ivar Nyberg. He was an instructor for four years at the U of New Mexico. Illustrations for children's books were his specialty.

HOGUE, Alexandre. Born Memphis, Mo 1898, living Tulsa, Okla 1976. Modern Texas painter, lithographer, teacher, "artist of the dust bowl." Work in Philbrook AC, GIL, Dallas MFA, Houston MFA, etc. References A76-MAL. Sources AAT-ALA-CAP-CON-MAP-TOB-TSF-TXF-WHO 70. No auction record. Signature example p 56 CON.

Hogue, son of a Presbyterian minister, was raised in Denton, Tex. "He knew the fine grazing lands and thriving ranches as they were then, and during the years he watched the grassy plains turn to hot, arid, and lifeless wasteland." CON. His mother secured lessons for Hogue beginning when he was nine, at the Teachers'

College class of Elizabeth Hillyer. He studied briefly at the Minneapolis AI and on three summer trips with Frank Reaugh. Otherwise self-taught, he spent four years in NYC before returning to Texas in 1925 to paint and teach. He was on the summer faculty of Texas State College for Women 1931–42, conducting field painting classes in Taos beginning 1932. He worked as technical aviation illustrator 1942–45, then as head of department of art, U of Tulsa.

As the artist of the dust bowl, he "painted the Texas panhandle, the dunes ridged by the dry wind where starving cattle left their tracks." This is "psychoreality, a kind of surrealism that compels the beholder to feel the heat, the despair and tragedy of the dust bowl." CON.

HOKEAH, Jack. Born western Oklahoma, 1902, living Anadarko, Okla 1967. Painter, one of the "Five Kiowas." Work in DAM, GIL, Joslyn AM, MAI, MNM, etc. Reference MAL. Source AIP. No current auction record or signature example.

With Asah, Hokeah was brought from the Fine Arts Club in Anadarko to the U of Oklahoma by Mrs Susie Peters one Sunday afternoon in 1926. They carried with them their paintings of Indian dancers done on brown paper bags and shoe box covers. Instructor Edith Mahier said, "I was seeing for the first time an Oklahoma art expression, true and fresh, and deserving of interest from educators." In the fall of 1926 Asah, Hokeah, Mopope, and Tsatoke were sponsored by Dr O B Jacobson of the university for art instruction by Miss Mahier in her office, away from "white art." The Kiowas gave recitals to support themselves, with Hokeah as an Eagle dancer. In 1927 Lois Smoky joined to make "the Five." Financial contributions came from an oil millionaire, Lew Wentz. The Kiowas were a sensation at the First International Art Exposition in Prague in 1928, with major books written about them in 1929 and 1950. During the Depression they decorated public buildings for the WPA.

Hokeah became an actor in NYC where in the 1930s he had exhibited his paintings. Later he worked for the Bureau of Indian Affairs, but he ceased painting.

HOLDREDGE, Ransom Gillet. Born NY (or England) 1836, died Alameda Cnty, Cal 1899. Cal painter of mountain landscapes with Indians and of seascapes. Work in Oakland Mus, HAR. No reference. Sources ANT 6/58,4/73-DCC-HON-PNW. Oil on canvas mounted on board 30×50" *Nocturnal Indian Encampment* with signature example estimated for sale 10/28/74 at $4,500 to $5,500 at auction in LA but did not sell. (See illustration 140.)

Holdredge came to California in the late 1850s as a draftsman in the Mare Island Navy Yard, San Francisco. He studied with local artists and began exhibiting landscapes about 1860 while working as head draftsman and signing his name to paintings as Holdridge. The local press referred to him as the ranking landscape painter of the day, praising his canvases that were in the bright Hudson River style. In 1874 he and Hiram Bloomer held a joint sale of paintings to finance European studies.

In 1876 Holdredge was said to have been acting as a field artist for *Scribner's* with Major Reno's troops at the time of the Custer massacre. He returned to San Francisco about 1880, painting darker landscapes in the Barbizon style and using a palette knife to gain a thick impasto. His landscape paintings continued to be well received and were reviewed as superior to Keith. Although Holdredge preferred portraiture, the

demand for his landscapes sent him sketching throughout California, the Northwest, Western Canada, and the Rockies. Holdredge is not named as a bohemian in the art circles of the day, but he was said to have become an alcoholic. His ability declined during the 1890s. He was buried at public expense.

HOLGATE, Edwin Headley. Born Allandale, Ont, Can 1892, living Westmount, Montreal, PQ, Can 1976. Modern Montreal painter on the West Coast in the 1920s, illustrator, muralist, teacher. Member RCA 1935, Can Group Ptrs 1933. Work in NGC, Sarnia AG, Art Assn Montreal, Le Havre (France). References A76-MAL. Sources CAH-CAN-DCA. Oil 15×17" *Landscape* dated 1960 sold 5/14/73 for $2,000 at auction in Toronto. Signature example p 118 "Temlaham." (See illustration 141.)

Son of a civil engineer, E H Holgate studied at the Art Assn of Montreal from 1904 to 1906 and in France with Lucien Simon beginning 1912 and again in 1920. "The Downfall of Temlaham" by Marius Barbeau published in 1928, a landmark book on Indians of British Columbia, contains four illustrations by Holgate along with illustrations by other major painters of the Canadian West Coast Indians in the 1920s—Emily Carr, A Y Jackson, Langdon Kihn, and Annie D Savage. The illustrations are stylistically compatible with the Canadian nationalist artists in the Group of Seven. Holgate had visited the Skeena River area in BC with Barbeau and A Y Jackson in 1926, sketching the Indian totem poles and villages. He used this West Coast Indian motif in large canvases and in an Ottawa mural called "the most important decoration ever entrusted to a Canadian artist." DCA.

In 1931 Holgate became the eighth

member of the Group of Seven, the only member besides Varley who painted nudes. He also painted portraits including Westerner sitters. During WWII, Holgate was an official artist for the Royal Canadian Air Force.

HOLLING, Holling C. Active 1935–48 as a NYC illustrator for The Platt & Munk Company. Wrote and with Lucille Holling illustrated "The Book of Indians" in 1935 and "The Book of Cowboys" in 1936. Reference MAS. No other source. No auction record. Signature example frontispiece "The Book of Indians."

Holling is happily reminiscent of Langdon Kihn in the perspective-less style and pastel colors of a painting that appears to be by rather than about an Indian, and also in the range of Indian cultures depicted.

HOLME, John Francis. Born Corinth, WVa 1868, died Denver, Colo 1904. Illustrator, engraver, printer, reporter. Work in Huntington Lib (San Marino, Cal), Ariz Hist Soc (Tucson), U of Ariz Lib. References A05 (obit)-BEN-MAL-SMI. Sources AHI 1/68-WHO 03. No auction record but the estimated price of a drawing 10×12″ showing the Schrogl ranch would be about $200 to $300 at auction in 1976. Signature example p 4 AHI 1/68.

Frank Holme was educated in Keyser, WVa public schools. He worked as a country newspaper printer until he was 16, on a civil engineer corps for a year, and then as reporter and artist on newspapers in Wheeling, Pittsburgh, Chicago, and San Francisco. As a sketch artist he caught the spirit of the time, appearing in the world press following his on-the-scene drawings of the Johnstown flood in 1889. His sketches included stage personalities and the Spanish-American War. In 1893 he had founded the private imprint Bandar Log Press named for Kipling's description of the organizational effectiveness of monkeys. In 1898 he founded the School of Illustration in Chicago for newspaper artists.

Holme spent two years in Asheville, NC to rest from tuberculosis, continuing the Bandar Log imprint while there. In 1903 his doctors sent him to Phoenix. The trip was paid for by the subscriptions of 150 friends, Booth Tarkington, Charles Dana Gibson, Mark Twain, etc.

When a painting exhibition was held in Chicago in 1903, every artist made and framed a tiny replica that was shipped to Holme in Phoenix in a Pullman chartered by William Randolph Hearst. When Holme died at 36, newspapers around the country carried his obituary, "the tall slender figure in black, with his overcoat flying loose, always striding somewhere." AHI notes, "Interest in Holme has increased rapidly. His illustrations, etchings, lithographs, when they come up, are snatched by collectors." Over 400 are in the U of Arizona collection.

HOLMES, William Henry. Born near Cadiz, Ohio 1846, died Washington, DC 1933. Important panoramist of the Grand Canyon, survey artist, scientific illustrator, archaeologist, art director. Member major scientific societies. Work in NGA, MNM, ACM, COR. References A31-BEN-DABS-ENB-FIE-MAL-SMI. Sources AHI 7/73,6/74-AIW-DCC-HAR-WHO 32. No auction record but the estimated price of a watercolor 16×20″ showing the rim of the canyon would be about $4,000 to $5,000 at auction in 1976. Signature example p 39 DCC. (See illustration 142.)

Holmes was educated at Georgetown, Ohio public schools and at McNeely Normal School in 1870. He was a teacher until 1872 when he moved to Washington, studying art under Theodore Kaufmann and sketching Smithsonian specimens. He was appointed field artist to the Hayden survey of the Yellowstone in 1872. Working as assistant geologist, he was on the Colorado survey in 1874. In 1875 he led the survey party in New Mexico and Arizona, then in Washington prepared the Philadelphia Centennial exhibits.

After spending 1879 in Europe traveling and studying art, he returned to accompany Major Dutton as a geologist in exploring the Grand Canyon. He produced double-paged panoramas that let you "step to the edge of 40 miles of outdoors" in "the most beautiful book by any of the government surveys." AIW. Holmes also traveled to Texas and Mexico in 1884. In 1886 he participated in a study of the Pueblo Indians, while acting as curator of aboriginal pottery for the US National Museum. He became head curator of anthropology in Chicago's Field Museum in 1894 and in the Smithsonian in 1897. In 1902 he was chief of the Bureau of American Ethnology, and in 1920 director of the National Gallery of Art.

HOLT, Percy William. Born Mobile, Ala about 1895, living Galveston, Tex 1941. Galveston landscape painter, designer, teacher, writer. References A41-MAL. Sources TOB-TXF. No current auction record or signature example.

Holt was raised in Galveston. He first studied with Birge Harrison, then attended the John Carlson School of Landscape Painting at Woodstock, NY, the pupil of Bellows, Speicher, F S Chase, and Dasburg. In 1922 he sketched in

France. From 1929 to 1931 he taught landscape painting at the U of Buffalo. He returned to Texas about 1928 and exhibited in Houston.

HOOD, Harry. Born Cupar, Scotland 1876, living Vancouver, BC, Can 1941. BC painter of landscapes, figures, and still lifes. Work in Vancouver City Mus. No reference. Sources CAN-WNW. No current auction record or signature example.

Hood studied drawing and design in South Kensington, London. He was president of the BC Society FA.

HOOPER, Will Phillip. Born Biddeford, Me about 1855, died probably Forest Hills, NY 1938. Eastern painter, illustrator, writer. Work in MNM, magazines, books. References A41 (obit)-BEN-FIE-MAL. Source AAC. No current auction record or signature example.

Hooper was the pupil of Benjamin Fitz in NYC and studied at the ASL and Mass Normal AS in Boston. He was an illustrator and writer of magazine articles. In 1903 he contributed to Frank Norris' stories of the new and old West, along with Remington, Leigh, and Leyendecker.

HOPKINS, Arthur. Born probably London, Eng 1848, died London 1930. English illustrator, engraver, watercolorist. Member Royal Society of Painters in Water Colours. References BEN-MAL. Sources AOH-BAW. No current auction record but a watercolor *Agitated Sea* sold in 1911 for £5 15s 6d at auction. Drawing example p 101 AOH *The Assassination of Gen Canby by Capt Jack* 4/11/1873.

Hopkins exhibited for the first time in London in 1872, then continued showing at the RA. He appears in 1873 as a staff illustrator for *ILN,* redrawing the Modoc Indian War sketches made by William Simpson. There is no indication that Hopkins visited the West.

HOPKINS, Mrs Frances Ann Beechey. Born England 1856, died London, Eng 1918. English genre painter in the Canadian Red River area in 1870, painter of the Canadian voyageurs. Work in ROM, Public Archives of Canada. References BEN-MAL. Source DCA. No auction record or signature example. (See illustration 143.)

The daughter of an admiral, Mrs Hopkins accompanied her husband to Canada where he worked for Hudson's Bay Company. She painted Canadian genre scenes that were exhibited in London at the RA and the Old Watercolour Society beginning 1872 when she may have been back in England.

Mrs Hopkins made a series of paintings of voyageurs, probably during Col Wolseley's Red River expedition in 1870. "Most of her work was untitled but she did sign with her initials FAH." DCA. About 1870 Knoedler & Co published a reproduction of a painting by Mrs Hopkins.

HOPKINSON, Harold. Born Salt Lake City, Utah 1918, living Byron, Wyom 1976. Traditional Western painter, illustrator, muralist. Work in Mormon temples. Reference A76. Sources COW-Cody *Enterprise.* No auction record or signature example.

Hopkinson was raised on a ranch in the Bridger Valley of Wyoming. After WWII he received his MA in art from the U of Wyoming and became an art instructor. He had additional training at Los Angeles Art Center and in Westport, Conn, with further studies under Ed Grigware, Conrad Schweiring, and Bob Meyer. He remembers seeing Remington and Russell calendars that influenced him to paint.

HOPPER, Edward. Born Nyack, NY 1882, died NYC 1967. Very important international painter of realism, etcher. Work in PAFA, BM, AIC, MMA, MOMA, WMAA, BMFA, etc. References A66-BEN-FIE-MAL-SMI. Sources AAR 3/74-AAT-AIC-ALA-ANT 10/60-APT-ARI-ARM-CAA-CON-DEP-HMA-190-MAP-M50-PIT-TSF-WHO 66. Watercolor $14 \times 20''$ signed and titled *Two Lights, Me* painted in 1927 sold 10/18/72 for $50,000 at auction of Burton colln. Signature example p 63 HMA.

Hopper was educated in public and private schools in NY. He was the pupil of the NY SA under Chase, Henri, and Kenneth Hayes Miller from about 1900 to 1906. Hopper made three European visits, returning in 1910 to a studio on Washington Square, his address at his death. After he exhibited in the 1913 Armory Show, sales were few. Hopper worked as a commercial artist until 1919 when a series of successful etchings let him return to oils: "My aim in painting has always been the most exact transcription possible of my most intimate impressions of Nature." A painting may be "no exact transcription of a place, but pieced together from sketches and mental impressions of things in the vicinity. The figures were done almost entirely without models." CON.

Hopper came to Santa Fe for the summer of 1925 at the suggestion of Sloan, as a change from other summers in Maine or Cape Cod. It is said that he "wandered among the Indians, adobe houses, and gaudy mountains, but he could find nothing to paint. One day the spell was broken; he had done the watercolor *Locomotive, D&RG."* TSF. In 1925 Hopper was just achieving acceptance as an artist. His painting technique was the same for New Mexico as for New England or New York.

HOPPIN, Augustus. Born Providence, RI 1828, died Flushing, LI, NY 1896. Humorous illustrator, boundary survey artist, author. Work in magazines and books. References BEN-DAB-FIE-G&W-MAL-SMI. Sources ALA-AOA-BOA-HUT-TEP. No current auction record. Signature example ⚹46 AOA.

Son of a China-trade merchant and younger brother of an artist, Hoppin was educated at Brown U and at Harvard Law School. Although admitted to the RI bar in 1850, Hoppin quit the law in favor of illustrating where he was an immediate success. He contributed to Washington Irving's "Sketch Book" by 1852. In 1854–55 he toured Europe and Egypt, providing himself with material for popular travel books he wrote and illustrated. "Some of the elaborate drawings surpass in finish, force, and beauty, anything of the kind produced in this country." BOA. In 1872 his drawings were used to demonstrate chemical engraving, the process that led to daily newspapers that were illustrated.

As a fledgling illustrator in 1850, Hoppin was an artist for the Bartlett survey of the boundary between Texas and Mexico. While the professional painter Henry Cleves Pratt drew elaborate landscape views, Hoppin's few sketches were consonant with his sense of humor. An example is *Prairie-Dog Town* with men passing as part of the wagon train shooting at the prairie dogs, the owls, and the snakes inhabiting the burrows. The Bartlett survey was constantly in turmoil, due to conflict with Washington and with the army corps. Hoppin did not remain to complete the work and was in Europe studying old masters when the Bartlett report was published.

HORD, Donal. Born Prentice, Wis 1902, died San Diego, Cal 1966. Western sculptor specializing in stone and wood Indian heads, monuments, façades. Member NA 1951, NSS, NIAL. Work in San Diego FA Gall, San Francisco MA, San Diego fountain and bas-relief, bronze memorial in Belgium. References A70 (obit)-BEN-MAL-SMI. Sources AAT-ALA-NA 74-WHO 66. No auction record but the estimated value of The Society of Medalists 1950 issue 3″ bronze medal *Man Must Sow / To Reap* signed with monogram would be about $100 to $150 at auction in 1976. Sculpture example p 201 AAT. (See illustrations 144 a & b.)

Beginning his career as a sculptor at 15, Hord studied at Santa Barbara School of the Arts, the modeling and wax casting pupil of Archibald Dawson of Scotland. He was awarded a scholarship to Mexico 1928–29 and later to the PAFA and to the Architectural Institute.

After 1929 he settled in San Diego where the Fine Arts Gallery has the bronze *Indian Chief* and the carved rosewood *Young Maize*. He preferred to work "out of doors in the hard California light," using mechanical tools to cut the "hard obsidian and diorite of the Southwest into shining Indian heads." ALA.

HORN, Trader. See Smith, Alfred Aloysius.

HORSFALL, Robert Bruce. Born Clinton, Iowa 1869, died probably Fairport, NY 1948. Illustrator, naturalist, animal and bird painter. Work in NY Zoological Soc, Amer M Nat Hist, U of Minn, Ill Mus. References A41-BEN-FIE-MAL-SMI. Sources POW-WHO 46. No current auction sale but the estimated price for a small watercolor of an American bird would be about $350 to $500 at auction in 1976. Signature example "Birds of the Rockies."

The pupil of L C Lutz and Thomas S Noble at Cincinnati AA from 1886–89, Horsfall was then awarded a scholarship for Munich's Bavaria König Academy and the Colarossi Academy in Paris from 1889–93. Horsfall exhibited in Chicago first in 1886 and also at the World's Columbian Expos in 1893. He made scientific illustrations for the American Museum of Natural History from 1898–99, for the Princeton Patagonia Report from 1904–14 and for "Land Mammals of the Western Hemisphere" from 1912–13. He was an illustrator for *Century* and *St Nicholas* from 1899 to 1921, for 30 "Nature Books," and for "Birds of the Rockies" and "Birds of California." In 1941 Horsfall was affiliated with the Paleontologic Dept of Princeton U and with the American Nature Assn in Washington.

HOSKINS, Gayle Porter. Born Brazil, Ind 1887, died Wilmington, Del 1962. Magazine and book illustrator specializing in military subjects, portrait painter, muralist, teacher. Work in Del museums, Custer Battlefield Nat Monument. References A62-MAL. Sources CUS-letter from Allen R Neville. No auction record or signature example. (See illustration 145.)

Hoskins studied at the AIC in 1904 with Vanderpoel and was the pupil of Howard Pyle in 1907. He began exhibiting in Wilmington in 1916 and taught at Wilmington AA. An illustrator of books like "Kazan," of magazines, and of advertising, Hoskins painted WWI and WWII subjects as well as historical scenes involving firearms. From 1928 to 1938 Hoskins specialized in Western subjects. His *The Battle of the Little Big Horn* was used for a 1930 calendar. In 1953 he painted *Custer's Last Fight,* employing a clay model of the battlefield taken from a contour map. Troop movements were indicated by Colonel Graham for whose "The Custer Myth" the painting was reproduced in color. It was also issued as a separate print.

HOUGHTON, Arthur Boyd. Born Bombay, India 1836, died Hampstead, London, Eng 1875. English Special Artist-illustrator, genre painter, caricaturist. Work in MFA, MIL, Victoria & Albert Mus, Tate, Art Gall of Melbourne. References BEN-ENB-MAL. Sources ANT 8/57-AOH-HUT-ILP-MIL. Oil 17½ × 13½" *Water Carrier* sold 10/2/73 for $100 at auction. In 1936, *Holborn in 1861* brought £35 14s at auction. The estimated price for a drawing 8×12" of an Indian spree would be about $1,000 to $1,500 at auction in 1976. Signature example p 52 AOH.

Houghton's father was secretary to the governor of Bombay. Despite the loss of an eye, Houghton studied art in London at Leigh's Academy. He was first a leading illustrator of ornate books and magazines, then in 1861 began exhibiting genre scenes at the RA as a part of the genteel Pre-Raphaelite Brotherhood. In 1869 this impulsive bohemian became the *Graphic*'s correspondent for the US, spending the fall in the East and arriving in Omaha by train in January 1870.

Several days at the neighboring Pawnee reservation showed the romantic artist that "the noble and uncorrupted savage" was gone except for the young. The Indian females were drudges. The grandeur of the West remained only in the landscape, although buffalo were still plentiful. Houghton participated in a hunt with Buffalo Bill: "The sport is Titanic—meat for gods and savages. How puny seem the home sports. The Indian is tigerlike in his ferocity when hunting the buffalo, his eyes gleam, his mouth foams, and his hideously painted countenance flows with the heat of his passion." In a jamboree, Houghton engaged in a drinking bout with an Indian chief, and the party danced to a cook pot drummed with a handgun. By February the artist was in Salt Lake City, and he had returned to England by summer. His early death from excessive drinking followed the childbirth death of his young wife.

The *Graphic* gave Houghton a short obituary. His work had been unfavorably received in America because in his Eastern sketches Houghton had been a social satirist, "an artist who did not know his place," exaggerating and emphasizing the unconventional. In 1881, though, Vincent Van Gogh collected Boyd Houghton's drawings of the American West in old *Graphic* issues, and wrote to his brother that Houghton "has something rather mysterious like Goya, with a wonderful soberness." AOH.

HOUGHTON, Merritt Dana. Born Otsego, Mich 1846, died Seattle, Wash 1918. Wyom sketch artist in watercolor and pen-and-ink of landscapes, mines, and ranches; teacher, photographer. Work in ACM, WYG (drawings). No reference. Source WYG. No auction record or signature example. (See illustration 146.)

Houghton settled in Laramie in 1875. He later lived in Saratoga and Encampment, working as a teacher. His drawings and maps are important historical records.

HOUSER, Allan C. Born Apache, Okla 1915, living Santa Fe, NM 1975. Chiricahua Apache painter, sculptor, muralist, teacher. Work in Joslyn AM (Omaha), MNM, Philbrook AC, murals in Indian schools, sculpture in Haskell Inst and Ariz St Capitol. References A53-MAS. Sources AHI 2/50-AIP-COW. No current auction record. Signature example AHI 2/50. (See illustration 147 a & b.)

Houser, whose Apache name is Haozous or Pulling Roots, is the great-nephew of Geronimo, the famous chief imprisoned at Fort Sill along with Houser's parents. When his father became a farmer, Houser could attend school only when not needed at home. He studied with Dorothy Dunn at the Indian Art School in Santa Fe and under Olaf Nordmark for murals in Fort Sill.

Houser became the leading Apache artist and has been called one of the most important artists of his day. He received a Guggenheim Scholarship in 1948. Figures of dancers and genre subjects are dynamically portrayed. He has been artist in residence at Inter-Mountain Indian School and an instructor at the Institute of American Indian Arts.

HOWARD, Robert Boardman. Born NYC 1896, living San Francisco, Cal 1976. Cal sculptor, painter. Work in Acad Science (San Fran), San Fran MA, Oakland MA, U Cal (Santa Cruz); murals in San Fran Stock Exchange, Yosemite, *Whale Fountain* (San Fran). References A76-MAS. Sources AAT-MCA-WHO 70. No auction record. Sculpture example p 201 AAT *Hawk* in redwood and copper.

Howard studied at the California School of Arts 1915–16, the ASL 1916–17, and in Europe 1919–22, the pupil of P W Nahl, Worth Ryder, X Martínez, and Kenneth Hayes Miller. He began as a designer of murals and sculpture in 1922. From 1929 to 1936 he designed murals at Yosemite National Park, for Ahwahnee Hotel and Camp Curry, then Badger Pass. Howard was instructor of sculpture at San Francisco AI 1945–54.

HOWE, Oscar. Born in Joe Creek, Crow Creek Reservation, S Dak 1915, living

Vermillion, S Dak 1976. Yanktonai-Sioux painter, illustrator, muralist, teacher. Outstanding Indian artist, 1966. Work in DAM, MAI, MNM, Montclair AM, Philbrook AC, etc. Reference A76. Sources AIP-LAF. No current auction record. Signature examples pp 157, 168 LAF.

Howe, Sioux name Mazuha Hokshina, Trader Boy, is descended from the Yanktonai head chiefs. He attended Pierre Indian School where he taught after graduating from Santa Fe in 1938. He served with the US Army in the European Theater for 3½ years. Howe's paintings were used in book illustration beginning 1942, won awards beginning 1947, and were exhibited beginning 1949. He earned his BA from Dakota Wesleyan U in 1952 and MFA from U of Oklahoma in 1953. He became artist in residence and professor of art at the U of South Dakota in 1957. Howe is Artist Laureate of South Dakota, a contributor to "North American Indian Costumes," "Indian Art of the United States" by d'Harnoncourt, and La Farge's "A Pictorial History of the American Indian."

HOWLAND, John Dare. Born Zanesville, Ohio 1843, died Denver, Colo 1914. Early Rocky Mountain painter specializing in fauna including buffalo. Work in ACM, Colo Hist Soc, DAM, Denver Country Club, HAR. No reference. Sources ACM-AIW-DAA-DCC-HAR-JNB-SPR. Oil on board 15×22" *Elk on the Plains* signed not dated sold 10/27/71 for $2,000 at auction. Signature example ⚡72 ACM.

Howland, grandson of the founders of Zanesville and son of a riverboat captain, ran away at 14. In St Louis he was befriended by a fur trader who let him join the American Fur Company voyages. He traveled up the Missouri to the fur posts, on buffalo hunts, trading with the Sioux Indians. At 15 he journeyed to the Pikes Peak gold mines. In 1861 he enlisted in the Colorado Volunteers, fighting in New Mexico and rising to Captain of Scouts. He also worked as sketch artist and correspondent for *Harper's Weekly,* earning funds for two years' study in Paris, the pupil of Dumaresq.

From 1867 to 1869 he served as Secretary of the Indian Peace Commission. He continued as correspondent for *Harper's* and *Leslie's,* contributing to the record of the Indian wars. In 1872 he returned to Europe for further study. Howland worked in Utah, then settled in Denver about 1873 where he founded the Denver Art Club in 1886. He also designed the Civil War monument at the Colorado State Capitol. Howland was thus one of the earliest artists resident in the Rockies, although he did not work as an artist until the Civil War.

HOXIE, Vinnie Ream. Born Madison, Wis 1847, died Washington, DC 1914. Sculptor of statues including the Indian Chief Sequoyah in the National Capitol. Work in Rotunda of Capitol, Farragut Square, City Hall (Brooklyn), Cornell U, etc. References A15 (obit)-DAB-FIE (as Vinner Ream Hoxie, corrected in notes)-MAL-SMI. Sources WHO 14-WOM 14. No auction record or signature example.

Vinnie Ream was educated at Christian Col in Missouri. At 15 she was a clerk in Washington, DC when she became the pupil of the sculptor Clark Mills. When she was 16, President Lincoln sat for her in the White House over a period of five months. When she was 19 the Congress awarded her a commission for $10,000 to make a full-length marble statue of Lincoln for the Rotunda. The first woman to sculpt for the US Government, she went to Rome to perform the work. "Abroad, her frontier spirit coupled with her artlessly ingratiating demeanor proved attractive." To obtain a commission for a bust of a cardinal, "she had merely put on her most beautiful white gown." DAB. In 1875, she received a $20,000 contract for the heroic bronze statue of Admiral Farragut.

She was married in 1878, giving up sculpture to become a popular Washington hostess. *Sequoyah,* the statue of the halfbreed who invented the Cherokee alphabet, was modeled for the state of Oklahoma at the end of her life. She had also sculpted the ideal figure of *The Indian Girl* and *The West.*

HUDDLE, William Henry. Born Wytheville, Va 1847, died probably Austin, Tex 1892. Important early Texas portraitist and historical painter. Work in Dallas MFA, State Capitol (Austin). Reference MAS. Sources COW-TEP-TOB-TXF. No current auction record but the estimated price of an oil 20×30″ showing the battle of San Jacinto would be about $12,000 to $15,000 at auction in 1976. Signature example p 197 TEP.

Huddle was educated in Virginia, enlisting in the Confederate cavalry in 1863. After the war he worked for his father in Paris, Tex as a gunsmith. At 18 he went to Lynchburg, Va to study portrait painting with his cousin Flavius Fisher. In 1870 he returned to Texas, again leaving in 1874 for study in NYC at the NAD and in 1875 at the ASL, the pupil of L E Wilmarth. In 1876 Huddle established his studio in Austin, making a sketching trip to Leadville, Colo in 1881.

In 1884 Huddle received a commission from the Texas Legislature to paint portraits of all of the past presidents and governors of Texas. As further preparation he studied in Munich 1884–85, then commenced the long task of completing the portraits. When the new Capitol was dedicated in 1888, 20 were ready. Hud-

dle received $7,000 for the work, achieving financial independence. In 1886 he had begun his historical paintings with the *Surrender of Santa Anna* and *David Crockett* (1889). For a man of strong physical appearance, his life was short, particularly for his self-appointed work of painting the thrilling history of Texas.

HUDSON, Grace Carpenter. Born near Ukiah in Potter Valley, Cal 1865, died there 1937. Important California painter specializing in Indian children, illustrator. Work in ANS, Field Mus, HAR. References A09-BEN. Sources ANT 4/73-DCC-HAR-JNB-POW-WAA. Oil 20×16″ *Indian Boy with Rabbit* signed G Hudson and inscribed Ukiah, Cal sold 5/22/73 for $6,000 at auction in Los Angeles. In 1907 her painting *Indians* had sold for $1,010 at auction in NYC. Signature example p 59 PB 5/22/73. (See illustration 148.)

Grace Carpenter, the daughter of a newspaperman-photographer, was educated in Ukiah elementary school. She studied at the Mark Hopkins Institute in San Francisco and was the pupil of Virgil Williams, at a time when San Francisco was an important art center. She returned to Ukiah, 100 miles north along the "Redwood Highway," to teach painting. She also acted as illustrator for *Sunset, Cosmopolitan,* and *Western Field.*

In 1890 she married John W N Hudson, Pacific Coast ethnologist for the Field Museum and researcher on the language and art of the Pomo Indians. Mrs Hudson was enabled to specialize in painting "les enfants Indiens Peaux-Rouges." BEN. The Hudsons made two extended European tours. In 1901 she painted children in Hawaii. In 1904 she was commissioned by the Field Museum to paint portraits of the Pawnee Indians including chiefs in Oklahoma. She is said to have lived and painted in Ukiah until her death.

HUGHES, Edward John. Born North Vancouver, BC, Can 1913, living Cobble Hill, BC, Can 1976. Modern painter of Can Northwest. Member Can Group of Painters 1948, Royal Can Acad Art. Work in NGC, AG Ont, Vancouver AG, Montreal MFA, Greater Victoria AG. References A76-BEN-MAL. Sources CAR-DCA. No auction record. Signature example ※126 CAR. (See illustration 149.)

Son of a trombone player, Hughes grew up in Nanaimo and Vancouver. He attended evening art classes in 1926 and from 1929 to 1935 studied at the Vancouver SA, the pupil of F H Varley and J W G MacDonald. He then was one of three artists commissioned to do the British Columbia murals at the San Francisco fair. After service as an artist during WWII, he received a scholarship in 1947 and in 1951 was discovered by a Montreal gallery that became his exclusive agent, providing financial security.

It is said that Hughes is not a primitive but that he has some qualities that belong to a child's world, and that his paintings look as if they had been carved out of linoleum. DCA. His technique is to make a 9×12″ field sketch in pencil, then in his studio do an 18×24″ watercolor to prepare for the 25×32″ final oil painting. His second stage used to be an elaborate pencil drawing he could himself sell because it was not covered by his exclusive gallery contract. DCA.

HULINGS, Clark. Living Santa Fe, NM 1975. Portrait, landscape painter, illustrator. Member SI. No reference. Source PER vol 3, ※3. No recent auction record. Painting example p 18, PER vol 3 ※3.

After a childhood in Spain, Hulings studied drawing and anatomy under Sigismund Ivanowsky, and at ASL with Bridgman. He left art to earn a degree in physics from Haverford College. Then ill health made it necessary for Hulings to move to the West, and he settled in Santa Fe.

At first children and animals in landscapes were his favorite subjects. In 1946 he moved to Louisiana where he became a successful portrait painter. By 1951 he was also a free-lance illustrator. After 1957 he returned to Santa Fe and to landscape painting.

HUMPHREY, Elizabeth B (Lizzie B). Born Hopedale, Mass before 1850, living probably NYC after 1867. Illustrator including Western scenes for BEY. References FIE-SMI. Sources BEY-WAA. No current auction record or signature example.

Miss Humphrey studied at the Cooper School of Design and was the pupil of Worthington Whittredge. She worked as an illustrator of widespread subjects, landscapes, still lifes, and figures. Early in her career she contributed four sketches to "Beyond the Mississippi," the 1867 travel book of the West. Her illustrations covered the period 1858 to 1865 and were placed in Nebraska, Texas, Colorado, and Utah. They were probably drawn about 1867 from photographs and other materials available in NYC, although she did later visit California where "she made some excellent sketches and paintings." FIE.

HUMPHRISS (or Humphries), Charles Harry. Born England 1867, living Pleasantville, NY 1940 or died 1934. Eastern sculptor specializing in Indians. Member NSS 1908, SIA. References A31-BEN-FIE-MAL-SMI. Sources BRO-JNB-WHO 40. Bronze 31½″ high *Indian Prayer* signed and dated 1900, incised "Gorham Co. Founders, 67″ sold 9/28/73 for $4,750 at auction.

Humphriss exhibited at the NY Academy of Design, PAFA, and in South America, winning an award at the Panama-Pacific Expos. His studio was in NYC in 1931. Other known bronzes were cast by Roman Bronze Foundry.

HUNT, Wayne. Born Bear Valley, Wis 1904, living Cornville, Ariz 1974. Traditional Western sculptor specializing in horses and cowboys, poet. Member CAA. No reference. Source COW-WAI 71. No auction record or signature example.

Where Hunt lives in Arizona, cattle ranching is still much the same as it was in 1900. Hunt specializes in sculpture of cowboy genre, "to preserve in bronze the cowboy and horses of my era." WAI 71. Known also as a poet, Hunt sculpts the cowboy doing traditional chores.

HUNTER, Russell Vernon. Born Hallsville, Ill 1900, died Roswell, NM 1955. New Mexico painter, museum director, teacher, writer. Work in MNM, Dallas MFA, Virginia MFA; murals in churches, public buildings. References A53-MAS. Source TSF. Oil *Still Life of Flowers* sold 10/17/69 for $135 at auction. No signature example.

Hunter studied at James Millikan U, Denver AA, AIC, and with S MacDonald-Wright. He began as an art instructor in Los Cerrillos schools near Santa Fe. During the 1920s he taught at State Teacher's College, NM and the Otis AI in Los Angeles, 1923–27. He then taught at the Roerich Museum in NYC until the Depression in 1931.

From 1935 to 1942 Hunter was WPA art director for New Mexico. From 1943 to 1948 he was regional director of the USO. From 1948 to 1952 he was administrative director of Dallas MFA, moving to Roswell Museum as director in 1952. In this time he continued to paint scenes of eastern New Mexico with its "unending flat horizon, windmills, thirsty cattle, and general stores," treated in an anecdotal simplified style. TSF. There was a retrospective exhibition at MNM in 1955.

HUNTER, Warren. Traditional Western painter active Bandera, Tex 1948, living San Antonio, Tex 1972. Work in USPO Alice, Tex. References A41-MAS. Source COW. No auction record or signature example.

Hunter's residence is also given as Helotes, Tex. He worked for the Fine Arts Section of the FWA during the Depression.

HURD, L P. Canadian watercolorist active near Fort William on the Ottawa River 1863–73. Work in ROM. No reference. Sources CAE-p 60 KEN 6/70 with signature example. No auction record. (See illustration 150.)

HURD, Peter. Born Roswell, NM 1904, living San Patricio, NM 1976. Modern Western painter, muralist, illustrator, writer. ANA 1941, NA 1942. Work in MMA, MNM, BM, DAM, Colo Springs FA Center, colln in Roswell Mus. References A76-BEN-MAL. Sources AAT-ACO-ALA-CAP-CON-COW-DAA-HAR-HMA-MAP-MCA-M57-NEU-OSR-WAI 71,72-WHO 70. Dry brush on paper 22×27¾" *La Neblina* with signature example, estimated for sale 3/10/75 at $1,400 to $1,600 at auction in LA but did not sell. Signature example p 113 CAP. (See illustration 151.)

Hurd was raised in New Mexico and was educated at NM Military Institute 1917–20. Appointed to the US Military Academy, he resigned in 1923. He attended Haverford College 1923–24 but left to be a private nonpaying pupil of N C Wyeth. He lived in Wyeth's barn at Chadds Ford, Pa for three years, also studying at the PAFA. Hurd worked as an illustrator, particularly for books. In 1929 he married Wyeth's daughter Henriette, a professional painter and sister of Andrew Wyeth.

By 1931 Hurd was living on a ranch in New Mexico. In 1935 he began painting in tempera. "An impeccable craftsmanship modeled the flanks of New Mexico hills and drew the cowboys raising dust in rodeos under a glittering June sky." CON. National recognition followed a *Life* article. During WWII he was a war correspondent for *Life*. By 1958 he was appointed to the President's Commission of Fine Arts. His official portrait of Pres Johnson for the White House colln was rejected by the President and is now in the National Portrait Gallery. In the 1960s Hurd turned to watercolors.

HURLEY, Wilson. Born Tulsa, Okla 1924, living Albuquerque, NM 1973. New Mexico painter, lawyer. Member Nat Acad of Western Art. No reference. Sources ACO-PER vol 3 ⋕3. No current auction record. Painting example PER vol 3 ⋕3 1972–73.

Hurley was raised on a northern Virginia farm. When he moved to New Mexico with his family in 1936, he was encouraged to paint by local artists.

Hurley was educated at West Point, graduating in 1945. He earned a law degree in 1951, practicing law in New Mexico for 14 years.

In 1965 Hurley began painting full-time, exhibiting throughout the Southwest. His oil 30×40″ *Cliff of the Moqui Stairs* was in the 1973 exhibition at Tucson Art Center.

HUTCHISON, D C. Born Arboath, Scotland 1869, died 1954. Illustrator of Western, historical, and adventure books. References A23-BEN. Source 50G. No recent auction record. Signature example p 168 50G.

He studied in Paris under Laurens. Hutchison came to NY to work as an illustrator. Some of the books he illustrated are "The Lonesome Trail," "Flying U Ranch," "With Kit Carson in the Rockies," etc.

HUTTON, William Rich. Born Washington, DC 1826, died Montgomery Cnty, Md 1901. Topographical watercolorist and sketch artist of Los Angeles area. Work in Huntington Lib (San Marino, Cal). Reference G&W. Source AIW. No auction record or signature example.

Hutton was in southern California during the Mexican War, as a member of the military. He sketched views of Los Angeles from 1847 to 1852. Such views are rare, in comparison with San Francisco scenes that accompanied the Gold Rush. Hutton also drew views of Monterey.

IMHOF, Joseph A. Born Brooklyn, NY 1871, died Taos, NM 1955. Early New Mexico "anthropologist-painter," lithographer. Work in ACM, ANS, MNM, HAR, Mus of Anthropology (UNM-60 paintings), Adams colln. No reference. Sources PAW-PIT-TAL-TSF-TWR. No current auction record but an oil 16×20″ *Indian Pueblo* was estimated 3/5/74 at $400 to $500 at auction and sold for $600. Signature example p 43 TWR. (See illustration 152.)

Imhof was a self-taught lithographer for Currier & Ives in NYC. To become an artist he went to Europe in 1891 where he was apprenticed for four years to artists in Antwerp, Brussels, Munich, and Paris. He met and sketched Buffalo Bill and his Indians in Antwerp. On his return to the US he studied the Iroquois in NY and Canada. He lived in Albuquerque from 1907 to 1912, recording data on the Pueblo Indians. He then left for further study in Europe but got no farther than NYC where he remained to work on inventions in photography.

In 1929 he settled in Taos, building his studio on the edge of the reservation facing the sacred Mountain behind the pueblo. He began collecting Indian artifacts, observing and recording ethnological data as a painter rather than with words. His large simple oils concentrate on fact at the expense of artistry in documenting his view of the importance of corn in the life of the pueblo people. Imhof had the first lithographic press in Taos, producing successful prints of anthropological value. He also taught the lithographic process. As an index of his personal reserve, Mrs. Luhan in TAL refers to her neighbor of twenty years as "the Grand Old Man of the Pueblos," and concludes, "no (biographical) information available."

INMAN, Henry. Born Utica, NY 1801, died NYC 1846. Eastern portrait and genre painter, illustrator, lithographer. A founding member NAD 1826. Work in MMA, COR, BMFA, NGA, State House (Pa), etc. References BEN-CHA-DAB-ENB-FIE-G&W-MAL-SMI. Sources AAR 3/74-ALA-ANT 5/49,3/53,11/58 (article), 12/66,4/67,1/69,3/73,4/74, 2/75-AWM-BAR-BOA-BOL-COR-HUT-ISH-KAR-KW1-M15-MSL-NA 74-NGA-NJA-PAF-STI. No current auction record but the estimated price of an Indian painting would be $5,000 to $7,000 at auction in 1976. Signature example, cover ANT 3/73.

Son of a merchant and brother of a commodore and an editor, Inman as a boy had drawing lessons from an itinerant painter. The family moved to NYC in 1812. At 13 Inman relinquished an appointment to West Point in favor of a seven-year apprenticeship to the portrait painter John Wesley Jarvis. Soon Inman was allowed to paint the sitter's costume and background, enabling Jarvis to schedule six portraits a week. In 1823 Inman established his own studio on Vesey Street, earning up to $9,000 a year. "Handsome" with a "genial personality," Inman moved to Philadelphia in 1831 despite his NYC success. The inducement was joining Cephas Childs as a lithographer plus the diversion from Sully to Inman of the commission for a painting of William Penn. ANT 4/74.

As lithographer Inman made copies of many of the Charles Bird King portraits in the Indian Gallery of McKenney and Hall, "a monument of American culture." AWM. In addition, Inman's range of subjects for easel paintings included Indians. Sully at an NA exhibition praised Inman to Dunlap for his landscape, figures, miniatures, and "then some Indians caught my eye." KAR. Inman returned to NYC in 1834 but his work declined in popularity as "weak and monotonous." He was working on a historical painting of Daniel Boone in Kentucky, on a Congressional commission, when he died of heart disease.

INNES (or Innis), John. Born London, Ont, Can 1863, died Vancouver, BC, Can 1941. Painter of Western Canada, railway survey artist, illustrator, cartoonist, etcher. Work in Hudson's Bay Company (England), David Spencer Ltd (Vancouver), U of BC, Eastman colln (Rochester, NY), Washington (*Harding in Canada* in DC). No reference. Sources CAE-CAN-DCA-WNW. No current auction record or signature example.

Son of a minister, Innes was educated at colleges in Ontario and England. He studied art in London, NYC, and Toronto before working with the survey parties of the Canadian Pacific. In 1885, while riding as a cowboy on his own High River, Alberta ranch, he began drawing cartoons for the Calgary *Herald*. He also operated the first Calgary telephone exchange before moving to Banff as owner of a newspaper. By the late 1890s he was back in Ontario as cartoonist and writer as well as illustrator for *Canadian Magazine*.

About 1905 Innes went to Vancouver by pack train, painting en route. His *Epic of the West* of 30 paintings was exhibited at Vancouver, Montreal, Leipzig, and London. "A singular and engaging personality not of the first-flight of Canadian painters," he was a "truthful, observant and, within limitations, exact recorder" of pioneer Western Canada. CAN. Between 1907 and 1913 he was in NYC as a Hearst artist. "In the cow camps," Innes said, "in the lodges of the long-dead chiefs, in construction camps, on the mountain tops, or out upon the Prairies criss-crossed with buffalo trails, I have learned the lore of Western Canada." DCA.

INNESS, George, Jr. Born Paris, France 1853 (or 1854), died Cragsmoor, NY 1926. Eastern animal and landscape painter, illustrator. ANA 1893, NA 1899. Work in MMA, Montclair AM, BMFA. References A26 (obit)-BEN-CHA-FIE-MAL-SMI. Sources ANT 10/74 - HUT - ISH - MSL - NJA - POW - WHO 26. Oil 12×16" *Tivoli* sold 2/19/71 for $3,780 at auction in London. Signature example p 563 ANT 10/74 *Coming Storm* signed "Inness Jr."

Inness, the son of one of the greatest American landscape painters, was the pupil of his father in Rome 1870–74. He studied in Paris in 1875, including a few months with Bonnat. In 1878 his father and he occupied a studio together in NYC when the *Evening Post* review noted he "is sure to make his mark as an animal painter because he understands the spirit of his brutes." His painting signature was "Inness, Jr." WHO 26.

Between 1881 and 1885 he illustrated articles for *Scribner's* and *Century* on big game hunting in the American West. He settled in Montclair, NJ in 1880. Between 1895 and 1899 he maintained a studio in Paris. Later he summered in Cragsmoor, NY and wintered in Tarpon Springs, Fla. In 1917 he had written an appreciation of the art and life of his father.

INNESS, George, Sr. Born near Newburgh, NY 1825, died Bridge of Allan, Scotland 1894. Important Eastern landscape painter in Cal 1890. NA 1853. Work in most major museums (20 paintings in AIC). References BEN-CHA-DAB - ENB - FIE - G&W - MAL - SMI. Sources ALA-AMA-BOA-HUT-KAR-KW1 and AAR 3,5,9,11/74-ANT 8/45, 5/46, 3/57, 11/59, 1/60; 4,12/61; 2,10, 11/62; 1/64; 5,11,12/65; 2/66, 1/67, 11/70; 1,2,3,11/72; 5,9,11/73; 4,5,6,11, 12/74; 1/75. Oil 48×72" *Niagara Falls* signed G Inness and dated 1884 was estimated for sale 10/16/74 at $70,000 to $85,000 at auction, but did not sell. Signature example p 201 KW1. (See illustration 153.)

The fifth of 13 children of a well-to-do grocer, Inness was raised in a country home near Newark, NJ. Unwilling to accept schooling or a job, Inness at 13 obtained art instruction from a drawing master. At 16 he worked at engraving briefly in NYC, then returned to Newark to study on his own, sketching from nature and copying prints. He was for one month the pupil of Gignoux in 1843 but could not accept instruction and was subject to epilepsy which interfered with sustained endeavor. About 1845 Inness took a NYC studio as a professional painter, tight and grandiloquent in style but somber in color. ENB. A patron sponsored the year 1847 in Italy. Inness returned to Europe regularly until 1854. His brushwork became looser and finally his style reached a very personal lyricism. Although indifferent to money, by the 1870s his income was "larger than that of any landscape painter living." DAB. Sometimes unequal in his paintings, he was also sometimes unequaled. BOA. Inness was a mystic who looked like a fanatic, "supertemperamental even for an artist." DAB. His first wife died six months after they were married. His second marriage at the age of 25 was long and happy and they had 5 children.

ANS's Inness, *Afterglow on the Prairie,* is thought to be an early work. Inness is not mentioned as having been West until late in his life when he used Keith's San Francisco studio, an important influence on Keith. (See George Inness, Jr entry.)

IRELAND, Leroy. Born Philadelphia, Pa 1889, died probably NYC 1970. NYC still-life painter in the Southwest. Work in Dallas AA, Mus San Antonio. References A41-BEN-FIE-MAL. Source ANT 5/70 illustrating *Still Life with Kachina Doll* and pueblo pottery, beads. No current auction record but the estimated price of a Western still life would be about $800 to $1,000 at auction in 1976. Signature example p 671 ANT 5/70.

Ireland studied at the PAFA, the pupil of W M Chase and Daniel Garber. He also studied with Emil Carlsen in NYC. His *God of the Snake Dance* is in the Dallas Art Assn.

IRWIN, Col De la Cherois Thomas. Born Carnagh House, Cnty Armagh, Ireland 1843 (or 1842), died probably Ottawa, Ont, Can 1928. Professional British and Can artillery officer; watercolorist of the Can West. Work in ROM *The Banff River* signed D Irwin. No reference. Source CMW. No auction record or signature example. (See illustration 154.)

Irwin was educated privately, then graduated from Staff College at Sandhurst in England where he probably received training in topographical drawing. He also studied watercolor painting with Callow and Needham in England. He came to Canada as a lieutenant with his battery in 1861, attended Ottawa Art School, and as Inspector of Artillery was in the West in 1878 supervising construction of gun batteries on Vancouver Island. He retired as lieutenant-colonel in 1882 to join the Canadian service, from which he retired in 1897. Irwin continued in public service activities in Ottawa through 1912.

ISAACS, Andrew. Born probably England about 1810, died probably NYC after 1859. Philadelphia landscape painter probably up the Missouri with Wimar in 1859. Reference G&W. Sources PAF-TAW-WIM. No auction record or signature example.

Isaacs was active in Philadelphia 1836–49 and in NYC 1850. PAF shows that paintings exhibited by Isaacs were mainly copies.

For May 28, 1859, the log of the steamer *Spread Eagle* listed as passengers "Messrs Wimar and Isaacs, artists." The trip was from St Louis to the headwaters of the Missouri with Indian supplies, the American Fur Company's outfit, and government surveyors. At Fort Union the artists transferred to the *Chippewa* for passage to Fort Benton. They returned to St Louis in September. Judging from Wimar's similar trip the previous year, Isaacs would have seen Yanktonai Indians, Sioux at Fort Pierre, the village of the Mandans, Assiniboines at Fort Union, herds of buffalo crossing the river, and the vast Western prairies. There is, however, no record of an Isaacs painting of the West or even of his sketchbook.

JACKSON, Alexander Young. Born in Montreal, Quebec, Can 1882, died probably Kleinberg, Ont, Can 1976. Important modern Canadian landscape painter, illustrator, teacher, writer; a founder of the "Group of Seven." Member ARCA 1914, RCA 1919 (resigned 1933, reelected 1953). Work in Tate (London), Dunedin (New Zealand), NGC, AG Toronto, AA Montreal, etc. References A73-BEN-MAL. Sources CAN-CAR-CAH-DCA. Oil *A Rocky Pool with Jack Pines* sold 3/26/70 for $8,000 at auction in Montreal. Signature p 85 CAR. (See illustration 155.)

A Y Jackson began to work for a Quebec lithographer while the pupil of Edmond Dyonnet in the evening classes at Montreal's Council of Art and Manufactures. He went to Europe on a cattle boat in 1905. In 1906–7 he worked in advertising design in Chicago, attending the AIC nights under Clute and Richardson. In 1907–9 he was again in Europe, at the Julien Academy under Laurens. In 1910 he returned to Montreal, working at photoengraving and painting at Sweetsburg. He made his third tour of Europe 1911–13.

When Jackson established his studio in Toronto through J E H MacDonald in 1913, all of the members of the Group of Seven were in place. Jackson shared his studio with Tom Thompson. In 1914 they painted together in the North Country, using bold Fauve colors and flat Post-Impressionist patterns. Jackson served in the Canadian Army beginning 1915, then painted for the Canadian War Memorials. Returning to Toronto, he painted in Algoma 1919. The Group of Seven had its first exhibition in 1920. The Canadian reviews were negative, on the theme of "Art Gone Mad," but in 1924 the Tate Gallery in England bought Jackson's *Halifax Harbor*. This was a triumph for the Group. Jackson painted the lower St Lawrence 1921, Jasper Park 1924, British Columbia 1925, the Arctic 1927 and 1930, Alberta 1937, Western

Canada 1943, Yellowknife 1949, etc. He illustrated books on Quebec and on the West Coast Indians along with the American painter W Langdon Kihn.

JACKSON, Everett Gee. Born Mexia, Tex 1900, living San Diego, Cal 1976. Modern Texas and Cal landscape, figure, and portrait painter, illustrator of books including Indian subjects, teacher. Work in Houston MA, FAG San Diego, LA Cnty MA, PAFA. References A76-MAL. Sources AAT-TOB-TXF-WHO 70. No current auction record. Initials example p 284 AAT.

Educated at Texas A&M College 1919–21, Jackson studied at the AIC 1921–23. He was in Mexico 1924–28, influenced by Rivera and Orozco. A painter and illustrator since 1926, he exhibited Mexican, Texan, and New Mexican scenes in Dallas and San Diego in 1926 and 1927. *Mexican Tropics* was reproduced in *International Studio* in 1927. He began teaching in Texas in 1929 and taught at San Diego State College 1930–63. Books he illustrated include a limited edition of "Ramona" by Helen Hunt Jackson in 1960. Jackson's special interest is Mayan sculpture. He was professor of art at the U of Costa Rica in 1962.

JACKSON, Harry Andrew. Born Chicago, Ill 1924, living Lost Cabin, Wyom and Camaiore, Italy 1976. Traditional Western painter and sculptor, muralist, "a master sculptor in the Remington tradition," writer. Member CAA, NSS, Nat Acad of Western Art. Work in ACM, Buffalo Bill Mus, Glenbow Fndn (Calgary), Mont Hist Soc, Whitney Gall Western Art, Wyom St Gall, Woolaroc Mus, Fort Pitt Mus. Reference A76. Sources ACO-AHI-C71 to 74-CAP-

COW-Cheyenne *Sun DAY Magazine*-EIT-JAC-OSR-PER vol 3 ✕3-WAI 71, 72-12/4/73 data from Harry Jackson. Bronze 16½″ *The Bronc Stomper* signed and dated 1959 sold 4/20/72 for $2,200 at auction. Signature example and photo JAC.

Jackson's mother ran a lunchroom near the Chicago Stockyards. Even as a child his only interests were horses and drawing. At 14 he ran away to Wyoming where he worked as a ranch hand and was encouraged by the painter Ed Grigware. In 1942 Jackson joined the Marines and was wounded in Pacific service. He later became a combat artist and entertainer. After the war he studied in NYC with Tamayo and Hans Hoffman. His one-man show in 1952 was of abstract expressionist paintings. By 1956 he was exhibiting as a realist. In Italy in 1957 on fellowships, he began on Western themes leading into *Range Burial* and *Stampede* bronzes that were in effect studies for murals. In 1950 he made an album of traditional music "Harry Jackson, the Cowboy, His Songs, Ballads, and Brag Talk."

Jackson's NYC show of Western bronzes and drawings was a 1960 success. He built a studio and established a foundry in Italy. Best-known for his bronzes, he has received substantial attention from national magazines such as *Life* and *Time*. In 1972 he wrote "Lost Wax Bronze Casting."

JACKSON, William Henry. Born Keesville, NY 1843, died NYC 1942. Survey artist, illustrator, important pioneer photographer, author. Work in GIL. References A47 (obit)-MAL. Sources AIW-ALA-AWM-GIL-PNW-POW-WHJ-WHO 42-WYG. No current auction record but the estimated price for an oil 20✕30″ showing covered wagons would be about $3,500 to $4,500 at auction in 1976. Signature examples and photo WHJ. (See illustration 156.)

Jackson graduated from public school in Troy, NY in 1858 where he began as a photographer before moving to Vermont in 1860. After service in the Civil War he traveled overland by wagon train to California in 1866, then back to Omaha, Neb where he set up a photographic studio in 1867. From 1870 to 1878 Jackson was the official photographer for the Hayden Survey of Territories, making the first photographs of Yellowstone Park in 1871 when the survey artists were Thomas Moran and William H Holmes. One photograph is of Moran painting. He also kept a sketchbook and executed some paintings such as 1873 self-portrait in the mountains. From 1879 to 1894 he was in business as photographer and publisher in Denver, following which he was on assignment for *Harper's* photographing around the world. He was with the Detroit Publishing Co from 1898 to 1924, and then retired at the age of 81.

He moved to Washington, DC and continued painting and writing about the "covered wagon days." When he was 93 he painted a series of Western scenes for the Department of the Interior. Jackson continued writing and painting through 1940.

JACOB, Ned. Born Elizabethton, Tenn 1938, living Denver, Colo 1976. Traditional Western painter, sculptor. Member CAA 1967, Nat Acad Western Art. Work in Nat Cowboy Hall of Fame, HAR. No reference. Sources AAR 11/74-AHI 11/71-C71 to 74-HAR-OSR-PER vol 3 ✕3-WAI 72. No auction record. Signature example p 29 OSR. (See illustration 157.)

When Jacob graduated from high school in New Jersey, he hitchhiked to Montana. He worked as a ranch hand, lived on the Blackfoot Indian reservation, and collected Indian artifacts. He is self-taught as an artist: "The extent of my art training has been thousands of hours spent at the drawing board and easel, punctuated by advice from artists." C71. He moved to Taos into Ufer's old studio, then in 1965 moved to Denver.

JACOBSON, Oscar Brousse. Born Västervik, Sweden 1882, living Norman, Okla 1962. Western landscape, Indian genre, and portrait painter, etcher, teacher, sponsor of the "Five Kiowas," writer on Indian subjects. Member Okla Hall of Fame. Work in McPherson AG (Kan), Bethany Col AG, St Cap (Okla), Okla Hall of Fame, U Okla, Broadmoor AA. References A62-BEN-FIE-MAL-SMI. Sources AAT-AIP (under Five Kiowas)-WHO 58. No current auction record. Signature example p 96 AAT *Trail Ridge in June.*

O B Jacobson was brought to the US when he was eight. He graduated from Bethany College in 1908, studied at the Louvre in Paris in 1914, and received a degree from Yale in 1916. He had been the pupil of Birger Sandzen, Weir, Albert Thompson, and Neimeyer. In 1908 he taught in Minneapolis, 1911–15 Washington State, 1915–45 U of Oklahoma. A lecturer nationally and for the Park Service, a technical advisor for the Public Works Administration and a museum director, Jacobson sketched in the Sahara 1925–26 and exhibited widely. He painted 500 landscapes in Oklahoma, Colorado, New Mexico, Wyoming, Utah, Nevada, Arizona, and California. "Nahquoey" was his Kiowa name. He wrote "Kiowa Art," "Les Peintres Indiens d'Amérique," and "Costumes Indiens de l'Amérique du Nord." Listed painting titles are *Prayer for Rain, Voices of the Past, Rio Grande, Grand Canyon.*

Jacobson was the sponsor of the "Five Kiowas," the Indian painters he guided into international prominence in 1928. With the help of Edith Mahier, he provided a studio for Asah, Hokeah, Mopope, Tsatoke, and Lois Smoky, supported them, publicized them, and hired them as muralists during the Depression.

JAMES, Rebecca Salsbury (Mrs William H James, formerly Mrs Paul Strand). Born London, Eng 1891, died Taos, NM 1968. Florals reverse-painted on glass, Indian subjects. Work in MNM, DAM. No reference. Sources TAL-TSF-7/68 obit Taos, NM. No current auction record but the estimated price of an oil on glass 24×18″ showing a Taos garden would be $600 to $700 at auction in 1976. Portrait photo obit above.

Rebecca Salsbury was the daughter of the manager of Buffalo Bill's Wild West Shows. She was married to Paul Strand, the modernist photographer, when they came to Taos in 1926. She began to paint, self-taught. Her friend Marsden Hartley had experimented with reverse painting on glass in 1916 and 1917. By 1930 she had developed a similar technique adding luminosity to her floral subjects and to her romantic Indian paintings. In 1932 she and Paul Strand exhibited paintings on glass and photographs of New Mexico at An American Place gallery in NYC.

In 1933 she became a permanent resident of Taos as Mrs James. The comparison is made between the flower paintings of Mrs James and the earlier paintings by her prestigious friend Georgia O'Keeffe. Mrs James had one-man shows and participated in the annuals of Painters of the Southwest. She also exhibited colcha embroideries and wrote a book on Taos personalities. Her newspaper obituary provides some discrepancy in dates: Came to Taos with Georgia O'Keeffe in 1928, married James in 1937, and resided permanently in Taos from 1964.

JAMES, Will (William Roderick James, William James Dufault, Joseph Ernest-Nepthali Dufault). Born St Nazaire de Acton, Quebec, Can 1892, died Los Angeles, Cal 1942. Traditional Western illustrator, sketch artist, painter, writer. Work in ACM, GIL. References A47 (obit)-MAL. Sources ANT 11/71-COW-GIL-ILA-ILP-TWR-WAI 71,72-WHO 42-WNW. Oil 28×22¼" *Smoky*, the frontispiece of James's book, was offered at auction 4/11/73 but did not sell. Signature example p 129 GIL.

Ernest Dufault, a French Canadian, came to Montana under the assumed name of Will James about 1911. He hid his true identity while he worked as a cowboy and rodeo rider. In WWI he was a Mounted Scout in the US Army in Cal. About 1922 Harold von Schmidt and Maynard Dixon staked "Bill" James while he prepared a portfolio for *Sunset*. The next year they paid his way to NYC so he could work for *Scribner's*. Cowboy books written and illustrated by James were issued every year. "Smoky" written in 1926 and filmed in 1934 was credited with helping influence public enthusiasm for Western art. About 1928 James acquired a 12,000-acre cattle ranch near Billings, Mont where he wrote, drew, and painted: "I just write till I'm tired an' then spell off 'nd draw till I get tired of that." COW.

In "Lone Cowboy" published in 1930 and made into a movie in 1933, James created his own life story that was accepted by WHO 42 and A47: Born in Montana, orphaned at four, brought up by a French-Canadian trapper called "Bopy" who taught James to read and write while working in the forest, until Bopy disappeared in a spring flood, after which James at 13 became a cowboy.

Near the end of his real life, James was an alcoholic. His death certificate was for "William Roderick James, a cowboy, author, and artist, father's name William James from Texas." COW. Even at the end, his life was a mystery.

JANSSON, Arthur August. Born White Mills, Pa 1890, living Pearl River, NY 1941. Eastern painter, designer, decorator for AMNH. Work in AMNH. References A41-MAL. Source LAF, with signature example p 194 *Impression of Northwest Coast Indian Life*. No current auction record.

Jansson was the pupil of W R Leigh, William Chase, and George Bridgman. He did the cover design for *Natural History Magazine* and the landscapes for the Eastman Pomery Akeley British East Africa Expedition 1926–27. LAF is critical of a detail of the Northwest Indian painting listed, where Jansson added "kilts" to normally nude males.

JARVIS, Miss M. Active about 1865 in NYC as an illustrator contributing three Western drawings to "Beyond the Mississippi," an 1867 book of travel from the Mississippi River to the Pacific Coast. No reference. Source BEY. No auction record or signature example.

Three of her illustrations are included in BEY, *End of the Bogus Laws* in 1859 in Kansas, *A Mexican Grist-Mill* in 1859 in New Mexico, and *A Prolific Country* in 1865 in Montana. It would appear that the drawings were made from photographs or other materials in NYC at the time.

JARVIS, W Frederick. Born Monroe Cnty, Ohio before 1900, living Dallas, Tex 1935. Texas landscape painter, craftsman, teacher. Member Soc Indep Artists. Work in private collns. References A33-MAL. Sources TOB-TXF. No current auction record or signature example.

Jarvis studied at the ASL and in Munich with Franz Mueller. He was the pupil of Silas Martin, Charles Bullette, and Madam Schille. Jarvis moved to Dallas about 1922, opening his studio in Bush Temple and teaching at the Merrick FAS. He also displayed art pottery.

After sketching trips to New Mexico and the Grand Canyon before 1928, his paintings recorded "impressions of the scenes in their vivid coloring." TXF.

JEFFERYS, Charles William. Born Rochester, Kent, Eng 1869, died probably York Mills, Ont, Can 1951. Important Canadian painter of history and landscape, illustrator, teacher, writer. Work in Royal Ont Mus, NGC, Imperial Oil colln, etc. References A53 (obit)-MAL. Sources CAH-CAN-DCA-NJA-WHO 50. No current auction record. Signature example p 62 CAN.

Educated in Toronto, Jefferys was a student of G A Reid in 1887 and became a member of the Toronto ASL in 1888. He worked as an apprentice with the Toronto Lithographing Co and was sent throughout Ontario to sketch city and industrial views for advertising reproduction. He then went to *The New York Herald* in 1892 as a rapid sketch artist, assigned to cover news events such as the Chicago railway strike of 1893. He kept in touch with Canadian art, continuing to contribute to the Toronto ASL calendar. His 1898 drawings were the Indians in combat with early French settlers, starting Jefferys on his role as one of Canada's few historical painters. When his wife died in 1900, he returned to Toronto.

Jefferys was classified with the Eastern Canadian artists who painted the Western landscape. His best-known subject was the prairies he first saw on a commission in 1901 and to which he went back for many years including 1907 and 1910. Jefferys illustrated the classic book "The Chronicles of Canada." He painted magazine illustrations as well, and from 1912 to 1939 was art instructor at the U of Toronto. From 1929 to 1933 he painted historic murals for hotels and the Royal Ont Mus. In 1942 he published the first of three volumes of "The Picture Gallery of Canadian History" with 2,000 drawings. A postage stamp based on a historical painting was issued in 1949. The Imperial Oil colln is comprised of 1,200 Jefferys drawings and paintings.

JEPPERSON, Samuel Hans. Born Copenhagen, Denmark 1854 (or 1855), died Provo, Utah 1931. Utah historical, landscape, and portrait painter, musician. No reference. Sources PUA-YUP. No auction record or signature example.

Jepperson's parents were Mormon converts. They emigrated from Denmark, taking three days by steamer to England, 36 days to Philadelphia, train to Iowa City, and three months by handcart for the 1,300 miles to Salt Lake City in 1857. They settled in Provo. Jepperson as a boy taught himself to play the violin. He began to consider music as his vocation. At 17 he was hired as a house painter, with art lessons from his employer and another worker.

After he had married, he continued painting, making sketching trips with the professional artists. He also became the friend and companion of George Henry Taggart. Later, lead poisoning from work as a house painter forced him to outdoors work as a farmer to provide food for his family. Nevertheless, he completed over 1,000 paintings, specializing in the history of Utah as his subject. He was essentially self-taught as a painter, a disciple of John Hafen with whom he had sketched.

JEWETT, William Smith (distinguish the William Jewett who was the "portrait factory" partner of Waldo in NYC, and William Jewett's son William Samuel Lyon Jewett). Born South Dover, NY 1812, died Springfield, Mass 1873. Portrait and landscape painter who became the first important Cal portrait painter. ANA 1845. Work in De Young Mus (San Fran), Sutter's Fort and St Capitol (Sacramento), Bowers Mem Mus (Santa Ana), Kahn colln. References FIE-G&W-MAL-SMI. Sources ANT 11/42 (article), 6/69-BAR-KAH-NA 74-SSF. No current auction record but the estimated price of a Western landscape would be about $1,500 to $2,000 at auction in 1976. No signature example.

W S Jewett studied at the NA as "a well-to-do young gentleman," becoming active as a successful NYC portrait painter after 1833. This he abandoned to join the "Hope Company" for the Gold Rush in 1849. Fortune was elusive. "It is difficult to say," he wrote, "which predominates here, mud or gold." When he did not find gold by 1850, he established painting studios in San Francisco and in Sacramento. With his technique hardened to suit the Western tastes, his portraits and Yosemite landscapes plus his real estate investments made him rich enough to buy a castle in the Pyrénées.

William S Jewett also signed portraits as W J Jewett. ANT 6/69 reproduced an oil *View of Sutter's Farm from Feather River* dated 1851. Jewett visited NYC to marry in 1869, returned to California in 1870, and went to Europe shortly before his death. His son William Dunbar Jewett was known in France as a sculptor.

JOHN, Grace Spaulding (early signature Grace Spaulding). Born Battle Creek, Mich 1890, died probably Houston, Tex 1972. Texas landscape, architectural, and portrait painter, writer and illustrator, muralist. Work in Houston Pub Lib, Hist Bldg (Austin), MFA of Hous-

ton, Princeton U; murals in Tex and Va bldgs. References A73 (obit)-MAL. Sources TOB-TXF-WAA. No current auction record or signature example.

Mrs John was educated in Beaumont, Tex. She studied at the St Louis SFA for two years, then at AIC, the ASL, the NAD, and the Parsons School, the pupil of Charles Hawthorne, Daniel Garber, and Emil Bisttram. She also studied at the Tiffany Foundation, in Europe in 1927, and in Mexico. Her 1924 exhibition in Houston included landscapes of *Buffalo Bayou* and cityscapes. One Houston mural was *The Peace Pipe*.

JOHNSON, Frank Tenney. Born near Big Grove, Pottawattamie Cnty, Iowa 1874, died Los Angeles, Cal 1939. Important traditional illustrator of Western life, particularly in moonlight; painter. ANA 1929, NA 1937. Work in NGA, Dallas AA, ANS, Fort Worth MA, Phoenix Munic AG, Denmark, and New Zealand. References A41 (obit)-BEN-FIE-MAL-SMI. Sources AAR 1/74-AHI 11/62-ANT 2/74-ARI-COW-CRS-DCC-EIT-HAR-JNB-NAD-POW-WAI 71,72-WHO 38. Oil 36¼ × 46¼" *Camp of the Blackfeet* signed F Tenney Johnson NA and dated 1938 was estimated to sell for $40,000 to $50,000 on 3/4/74 at auction and sold for $50,000. Signature example p 33 ARI. (See illustration 158.)

Johnson, born on a ranch near Council Bluffs on the Missouri River, was educated in Oconomowoc, Wis. At 14 he ran away to apprentice himself to the panoramic painter F W Heinie in Milwaukee. At 15 he studied with the former Texas ranger Richard Lorenz. He then painted portraits and worked on the staff of the Milwaukee newspaper. In 1902 he went to NYC to study at the ASL with Henri, Chase, Kenneth Hayes Miller, and Mora. He became a newspaper and fashion artist.

In 1904 Johnson spent the summer on

a ranch in Hayden, Colo, observing cowboy life. As a successful illustrator, he worked on the Zane Grey books of the West. In 1920 Johnson followed his friend Clyde Forsythe to Alhambra, Cal where they shared a studio that became a meeting place for leading Western artists, Russell and Borein, as well as Norman Rockwell and Dean Cornwell. Johnson's "moonlight" technique of painting Western scenes under the stars was nationally famous when he died at the height of his career due to spinal meningitis possibly contracted from a kiss.

JOHNSON, Garrison. Artist and anthropologist active in Palm Springs, Cal about 1950. No reference. Source, pair of watercolor and crayon drawings of Apache devil dancers. No auction record or signature example. (See illustration 159.)

JOHNSON, Harvey W. Born NYC about 1920, living Santa Fe, NM 1976. Traditional Western painter, illustrator, teacher. Member CAA 1966. Reference A76. Sources AHI 11/71-C71 to 74-COW. No auction record. Signature example C71.

H W Johnson was raised in California, his father a sculptor and his mother a landscape painter. He was the pupil of his aunt who was the sister-in-law of Augustus Saint-Gaudens the sculptor. After WWII he studied at the ASL in NYC for three-and-a-half years, then worked in NYC at art studios and at Western artwork for pulp magazines. He has been an instructor at the Famous Artists School in Westport, Conn since 1954, traveling extensively in the West to make his paintings as authentic as possible in every detail. He works from his sketches, reference books, his collection

of Western artifacts, and his photo reference library. A quiet-spoken, gentle man known as Bud, he expects to devote all his time to painting Western historical scenes. C74.

JOHNSON, Jonathan Eastman. Born Lovell, Me 1824, died NYC 1906. Very important Eastern portrait and genre painter. NA 1860, SAA. Work in MMA, BMFA, ACM, COR, White House, NY PL, NYHS. References A05-BEN-CHA-DAB - ENB - FIE - G&W - MAL - SMI. Sources AAR 9/73; 5,7/74-AIW-ALA-AMA-ANT 11/48, 11/50, 11/55; 5, 12/56; 9/57; 6,8/59; 6,8/61; 4/62; 1, 8/64; 1,10/66; 2,11/67; 5,6/68; 9, 11/70; 6,9,10/71; 3,5,9/72; 3,4,10,11/73; 6,7,8,9,11/74-ARI-BAR-BOA-BOL-COR-DWF-HUT-ISH-KAR-KEN-KW1-MAP-MSL-M19-NGA-PAF-STI-WHO 06. Oil 40½×67⅞" *Washington Crossing the Delaware* signed E Leutze but painted in 1851 by Johnson after Leutze, sold 10/25/73 for $260,000 at auction. Signature example p 683 ANT 11/67.

Eastman Johnson, the son of Maine's Secretary of State, was educated in Augusta, Me public schools. In 1840 he was a lithographer in Boston. Beginning 1841 he drew crayon portraits of notables while moving from Augusta to Washington, DC. In 1849 Johnson went to Düsseldorf, working with Leutze for two years before setting off to make museum copies in Italy and France. He then took a studio at The Hague for four years, sending his genre paintings back to NYC for sale and declining appointment as official Dutch portrait painter. Instead, he opened a studio in NYC in 1858. He concentrated on distinctively American subjects, traveling in the South to study Negro life and following with genre paintings of farming and fishing. As a portrait painter he had as subjects the eminent Americans of the day. His "flesh tones in the sixties were those of living matter and his painting of costume had a delight in textures." ALA.

Johnson made two trips to the West of his time. He went to the Wisconsin shore of Lake Superior to visit his sister in the summer and fall of 1856, and again in 1857. "While at Great Portage, he sketched the Sioux—old men and women, young squaws and children, and we have never seen the savage melancholy so truly portrayed. We hope that Johnson will do for the aborigines what he has done for the negroes." BOA. When he contemplated a third Western trip in 1860, the NY *Tribune* wrote, "We regret to learn that Mr Eastman Johnson intends going off on an extended tour of the North-west for the purpose of making sketches among the half-breeds and Indians who live beyond the confines of civilized life." Johnson did not go.

JOHNSTON, Francis Hans (or Frank H or Franz). Born Toronto, Ont, Can 1888, died Midland, Ont 1948. Important Can landscape painter of the North Country and the Rockies, illustrator, commercial artist, teacher. Original member Group of Seven, 1920. Work in NGC, AG Ont, Winnipeg AG, etc. Reference MAL. Sources CAH-CAN-CAR-DCA. Oil on board 27½×39″ *Land of Contentment* sold 5/14/73 for $5,800 at auction in Toronto. Signature example p 89 CAN.

Johnston studied at the Ontario School of Art and Design, the Pennsylvania School of Art, and later attended life classes at the Graphic Arts Club. He worked as a commercial artist in Toronto by 1912, with commissions from Grip Limited, the engraving house that was the center for the young painters who began to take joint sketching trips into northern Ontario. During WWI he was with the Canadian War Records Office, painting the Air Force in training. After Tom Thomson who had most strongly

influenced modern Canadian art died in 1917, the Group of Seven was formed with Johnston as an original member. Johnston painted with the Group in northern Ontario. The first Group exhibition was in Toronto in 1920, stating its "vision concerning art in Canada." Johnston, least affected by the Group, quit as early as 1922.

After teaching in Winnipeg and Toronto, Johnston specialized in tempera paintings of northern Ontario. He also painted in the West including the Rockies, regarded as one of the important Eastern interpreters of Western Canada. His Western landscapes were exhibited in Paris in 1927. About then, he changed his given name to Franz to suit a NYC friend who was a numerologist. DCA. Full commercial success came soon after.

JOHNSTON, Walt. Born Washington, DC 1932, living Albuquerque, NM 1972. Traditional Western painter, lithographer. No reference. Source CAP. No auction record. Signature example p 119 CAP.

Johnston's gallery catalog states his belief that the facts of his "early training are of little importance. His work either has meaning or it does not. Not a member of any 'school,' when he finds a place about which he can honestly say something, he paints it with as much realism as he can." He considers himself a genre painter.

JONSON, Raymond. Born Chariton, Iowa 1891, living Albuquerque, NM 1976. Western Transcendentalist painter, teacher, gallery director. Work in LA Cnty MA, MOMA, MNM, Vanderpoel colln, MFA Houston, GIL. References A76-FIE-MAL. Sources ALA-CAH-

PIT-TSF-WHO 62. No current auction record. Signature example p 135 PIT *Cloud Forms and Mesas.*

Jonson was a student of the Portland AS 1909–10, the Chicago AFA 1910–12, and the AIC, a pupil of B J O Nordfeldt. From 1913 to 1919 he executed settings and lighting effects for the Chicago Little Theatre, evolving simplified designs. He was a teacher at Chicago AFA from 1918 to 1921.

He visited New Mexico in 1922, finding Taos too restrictive. In 1924 he moved to Santa Fe where he painted in the cubist manner of rearranging nature. Beginning in 1927 Jonson became abstract and then transcendentalist, "claiming indifference to social, economic, or political problems." ALA. He was a professor at the UNM 1934–54, thereafter professor emeritus and director of Jonson Gallery. Jonson moved to Albuquerque in 1949. In 1960 an exhibition of Albuquerque paintings was called "a tribute to Jonson. He has been a one-man task force for modern art isolated in New Mexico for 40 years. During this time he has painted more than 1,500 works. Modern art in this remote city relates to New York as New York related to Paris in the 1930s." TSF.

JORGENSEN, Christian. Born Oslo, Norway 1860, died Piedmont, Cal 1935. Cal landscape and mission painter. Work in Yosemite Nat Park, ANS. No reference. Sources HON-JCA. No auction record or signature example.

Known by 1883 for his paintings of Western landscapes and California missions, Chris Jorgensen founded the Carmel artist colony with George Sterling. In 1889 he built his studio in Yosemite and lived there until about 1908. He also painted the Grand Canyon and San Francisco. According to JCA, the best-known Chris Jorgensen subjects were "the High Sierras and the Big Trees."

JOULLIN, Amedee (not "Miss" Jouillin). Born San Francisco, Cal 1862, died there 1917. Cal painter specializing in San Fran and Western subjects including Southwest Indians. Member French Acad 1901 (or 1900). Work in Elks Club (Oakland, Cal), Bohemian Club (San Fran), Olympic Club (San Fran). References A17 (obit)-BEN-FIE-MAL-SMI. Sources AIW-BWB-JNM-POW. Oil *Still Life with Roses* 22×34″ with signature example LR sold 11/7/75 for $250 at auction.

Joullin was the friend and pupil of Jules Tavernier at the Art School of San Francisco during Tavernier's hectic residence between 1874 and 1884. In the 1890s Joullin was a specialist in portraits. BWB. Joullin also painted landscapes around San Francisco. And, "enamoured of New Mexico, the desert flora, and particularly the Indians," he and his wife Lucile who also painted "spent much time traveling over the wide spaces of NM and associating in most primitive simplicity with their Indian friends." JNM.

Joullin lived and studied in Paris in 1900 and 1905, the pupil of Bouguereau and Robert-Fleury at the Julien Academy and at the École des Beaux-Arts. He was said to have been an "officer of Public Instruction" in France in 1905. BEN. A05 listed Joullin as resident in San Francisco in 1905, a member of the Bohemian Club. AIW terms him a well-known California artist. POW mentioned exhibits at the NAD in NYC in 1901 and medals won at the St Louis Expos in 1904.

JOULLIN, Mrs Lucile (or Mrs Lucile Joullin Benjamin). Born Geneseo, Ill 1876, died San Francisco, Cal 1924. Cal landscape painter specializing in Indian subjects. Work in Bohemian Club (San Fran). References A24 (obit as Benjamin)-BEN-FIE (as Benjamin)-MAL-

SMI. Source BDW-JNM-WAA. No auction record. Signature example frontispiece JNM.

Mrs Benjamin studied at the AIC, the pupil of John Vanderpoel, Fred Freer, and Ralph Carlson, and with Arthur Mathews at the San Francisco AA. In 1919 she was an instructor at Mills College.

The widow of Amedee Joullin, she had painted Southwest Indians with him. After he died in 1917, she lived in Isleta, NM painting Indian subjects.

JUDSON, William Lees. Born Manchester, Eng 1842, died Los Angeles, Cal 1928. Landscape painter of Cal desert and coast, Indians and cowboys, missions; author, teacher. Work in ANS, Stenzel colln. References A29 (obit)-FIE-MAL-SMI. Sources AAR 11/74-JCA-PNW-WHO 28. No current auction record. Signature example p 13 PNW.

Judson was brought to the US at 10. He studied with his father John Randle Judson and with John Beaufain Irving in NYC. In Paris he was the pupil of Boulanger and Lefebvre. In 1861 he enlisted in the Illinois State Militia, serving in the commissary department to the end of the Civil War. From 1865 to 1867 he was a farmer in Ontario, where he married in 1868 and resumed his work as an artist. HON shows an 1867 watercolor of Indian ponies.

Until 1890 Judson painted in NYC, Toronto, and London, Can, winning an award at the Indian Exhibition in London in 1886. He was in Chicago 1890–93 and thereafter in California. From 1896 to 1901 he was professor of drawing and painting at the U of Southern California. He continued as dean 1901–20. Judson was the author of "Building of a Picture." Judson and Francisco were the leading LA painters around 1910.

JUMP, Edward. Born France 1838, died Chicago 1883. California genre and portrait painter, illustrator, caricaturist. Reference G&W. Sources AIW-COS-HON-OCA. No auction record. Signature example plate 63 COS.

Jump during his 45 years lived in Europe, Australia, and North America. In the US he lived in NY, Cincinnati, St Louis, Chicago, San Francisco, and Washington. When he moved to San Francisco about 1852, he accompanied Hutchings on an 1857 trip, made labels for whiskey bottles, then turned to lithographs which he signed on the stone. He specialized in crowd scenes where his talent as caricaturist provided well-drawn individual figures. He also illustrated for "Beyond the Mississippi" in 1867, one of the few illustrators to have been West.

By 1868 he was painting portraits in Washington, earning $500 a week. Next he was a staff artist for *Leslie's* in NYC. By the early 1870s he was in St Louis where he married a member of a visiting French opera company. In 1874 he had a California sketch in *Leslie's,* and in 1879 he was *Leslie's* correspondent in Leadville with a series of illustrations on the mines. In 1882 *Leslie's* credited a St Louis scene to Jump. His death occurred by suicide in Chicago in 1883—COS noted that one of his California lithographs had been "The Last Jump," a self-portrait in a balloon.

KABOTIE, Fred. Born Shungopovi, Second Mesa, Ariz 1900, living there 1976. Hopi painter, illustrator, teacher, writer, lecturer. Work in COR, GIL, MAI, MNM, MOMA, Philbrook AC, Colorado Springs FAC. References A76-MAL. Sources AHI 2/50,7/51-AIP-LAF. No auction record. Painting example p 125 LAF.

Kabotie's Hopi name is Nakayoma, Day After Day. In 1906 his family and other Hopis of Oraibi founded Hotevilla to preserve Hopi ways. In 1913 the children were forced into a government school. Kabotie was sent away to Santa Fe Indian School as discipline. There he developed his art to such an extent that by 1920 he had become an influential Hopi painter, setting a new pattern of modeling in color with occasional shadows rather than the usual flat colors. He graduated from Indian School in 1924, then attended summer sessions at Alfred and studied with Olaf Nordmark.

He began as an illustrator in 1920, recording Indian dances for scientific purposes, and illustrated books beginning 1925. He was commissioned by MAI in 1928 to paint Hopi life and customs, and in the 1930s by the Peabody Museum to reproduce Awatovi prehistoric murals in original size on panels in fresco. Kabotie taught in Hopi High School beginning 1937, received a Guggenheim Fellowship 1945–46, and represented the US as goodwill envoy to India in 1960. He has done little painting since 1959.

KAHLER, Carl (Karl). Born Linz, Austria 1855, living NYC 1924. International painter of genre. References A24-BEN-FIE. Source ANT 7/65. Oil 30×40" *My Studio* sold 2/28/72 for $550 at auction. In 1899 *The Happy Family* sold for $470, and in 1907 *The Artist's Studio in Melbourne* sold for $525, both at auction. No signature example. (See illustration 160.)

Kahler first exhibited in Berlin in 1880, then in Dresden, Vienna, and Munich where he was active. He traveled much, including Australia. Kahler's studio was in NYC in 1891, when he completed a Western painting 48×60" *Prairie Fire,* and again in 1921–24. He exhibited in Philadelphia in 1921.

KANE, Paul. Born Mallow, Cnty Cork, Ireland (not Toronto, Ont, Can) 1810, died Toronto 1871. Very important Can painter of Indian genre, landscapes. Work in Royal Ont Mus (100 oils and 300 sketches), Montreal MFA, NGC, AG of Ont, Stark Fndn (200 sketches in Orange, Tex), etc. References G&W-MAL-SMI. Sources AAR 11/74-AIW-ANT 3/71,6/71,12/71-CAH-CAN-CAR-DCA-FRO-LAF-POW. No current auction record but the estimated price of an oil 20×30" showing buffalo near Saskatchewan would be about $40,000 to $50,000 at auction in 1976. It is said that more than 200 works were offered for sale as a lot from 1935 to 1952 at $250,-000, and later bought by a Texan for $100,000. Signature example p 788 ANT 6/71. (See illustration 161.)

Kane, brought to Toronto (then York) about 1818, was the son of a soldier turned wine merchant. When he was 16 he was apprenticed and worked for 10 years as a furniture decorator. During this time he was in 1830 the pupil of Thomas Drury, the drawing master of Upper Canada College. Kane also painted portraits, some not signed. He also painted portraits in Detroit in 1836 and in Mobile in 1840. From 1841 to 1843 Kane traveled in Europe to learn to paint by copying masterpieces. In London, Kane met Catlin, thereafter taking as his own goal the painting of a gallery of Canadian Indians. He returned to Mobile in 1843 and to Toronto in 1845.

For the next three years Kane made his way to Vancouver and back, by river boat, canoe, horseback, sloop, and snow-shoes. He sketched in pencil, expanded to watercolor, and sometimes made oil sketches on paper from life. He moved from place to place where Indians were, walking up to an Indian chief and without a word beginning to sketch. He recorded Indian rituals and the spectacular landscape. Back in Toronto in 1848, he completed 100 canvases by 1856, at the same time writing his immediately successful "Wanderings of an Artist among the Indians of North America," published in 1859 with his own paintings as illustrations. More fortunate than Catlin, he sold the 100 canvases to a patron. Substantially all of his work including the simplest sketch remains in museum collections. Kane became blind in 1866.

KAUBA, Carl. Born Austria 1865, died probably Vienna, Austria 1922. Austrian sculptor of Western American bronzes specializing in Indians. Work in Harmsen, Anschutz collns. No reference. Sources ANT 8/61,10/62;3,6,9/74-DCC-JNB. Bronze, dark patina, with applied enamel and bronze decoration, on a marble base, 26½″ high *Chief Wolf Robe* signed C Kauba was estimated at $10,000 to $12,000 for auction 9/28/73 but did not sell. In the same sale, bronze, gold patina, on marble base, 11″ high *Taking Aim* signed C Kauba and stamped GERSCHUTZT sold for $3,900. Signature example ✳119 PB 9/28/73.

Kauba was the pupil of Carl Waschmann and Stefan Schwartz in Austria. He traveled widely in the American West, sketching and modeling, about 1895. He returned to Vienna where his Western bronzes were cast for the American market between 1895 and 1912. Small and medium bronzes were sometimes polychromed at the foundry. It is said

that there were two Kaubas, father and son, and that the son modeled the small polychromed bronzes.

KAUFMANN. Theodore (Theodor Kauffman). Born Uelzen (Nelsen), Hanover, Germany 1814, died probably Boston after 1887. Military and historical painter, portraitist, teacher, writer. References BEN-CHA-FIE-G&W-SMI. Sources HUT-KW1,2-WHI. No current auction record but the estimated price of an oil 20×30″ showing an Indian attack would be about $4,000 to $5,000 at auction in 1976. Signature example fig 34 WHI.

Kaufmann studied art in Europe, the pupil of Hess and Kaulbach in Munich. He worked in Hamburg and Dresden, exhibiting historical paintings in Dresden and Vienna. After taking part in the revolution of 1848, he came to the US in 1850, establishing his studio in NYC. He fought with the North in the Civil War and was best known for his Civil War paintings of the exploits of Adm Farragut and Gen Sherman. His 1867 *Railway Train Attacked by Indians* was painted in NYC. He is recorded as the teacher of Thomas Nast in NYC about 1855 and of W H Holmes in Washington, DC in 1872. In 1871 he had published his "American Painting-Book." He then settled permanently in Boston.

KEITH, William. Born Old Meldrum, Aberdeenshire, Scotland 1839 (or 1838), died Berkeley, Cal 1911. Important Cal landscape painter of the Rocky Mtn School, portraitist, illustrator, wood engraver. Work in ACM, COR, LA Cnty MA, E B Crocker AG (Sacramento), NGA, AIC, BM, Kahn colln, etc. References A11 (obit)-BEN-DAB-FIE-G&W-MAL-SMI. Sources AIW-ALA-ANT

10/62,11/68,1/69,2/72,1/75-BOL-BWB - COW - HAR - HON - JCA - JUT - KAH-KW1-MSL-PNW-POW-SSF-TAW-TWR-WHI-WHO 10. Oil 46×30" *Mountain Landscape* (Cal) signed W Keith dated SF '03 sold 5/22/73 for $4,000 at auction. The same sale had 30×38" *Moon and Figures* selling for $400 at auction. Oil 34×56½" *King's River Canyon* estimated for sale 3/10/75 at $10,000 to $12,000 at auction in LA, but did not sell. Signature example pl 101 TAW. (See illustration 162.)

Brought to NYC in 1850, Keith was apprenticed to a wood engraver in 1856, working for *Harper's.* In 1858 (or 1859) he visited California for *Harper's,* then after a trip to Great Britain settled in California as an engraver in 1862. He began exhibiting paintings in 1864 in San Francisco where he opened his studio, after having been taught painting by his wife. The Northern Pac RR commissioned landscape paintings along its route about 1868. In 1869–70 he studied in Düsseldorf. In 1871–72 he shared a studio in Boston with William Hahn, returning to California in 1872. A nature lover, there was "scarcely a mountain in three-fourths of California where he had not kept vigil for days at a time, studying every detail of color, flower, rock, forge, shadow, and sunshine." Keith became Thomas Hill's rival in monumental landscapes, saying, "I'd be satisfied if I could reach the power and success of Tom Hill." ALA.

When George Inness visited California in 1890, he worked in Keith's studio for many weeks. They made sketching trips together. The result for Keith was an influenced style reflecting the subjective rather than the spectacular. His *Majesty of the Oaks* sold at auction in NYC in 1903 for $2,300 and about the same time *Glory of the Heavens* sold at auction in San Francisco for $12,000. The 1906 earthquake and fire destroyed 2,000 of Keith's works. California's most industrious painter, of medium height with un-

ruly curly hair, Keith had his studio next to the live oaks on the Berkeley campus where it was the center of the university-oriented California culture. He condemned hunting and fishing for sport. KW1.

KELLER, Arthur Ignatius. Born NYC 1866 (or 1867), died Riverdale, NY 1924. Eastern illustrator and painter. Member SI 1901. Work in Munich Acad. References A25 (obit)-BEN-DAB-FIE-MAL-SMI. Sources ILA-MSL-POW-WHO 22. No current auction record. Signature example p 58 ILA.

Keller began work as a lithographer as a youth. At 17 he became the pupil of Wilmarth at the NAD. At 20 he went to Munich as the pupil of Löfftz. He returned to NYC about 1890, as a painter in oil and watercolor. When his paintings did not sell, he was forced to begin illustration, starting with newspapers, then progressing to books and magazines as part of the "golden age of American illustration," along with Abbey, Rinehart, Pyle, and Remington. "Circumstances diverted him into illustration but he was essentially a painter." He "used the model conscientiously for the figure, and obtained his facial expression by posing his model before a mirror and conjuring up the mood." DAB.

He did illustrations for Owen Wister's "The Virginian," for Bret Harte stories, and for "Picturesque California." He had extensive firsthand experience in the West, at the same time as Gilbert Gaul, J Carter Beard, and Joseph Henry Sharp.

KELLER, Clyde Leon. Born Salem, Ore 1872, living Portland, Ore 1941. Pacific coast landscape painter, teacher. Work in Liberty Theater, BPOE, and Press Club in Portland, Herbert Hoover colln, F D

Roosevelt colln, Pub Gall (Norway). References A41-BEN-FIE-MAL-SMI. Source WNW. No auction record or signature example.

Keller studied with Bridges in Munich, E W Christmas in London, and Knowles in Boston. He painted in oil and watercolor. Typical titles were *Site of the Bonneville Dam, California Marshes, Columbia River, The Tualatin, Battleship Oregon.*

KELLEY (signs as Ramon), Ramon. Born Cheyenne, Wyom 1939, living Denver, Colo 1976. Painter of Southwestern scenes and Mexican subjects. Work in Gillette Lib (Wyom), Harmsen colln. Reference A76. Source HAR. No current auction record. Signature example p 119 HAR.

Of Mexican-American descent, Kelley worked as a ranch hand and served in the Navy before studying at the Colorado Institute of Art in Denver. He went on sketching trips in Taos. *American Artist Magazine* published his article 3/69. Kelley is regarded as especially successful with portraits of children and older people.

KEMBLE, Edward Windsor. Born Sacramento, Cal 1861, died Ridgefield, Conn 1933. Illustrator and cartoonist specializing in Negro subjects, writer. References A33 (obit)-BEN-FIE-MAL-SMI. Sources ALA-ILA-ILP-MSL-PNW-WHO 32. No auction record. Signature example p 13 PNW, p 28 ILA.

Son of the founder of *Alta Californian,* Kemble was educated in NYC public schools. Self-taught, his artistic talent was natural enough so that he was a successful contributor to periodicals by 1881. In the 1880s his Western illustrations were of Indians, soldiers, and barracks life. PNW reproduces *Uncle Sam's Wards,* the reservation Indians. After Kemble drew Negro characters for "The Thompson Street Poker Club" in *Life,* he became the specialist in such illustrations. His work was frequently humorous and in the nature of caricature.

KEMEYS, Edward. Born Savannah, Ga 1843, died Georgetown, DC 1907. First American sculptor specializing in Western animals. Work in Fairmount Park (Philadelphia), Champaign (Ill), London, Central Park (NYC), Omaha, AIC, NGA. References A05-BEN-DAB-FIE-MAL-SMI. Sources ALA-AMA-ANT 12/61,9/72 - HUT - MSL - NJA - POW - WHO 06. Bronze *Stag* reddish-brown patina 16¾" high signed E Kemeys with wolf monogram sold 10/31/75 for $1,-300 at auction. Signature example p 392 ANT 9/72. (See illustration 163.)

Kemeys was educated in public schools in Scarborough, NY and NYC. After serving throughout the Civil War he failed as a farmer in Illinois. Returning to NYC he worked as a woodsman in Central Park. When he saw a sculptor in the zoo, he bought wax and by 1870 was modeling animals, self-taught. His *Wolves* was sold to Fairmount Park in 1872, providing funds for a Western trip to study animals.

In the West he dissected and modeled all of the game animals, also learning Indian lore. He hunted buffalo with the Indians, inside a wolf skin. His work was unique because the inroads of civilization soon destroyed what he had seen. In 1877–78 Kemeys was in London and Paris, studying the methods of the French sculptor Barye: "In anatomical knowledge, Kemeys appears little behind, and if he be Barye's inferior in conception, he compensates by a fine discrimination of animal individuality." HUT. As the base for his trips into the West, Kemeys kept a Chicago studio, moving from there to make studies in Arizona, for example, for his smaller works. His specialty included the Indian, but his Indian heads were evaluated as ethnographic rather than artistic.

KENDERDINE, Augustus Frederick. Born near Blackpool, Lancashire, Eng 1870, died Emma Lake, Saskatchewan, Can 1947. Painter of the Western Can prairies and of Indian portraits, illustrator, teacher. Work in NGC, U Saskatchewan (Regina), Glenbow Fndn (Calgary, 25 major oils plus 116 minor works), Queen's Park Gall (Manchester, Eng), etc. Reference MAL. Sources CAH-CAN-DCA. No auction record or signature example.

Gus Kenderdine studied at the Manchester School of Art, the pupil of his godfather Augustus Lafosse, and at Julien Academy with Lefebvre. He exhibited at the RA in 1901, specializing in hunting scenes.

In 1907 he emigrated to Lashburn, Saskatchewan, settling on a homestead-ranch in a remote area five days from town. He painted in his spare time. About 1920, when he left paintings for framing, he was discovered by the president of the U of Saskatchewan and hired as instructor in Saskatoon. In 1921 he exhibited *The Saskatchewan River at Yankee Bend*. In 1933 the Canadian Government commissioned two 21' canvases. He also illustrated a school reader and in 1935 founded a summer school of art at Emma Lake in northern Saskatchewan. His paintings were in "softly modulated tones and colors" suggesting the French countryside rather than the "breeze-swept plains," but "beautiful as pure decoration." CAN.

KENSETT, John Frederick. Born Cheshire, Conn 1816 (or 1818), died NYC 1872. Very important landscape painter, the first of the Hudson River School to visit the West. NA 1849. Work in ACM, MMA, BM, BMFA, City AM of St Louis, DAM, DIA, COR, etc. References BEN-CHA-DAB-ENB-FIE-G&W-MAL-SMI. Sources AAR 9/73, 5/74-AIW-ALA-ANT 9/45,6/47,1/49, 2/61,10/62;7,11/64;5,10/68;1,6,9/69; 3,5,7/71;1,4/72;3,8/74-BOA-DCC-HUD-HUT-KAR-KW1-M19-MIS-NA74-PAF-POW-STI-TAW. Oil 40¼ × 34" *The Flume, Franconia Notch, NH* signed with initials but not dated sold 10/28/71 for $15,000 at auction. Oil 7½×18" *Snowy Range, and Foothills, from the Valley of Volmount, Colo* signed on the reverse but not dated sold 9/13/72 for $3,700 at auction. Monogram p 74 ANT 6/69.

Kensett began as an engraver, the pupil of his father Thomas Kensett until 1829, his uncle Alfred Daggett in New Haven until 1838, and Peter Maverick in NYC until 1840. Determined to become a landscape painter, he then set off on the traditional European tour to study the great art collections, under the guidance of A B Durand and accompanied by Casilear and Rossiter. After seven years of living in France and England, walking the Rhine, painting in Rome, he returned to NYC in 1848. He was an instant success as a painter, both in recognition and sales. His life was convivial, this romantic-looking bachelor with high forehead and sensitive expression. The style he developed by 1848 he retained for life, providing ready sales to the collectors of the day. He died at the height of his career, after attempting to rescue the drowned wife of Vincent Colyer.

As an example of his Western experience, ANT 1/72 shows *Indians in a Forest Scene* dated 1849 while Kensett was in NYC. Kensett made a trip up the Mississippi in 1854 and the Missouri in 1857 (or 1856), the first of the Hudson River School painters to record the Western landscape. MIS illustrates a Kensett painting *Upper Mississippi* dated 1855.

He is said to have traveled to Colorado in 1866 (with Whittredge and S R Gifford according to KAR but not KW1 or TAW). In 1870 he went West again, this time in the company of Whittredge and Sanford Gifford, to Colorado and the Rockies.

KERN, Benjamin Jordan. Born Philadelphia, Pa 1818, killed by Ute Indians in the Colo Rockies 1849. Sketch artist for the 1848 Frémont expedition. No reference. Sources AIW-SUR. No auction record or signature example.

Dr Kern was the oldest of three brothers with sketching ability who participated in the railway surveys. He was the first to die.

Frémont's expedition failed to cross the Rockies. Eleven of the members of the party succumbed to the cold and starvation, the surviving 21 abandoning their gear and notes to retreat to Taos. Benjamin Kern and the "Mountain Man," "Old" Bill Williams, returned to recover the gear and notes but were killed by Utes who had themselves been savaged by US troops a few days earlier. Benjamin Kern thus became the first of the few artists who were murdered by Indians, and it must be said that, while the circumstances of his death are clear, he did not really qualify as a professional artist. (See Edward and Richard Kern entries.)

KERN, Edward Meyer. Born Philadelphia, Pa 1823, died there 1863. Survey artist, topographer, landscape painter, teacher. Work in BMFA, Huntington Lib (San Marino, Cal), US Naval Academy, Smithsonian Inst. Reference G&W. Sources AIW-ANT 10/62-KW1-PAF-SUR. Oil 15×20″ *The Indian Camp* sold 2/20/65 for $575 at auction. Signature example p 218 KW1.

Edward Kern, youngest of three brothers who were survey artists, exhibited as a painter in Philadelphia in 1841. The first of the brothers to travel West, he served as topographer with Frémont's third expedition and as Frémont's Mexican War lieutenant from 1845 to 1847, although he was listed in the Philadelphia directory as a drawing teacher during this time and up to 1853. Frémont's party crossed the Plains and the Rockies to Salt Lake City and California. Kern River was named for him by Frémont. In 1848–49 the three brothers were with Frémont's fourth expedition that attempted a winter crossing of the Colorado Rockies. Eleven lives were lost en route, and Benjamin Kern was killed by Indians while returning to the Rockies to recover the expedition's notes and collections.

The two surviving brothers participated in the 1849 Simpson expedition to the Navaho country. Edward Kern accompanied a military tour under Lt John Pope in 1851. From 1853–56 he was "photographist" and artist for the Ringgold expedition in the North Pacific. From 1858-60 he was with the Navy expedition to establish a route from California to China. He served in the Civil War. An epileptic and a bachelor, his early death was attributed to the hardships experienced during Frémont's attempted winter crossing of the Rockies. (See Richard and Benjamin Kern entries.)

KERN, Richard Hovenden. Born Philadelphia, Pa 1821, died near Sevier Lake, Utah 1853. Survey artist, topographer, landscape painter. Work in ACM, Huntington Lib (San Marino, Cal). Reference G&W. Sources AIW-DWF-FRO-PAF-SUR-TSF. No current auction record but the estimated price of a drawing 8×10″ showing a view of Fort Smith would be about $600 to $800 at auction in 1976. Drawing examples p 57 FRO.

Richard Kern was one of three Philadelphia brothers who were survey artists in the West. He exhibited landscapes and figure studies beginning 1840 while working as a drawing master in Philadelphia. Along with his older brother Benjamin, he joined the youngest brother Edward on Frémont's 1848–49 expedition that attempted a winter crossing of the Colorado Rockies, resulting in Benjamin's death (see his entry).

The two surviving brothers were with the Simpson expedition into Navaho territory in the fall of 1849. The reports included 72 plates credited to Richard Kern, some "after sketches by E M Kern," with about 40 of the plates involving Indian genre. The best-known plate was *View of El Paso from the East*. He also painted Jemez and Sandia Pueblos, as well as the Jemez Green Corn Dance. Careful detail was said to be characteristic of his work. In 1851 he was on the Sitgreaves expedition down the Colorado River. In 1853 he joined the Gunnison party to survey the central rail route, along what was the Santa Fe trail. After two-and-a-half months the party reached central Utah, Gunnison noting, "The great mountains have been passed and a new wagon road open across the continent, for 700 miles across an untrodden track." AIW. At that point Gunnison and Kern while exploring with an escort were killed by Paiute Indians. Richard Kern was thus the second of the three brothers to die from Indian attack, a rare occurrence for an artist in the West. Kern's sketchbook was recovered, and J M Stanley redrew the sketches for the plates in the report. (See Edward Kern entry.)

in oil and watercolor, muralist. Work in Jefferson Nat Expansion Mem (St Louis), Wyom St colln, Dept of Interior, Teton Nat Park, collns of 15 Western governors. Reference A76. Sources AHI 5/72-WYG-11/30/70 letter from Mrs Roy Kerswill. No auction record. Signature example *In Wyoming* summer/73 (article).

Kerswill studied at Plymouth College of Art in England when he was 15. After serving in the Royal Navy 1942–45, he toured Europe as an itinerant artist painting portraits in charcoal and watercolor. The year 1947 he spent in the Yukon and Alaska, then took a 7,000-mile canoe trip from British Columbia to New Orleans. About 1949 he worked in Calgary as an artist for Hudson's Bay Company, and about 1950 in Denver as space concept artist for Martin Marietta Company.

"That bearded guy who wears those mountain-climbing knickers" moved to Jackson Hole, Wyom in 1960 in order to paint full-time. By 1967 two of his oils *Wintering with the Elk* and *Trail West* sold for $2,500 each, and advance commissions for 1968 were $30,000. His procedure is to paint a watercolor on the spot outdoors, complete it in his studio, then perfect it in a series of oil paintings. He calls himself "a Painter of the West," a romantic about the men, horses, and mountains. For detail, Kerswill relies on his reference library—Borein for longhorn cattle, Remington or Russell for Indians, Eggenhofer for Western vehicles. The motto in his studio is "Luck—is what happens when preparation meets opportunity." *Arizona Living* for 10/19/73 indicates that Kerswill sketched in a Mexican silver mining town that summer and that he winters near Phoenix.

KERSWILL, Roy. Born Bigbury, Devon, Eng 1925, living Teton Village, Wyom 1976. Traditional Western painter

KEY, John Ross. Born Hagerstown, Md 1832, died Baltimore, Md 1920. Landscape painter and illustrator, in San

Francisco 1870–73. Work in ACM, Kahn colln (Oakland, Cal), Phila Centennial Expos, reproduced in Prang prints. References A20 (obit)-BEN-FIE-G&W-MAL-SMI. Sources ANT 3/73-BOA-HON-HUT-KAH-PAF. Oil 22½×49" *Drewry's Bluff 1865* sold 4/11/73 for $9,500 at auction. Signature example p 423 ANT 3/73.

Grandson of Francis Scott Key, he studied in Munich and Paris before establishing his studio in Boston. He had worked in 1854 as a draftsman for the US Coast and Geodetic Survey. In 1863 he had sketched the siege of Charleston for the Federal Corps of Engineers.

In 1870 his studio was in San Francisco where he painted landscapes of northern California. These paintings were reproduced as chromos by Prang in the 1870s. Key's 1870 press review of a San Francisco exhibition listed such subjects as Lake Tahoe, Mariposa Big Trees, Point Lobos, and Yosemite Half Dome. At the Philadelphia Centennial, Key exhibited *The Golden Gate, San Francisco,* showing it again in Boston in 1877 along with 100 other Key paintings. The press review said his "charcoal drawings are among the best ever shown in Boston, firm and masterly, strong and graceful." HUT.

KIDD, Steven R. Born Chicago, Ill 1911, living probably NYC 1966. Illustrator who began with pulp Westerns, teacher. Member SI. Work in Pentagon, Air Force Hist Mus, NY News Bldg. No reference. Sources ILA-IL 60. No current auction record. Signature example ⚹54 IL 60.

Kidd studied at the AIC. At 18 he sold his first illustrations to *Two Gun Western Stories.* When he moved to NYC he was the pupil of George Bridgman at the ASL and of Harvey Dunn for 10 years at the Grand Central School of Art. Kidd specialized in line drawings in ink, particu-

larly for the fiction page of the *NY News* syndicate. During WWII he was an official Army artist. Later he painted illustrations of US air activities in the West. He has taught at the Newark School of Fine and Industrial Art and at the ASL.

KIHN, William Langdon (or mistakenly Wilfred Kilm). Born Brooklyn, NY 1898, died probably Hadlyme, Conn 1957. Painter specializing in Indian portraits, illustrator. Member RSA. Work in U of Okla, Wellcome Hist Mus (London, Eng), Litchfield Mus (Conn), Royal Ont Mus, NGC. References A59 (obit)-BEN-FIE-MAL-SMI. Sources CAN-CUS-WHO 57-7/75 data from Helen Kihn. No auction record. Signature example p 43 LAF *Iroquois Harvest.* (See illustration 164.)

Kihn studied at the ASL 1916–17, had private teachers, and was the pupil of Homer Boss and Winold Reiss. In 1920 Reiss took Kihn on a field trip to Montana and NM, the first time Kihn "had been West of Hoboken." His one-man exhibitions began with the MNM in Santa Fe in 1921, the year Kihn spent three months for 60 portraits among the Blackfeet. His next one-man show was in 1922 in NYC, and it practically sold out. The Canadian Pacific Rys sent Kihn to Banff and Vancouver and the Northwest to paint Totem Pole Indians, and "from then on it was Indians, Indians." Between 1935 and 1949 Kihn embarked on a commission to survey all of the North American Indians. He painted for the *National Geographic* American Indian series in 1937 with 24 works on *When Red Men Ruled Our Forests,* in 1940 with 25 works on *Red Men of the Southwest,* in 1944 with 16 works on *Indians of Our Western Plains,* in 1945 with 16 works on *Totem Pole Builders,* etc. He illustrated numerous books on Indians and was a contributor to popular national magazines. The AMNH in NYC exhibited 60 Indian portraits in 1952. In 1953 he was a partner in the Guy Wiggins-Langdon Kihn Art School in Essex, Conn.

Kihn was also accepted as authoritative on Indian lore of the Canadian West Coast. His "portrayal and interpretation of Indian subjects, highly individualistic in style, has stirred the admiration of the art world for its pure beauty, and of scientists for its truth. Some of Kihn's paintings are of the Nootka (totem pole) Indians of Vancouver Island." CAN. Kihn said he had painted 500 Indian pictures (an understatement), visited 35 tribes, and covered the area from the Atlantic to the Pacific and from the Mexican border to the Arctic.

KIMMEL, Lu. Born Brooklyn, NY 1905, died Queens, NY 1973. Illustrator for national magazines including Western subjects, painter, teacher. Member SI. Work in Amer Red Cross (DC). References A41-MAL. Source interview Mrs Kimmel 6/75. No auction record or signature example. (See illustration 165.)

Kimmel studied at Pratt Institute and was the pupil of Pruett Carter and George Luks. He began as a free-lance illustrator for magazines and books—*The Saturday Evening Post, This Week, Scribner's, Country Gentleman, Woman's Day.* His specialty was Western subjects, particularly in his work for paperback books, although Kimmel never went West.

In 1933 Kimmel won the Red Cross poster competition. He painted from models until the end of the 1940s when the fashion was to work from photographs. In the early 1950s he returned to school to obtain the degree that enabled him to teach commercial art at Hunter College and at Commercial Illustration School in NYC.

KING, Charles Bird. Born Newport, RI 1785, died Washington, DC 1862. Very important portrait painter specializing in Indians. Honorary NA. Work in the White House, Smithsonian Inst, National Mus (Copenhagen), Peabody Mus (Harvard), COR, Maryland Hist Soc, Redwood Lib (Newport, RI). References BEN-FIE-G&W-MAL-SMI. Sources ALA-ANT 6/53,8/57,11/66,6/68,5/70; 10,11/72;2/74-AOW-BAR-BOA-DAA-DBW-DCC-HAR-HUT-150-ISH-KW1-M19-STI-TEP-WES. Oil 17½×13¾" on panel *Wab-bawn-see, Cause of Paleness, Powerful Chief of the Potawatomies,* signed C B King, Washington 1835, on the reverse, sold 4/11/73 for $26,000 at auction. The auction sale 5/21/70 included an Oto chief sold for $9,000, a Seneca chief sold for $27,000, and a Sioux chief sold for $11,000. Signature p 32 PB 10/25/73.

King was as a boy the pupil of Samuel King in Newport, then of Edward Savage in New York, and finally of Benjamin West in London for seven years along with Thomas Sully. After failing with a Philadelphia studio he opened in 1812, King moved to Washington, DC in 1816 where he was the "principal artist-in-residence less by his painting skill than by a bachelor's pleasant manner while eating out." King thus "smiled his way to success as a mediocre portraitist," although as a still-life painter he "made loveliness out of ruined things." BAR.

In 1821 King was commissioned by Thomas L McKenney, Superintendent of Indian Trade, to paint portraits of eight Western Indians brought to Washington "to visit their Great White Father" to become impressed with his strength. King went on to paint about 90 portraits of Indians visiting Washington, to comprise by 1837 the nucleus of the National Indian Portrait Gallery. All but three of these were lost in the Smithsonian fire in 1865. Today these paintings exist in the many replicas King is said to have painted, as well as copies known to have been made by Henry Inman and others. In addition the portraits were duplicated in "faithful and colorful lithographs" illustrating McKenney and Hall's three-volume work published 1836–44. And finally, the lithographs themselves were widely copied, as in the paintings by the Unknown Primitive about 1870 illustrated in KEN 6/70.

KINGSLEY, Rose. Born probably London, Eng 1845, died England 1925. Amateur sketch artist, illustrator, writer active Colo Springs, Colo 1871, 1874. No reference. Sources GOD-KW1-NEW-SPR. No auction record or signature example.

Daughter of Canon Charles Kingsley who wrote "Westward Ho!" and "Water Babies," Rose Kingsley arrived in Colorado Springs in Nov 1871, a "tall, angular, ruddy spinster of 26 in heavy tweeds, a shapeless felt hat, wool stockings, and stout coarse shoes." NEW. She lived that winter in a shack with her brother and spent the spring of 1872 in New Mexico. Mt Rosa (11,499 feet) near Colorado Springs was said to have been named for her although she did not claim to have climbed to the summit.

To describe her Western experiences, Miss Kingsley wrote "South and West" published in London in 1874. The illustrations were drawn from her sketches: *Prairie Dogs, A Prairie Ranch, Mule Team Refusing to Cross a Trestle, Indians with Papoose, Pikes Peak,* etc.

KIRKHAM, Reuben. Born 1850, active beginning 1866 in Salt Lake City, died Logan, Utah 1886. Pioneer Utah painter of landscapes real and imagined. Work in Springville AM (Utah). No reference. Sources JUT-YUP. No auction record

but the estimated price of an oil $20 \times 30''$ showing a fantastic landscape would be $300 to $500 at auction in 1976. Painting example p 14 YUP.

Kirkham arrived in Utah in 1866, settling in Logan. Along with Alfred Lambourne, he was a scenic artist for the Salt Lake Theatre. Lambourne and Kirkham in the 1870s painted a large panorama of American scenes that Lambourne toured with, giving lectures. Kirkham in 1884–85 traveled with 19 panoramic paintings illustrating The Book of Mormon. It is said that Kirkham's invented landscapes are reminiscent of Ottinger's paintings of the Incas.

KIRKLAND, Forrest. Born Mist, Ark 1892, died probably Dallas, Tex 1942. Texas watercolor painter, commercial artist. References A41-MAL. Source TOB. No auction record or signature example.

Kirkland studied commercial art at the School of Applied Art in Battle Creek, Mich and worked for an engraver in Dallas. After WWI service in France he established his own commercial art studio and studied briefly with E G Eisenlohr. By 1930 he was winning Dallas watercolor awards. In 1935 Kirkland "completed paintings of all Indian pictographs on the rocks at Paint Rock, Texas." TOB. Typical titles of later paintings are *Mayer Springs, Fort Davis, Rock Pile Ranch, Pecos Valley, Lower Rio Grande, Hueco Tanks, Panhandle.*

KISSEL, Eleonora. Born Morristown, NJ 1891, died probably Taos, NM 1966. Taos landscape and portrait painter, etcher. Work in MNM, HAW. References A47-MAL. Sources AAT-TAL. No current auction record. Signature examples p 100 AAT *Winter Landscape NM,* pl 35 TAL.

Ms Kissel was a member of NA Women PS and the Taos Heptagon. In 1941 she was listed as resident in NY with her studio in Taos.

KITTELSON, John Henry. Born Arlington, SD 1930, living Fort Collins, Colo 1976. Traditional Western Sculptor in wood, bronze, and ceramics, painter. Member CAA. Reference A76. Sources AHI 11/71-C71 to 73-COW-OSR-WAI 72-WHG-11/27/73 data from John Kittelson. No auction record. Signature example p 37 *The Western Horseman* 7/71.

Kittelson was born on a small farm in South Dakota. He became a saddlemaker at 13, left home at 14 to work as a cowboy in South Dakota, Montana, Nebraska, Wyoming, and Colorado. When he settled down in the shadow of the Rockies in Poudre Valley near Bellvue, Colo, he returned to leathercraft in saddles and belts. His last major leatherwork was the 1957 Cheyenne Frontier Days trophy plaque. He began painting in oil about 1956 using his Tepee Bar brand with his signature. Self-taught as a sculptor, he "got serious" about his whittling and started selling small woodcarvings, mainly horses. By 1966 he was one of the first seven artists elected to the CAA. In 1970 he began in bronze because "bronzes bring the big money." He still ropes and rides.

His woodcarving procedures are described in *Arizona Living* 10/26/73. He buys an entire linden tree and lets it sit up to three years until it's cured, then has it kiln-dried. Without a sketch he roughs with a bandsaw and starts chiseling. "You have a lot of whittlers, but I'm a chiseler." By 1969, "I could have worked 24 hours a day and not fill all the orders."

KLEIBER, Hans. Born Cologne, Germany 1887, died Dayton, Wyom 1967. Traditional Western etcher, painter, illustrator. Member Assoc Amer Artists, Amer Artist Group. Work in Lib Cong, Wyom St AG, U of Wyom, St Lib of Cal. References A41-MAL. Sources AAT-WAN-WYA-WYG. No current auction record. Drypoint example p 286 AAT *Crossing the Platte.*

Kleiber came to Wyoming from Germany in 1906 when he was 19. In 1907 he entered the US Forestry Service as a Ranger, with duties throughout the Northwest. When he resigned in 1924, it was to devote his entire time to art, despite his lack of formal art instruction. By 1929 he was exhibiting as an important Wyoming painter and he was selling illustrations. By 1931 he was listed in the American Art Annual, having won a silver medal for etching.

KLEPPER, Frank Earl (or Frank L). Born Plano, Tex 1890, living Dallas, Tex 1953. Texas landscape painter, muralist, etcher, teacher. Work in Dallas MFA, Ark St AA, West Texas AA, Vanderpoel colln. References A53-FIE-MAL. Sources TOB-TXF. No current auction record or signature example.

Klepper studied at the AIC, the American Art Training Center in Paris, and with Henry B Lachman in Bellevue, France. When he returned to Texas, typical 1920s subjects were *Texas Plume, The Pueblo, Morning at Mossy Bank.* By the 1930s he specialized in landscapes and Negro subjects. His hobby was collecting objects relating to goats.

KLINKER, Orpha. Born Fairfield, Iowa 1895 (or 1891), died Hollywood, Cal 1964. Desert painter, illustrator of Indian books and pioneer portraits, etcher. Member Acads of Brazil, Argentina, Mexico, etc. Work in LA City Hall, MMA, LA AA. References A66 (obit)-MAS. Sources SCA-WAA. No auction record or signature example.

Ms Klinker was educated at the U of California LA. She was the pupil of John Hubbard Rich, Edgar Payne, Paul Lauritz, Anna A Hills, Mildred Brooks, Will Foster, and studied at the Julien Academy in Paris, the pupil of Morriset, and at the Colarossi Academy. In 1937 she painted a series of 40 California pioneer subjects as illustrations for *Los Angeles Sunday Times Magazine*. By 1959 she had illustrated a variety of books including "Enchanted Pueblo." She gave art lectures on early California.

KLOSS, Gene (Mrs Phillips Kloss, née Alice Geneva Glasier). Born Oakland, Cal 1903, living Taos, NM 1976. Taos landscape etcher, painter in oil and watercolor. ANA 1950, NA (graphics) 1972. Work in NGA, MMA, MNM, Dallas MFA, PAFA, HAW, AIC, Mus of Tokyo, etc. References A76-MAL. Sources AAR 11/74-AAT-ACO-CAPTAL-TSF-WHO 70-WOM 64. No current auction record. Signature example p 122 CAP. (See illustration 166.)

Gene Kloss received her AB from the U of California in 1924. She studied at the California SFA 1924–25, becoming a summer visitor to Taos, NM in 1925 while living in Oakland. In 1929 she became a permanent resident of Taos. She began winning awards in the 1930s, with one-artist museum shows beginning 1950s. Her work was included in "Fine Prints of the Year" and "100 Best Prints of the Year." In 1938 her work was exhibited in Paris as a leading New Mexico artist along with Blumenschein, O'Keeffe, and Sloan. Her prints of New Mexico landscape and genre scenes are her most

popular, displaying a sensitive simplicity with sharp contrasts in tonality to emphasize the immensity of the West.

KNAPP, Mrs Martha Severance. Born Middlebury, Vt 1827, died Portland, Ore 1928. Amateur painter of Alaska landscape and Indians 1889–93. Work in Alaska Hist Lib and Mus (Juneau). No reference. Source and painting example p 576 ANT 6/60. No auction record.

Mrs Knapp was educated at Burr Seminary in Manchester, Vt. She worked as a schoolteacher in Middlebury while painting and teaching art. In 1865 she married Lyman E Knapp, publisher, lawyer, and politician who was appointed Governor of Alaska in 1889. The Knapps lived in Sitka which had been a Tlingit Indian village and then Russian colonial capital. They visited Wrangell, a totem-pole village. Mrs Knapp painted Sitka and Wrangell in oil and watercolor and sketched the Indians in "gay blankets." ANT. In 1893 the Knapps moved to Seattle.

KNATHS, Otto Karl. Born Eau Claire, Wis 1891, died probably Provincetown, Mass 1971. Important international abstract-expressionist painter. NA 1971. Work in MMA, AIC, DIA, PAFA, WMAA, MOMA, etc. References A73 (obit)-BEN-MAL. Sources AAR 3,5/74-AAT-ALA-APT-ARI-ART 1/63-CAA-190-M50-NA 74-NEU-WHO 70. Oil 49×39" *The House Painters* signed "Knaths" and inscribed 1925 sold 3/21/74 for $6,000 at auction after a presale estimate of $1,500 to $2,000. Oil 24×18" *Cowboy* signed and dated 1947 sold 1/29/74 for $450 at auction. Signature p 295 NEU.

Karl Knaths graduated Portage, Wis high school in 1910. He studied for five years at the AIC, leaving to work on the railroad during WWI after having seen the Chicago exhibit of the 1913 Armory Show. In 1919 he visited NYC en route to Provincetown where he made his permanent home. He was an original exhibitor with the American Abstract Artists group in 1936. "Knaths' work stems from Cézanne, Braque, and Picasso; he has achieved an American idiom based on their forms, but with an added flavor of Expressionism." ARI.

KNEE, Gina (Mrs Alexander Brook). Born Marietta, Ohio 1898, living Sag Harbor, NY 1976. Abstract painter, graphic artist. Work in Phillips colln (DC), MNM, DAM, Santa Barbara MA, Buffalo FAA. References A76-MAS. Sources AAT-TSF-WAA. No current auction record. Signature examples p 98 AAT *Landscape Abstraction in Blue,* p 89 TSF. (See illustration 167.)

Gina Knee came to Santa Fe in 1930, after seeing a NYC exhibition of Marin's Taos watercolors. She studied one summer with Ward Lockwood and taught at a girl's school. Her watercolors at first showed the influence of Marin, and later incorporated Klee symbolism to produce abstracted Indian and landscape motifs. She remained in Santa Fe for 15 years, with one-artist exhibitions beginning in 1942. "Up to 1945," she said, "I painted everything I could see: Indian dances, the Spanish Americans—the desert and mountains—but after a few years I started trying to express in the forms their spirit, or sound, or smell." Gina Knee is married to the artist Alexander Brook.

KNOX, Susan Ricker. Born date unknown Portsmouth, NH, living NYC 1959. Painter, especially of children.

Work in Brooks Mem AG, Cornell colln (Mt Vernon, Iowa), U of the South (Sewanee, Tenn). References A59-BEN-FIE-MAL-SMI. Sources INS 4/17-WAA-WOM. No auction record. Painting example p LXVIII INT.

Susan Knox studied at the Drexel Institute, Philadelphia, and Cooper Union Art School in NY. She was a pupil of Howard Pyle, Douglas Volk, and Clifford Grayson. Her studies were continued abroad in Spain, Italy, Paris, and London. About 85 paintings done in the Southwest are in a private collection in Massachusetts. These include many scenes of Mexican and Indian mothers and children.

KNUDSON, Robert. Born Minnesota 1929, living Williams, Ariz 1974. Ariz painter of Western landscapes including Indians, teacher. Work in Mus No Ariz, Wm Penn Mem Mus. No reference. Sources AHI 7/72-Baker Gall exhib cat-WAI 71,72. No auction record. Signature p 13 AHI 7/72.

Knudson graduated from the Minneapolis Art Museum school in 1950. He painted in his spare time, working in advertising art, color photography, and business management until 1963. Since then he has been an instructor at the Kachina School of Art in Phoenix and also in Sedona and Prescott in the summers. His specialty is the ancient culture of the Hopi and the Navaho: "It has great space, dynamic forms. The people and the land complement one another." WAI 72.

KOERNER, H T. Born probably 1855, died 1927. German painter, illustrator, writer working in the US, including Indian subjects. Work in Buffalo Hist Soc (*Halfmoon on the Hudson*). No other reference, source, auction record, or signature example. Source 1/29/75 letter from Steve Wunderlich, Buffalo Hist Soc.

KOERNER, William Henry David (or Dethlep, or Dethlef). Born Lun (Schleswig-Holstein), Germany 1878, died Interlaken, NJ 1938. Very important Western illustrator. Work in ANS. References A41 (obit)-MAL-MAS. Sources AAR 5/74-ANS-ANT 1/73-BAW-COW-ILA-150-PAW-WAI 72-"W H D KOERNER" ©1969 ACM-"W H D Koerner and Montana" ©1971 The Montana Hist Soc. Oil 25×44″ *Rustlers* signed W H D Koerner and dated 1928 sold 10/27/71 for $21,000 at auction. Signature p 97 ILA. (See illustration 168.)

Koerner was brought to Clinton, Iowa in 1880. In 1896 he was hired by the *Chicago Tribune* as staff artist at $5 a week, sketching spot news. He attended the AIC and the Francis Smith Art Academy. In 1904 he was art editor of a literary magazine in Battle Creek, Mich. From 1905–7 Koerner studied at the ASL in NYC. In 1907 he moved to Wilmington, Del, working as an illustrator while the pupil of Howard Pyle until 1911, along with N C Wyeth and Harvey Dunn. By the 1920s he was one of the best-known magazine and book illustrators. Study with Frank Breckenridge had provided the use of "broken color," a "commercial impressionism." His palette became full and vibrant.

In 1922 Koerner was given the commission to illustrate Emerson Hough's "The Covered Wagon," published serially by *The Saturday Evening Post*. By 1924 he was spending his summers in a log cabin near the Crow Indian Reservation in southern Montana. He also visited California and the Southwest. Koerner became truly the "illustrator of the Western myth, of symbols of an earlier less complicated, infinitely more moral land of ample time and room to roam." ACM. Koerner received $1,000 for cover illustrations for the *Post*. His painting garb was a smock over his knickers and golf socks with saddle shoes. After his death, hundreds of paintings were in his studio, along with drawings, sketchbooks, and artifacts. His widow kept the studio intact until 1962, when exhibitions demonstrated that Koerner had been an important Western painter.

KOPPEL, Charles. Active 1853–65. Railway survey artist in California in 1853. Work in ACM. Reference G&W. Sources AIW-ANT 9/43. No auction record. Lithograph example p 131 ANT 9/43 *Los Angeles*.

Of the 11 railway survey artists engaged on the work for the 12-volume "Reports of Explorations and Surveys to Ascertain the Most Practicable and Economic Route for a Railroad from the Mississippi River to the Pacific Ocean" published from 1855 to 1861, the best-known was John Mix Stanley and the least was Charles Koppel. The party to perform the California portion of the survey was commanded by Lt R S Williamson with William P Blake as the geologist and Koppel as the official artist.

In June 1853 the party arrived in San Francisco after sailing from NYC. The survey was especially to explore the passes of the Sierra Nevada. Work began July 10 at Benicia and was completed at San Diego Dec 19. The report credits Koppel with field sketches for 21 full-page lithographs and 26 woodcuts. The view of Los Angeles taken November 1 is the most popular. Two of the sketches were of the desert. One was *Tejon Indians*. There is no other data on Koppel except for a portrait of Jefferson Davis, the Secretary of War who in 1853 supervised the survey. The portrait was made as a lithograph, released in 1865.

KRANS, Olaf (or Olof, Olaf Olson). Born Selja, Västmanland, Sweden 1838, died Altoona, Ill 1916. Important primitive Illinois genre and portrait painter. Work in State Memorial (Bishop Hill, Ill). Reference G&W. Source ANT 2/43,11/50,3/65,1/71,2/72. No current auction record but the estimated price of an oil 20×30″ showing women binding grain would be about $10,000 to $12,000 at auction in 1976. Signature p 327 ANT 2/72.

In 1845 a site named Bishop Hill in Illinois was selected for the establishment of a religious colony of Swedish Jansenists. The first immigrants arrived in 1846. Olaf Olson was brought to the colony by his parents in 1850. He grew up in Bishop Hill, working as a house painter. After the Civil War he changed his name to Krans, moving to Galesburg in 1865 and to Galva, Ill about 1867.

Krans then worked as a decorative painter as well as on houses and signs. In the 1890s he painted the scenes of Bishop Hill that he remembered or was told about, "breaking prairie, sowing grain, planting corn, haying, harvesting." He also painted portraits of the colonists, working from photographs. In 1896 he gave these paintings to the village on its 50th anniversary. An important folk artist, he continued painting into the 1900s.

KRIEGHOFF, Cornelius David. Born Amsterdam, Holland 1815 (not Düsseldorf, Germany 1812), died Chicago, Ill (not Canada) 1872. Very important Canadian genre painter specializing in Indians and settlers of lower Canada. Work in ACM, Beaverbrook AG (NB), AG Ont, NGC. References BEN-G&W-MAL. Sources ANT 1/51,10/56,10/58, 12/63,7/64,7/67,9/67,1/69-*Art News* 11/49-CAH-CAN-CAR-DCA-KEN. Oil *Settler's Homestead* sold 10/14/71 for $28,000 at auction in Montreal. Signature p 29 KEN 6/70. (See illustration 169.)

Krieghoff's father was a wallpaper-maker in Düsseldorf and later near Schweinfurt in Bavaria. Educated in Rotterdam, Holland, Krieghoff studied art at Düsseldorf before traveling in Europe as an itinerant artist-musician. Emigrating to the US in 1837, he enlisted in the Army as a skilled mechanic. It is said that Krieghoff may have made drawings during the Seminole War in Florida. When he was discharged in 1840 in NYC, he married a French-Canadian girl from Longueuil near Montreal.

Soon afterward, Krieghoff went to Canada. He was in Toronto in 1846, Longueuil painting Caughnawaga Indians in 1847, then Montreal in 1849, and in 1853–54 to Quebec. He matured as a painter in Quebec from 1854 to 1868, adapting to rustic lower Canada the Düsseldorf Academy style of placing little figures on an elaborately decorated stage. His renderings of the habitant as a jolly peasant were popular souvenirs for the British officers in Quebec, although less acceptable to the Quebeckers. He and Paul Kane were the most important Canadian painters of the time, Krieghoff leaving detailed records of the Indian encampments of Lorette. He is said to have visited Europe about 1860. In 1868 he moved to Chicago where he remained except for a visit to Canada in 1871. There were many editions of Krieghoff paintings. Some were mounted on canvas and heavily varnished.

KROLL, Leon. Born NYC 1884, died there 1974. Eastern landscape, figure, genre painter of realism, muralist, lithographer. ANA 1920, NA 1927. Work in MMA, WMAA, AIC, MOMA, Detroit IA, DAM, PAFA, MNM, etc; murals in public buildings. References A73-BEN-FIE-MAL-SMI. Sources AAT-AIC-ALA-AMA-ANT 4/74-ARM-CAA-CON-

138. Henry George Hine. *Buffalo Hunt on the Prairies*, watercolor with gouache 8¼ x 22⅜″ signed (LL) H G Hine and dated 1847. English illustrator depicting the Canadian West. CREDIT, ROYAL ONTARIO MUSEUM, TORONTO.

139. Malvina Hoffman. *No Man Is an Island/Every One to His Brother*, bronze medal 3″ diameter signed MH and dated 1955. M H for mud head. CREDIT, THE AUTHORS.

140. R C Holdredge. *California Mountains with Indians*, oil on canvas 20 x 36″ signed LL. The ranking California landscape painter of the 1860s. CREDIT, THE AUTHORS.

141. E H Holgate. *Totem Poles, Gitsegiuklas*, oil on canvas 32 x 32″ signed (LR) E Holgate. In the Skeena River area with the ethnologist Barbeau in 1926. CREDIT, THE NATIONAL GALLERY OF CANADA, OTTAWA.

142. W H Homes. *Mesa Encantada*, watercolor 9½ x 13¾″ signed LL and dated 1917. You "step to the edge of 40 miles of outdoors" in his panoramas. CREDIT, MUSEUM OF NEW MEXICO.

143. Frances Ann Hopkins. *Lake Superior*, oil 24½ x 40″ painted about 1870. Painter of the Canadian voyageurs, shown in the center of the near canoe. CREDIT, ROYAL ONTARIO MUSEUM, TORONTO.

144. Donal Hord. *Man Must Sow/To Reap*, bronze medal 3″ diameter signed DH and dated 1950. He worked "in the hard California light" to model "shining Indian heads." CREDIT, THE AUTHORS.

5. Gayle Hoskins. Sketch for *Battle of Little Big Horn*, oil board 11 x 18″ signed (LR) Hoskins. Final version was d as a calendar for Brown & Bigelow in 1930. CREDIT, E AUTHORS.

146. Merritt D Houghton. *Fort Steele Tie Loading Plant*, watercolor signed LL and placed at Grand Encampment. Wyom. Important genre records. CREDIT, WYOMING STATE ARCHIVES AND HISTORICAL DEPARTMENT.

147. Allan Houser. *Apache Fire Dancer/Buffalo Hunt*, bronze medal 3″ diameter signed (LR) Houser and dated 1959. The leading Apache artist. CREDIT, THE AUTHORS.

148. Grace Hudson. *Grasshopper Dance*, oil on canvas 30 x 21″ signed (LL) G Hudson. Important California painter of Indian children. CREDIT, THE ANSCHUTZ COLLECTION.

149. E J Hughes. *Beach at Savary Island, British Colum* oil on canvas 20⅛ x 24″ signed LL and dated 1952. Qual of a child's world. CREDIT, THE NATIONAL GALLERY CANADA, OTTAWA.

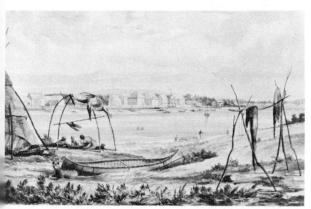

150. L P Hurd. *Fort William*, watercolor 8½ x 12¹³/₁₆″ painted about 1863. Originally owned by Chief Factor of Hudson's Bay Company. CREDIT, ROYAL ONTARIO MUSEUM, TORONTO.

151. Peter Hurd. *Study for The Plainsman*, egg tempera on board 39 x 75″ signed LL. He lived in Wyeth's barn and married Wyeth's daughter. CREDIT, THE ANSCHUTZ COLLECTION.

52. Joseph Imhof. *The Camoufleurs (Deer Dancers at San uan Pueblo)*, oil on canvas mounted 30½ x 46½″. Painter of Corn in the Life of the Pueblo Indians." CREDIT, THE NSCHUTZ COLLECTION.

153. George Inness, Sr. *Afterglow on the Prairie*, oil on canvas 14 x 21″. Sometimes unequal and sometimes unequaled. CREDIT, THE ANSCHUTZ COLLECTION.

4. De la Cherois Thomas Irwin. *The Banff River, Canada*, tercolor 9 x 14″ signed (LR) D Irwin. Canadian artillery cer on Vancouver Island 1878. CREDIT, ROYAL ON-RIO MUSEUM, TORONTO.

155. A Y Jackson. *Alaska Highway between Watson Lake and Nelson*, oil on panel 10¼ x 13¾″ signed LR. First international recognition for the Group of Seven. CREDIT, THE NATIONAL GALLERY OF CANADA, OTTAWA.

156. W H Jackson. *Hat Creek Station in 1877*, watercolor 9½ x 14¾″ signed LR and dated 1939. Pioneer photographer painting the scene he sketched 62 years before. CREDIT, DENVER PUBLIC LIBRARY, WESTERN HISTORY DEPARTMENT.

157. Ned Jacob. *Grandfather, Give Us Your Children*, oil on canvas 24 x 48″ signed LL and painted 1974. CAA member trained only by ''thousands of hours at the board and easel.'' CREDIT, THE ARTIST.

158. Frank Tenney Johnson. *Riders of the Dawn*, oil on canvas 48 x 60″ signed (LL) F Tenney Johnson. Impressionist technique and moonlight subjects. CREDIT, THE ANSCHUTZ COLLECTION.

159. Garrison Johnson. *Apache Dancers*, cray and gouache 16 x 14″ signed LR. Anthropologis Palm Springs 1950. CREDIT, THE AUTHORS.

160. Carl Kahler, *Giant of the Ages*, oil on canvas 48 x 60″ signed LR. International painter depicting smoke along the prairie tracks. CREDIT, THE AUTHORS.

161. Paul Kane. *Indians Playing at Alcoloh*, oil on canva x 29″. Just walked up to Indian chiefs and began to ske CREDIT, THE NATIONAL GALLERY OF CANADA, TAWA.

163. Edward Kemeys. *A Panther and Cubs*, bronze group 26½" high signed LL and dated 1907. He hunted buffalo with the Indians. CREDIT, THE METROPOLITAN MUSEUM OF ART, ROGERS FUND, 1907.

162. William Keith. *The Falls of Yosemite*, oil on canvas 26 x 13" signed (LL) W Keith and dated 1879. "If I could reach the power and success of Tom Hill." CREDIT, THE METROPOLITAN MUSEUM OF ART, GIFT OF MRS SCOTT SCAMMELL, 1952.

165. Lu Kimmel. *Conference in the Cabin*, grisaille on canvas 35 x 53" signed (CR) K and dated 1939. K is for Kimmel, too. CREDIT, THE AUTHORS.

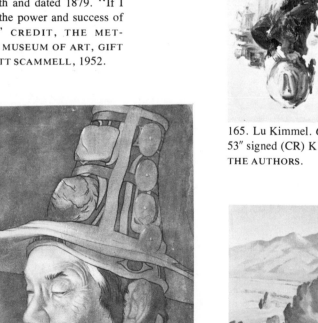

54. Langdon Kihn. *He-Knows-the-Sky, Alimlarhae, Old Chief of the Skeena*, crayon, pastel, pencil on aper 20 x 15" about 1926. Painted 35 tribes from the rctic to Mexico and coast to coast. CREDIT, THE UTHORS.

166. Gene Kloss. *Taos Scene*, signed LR. She emphasizes the humanity of the West. CREDIT, MUSEUM OF NEW MEXICO.

167. Gina Knee. *Canyon de Chelly*, oil on canvas 15 x 18″ signed LR and painted about 1939. Drawn to Taos by a NYC exhibition of Marin watercolors of New Mexico. CREDIT, THE AUTHORS.

169. Cornelius Krieghoff. *Indians Running a Rapid*, oil on canvas 10¾ x 15″ signed (LR) C Krieghoff and dated 1855. With Paul Kane, the important Canadian painter of his time. CREDIT, THE NATIONAL GALLERY OF CANADA, OTTAWA.

171. Mort Kunstler. *Table Stakes,* tempera on board 16½ x 18½″ signed (LL) M Kunstler. An illustration for *Saga.* CREDIT, THE AUTHORS.

172. (Right) R L Lambdin. *The Green Curse*, wash, crayon, ink on paper 14 x 10″ signed LL. An illustrator for Western newspapers who moved East in 1917. CREDIT, THE AUTHORS.

168. W H D Koerner. *Ceremony of the Sun Horse*, oil on canvas 28 x 40″ signed LR and dated 1931. The illustrator of the Western myth painting in knickers and saddle shoes. CREDIT, RUTH KOERNER OLIVER.

170. Otto Kuhler. *Decay at Delagua*, oil 17½ x 23½″ signed (LR) O Kuhler 1963. One of the series "Land of Lost Souls." CREDIT, DENVER PUBLIC LIBRARY, WESTERN HISTORY DEPARTMENT.

173. Alfred Lambourne. *Autumn*. Painter of unexplored lands, with 610 works before 1900. CREDIT, CORPORATION OF THE PRESIDENT OF THE CHURCH OF JESUS CHRIST OF LATTER-DAY SAINTS, 1975.

174. Tom Lea. *Snake Dancers*, oil 61 x 41″ signed LL and dated 1932. The writer of ''The Brave Bulls'' and j''the Wonderful Country.'' CREDIT, MUSEUM OF NEW MEXICO.

175. Harry Learned. *Robinson, Colorado*, oil 10 x 15″ signed LC and dated 1886. An itinerant painter of theater scenery. CREDIT, DENVER PUBLIC LIBRARY, WESTERN HISTORY DEPARTMENT.

177. A C Leighton. *High River, Alberta*, oil on canvas 24¼ 30½″ signed LR. Known for watercolors of Canadian airies and Rockies. CREDIT, THE NATIONAL GALLERY CANADA, OTTAWA.

176. W R Leigh. *A Close Call*, oil on canvas 35 x 30″ signed LR and dated 1943. Purple horses with yellow bellies from an important illustrator. CREDIT, THE ANSCHUTZ COLLECTION.

179. Chester Loomis. *Antelope Hunters*, oil on canvas 23 x 36″ signed LL and dated Texas 1887. Eastern painter and illustrator. CREDIT, THE ANSCHUTZ COLLECTION.

178. Ward Lockwood. *Landscape with Horses*, oil on canvas 30 x 40″ signed (LR) Lockwood and painted about 1934. New Mexico regionalist whose work became more abstract. CREDIT, THE ANSCHUTZ COLLECTION.

180. Robert Lougheed. *Whistle Stop*, signed LR. Designed the six-cent buffalo stamp and the "Flying Red Horse." CREDIT, THE ARTIST.

181. Orson Lowell. *A Son of John Brown*, pen and 17 x 11″ signed LR. "Greatface no fight," he tested. "Greatface Quaker Indian." CREDIT, AUTHORS.

182. J E H MacDonald. *Mount Lefroy*, oil on canvas 21 x 26¼″ signed LL and dated 1932. He saw the Scandinavian paintings that influenced the Group of Seven. CREDIT, THE NATIONAL GALLERY OF CANADA, OTTAWA, VINCENT MASSSEY BEQUEST, 1908.

183. H A MacNeil. *Hopi/Prayer for Rain*, bronze medal 3″ diameter signed. "The red man as worth as the athletes of ancient Greece." CREDIT, THE AUTHORS.

184. William W Major. *Brigham Young's Family*, oil on canvas 26 x 34″ painted 1845–51. The first artist in the Salt Lake valley. CREDIT, CORPORATION OF THE PRESIDENT OF THE CHURCH OF JESUS CHRIST OF LATTER-DAY SAINTS, 1975.

185. Beatrice Mandelman. *Taos Valley*, oil on canvas 20 x 24″ signed (LL) B Mandelman. "Technical ability more masculine than feminine." CREDIT, THE AUTHORS.

186. J N Marchand. *The Prospectors*, pastel on board 19 x 17″ signed LL and dated 1907. A Western illustrator born on the frontier and trained in Munich. CREDIT, THE AUTHORS.

187. John Marin. *Canyon of the Hondo, New Mexico*, watercolor 15 x 20″ signed (LR) Marin and dated 1930. Made modernism acceptable in the Victorian West. CREDIT, THE ANSCHUTZ COLLECTION.

188. George B Marks. *Makin' a Break*, oil on canvas 21 x 32″ signed (LL) G B Marks and dated 1974. CAA member painting the life of the contemporary cowboy. CREDIT, THE ARTIST.

189. T Mower Martin. *Summer Time*, oil on canvas 61½ x 53″ signed (LR) Mower Martin and dated 1880. Considered out-of-date in 1886 in the Canadian East. CREDIT, THE NATIONAL GALLERY OF CANADA, OTTAWA, THE ROYAL CANADIAN ACADEMY DIPLOMA COLLECTION.

190. María and Julián Martínez. *Blackware Food Bowl*, 4½ x 10″ signed Marie and Julian about 1925. The Potter of San Ildefonso. CREDIT, THE AUTHORS.

192. Marmaduke Matthews. *Nanaimo, BC, from the West*, watercolor with gouache 13⅜ x 27″ signed (LR) M Matthews and dated 1889. Transplanted Englishman with traditional style. CREDIT, ROYAL ONTARIO MUSEUM, TORONTO.

191. Arthur F Mathews. *California Landscape*, oil on canvas 26 x 29⅞″ signed LR. Important as a Western teacher. CREDIT, THE METROPOLITAN MUSEUM OF ART, GIFT OF HENRIETTA ZEILE, 1909.

193. Jan Matulka. *Indian Dancers*, oil on canvas 26 x 16″ painted about 1918. Witnessed the rise of Cubism in Europe. CREDIT, THE ANSCHUTZ COLLECTION.

194. Herman Matzen. *Buffalo Bookends*, bronze 6½ x 6½″ signed HNM and dated 1915. Matzen made monuments. CREDIT, THE AUTHORS.

195. Frank McCarthy. *Behind Bars*, oil on board 20 x 14″ signed LR. "Strong, dramatic, masculine illustration." CREDIT, THE AUTHORS.

196. Solomon McCombs. *Shield Dance*, acrylic or board 37 x 28″ signed (LC) McCombs and dated 1968 Designs in Presidential parades. CREDIT, THE AUTHORS.

197. Frank Mechau. *Horses at Night*, oil mural 62 x 144″ signed Mechau Colorado and dated 1934. Caused controversy with an "imaginative reconstruction of a massacre." CREDIT, DENVER PUBLIC LIBRARY, WESTERN HISTORY DEPARTMENT.

198. (Right) Lon Megargee. *Grand Canyon*, oil on canvas 68 x 47″ signed LR and dated 1925. Illustrator of humorous aspects of cowboy life. CREDIT, THE ANSCHUTZ COLLECTION.

9. Ivan Messenger. *Desert Landscape*, watercolor on per 14 x 16″ signed LC. Active Julian, Cal in 1940s. EDIT, THE AUTHORS.

200. (Right) W L Metcalf. *Zuni*, gouache grisaille on board 9 x 6½″ signed LR and dated 1881. "The Ten" New England impressionist when he was a Special Artist-Correspondent. CREDIT, THE AUTHORS.

201. A J Miller. *Indian Scout*, oil 17½ x 23¼" signed LR and dated 1851. The only painter in the West of the mountain men. CREDIT, DENVER PUBLIC LIBRARY, WESTERN HISTORY DEPARTMENT.

202. Fred R Miner. *The Artist's Cabin*, oil on canvas 2 30" signed LR. Influenced by Wendt and the South California landscape school. CREDIT, THE AUTHORS.

203. G B Mitchell. *Red Cloud's Daughter*, charcoal and pencil drawing on paper 24 x 16" signed LR and drawn about 1938. For 25 years he painted Indian genre particularly Blackfoot. CREDIT, THE AUTHORS.

204. Thos J Mitchell. *Indian Pueblo, Taos, NM*, oil canvas 36 x 40" signed LR. Painted for Public Works of Project. CREDIT, THE AUTHORS.

DEP-190-ISH-MAP-M50-M57-NEU-PIT-TSF-WHO 70. Oil 26×32" *Landscape, Santa Fe* signed Kroll and dated 1917 sold 5/26/71 for $3,300 at auction. Oil 26¼×32" *Bass Rocks* with signature example and dated 1912 sold 12/8/71 for $4,250 at auction.

Kroll worked his way through the ASL as a janitor, the pupil of Twachtman, encouraged to paint by Homer. He made mechanical drawings for a living before winning a NAD scholarship for study under Laurens at the Julien Academy in Paris. In NYC his aggressive enthusiastic realism made him a quick popular success. By 1912 he was winning important national awards. He exhibited at the 1913 Armory Show. In the 1920s he was a leading figure, painting in a full, lush style mixing sentimentality and voluptuousness under academic restraints such as dynamic symmetry. Kroll idealized the human form.

Kroll was painting in Colorado Springs in 1917. As a summer visitor he joined Henri and Bellows in Santa Fe that year, painting "the local scene with relish that reflected his great enthusiasm for life." TSF. In 1919 he was selected as a New Mexico painter for a Paris exhibition.

KUCHEL, Charles Conrad. Born Zweibrücken, Switzerland 1820, living 1865 San Francisco, Cal. Lithographic artist. Reference G&W. Sources ACM-COS-OCA. No auction record. Signature example plate 48 COS.

After coming to the US, Kuchel worked for P S Duval in Philadelphia in 1846. By 1853 he was in San Francisco, a partner in Kuchel & Dresel, lithographers. The firm's outstanding work was a series of California views of the important cities and mining towns during 1855–58. These views were medium in size and many were surrounded by a border of smaller scenes. All of the views were drawn and lithographed by the firm, printed by Britton & Rey, and published by a local merchant such as a bookseller. Some of the lithographs indicate that Kuchel was the artist of the sketch as well as the drawing on the stone.

KUHLER, Otto. Born Remscheid near Cologne, Germany 1894, living Santa Fe, NM 1976. Colo landscape painter, Santa Fe etcher, railroad equipment designer. Member Nat Acad Western Art. Work in DPL. References A76-MAS. Sources "The Land of Lost Souls" published by DPL 1964-9/22/74 article *Post* (*Empire*)-PER vol 3 ⅗3. No auction record. Signature example p 26 PER vol 3 ⅗3. (See illustration 170.)

Educated as a mechanical engineer, Kuhler served in the German Engineer Corps in WWI. When the postwar inflation wiped out the family fortune, Kuhler emigrated to Pittsburgh in 1923. He moved to NYC in 1928 and was engaged as design consultant to the American Locomotive Co in 1931. Nearly 100 patents resulted.

In 1947 Kuhler bought the KZ Ranch near Bailey, Colo, raising cattle and painting landscapes. In 1964 he gave the DPL a series of paintings re-creating the coal mines and villages that were functioning in the early 1900s.

KUHN, Robert F. Born Buffalo, NY 1920, living Roxbury, Conn 1976. Illustrator specializing in animals including the West. Work in Nat Cowboy Hall of Fame, magazines like *Field and Stream* and *Argosy*. Reference A76. Sources ILA-IL 60-PER vol 3 ⅗3-May 1975 data from Bob Kuhn. No auction record. Signature example IL 60.

Bob Kuhn studied at Pratt Institute in Brooklyn and was influenced by animal illustrator Paul Bransom. Kuhn drew in zoos and then began traveling widely, Newfoundland, Western Canada, Alaska, the American West, and Africa. He started with illustrations for *Field and Stream*. His *Argosy* drawing shown in IL 60 is a Western featuring a dog.

Kuhn has hunted the animals he paints. Beginning 1949 he was a regular contributor to Remington Arms Company for wildlife calendars. He "quit illustrating in 1970 and now paints easel pictures of big game, mostly African but some North American. Some of his best portrayals have been achieved after he successfully hunted his game." KUHN.

KUHN, Walt (Walter Francis). Born Brooklyn, NY 1880 (or 1877), died NYC 1949. Modern Eastern painter specializing in clown portraits. Work in BM, AIC, ACM, MOMA, WMAA, DAM, Dublin Mus. References A53 (obit)-BEN-FIE-MAL. Sources AIC-ALA-ANT 12/54,10/64-ARI-ARM-CAA-CAP-CON-DAA-DEP-190-M57-NGA-STI-WHO 48. See "Walt Kuhn: An Imaginary History of the West" ©1964 Colo Springs FAC. Oil 40×30" *Bareback Rider* signed Walt Kuhn dated 1926, and titled on stretcher, sold 3/14/73 for $35,000 at the Edith G Halpert auction. Signature pl 1 "Walt Kuhn."

Kuhn was educated in Brooklyn. He owned a bicycle shop, barnstorming as a professional rider. He made his first trip West in 1899, selling cartoons to *The Wasp* in San Francisco and doing decorations such as a painted back-bar for a saloon. In 1901 he studied at the Colarossi Academy in Paris and the AFA in Munich. He continued as cartoonist for *Life, Puck, Judge,* and NY newspapers. In 1910 he became a painter, gaining his first one-man exhibition the same year. He continued his association with the theatrical world, best known for his portrayals of circus people. Cézanne was his most important influence. With A B Davies he organized the 1913 Armory Show which accomplished what Kuhn had hoped, to mark the starting point of the new spirit in art, as far as America was concerned.

The West was a major interest for Kuhn. Between 1918 and 1920 he made 29 paintings he called his *Imaginary History of the West*. After rejection by MMA, the series became part of the Colorado Springs collection. Kuhn had as source material 59 Western books. Each painting was "from memory from material gathered out of" the books. The critical reaction to the paintings was, "They are ironical and amusing, the true comic touch." In 1936 Kuhn was commissioned to design the interior of a Union Pacific club car as "The Frontier Shack," and in 1937 another as "Little Nuggett."

KUMMER, Julius Hermann. Born Dresden, Saxony, Germany 1817, died probably St Louis, Mo after 1869. Landscape painter of the Western Plains and the Rocky Mountains during the 1860s, lithographer. Work in Dresden Mus. References BEN-G&W. Source ANT 6/69. Oil 25×32" *Sunset Landscape* 1857 sold 1/14/70 for $170 at auction. Painting example p 740 ANT 6/69 *May Day, 1859*.

Kummer studied at the Dresden Academy 1832–35. Six of his landscapes of the Dresden vicinity are in the museum there. A refugee of the Revolution of 1848, he emigrated to NYC, moving to Brooklyn and Boston before settling in St Louis after 1860. In 1868 his *Twelve Views of the Rocky Mountains* were reviewed in a St Louis newspaper.

KUNIYOSHI, Yasuo. Born Okayama, Japan 1893, died NYC 1953. New York realist painter, lithographer, teacher. Honorary associate, Nat Inst. Work in MMA, MOMA, WMAA, BM, Detroit IA, AIC, etc. References A53-BEN-FIE-MAL. Sources AAR 9/73-AAT-AIC-ALA-ANT 3/75-APT-ARI-CAA-CON-DEP-190-MAP-M50-M57-STI-TSF-WHO 50. Oils 28×42" *Little Joe with Cow* with signature example and dated '23 sold for $220,000; 40¼×65" *Circus Girl, Resting* with signature example and dated '31 sold for $160,000 at auction 3/14/73 of the Halpert colln.

Kuniyoshi was sent from Japan by his father to learn textile production at 13. He became a night student at the LASA 1908–10, NAD 1912, Indep SA 1914–16, and ASL 1916–20 under Kenneth Hayes Miller. In 1917 he began exhibiting paintings of cows and people in Maine, making an immediate impression due to the studied naïveté and humor. In 1922 his subjects were children, and in 1924 women and the sea, as examples of "American studio painting," the popular style of the time. In 1925 and 1928 he visited France and Italy. In 1935 his Guggenheim Fellowship permitted travel to Mexico and Japan. His later paintings reflect social content with greater complexity in composition and color. He taught at the ASL beginning 1933 and the New School beginning 1936.

Kuniyoshi was a Taos summer visitor in 1935, as a part of his Guggenheim: "He found the picturesqueness overpowering and did little painting." TSF. When he returned to Taos in 1941, he made a series of pencil drawings giving a direct impression of the open landscape, quite different from the sophisticated Eastern work.

KUNSTLER, Morton. Born Brooklyn, NY 1931, living Oyster Bay Cove, NY 1976. Eastern illustrator of realism in historical, animal, and Western subjects.

Member SI 1955. Work in Favell Mus (Oregon), San Matteo Cnty Hist Soc (Cal), Air Force Mus. No reference. Sources ※59 IL 60 with signature example-March 1975 data from M Kunstler. No auction record. (See illustration 171.)

Kunstler went to Brooklyn public schools and attended Brooklyn College and the U of California at LA before studying art at Pratt Institute, the pupil of Ajootian. His first job was as apprentice in a commercial art studio. After four months he painted three Westerns as samples for the paperback houses and sold all three. Since then, Kunstler has been a free-lance illustrator, in historical subjects on commission from major adventure magazines and agencies.

For Westerns, Kunstler's practice is to paint a complex subject intended for sale as fine art, planning the painting so that it can be divided into two or three sections to allow additional commercial sales of transparencies of those sections before the gallery sale of the painting.

KURZ, Rudolph Friedrich. Born Bern, Switzerland 1818, died there 1871. Swiss painter important because of travel in the American West 1847–52. Work in Bern Historical Mus (colln of uncataloged drawings), GIL, Peabody Mus (Harvard), DAM. References BEN-G&W. Sources AIW-AOW-COW-DBW-FRO-GIL-KW1,2-LAF-MIS-POW-TAW. No current auction record but the estimated price of a wash drawing 14×20" showing an Indian girl cooking would be about $7,000 to $8,000 at auction in 1976. Signature p 111 POW.

When Friedrich Kurz first thought of travel to North America, Bodmer told him to become more proficient "in the drawing of natural objects and animals." By the time Kurz was 29 he had had 12 years of European study, including having been the pupil of J Valmar in Bern and of S Fort in Paris. He landed in New Orleans at the end of 1846. He spent 1847 based in St Louis, including short sketching trips west into Indian territory. In 1848 he started up the Missouri, settling at St Joseph, then a frontier town where Indians came to trade. Kurz painted and sketched the Potawatomi, Fox, Oto, Iowa, and Kickapoo. He noted the gold seekers replacing the fur traders in 1849. In 1850 he married the 16-year-old daughter of an Iowa chief: "Her mother served hot coffee, fried meat, and bread. Next day I purchased her outfit." But in the spring, "I found my bird had flown. That was the end of my romantic dream of love and marriage with an Indian maiden. Brief joy!" POW.

Kurz boarded a fur boat to seek new scenes. He ended in Fort Berthold, western North Dakota, which was "alive with Indians," Mandans and Crows. For two weeks he sketched and compiled a Mandan dictionary but the Indians threatened his life, believing his sketching caused cholera. He wintered at Fort Union, then returned to Bern where he painted pastels and oils from his American sketches. From 1855 to 1871 Kurz taught drawing in Bern. In 1946 a sketchbook of his drawings was cut apart by a NYC dealer for sale of the pages separately.

LACHER. See Gisella Loeffler.

LACKEY, Vinson. Born Paris, Tex 1889, died probably Oklahoma 1959. Architectural painter, designer, draftsman. Work in GIL. No reference. Source GIL. No auction record but the estimated price of an oil 20×30" of Indian territory near Fort Washita would be about $400 to $600 at auction in 1976. Signature p 217 GIL.

Lackey was educated at the U of Oklahoma. He worked for 20 years as head of layout inspection at Douglas Aircraft in Tulsa. In the 1940s he was commissioned to research for the Gilcrease collection the government buildings that existed before Oklahoma became a state. Lackey painted more than 100 of these views, concentrating on the buildings and terrain rather than genre.

LAMBDIN, Robert Lynn. Born Dighton, Kans 1886, living Westport, Conn 1966. Illustrator who worked for Western newspapers and Eastern magazines; painter, muralist. Member Artists Guild, Nat Soc Mural Ptrs. Murals in Conn public and industrial buildings, NYC hospital. References A62 - MAL. Source p 97 ILA with signature example. No auction record. (See illustration 172.)

Lambdin studied for a year at the Denver School of Art with Henry Read and at the Kansas City AI with C A Wilimovsky. He began in the art department of the *Rocky Mountain News.* After working for the *Denver Republican,* he moved to the *Kansas City Star* as illustrator of feature stories.

When Lambdin settled in NYC in 1917, he was an ink-drawing illustrator for national magazines and juvenile books. Later he worked in half-tone washes and oil paintings. ILA. His subjects frequently included Westerns based on his own experiences.

LAMBOURNE, Alfred. Born in England 1850, died Salt Lake City, Utah 1926. Pioneer Utah landscape painter. Work in Utah MFA. No reference. Sources JUT-PUA-YUP. No auction record but the estimated price of an oil 20×30" showing Bryce Canyon wall would be about $1,000 to $1,200 at auction in 1976. (See illustration 173.)

As LDS converts, Lambourne's family emigrated to St Louis in 1860. They collected supplies and equipment enabling them to join an ox-team train for Salt Lake Valley in 1866. Lambourne kept a sketchbook while crossing the Plains. He became the pupil of Ottinger at Deseret Academy and the travel companion of the photographer Savage. In the course of his painting, Lambourne rode horseback to Bryce Canyon, Green River, the Uinta Mountains. Some lakes he named. It is said that explorers of the time did not claim discoveries in an area until they ascertained whether Lambourne had already painted there.

Lambourne was a prominent Utah artist of the 1880s, painting in most of the Western states. He was considered to be essentially self-taught. Up to the turn of the century his journal listed 610 works including a panorama of a transcontinental journey. He was also a scenic painter for the Salt Lake Theatre and a muralist for the LDS Church. After 1900 he turned to books and poetry, some of which he illustrated.

LAMSON, J. Born probably Sebec, Me about 1825, living California 1860. Itinerant Cal sketch artist, miner, merchant. Work in Cal Hist Soc. Reference G&W.

No other source, auction record, or signature example.

Lamson was in California 1849–52 and again 1856–60. His drawings were commissioned by mine and home owners.

LANE, Remington W. Active in Colorado and Utah 1893, as *Harper's Weekly* illustrator. No reference. Source AIW. No auction record or signature example.

Lane was a member of the Moorehead archaeological expedition that went from Durango, Colo to Bluff City, Utah. Seven of Lane's sketches were in his article "An Artist in the San Juan Country," printed 12/9/93.

LANING, Edward. Born Petersburg, Ill 1906, living NYC 1976. Modern Eastern painter, muralist, teacher. NA 1958, Nat Soc Mural Painters. Work in WMAA, MMA, Wm Rockhill Nelson GA (Kansas City); murals in libraries, hotels, post offices, etc. Reference A76. Sources CAA-DEP-MAP-WHO 70. No auction record. Signature p 74 MAP *The Corn Dance*.

Laning studied at the AIC in the summers of 1923–24, at the U of Chicago 1925–27, at the ASL in NYC 1927–30, and at the AFA in Rome 1929 and 1931. He was considered to be the pupil of Kenneth Hayes Miller, painting "the same subjects in the early '30s, borrowing his mentor's mannerisms." DEP.

Laning was an instructor at ASL 1932–33 and again beginning 1952. He was an artist-correspondent for *Life* 1943–44 and head of department of painting, Kansas City AI 1945–50. His *The Corn Dance* is a rare "social protest" painting of the serious Pueblo ritual diminished by the uninvolved tourists. MAP.

LAPHAM, J M. Active California 1852–58. Landscape artist for lithographers. Reference G&W. Sources COS-OCA. No auction record. Signature example p 41 OCA.

OCA shows *Mammoth Arbor Vitae* drawn from nature by Lapham and lithographed by Britton & Rey, San Francisco.

LAPLACE, Cyrille Pierre Théodore. Born France 1793, died there 1875. Topographical artist, naval officer. Reference G&W. No source, auction price, or signature example.

Laplace was a French officer in California in 1839 while commanding an around-the-world expedition. A sketch of the San Carlos Mission in Carmel appears as an illustration in Laplace's book written about the voyage. He later became vice-admiral of the French fleet.

LARGE, Virginia. Born Portland, Ore 1914, living Saratoga, Wyom 1974. Painter of Western scenes. Source WYA. No current auction record.

Mrs Large was a pupil of the AIC.

LARSEN, Bent Franklin. Born Monroe, Utah 1882, died Provo, Utah 1970. Modern Utah realist landscape painter, teacher. Work in Springville AA, Utah St Col, Weber Col, BYU. References A59-BEN. Source YUP. No current auction record but the estimated price of an oil 20×30″ showing a canyon lake would be $500 to $600 at auction in 1976. Signature p 28 YUP.

Larsen was educated at Snow College and BYU (AB). He was a public school principal 1901–6, an art supervisor

1907–8, and a director of art 1908–12. He received his MA from U of Utah in 1922, then studied at the AIC 1922, Julien Academy in Paris 1924–25, Académie de la Grande Chaumière, Colarossi, and Académie André Lhote in 1929–30. He was one of the last Utahans to study in Paris. YUP. He taught at BYU 1931–53, then becoming professor emeritus. Though he was considered a "painter of hearty landscapes, there is an abstract quality in the unusual close-up studies." YUP.

LA RUE, Walt. Born Canada about 1925, living Burbank, Cal 1973. Traditional Western painter specializing in cowboy genre. No reference. Source COW. No current auction record. Signature p 197 COW.

La Rue was brought up in Montana and educated in California where he worked on mountain pack outfits in the summers. He became a wrangler in Montana. A success at "rodeoing" for 15 years, he had drawn the covers on the official rodeo publication and had sold cartoons. He is self-taught except for six months' study at Otis AI in Los Angeles. He has also worked as a stuntman for Western movies. This he credits with giving him the equivalent of actual experiences in the old West.

LASALLE (Lassell), Charles. Born Greenwood, Mass 1894, died Scottsdale, Ariz 1958. Western genre painter, illustrator. Work in Valley National Bank, Ariz. Reference MAL. Sources BDW-Chas LaSalle (Retrospective Catalog), Maxine Olmstead, Scottsdale Arts Festival, 1971-ILA-WAI 71. No auction record. Signature example ILA p 150.

LaSalle was one of the top producers during the "golden age" of illustrators, the '20s, and '30s. A pupil of Fenway Art School in Boston and later of Harvey Dunn, LaSalle had work in *The Saturday Evening Post, Collier's, Redbook,* etc.

Six-foot-two, "tidy, handsome, manly, gregarious, friendly" (Retrospective) LaSalle had been born Charles Louis Lassell, but people continually miscalled him LaSalle, so he changed his name just to be accommodating. A trip, hoboeing through Texas when he was 19, made him an ardent Westerner in spirit, but he didn't move West until 1954 when his health demanded a dry climate. His last four years were spent painting Western scenes for galleries and exhibitions.

LATHAM, Barbara (Mrs Howard Cook). Born Walpole, Mass 1896, living Ranchos de Taos, NM 1976. Painter, illustrator, author, graphic artist. Work in MMA, MNM, Philadelphia Mus, Dallas MFA. References A76-MAL. Sources AAT-TAL-TSF-WAA-W64. No current auction record. Wood engraving example p 294 AAT.

Miss Latham studied at the Norwich (Conn) AS, at Pratt Institute in Brooklyn, and at the ASL in Woodstock. She came to Taos in 1925. Her Taos paintings are landscapes of the Talpa Valley, "delicate and exquisite in color and directly joyous." She "treated the everyday occupations of her neighbors in a pleasant, realistic manner, with special attention to the seasonable pastoral pattern of life." After WWII her "style of painting combines surrealism and meticulously rendered still-life arrangements." TSF. Her reputation at the time was based on her illustrations for Christmas cards and juvenile books such as "I Like Caterpillars."

LATIMER, Lorenzo Palmer. Born Gold Hill, Placer Cnty, Cal 1857, died probably Berkeley, Cal 1941 (MAS lists Latimer as living 1948). Nev and Cal watercolorist, teacher. Reference MAS. Source BDW. No auction record or signature example.

Son of California pioneers, Latimer was educated at an Oakland military academy. He studied at the San Francisco School of Design, then painted watercolors in Nevada where he was teaching in 1921. Latimer also taught in California at Mark Hopkins AI and the U of California at Berkeley.

LATOIX, Gaspard. Active late 19th century, specializing in traditional action paintings of Indians. Work in ANS. No reference. Source ANT 10/67 illustrating four watercolors of Indians, two on horseback in winter and two preparing to ambush a wagon train. Oil 14×18″ *Indian Pueblo* is said to have sold in 1968 for $2,600 at auction. An oil 26×20″ *Navajo on a Horse* signed but not dated sold 9/24/70 for $325 at auction. Painting examples pp 414–15 ANT 10/67.

LAUDERDALE, Ursula. Born Moberly, Mo about 1880, living Dallas, Tex 1933. Texas painter, teacher. Work in City Temple (Dallas). References A33-BEN-MAL. Sources TOB-TXF. No current auction record or signature example.

Mrs Lauderdale was educated at St Mary's Academy, Goetz Conservatory of Music in Moberly, and the Sargent School of Dramatic Art in NYC. She studied at the ASL and was the pupil of Michael Jacobs, William DeVol, Maurice Braun, and Robert Henri. The summer of 1926 was spent in New Mexico near the Penitentes sect, in Santa Fe where she sketched in pastel, and in Taos, exhibiting *Indian Wild Flowers*. Mrs

Lauderdale was dean of the Southwestern Chautauqua and art director of Trinity U in Waxahachie.

LAURITZ, Paul. Born Larvik, Norway 1889, living Los Angeles, Cal 1976. Cal landscape and desert painter. Member RSA. Work in Vanderpoel colln, U Chicago, San Diego FAG, Joslyn MA (Omaha), LA City Col, etc. References A76-MAL. Sources DIG 11/44-SCA. No auction record. Painting example p 15 *The Art Digest* 11/1/44.

Self-taught, Lauritz was winning California awards by 1920. After beginning as a painter of marines and snow scenes, he changed about 1940 to panoramic landscapes of California valleys and of the desert, becoming "one of Southern California's favorite landscape artists." DIG.

LAVENDER, Eugénie Aubanel (Mrs Charles Lavender). Born Bordeaux, France 1817, died Houston, Tex 1898. Painter of religious subjects and Texas landscapes. Work in Incarnate Word Acad and St Patrick's Cathedral (Corpus Christi). References G&W-MAS. Sources BAR-TEP-TOB-WAA. No current auction record. Portrait example p 96 TEP.

Daughter of French nobility, Mrs Lavender studied at the École des Beaux-Arts in Paris, the pupil of Paul Delaroche and Ary Scheffer. She won an award by 1838 and married a science professor in 1846. Attracted to Texas, they emigrated with their two children in 1852. From New Orleans they outfitted two prairie schooners, sketching and hunting en route to Dallas. They lost one wagon in a flood, were captured by Indians, fought against prairie fires, and experienced the birth of a third child while alone on the plains.

When they settled in Waco, they were the seventh family. Mrs Lavender painted local landscapes, making her own colors from vegetables and clay. After a year they moved to Corpus Christi where her religious paintings are found. She also painted portraits of Texas pioneers and French historical scenes.

LAWRENCE, Sydney M (Laurence, Lawarence). Born Brooklyn, NY 1865 (or 1860), living Anchorage, Alaska 1931, died 1940. Painter of Indians, Alaskan landscapes. References A31-BEN-MAL. Sources ANT 11/73-ARC-JNB. No current auction record but the estimated price of an oil 20×30″ showing Indians on the plains would be about $2,000 to $3,000 at auction in 1976. Signature ✳27 JNB.

The surname is shown as "Laurence" in some references and as "Lawarence" in ANT illustration. BEN ascribes him to the English School, crediting him with an honorable mention in 1894 at the Salon des Artistes Français. ARC illustrates *The Top of the Continent* as "nearly six feet high and eight feet wide." A similarly described painting was said to have been sold for $40,000.

LAWSON, Ernest. Born Halifax, Nova Scotia, Can (not San Francisco, Cal) 1873, died Miami Beach, Fla 1939. Eastern Impressionist landscape painter in Colorado Springs, Colo 1927–28, teacher. ANA 1908, NA 1917, member The Eight 1908. Work in NGA, Montclair AM, MMA, MNM, BM, City AM (St Louis), COR, Columbus Gall FA (Ohio), etc. References A41 (obit)-BEN - DABS - FIE - MAL - SMI. Sources AAR 1/74-AIC-ALA-ANT 4/56,10/59, 4/60,11/61,10/62,11/64; 7,9/65; 3,4,6/66; 4,6,12/67; 2,3,10,11/69; 9/72; 3,4,

11,12/73; 11,12/74; 3/75 - ARI - ARM-CAA-CAN-CAR-COR-DEP-IMP-190-ISH-M31-NA 74-SHO-WHO 38. Oil *Colorado Landscape* sold 10/22/69 for $5,500 at auction. Oil 25×30″ on canvas *Green and Gold* signed but not dated was estimated for sale 5/23/74 at $10,000 to $12,000 at auction, and sold that day for $15,000. Signature example p 947 ANT 12/73 *Geneses*.

Son of a doctor, Lawson was raised in Ontario, Can. He joined his parents in Kansas City, Mo in 1888, studying stippling cloth at the Kansas City AI. In 1889 he accompanied his father to Mexico City where he worked as a draftsman and attended Santa Clara Art Academy. In 1891 he studied at the ASL and with the Impressionists Twachtman and Weir at Cos Cob, Conn. From 1893 to 1895 Lawson was in Paris, beginning at the Julien Academy with Laurens and Constant but proceeding on his own. He settled in Washington Heights in 1898, then a rural section of NYC, developing a personal style that remained relatively constant, without obvious periods. His emphasis was on jeweled colors, applied with palette knife, brush, and even his thumbs, in a thick but smooth impasto. While he exhibited as a member of the socially concerned "Eight," he painted cheer and beauty.

Lawson was in France 1903–4, NYC 1906, Spain 1916, NYC 1920, LI 1923, Nova Scotia 1924, and Kansas City 1926. He taught at Broadmoor Academy in Colorado Springs in 1927, painting mountain landscapes and dead mining towns, and exhibiting there in 1928. Although Lawson was a successful and collected painter, both his health and his finances were poor late in his life. When his body was found off Miami Beach, the verdict was suicide.

LAWSON, Robert. Born NYC 1892, died Westport, Conn 1957. Book illustrator including Indian subjects, etcher, writer. References A59 (obit)-MAL. Source WHO 56. No auction record but the estimated price of Lawson etchings is about $60 to $80 at auction in 1976. No signature example.

Lawson was educated at Montclair, NJ high school 1907–11. He studied at the NY School of Fine and Applied Art 1911–13 and was the pupil of Howard Giles, R Sloan Bredin. Beginning 1914 Lawson worked as a book illustrator, including "Seven Beads of Wampum" for Putnam. His list of titles was lengthy, encompassing the major publishers. He was also an etcher after 1929, winning an award from the Society of American Etchers in 1931 as well as awards from the American Library Association. In WWI he had served in the camouflage section of the Army.

LEA, Tom. Born El Paso, Tex 1907, living there 1976. Modern Texas painter, illustrator, writer. Work in Dallas MFA, El Paso MA, MNM, St Capitol (Austin), Pentagon; murals in public buildings. References A76-MAS. Sources AHI 3/72-COW-CRS-T20-WHO 70. No current auction record. Signature pl 20 CRS. (See illustration 174.)

Lea was educated in El Paso public schools. He attended the AIC 1924–26, working in Chicago 1926–33 as a mural painter, commercial artist, teacher, and studio assistant to John Norton. In 1930 he studied in Italy. From 1933 to 1935 he was on the staff of the Laboratory of Anthropology in Santa Fe, NM. He returned to El Paso in 1936, painting murals in Texas and in Washington. Commissions for Western illustrations were received from *The Saturday Evening Post* and *Life*. During WWII, Lea was a correspondent for *Life* in Europe and in the Pacific.

In 1945 *Life* commissioned a picture story on beef cattle. Lea followed this

with his first novel "The Brave Bulls" in 1949 and then "The Wonderful Country" in 1952. His two-volume history "The King Ranch" was published in 1957.

LEAMING, Charlotte. Born Chicago, Ill 1878, living Colo Springs, Colo 1941. Colo animal and landscape painter, book illustrator, teacher. References A41-MAL. Source SPR. No auction record or signature example.

Miss Leaming graduated from the AIC, the pupil of Frederick Freer, of William Chase and Albert Herter in NYC, and of Frank Duveneck in Cincinnati. She established her studio in Chicago where she was publicized as a woman animal painter. She used models in the Chicago Stock Yards as well as buffaloes, lions, and a ram. She worked as art teacher at the AIC from 1899 to 1905, in Oak Park (Ill) schools 1905–6, and Chicago AFA 1909–10.

With her sister Susan she settled in Colorado Springs in 1911, teaching at the Colorado Springs AFA and associated with Colorado College. A listed painting in 1916 was *Pike's Peak from the Denver Highway*.

LEARNED, Harry. Active 1874–96. Pioneer Colorado landscape painter. Work in DAM, HAR, ACM, St Hist Soc Colo. No reference. Sources DAA-DCC-DPL-FRO. No auction record but the estimated price of an oil 20×30″ showing a Summit mine would be about $1,200 to $1,500 at auction in 1976. Signature p 54 DAA. (See illustration 175.)

Learned was an itinerant scenic painter who settled in Denver in 1874. In 1881 he was in Denver painting scenery and the drop curtain at the Greeley Opera House. In 1893 he was a charter member of the Art Club of Denver along with Harvey Young and Charles Partridge Adams. He was "active in Colorado as late as 1896, primarily in the Summit County area, where, supposedly, he had relatives who owned a mine." DAA. His painting *Iron Mask Mine* in DAM indicates a continuing interest in the 19th-century depiction of Colorado mines, providing a scarce and important historical documentation. Learned may be compared to the pioneer Utah painters who also decorated scenery for the theater.

LEE, Charlie. Born near Four Corners area, Ariz 1926, living Shiprock, NM 1967. Navaho painter, illustrator, silversmith. Work in GIL, MAI, MNM, Philbrook AC, Smithsonian Inst. No reference. Sources AHI 2/50-AIP. No auction record or signature example.

Lee's Navaho name is Hushka Yelhayah, the Warrior Who Came Out. As a child he lived on the reservation, herding sheep and tending horses. He studied art and music at Santa Fe, graduating 1946. His outstanding paintings involve horses. Lee painted side by side with Harrison Begay, demonstrating the same air of delicacy and calm.

While soloist for a Santa Fe choir, he was influenced to attend Central Bible Institute in Springfield, Mo. He became active as a Christian minister on the Navaho reservation.

LEE, Joseph. Born probably Oxfordshire, Eng 1828, died San Francisco, Cal 1880. San Francisco marine and landscape painter, ornamental painter. Work in Oakland AM, M H De Young Mem Mus, LA Cnty MNH, Cal Hist Soc, SF Maritime Mus. No reference. Sources ANT 6/69 (article),5/73-HON. No current auction record but the es-

timated price of a Western landscape would be about $1,500 to $2,000 at auction in 1976. Signature example p 869 ANT 5/73.

Said to have been an English remittance man, Lee appeared in San Francisco in 1858 as a prize-winning sign and ornamental painter. His identified paintings numbered about 60 as of 1969, with 15 landscapes, 12 seascapes and 45 ship portraits. The paintings date from about 1867. Renderings are realistic, with extreme detailing. Lee understood the interest created by figures in paintings, populating all with little people in action and accurate to the cut of the clothes. In the landscapes the animals are fine. In the marines the ships are headed left, at speed, with every line and pulley. Lee died of "gangrine of the lungs." ANT 6/69.

LEE, Robert M. Born Alamogordo, NM 1933, living New Mexico 1973. Traditional Western painter. No reference. Sources COW-OSR. No auction record. Signature p 31 OSR.

Bob Lee is third-generation New Mexican, raised with horses, cattle, and cowboys. His grandfather, uncle, and he were all state senators. His family have been ranchers, cattlemen, and horse breeders. Lee has served on the NM State Racing Commission and the NM Cattle Growers Association.

"In ranch work, Lee is exposed to a wealth of subject matter for his art; his pictures are of scenes, and of characters, and incidents he knows about." OSR.

LEFRANC, Margaret (Mrs Margaret Schoonover). Born NYC 1907, living Miami, Fla 1962. Painter and illustrator of the Southwest, graphics artist, teacher. Work in *Southwest Review* and books on

Southwestern Indians. References A62-MAS. Source WAA. No current auction record or signature example.

Miss Lefranc was educated at NYU and studied in Paris with Schoukaieff, Bourdelle, and Lhote. She illustrated "Maria, the Potter of San Ildefonso" and "Indians on Horseback" in 1948, "Indians of the Four Corners" in 1952.

LEFTOWICH, Bill. Traditional Western painter active in Pecos, Tex, living Lubbock, Tex 1971. No reference. Source COW. No auction record or signature example.

Leftowich was director of publicity at Lubbock Christian College in 1971.

LEGGETT, Mrs Lucille. Born Tennessee 1896, living Santa Fe, NM 1952. New Mexico painter of Western buildings, ghost towns, and the desert. Work in MNM. No reference. Source BDW. No auction record or signature example.

Mrs Leggett moved to New Mexico in 1914. She studied in El Paso, Tex and painted in Capitan, Carrizozo, Ruidoso, and Santa Fe, NM. Favorite subjects were buildings such as ranches, adobes, and village churches.

LEHNERT, F (perhaps Pierre Frédéric Lehnert). Active in Mexico about 1840. Reference BEN (as PF Lehnert). Source GIL. No auction record but the estimated price of an oil 20×30″ showing a mule train would be about $2,500 to $3,000 at auction in 1976. Signature p 135 GIL.

Two colored lithographs published in Mexico about 1840 depict the genre of ranch life in Mexico. The first is *Ar-rieros,* Mexican muleteers, loading the animal. The second is *Hacendado Y Su Mayordomo,* the landowner with his lady and manager all in formal riding gear.

The reference BEN lists Pierre Frédéric Lehnert, a French animal painter who was also a lithographic artist. A student of Bouton, he exhibited in the Paris Salon around 1840.

LEIGH, William Robinson. Born Berkeley Cnty, WVA 1866, died NYC 1955. Important traditional Western painter, illustrator, sculptor, writer. NA 1955. Work in GIL, ANS, HAR, Dublin Mus, AMNH, Frank Phillips Mus (Bartlesville, Okla). References A53-BEN-FIE-SMI. Sources ACO-AHI 7/56,11/62-AIW-ANT 6/48,6/68,7/71,2/72,10/72,3/75-BAW-COW-CUS-EIT-GIL-GWP-HAR-HMA-JNB-MSL-PAW-POW-WAI 71,72-WHO 54. Oil 22½×28¼″ *The Pool at Oraibi* signed W R Leigh and dated NY 1917 sold 4/11/73 for $23,000 at auction. In 1945 *Rustling* sold for $410 at auction in NY. Signature p 21 GWP. (See illustration 176.)

Son of impoverished Southern aristocrats, W R Leigh was educated privately. He studied art under Hugh Newell at Maryland Institute in Baltimore from 1880 to 1883. He then went to the Raupp-Royal Academy in Munich 1883–84, the pupil of Gysis 1885–86, of Löfftz 1887, and of Lindenschmid 1891–92. He painted six cycloramas (murals in the round) during 1891–96. Leigh returned to NYC in 1896, after 13 years in Europe, becoming an illustrator for *Scribner's* and *Collier's* and painting portraits, landscapes, and compositions with figures and animals. He was not successful despite his courtly manner, this "big man with big mustaches and a goatee." COW.

In 1906 Leigh persuaded the Santa Fe Railroad to give him free transportation for his first trip West, in exchange for a painting. Five more paintings were commissioned, permitting Leigh to make an elaborate sketching trip through Arizona and New Mexico. His critics who had not seen the West said that the resulting paintings were of "purple horses with yellow bellies," a "ridiculously false color," and only illustrations. It was not until the 1940s that Leigh's Western work was completely accepted. In that period of 40 years, he had depicted "every facet of the West, from wild horses to Navahos and from wolf hunts to burro trains." COW. He also painted African wild animals, participating in 1926 and 1928 expeditions for the AMNH. After his death the contents of his studio were given to GIL, which exhibited 534 oils, 344 charcoals, and many sketches in a special gallery.

LEIGHTON, Alfred Crocker. Born Hastings, Eng 1901, died Calgary, Can 1965. Watercolor painter of the Canadian West, illustrator, teacher, art director. Member Royal Soc Brit Artists 1929, ARCA. Work in Vancouver AG, Edmonton Mus, AA Montreal, and museums in Hastings, Brighton, Hull, Glasgow. References A66 (obit)-MAS. Sources CAH-CAN-DCA. No current auction record. Signature example "A Portfolio of Paintings by A C Leighton." (See illustration 177.)

Established as a London, Eng painter 1920–27, Leighton visited Canada in 1925. During his second visit in 1928, the Canadian Pacific Ry commissioned a series of paintings of the prairies and the Rockies. The paintings were done out of doors and they sold. By 1930 he was teaching at Calgary Inst of Tech. His paintings were exhibited and publicized. In 1936, 100 watercolors were exhibited in Montreal. Leighton worked in oil and pastel as well as watercolor. His commissions included paintings for English railways and Vickers in London. He was an illustrator of books, a contributor to magazines, a lecturer on art appreciation, the art director of Alberta, and the founder of the Banff SA.

LEIGHTON, Mrs Kathryn Woodman. Born Plainfield, NH 1876, died probably Los Angeles, Cal 1952. Portrait painter of Amer Indians, especially Montana Blackfeet. Work in GIL. References A53-MAL. Sources BDW-WHO 46. No auction record or signature example.

Mrs Leighton graduated from Kimball Union Academy (Meriden, NH) in 1895 and from Massachusetts Normal Art School. She married Edward Everett Leighton of Los Angeles in 1900. Influenced by Charles Russell, she spent summers on the Reservation painting Blackfeet portraits, many of which bear the sitter's mark. Mrs Leighton also painted the Sioux, Cherokee, Western landscapes, and flowers.

LEITCH, Richard P. English painter and illustrator, active in London in the middle of the 19th century. Watercolors in Albert and Victoria Mus (London). Reference BEN. Sources GOD-PAF. No auction record. Signature example p 89 GOD.

Source GOD reproduces sketches by R P Leitch, J Cooper, and T W Wilson from "The North West Passage by Land" by Milton and Cheadle who sailed from Liverpool in 1862. They traveled by train and boat to St Paul, then as explorers went north into Manitoba and west across the Canadian Rockies to British Columbia. Leitch did not accompany the authors but evidently sketched from photographs and other materials available in London. Leitch's exhibits at PAFA were European watercolors from a London address in 1858.

LE MOYNE (Lemoine), Jacques de Morgues. Born Dieppe, France before 1540, died London, Eng 1588. French watercolorist in Florida 1564. Work reproduced in De Bry's "Voyages." References BEN-G&W-MAL. Sources ALA-ANT 7/58-ISH-POW. No current auction record or signature example.

Le Moyne went to Florida as a colonist with Laudonnière in 1564. When the Spanish admiral Menéndez had the settlers slaughtered in 1565, Le Moyne escaped to a French ship. Brought to England, he married, wrote a journal concerning his experiences, and painted about 40 watercolors from memory as illustrations. Le Moyne could not find a publisher for his pictures of America and became a watercolorist of English still lifes and animals. After his death, however, his widow arranged with the German Theodore de Bry for 43 engravings, released in 1591 along with the journal. The reproductions represent the beginning of the European tradition of the decorative Indian, with the "elegance of a royal masque of the period." ANT. "Even the portrait of King Saturiona except for his attire and tattooing shows no racial characteristic." BAR. "Only one of Le Moyne's original paintings is known to exist, in gouache on vellum, measuring 7×10⅛"." POW.

LENDERS, Emil W. Born Germany date unknown, died Oklahoma City, Okla 1934. Wildlife painter, particularly the buffalo. References A36 (obit)-MAS. No source, auction record, or signature example.

LENT, Frank T. Active 1880s in Colo Springs, Colo as landscape painter, architect. No reference. Sources NJA-SPR. No auction record or signature example.

Lent studied with Bruce Crane. He lived in New Brunswick, NJ where he painted marine views. In Colorado Springs he gave up the design of residences for landscape paintings such as *Plains from the Mountains near Glen Eyrie* and *Stormy Day at Glen Ayries Crags*.

LEUTZE, Emanuel Gottlieb. Born Gmund, Wüttemberg, Germany 1816, died Washington, DC 1868. Very important historical and portrait painter. NA 1860. Work in COR, DPL, Smithsonian Inst, MMA; murals in the Capitol. References BEN-CHA-DAB-ENB-FIE-G&W-MAL-SMI. Sources AAR 9/73,11/74-AIW-ALA-AMA-ANT 2/40,9/70,11/73,11/74,2/75-BAR-BOA-COR-DBW-DUS-GIL-HUT-ISH-M19-POW-STI-WES-WHI. Oil 37½×50" *Cromwell and Milton* 1855 sold 6/20/73 for $5,180 at auction in Düsseldorf. This is not relevant to the price of a Western painting. Eastman Johnson's replica of *Washington Crossing the Delaware* signed by Leutze sold 10/25/73 for $260,000 at auction. Signature example p 242 GIL.

Leutze was the son of a mechanic who emigrated for political reasons to Virginia and then to Philadelphia. Leutze studied drawing with John A Smith in Philadelphia, beginning to paint portraits about 1837. By 1840 he was successful enough to become the pupil of Lessing in Düsseldorf. By 1842 he had learned the fashionable style of painting historical scenes in a huge and realistic format. When his first attempt was bought by the Düsseldorf Art Union, he maintained his studio there for almost 20 years. In 1848 he began his most famous work *Washington Crossing the Delaware,* 12'5"× 21'3". He used American visitors as models. Whittredge posed as Washington: "Clad in full uniform, I was nearly dead. They poured champagne down my throat and I lived through it." M19. The studies for the ice on the river were made at the Rhine. The painting was intended to encourage German radicals after their failure in the Revolution of 1848.

In 1859 Leutze returned to the US to paint *Westward the Course of Empire Takes Its Way* as a mural in the Capitol's House of Representatives. Completed in 1862, it was based on a sketching trip to the Rockies and involved a return to Germany for advice on mural techniques. The critical view was that his combination of history and allegory produced confusion increased by the realism of the treatment. This was the climax of the Düsseldorf era in American art.

LEWIS, Edmonia. Born Greenbush opposite Albany, NY 1843 (or 1845), living Rome, Italy 1898. Black American neoclassic sculptress. Work in Phila Centennial Exhibition (1876). References BEN - FIE - MAL - SMI. Sources ALA - ANT 11/72-BOA-HUT-MSL-WAA. No current auction record or signature example.

Edmonia Lewis, of Negro and Indian descent, was comparatively untaught in sculpture. Her first exhibition at the Soldier's Relief Fair in Boston in 1865 was "an inspiration to have emanated from the unpracticed hands of a dusky maiden." BOA. After showing the statue *The Freedwoman* in 1867, she settled permanently in Rome. There, "in her coarse but appropriate attire, with her black hair loose, and grasping in her tiny hand the chisel, and with her large, black, sympathetic eyes brimful, Miss Lewis is unquestionably the most interesting representative of our country in Europe." BOA. In the Centennial rotunda, the neoclassic marbles called the "swarm from the Carrara hive" included *Dying Cleopatra* by Miss Lewis. ALA.

An 1871 review referred to her sculpture groups that illustrated Longfellow's *Hiawatha.* One "represents Minnehaha seated, making a pair of moccasins, and Hiawatha by her side with a world of love and longing in his eyes. No happier illustrations of the poem were ever made." Another view called "her works those of a girl. By and by, she will leave the prettinesses of poems, and give us Red Jacket, and, it may be, Black Hawk and Osceola." BOA.

LEWIS, Henry. Born Newport (or Scarborough), Eng 1819, died Düsseldorf, Germany 1904. Important panoramist of the Mississippi, landscape painter. Work in City AM (St Louis), Minneapolis IA, Missouri Hist Soc, ACM, Minnesota Hist Soc. References A05 (obit)-BEN-G&W-MAL-SMI. Sources ALA-ANT 7/43, 12/49,4/52,2/56,4/69-BAR-MIS-PAF-POW - TEP - WES - WIM. Oil 28×40" *Moonlit Landscape near Düsseldorf* sold 4/26/68 for $200 at auction in London. This is not relevant to the price of a Western painting. Signature example p 332 ANT 4/52.

Lewis was brought to Boston at 10 and apprenticed to a carpenter. He settled in St Louis at 17, working as a stage carpenter and scenery painter. At 25 he was a serious landscape painter, sharing a St Louis studio with the portraitist James F Wilkins. In 1845 the St Louis newspapers reviewed his landscapes as of more than ordinary merit. In 1846 he submitted to the American Art-Union a view of St Louis from the Illinois shore. In 1847 he traveled up the Mississippi to the Falls of St Anthony, producing a large number of paintings "of the wildest American scenery, the Indian's hut and the white man's cabin in a pale blue atmosphere peculiar only to these high northern latitudes." ANT. During this trip Lewis envisioned his river panorama to compete with Banvard's 425-yard "newsreel."

In 1848 Lewis went back up the river, filling more 5⅛ ×3¾" notebooks with sketches for "a gigantic and continuous painting of the Mississippi River from the Falls of St Anthony to where it empties into the Gulf of Mexico." ANT. In Cincinnati, Lewis with four other artists painted his panorama four yards high and 1,325 yards long. He began his exhibition tour in Cincinnati in 1849, ending in Europe in 1851. The panorama was then sold to a planter from Java. Lewis remained in Europe.

In 1853 he published in Düsseldorf "Das Illustrierte Mississippithal" with 78 scenes that are "the most extensive set of lithographic views of the Mississippi Valley published during the 19th century." ANT. Lewis served as American consular agent. He also continued to paint landscapes and still lifes as well as American views he sent back for sale in the river towns.

LEWIS, James Otto. Born Philadelphia, Pa 1799, died NYC 1858. Important painter of Indian portraits, stipple-engraver. Work in ACM, GIL. References BEN-FIE-G&W-MAS-SMI. Sources ALA-ANT 5/47,1/49,10/66-GIL-POW. No current auction record but the estimated price of an oil 30×25″ portrait of a Fox chief would be about $13,000 to $15,000 at auction in 1976. Lithograph after Lewis p 40 GIL.

Lewis began engraving in Philadelphia when he was about 16. In 1819 he went West as a touring actor. After quitting the troupe in St Louis to work as an engraver 1820–21, he watched Chester Harding paint Indian portraits. From 1823 to 1834 Lewis was resident in Detroit. He painted the *Shawnee Prophet* portrait for Gov Lewis Cass, through whom Lewis was commissioned by the US Indian Department "to attend the different Indian Councils, for the purpose of taking portraits of the distinguished chiefs." He began with the treaty meeting at Prairie du Chien (now Wis) in 1825

where he sketched about 50 of the chiefs. The portraits included the Fox chief Cut-Taa-Tas-Tia who "appeared in Council in his war dress, wearing a sword, from the hilt of which hung five human scalps, the terrible trophies of his success and valor in battle." Of another, Lewis wrote, "In very early life he visited the carousels of slaughter and delighted to bathe his tomahawk and scalping knife in the blood of his victims. His mercies were those of the grave."

Through 1827 Lewis worked as an engraver and copperplate printer while attending Indian councils at Fond du Lac, Butte des Morts, Fort Wayne, and elsewhere in Wisconsin and Indiana. Thereafter he held himself out as a miniature, portrait, and landscape painter while continuing to work on his Indian portraits. He produced a unique document, excusing himself to his critics with "the great and constantly recurring disadvantages to which the artist is necessarily subject while travelling through a wilderness." The quotes are from Lewis' "The Aboriginal Port-Folio" published in 1835 in Philadelphia with 80 lithographed Indian portraits, issued in installments at a cost of $2 each. The original edition is the first published collection, the rarest work on Western Indians, although overshadowed by Catlin and C B King. Lewis died in obscurity in NYC, his paintings termed "little more than stilted." POW. No actual painting remains, so that negative judgments were based on the lithographs drawn from the paintings.

LEWIS, Minard. Born Maryland about 1812, living NYC 1860. Panoramist of the "Overland Route," scene painter. Reference G&W. Sources AIW-KW1. No auction record or signature example.

Lewis collaborated with T C Bartholomew in Boston in 1838 to paint a panorama of Boston in the Revolutionary

War. In 1841 he painted a Niagara Falls panorama and model. In 1847–48 he lived in NYC. In 1850 the *New York Tribune* advertised a 40,000-foot canvas by Lewis based on an 1849 trip Lewis made from St Joseph, Mo to California, the "Overland Route to the Pacific." This was one of the gold rush panoramas intended for exhibition in the East and in Europe. A rare "authentic pictorial record" of the route, it has since been lost. AIW.

Lewis exhibited paintings at the American Art-Union in 1851 and 1852. By 1857 he was again in Boston, "collaborating with several other artists on scenes from a stage version" of Dr King's pioneering expeditions toward the North Pole.

LEWIS, Thomas L (distinguish Thomas Lewis in MAS). Born Bay City, Tex 1907, living Taos, NM 1974. Taos painter, etcher, gallery owner. Work in GIL, Swope Mus (Terre Haute), U of Ariz AM, Witte Mus (San Antonio). No reference. Sources COW-HAR. No current auction record. Signature example p 125 HAR.

At 19 Lewis was painting Southern landscapes and Negro subjects. By the time he was 24 he was painting the Western deserts in sepia tones. After service in WWII, Lewis opened the Taos Art Gallery where he represents other artists, like William Moyers and John D Free. His own postwar painting was influenced by sketching with Bert Phillips.

LILLYWHITE, Raphael. Born Woodruff, Ariz 1891, died Evanston, Wyom 1958. Traditional Western painter, teacher. Work in Colo MNH (Denver), HAR. No reference. Sources COW-HAR-WYA. No current auction record.

Signature example p 127 HAR *Return of the Stray*.

Raised as one of 15 children of a Mormon who operated an Arizona trading post, Lillywhite was educated in Mormon schools and graduated from the U of Utah. He also studied art with Gonzáles and Ed Tigera in Sonora, Mexico. After he married in 1924, he settled near Walden, Colo where he painted scenes of ranch life and of the Old West. From 1940 to 1942 he painted 13 habitat backgrounds of bird and mammal groups at the Colo MNH in Denver. Two that are noted in HAR are *Alaska Tundra* and *Bering Strait*. In 1943 he moved to Laramie, Wyom where his wife died. Lillywhite remarried in 1946.

LINDEBERG, Carl. German painter before 1953. Work in Karl May Mus, Dresden. No reference. Sources CUS-MWS W/74. No current auction record but the estimated price of a Western with Indians would be about $1,500 to $1,700 at auction in 1976. No signature example.

The Lindeberg painting *Gall's Warriors Gathering for the Final Rush* is a variant of the Custer battle. MWS points out that the cluster of figures in the background of the Lindeberg painting is a copy of a C M Russell watercolor, *The Custer Fight,* that was reproduced in color both in *Scribner's* in 1905 and as a print. The remaining three foreground figures of mounted Indians are copied from the Remington oil *The Pony War Dance.*

LINDNEUX, Robert Ottokar. Born NYC 1871, died Denver, Colo 1970. Western genre and portrait painter. Member RSA. Work in ACM, Buffalo Bill Memorial Mus, Colorado St Hist Mus, GIL, Northwestern U, U of Okla,

Frank Phillips Mus. References A62-FIE. Sources COW-GIL-HAR-WHO 54. Oil *On the Chisholm Trail* 30×42¼" signed and dated 1939 sold 3/4/74 for $2,000 at auction in Los Angeles. Signature example p 60 COW.

An orphan, Lindneux was educated privately by an aunt. He studied art abroad as a pupil of Vautier at Düsseldorf Academy, Mokacsy at École des Beaux-Arts in Paris, and Franz Stuck Academy in Munich. In Paris in 1892, Lindneux saw Buffalo Bill perform with his Wild West Show, then met Rosa Bonheur who had just completed a full-length portrait of Buffalo Bill. When Lindneux returned to the US in 1893 en route to the West, he painted portraits in Boston for a year to finance his journey.

From 1894–97 he painted around Denver, then worked farther West into Montana where in 1899 he joined C R Russell in his Great Falls studio. In 1909 he established his own studio in Denver. He called himself "the historian of the West," was considered eccentric, and lectured on Indians. He exhibited widely around the US and London, Paris, Berlin, Vienna, Munich, Budapest. Lindneux's subjects included Indian portraits, *Fort Lyons 1863, Hay-o-wei-Buffalo Bill Duel,* and Wild Bill Hickok's portrait. On top of Lookout Mountain at Buffalo Bill's grave there is a huge portrait of Buffalo Bill by his friend Lindneux, "one of the most flamboyant of American painters."

LINDSAY, Andrew Jackson. Born probably in the South about 1820, died place unknown 1895. Military topographical artist who traveled overland to Oregon in 1849. Reference G&W. No source, auction record, or signature example.

As a cadet from the South, Lindsay was educated at West Point 1839–41. Resigning to join the Army in 1841, he was appointed First Lieutenant in the Mounted Rifle Regiment in 1846. Participating in the 1849 expedition of the Regiment from Ft Leavenworth to Oregon, Lt Lindsay was credited with a series of sketches illustrating the trip. The Civil War in 1861 ended his service in the West. He joined the Confederate Army.

LINDSAY, T C. Active in Cincinnati beginning 1860 as landscape painter. Work in Cin AM. Reference G&W. Source ANT 12/72 with painting example p 1093 watercolor 20×32" of mounted Indians. No auction record.

LION, Henry. Born Fresno, Cal 1900, died Los Angeles, Cal 1966. Traditional Western sculptor, painter, writer. Sculpture in GIL, Earl C Adams colln, figures and fountains (Los Angeles City Hall), Ebell Club (LA), Fed Bldg (LA). References A62-MAL. Sources ANT 5/65-GIL-TWR. No current auction record. Sculpture example p 549 ANT 5/65.

Lion studied at Otis AI and was the pupil of S MacDonald-Wright. He became a teacher at the Hollywood Art Center and wrote "Sculpture for Beginners." He sculpted a 30" figure of C M Russell, then used a Russell sketch to do a 35" sculpture of *Lewis and Clark with Sacajawea,* cast by Roman Bronze Works. A prolific sculptor, Lion is represented in Los Angeles with the *Pioneer Fountain,* a figure, bronze doors, and bas-relief eagles.

LITHGOW, David Cunningham. Born Glasgow, Scotland 1868, living Albany, NY 1935. Painter of landscapes and portraits. Work in Albany Mus. References BEN-MAL. No current auction record but the estimated value of an oil 30×20″ showing an Indian moonlight tryst would be about $400 to $500 at auction in 1976. No signature example.

Lithgow emigrated to NYC in 1888, then moved to Albany. At least two Indian subjects exist.

LOCHRIE, Elizabeth Davey. Born Deer Lodge, Mont 1890, living Butte, Mont 1976. Montana painter specializing in Indian portraits, sculptor. Work in Butte schools; murals in hospital and post offices; bronze portrait panels. References A76-MAS. Sources MON-WAA-WNW-W64. No current auction record. Signature example p 91 MON.

Raised in an early Montana settlement with "braid" Indian neighbors, Mrs Lochrie was educated in the Butte high school. She studied art education at Pratt Institute in Brooklyn until 1911, then married in Deer Lodge. In 1924–25 she painted 18 children's murals for the state hospital.

After 1931 when Mrs Lochrie was adopted a Blackfoot as Net-chi-take, Lone Woman, she specialized in Indian portraits. A realist, she feels that the subject's face is the key to the personality that must be shown. From 1937 to 1939 Mrs Lochrie painted historical murals in post offices in Idaho and Montana. She studied the summers of 1943–44 at Glacier National Park with Winold Reiss, the Indian painter. As a lecturer, she talked on Indian portraiture.

LOCKWOOD, John Ward. Born Atchison, Kan 1894, died Taos, NM 1963. Contemporary Taos painter, illustrator, printmaker, teacher. Work in WMAA, MNM, ANS, U of Kan (colln), DAM, Dallas AM, PAFA, Phillips Mem Gall (Washington). References A66 (obit)-MAL. Sources AAR 3/74-ALA-MAP-M50-PIT-TAL-TSF-WHO 62-obit Fort Worth Star-Telegram 7/7/63. No current auction record. Signature example p 143 PIT Cisneros Store. (See illustration 178.)

Ward Lockwood studied at the U of Kansas 1912–14, the PAFA 1914–16, and, after service in WWI, in Paris at Académie Ranson. A friend of Kenneth Adams, Lockwood was drawn to Taos in 1926 because it was cheap. He was considered a follower of Dasburg in his simplified landscapes. He also worked with Marin during Marin's visits in 1929 and 1930, and spent the summers of 1932–33 at Colorado Springs FAC with Boardman Robinson.

During the Depression, Lockwood painted government-sponsored murals in New Mexico. With the U of New Mexico 1936–37, he was professor at art at U of Texas 1938–49 and U of California at Berkeley 1949–61. A "regionalist" of New Mexico in the 1930s, his work became increasingly abstract. He received more than 45 one-man shows.

LOEFFLER, Gisella (Mrs Gisella Loeffler Lacher). Born Vienna, Austria (Wertherburg, Austria-Hungary) 1900, living Taos, NM 1947. Painter, decorator, illustrator. Work in Missouri schools, MNM, HAW, Encyclopaedia Britannica colln. References (under Lacher) A41-MAL. Source TAL. No current auction record. Signature example pl 40 TAL.

Mrs Lacher was the pupil of Mary McCall and Hugh Breckenridge. She was listed as resident of Kirkwood, Mo in 1941. In Taos she illustrated juvenile stories of Indians, "funny little painted children and the sunny, reassuring life." TAL.

LOEMANS, Alexander F. Born probably France, date unknown, living Vancouver, Canada, 1894. Landscape, portrait painter, active 1882–94. No reference. Sources ANT 12/74-CAE. No auction record. Signature example ANT 12/74 p 925.

Very little is known about Loemans. It is thought that he was born in France, and that he was in Boston about 1880 and in Canada from 1882 to 1894. He was the stepfather of J R Seavey (see listing), an important Canadian artist and educator.

Loemans worked in oils. He painted scenes of the Rocky Mountains with Indians, the Sierra Nevada Mountains, Canadian landscapes and portraits. The painting shown in ANT is of the Andes.

LOFT, P. New England watercolorist of Mass lumber mill scenes dated 1860 who was a Cal gold miner about 1865. Reference G&W. Source ANT 12/44. No auction record. No signature visible on watercolors in ANT.

His work included *Mining Settlement of Chaparall Hill, Sierra County, California* and *Mining Town of Donnieville, Sierra County, California*. Loft was said to be a "far better painter of pictures than a miner of gold. It is probable that in Massachusetts he was a lumberman." ANT. Compare P Toft, the Danish watercolorist, in his chronology shown in TAW. Toft is a unique omission from G&W.

LONE WOLF. Born on the Blackfoot Reservation, Mont 1882, died probably Tucson, Ariz about 1965. Blackfoot commercial artist, painter, illustrator, sculptor. Work in GIL, HAR, U of Neb A Gall, Santa Fe RR (Chicago). Reference MAL. Sources AIP-COW-HAR-

MWS 10/60-WAI 71-WHO 48 (listed under James Willard Schultz). No current auction record but the estimated price of an oil 20×30″ showing Will Rogers roping would be about $3,000 to $3,500 at auction in 1976. Signature example "Bird Woman" below.

Lone Wolf in Blackfoot is Nitoh Mahkwii. His given name was Hart Merriam Schultz, the son of James Willard Schultz and Fine Shield Woman. His father was the author of many books with Indian subjects, beginning with "My Life as an Indian" in 1907. Lone Wolf was educated in Indian schools. He began painting when he was 11, amusing his fellow cowboys with sketches while he worked as a range rider. It is said that he was taught art by Thomas Moran who did encourage Lone Wolf's career as an artist.

Lone Wolf left the reservation in 1904. He attended Los Angeles ASL in 1910 and studied in Chicago 1914–15. He illustrated his father's books with paintings signed with a line drawing of a wolf's face. His style was in the school of Remington and Russell. The 1918 dedication of James Willard Schultz's "Bird Woman" is to his son Lone Wolf: "Born near the close of the buffalo days he was, and ever since with his baby hands he began to model statuettes of horses and buffalo and deer with clay from the riverbanks, his one object has been the world of art."

LONG, Stanley M. Born Oakland, Cal 1892, died San Carlos, Cal 1972. Traditional Western watercolor painter, illustrator, teacher. Work in Prudential Life Ins, Shasta City Mus. References A73 (obit)-MAS. Sources AHI 3/72-COW-USM. No auction record but the estimated price of a watercolor 16×20″ showing wild mustangs would be about $500 to $600 at auction in 1976. Signature examples USM, p 104 COW.

Raised with horses on a ranch in Napa County, Long studied at the California IFA and at the Mark Hopkins IA in San Francisco from 1901 to 1904. He then attended the Julien Academy in Paris on a scholarship. His paintings are in watercolor "because of the extemporaneous feeling, the airiness, the activity, and the lightness." COW. He specialized in horses and riders participating in Western range life. Long was a high school art teacher and illustrated magazines, newspapers, and books including "The Black Military Experience in the American West."

LOOMIS, Chester. Born near Syracuse, NY 1852, died Englewood, NJ 1924. Eastern painter and illustrator in Texas 1887, muralist. ANA 1906, Nat Soc Mural Ptrs. Work in ANS, Herron AI; murals in Cornell U and Englewood Pub Lib. References A25 (obit)-BEN-FIE-MAL-SMI. Sources ANS-ANT 2/75. No auction record. Signature example p 27 ANS "Chester Loomis/Texas 1887." (See illustration 179.)

Loomis studied with Harry Thompson and in Paris with Bonnat.

LOOMIS, Pascal. Born Hartford, Conn 1826, died San Francisco, Cal 1878. San Francisco landscape and dog painter, wood engraver. Work in Honeyman colln. Reference G&W. Source HON. No auction record or signature example.

Loomis worked as a wood engraver in NYC from 1848 to 1859. His firms were Loomis & Annin (1858–59) and Hewet & Loomis (1859). The San Francisco engraving company was Eastman & Loomis (1860 and after). It is thought that he may have been listed in the 1850 NYC census as Caspar Loomis, married

with one child, and in the 1860 NYC census as Parker Lumas, married with three children.

In addition to his engraving in San Francisco, Loomis exhibited landscapes at the Mechanics Fair of 1876. He was also a dog painter. His landscape drawings in HON are dated 1862–74.

LOPP, Harry Leonard. Born Highmore, SD 1888, living Somers, Mont 1966. Staff artist in Glacier Nat Park 1936–41, 1960. Work in Hodgson Mem and in restoration of Russell colln (Great Falls), Truman and J Edgar Hoover collns. Reference A66. No other source, auction record, or signature example.

Lopp studied at Union College (Lincoln, Neb) with P J Rennings, at U of Washington (Seattle), with Prof Updyke, and with Roland Gissing. He became staff artist in Glacier National Park for Great Northern RR 1936–41 and for Knutson Corp 1960. As a lecturer, he spoke on color psychology.

LORENZ, Richard. Born Voigtstaedt, Weimar, Germany 1858, died Milwaukee, Wis 1915. Important European-trained Western painter, illustrator, teacher. References A15 (obit)-BEN-FIE-MAL-SMI. Sources COW-CUS-HAR-WHO 14. No current auction record but the estimated price of an oil 20×30″ showing an Indian attack would be $3,000 to $4,000 at auction in 1976. Signature example p 39 CUS.

Lorenz began the study of art in Weimar at 15. He was the pupil of Brendel, Thedy, and Hagen from 1874 to 1886, winning the Carl Alexander prize at Weimar in 1884 and exhibiting in Berlin and Munich. Lorenz emigrated to Milwaukee in 1886. He worked with

William Wehner painting panoramas, specializing in horses.

In 1887 Lorenz quit Milwaukee to travel in the West. It is said that he became a Texas ranger during the "lawless" days of the frontier, getting an understanding of cowpunchers and "bad men." Lorenz returned to Milwaukee about 1890, teaching at the new School of Art and painting Western subjects from his sketches. Frank Tenney Johnson as Lorenz's most famous pupil credited him with the influence toward Western subjects. Lorenz visited Montana about 1898. His *Last Glow of a Passing Nation* was Custer's Last Stand from the viewpoint of the Sioux Indians. A Lorenz retrospective was held at the Milwaukee Art Center in 1966. It included 103 works, more than half Western.

LOTAVE, Carl G (not Lotare). Born Jönköping, Sweden 1872, died Colorado Springs, Colo (or NYC) 1924. Colo Springs painter of Indian subjects and portraits, muralist. Work in MNM, Pioneers' Mus (Colo Springs); murals St House NM. References A25 (obit)-BEN-FIE-MAL-SMI. Sources SHO-SPR. No current auction record. Signature example p 33 SHO.

Lotave studied in Stockholm, the pupil of Anders Zorn and Anton-Mathias Bergh, and also in Paris. He emigrated to Kansas in 1897 as painting instructor at Bethany College. He settled in Colorado Springs in 1899 where he exhibited in 1900. "An artist with a meteoric career, flashing across Colorado's sky for a brief period," he painted portraits, did ceiling decorations and murals, and illustrated for *Mountain Sunshine* magazine and *The Gazette*. SPR.

"The high tide of achievement in his temperamental and eccentric career in the West" was the Indian room in Denver with its simulated windows looking upon Indians and wildlife. SPR. He

was also special painter of the Indian for the Smithsonian Institution and creator of the *Cliff Dwelling* and *Pueblo Indian* frescoes in the Archaeological Museum in Santa Fe. His most famous portraits were Marshal Joffre and other WWI celebrities. When Lotave died, a memorial was placed on Pikes Peak where his ashes were strewn.

LOUGHEED, Robert Elmer. Born Massie, Ontario, Can 1910, living Santa Fe, NM 1976. Traditional Western painter, animal painter, illustrator. Member CAA, Nat Acad Western Art. Work in Cowboy Hall of Fame, Montreal AA Gallery. Reference A76. Sources C71 to 74-COW-HAR-OSR-PWA-PER vol 3 ✕3. No auction record. Signature example C74. (See illustration 180.)

Lougheed was raised on a farm in central Canada. At 19 he was a mail-order and newspaper illustrator for the *Toronto Star,* studying at night at the Ontario College of Art and then the École des Beaux-Arts in Montreal. At 25 he came to NYC as the pupil of DuMond and Cornwell, taking off in the fall to tour the West, particularly the old Bell Ranch country of New Mexico. He has continued to work as a commercial artist, having painted Mobil's "Flying Red Horse," as well as calendar scenes. His illustrations appeared for more than 30 years in national magazines such as *National Geographic, Sports Afield,* and *Reader's Digest.* In 1970 he was commissioned by the Post Office Department to design the six-cent buffalo stamp for the Wildlife Conservation Series. Books he has illustrated are "Mustang," with the paintings in the Cowboy Hall of Fame, and "San Domingo." Among his honors are the Western Heritage Award in 1966 and the National Cowboy Hall of Fame's gold medals for painting in 1969 and 1972.

LOVELL, Tom. Born NYC 1909, living Norwalk, Conn 1976. Painter including Western subjects, historical illustrator. Member SI, Nat Acad Western Art. Work in New Britain Mus, US Marine Corps HQ, Nat Cowboy Hall of Fame, US Merchant Marine Acad, Va Mil Inst. References A76-MAS. Sources ILA-IL 59,62,63-PWA-PER vol 3 ⌗3. No current auction record. Signature example p 189 ILA.

Lovell studied at Syracuse U, the pupil of Hibbard Kline. While still in college, he began illustrating for pulp magazines including Westerns. By 1940 he was a leading illustrator with his work appearing in many national magazines. In WWII he was in the Marine Corps Reserve, completing a series of historical paintings for the Marines by 1945. He painted a series of historical works for the *National Geographic* 1965–68, and another series for Abell-Hanger Foundation 1969–73. In 1974 his Western oil *Tumbleweed Serenade* was issued as a print.

LOWELL, Orson Byron. Born Wyoming, Iowa 1871, died New Rochelle, NY 1956. Eastern illustrator of books and magazines, cartoonist, painter, writer. Member SI 1901, Artists Guild. Original drawings in Cincinnati Mus, La Crosse AA (Wis), Maryland Inst (Baltimore), Mechanics' Inst (Rochester), Vanderpoel AA (Chicago), schools. References A59 (obit)-FIE-MAL-SMI. Sources AAC-DIC-WHO 56. No auction record. Signature example p 270 DIC. (See illustration 181.)

Orson Lowell was graduated from Chicago public schools in 1887. He studied at AIC, the pupil of Vanderpoel and Grover, until 1893 when he moved to NYC. He drew illustrations for many periodicals, novels, and texts in addition to designing covers, advertising, and posters. His jobs included cartoonist for *Life*

1907–17, *Judge* 1915–23, a news service 1937–38, and *The Churchman* 1943–46. He was on the staff of *The American Girl* 1935–45.

His drawing techniques are detailed and illustrated pp 270–71 DIC. It is said that he "painted with his pen" through changes in stroke, as compared to the bolder more uniform strokes of his contemporary Charles Dana Gibson. His work included many Western subjects.

LUDEKENS, Fred. Born Hueneme, Cal 1900, living Belvedere, Cal 1976. Military and Western illustrator, painter, advertising exec. Member SI, Art Dir Club. Work in books, magazines. References A76-MAS. Sources COW-ILA-IL 36,42-PIT-POI-WHO 70. No current auction record. Signature example p 190 ILA.

After a childhood in Victoria, BC, he was educated in California public schools. Ludekens was self-taught in art except for brief study with Otis Shepard at the U of California Extension. He began with an outdoor advertising agency, then was an advertising illustrator in San Francisco. From 1939–41 he was an agency art director, then until 1955 was a free-lance illustrator for magazines. He illustrated the book "Ghost Town" and a Western serial for *The Saturday Evening Post*. Ludekens became associate creative director of an advertising agency in 1955 and a co-founder of the Famous Artists School in Westport, Conn.

LUNDBORG, Florence. Born San Francisco, Cal about 1880, died probably NYC 1949. Cal and NYC illustrator, portrait and mural painter. Work (murals) in Pan-Pacif Intern Expos (1915), schools. References A53 (obit)-FIE-MAL-SMI. Sources PPE-WAA-WHO

46. No current auction record or signature example.

Miss Lundborg studied at the Mark Hopkins IA, in Paris, and in Italy. Among the books she illustrated was "Yosemite Legends." Her address in 1915 was San Francisco, in 1923 Paris, and in 1933 NYC.

LUNGKWITZ, Carl Hermann Frederick. Born Halle an der Saale, Germany 1813, died Austin, Tex 1891. Important pioneer Texas landscape painter, lithographic artist, photographer. Work in ACM, San Antonio PL, Witte Mus (San Antonio). References BEN-G&W-MAS. Sources AIW-ANT 6/48-BAR-TEP-TOB-TXF. No current auction record but the estimated price of an oil 20×30″ showing a view of Austin would be about $3,000 to $3,500 at auction in 1976. Signature example pl 41 TEP.

Hermann Lungkwitz, the son of a stocking manufacturer, used a legacy when he was 25 to study at Akademie der Bildenden Künste at Dresden. He became the friend and brother-in-law of 14-year-old Richard Petri. Both were pupils of Ludwig Richter. Lungkwitz took the usual Alps sketching tour in 1843. He settled in Leipzig where his father bought wool, then returned to Dresden in 1849. Involved in radical politics, he joined Petri and Richard Wagner behind the barricades in the revolution. As political refugees, Lungkwitz and Petri emigrated to a German settlement at New Braunfels, Tex in 1851. Because they could not support themselves as artists in the rigors of pioneer life, they moved to Fredericksburg in 1854 where they built a log house. Petri painted genre and Indian scenes, Lungkwitz landscapes. From today's viewpoint, "they are so obviously European in technique that they seem culturally homeless in the Texas of 1850." BAR. When Petri drowned in 1857,

Lungkwitz had increasing financial difficulty.

In 1866 Lungkwitz moved to San Antonio, opening a photographic studio with the painter von Iwonski. He continued to paint landscapes, lightening his dark Dresden palette with newer luminous colors. In 1870 he was appointed official photographer in the land office in Austin. He became a drawing master as well, painting quiet, rugged landscapes around Austin. When he died of pneumonia, there were only 72 paintings and 40 pencil sketches definitely ascribed to him.

LUNGREN, Fernand Harvey (not Lundgren). Born Hagerstown, Md (or Toledo, Ohio) 1859 (or 1857), died Santa Barbara, Cal 1932. Painter and illustrator specializing in the Southwest desert including Indians. Work in Earl C Adams colln, Stenzel colln, Santa Barbara St Col. References A32 (obit)-BEN-FIE-SMI. Sources AAR 11/74-AIW-ANT 1/54,5/66-NJA-PNW-POW-TWR-WHO 08. Oil 28×18″ Snowy Evening sold 11/15/67 for $200 at auction. This would not be relevant to the price of a Western painting in 1976. Signature example ✕86 TWR.

Lungren attended the U of Maryland. At 19 he was influenced by Kenyon Cox to quit college to paint. Lungren studied briefly in Cincinnati and was the pupil of Thomas Eakins in Philadelphia. At 20 he became an illustrator in NYC for Scribner's Magazine, Harper's, Century, and St Nicholas. His specialty was painting night effects on city streets. He studied privately in Paris for two years, returning to Cincinnati in 1892.

Lungren met both Farny and Sharp who were already painting Western subjects. He sketched in New Mexico for the Santa Fe railroad in 1892 and in Arizona in 1893. Thereafter, Lungren devoted himself to the Southwestern desert, especially the ceremonies and folklore of the Moquis, Navaho, and Apache. He became a priest of the Snake-Antelope fraternity of the Moquis. His first Western illustrations were in 1895. *Thirst* published in 1896 depicted a dying man with a dead horse. It was his best-known work. In 1900 a series of his paintings was reproduced and widely sold. He moved to California in 1903 where he painted Death Valley and the Mojave Desert. His illustrations in this period were black and white. Lungren distinguished between these illustrations left with the publishers and his "art work" he sold to friends. He settled in Santa Barbara in 1907.

LYNCH, Brandon. Magazine illustrator active about 1950 who included Indian subjects. No reference. Source, illustrations for 1948 article in *Cavalier* magazine, *Did a Woman Die with Custer?* No auction record. Signature example in article above.

MABRY, Jane. Painter active in Albuquerque, NM 1958–73, specializing in pastel portraits of Indians. No reference. Source NMX 9,10/73. No auction record. Signature example p 32 NMX.

Descendant of New Mexican pioneers, Ms Mabry was the pupil of Gerald Cassidy. She worked as staff artist for the National Park Service. "The modern Indian looks to the future," she is quoted. "When I paint, I go back into the pueblos and seek out the old, beautiful faces." NMX.

MACDONALD, James Edward Hervey. Born Durham, Eng 1873 of Canadian parents, died Toronto, Ont, Can 1932. Important Can landscape painter in the Rocky Mtns 1924; teacher, muralist, poet. Original member Group of Seven 1920. Work in NGC. Reference MAL. Sources CAH-CAN-CAR. No current auction record. Signature example ⚹84 CAR. (See illustration 182.)

Brought to Hamilton, Ont at 14 and then to Toronto at 16, MacDonald studied commercial art in the Ontario School of Art and Design. Fine art and sketching trips came through the Toronto ASL. He worked as a graphic designer for Grip Ltd in Toronto from about 1895 and for Carlton Studios in London from 1904 to 1907. When he returned to Toronto and to Grip Ltd, he sketched landscapes near Toronto, in northern Ontario in 1909, and Georgian Bay 1910. His exhibition of sketches at the Arts and Letters Club in 1911 led MacDonald to Lawren Harris who persuaded MacDonald to give up commercial work for painting. In 1912 Harris and MacDonald painted and exhibited together, fixing on native Canadian subject matter. When they saw a Buffalo exhibition of contemporary Scandinavian painting in 1913, they had found the freer technique they needed for their similar northland. Harris and MacDonald became the core of the Canadian painters who formed the Group of Seven.

MacDonald first visited the Rockies in 1924 on a summer tour, then returned to his teaching at the Ontario College of Art. He went back to the Rockies each summer but it was "only in 1932 at the end of his life that he achieved success with his mountain canvases, by moving down into the intimate detail." CAH.

MACDONALD, James Williamson Galloway ("Jock"). Born Thurso, Scotland 1897, died Toronto, Ont, Can 1960. Modern landscape painter of the Can West Coast, designer, teacher. Member Can Group Painters. Work in NGC, Vancouver AG, U BC, Imperial Oil colln; murals in Hotel Vancouver. References A62 (obit)-MAL. Sources CAH-CAN-WNW. No current auction record but the estimated price of an Indian village painting would be $4,500 to $5,000 at auction in 1976.

After study in commercial design at the College of Art in Edinburgh, he was apprenticed as an architectural draftsman. He then worked as a textile designer in England 1922–25 before coming to Vancouver where he taught design at the School of Art beginning 1926. Accompanying Varley, he began to paint for the first time. When the school failed in 1935, he moved to a remote cove where he studied the Indian arts in their environment. When he returned to Vancouver in 1936, his styles emphasized designs, then nature à la Emily Carr, then abstract à la Harris, then surrealism.

As a landscape painter he was regarded as an "adept if somewhat heavy-handed interpreter of the Western scene. His brushwork is broad and his subjects are decorative." CAN. MacDonald moved to Toronto in 1947 to become professor of painting at Ontario College of Art.

MACDONALD, L W. Active 1881 as *Leslie's* magazine illustrator in Kerrville, Tex. No reference. Source CAP. No current auction record.

CAP illustrates MacDonald's sketch of Texas cowboys driving a herd to the Mississippi for shipment by boat to the East. A second sketch shows the cowboys checking a stampede during a lightning storm.

MACK, Leal. Born Titusville, Pa 1892, died Taos, NM 1962. Taos painter. Work in Harwood Fndn (Taos). No reference. Sources BDW-HAR-HAW. No auction record or signature example.

MACLEOD, Pegi Nicol (Mrs Margaret Nichol MacLeod, Pegi Nicol). Born Listowel, Ont, Can 1904, died NYC 1949. Can modern painter in Alberta 1927 and among the Skeena River Indians 1928. Work in NGC. No reference. Sources CAN-CAR-C30-4/75 data from Jane Pappidas. No current auction record. Signature example ✗107 CAR. (See illustration 213: Pegi Nicol.)

Mrs MacLeod studied for three years with Franklin Brownell in Ottawa and for one year at the École des Beaux-Arts in Montreal. Her Western experience was early. In 1928 she accompanied the ethnologist Marius Barbeau to the Skeena River area in British Columbia as an Eastern painter who recorded her "impressions of the West, and especially that portion beyond the Rockies," at the same time as Holgate, Annie D Savage, Jackson, and the American Langdon Kihn. CAN. In 1931 she won the Willingdon Prize for her landscape *The Log Run.*

About 1931 she moved to Montreal where she exhibited. When her studio burned, she went to Ottawa in 1932 and

Toronto in 1934. Her specialty was "children, floating, parading, packaged in cellophane, all swirling in decorative shapes and colors." C30. She married an engineer in 1936 and moved to NYC where she continued to paint but without impact on the NY scene. Summers from 1940 to 1948, she returned to Canada to teach at the U of New Brunswick. She died of cancer. Her work was included in "Canadian Paintings in the Thirties" as exhibited at the NGC in 1975.

MACMONNIES, Frederick William. Born Brooklyn, NY 1863, died NYC 1937. Very important international sculptor, painter. NA 1906, NSS. Works in City Hall Park (NYC), Prospect Park (Bklyn), Boston PL, World's Columbian Expos, MMA, Washington Arch (NYC), Congressional Lib, Bklyn Arch. References A38 (obit)-BEN-DAB-ENB-FIE-MAL-SMI. Sources ALA-AMA-ANT 10,12/74-DEP-GIL-ISH-M19-MSL-NSS-SCU-WHO 36. Bronze 27¼" high *Nathan Hale* about 1890 by Roman Bronze Works sold 10/21/72 for $4,000 at auction. The M19 bronze *Nathan Hale* is 28½".

F W MacMonnies dropped out of school when his father's grain business failed. At 16 he became studio boy for Augustus Saint-Gaudens, the leading sculptor of the day. He was enabled to watch the modeling, plaster and bronze casting, and marble cutting. While Saint-Gaudens was away, MacMonnies copied a bas-relief sculpture that led to assignments of assisting in actual sculpture. MacMonnies attended the NAD and the ASL at night. He met the outstanding artists of the day. At 20 he became the pupil of Falguière at the École des Beaux-Arts in Paris. By the time he was 25 "the volume, variety, and quality of his work was astounding." DAB. He made figures, fountains, portrait statues, and groups. His best-known work was

Bacchante and the Infant Faun, forced out of Boston because its "wanton drunkenness was considered the supreme insult to American motherhood." M19. MacMonnies' *Fountain* was the sensation of the World's Columbian Exposition in Chicago in 1893. He represented a departure from the classical mode.

After 1900 he suffered a breakdown. He took up painting under an assumed name, winning medals. After 1905 he returned to sculpture. He made a pioneer memorial for Denver. GIL has an undated bronze of *Buffalo Bill and His Dog*. "Tall and lean, too energetic ever to put on an extra pound, with tousled and unruly hair, he was an arresting figure." DAB. He returned to NYC in 1915.

MACNEIL, Hermon Atkins. Born Everett (Chelsea), Mass 1866, died (probably College Point) NYC 1947. Important sculptor including Indian subjects. NA 1906, NSS. Work in MMA, COR, AIC, US Supreme Ct Bldg, McKinley Arch (Columbus, O), Mo St Capitol, Flushing (NY). References A53 (although dead)-BEN-ENB-FIE-MAL-SMI. Sources AMA-ANT 5/65-GIL-MSL-NAD-NSS-POW-SCU-SSF-WHO 48. Bronze, dark patina 36" high *The Sun Vow* stamped Roman Bronze Works NY estimated for sale 10/28/74 at $12,000 to $14,000 for auction in LA, and sold for $14,000. Signature example p 300 NSS. Medal illustration p 234 A31. (See illustrations 183 a & b.)

MacNeil studied at the Massachusetts Normal Art School in Boston in 1886. Until 1888 he worked as the first drawing instructor at Cornell U and taught at Pratt. He then went to Paris, the pupil of Falguière at the École des Beaux-Arts and of Chapu at the Julien Academy. He returned to the US in 1891, working as an assistant to Philip Martiny on architectural sculpture for the World's Colum-

bian Exposition in Chicago in 1893. He taught at the AIC for three years. Because of a dislike for conventional studio models, he made "several trips" West to study the Indians, feeling "that the red man is as worthy of the sculptor's interest as were the athletes of ancient Greece." AMA.

In 1896 MacNeil won the Rinehart Roman scholarship letting him study in Rome until 1899. While in Rome in 1898, he made *The Sun Vow*, "one of the greatest statues of Indians, representing a Sioux youth as he is taking the oath of allegiance to his tribe." AMA. Just before WWI, MacNeil designed the US quarter dollar with the obverse depicting Columbia guarding the US gateway and the reverse representing an active eagle to indicate preparedness. By 1923 NSS noted that "in former years he has made a specialty of Indian subjects but more recently of large monumental works." His wife, Carol Brooks MacNeil, was also a recognized sculptor.

MADAN, Frederic C. Born Brooklyn, NY 1885, living Irvington-on-Hudson, NY 1948. Illustrator for magazines including pulp Westerns. Member SI. Reference A41-MAS. Source, magazine credits. No auction record or signature example.

MAGAFAN, Ethel. Born Chicago 1916, living Woodstock, NY 1976. Painter, muralist. NA 1966. Work in DAM, Newark Mus, MMA, Senate Chamber, Holland. References A76-MAL. Sources AAT-M50-SHO-WAA-WHO 70-W64-WYA. No current auction price but *Lonesome Valley* was offered at $900 when awarded honorable mention in the MMA exhibition "American Painting

Today 1950." Signature example p 69 SHO *High Meadow*.

In A41, Magafan was listed as resident of Redstone, Wyom, having studied with Frank Mechau, Boardman Robinson, and Peppino Mangravite at Colorado Springs FA Center. She has been awarded many fellowships and scholarships, has won many awards including purchase prizes, and has had many one-man shows. The twin sister of the painter Jennie Magafan, she is the wife of the painter Bruce Currie.

MAHIER, Edith. Born Baton Rouge, La 1892, living Norman, Okla (summer Baton Rouge) 1934. Okla painter, teacher, instructor of the "Five Kiowas" at the U of Okla 1926. References A33-FIE-MAL. Sources AIP-WAA. No auction record or signature example.

Miss Mahier studied at Newcomb Memorial College School of Art, the pupil of Ellsworth Woodward, at NY School of Fine and Applied Art, the pupil of George Bridgman and Will Stevens. By 1919 she was listed as at the U of Oklahoma. She was the key to the acceptance of the Five Kiowas at the U of Oklahoma, passing first judgment on the work of Asah and Hokeah as brought to her on Kraft bags and box covers: The paintings "looked like Leon Bakst, an Oklahoma art expression true and fresh and deserving of interest." AIP. When the Five Kiowas were passed on to O B Jacobson for final decision, he gave them Miss Mahier's office as their studio, assigning her as instructor and coach. Asah said she understood the Kiowas. She felt design and color were innate for the Kiowas because their "rhythm was a natural living thing." AIP.

MAILS, Rev Thomas E. Born Cal about 1920, living Laguna Niguel, Cal 1974. Painter of Indians, illustrator, writer on Indian and religious subjects, minister. No reference. Source, jacket biography for "Dog Soldiers, Bear Men and Buffalo Women" 1973-catalog sheet for "The People Called Apache-interview *The Seattle Times* 1/13/74 *Magazine*. No auction record. Signature example "Dog Soldiers."

Mails studied at the California College of Arts and Crafts. In WWII he served as an engineering officer with the US Coast Guard. After working in theater and residential design in Oakland and San Francisco, he opened an architectural office in Seattle in 1947. Entering Luther Theological Seminary in St Paul in 1955, he became pastor of a Pomona, Cal church. Mails has written 18 books on religion.

As an admirer of Indian life-style and religion, Mails traveled the Southwest, buying artifacts, researching the culture, and sketching in charcoal and ink. He believed the Indians had attained a golden age of adjusting to nature and worshipping a supreme being. The Indians "lived as Christ tells us how to live." *Times*. The result was his book "The Mystic Warriors of the Plains," with Mails using his own artifacts as models. "The People Called Apache" was called equally authentic in text and art.

MAJOR, William Warner. Born Bristol, Eng 1804, died southern England 1854 (or 1853 in London). Pioneer Utah landscape and portrait painter. Work in Beehive House (Salt Lake City). Reference G&W. Sources ANT 2/75-FRO-JUT-PUA-YUP. No current auction record. Painting example p 286 ANT 2/75 *Brigham Young's Family*. (See illustration 184.)

Major was an English artist who was converted to the LDS Church in 1842.

He worked in the LDS ministry in England. In 1844 he emigrated to Nauvoo, Ill, the Mormon town. There he painted the assassination of Joseph Smith and the Mormon sufferings before they were driven out in 1846. In 1848 he was part of 1,229 emigrants who traveled to Salt Lake City in 397 wagons with 1,275 oxen, all as recorded each day by a writer and by Major to sketch the scenes. The first artist in the Salt Lake valley, he remained in Utah for five years, traveling to the principal settlements to record the landscape and to paint portraits of the settlers and the Indians. There were also small watercolors with portraits in profile.

Very few of Major's paintings are known today. He was said to have been "a diligent man attending to all the duties expected of him, ever ready to go or come at the bidding of those whose right it was to command him. Brother Major was the perfect master of his temper." PUA. He died while on a mission to England for the church.

MANDELMAN, Beatrice (Mrs Louis Ribak). Born Newark, NJ 1912, living Taos, NM 1976. Taos painter, graphic artist, teacher. Member Nat Serigraph Soc. Work in MMA, MOMA, MNM, Bklyn Pub Lib. References A76-MAS. Sources TAL-WAA. No current auction record. Painting example pl 41 TAL. (See illustration 185.)

Beatrice Mandelman studied at the Newark School of Fine and Industrial Arts and at the ASL. During the Depression she was graphic arts director, WPA Federal Art Project, NY. In 1947 she and her husband were called "outstanding among the new Taos painters. Her paintings have an authoritative technical ability that is more masculine than feminine." TAL. In 1959 she was an instructor at the Taos Valley Art School.

MARCHAND, John Norval. Born Leavenworth, Kan 1875, died Westport, Conn 1921. Traditional Western illustrator, painter, sculptor. Member SI. Work in Earl C Adams colln, ANS, HAR. Reference A09. Sources HARKEN-RUS-TWR. Oil *End of the Trail* sold 10/1/69 for $650 at auction. Signature example p 137 HAR. (See illustration 186.)

J N Marchand's birthplace in Kansas was Western frontier country when he was young, providing an opportunity to observe the cowboy and the Indian. At 16 he, and his family, moved to St Paul where he attended high school, worked for the *Minneapolis Journal,* and studied at the Harwood Art School. At 20 he became a staff artist for the *New York World.* From 1897 to 1899 he and the painter Albert Levering studied at the Munich Academy.

When he returned to NYC, Marchand worked as a book and magazine illustrator. He made sketching trips West for material. In 1902 he met Charles Russell while in Montana with Will Crawford. It was Marchand's suggestion that Russell come to NYC and he acted as host to Russell in NYC at the studio Marchand shared with Levering and Will Crawford. Marchand illustrated 35 books including "Girl of the Golden West" and "Arizona: A Romance of the Great Southwest." His magazine illustrations were numerous, too, in his abbreviated career. TWR lists a 9″ *Bust Portrait of Charles M Russell* signed Marchand and dated 1905.

MARCOU, Jules. Born Salins, France 1824, died Cambridge, Mass 1898. Survey geologist, sketch artist. Reference DAB. Source AIW. No auction record or signature example.

Marcou dropped his college study of mathematics in France because of poor health at 20. He led an outdoor life, finding his place in geology as an authority on fossils. He published his first work at 21, becoming professor of mineralogy at 22 and traveling geologist for a Paris museum at 24. The same year he accompanied Louis Agassiz on an expedition to Lake Superior in the US. He returned to Europe in 1854, working as professor of paleontology in Zürich from 1856 to 1860 when he settled in Cambridge, Mass. He was "a man of striking personality, tall and erect, with long, flowing beard." DAB.

He continued to work as a field geologist when he could. In 1875 he was a geologist on Lt Williamson's survey party in California, along with William P Blake. The survey began above San Francisco with much of the work in the California deserts and in the Sierra Nevada Mountains. Charles Koppel was the official artist but Blake was credited with many of the illustrations in the official report. "Blake also re-drew a number of geological cross-sections from original sketches by Marcou." AIW.

MARIN, John. Born Rutherford, NJ 1870 (or 1872), died Cape Split, Me 1953. Very important international watercolorist. Member ANA. Work in ACM, ANS, MNM, MMA, MOMA, BM, LAMA, Ariz St U, AIC, DAM. References A53-BEN-FIE-MAL-SMI. Sources AAR 9/73,3/74,5/74-ANS-ALA-APT-ARI-ARM-CAA-DEP-HAR-HMA-190-ISH-MSL-NEU-PIT-STI-TAL-TSF-WHO 52. Watercolor 15× 21″ *Movement: Boat off Deer Isle, Maine No 7* signed and dated '26 sold 3/14/73 for $47,500 at auction as part of the Halpert colln. Signature example p 44 ANS *Canyon of the Hondo*. (See illustration 187.)

Marin was educated at Hoboken Academy and Stevens Prep. He was sketching at 14 and painting sensitive watercolors at 15. His family influenced him to attend Stevens Institute to become an architect. He opened an office in 1893 but abandoned it to sketch and paint watercolors on his own. Marin studied at PAFA with Thomas Anshutz from 1899 to 1901 but missed classes to sketch the city. From 1901 to 1903 he attended the ASL in NYC under DuMond, then worked as a free-lance architect while trying to resolve his light pattern technique by painting 100 9×12″ canvases in oils of the North River, the Palisades, and Manhattan. In 1905 his family sent him to Europe where he studied etching. When he returned in 1909, he had his first one-man exhibition at Stieglitz's "291" gallery. From that point he maintained his long span as the dean of American watercolor, the master of capturing the fluidity of motion and of the simplification of nature into semiabstract compositions.

Marin visited Taos the summers of 1929 and 1930 when he was almost 60. The first exhibition of his Western watercolors was an event in 1936 at the Museum of Modern Art. His friends even identified his sites by means of a map that showed his haunts. Actually, he had painted about 100 New Mexico watercolors without any effect on him that would compare to the impact of the West on Hartley. Marin's Taos landscapes did not capture him as did Maine. His Indians dancing were technically adept but not penetrating. More important to New Mexico art than Marin's watercolors, however, was his influence. Along with Dasburg, he made modernism acceptable in this part of the Victorian West.

MARKS, George B. Born Conrad, Iowa 1923, living Albuquerque, NM 1976. Traditional Western painter, sculptor. Member CAA. Reference A76. Sources AHI 11/71-COW-C71 to 74-OSR-WAI 72. No current auction record. Signature example p 24 C73 *The Noon Break.* (See illustration 188.)

Marks was influenced toward the West by his grandfather's stagecoach experiences, told while Marks was growing up on an Iowa farm. This was near Sidney, Iowa where there was rodeoing every summer. Marks served three years in the Marine Air Corps during WWII, then spent five years studying art at the U of Iowa. In the summers he worked in the West for the experience and the proximity to historical sites. To paint the West, Marks moved to Albuquerque where he also continued his studies.

His specialty is painting the life of the contemporary cowboy. He finds that most of the men are willing to pose for him because they are as interested in his work as he is in theirs. Favorite ranches are the Lee Ranch south of Magdalena and the N-Bar Ranch in Montana. He also sketches back of the chutes at rodeos.

MARLATT, H Irving. Born Woodhull, NY probably before 1867, died Mt Vernon, NY 1929. Landscape and portrait painter including Indian subjects, illustrator. Work in Mt Vernon Pub Lib. References A29 (obit)-MAL. Source KEN. No current auction record but the estimated price of an oil 20×30″ showing Indians at a ford would be $1,000 to $1,200 at auction in 1976.

One recorded Western painting dated 1887 shows mounted Indians crossing a stream in the Rockies. Marlatt painted many cover illustrations for the *Literary Digest.*

MARPLE, William L. Born 1827, active in California mid-19th century, died 1910. Cal painter. Work in Oakland AM, Cal St Lib (Sacramento). No reference. Sources BDW-KEN. No current auction record but the estimated price of an oil 20×30″ showing a Cal landscape would be about $600 to $800 at auction in 1976. No signature example.

One recorded painting depicts wheat farming in the San Joaquin valley.

MARRYAT, Francis Samuel. Born London, Eng 1826, died there 1855. English topographical artist in San Fran 1850–53, author. Work in ACM, Kahn colln, Oakland, Cal. Reference G&W. Source COS-KAH. No auction record. Lithograph example ⅛1382 ACM *San Francisco* 1851.

"Frank" Marryat was the son of the English author Capt Frederick Marryat. He served in the Royal Navy from about 1843 to 1848. In 1849 he came to California, bringing a gamekeeper and bloodhounds. He settled in 1850 in San Francisco where he remained until 1853 except for a brief trip home in 1852. Marryat occupied himself as miner, innkeeper, author, and actor. In 1851 he drew a view of San Francisco for reproduction in London, and in 1930 there were exhibited in NYC seven small watercolors of San Francisco that were signed and dated 1850.

Marryat's book published in NY and London the year of his death at 29 was an account of California, "Mountains and Molehills, or recollections of a burnt journal. By Frank Marryat. With illustrations by the Author." His premature death was precipitated by yellow fever contracted during his 1853 honeymoon trip to San Francisco.

MARTIN, Fletcher. Born Palisade, Colo 1904, living Guanajuato, Mex 1976. Modern Western painter, muralist, illustrator, lithographer, teacher. ANA 1969.

Work in Britannica colln, DAM, LA County MA, MMA, MOMA, MNM. References A76-MAS. Sources AAT-ALA-CAA-CAP-CON-M50-WHO 70-WNW. Oil *Two Sisters* 1956 sold 5/21/69 for $600 at auction. Signature example p 77 CON.

The son of an itinerant newspaper man, Martin began as a printer at 12. He graduated from Clarkston (Wash) high school in 1921, then worked as a harvester, a lumberjack, and a professional boxer before serving in the US Navy 1922–26. He was self-taught as a painter, becoming successful as a muralist after assisting in decoration and getting federal mural assignments during the '30s.

Martin had his first exhibition in 1934. He taught painting at the Art Center School in Los Angeles 1938–39, was artist-in-residence at U of Iowa 1940–41, and was director of painting at Kansas City AI 1941–42. During WWII he was an artist-correspondent for *Life*. In 1948–49 he taught at the ASL, and continued teaching from year to year at various institutions. His approach to teaching is that the important thing is to maintain interest while students avoid formal study, because art can't be taught. Husky and laconic, Martin is somber-looking with drooping red mustachios. His specialty as a painter is in catching the essence of speed, as in his rodeo subjects. His work has been reproduced in national magazines and has illustrated reissues of famous novels.

MARTIN, John Breckinridge. Born near London, Ky 1857, living Dallas, Tex 1935. Texas painter of pastel landscapes, writer. References A33-MAL. Sources TOB-TXF. No current auction record. No signature example.

After growing up without having seen a town until 1874, he moved to Texas in 1876, living in Sherman, working as a cowhand in Cook County, moving to Fort Worth in 1881, then settling in Dallas in 1888. He worked with Hulburt Portrait Company which specialized in family paintings.

Self-taught as an artist, J B Martin went on sketching trips with the Onderdonks. His subjects were as remembered, *Spanish Longhorns* rather than the cattle of the 1920s. "He might add a few extra thorns to the cacti, in remembrance of the pricks they have given him." TOB. Other 1934 paintings were *My Old Home* and *Texas Flowers*. In 1935 Thomas Hart Benton called Martin's work "some of the finest paintings he had ever viewed." TOB. Martin also wrote on the subject of art.

MARTIN, Kirk. Born probably Palisade, Colo 1906, living Yucca Valley, Cal 1975. Traditional Western painter, wood-block printer specializing in horses. No reference. Source COW. No current auction record. Signature and monogram p 70 COW.

Kirk Martin, the younger brother of Fletcher Martin, was the son of a Colorado newspaper printer. He was himself trained as a printer when he was 10, along with Fletcher. See Fletcher Martin entry.

MARTIN, Thomas Mower. Born London, Eng 1838, died Toronto, Ont, Can 1934. Important early Canadian railway survey artist, landscape painter specializing in Western Canadian watercolors, illustrator, teacher. Member RCA. Work in NGC, Hope House (British Columbia), Windsor Castle, Stenzel colln. References MAL-SMI. Sources CAH-CAN-PNW. Oil $28\frac{1}{8} \times 43\frac{1}{2}''$ *Indian Encamp-*

ment on a River 1881 sold 1/30/69 for $1,440 at auction in London. Painting example p 14 PNW. (See illustration 189.)

Martin was educated at the Enfield Military College in England. He studied at the South Kensington Art Galleries. When he emigrated to Canada in 1862, he failed as a homesteader and in 1863 became the first full-time professional artist in Toronto. He was a founder of the Ontario Society of Artists in 1872, director of the Ontario School of Art in 1877, an original member of the RCA in 1879, and a founder of the Toronto Society of Artists in 1885. He lived in NYC around 1884 and exhibited at the NAD.

Thirty years after the explorer-painter Paul Kane, Martin led a new flow of painters into the Canadian West. In the late 1860s he crossed Canada painting watercolors later reproduced as book illustrations. He had traveled along the proposed right-of-way of the Canadian Pacific, so that his large studio paintings were used as railway publicity. Ten subsequent sketching trips took him through to the Pacific Coast, Vancouver Island, and Washington State. "Largely self-taught" as a painter, his work was "contrived and over-elaborate" and by 1886 was "considered out-of-date in the east." CAH.

MARTÍNEZ, Crescencio. Born New Mexico date unknown, died there 1918. One of the first Rio Grande painters. Work in MNM, Fndn Mus (Taos). Sources AHI 2/50-AIP. No auction record or signature example.

Martínez, Indian name Te E or Home of the Elk, was the janitor at San Ildefonso Day School before 1910. He was experienced in painting pottery. At the school he obtained crayons with which he made drawings on the ends of cardboard boxes. Dr. Edward L. Hewett noted his talent and gave him paper and watercolors.

He painted steadily for two years, participating in the beginning of the Pueblo watercolor movement. Martínez was commissioned to do a series of paintings, which he began in 1917, for the Museum of NM and the School of American Research illustrating the costumed dances of San Ildefonso's summer and winter ceremonies. WWI interrupted this commission and Martínez moved to Santa Fe, where he groomed and fed horses. He was the father of José Miguel Martínez, who painted infrequently in the 1950s. AIP.

MARTÍNEZ, Julián. Born New Mexico 1897 (not 1879), died there 1943 (or 1944). Among the first Rio Grande painters, important ceramic artist, muralist. Work in ACM (under Maria Povella), DAM, GIL, MAI, MNM, Riverside Mus. References A47 (obit)-MAL. Sources ACM (under Maria Povella)-AHI 2/50-AIP-LAF. No auction record. Ceramic example and photo p 255 LAF. (See illustration 190.)

Julián Martínez, Indian name Pocano (or Po-ea-no), was self-taught as an artist. His wife was María, the internationally known "potter of San Ildefonso." His sons were John D Martínez and Popovi Da, who legally changed his name from Tony Martínez.

Martínez was painting watercolors and decorating his wife's pottery before 1920. The pottery designs were simpler but his paintings were also developed from similar styles, for example, romanticized birds in brilliant colors. His typical work included symbolic designs and geometric figures. He also had periods of less successful realistic paintings. The economic importance of the Martínez process of producing blackware was substantial for the agriculturally poor San Ildefonso Pueblo.

MARTÍNEZ, María (or Marie) Montoya. Born San Ildefonso Pueblo, NM 1881, living there 1976. "The Potter of San Ildefonso." Work in Lab of Anthropology, AMNH, MNM, ACM, Century of Progress Expos (Chicago 1934). Reference A41. Sources AHI 2/50,3/74-AIP-LAF-MAR. No current auction record. Photo p 255 LAF. (See illustration 190.)

In 1904 María Montoya, who was entirely self-taught as a potter, married Julián Martínez, a painter who was one of the first Rio Grande artists. At this time pottery making in San Ildefonso was for home use. About 1908 María's pots were polychromed by Julián and some were sold at the MNM and as curios. About 1912 María and Julián learned to make plain black pottery, and by 1915 they had learned to make large pots that were plain black. About 1919 Julián invented the black-on-black decoration that he taught to the other San Ildefonso potters in 1921, initiating an industry rewarding for the entire Pueblo. About 1923 María began signing the pots, first as "Marie" and then as "Marie and Julian." In the beginning the pot was matte black and the design shiny, but this was reversed by 1923.

María's life was changed by being hired as a demonstrator at the MNM, at Chicago's Century of Progress Exposition in 1934, and the Golden Gate Exposition in 1939. In contrast, success exposed Julián to liquor and the Pueblo to tourists. The two sons became artists. After Julián died in 1943, the younger son Popovi Da continued the decorating.

MARTÍNEZ, Pete. Born Porterville, Cal 1894, living Tucson, Ariz 1968. Traditional Western painter specializing in horses. No reference. Source COW. No current auction record or signature example.

Pete Martínez worked as a jockey at 14. He became a cowboy in Nevada and served in the horse cavalry in WWI. For 23 years he was a horseback riding instructor at a summer camp in Pennsylvania. In 1935 he opened a riding stable in Tucson.

Martínez had studied art in San Francisco and at the PAFA. In the 1930s he shared a sales counter with his friend Olaf Wieghorst to display their horse drawings at Madison Square Garden in NYC. When he moved to Tucson he operated an art studio in addition to his riding stable. His paintings featured his recollections of his cowboy days.

MARTÍNEZ, Xavier (Xavier Tizoc Martínez y Orozco). Born Guadalajara, Mexico 1869, died Carmel, Cal 1943. San Fran painter, illustrator, etcher, teacher. Work in M H De Young Mem Mus (San Fran), Oakland AM, AM (Guadalajara), MCA. References A41-BEN-FIE-MAL-SMI. Sources A A R 3/74-B W B-C O W-MCA-WHO 42. No current auction record but the estimated price of a charcoal drawing $18 \times 24''$ showing desert water would be about $200 to $250 at auction in 1976. Monogram example p 78 MCA.

Martínez, a descendant of the Aztecs, was educated at the Liceo de Varones in Guadalajara. Brought to San Francisco by foster parents, he studied at Mark Hopkins Inst as the pupil of Arthur Mathews up to 1895 and at the École Nationale et Speciale des Beaux-Arts in Paris from 1897 to 1901, the pupil of Gérôme and Carrière. He had opened his studio in San Francisco in 1892.

Beginning in 1901 he lived flamboyantly in San Francisco's bohemian Italian Quarter. As "Marty" Martínez he was most colorful of the bohemians with his "corduroy coat, baggy trousers, black velvet beret, and flowing red bow tie." BWB. In later years he added "a crimson band about his ample middle." BWB. After his "vivid" paintings were lost in the 1906 earthquake and fire, he established his studio in the Piedmont hills. Beginning 1908 he was professor of painting at California School of the Arts and Crafts in Berkeley, remembered for his tie and his strictness with students. At the NY World's Fair in 1940, Martínez was selected as one of the 600 foreign-born Americans making outstanding contributions to culture. In 1974 a Martínez retrospective in Oakland included California and Southwestern desert landscapes.

MASTERSON, James W. Born Hoard, Wis 1894, living Miles City, Mont 1970. Montana illustrator, painter, sculptor, writer. Work in Mont schools, banks, lib. Reference A70. Source, "It Happened in Montana" illustrated and written by Masterson. No current auction record or signature example.

Masterson studied at the Chicago AFA, the AIC, and the San Jose Art School (Cal). He became an instructor in Custer County Junior College and received a fellowship in 1962.

MATHEWS, Alfred E. Born Bristol, Eng 1831, died near Longmont, Colo 1874. Important Western landscape, portrait, and panorama painter, lithographic artist. Work in DAM, ACM, City AM (St Louis), DPL, Lib of Congress, Neb St Hist Soc, Mariners Mus (Newport News). Reference G&W. Sources AIW-ANT 6/66-DBW-MIS-POW-WES. No current auction record. Drawing example plates 31–38 AIW.

Son of a book publisher, Mathews was brought to Rochester, Ohio at the age of two where he was raised in a musical and artistic family. At 14 he was a typesetter. By the time he was 25 he was an itinerant bookseller in New England, also making landscape drawings: "I fill up odd times with such work and find it profitable." AIW. At the outset of the Civil War, he was teaching school in Alabama. During the war Grant himself commended Mathews for his Union services as a topographical artist. About 1864 Mathews painted a panorama of the war in the deep South and exhibited throughout the North. By 1865 Mathews was sketching Nebraska City, Neb as a busy freighting center. By 1866 lithographs of his Western sketches were available in the book "Pencil Sketches of Colorado," which originally sold for $30 and is now rare.

Mathews remained in Colorado through 1866, sketching the Pikes Peak region and the southern Colorado mines. In 1867 he drew scenes for his book "Pencil Sketches of Montana." This he lithographed himself that winter in NYC where he also began his panorama of the Rockies that he exhibited in 1868 in Colorado and Montana: "Receipts were from $58 to $117 per night, and sometimes we had to close the doors and refuse to admit more." AIW. In 1869 the panorama itself was sold in Denver, and his third book, "Gems of Rocky Mountain Scenery," was published: "The artist made many excursions, about 6,000 miles, performed (almost) entirely alone, and principally with ponies." AIW. In 1870–71 Mathews traveled in the East and in England, publishing "Canyon City, Colorado, and Its Surroundings" to seek emigrants for his own land venture. In 1872–73 he sketched for lithographs in California. His books and lithographs are rare and valuable. None of the original Western sketches is known to exist.

MATHEWS, Arthur Frank. Born Markesan, Wis 1860, died San Francisco, Cal 1945. Cal painter, muralist, teacher. Work in MMA; murals in Oakland Lib (Cal), Cal St Capitol, U of Cal Lib, Lib of

Stanford U, Masonic Temple (San Fran). References A41-BEN-FIE-MAL-SMI. Sources ANT 4/74-BWB-M57-WHO 44. No current auction record. Portrait example p 660 ANT 4/74. (See illustration 191.)

Mathews was educated in San Francisco and Oakland schools, then worked as an architect until 1882. He studied art in Europe 1884–89, the pupil of Boulanger in Paris. When he returned to San Francisco, he reorganized the California School of Design, continuing as director until 1906.

MATHIES, J L D. Active 1816–48. Early portrait painter including at least one Indian subject. Reference G&W. No current auction record or signature example.

Mathies was painting portraits in Canandaigua, NY in 1816. He and William Page operated an art gallery in Rochester, NY from 1825 to 1826. Mathies remained in Rochester as an innkeeper, grocer, and patent agent. Before 1838 he painted the portrait of Red Jacket that hung in Mathies' Clinton Hotel. He may have moved to NYC to paint a view of the East River that was exhibited at the NAD in 1848.

MATTHEWS, Marmaduke. Born Barcheston, Warwickshire, Eng 1837, died probably Toronto, Can 1913. Can landscape watercolorist in the Rockies and the Pacific Northwest on visits beginning 1888. Founding member and secretary, RCA 1879. Work in AG Ont, ROM. Reference MAL. Sources CAH-CAN. No auction record or signature example. Photograph p 23 CAN in group, seated in profile with full beard and Edwardian garb. (See illustration 192.)

Matthews studied with T M Richardson at Oxford and moved to Toronto in 1860. In 1872 he joined with W L Fraser in forming the Toronto artists' society, even though Fraser "did not admire" Matthews' work. CAN. It was felt that Matthews was a transplanted Englishman who worked in the traditional English watercolor style, not relevant to the history of Canadian art. CAH.

Matthews visited the Rockies and the Pacific Northwest frequently beginning 1888. "Some of his western pictures have a sweep that almost compensates for the obsessive detail." CAH.

MATULKA, Jan. Born Prague, Czechoslovakia 1890, living NYC 1966. Eastern abstract painter, illustrator, printmaker, teacher. Work in WMAA, NY Pub Lib, PAFA, San Fran MA, Detroit IA, Yale U AG, Cincinnati AM, BM, AIC, ANS. References A62-BEN-MAL. Sources ANS-CAA-DEP-ILP-190. No current auction record or signature example. (See illustration 193.)

Matulka who studied at the NAD with G W Maynard was said to have been one who based his own teaching at the ASL on having witnessed the rise of Cubism in Europe. He had won a NAD scholarship in 1927, had studied in Paris, and had traveled in Europe. In the late 1920s Matulka had been involved in Mechanistic painting. By 1930 he and Stuart Davis were independently working toward a new type of Cubism based on distortions of natural forms.

Indian Dancers in the ANS colln is an example of Matulka's contemporary style. He lived and exhibited in Paris 1951–55.

MATZEN, Herman N. Born Loit Kjerbeby, Denmark 1861, died probably Cleveland, Ohio 1938. Ohio sculptor of monuments, teacher. Member NSS. Sculpture

War and *Peace* (Indianapolis), Schiller (Detroit), Cleveland Cthse and City Hall, Akron Cthse, memorials, etc. References A41 (obit)-BEN-FIE-MAL-SMI. Source WHO 38. No current auction record but the estimated price of a pair of buffalo-skull bookends would be about $400 to $500 at auction in 1976. No signature example. (See illustration 194.)

Matzen was brought to the US as a boy. He was educated at the German-American Seminary in Detroit, began working as a sculptor in 1893, and studied at the Munich AFA and the Royal AFA in Berlin in 1896. Typical sculpture titles were *Law, Justice, Moses, Gregory, Cain and Abel,* etc. Matzen taught at the Cleveland School of Art.

MAURER, Louis. Born Biebrich-on-the-Rhine, Germany 1832, died NYC 1932. Lithographic artist for Currier & Ives, lithographer, painter. Work in ACM, Buffalo Bill Mus. References A32 (obit)-FIE-G&W-MAL. Sources ALA-ANT 10/58,1/74-C&I-DEP-KW1-POW-STI. Oil 23×30″ *River Landscape* sold 3/14/68 for $800 at auction. Signature example plate 175 C&I.

In Germany, Maurer studied mechanical drawing, attending school in Mainz where he also took courses in animal anatomy. He helped his father at cabinet-making, was apprenticed to a lithographer, and carved ivory. Brought to NYC with his family in 1851, he became a staff artist for Currier & Ives at $5 a week, a master of horse and outdoors prints. His assignment until 1860 was to design, draw, and/or lithograph in any subject, alone or in combination with the other artists, so that Fanny Palmer might do the backgrounds, he the figures, and John Cameron the lithographing with his own variations. Maurer's most famous series was *The Life of a Fireman.* He also specialized in the American trotting horse.

When Maurer and Arthur Fitzwilliam Tait were assigned to Indian subjects, they worked out of the Astor Library, plagiarizing Bodmer and Catlin. When Maurer wanted to marry in 1860, he had to change employers to obtain $25 a week. In 1872 he formed a commercial lithography firm, retiring successfully in 1884. He collected sea shells as a savant in conchology, flutes as a recitalist, and guns as a marksman. At 50 he studied in the Gotham Art School, later becoming the pupil of Chase at the NAD. During the latter half of his life, he considered himself to be a painter. He made two extensive trips West, the first in 1885 as the guest of Buffalo Bill. The second trip produced Rocky Mountain landscapes and paintings of Western animals. He had his first one-man show in NYC in 1931, at the age of 99. Though an artist of great accomplishment, he is mentioned in some of the references only as the father of Alfred H Maurer, the Fauve painter.

MAUZEY, Merritt. Born Clifton, Tex 1897 (or 1898), died Dallas, Tex 1975. Texas painter, illustrator, lithographer, author. Member SAGA. Work in MNM, Bklyn Mus Mem colln, Wicht Pub Lib (Boston), Pa St U. References A73-MAS. Sources AAT-CAP. No current auction record. Signature example p 129 CAP.

In 1946 he was awarded a Guggenheim Fellowship for creative lithography. Mauzey's prints have been exhibited nationally and in six overseas tours. They were also included in "The Artist in America" and "Prize Prints of the 20th Century." Mauzey has illustrated magazines and books such as his own "Texas Ranch Boy" (1955).

MAY, Philip William. Born Wortley, Leeds, Eng 1864, died St John's Wood, London, Eng 1903. English illustrator, caricaturist. Work in City Art Gall (Leeds), Victoria and Albert Mus. References BEN-ENB-FIE. Sources ALA-AOH. Drawing 9¼ ×6⅜" *Robust Artist* sold 5/25/71 for $100 at Christie auction. No signature example.

Phil May's father died when he was nine. He became an office boy when he was 12. At 15 he was a touring actor. At 17 he moved to London where he was a self-taught caricaturist and a designer of theatrical costumes. When he was 20 his political cartoons were published, and at 21 he was hired as a staff artist in Australia. From 1888 to 1890 he copied old masters in Rome, and then returned to London as a leading cartoonist and social commentator.

May was the *Daily Graphic* special artist for four weeks in 1893, starting in NYC and then covering the World's Columbian Exposition in Chicago where he was said to have made drawings of Buffalo Bill's Wild West Show. Many albums of May's drawings followed.

MAYER, Frank Blackwell. Born Baltimore, Md 1827, died Annapolis, Md 1899. Historical, genre, and portrait painter who made one trip West in 1851. Work in Peabody Inst (Baltimore), Minn Hist Soc, Cincinnati AM, COR, MMA. References BEN-CHA-FIE-G&W -MAL-SMI. Sources AIW-ALA-BAR-COR-HUT-M57-PAF-POW. No current auction record or signature example.

Mayer was a Baltimore student of Alfred Jacob Miller. Mayer traveled to Minnesota via Nashville, Tenn in 1851, keeping a diary and sketching Indians at Traverse des Sioux "under favorable conditions for observing their festivals and manners. He made a large collection of life studies of the Indian character, with a journal of his experiences among them. The majority of these sketches will no doubt at some time be of much historic value." HUT. A few of the sketches were published then in Schoolcraft's "History of the Indian Tribes." In 1932 the full Minnesota diary and sketches were published as "With Pen and Pencil on the Frontier in 1851."

Mayer maintained his studio in Baltimore until his Paris studies from 1864 to 1869, the pupil of Gleyre and Brion. He exhibited in the Paris salons. In 1870 he settled in Annapolis, well known as a painter of Colonial subjects. Today his genre scenes are regarded as "spotty and uncoordinated." Even his Indian painting is "almost amateur in the uncertainty of design and of drawing," but it is certainly important ethnologically. BAR. It was copied by F D Millet for his Minnesota murals. (See F D Millet entry.)

MAYS, Paul Kirtland. Born Cheswick, Pa 1887, died Carmel, Cal 1961. Muralist, painter, illustrator. Member Nat Soc Mur Ptrs. Work in The White House, Oberlin Col; murals Gall Contemp Art (Phila), U of Penn, PO, San Francisco hotel, etc. References A62 (obit)-MAS. Source WHO 54. No current auction record or signature example.

Mays studied at the ASL 1907–10, at the Hawthorne School of Provincetown (Mass) 1911, and 1923–24 at the Newlyn School of Painting (London) and Colarossi Academy (Paris). He studied with William Chase, J C Johansen, Alexander Robinson, Ernest Proctor, Harold Harvey, and Henry Keller. His paintings included *Taos, NM* at the U of Penn, and his murals *Indian Legends* at the Gallery of Contemporary Art and *Buffaloes and Antelopes* (1951) at Bryn Athyn Library. He also illustrated an edition of "Benjamin Franklin's Autobiography."

MCAFEE, Ila Mae (Mrs Elmer Turner). Born Gunnison, Colo 1897 (or 1900), living Taos, NM 1974. Western animal painter, juvenile illustrator of animals, muralist, textile designer. Work in GIL, DAM, MNM, Baylor U, Koshare Mus (Colo), murals in post offices. References A62-MAS. Sources GIL-TAL-TSF-WAA. No auction record. Signature example pl 44 TAL.

Mrs Turner was educated at Western State College in Gunnison. She studied art at Colorado State Normal School, at the ASL and NAD. She then painted murals in Chicago under James E McBurney. In 1926 she married the landscape painter Elmer Turner and moved to Taos, becoming a permanent resident in 1930.

Mrs Turner paints mainly animals, wild and domestic. She "has a profound understanding of animals. Not a picture lacks one. Her portraits of horses are so recognizable that one knows the originals when one sees them." TAL.

MCARDLE, Henry Arthur. Born near Belfast, Ireland 1836, died San Antonio, Tex 1908. Important Texas historical, military, and portrait painter. Work in Texas govt buildings. References G&W-MAS. Sources AIW-BAR-POW-TEP-TOB-TXF. No current auction record but the estimated price of an oil 20×30″ showing destruction of a bridge would be about $7,000 to $8,000 at auction in 1976. Signature example opp p 188 TEP.

McArdle studied drawing in Belfast, the pupil of Prof Sauveur. Brought to Baltimore at 15, he was the pupil of David A Woodward at the Maryland Institute for the Promotion of the Mechanic Arts, winning prizes in 1860. In the Civil War he was a draftsman in the Confederate engineering corps designing gunboats. Later he was a topographer for Gen Lee.

After the war, McArdle settled in Independence, Tex as professor of art at Baylor Female College. In 1875 he painted *Lee at the Wilderness* which was accidentally burned before he received the $8,000 appropriated for it by the state. His influences were Meissonier and James Walker. In 1876 he began *Dawn at the Alamo,* an oil 7′×12′ symbolizing the birth of Texas' independence. It was completed in 1883. He then began *The Battle of San Jacinto,* completed 1888, which portrays the moment when the Texas army commanded by Gen Houston led the charge against the Mexicans, 1836. McArdle's interest was in historical accuracy: "In every part of my work I have arrived at natural action and historic truth which implies the necessity of models for every portion of my painting." The hundreds of faces are individual portraits. The uniforms and arms were equally researched. After McArdle moved to San Antonio in 1889, his "financial condition" remained "desperate." His income was from teaching and portraiture. The State of Texas which had hung his *Dawn* and *Battle* in the Senate Chamber did not pay for them until McArdle had been dead for 19 years. The appropriation was $25,000, half of the appraised value, although "the last-named picture alone contains *any* money's worth of melodramatic incident —enough to have occupied the painter for 30 years." TEP.

MCCALL, Robert Theodore. Born Columbus, Ohio 1919, living NYC 1970. Illustrator specializing in aviation subjects, painter. Member SI. Work in USAF colln. Reference A70. Sources AHI 4/73-ILA-IL 61,62,63. No current auction record. Signature example p 25 AHI 4/73.

McCall studied at Columbus FAS and the AIC. In WWII he was an Army Air Corps instructor. He worked for three years as an illustrator in Chicago, then moved to NYC about 1948. For USAF paintings he has been flown to Europe, Africa, and Asia. His Western cityscape is half sky, with a plane included, as shown in AHI with which his Western work is identified. McCall's magazine illustrations are for stories and advertising. Series of full-color paintings have been commissioned by *Life,* General Electric, USAF, NASA.

His technique is to start with compositional scribbles, then paint on a gesso-covered Masonite panel, using casein underpainting and oil overpainting and glazing. Listed titles are *Along the Beaver Stream, War Party, An Old-Time Mountain Man, The Attempt on the Stage.* "Why does an Easterner do Western paintings? My milieu was settled" by Buffalo Bill in a Wild West show, Will James and N C Wyeth, and the Western movies. MAC.

MCCARTHY, Frank C. Born NYC 1924, living Sedona, Ariz 1976. Important Western illustrator, painter. Reference A76. Sources AAR 11/74-CUS-ILA-IL 60,62,63-MAC. No current auction record. Signature example MAC. (See illustration 195.)

McCarthy grew up in Scarsdale, NY. At 14 he studied summers at the ASL under George Bridgman and Reginald Marsh and after he graduated from Scarsdale high school he studied illustration at Pratt Inst in Brooklyn. He made a short stay as an artist with a NYC studio, then established his own studio in 1948. In 1949 he toured the American and Canadian West, 14,000 miles of sketching and photography. Before 1950 he had obtained commissions from *American Weekly.* He had also done paperback book covers, and "over the years I have painted hundreds." MAC. These led to illustrations for magazines and to advertising and movie company illustrations. "McCarthy does strong, dramatic, masculine illustration. His pictures are always exciting to look at." ILA.

In 1969 McCarthy began painting Westerns for galleries. The response was immediate so that by 1971 McCarthy did no more commercial work. His intent is to "paint to achieve visual impact," to arrange a Western setting and then place into it the appropriate historical characters and vehicles. Events are not specific.

MCCARTY, Lea Franklin. Born probably California 1905, living Santa Rosa, Cal 1958. Painter specializing in Western gunmen, portraiture, sculptor, author. Reference Who's Who Western Art 1956. Sources AHI 11/58-COW. Sculpture Jack London Square (Oakland), busts, Wyatt Earp plaque (Tombstone). No current auction records. Signature example, cover AHI 11/58.

Son of a Texas minister and a Chicago art teacher, McCarty studied at the Chouinard AS in Los Angeles and privately in California. He began as a sculptor of statues and bronze busts. As a painter he was a portraitist.

After years of immersion in Western history, McCarty in 1956 commenced his portrait series *Gunslingers of the Old West.* After collecting the old tintypes such as Billy the Kid standing in front of Fort Sumner, interviewing the living witnesses including Wyatt Earp's deputy, and using the Hunter-Rose photograph collection at the Bandera Museum, McCarty took three years "to set the gunfighters down accurately as they actually appeared and dressed, to set them down for the first time. I get at the original photograph. Next, I make a careful documentary study of his clothing down to the most minute detail. Then I find somebody who is his build and height to pose while I paint the body, then go back to the old photograph of his head." AHI.

In addition to the expected killers, McCarty's series included Pearl Hart and Pauline Cushman.

ited at the PAFA and the NAD. In 1859 he offered for sale at the PAFA the sketch *A Mother Defending Her Children from the Indians.*

MCCLUNG, Mrs Florence Elliott. Born St Louis, Mo 1896, living Dallas, Tex 1964. Texas landscape painter, printmaker, teacher. Work in MMA, Dallas MFA, Lib Cong, Mint MA (NC), High MA (Atlanta, Ga), Delgado Mus (New Orleans), etc. References A62-MAL. Sources AAT-M57-TEW-TOB-WAA-W64. No current auction record but the published estimate for prints is $80 to $125. Painting example p 113 AAT *Lancaster Valley, Tex.*

Mrs McClung was brought to Dallas in 1899 and educated as a pianist. She studied art at Texas State College for Women, Colorado School of Fine Arts, and with Frank Reaugh, Frank Klepper, Olin Travis, Alexandre Hogue, and Thomas Stell. In NYC she studied with Martha Simkins, and at Cincinnati Art Institute with Charles McCann. She studied in Taos, and received her degree from Southern Methodist U in 1939. At Trinity U in Waxahachie, she was head of the art department 1929–41. "Although not a native Texan, she has lived here since she was three and feels she qualifies." TOB.

MCCLURG, Trevor. Born probably Pennsylvania 1816, died probably NYC 1893. Portrait, genre, and historical painter. Reference G&W. Source PAF. Oil 24×18" *An Indian Brave* sold 11/15/67 for $325 at auction. No signature example.

McClurg was active in Pittsburgh from about 1845 to 1859 when he moved to NYC where he lived 1861–65. He exhib-

MCCLYMONT, John I. Born Manchester, Eng 1858, died probably Colo Springs, Colo 1934. Colo portrait, landscape, and genre painter. Work in AS of Dundee (Scotland), Colo Spr FAC, Masonic Temple (Washington), Colo St Capitol, Vassar Col. No reference. Sources SHO-SPR. No auction record. Signature example p 22 SHO *Portrait of Francis Drexel Smith.*

Raised in Kirkcudbrightshire, Scotland, McClymont was educated in the parish school and privately. From 18 to 21 he studied at Edinburgh SA, then spent four years at the RSA. His specialties were portraits and interiors. When he emigrated to Colorado Springs at the turn of the century, he became a leading painter in the area. Called "Portrait Painter of the State's Builders," many of his likenesses were from photographs. His landscapes included *July Moon* and *Dawn on the West Side of Pikes Peak.*

MCCOMAS, Francis John. Born Fingal, Tasmania 1874, died Pebble Beach, Cal 1938. Cal and Southwestern desert landscape painter in watercolor, muralist. Work in MMA, San Francisco Mus, Portland Mus, Cal Hist Soc (San Francisco), etc. References A41 (obit)-BEN-FIE-MAL-SMI. Sources ARM-ISH-MCA-WHO 26. Watercolor 24×32" *Landscape* 1906 sold 1/11/68 for $110 at auction, and the published estimate is $150 to $200. Painting example p 59 MCA.

McComas was educated at Sydney Technical College in Australia. He emigrated to the US in 1898, and by 1915 was recognized to the point of being named to the jury of the Panama-Pacific Expos. His work had been accepted for the epochal NY Armory Show in 1913: ✕959 *Monterey Evening,* ✕960 *California Landscape,* and ✕961 *Arizona Desert.*

McComas' best-known work was of the Southwestern desert beginning 1909. ISH uses McComas' desert scenes to contrast with Benson's Eastern fishing streams to illustrate the individuality of the realistic painters of the day.

MCCOMBS, Solomon. Born west of Eufaula, Okla 1913, living Arlington, Va 1968. Important Creek painter working as illustrator and designer. Work in DAM, GIL, MNM, Philbrook AC. Sources AIP-MNM. No auction record or signature example. (See illustration 196.)

McCombs' father was pastor of Tuskegee Indian Baptist Church. His great-grandparents traveled the "trail of tears" from Georgia to Oklahoma. He graduated high school in 1937, attended Bacone College where he studied under Acee Blue Eagle. He also studied under Frank von der Lauchen in 1944 while working as illustrator and draftsman in Tulsa. He has exhibited in Philbrook's "Indian Annual" beginning with its inception in 1946.

He moved to Washington to work for the General Services Administration 1950–56 and for the State Department beginning 1956. He toured the Far East and Africa for the State Department in 1954, lecturing on American Indian art and culture. His painting was a part of Pres Kennedy's inaugural parade, and he designed the American Indian float for Pres Johnson's parade. The tempera *Creek Indian Mother* won the MNM purchase award in 1962.

MCCORMICK, Howard. Born Hillsboro, Ind 1875, died NYC 1943. New Jersey painter specializing in Indian habitat groups for museums, muralist, illustrator, engraver. Member ANA (graphics) 1928. Work in AMNH, NJ St Mus, John Herron AI, Mus Sci and Ind (NYC), etc. References A47 (obit)-BEN-FIE-MAL-SMI. Sources NA 74-NJA-WHO 42. No current auction record but the published estimate for prints is $75 to $100. No signature example.

McCormick was educated in public schools in Newcastle and Indianapolis, Ind. He studied at the Indianapolis SA and the NY SA, the pupil of Forsyth and Chase, and in Paris at the Julien Academy, the pupil of Laurens. He was a resident of Leonia, NJ. Principal works were the Hopi, Apache, and Navajo habitat group at the AMNH, *Hopi World* in gesso at Herron, and six murals plus a habitat group of NJ Indians at NJ State Museum. His wood engravings were published in numerous magazines.

MCCOUCH, Gordon Mallett. Born Philadelphia, Pa 1885, died Ticino, Switzerland 1962. Illustrator, including Western and outdoor subjects; international painter and printmaker. Work in Swiss museums. References A62 (obit)-BEN-FIE (as D W)-MAL. Sources NCW-illustration in *The Outing Magazine* 1903 *Clearing the Tote-Road.*

McCouch was educated at Chestnut Hill Academy. He studied at the Pyle School of Art 1903, and is photographed in NCW with Pyle, Wyeth, and Allen True. All of the Pyle students did Western illustrations in this period. McCouch went on to the Royal Acad of Art in Munich, the pupil of Heinrich von Zügel. He became a member of the Gesellschaft Schweizerischer Maler, Bildhauer und Architekten, exhibiting internationally.

MCDERMOTT, John R. Born Pueblo, Colo 1919, living probably Cal 1966. Illustrator. No reference. Sources ILA-IL 59,63. No auction record. Signature example p 225 ILA (monogram MCD).

Educated in high school in Hollywood, McDermott worked as an animator for Disney until WWII. A combat artist in the service, he made Marine Corps drawings that gained him a start as an illustrator for *Blue Book*. His *Venture* illustration was an Indian portrait. McDermott has also made documentary movies of the Civil War and WWI. In the 1950s he specialized in illustrations of action subjects including Westerns.

MCEWEN, Katherine. Born Nottingham, Eng 1875, living Dragoon, Ariz 1941. Painter of Arizona and Alaska landscapes. Member Nat Soc Mural Ptrs. Work in DIA (watercolors), frescoes and murals in Cranbrook School for Boys (Mich). References A41-FIE-MAL. Source WAA. No current auction record or signature example.

A long-time resident of Detroit, Ms McEwen was the pupil of Chase, Miller, Wicker, and Woodbury.

MCGREW, Ralph Brownell. Born Columbus, Ohio 1916, living Quemado, NM 1976. Important contemporary painter of Indians, sculptor, author. Former member CAA, Am Inst FA, Nat Acad Western Art. Work in ANS, Cowboy Hall of Fame, U Santa Clara, Read Mullan Gall Western Art, Mus No Ariz. Reference A76. Sources AHI 7/69,5/73-C71 to 73-EIT-HAR-OSR-WAI 71,72-PER vol 3 ⌗3. No auction record. Signature example p 7 AHI 5/73.

McGrew was educated in Alhambra,

Cal, the high school art pupil of Lester Bonar. He concentrated on portraiture at Otis AI in Los Angeles, the pupil of Ralph Holmes. He also studied with Edouard Vysekal and E R Shrader. His first job was as a movie set decorator.

He soon went to Palm Springs, Cal to become a desert painter: "There is a great difference in natural colors in the desert you can't find anywhere else." WAI 72. His technique is quite literal. "Sketching in the Indian country with Jimmy Swinnerton began my consuming interest in the Navahoes." AHI. He moved to Cottonwood near the Indians, a quiet "loner" living in a remote area with the horses he loves. His paintings are immediately recognizable because of the subject matter, the poetic realism of the sympathetic treatment, and the heavily varnished thin oils on a white ground to make the painting look wet. "McGrew has been able to leave the social-protesting smog-polluted world and send back messages about human values." C71. In 1974 "Browny" was living on the western edge of New Mexico, between the Apache and Navaho reservations.

MCILROY, Carol. Born 1924, living Albuquerque, NM 1976. Painter. Work in Hobbs U, American Bank of Commerce (Albuquerque). Reference A76. Sources NMX 9,10/73-Letter from artist 10/10/75. No auction record. Signature example p 33 NMX 9,10/73.

Ms McIlroy was raised in the state of Washington. She studied at U of Colorado, U of New Mexico with John Pellew, and with Joe Morello in Albuquerque. "I have no interest in leaving New Mexico," she is quoted. "My lifetime won't be long enough for the paintings I want to do here." NMX. Since 1951 Ms McIlroy has been painting Western themes in an impressionistic style, landscapes, ghost towns, Indians, and ranch life. "I try to 'write' in pigments the story of the West." Letter 10/10/75.

MCILVAINE, William, Jr. Born Philadelphia, Pa 1813, died Brooklyn, NY 1867. Landscape painter in watercolor, author. Work in NYHS, BMFA. Reference G&W. Sources COS-FRO-KW1-PAF. No auction record. Signature example p 231 KW1 *Panning Gold, Cal.*

After graduating U of Penn in 1832, McIlvaine studied art in Europe. He was in business with his father in Philadelphia until 1845 when he became a professional painter. In 1849 he visited the California gold fields, the subject of his 1850 book, "Sketches of Scenery and Notes of Personal Adventure, in California and Mexico. Containing Sixteen Lithographic Plates."

A panorama based on McIlvaine's views was painted by Russell Smith and exhibited in Philadelphia in 1850 and Baltimore in 1851. McIlvaine moved to NYC about 1856. In the Civil War he served as a member of the NY 5th Regiment of Volunteers.

MCILWRAITH, William Forsythe. Born Gault, Ont, Can 1867, died Fishkill, NY 1940. Pacific Northwest painter, illustrator, etcher, commercial artist. Reference MAS. Sources PNW-WNW. No auction record but the estimated price of a watercolor 16×20″ showing Indians fishing would be about $600 to $800 at auction in 1976. Signature example p 15 PNW.

McIlwraith studied at the ASL in NYC where he became a commercial artist in 1896. From 1911 to 1923 he did not paint at all while working as a farmer at Hood River, Ore. After 1923 he established himself in Portland, Ore as a commercial artist, watercolor painter, etcher, and illustrator. He avoided exhibitions of his work, selling paintings only through friends, so that he is listed primarily as an etcher. Some of his etchings were published as calendar art.

His specialty was scenes along the Northwest rivers, the Willamette and the Columbia. He recorded the Cecilo Indians' fishing sites, sometimes continuing a view in several paintings and etchings.

MCLEARY, M. Active 1827 in the northern Great Lakes region. Watercolor drawings of the Chippewa Indians. No reference. Source ANT 11/57. No auction record but the estimated value of a watercolor 8×10″ showing Indians hunting would be about $700 to $900 at auction in 1976. Signature example p 455 ANT 11/57.

A scrapbook compiled in connection with McKenney's "Tour of the Lakes" in 1827 contains a watercolor portrait of Key-way-no-wut, Going Cloud, "by Mr. McLeary of the garrison at the Sault de Marie. It is said to be an excellent likeness." Also in the scrapbook is an unpublished watercolor *Indian Method of Taking Fish* addressed to "the Colonel" and signed "M McLeary St Maries—1827." McKenney was compiling the paintings of Indians for the U S Government's Indian Office.

MCMURRY, Leonard. Born Texas Panhandle, 1913, living Oklahoma City, Okla 1975. Sculptor. Work in Oklahoma City Civic Center, Nat Cowboy Hall of Fame, Indian Hall of Fame (Anadarko, Okla). No reference. Source PER vol 3, ✳3 with sculpture example.

After attending a series of schools and colleges in Texas, McMurry enrolled in Washington U, St Louis. He studied sculpture under Carl C Mose and earned a degree in fine arts. He served in WWII, and after the war returned to sculpture, a pupil of Ivan Meštrović.

He has completed four monuments including the *Eighty Niner* for Oklahoma City, and the National Cowboy Hall of Fame has many portrait busts in its collection. He has sculpted a series of portraits of the main characters of the Battle of the Little Big Horn: Rain-in-the-Face, Sitting Bull, Col Custer, etc.

MCMURTRIE, William Birch. Born Philadelphia, Pa 1816, died Washington, DC 1872. Topographical artist for Pacific Coast Survey 1849–53, landscape and portrait painter in Philadelphia. Work in Honeyman and Karolik collns. Reference G&W. Sources ANT 10/62-FRO-HON-KW1-PAF. No current auction record. Watercolors reproduced p 234 KW1, p 396 ANT 10/62.

Son of a scientist and teacher, McMurtrie was named for the painter William Russell Birch. He applied but failed to obtain appointment to the 1838 Pacific Ocean Survey. After exhibiting oil paintings until 1845, he was hired, in 1848, as a topographical draftsman starting at $15 per month. He served from 1849 to 1853 on the ship *Ewing* for the Pacific Coast Survey. Some of the drawings and watercolors of this period are listed in KW1, including scenes in Oregon, Washington, and Idaho. McMurtrie's 1850 view of San Francisco from Telegraph Hill was lithographed and published by N Currier in 1851. While in San Francisco he secured a salary increase to $1,000 per year because of the Gold Rush inflation: "The unprecedented state of things compels me to exercise the greatest economy and privation, to obtain food and cloth-ing of the most indifferent quality." KW1.

The drawings and watercolors listed in HON are 1855–58, with scenes from San Diego to British Columbia. Between 1854 and 1858 McMurtrie may also have been in Colorado. From 1851 to 1870 he again exhibited paintings in the East. In 1859 he returned to the Coast Survey, working in the South and East.

MEAD, Ben Carlton. Born Bay City, Tex 1902, living probably Amarillo, Tex 1967. Texas illustrator specializing in the Southwest, muralist, commercial artist. Mural in Panhandle Plains Hist Soc (Canyon, Tex). No reference. Sources COW-TOB-*Amer Book Collector* summer/67 with signature example p 21. No auction record.

Mead's family moved frequently in Texas where his father opened yards for lumber companies. Educated in Amarillo, Mead studied at the AIC, with instruction in illustration from Jerome Rozen and Charles Schroeder. His first job was as a designer for a San Antonio advertising agency. He then opened his own commercial art studio in San Antonio, concentrating on illustrating for books, magazines, and newspapers. By 1935 he had illustrated 10 books. His subjects were traditional Southwestern genre, such as Mexican bandits, Texas Rangers, pioneer mother, old prospector, Indians, buffalo hunters, etc. "His ranch home is 12 miles south of Amarillo in the Palo Duro Canyon. There is atmosphere here—the kind Mead paints into his pictures. A young Indian, who tends the paint-ponies, lives in a tepee just back of the ranch house, adding a bit of true western color." TOB. By 1967 the books Mead had illustrated numbered 17, and some of the books were resold "for relatively high prices" because they contained the illustrations. ABC.

MEAKIN, Louis Henry. Born Newcastle, Eng 1850 (or 1853), died Boston, Mass 1917. Ohio landscape painter in the US and Can Rockies, etcher, teacher, curator. Member ANA 1913. Work in Cincinnati Mus, Indianapolis AA, AIC. References A17 (obit)-BEN-FIE-MAL-SMI. Sources CIN-NA 74-WHO 16. No current auction record or signature example.

Brought to the US as a child, Meakin studied at the Art Association of Cincinnati (then the School of Design) and in various schools in Germany, France, Italy, and Holland, including the Munich Academy 1882–86 and in Paris. He painted with William Picknell in France. When he returned to Cincinnati, he became an instructor at the Art Academy and painting curator at the Museum. Painting titles were *Landscape, Eden Park, In the Selkirks, Canada, Canadian Rockies, In British Columbia.* A studio portrait of Meakin is reproduced opp p 320 A17.

MEANS, Elliott Anderson. Born Stamford, Tex 1905, died NYC 1962. Painter, illustrator, and sculptor of Western and religious subjects. Member SI, Artists Guild. Relief sculptures in Govt Printing Bldg (DC), Welfare Island (NYC), post offices. References A66 (obit)-MAL. Sources SCA-book illustrations-*My Southwest* exhibition catalog 5/10/60 Grand Central Art Galleries, NYC. No auction record. Signature example catalog above.

Elliott Means as a child traveled in a covered wagon from Texas to the New Mexico homestead where he experienced a Pancho Villa raid. He was educated in El Paso before taking to the road as hobo, Oklahoma wheat-field worker, sign and mural painter on the Pacific Coast. After study at the BMFA school, he moved to NYC where he designed for expositions before becoming a sculptor and illustrator of magazines and books including the Bible. Typical painting titles were *Chaps and Spurs, Saloon on a High Hill, Birds on the Windmill, Corral, Cavalry and the Airplane.*

MECHAU, Frank Albert, Jr. Born Wakeeny (or Wakenny), Kan (or Glenwood Springs or Denver, Colo) 1903 (or 1904), died Denver, Colo 1946. Important modern Western painter, muralist, illustrator, teacher. ANA 1937. Work in Colo Spr FAC, ANS, DAM, DPL, DIA, PAC, MOMA, MMA; murals in post offices. References A47 (obit)-BEN-MAL-MAS. Sources AAT-ALA-CAP-CON-DAA-MEC-SHO-WHO 46. No current auction record but the estimated price of an oil 20×30″ showing wild horses would be about $4,000 to $5,000 at auction in 1976. Signature example p 7 MEC. (See illustration 197.)

Mechau was raised in Glenwood Springs, Colo. To finance his art education, he was a prize fighter and a railroad cattle hand. He studied at Denver U 1923–24 and the AIC 1924–25. From 1925 to 1929 he was in NYC, "studying" in the museums. From 1929 to 1931 he was in Europe, greatly influenced by the Cubists, particularly Léger. He began as a painter and teacher in Denver in 1931. His career was helped in 1934 with commissions for Federal Art Project murals. The same year, he received a Guggenheim fellowship.

In 1936 Mechau's study *Dangers of the Mail* for a post office mural caused a national controversy. The painting depicted Indians scalping nude white women after overturning a stagecoach and murdering the white men. Despite criticism as "mural turpitude," the work was painted in accordance with the study. Mechau said, "No artist ever wished to be considered an ethnologist. My intention was to create an imaginative reconstruction of a massacre." CON.

He was painting instructor at Colorado Springs FAC 1937–38 and director of art classes at Columbia 1939–43. In 1944 he began a 20,000-mile trip as artist-correspondent for the Army and for *Life,* painting scenes of Pacific army bases. When he died after only 15 years of painting, he had completed about 60 works. His practice was to proceed slowly from a thumbnail sketch, with many variations and enlargements that have also been preserved. "He changed the documentation of western life from a handpainted photographic rendering to a magnificent exploration of line, space and color." MEC.

MEEKER, Joseph Rusling. Born Newark, NJ 1827, died St Louis, Mo 1889 (or 1887). Landscape painter specializing in Louisiana bayous, portraitist. Work in City AM (St Louis), Tulane U Lib. References BEN-CHA-FIE-G&W-MAL-SMI. Sources ANT 12/49,11/61-KW1-MIS-NJA-PAF-WES. No current auction record but the estimated price of an oil 20×30″ showing a swamp interior would be about $2,500 to $3,000 at auction in 1976. Signature example p 105 MIS.

Meeker studied at the NAD 1845–46, drawing from casts. He was influenced as a landscapist by the paintings of his teacher, Asher B Durand. As a portraitist he was the pupil of Charles Loring Elliott. He painted in Buffalo, NY, then moved to Louisville, Ky in 1852. In 1859 he settled in St. Louis after traveling through a dozen other cities.

During the Civil War, Meeker served as paymaster in the Union Navy. While in Louisiana he sketched in the bayous and "fell in love with the mystery, the deadly stillness, the pale light of these somber swamps, which became the themes of his art." ANT 11/61. After the war he returned to St Louis, active there and in Wisconsin, with his paint-

ings including Indian portraits. His bayou works were dated from 1871 to 1879, painted in St Louis.

MEGARGEE, Alonzo. Born probably Philadelphia, Pa 1883 (or 1891), died probably Cottonwood, Ariz 1960. "Humorous" Western painter, illustrator, graphic artist. Work in ANS, MNM. References A41-MAL. Sources COW-SCA-WAI 71,72. No current auction record or signature example. (See illustration 198.)

Lon Megargee left Philadelphia at 13 for Arizona where he worked as "an exhibition roper in a Wild West show, a bronc buster, a fireman, a poker dealer, a police captain, and a rancher." WAI 72. Although he had not previously painted, he obtained a commission for $7,000 from the first governor of Arizona about 1911 for official paintings for the capitol building.

Megargee studied at the PAFA, the NAD, the ASL, Pratt Institute AS in Brooklyn, and Cooper Union AS. He began exhibiting at the Dallas MFA in 1936. He became best known for his illustrations for ads for Arizona Brewing Co featuring humorous aspects of cowboy life. After his death, *The Saturday Evening Post* published a double-page reproduction of Megargee's *Cowboy's Dream.*

MEGILP. Apocryphal artist before 1880 quoted in KEN 6/71 as having been west of the Mississippi: "Give me the music of the rifle in the untrodden wilderness, and let me gossip with the red-man, the bison, and the bear."

In art, "megilp" is the mixture of linseed oil and mastic varnish that was widely used in the 19th century to provide a butter-smooth vehicle for oil colors. Unfortunately it caused the paintings to fail with age. Also known as Macgilp and McGuilp, Megilp in this KEN reference may be a coined name.

MEIGS, John Liggett. Born Chicago, Ill 1916, living San Patricio, NM 1976. Modern Western painter, lithographer, author. Work in Roswell Mus (NM), U Texas (Austin), W Tex Mus (Lubbock), MNM. Reference A76. Sources CAP-COW-OSR. Tempera on board 15¾ × 13¾" *Scene in a Western Town* estimated 10/28/74 for sale for $400 to $500 at auction in LA, and sold for $175. Signature example p 184 COW.

John Meigs was raised in San Antonio and educated at the U Redlands. He worked as a newspaperman in Los Angeles and in architectural design until 1951 when he became a full-time painter, collaborating with Peter Hurd on the Pioneer frescoes at Texas Tech U. He acknowledges Hurd as his influence. He also studied in Paris at the Grande Chaumière Academy.

Meigs is the author of books on Peter Hurd lithographs (1970) and sketchbook (1971) as well as "The Cowboy in American Prints" (1972). He lectures on American Realist graphics and is a consultant on museum acquisitions. As a painter, "My object is to record the West through its people, its buildings, its landscape and to preserve, as artists have for centuries, some small part of 'how it is in your own time.'" COW.

MELROSE, Andrew W. Birthplace unknown 1836, died West New York, NJ 1901. New Jersey landscape painter who incorporated Indians in scenes and who was said to have painted in the West. Work in NYHS, Oberlin Col. Reference G&W. Source, *On the Mississippi* or *The March of American Civilization* ❋111

PB 9/28/73-AAR 11/74-ANT 11/55, 10/58,10/62; 4,11/67,11/69,10/70. Oil 22×36" *New York Harbor and the Battery* signed but not dated sold 10/25/73 for $37,500 at auction. Signature example p 681 ANT 11/67.

Andrew Melrose's studio was in West Hoboken and Guttenberg, NJ in the 1870s and 1880s. "His subjects include views in North Carolina, the Hudson Valley, the Berkshire Hills, NYC, Cornwall (England), Lake Killarney (Ireland), and the Tyrolese Alps." G&W. ANT 10/58 claims that Melrose also painted in the West. In his early paintings Melrose painted in a tight Hudson River style, but by 1887 he is said to have revealed the influence of the French Impressionists with broader brush strokes and a lighter palette. ANT 11/67.

MERRICK, William Marshall. Born Wilbraham, Mass 1833, living Chicago, Ill 1902. *Harper's Weekly* illustrator in 1866, draftsman. No reference. Source AIW. No auction record. Drawing example *Harper's Weekly* 1/27/66 p 56.

William M Merrick was living in Atchison, Kans in 1866 when *Harper's Weekly* published his Atchison sketches on Butterfield's Overland Mail-Coach and on the railroad to Pikes Peak.

MERRILD, Knud. Born Odum (Jutland), Denmark 1894, died Copenhagen, Denmark 1954. Modern Cal painter, printmaker, muralist, sculptor, writer. Work in MOMA, Phila MA, LAMA, San Diego FAS, Pomona Gall (LA), Arts & Crafts Mus (Copenhagen). References A53-MAL. Sources ALA-BDW-SCA. No current auction record or signature example.

Merrild studied at the Arts & Crafts

School of the Royal AFA in Copenhagen where his "unconventional forms" caused his expulsion. ALA. He emigrated to the US where he worked as a house painter and decorator, living in Taos and Los Angeles. His one-man show at the MNM was in 1923. In the mid-30s efforts toward "absolute beauty," he contributed *Synthesis* and *Mirage*. ALA. Designs he developed were executed in various crafts: *Man and Horse* and *Leaping Deer* were in silk embroidery for the Copenhagen Museum of Art and Industry. Murals were painted for LA buildings. He wrote "A Poet and Two Painters" as a memoir of his friend D H Lawrence (1938).

MESSENGER, Ivan. Born Omaha, Neb 1895, living San Diego, Cal 1975. Western landscape painter. Reference MAS. Source SCA. No auction record or signature example. (See illustration 199.)

Messenger earned his MA at Stanford U in 1921. He taught romance languages there and at the U of Texas. He painted watercolors in Mexico in 1922 and 1932 and in South America 1936–37.

METCALF, Willard Leroy. Born Lowell, Mass 1858, died NYC 1925. Important Eastern Impressionist landscape painter who sketched in the Southwest 1881–83, illustrator, teacher. Member of "The Ten American Painters." NIAL 1924. Work in COR, BMFA, MNM, NGA, PAFA, AIC, MMA. References A25 (obit)-BEN-DAB-ENB-FIE-MAL-SMI. Sources AAR 1,5/74-AIW-ALA-AMA-ANT 10/65,8/67,12/68,5/70,8/72; 1,9/73, 12/74-DEP-ISH-IMP-MSL-NEU-WHO 24-letter 3/76 Ede Veer. Oil 50×60″ *Indian Summer Vermont* 1922 sold 12/8/71 for $13,000 at auction. Signature example p 396 ANT 10/65. (See illustration 200.)

Metcalf was educated in Lowell and Newton public schools. At 12 he worked in a Boston store. At 17 he was apprenticed to a wood engraver and became the pupil of the landscapist G L Brown, with life classes at Lowell Institute at night. He then studied at the Massachusetts Normal AS and the BMFA. From 1883 to 1889 he was in Paris, the pupil of Boulanger and Lefebvre at the Julien Academy, sketching in Giverny near Paris and in North Africa. He moved to NYC in 1889, working as a magazine and book illustrator, teaching at Cooper Union and the ASL. In 1898 he was a founding member of "The Ten American Painters" who exhibited together for 20 years, popularizing American Impressionism.

Before his trip to France, Metcalf spent most of the years 1881 to 1883 in the Southwest. He worked in oil, watercolor, and crayon in New Mexico, Arizona, and Texas. *Harper's Magazine* published Pueblo illustrations dated "Zuni '81" showing the famous ethnologist Cushing in Indian garb. There were also El Paso sketches in 1882, and Metcalf was reported in Chicago in 1883 returning from Zuni sketching.

His painting style is said not to follow consistently any particular school and that it was his occasional use of "broken color" and his close association with Robinson and Twachtman that gave him the impressionist label.

MEUTTMAN, W. Painter active 19th–20th centuries. No reference. Source oil 14¼×10¼″ *Indian Burial* with signature example but not dated sold 4/20/72 for $450 at auction.

MEWHINNEY, Mrs Ella Koepke. Born Nelsonville, Tex 1891, living Holland,

Tex 1962. Texas landscape and flower painter. Work in Witte Mem Mus (San Antonio). References A62-MAL. Sources TOB-TXF-WAS. No current auction record. No signature example.

Mrs Mewhinney was educated at Texas Presbyterian College where she studied art with Mollie Bishop in 1908. She taught art in Bartlett, Tex, studying again in 1911 at the American Woman's League of St Louis. In 1913 she studied in Chicago. In 1919 she was at the ASL, the pupil of George Bridgman. In 1925 she studied at Colorado Springs' Broadmoor Academy with Randall Davey and Robert Reid. Her large oil of cactus *Under Texas Skies* was the center of the Texas exhibit at the Chicago Century of Progress Exposition.

MEYER, Richard Max. Active 1891 to 1898 in Portland, Ore. Painter, teacher, photographer. Work in Stenzel colln. No reference. Source PNW. No auction record but the estimated price of an oil 20×30″ showing an Indian genre subject would be about $750 to $900 at auction in 1976. Signature example p 15 PNW.

Meyer was listed in the Portland directory as both artist and photographer during this period. He painted in oil and in watercolor.

MEYERHEIM, Paul Friedrich. Born Berlin, Germany 1842, died there 1915. German genre and animal painter whose 1873 painting *Exhibition of Savages* was the original of the print *A Wild Indian Show* published in 1876. Member Berlin Acad 1869. Work in NG Berlin, Suermondt Mus (Aix-la-Chapelle), Danzig Mus. References BEN-CHA-MAL. Sources HUT-IND. Oil 23¾×27¾″ *Girl by a Well* sold 11/15/72 for $960

at auction in Cologne. Signature example BEN.

Paul Meyerheim was the pupil of his father Friedrich Eduard Meyerheim and studied at the Berlin Academy 1857–60. He traveled through Germany, Switzerland, Belgium, and Holland, remaining a year in Paris for further study. Meyerheim was interested in the circus, painting *Snake Charmer in Menagerie* in 1864 and *Circus Riders before Performance* in 1869 before depicting his wild Indian *Savages*.

MEYERS, Robert William. Born NYC 1919, died Cody, Wyom 1970. Traditional Western painter, illustrator. Member CAA. Reference A73. Sources COW-C71,73-*The New York Times* 11/22/70 (obit). No auction record but the estimated price of an oil 20×30″ showing contemporary Wyoming ranch genre would be about $1,000 to $1,500 at auction in 1976. Signature example C71.

Bob Meyers was influenced toward the West by movies he saw as a boy in Bogota, NJ. He studied at the NAD with Ivan Olinsky, at the Grand Central AS, and at the Traphagen School of Fashion. He became a successful commercial artist and illustrator, specializing in Western subjects for national magazines such as *True, Argosy,* and *The Saturday Evening Post.* He received one-man shows at the Society of Illustrators in 1955–56 but felt, "There must be more to life than just being a paint brush." *Times.*

In 1960 he moved his family to the 300-acre Circle M Ranch on the South Fork of the Shoshone River near Yellowstone Park, 50 miles from town. He became an active cattle rancher and operator of a dude ranch as well as a teacher of art classes. He also "painted his beloved ranch, his family at work. He painted the life of the West." C71. When he threatened trespassing hunters and fishermen, he was murdered by an unknown sniper while his wife and he were digging post holes for a fence. The county sheriff found no clue.

MEYERS, William Henry. See Myers.

MILLER, Alfred Jacob. Born Baltimore, Md 1810, died there 1874. Very important Eastern landscape and portrait painter who sketched Rocky Mountain Indians in 1837. Work in Joslyn AM (Omaha), GIL, Walters Art Gall, Boston Athenaeum, DAM, U of Wyom, ANS, MNM, ACM, BMFA. References BEN-CHA-FIE-G&W-MAL-SMI. Sources ACO-ANT 11/61,3/69,11/71,1/72,1/73,11/74-AOW-AWM (large number of Miller reproductions)-BAR-COW-DAA-DBW-DCC-DWF-FRO-GIL-GOD-HAR-HON-HUT-150-KAR-KW1-LAF-PAF-PAW-POW-TAW-TEP-TWR-WES-WHI. Oil 40×32″ *Trappers' Camp* sold 10/24/68 for $45,000 at auction. Signature example p 221 ANT 1/72. (See illustration 201.)

Miller's well-to-do parents encouraged his drawing at Dr Craig's school. In 1831–32 he studied portraiture with Thomas Sully. In 1833 a patron sponsored a European tour with study at the École des Beaux-Arts in Paris and the English Life School in Rome. His portrait studio, opened in Baltimore in 1834, was not successful. In 1837 he moved to New Orleans where he was selected by Capt William Drummond Stewart as artist to record a journey to the Rocky Mountains. In mid-May the expedition left Missouri by wagon along what was to become the Oregon Trail. Miller's only duty was to sketch what interested him, the first white artist in the area. The wagon train crossed the Continental Divide through the South Pass, camping for a month at the rendezvous of the moun-

tain men and their Indian allies in what is now southwestern Wyoming. By mid-October, Miller and Stewart were back in St Louis. Miller had made about 166 sketches in the West, to which he never returned. These anecdotal sketches provided only impressions of the subjects, with no ethnological detail, but Miller's importance is unquestioned. He was the only artist in the West at the time of the mountain men. His paintings were the first made of the "interior West," except for Seymour's.

In 1838 Miller was in New Orleans and Baltimore, resuming his portrait painting and developing his Western sketches into 18 large oils. From 1840 to 1842 he lived in Capt Stewart's Murthly Castle in Scotland, painting oils as decorations depicting favorite episodes from the trip. He also delivered a portfolio of 83 small drawings and watercolors. Miller spent the rest of his life in Baltimore, a typical artist of the time except for his fame for Indian subjects. Every year he painted Indian scenes for the local trade, the 425 such pictures becoming more formal and decorative with the years, the authenticity diminishing. In 1858 he began copying his field sketches for what became the Walters Gallery. This involved 200 watercolors at $12 each, including *The Trapper's Bride* "which Miller copied and sold to a good many purchasers besides Walters." AWM. Another group of 80 watercolors was copied for an Englishman for $25 each in 1867. Miller's top price was $200, for a 48× 32″ Rocky Mountain oil.

MILLER, Ralph Davison. Born Cincinnati, Ohio 1858, died Los Angeles, Cal 1945. Western landscape painter. Reference A47 (obit). Sources BDW-SCA. No auction record or signature example.

Self-taught in art except for instruction from Bingham, Miller was educated in Cincinnati and Kansas City. In the 1880s he was painting in New Mexico. Beginning 1890 he settled in Los Angeles specializing in still life, landscape and marine subjects.

MILLET, Francis Davis. Born Mattapoisett, Mass 1846, died on the *Titanic* 1912. Painter, muralist, artist-correspondent, author. ANA 1882, NA 1885. Chevalier, Legion of Honor 1900. Work in MMA, Union League Club (NYC), and Tate Galleries (London); murals in World's Columbian Expos, Minn and Wis capitols, Baltimore custom house, Cleveland federal building. References A13 (obit)-BEN-CHA-DAB-ENB-FIE-MAL-SMI. Sources ALA-AMA-BAR-ISH-M57-MSL-SCU-WHO 12. Oil 14× 10" *Fastening the Strophion* sold 6/3/71 for $650 at auction. No signature example.

Millet served as a drummer in the Civil War. He graduated from Harvard in 1869, then worked as a lithographer to pay for his study at the Royal Academy in Antwerp 1871–73. He also studied painting in Rome and Venice. In 1876 he exhibited at the Philadelphia Centennial, then collaborated on murals for Boston's Trinity Church with John La Farge. In 1877 he was artist-correspondent for the Russo-Turkish War. In 1884 he formed a "Bohemian" colony in England with E A Abbey and J S Sargent. He was director of decorations and master of ceremonies at the World's Columbian Exposition of 1893. He was artist-correspondent during the Spanish-American War. Millet went down with the *Titanic* while traveling in his capacity as director of the American Academy in Rome.

Many of Millet's paintings and murals were historical, showing, for example, mail delivery in the West and in Alaska. In his Minnesota mural his depiction of Sioux Indians was drawn from the 1851 work of Frank Blackwell Mayer.

MILLET, Jean François. Born Gruchy, near Gréville, France 1814, died Barbizon, France 1875. Very important French painter of peasant life. Legion of Honor. Work in Louvre, MNM, MMA, AIC. References BEN-CHA-ENB-MAL. Sources AIC-ALA-AMA-ANT 9/43-ARI-BAR-CAH-DEP-HUD-ISH-KW1-PAF-POW. Oil 40×32" *Portrait of M de Witt* sold in 1968 for $99,000 at auction in England. Signature example p 108 ANT 9/43.

Millet was raised as a peasant. He became the pupil of Mouchel on the strength of untutored drawings but went back to work the farm when his father died in 1835. After returning to art he became the pupil of Delaroche. His first success was in 1844. In 1848 a commission enabled him to move to Barbizon, but he was not financially secure until 1860. Millet was a major influence on American artists like William Morris Hunt who "taught that art is found inside the artist himself rather than outside him in the subject." BAR. Millet through Hunt popularized the Barbizon school in America.

In 1850 Karl Bodmer who was then the best known of the Barbizon artists engaged the struggling Millet to make a hundred Indian drawings for an American publisher. Millet worked from Bodmer's own sketches without having seen an Indian. When the publisher found that the work was by Millet rather than Bodmer, he canceled the commission. By 1879 Millet had died a famous artist while Bodmer, whose vogue had passed, was obliged to sell some of his Millet drawings including Bodmer-Millet lithographs of Indians. In 1887 more than 20 Indian drawings by Millet were exhibited. In 1889 and 1892 Bodmer sold the last of his Millet Indian lithographs: "The whereabouts of the original drawings on which the two collaborated is unknown. To an American who had seen and known Indians, the Millet drawings might not seem quite authentic. The figures of pioneers and settlers in some of them resembled French peasants." ANT.

MILLS, John Harrison (not Harrison W Mills). Born near Buffalo, NY 1842 (not Denver, Colo 1841), died there 1916. Landscape, genre, and portrait painter, engraver, sculptor, poet. Work in Albright Gall (Buffalo), Pioneers' Mus (Colo Springs). References A17 (obit)-BEN-MAL-SMI. Sources AIW-SHO. No auction record but the estimated price of an oil 20×30″ showing a genre Denver scene would be about $1,200 to $1,500 at auction in 1976. Signature example p 14 SHO.

Mills, born on a farm, was the pupil of John Jamison, a Buffalo bank-note engraver, in 1857. He became the pupil of the sculptor William Lautz in 1858. His portraits begun in 1859 were encouraged by Lars Sellstedt and W H Beard. Wounded at the second battle of Bull Run, he returned to Buffalo where he exhibited paintings and a bust of Lincoln he had made from studies while guarding Lincoln's body in Buffalo.

In 1872 Mills settled in a log cabin near Longs Peak, Colo before moving to Denver as an artist, illustrator, and teacher. "His genre scenes tend to fall into the initial settlement period characterized by romantic painting based upon regional subject matter." SHO. He was also a portraitist and the organizer of Denver's first art school, the Colorado Academy of Fine Arts. His Colorado illustrations were published in *Leslie's* in 1873, in *Scribner's* 1878, and in *Cosmopolitan* 1888. Mills had left for NYC in 1883.

MINER, Frederick Roland. Born New London, Conn 1876, living probably Pasadena, Cal 1933. Southern Cal landscape painter, photographer, writer. Work in Union League Club (LA), Glendale Sanitarium (Cal). References A33-BEN-FIE-MAL. Source SCA. No current auction record or signature example. (See illustration 202.)

Fred R Miner studied at the ASL and was the pupil of William Wendt and John Carlson. He settled in California by 1897, returning to New York and Connecticut in 1911, 1916, 1921, and 1925. Miner's book "Outdoor California" with his own photos and paintings as illustrations was published in 1923.

MIRABEL, Vicente. Born Taos, NM 1918, died Battle of the Bulge, WWII 1945. Leading Taos Pueblo painter. Work in City AM (St Louis), MAI, U of Okla. Sources AHI 8/52-AIP. No auction record but the estimated price of a watercolor 16×20″ showing a Turtle Dance would be about $600 to $800 at auction in 1976. Signature example p 22 AHI 8/52.

Mirabel, called Chiu Tah or Dancing Boy, graduated from the Santa Fe Indian School. He was assistant painting instructor at the school when he entered the army, at which time he was regarded as the most promising of the Taos Pueblo artists.

MITCHELL, Alfred. Active 1887–89 in Colorado as illustrator for *Harper's Weekly* specializing in mining subjects. No reference. Source AIW. No auction record or signature example.

MITCHELL, Alfred R. Born York, Pa 1888 (or 1886), died probably San Diego, Cal 1972. California landscape painter, teacher. Work in Reading Mus (Pa), San Diego FAS, San Diego Mus of Man, U WVA. References A62-FIE-MAL-SMI. Source ASD. No auction record but the estimated price of an oil 20×30″ showing a California landscape would be $400 to $500 at auction in 1976. Painting example ASD.

Mitchell came to San Diego at 16. He prospected for gold and drove express stages in Nevada. He studied art under Maurice Braun at the San Diego AA, then attended the PAFA, the pupil of Garber and Pearson, and went to Europe on a scholarship in 1920. Later he also studied with Philip Hale and Blashfield before returning to San Diego where he was still teaching painting in 1970.

MITCHELL, Arthur. Born Trinidad, Colo 1889, living there 1974. Traditional Western painter, illustrator. No reference. Sources HAR-PER vol 3 ⚹3. Two oils 24×17¼" *Wounded Cowboy* and 24×20" *Cowboy on Horse* sold 10/27/71 for $160 the pair at auction. Signature example p 145 HAR.

Mitchell was raised on a Colorado homestead, becoming a cowhand at 18 in northern New Mexico. After serving in WWI he studied at the Grand Central School of Art under Harvey Dunn, establishing his studio in NYC. About 1928 he moved to Leonia, NJ, working as a magazine and book illustrator. The neighbor of Charles Chapman, Frank Street, and Grant Reynard, he painted 160 covers for Western pulp magazines. About 1946 Mitchell returned to Colorado, teaching at Trinidad State Junior College. He founded the Baca House Pioneer Museum.

MITCHELL, George Bertrand. Born East Bridgewater, Mass 1872 (or 1873), died Mystic, Conn 1966. Painter specializing in Blackfoot Indians of Canadian Rockies, illustrator, writer. Work in Glasgow (Scotland), Etaples (France), Marine Hist Assn (Mystic). References A62-BEN-MAL. Source 1966 news

release Rutherford Art Studio. No auction record but the estimated price of a watercolor 20×16" showing a Blackfoot dance would be about $800 to $900 at auction in 1976. No signature example. (See illustration 203.)

G B Mitchell began his studies at Lowell Institute of Design (Boston) as a textile designer. Summer jobs at Provincetown, Mass brought him into contact with artists. He transferred to Artist Artisans in NYC and Cowles Art School in Boston before going to Paris for three years at the Colarossi, the Beaux-Arts, and the Julien Academy under Laurens and Constant. On returning to NYC he became art manager for McClure Publications for seven years.

As vice president of the advertising agency representing the Canadian Pacific Railway and Steamship Lines, he toured the Orient in 1924 and commenced his 25-year involvement with the Blackfoot Indians of the Stoney Reserve in the Canadian Rockies. Admitted as a blood brother and named O-Ha-Ze-Na-Na, Spotted Cloud, he exhibited paintings and film of the Indians, writing and illustrating to foster travel. He also collected Indian regalia, Western garb, and firearms.

MITCHELL, Thomas John. Born Rochester, NY 1875, living there 1941. Eastern landscape painter. Work in Memorial AG, Univ Club, Iolo Sanitarium (all Rochester). References A41-BEN-MAL. Source, painting *Indian Village, Taos, NM* in Memorial AG. No auction record but the estimated price of an oil 20×30" showing the Taos Pueblo would be about $750 to $1,000 at auction in 1976. No signature example. (See illustration 204.)

Mitchell was the pupil of the Mechanics Institute and the Art School in Rochester. A17 through A41 indicate Rochester residence, studio, clubs, exhibitions, and collections. There is no reference to Mitchell in TAL or TSF, but his Taos paintings bear a WPA plate indicating a visit West in the mid-1930s.

MIZEN, Frederic Kimball. Born Chicago, Ill 1888, died there 1964 (or 1965). Portrait painter, Taos Indian painter, and illustrator, teacher. Work in ANS, HAR. References A41-MAL. Sources HAR-ILA-WHO 62. No auction record but the estimated price of an oil 20×30″ showing an Indian ceremony would be about $1,200 to $1,500 at auction in 1976. Signature example p 147 HAR. (See illustration 205.)

Mizen's father had been secretary to generals stationed in the West. Mizen was educated in Chicago public schools with summers spent in the West with his father. He became the pupil of Walter Ufer at the J Francis Smith Academy of Art in Chicago 1904–6. He next studied at the AIC in the evenings, the pupil of Vanderpoel and Clute. At 20 he was a Sears catalog illustrator. He became known for his 14 years of billboard advertisements, including the first such ad for Coca-Cola, as well as covers for *The Saturday Evening Post, American,* and *Collier's.*

In Taos in 1935 he again studied with Ufer, receiving a commission from the Santa Fe Ry for Indian paintings and Southwest landscapes. In 1936 he founded the Mizen Art Academy in Chicago, limiting his own paintings to portraits after 1939. Summers were spent in Taos, painting and teaching. From 1952 to 1960 he was chairman of the art department at Baylor U.

MÖLLHAUSEN, Heinrich Balduin. Born near Bonn, Germany 1825, died Berlin, Germany 1905. Railway survey, topographical, and sketch artist, author called "the German Fenimore Cooper." Work in Staatliches Mus für Völkerkunde (Berlin), ACM, Oklahoma Hist Soc, US Nat Mus (Washington). References DAB-G&W. Sources AIW-POW-SUR-TEP. No auction record but the estimated value of a sketch 8×10″ showing the Grand Canyon would be $2,000 to $2,500 at auction in 1976. Drawing examples plates 11 to 16 AIW.

Möllhausen's father Heinrich, a retired Prussian officer, roamed the world as a civil engineer, including mapmaking in Texas in 1840. Möllhausen attended the Gymnasium at Bonn until 14, became a farmer in Pomerania, and fought in the Revolution of 1848. In 1849 he sailed for the US, becoming a hunter in Illinois. In 1851 he joined Prince Paul of Württemberg in an expedition to the Rockies. The party turned back at Laramie, Wyom due to difficulties with Indians and weather. Möllhausen was left to winter on his own on Sandy Hill Creek, Neb, in mortal danger from wolf packs, ill health, ice, and Pawnees before rescue by friendly Otos.

In the fall of 1852 he returned to Germany with a consignment of animals for the Berlin zoo. By May 1853 he was in Washington, appointed topographer to Lt Whipple's railway survey along the 35th parallel. The expedition proceeded from Arkansas through Texas, New Mexico, Arizona, and the coast range to Los Angeles in March 1854. Möllhausen was the illustrator of the Whipple report, depicting Navaho and Mohave Indians as well as landscape. He was in Germany by the end of the summer, obtaining sponsorship of the King of Prussia and completing his diary. In 1857 his friend from the Whipple survey, Lt Ives, appointed him as artist for an expedition to explore the Colorado River. By April 1858 they reached the Grand Canyon, before returning east by the Santa Fe trail. The Ives report was illustrated by Möllhausen and von Egloffstein, the topographer. For the rest of his life

Möllhausen concentrated on his writing in Germany, producing 178 volumes. The earlier books are adventure stories taking place in America: "In view of his splendid portrayals of Indian and pioneer life, there is none who deserves so much the title of 'The German Cooper.'" DAB. Most of Möllhausen's original sketches were burned during the attack on Berlin in 1945.

MOMADAY, Alfred Morris. Born Mountain View, Okla 1913, living Jemez Pueblo, NM 1976. Important Kiowa painter, medalist, teacher. Work in GIL, MAI, MNM, Philbrook AC. Reference A76. Source AIC-LAF-PWA 3/75-WHO 70 (under Navarre Scott Momaday). No auction record. Signature example p 140 LAF *Apache Fire Dance*. Portrait photo p 5 PWA 3/75.

Al Momaday (Huan Toa or War Lance) is the grandson of the first Kiowa judge, on the one side, and a Kiowa medicine man. He was educated at Bacone Col, NMU, and UCLA. He became principal and art teacher at Jemez Day School 1947–67, initiating an arts and crafts program that brought international recognition. He also directed arts and crafts for expositions and fairs.

Momaday was designated outstanding Indian artist in 1956 and again in 1962. In 1975 he was commissioned to create a medal honoring his own son, Dr N Scott Momaday, the first American Indian to win a Pulitzer Prize for literature.

MONAGHAN, Eileen. See Whitaker, Eileen.

MONTOYA, Alfredo. Born probably San Ildefonso Pueblo, NM before 1890, died probably there 1913. The first of the modern Pueblo painters. Work in MAI, MNM. Sources AHI 2/50-AIP. No auction record or signature example.

Montoya's Indian name was Wen Tsireh, Pine Tree Bird. In 1911 he attended San Ildefonso school where his teacher Elizabeth Richards encouraged him to paint Indian subjects as an Indian, departing from government edict opposing Indian customs. The result was splendid Montoya drawings depicting ceremonial native dances, setting the pattern for the later Rio Grande painters. The drawings were exhibited in England.

About 1915 Montoya worked on Pajarito Plateau excavations for the School of American Research. His tubercular condition precluded digging so he became a recorder, drawing replicas of the unearthed ceremonial life. He was "perhaps the young man from San Ildefonso who initiated modern pueblo painting." AIP.

MONTOYA, Gerónima Cruz. Born San Juan Pueblo, NM 1915, living Santa Fe, NM 1976. Pueblo painter, important teacher, lecturer. Work in De Young MA, Hall of Ethnology, MAI, MNM. Reference A76. Sources AHI 2/50-AIP. No auction record or signature example.

Gerónima Montoya's San Juan name is Po Tsunn or Shell. Her mother was a potter. She graduated Santa Fe Indian School in 1935, attending NMU and Claremont before receiving her BS from St Joseph's in 1958. She studied art under Dorothy Dunn, Alfredo Martínez, and Kenneth Chapman, acting as assistant to Dorothy Dunn at Santa Fe Indian School 1935–37. She served as chairman of the art department at the school 1937–61, with credit as the teacher who most encouraged Indian artists. Since 1961 she has been concerned with adult education at San Juan Day School, San Juan Pueblo.

Her own career as a painter has been subordinated to her role as a teacher. Her exhibitions and purchase prizes on the national level did not begin until about 1954.

MOODY, Edwin. Active 1850–61 in San Francisco. Lithographic artist, marine and topographical painter. Reference G&W. Sources COS-OCA. No auction record. Signature example pl 87 COS.

Moody appears as the lithographic artist in Sept 1850 for *View of San Francisco from Telegraph Hill,* Peirce & Pollard, and as the original artist in July 1851 for the powerful *Wreck of the Steamship Union on the Coast of Lower California.* Moody was listed in the San Francisco CD for 1861.

MOON, Carl. Born Wilmington, Ohio 1879, died probably Pasadena, Cal 1948. Book and magazine illustrator, painter, writer on Indian subjects, photographer. Work in Smithsonian Inst, Huntington Lib (San Marino, Cal), Montclair AM, Lib Cong, AMNH. References A53 (obit)-MAL-SMI. Sources 50G-ILP-WHO 48. No current auction record or signature example.

Son of a doctor, Moon graduated from Wilmington high school, a member of the Ohio National Guard in 1897. From 1904 to 1907 he ran a photographic studio in Albuquerque where he made the first collection of photographs and paintings of the Pueblo Indians. From 1907 to 1914 he was at the Grand Canyon headquarters of Fred Harvey, in charge of the art business. For the AMNH and for Harvey, Moon made a historic collection of pictures of American Indians. He also collected Indian prints for the Library of Congress and for the Montclair Museum.

As a painter he had studied with Thomas Moran, Frank Sauerwein, and Louis Akin. When he married in 1911 and moved to Pasadena in 1914, he began working with his wife as co-writer and as illustrator: "Lost Indian Magic" (1918), "Wongo and the Wise Old Crow," "The Flaming Arrow" (1927), "Painted Moccasin" (1931), and many other Indian and Mexican stories for children. He also painted 24 Indian studies for the Huntington Library, four for the Otto Vollbehr colln (Charlottenburg, Germany), and 26 oil paintings of Indians of the Southwest for the Smithsonian.

MOORE, John W (or John Marcellus, or "Tex"). Born near Fort Worth, Tex 1865, living Wichita Falls, Tex 1948. Self-taught painter of the West in Texas and Yellowstone. Work in Ft Worth AM, Santa Fe RR colln. Reference MAS. Source TOB. No current auction record. No signature example.

Tex Moore's father started the Abilene Trail. Moore worked as a cowboy when the range was "open" and drew by the chuckwagon fire at night. He was a Texas Ranger and an Indian Scout with Gen Crook in the campaign against Geronimo's Apaches.

Encouraged by Remington, Moore painted cowboy genre scenes and landscapes of Colorado, Montana, and Wyoming. About 1885 he opened a studio near Yellowstone Park. The Santa Fe Railroad commissioned a painting of the Grand Canyon. In 1935 Moore returned to Texas, establishing his studio in Wichita Falls. That year the Texas Legislature in its Resolution 48 designated him the "Official Cowboy Artist of the Lone Star State."

MOORE, Tom James. Born Dallas, Tex 1892, living Hamilton, Mont 1948. Montana painter, printmaker, muralist. Work in NY World's Fair (1939); mural Kalispell, Mont. References A41-MAS. Sources AAT-WNW. No current auction record. Signature example p 123 AAT *Saturday Night Dance*.

Moore studied at the Cincinnati AA, the pupil of Frank Duveneck, and with George Luks and John Sloan. He worked as staff artist with the US Public Health Service, Rocky Mountain Laboratory, in Hamilton.

MOPOPE, Stephen. Born near Red Stone Baptist Mission, Kiowa Reservation, Okla 1898 (not 1900), living Fort Cobb, Okla 1967. Painter, one of the original "Five Kiowas." Work in GIL, MAI, MNM, Philbrook AC; murals in public buildings. References A41-MAS. Sources AIP-COW-LAF-2/8/74 letter from J K Reeve, Philbrook AC. No current auction record. Painting example p 257 LAF. (See illustration 206.)

Mopope's Kiowa name is Qued Koi or Painted Robe. His grandfather was Spanish, kidnapped from a wagon train. Educated up to 7th grade in mission school, his granduncles taught him to paint on tanned skins. In 1926 he was a member of Mrs Susie Peters' Fine Arts Club. Along with Asah, Hokeah, and Tsatoke he was brought to Dr O B Jacobson at the U of Oklahoma art school for special training under instructor Edith Mahier.

The work of the "Five Kiowas" created a sensation in 1928 at the First International Art Exposition in Prague. The acclaim carried on until the great Depression. Mopope had continued as an artist and was honored with a one-man show at the American Indian Exposition in Anadarko in 1965.

MORA, Francis Luis. Born Montevideo, Uruguay 1874, died probably NYC 1940. Eastern painter in oil and watercolor, illustrator, muralist, etcher, teacher. ANA 1904, NA 1906. Work in White House (Harding portrait), MMA, Newark AM, NAD, Royal Art Gall (Ottawa); murals in post offices. References A41-BEN-FIE-MAL-SMI. Sources ANT 10/71,12/74-COW-HAR-INS 1/08,5/08-M57-MSL-NJA-TWR-WHO 40. Oil 77×42" *Portrait of Patty Mora* 1931 sold for $1,500 at auction. Signature example p cvii INS 1/08. (See illustration 207.)

F Luis Mora, son of the Spanish sculptor Domingo Mora, was educated at Manning's Seminary in Perth Amboy, NJ and public schools in NYC and Boston. He was the pupil of his father, of Benson and Tarbell at the Boston MFA School, and of Mowbray at the ASL. Beginning 1892 Mora was an illustrator for the leading magazines. Two years later he was included in major fine arts exhibitions. His first important mural commission was in 1900.

He was the older brother of Jo Mora who was in the West in 1900 for ethnological studies of Indians. F Luis Mora also traveled and painted in the West. His *Indian Family* is in the Harmsen collection.

MORA, Joseph Jacinto. Born Montevideo, Uruguay 1876, died Monterey, Cal 1947. Sculptor, painter, illustrator, muralist, author. Member NSS. Work in Valley Nat Bank (Phoenix), Casa Serrano (Monterey), 13 dioramas in Will Rogers Mem Mus (Claremore, Okla), Indian plaque Rainbow Natural Bridge, Sutter's Fort Hist Mus (Sacramento). References A41 - BEN - FIE - MAL-SMI. Sources AHI 9/52 (9 paintings reproduced) - BWB - COW - TWR - WHO 48. No auction record as sculptor or painter. Signature example p 17 AHI 9/52.

Jo Mora graduated from Pingry Acad

in Elizabeth, NJ in 1894. He was the pupil of his father and studied at both the ASL and Chase's School in NYC as well as Cowles Art School in Boston. He worked as an artist for Boston newspapers until 1900 when he went to Mexico, beginning a horseback tour to gather material for a book while painting and sketching. He stopped at the large ranches, joining in the work, until he reached San Jose, Cal where he sketched the missions. He was the illustrator of children's books in 1901–2.

From 1902 to 1907 he lived with the Hopi and Navaho Indians in Arizona and New Mexico. He learned the languages and painted an ethnological record, particularly of the Kachina ceremonial dances. He then established his studio in Pebble Beach, Cal where he executed many sculpture commissions including heroic bronzes. He published his humorous Jo Mora maps and wrote two books, "Trail Dust and Saddle Leather" and "Californios." The first book was about the horse in America, with his own illustrations. He also painted a watercolor series, "Horsemen of the West."

MORAN, Edward. Born Bolton, Lancashire, Eng 1829, died NYC 1901. Eastern marine painter who used Indian figures. Cited DAB and G&W as ANA but not listed NA 74. Work in Phila MA, MMA, BMFA, DAM. References A03 (obit) - BEN - CHA - DAB - ENB - FIE - G&W-MAL-SMI. Sources ANT 1/64; 3, 6/68; 4, 8/70; 2/71; 9, 11/72; 4/73- BOA - COW - DAA - EDW - HUT - KW1- M31-MOR-MSL-PAF-POW. Oil 38½ × 26½" *Bringing in the Catch* signed but not dated sold 9/13/72 for $6,250 at auction; an oil of identical specification was estimated 1/24/74 at $6,000 to $7,000 for sale at auction, and sold that date for $6,750. Oil 16×22" *The First Landing* signed and depicting Indians as observers was estimated 3/4/74 at $1,000 to $1,500 for sale at auction. Signature example *The First Landing* above.

The older brother of Thomas and Peter, Edward Moran was raised as a hand-loom weaver. When his family emigrated to Maryland in 1844, the penniless Moran walked to Philadelphia to improve his employment. Talent for drawing led him to the landscape painter Paul Weber and to the marine painter James Hamilton. Moran opened his own Philadelphia studio in an attic over a cigar store. By 1857 he was established as an artist, the teacher of brother Thomas, and on the way to becoming the leading marine painter. When he was dissatisfied with the placement of his paintings at the PAFA in 1868, he expressed his objection by using "varnishing day" to coat the paintings with an opaque red of beer and porter. He had been to England in 1862, and in 1871 he exhibited 75 paintings for charity before settling in NYC in 1872. His studio was a center of artistic life of the time. Edward Percy and John Leon were his sons.

His important series was 13 large paintings illustrating the marine history of the US. The sixth painting was *Henry Hudson Entering New York Bay 1609.* "The interest centers in the effect upon the natives, the mingled fear and defiant surprise of the Indian warrior heightened through the grouping of the squaw and Indian dog, with the Indian hut in the background." EDW. The series was exhibited at the MMA in 1904, at the NGA in 1907, and at the PAFA.

MORAN, Peter. Born Bolton, Lancashire, Eng 1841 (or 1842), died Philadelphia, Pa 1914. Landscape and animal painter in oil and watercolor, etcher, illustrator. Work in ACM, Parrish AM (LI, NY), MMA, Peabody Inst (Baltimore). References A15 (obit) - BEN - CHA - DAB - FIE - G&W - MAL - SMI. Sources ACM-AIW-ANT 5/65,7/68,1/

69,3/72-BOA-HUT-KW1-MSL-PAF-PCN-POW-SPR-TAW-WHO 14-"The Moran Family" 1965 Heckscher Mus (Huntington, NY). Watercolor 11×17" *The Homesteaders* sold 4/20/72 for $1,000 at auction. Signature example p 252 PCN. (See illustration 208.)

Peter, the youngest of the four Moran brothers, was brought to the US at 3. He graduated from Harrison Grammar School in Philadelphia in 1857 and was apprenticed to Herline and Hersel, lithographic printers. He soon became the pupil of his brothers Edward and Thomas in their Philadelphia studio. Peter's interest was in animal subjects rather than marines or landscapes like his more famous brothers. He copied Rosa Bonheur and Van Mercke. In 1863 he returned to England to become the pupil of Landseer but left after seeing Landseer's work. He maintained his studio in Philadelphia for the rest of his life, making "his mark as a competent and prolific etcher." DAB. In addition to his art, he was said to have been involved in the theater as a scene painter and bit player.

While Thomas Moran made his first trip West in 1871, Peter Moran had already been in New Mexico in 1864. Peter accompanied Thomas on a trip to the Tetons in 1879, taking the Union Pacific west to Donner Pass, then traveling south and east to the Teton River. Peter was also with Capt Bourke on the ethnographic trip to Indian pueblos in New Mexico and Arizona in 1881, as mentioned in "The Snake-Dance of the Moquis of Arizona." ACM illustrates 19 Southwestern works on paper, giving dates of 1879 to 1890. In 1890 Peter Moran (along with Julian Scott, Gilbert Gaul, Walter Shirlaw, and Henry R Poore) was a special agent for the government to take the census among the Indians. The report "Indians Taxed and Indians Not Taxed" included three illustrations by Peter Moran on the Shoshone Agency in Wyoming, published "just at the time the frontier in American history had ceased to exist." AIW.

MORAN, Thomas. Born Bolton, Lancashire, Eng 1837, died Santa Barbara, Cal 1926. Very important panoramic Western landscape painter, illustrator, etcher. ANA 1881, NA 1884. Work in MNM, MMA, Nat Cowboy Hall of Fame, NGA, the Capitol (DC), GIL, Wilstach Gall (Philadelphia), Buffalo FAA, Carnegie Inst, ANS, Walker AG (Minneapolis), etc. References A26 (obit) - BEN - CHA - DAB - ENB - FIE - G&W-MAL-SMI. Sources AAR 9/73-AIW-ALA-AMA-ANT 1/49,2/51,4/53, 11/62,12/64,5/66; 5,11/67; 4,11/68; 3/69; 1,6/70; 4/71; 5,8/72; 4/73; 4,6, 7, 12/74-ARC-BAR-BOA-COW-DBW-DCC - FRO - GIL - GOD - HAR - HMA - HUD-HUT-ISH-150-JNB-KW1-MCA-M19-MSL-NGA-NJA-PAF-PAW-POW-SHO-SPR-TAW-TSF-TWR-WAI 71,72-WES-WHI-WHO 26. Oil 80×63" *The Mountain of the Holy Cross, Colorado* signed and dated 1875 sold 4/8/71 for $110,000 at auction of Huntington Hartford property. Signature example p 200 GIL. (See illustration 209.)

Moran was the son of a hand-loom weaver, the brother of Edward and Peter. His family emigrated in 1844 to Philadelphia where in 1853 he was apprenticed to a wood engraver, sketching designs on the blocks. As the pupil of Edward, he began to paint, making his first etchings in 1856 when he took space in Edward's studio. After exhibiting an oil in 1858, he made his first sketching trip westward in 1860, to Lake Superior. In 1861 and 1862 he went to England with Edward, both brothers falling under the influence of Turner whose pictures they copied. In 1866 and 1867 Moran went to Europe, meeting another influence, Corot, and making studies of Venice.

In 1871, when Moran was 34, he found the subject matter for the rest of his life. He accompanied the geologist Dr F V Hayden on a surveying expedition to the Grand Canyon of the Yellowstone. When he returned, he moved his studio to Newark and began on huge Western paintings. In 1872 he visited the Yosemite and California. In 1873 he painted the Grand Canyon of the Colorado, and Congress bought this and the Yellowstone painting for $10,000 each. In 1874 he painted the Mountain of the Holy Cross. In 1879 he went to the Tetons with his brother Peter, after Florida and Wisconsin jaunts. From 1881 to 1911 Moran traveled almost every year, to Colorado, New Mexico, Europe, Mexico, Florida, Arizona, Wyoming, Idaho, Utah, etc. In contrast with Bierstadt, who died rejected, Moran's Western paintings with the distinctive monogram developed in 1873 and the thumbprint affixed from 1911 remained in demand. Moran painted his emotions as landscape: "I place no value upon literal transcriptions from Nature. All my tendencies are toward idealization. A place as a place has no value in itself for the artist. While I desire to tell truly of Nature, I do not wish to realize the scene literally but to convey its true impression." AIW. Still debunking modern art on his deathbed at 90, he saw his own yet-to-be painted landscapes on the ceiling and talked of them. Mt Moran was named for him.

MORANG, Alfred Gwynne. Born Ellsworth, Me 1901, died probably Santa Fe, NM 1958. Santa Fe nonobjective painter, illustrator, etcher, lecturer, writer, teacher. Work in MNM (Santa Fe), Eastern NM Col, Canyon Mus (Tex). Reference A59 (obit). Source TSF. No auction record. No signature example.

Alfred Morang was educated at Fremond U, earning a master's degree in Fine Arts, and was the pupil of Henry B Snell and Carroll S Tyson. He was an illustrator for magazines and books. In 1939 he moved to Santa Fe. The next year, he was the author of "Transcendental Painting." He founded the

334

Morang School FA in Santa Fe and was the producer of "The World of Art" on the Santa Fe radio station. Morang was survived by his former wife, Dorothy Morang (see entry).

MORANG, Mrs Dorothy (Alden Clark). Born Bridgton, Me 1906, living Santa Fe, NM 1966. Santa Fe nonobjective painter and museum curator, craftsman. Work in MNM, Canyon Mus (Tex). Reference A66. Sources WAA-W64. No auction record. No signature example.

Mrs Morang studied at the NE Conservatory of Music in Boston in 1928, after having taught in West Bridgton, Me 1922–23. She was a piano teacher and soloist in Maine 1928–36. She married the painter Alfred Morang in 1930. They moved to Santa Fe in 1939. The pupil of her husband, of Raymond Jonson, and of Emil Bisttram, she painted with the WPA Art Project in Santa Fe 1939–41. In 1942 she began working with the Museum of New Mexico.

MORGAN, Robert F. Born Helena, Mont 1929, living there 1969. Montana wildlife painter, sculptor, museum curator. No reference. Source MON. No auction record. Signature example center section MON.

Bob Morgan studied art in Helena high school, the pupil of Mabel Bjork. He worked as a commercial artist while the pupil of Jack Beauchamp at Carroll College. In 1960 he became curator at the museum of the Montana Historical Society. As a painter he "fills an average of 15 sketch books a year." MON. His specialty is wild birds, particularly ducks and geese.

MORRIS, Edmund Montague. Born Perth, Ont, Can 1871, died probably Toronto, Ont, Can 1913. Can painter specializing in Indian studies. Co-founder, Can Art Club. Work in Royal Ont Mus, AG of Toronto. Reference MAL. Sources CAH-CAN. No current auction record. Painting example p 121 CAH.

Edmund Morris was a member of the Toronto ASL which provided classes and sketching trips. He then studied at the ASL in NYC and at the Julien Academy in Paris, returning in 1896. In 1907 he was co-founder of the Canadian Art Club, intended to stimulate a spirit of nationalism in art and to hold exhibitions with standards of excellence. When Morris became a member of the board of the Art Gallery of Toronto, the Gallery absorbed functions of the Club. After Morris' death by drowning, the Club disbanded.

One of the Eastern painters who was recognized as an interpreter of the scenery and genre of Western Canada, Morris was "well known for his authentic Indian studies, many of which are in the collections of the Royal Ontario Museum." CAN. In 1906 he had gone with a government commission to James Bay, and in 1907 he completed a large series of Indian portraits. He sketched in the West in 1910, using "dark Dutch tonalities, strangely modern." CAH.

MORRIS, Ernest. Born probably California 1927, living Templeton, Cal 1968. Traditional Western painter, braider of rawhide lariats. No reference. Source COW. No auction record or signature example.

Influenced by Russell, Will James, and Borein as a painter, Morris specializes in scenes of the old West and the California vaquero.

MORRIS, Mrs Florence Ann. Born Nevada, Mo 1876, living Roswell, NM 1947. New Mexico painter of Indian history, portraits, and landscapes. Member NM Archaeol Soc. Work in MA & Archaeology (Santa Fe), MNM, US Bldg (Sorbonne), Women's Club Bldg (Sorbonne), Women's Club Bldg (Paris), Will Rogers Mem Lib, etc. References A47-BEN-MAL. Source WHO 44. No current auction record or signature example.

Educated in Missouri public and private schools, Mrs Morris studied with W C Rollins, A J Hammond, and L Brezoli, in Paris, Antwerp, and Florence. She married Richard E Morris in 1895. Her first listed award was in 1925 in New Mexico. Named painting titles were *The Papoose*, portrait of *Will Rogers, New Mexico Landscape, Old Baldy, Shasta Tribe, Ancient Acoma, Zuni Water Carriers*.

MORRIS, George Lovett Kingsland. Born NYC 1905, died there 1975. Eastern abstract painter and sculptor, teacher, writer. Work in MMA, WMAA, Phila MA, COR, NC Mus Art (Raleigh). References A73-BEN-MAS. Sources ALA-CAA-M50-M51-190-WHO 70-"George L K Morris/A Retrospective Exhibition," Hirschl & Adler Galleries (NY 1971). Oil *Wall Painting* 45¼ × 54¼" with signature example LR and dated 1936–44 sold 3/14/73 for $14,000 at auction.

George L K Morris graduated from Groton School in 1924 and Yale in 1928. He studied painting from 1928 to 1930 at the ASL with John Sloan and Kenneth Hayes Miller and at the Galerie Moderne in Paris with Léger and Ozenfant. Morris was an editor of literary magazines, exhibited paintings in NYC beginning 1933, and taught at the ASL in 1945. A founder of Abstract American Artists in 1936, his early work "spoke the same language as" Hans Arp. ALA. His inspiration came from Europe, but his flavor was American. The retrospective catalog included *Indian Concretion* (1938), *Indian Composition* (1939), *Arizona Altar* (1949), etc.

MOSER, John Henri. Born Wabern, Switzerland 1876, died Logan, Utah 1951. Utah painter of impressionist landscapes, historical and portrait painter, muralist, teacher. No reference. Sources PUA-YUP. No auction record but the estimated price of an oil 20×30″ showing a Utah landscape would be about $400 to $500 at auction in 1976. Signature example p 6 YUP.

Henri Moser was brought to Utah by covered wagon when he was 12. He worked on a farm, then for 10 years in a printing shop. In 1905 he studied art at Brigham Young University, the pupil of Alma B Wright. From 1908 to 1910 he studied in Paris, the pupil of Laurens and Simon, where he was influenced by Picasso. From 1911 to 1917 he taught art in Utah colleges. He then bought a ranch, farming and painting, until he returned to teaching.

Moser painted 1,197 recorded works, "an extremely uneven body of paintings. He produced incandescent canvases. It is always summer, always high noon, all hues at full saturation." YUP.

MOSLER, Henry. Born NYC (not Cincinnati) 1841, died same 1920. International genre painter, Civil War artist-correspondent. Chevalier, Legion of Honor. ANA 1895. Work in COR, MMA, Luxembourg (Paris), PAFA, Cincinnati AM, Sydney (Australia), Grenoble (France). References A20 (obit)-BEN-CHA-DAB-ENB-FIE-G&W (see Henry Mosler, Jr.)-

MAL-SMI. Sources AIW-ANT 4/65-COR-ISH-KW 1,2-MSL-M31-WHO 20. Oil 45×62½″ *A Peasant Wedding* 1883 sold 2/18/70 for $2,400 at auction in London. Signature example p 442 ANT 4/65.

Son of a lithographer, Mosler moved to Cincinnati in 1851, Nashville in 1854, and back to Cincinnati in 1855. Self-taught in wood-engraving and painting, he became a draftsman on a comic weekly in 1855. From 1859–61 he was the pupil of James H Beard. From 1861–63 he was *Harper's Weekly*'s special artist with the Army of the West. He studied at the Düsseldorf RA 1863–65, the pupil of Mücke and Kindler. In 1865 he was the pupil of Hébert in Paris. He returned to Cincinnati from 1866 to 1874 when he went to Munich as the pupil of Wagner and von Piloty. In 1877 he settled in Paris except for rare trips to America. The first painting by an American to be bought by the Luxembourg Museum was his, in 1879. In 1894 he established his studio in NYC.

In 1886 Henry Mosler "of France" was reported in Santa Fe, to tour New Mexico for six weeks with fellow painters Worrall of Topeka and Webber of Cincinnati. He was said to have "two commissions for Indian paintings that were to pay him $25,000 each." AIW.

MOYERS, William. Born Atlanta, Ga 1916, living Albuquerque, NM 1976. Traditional Western painter, illustrator, sculptor, writer. Member CAA. Sculpture in GIL. Reference A76. Sources AHI 11/71-COW-C71 to 74-HAR-OSR-WAI 71,72. No auction record. Signature example p 186 COW. Portrait photo C72. (See illustration 210.)

Moyers' father, a lawyer who was an authority on Western history, moved to Texas and in 1930 to Alamosa, Colo. Moyers was raised on a ranch. Rodeo prizes helped support his education at

Adams State College. He studied at Otis AI in Los Angeles and worked at Walt Disney Studios for a year before returning to Colorado to teach school. While still in the Army in 1945, he won the Limited Edition Club competition to illustrate "The Virginian." He became a successful NYC artist, influenced by Remington, Russell, Will James, Eggenhofer, and Von Schmidt. He has illustrated more than 150 books.

When Moyers moved to Albuquerque about 1965, he concentrated on paintings and bronzes, specializing in the genre of the cowboys of his own youth.

MOYLAN, Lloyd. Born St Paul, Minn 1893, living Gallup, NM 1948. Painter specializing in Southwest Indians, museum curator, muralist. Work in MNM, Penrose Pub Lib; murals in public buildings in Colorado and New Mexico. References A41-MAS. Sources AAT-SHO-SPR. No auction record but the estimated value of an oil 20×30" showing Navaho genre would be about $1,200 to $1,500 at auction in 1976. Signature example p 48 SHO.

Moylan studied at the Minneapolis AI, the ASL, and the Broadmoor AA in Colorado Springs. He taught at Broadmoor 1929–31 and later became curator of the Museum of Navaho Ceremonial Art in Santa Fe.

MOZLEY, Loren Norman. Born Brockport, Ill 1905, living Austin, Tex 1962. Taos painter, printmaker, writer, teacher. Member Taos Heptagon. Mural in Fed Bldg (Albuquerque). References A62-MAS. Source T20. No current auction record. No signature example.

Mozley studied at the U of New Mexico and in France at the Colarossi and Chaumière academies. In 1936 he wrote about John Marin for the catalog of MOMA. A teacher in the art department of the U of New Mexico in 1941, he became associate professor at the U of Texas in Austin.

MRUK, Walter (Wladyslaw R Mruk). Born Buffalo, NY 1883, died there 1942. Modernist Santa Fe painter, member Los Cinco Pintores. Work in MNM. No reference. Sources LOS-TSF. No current auction record. Signature example p 84 TSF.

Mruk studied at Albright AI in Buffalo, at the ASL, and in Denver with John Thompson. He came from Buffalo to Santa Fe in 1920, becoming a forest ranger in Frijoles, NM until about 1923. He sold newspaper cartoons and exhibited at the museum in Santa Fe. Along with Bakos, Ellis, Nash, and Shuster he formed Los Cinco Pintores in Santa Fe to provide an exhibition group like the Taos SA and "to bring art to working people." In 1924 he exhibited with the New Mexico Painters society in NYC. Mruk and Will Shuster in 1925 were lowered into the Carlsbad Caverns in buckets, in order to paint the unexplored caves by lantern light. The Museum of New Mexico in the late 1920s had an exhibition alcove reserved for "the modernists" including Mruk and Bakos whose work was regarded as similar.

Mruk's New Mexico paintings are few in number and they "express a feeling of agitation that appears to be a personal summation of the artist's emotional indecision." TSF. Mruk returned to the East from 1926 to 1928 for further study with John Thompson. He remains the least known of Los Cinco Pintores.

MUELLER, Michael J. Born Durand, Wis 1893, died Bend, Ore 1931. Painter specializing in Northwest landscapes, teacher. References A31 (obit)-MAL. No source. No auction record or signature example.

Mueller was the pupil of Sergeant Kendall, Ezra Winter, and Eugene Savage. He graduated from the School FA at Yale U and attended the American Academy in Rome on a fellowship. He was professor of painting at the U of Oregon.

MULFORD, Stockton. Painter active in NYC 1923–34. Traditional Western illustrator for pulp magazines. References A27-MAL. Source, cover *Western Story Magazine* 9/22/23 with signature example. No auction record but the estimated price of an oil 20×30" showing nostalgic cowboy genre would be about $800 to $1,000 at auction in 1976. (See illustration 211.)

Mulford was listed as a member of the Guild of Free Lance Artists and the Artists' Guild of the Authors' League of America. Mulford was an illustrator for Zane Grey stories.

MULLEN, F E (or E F). Active in 1860s as book illustrator. "Beyond the Mississippi" published in 1867 credits F E Mullen with two illustrations. The first is *Comanche Greeting* placed in Texas in 1859: "When a Comanche would show special fondness for an Indian or white man, he folds him in a pair of dirty arms and rubs a very greasy face against the suffering victim's." The second is *Penitentes Lashing Themselves* placed in New Mexico in 1859.

BEY is not the most accurate source for names. Neither illustration is signed. The reference G&W lists E F or E J Mullen as an illustrator for *Vanity Fair* about 1860 and for books published in the 1860s.

MULLER, Dan. Born Choteau, Mont 1888, living Port Washington, Wis 1966. One of the 50G Western illustrators, writer, adopted son of Buffalo Bill. Reference MAS. Sources ABC,v18,#4-HAR (under Stefan)-MWS 10/66 (article). No auction record. Signature example MWS.

Muller's father was a quarter-blood Piegan Blackfoot, a free-lance scout in Dakota with Buffalo Bill. Raised on the Cross-Up Ranch near the headwaters of the Teton, Muller was influenced toward art by meeting Charles Russell. At 9 he went to live with Buffalo Bill in North Platte, Neb. Discouraged by teachers from taking formal art instruction in order to protect his personal style, Muller continued drawing and painting. He traveled with the Buffalo Bill Shows in 1911 and 1912, joining in a Cody film on the West in 1913.

When Cody died in 1917, Muller rode from Canada to Mexico before settling in Elko, Nev. In WWI he broke horses for the Army and taught riding, then opened a sign shop in Chicago. In 1920 he sold landscapes to tourists in Yellowstone Park. Failing to catch on as a NYC illustrator, he went back to working for cow outfits. In Chicago in 1930, his Western paintings started to sell. He received commissions for murals for the Chicago Fair and became writer-illustrator for *Esquire* in 1933. Returning to Nevada in 1935, he again painted for the tourist trade. His three published books were "Horses" in 1936, "Chico" in 1938, and "My Life with Buffalo Bill" in 1948.

MULVANY (or Mulvaney), John. Born Ireland 1844, died NYC 1906 (or 1904). First painter of *Custer's Last Rally,* Western painter of 1870s, portraitist. Work in Cincinnati AM, Memphis Mus (Tenn). References BEN-FIE-MAL-SMI. Sources AIW-BAR-CUS-ISH-MWS W/74-POW. No current auction record but the estimated price of an oil 20×30″ showing Western genre would be $3,000 to $3,500 at auction in 1976. Painting example pl 55 AIW.

Mulvany emigrated to NYC at 12 (or 20). He served in the Union Army. After the war he studied in Düsseldorf, in Munich as the pupil of Wagner and Piloty for battle scenes, and in Antwerp the pupil of the military painter De Keyser. Mulvany returned to the US to live in St Louis, Chicago, and Cincinnati. After the Chicago fire in 1871, he moved to Nebraska. In 1876 he exhibited *The Preliminary Trial of a Horse Thief* at the NAD.

In 1879 Mulvany's studio was in Kansas City. He had visited the Custer battlefield of 1876, sketching the landscape and the Sioux, consulting with Army officers, and obtaining likenesses of Custer and his men. The resulting painting about 11×20′ was enthusiastically viewed by the Kansas City press in March 1881. The next month Mulvany and *Custer's Last Rally* were in Boston where changes were made in Custer's figure. The painting was on view in NYC in the summer, evoking from the poet Walt Whitman: "Altogether a Western phase of America, the frontiers, culminating typical, deadly, heroic to the uttermost; nothing in the books like it." The exhibition in Chicago included other Western paintings, one called *The Scouts of the Yellowstone. Custer's Last Rally* was widely shown, was lithographed in color, and was owned by H J Heinz after 1900. The painting is now in the Memphis Museum (Tenn). This was the first in a parade of paintings of Custer's final moments. It influenced major American artists like Remington and Russell. AIW. Mulvany continued painting Western, genre, and Civil War scenes. He was sketching in Colorado in 1890 but specialized more in portraiture as his talents declined. He became an alcoholic derelict, committing suicide by drowning in 1906.

MUNGER, Gilbert Davis. Born Madison, Conn 1837 (or 1836), died Washington, DC 1903. Landscape painter in the Rockies after the Civil War, engraver. Work in Berlin Mus. References A03 (obit) - BEN - G&W - MAL - SMI. Sources ANT 12/73-KEN 6/70. Oil 10¾ × 18″ *Summer Landscape* sold 11/2/72 for $1,440 at auction in London. Oil 19×34″ *Bay of San Fran* 1871 sold 8/7/73 for $1,450 at auction in Mass. Signature example p 68 KEN 6/70.

Munger was educated in New Haven. At 14 he began working in Washington as an engraver for the Smithsonian Institution. He founded the Bureau of Lithography and shared quarters with William H Dougal in 1860. Two years were spent with Prof Louis Agassiz in the Indian Ocean. He served in the Civil War as a lieutenant of engineers building the defenses for Washington.

After the war Munger sketched and painted in the Rockies. He was in the Yosemite Valley soon after it was open, painting in oil on cardboard approximately 20×27″. It is said that the "landscapes brought him a fortune from English collectors." A03. His *Niagara Falls* was sold to the Berlin Museum for $5,000. A landscape featuring the Great Salt Lake was dated 1877, perhaps painted in Europe where he lived for 17 years. He became a friend of Sir John Millais in England. His studio was in Barbizon, France near Paris until 1893.

MURDOCK, John. Birthplace unknown 1835, died probably in the East 1924. Portrait and landscape painter, active in San Francisco, Cal 1856. Reference G&W. Sources COS-KEN 6/71-PAF. No current auction record or signature example.

Murdock was in St Louis in 1854. Later he moved to San Francisco where he painted portraits and sketched a ranch scene showing an Indian as a laborer. PAF listed an 1862 exhibition of a Baltimore scene painted by Murdock in combination with Thomas W Richards.

MURPHY, Hermann Dudley. Born Marlborough, Mass 1867, died Lexington, Mass 1945. Landscape and portrait painter, illustrator, teacher, frame designer. ANA 1931, NA 1935. Work in AIC, Albright Art Gall, Dallas MFA, Cleveland AM, Boston MFA, Springville (Utah) AA. References A47 (obit)-BEN-FIE-MAL-SMI. Sources AIC-ARM-WHO 44. No auction record or signature example.

H Dudley Murphy was educated at Chauncy Hill School in Boston 1880–85 and studied at the Boston Museum school and in Paris at Julien Academy with Laurens and Constant. He became the artist for the Nicaraguan Canal expedition 1887–88 and worked as an illustrator for books and magazines 1888–94 before exhibiting paintings beginning 1895. His hobby was sailing canoes.

MUTZEL, Gustav. Born Berlin, Germany 1839, died there 1893. German painter and illustrator of animals. Reference BEN. Source BAW. No current auction record. Signature example p 431 BAW.

Mutzel studied at the École des Beaux-Arts in Berlin. He was best known for his animal drawings used as illustrations, for example "Lives of Animals" by Brehm. An engraving was made from his *Bison Family Group with New-Born Calf.*

MYERS, Frank Harmon. Born Cleves, Ohio 1899, died Pacific Grove, Cal 1956. Ohio landscape, marine, and portrait painter, teacher. Work in MNM, U of Cincinnati, Miami U (Ohio), Cincinnati schools. References A59 (obit)-BEN-MAL. Source TSF. No current auction record but the estimated price of an oil 20×30″ showing Santa Fe valley would be $400 to $500 at auction in 1976. Signature example p 96 TSF.

Myers studied at the Cincinnati AA with Duveneck, Wessel, and Weis, at the PAFA with Garber, Breckenridge, and Joseph Pearson, and at Fontainebleau SFA with Despujols and Gourguet. He taught drawing and painting at Cincinnati AA for 15 years and at U of Cincinnati. Myers also lectured on techniques of marine painting. He spent 1932–33 in Santa Fe, painting realistic landscapes.

MYERS (or Meyers), William Henry. Birthplace unknown 1815, self-taught sketch artist in Cal mining camps in 1849. Work in F D Roosevelt Lib. Reference G&W. Source AIW. No auction record or signature example.

Myers was a gunner on the US sloop-of-war *Dale* who kept a watercolor sketchbook of his 16 years in California. He depicted the voyage to California via Cape Horn, the American conquest of California in 1847, and scenes in the diggings. A panorama based on Myers' sketches was painted in 1849 by Thomas B Glessing of Philadelphia and exhibited in NYC. The original sketchbook is owned by the Franklin D Roosevelt Library, the President having reproduced some of the sketches in his "Naval Sketches of the War in California," NY 1939.

NAHA, Raymond. Born Polacca (Hopi Reservation), Ariz 1933, died probably San Carlos, Ariz 1976. Traditional Hopi painter in acrylics. Work in MAI, Mus No Ariz. Reference A73. Sources AHI 8/66,3/74-AIP. No auction record. Signature example p 7 AHI 3/74.

As a high school student Naha was the pupil of the well-known Hopi artist Fred Kabotie. Naha won the grand award at the Scottsdale Indian Arts & Crafts Show.

NAHL, Charles Christian. Born Cassel, Germany 1818, died San Francisco, Cal (not Brooklyn) 1878. Important Cal history, genre, and portrait painter, illustrator, lithographer. Work in European museums, ACM, BMFA, Crocker AG (Sacramento), BM, Stanford, Kahn colln (Oakland, Cal). References BEN-G&W-MAL. Sources AAR 11/74-ANT 3/66 - AOW - BAR - COS - COW - DWF-HON-150-KAH-KW1-SSF-STI. Oil 42× 51″ Vaqueros Roping a Steer with signature example on rock, dated 1866, estimated for sale 3/4/74 at $14,000 to $16,000, sold for $60,000 at auction in LA.

Charles Nahl was an important gold-rush painter, descendant of German artists for 300 years and himself trained in Cassel and in Paris, with Paris exhibitions in 1847–48. Following the 1848 French revolution, the Nahl family, consisting of the much-married mother and five children, emigrated to NYC, where Nahl painted and exhibited. In 1851 Nahl and his half-brother Arthur set sail for California, traveling across the Isthmus of Panama and then to San Francisco. They worked in the mines, accumulating more sketches than gold. In 1852 Nahl moved to Sacramento, painting portraits for gold dust and illustrating books and newspapers until the fire that swept the town destroyed his accumulated sketches.

Later in 1852 the Nahl brothers moved to a permanent home in San Francisco, opening an art and photography studio at 79 Broadway. One patron was Charles Crocker. Charles Nahl also made many drawings for lithographers and illustrations that won him the title of "the Cruikshank of California." His genre works were "authentic representations of humorous and pathetic incidents in the flats of the mining country." AOW. Few of Nahl's oil paintings have survived; of these the masterpiece is Sunday Morning in the Mines, 1872. Charles and Arthur operated a gallery and studio where Charles designed the bear on the state flag. A shy bachelor, Charles lived with his mother and his sister until his death from typhoid fever.

NAHL, Hugo Wilhelm Arthur. Born Cassel, Germany 1833 (not 1820), died San Francisco, Cal 1889. Cal genre and landscape painter, illustrator, engraver, pioneer photographer. Work Kahn colln, Oakland AM, ACM. References BEN-G&W. Sources ANT 11/65-AOW-COS-KAH-SSF-12/5/73 letter Marjorie Arkelian, Oakland AM. No current auction record. Painting example p 702 ANT 11/65 Californians Catching Wild Horses with the Reata.

Arthur Nahl traveled with and was overshadowed by his older half-brother Charles Nahl. Arthur Nahl is listed in the San Francisco family firm of commercial artists as "& Bro" from 1856 to 1862, then "Nahl Brothers" art and photographic gallery until 1871, then "H W Arthur Nahl, landscape painter." He was part of the photographic study at Palo Alto of the horse in motion, but his 1857 painting of vaqueros catching wild horses still depicted horses in carousel poses.

Arthur Nahl was a frequent exhibitor at the San Francisco AA during the 1870s and designed the state seal. He visited Europe in 1881. Some of his paintings were signed jointly with Charles Nahl, eg, the huge *Royal Family of the Sandwich Islands on Horseback* exhibited in 1858 which shocked San Francisco viewers because the royal women were depicted riding astride.

NAILOR, Gerald A (or Lloyde). Born Pinedale, NM 1917, died Picuris Pueblo, NM 1952. Navaho painter, illustrator, designer. Member Indian Art Colony. Work in DAM, MAI, MMA, NGA; murals in public buildings in Ariz, Colo, and DC. References A53 (obit)-MAS. Sources AHI 2/50-AIP. No auction record but the estimated price of a watercolor 20×16″ showing a Navaho woman riding would be about $700 to $900 at auction in 1976. Signature example p 13 AHI 2/50.

Nailor, Navaho name Toh Yah or Walking by the River, attended mission schools. He went to public school on a scholarship, graduated Albuquerque Indian School, and attended Santa Fe Indian School for supplementary courses. He studied under Dorothy Dunn, Kenneth Chapman, and the Swedish muralist Olaf Nordmark. In 1937 Nailor shared a studio in Santa Fe with Allan Houser.

NAPPENBACH, Henry. Born Muende, Bavaria, Germany 1862, died NYC 1931. San Francisco and NYC illustrator, cartoonist, engraver. Work in Bohemian Club (San Fran), Oakland AM. References A31 (obit)-MAL. Sources BDW - BWB - KAH. No auction record. Painting example p 38 KAH.

"Nap" studied in Munich where a San Francisco printer hired him to come to California as an engraver in 1885. Hearst employed him as a staff artist in 1893.

Nap also drew for the weekly *Wasp* and painted landscapes and city views around San Francisco, in Hawaii, and in the Sandwich Islands. He was transferred to NYC in 1918 to manage the *American* color art department. He also continued as an illustrator, completing thousands of sketches.

NARJOT, Erneste Étienne de Francheville. Born St Malo, Brittany, France 1827 (or 1826), died San Francisco, Cal 1898. Cal genre and mural painter. References G&W-MAL. Sources AAR 9/73-BAR-COW-CRS-HON-POW-WHI. No current auction record but the estimated price of a large oil of a skirmish with Indians would be about $7,500 to $8,000 at auction in 1976. Signature example p 38 AAR 9/73 *Gold Rush Camp* 1882.

Son of a painter, Narjot studied in Paris when he was 16. He emigrated to San Francisco via Cape Horn as a gold seeker in 1849. *Placer Mining at Foster's Bar* dated probably 1851 helps locate his activities. After three years he joined an expedition to mine gold in Mexico where he settled, married, and painted. When he returned to San Francisco in 1865 it was to establish a studio as a painter of genre scenes of the mining camps, portraits, military skirmishes, and murals. He was in demand as a fresco painter for churches and public buildings, but his career was ended by paint dropping into his eyes while decorating the ceiling of the Leland Stanford tomb in Palo Alto.

Many of Narjot's paintings were burned at the San Francisco AA during the 1906 earthquake and fire. Two of the known paintings depicted the US Army's attempt to use camels on a march from Texas to California in 1857 (see also Gwinn Heap). An 1867 painting shows an engagement between US troops and Apaches under Cochise.

NASH, Willard Ayer. Born Philadelphia, Pa 1898, died Los Angeles, Cal 1943. A "Santa Fe Modernist" painter, etcher, teacher. Work in DAM, LA Cnty MA, U NM, MNM. References A41-FIE-MAL. Sources DIG 3/15/37-LOS-PET-PIT-TSF. No current auction record. Painting example DIG.

Willard Nash was the pupil of John P Wicker at the Detroit AS. He had been the highest paid boy soprano in the US, acted on the Detroit stage, boxed as an amateur, and earned more as a commercial artist at 16 than he did as a fine artist at 39. Nash came to Santa Fe in 1920, joining Los Cinco Pintores under the leadership of Bakos as a modernist exhibition group. Cézanne appealed to Nash as an influence, as did the Fauve colors and Marin's simplifications. In the late 1920s Nash's abstract work was shown in "The Modernists" alcove at the Mus of NM. The same group was shown at the Whitney in NYC in 1932 and 1935. In 1936 Nash moved to California. He taught at Broadmoor AA in Colorado Springs, at San Francisco AS, and at the Art Center School in LA.

DIG classifies Nash periods as early Whistleresque impressionism, vivid New Mexico decorations, cubism, and simplified nudes. His February 1937 exhibition in Hollywood combined New Mexico landscapes and movie star portraits. It was attended by the celebrities and reviewed favorably in both the art and gossip columns.

NASON, Daniel W. Born probably Epping, NH about 1825, living probably Boston, Mass 1891. Sketch artist for *Gleason's* during the Gold Rush. Work in New England Pioneer Assn (Boston). Reference G&W. No other source, auction record, or signature example.

Nason went to California as a member of the New England Pioneer Association, remaining 1849–52. Gleason's *Pictorial and Drawing-Room Companion* printed Nason's California sketches in 1851.

NAST, Thomas. Born Landau, Germany 1840, died Guayaquil, Ecuador 1902. Very important cartoonist, first American caricaturist, illustrator, painter. Work in BMFA, Colo Springs Crthse, MMA. References A03 (obit)-BEN-DAB-ENB-FIE-MAL-SMI. Sources AIW-ALA-ANT 2/75-AOA-HUT-KW1,2-MSL-NJA-SPR-WHO 99. No current auction price. Signature example p 252 KW1. (See illustration 212.)

Son of a trombone player in the Bavarian Army, Nast was brought to NYC when he was 6. Self-taught except for brief study with Theodore Kaufmann and at the NAD, he furnished sketches for *Leslie's* when he was 15, beginning with a prize fight in Canada. In 1860 he went to Europe as the correspondent of the *NY Illustrated News* with Garibaldi's army. Returning in 1862 he became a major field artist of the Civil War, sending drawings to *Harper's* with which he worked for 25 years. Occasional oils were exhibited beginning 1868. After the war his *Harper's* contributions became cartoons with "great influence on the politics of the time," toppling Boss Tweed in 1871. A03. He invented the Democratic donkey and the Republican elephant as symbols. The wood engravers of the 1870s generally reduced all reproduced art to the same level, and "Only the bold lines of Thomas Nast bear any individuality during this period." AIW.

As a Western artist Nast did contribute to "Beyond the Mississippi" published in 1867, along with other Civil War field artists. Most of the illustrations in this book were copied from other than original sources. Nast was also a familiar cartoonist of the Indian, a Tammany symbol. When he lectured at the Colorado

Springs Opera House about 1895, he drew himself on a bucking bronco, with a descending spiral line to make "Colorado Springs."

NEAGLE, John. Born Boston, Mass 1796, died Philadelphia, Pa 1865. Very important Philadelphia portrait painter. Hon NA 1828. Work in BMA, DIA, MMA, COR, BMFA, Boston Athenaeum. References BEN-CHA-DAB-FIE-G&W-MAL. Sources ALA-AMA-AOW-BAR-BOA-COR-HUT-150-ISH-KAR-KW1-M15-NCB-NGA-PAF-TEP. Oil 30×25" *Portrait of James Ash* 1824 sold 3/19/69 for $12,500 at auction. Signature example p 50 AOW.

Neagle was raised in Philadelphia. In grammar school he received drawing instruction from Edward Petticolas, then attended the drawing school of Pietro Ancora before apprenticeship in 1813 to Thomas Wilson, a coach painter who was himself taking lessons from Bass Otis. Otis introduced Neagle to Sully. In 1818 Neagle traveled over the mountains to Lexington, Ky but found Jouett established there as a portrait painter. New Orleans was also unprofitable, so Neagle returned to Philadelphia in 1820 where he had all the sitters he wanted. His first price was $15, increasing to $100 as he matured. In 1826 he married Sully's stepdaughter and also painted *Pat Lyon the Blacksmith,* his most famous portrait. "He was at his most irresistibly sentimental in painting children, and his limpid small studies of papooses are lovable creatures." ALA. The work of Allston, Vanderlyn, Morse, and Neagle indicated that "art had come of age in America by the 1820s." ALA.

In 1821 a delegation of Indians visited Philadelphia as a part of the grand tour given them to emphasize the strength of the United States. Neagle painted the portraits of at least four Indians, as exhibited at the PAFA in 1822. "Neagle had an Indian-like facial expression himself." AOW. In 1839 a lithographic reproduction of a Neagle portrait was the frontispiece for a pioneer scientific study of Indians.

NEAL, David Dalhoff. Born Lowell, Mass 1838, died Munich, Germany 1915. International historical and portrait painter with early work in San Francisco. ANA. Work in German museums, AIC. References A15 (obit)-BEN-CHA-DAB-ENB-FIE-G&W-MAL-SMI. Sources BAR-COS-HUT-ISH-STI-WHO 14. No recent auction record or signature example.

Neal was educated in the academy at Andover, then before he was 21 went to San Francisco via New Orleans and the Isthmus. Although Neal was essentially self-trained as an artist, a rich Californian in 1861 saw talent in Neal's drawings on wood and his occasional portraits. He sponsored Neal's art education as the first American to study at the Bavarian Royal Academy in Munich. In 1862 Neal married his teacher's daughter Marie Ainmiller. From 1869–76 Neal worked in the atelier of the historical painter Karl von Piloty. In 1876 he completed *The First Meeting of Mary Stuart and Rizzio* and was the first American to receive the highest medal of the Academy. The painting was exhibited in Munich, London, Boston, and Chicago and has been widely reproduced. Subsequent historical paintings evoked equal enthusiasm. Neal's later years were devoted to portrait painting. He divided his time between Europe and America but Munich continued to be his home.

Neal is one of the Munich Americans who "mastered the Munich technique and assimilated the Munich ideals so thoroughly that they reveal no trace of anything distinctly American." DAB. Compare the COS listing of the Western

Neal as a "San Francisco painter of good portraits that were lithographed, including Captain John Paty."

NEHLIG, Victor. Born Paris, France 1830, died NYC 1909. Portrait and genre painter, historical painter using Indian subjects. ANA 1863, NA 1870. Work in NY Hist Soc. References A09-BEN - CHA - FIE - G & W - MAL - SMI. Sources ANT 9/55-BOA-HUT-PAF-WHO 08. Oil 89×74½" *Pocahontas and John Smith* with signature example and dated NY 1870 sold 4/7/71 for $4,250 at auction.

Nehlig studied under Cogniet and Abel de Pujol in Paris. He emigrated to NYC in 1850. He was immediately successful. BOA in 1867 termed his work the equal of the best French painters, and hoped that Nehlig would enter into the field of historical painting. In 1871 Nehlig exhibited *Mahogany Cutting* at the NAD, based on a trip to Cuba. He visited Europe in 1872. Nehlig's later historical paintings did specialize in Indian subjects such as Pocahontas and Hiawatha.

NEPOTE, Alexander. Born Valley Home, Cal 1913, living Millbrae, Cal 1976. Cal semiabstract painter, teacher. Work in San Francisco MA, MMA, Pasadena AM, DAM, MCA, LA Cnty MA. References A76-MAS. Sources ASF-CON-DAA-MCA. No auction record. Signature example pl 98 MCA.

Son of a truck-gardener of Italian birth, Nepote was raised on a farm in Shasta County. After a trip to Italy in 1929, he graduated from Santa Rosa high school in 1932. One year as a truck-gardener was followed by enrollment in the California College of Arts and Crafts in Oakland. He was graduated from the course in Applied Arts in 1936,

earning a teacher's certificate in 1939. During WWII, Nepote worked as an engineering draftsman in the shipyards. He received his master's degree from Mills College in 1942. By 1945 Nepote was teaching at California College of Arts and Crafts. In 1950 he became professor of art at San Francisco State College.

"Anyone not knowing him well would most likely draw the conclusion that he is easy-going. Alexander is really a very earnest and hard-working person." ASF. His oil in DAA is described as "semiabstract interpretation" of "patterns of melting snow in a creek bed." DAA.

NESEMAN (or Nesemann), Enno (or Eno). Born Marysville, Cal 1861, died probably Berkeley, Cal 1949. Painter of California genre. Member SIA. Work in De Young Mem Mus (San Francisco). References A53 (obit)-BEN-FIE-MAL. Source POW. No current auction record or signature example.

Neseman was the pupil of Alfred Hart, the California landscapist. His best-known painting was *The First Discovery of Gold in California at Sutter's Mill*. His studio was in Berkeley.

NESTLER, Al. Landscape painter active in the Southwest in the 20th century, died before 1971. No reference. Source p 42 AHI 10/71, with signature example.

The book "Al Nestler's Southwest," published by Northland Press, was reviewed as, "forty years of it, presented through the perceptive eye and skilled hand of a fine landscape painter." AHI.

NEUHAUS, Eugen. Born Barmen, Rhine Prov (or Wuppertal), Germany

1879, died probably Orinda, Cal 1963. Cal landscape painter, writer, teacher. Work in "public and private collns." A62. References A62-FIE-MAL-SMI. Sources AIW (as writer)-ALA (as writer)-MCA-WHO 54. No current auction record. Signature example pl 65 MCA.

Neuhaus graduated in 1899 from the Royal Art School in Kassel, Germany and in 1902 from the Royal School for Applied Arts in Berlin. He emigrated to the US in 1904 and became a member of the faculty U of California beginning 1907. His landscapes were exhibited nationally.

As an art historian, the Westerner Neuhaus was among the first to recognize Taos as a focal point in American art life. He was "practically the only art historian to devote any consideration to the painters of Indian and frontier life." AIW. "The History and Ideals of American Art" is his definitive work, while "Art of the Exposition" is most known.

NEWBERRY, John Strong. Born Windsor, Conn 1822, died New Haven, Conn 1892. Exploration expedition sketch artist, medical doctor, geologist, paleontologist, educator. References DAB - ENB-G&W. Sources AIW-SUR. No auction record or signature example.

Raised in Cuyahoga Falls, Ohio, a coal mining town founded by his father, Newberry graduated from Western Reserve College in 1846 and Cleveland Medical School in 1848. From 1849 to 1851 he studied medicine and geology in Paris. After practicing medicine 1851–55 in Cleveland, he was named assistant surgeon on Lt Wilkinson's railway survey expedition seeking passes in the Sierras 1855–56. The next year he was physician and naturalist on Lt Ives's military exploration of the Colorado River.

In 1859 Dr Newberry was geologist on Capt Macomb's exploring expedition from Santa Fe to the Colorado River. Three of Dr Newberry's landscape sketches were reproduced in the official report. Another 11 were redrawn by J J Young as watercolor illustrations for the report. The greater part of the text was Dr Newberry's geological data. After service with the US Sanitary Commission during the Civil War, Dr Newberry became professor of geology and paleontology at Columbia's School of Mines. A cheerful, buoyant, and sensitive man, he wrote many scientific articles and books, receiving academic honors.

NEWSAM, Albert. Born Steubenville, Ohio 1809, died near Wilmington, Del 1864. Portrait draftsman in crayon, lithographer. Lithograph in McKenney and Hall colln. References BEN (as Newseam) - DAB - FIE - G&W - MAL - SMI. Sources BOL-DBW-PAF. No current auction record. No signature example.

A deaf-mute from birth, Newsam was a small child when his father, an Ohio River boatman, drowned. When Newsam was 10 and evidencing talent for drawing, a pretended deaf-mute assumed his custody to aid begging. In Philadelphia in 1820 Newsam's talent was recognized in street sketches. His companion was bribed by a bishop to permit Newsam to enter the Asylum for the Deaf and Dumb. Newsam remained a state ward until 1826 and a monitor until 1827, the pupil of Bridport and Catlin, exhibiting chalk drawings at the PAFA beginning 1824 along with the major painters of the day. Lambdin taught him portraiture but stopped because Newsam lacked the necessary faculty of being able to animate the sitter with conversation.

In 1827 Newsam was apprenticed to the Philadelphia engraver Col Cephas G Childs. P S Duval was brought from France, teaching Newsam the new process of commercial lithography. Aided by study at the PAFA, Newsam was at the head of American portrait lithographers when his apprenticeship ended in 1831. This is the same year that Henry Inman, an important NYC portrait painter, came to Philadelphia to join Col Childs. Both Inman and Newsam made portrait drawings for the Indian Gallery of McKenney and Hall. The portrait of *Shau-Hau-Napo-Tinia, an Ioway Chief* as lithographed by Newsam is regarded as unusually handsome, commanding a premium price today. Newsam became partly blind in 1857, partly paralyzed in 1859 when he was hospitalized, removed to the city almshouse in 1860, and transferred to the Living Home in 1862 through contributions.

gomery while refusing to be called Mrs Montgomery, causing her social ostracism. Joining a group of other "free spirits," they formed a colony to emigrate to Thomasville, Ga in 1870, and two years later Elisabet and her husband moved to Texas where they purchased a plantation near Hempstead.

After years devoted to the children and to the failing plantation, they moved to Austin where Miss Ney built a studio that is now the Elisabet Ney Museum. Despite appearance as a "modern woman, with bobbed hair, wearing a tunic of black velvet and leggings, maintaining a separate establishment from her husband," she received statewide recognition. TXF. She worked steadily at portrait busts and statues of Texans. When she visited Germany in 1895, it was a "triumphal return." DAB.

NEY, Elisabet. Born Westphalia, Germany 1830, died Austin, Tex 1907. Portrait and statuary sculptor of prominent Texans. Work in St Capitol (Austin), Natl Hall (DC), Elisabet Ney Mus, Fort Worth MA, St Cemetery (Austin), and in Europe. References A05-BEN-DAB-FIE-MAL-SMI. Sources MSL-TEP-TOB-TXF-WAA. No current auction record. No signature example.

Daughter of a sculptor of religious works, she used a hunger strike in 1852 to win approval to attend the all-male Academy of Fine Arts in Berlin. After two years she was accepted as pupil of Christian Rauch, the Berlin master. When he died in 1857 "her extraordinary gifts, unusual beauty, and indomitable will carried her to heights of popularity." DAB. "She was the rage of Berlin, this lovely girl, with short red, curly hair, marvelously fair skin." TXF. She modeled royalty, including King Ludwig II of Bavaria, and herself sat for portraits. In 1863 she married the Scotch medical doctor Edmund Montgomery. As an independent artist she lived with Dr Mont-

NICHOLS, Henry Hobart. Born Washington, DC 1869, died NYC 1962. Academic landscape painter, illustrator. NA 1920. Work in NGA, AMNH, COR, MMA, New Zealand AM. References A66 (obit) - BEN - FIE - MAL - SMI. Sources IL 2/95-WHO 62. Oil $300 at auction 1970–71. Signature example p 118 IL 2/95 *An Old Zuni Spinner* signed "H H Nichols," also p 378 *A Puebloan Woman Polishing Pottery* signed "H H Nichols Sc." The notation Sc indicates that Nichols engraved the illustration, so that he need not have drawn the original from life.

Nichols was educated in Shortledge College of Pennsylvania and studied at the ASL in Washington as well as in Paris at the Julien Academy and with Castellucho. He was president of the NA from 1939 to 1949. In 1945 "a snow scene by Hobart Nichols proved that the academic naturalists are always with us; and artists of greater originality seemed caught in the meshes of their own style." ALA.

NICOL, Pegi. See MacLeod. (See illustration 213.)

NICOLS, Audley Dean. Born Pittsburgh, Pa date unknown, active in El Paso, Tex 1919–35. Painter of the Southwestern desert, illustrator, muralist. Murals in Pittsburgh public buildings, El Paso hotel. No reference. Sources TOB-TSF. Two oils 12×20″ *Arizona Landscape* with signature example sold 4/7/71 for $1,200 the pair at auction.

Nicols was raised in Pittsburgh. His mother had been an art instructor. An aunt originated Rookwood pottery. Nicols studied at the ASL and the Metropolitan School FA, the pupil of Blashfield, Cox, and Mowbray. He also studied in Europe. In his early career he was a NYC illustrator for national magazines.

While touring the US, Nicols stopped to visit in El Paso and settled there. His specialty is "paintings of desert scenes in Texas, Arizona, California, the cowboy, longhorn, the covered wagon, the Rocky Mountains." TOB.

NOBLE, John. Born Wichita, Kans 1874, died NYC 1934. International painter known for the gray Brittany horse and the American buffalo. ANA 1924, NA 1927. Work in St Capitol (Okla), NGA, Smithsonian, COR, BM, Delgado Mus (New Orleans), etc. References A36 (obit) - BEN - MAL - SMI. Sources AAC-COR-INS 12/28-MSL-NA 74-TOB-WHO 32. No current auction record. No signature example.

Raised on the Osage Indian Reservation, Noble was part of the Oklahoma land run and worked as a Texas sheepherder while sketching and painting as a cowboy artist. He studied at the Cincinnati Academy of Fine Arts, then went to Paris to study at Julien Academy and the École des Beaux-Arts where he was known as Wichita Bill, the Kansas Cyclone with cattleman's hat and rattlesnake tie. In Brittany he identified with the gray horses, the plodders for work. By 1908 his Brittany paintings were successful in France. When he moved to London he became famous immediately. His return to the US completed his international acceptance.

To Noble, who in his youth had seen one herd of 3,000 buffaloes, the goal was "to paint one buffalo standing alone, kneedeep in the prairie grass, under the moon" to represent "all those millions that are gone." TOB. Noble "never used models nor painted with the object before him, his theory being that an artist should be creative, not a copyist." A36. Irving Stone based a book, "The Passionate Journey," on his life.

NONNAST, Paul E. Born Carlisle, Pa 1918, living Philadelphia, Pa 1966. Magazine illustrator, teacher, photographer. Work in *The Saturday Evening Post* and others. No reference. Sources IL 42-ILA. No auction record. Signature example p 227 ILA.

Nonnast, restricted in physical activity as a young man, studied at the Philadelphia Museum School of Art, graduating in 1940. He worked as a lithographer and for a newspaper before entering freelance advertising illustration in 1942. His work was immediately recognized in IL 42. From 1943 to 1946 he was a teacher of illustration at Moore Institute of Art in Philadelphia. In 1947 he began magazine illustrating with *The Saturday Evening Post* including Western subjects.

NORDFELDT, Bror Julius Olsson. Born Tullstorp, Sweden 1878, died Lambertsville, NJ 1955. Modernist painter, graphic artist, teacher. Member Taos SA, Santa Fe Artists. Work in Nat Mus (Sydney), Nat Mus (Norway), Bibliothèque d'Art (Paris), Toronto Mus, AIC, MNM, ACM, ANS, MMA. References A53 - BEN - FIE - MAL - SMI. Sources AAT-ARI-CAA-M50-MSL-PET-PIT-TSF-WHO 52. Oil on Masonite 26×20" *What Do You Mean—Abstract?* signed, titled, and dated 1936 on the reverse sold 1/26/72 for $150 at auction. This price would not be relevant for a Western subject. Signature example p 78 TSF. (See illustration 214.)

B J O Nordfeldt adopted his mother's surname after he emigrated to Chicago in 1891. He worked as a typesetter, then studied at the AIC beginning about 1896 and as Albert Herter's assistant in NYC. He spent one year in Paris, part at the Julien Academy with Laurens, who was too academic for Nordfeldt. He also studied at the Oxford Extension College in England with F M Fletcher to learn woodblock techniques. He won international awards beginning 1906, mainly for etchings, with one-man exhibitions beginning 1912. Early in 1918 he served as a Navy camouflage painter in San Francisco.

Later in December 1918 Nordfeldt moved to Santa Fe. He was considered a romantic expressionist, selecting simple subject matter he then invested with mystery. His portraits of Spanish-Americans and his still-life paintings incorporating santos were sympathetic. After 1929 he painted Santa Fe landscapes at the urging of his friend Russell Cowles. His importance as a pioneering modernist, however, was in his repainting Indian subjects similar to those of the traditional Indian painters like Couse, but treating the Indians not with Hiawathan nostalgia but rather with distortion and abstraction for color and design values only. He also adopted Indian pottery and textile designs in his influential experiments. Nordfeldt left Santa Fe in 1940 when he was 62, and is said to have destroyed many Santa Fe paintings before leaving.

NUMKENA, Lewis, Jr. Born Moenkopi, Ariz 1927, living Tuba City, Ariz 1967. Hopi artist. Sources AHI 2/50-AIP. No auction record. Signature example p 16 AHI 2/50.

Numkena, the son of a village leader, was educated at Santa Fe Indian School. His work has been published in *Arizona Highways* and has won awards in exhibitions in Museum of Northern Arizona, Museum of New Mexico, and Philbrook Art Center.

OBERHARDT, William. Born Guttenberg, NJ 1882, died probably Pelham, NY 1958. Eastern portrait illustrator, portrait painter, lithographer, sculptor. ANA (graphics) 1945, member SI. Work in NY Pub Lib, Lib of Congress, War Dept, Comn of FA. References A59 (obit) - BEN - FIE - MAL - SMI. Sources AAC-AAT-CAP-ILA-WHO 58. No current auction record. Signature example p 134 CAP.

Oberhardt studied at the NAD 1897–1900 and then at the Munich AFA 1900–3, the pupil of Marr and Herterich. "Early in his career as an illustrator, he found his greatest interest in delineating the human head." ILA. He worked directly from the sitter rather than photographs. From 1908 to 1956 he drew hundreds of portraits of the celebrities of the day, from Presidents to other famous artists. Charcoal and the lithographic crayon were his favorite media. His lithographs included cowboy portraits.

O'BRIEN, Lucius Richard. Born Shanty Bay, Lake Simcoe (or Bairie), Ont, Can 1832, died Toronto, Ont, Can 1899. Important early landscape painter of the Canadian West, illustrator. Charter member RCA 1880. Work in RCA, NGC, Parliament bldgs (Toronto). References A00 (obit) - BEN - MAL - SMI. Sources ANT 3/73-CAH-CAN-CAR. Oil 23½ × 41½" *Indians Fishing in Canoes* 1877 sold 3/15/67 for $2,660 at auction in London. Signature example p 398 ANT 3/73. (See illustration 215.)

O'Brien, the son of a retired British lieutenant-colonel of Irish descent, was educated at Upper Canada College, Toronto. He was employed by an architect at 16 before becoming a civil engineer. When he was 40 he quit as an engineer in order to paint full time. His first exhibition was with the Ontario Society of Artists in 1873. Starting with the landscape in Ontario and Quebec, he painted

as a self-taught watercolorist, emphasizing the literal topographic features. Queen Victoria commissioned two views of Quebec. In 1880 he was the first RCA president, a conservative and gentlemanly aspirant to the upper classes. CAH.

In 1882 O'Brien was art editor and an illustrator for "Picturesque Canada" which followed the publication of "Picturesque America." By this time O'Brien had painted in the Rockies and Selkirks of Western Canada, following the Canadian Pacific Railway. One of the few native Canadians among the artists then, O'Brien was encouraged by Albert Bierstadt. His realistic paintings were influential in the settlement of Western Canada and in showing "the possibilities offered for commercial exploitation." CAR. He painted in Western Canada again in 1888, giving "Canadians of the time a fascinating new Eden-like image of their country." CAH.

OERTEL, Johannes Adam Simon. Born Fürth, Bavaria 1823, died Vienna, Va 1909. ANA 1856. Designed ceiling decorations for House of Representatives, NGA, Nat Cathedral and other churches; religious art including paintings and ecclesiastical woodcarvings; portraits, Civil War subjects, and Western scenes. References BEN-DAB-FIE-G&W-MAL-SMI. Sources ANT 5/68 - BAR - BOA - KW2 - PAF - STI - WHI - WHO 08. Oil 19½ × 26½" *The Return from the Hunt* sold 11/20/69 for $850 at auction. Signature example p 79 KW2. (See illustration 216.)

Oertel was in religious training from the time he was 13 so that he could become a missionary. When he was persuaded that his real talent was in art, he studied with a Munich engraver. He emigrated to Newark, NJ in 1848, settling down to teaching drawing and to establishing a family. As early as 1852 when he was confirmed in the Episcopal Church, his intent was to design a series of four paintings to illustrate the redemption of mankind. This goal he set aside while from 1852 to 1857 he made banknote engravings of decorative scenes including Indian subjects—*The War Path* (1855) fig 28 WHI probably relates to this usage. During 1857–58 he designed ceiling decorations for the House of Representatives in Washington and in 1862 he sketched with the Army for material for paintings.

His most famous painting was *Rock of Ages* widely reproduced in photos and chromos. Faulty copyrighting minimized Oertel's royalties. In 1867 Oertel was admitted as a deacon, and in 1871 ordained priest. He served Southern congregations. Painting remained his other interest. He was instructor in fine arts at Washington U in St Louis 1889–91, painting some Western subjects. In 1895 his sons sponsored his completing the series on redemption. In 1902 the paintings were given to the U of the South, in Sewanee, Tenn.

showing US Army uniforms for the period 1888–1906 as well as military plates for "Pageant of America" and "Chronicles of America." By order of the government, he collected US Army uniforms for the period 1775–1906.

The most elaborate junket to the West was Frank Leslie's in 1877. The party of 12 included the staff artists Harry Ogden and Walter R Yeager as well as writers and a photographer. The result was about 200 illustrations published in *Leslie's*. They were mostly Western, with many taken from Ogden sketches. The trip featured genre views of Cheyenne, Colorado Springs, Salt Lake City, Virginia City, Sacramento, and San Francisco. The emphasis was on people doing things rather than landscape. Minimized were the Indians, even as compared to the Chinese railway workers. Mrs Leslie wrote about the Chinese: "Ill as their odor may be in Caucasian nostrils, their cleanly, smooth, and cared for appearance was very agreeable in contrast with the wild, unkempt, and filthy red men." AIW.

OGDEN, Henry Alexander (or Harry). Born Philadelphia, Pa 1856, died Englewood, NJ 1936. Western artist-correspondent for *Leslie's* in 1870s, painter of military and historical subjects, illustrator, author. References A38 (obit)-BEN - FIE - MAL. Sources AIW - p 330, ANT 5/51 with signature example-WHO 36. No current auction record.

Ogden was educated in a Brooklyn high school. He studied art at the Brooklyn Institute, the Brooklyn Academy of Design, the NAD, and the ASL. He worked as staff artist for Frank Leslie 1873–81 and in NYC as a lithographic artist for a Cincinnati printer 1881–1932. As a boys' book illustrator, he painted for "Our Army" in 1906, "Famous Regiments" in 1914, and "Our Flag" in 1917. He made 71 color plates

O'HARA, James Frederick. Born Ottawa, Ont, Can 1904, living La Jolla, Cal 1976. Lithographer, woodcutter, teacher, author. Prints in NGA, MMA, MNM, Cincinnati MA, Stadtmuseum (Karlsruhe, Germany). References A76-MAS. Source CAP. No current auction record. Signature example p 137 CAP.

Frederick O'Hara studied at the Massachusetts SA 1922–26, at the BMFA School 1926–29, and at the Inst Bellas Artes (Toledo, Spain) 1929–31. He has exhibited nationally and in England, Japan, and Germany. A teacher of art since 1948, O'Hara has been visiting professor at the U of New Mexico. He has also served on the art advisory committee of the Archaeological Institute in Santa Fe. His work has been included in collections of Western graphics.

O'KEEFFE, Georgia. Born Sun Prairie, Wis 1887, living Abiquiu, NM 1976. Very important Western modernist painter. Member, honorary academies. Work in ACM, ANS, MMA, MNM, MOMA, WMAA, BM, AIC, BMFA, etc. References A76-BEN-FIE-MAL. Sources AAR 9/73, 3/74-ALA-ANS-APT-ARI-CAA-DEP-HAR-HMA-190-ISH-MAP-NEU - OKE - ACM-AIC-BMC-PIT-SCU-STI-TAL-TOB-TSF-TXF-WAA-W64-WHO 70. Oil 36×30" *Poppies* 1950 sold 3/14/73 for $120,000 at auction of the Halpert colln. It is not Miss O'Keeffe's practice to sign her paintings. Portrait photos in OKE catalogs. (See illustration 217.)

Miss O'Keeffe was born on a Wisconsin farm and grew up in Virginia. She was educated at Sacred Heart Academy (Wis) 1900–1, Madison high school (Wis) 1901–2, and at Chatham Episcopal Institute (Va) 1902–4. Her art studies were at AIC with Vanderpoel 1904–5 and ASL with Chase 1907–8. She began working in 1909 as an illustrator for advertising companies, then became supervisor of art in the Amarillo, Tex public schools 1912–14, instructor in art at the U of Virginia 1913–16, and head of the art department West Texas State Normal College 1916–18. When Stieglitz saw the sketches of the young art teacher in 1916 he said, "Finally a woman on paper." She had become the pupil of Arthur Wesley Dow 1914–16 who led her to forms derived from nature and to subtle color contrasts. Stieglitz gave her the first exhibition in 1916, was her dealer and her husband. Her paintings were said to embody the feminine principle and she herself the symbol of the new uninhibited woman.

When she visited Taos in 1919 her art became more mystical and visionary, flavored with symbolism. She returned to New Mexico each summer, moving permanently in 1946. Miss O'Keeffe has spent the rest of her life communicating the essence of the West on simplified, pu-

ritan, austere canvases. "When she first saw bones on the arid earth of New Mexico, she thought of them as a kind of wildflower which had been purified by the wind and rain so that they evoked no association of death but rather a feeling of pristine splendor." TSF. There have been many retrospective one-artist exhibitions, beginning in 1927.

OLSON, J Olaf. Born Buffalo, Minn 1894, living NYC 1941. Landscape watercolor painter, in the West 1929. Work in BM. References A47-BEN-FIE-MAL. Source, Western watercolors dated 1929 were part of a lot as ※480 Morgan colln sold 5/30/74 at auction. Watercolor *Chiogga Boats* sold 5/22/72 for $180 at auction in Los Angeles. No signature example.

Olson was the student of F Tadema and George Bellows.

OLSON, Merle. Born Snowflake, Ariz 1910, living Big Fork, Mont 1974. Montana landscape and Indian portrait painter, sculptor. No reference. Sources BRO-MON. No current auction record. Signature example p 133 MON.

Mrs Olson was raised in Arizona where she studied music. Later she ran a beauty shop in El Paso. In 1941 she opened an art studio in Salt Lake City after taking a correspondence course and studying briefly at art school. From 1952 to 1954 she lived with her family on a Montana ranch, then settled at Flathead Lake in 1962. She seldom paints on location, preferring to work from quick sketches and color slides. Her work is realistic. "When I do a landscape I look for freshness. I don't like to paint a dreary picture." MON.

OLSTAD, Einar Hanson. Born Lillehammer, Norway 1876, living North Dakota 1951. Painter of ND Badlands. No reference. Source BDW. No auction record or signature example.

Olstad was brought to South Dakota as a baby. At 60 he began painting the cowboy genre and landscapes familiar to him when he had been a young homesteader in the North Dakota Badlands.

ONDERDONK, Julian. Born San Antonio, Tex 1882, died there 1922. Texas landscape painter. Work in Dallas MFA, Ft Worth AA, MFA of Houston, San Antonio Art League. References A22 (obit) - BEN - FIE - MAL - SMI. Sources AAR 5/74 - ANT 12/71 - COW - TEP - TOB-T20-TXF. Oil 12¾ × 16¾" *Morning on a Hilltop* in southwest Texas sold 4/15/70 for $925 at auction. Signature example p 17 AAR 5/74 *Blue Bonnets at Summer*.

Julian Onderdonk was the son of the important Texas landscapist, Robert Onderdonk. He was his father's pupil at 16. Sponsored by a Texas patron, he studied at the ASL when he was 19, the pupil of Cox, DuMond, and Henri. He also studied with Chase on Long Island. In 1902, having lost his Texas patron because he married, he asked $18 for 12 paintings at a Fifth Avenue dealer in NYC, and was glad to accept $14 for the lot.

In 1909 Julian Onderdonk returned to the family studio in San Antonio. He painted "the bigness of Texas, dusty roads, the blooming cactus or hillsides of blue lupine, rolling gulf clouds, aged liveoaks, and the gray brush in winter." TXF. "His style changed somewhat in his later years." TOB. Onderdonk was heavy-set with dark eyes and hair, quiet and serious, "a strong personality." TXF. When he died at 40, "five of his pictures were on the way to NY. He also had orders ahead for $20,000 worth of work." TOB. He was known as the painter of the bluebonnet flowers of Texas.

ONDERDONK, Robert Jenkins. Born Catonsville, Md 1852, died San Antonio, Tex 1917. Important Texas landscape and portrait painter, "the dean of Texas artists," teacher. Work in Fort Worth MA, Dallas AA, San Antonio Art League, Confederate Mus (Richmond, Va), State Senate (Austin). References A17 (obit) - BEN - FIE - MAL - SMI. Sources ANT 6/48,12/71-HMA-TEP-TOB-TXF. No current auction record but the estimated price of a substantial oil showing a San Antonio street scene would be about $2,500 to $3,000 at auction in 1976. Signature example p 205 TEP.

Onderdonk was educated at the College of St James in Maryland where his father was headmaster. At 20 he studied for two years at the NAD under Wilmarth, then at the ASL under Shirlaw and Beckwith. He was the private pupil of A H Warren, then known as "the Corot of America," and in 1878 concluded his art studies with Chase in his Munich period.

To earn funds for a European trip he never made, Onderdonk was persuaded to establish his studio in San Antonio in 1878. By 1881 he was married, living near Pedro Spring, taking the mule car to his studio in the city. He always carried with him a wood panel such as the top of a cigar box so he could paint small scenes. For his studio classes he charged $3 per month. He moved to Dallas in 1889 when offered $100 a month to teach. After his father-in-law died in 1896, he returned to San Antonio where he remained except for a trip to St Louis in 1899 to try commercial painting on tile. Not ambitious, not robust, not careful in signing his paintings, he received commissions for hundreds of portraits without being able to earn a suitable living. Even his epic *Davy Crockett's Last Stand* brought him only to say, "No one cares for historical pictures." TEP.

O'NEIL, John. Born Kansas City, Mo 1915, living Houston, Tex 1976. Modern painter in acrylic and pastel, teacher, writer. Work in DAM, Dallas MFA, Lib Cong, U Mich MA, Seattle AM, Philbrook Art Center (Tulsa), Joslyn MUS (Omaha, Neb). References A76-MAS. Sources AAT-DAA-WHO 70. No auction record. Painting example p 129 AAT *The Goat Ranch* 1939.

O'Neil earned his BFA 1936 and MFA 1939 from U of Oklahoma where he was professor of painting 1939–65. He studied at Colorado Springs FAC 1936–37 with H V Poor, Paul Burlin, and Boardman Robinson, at the Taos SA 1942 with Emil Bisttram, and in Italy 1951–52. Beginning 1965 O'Neil was chairman of the Department of Art at Rice U. He has exhibited internationally, winning more than 20 awards.

OQWA PI (or Oqua Pi, Abel Sánchez). Born San Ildefonso Pueblo, NM about 1899, living Santa Fe, NM 1967. Pueblo painter, muralist, farmer. Work in AMNH, BM, DAM, MAI, MNM, Riverside Mus. Sources AHI 2/50-AIP. No current auction record or signature example.

Oqwa Pi was educated at Santa Fe Indian School. Painting by 1920, he was a part of the San Ildefonso movement. It is said that his paintings have retained a great simplicity, with individual traits such as heads depicted relatively large. His color is fresh and his action is vivid.

He is quoted, "As I found that paint-

ing was the best among my talents, I decided to do my best to win me fame as an Indian artist. I have raised a big healthy family for my painting brought in good income." AIP.

ORMES, Mrs Manly D. Born probably Philadelphia, Pa about 1865, living Colo Springs, Colo 1923. Painter of Colo landscape. No reference. Sources NEW-SPR. No auction record or signature example.

Wife of a minister-librarian, Mrs Ormes studied watercolor painting at the PAFA. After Ormes moved to Colorado Springs in 1890, she continued in watercolors, exhibiting at Colorado College in 1900. By 1920 she was painting landscapes in oil. "Her talent burgeoned out into amplified heightened, brighter, accented lights." SPR. Subjects included Cheyenne Cañon, Red Rock Cañon, Camerons Cone, Monument Valley, Pikes Peak, and the Rampart range.

OSGOOD, Samuel Stillman. Born probably New Haven, Conn 1808, died California 1885. Cal portrait and historical painter. ANA (not listed NA 74). Work in NYHS. References BEN-FIE-G&W-MAL-SMI. Sources ALA-BAR-BOA-PAF. No current auction record or signature example.

Middle brother of three painters, Osgood was raised in Boston where he studied painting. Osgood painted portraits in Hartford and Boston as a leading practitioner. He visited Charleston in 1829, married the poetess Frances S Locke, and studied in Europe 1835–39. Osgood then moved to NYC where he painted except for residence in Philadelphia 1847–49 and trips to Europe and New Orleans after his wife's death in 1851.

He exhibited in NYC, Boston, and Philadelphia.

About 1869 Osgood moved to California where he "made a fortune with a continuation of his commonplace semi-photography" style of hard-edged portrait painting. BAR.

OTIS, Fessenden Nott. Born Ballston Springs, NY 1825, died New Orleans, La 1900. Landscape artist, writer, doctor. Work in ACM. References DAB-G&W. No other source, auction record, or signature example.

At 18 Otis studied landscape drawing when incapacitated due to an accident. He wrote the popular "Easy Lessons in Landscape." After returning to medical school and graduating in 1852, he became a ship's surgeon in Panama and in the Pacific.

In 1855 Otis drew a view of San Francisco that was published through a Parsons lithograph. He married in 1859 and settled into medical practice in NYC where he became police surgeon and an authority on genito-urinary diseases, a "charming, enthusiastic, and honest gentleman." DAB.

OTNES, Fred. Born Junction City, Kans 1925, living probably West Redding, Conn 1966. Eastern magazine and advertising illustrator including Indian subjects. No reference. Sources ILA-IL 62. No auction record. Signature example p 227 ILA.

Otnes studied at the American Academy and the AIC. His illustrations have appeared widely in magazines both for features and for advertising. ILA shows the illustration for "Ride Against the Sioux," a story for *The Saturday Evening Post*.

OTTER, Thomas P. Active in Philadelphia, Pa 1855–67. Painter and engraver. Work in Wilstach colln (Fairmount Park, Philadelphia), W R Nelson Galley of Art (Kansas City, Mo). References BEN-FIE-G&W-MAL. Sources ANT 12/65 - DBW - DWF - PAF - WES - WHI. No current auction record but the estimated price of a substantial oil showing a Western-related subject would be about $4,000 to $5,000 at auction in 1976. Painting example fig 33 WHI.

Otter's *On the Road* is a part of many Western exhibitions and has been reproduced in great quantity. Painted in 1860 it placed the covered wagon in contrast with the railroad train to demonstrate improvements in transportation means to open the West. Otter exhibited at the Boston Athenaeum and the PAFA which listed *On the Road* as for sale in 1860. *Moonlight* was also dated 1860, and *On the Beach* was exhibited at PAFA in 1862.

OTTINGER, George Morton. Born Bedford, Springfield Township, Pa 1833, died Salt Lake City, Utah 1917. Pioneer Utah painter of Western genre, landscapes, Aztec historical scenes, portraits; illustrator, teacher. Work in LDS temples. Reference A15 (as F M Ottinger). Sources AIW-PNW-PUA-YUP. No current auction record. Painting examples pp 10, 12 YUP. (See illustration 218.)

Of Quaker descent and raised in NYC, Ottinger ran away at 17 to become a sailor on a whaling ship and a gold seeker in California. When he returned to NYC at 20, he studied art briefly with Robt W Weir. At 25, he tinted photos in Kentucky. His mother joined the LDS Church so he took her by wagon train to Salt Lake City in 1861, remaining himself when he was urged to paint theater scenery. He married, bought a house from Brigham Young for $125, and settled down as painter, fire chief, in charge of the waterworks, adjutant general of the National Guard, president of the Deseret Academy FA in 1863, tinter of photos for the firm of Savage and Ottinger (Ambrotypes), and Shakespearean actor.

Ottinger's photography business flourished, so that he could travel to Europe by 1879. His painting income, however, was poor. Nominal prices for portraits and landscapes were $20 to $50, but in 1872 he wrote, "In the last eight years I have painted 223 pictures which have been sold for $3,415 or a little over $15 each. Deducting $7 each for supplies, my work then was not worth much." PUA. His two principal painting subjects were Western scenes and his series of allegorical and historical interpretations of the history of Mexico. The painting he sent to the Philadelphia Centennial was *Montezuma Receiving News of the Landing of Cortez*. Ottinger remained active as a painter until the end of his life.

OWEN, Bill. Born Gila Bend, Ariz 1942, living Flagstaff, Ariz 1976. Arizona painter of contemporary cowboy genre, sculptor. Member CAA 1973. Reference A76. Sources C74-PWA-letter Bill Owen 11/75. No auction record. Signature example painting *Laying a Heel Trap* PWA.

Owen's family has been in ranching so that he grew up as a working cowhand. Without formal art training, he decided about 1969 to paint full time. Living in the high country above the Mogollon Rim, he works in pastel, ink, and pencil as well as oil. He also modeled clay for bronze sculpture in 1973. Owen's paintings have been used as magazine covers for *Western Horseman* and *National Cattlemen* and his work has been reproduced by the Franklin Mint.

PAAP (or Pape), Hans. Born Hamburg, Germany 1894 (or 1890), died on a Pacific island 1966. New Mexico and California painter, art director, engraver. References BEN (Pape)-MAS (Pape). Sources BDW (Pape)-Helen L Card catalog no 5-SCA. No current auction record. An oil *Taos Indian* 21×19″ was illustrated and priced at $475 on p 56, Helen L Card catalog no 5 in 1964.

BEN lists "Pape" as having been the pupil of P von Halens and working as painter-engraver in Münster, Westphalia. Helen Card records Paap as born in Germany in 1890, painting around the world, settling in Taos, and living in 1964. Moure places Paap as a motion-picture art director in Berlin before WWI. He painted in Brazil and Argentina until he emigrated to Hollywood in 1928. He began exhibiting in California that year and later painted in Taos and Santa Fe.

PALENSKE, Reinhold H. Born Chicago, Ill 1884, died probably there 1954 (or 1953). Graphic artist, painter. Work in Lib Cong, NY Pub Lib, Royal Gal (London), Ft Worth AC Mus. References A53-MAS. Sources AAW-CAP. No current auction record. Signature example p 139 CAP *Over the Pass*.

Palenske studied at the AIC, the pupil of W Reynolds. His work was reproduced in *The Spur* and in the *Washington Star* and *Chicago Daily News*.

PALEY, Robert L. Active Colo Springs, Colo 1890s–1906, later moving to Boston. Colo illustrator. No reference. Source SPR. No auction record or signature example.

Paley sketched for Colorado publications and illustrated "Myths and Legends of Colorado" (1906) by Mrs Louise M Smith. He settled in Boston and by 1923 was illustrating for *The Saturday Evening Post*.

PALMER, Frances Flora. Born Leicester, Eng 1812, died Brooklyn, NY 1876. Lithographic artist, watercolorist. Lithographs in major museums. References BEN - FIE - G&W - MAL. Sources ACM-AWM-ALA-BAR-C&I-COS-GIL-KW1-STI-WAA-WES. Auction prices for C&I lithographs are listed in guides; estimated price for a watercolor from which a lithograph had been taken would in 1976 be about $1,500 to $2,500 at auction. Lithograph examples including *The Rocky Mtns/Emigrants Crossing the Plains* ✕1516 ACM.

A wellborn Englishwoman, Fanny Bond Palmer came to the US about 1840. She lived in Brooklyn with her husband who was also a lithographer. They worked together from 1846 to 1849, but her husband's irresponsibility forced her to support the family as a Currier & Ives artist. She made original paintings for reproduction and also was able to draw work from field sketches directly on the lithographic stone, depicting, for example, "transcontinental trains in hard, prim watercolor." ALA.

There is no record of Fanny Palmer traveling West but she is included in Western source books because of subjects like the McMurtrie *View of San Francisco* for N Currier, and *Across the Continent* for C&I with covered wagons and Indians as background for the "Through Line" train. She was described by Louis Maurer as a "small, frail woman with large, dark eyes, plain in appearance, but of perfectly delightful manners." Maurer, who lived to be a hundred, reported just before she died at 64 that her "back became so very stooped from overwork that she looked almost deformed." KW1.

PANABAKER, Frank S. Born Hespeler, Ont, Can about 1895, living Ancaster, Ont, Can 1976. Eastern Can landscape painter, in the Can West; author. Assoc member RCA. Work in AG Toronto, AG Hamilton, AG London (Ont), Thomson Gal (Owen Sound, Ont). References A76-MAL. Source CAN. No current auction record. Painting example p 178 CAN, *The Fallen Monarch.*

Panabaker studied at the Ontario College of Art in Toronto and in NYC at the Grand Central School of Art and the ASL. He wrote "Reflected Lights" in 1957 and was trustee of the NGC 1959–66. Panabaker is listed as one of the Eastern painters who is an interpreter of "the scenery and life of Western Canada." CAN. He has exhibited both in Canada and the US.

PARADISE, Philip Herschel. Born Ontario, Ore 1905, living Cambria, Cal 1976. Painter sculptor, illustrator, graphic artist, teacher. ANA 1953 (aquarellist). Work in Lib Cong, PAFA, Cornell U, Spokane AA, etc. References A76-MAS. Sources AAT-WHO 70. No current auction record. Signature example p 132 AAT *Indian Threshers.*

Phil Paradise graduated from Chouinard AI in Los Angeles in 1927. He also studied with F Tolles Chamberlain, Rico Lebrun, and Leon Kroll. He taught at Chouinard 1932–40, was a film art director at Paramount Studios 1941–48, lectured at U of Texas at El Paso and Scripps College, and became director of the Cambria Summer Art School. Paradise was an illustrator for magazines

such as *Fortune, Westways,* and *True.* His work including Western subjects has been reproduced.

PARIS, Walter. Born London, Eng 1842, died Washington, DC 1906. Watercolorist, architect. Work in COR, Pioneers' Mus (Colo Springs, Colo). References A05-BEN-DAB-FIE-MAL-SMI. Sources COR-DCC-KW1-NEW-SHO-SPR. Watercolor 10×6" *A Stroll by the Capitol* sold in 1971 for $650 at auction. Signature example p 15 SHO.

Paris studied at the RA, after having been apprenticed at 15 to an architect. From 1863 to 1870 he worked as an architect for the British Government in India. When he returned to England, he studied painting under Robotham and Naftel. He moved to Colorado Springs on the advice of his doctor about 1872, acting briefly as a member of the F V Hayden US Geological Survey. Becoming the first artist resident in Colorado Springs, Paris painted watercolors of the Colorado landscape, including views of the Springs and of Pueblo until 1876. These were "exquisitely dainty paintings, done painstakingly with minute attention to detail." DAB. "Paris attributed this exactitude to his years in the field of architecture." DCC.

A large and pompous man with square-cut beard and British accent, Paris founded the famous Tile Club when he set up his studio in NYC in 1876. Members were artists like Abbey, Millet, Augustus Saint-Gaudens, Vedder, and Alden Weir. Paris later moved to Washington. His favorite subjects were rural English scenes and flower studies. He was also a distinguished amateur violinist.

PARISH (or Parrish), Charles Louis. Born probably NYC about 1830, died there 1902. Sketch artist, lithographic artist, businessman. Work in HON. Reference G&W. Sources ANT 1/54-HON. No auction record but the estimated value of a drawing of a Cal town would be $400 to $500 at auction in 1976. Signature example p 41 ANT 1/54.

Parish was apprenticed to a builder and architect. In 1850 he sailed around the Horn to join the gold rush as an entrepreneur. In Jackson, Cal he made mining equipment. Drawings of coastal cities in South America by this self-taught artist are dated 1852. The views of California towns such as Jackson, Volcano, and Mokelumne Hill are assumed to be about 1854. In this period Parish also owned a toll bridge at Big Bar, Cal.

PARKER, James K. Born probably Hawaii about 1880, died Hawaii 1963. Primitive painter of Parker Ranch cowboy genre in Hawaii. No reference. Source COW. No auction record but the estimated price of a major oil showing nostalgic Hawaiian cowboy genre would be $800 to $900 at auction in 1976. Signature example p 219 COW.

Parker began painting at 70, depicting life on the ranch as he remembered it. Parker Ranch was 262,000 acres with 42,000 cows, having been founded about 1820. The cowhands were Mexican vaqueros called "paniolas."

PARKINSON, William Jensen. Born Hyrum, Utah 1899, living Salt Lake City, Utah 1965. Utah painter, decorator, illustrator. Work in Utah schools and public buildings. References A41-MAS. Source YUP. No current auction record. Signature example p 30 YUP.

Parkinson was essentially self-taught, although he studied at U of Utah with A B Wright in 1924, with correspondence schools in 1934, and with Ralph Pearson in 1946. He has taught in a Utah school and art center, and was a department store decorator in 1946. Some of his work was for the "Index of American Design." It is said that he was "one of the few Utahans to venture into surrealism. His later work is largely tense and detailed portraiture." YUP.

PARRISH, Anne Lodge (Anne Willcox). Born probably Philadelphia, Pa about 1850, living Colorado Springs, Colo until about 1900. Portrait painter, etcher. Work in Pioneers' Mus, El Paso Club, Cheyenne Mountain Country Club, all in Colorado Springs, Colo. No reference. Sources GOD-NEW-SHO-SPR. No current auction record but the estimated price of a major portrait of a prominent Colorado figure of the 1880s would be about $400 to $500 at auction in 1976. Signature example p 20 SHO.

Both Tom and Anne Parrish had been Philadelphia portrait painters. They opened a studio in Colorado Springs and conducted art clases about 1880. Anne Parrish's brother was William J Willcox who owned the Broadmoor Dairy Farm that was held in partnership with Count James Pourtales after 1885. Tom Parrish was a civic leader, the count's partner in Cripple Creek mining ventures in 1891–92 and publisher of the *Colorado Springs Gazette* in 1896–98. His brother was Stephen Parrish, the Philadelphia etcher who was the father of Maxfield Parrish.

Colorado portraits by Anne Parrish are dated between 1880 and 1900. Her daughter Anne, raised in Colorado Springs, was the novelist who wrote "The Perennial Bachelor."

PARRISH, Charles Louis. See Parish.

PARRISH, Jean. Born New Hampshire (or Windsor, Vt) about 1920, living Albuquerque, NM 1973. Southwestern landscape painter. No reference. Source NMX 9,10/73-catalog from the artist. No auction record. Painting example p 32 NMX. (See illustration 219.)

Miss Parrish, daughter of the important illustrator Maxfield Parrish, moved from New England to New Mexico in 1937. Self-taught, she began to paint in 1948 when she felt able to express herself apart from her father's distinctive style. In New Mexico she saw the "shape of the land. When I paint I try to mirror the way light sculptures the earth, the way shadows fall." NMX. Her studio faces the west slopes of the Sandia Mountains.

where he was influenced as a colorist. He painted Southwestern landscapes in a style already distinctive in his 1902 illustrations for *Century*. Third, he went to Italy. Recovered physically, he settled in Windsor, Vt.

Parrish was best known as an illustrator for children's books and magazines. Some of these illustrations, as the 1927 *Pueblo Dwelling* for "The Home University Bookshelf," were based on his Southwestern experiences. Reproductions of his illustrations were widely collected. A favorite work *The Dream Garden* was designed by Parrish and executed in Favrile glass by Tiffany as a mosaic mural in 1915. "Insider" favorites were the paintings in the bar of the St Regis in NYC and in the Palace Bar in San Francisco.

PARRISH, Maxfield. Born Philadelphia, Pa 1870, died Plainfield, NH 1966. Unique Eastern illustrator and painter in Ariz 1902, noted as colorist of "Maxfield Parrish blue." ANA 1905, NA 1906. Work in City AM (St Louis), murals in hotels, clubs, and public buildings. References A66-BEN-FIE-MAL-SMI. Sources AAR 9/73 - ALA - AMA - ANT 12/73 - DEP-ILA-ILP-ISH-JCA-MSL-NA 74-POW-WHO 66. Oil on paper 22×16″ *The Giant Amused* (a *Collier's* cover 7/30/10) signed with initials and dated 1908 sold 5/22/73 for $2,500 at auction. Signature example p 64 ILA. (See illustration 220.)

The son of the Philadelphia etcher and landscape painter Stephen Parrish, Maxfield Parrish was educated at Haverford College 1888–91. He studied art at the PAFA and was the pupil of Howard Pyle at Drexel Inst, Philadelphia. Early in his career he had typhoid fever, requiring recuperation away from the East. First, he went to Saranac in the Adirondacks where the winter forced him to give up his water-base inks in favor of oils. Second, he went to sunny Arizona

PARRISH, Thomas. Born Philadelphia, Pa 1837, died Colo Springs, Colo 1899. Colo landscape and portrait painter, illustrator, etcher, teacher, publisher, land speculator. No reference. Sources GOD-NEW-SHO (p 6)-SPR. No auction record or signature example.

A member of the Philadelphia family of artists, Parrish studied drawing in Philadelphia and etching with his brother Stephen. He moved to Colorado Springs with his wife, soon after the arrival of the Springs' first artist, Walter Paris, in 1871. He sketched and speculated in real estate.

After his wife died, he returned to Philadelphia. He studied at the PAFA, painted and etched, and married the portrait painter Anne Lodge. When he came back to Colorado Springs about 1880, he was more of a civic leader, land gambler, and publisher than artist. His etchings included *Dawn from the Foot Hills* and *Cherokee Rose*. His *Rocky Mountain Canary* was the cover for a scenic booklet, and he illustrated Ernest Whitney's "Legends and Myths of the Pike's Peak

Region." His medium was watercolor, and with his wife he conducted an art studio. In Colorado Springs, however, his fame rests on his associations with the legendary Count Pourtales. His daughter Anne Parrish became a noted novelist.

PARROTT, William Samuel. Born Missouri 1844, died near Goldendale, Wash 1915. Northwestern landscape painter, teacher. Work in the FA Mus of San Francisco. References A15 (obit)-BEN (as Parrot)-FIE-MAL-SMI. Sources WHI-WNW. Oil 9×12″ *Mt Hood from Bull Run Lake, Oregon* sold 10/01/69 for $350 at auction. No signature example.

Parrott was brought to Oregon in 1847 and to Washington in 1859. His studio was in Portland, Ore for 20 years. The painting in WHI was *Shoshone Falls, Snake River, Idaho*.

PARSHALL, DeWitt. Born Buffalo, NY 1864, died Santa Barbara, Cal 1956. Landscape painter of the Grand Canyon. ANA 1910, NA 1917. Work in MMA, Seattle AM, San Diego MFA, Toledo Mus, Worcester AM, WMAA, Detroit IA, LA MA. References A59 (obit)-BEN-FIE-MAL-SMI. Sources HAA-SCH-WHO 50. No current auction record. No signature example. Studio photo opp p 497 A17. (See illustration 221.)

DeWitt Parshall was educated at DeVeaux school in Niagara Falls, NY 1877–81, receiving his BS from Hobart College in 1885. He then became the pupil of the Julien and Cormon academies in Paris 1886–92 and studied privately with T Alexander Harrison. By 1899 his studio was in NYC. As his interest centered on Western landscape, he became a member of the Society of Painters of the West and vice president of the Santa Barbara MA. Paintings in museum collections include *Great Abyss, Granite Gorge, Isis Peak, Hermit Creek Canyon, Grand Canyon, Platform Rock,* and *Night—Grand Canyon.*

In 1901 the important critic Sadakichi Hartmann called Parshall one "who approaches mountain scenery with the spirit and treatment of the modern landscape school," the only younger painter of note since the Barbizon school replaced the Rocky Mountain school in 1860. HAA. In 1911 Charles de Kay noted that the "extraordinary colouring of the landscape in the West prevented artists from attempting to reproduce it since they feared it would not be accepted in the East as true to facts," and listed Parshall among the expressive landscape painters. SCH.

PARSHALL, Douglass Ewell. Born NYC 1899, living Santa Barbara, Cal 1976. Cal landscape and figure painter, teacher. ANA 1928, NA 1969. Work in De Young Mus (San Fran), Detroit IA, San Diego Gall FA, NGA, Kansas City MA. References A76-BEN-FIE-MAS. Source WHO 68. Oil 24×28″ *Village Scene, Taxco, Mexico* with signature example, estimated for sale 5/27/74 at $300 to $500 at auction in LA and sold for $500.

Parshall was the pupil of his father, DeWitt Parshall. He also studied at the ASL and the Santa Barbara School of Arts. From 1942 to 1944 he was technical illustrator for Douglas Aircraft. His paintings include *Fiesta at Taos* in the Kansas City MA. Beginning 1967 he has been instructor in portraits at the Santa Barbara AI.

PARSONS, Charles H. Born Rowland's Castle, Hampshire, Eng 1821, died

Brooklyn, NY 1910. Lithographic artist, illustrator specializing in marine scenes, marine and landscape painter in watercolor and oil, art director. ANA 1862. Drew on the stones for many C&I lithographs in major museums. References A09 - BEN - CHA - FIE-G&W-MAL-SMI. Sources ACM - AIW - ANT 3/71 - COS - HUT - KW1 - NJA - WES - WHO 10. No current auction record but the estimated price for a watercolor of San Fran would be about $1,000 to $1,500 at auction in 1976. Painting examples p 361 ANT 3/71 a pair of watercolor ship portraits that were the originals of lithographs.

Parsons was brought to the US at nine, was an apprentice at 12 with the lithographers George Endicott & Company in NYC, and a regular employee from 1835 to 1861. During this period he made lithographs for C&I working both in watercolor and on the stone, and he was also a pupil of and exhibitor at NAD. From 1861 to 1889 Parsons was the head of *Harper's* art department. According to Pennell, Parson's "name will never be forgotten as one who helped greatly to develop American art." At one point Parsons as art director had Edwin Austin Abbey doing the foreground figures on a given illustration, W A Rogers doing the middle-distance figures, and T R Davis the architectural features. In 1885 Howard Pyle said Parsons showed him engravings of illustrations of a parade not yet held!

In 1878 Parsons visited Britton & Rey, pioneer San Francisco lithographers and former Eastern sketching partners, and probably made the sketch for *City of San Francisco*. C&I. After his retirement in 1889, Parsons painted in oil and watercolor including some Westerns.

PARSONS, Ernestine. Born Booneville, Mo 1884, died Colorado Springs, Colo 1967. Painter, teacher resident in Colorado Springs. Work in CSFAC, Fort Car-

son. References A70 (obit) - MAS. Sources SHO-WAA. No current auction record but the estimated price of a substantial oil showing a Colorado mine would be about $500 to $700 at auction in 1976. Signature example p 41 SHO.

Ernestine Parsons was educated at Colorado College and Columbia U. She studied at Broadmoor AA, the ASL, and the CSFAC with Randall Davey and Paul Burlin. She was a teacher at Colorado Springs high school and exhibited since 1927.

PARSONS, Orrin Sheldon. Born NYC (or Rochester) 1866, died Santa Fe, NM 1943. Early impressionist Santa Fe landscape painter, museum director. Work in MNM, U NM, ANS. References A47 (obit)-BEN-MAL-SMI. Sources COW-PIT-SUG-TSF. Oil on panel 32×24" *Glory of the Aspens* was estimated at $600 to $800 for sale 3/4/74 at auction, brought $600, and was estimated again at $800 to $1,000 for sale 10/28/74 at auction in LA, and sold for $800. Signature example SUG. (See illustration 222.)

Sheldon Parsons studied at the NAD with Chase, Will Low, and Edgar Ward. He was a successful NYC portrait painter of national celebrities between 1895 and 1912. When his wife died Parsons came to Santa Fe in 1913, one of the earliest of the resident artists. He painted happy, serene, impressionist landscapes. In 1918 Parsons was the first director of the Museum of New Mexico. In Santa Fe, Parsons painted "town plazas, Indian villages, desert, and mountains. His work began to show a greater freedom in handling forms and a stronger sense of color." PIT.

PAXSON (or Paxon), Edgar Samuel. Born East Hamburg, NY 1852, died

Missoula, Mont 1919. Important pioneer Montana painter, illustrator, muralist specializing in Western Indian and settler life. Work in ANS, U of Mont, murals in Whitney Gall of Western Art (Cody, Wyom), Mont Cnty Cthse and State Capitol. References A21-FIE-MAL. Sources ANT 4/69,11/73 - COW - CUS - DCC - HAR - JNB - PAW - PNW - POW - TWR-WAI 71,72-WHO 20-WNW. Oil 20×40" *Buffalo Hunt* signed E S Paxson and dated 1902 sold 10/27/71 for $10,000 at auction. Signature example p 780 ANT 11/73. (See illustration 223.)

Paxson was educated in a log schoolhouse with one year at Friends' Institute in East Hamburg. He became his father's helper as a sign painter and decorator. In 1877, the year after Custer's battle, he went to Montana, leaving his wife and child in Buffalo. He worked at odd jobs in Montana, on a cattle ranch, as a meat hunter, as a dispatch rider, as a stage driver, and as a scout in the Nez Percé war 1877–78. In 1879 he brought his family to Deer Lodge, where he began to paint in oil while working as a commercial artist, painting signs, decorating saloons and theater sets. In 1881 he moved to Butte where there was more demand for his services.

He served in the Montana National Guard for 10 years, spending eight months in the Philippines during the Spanish-American War. In 1905 he settled in Missoula. His most famous painting was *Custer's Last Battle on the Little Big Horn,* 6×10' and took six to eight (or 20) years to paint. It was nationally exhibited, producing recognition for Paxson, although his small watercolors were considered more successful artistically. His dress and grooming were in the frontier style, with long hair, full mustache, and pointed goatee.

PAYNE, Edgar Alwin. Born Washburn, Mo 1882, died Los Angeles, Cal 1947.

Western landscape painter, muralist. Work in Neb AA, Chicago Munic Art Comn, ANS, Herron AI (Indianapolis), NAD; murals in theaters and public buildings. References A47(obit)-BEN-FIE-MAL-SMI. Sources AAR 11/74-COW-HAR-HON-PAW-WAI 71, 72-WHO 42. Oil 20×24" *Monument Valley Promontory* with signature example, estimated $1,500 to $2,000 for sale 3/10/75 for auction in LA, and sold for $1,000. (See illustration 224.)

Edgar Payne was a member of the Alumni Association of the AIC but considered himself to have been self-taught. He had begun as a house and sign painter and as a decorator, becoming a member of the Chicago Society of Artists. In 1911 a sketching trip West took him to Laguna Beach, Cal where he settled in 1917. Later sketching trips were into the Sierras, which he learned so intimately that a lake was named for him. Payne had married Elsie Palmer, a fellow Chicago artist, in 1912.

In the 1920s Payne traveled in Europe, winning an honorable mention in the 1923 Paris Salon. When he returned to California, he wrote a successful book on landscape painting and made a movie about the Sierras. His paintings were said to have been "post-impressionistic in manner." PAW. He had also painted in Arizona and New Mexico, the Grand Canyon, Canyon de Chelly, and the mesas. Payne was listed as living in NYC in 1934 and in Los Angeles by 1941.

PEABODY, Ruth Eaton. Born Highland Park, Ill 1898, died Laguna Beach, Cal 1967. California painter and sculptor. Work in San Diego FAS; monuments in Laguna Beach. References A53-MAL. No other source. No auction record or signature example.

Ruth Peabody studied at the AIC and was the pupil of Eleanor Colburn. Her awards began with 1926. They included watercolor and oil painting as well as sculpture.

PEALE, Charles Willson. Born St Paul's Parish, Queen Anne Cnty (or Chestertown), Md 1741, died Philadelphia, Pa 1827. Very important Philadelphia portrait painter specializing in Geo Washington, Lewis and Clark illustrator, Indian silhouettist. Work in PAFA, MMA, Peale Mus (Balt), Washington and Lee U, U Ariz Art Gall, Winterthur Mus. References BEN-CHA-DAB-ENB-FIE-G&W-MAL-SMI. Sources AAR 11/74-ALA-AMA-ANT 6/43; 9/45; 6/47; 2/49; 4/50; 1,6/51; 3,12/54; 8/57; 5/58; 7,12/61; 1,11/62; 2/66; 1,4/67; 6/68; 2,4/69; 3/71; 1,5,10,11/72; 1,9,11/73; 5,10,11/74; 3/75 - AOW - BAR - BOA - ISH-KW1-M19-MSL-NJA-PAF-POW-STI-TEP. Oil 26×22″ *Study for "The Artist in His Museum"* painted in 1822 but not signed, sold 10/27/71 for $60,000 at auction. Painting example p 71 AAR 11/74.

Son of a schoolmaster, Peale was apprenticed at 13 to an Annapolis saddler. At 20 he established himself as a saddler, but his activities as a patriot led his Tory creditors to put him out of business in 1764. He became the pupil of John Hesselius and met Copley in Boston. In 1767 his neighbors sponsored a trip to England where he painted portraits and miniatures as the pupil of West. His studio was successfully established in Annapolis in 1769. When he moved to Philadelphia in 1776, he soon was in active service as a captain of the 4th Battalion. After the war he was a politician until 1780, voting for the abolition of slavery. He continued to paint during this period and also engraved mezzotint plates of some of his portraits. By the 1800s he was painting only as an avocation. His style changed radically from highly decorative to vividly realistic. Peale was best known as the painter of George Washington, working seven times from life beginning in 1772, completing 60 portraits in all. Peale survived three wives and had 17 children, some of whom were famous painters and naturalists.

In 1805 a group of 27 Indian chiefs from 12 tribes was given a government-sponsored tour of Eastern cities. When they visited Peale's museum in Philadelphia, Peale cut about 12 silhouettes of the Indians, sending the mounted "blockheads" to his friend President Jefferson. Peale's museum displayed specimens brought back by Lewis and Clark in 1808. Peale made several renderings of animals as illustrations for the expedition's report, but none was used.

PEALE, Titian Ramsay. Born Philadelphia, Pa 1799 (or 1800), died there 1885. Artist in the Rockies in 1819–20, pioneer naturalist. Work (50 sketches) in Amer Philos Soc (Phila), ACM. References BEN-DAB-ENB-FIE-G&W-MAL-SMI. Sources AAR 5/74-ANT 1/49, 10/54, 8/60, 6/62, 11/64-AOW-BAR-COW-FRO-150-PAF-WHI. Watercolor 6¼×9″ *Sioux Lodge* with initials as signature example, titled, and dated 1819 sold 10/19/72 for $12,500 at auction.

Titian Peale, the youngest son of Charles Willson Peale, was named for his older brother who had died in 1798. As a youngster, he worked in a cotton-spinning factory. At 17 he attended the U of Penn to study anatomy, taxidermy, and specimen drawing. Two years later he joined an expedition to collect Georgia coast fauna. In 1819 he was assistant naturalist for Maj Long's expedition to the Rockies. When he returned he was assistant manager of the Philadelphia Museum. He went to Florida in 1823 to illustrate "American Ornithology" and "American Entomology." Eight years later he traveled to Colombia for his own

"Lepidoptera Americana." The next year he became manager of the museum. From 1838 to 1842 he was a member of the expedition to the South Seas. From 1849 to 1872, after financial difficulties at the museum, he was an examiner in the US Patent Office.

His Western experiences were limited to the 1819–20 Long expedition where he was assistant to the naturalist Thomas Say and junior to the established artist Samuel Seymour. He wintered 1819–20 near Omaha, Neb, collecting animal and insect specimens and making field sketches of buffalo as well as the first rendering of a tepee. In 1820 the expedition moved westward to the Rockies. Peale sketched a Pawnee Indian fort on the Platte. In the report on the expedition, he was credited with 122 sketches.

PEARCE, Mrs Helen Spang (Mrs Helen Spang Ancona). Born Reading, Pa 1895, living Albuquerque, NM 1964. New Mexico landscape painter. Work in MNM. Reference A62. Sources WAA-W64. No auction record or signature example.

Mrs Pearce graduated from Philadelphia School of Design for Women in 1923. She studied at the U of New Mexico 1941–44 with Raymond Jonson, Kenneth Adams, and Randall Davey, at the Pasadena City College in 1952 with Kenneth Nack, and with George Bridgman, Henry Snell, Leopold Seyffert, and Lucile Howard.

PEASE, Lucius Curtis (Lute). Born Winnemucca, Nev 1869, died Maplewood, NJ 1963. Artist-correspondent in Alaska 1897–1901, cartoonist, portrait painter. Work in Stenzel colln. References A62-MAL. Sources NJA-PNW-WHO 58. No current auction record but the estimated price of an oil showing Alaskan gold-rush genre would be $900 to $1,100 at auction in 1976. Signature example back cover PNW.

Lute Pease graduated from Malone (NY) Academy in 1887 with little formal art training. The same year, he was a rancher in Santa Barbara County, Cal. From 1897 to 1901 he was a prospector and gold miner in Alaska as well as the Yukon-Nome correspondent for a Seattle newspaper, sketching in crayon and watercolor. From 1901 to 1902 he served as a US Commissioner for Alaska.

When he left Alaska he was political cartoonist and reporter for the *Portland Oregonian* 1902–5. In 1906 he was editor and illustrator for *Pacific Monthly,* resigning when the publication merged into *Sunset Magazine* in 1913. Moving to Newark, NJ, he was an editorial cartoonist for more than 30 years, drawing about 70,000 cartoons and winning a Pulitzer Prize. Pease also painted genre, portrait, and landscape subjects in oil, including scenes of Alaska and the Pacific Northwest. He exhibited oils at the NAD.

PEASE, Nell Christmas McMullin (or McMillan). Born Steubenville, Ohio 1883, living Maplewood, NJ 1963. Illustrator for *Pacific Monthly,* portrait painter. References A41-MAS. Source PNW. No current auction record or signature example.

Nell Pease studied at the Corcoran School of Art and was the pupil of Howard Helmick. She married Lute Pease in 1905. When he was editor of *Pacific Monthly* in Portland, Ore from 1906 to 1913, she painted illustrations and covers. They moved to New Jersey in 1914.

PECK, Henry Jarvis. Born Galesburg, Ill 1880, living Warren, RI 1941. Illustrator of historic Western subjects, painter, etcher, writer. References A41-MAL. Sources, illustrations for article on Davy Crockett-NCW. No auction record or signature example.

Peck was the pupil of Eric Pape and Howard Pyle. He studied at the Rhode Island School of Design.

PECK, Orin. Born Delaware Cnty, NY 1860, died Los Angeles, Cal 1921. Cal genre, landscape, and portrait painter. Work in World's Columb Expos (1893). References A21 (obit)-BEN-FIE-MAL-SMI. Source, *Scene in the Garden of the Santa Barbara Mission* listed A21. No auction record or signature example.

Peck studied in Munich with N Gijsis and Loefftz. He supervised the artwork for the northern California Hearst ranch and painted Hearst portraits.

PEIRCE, Gerry. Born Jamestown, NY 1900, living Tucson, Ariz 1962. Arizona painter, illustrator, etcher, teacher. Work in Joslyn AM, IBM, BMFA, MNM, MMA, Lib Cong, Denver AM, etc. References A62-MAS. Source AAT. No current auction record but the published estimate for prints is $80 to $100. Drypoint example p 307 AAT *Hilltop*.

Peirce studied at the Cleveland IA and the ASL. He illustrated "Plants of Sun and Sand" in 1939 and taught in Tucson.

PEIRCE, Joshua H. Active 1841–59. Miniaturist and landscape painter. Reference G&W. Source COS. No auction record or signature example.

Peirce was in NYC in 1841–42 as a miniaturist. About 1841 in NYC he made portraits for G W Lewis. He lived in Boston in 1843, exhibiting miniatures at the Boston Athenaeum, and worked with Sharp & Peirce in Boston from 1846–49.

In 1849 Peirce was in San Francisco, painting a view of the city and the harbor beyond, all with a miniaturist's detailing. He was active throughout the 1850s as an artist for lithographers and as a lithographer for his firm (Peirce & Pollard). COS.

PEIXOTTO, Ernest Clifford. Born San Francisco, Cal 1869, died NYC 1940. International painter, illustrator, muralist, printmaker, teacher. Member ANA 1909, officer Legion of Honor 1924, SI 1906. Work in NGA, Hispanic Soc NY; murals in NYC banks and club. References A47 (obit)-BEN-FIE-MAL-SMI. Sources AMA-BWB-MSL-NA 74-WHO 40. No current auction record. Signature example p 123 *Harper's New Monthly Magazine* vol xciv Dec 1896.

Educated in San Francisco, Peixotto studied in Paris with Constant, Lefebvre, and Doucet. When he returned to San Francisco in 1895, Peixotto was one of the earliest artists to contribute drawings for *Lark*. He was also a contributor of illustrations to *Overland Monthly* and wrote and illustrated "Romantic California" (1911), "Our Hispanic Southwest" (1916), etc. He wrote for and illustrated national magazines such as *Scribner's*. During WWI, Peixotto was one of eight painters chosen to sketch soldiers in action. He settled in NYC after the war, teaching mural painting.

PENA, Tonita. Born San Ildefonso Pueblo, NM 1895, died there 1949. Among the first of the Rio Grande artists, muralist, teacher. Work in AMNH,

City AM (St Louis), COR, DAM, GIL, MAI, MNM, Philbrook AC, Southwest Mus. Sources AHI 2/50-AIP. No auction record or signature example.

Tonita Pena (Quah Ah or White Coral Beads) was brought up by her aunt, a potter. She was educated in San Ildefonso Pueblo Day School and at St Catherine's Indian School in Santa Fe. At the age of 21 she was a successful artist, the only woman painter of her generation and an original participant in the watercolor movement with Awa Tsireh, Fred Kabotie, and Oqwa Pi. Her work was compared to the painters of the figures on Greek vases. In addition to her art, she was a housewife, married first at 14 and married twice again, with six children.

Tonita Pena was one of the artists who copied the Pajarito murals before restoration. Murals by her were commissioned for the Society of Independent Artists in 1933 and for the Chicago World's Fair. She was art instructor at the Santa Fe and Albuquerque Indian schools. Her favorite subjects were children and animals. She was referred to as "the grand old lady of Pueblo art."

PÉNÉLON, Henri. Born Lyon, France 1827, died probably France 1885. French fresco painter, portraitist, and photographer in southern California beginning about 1853. Work in Bowers Memorial Mus (Santa Ana). Reference G&W. Sources ANT 11/53-COW-FRO-PAW. No auction record. Painting example p 141 FRO.

Pénélon's one known portrait is of Don José Sepúlveda, an important ranch owner of early California. Don José was the importer of a black mare from Australia. His costume and saddlery are preserved with the equestrian portrait that was painted about 1856. Pénélon also applied frescoes to the Plaza Church in Los Angeles.

PENFIELD, Edward. Born Brooklyn, NY 1866, died Beacon, NY 1925. Eastern decorative illustrator, painter, art editor, writer, teacher. Member SI 1901, Artists Guild. Murals at Harvard and Rochester Country Club, magazine covers for *Collier's* and *Harper's,* the inaugurator of poster art in US. References A25 (obit)-BEN-DAB-FIE-MAL-SMI. Sources AAC-ALA-BAW-ILA-WHO 24. No current auction record. Signature example p 262 BAW, monogram p 29 ILA.

Penfield studied at the ASL. At 24 and for 10 years he was art editor and illustrator for *Harper's Magazine, Harper's Weekly,* and *Harper's Bazaar.* During this period he drew *Bandit Group Stages Train Hold-up* for *Harper's Weekly* (1892), as reproduced in BAW.

After 1901 Penfield devoted himself to art, mainly commercial. His style was art nouveau, pioneering this influence in the US. He was the originator of the poster in the US, and used drawing textures that were new in printing. Favorite subjects were horses and carriages, cats, old uniforms. "He was quiet, modest, and retiring to the point of secretiveness. His health was not strong, though his art was always robust." DAB.

PERCEVAL, Don Louis. Born Woodford, Essex, Eng 1908, living Santa Barbara, Cal 1973. Traditional Western illustrator, painter, author. No reference. Sources AHI 9/63,3/74-COW-TWR. No current auction record. Signature example p 5 AHI 9/63.

Perceval was raised in Los Angeles. At 19 he illustrated his first book. He returned to England about 1930, studying at the Heatherly Art School in London and at the Royal College of Art. He visited Spain before serving in the Royal Navy during WWII.

After the war Perceval was an instructor at Chouinard Art School in Los Angeles and at Pomona College. He became an expert in the history of cattle brands, as well as costume, saddlery, and equipment of horsemen and horses. He has been a popular illustrator of books and magazines.

PERILLO, Gregory. Born Staten Island, NY date unknown, active 1973 as painter of the Amer Indian. Work in Denver MNH, Pettigrew Mus (S Dak), Mus No Amer Ind (Fla), and St Michael's Col (N Mex). No reference. Sources ANS-1973 Perillo catalog *Indian Heads/Face to Face with the American West*. No auction record. Signature example Perillo catalog.

Son of an Italian immigrant, Perillo served in the US Navy before studying at Pratt Institute, ASL, and School of Visual Arts. He worked as an artist for the State Department, then traveled to Nevada, Wyoming, and Arizona to live on Indian reservations. He was an authority on Indian history. Painting titles include *Buffalo Robe, Navajo Madre, Little Urchin (Apache), Half Breed, Warrior (Blackfoot)*.

PERKINS, Granville. Born Baltimore, Md 1830, died NYC 1895. Eastern book and *Harper's* illustrator, scenery and marine painter. References BEN-FIE-G&W-MAL-SMI. Sources ANT 5/58,12/68-AOA-BEY-PAF. Oil 18×22″ *Florida Landscape* signed and dated 1888 sold 4/20/72 for $2,800 at auction. Signature example ✗144 PB 4/20/72.

Perkins was the pupil of the marine painter James Hamilton in Philadelphia. He painted in Baltimore, Richmond, Philadelphia, NYC, Florida, and Cuba, exhibiting at the PAFA in 1856 and at the NA after 1860.

He drew five illustrations for "Beyond

the Mississippi," from *Indian Mode of Burial* in Kansas, 1858, to *El Capitan* in California, 1865. The latter reproduction is credited as after a photograph by Watkins of San Francisco, and it is assumed that all of Perkins' BEY drawings were made from photographs and other reference materials in the East rather than on the spot.

PERRY, Enoch Wood. Born Boston, Mass 1831, died NYC 1915. Eastern genre and portrait painter in California, Utah, and Hawaii 1862–65. ANA 1868, NA 1869. Work in MMA, the Cabildo (New Orleans), Buffalo AFA. References A16 (obit)-BEN-CHA-DAB-FIE-G&W-MAL-SMI. Sources AAR 11/74-ALA-ANT 6/43,4/45,6/49,12/54,5/55, 3/56,11/68-HUT-M57-NA 74-PAF-WHO 14-YUP. Oil 20½×35½″ *Mule Train Crossing the Andes* 1872 sold 3/20/73 for $1,125 at auction in London. In 1945 *Vaccination* had sold for $325 at auction. Signature example p 423 ANT 6/49.

At 17 Perry worked in a New Orleans grocery store, saving $1,100 in four years —"no slight achievement in a city presenting so many temptations to prodigality." DAB. He was in Europe from 1852 to 1860, first as the pupil of Leutze in Düsseldorf for two years, next as the pupil of Couture in Paris for one year, and finally as US consul in Venice for three years. In 1860 he established his studio successfully in New Orleans, painting likenesses of notables. He went to San Francisco in 1862, to Hawaii in 1863 where he painted the kings' portraits, and to Utah in 1864. Perry settled in NYC in 1865, attaining "a place very nearly at the head of our American genre painters." HUT. His works are regarded as faithful records of American interiors of the time.

Wherever he was, Perry obtained his portrait commissions from the most important personalities, at the height of their power. A pioneer Utah painter noted in 1866 that "a gentile artist (Perry) had received $1,000 in gold for a portrait of Brigham Young." YUP. Perry in Utah "sold in four months portraits and landscapes for more than $11,000," while pioneer painter Ottinger sold in eight years 223 pictures "for $3,415, or a little over $15 each." YUP.

PESCHERET, Leon Rene. Born Chiswick, Eng 1892, died probably Whitewater, Wis 1961. Illustrator, color etcher, designer, writer. Work in *Arizona Highways,* books; etchings in Brit Mus, Lib Cong, Cabinet du Roi (Brussels). References A62-FIE-MAS. Sources AAT-ACO. No current auction record or signature example.

Pescheret studied at the AIC and at the Royal College of Engraving in Kensington, England. His color etching in ACO was *Yucca, Arizona.*

PETEK, Poko. Southwestern painter, died 1972. Specialty, oils of Indian ceremonial dances. Work in MNM-Read Mullan Gallery. No reference. Sources AHI 11/62; 6,7/72. No current auction record but the estimated price of an oil of Apache dances would be $1,500 to $1,800 at auction in 1976. Monogram p 25 AHI 11/62.

She had completed a series of oils of Indian ceremonial dances: *Rain Dancers —Santa Clara, Corn Dance—Santo Domingo,* Apache sunrise ceremonies, Zuni *Long Hair Procession, Navaho Fire Dancers, Zuni Turkey Dancers.*

PETERS, Charles Rollo. Born San Francisco, Cal 1862, died there 1928 (or 1927). Cal painter of nocturnal landscapes. Work in Earl C Adams colln, Kahn colln. References A23-BEN-FIE-MAL-SMI. Sources BWB-KAH-TWR-WHO 26. No current auction record. Painting example p 40 KAH.

The son of a wealthy businessman, Peters was educated at Urban Academy. Before 1880 he studied at the California School of Design, the pupil of Virgil Williams. In 1885 he studied with Jules Tavernier in San Francisco, going on to Paris for six years of study at the École des Beaux-Arts with Gérôme and with Boulanger and Lefebvre. When he returned to San Francisco in 1890 he was a member of the Bohemian Club with the fun-loving Tavernier, Joullin, Joe Strong, and Julian Rix.

In Europe, Peters had painted night scenes. These became his specialty as he settled into the Carmel art colony with Maynard Dixon and Jo Mora to enjoy the "carefree, unfettered—and inexpensive—life." BWB. His favorite locations were the adobe houses around Monterey and the Old California missions in the moonlight. Typical titles were *The San Juan Mission* and *After the Gringo Came.* Peters' second wife was the artist Constance Evans Owens, with whom he spent his later years in Europe.

PETERS, Leslie H. Born Great Falls, Mont about 1916, living there 1974. Montana painter of wildlife landscapes. No reference. Source MON. No auction record. Signature example p 158 MON.

Educated at U of Montana, Peters studied sculpture for a year at the U of Oregon. After working in a Great Falls gas station for another year, he served with the 11th cavalry on the Mexican border 1940–42 and with the 13th Armored Division in Europe. In 1945 he studied in NYC, at the ASL days and Central Park School of Art at night. Back in Montana he painted the larger wildlife, influenced by Russell and Rungius and by study with Charlie Beil in Banff. Favorite subjects are elk, mule deer, moose, buffalo, and mountain sheep.

The important thing about painting wildlife is "how the light hits them, what their attitude is, how they move. A photograph might be the truth, but it isn't what your eye sees." MON. Peters works only in daylight and may be painting as many as six canvases at a time, changing off.

PETICOLAS (or Petticolas), Edward F. Born Pennsylvania 1793, died probably Virginia about 1853. Eastern portrait and landscape painter. References BEN-FIE-G&W-MAL-SMI. Sources BOA-ISH. No auction record or signature example.

Son of Philippe Abraham Peticolas and brother of Theodore F Peticolas, Edward Peticolas grew up in Philadelphia where he was an early influence on the younger John Neagle. Peticolas had some instruction from Thomas Sully. When his family moved to Richmond, Va in 1804, he continued his studies and was painting miniatures by 1807. He made three European trips and married the artist Jan Pitfield Braddick.

PETRI (or Petrie), Frederick Richard. Born Dresden, Germany 1824, died Fredericksburg, Tex 1857 (or Austin, Tex 1858). Texas pioneer painter, illustrator of genre, portrait and religious subjects. Work mainly in private collections. References BEN-G&W. Sources ANT 6/48-BAR-TEP-TOB-TXF. No current auction record but the estimated price of an oil showing Comanche Indians would be about $5,000 to $6,000

at auction in 1976. Signature example p 456 ANT 6/48.

Richard Petri, son of a prosperous shoemaker, studied at the Dresden Academy from 1838 to 1844, the pupil of Richter and Hübner. As a German romantic in the Düsseldorf manner, he painted religious and allegorical subjects. With the older painter Hermann Lungkwitz who married Petri's sister, he joined the liberal revolution of 1848. The painters emigrated to West Virginia as political exiles in 1850, then settled in Texas to suit Petri's health, frail beyond the artistic appearance of his "slight build, grave blue eyes, and slender expressive fingers." TEP. Petri never married.

Joining the German colony at New Braunfels, Petri drew portraits in crayon, watercolor, and tempera. He also painted miniatures, making his own pigments. To relieve the hardships of frontier life, the family moved to Fredericksburg, Tex in 1854. Here Petri sketched Caddo, Lipan, and Comanche Indians, drawing portraits he presented to the Indians to induce them to be friendly. "His drawings of these Indians depict the character, early dress, and dances with such accuracy that they are historical documents." TOB. He also recorded the genre of the settlers, his sisters in gowns milking cows in *The Pioneer Cowpen,* the family *Going Visiting* in an oxcart. Petri died at the age of 34 in a swimming accident.

PETTRICH, Ferdinand Friedrich August. Born Dresden, Germany 1798, died Rome, Italy 1872. European sculptor in the US to model Indians. Sculpture in Rome; drawing in Newberry Lib (Chicago). References BEN-G&W-MAL. Sources ANT 8/48-DCP-PAF. No current auction record. Drawing example p 100 ANT 8/48.

Son of a German sculptor, Pettrich studied at the École des Beaux-Arts in

Dresden in 1816 and then with his father. Later he went to Rome as the pupil of the master Thorwaldsen. In 1835 he traveled to Washington, DC on commission from Pope Pius IX to model North American Indians. In 1838 Pettrich billed the US Government for models he had made for statues to decorate the Capitol. After initial refusals, an appropriation of $600 was made "to Ferdinando Pettrich for models." DCP. When Pettrich's *The Dying Tecumseh* was exhibited in the Capitol, it was not bought by the government.

Pettrich was in Washington in 1842 to sketch Keokuk when the chief was visiting the Capitol. Keokuk in the sketch is wrapped in a toga in the European heroic tradition of the time. Pettrich exhibited at the PAFA from 1843 to 1845 and again in 1865. He was in Rio de Janeiro about 1847. When he returned to Rome the Pope granted him a pension.

PHILBRICK, Stacey. Painter of *Grand Canyon* dated 1915 in the ANS colln. No reference, other source, auction record, or signature example. (See illustration 225.)

PHILLIPS, Bert Greer. Born Hudson, NY 1868, died San Diego, Cal 1956. First artist permanently resident in New Mexico, traditional Taos painter and illustrator specializing in Indian subjects. Member Taos SA 1912. Work in ANS, MNM, Philbrook AC, GIL, HAR; murals in public buildings. References A41-BEN-FIE-MAL. Sources AIW-AMA-ANS-COW-DCC-HAR-HMA-JNB-PET-PIT-TAL-TSF-WHO 50. Oil 30¼ × 25¼" *Kneeling Indian* signed but not dated sold 1/24/73 for $9,000 at auction. Signature example p 171 PIT. (See illustration 226.)

Phillips won art prizes as a child. He studied in NYC at the ASL and the NAD about 1889, maintaining a studio in NYC. In 1894 he painted watercolor landscapes in England. In Paris in 1895, he was the pupil of Laurens and Constant at the Julien Academy, along with Ernest Blumenschein who was six years younger. At the Academy he met the established Cincinnati artist Joseph Sharp who extolled the "fresh material" of Taos to cure Blumenschein's complaint, "We were ennuied with the hackneyed subject matter of thousands of painters."

Back in NYC in 1897 Blumenschein shared a studio with Phillips. Blumenschein received a magazine commission for illustrations of Gallup, NM and Arizona, which he visited until early 1898. In the summer of 1898 Phillips and Blumenschein made a sketching trip into Colorado. They bought a covered wagon to travel to Mexico but a broken wheel near Taos was the accident that led to the founding of the art colony. Phillips stayed in Taos, in love with his subject. He was one of the six founders of the Taos SA in 1912, organized to promote the sale of painting through traveling exhibitions. Phillips was successful as a painter, remaining idealized and visionary even after some of his fellows (including Blumenschein) became modernist. Phillips continued to paint "in a world part Hiawatha and part Zane Grey," in a manner that "arouses a nameless nostalgia for something we have lost." TSF.

PHILLIPS, Claire Dooner. Born Los Angeles, Cal 1887, living Prescott, Ariz 1962. Arizona landscape painter. Work in Prescott school and club. References A62-MAL. Sources WAA-A41 listing of *In Lonesome Valley* and *When Verbenas Bloom*. No auction record or signature example.

Ms Phillips graduated from Stanford U

and studied at Columbia's Teachers College with Arthur Dow. She began winning awards in Arizona in 1928.

PHILLIPS, Gordon. Born Boone, NC in 1927, living Crofton, Md 1976. Painter, sculptor, illustrator. Reference A76. Sources AHI 3/72-PWA-letter Kennedy Galleries 10/11/75. No auction record. Signature example p 30 AHI 3/72. (See illustration 227.)

After serving in the Navy, Phillips enrolled in the Corcoran School of Art in Washington, DC. As a commercial artist his work appeared in *Look, Time, Life, Newsweek,* in addition to Western illustrations for Western magazines. Over a period of fifteen years he traveled and collected Western regalia to use as props.

Since 1959 he has devoted his time to painting scenes of the West. Although Phillips' paintings are carefully researched and his style is realistic, he says "The ultimate objective, however, is to 'paint beyond the detail,'" so that "each time a person looks at the painting he will see something new."

PHILLIPS, Walter Joseph. Born Barton-on-Humber, Eng 1884, died Calgary, Alta, Can 1963. Painter of Can West, illustrator, printmaker, writer, teacher. ARCA 1921, RCA 1933 (as an engraver, the only one so recognized). Work in Brit Mus, Lib Cong, Natal (South Africa), AIC, MNM, AG Toronto, Royal Ont Mus, etc. References A53-BEN-MAL. Sources CAH-CAN. No current auction record. Monogram example p 180 CAN. (See illustration 228.)

W J Phillips studied at the Birmingham Municipal School of Art, the pupil of E R Taylor. He moved to Winnipeg in 1913 where he painted in water-

color as an artist of Western and British Columbia scenes. He wrote "The Technique of the Colour Woodcut," after beginning in graphics as an etcher, and his "exquisite colour prints" evidence study of the Japanese. CAN. In 1937 Phillips illustrated "Colour in the Canadian Rockies." He has taught art history and printmaking at the U of Wisconsin, U of Alberta, U of Manitoba, and the Banff School of Fine Art.

PHILLIPS, Walter Shelley. Birthplace unknown 1867, died 1940. Western illustrator, writer. No reference. Source ABC vol 18 ✕4 "Tentative Bibliographic Check Lists of Western Illustrators." No auction record or signature example.

Phillips is listed as active in Chicago before 1900. He wrote and illustrated "Totem Tales" in 1896.

PHIPPEN, George. Born Iowa 1916, died probably Skull Valley, Ariz 1966. Traditional Western painter, sculptor. First president, CAA. Sculpture in Phoenix AM. No reference. Sources ACO-AHI 3/66 - C73,74 - COW - OSR - WAI 71,72. No current auction record. Signature example p 144 COW.

Raised on farms in Iowa and Kansas, Phippen taught himself to paint while in service in WWII. He then moved to Santa Fe where he studied with Henry Balink for three months. Successful as a commercial artist and illustrator, he began oil painting in 1948 while selling works for Christmas cards and calendars. Phippen was called "The Cowboy's Artist" because his "cowboys look like men we have all known. They aren't handsome but they sure did know cow." OSR.

In 1958 Phippen was commissioned to sculpt a famous quarterhorse. He continued to sculpt, specializing in modeling of

205. Frederic Mizen. *The Dancing Lesson*, oil on canvas 24 x 30″ signed LR. Grew up on Western army posts. CREDIT, THE ANSCHUTZ COLLECTION.

206. Stephen Mopope. *Mounted Warrior*, tempera on board 14 x 11″ signed (LL) Mopope. One of the "Five Kiowas," sensations in Prague in 1928. CREDIT, THE AUTHORS.

07. F Luis Mora. *Grand Canyon*, pencil on paper 3½ x 5½″ gned (LL) FLM dated 1911. A page from Mora's New exico sketchbook. CREDIT, THE AUTHORS.

208. Peter Moran. *New Mexico Mountain*, watercolor on paper 3¼ x 7″ initialed LL and dated 1888. The youngest Moran brother and first in the West. CREDIT, THE AUTHORS.

209. Thomas Moran. *The First Night's Camp on the Mountain*, watercolor 9¾ x 7⅞" signed T Moran with monogram TM and dated 1895. He painted his emotions as landscapes. CREDIT, DENVER PUBLIC LIBRARY, WESTERN HISTORY DEPARTMENT.

210. William Moyers. *Ropes and Broncs Don't Mix*, bronz 16" high signed Wm Moyers and dated 1974. Depicts th cowboys of his own youth. CREDIT, THE ARTIST.

211. Stockton Mulford. *The Code of the West*, oil on canvas 29 x 25½" signed LR. An illustration for Zane Grey. CREDIT, THE AUTHORS.

212. Thomas Nast. *Tammany Indian* and *Self-Portrait*, tw drawings on paper 4½ x 7" and 2 x 3½". Frequent cartooni of the Indian, Tammany variety. CREDIT, THE AUTHORS.

213. Pegi Nicol. *Fort St James Boy*, oil on wood 24 x 24″ signed LL and painted before 1930. Painter of children, in British Columbia with Barbeau in 1928. CREDIT, THE AUTHORS.

214. B J O Nordfeldt. *Corn Dance, San Ildefonso*, oil on canvas 33½ x 43″ signed (LR) Nordfeldt and painted 1919. Not Hiawatha but modern designs. CREDIT, THE ANSCHUTZ COLLECTION.

216. J A S Oertel. *An Apparition*, oil on canvas 12 x 20″ signed (LR) Oertel and dated 1881. Religious painter of *Rock of Ages*. CREDIT, THE AUTHORS.

5. L R O'Brien. *A British Columbian Forest*, watercolor ½ x 30⅛″ signed LL and dated 1888. "A fascinating new Eden-like image" of Western Canada. CREDIT, THE NATIONAL GALLERY OF CANADA, OTTAWA.

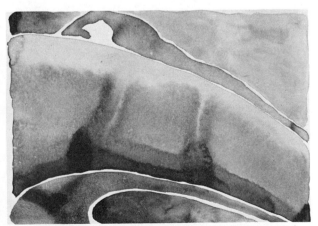

217. Georgia O'Keeffe. *Pink and Green Mountains*, watercolor on paper 9 x 12″ painted 1917. The essence of the West in puritan paintings. CREDIT, THE AUTHORS.

218. G M Ottinger. *The Romance of Spain and Mexico*, oil on canvas 40 x 31″ signed on reverse and dated 1876. Pioneer Utah painter whose yearly art income averaged $225. CREDIT, THE AUTHORS.

219. Jean Parrish. *Pecos Valley*, oil 18 x 24″ signed LR and painted 1973. She shows the "shape of the land." CREDIT, THE ARTIST.

221. DeWitt Parshall. *The Darkness He Called Night* (or *Night, Grand Canyon*), oil on canvas 40 x 50″ signed on the reverse and dated 1922. Painter of the Grand Canyon. CREDIT, THE AUTHORS.

220. Maxfield Parrish. *The Prospector*, oil on paper mounted on wood 15¼ x 14¼″ signed (LR) MP and painted 1911. The sky is Maxfield Parrish blue. CREDIT, THE AUTHORS.

222. Sheldon Parsons. *Springtime in Santa Fe*, oil 48 x 6 signed LL and painted 1928. In Santa Fe by 1913, painti happy landscapes. CREDIT, THE ANSCHUTZ COLLECTIO

224. Edgar Payne. *Sierra Lake*, oil on canvas 14 x 17″ signed LL. Another Sierra lake was named for Payne. CREDIT, THE AUTHORS.

223. E S Paxson. *Once We Were Great*, gouache 22 x 16″ signed LR and dated 1906. Pioneer Montana decorator who painted Indian and settler genre. CREDIT, THE ANSCHUTZ COLLECTION.

225. Stacey Philbrick. *Grand Ganyon*, oil 36 x 51″ signed LL and dated 1912. CREDIT, THE ANSCHUTZ COLLECTION.

226. Bert Phillips. *Captain of the Buffalo Dance*, oil on canvas 40 x 30″ painted before 1916. "A nameless nostalgia for something lost." CREDIT, THE ANSCHUTZ COLLECTION.

227. Gordon Phillips. *When the Wind Blows Cold*, oil on canvas 20 x 26″ signed LR and dated c. 75. Illustrator turned fine artist, painting and sculpting only the Western scene. CREDIT, KENNEDY GALLERIES INC NYC.

228. Walter Phillips. *Silver Plains, Manitoba*, watercolor 14 x 20⅞″ signed (LL) W J Phillips and dated 1930. The Canadian big sky. CREDIT, THE NATIONAL GALLERY OF CANADA, OTTAWA.

229. Lucien Powell. *Grand Canyon, Colorado*, gouache on paper 25½ x 35½″ signed LL and dated 1906. Spirited paintings by a pessimist. CREDIT, THE AUTHORS.

230. Hiram Powers. *California*, marble 71″ high signed and dated 1858. Allegorical of the state with divining rod and quartz crystals. CREDIT, THE METROPOLITAN MUSEUM OF ART, GIFT OF WILLIAM B ASTOR, 1872.

231. Lorus Pratt. *Harvest*. "He would paint a picture for a sack of onions." CREDIT, CORPORATION OF THE PRESIDENT OF THE CHURCH OF JESUS CHRIST OF LATTER-DAY SAINTS, 1975.

232. Norman Price. *The Passing of Bear Moon*, pen and ink drawing 8 x 12" signed LR. He learned from "sing-song and assault at arms." CREDIT, THE AUTHORS.

233. Burt Procter. *Show Them the Way*, oil on canvas 25 x 33" signed LL and dated 1932. Reputation based on depicting horses. CREDIT, THE AUTHORS.

234. A Phimister Proctor. *Buffalo*, bronze statuette 13¼" high signed and dated 1912. "Few major cities did not have Proctor's life-size figures." CREDIT, THE METROPOLITAN MUSEUM OF ART, BEQUEST OF GEORGE D PRATT, 1935.

236. Hanson Puthuff. *Grand Canyon from Maricopa Point*, oil on canvas 60 x 72" signed (LL) H Puthuff. "Realistic reproduction of landscape." CREDIT, THE ANSCHUTZ COLLECTION.

235. Robert Prowse. *The Doom of Red Mullet* (or, *Trailed to His Lair*), gouache on board 14 x 10" signed (LL) R Prowse. Illustrator for English *Buffalo Bill Magazine*. CREDIT, THE AUTHORS.

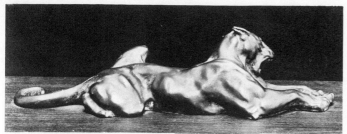

237. Arthur Putnam. *Snarling Jaguar*, bronze 2¾″ high signed Putnam and dated 1906. He drew from his imagination. CREDIT, THE METROPOLITAN MUSEUM OF ART, ROGERS FUND, 1909.

238. Howard Pyle. *Trapper Descending the Rapids*, oil on canvas 19½ x 13″ signed LR. Rare early Western attributed to the leading teacher of illustrators. CREDIT, THE AUTHORS.

239. William Ranney. *Trapper Crossing the Mountains in Winter*, oil on canvas 30 x 25″ painted about 1853. Dramatic stories about the white hunters and pioneers. CREDIT, THE ANSCHUTZ COLLECTION.

240. Leonard H Reedy. *Indians Attacking Wagon Train*, oil on canvas 20 x 30″ signed LL. Chicago's "Cowboy Painter" who roamed the great plains in his youth. CREDIT, THE AUTHORS.

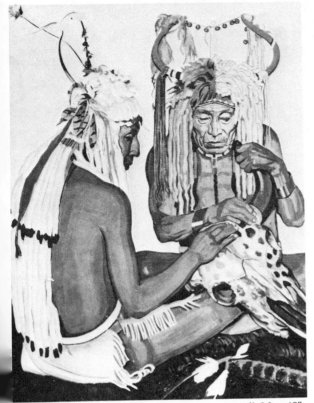

241. Winold Reiss. *Buffalo Skull Ceremony*, oil 36 x 48".
The Blackfeet scattered his ashes at the foot of the Rockies.
CREDIT, W TJARK REISS.

242. Frederic Remington. *Arresting Cattle Thieves*, grisaille
19 x 26" signed (LR) Remington and published as an illustration 1889. The Eastern view of the West in confident, illustrative paintings. CREDIT, DENVER PUBLIC LIBRARY,
WESTERN HISTORY DEPARTMENT.

243. Frederic Remington. *Comin' Through the Rye*, bronze
27¼" high signed and modeled about 1902. A life-size replica was exhibited 1904–5. CREDIT, THE METROPOLITAN
MUSEUM OF ART, BEQUEST OF JACOB RUPPERT, 1939.

244. Sidney Riesenberg. *Empty Saddle*, oil on canvas 39 x
27" signed LL and painted about 1917. Illustrator for *Pacific
Monthly* who worked at Yonkers Museum of Art. CREDIT,
THE AUTHORS.

245. Mary G Riley. *The Arroyo, Arizona*, oil on board 12 x 14″. Eastern landscape painter. CREDIT, THE AUTHORS.

246. Peter Rindisbacher. *War Party at Fort Douglas Discharging Their Guns in the Air as a Token of Their Peaceable Intentions*, watercolor, gouache, ink 10⁷/₁₆ x 12⅞″ signed (LR) P Rindisbacher and painted about 1823. CREDIT, ROYAL ONTARIO MUSEUM, TORONTO.

247. Julian Rix. *California Sunset*, oil on canvas 24 x 14″ signed LR and dated 1885. Good-natured bohemian who liked to travel. CREDIT, THE AUTHORS.

248. C D Robinson. *Grand Canyon*, 115 x 131″ painted in 1912 Spent 19 summers in Yosemite and the Sierras. CREDIT, TH ANSCHUTZ COLLECTION.

250. Randolph Rogers. *The Last Shot* (or, *Last Arrow*), bronze group statuette 45″ high signed and dated 1880 in Rome. Expatriate neoclassical sculptor of ideal figures. CREDIT, THE METROLOPITAN MUSEUM OF ART, BEQUEST OF HENRY H COOK, 1905.

249. Fred Rodewald. *Real Western* cover, oil on canvas 30 x 21″ signed (LL) F Rodewald and painted about 1935. Eastern illustrator and teacher. CREDIT, THE AUTHORS.

51. W E Rollins. *Harvest Dance at Walpi*, oil on canvas 46 x 69″ signed LL. Dean of the Santa Fe art colony. CREDIT, HE ANSCHUTZ COLLECTION.

252. Julius Rolshoven. *Pueblo Ceremony*, oil on board 12 x 16″ painted about 1918. He painted his outdoor studies in a tent. CREDIT, THE AUTHORS.

253. Clarence Rowe. *Registering the Mine*, pen and ink drawing 12 x 13″ signed LR. Early 20th-century Western illustrator. CREDIT, THE AUTHORS.

254. Charles M Russell. *Indians on Horseback*, watercol signed (LL) C M Russell with skull and dated 1889. Worl less as a sheep herder and night wrangler. CREDIT, DENV PUBLIC LIBRARY, WESTERN HISTORY DEPARTMENT.

255. Charles M Russell. *Smoking Up*, bronze statuette 11¾″ high signed C M Russell. By 1911, he sold for "dead men's prices." CREDIT, THE METROPOLITAN MUSEUM OF ART, GIFT OF MRS GEORGE S AMORY, 1964.

256. Betty Sabo. *Pueblo in the Snow*. Trained to see how the world is made. CREDIT, THE AUTHORS.

57. Jules Émile Saintin. *The Sioux Family*, oil on canvas 10 8″ signed (LR) J E Saintin and dated 1864. French painter in YC depicting Indian costumes and customs. CREDIT, THE UTHORS.

258. Mrs A H Sander. *Indian Head Bookends*, bronze 5¾ x 4″ signed. 20th-century Fort Worth sculptor. CREDIT, THE AUTHORS.

259. Percy Sandy. *Apache Raid*, tempera on board 18 x 22″ signed (LR) Kai Sa and placed Taos, NM. Zuni illustrator for Bureau of Indian Affairs. CREDIT, THE AUTHORS.

260. F P Sauerwein. *The First Iron Horse*, oil on canvas 31 52″ signed (LL) F P Sauerwein and painted about 190 Competent, straightforward, and naturalistic. CREDIT, TH ANSCHUTZ COLLECTION.

261. Sam Savitt. *Roping a Wild One*, pen and ink drawing 12 x 20″ signed (LC) S Savitt and dated 1946. Illustrated more than 90 books, some he wrote. CREDIT, THE AUTHORS.

262. Harry Schaare. *Off Brand*, mixed media on board 16 x 18″ signed (LC) Schaare. Magazine illustrator in 1950s style. CREDIT, THE AUTHORS.

263. Al Schmidt. *Oregon or Bust*, watercolor on paper 10 x 14″ signed (LR) A Schmidt. Western illustrator raised in Missouri. CREDIT, THE AUTHORS.

264. Fritz Scholder. *Crow Chief*, signed (UR) Scholder. The modern Indian—beauty, dignity, and maddening absurdity. CREDIT, MUSEUM OF NEW MEXICO.

265. Charles Chreyvogel. *My Bunkie*, oil on canvas 25¼ x 34″ signed (LR) Chas Schreyvogel. The classic that couldn't be sold. CREDIT, THE METROPOLITAN MUSEUM OF ART, GIFT OF FRIENDS OF THE ARTIST, 1912.

266. Remington Schuyler. *Plains Rifleman*, oil on canvas 38 x 25″ signed LR. European-trained illustrator of Indian and Western subjects with a touch of Deco. CREDIT, THE AUTHORS.

267. John Scott. *The Mammoth Bear*, acrylic on board 20 x 16″ signed (LR) J S and painted 1964 for *Sports Afield*. Illustrator of outdoor subjects. CREDIT, THE AUTHORS.

268. C H Sells. *Squaws with Jugs and Threshing Baskets*, oil on canvasboard 10 x 14″ signed LR and painted about 1890. Pastiche of Papago, Paiute, and Plains. CREDIT, THE AUTHORS.

cowboy scenes. When he died of cancer his Skull Valley studio was made into a public gallery and his widow wrote a book of recollections of the artist.

PIERCE, Martha. Born New Cumberland, WVa 1873, living Wayne (summers Lincoln), Neb 1941. Nebraska landscape painter, teacher. Work in St Teachers Col (Wayne). References A41-MAL. Source, A41 listing of *Road, Black Hills, South Dakota*. No auction record or signature example.

Ms Pierce studied at the Chicago AFA, with J W Reynolds, J Norton, L Welson, Carl Werntz, at the AIC, and at NYU with J P Haney. She was head of the art department at State Teachers College.

PIERCY (or Peircy), Frederick. Born Portsmouth, Eng 1830, died London, Eng 1891. English painter who wrote and illustrated a book on his 1853 trip to Salt Lake City. Work in BMFA, NY Pub Lib, Mo Hist Soc. References BEN-G&W. Sources AAR 11/74-AIW-ANT 3/54,2/75-DBW-DCC-FRO-KW1,2-MIS-POW. No current auction record but the estimated price of a gouache drawing showing a view of Salt Lake City would be about $1,500 to $2,000 at auction in 1976. Watercolor example p 38 KW2.

Piercy exhibited portraits and landscapes in London from 1848 to 1880 when he suffered from paralysis. In 1853 he traveled from Liverpool to Salt Lake City. His route was via New Orleans, Natchez, St Louis, Nauvoo, Ill, and then overland on the path of the Mormon pioneers. His illustrated book was "Route from Liverpool to Great Salt Lake Valley" published in 1855. Rare now, the book is a basic source of authentic data for the Mormon migration. It had been commissioned by the Latter Day Saints in England to show the points of interest on the journey taken by the 20,000 Mormons who emigrated via Liverpool between 1840 and 1855. Piercy made pencil sketches—generally hurried—during the trip and expanded them into wash drawings for the engraver. The book was published in England for the work of the church.

PILLSBURY, Tom G. Born Enid, Okla about 1915, living Truth or Consequences, NM 1975. New Mexico painter. Reference MAS. Source, letter from artist 10/18/75 and undated exhibition catalog with signature example. No auction record.

Pillsbury studied art at Phillips U in Enid when he was 16, then at Nebraska U and Chicago art schools. He lived in Taos and studied with Emil Bisttram in the 1930s. Later he studied with Fred Brandrif in Laguna Beach, Cal.

Pillsbury's paintings show the old shacks, barns, windmills, and the pueblos of the West in a realistic style.

PITMAN, Theodore B. Birthplace unknown 1892, died 1956. Painter, illustrator, maker of museum dioramas, sculptor. No reference. Sources ANT 8/68-CUS-MWS W/74. No current auction record. Painting examples p 61 MWS W/74, signature example p 55 CUS.

Educated at Harvard, Pitman served as artillery captain in WWI and OSS colonel in WWII. His first *Custer* was commissioned for "The Frontier Trail" in 1923. His second *Custer* was for "Firearms in the Custer Battle," 1953. It shows Custer with the correct English Bulldog revolvers, wearing a blue shirt and with hair cut short.

PLATT, George W. Born Rochester, NY 1839, died Denver, Colo 1899. Trompe l'oeil still-life and landscape painter, topographical draftsman. Reference G&W. Source STI. No current auction record or signature example.

Educated at the U of Rochester, Platt "spent several years in the West as draftsman with John Wesley Powell's geological surveys." G&W. This would have placed Platt in the explorations of the canyons of the Colorado in the early 1870s, and also in contact with the Indians in view of Powell's ethnological interests. In the late 1870s Platt studied for five years at the PAFA, at the same time as Peto and while Harnett was exhibiting at the PAFA. Later Platt studied in Italy and Munich. When he returned to the US his studio was in Chicago in the 1880s.

At the St Louis Exposition of 1888, the painting *Vanishing Glories* later attributed to Harnett was exhibited by Platt. It was a Western trompe l'oeil, "with cowboy outfit, bowie knife, saddle, sombrero, and rifle." Platt's palette was "neutral tones—blacks, grays, and browns." His lighting was soft and even so that his work lacked "dramatic intensity." STI. During the 1890s Platt was in Denver.

PLEISSNER, Ogden Minton. Born Brooklyn, NY 1905, living NYC 1976. International painter, illustrator, artist-correspondent. NA 1940. Work in ACM, MMA, Nat colln FA, BM, C R Smith colln, WMAA, LA Cnty MA. References A76-BEN-MAL. Sources ANT 8/70,3/74,2/75-CRS-DIC-M50-M57-NA 74-NEU-WHO 70-WYA. Oil 22×28" *Conversation* showing figures on a French street, signed but not dated, sold 5/24/72 for $5,000 at auction. Signature example ✕251 PB 3/4/74.

Pleissner was educated at the Brooklyn Friends School. He studied at the ASL, the pupil of F J Boston, Bridgman, and

DuMond. In 1932 the MMA purchase of an oil made him its youngest artist. He began painting in watercolor in the 1930s. In WWII he painted for the US Air Force and also for *Life*. He has since then specialized in realistic watercolors of city subjects in France, Italy, and Spain.

According to CRS, Pleissner's first painting subject was the Grand Tetons in Wyoming. WYA lists him as a painter who has worked in Wyoming. Fond of the outdoors, he made many Western hunting and fishing trips he combined with painting.

POGZEBA, Wolfgang. Born Planegg, Germany 1936, living Denver, Colo 1975. Painter, etcher, and sculptor. Work in MNM, Lubbock Chamber of Commerce. No reference. Sources CAP-EIT-WAI 71. No current auction record. Signature example p 141 CAP.

Pogzeba maintains his studio in Denver. WAI 72 included an oil *Blackfoot Indian Encampment* and a bronze. The graphics reproduced in CAP are traditional cowboy genre.

POHL, Hugo David. Born Detroit, Mich 1878, died San Antonio, Tex 1960. Texas landscape and historical painter, muralist. Work in City of San Antonio colln, Atelier AG (San Antonio), Union Pac RR colln; murals in Int Harvester Co (Chicago). References A62 (obit)-BEN-MAL. Sources TOB-TXF. No current auction record or signature example.

At 11 Pohl studied with Julius Melchers, and later at the Detroit Museum of Art with Joseph Gies. He studied in NYC, in Paris at the Julien Academy with Laurens, in Munich, Amsterdam, and Rome. After painting in Detroit briefly, he moved to Chicago where he spent 18 months on the Harvester murals.

In 1918 he built a traveling studio onto an auto in order to tour the West. Pohl bought a ranch in the Colorado Rockies, painting mountain landscapes. In 1919 he painted Indians in New Mexico and Arizona. Pohl then moved on to California, "and for 17 weeks I camped in the yards of the San Luis Rey Mission, until I felt and lived the life in spirit." TOB. "His paintings of the old Spanish missions were reproduced in" a national magazine. TXF. After working as director of the Art League of Washington and painting in France, he settled in Texas, joining the San Antonio art colony.

POINT, Father Nicolas, SJ. Born Rocroy (near Belgium), France 1799, died Quebec, Can 1868. Amateur painter of Rocky Mountain Indian genre of the 1840s, priest, author. Work in Jesuit Provincial House (St Louis), Jesuit Archives (Rome), Col Sainte-Marie (Montreal). Reference G&W. Source WIL. No auction record. Painting examples throughout "Wilderness Kingdom" copyright 1967 Loyola U Press.

Point was educated in Rocroy 1810–12 and found work as a clerk. He returned to school in 1815. Becoming a Jesuit in 1827, he was prefect at St Acheul before it was burned by a mob, then was sent to Brigg where he was ordained a priest in 1831. After service in Switzerland and Spain, he was sent to St Mary's, Ky in 1835. A good schoolmaster, zealous and prudent, he was chosen to establish a new Louisiana college in 1837. When he failed as superior, he was sent to Westport, Mo in 1840, erecting a church for the 25 families who were residents.

In 1841 Point joined Father de Smet's group on its journey to the Rockies. They were part of a caravan led by John Bidwell and Thomas Fitzpatrick. Point was diarist for de Smet. On arrival the missionaries were welcomed by the Flatheads who had requested them. A mission center was built near Missoula, Mont, but Point spent the winter with the Indians in their village to continue their religious instruction. In 1842 Point started a mission near the Coeur d'Alêne Indians, but with little success. Point's health failed by 1844, although he spent the winter of 1846 negotiating with the difficult Blackfeet. His request for transfer to Canada was granted in 1847. After reorganizing one mission, he retired to Windsor, Ont where in 1859 he wrote his "Wilderness Kingdom" and illustrated it with hundreds of paintings that are the only existing depictions of the intimate lives of the Rocky Mountain Indians. Other sketches by Point were redrawn for the lithographs in Father de Smet's "Oregon Missions and Travels over the Rocky Mountains in 1845–46."

POLELONEMA, Otis. Born Shungopovi, Ariz 1902, living Second Mesa, Ariz 1967. Early Hopi painter. Work in DAM, GIL, MAI, MNM, Philbrook AC. Reference MAL. Sources AHI 2/50-AIP. No auction record or signature example.

Polelonema means Making Ball. He is also called Lomadamocvia or Springtime. He was educated at Santa Fe Indian School 1914–20 and at Santa Fe high school. He began painting in 1917 and was active in the WPA art project.

POLITI, Leo. Born Fresno, Cal 1908, living probably Los Angeles, Cal 1972. Illustrator, painter, cartoonist, sculptor. Murals in U of Fresno theater. References A41-MAS. Source p 37 AHI 12/72 with signature example. No current auction record.

Politi studied at the Art Institute in Milan on a national scholarship in 1924. He was the art editor of Viking Press, illustrating "Little Pancho" in 1938 and the weekly "Jack and Jill" in 1939.

POLK, Frank. Born Arizona 1909, living Mayer, Ariz 1976. Traditional Western sculptor of cowboy genre. Member CAA. Work in private collections. Reference A76. Sources AHI 11/71-C71 to 74-OSR-WAI 71. No current auction record. Signature example p 38 OSR.

Polk was raised in Mayer and Phoenix, Ariz. He entered his first rodeo at 10 with a trained burro and toured nationally at 16. He became a rodeo personality, voted best all-around cowboy in a 1946 Arizona show. "He has worked for almost every major cattle ranch in Arizona," plus "singing on the radio, guitar picking, dude wrangling, and doing stunt bits in Western movies" of the mid-30s. C71.

He was first known as a cowboy whittler. Later he carved rodeo scenes in basswood he then had bronzed. WAI 71. In California he was encouraged to become a sculptor in bronze, specializing in subjects based on his experience, rodeo scenes and modern cowboys.

POMAREDE (or de or de la), Léon. Born Tarbes, France 1807, died St Louis, Mo 1892. Mississippi River panoramist, landscape and religious painter, muralist. Murals in St Louis buildings. References BEN-FIE-G&W. Sources ANT 7/43,11/45,7/48,12/49-BAR-MIS-POW-TEP-WIM. No current auction record but the estimated price of an oil showing a view of St Louis would be about $2,000 to $2,500 at auction in 1976. Painting example p 111 MIS.

Pomarede emigrated to New Orleans in 1830, after probably having studied in "the best schools of Paris." MIS. He became the pupil of the scenic painters Develle and Mondelli whose daughter he married. His studio was in St Louis 1832–37 and after 1843 when he was the partner of T E Courtenay. Beginning 1851 Pomarede specialized in religious paintings and in murals. He died as the result of a fall from a church scaffolding.

In New Orleans and St Louis, moving panoramas were popular entertainment. Mondelli offered a scenic view of the port of New Orleans in 1830, the year Pomarede arrived. In 1846 Banvard completed the first of the Mississippi panoramas, "painted on three miles of canvas," and unwound from one cylinder to another so that the painting went up the river to the Missouri on one showing, down river to New Orleans on the next. Léon Pomarede assisted Henry Lewis on the largest panorama until a quarrel launched Pomarede on his own panorama, "The Mississippi River and Indian Life." Pomarede had help from his partner Courtenay and from the young Charles Wimar. Opening just after Lewis' work in 1849, Pomarede gave St Louis "a war of panoramas." ANT 7/43. The entertainment was also successfully shown in New Orleans and the East until destroyed in a Newark fire in 1850. The only remaining piece is "significantly, an Indian signed by Pomarede." TEP.

POOR, Henry Varnum. Born Chapman, Kan 1888, died probably New City, Rockland Cnty, NY 1970. Painter, illustrator, muralist, potter 1920–30, craftsman. NA 1963. Work in MMA, WMAA, BM, LAMA, Dallas MFA; frescoes Dept of Justice, Interior Dept (Washington); ceramic murals. References A73 (obit)-BEN-FIE-MAL. Sources AAR 1,5/74-AAT-AIC-ALA-ANT 2/72-ARC-ARI-ART 3/63-CAA-MAP-MCA-M50-M57-NA 74-SHO-WHO 70. Oil 12×15" *Still*

Life sold 11/29/66 for $450 at auction. In M50, oil *This Is the Life* offered for sale for $2,000 at retail. Signature example p 82 MAP.

The son of a banker, Poor graduated from Stanford in 1910. He toured Europe on a bicycle, studied at Slade School in London with Walter Sickert and Julien Academy in Paris with Laurens in 1911. Poor taught at Stanford and at Mark Hopkins IA in 1917–19. He went to NY in 1921 where he became successful at pottery when his paintings did not sell. Poor returned to painting after 1930. In 1935 he was commissioned to paint Washington, DC murals at about $20 psf. The mural reproduced p 82 MAP included one panel *Surveying New Lands* with Pueblo Indians in a Southwestern background. The mural for the Department of Interior was *Conservation of American Wild Life* and for Pennsylvania State College *Land Grant Mural* (1941). In 1945 Poor wrote and illustrated "Artist Sees Alaska." He also illustrated "Call of the Wild."

graduating in 1883 he went to Europe for 2½ years, the pupil of Lumenais and Bouguereau. His studio was established in Philadelphia. His work was reproduced in Germany and was the subject of a William Dean Howells poem. In 1891 he returned to Paris. In 1892 he was in England, sketching foxhunting, but he returned home to become a professor at PAFA. His series of books on art criticism began in 1903.

Poore's mining illustration appeared in *Harper's Weekly* in 1878 when he was probably in Colorado. This is about the time he was studying with Peter Moran who was also in the West before 1880. Poore is recorded as in Taos in 1882, painting a burro train leaving the Pueblo. CHA. He is listed as visiting Taos in 1888. TSF. In 1890 he was the illustrator and reporter for 16 New Mexico Pueblos in the census document "Report on Indians Taxed and Indians Not Taxed." Also participating was Peter Moran, along with Julian Scott, Gilbert Gaul, and Walter Shirlaw.

POORE, Henry Rankin. Born Newark, NJ 1859 (or 1858), died Orange, NJ 1940. Genre and landscape painter in the West probably by 1878, illustrator, writer, teacher. ANA 1888. Work in Buffalo AFA, City AM (St Louis), Indianapolis AA, Worcester AM. References A47 (obit)-BEN-CHA-FIE-MAL-SMI. Sources AAT-AIW-AMA-ANT 12/67,10/71-DEP-ISH-NA 74-NCB-NJA-POW-TSF-WHO 40. Oil 20×30" *Landscape* sold 2/20/69 for $150 at auction. This is not relevant for a Pueblo painting. Signature example NCB.

Poore was raised in California, intended for the ministry. When he saw the Philadelphia Centennial art display, he entered the NAD for a year, then became the pupil of Peter Moran at the PAFA until 1880. He used his art earnings to study at the U of Pennsylvania. After

POP CHALEE (Hopkins, Merina Lujan). Born Castle Gate, Utah 1908, living Manhattan Beach, Cal 1968. Taos Pueblo painter. Work in Gil, Mus N Ariz, Mus NM, Stanford U; murals in Albuquerque Airport Terminal. No reference. Sources AHI 2/50-AIP-COW. No current auction record. Signature example AHI 2/50.

Pop Chalee means "Blue Flower." She was graduated from Santa Fe Indian School, intending to teach art, and was active in radio work in the 1950s. Her mother was East Indian. Her style combines Oriental and Amerindian motifs: "This is best illustrated in her paintings of forest scenes, with three or five trees in the background, delicate and unreal in their leafing, and in front of, between, and above them whimsical portrayals of rabbits, deer, birds, and other delightfully depicted forms of life. Pop Chalee has also painted fanciful horses with long and delicate manes and tails which cover her paintings like string." AHI.

Colorado landscape of the mouth of Cheyenne Canyon, dating the oil as about 1924. Living in Greenwich beginning in the 1930s, Potter specialized in painting scenes in old European towns.

PORAY, Stan Pociecha. Born Kraków, Poland 1888, died probably Hollywood, Cal 1948. Painter including Western genre, decorator, teacher. Work in Imperial Red Cross (Tokyo), LA Comcl Club, LA Mus, etc. References A53 (obit)-BEN (as Stanislas de Poray-Pstrokowski)-MAL. Source, oil 36×35" *Cowboy* signed with initials but not dated, offered for sale 10/28/74 at the esitmated price of $800 to $1,000 for auction in Los Angeles, but did not sell. Monogram example in above.

Poray was a pupil of the Academy of Fine Arts in Poland and a member of the Society of Polish Artists in Paris. A41. Poray-Pstrokowski according to BEN was a genre painter born in Kalisz, Poland in the 19th century, the pupil of W Gerson, and an exhibitor in Paris in 1905. Also according to BEN, Wojciech Guerson (or Gerson) taught fine arts at his own academy in Warsaw, Poland.

POTTHAST, Edward Henry. Born Cincinnati, Ohio 1857, died NYC 1927. Eastern impressionist painter of figures, landscapes, and marines, illustrator. ANA 1899, NA 1906. Work in Cincinnati AM, AIC, BM. References A27 (obit)-BEN-FIE-MAL-SMI. Sources AAR 11/74-ANT 3/62,7/65,2/66;4,5/67;12/72,11/73,11/74-DBW-HMA-ISH-MSL-NA 74-WHO 26. Oil 12¼×16" on board *In the Surf* sold 5/24/72 for $10,000 at auction. Oil 40×50" *In the Far Northwest, Montana* about 1913–14 sold 10/22/69 for $4,750 at auction. Oil 12×16" *The Grand Canyon* sold 1/27/65 for $875 at auction. Signature example p 45 HMA.

Potthast was educated in the public schools. He became a pupil of the Cincinnati AA and studied in Antwerp, Munich, and Paris. HMA shows the oil *Grand Canyon* dated 1910.

POTTER, William J. Born Bellefonte, Pa 1883, died Greenwich, Conn 1964. International landscape painter. Work in BM, Hispanic Mus (NYC), Herron AI (Indianapolis), and museums in Sydney, Rouen, and Madrid. References A66 (obit)-BEN-FIE-MAL-SMI. Sources SHO-WHO 58. Painting sold 1970–71 for $100 at auction. Signature example p 40 SHO.

Potter studied sculpture at the PAFA, then went to London to learn drawing as the pupil of Walter Sickert. In the 1920s he taught at the Broadmoor AA in Colorado Springs, Colo. SHO illustrates a

POWELL, Arthur James Emery. Born Vanwert, Ohio 1864, died probably Dover Plains, NY 1956. Eastern painter. ANA 1921, NA 1937. Work in Milwaukee AI, Nat Arts Club (NYC); murals in public buildings. References A53-BEN-FIE-MAL-SMI. Sources NA 74-WHO 50. Oil 48×60" *Gunsight Pass, Glacier National Park* with signature example but not dated sold 5/26/71 for $600 at auction.

Powell was educated in public schools. He studied at San Francisco School of Design, the St Louis SFA, and the Julien Academy in Paris, the pupil of Toulouse and Ferrier.

POWELL, Asa L. Born Tulerosa, NM 1912, living Kalispell, Mont 1973. Traditional Western painter of northwestern Montana genre, writer. No reference. Source COW-MON. No current auction record. Signature example p 109 MON.

"Ace" Powell, son of a cowboy and a teacher, was raised in Apgar, Mont on the south end of Lake McDonald. His father was a stable boss, guide, and packer in Glacier National Park. At 10 Powell was a working wrangler. He went to high school in Browning and attended Montana State U. Powell worked as a cowboy, breaking and wrangling horses east of Glacier Park.

As a boy, Powell had watched Charles Russell paint in Bull's Head Lodge in Apgar. In 1938, after a few private art lessons, Powell became a self-taught artist, sketching and painting what he knew best, the cowboy and the Indian with their horses in the region around Glacier Park. He also wrote and illustrated a 1965 book "The Ace of Diamonds" containing his recollections and anecdotes.

POWELL, H M T. Active California 1850s. Writer and illustrator. Reference G&W. Source AIW. No auction record or signature example.

Powell wrote and illustrated the book "Sante Fe Trail to California." In the 1850s he painted a view of Los Angeles, and he also painted portraits.

POWELL, Lucien Whiting. Born Levinworth Manor, Upperville, Va 1846, died Washington, DC 1930. Painter of Western landscapes and of Venice. Work in NGA, COR, Carnegie Lib and Congressional Club (DC), etc. References A30 (obit)-BEN-FIE-MAL-SMI. Sources POW-WHO 30. Oil 30×50″ *Virginia Skating Scene* about 1868 sold 11/17/72

for $950 at auction. No signature example. (See illustration 229.)

Lucien Powell entered the Confederate Army when he was 17. After the war he studied in Philadelphia with Thomas Moran and in the PAFA. He also studied in NYC, at the London School of Art with Fitz about 1875, in Rome and Venice, and in Paris with Bonnat. Powell became known as a painter of Venetian scenes when he returned to Europe about 1890. The influences on his work were Thomas Moran and Turner; Powell had made a study of the latter's paintings. Powell painted in oil and watercolor, but it was felt that his "fresh and spirited" watercolors were superior. DAB.

In 1901 Powell visited the American West. The trip resulted in large and imposing oils and colorful watercolors of the Grand Canyon including *The Afterglow* (COR), *Grand Canyon of the Yellowstone River* (NGA), and an oil in the colln of Theodore Roosevelt. In 1910 Powell went to the Holy Land. He was pessimistic by nature and apparently did not enjoy his career as an artist although having a wealthy woman as his patron had eliminated economic concerns.

POWERS, Hiram. Born near Woodstock, Vt 1805, died Florence, Italy 1873. Expatriate neoclassical sculptor of the *Greek Slave,* the best-known work of the mid-century. Honorary NA 1837. Work in COR, MMA, Smithsonian Inst, etc. References BEN-DAB-ENB-FIE-G&W-MAL-SMI. Sources ALA-AMA-ANT 8/47,3/48,2/57,11/72,3/75-BAR-BOA-COR-HUT-KW1-M19-NA 74-PAF-SCU. Marble sculpture 23½″ high *Bust of Princess Mathilde Demidoff* (1846) sold 4/22/69 for $3,564 at auction near Florence. Sculpture example ANT 11/72 (article) pp 868–75. (See illustration 230.)

Powers was born on a poor hillside farm, the eighth of nine children. When the family moved to Cincinnati, Powers from ages 17 to 23 worked in a clock and organ factory. He then ran the wax-works department of the Western Museum, modeling wax figures and making clockwork mechanisms to move them. In 1834 he went to Washington, DC where for two years he made portrait busts of political celebrities. By 1837 he was able to settle in Florence where he executed portrait busts in marble. For his life-size studio figures, he specialized in "ideal" nude female figures. *Eve Before the Fall* preceded the *Greek Slave* in 1843 which had at least six marble reproductions. The original was sold for about $6,000 and was exhibited widely despite being banned in Boston. Powers became the autocrat of sculpture, a vitriolic critic of others though dogmatic himself, a patriot who never went home, a sculptor of single pieces because they were more profitable than groups.

His 1858 version of the ideal female figure was *California,* sold to W B Astor but given to the MMA when critic Tuckerman noted that the statue illustrated the "deceitfulness of riches." BOA. In 1872 he carved an Indian maid as *The Last of the Tribe.* Powers' pupils were his sons Longworth and Preston. *Closing Era* in Denver was by Preston Powers, depicting an Indian standing over a buffalo.

PRANISHNIKOPF (or Pranishnikoff), Ivan P. Russian painter active in NYC 1875–76, died probably Paris, France about 1910. Painter exhibiting in France, *Harper's* illustrator. Chevalier, Legion of Honor. Reference BEN. Sources AIW-AOA. Oil 23×29" *Russian Peasants* sold 7/22/70 for $384 at auction in London. In 1900, *Herd of Wild Steers* sold for 340 fr at auction in Paris. Signature example ✕210 AOA *The Hayden Survey.*

"He had occasional Western illus-

trations appearing in various (American) periodicals for many years." AIW. In May 1876 an illustration *Red Cloud Agency—Distributing Goods* is thought to have been taken from a photograph. Also in *Harper's Weekly* is an October 1876 view of Denver. The signature on the illustrations is I P Pranishnikopf. The Russian painter exhibiting in Paris in 1889 is Ivan Pranishnikoff.

PRATT, Henry Cheever (or Cheeves). Born Orford, NH 1803, died Wakefield, Mass 1880. Portrait, landscape, and panorama painter, Texas survey artist 1851–53. Work in Orford Mus (NH), MMA, Brown U Lib, Peabody Mus of Salem, U Texas (Austin), ACM. References BEN-FIE-G&W-MAL-SMI. Sources AIW-ALA-ANT 3/65,5/72,11/72,2/75-BOA-KW1-PAF-SUR-TEP. No current auction record but the estimated price of a major oil showing an El Paso street would be about $4,000 to $5,000 at auction in 1976. Painting example p 157 TEP.

Samuel F B Morse while painting portraits in Vermont saw the 14-year-old Pratt's self-taught drawings on a barn door. He persuaded Pratt's parents to have the boy become the pupil of Samuel Finley. In 1819 Morse took Pratt to Charleston, SC as his assistant. Drawing was taught with crayon, then painting with a palette limited to black, white, and umber. Morse and Pratt made a second trip to Charleston in 1820. In 1821 they went to Morse's home in New Haven, Conn and to Washington for Morse's painting of the House of Representatives. Pratt's earliest painting was 1822. By 1825 he had his own Boston studio, earning his livelihood painting portraits and exhibiting annually at the Boston Athenaeum. His sketching trips were to neighboring mountains and islands, sometimes in the company of his friend Thomas Cole.

In 1851 Pratt joined the survey party appointed by President Taylor to establish the western boundary of Texas. He painted the portraits of John Bartlett, survey leader, and James Magoffin of Magoffinville. Quoting Bartlett's report, "Besides the portraits of Indian tribes and illustrations of their manners, Mr Pratt has made many hundred sketches from ocean to ocean along the boundary line, panoramic views I have been compelled to omit as it would detract to reduce them." TEP. As the result, Bartlett who was an amateur artist "employed his own sketches very nearly to the exclusion of those of Pratt." AIW. In subsequent years Pratt refined these sketches into major oils.

PRATT, Lorus. Born Salt Lake City, Utah 1855, died probably there 1923 (or 1924). Pioneer Utah portrait and landscape painter, muralist. Work mainly in Pratt family; murals in LDS temples. References A24 (obit)-BEN-MAL. Sources PUA-YUP. No current auction record. Painting example p 22 YUP. (See illustration 231.)

Pratt was the fourth of six children of the third wife of Orson Pratt, a member of the first party to enter the valley. Pratt studied at Deseret U, the pupil of Dan Weggeland and Ottinger. He also taught English at the university. In 1876 Pratt studied art in NYC where he was exposed to European painting. He went to England in 1879 for the LDS Church. About 1885 he studied at the Julien Academy in Paris, the pupil of Constant and Doucet.

Returning to Salt Lake City about 1890, he painted scenes in LDS temples. Finding art unprofitable, he worked at other jobs to support his family, trading his paintings for services such as doctors' fees: "He would paint a picture for a sack of onions." PUA. Pratt's son Lorus Pratt and his grandson Louis Hand were both artists.

PRENDERGAST (or Pendergast), John. Englishman active as amateur painter in California 1848–51. Reference G&W. Source COS. No auction record or signature example.

Prendergast was in Hawaii before coming to San Francisco in 1848. His drawings were used as illustrations for early California books.

PREUSS, Charles. Active 1845–53 as topographical draftsman and artist with Western surveys. Work in Frémont's 1845 report. References DAB (under Frémont)-G&W. No other source, auction record, or signature example.

Under Frémont, DAB states that Preuss was topographer on Frémont's second expedition of 40 men who left the Missouri River May 1843 with Thomas Fitzpatrick as guide. The party, joined by Kit Carson, followed the Oregon trail, reaching the Columbia River by November. Turning south, the party moved through Oregon into Nevada by January 1844. They crossed the Sierras into California in mid-winter and ascertained the "feeble hold" that Mexico had on the territory. The party followed the Spanish trail from Los Angeles to Santa Fe to the Arkansas River, arriving in St. Louis in August 1844, "one of the sensations of the day." The official report with Preuss's illustrations was printed in a run of 10,-000.

PRICE, Clayton S. Born Bedford, Ia 1874, died Portland, Ore 1950. Traditional Western painter-illustrator turned muralist. Work in DIA, LACMA, MMA, MOMA, Portland (Ore) AM. References A40-MAL. Sources CAA-COW-NEU-PNW-WNW-WYA-MOMA "Fourteen Americans." Oil 15¾ ×11¾" *Madonna* sold 2/20/69 for $200 at auction. Signature example p 386 NEU.

Price was born on a ranch. He worked as cowhand and ranchman, chiefly in Wyoming, until about 1918. "I arrived near the old town of Buffalo about the year 1888. For 20 years lived there and in the Big Horn Basin, most of the time 150 miles from the railroad. Those were wonderful days." In 1905 a wealthy cattleman sent him to the St. Louis School of Fine Arts for one year. He met C R Russell who said, "You're just as good an artist as I am—all you need is the name." Price "painted the subjects he knew best, cattle, horses, and the western riders on the plains." COW.

Price moved to Portland, Ore in 1909 as illustrator for *Pacific Monthly*. The years 1910–14 were spent as a cook in Canada. He saw the modern paintings in the 1915 Pan-Pac Int Expositions and in 1918 in Monterey, Cal, began devoting himself to serious painting. He chose the life of a recluse, still concerned with the appearance of things down to the minutest detail for his drawing, but in his painting searching for the truth behind the appearance. His experiments are all "in the direction of the thing behind the form. The final painting is of no concern to Price and may be scraped away or painted over." MOMA.

PRICE, Julius Mendes. Born London, Eng 1857, died there 1924. English Special Artist-illustrator, painter. Work in Liverpool Mus. Reference BEN-MAL. Sources AOH-12/14/73 letter Edward Morris, Walker AG (Liverpool). No current auction record but *Portrait of a Lady* dated 1901 sold for £16 16s at auction in 1910. No signature example.

Price studied at the University College School and the École des Beaux-Arts, Paris. He exhibited at the Salon and the RA. He covered the Bechuanaland Campaign from 1884 to 1885 for the *Illus-trated London News,* then from 1890 to 1891 joined an expedition to Siberia. In 1895 he toured the Australian gold fields, and in 1897 reported the Greco-Turkish War.

In 1898 Price went to the Klondike over the Chilcoot Pass to Dawson, as reported by him in *ILN* and in his two books. In 1904–5 he was with the Russian Army in Manchuria, and in WWI he was on the French and Italian fronts. He also exhibited easel paintings in the Paris expositions, winning the bronze medal in 1900.

PRICE, Norman Mills. Born Brampton, Can 1877, died probably NYC 1951. Historical illustrator including Indian subjects. Member SI, Artists Guild. Illustrations in historical books and juveniles. References A31-MAL. Sources AAC-CAN-ILA-ILG-ILP. No current auction record. Signature example p 66 ILA. (See illustration 232.)

Norman Price studied at the Toronto ASL which provided life and composition classes plus weekend sketching. He also sketched at the Mahlstick Club organized in 1899, where Saturday night composition class was followed by "a sing-song and assault-at-arms" with "all the members' bicycles parked in the lower hall." CAN. Price also belonged to the Little Billee Sketch Club that met over McConkey's restaurant. In 1904 he contributed a *Fruit Farm* painting to the Toronto Art League calendar. About 1901 Price had gone to England to study, the pupil of Cruickshank, and to Paris, the pupil of Laurens.

By 1912 Price was in NYC, illustrating frontier and Indian subjects for historical novels such as those of Robert W Chambers. "His pen-and-ink drawings were especially effective, exhibiting a full range of values and textural effects." ILA.

PRIOR, Melton. Born London, Eng 1845, died there 1910. English Special Artist-illustrator. Work in Glenbow Fndn (Calgary), Royal Ontario Mus (Toronto). References BEN-MAL. Source AOH. No current auction record. Signature example p 42 AOH.

Prior was the pupil of his father William Henry Prior, a landscape painter. He worked as an artist for *Illustrated London News* from the time he was 23 until his death, covering more than 25 campaigns, revolutions, royal tours, and foreign weddings.

There were four trips to the US and Canada. The first was in 1876 for the Philadelphia Centennial and continued with a record 3½-day cross-country "Lightning Express" train trip that produced 11 *ILN* Pullman sketches. The second trip was in 1878 with sketches near Leadville, Colo and in the Dakota Territory. The third trip was in 1888, trans-Canada en route to Australia. The last was seven days across Canada with a royal party including *Indian Chiefs at Pow-wow* in 1901. Prior became a familiar figure over much of the world.

PROCTER (or Proctor), Burt. Born Gloucester, Mass 1901, living Corona del Mar, Cal 1976. Traditional Western painter specializing in horses. Member Nat Acad Western Art. Work in Adams colln. Reference A76. Sources AHI 11/62-COW-EIT-PER vol 3 #3-TWR-WAI 71. No current auction record. Signature example p 14 AHI 11/62. (See illustration 233.)

Son of a newspaper reporter, Procter traveled West at 17, attending Stanford U to study mining engineering. He also visited Wyoming and worked at the Grand Canyon. He became a commercial artist in Los Angeles, then moved to NYC where he was an art director and illustrator for five years. He studied with Harvey Dunn and Pruett Carter.

Returning to the West as a mining engineer, Procter decided to devote full time to painting. His technique is like his teachers'—he makes a small sketch for form, then a small color key, then a simplified painting combining form and color to define the final painting. His subjects have broadened to include marines, Asia, and South America but his reputation is based on painting horses. In 1973 his work was shown in the First Annual Competition of the National Academy of Western Art.

PROCTOR, Alexander Phimister. Born Bozanquit, Ont, Can 1862, died Palo Alto, Cal 1950. Important animal, Western, and figure sculptor, painter. ANA 1901, NA 1904, NSS. Work in Prospect Park (Brooklyn), MMA, BM, Washington (DC) bridges, Civic Center (Denver), Pony Express Trail markers. References A53 (obit)-BEN-ENB-FIE-MAL-SMI. Sources ALA-AMA-ANT 4,9/45;1/62,5/68,12/74-CAN-MSL-NA 74-NSS-PNW-POW-SCU-TOB-WHO 50-WNW. Bronze 28" *Riding Down the Buffalo* with signature example and dated 1917 Gorham Co sold 4/7/71 for $9,-000 at auction. (See illustration 234.)

Proctor was raised in Denver where he knew legendary frontier personalities. At 14 he was spending his summers hunting and trapping in the Rockies, a self-taught sketch artist on Western subjects. He also began modeling animals, working alone. In 1887 he went to NYC for formal training at the NAD and the ASL. His first important exhibition was at the Columbian Exposition in 1893, following which he studied in Paris for a year until Saint-Gaudens hired him as an assistant. In 1895 he won a Rinehart Scholarship for study in Paris at the Julien and

Colarossi academies, the pupil of Puech and Injalbert.

Success came by 1900. Proctor spent his summers in the Northwest, hunting and making studies for his winters in NYC. Theodore Roosevelt commissioned the *Bison Heads* over the mantel in the state dining room of the White House. Many of his monuments were recast by the foundries Roman Bronze and Gorham Bronze in sizes reduced to eight to 35″ high. Proctor also made pen and ink drawings, crayon drawings, small oils, and Western animal etchings. "During his lifetime, there were few major cities which did not have Proctor's life-size bronze figures." PNW.

PROWSE, Robert. Illustrator active 1910–20 as designer of covers for English *Buffalo Bill* magazines. No reference, other source, auction record, or signature example. (See illustration 235.)

PRUITT, A Kelly. Born Waxahachie, Tex 1924, living Presidio, Tex 1976. Traditional Western painter, illustrator, sculptor, author. Work in MNM, Diamond M Mus (Snyder, Tex). Reference A76. Source COW. No current auction record. Painting and sculpture examples p 117 COW.

Pruitt's father was an oil-field pipeline walker who picked cotton in the Depression. At 13 Pruitt became a working cowboy in Texas. In WWII he served with the cavalry in Asia. After experience in the Merchant Marine, he started painting.

By the 1960s his life had become the subject of a movie, "A Lamp Out of the West" and an autobiography. His illustrations for his own articles have appeared in *Cattleman* and *Paint Horse* magazines. His wax sculptures are cast in bronze.

PUTHUFF, Hanson Duvall. Born Waverly, Mo 1875, died Corona del Mar, Cal 1972. Cal landscape and portrait painter. Work in Denver Munic colln, LA Cnty colln, Phoenix Munic AG, backgrounds for AMNH (1937) and No Amer Hall (LA Mus 1938). References A41-BEN-FIE-MAL-SMI. Sources AAR 11/74-WHO 52. No auction record or signature example. (See illustration 236.)

Hanson Puthuff graduated from University Art School in Denver in 1893 and also studied in Chicago. After working as a designer of stage settings, he was winning awards in Los Angeles by 1909. In the 1920s he was a diorama background designer for the Museum of History, Science, and Art in Los Angeles. His painting was "realistic reproduction of the local landscape using typical colors and forms." AAR.

PUTMAN, Donald. Born in state of Washington 1927, living Hermosa Beach, Cal 1973. Traditional painter including Old Western subjects. No reference. Sources ACO-WAI 71,72. No current auction record. Painting examples ACO *49er* and WAI 71 ⚔69 *Don't Answer*.

Putman studied at Los Angeles Art Center College of Design, where he became a teacher in 1962. He began traveling abroad at 18, was a college athlete, served in the Navy, worked as a circus acrobat and clown, and painted backdrops and designed scenery for MGM. His subject matter ranges from the Old West, buffalos, Indian dancers, the circus, to the race track. Putman "considers himself an illusionist." WAI 71.

PUTNAM, Arthur. Born Waveland, Miss 1873, died Paris, France 1930.

Sculptor specializing in Western animals. Member NSS 1913. Work in MMA, BMFA, Adams colln, Fine Arts Soc (San Diego). References A30 (obit)-BEN-DAB-FIE-MAL-SMI. Sources ARM-BWB-SCU-TWR-WHO 30. Bronze 3½" high 13¾" long *Jaguar* dated 1911 sold 12/11/70 for $378 at auction in London. Bronze dark patina 14" high *Puma Descending a Rocky Ledge* with monogram example and cast 1905, estimated for sale 10/28/74 at $1,000 to $1,200 at auction in LA. (See illustration 237.)

Putnam was brought up in Omaha, with only a brief education at military school. After odd jobs, when he was 20 he worked for a few months with the sculptor Rupert Schmidt in San Francisco. He then studied by himself until 1897–98 when he was the pupil of Edward Kemeys in Chicago.

By 1900 Putnam was receiving commissions for architectural decorations. In 1903 he began a series of large bronze figures from California history. In 1905 he went to Europe to study bronze casting. He exhibited in Rome in 1906 and Paris in 1907 when he returned to San Francisco. His specialty was animals of the West, particularly pumas and cougars. He said he "drew less well from a model than from his imagination" because the model "disturbs by thrusting individual peculiarities between conception and work." His sculpture "won high praise from modernists who oppose academic ideals." DAB. In 1911 Putnam suffered a brain tumor that prevented further work, even though he received a gold medal for 14 bronzes exhibited at the Panama-Pacific Exposition in 1915.

PYLE, Howard. Born Wilmington, Del 1853, died Florence, Italy 1911. Very important illustrator, muralist, author, teacher. ANA 1905, NA 1907. Work in Pyle Mem Gallery in Wilmington Inst Lib, where there is a replica of his living room with its murals in addition to rooms containing his oils and his sketches. References A13 (obit)-BEN-DAB-ENB-FIE-MAL-SMI. Sources AIW-ALA-AMA-CAN-COW-GIL-ILA-ILP-ISH-MSL-NA 74-WHO 10. Oil 24×16" *Jackson's Brigade Standing at Bull Run* signed H Pyle as a 1904 *Harper's Monthly* illustration sold 5/22/72 for $2,400 at auction. Signature example p 30 ILA. (See illustration 238.)

Pyle was educated at Friends' schools. When he indicated skill at drawing, he was for three years the pupil of Van der Weilen in Philadelphia. After an interval of work in his father's leather business, he went to NYC in 1876 to seek a career as an illustrator. After months of discouragement, advice from Abbey, Frost, and F S Church aided him in his first sale, a double-page spread for *Harper's Weekly* in 1878. When he returned to Wilmington in 1880 he was fully established as an illustrator.

A large and jovial man, he specialized in historical subjects and in pictures for the children's books he wrote. GIL reproduces *George Rogers Clark on His Way to Kaskaskia*. From 1894 to 1900 he taught illustration at Drexel Institute in Philadelphia to such painters as Maxfield Parrish. In 1900 he established his own school in Wilmington, with a limited number of students and no charges. He trained W H D Koerner, Arthurs, and Schoonover. His pupil N C Wyeth taught Peter Hurd who guided John Meigs. His pupil Harvey Dunn taught Von Schmidt who helped Will James and William Moyers. Pyle could well be called both America's most important illustrator and most important teacher of illustrators.

QUIGLEY, Edward B. Born Park River, ND 1895, living Portland, Ore 1968. Traditional Western painter, illustrator, woodcarver, muralist. Work in Merrihill MFA (Goldendale, Wash). No reference. Sources COW-JNB-WNW. No current auction record. Signature example ⅩⅩ40 JNB.

"Quig" was raised in North Dakota and Idaho. He studied at the AIC and the Chicago AFA. As a commercial artist, he became art director for Chicago publishing companies. His specialty was animals.

In the early 1930s, while traveling in northern Washington, he sketched ranch life, Yakima Indians, and wild horses. This led to a successful career as a painter of cowboy genre. He is said to use a palette with only eight colors in order to avoid being restricted by details.

QUINTANA, Ben. Born Cochiti Pueblo, NM 1923, died WWII Pacific Theater 1944. Pueblo painter, muralist. Work in GIL, MAI, Philbrook AC. Sources AHI 8/52-AIP. No auction record but the estimated price of a watercolor 16×20″ showing Koshare clowns would be about $700 to $900 at auction in 1976. Signature example AHI 8/52.

Ben Quintana (Ha A Tee) was educated at Santa Fe and Cochiti Pueblo Indian schools. His art instruction was from Tonita Pena and Geronima Montoya. At 15 he won a poster contest. At 17 he won a $1,000 first prize in a poster contest against 52,000 entries. At 21 he was killed in combat at Leyte in the Pacific during WWII.

QUINTANA, Joe A. Born Cochiti Pueblo, NM date unknown. Pueblo painter. Work in Mus of Northern Ariz (Katherine Harvey colln, Flagstaff). Sources AHI 8/52-AIP. No auction record but the estimated price of a watercolor 16×20″ showing a clown corn dance would be about $500 to $700 at auction in 1976. Signature example AHI 8/52.

QUIRT, Walter W. Born Iron River, Mich 1902, living Minneapolis, Minn 1966. Surrealist and abstract painter, teacher. Work in MOMA, WMAA, Newark Mus, Walker Art Center. References A66-MAL. Sources ALA-CAA-M50-NEU. Oil 40×28″ *Two Women* dated 1954 sold 1/27/65 for $775 at auction. Oil 16×20″ *Early Indians* sold 6/16/71 for $125 at auction. In M50, *Man Meets Woman, Tips Hat* was offered for sale at $1,200. Signature example plate 21 M50.

Quirt studied at the Layton School of Art 1921–23. He taught there 1924–29. His first exhibition was in 1936 when he did easel paintings for the Federal Arts Project. In 1941 Quirt taught at the American Artists School in NYC. In 1966 he was professor of art at the U of Minnesota where he had begun teaching in 1945. In the mid-30s Quirt wrote about his "Social Surrealism" paintings exposing "the real human being" from "behind a smoke screen of patriotic anecdote." ALA.

RABORG, Benjamin (or BOF). Born Missouri 1871, died San Francisco, Cal 1918. California painter of Indian scenes, portrait and landscape painter. Work in Stenzel colln. No reference. Sources ANT 10/68-PNW. No current auction record but the estimated price of an oil showing Indians would be about $900 to $1,100 at auction in 1976. Signature example p 19 PNW.

Raborg appears to have traveled from Chicago to San Francisco about 1895, based on locations indicated by labels affixed to paintings. It is said that his style changed and that his quality varied considerably. PNW. After the San Francisco earthquake, Raborg received commissions for redecorating Nob Hill homes. By the time he was killed in a cable car accident, his work was no longer in demand. Both PNW and ANT illustrated Indian scenes painted in oil in 1895.

RABUT, Paul. Born NYC 1914, living Westport, Conn 1976. Illustrator expert in American Indian culture, particularly of the Northwest; painter, teacher. Member SI. Work in USA Medical Mus (Washington), US Postal Service colln, Gen Elec colln. Reference A76. Sources ILA-IL 42. No current auction record. Signature example p 143 IL 42.

Rabut was educated at City College NY. He studied at the NA and the ASL in NYC, the pupil of Jules Gottlieb, Harvey Dunn, and Lewis Daniel. Rabut began exhibiting in 1941, and in IL 42 received the Art Directors Club medal for a historical stockade scene with Indians. Major magazine commissions followed. In 1970 Rabut designed a six-cent commemorative postage stamp as a *Haida ceremonial canoe,* and in 1972 designed the 11-cent airmail commemorative stamp *City of Refuge.*

RACINE, Albert (or Apowmuckcon, Running Weasel). Born Browning, Mont 1907, living there 1969. Woodcarver, sign painter, gallery owner. Work in Mus of the Plains Indian (Browning), Methodist Mission (Browning). No reference. Sources AIP-MON. No current auction record or signature example.

A Blackfoot, Racine was raised on an isolated ranch where his grandmother told stories of the "old days." He attended Haskell Institute in Lawrence, Kans 1921–22 and graduated from Browning high school 1928. His first job was as sign painter for Glacier Park Hotel Company where he had the opportunity to study with Winold Reiss and Edward Everett Hale, Jr, painters, and sculptors Adrian Voision of France and Carl Hutig of Germany. He had begun painting in 1926, and in 1936 became a woodcarver when he made an altarpiece in relief.

From 1940–42 Racine worked in Seattle, then served in WWII. After the war he painted signs and carved on the West Coast, studied for a year at the College of Puget Sound, worked as an illustrator for the US Navy for six years, and returned to Montana in 1960. He settled in Browning in 1961. His intent is "to tell a story with each carving," stories of the old days. MON.

RAE, John. Born Jersey City, NJ 1882, living North Stonington, Conn 1954. Illustrator, portrait painter, teacher. Member SI, 1912. Work in Lib Cong. References A41-BEN-FIE-MAL-SMI. Sources AAC-WHO 54. No current auction record but the estimated price of an illustration from "American Indian Fairy Tales" would be $1,000 to $1,200 at auction in 1976. No signature example.

Rae went to Pratt Institute high school in Brooklyn up to 1900. He studied art at the ASL, the pupil of Kenyon Cox and

387

DuMond as well as Pyle. A painter of portraits of celebrities like Sandburg and Einstein, he taught portrait painting at Catau-Rose Institute of Fine Arts. Later, he taught design and painting at Rollins College in Florida.

Rae began illustrating his own books in 1916. Best known were the children's books such as "The Big Family." The very successful "American Indian Fairy Tales" in its 11th edition in 1921 was adapted by W T Larned from the Schoolcraft legends illustrated by Seth Eastman in 1850.

RALSTON, James Kenneth. Born Choteau, Mont 1896, living Billings, Mont 1976. Western historical painter, illustrator, muralist, sculptor, author. Work in Jefferson Nat Expansion Mem (St Louis), Custer Battlefield Nat Monument, Montana Hist Soc. References A76-MAL. Sources COW-CUS-HARMON-USM-WNW-WYG-*Denver Post* magazine 12/17/67. No current auction record. Signature example USM. Portrait photo p 96 MON.

J K Ralston began painting in oil at 14 and at 18 was receiving landscape commissions. His father had come to Montana in a covered wagon, had succumbed to the gold fever, and had settled on his own ranch along the Missouri. Ralston worked as a cowpuncher, but took the winter of 1917 to study at AIC. In 1920 he returned to AIC for a second winter, after selling his herd to pay for the study. He married the country schoolma'am and from 1923 to 1930 worked as a commercial artist in Seattle, Wash. After his father's death he ran the ranch until the drought and the depression in 1935.

Demand for Ralston paintings increased in the early 1940s. His *After the Battle* has been seen in its original form by more than 2,000,000, unveiled in 1955 at the Montana Historical Society, then hung at the Custer National Monument, then displayed on the Montana Centennial train, then shown at the World's Fair in Europe, and then taken to Paris by the government to popularize the West. The canvas is $4\frac{1}{2} \times 18$ feet, depicting 39 recorded incidents that occurred immediately after Custer's stand. Ralston's goal is to make the Old West live again on canvas, and he considers himself lucky he was there "to see and be a part of it." MON.

RAMÓN. See Kelley, Ramón.

RAMSEY, Lewis A. Born Bridgeport, Ill 1873, died Hollywood, Cal 1941. Utah landscape and portrait painter, muralist, sculptor. Work in LDS temples and public buildings. References A41-BEN-FIE-MAL. Source YUP. No current auction record. No signature example.

Ramsey moved to Utah at 12 as a convert. He studied with John Hafen and at 16 taught penmanship in Brigham Young U. At 17 he studied at the AIC before working in Boston and NYC as a calligrapher and a photo retoucher. He studied under Douglas Volk, then went to the Julien Academy in Paris, the pupil of Bouguereau and Laurens from about 1897 to 1903.

After travel in Europe, Ramsey taught at LDS U 1903–5. He was in Chicago until 1908 when he settled in Utah except for a 1916 mission in Hawaii decorating a temple. "A thoroughly romantic personality, Ramsey would give as wedding presents to his friends paintings of red-headed nymphs cavorting in the forest." YUP. In the early 1930s Ramsey moved to Hollywood where he painted portraits of movie stars for art cards.

RANNEY, William Tylee. Born Middletown, Conn 1813, died West Hoboken,

NJ 1857. Very important painter of Southwestern hunters and trappers; portrait, historical, and sporting painter. ANA 1850. Work in N Car MA (Raleigh), BMFA, ANS, CRS, COR, J B Speed AM (Louisville), NAD. References BEN-DAB-FIE-G&W-MAL-SMI. Sources AIW-ALA-ANT 2,5/45; 3/50, 2/53,1/56,6/59,9/72,5/73,9/74-BAR-BOA-COW-CRS-DBW-DCC-GIL-HON-KAR-KW1-M19-NJA-PAF-POW-TAW-TEP-WES-WHI-RAN. Oil 14×20″ *Prairie Burial* initialed "WR" as a study for the 1848 painting, sold 3/16/67 for $4,250 at auction. Signature example pl 20 RAN. (See illustration 239.)

William Ranney, son of a captain in the West Indies trade, was apprenticed from 1826 to 1833 to a tinsmith in Fayetteville, NC where he had relatives. He interrupted his painting studies in Brooklyn, NY to enlist in the Texan Army in 1836 to avenge the Alamo. While serving as paymaster, he was deeply influenced not by the military but rather by the trappers and hunters gathered in Texas. Their garb and anecdotes were remembered as romantic prairie life for the rest of Ranney's career. He was back in Brooklyn in 1837, established as a portrait painter by 1838. In 1843 his studio was in Manhattan. By 1848 he was in Weehawken, and by 1853 in West Hoboken, NJ where his studio was "so constructed as to lead a visitor to imagine he had entered a pioneer's cabin or border chieftain's hut." BOA. Ranney was a sportsman, playing with the NY Cricket Club until 1854. He was described as a "glorious fellow" by Mount, and his artist friends rallied to the support of his family after his death from consumption. Paintings for a benefit auction were donated by 95 artists including Church, Bierstadt, Tait, Kensett, Inness, and the Harts.

Ranney's Western paintings did not begin until almost 10 years after his return from Texas. His approach was to tell a dramatic story about the white hunters and pioneers, ignoring the panoramic landscape and minimizing the role of the Indians. He was an important member of the new American genre school, and the leader of the school, Mount, thought enough of Ranney to complete paintings left in Ranney's studio. Ranney's work was reproduced at the time by the American Art-Union.

RASCHEN, Henry. Born Oldenburg, Germany (or Mendocino Cnty, Cal) 1854 (or 1856, or 1857), died Oakland, Cal 1937 (or 1938). Important California Indian painter during 1880s. Work in Anschutz, Kahn, Harmsen collns. No reference. Sources ACO-ANT 6/55,7/69, 5/71,3/73-DCC-HAR-KAH-PAW. Oil 12½×9¼″ *Tahana, Chief of the Sonomas, California* signed H Raschen and titled on reverse, sold 10/27/71 for $8,000 at auction. Signature example p 468 ANT 3/73.

Raschen emigrated with his family to Fort Ross, Cal in 1868. He was the pupil of Virgil Williams at the San Francisco AA and was influenced by Charles Nahl. In 1875 he studied in Munich along with Chase and Shirlaw, the pupil of Loefftz, Streihuber, Barth, and Dietz. He traveled in Italy and France before returning to San Francisco in 1883. From 1883 to 1890 he specialized in Indian paintings based on California sketching trips taken with C Von Perbandt, a landscape painter. In this period he accompanied Gen Miles on an expedition to capture Geronimo. From 1890 to 1894 his studio was again in Munich where he was a successful painter and teacher. After having come back to San Francisco in 1894, he won the gold medal at the Munich exposition in 1898. He visited Geronimo imprisoned at Fort Sill, Okla. Raschen moved to Oakland after the 1906 San Francisco fire. His California patron was Mrs Phoebe Hearst.

PAW says that Raschen was born in Mendocino County, Cal in 1857, that he was a member of the Bohemian Club until 1892, and that he painted Southwestern as well as California Indians before his death in 1938.

RAVLIN, Grace. Born Kaneville, Ill 1885, living there 1943. International painter. Assoc, National Society FA, Paris, 1912. Work in collection of French Govt, AIC, Newark AM, LAMA, Vanderpoel colln. References A41-BEN-FIE-MAL-SMI. Sources AIC-TSF-WAA-WHO 42. No current auction record but *La Plage* sold in 1942 for 600 fr at auction. No signature example.

Miss Ravlin studied at the AIC, the PAFA under Chase, and the Simon-Ménard Cours in Paris. She was winning international awards by 1911. Her listed work is European in subject. TSF shows her as having come to Taos in 1934.

RAY, Joseph Johnson (or J A). Active 1906–8 as Cal genre painter, illustrator. No reference. Sources GIL-SCA. No current auction record, but the estimated price of an oil of mining genre would be about $500 to $600 at auction in 1976. Signature example p 244 GIL *Prospector's Departure*. Ray moved to Riverside, Cal from Philadelphia about 1906. He exhibited in Los Angeles in 1907–8.

RAY, Robert Donald. Born Denver, Colo 1924, living Taos, NM 1976. Taos painter, sculptor, printmaker, gallery owner. Work in Baltimore MA, BM, DAM, MNM, Columbia MA (SC). Reference A76. Sources HAR-PIT. No current auction record. Signature example p 165 HAR.

Ray was educated at Drake U in Des

Moines, Iowa. After service in WWII he transferred to art, graduating from the U of Southern California in 1950, then going on to study at the Centro Estudios Universitarios in Mexico City, the pupil of Justino Fernández. After travel in Europe, a grant from the Wurlitzer Foundation brought him to Taos in 1954.

In Taos, Ray considers himself influenced by the unique light, "a particularly crystalline quality not found anywhere else." HAR. His painting *New Mexico* was reproduced in NMX. Recent work includes explorations of light in glass sculpture.

READ, Thomas Buchanan. Born near Guthriesville, Chester Cnty, Pa 1822, died NYC 1872. International portrait and historical painter, illustrator, sculptor, important poet. Work in Peabody Inst (Baltimore), PAFA, Cincinnati AM, Smithsonian Inst. References BEN-CHA-DAB-FIE-G&W-MAL-SMI. Sources ALA-ANT 11/54,11/55,10/72, 3/73,8/74-AOA-BAR-BOA-HUT-KW1-MSL-NJA-PAF-TEP. Oil 30×22″ *Portrait of Gen Philip Sheridan* sold 1/22/71 for $2,100 at auction. Signature example p 660 ANT 10/72.

Read at 10 ran away from a stern master to reach his sister in Cincinnati, earning his travel cost as a grocer's helper and a cigar maker. He painted canal boats, chiseled tombstones, painted signs and itinerant portraits, and played female parts in a theatrical troupe. His patron Nicholas Longworth provided a Cincinnati studio where Read painted a portrait of Gen Harrison, launching a successful career that moved to NYC, Boston, and to Philadelphia in 1846. By 1855 he was a leading American poet. In the Civil War, he served as a public-relations major on the staff of Gen Lew Wallace.

Five feet tall and 100 pounds, Read

was modest and sincere. His romantic paintings included Indian subjects like *Hiawatha's Wooing*. Famous in his time, neither his painting nor his poetry is in vogue in the 1970s.

REANEY, Thomas A. Born Valjean, Sask, Can 1916, living Colorado Springs, Colo 1971. Painter. Work in Cranbrook AA, Princeton U, Colo Springs FAC. No reference. Source SHO. No current auction record. Example of initials p 71 SHO.

Reaney was the pupil of Zoltan Sepeshy at Cranbrook Academy of Art in the 1930s.

REAUGH, Charles Franklin. Born Jacksonville, Ill 1860, died Dallas, Tex 1945. Texas painter, teacher. Work in U of Texas (Austin), Dallas MFA, Ft Worth AM, Texas Tech Lib (200 works in Lubbock), Panhandle Plains Hist Mus (500 works in Canyon). References A41-BEN-FIE-MAL-SMI. Sources AIW-COW-GIL-POW-TEP-TOB-T20-TXF. No current auction record but the estimated price of an oil showing longhorns would be $10,000 to $12,000 at auction in 1976. Signature example p 279 GIL.

Frank Reaugh (pronounced Ray) traveled to Terrell, Tex at 15 in a covered wagon with his parents. A farmer, he plowed the prairie, his only schooling coming from his mother. Self-taught as a sketch artist, he saved for a year's study at the St Louis School of Fine Arts in 1883. Back in Terrell he painted, and organized a school. By 1888 he had accumulated funds for study at the Julien Academy in Paris, the pupil of Doucet and Constant along with Abbott Thayer and Anton Mauve. In 1891 Reaugh returned to Texas, moving with his parents to Dallas in 1903.

This was the time of the end of the open range, the finish of the era of the longhorn. On his old ranch home in Terrell, Reaugh's "little ranch was the only fenced ground. All around was pasture stocked with longhorn steers that had never seen a man on foot before. People walking were sometimes treed by them. This would have happened more often if there had been more trees." TOB. His first studio was called "The Iron Shed." In one half he lived bachelor style, "never married though claims to have had about 200 sweethearts." TXF. The other section was like a curiosity shop, presided over by this big man with a mop of hair, a full beard, a flowing tie, and a working smock. He sketched in pastels of his own design, believing that dry colors reproduced the Texas atmosphere. His paintings and sketches numbered 6,000 to 7,000, almost all of them landscape and cattle that romanticized a departed way of life. As early as 1892 the railroads were renting his paintings for Northern advertising devices, and Reaugh became a Texas institution called the "Dean of Texas Artists," and the "Rembrandt of the Longhorn."

REDWOOD, Allen C. Born probably in the South 1844, died Asheville, NC 1922. Magazine illustrator of the Civil War, the West, and the Spanish-American War, writer. Work in *Leslie's Weekly, Harper's Weekly, Harper's Magazine,* and *Century.* No reference. Sources AAR 11/74-AIW-CIV-NJA-TWR. Watercolor on tan paper mounted on canvasboard 18×24" *Officer's Mess—US 9th Cavalry* signed, dated 1898, and titled on the reverse, sold 4/11/73 for $4,000 at auction. Signature example, center CIV.

Rising from the ranks to become a major, Redwood served in the Confederate Army in the Civil War which he wrote about and sketched. In 1882 he traveled

West through Idaho to the state of Washington. By the 1890s Redwood was regarded as a Western illustrator and probably made other Western trips.

Harper's sent Redwood to Cuba to cover the Spanish-American War in 1898. He drew scenes of the 9th Cavalry, a black troop also sketched by Remington.

REED, Doel. Born Logansport, Ind 1894, living Taos, NM 1976. Taos painter, printmaker, writer, teacher. NA 1952 (graphics). Work in Bib Nat (Paris), Vict and Albert Mus (London), NY Pub Lib, Lib Cong, MNM, MMA, etc. References A76-BEN-MAL. Sources AAT-HAR-HAW-NA 74-WHO 70. No current auction record. Signature example p 167 HAR.

After working briefly in architecture, Reed studied at the Art Academy of Cincinnati 1916–17 and 1919–20, the pupil of L H Meakin, J R Hopkins, and H H Wessel. From 1917–19 he served in WWI, was injured and hospitalized. Reed became a teacher of art at Oklahoma State U, remaining from 1924 to 1959, with 1926 and 1930–31 set aside for further study in France.

In 1959 Reed settled permanently in Taos where he had previously spent his summers. He sketches on field trips, completing the paintings in his studio. In 1967 he wrote "Doel Reed Makes an Aquatint."

REED, Earl Meusel. Born Milford, Neb 1895, living Mills, Wyom 1974. Painter, illustrator, teacher. Work in U of Neb, U of Wyom, Queens Col (NYC), Casper Col Lib (Wyom), PAFA. Reference A53. Sources WYA-data from Earl M Reed. No current auction record or signature example.

Earl M Reed studied at the U of Nebraska Art Department. At 19 he worked in commercial art in Chicago until WWI. While in France he made a series of drawings for the Red Cross. After the war he worked as a commercial illustrator in Milwaukee, then studied at the PAFA 1923–25, the pupil of Daniel Garber, Leopold Seyffert, and George Harding. Believing that "people are more valuable than pictures," Reed worked in social service with the youth of South Philadelphia for 10 years, as an instructor at College Settlement.

He moved to Wyoming in 1933. As the partner of Olaf Moller he shared a log cabin studio in the Teton Mountains 1940–41. From 1953 to 1958 when he retired, he taught at Casper College. Since then he has been a private art instructor and has painted Indian subjects, Western scenes, and waterfalls, as well as watercolors of wildflowers.

REED, Marjorie. Born Springfield, Ill 1915, living Tombstone, Ariz 1975. Traditional Western painter specializing in horses, illustrator. Work in "Colorful Butterfield Overland Stage." No reference. Source COW. No current auction record. Signature example p 195 COW.

Marjorie Reed is the daughter of a commercial artist. She was raised in Los Angeles, the pupil of her father in designing Christmas cards. At 14 she worked for Walt Disney. She studied at the Chouinard Art School and the Art Center School in Los Angeles, as well as with Jack Wilkinson Smith of Alhambra for two years.

Miss Reed said that Charles Russell called her "the poorest cowboy." COW. She has visited ranches throughout the West and has made pack trips into the Tetons. A series of 20 paintings of the 1858 Butterfield Overland Stage from St Louis to San Francisco was incorporated in the "Colorful Stage" book.

REEDY, Leonard Howard. Born probably Chicago, Ill 1899, died probably there 1956. Chicago's "Cowboy Painter" of the Old West. Work in Adams colln, 1970 calendar cover, Santa Fe Ry colln. No reference. Sources TWR-WAI 71. Watercolor 8½×11" *Roundup in Electrical Storm* with signature example, estimated for sale 10/28/74 at $300 to $400 at auction in LA but did not sell. (See illustration 240.)

Reedy studied at the AIC and the Chicago Academy FA. He "spent much of his youth in the West, living with the Indians, roaming the great plains and desert country, and working for a while as a ranch hand." TWR. The work in the Adams colln is *Covered Wagons,* 8¼×11¼" watercolor over pencil on paper. WAI 71 lists *Glad You Made It,* 11×8" watercolor on paper. It is said that in Chicago, restaurants have framed Reedy paintings and drawings received in lieu of cash.

REGAMEY, Félix Élie. Born Paris, France 1844, died Juan-les-Pins, France 1907. French Special Artist-illustrator, painter of portraits, history, and genre, engraver. References BEN-MAL. Source AOH. No current auction record but a watercolor *Portrait of a Man in His Office* sold for 550 fr at auction in 1942. Signature example *ILN* 1871.

Regamey was one of three brothers who were the pupils of their father, L P G Regamey. He also studied with Léococq de Boisbaudran at École des Beaux-Arts, Paris. He became a Special Artist in 1871, traveling for *ILN, Harper's Weekly,* and *Monde Illustré,* covering West African native life, South African diamond fields, the marriage of the Emperor of China, and the first Japanese railroad.

Regamey worked in the US from 1874 to 1876, with the drawings including Shoshone, Gros-Ventre, and Sioux Indians. He was also in the US in 1880, making Western sketches that were unpublished until 1891 when the final defeat of the Sioux evoked new French interest in Indians. When Regamey returned to France in 1881, he was named Inspector of Drawing for the Paris schools.

REID, Robert. Born Stockbridge, Mass 1862, died Clifton Springs, NY 1929. Impressionist painter of portraits and figures, muralist, teacher. ANA 1902, NA 1906, NIAL, member Ten American Painters. Work in COR, NGA, MMA, BM, DIA, etc; murals World's Columb Expos (1893), Lib Cong, Appellate Cthse (NYC), Mass St House (Boston), etc. References A30 (obit)-BEN-DAB-ENB-FIE-MAL-SMI. Sources AAR 1,5/74-ALA-AMA-ANT 4/72-COR-DEP-ISH-M31-MSL-NA 74-SHO-SPR-STI-WHO 28. Oil 12×20" *Reverie* 1890 sold 1968 for $5,000 at auction. Signature example p 169 AMA.

Son of a schoolmaster, Reid was educated at Phillips Academy in Andover, Mass. He studied at the School of the MFA, Boston from 1880 to 1884, acting as teaching assistant the last three years, then briefly at the ASL in NYC before going to Paris to study 1884–89 at the Julien Academy, the pupil of Boulanger and Lefebvre. On his return to NYC he was immediately successful, painting portraits and figures, teaching at the ASL and Cooper Union, selected to decorate the main domes at the Columbian Exposition 1892–93, and joining in 1898 as one of the Ten American Painters, the leading impressionists of the day. An important part of his effort was devoted to murals, with five years spent on 20 stained-glass church windows alone.

From 1920–27 Reid taught figure drawing and painting at Broadmoor Art Academy in Colorado Springs, Colo. His purpose was to sketch in the Rockies and the Garden of the Gods, as in *Mountain Scene* p 25 SHO. When a stroke paralyzed his right side, he taught himself to paint with his left hand, exhibiting in 1928.

REIFFEL, Charles. Born Indianapolis, Ind 1862, died San Diego, Cal 1942. Cal landscape painter, muralist. Work in COR, San Diego FAG, Phoenix Munic colln, etc. References A41-BEN-FIE-MAL-SMI. Sources SCA-WHO 42. No auction record or signature example.

Self-taught by some accounts, Reiffel had studied with Carl Marr in Munich and traveled widely in Europe to sketch and study in museums. After 6 years that included commercial art in England, he worked in Buffalo, NYC, and Silvermine, Conn. He began winning awards in 1908. In 1925 he settled near San Diego. Some of his listed paintings were *In the San Filepe Valley, In Banner Valley, Mountain Ranch, Desert Below Julian.*

REINHART, Benjamin Franklin. Born near Waynesburg, Pa 1829, died Philadelphia, Pa 1885. Eastern historical, genre, and portrait painter. ANA 1871. Work in COR. References BEN-CHA-DAB-FIE-G&W-MAL-SMI. Sources ANT 9/58,6/72-HUT-NA 74-PAF-WHI (as Rinehart). No current auction record. Signature example p 183 ANT 9/58.

Reinhart began painting portraits at 16, following a few lessons in mixing and applying paint. From 1847 to 1849 he studied at the NA in NYC, then visited "Ohio and several cities of the West" to paint portraits. HUT. From 1850 to 1853 he studied in Düsseldorf, Paris, and Rome, learning "grand composition" to become a historical painter. On his re-

turn to the US he painted portraits in New York, Ohio, and New Orleans.

From 1861 to 1868 Reinhart lived in London where he was a successful painter of English genre subjects and of portraits of the nobility. During this period he painted *The Emigrant Train Bedding Down for the Night* 1867 shown as fig 36 WHI. After 1868 his studio remained in NYC where he painted cabinet-sized genre and historical works including *Pocahontas*. At least 45 of his paintings were reproduced.

REISS, Fritz Winold. Born Karlsruhe, Germany 1888 (or 1886), died Carson City, Nev 1953. Indian painter, illustrator, muralist, designer. Member SI. Work in Louis W Hill colln, Cincinnati Union Terminal, Woolaroc Mus (Okla), Minneapolis IA, ANS. References A53-FIE-MAL. Sources AAR 11/74-ANT 10/72-WYG-"American Indian Portraits by Winold Reiss" USIS-data from Tjark Reiss. No current auction record. Signature example p 533 ANT 10/72. (See illustration 241.)

Winold Reiss was raised in the Black Forest where he was the pupil of his father, a landscape painter. Reiss also studied with von Stuck at the Royal Academy in Munich and with Diez at the Art School in Munich. Inspired by the novels of James Fenimore Cooper, he came to the US in 1913 expressly to paint the American Indian.

After a delay due to WWI, Reiss began in 1919 to paint his collection of Indian portraits, including 81 for the Great Northern RR that were exhibited nationally and in Europe. The Blackfeet initiated him into the tribe as "Beaver Child," in reference to the intensity of his painting, and were the subjects of many book illustrations for which Reiss was commissioned. He also did portraits of Negroes and Western landscapes such as the Grand Canyon. In 1941 he was assistant professor of mural painting at NYU, and had constructed tens of murals depicting the Indian in theaters, restaurants such as Longchamps in NYC, hotels, clubs, and the Cincinnati Union Terminal. Some of the murals were made in glass mosaic. When Reiss died, the Blackfeet scattered his ashes at the foot of the Rockies. His Indian portraits have been widely reproduced.

REMINGTON, Frederic Sackrider. Born Canton, NY 1861, died Ridgefield, Conn 1909. Very important Western illustrator of the turn of the century, painter, sculptor, and author. ANA 1891, NIAL. Work in ANS, ACM, Remington Art Mus (Ogdensburg), Ogdensburg Pub Lib, NY Pub Lib, MMA, AIC, GIL, etc. References A10 (obit)-BEN (signature) - DAB - ENB - FIE - MAL - SMI. Sources AAR 9/73;1,3,5/74-ACO-AHI 11/62-AIW-ALA-AMA-ANT 4,9/45;8, 12 / 47;6 / 48;12 / 53;5 / 54;8,10 / 59;6,7, 12/61; 12/65; 6,7/67; 3,6,9/68; 6,11/69; 2,3/70; 2,7/71; 12/72; 3,10/73; 4,8,10/ 74;1,2/75-AOA-ARI-BWB-CAN-CAP-COW-CUS-DBW-DCC-DWF-EIT-GIL-GWP-HMA-150-ILA-ILP-IND-ISH-JNB-KEN-M19-M31-M51-MSL-NA 74-PAW-PNW-POW-SCU-TEP-TSF-TWR-WAI 71,72-WES-WHO 08. Oil 27¼ × 40¼" *Coming to the Call* with signature example and not dated but an 8/19/05 illustration in *Collier's Weekly* sold 12/ 10/71 for $105,000 at auction. Bronze, brown patina, 28½" high and 33½" long *Coming Through the Rye* signed and dated 1902, incised "Cire Perdue Cast/Roman Bronze Works NY" sold 10/19/72 for $125,000 at auction. (See illustrations 242, 243.)

Remington was raised in Canton where his father published the *Plaindealer*. He was educated at the Vermont Episcopal Institute and studied at Yale Art School 1878–79. He played football on the team with sports immortal Walter Camp. When his father died in 1880, he made a trip to Montana. One Western sketch was published in *Harper's Weekly* in 1882. He joined a Yale classmate in 1883 as a gentleman Kansas sheep rancher, riding to the Southwest in the summer. Selling the ranch in 1884, he again visited the Southwest, sketching Indians and Mexican vaqueros. After finding his first customer for paintings in Kansas City, he sketched in Arizona, Texas, and Oklahoma in 1885 before studying at the ASL in NYC. By 1886 he was an illustrator for *Outing* and *Harper's Weekly*.

In 1895 he began modeling figures to be cast in bronze, starting with *Bronco Buster*. The same year, he wrote his first illustrated book. One book became a play. From his home in New Rochelle, NY, he traveled to North Africa, Russia, Germany, England, Mexico, and to Cuba as a correspondent.

When he was a Kansas rancher he looked "like some Greek god in modern clothes. He was over six feet tall, blond, and wore a small mustache. Later in life he became very heavy." DAB. This is from a description of Remington by the wife of a friend. More accurately, he was little above average height, and sturdy. "In his confident, polished illustrative paintings and drawings, Remington summed up the eastern view of the West at the turn of the century." TAW. His subject matter ranged from cavalry to Indians, frontier scenes, Mexicans, wildlife, cowboys, and scenes in Canada as well as non-Western subjects from Africa to the Far East.

REMINGTON, S J. Active 19th century. No reference. Source, oil 20×32" *Mount Hood, California* signed, titled on stretcher, offered 1/27/71 for auction but did not sell. Oil 29½×45½" *Moun-*

tainous Landscape with a Cataract sold 10/21/71 for $375 at auction. No signature example.

RETTIG, John. Born Cincinnati, Ohio about 1860, died probably there 1932. Theatrical scenery designer, painter. References A32 (obit)-BEN-FIE-MAL. Source p 332 IL 2/95 (article) with signature example. No auction record.

Rettig began fresco painting when he was 15. He studied at the Cincinnati Art School, the pupil of Duveneck and Potthast, and in Paris with Collin, Courtois, and Prinet. When Rookwood pottery began to be sold commercially, Rettig participated in the modeling and decoration in Cincinnati. Thereafter he dedicated himself to the painting of scenery, adding a "new value and significance." IL 2/95. He produced open-air pageants in Cincinnati and NYC, going to North Africa to prepare for "Babylon" and in 1891 to Mexico and the Southwest for "Montezuma." IL 2/95 on p 335 reproduces a fine study of a Southwestern Indian.

REUSSWIG, William. Born Somerville, NJ 1902, living probably NYC 1973. Eastern illustrator specializing in adventure, the Old West, and sports; author. Reference MAL. Sources CUS-ILA-ILG-USM. No auction record. Signature example p 154 ILA.

Reusswig was educated at Amherst College and studied at the ASL. At 23 he sold his first illustration to *Collier's*. ILA reproduces his *True* illustration of the Donner party in the Sierra Nevadas 1846–47. He wrote and illustrated "A Picture Report of the Custer Fight." Reusswig is married to Martha Sawyers, also an author-illustrator important in the 1930s and later.

REVERE, Joseph Warren. Born Boston, Mass 1812, died Hoboken, NJ 1880. Cal sketch artist 1849, Navy and Army officer, writer. Illustrations in "A Tour of Duty in California" (1849). References DAB-G&W. No other source, auction record, or signature example.

Son of a doctor and grandson of Paul Revere and subject to wanderlust, Joseph Warren Revere enlisted in the Navy as a midshipman in 1828. He experienced a three-year Pacific cruise, a year of hunting pirates in the Caribbean, and trips to the African coast, the Mediterranean, and Russia. In 1836 he carried dispatches overland from Lisbon to Paris and back to Gibraltar. After a cruise to China he led a landing party in California to join the fight against Mexico in 1846, raising the American flag at Sonoma. As agent for naval timberland, he was back in California for the 1849 Gold Rush. He resigned in 1850 to operate a Sonoma ranch and to run trading voyages to Mexico. Wounded as a Mexican colonel, he returned to Morristown, NJ until the Civil War. By 1862 he was a general in the Union Army, then was court-martialed and dismissed when he ordered his division to retreat at Chancellorsville. The sentence was revoked by Lincoln.

In 1849 Revere had written "A Tour of Duty in California." The illustrations were views of California taken from Revere's own sketches. He also wrote "Keel and Saddle" (1872).

REYNOLDS, James E. Born Taft, near Bakersfield, Cal 1926, living Oak Creek Canyon, near Sedona, Ariz 1976. Traditional Western painter, illustrator. Member CAA 1969. Work in The Arizona Bank. Reference A76-(distinguish James Reynolds listed MAL as working NYC 1933). Sources ACO-AHI 11/71-COW-C71 to 74-EIT-OSR-PWA-WAI

71,72. No current auction record. Signature example C71.

Reynolds as a boy spent his summers at his grandmother's hotel in Washington, Cal near Nevada City and the Donner Pass. After service in the Navy in WWII he studied at the Allied Arts School in Glendale, for five years the pupil of Arthur Beaumont, Charles Payzant, and Stan Parkhouse working in watercolor. After a try at ranching, he became an illustrator for the movie studios for 15 years. In his spare time, he traveled through the West, painting in oil and sketching.

In 1968 Reynolds moved to Arizona to paint scenes of the West, with summers in Montana. "Big Jim looks cowboy enough for two or three fellows. Detail and authenticity are important in his work." OSR. In *The Supply Wagon,* "note the differences between the outrider's horse and the wagon horses." PWA. Reynolds thinks John Singer Sargent was the greatest painter. "I just paint as honestly as I can." WAI 71. His greatest public exposure came from Marlboro's 1974 Christmas advertising.

RHEES, N (or Morgan L). Active early 20th century. No reference. Source, oil 36×60" *The Wounded Rider* signed but not dated, showing a cowboy with an arrow in his back, sold 12/10/70 for $650 at auction. No signature example.

MAL lists Morgan L Rhees as active 1888.

RHIND, John Massey. Born Edinburgh, Scotland 1860 (or 1858), died probably NYC 1936. Sculptor of architectural elements, portrait busts. Founding member NSS 1893, Assoc RSA (Edinburgh). Work in Newark (NJ), Philadelphia, Jersey City, Pittsburgh, Butler AI (Youngstown, Ohio); decorations for buildings. References A38 (obit)-BEN-FIE-MAL-SMI. Sources AMA-MSL-WHO 14. Bronze 37¼" high *Benjamin Franklin* 1901 sold 11/3/71 for $725 at auction. Bronze, brown patina 22½" high *Waiting for the Peace Parley* signed and dated 1919 estimated 9/28/73 at $2,500 to $3,500 but did not sell at auction. Bronze, brown patina 23" high *Indian Chief* signed and dated 1919 was estimated at $1,000 to $1,500 for sale at auction 10/31/75, and sold for $4,250. Sculpture examples p 385 AMA (Carnegie bust), p 279 A98 (Indian Chief).

Son of a Scotch sculptor who was a member of the Royal Society of Artists, Rhind studied in Lambeth, the pupil of Delau, at the Royal Academy, and in Paris. He emigrated to the US in 1889, at a time when his work was primarily architectural. His frieze figures were considered "the finest examples of architectural sculpture in the US." MSL. When he went on to portrait busts, his best-known sculpture was his bust of Carnegie that was distributed to libraries. As early as 1898 Rhind's exhibition pieces included *Young Indian* and *Indian Chief.*

RIBAK, Louis Leon. Born Russian Poland 1903 (or 1902), living Taos, NM 1976. Painter, muralist, teacher. Work in MMA, WMAA, BM, MNM, Newark AM. References A76-MAL. Source TAL. Charcoal drawing *Nude Reading* sold 4/15/70 for $100 at auction. Signature examples p 134 AAT, pl 49 TAL.

Ribak studied at the PAFA with Daniel Garber, at the ASL with John Sloan and the Educational Alliance AS in NYC. In 1947 he and his wife Beatrice Mandelman were called "outstanding among the new Taos painters. Ribak is full of change and variable moods." TAL. In 1959 he was director and instructor in the Taos Valley Art School.

RICE, William Seltzer. Born Manheim, Pa 1873, living Oakland, Cal 1962. California landscape painter, illustrator, woodblock printer, teacher, writer. Work in Cal St Lib, Cal Col of Arts and Crafts, Golden Gate Park Mus. References A62-BEN-FIE-MAL. Source AAT. Pastel 24×19" *Portrait of an Indian Girl* signed but not dated, sold 5/22/72 for $300 at auction. Signature example p 64 PB 5/22/72.

Rice studied at the Pennsylvania Museum School of Industrial Arts, was the pupil of Howard Pyle at Drexel Institute (Philadelphia), and graduated from the California College of Arts and Crafts. His work in public collections included *Glacier, High Sierras* and *Old Adobe—Monterey*. He wrote books on block printing and taught at the U of California Extension Division.

RICHARDS, Frederick De Bourg (or De Berg). Born Wilmington, Del 1822, died Philadelphia, Pa 1903. Pennsylvania landscape painter, etcher. References A00-FIE-G&W. Sources ANT 10/52,9/72-PAF. Oil 10×21" *Lake Maggiore, Italy* signed and dated '80 sold 11/28/73 for $200 at auction in Los Angeles. Oil 16×26" *Indian Encampment in the Rockies* sold 4/15/70 for $175 at auction. Signature example p 379 ANT 9/72.

Richards was in NYC 1844–45, in Philadelphia 1845–66, and in Paris 1868. In his paintings exhibited at PAFA, a view near Rome, Italy is dated 1856. At the Brooklyn Art Association, he "exhibited" *Bear Creek Cañon* in 1875, *Pikes Peak at Sunrise from the Plains* in 1876.

RICHARDS, Lee Greene. Born Salt Lake City, Utah 1878, died there 1950. Utah portrait painter. Member Salon d'Automne. Work in Utah St Cap, U of Utah BYU (32 oils). References A33-BEN-FIE-MAL. Sources PUA-YUP. No current auction record but the estimated price of a portrait would be about $400 to $500 at auction in 1976. Monogram example p 22 YUP.

Richards was one of the "20th Ward Group" of artists, including Mahonri Young and Alma B Wright, neighbors of the pioneer Utah painter George M Ottinger. Influenced toward the English 18th-century painters by his grandmother, he studied with James T Harwood. At 18 he visited England and France on an LDS mission. After three years as a bank clerk in Utah, he had saved enough to study in France. He was the pupil of Laurens at the Julien Academy in 1901, of Bonnat at the École des Beaux-Arts in 1902, and had his own studio in Paris in 1903.

After returning to Utah in 1904, Richards immediately received portrait commissions. His early work was brilliant and bravura. Later he became involved in gray tonalities and in a simplified palette that added only yellow ochre and red. "The long list of men and women who sat for Mr Richards' portraiture reads like a 'Who's Who' of the intermountain region." PUA. He visited Paris again 1908–9 and 1920–23. He taught at the U of Utah 1938–47.

RICHARDT, Ferdinand Joachim. Born Brede (Seeland), Denmark 1819, died Oakland, Cal 1895. Danish landscape painter in NYC and Cal beginning 1850s. Work in Thorwaldsen Mus (Copenhagen), NYHS (14 paintings), NY Pub Lib. References BEN-G&W-MAL. Source ANT 10/68; 7/70 (with signature example p 2 *View on the Mississippi 57 Miles above St Anthony Falls,*

Minneapolis signed Ferd Richardt and dated 1858); 3/75. Oil *View of Frederiksborg, Denmark* dated 1849 sold 1968 for $1,000 at auction.

Richardt was said to have been painting in NYC 1856–59. Niagara Falls was a popular Richardt subject.

RICHMOND, Leonard. Active 20th century as English landscape and figure painter, art critic, living in London, England in 1934. References BEN-MAL. Source, oil 40×50¼" *Western Landscape* sold 1/24/74 for $200 at auction. Oil 21½×27¾" *Pidgeon Point Lighthouse, Pescayero, California* estimated 3/4/74 at $600 to $800 for auction in Los Angeles but was not sold. Signature example in *Pidgeon Point Lighthouse* above.

Richmond studied at the Taunton School in London. He worked in England, France, Italy, and particularly Canada as well as in California.

RICHTER, Albert B. Born Dresden, Germany 1845, died there 1898. German Special Artist-illustrator, important painter of big-game hunting. Reference BEN. Sources AOH-MEI. No current auction record but the estimated price of an oil 20×30" showing California vaqueros would be about $3,000 to $4,000 at auction in 1976. Signature example pl xxx vol xvi MEI.

Richter was a pupil of the Dresden Academy, then of A Zimmermann at Vienna and Munich. He lived in Austria for 14 years, hunting big game in Bavaria, Hungary, and Russia, as well as Corsica, Sardinia, Algeria, Tunis, and Morocco.

In 1877 Richter became a Special Artist for *Illustrierte Zeitung,* traveling to the US in 1878 to paint horses for battle murals in St Paul and Chicago. The Western illustrations resulting from the US trip were not published in Germany until the 1890s. The drawings included Indian and pioneer life in the Northwest, an account of the Battle of Little Big Horn, and a popular view of the German settler bringing his Christmas tree and buck home to his wife and child in the wilderness cabin. On his return to Europe, Richter established his studio in Dresden.

RIDDLES, Leonard. Born Walters, Okla 1910, living there 1967. Traditional Comanche painter, muralist, teacher. Work in Dept of Interior, U of Okla, Philbrook AC; murals in Indian schools. Source AIP. No auction record or signature example.

Riddles (Black Moon), whose father was a white man, graduated from Fort Sill Indian School in 1941. He had instruction from Olaf Nordmark, the muralist. He paints the Comanche people authentically, considering a painting successful if it is accepted by his elders and friends. He is active in Indian affairs as historian.

RIESENBERG, Sidney H. Born Chicago, Ill 1885, living Hastings-on-Hudson, NY 1962. Illustrator specializing in Western subjects, painter, teacher. Work in Stenzel colln, Hudson River Mus (Yonkers), Vanderpoel colln (Chicago). References A62-MAL. Sources AAC-PNW. Oil 30¼×45¼" *An Achievement of the Medal of Honor* signed and dated 1910 was estimated 10/28/74 at $3,000 to $3,500 for auction in Los Angeles. Signature example in tight style *An*

Achievement above, in looser style p 19 PNW *Shooting Up the Town.* (See illustration 244.)

After studying at the AIC, Riesenberg worked at the Museum of Art in Yonkers about 1905. He made two trips West between 1905 and 1909, selling several cover illustrations to *Pacific Monthly* magazine. Other illustrations were published in *The Saturday Evening Post, Harper's, Collier's,* and *Scribner's.* In WWI he designed posters for the Marines and for Liberty Loan campaigns. In 1927 he illustrated the book "With Whip and Spur," and in 1929, "Pioneers All."

As an easel painter Riesenberg was an impressionist, exhibiting widely beginning with the NAD in 1930. He taught art classes in Westchester, NY.

RIGER, Robert. Born NYC 1924, living there 1971. Eastern illustrator including Western subjects, writer, TV director and producer. No reference. Sources ILA-IL 59, 60-WHO 70. No auction record. Signature example ✗267 IL 59.

Riger studied at the High School of Music and Art in NYC and, after service in the Merchant Marine in WWII, at Pratt Institute until 1947. He worked as layout artist on *The Saturday Evening Post* and as a commercial artist. When *Sports Illustrated* was founded, Riger began his series of action drawings of athletes. He also wrote on sports beginning 1960. His best-known book was "Run to Daylight" with Vince Lombardi in 1963. Riger became director-producer for ABC Sports in 1964.

Before he began his involvement with sports, Riger was an illustrator of action subjects including Westerns.

Riger drew the prize-winning illustrations for the 1958 Houghton Mifflin book "Riders of the Pony Express" by Ralph Moody.

RILEY, Kenneth Pauling. Born Missouri 1919, living Tombstone, Ariz 1973. Painter, illustrator. Work in West Point Mus, White House colln, Air Force Acad, Custer Mus. Member Nat Acad of Western Art. No reference. Sources AAR 11/74-ILA-IL 60, 62-PER, vol 3 ✗3. No auction record. Signature example pp 55, 192 IL 62.

Riley spent his boyhood in Kansas and studied at the Kansas City Art Institute with Thomas Hart Benton, at the ASL with Frank DuMond, and at the Grand Central School with Harvey Dunn. His work has appeared in *The Saturday Evening Post, Reader's Digest, Life,* etc. Riley's forte is color, as shown in his *National Geographic Society* illustrations of the Indian and French Canadian massacre at Deerfield in 1704.

RILEY, Mary G. Born Washington, DC 1883, died probably there 1939. Landscape painter. Work in COR. References A41 (obit)-BEN-FIE-MAL. Sources COR-WAA. No auction record or signature example. (See illustration 245.)

Miss Riley was the pupil of Birge Harrison and Henry B Snell. In Arizona she painted *The Arroyo,* not dated.

RINDISBACHER (Rhindesberger), Peter. Born Upper Emmenthal, Canton Bern, Switzerland 1806, died St Louis, Mo 1834. Very important 1820s watercolor painter of Indians and frontier life in Canada and US, the first pioneer artist recording genre of Western Indians. Work in ACM, GIL, Pub Archives of Canada, US Military Acad Mus (18 watercolors), ROM, Peabody Mus (Harvard U), DAM. References BEN-G&W. Sources ANT 8/48,1/49-AOW-AWM-CAE-COW-DAA-DBW-DCC-DWF-

FRO-GIL-150-PAF-POW-WES. Watercolor 6⅝×9⅝″ *Two of the Companies Officers Traveling in a Canoe* sold 5/14/73 for $10,000 at auction in Toronto. Signature example p 146 GIL. (See illustration 246.)

Peter Rindisbacher, son of a veterinary surgeon, was brought by his parents to the Earl of Selkirk's Red River Colony in 1821. The colony was part of a 116,000 square mile grant from the Hudson's Bay Company to settle the prairie of southern Manitoba and Saskatchewan and northern Minnesota and North Dakota. Rindisbacher was transported by ship to the shore of Hudson's Bay, then south across the wilderness to what is now Winnipeg. With only one summer of art study with Jacob S Weibel in the Swiss Alps when he was 12, Rindisbacher sketched the sights en route: icebergs, Eskimos, Indians, the landscape. In the five years Rindisbacher lived in Canada, he continued to sketch the people and their activities, the settlers, trappers, and Indians. About 1822–23 he was commissioned to paint views at British forts. His technique was to draw a subject in pencil, then copy the scene in watercolor. There was growing demand for his work, some of which was lithographed in London.

The severe winter of 1825–26 discouraged the Swiss settlers who moved south to Gratiot's Grove in Wisconsin. Rindisbacher continued to paint, selling paintings to Indian Commissioner Atwater for $130 that became famous in reproduction both by McKenney and Hall in "Indian Tribes" and by Murray in "Travels." "My Swiss artist Rhindesberger" as Atwater described him, referring to a portrait of *Keokuck* and the *Sac and Fox War Dance*. In 1829 Rindisbacher moved to St Louis where he painted miniature portraits and landscapes in addition to Western illustrations for *The American Turf Register and Sporting Magazine*. At his death

when he was 28, he was "beginning to achieve national recognition." AOW. About 100 works survive.

RISHELL, Robert. Born Oakland, Cal about 1925, living there 1976. Traditional Western painter. Work in Nat Cowboy Hall of Fame. Member of Nat Acad of Western Art. Reference A76. Sources COW-PER vol 3 #3. No current auction record. Signature example p 190 COW.

Rishell who demonstrated artistic ability while in elementary school began art studies when he was about 14. After he graduated from high school he became the pupil of Xavier Martínez at the California College of Arts and Crafts in Oakland. He married a fellow student, Dorothy Olsen.

Rishell specializes in horses and portraits. He paints horses in repose rather than in violent action. "Trying to stop a horse in action is like trying to stop a wave in action." COW. He also paints horse portraits and in the 1960s painted Navaho Indians with their horses. A distinguishing feature of his work is said to be his use of light.

RITSCHEL, William (or Wilhelm). Born Nürnberg, Bavaria, Germany 1864, died probably Carmel, Cal 1949. Cal marine painter. ANA 1910, NA 1914. Work in PAFA, Ft Worth Mus (Tex), AIC, Detroit Art Club, City AM (St Louis), Smithsonian Inst, etc. References A53 (obit)-BEN-FIE-MAL-SMI. Sources AMA-ANT 8/58-DEP-INS 7/28-NA 74-WHO 50. Oil 12×16″ *Calif Coast* sold 11/6/68 for $425 at auction. Signature example p 81 INS 7/28 *Spell of the Cypress*.

Ritschel was educated in a Latin and

technical school in Germany. He studied at the Royal Academy in Munich, the pupil of F Kaulbach and C Raupp, before coming to the US in 1895. He exhibited widely and was accepted in the Salmagundi Club by 1901. Listed painting titles included *Across the Plains, Arizona* and *Desert Wanderers*.

RIX, Julian Walbridge. Born Peacham, Vt 1850, died NYC 1903. California landscape painter, illustrator. Work in COR, Minneapolis and Toledo AM, Harmsen colln. References A05 (obit)-BEN-DAB-FIE-MAL-SMI. Sources AIW-AOA-BWB-COR-DCC-NJA-POW. Oil 20×36" *Foggy Morning near San Rafael* with signature example and dated '18 ('78?) offered 5/27/74 at an estimated price of $800 to $1,000 at auction in Los Angeles, and sold for $1,500. (See illustration 247.)

Rix, a descendant of early Massachusetts settlers, was brought to San Francisco by his family when he was 4. He indicated an interest in painting while working as an errand boy in a paint store. When his parents would not help him toward art school, Rix became a sign and decorative painter. By 1875, he had progressed in painting to the point where he made black and white landscapes. He was a member of the Bohemian Club, an associate of the unconventional artists of the day, Tavernier, Strong, and Joullin. He was particularly influenced by the "bohemian of Bohemians," Jules Tavernier with whom he shared a studio, in the landscape usage of "deep shadows, gray skies, and shady trees." DAB. Rix specialized in etchings such as *Golden Gate*. In 1888 he provided illustrations for "Picturesque California."

Rix became known nationally when he moved East in 1888, first to Paterson, NJ, and then to NYC. "He was an independent worker and thinker, not shown at the annual exhibitions. He ranked among the best landscape painters of the day." A05. He was described as an extremely good-natured bohemian who liked to travel, and his aim was to put feeling and atmosphere into his work. He never married.

ROBBINS, Charles D. California painter active in the 1880s, probably in San Francisco. No reference. Listed in PNW as one of a group painting at the same time as J E Stuart, along with Hill, Keith, Hamilton, Denny, and Arthur Nahl. No other source. No current auction record or signature example.

ROBERTS, Jack. Born Oklahoma City, Okla 1920, living Carbondale, Colo 1975. Traditional Western painter, illustrator. Work in ANS and on life insurance calendars. No reference. Sources COW-ILP. No current auction record or signature example.

Roberts worked as a cowboy in Burns, Colo. He studied art at the U of Oklahoma and at the American Academy of Art in Chicago. The pupil of Harvey Dunn at the Grand Central School of Art in NYC, he considers Dunn to have been "the greatest artist of his generation." COW. Specializing in historical Westerns, Roberts regards the mountain men and hunters as more satisfying subjects than present-day cowboys.

ROBINSON, Alfred. Born Mass 1806, died probably Cal 1895. Cal sketch artist. Reference G&W. No other source, auction record, or signature example.

Robinson was in California 1829–37 and 1840–42 as the agent for Bryant & Sturgis, Boston merchants, and after

1849 as representative of Pacific Mail Steamship Company. His sketches from 1829 to 1842 were used for seven lithographs in "Life in California" (1846), published anonymously.

ROBINSON, Boardman. Born Somerset, NS, Can 1876, died Colorado Springs, Colo 1952. Colorado Springs painter, muralist, illustrator, cartoonist, teacher. Work in CSFAC, AIC, MMA, DAM, Dallas MFA, WMAA, LA Cnty MA, ACM, MNM. References A53 (obit)-FIE-MAL-SMI. Sources AAT-ALA-ARM-CAA-CAH-DEP-190-M57-NEW-SHO-WHO 52. Three paintings oil on board each about 16×12" signed with initials, sold 5/3/72 for $550 at auction. Signature example p 37 SHO.

Educated in Canada and England, Robinson came to the US in 1894 and studied with E W Hamilton 1894–97 at the Boston Normal Art School. From 1898 to 1900 he studied in Paris at the academies Colarossi, des Beaux-Arts, and Julien. After painting for six years in Paris and San Francisco, he became the cartoonist for the NY *Morning Telegraph* 1907–10 and *NY Tribune* 1910–14, where he developed a powerful crayon technique that became the radical style. His drawings and cartoons were exhibited in the 1913 Armory Show. In 1915 he went to Russia with John Reed for *Metropolitan Magazine*. From 1915 to 1920 he was on the staff of *The Masses, Liberator,* and *Harper's Weekly*. Robinson was an instructor at the ASL 1920–30.

In 1930 the "choice for art teacher at Fountain Valley School in Colorado Springs was the New York Socialist, Boardman Robinson. He was taken to the local Republican bosom like a prodigal son and even made instructor at Broadmoor. Soon after, Broadmoor found itself without a head. The board considered both Robinson and Randall Davey, but Davey withdrew from the running because of the decline of polo at Broadmoor." NEW. The Southwest then received a "muscular treatment in Robinson's lithographs of Colorado." ALA. The Los Angeles Museum has *In New Mexico*.

ROBINSON, Charles Dorman. Born Vermont (or Monmouth, Me) 1847, died San Rafael, Cal 1933. Cal landscape and marine painter, specializing in Yosemite Valley and the High Sierras, illustrator. Work in Cal Hist Soc, San Fran Maritime Mus, Soc Cal Pioneers (all San Fran), Crocker AG (Sacramento), Oakland AM. References A17-BEN-FIE-MAL-SMI. Sources BDW-KAH-WHO 20. No auction record. Signature example p 41 KAH. (See illustration 248.)

Son of a Gold Rush theatrical producer, C D Robinson was educated in California public schools and in the academy in North Troy, Vt. In 1860 he won an award at the Mechanics Fair in San Francisco. He then lived in Vermont 1861–73, and was the pupil of William Bradford 1862, of George Inness and M F H de Haas 1863, of Gignoux and Cropsey in Newport, Vt 1866–67.

Robinson lived in Iowa 1873–74 and then settled in San Francisco where he became known as the "dean of Pacific Coast artists." WHO 20. After beginning as photo retoucher, he wrote and illustrated for *Overland Monthly* and *Century*. Nineteen summers were spent in Yosemite Valley and the High Sierras. 84 of his paintings are in collections in Great Britain. Robinson was in Paris 1899–1901, the pupil of Boudin and of the methods of Segantini. He offered the Paris Exposition in 1900 a painting of Yosemite that was 50×400′ and weighed 50 tons. When it was not exhibited, Robinson cut the panorama into salable sections to earn his passage home.

ROCKWELL, Cleveland. Born Youngstown, Ohio 1837, died Portland, Ore 1907. Marine survey artist, topographical artist, mapmaker. Work in Stenzel colln, Flavel Mus (Astoria, Ore). Reference A05. Source PNW. No auction record. Signature example p 21 PNW.

Educated at the Polytechnic School at Troy, NY, and the U of NY, Rockwell studied art from time to time, as a boy, in NYC, and in England. He worked for the Coast Geodetic Department until the Civil War when his talent as a mapmaker made him in demand at general headquarters such as the staff of Gen Sherman on his march through Georgia.

After the war Rockwell returned to the Geodetic Survey and was assigned to California. In 1868 he was in Oregon as chief of the Northwest section, personally surveying the Oregon coast in the area of the Columbia and Willamette rivers. The silhouette illustrations in "Pacific Coast Pilot, Vol No 1" are his. Aside from the survey illustrations, Rockwell also painted the coastal and river scenery in oil and watercolor. The work is of historic interest, the ocean fishing fleet, the river seine fishing, "the floating canneries, the early steam boats, the picturesque and long-gone fish wheels." PNW. Rockwell also painted ship portraits on commission.

ROCKWELL, Norman Percevel. Born NYC 1894, living Stockbridge, Mass 1976. Very important Eastern illustrator, painter. Member SI. Work in MMA, *The Saturday Evening Post*. References A76-BEN-FIE-MAL. Sources AAC-ANT 6/72,1/73,11/74,3/75-COW-DIC-ILA-ILG-IL32,42,59,61-POI-ROC-WHO 70. Oil 43×34" *The Convention,* signed, a cover illustration for 5/3/41 *Sat Eve Post,* sold 12/13/72 for $11,000 at auction. Signature examples ROC.

When Norman Rockwell was 9, his genteel middle-income family moved to Mamaroneck, NY. His grandfather was Howard Hill, an unsuccessful English artist. As a high school freshman, he studied at the Chase School of Art. The next year he left high school for the National Academy of Art, earning his way through odd jobs that included designing cards for Arnold Constable and teaching painting to Ethel Barrymore—"me, a long, gawky kid bending over graceful Ethel Barrymore, guiding her shapely hand across the paper . . . my great Adam's apple churning up and down my neck." ROC. At 16 he transferred to the ASL to learn to "paint storytelling pictures." He was the pupil of Bridgman for life class and of Fogarty for illustration. At 17 he was illustrating books, and at 18 was art director for *Boys Life.* When his parents moved to New Rochelle, NY, he shared a studio there with the established illustrator Clyde Forsyth. At 22 he sold his first five covers to George Horace Lorimer of *The Saturday Evening Post*—the beginning of 318 such covers in a career that made Rockwell the most popular living American artist.

His procedure was to pencil a loose 2×3" sketch on a scrap of paper. Second, make individual drawings or (after 1937) photographs of each element of the painting, using the models and props he gathered, on the spot or in a simulated background. Third, do a full-size charcoal drawing. Fourth, make color sketches for the final painting—or, project a photograph onto a white canvas, draw with charcoal, and paint. Rockwell is not a Western artist and had not been West when he painted his 8/13/27 cover of the "old-timey" cowboy with his nostalgic gear. The 4/23/38 cover was a bedraggled Indian. The 9/25/54 cover showed the rancher's son off to college. In 1966 Rockwell did a promotional series for the movie "Stagecoach." In 1969 Rockwell went to Arizona for a painting of Glen Canyon Dam that included the neighboring Navahos. His portrait of the actor John Wayne hangs in the Cowboy Hall of Fame.

RODEWALD, Fred C. Illustrator active in NYC, painting covers for pulp Western magazines in 1930s and working for Macmillan Co in 1948. Reference MAS. Sources ILG-cover *The Flaming Frontier* for *Real Western* magazine. No current auction record but the estimated price of a Western illustration would be about $800 to $1,000 at auction in 1976. No signature example. (See illustration 249.)

ROERICH, Nicholas Konstantin. Born Leningrad, Russia 1874, died Naggan, India 1947. International painter, writer, traveler, designer of ballet and opera sets. Work in the Louvre, Luxembourg, Victoria and Albert Mus, Roerich Mus (NY). References BEN-ENB-FIE-MAL. Sources NMX 11/75-TSF-WHO 48-Nicholas Roerich Catalog, Kingore Gal, NY 1920–21-letter 11/18/75 Sina Fosdick, Dir, Nicholas Roerich Mus. Oil on canvas 35¼ ×53¼″, scene for "Ivan the Terrible" sold 1969 at Sotheby's London for $624. No signature example.

Born a member of the Russian aristocracy, he was sent to the University in Petrograd to study law. He was simultaneously permitted to attend the Imperial Academy of Arts. At the end of three years he had graduated from the law school and had also had a painting of his accepted by the leading art gallery in Moscow. Family opposition to his becoming an artist ceased and he went to Paris in 1900 for a year's study.

Roerich was a world traveler, spending 1901–4 painting through Russia before coming to the US in 1920. He also spent five years in Central Asia, and headed an expedition through China and Mongolia in 1934 for the Department of Agriculture looking for a drought-resistant grass.

Roerich had visited Sante Fe in 1921. TSF. He did two series of paintings, the Grand Canyon Series and the Arizona Series. One of these paintings, *The Bridge of Glory*, is in the Roerich Museum, NY. Letter Roerich Museum.

ROETTER, Paulus. Born Nürnberg, Germany (or Thun, Switzerland) 1806, died St Louis, Mo 1894. Botanical and landscape painter illustrating Texas boundary report in 1859. Work in Mo Hist Soc (St Louis), U of Texas (Austin), Mo Botanical Gardens (St Louis). Reference G&W. Sources MIS-TEP. No auction record. Signature example 113 MIS.

After studying art in Germany and possibly France, Roetter painted miniature landscapes and taught art in Switzerland 1825–45. He emigrated to the US to form a socialistic colony, but settled in St Louis as the first drawing teacher at Washington U and as an evangelical minister. When George Engelmann of St Louis prepared the section on cactus for the Emory "Report of the US and Mexican Boundary Survey" in 1859, Roetter drew the 61 illustrations. It is not said that the Roetter drawings were made on the spot.

Roetter was in the Home Guard during the Civil War, after which he worked with the famous Louis Agassiz at Harvard.

ROGERS, Charles A (or D or H). Born New Haven, Conn about 1840, living Los Angeles, Cal 1913. Cal landscape and Chinatown painter. Reference G&W. Sources BDW-SCA.

Rogers studied in NYC where he lived for 15 years before training in Munich, Paris, and Rome. He may be the same Charles Rogers who painted a San Francisco panorama about the California Vigilance Committee in 1856 and worked at the Lyceum Theater there in 1859. As Charles A, he is said to have lived in California from 1866.

Rogers is recorded as a landscape painter in San Francisco in 1880. The 1906 fire destroyed 150 of his paintings of Chinatown and he moved to Los Angeles soon after. Rogers sketched in Yosemite in the summer of 1911. It is apparent, though, that there may be more than one Charles Rogers.

ROGERS, Randolph. Born Waterloo, NY 1825, died Rome, Italy 1892. Expatriate neoclassical sculptor of ideal figures, portrait busts, and monuments. Work in MMA, the *Columbus* doors in the Capitol, Washington monument (Richmond), Lincoln (Phila), Seward (NYC), etc, with about 200 casts in the U Mich MA. References BEN-DAB-FIE-G&W-MAL-SMI. Sources ALA-AMA-BOA-HUT-M19-PAF-SCU. No current auction record. Sculpture examples pp 26, 27 SCU. (See illustration 250.)

Son of a carpenter moving West, Rogers was raised in Ann Arbor. From ages 18 to 23 he worked in a NYC wholesale dry goods store. With his employers as patrons he studied at the Academy of St Mark in Florence, the pupil of Bartolini 1848–51. In his studio established in Rome, Rogers by 1853 had modeled his famous *Nydia,* the blind flower girl listening for the Pompeian lava. About 100 replicas were made. In the US 1853–55, Rogers secured the commission for the *Columbus* doors he modeled back in Rome and had cast in bronze in Munich. In 1867 he obtained orders for 50-foot granite monuments,

one at $50,000 for Rhode Island and the second at $75,000 for Michigan with a warlike Indian on the summit.

A powerful man with a long beard, the convivial Rogers entertained visiting celebrities and royalty. He was paralyzed by 1882. His final works included the 45″ bronze *Last Arrow,* an Indian on a rearing horse with a wounded Indian on the ground.

ROGERS, William Allen. Born Springfield, Ohio 1854, died Washington, DC 1931. Cartoonist, important Western artist-correspondent for *Harper's Weekly,* teacher, illustrator. Member SI. Work in Lib Cong, *Harper's Weekly, Harper's Magazine, Life, St Nicholas, Century, Washington Post, NY Herald.* References A31 (obit)-BEN-FIE-MAL. Sources AIW-AOA-CAP-IND-POW-WHO 32. No current auction record but the estimated price of a Western illustration would be about $3,000 to $4,000 at auction in 1976. Signature example pl 38 CAP.

Rogers whose mother was an amateur painter attended Worcester Polytechnic Institute. He worked as a railway clerk at 13. A fellow employee taught him to sketch with chalk. At 14 Rogers drew cartoons for a Dayton paper. From 1870 to 1877 he was engraver and artist in various cities. In 1877 he went to work for *Harper's.* Sent to cover President Hayes's visit to Minnesota in 1878, Rogers left for Dakota Territory without authorization from *Harpers',* tempted by stories of the Western plains. He took the train to Bismarck, then spent three weeks at Standing Rock Indian Agency 65 miles south. Some of his most famous illustrations of Indians resulted, including *Indian Dance After Distribution of Rations* and *An Indian Chief Having His Hair Dressed.* On the way back he sketched in Fargo and via riverboat in Winnipeg, where, "From the 19th century I had dropped as from the clouds, into the 17th or 18th." AIW.

In 1879 *Harper's* sent Rogers to Colorado and New Mexico, along with the writer A A Hayes. They went by rail to Pueblo, Colo, then by buckboard to a cattle ranch where Rogers proved poor at drawing animals. They descended in a silver mine bucket before visiting Leadville, and viewed the Santa Fe trail. Back in NYC, Rogers as the Western specialist on the staff redrew a Remington sketch for *Harper's* in 1882. He apparently made another trip to the Dakotas in 1890, sketching the genre of the wheat fields that replaced the buffalo. As the mining artist, he went to Cripple Creek, Colo in 1893 to cover the discovery of gold. In 1896 he made *Sketches in Santa Fe*. In 1898 he covered the Omaha Exposition including the Indian congress, continuing on to Oregon and California before returning via the Southwest. He had made six Western trips over 21 years. Rogers thereafter worked primarily as a newspaper cartoonist, following Thomas Nast at the *New York Herald* where he remained for 19 years.

ROHLAND, Paul. Born Richmond, Va 1884, died probably Sierra Madre, Cal 1953. NY and Cal painter specializing in still life and landscape. Work in WMAA, MNM, Davenport Munic AG, Barnes Fndn, Honolulu Acad Arts; murals in POs. References A53 (obit)-BEN-MAL. Sources AAT-ARM. No auction record. Signature example p 134 AAT *Western Town*.

Rohland studied at the ASL and was the pupil of Robert Henri.

ROLLINS, Warren Eliphalet. Born Carson City, Nev 1861, died Winslow, Ariz 1962. Early member of Santa Fe artists colony, painter of Indians, teacher. Work in MNM, ANS, Harmsen colln, Oakland AM, Santa Fe RR; murals in MNM and public buildings. References A59-MAL. Sources AIW-DCC-HAR-KAH-PIT-TSF. Oil 20¼×30" *New Mexico Landscape* signed but not dated, sold 10/21/71 for $375 at auction. Oil 46×68" *Indians at the Grand Canyon* 1908 estimated for sale 10/28/74 at $7,000 to $9,000 for auction in LA. Signature example p 169 HAR. (See illustration 251.)

Warren E Rollins was raised in California. He was the pupil of Virgil Williams at the San Francisco School of Design, becoming assistant director of the school. In 1887 after further study in the East he moved to San Diego. He began to specialize in Indian subjects, traveling through the Western states. In 1900 he was in Arizona painting Hopi Indians. He also worked at the Chaco Canyon ruins in northern New Mexico and had a studio near El Tovar at the Grand Canyon.

Rollins was an early member of the Santa Fe art colony, along with Carlos Vierra, Gerald Cassidy, Kenneth Chapman, and Sheldon Parsons, arriving in 1915 through his friendship with E I Couse. He had previously spent years at Pueblo Bonita, NM. According to AIW and HAR, Rollins had the first formal exhibition in Santa Fe, showing Indian paintings before 1910 so that he was properly regarded as the "dean of the Santa Fe art colony." Rollins had a period when he favored working in crayon, an oddity matched by other Western painters like Groll and Kihn. In the 1940s, Rollins moved to Baltimore where he drew crayon seascapes.

ROLSHOVEN, Julius. Born Detroit, Mich 1858, died NYC 1930. International painter. ANA 1926, Taos SA. Works in Detroit IA, Cincinnati AM,

BM, MNM, Harmsen colln. References A31 (obit)-BEN-DAB-FIE-MAL-SMI. Sources AMA-ANS-ANT 12/69-MSL-TSF-WAI 72-WHO 30. Oil 19×15" *Portrait of Indian Woman* sold 4/20/72 for $1,000 at auction. Signature example p 36 ANS *Indian Market*. (See illustration 252.)

Rolshoven began his study of art at Cooper Union in NYC in 1877, then in 1878 in Düsseldorf with Hugo Crola, and in 1879 in Munich with Loefftz where he remained until 1882 as a "Duveneck boy." In 1882 he started studies in Paris with Robert-Fleury and Bouguereau. He exhibited in the principal European cities. By 1890 he was teaching in Paris, and in 1896 in London. His chief interest was in depicting the effects of light. In 1912 his North African paintings were exhibited in Detroit.

During a visit to the West in 1914 Rolshoven became interested in the Indians of New Mexico. Spending the war years in the US, he arrived in Santa Fe in 1916 "dressed in fashionable white traveling clothes, followed by a wagon loaded high with luggage." TSF. As a world-rank painter, a studio was provided for him in the old Palace. Rolshoven made his accommodations to the harsh New Mexico light by setting up his outdoor studies in a tent, providing the subdued effects he wanted for the large number of Indian portraits and genre scenes he painted in oil and pastel. He exhibited with the Taos Society of Artists in 1922. It was said of Rolshoven that he had "the artistic temperament, making it difficult for him to adapt himself to routine work." DAB. He believed that he should demand from the American public at least as much as was given to foreign artists.

ROOK, Edward Francis. Born NYC 1870, died probably Old Lyme, Conn 1960. Eastern landscape, genre, and flower painter. ANA 1908, NA 1924. Work in PAFA, Cincinnati AM, COR, Portland (Me) AM. References A47-BEN-FIE-MAL-SMI. Sources ARM-COR-NA 74-WHO 50. No current auction record or signature example.

Rook studied in Paris, the pupil of Constant and Laurens. He began winning medals in 1898 for paintings that included Western landscapes. Two of his paintings were exhibited at the 1913 Armory Show.

ROPER, Edward. Born Kent, England 1857, died England 1891. Artist, illustrator, writer. Work in Vancouver City Archives, Pub Archives of Canada (Ottawa), British Columbia Archives (Victoria). No reference. Sources CAE-KEN 6/70. Watercolor 14×12" *The Field Hotel* sold 12/7/71 for $1,323 at auction in London. *A Sketch Book 1883–1887* sold 3/26/70 for $950 at auction in Montreal. Signature example p 70 KEN 6/70, a watercolor *Indian Burial Ground*.

Roper visited the US and Canada several times. In 1887 he painted in British Columbia. His last visit in 1890 was spent in the Yukon. He wrote and illustrated "By Track and Trail Through Canada."

ROSE, Guy. Born San Gabriel, Cal 1867, died Pasadena, Cal 1925. Cal impressionist landscape painter, illustrator. Work in Oakland AM, LA County MA, Cleveland MA, San Diego FAG. References A26 (obit)-BEN-FIE-MAL-SMI. Sources AAR 11/74-BDW-WHO 24-SCA. No current auction record. Signature example p 139 AAR 11/74.

Rose was educated at Los Angeles high school and studied at San Francisco Art School, the pupil of Emil Carlsen in

1885, before attending the Julien Academy to study with Lefebvre, Constant, and Doucet. In 1891 Rose began as a magazine illustrator in NYC, then returned to Paris in 1893 until lead poisoning interrupted his painting. He taught at Pratt Institute in NYC 1896–1900, then settled in France where he knew Claude Monet and the Impressionists in Giverny. Rose came back to Los Angeles, painting there again from 1914 to 1920. In Southern California, Rose is considered the equal of any American painter of his time. Rose's wife was the fashion illustrator Ethel Boardman Rose.

ROSENBAUM, David Howell, Jr. Born Brigham City, Utah 1908, living there 1974. Modern Utah painter, teacher. Work in WPA Allocations (Utah). References A41-MAS. Source YUP. No current auction record or signature example.

Rosenbaum studied at the Utah State Agricultural College, the pupil of Calvin Fletcher in 1931. He painted in Utah until 1938 when he went to NYC to study at the ASL. He also entered the American Artists' School in NYC, the pupil of Sol Wilson, Moses Soyer, and Jean Liberté. In 1941 he taught at the Utah Art Center. In 1942 he served in WWII's Seabees, painting in Guadalcanal.

One of the few Utah artists "who might be called expressionists," Rosenbaum painted "some of Utah's most powerful landscapes, bold in color, dynamic in composition. He was a solitary and intense individual." YUP.

ROSENTHAL, Doris (Mrs Jack Charash). Born Riverside, Cal about 1895, died probably Oaxaca, Mexico 1971. Modern painter specializing in Mexican Indians, lithographer, teacher. Work in MMA, MOMA, Colo Spr FAC, Lib Cong, San Diego FA Gallery, Cranbrook AA. References A73 (obit)-BEN-MAL. Sources AAT-AIC-CON-M50-M51-WAA-WHO 70-WOM 64. Oil 21×28″ *Las Peinades* signed but not dated sold 5/22/73 for $350 at auction. In M50, *Nixtamal y Postole* was illustrated and offered for sale for $1,000 in 1950. Signature example ✗94 CON.

Doris Rosenthal was educated at LA State Teachers College. She was at Columbia U 1912–13. She studied at the ASL 1918–19, the pupil of Bellows and Sloan. In 1920–21 she studied in Europe, following which she became a NYC teacher. In 1931 she received the first of her grants for painting in Mexico. Her work was included in "50 Prints of the Year" 1932. By 1934 she was exhibiting in the most important national and international shows. Articles with illustrations of her work have appeared in such national magazines as *Life, The New Yorker,* and *Art News.* Her specialty was "Old Mexico, its color, its people and children and landscape with intriguing intimacy." CON.

ROSSI, Paul A. Born Denver, Colo 1929, living Tucson, Ariz 1974. Traditional Western painter, illustrator, sculptor, writer, museum director, Western historian. No reference. Sources ACO-AHI 3,4/72; 1/73-COW-GIL-USM-WAI 71-12/28/73 data from Florence R Rossi. No current auction record. Signature example p 3 AHI 3/72.

Rossi, the descendant of Italian pioneer ranchers, was educated in Denver and attended Denver U 1947–51. The summers of 1946–50 he worked on cattle ranches. During the Korean War he served in the Air Force. Rossi was with the Colorado State Historical Society until 1956, as acting curator. He resigned to open his own commercial art studio in

1956. From 1959 to 1961 he was designer and illustrator for Martin Aircraft Co in Denver. Rossi worked from 1961 to 1972 at the Gilcrease Institute in Tulsa. He was museum director beginning 1964, editor of *The American Scene* and co-author of "Art of the Old West."

In 1972 Rossi established his own studio in Tucson to devote full time to painting. He is considered an authority on Western military history, having supplied the illustrations for *The Buffalo Soldier* and the saddle drawings for *The Vaquero* in the *American Scene* magazine. His 1974 bronzes include a series of 12 *Great Saddles of the West*.

ROSSITER, Thomas Pritchard. Born New Haven, Conn 1818, died Cold Spring, NY 1871. Eastern portrait and historical painter. ANA 1840, NA 1849. Work in NGA, COR, MFA, MMA. References BEN - CHA - DAB - FIE - G&W - MAL-SMI. Sources AAR 11/74-ANT 4/57; 7,10/70; 5/72-ALA-BAR-BOA-HUD-HUT-ISH-KAR-KW1-PAF-WHI. Oil 44×39" *An Allegory of War, 1866* sold 9/24/70 for $100 at auction, no indication of the auction price for a frontier landscape. Signature example ✳45 HUD.

Rossiter, the descendant of a 1630 settler, studied under Nathaniel Jocelyn in New Haven. At 20 he was a portrait painter in his own studio. In 1840, when he was 22, he was one of the young men who accompanied Durand to Europe, along with Kensett and Casilear. After visiting England, Rossiter spent a year with Kensett in Paris. In 1841 he went with Cole to Rome where he spent five years. In 1846 he opened his studio in NYC, before moving in with Kensett and Louis Lang in 1851.

It was in the NYC period that Rossiter painted *Opening of the Wilderness* which depicted the meeting of railroad trains on the frontier. KAR p 467. From 1853 to 1856 he was in Paris. In 1856 he returned to NYC, painting portraits. In 1857 he began his series of historical paintings, including important representations of the life of Washington.

ROULAND, Orlando. Born Pleasant Ridge, Ill 1871, died probably NYC 1945. Eastern portrait painter. ANA 1936. Work in U of Texas and St Capitol (Austin), NGA, Montclair AM, AMNH. References A47 (obit)-BEN-FIE-MAL-SMI. Sources TOB-WHO 44. No current auction record or signature example.

Rouland was the pupil of Max Thedy in Germany and of Laurens and Constant at the Julien Academy in Paris. He studied in London, NYC, and Marblehead, Mass. He painted portraits of personages like Theodore Roosevelt, Thomas A Edison, and Mme Melba. Included were some Westerners, for example, the Sam Houston portrait painted in 1912 for the Gallery of the Senate in Texas.

ROWE, Clarence Herbert. Born Philadelphia, Pa 1878, died Cos Cob, Conn 1930. Illustrator in watercolor including Western subjects, etcher. Member SI, Guild of Free Lance Artists of the Authors' League of Amer. References A30 (obit)-BEN-FIE-MAL. Source, magazine illustrations of West. No auction record or signature example. (See illustration 253.)

Clarence Rowe studied at the PAFA, the pupil of Max Bohm. He studied in France on a scholarship, the pupil of Bouguereau and Ferrier. In addition to his work in illustration, Rowe exhibited internationally.

RUNGIUS, Carl Clemens Moritz. Born Berlin, Germany 1869, died probably

NYC 1959. Painter specializing in Western American big-game subjects, illustrator, etcher. ANA 1913, NA 1920. Work in NY Zoological Soc, Shelburne Mus (Vermont), Glenbow Fndn and Riveredge Fndn (Calgary), Harmsen colln. References A62 (obit)-BEN-FIE-MAL-SMI. Sources AMA-ANT 10/67; 10,11/71; 10/73; 1,6/74-COW-HAR-JNB-NA 74-POW-WAI 71,72-WHO 50. Oil 31×40″ *Pack Horses on a Trail* sold 3/19/69 for $5,250 at auction. Oil *Throwing a Steer* sold in 1937 for $400 at auction. Signature example p 171 HAR.

Carl Rungius was educated at the gymnasium Burg bef Magdeburg und Glessen. He studied at Berlin Art School, School of Applied Arts, and Academy Fine Arts, the pupil of Paul Meyerheim. He began painting in Berlin in 1889. When he emigrated to the US in 1894, he established his studio in NYC. His summer home and studio were in Banff, Alberta, Canada. The first sketching trip was to Wyoming and Yellowstone Park in 1895.

Rungius traveled from Arizona to Alaska, hunting, sketching, and painting. He specialized in big game, moose, caribou, and bear, as well as mountain sheep, goats, elk, deer, and antelope. He also painted the cowboys he met, while leaving to others the Indians and Pueblos. His work is today a valuable record of the animals and their environment at the time. He painted directly from nature. The Glenbow Foundation maintains his Rockies studio as a museum.

RUSH, Olive. Born Fairmount, Ind 1873, died Santa Fe, NM 1966. Modernist Santa Fe painter, portraitist, muralist, illustrator. Work in BM, John Herron AI, MNM, Houston MFA, Witte Mem Mus. References A62-BEN-FIE-MAL-SMI. Sources AHI 8/67-TSF-WHO 31-WOM. No current auction record. Signature example p 64 TSF.

Miss Rush was educated at Friends Academy. She studied at the Corcoran SA, at the ASL under Twachtman and Mowbray, at the Howard Pyle School of Illustration, and with the (Richard) Miller Class for Painters in Paris. She did cover designs for the *Ladies' Home Journal* and illustrations for *Scribner's, Collier's* etc. She specialized in portraits of children and women and in frescoes for private homes.

She made her first visit to Santa Fe with her father in 1914 when she was 41. She became a resident in 1920. Miss Rush experimented with different styles of painting during her career, decorative landscapes and decorative cubism and expressionism, all delicately handled. Her work became freer as she got older.

RUSSELL, Charles Marion. Born Oak Hill, St Louis, Mo 1864, died Great Falls, Mont 1926. Very important Western painter specializing in Indian genre, illustrator, sculptor, writer, *the* "cowboy artist." Work in Montana Hist Soc (Helena), Trigg-Russell Gall (Great Falls), ANS, MNM, GIL, ACM, Whitney Gall (Cody, Wyom), Nat Cowboy Hall of Fame (Okla City), etc. References A26 (obit)-BEN-FIE-MAL-SMI. Sources AAR 1,5/74-ACO-AHI 3/66-AIW-ANT 12/44; 12/50; 10,11/51; 3, 12/52; 12/53; 1,5,11/54; 2/56; 8/57; 5/58; 1/60; 1,5,9,12/61; 7,10/62; 8, 10/64; 8,9/65; 3,7,8,10/66; 8,10/67; 8, 10/68; 1/69; 7,8/71; 2,3,7/74; 2/75-AOW-ARI-COW-CRS-CUS-DBW-DCC-DWF-EIT-GIL-GWP-HAR-HMA-HON-150-ILA-JNB-KEN-PAW-PNW-POW-REN-RUS-STI-TAW-TEP-TWR-WAI 71,72-WHO 26-WNW. Oil 24×36″ *Death of a Gambler* signed and dated 1904, bearing skull symbol and "copyright" sold 10/27/71 for $100,000 at auction. Signature example p 224 AOW. (See illustrations 254, 255.)

Russell attended Clinton and Oak Hill schools beginning 1872. A poor student, he was sent to military school in New Jersey for a term in 1879, then was permitted by his well-to-do father to travel to remote Montana to work as a sheepherder. "I did not stay long, but I did not think my employer missed me much. I soon took up with a hunter and trapper named Jake Hoover. This life suited me. I stayed about two years. (In 1881) I struck a cow outfit coming in to receive 1,000 dougies. The boss hired me to night-wrangle horses. I was considered worthless. For 11 years I sung to the horses and cattle. In 1888, I stayed about six months with the Blood Indians. In the spring of 1889 I went back to the Judith, taking my old place as a wrangler. In the fall of 1891, I received a letter from 'Pretty Charlie,' a bartender in Great Falls, saying I could make $75 a month and grub. When I arrived I was introduced to Mr G who pulled a contract as long as a stake rope for me to sign. Everything I drew, modeled or painted in a year was to be his. I balked. I put in with a bunch of cowpunchers, a roundup cook and a prize fighter out of a job, and we wintered. Next fall I returned to Great Falls, took up the paint brush and have never 'sung to them' since." *The Outing Magazine* 12/04

Even when he was "singing" to the stock, "Kid" Russell was sketching and painting, expanding his self-taught talent. Hard-drinking and pleasure-loving, bull-necked and lantern-jawed, he gave his pictures to any friend who wanted one. In 1888 his *Caught in the Act* was published in *Harper's Weekly*. In 1890, 14 of his oils were reproduced in NYC. In 1893, saloon keepers were the first Russell collectors. When he married in 1896, his wife became his business manager. By 1904 he was sculpting in bronze. By 1911 his works were selling in NYC for what he called "dead men's prices." AOW. In his thousands of pictures, the

favorite subject was Indians. At least 49 showed the buffalo hunt. Many were of Indian women; white women were rarely shown.

RUSSIN, Robert I. Born NYC 1914, living Laramie, Wyom 1976. Modern sculptor, teacher. Member NSS, Sculptors Guild. Work in U of Wyom, Wyom Highway Bldg, Roosevelt U, Lincoln Hwy, Fed Bldg in Denver. References A76-MAL. Sources WHO 70-WYG-*Denver Post* magazine 12/8/68. No current auction record. Signature example *Post* above.

Russin graduated from the College of the City of NY in 1933 and received his master's degree in 1935 when he became a fellow at Beaux-Arts Industrial Design. He taught sculpture at Cooper Union 1944–47 and was professor of art at the U of Wyoming beginning 1947. His work includes 8' metal figures Evanston (Ill) PO 1939, three life-size carved figures Conshohocken (Pa) PO 1940, Benj Franklin monument U of Wyoming 1957, etc.

RYAN, Tom. Born Springfield, Ill 1922, living Lubbock, Tex 1974. Modern Western painter, illustrator. Member CAA. Work in Harmsen colln, Cowboy Hall of Fame. No reference. Sources ACO-AHI 10/71-CAP-COW-C71 to 73-HAR-OSR-WAI 71,72. No current auction record. Signature example p 57 C73.

Ryan was educated at Springfield Junior College. He studied at St Louis School FA before service in WWII with the Amphibious Fleet in the South Pacific. After working as an artist for a Springfield agency, he studied for three years at the American Academy of Art in Chicago, the pupil of Sturba and Mosby.

Moving to NYC, he studied at the ASL, the pupil of Frank Reilly and the assistant of Dean Cornwell.

After Ryan had won a publishing-house commission, he began sketching in the Southwest as research for eight years of Western illustrations for book jackets. He moved to Lubbock and from 1954 to 1962 painted Western historical scenes for a NYC gallery. After 1964 he painted Western genre for national calendars. "Tom is a fine portrait painter and this lends a strength to his work. His efforts have attracted a lot of folks who never paid much attention to cowboy art before." OSR. He is known for his "highly realistic style and meticulous detail." HAR. He specializes in painting the present-day cowboy, sketching at the 6666 Ranch near his home. Ryan's 1974 illustrations for cigarette ads are the epitome of Western nostalgia.

RYDER, Albert Pinkham. Born New Bedford, Mass 1847, died Elmhurst, LI, NY 1917. Very important Eastern romantic painter. ANA 1902, NA 1906. Work in MMA, BM, AIC, NGA, Phillips colln (Washington), Worcester AM, BMFA, DIA, etc. References A17 (obit)-BEN - CHA-DAB-ENB-FIE-MAL-SMI. Sources AAR 11/74-AIC-ALA-AMA-ANT 11/74-ARI-ARM-ART 8/47-BAR-DAA-DEP-HUD-INS 10/29-ISH-190-MAP-MSL-M19-M31-NA 74-NGA-RYD-STI-WHO 16. Oil 13½×10" *Marine* sold 6/27/72 for $40,320 at auction in London. Oil 11×16" *Homeward Plodding* sold 1968 for $15,000 at auction. Signature example pl 64 RYD.

Son of a custom-house officer, Ryder was educated at New Bedford grammar school. He began experimenting on his own with landscape painting. When he moved to NYC with his family about 1870, he became the pupil of William E Marshall, portraitist and engraver. In 1871 he studied at the NAD. By 1873 he exhibited small naturalistic landscapes at the NAD. Tall and heavy with a full reddish-brown beard, he was normally sociable, a founder of the Society of American Artists in 1877. He made several trips abroad, just for the sea voyage and with no effect on his art. After about 1880 he became a romantic, taking his subjects from religion and literature. His paintings were the product of his mind's images, not painted directly from reality but simplified and redesigned. These paintings were not popular and were not exhibited. He became unworldly, dressed like a tramp, living in a studio in complete disorder, sleeping on the floor. His paintings were worked on for years. Some were still in his studio at his death although he painted little after 1900.

The DAB article on Blakelock states, "The rich color schemes and enamel-like technique of Ryder fixed his attention. Ryder had sometimes used Indian figures and groups imaginatively as vehicles for moods. Blakelock followed suit." In his lifetime, Ryder made only about 160 paintings. There are many forgeries of his paintings.

SABO, Betty. Born Kansas City, Mo 1928, living Albuquerque, NM 1976. Landscape painter. Reference A76. Source p 34 NMX 9,10/73. No auction record or signature example. Painting example *Winter Night in Taos* shown NMX. (See illustration 256.)

With most of her life having been spent in New Mexico, Ms Sabo studied at the U of New Mexico. She was the pupil of Carl Von Hassler who taught her that a "good artist must train himself to see how the world is made. He must be a historian, biologist, botanist, as well as a painter." NMX. A realist, she sketches on location and finishes her paintings in the studio. She is known for snow scenes, particularly of an old mission at night with warm window lights in the tiny adobe houses clustered around.

SAINTIN, Jules Émile. Born Lemée, Aisne, France 1829, died Paris, France 1894. French historical, genre, and portrait painter who spent 1856–66 in NYC specializing in Indian subjects. ANA 1861, Chevalier Legion of Honor 1877. Work in museums of Nice and Saint-Brieuc, BMFA. References A10 (list p 400)-BEN-G&W-MAL-SMI-von Boetticher-Thieme und Becker. Sources HUT-KW2-PAF-WCE. Oil 29½×19½" *At the Window* 1870 sold 11/2/73 for $3,682 at auction in London. Chalk drawing 10¾×16¼" *Indian with Ear to Ground* p 42 KW2. (See illustration 257.)

Saintin was the student of Drolling, Le Boucher, and Picot at the École des Beaux-Arts in Paris in 1845. He exhibited in the Paris Salon beginning 1848, winning medals 1866, 1870, and 1886, and in Vienna 1882. About 1853 Saintin moved to NYC where he painted portraits of French sitters and also depicted the costumes and customs of Indians. KW2 lists as his best-known work *The Pony Express Carrying Mail from Placerville, Cal to St Joseph, Mo. The Sioux Family* was painted in 1864. He exhibited at the NA, Boston Athenaeum, and PAFA which listed *California Overland Mail Attacked by Indians* in 1867 by which date Saintin was in Paris.

Saintin had returned to Paris in 1865. He was described there in 1867 as "white gloved hands on hips, bright red cheeks emphasizing the yellow of his hair and thick mustaches." KW2. When he died in Paris after a long illness, he bequeathed to the NAD the paintings in his Paris studio. There is no record of Saintin having visited the West.

SAINT-MÉMIN, Charles Balthazar Julien Fevret de. Born Dijon, France 1770, died there 1852. Important early portrait and landscape painter in the East, engraver. Work in COR, NY Hist Soc, Winterthur Mus, Peabody Mus (Salem), MMA. References BEN-DAB-FIE-G&W-MAL-SMI. Sources AAR 11/74-ALA-ANT 3/26, 7/42, 2/45, 10/48, 2/49, 4/52, 8/57, 7/58, 7/59, 7/61, 7/64, 6/66; 1, 11/73; 6, 7/74 - AOW - BAR - BOA-BOL-DBW-DWF-NJA-PAF-WES. No current auction record but the estimated price of an Indian watercolor portrait would be about $10,000 to $15,000 at auction in 1976. Signature example p 17 AOW.

Saint-Mémin, of the lesser French nobility, was educated privately. He attended military school in Paris where he studied art and drew portraits "with an exactitude perfectly geometrical." BOL. After graduating in 1785 he followed a military career until the French Revolution forced emigration. The family came to NYC where Saint-Mémin in 1796 made and sold engravings of his landscape sketches. He soon turned to portraiture. He used a physiognotrace, a wooden-framed device to produce an exact life-size profile of the sitter in pencil on red paper. The picture was filled in with crayon or watercolor, "delicate and sure." ALA. Afterward the drawing was by pantograph reduced to a 2″ miniature on a copper engraving plate. The charge was $33 for the drawing, the plate, and 12 proofs. At least 800 of these profile engravings were completed, including the last portrait of Washington from life. Saint-Mémin worked in NYC until 1798, then Burlington (NJ), Philadelphia, Baltimore, Annapolis, Washington, Richmond, and Charleston. From 1812–14 he painted in oils before returning to France.

In Washington in 1804, Saint-Mémin made "the earliest known portraits of Plains Indians." AOW. President Jefferson had invited a group of 12 Osage chiefs to visit their Great White Father. "The finest men we have seen," their head chief White Hair was more than six feet tall and muscular, in contrast with the short, fat, balding Saint-Mémin who was commissioned by the British Government to make profile portraits of the Indians. At least five of the Indian portraits survive, measuring $21\frac{1}{2} \times 15\frac{1}{2}$″ on paper that is now pink.

SALINAS, Porfirio. Born Bastrop, Tex 1910, living probably Austin, Tex 1970. Traditional Southwestern landscape and genre painter. Work in private collns. Reference A70. Sources COW-NYG-undated exhibition catalog Texas Art Gallery (Dallas). No current auction record. Signature example p 487 NYG *Blue Bonnet Time*.

Born in a piney woods town, Salinas was raised in San Antonio. Selling art supplies, he met Robert Wood and José Arpa who took him on field trips. This was the extent of his art education. His earliest commissions were sign painting on beer trucks and Christmas cards. Salinas' subjects are restricted to the Southwest, bluebonnets, prickly cactus, rugged landscapes, sunny villages, bull fights. His paintings are untitled: "They are whatever they say to the viewer." As a state present, Pres Johnson gave a Salinas painting to the Pres of Mexico.

A painting of the hill country intended as a gift for Pres Kennedy was retained by Salinas, as was the allegorical painting after Kennedy's death, a lone horse against ominous clouds.

SALISBURY, Cornelius. Born Richfield, Utah 1882, died Salt Lake City, Utah 1970. Utah painter, teacher. Work in Utah St and school collections. No reference. Source YUP-letter Charles T Howard 10/22/75. No current auction record. Signature example p 32 YUP.

Cornelius Salisbury studied with J F Carlson 1904, at U of Utah 1905, at Brigham Young U 1907–8 (pupil of Eastmond), at ASL in NYC 1908, at Pratt Institute (Brooklyn) 1909–10, at Corcoran SA 1916–18, and at Broadmoor AA 1927. He also taught at colleges, schools, and privately between 1907 and 1943. His wife was the painter "Rose" Howard Salisbury.

Salisbury "painted many of the landmarks and buildings in Salt Lake City that were built by Brigham Young and the old pioneers years ago." He also painted mining ghost towns and landscapes, especially of the Wasatch Mountains. "He was a very exacting and meticulous painter." Letter.

SALISBURY, Paul. Born Richfield, Utah 1903 (or 1904), died Provo, Utah 1973. Traditional Western painter, illustrator. Work in *Western Horseman, Desert Magazine*. No reference. Sources COW-WAI 71-YUP-letter Charles T

Howard 10/22/75. No current auction record but the estimated price of a Western painting would be about $1,000 to $1,500 at auction in 1976. Signature example p 211 COW.

Paul Salisbury was raised on his father's ranch near the Kanosh Indian Reservation in southern Utah. He studied with Cornelius Salisbury, his uncle, at West High School in Salt Lake City. In his magazine cover illustrations he was influenced by the work of Frank Tenney Johnson.

SALISBURY, Rosine Howard. Born New Brunswick, Can 1887, died Salt Lake City, Utah 1975. Utah painter, teacher. Work in Utah schools. No reference. Source YUP-letter from Charles Howard 10/22/75. No current auction record. Signature example p 32 YUP.

"Rose" Salisbury studied with Harwood and Richards in Utah, with Evans and Frazer at U of Utah in 1914, and in California 1922 and 1928. She taught at Utah colleges and schools between 1922 and 1944. Mrs Salisbury painted landscapes of the mountains and "she liked to paint the Utah flowers that grew in her garden and did quite a few portraits and still-lifes." Letter 10/22/75. She worked in both oils and watercolors. Her husband was Cornelius Salisbury.

SAMPLE, Paul Starrett. Born Louisville, Ky 1896, died probably Norwich, Vt 1974. New England realist landscape and genre painter. NA 1941. Work in MMA, White House, BM, BMFA, PAFA, Smithsonian Inst, etc. References A73-BEN-MAL. Sources AAT-ALA-CON-MAP-M51-NA 74-NYG-WHO 70. Oil 34×36" *Good Farming—Good Living* sold 12/13/72 for $2,100 at auction.

Signature example p 157 MAP *Janitor's Holiday*.

Son of a construction engineer who moved frequently, Sample entered Dartmouth in 1916. After the interruption of a year of service in the Navy, Sample returned to Hanover where he became an intercollegiate boxing champ and played the saxophone before graduating in 1921. Four years in the Adirondacks recuperating from tuberculosis turned Sample toward art. At 30 he became the pupil of Jonas Lie, and an immediate success.

He went to California in 1926 but "couldn't stomach painting a lot of High Sierras and desert flowers, the only pictures that were sold." MAP. He worked as professor of fine arts at U of Southern California 1926–38, beginning to paint without knowing how his work would develop and maturing into a realistic painter of the "richness of living." CON. Sample became artist in residence at Dartmouth 1938–62 and a nationally recognized painter.

SAMUEL (or Samuels), William M G. Born probably Missouri 1815, died probably San Antonio, Tex 1902. Early self-taught Texas painter of townscapes and portraits. Work in Witte Mus (San Antonio). Reference G&W. Sources ANT 6/48-TEP. No current auction record but the estimated price of a major Texas townscape would be about $2,500 to $3,000 at auction in 1976. Signature example opp p 28 TEP.

When Samuel came to Texas in the late 1830s, he manufactured cement in a lime kiln. He fought in the Indian Wars and was noted as a dead shot. In the Mexican War he served in Gen Wool's Army of Chihuahua. Samuel worked for the local San Antonio government for many years. When he was stationed in the Bexar County Courthouse in 1849, he made four oil paintings of views from the courthouse windows. These views showed each side of the plaza with the activities of the time. In 1930 the discolored paintings were still on the courthouse walls, along with a Samuel self-portrait and portraits of such notables as Sam Houston, Big Foot Wallace, and Deaf Smith. The paintings were then "discovered" and placed in the Witte Museum.

Samuel was a home officer in the Civil War. He became justice of the peace, county court commissioner, peace officer, notary public, and deputy sheriff. He was "a stalwart officer of the law and rid San Antonio of some of its worst characters." TEP.

SÁNCHEZ Y TAPIA, Lino. Active 1827 –28 in Texas. Mexican survey artist, military draftsman. Work in GIL (38 watercolors). No reference. Sources GIL-TEP. No current auction record but the estimated price of a watercolor of Indians would be about $2,500 to $3,000 at auction in 1976. Signature example p 8 TEP.

In 1827 Mexico sent a boundary survey to Texas. The chief scientist was Don Manuel Meier y Teran. Dr Jean Louis Berlandier, a Swiss botanist, and José María Sánchez y Tapia, the mapmaker, both sketched. Lino Sánchez refined their sketches into watercolors and made his own paintings. The party moved from west to east across southern Texas, describing the settled places by word and by watercolors of Mexicans, Indians, and rancheros. These depictions of the Indians are quite romantic and civilized, with details of clothing and of implements.

SANDER (or Sanders), A H (or Mrs). Born place unknown 1892, living Fort Worth, Tex 1948. Texas sculptor. Work in Dallas MFA. Reference MAS. Source, pair bronze bookends 6×4" *Indian Head* signed A H Sander Sc but not dated, cast by Griffoul, Newark, NJ. No auction record or signature example. (See illustration 258.)

SANDERSON, William. Born Latvia 1905, living Denver, Colo 1969. Contemporary Colo painter of social comment, illustrator, teacher, designer. Work in DAM. No reference. Source DAA. No auction record. Signature example p 95 DAA *Composition with Fried Eggs*.

Sanderson studied at the Fach and Gewerbe Schule in Berlin before emigrating to NYC. He studied at the NAD 1923–28, the ASL, and traveled in Turkey, Greece, Poland, Germany, France, and England. In 1938–39 Sanderson was editorial artist for *PM Newspaper* in NYC and from 1939–42 was an advertising art director. Beginning 1946, Sanderson taught at U of Denver SA. A favorite subject for his paintings was the working man, for example, Western farmers.

SANDHAM, J Henry. Born Montreal, Can 1842, died London, Eng 1912 (or 1910). Historical, portrait, marine and landscape painter, illustrator including Western subjects. Charter member, RCA 1879. Work in Parliament Bldgs (Ottawa), Lexington Town Hall, NGC, Phila Centennial Exhib, World's Columb Expos. References A12 (obit)-BEN-CHA - DAB - FIE - MAL - SMI. Sources AIW-CAH-CAN-GOD-HON-POW. No current auction record but the estimated price of an oil showing a California mission would be $2,500 to $3,000 at auction in 1976. Signature example p 229 GOD.

Henry Sandham, the son of an English house decorator, was educated in Montreal public schools. Although untrained in art, he successfully retouched photographic portraits in the Notman studio that employed so many who became important Canadian artists. After he achieved a partnership in the studio, he tried sketching landscapes. By 1870 he was a known portrait and landscape painter. He was made a charter member of the RCA in 1879, the year his marine painting was purchased by the NGC. Sandham took the artist's tour of England and France in 1880 before moving to Boston. He made a second tour in 1884.

In his Boston studio, Sandham succeeded as a magazine and book illustrator. "Picturesque Canada" contained his work in 1882. He traveled to the West in 1883 for *Century* illustrations and for *Art Amateur* in 1885 when he also illustrated Roosevelt's "Hunting Trips of a Ranchman." He made drawings for Poe's "Lenore" in 1886 and for Helen Hunt Jackson's famous "Ramona," going to California again in 1902 for her books on missions. As a painter he specialized in historical subjects: *The Dawn of Liberty* in Lexington, *Founding in Maryland* shown in 1893, and *The March of Time* concerning the Civil War in 1889. He moved to London in 1901.

SANDOR, Mathias. Born Hungary 1857, died NYC 1920. Portrait, landscape, and Indian painter, commercial artist. Work in Harmsen colln. References A20 (obit)-BEN-FIE-MAL-SMI. Sources KEN - WHO 20. Oil 24×20″ *Landscape* sold 5/20/66 for $150 at auction. Oil *Home of the Hopi Indians* offered 4/20/72 but passed at auction. Signature example p 46 KEN 6/70.

Sandor was educated in high school in Hungary. He emigrated to the US in 1881, establishing himself as a commercial designer and portrait painter. He studied at the ASL 1885–86 and in Paris at the Julien Academy 1889–90, the pupil of Flameng and Ferrier. After 1890 he was a portrait, miniature, and landscape painter with his studio in NYC. He also painted in the Southwest, particularly the life of the Hopi Indians.

SANDUSKY, William H. Born probably Columbus, Ohio 1813, died probably Galveston, Tex 1846. Survey and topographical draftsman, mapmaker, printmaker. Work in Austin Pub Lib (Tex). No reference. Source TEP. No auction record. Print shown p 149 TEP.

Sandusky settled in Austin in 1838. In 1839 he drew views of Austin that he reproduced and colored. In 1840 he became secretary to President Mirabeau Lamar. In 1841 Sandusky moved to Galveston after an appointment in the coastal survey of Texas. In 1845 Sandusky was named import inspector.

His prints of Austin have historical importance. They were also published in the newspaper of the day.

SANDY, Percy Tsisete (or Kai Sa, Red Moon). Born Zuni Pueblo, NM 1918, living Taos, NM 1974. Zuni painter, illustrator, muralist. Work in GIL, MAI, Mus No Ariz, MNM, Okla U MA, Philbrook AC, SE Mus. No reference. Source AIP. No auction record or signature example. (See illustration 259.)

Percy Sandy was educated at Zuni Pueblo Day School where he began painting. He attended the Black Rock school before receiving formal art instruction while at Albuquerque where he graduated in 1940. His aim as an artist was to depict the customs of his people. AIP. He also attended Santa Fe Indian School and Sherman Institute in Riverside, Cal.

Sandy's illustrations were in "Sun Journey" by Clark in 1945 for the Bureau of Indian Affairs. He painted three murals before being injured in a 1959 accident that periodically prevented painting. He had many exhibitions and a one-man show.

SANDZÉN, Sven Birger. Born Bildsberg, Sweden 1871, died Lindsborg, Kan 1954. Impressionist landscape painter of the Rockies, graphic artist, teacher. Work in Sandzén Mem Gall (Lindsborg), Stockholm AM, Bibliothèque Nat (Paris), AIC, BM, MNM, etc. References A53-BEN-FIE-MAL-SMI. Sources AAT-SHO-TSF-WHO 52-article p 56 *The Mentor* about 1924. No current auction record. Signature example p 31 SHO.

Son of a Lutheran minister, Birger Sandzén received all of his art education in Europe. He was an 1890 graduate of the College of Skara in Sweden with further study at U of Lund. The pupil of A Zorn and R Bergh, he studied painting at the art school of Stockholm's Artists' League, then with Aman-Jean in Paris. He emigrated to Kansas in 1894, to teach aesthetics and painting at Bethany College, as professor until 1945 and thereafter as professor emeritus. He accumulated a collection of 500 of his own Western paintings and drawings.

He first painted in the Colorado Springs area about 1916, teaching at Broadmoor 1923–24. He also taught at Denver and at Utah State College. Sandzén was primarily a landscape painter specializing in Rocky Mountain scenes. His style was after Van Gogh, with masses of paint and impressionist palette. Sandzén was also a frequent visitor to Santa Fe and Taos, beginning 1918. In 1922 he exhibited with the Taos Society of Artists in NYC, alongside the New Mexico painting giants of the day.

SANTEE, Ross. Born Thornburg, Iowa 1889, died Globe, Ariz 1965. Illustrator of Western genre in black and white drawings, watercolorist, writer. Work in Read Mullan Gall Western Art (Phoenix). References A41-MAS. Sources AHI 10/71; 3,9/72-COW-WAI 72-article in *Arizona and the West* ⅜/65. No current auction record. Signature example p 42 AHI 10/71.

Of Swedish descent, Santee was raised in Iowa and went to high school in Moline, Ill. He studied for four years at the AIC to be a cartoonist. Although he was befriended by Thomas Hart Benton, who advised him to study Daumier's work, Santee was unsuccessful as a commercial artist in NYC. In 1915 while visiting his mother in Arizona, he took a job on his uncle's ranch as wrangler and cowhand. After two years, his black and white sketches of ranch life were accepted by the St Louis *Post Dispatch*. This encouraged Santee to return to the AIC in 1919 as the pupil of Bellows. Following Bellows' advice to try the NYC art world again, he began writing short stories he illustrated with his bold black drawings. His Western books started in 1926 with "Men and Horses." In 1928 he wrote "Cowboy."

When he married, he built a home in Wilmington, Del to be near his wife's ailing mother, commuting to Arizona at roundup time to make a portfolio of sketches. From 1936 to 1941 he lived in Phoenix, editing a state guide to Arizona for the WPA. At this time he met Raymond Carlson, editor of *Arizona Highways,* the magazine that for the rest of Santee's life was the primary outlet for drawings, watercolors, and stories. A tall, balding man, he modeled as a tough-looking tenderhearted character for a Rolf Armstrong painting. When his wife died in 1962, he returned to Arizona to study oil painting with Ted De Grazia.

SAUERWEIN (or Sauerwen, Frank Paul), Frank Peters. Born Baltimore, Md (or Yonkers, NY or in NJ) 1871, died Stamford, Conn 1910. Western realistic painter. Work in Adams colln, Harmsen colln, MNM, ANS, Southwest Mus (LA), Panhandle-Plains Hist Soc (about 40 paintings, in Canyon, Tex). References A05-G&W (father). Sources AIW-DCC-PAW-PET-SPR-TSF-TWR. Pair of oils 6×8″ and 5½×7½″ on canvas-board *Studies of Western Horses* both signed sold 5/22/72 for $500 the pair at auction. This would not reflect the price of a Western painting at auction today. Signature example p 42 TWR. (See illustration 260.)

He was brought up in Philadelphia, the pupil of his father, Charles D Sauerwein, who studied in Europe and was living in Baltimore in 1871 (G&W). Sauerwein studied at Philadelphia School of Industrial Arts, then PAFA and AIC.

Sauerwein moved to Denver about 1891 because of tuberculosis. In 1893 he began to sketch Indians in the Rockies. He was in Colorado Springs in 1893, traveling with Charles Craig to the Ute Reservation. After a European trip he visited Taos in 1899, Santa Cruz and Santa Fe in 1900, Taos in 1902 and 1903. He apparently lived in California in 1905, then from 1906 to 1908 resided in Taos where he bought a house. Too ill to paint, he went to Connecticut to attempt a cure. Sauerwein was an important painter in the West of his time, a most competent, straightforward, and naturalistic recorder of the landscape and of Indian life.

SAUL, Chief Terry (AIP states "Chief" is the given name). Born Sardis, Okla 1921, living Bartlesville, Okla 1970. Choctaw-Chickasaw painter, illustrator, commercial artist. Work in DAM, GIL, Philbrook AC, etc. No reference. Sources AIP-COW. No current auction record or signature example.

C Terry Saul, Indian name Tabaksi, Ember of Fire, attended Jones Male Academy before graduating Bacone high school and college in 1940, the pupil of Acee Blue Eagle and Woody Crumbo. After five years of military service in WWII, he earned his BFA in 1948 and MFA in 1949 from Oklahoma, with further study at the ASL 1951–52 under Baer. His work was published beginning with *Art Digest* in August 1947. Saul owned an arts studio in Bartlesville in 1950 and has worked as an artist for industrial companies since 1952.

In 1963 Saul was quoted, "Each painting should be a departure from the one before." AIP. He had in 1961 begun on a technique of engraving a panel of oil painted on gesso.

SAVAGE, Annie Douglas. Born Montreal, PQ, Can 1896, died probably there 1971. Montreal painter who was West of the Rockies in the 1920s, illustrator, teacher. Member Can Group Ptrs. Work in AG Toronto, AA Montreal, Montreal MFA, U Toronto, Can Embassy (Washington). References A62-MAS. Sources CAH-CAN. No auction record or signature example. Illustration shown p 223 "The Downfall of Temlaham" by Barbeau, Macmillan 1928, *Where the Native "Paradise Lost" of Temlaham Used to Stand.*

Ms Savage studied at the Art Association of Montreal and the Minneapolis Society of Design. She was a "beloved" teacher (CAH) and supervisor of art for Montreal public schools. Her illustration for the Barbeau classic of Canadian West

Coast Indian lore was a landscape of the Upper Skeena River near Hazelton. It placed her among the Barbeau circle of Emily Carr, Jackson, Holgate, Pegi Nicol, and the American Langdon Kihn.

SAVITT, Sam. Born Wilkes-Barre, Pa, living North Salem, NY 1975. Illustrator and writer specializing in horses. Work in magazines and books. No reference. Source, Western illustration of cowboy genre. Signature example, cover of "Trotter" below. (See illustration 261.)

Sam Savitt graduated from Pratt Institute in Brooklyn, NY. He traveled and worked as a ranch hand throughout the West, and then spent four and a half years in the Army. After the war he returned to the study of art at the ASL and NYU.

"Sam Savitt's illustrations have appeared in national magazines and in over 90 books, some of which he wrote himself. He lives with his wife on a small farm where his favorite pastime is riding and schooling horses." "The Gallant Gray Trotter" by John T. Foster, 1973, Dodd, Mead & Company. Other books he has both written and illustrated include "Around the World with Horses," "There Was a Horse" and "Rodeo."

SAWYER, Edward Warren. Born Chicago, Ill 1876, died Clos Vert La Palasse, Toulon, France 1932. Sculptor specializing in medals including Indian subjects. Member NSS. Medals in Luxembourg Mus (Paris), AIC, US Mint (Phila), Mass Hist Soc, Buffalo Bill Mus (Cody, Wyom). References A32 (obit)-BEN-FIE-MAL-SMI. Source NSS. No current auction record. Signature example p 311 NSS.

Sawyer studied at the AIC. He was a pupil of Verlet at the Julien Academy in Paris, and also Injalbert, Frémiet, and Rodin, as well as Laurens. After 1900 he lived permanently in France.

During two visits to the US about 1912, he made a series of 40 bronze medals of various Indian tribes. These medals were exhibited in NYC in 1923. They became the property of the American Numismatic Society of New York. His *Buffalo* which had won a prize at the St Louis Exposition in 1904 is in the Buffalo Bill Museum.

SAWYER, Philip Ayer. Born Chicago, Ill 1877, died probably Clearwater, Fla 1949. Portrait painter, etcher, teacher, critic. Work (prints) in Smithsonian Inst, Lib Cong, NY Pub Lib. References A53 (obit)-BEN-FIE-MAL. Sources BDW-WBB. No current auction record. The published estimate for prints is $30 to $40. Oil *A Congress of Rough Riders* 5'10"×9' with signature example and date 1929 is shown p 64 WBB.

Sawyer studied at the AIC, at Purdue U, at the Yale School FA, and with Léon Bonnat in Paris. He was living in Tiskilwa, Ill in 1934 and in 1947 was teaching portraiture at the Clearwater Art Museum.

SCHAARE, Harry J. Born Jamaica, LI, NY 1922, living Westbury, LI, NY 1975. Eastern illustrator of paperback book covers and magazines, marine watercolorist. Member SI 1960. Work in Air Force art colln, War Memorial (Indianapolis), SI colln. No auction record or signature example. (See illustration 262.)

Schaare attended the NYU School of Architecture for the year 1940, then transferred to Pratt Institute for illustration. He served as a European Theater pilot in WWII. Max Herman, Ajoutian, and Costello were his teachers at Pratt where he graduated in 1947. After working briefly in commercial art studios, Schaare established his own studio. By 1951 he was doing paperback covers including Westerns. These illustrations were not returned to the artists at that time, and Schaare is sure the original art was resold in Mexico or Europe for more than the $350 he received. In 1953 he broke into the ranks of *The Saturday Evening Post* illustrators, for fiction including Westerns. Since 1971 Schaare has spent leisure time on marine watercolors.

SCHAEFER, Mathilde (Mrs Mathilde Schaefer Davis). Born NYC 1909, living Scottsdale, Ariz 1962. Arizona sculptor. Work in IBM colln, Mus No Ariz, Katherine Legge Mem (Hinsdale, Ill). Reference A62. Sources AAT-WAA. No auction record. Sculpture example p 229 AAT Tufa Stone *Maricopa Girl*.

Ms Schaefer studied with Raoul Josset, Walter Lemcke. She began exhibiting at the AIC in 1938 and was instructor of pottery and sculpture at the Desert School of Art in Scottsdale.

SCHAFER (or Schaeffer), Frederick Ferdinand. Born Germany 1841, died probably Oakland, Cal after 1917. Pacific Coast painter of landscapes and Indian scenes. Work in Stenzell and Honeyman collns. No reference. Sources HON-PNW. No current auction record but the estimated price of a West Coast Indian scene would be $2,000 to $3,000 at auction in 1976. No signature example.

Schafer became a naturalized citizen of the US in 1884 while he had his studio in San Francisco. He was a member of the San Francisco Art Association in 1880 and 1889. He was listed in the Oakland City Directory from 1905 to 1917.

From labels on his paintings it is known that he visited Montana, Idaho, Wyoming, Oregon, Washington, and British Columbia. His paintings were seldom dated. His early style in oil was "dark tones appropriate for the region depicted." PNW. Later views were "impressionist." HON. "According to people who knew him, he fought against alcoholism, not always successfully." PNW.

SCHALDACH, William Joseph. Born Elkhart, Ind 1896, living Tubac, Ariz 1964. Etcher, painter, illustrator, writer. Fellow, AMNH. Work in Vanderpoel colln, NY Pub Lib, MMA, Lib Cong, etc. References A62-MAL. Sources AAT-AHI 2/64-SPT. A pair of watercolors *Birds* sold 5/15/70 for $120 the pair at auction. Signature example p 50 SPT.

Schaldach studied at the ASL and was the pupil of Harry Wickey. He was living in Connecticut in 1937 when he was invited by his friend Ray Strang, the painter, to spend the winter in a cottage on Strang's ranch in Arizona. He returned to Connecticut and it wasn't until 1948 that he went back to Arizona as a winter visitor. For eight years he wintered in Sasabe, Ariz and he made Arizona his residence in 1956. Schaldach's specialty is writing and illustrating wildlife subjects, both in his books and in articles in national magazines. His habitat is the Sonoran desert with its plants and mammals, missions and Indians, in southern Arizona, Mexico, and lower California.

SCHATZLEIN, Charles. Watercolorist active in Montana in 1890s. No reference. Source, watercolor 12×8¾" *White Bird—Nez Percé Chief* signed Chas Schatzlein and dated Butte Mont—10–93, estimated 10/28/74 at $800 to

$1,000 for sale at auction in Los Angeles. Signature example *White Bird* above.

Schatzlein is identified in "Good Medicine" as a resident of Butte, Mont, an art collector and decorator who was a friend of Charles Russell at least 1899–1910. The 7/9/10 letter from Russell (p 87) invites "Dutch" to "come up to the lake and bring your paint box."

SCHELL, Francis H. Born probably Germantown, Pa 1834 (or 1830), died probably there 1909. Military painter, engraver, illustrator, for *Frank Leslie's Magazine,* art director. Work in "Beyond the Mississpppi," magazines. References A09 (obit)-BEN-G&W-MAL-SMI. Sources AIW-AOA. No current auction record but the estimated price of a Western drawing would be $400 to $450 at auction in 1976. Signature example ⚹171 AOA.

Frank Schell was raised in Philadelphia. He worked there as a lithographer when he was 16. During the Civil War he was one of the important *Leslie's* illustrators, along with William and Alfred Waud, Edwin Forbes, Henri Lovie, and W T Crane. In 1867 he, the two Wauds, Forbes, J Becker, J R Chapin and Thomas Nast were illustrators for "Beyond the Mississippi" which included views from the Mississippi River to the Pacific Coast from 1857 on. Some of these illustrations were drawn from 1866 photographs along the Union Pacific right of way.

After the war Schell became head of *Leslie's* art department. Later he joined Thomas Hogan to form Schell and Hogan, illustrators for 30 years.

SCHEUERLE, Joe. Born Vienna, Austria 1873, died South Orange, NJ 1948.

Painter of Indian portraits, illustrator, lithographer. Work in Boileau colln (Birmingham, Mich). Reference MAS. Source, "Three Decades of Plains Indians," MWH Fall/71, with signature example on cover. No current auction record but the estimated price of an Indian portrait would be about $2,000 to $2,500 at auction in 1976.

Raised in Stuttgart, Germany, Scheuerle was brought to Cincinnati when he was 9. His education stopped in grade school. After apprenticeship to a lithographer, he was employed as a commercial artist. In 1896 he sketched stage Indians for Wild West posters. When he studied at the Cincinnati Art Association, he painted with Duveneck, Farny, and Sharp. In 1900 he moved to Chicago as an illustrator, meeting Col Cody to prepare Buffalo Bill posters.

Beginning in 1906 Scheuerle made summer trips West: visiting the Oglala Sioux in 1909, Crow and Blackfoot in 1910, Cheyenne in 1911, etc. There are 200 portraits in the Boileau collection, many with cartoons and descriptions on the reverse to fix the circumstances. His sketches were used by the Great Northern railroad for the opening of Glacier National Park in 1910. In the West he was the peer of more famous artists, Charles Russell and Henry Cross, for example. At home he entertained Russell, Gollings, and DeYong as well as William S Hart, Will Rogers, and the Indians he had met in the West. He moved back to Cincinnati during WWI, then on to NYC in 1923. A friendly and modest man, he shunned publicity and retained his portrait collection as long as he lived. When the collection was finally exhibited it could be noted that many of Scheuerle's Indians had also sat for other artists, offering stylistic comparisons.

SCHIMMEL, William Berry. Born Olean, NY 1906, living Paradise Valley,

Ariz 1976. Traditional Western painter, illustrator, teacher, writer. Work in Phoenix FAM, Cincinnati AM, U NCar, Phoenix Pub Lib. Reference A76. Sources AHI 11/62-COW-WAI 71,72. No current auction record. Signature example p 26 AHI 11/62.

Schimmel was educated at Rutgers U. He studied at the NAD and was the pupil of Gerry Pierce and Roy Mason. From 1935 to 1938 he was art director of a major advertising agency in NYC. He has taught in Arizona, Wyoming, Colorado, Minnesota, Texas, and Washington. In 1958 he wrote "Watercolor, the Happy Medium."

SCHIMONSKY (or Tzschumansky), Stanislas. Painter of Indian scenes in Nebraska in 1854. Reference G&W. No other source, auction record, or signature example.

SCHIWETZ, Edward M. Born Cuero, Tex 1898, living College Station, Tex 1975. Texas watercolor painter in architectural and industrial subjects, illustrator. Work in Dallas MFA, MFA of Houston, Ft Worth AA; industrial paintings for Standard Oil, Union Oil, Humble Oil, Dow Chemical, and Monsanto Chemical. References A62-MAL. Sources TOB-T20. No current auction record. Signature example "Buck Schiwetz's Texas."

Schiwetz was educated in architecture at Texas A&M College, the pupil of Joseph Kellogg. As a painter he was largely self-taught, although he did study at the ASL. He was exhibiting widely by 1930. His illustrations appeared in leading magazines, for example, *Architectural Record, Architectural Forum,* and *Pictorial Review*. He wrote and illustrated "Buck Schiwetz's Texas" in 1960. His prints were included in the portfolio "Twelve from Texas."

SCHLEETER, Howard Behling. Born Buffalo, NY 1903, living near Santa Fe, NM 1963. Western abstract painter, muralist, illustrator, teacher. Work in ENB, U NM, MNM, Research Studio colln, Inst Religion (Utah); murals in public buildings in New Mexico. References A59-MAL. Sources CON-TSF. No current auction record. Signature example pp 96–7 CON.

Schleeter, the son of a commercial artist, was educated in Buffalo, studying briefly at Albright AS. He considered himself largely self-taught. He came to Albuquerque in 1929. His style in the 1930s was abstract but never departing from patterns found in nature. His paint was laid on thick to provide a raised fabricated texture. The Federal Arts Project 1936–42 gave him an opportunity to work on murals in New Mexico. He was instructor in art at Las Vegas Art Gallery 1938–39 and at the U of New Mexico 1950–51, 1954. He was the proponent of art that is a personal interpretation by the artist, not an imitation of nature, the same freedom allowed to a musical composer.

SCHMIDT, Albert H. Born Chicago, Ill 1883, died there 1957. Early member of Santa Fe art colony, painter. Work in MNM, Chicago Munic Art Comn. References A19-MAL. Source AIW. No current auction record or signature example.

Schmidt was the pupil of C F Browne at the AIC. He also studied at the Julien Academy in Paris and was the pupil of Henri Martin. The "modern period" of the Santa Fe art colony about 1918–19 included Gustave Baumann, Randall

Davey, Fremont Ellis, John Sloan, Will Shuster, Josef Bakos, Theodore Van Soelen, and, after 1922, Schmidt. AIW.

SCHMIDT, Alwin E. Born Des Peres, Mo 1900, living Bethel, Conn 1962. Illustrator for slick magazines and children's books, including action Westerns. Member SI. Work in *Collier's, Redbook, Liberty* magazines. Reference A62. Source, watercolor of Indian attack. No current auction record or signature example. (See illustration 263.)

Al Schmidt studied at the St Louis School of Fine Arts and with Fred Carpenter. He was exhibiting at the City Art Museum of St Louis as early as 1922.

SCHOLDER, Fritz. Born Breckinridge, Minn 1937, living Scottsdale, Ariz 1976. Mission Indian painter specializing in modern Indian portraits, printmaker. Work in ANS, MNM, BM, Houston MFA, Phoenix AM, San Diego Gallery FA, Dallas MFA, Dartmouth U. Reference A76. Sources AHI 1/74-AIP. No current auction record. Signature example p 3 AHI 1/74. (See illustration 264.)

Scholder was educated in public schools in North Dakota and Wisconsin. He has been painting since 1950, encouraged by Oscar Howe. He studied at the U of Kansas and Wisconsin State U and was the pupil of Wayne Thiebaud at Sacramento City College. He received his BA from Sacramento State College in 1960 and his MFA from U of Arizona in 1964 while assistant instructor and the recipient of national scholarships. After 1964 he was instructor at the Institute of American Indian Arts.

In the 1950s Scholder was a colorist. During the 1960s he concentrated on the image of the Indian, "to expand his richly colored canvases to include the complex human situation of the modern Indian, a compound of beauty, dignity, and maddening absurdity." AHI. In 1973 as artist-in-residence at Darmouth, he completed a series of 17 untitled Indian portraits.

SCHÖNBORN, Anton. Born Germany, date unknown, died Omaha, Neb 1871. Survey topographical artist who depicted Western forts 1859–71, mapmaker, meteorologist. Work in ACM (11 small 1870 watercolors of forts). No reference. Sources FRO-KEN 6/71-"Anton Schönborn, Western Forts" 1972 ACM. No current auction record but the estimated price of drawings of Western forts would be about $900 to $1,100 at auction in 1976. Signature example p 19 KEN 6/71.

Schönborn who spoke five languages was meteorologist and artist on Capt Raynolds' 1859 expedition to explore the upper Yellowstone River. Jim Bridger was guide and Dr Hayden was geologist. The party reached the Absaroka Mountains, then wintered at the Upper Platte Indian Agency before completing their task in Omaha in 1860. KEN shows three pen and ink drawings of Wyoming forts dated 1867 and noted as "from a sketch" by named Army officers. Early in 1871 Schönborn was in Omaha, commissioned by the Quartermaster Dept to make plans of barracks. It is thought that he made many paintings of forts, with copies as requested, and of other Western scenes.

In June 1871 Schönborn was a member of Dr Hayden's fifth survey, a record of the Yellowstone basin. Henry W Elliot was artist, W H Jackson photographer, and Thomas Moran was a guest. The party returned to Omaha in October. His paintings were "strictly representational," from "a bird's-eye view," with "their charm in their directness and immediacy." ACM. Schönborn committed suicide.

SCHOOLCRAFT, Henry Rowe. Born Albany Cnty, NY 1793, died Washington, DC 1864. Important ethnologist of Indians, explorer, author, topographical artist. References DAB-ENB-G&W. Sources KW1-POW-TEP. No current auction record or signature example.

Schoolcraft, son of the manager of a glass factory, was educated in Hamilton common school, Union and Middlebury colleges. In 1817–18 he visited the Missouri lead mines in Indian territory. In 1820 he was geologist on the Cass expedition to the upper Mississippi copper region. After he was appointed Indian agent in 1822, he married the granddaughter of an Indian chief, exploring Indian culture with her.

In 1851 Schoolcraft on a commission from Congress began his six-volume "Historical and Statistical Information Respecting the History, Condition, and Prospects of the Indian Tribes of the United States." The illustrations were by Seth Eastman. Schoolcraft also recorded "The Myth of Hiawatha" that was popularized by Longfellow. He used his own illustrations in his 1853 "Scenes and Adventures."

$375 (not a representative price) at auction. Oil 16×38" *We Went Into Camp* was estimated at $1,500 to $2,500 for sale 10/20/75, and sold for $3,200 at auction. Signature example p 69 ILA.

Frank E Schoonover was educated for nine years at the Model School in Trenton, NJ. He entered Drexel Institute in Philadelphia in 1896, becoming the pupil of Howard Pyle in composition class in 1897. In 1899 when he received his first commission for illustration, he established his studio in Wilmington close to Pyle, one of the "new generation—Violet Oakley, Jessie Willcox Smith, N C Wyeth, and Maxfield Parrish." ALA.

When he was involved in Indian and Western subjects in 1903, he made his first trip to the Hudson's Bay area, traveling by snowshoe and dog team. In 1911 he went to the Mississippi bayous for pirate background, then in the summer to Hudson's Bay for data on the life of the Indians. He wrote articles on the Canadian trappers and has illustrated books and magazines such as *Scribner's, Harper's, Century, Collier's,* and *McClure's.* In 1919 he painted WWI subjects for the *Ladies' Home Journal.* From 1920 to 1930 he illustrated a series of children's book classics. In 1930 he began designing stained-glass windows. In 1942 he founded his own art school. Schoonover was also active as a regional landscape painter of the Delaware and Brandywine valleys.

SCHOONOVER, Frank Earle. Born Oxford, NJ 1877, died probably Wilmington, Del 1972. Illustrator specializing in Indians and trappers, landscape painter, teacher, writer. Member SI 1905. Work in Wilmington Soc FA, magazines, and books. References A41-FIE-MAL-SMI. Sources ALA-ANT 11/69,6/74-COW-ILA-WHO 52. Oil 36×26" *The Good Catch* painted in 1913 sold 1/29/70 for

SCHOTT, Arthur. Born 1813, died Washington, DC 1875. Survey artist in Texas 1849–55, frontier naturalist. Work in "Report on the US and Mexican Boundary Survey" in 1857–59. Reference G&W. Sources AIW-SUR-TEP. No current auction record but the estimated price of an Indian drawing would be $900 to $1,100 at auction in 1976. Drawing example p 161 TEP.

The Gadsden purchase required a new survey of the Mexican boundary. The leader of the expedition, Maj Emory, enlisted three artists to prepare views of the West Texas landscape and its people for publication in the report. These artists were Arthur Schott who was first assistant surveyor under Emory, A de Vaudricourt, and J E Weyss (or Weiss). Toward the end of the survey the expedition was divided into two groups. One group traveled west and the other, the group Schott was with, traveled east from Ft Yuma, Ariz.

Schott prepared 226 drawings, 25 in color. His Indian portraits were particularly successful: *Yumas, Co-Co-las,* and *Lipans* of the Rio Grande area. His townscape *Military Plaza—San Antonio* was the frontispiece in vol I. His bird drawings were "a delight." TEP. From 1858 to 1866 Schott was a resident of Washington, DC, reporting on the geology of the Rio Grande area. He is listed variously in the city directory as "naturalist, engineer, physician, and a well-known professor of German and music." AIW.

SCHREIBER, Georges. Born Brussels, Belgium 1904, living NYC 1976. Eastern painter, illustrator, lithographer, writer. Work in MMA, WMAA, Tol Mus, Bibliot Nat (Paris), Lib Cong. References A76-BEN-MAL. Sources ARI-CAP-CON-WHO 68. Oil 31×35½″ *Circus* offered for auction 12/13/73 with price estimated at $2,500 to $3,000 but did not sell. Oil *Returning Home* sold in 1944 for $850 at auction. Signature example pl 59 CAP.

Schreiber was educated at the German Real Gymnasium in Brussels 1913–18 during the German occupation in WWI. He studied at the Arts and Crafts School in Elberfeld, Germany 1920–22, at the Academy FA in Berlin 1922, and in London, Florence, Rome, and Paris from 1923 to 1928 when he emigrated to NYC. Within six months he had sold cartoons and drawings to the NY newspapers. An author and illustrator of children's books and a teacher at the New School in NYC, he had also been a war correspondent and poster designer in WWII.

CAP shows lithographs of Texas. As a newcomer to the US, Schreiber had in a two-year trip visited each of the 48 states in order to paint the essential meaning of America. His desire is "the projection of humanity but he puts on vibrant color as well." CON.

SCHRECH (or Schreck), Horst. Born Herisau, Switzerland 1885, living El Paso, Tex 1935. Texas painter of animals, veterinarian. No reference. Sources BDW-TOB. No auction record or signature example.

Schrech began as a photographic apprentice before emigrating to Canada as a farmer in 1906. In 1916 at Indianapolis he graduated in veterinary medicine, having earned his way by making anatomical drawings. In WWI he was assigned to recruiting posters and illustrations. After the war he studied at the Beaux Arts Institute of Design in NYC, specializing in architectural problems. His Texas painting subjects were animals, still lifes, and landscapes.

SCHREYVOGEL, Charles. Born NYC 1861, died Hoboken, NJ 1912. Very important genre painter specializing in Western military life, illustrator, lithographic artist, sculptor. ANA 1901. Work in MMA, CR Smith colln, Harmsen colln, Anschutz colln, GIL. References A13 (obit) - BEN - FIE - MAL - SMI.

Sources AAR 3/74-ACO-AIW-ANS-ANT 4,12/59; 8/61,6/68,12/74-COW-CRS-CUS-DCC-EIT-GIL-150-KEN-M31-NA 74-NJA-POW-WAI 71,72-WHO 10. Oil 20×16″ *Dead Sure* dated 1902 sold 1/27/65 for $7,750 at auction. Oil *A Beeline for Camp* sold 4/28/71 for $29,500 at auction in Philadelphia. Bronze, dark patina 12×18″ *The Last Drop* signed Chas Shereyvogel (sic) sold 10/31/75 for $16,000 at auction. Signature example p 177 POW. (See illustration 265.)

A poor boy on the East Side of NYC, Schreyvogel sold newspapers and worked as an office boy while being educated in the public schools. When his parents moved to Hoboken, he carved meerschaum and was apprenticed to a gold engraver, then became a die sinker, and finally, in 1877, a lithographer. By 1880 he was a lithographic artist and teaching drawing. By 1887 he had patrons enabling him to study in Munich for three years, the pupil of Carl Marr and Frank Kirchbach. When he returned he existed as a lithographic artist while unsuccessful with portraits, landscapes, and miniatures on ivory.

After sketching the Buffalo Bill show personnel in New York, he was able to spend 1893 in the West. For five months he sketched in Colorado at the Ute Reservation, then went to Arizona to sketch the cowboys. When he came back to Hoboken with a collection of gear, he continued as a lithographic artist while his paintings of Western Army life did not sell. One of these paintings was *My Bunkie* which he could not dispose of either as a painting or for lithography in 1899. Offered to a restaurant on consignment, it was hung in a dark corner, so Schreyvogel took it back and entered it in the 1900 National Academy exhibition without leaving his address.

When *My Bunkie* won the highest prize of $300, no one at the Academy had until then heard of Schreyvogel or knew where he lived. Immediately suc-cessful, Schreyvogel went West again in 1900, sketching troopers and Indians in the Dakotas for the series of paintings on the Western Army. In 1903 Remington who was the most important Western illustrator called Schreyvogel's work "half baked stuff" but the soldiers depicted spoke up for Schreyvogel. His output was limited to relatively few major works per year (for example, 13 in the two years 1900–1) because of the number of his research trips and the size of the paintings, but reproductions were widely published. One set of these was in the form of "platinum prints," that is, large photographs. When he died in 1912 from blood poisoning after a chicken bone stuck in his gum, he left relatively few Western oils. There were clay models that were later cast in bronze.

SCHUCHARD, Carl. Born Hesse-Cassel, Germany 1827, died Mexico 1883. Survey and topographical artist. Sketches in survey report. Reference G&W. Sources AIW-TEP. No current auction record or signature example.

Educated as a mining engineer in Kassel and Hersfeld, Germany, Schuchard emigrated to California during the '49 gold rush. Failing to find gold, he moved to Texas as a surveyor. His landscape view near Fort Yuma appears in the *Journal* of Lt Sweeney, 1851 or 1853. TEP.

When Congress in 1853 authorized the surveys to establish a railway route to the West, the southern or 32nd parallel survey was by Capt Pope eastward from Fort Yuma early in 1854. No survey artist accompanied Capt Pope. About 1856 Schuchard worked for a private survey for the Southern Pac RR along a similar route, providing 32 sketches. The originals were destroyed in the 1864 fire in the Stanley Gallery at the Smithsonian. Three of these sketches survive as commercial lithographs made in Cincinnati. Schuchard "spent much of his later life in Mexico." AIW.

SCHULTZ, Hart Merriam. See Lone Wolf.

SCHUMANN, Paul R. Born Reichersdorf, Germany 1876, living Galveston, Tex 1941. Texas marine and landscape painter, teacher. Work in Vanderpoel AA (Chicago), Rosenberg Lib (Galveston), AA Springfield (Ill). References A41-MAL. Sources TOB-TXF. No recent auction record. Signature example p 56 TXF.

Born in a watermill, he was brought to Galveston when he was five and was educated in the public schools. He studied with the marine painter J Stockfleth. Typical Schumann titles would be *Oyster Sloops, The Heavy Sea,* and *The Gulf.* He also painted Southwestern landscapes, *A Bit of New Mexico* and *The Hill Country.*

SCHUYLER, Remington. Born Buffalo, NY 1887, living Buckingham, Pa 1953. Illustrator for Boy Scouts including Indian subjects, painter, writer. Member SI. Work in schools, city of New Rochelle colln, Clyde Steamship Line colln. References A53-MAL. Source AAC. No auction record or signature example. (See illustration 266.)

Schuyler studied at the ASL and in Paris at the Julien Academy, the pupil of Bridgman, Pyle, Laurens, and Bashet. His work included *Siwanoy Indians* and *Approach Sign,* as well as six Indian panels for the Clyde Steamship Line. His illustrations were used as magazine covers. Schuyler wrote and illustrated "Art" in 1944 and "Sculpture" in 1945.

SCHWIERING, Conrad. Born Boulder, Colo 1916, living Jackson Hole, Wyom 1976. Western landscape painter, author. Member Nat Acad of Western Art. Reference A76. Sources COW-WYG-PER vol 3 ⅜3. No current auction record. Signature example WYG color folder.

Schwiering's father was dean of education at the U of Wyoming. Schwiering took a minor in arts at the university, studied under Robert A Grahame and Raphael Lillywhite of Denver. Bert Phillips of Taos recommended continued study under "the painter you admire most," so Schwiering went to the ASL in NYC to work with Charles S Chapman.

After WWII, Schwiering settled in Jackson Hole and built his studio. One of the most successful Western artists, he has sold more than 1,000 paintings. "Research is very important for an artist. I plan on going out every day to sketch these mountains no matter what sort of weather is brewing. Because this is really what a mountain painter does—he catches, if he can, the essence of the moods as they come across the mountains, hoping he can pass them on to others." When asked how long it takes to do a picture, Schwiering replied, "Oh, I'd say about two weeks and 35 years." WYG color folder.

SCOTT, Charles Hepburn. Born Newmilns, Scotland 1886, died probably Vancouver, BC, Can 1962. Canadian West Coast painter, etcher, teacher. Member, Can Group Ptrs; Assoc RCA. Work in Vancouver AG. References A62-MAS. Sources CAH-CAN-WNW.

No current auction record or signature example.

Scott studied at the Glasgow School of Art, then visited galleries and sketched in Belgium, France, Holland, Germany, and Italy. He was in Canada and exhibiting by 1925. Lecturer on art education at the U of British Columbia, he was also director of the Vancouver School of Art where his assistants were F Horsman Varley, J W G Macdonald, and J L Shadbolt. Scott was the author of "Drawings of the B C Coast" and was a recognized Canadian etcher.

SCOTT, Harold Winfield. Born Danbury, Conn about 1898, living Croton Falls, NY 1975. Illustrator of pulp Western magazines. Reference MAL as Harold W Scott. Source, data from the artist. No auction record or signature example.

H Winfield Scott grew up in Montana where his father was in the horse business. After his father died, the family moved to Brooklyn, NY. Scott studied piano and gave recitals at 16. He worked as an auto mechanic and during WWI as an airplane mechanic. His arm was shattered in military service. By 1923 he had graduated from Pratt Inst, the pupil of Max Hermann.

In the 1930s and 1940s Scott painted "several hundred" covers in addition to story illustrations for the pulp Western magazines. He also did illustrations for the slick magazines but claims to have been known best as "a whirlwind painter of rootin' tootin' cowboys."

SCOTT, James Powell. Born Lexington, Ky 1909, living Tucson, Ariz 1974. Painter, illustrator, lithographer, teacher. Work in Little Rock AM (Ark). References A62-MAS. Source, illustrations for "Dusty Desert Tales." No auction record or signature example.

James P Scott studied at the AIC and with Anisfeld, Ritman, and Chapin. He exhibited at the AIC beginning 1930. He is professor of art at the U of Arizona in Tucson.

SCOTT, Jessie. Born Portis, Kan 1912, living Haxtun, Colo 1975. Western landscape painter, watercolorist, muralist. Work in Wyom State Mus. No reference. Sources WYG-data from artist 1973. No current auction record or signature example.

When Mrs Scott was six her family moved to Haxton, Colo. She was educated at the U of Colorado. Although she was always interested in painting, she had little opportunity in her remote location to study art. In 1953 she enrolled in the Famous Artists School of Painting and later studied with William Sanderson at U of Denver. Her preferred medium is watercolor. Her subjects range from prairie windmills to portraits to pueblos.

SCOTT, John. Born Camden, NJ 1907, living Ridgefield, Conn 1975. Illustrator specializing in men's subjects like hunting and fishing. No reference. Sources ILA-3/13/75 data from John Scott. No auction record. Signature example p 231 ILA. (See illustration 267.)

At the age of 16, Scott studied illustration in Philadelphia. Before WWII he concentrated on drawings and paintings for pulp Western magazines published by Street & Smith and by Dell. His estimate of the number of such Western illustrations and covers is "thousands." ILA. During WWII, Scott was a staff artist for *Yank* magazine. After the war he turned to the slick magazines such as *This Week* and *Woman's Day* as well as Canadian publications *Chatelaine* and *Toronto Star*. By the 1960s he was specializing in men's magazines, particularly wildlife assignments for *True* and *Sports Afield*.

In recent years Scott has painted murals for the Mormon Church including the new Mormon Temple in Washington, DC, as well as Salt Lake City and Independence, Mo. He has also completed a series of large paintings on the story of Texas oil and is preparing a series on the early days of the American West. His paintings on hunting and fishing were commissioned by the Garcia Corporation. Like all of the Western illustrators working before 1950 who were able to retain their original paintings, he has found that the old paintings have a ready market today.

and historical genre paintings. Later he moved to Plainfield.

In 1890 Scott was appointed the primary special agent to illustrate the "Report on Indians Taxed and Indians Not Taxed," along with Peter Moran, Gilbert Gaul, Walter Shirlaw, and Henry R Poore. He worked three years on the Kiowa, Comanche, Wichita, and other Oklahoma Indians, the Pueblos of New Mexico and Arizona, and the Navahos. Three quarters of the illustrations in the report were by Scott, including portraits of a Shoshone chief and a Pueblo maiden and *Issue Day* at the Oklahoma agency. Some of the original portraits are in the U of Pennsylvania MA. Scott also illustrated "The Song of the Ancient People," interpreting Moqui-Zuni thought. In "Indians Taxed," he had written the textual material on the Moqui Pueblos in Arizona.

SCOTT, Julian. Born Johnson, Vt 1846, died Plainfield, NJ 1901. Important Western artist-correspondent for "Indians Taxed," military and portrait painter, illustrator. ANA 1870 (or 1871). Work in U Penn MA, Div of Ethnology (Smithsonian), State House (Vt), Union League Club (NYC). References A03 (obit) - BEN - CHA - FIE - MAL - SMI. Sources AIW - BOA - HUT - NA 74-NJA-POW-WHO 99. Oil 12×18" *Civil War Encampment* dated 1874 sold Oct 1970 for $900 at auction. Signature example SPB 5/22/73 LA.

Scott at 15 enlisted in the Third Vermont Regiment as a Civil War musician. The first recipient of the Congressional Medal of Honor for battlefield bravery, he was appointed to the staff of Gen "Baldy" Smith, becoming a colonel. Wounded, he amused himself by sketching on the hospital walls. A NY merchant became his patron, arranging studies at the NAD 1863–64, with Leutze until 1868, and a visit to Paris in 1866. He had opened his studio in NYC in 1864, successfully selling Civil War

SCRIVER, Robert Macfie. Born Browning, Mont 1914, living there 1976. Traditional Western sculptor specializing in animals. Member CAA, NSS, Nat Acad of Western Art. Work in Glenbow Fnd (Calgary), Whitney Gal Western Art (Cody), Mont Hist Soc (Helena), Cowboy Hall of Fame (Okla City), Panhandle Plains Mus (Canyon, Tex). Reference A76. Sources COW-C71 to 74-EIT-MON-OSR-PER vol 3 ⅗3-WAI 71. No current auction record. Sculpture example C74.

Scriver, whose father owned the Browning Mercantile Company, taught music until 1951 when he earned his master's degree at Vandercook School of Music. Dissatisfied although listed in "Who's Who in Music," he became a taxidermist, sculpting his own mounts. In 1956 he established his own Museum of Montana Wildlife including a gallery for his clay sculpture and dioramas. In 1962 he had his work cast in bronze for exhibition nationally and in Europe.

In 1967 he discontinued taxidermy for full-time sculpture. His influence is Malvina Hoffman. Like her, he familiarized himself with the casting process. His Bighorn Foundry now follows the cire perdue process. Commissions have involved heroic bison and cowboy figures. Scriver has remained in Browning near the Glacier National Park: "All my friends are either cowboys or Indians. I don't know about any other kind of people." OSR.

SEARS, Philip Shelton. Born Boston, Mass 1867, died Brookline, Mass 1953. Boston sculptor of busts, memorials, statues. Member NSS. Work in White House, BMFA, St House (Boston), Am Ind Mus (Harvard), Indian Statue (Harvard, Mass). References A53-BEN-FIE-MAL-SMI. Sources AAT-WHO 50. No auction record. Sculpture example p 227 AAT *Pumanangwet* (*He Who Shoots the Stars*).

Sears practiced law in Boston 1892–98 after graduating from Harvard Law School. Beginning 1919 he worked as a sculptor. He studied at the BMFA School and with Daniel Chester French.

SEAVEY, Julian Ruggles. Born Canada (or Boston, Mass) 1857, died Hamilton, Ont, Can 1940. Canadian painter, illustrator, teacher. Work in NGC. Reference MAS. Sources CAE-KEN-STI. No current auction record but the estimated price of a Western landscape would be $800 to $900 at auction in 1976. Signature example p 30 KEN 6/71.

Seavey studied in Paris, Rome, and Germany before settling in Hamilton in 1884. He soon went to London, Ont to be Art Director of Hellmuth Ladies College, and then Alma College in St Thomas. He returned to Hamilton in 1908 where he continued in art education.

Early works by Seavey were mainly trompe l'oeil and landscapes. Later he did historical and book illustrations and flower studies.

Seavey traveled in the American Northwest. KEN illustrates a historical painting of Bridger's Pass in Wyoming before the building of the Union Pacific railroad.

SEDGWICK, Francis (or Frances) Minturn. Born NYC 1904, living Santa Ynez Valley, Cal 1968. Sculptor of Western monuments, museum official. Works in Colma, Cal (*Pioneer Monument*), others in England, San Francisco, Washington. Reference A66. Source COW. No current auction record or signature example.

Sedgwick was educated at Harvard U and at Trinity College (Cambridge U). He was Vice President of the Museum of Art in Santa Barbara, Cal where his heroic statue of a cowboy is at the Earl Warren Showgrounds.

SEFFEL, E A, Jr. Trompe l'oeil painter in California 1895. No reference. Source, p 483 ANT 6/55 showing an oil 20×30″ signed and dated *Pleasure and Chance* with a pistol above playing cards, dice and a cup, liquor and a glass, cigarettes and matches, currency and coins, pipe and tobacco. DBW lists the same titled oil painting as ⚡87. No current auction record. Signature example ANT.

SELLS, C H. No biographical data as an artist. One painting signed by Sells is on a patent stretcher dated 1888. (See illustration 268.)

Possibly Cato (Hedden) Sells born

Vinton, Iowa about 1864, an Iowa lawyer and politician who moved to Cleburne, Tex in 1907 and was appointed by Pres Wilson as Commissioner Indian Affairs, 1913–21. Scenes of Sells' paintings are Southwest Indian genre.

SELTZER, Olaf Carl. Born Copenhagen, Denmark 1877 (or 1881), died Great Falls, Mont 1957. Important traditional Russell-school Western painter, illustrator, miniaturist. Work in GIL (234 paintings), ACM, collns of Harmsen, Eiteljorg-Stenzel, Masonic Lib (Helena). No reference. Sources ANT 5/61, 12/62, 12/64, 6/69, 8,11/74; 1/75-COW-CUS-DCC-GIL-HAR-JNB-PNW-WAI 71,72-WNW. Oil 20×30″ *Buffalo Herd and Wolves* signed but not dated sold 10/23/73 for $17,000 at auction. Signature examples GIL. (See illustration 269.)

When he was 12 Seltzer studied sketching at the Danish Art School and Polytechnic Institute in Copenhagen. When Seltzer was 14 he emigrated to Great Falls, Mont with his mother. Seltzer worked briefly as a cowboy. He was hired as an apprentice machinist for the Great Northern Railroad, then as a locomotive repairman. In his spare time Seltzer made sketches in ink. At 20 he began to paint in oil, encouraged by a Canadian patron. His style was similar to his neighbor Charles Russell, who had encouraged him and who painted with him on trips.

At 44 Seltzer became a full-time painter when he was laid off by the railroad. He was immediately successful as a Russell disciple, going to NYC in 1926 to complete some of Russell's commissions. In 1930 he was engaged by a wealthy patron, Dr Philip Cole, to paint a series of miniatures on Montana history. After 100 works painted under a magnifying glass, his sight weakened so that thereafter he could paint only in bright light. Nevertheless he completed over 2,500 paintings. Ranked as an important Western painter today, in his lifetime Seltzer appeared colorless under the shadow of the personality of Charles Russell.

SETON, Ernest Thompson. Born Ernest Thompson ("Seton" was adopted) in South Shields, Eng 1860, died near Santa Fe, NM 1946. Animal painter, illustrator, sculptor, writer. Member NIAL. Work in MNM. References A47 (obit)-BEN-FIE-MAL-SMI. Sources ILP-MSL-POW-WHO 46. No current auction record or signature example.

As a child Seton lived in the Canadian wilderness from 1866 to 1870. He studied at Toronto Collegiate Institute and at the Royal Academy in London, then traveled on the American plains from 1882 to 1886. As official naturalist he wrote and illustrated "Mammals of Manitoba" in 1886 and "Birds of Manitoba" in 1891, beginning an impressive list of animal and Western books including "Wild Animals I Have Known" in 1898, "The Birchbark Roll" in 1906, "Indian Lore" in 1912, "Woodcraft Indians" in 1915, "Gospel of the Red Man" in 1936.

From 1890 to 1896 Seton had studied art in Paris, the pupil of Bouguereau and Gérôme. He was an illustrator of the Century Dictionary, delivered over 3,000 lectures on Indians and woodcraft, and was Chief Scout of the Boy Scouts until 1915. He also founded the College of Indian Wisdom on 2,500 acres near Santa Fe, for conservation of Indian lore and crafts.

SEWARD, Coy Avon. Born Chase, Kan 1884, died probably Wichita, Kan 1939. Lithographic artist, watercolorist, printmaker on Wichita history, writer. Work in Lib Cong, AIC, RI Sch of Des, Bibliot

Nat (Paris), Cal St Lib, etc. References A41-FIE-MAL. Source WHO 38. No auction record or signature example.

After being educated at Chase high school, Seward studied at Washburn College and Bethany College (both Kan) and was the pupil of Reid, Stone, and Sandzén. He was with Western Lithograph Co in Wichita. His listed works included *Wichita in 1869* and he exhibited watercolors at the PAFA in 1925. His writings were on printmaking.

SEWELL, Amos. Born San Francisco, Cal 1901, living Westport, Conn 1975. Illustrator specializing in rural subjects including the frontier. Member SI. Work in *Sat Eve Post,* etc. Reference A70. Sources ILA-POI. No auction record. Signature example p 40 POI. (See illustration 270.)

Sewell worked in a San Franciso bank while studying nights at the California School of Fine Arts. He moved to NYC by working on a lumber boat via the Panama Canal. Further study was with Guy Pène du Bois, Harvey Dunn, and Julian Levi at the ASL and the Grand Central School of Art. Sewell began as a dry-brush illustrator for the pulp magazines.

In 1937 Sewell received his first slick magazine assignment, from *Country Gentleman.* Later work was for covers for *The Saturday Evening Post,* for textbooks, and for advertising illustrations. POI shows Sewell's technique in charcoal, where he worked large and achieved textures by rubbing in some areas while leaving others granular.

SEYMOUR, Samuel. Born England about 1775, active 1796–1823 Philadelphia, living in NYC 1823 and perhaps also in the West. Landscape and portrait painter, engraver, in the West 1820. Work in Beinecke Lib (Yale), NY Pub Lib. References BEN-FIE-G&W-MAL-SMI. Sources AIW-ANT 2/45-AOW-AWM-COW-FRO-150-KW1-MIS-PAF-POW-SPR-WES-WHI. No auction record. Monogram example p 39 AOW, sepia field sketch of Indians 1820.

An important engraver of the day, Seymour was the first official painter for a Western exploration, the Long expedition to the Rocky Mtns in 1819. His duties were to "furnish sketches of landscapes of grandeur, to paint miniature likenesses of distinguished Indians and groups of savages." The expedition left Pittsburgh in April 1819, traveling by river boat to St Louis, up the Missouri to the Yellowstone, then overland. Seymour made the first field drawing of a Plains Indian dance group, the first painting of the interior of a Plains lodge, and on June 30, 1820 the first painting of the Rockies and Longs Peak. In July 1820 Seymour sketched the headwaters of the Platte River. Seymour returned home via New Orleans with Maj Long and Titian Ramsay Peale, the expedition's young naturalist.

The published account of the Long expedition was illustrated by Seymour and Titian Peale. Seymour had made 150 landscape views of which 60 were finished and 11 were published. Some of the paintings were displayed at Peale's Museum in 1832 and may have been sold at auction in 1854. Other Seymour pictures are attributed to a second Long expedition in 1823 to the upper Mississippi. Though Seymour was the first artist in the Rockies, his work is not widely known because so few pieces have survived and the ones that have are delicate drawings rather than bold portraits of Indians.

SHADBOLT, Jack Leonard. Born Shoeburyness, Essex, Eng 1909, living

Vancouver, BC, Can 1976. Modern Vancouver painter, teacher, writer. Work in AG Toronto, NGC, Montreal MFA, Seattle AM, Vancouver AG; murals in Can public buildings. Reference A76. Sources CAH-CAN-CAR. No current auction record. Painting example plate 127 CAR. (See illustration 271.)

Shadbolt was brought to Vancouver at the age of 3 and in 1934 studied with Varley. In 1936 he studied in London at Euston Rd Group, the pupil of Victor Pasmore and William Coldstream, in Paris with André Lhote, and in 1947 in NYC at the ASL. As a young man living in British Columbia, he was influenced by Emily Carr. He became head of drawing and painting at the Vancouver School of Art and a writer of articles on contemporary Canadian art. In 1956–57 he painted in France. His earlier style was "forceful" and "animistic." By 1960 he remained concerned with nature, but in a "more festive" manner. CAR.

Shadbolt's "strong work" began in 1948 with surrealistic images based on northwest-coast Indian themes, in dark, earthy tones. CAH. After 1957 his colors became more vivid, with subjects taken from landscape experiences.

SHAPLEIGH, Frank Henry. Born Boston, Mass 1842, died Jackson, NH 1906. Eastern landscape painter, the "painter of places." Work in private collections. References A03 (A05 lists Sharp's data for Shapleigh)-BEN-CHA-FIE-MAL-SMI. Sources ANT 10/52; 11/61 (bio); 6,8 (article)/66; 11/67; 7,12/69; 5/70; 11/73; 1,3/74; 2/75 - HUT - WHO 06. Oil 22×36" *View of a Town* dated 1878 sold 8/7/73 for $1,500 at auction in Massachusetts. Oil 22×36" *Mt Washington* sold 1/28/70 for $350 in NYC. Signature example p 776 ANT 6/66.

Educated in Boston public schools, Frank Shapleigh studied at Old Lowell Inst Drawing School. He was a nine-month volunteer with the 45th Mass Regiment, in the North Carolina campaign of the Civil War until 1863. Mustered out, he established his studio in Boston as a portrait painter. To develop his interest in landscape painting under the Barbizon influence then popular in Boston, he went to Paris in 1866. The pupil of Lambinet, he returned to Boston in 1869 after sketching trips in Switzerland and Italy. His work involved mainly New England scenes, although he traveled from Maine to Florida and Cape Cod to California. He dated and placed each canvas. He went to the White Mountains in New Hampshire on his honeymoon in 1873, opening his summer studio there in 1876. Many of his New Hampshire paintings were on commission for the tourist trade, hastily done and showing mountain passes like the West. Shapleigh's winter studio was in St Augustine, Fla after 1886. Again, he provided the tourists with paintings of the scenery along the routes they took.

Shapleigh was an early visitor to the Rockies and beyond. "His studies of the Yosemite Valley were especially popular in Boston." ANT 11/61. A man satisfied with his abilities and his world, he preferred Corot to the new impressionists when in Paris in 1894. He stopped painting 1895.

SHARER, William E. Born New Mexico date unknown, living Santa Fe, NM 1975. Painter. Member Nat Acad of Western Art. No reference. Source PER vol 3 ⅗3. No auction record or signature example. Painting example p 60, PER vol 3 ⅗3.

Sharer spent his childhood in Roswell, NM and following a tour of duty in the Marines, enrolled in American Academy of Art in Chicago. He studied under William H Mosby and Joseph Vanderbrouck. He returned to the West, first to Colorado, then to Taos, NM, then finally to Santa Fe where he built his studio. He won the Stacey Scholarship Award in 1971 and has been awarded exhibition prizes.

SHARP, Joseph Henry. Born Bridgeport, Ohio 1859, died Pasadena, Cal 1953. Very important Taos painter specializing in Indian portraits, illustrator, teacher, "the father of the Taos art colony." Member Taos SA. Work in ACM, Wyom St AG, Bradford Brinton Mem (Big Horn), ANS, MNM, Cincinnati AM, U of Cal, Smithsonian Inst, Houston MFA, Woolaroc Mus (Bartlesville, Okla). References A47-BEN-FIE-MAL-SMI. Sources AAR 1,3,11/74-AIW-AMA-ANT 11/55, 12/56, 11/58, 4/68, 11/72; 3,6/74-COW-CRS-DCC-GIL-HAR-HMA-150-PAW-PIT-PNW-POW-TAL-TSF-TWR-WAI 71,72-WHO 50-WNW. Oil 23¼×29¾" *Indian Encampment* signed but not dated sold 4/11/73 for $8,500 at auction. The estimated price of a pastel and gouache 10½×15½" *Indian Encampment* with signature example but not dated was $8,000 to $10,000 for auction 3/4/74, and sold for $8,500. (See illustration 272.)

Sharp was educated in public schools in Ironton and Cincinnati, Ohio, where he was raised, "interested in Indians before becoming an artist." At 14, deaf from an accident, he left public school to study art at McMicken School of Design and later at the Cincinnati Art Academy. He had a studio in the same building as Farny, who first "made me feel I didn't exactly have a right to paint Indians," then "gave me books on Pueblo Indians." At 22 he studied for a year with Charles Verlat in Antwerp. At 24 he made a sketching trip to Santa Fe, California, and the Columbia River, sketching the Indian tribes in 1883 to record the disappearing cultures. At 27 he returned to Europe to study with Karl Marr in Munich in 1886 and to accompany the Cincinnati master Duveneck to Italy and Spain. From 1892 to 1902 he taught life classes at the Cincinnati Art Academy.

In 1893 Sharp made his first visit to Taos. His sketch and commentary *The Harvest Dance of the Pueblo Indians* was published in *Harper's Weekly*. In 1895–96 he was at the Julien Academy in Paris, studying with Laurens and Constant, meeting Phillips and Blumenschein, influencing them toward Taos. Beginning about 1900 Sharp used his summers to sketch Indians as a "latter-day George Catlin," completing the paintings in the winters. In 1901 the government commissioned him to build a studio and cabin at the foot of the Custer battlefield in Montana. Sharp painted about 200 of the Indians who battled Custer. A collection of 80 of his Indian paintings was bought for the U of California, with a commission for 15 more each year for five years. These works are part of the anthropology department, illustrating the objectivity of Sharp's view of the Indians and his respect for scientific accuracy. Sharp had become a permanent resident in Taos, NM in 1912.

SHARP, Louis Hovey. Born probably Illinois 1875, died Los Angeles Cnty, Cal 1946. Western landscape painter. Work in ANS. No reference. Source SCA. Oil 36×51" *Inner Gorge, from Plateau, Grand Canyon* signed and dated '24, estimated 10/28/74 at $2,000 to $2,500 for auction in Los Angeles but did not sell. Signature example *Inner Gorge* above. (See illustration 273.)

Sharp studied at the AIC and sketched on the Hopi Reservation in Arizona. In 1914 he settled in Pasadena with his Russian wife. For the next 15 years he painted in California, at the Grand Canyon, and in Taos, NM. Sharp moved to the Austrian Tyrol in 1929.

SHAW, Joshua. Born Bellingborough, Lincolnshire, Eng 1776 (or, about 1777), died Burlington, NJ 1860. English romantic landscape painter who emigrated to US in 1817, engraver's artist, writer, inventor. Work in MMA, BMFA, Victoria and Albert Mus. References BEN - FIE - G&W - MAL - SMI. Sources ALA-ANT 7/64,8/70-BAR-HUD-KAR-M15-M19-NJA-PAF-WHI. Oil 27½×44" *Sunset on the Mohawk* sold 4/19/72 for $2,500 at auction. Signature example ⊁64 M19.

Shaw was a sign painter in Manchester, England while studying art. He established himself as a landscape painter in Bath from 1802 to 1817, exhibiting in London at the Royal Academy and the British Institution. He was considered in the school of Gainsborough and 18th-century France.

Shaw came to the US when American landscape art was achieving importance. Competent engravers made reproductions available to many. "A conceited English blockhead" the American painter-critic Dunlap called Shaw when they met while Shaw was sketching in the South and soliciting orders for his 1819 series of etchings, "Picturesque Views of American Scenery." As Shaw's English work was considered derivative, so were his engraved views regularly copied by American amateurs. Shaw traveled through all of the states, making watercolors and drawings of the popular views, including Indians and the frontier. His studio was in Philadelphia from 1817 to 1843 when he moved to Bordentown, NJ. His painting ended in 1853 when he was paralyzed. He later had received large payments from the American and Russian governments for inventions concerning naval guns.

SHAW, Stephen William. Born Windsor, Vt 1817, died San Francisco, Cal 1900. Pioneer painter of West Coast portraits, teacher. References A98-BEN-FIE-G&W-MAL. Sources ANT 7/46-COS-POW. No recent auction record or signature example.

Shaw was self-taught as a portrait painter. He became the director and an instructor at the Boston Athenaeum before moving to California in 1849 via New Orleans and Panama. Beginning in 1850 in San Francisco, he painted more than 200 portraits of Masonic officers alone. He also took part in the New Guinea expedition that discovered Humboldt Bay. He is recorded as the lithographic artist for Kuchel & Dresel of *Lachryma Montis. Residence of General M G Vallejo, near Sonoma, California,* not dated but about 1857.

SHAW, Sydney Dale. Born Walkley, Eng 1879, died probably Pasadena, Cal 1946. NY and Cal painter, principally landscapes (including the West) and street scenes. Work in ARM. References A41-BEN-FIE-MAL-SMI. Sources ACM-ARM-SCA-WHO 28. No current auction record but a published estimate is $600 to $800. No signature example.

Shaw was brought to the US in 1892. He studied at the ASL and in Paris at Colarossi Academy and École des Beaux-Arts. In 1913 Shaw exhibited at the most important Armory Show. His three paintings were *California, Southwestern Country,* and *Topanza.*

SHEBL, Joseph J. Born Crete, Neb 1913, living Salinas, Cal 1968. Traditional Western sculptor in bronze of historical subjects, particularly concerning animals. No reference. Sources AHI 3/72-COW. No current auction record. Signature example p 174 COW.

Shebl is a medical doctor and radiologist.

SHEETS, Millard Owen. Born Pomona, Cal 1907, living Gualala, Cal 1976. Modern Cal painter, illustrator, muralist, designer, teacher. NA 1947 as watercolorist. Work in more than 70 museums: MMA, AIC, LAMA, the White House, etc. References A76-BEN-MAL. Sources AAT - ARI - CAA - CON - COW-MCA-WHO 70. Watercolor *Old Mission, Mexico* estimated at $350 to $450 for auction 5/27/74 in Los Angeles, and sold for $375. In 1950, *Tropical Squall* was offered at $1,200. M50. Signature example pl 8 M50.

Millard Sheets studied at the Chouinard AI in Los Angeles 1925–29, the pupil of F T Chamberlain and Clarence Hinkle. He began teaching at Chouinard AI in 1929. Since then, he has taught in 16 schools and has traveled in Europe, Central America, and Mexico. His first one-man exhibition was in 1929, while he was still in Chouinard. In WWII he was *Life* correspondent in the Burma-India theater. Sheets has also done the architectural design for many buildings, executed murals in public buildings, illustrated for national magazines, handled production design for Columbia Pictures, and headed the art department at Scripps College. " 'Day is here!' his pictures cry, 'with life, color, and beauty.' " CON. "Cubism and the Impressionists have been synchronized here." ARI.

SHEETS, Nan Jane (Mrs Fred C Sheets). Born Albany, Ill 1885, living Oklahoma City, Okla 1976. Okla landscape painter, printmaker, writer, museum director. Work in Okla AC, U Okla AM, Philbrook AC, Cowboy Hall of Fame. References A76-BEN-FIE-MAL. Sources AAT-WAA. No current auction record. Painting example p 147 AAT oil *Church at Talpa, NM*.

Nan Sheets studied at Valparaiso U, U

of Utah, and Broadmoor AA, with J F Carlson, Robert Reid, E L Warner, Sandzén, H H Breckenridge. She wrote a weekly newspaper column from 1934 to 1962, directed the Fed Art Program in Oklahoma 1935–42, and was director of Oklahoma Art Center 1935–65.

SHELDON-WILLIAMS, Inglis. Born Elvetham, Surrey, Eng 1870, died Tunbridge Wells, Eng 1940. Canadian genre painter, English Special Artist-illustrator, portrait and landscape painter, author. Work in U of Saskatchewan, Regina Pub Lib Art Gal (Canada), Glenbow Fnd (Calgary). Reference MAL. Sources AOH-CAH. No current auction record but the estimated price of a gouache 7×10″ showing an Alberta cowboy roping would be about $700 to $900 at auction in 1976. Signature example p 175 AOH.

Sheldon-Williams was of the impoverished smaller English gentry, a family of struggling painters. At 13 he was in Merchant Taylor's public school, and at 17 his mother shipped him to Canada to find a place for the family. He arrived at Cannington Manor in southeast Saskatchewan, a self-contained English colony of gentlemen farmers where he filed for a homestead. To gain funds he worked as a ranch hand in Alberta during the summer of 1887, built his cabin at the Manor during the winter, and was ready when his family emigrated in 1888. When his mother died in 1890 he returned to England to take art lessons.

While in Canada he had made drawings and watercolors of prairie life that were published in England in the *Daily Graphic* beginning in 1890. He became an art student at the Slade School in London in 1896. In 1899 he started as Special Artist for the *Sphere,* and after 1904 made extended visits to Canada during which he painted Indian and ranch scenes. He taught at Regina College 1913–17. He outlived all the other Specials.

SHEPHERD, J Clinton. Born Des Moines, Iowa 1888, living Palm Beach, Fla 1962. Traditional Western painter, illustrator, sculptor of Western life and animals, lecturer. Member NSS. Work in John Herron AI. References A62-BEN-FIE-MAL. Sources AAC-ANT 9/44, 9/45, 10/62 - JNB - NSS. Oil 23¾ × 29½" *Moving Day on the Reservation* signed but not dated sold 5/23/72 for $400 at auction in Los Angeles. Signature example ⚒49 JNB.

Shepherd studied at the U of Missouri, at the Kansas City SFA, at the AIC, and with Harvey Dunn and Walter Ufer. At the NSS exhibit in 1923 he showed bronzes *The Broncho Twister, The Cayuse, The Maverick, The Night Herd.* In 1924 he was listed as a magazine illustrator living in NYC. AAC.

SHEPPARD, William Ludwell. Born Richmond, Va 1833, died there 1912. Illustrator including Western scenes redrawn for *Scribner's,* painter, sculptor, teacher. Work in Confederate Mus (Richmond), Valentine Mus (Richmond), St Capitol Bldg (Richmond); monument and statue in Richmond. References A13 (obit)-BEN-G&W-MAL-SMI. Sources AIW (as W L Snyder)-ANT 1/73-AOA-BAR-CIV-KW2-*Scribner's Monthly* p 280 July '73. No current auction record. Signature example p 161 ANT 1/73.

After having been educated in Richmond, W L Sheppard worked in art as a hobby until attention came to him through tobacco labels he had designed. He then studied art in NYC and Paris until the Civil War when he enlisted as an officer in the Richmond Howitzers. During the war Sheppard made sketches of Confederate military life which he later refined to "sensitive watercolors" quoting ANT or "pitiful in their technical inadequacy." BAR

Between 1867 and 1890 his drawings featuring Southern genre and Virginia landscapes were in *Harper's, Leslie's,* and others. In 1873 J Wells Champney (AIW p 314 as T Willis Champney) sketched in the Southwest for *Scribner's,* and the illustrations were redrawn by Sheppard (ascribed in AIW to W L Snyder) probably in NYC. The redrawings included *Kansas Herdsman, Indian Grave, A South-Western Ferry, A Creek Indian Woman, A School Among the Creeks,* and *Indian Ball-Player.* Sheppard also illustrated books such as "Dombey and Son" by Dickens in 1873 and parts of "Picturesque America" 1872–74. He studied again 1877–78 in London and Paris, the pupil of Paul Soyer. While in London he copied for the state of Virginia a series of portraits of Englishmen involved in Virginia history.

SHERMAN, Lenore Walton. Born NYC 1920, living San Diego, Cal 1976. Traditional Western painter, lecturer. Work in San Diego Law Lib. Reference A76. Source COW. No current auction record. Signature example p 116 COW.

L Sherman worked as a ventriloquist and comedienne before studying painting about 1950. She was the pupil of Leon Franks, Hayward Veal (English impressionist), Orrin A White, Sergei Bongart, J C Wright (watercolor), Ejnar Hansen (portraiture). She has also taught in California.

SHIRLAW, Walter. Born Paisley, Scotland 1838, died Madrid, Spain 1909.

Important artist-correspondent for "Indians Taxed," painter of genre and portraits, illustrator, muralist, engraver. ANA 1887, NA 1888, a founder of SAA 1877. Work in Lib Cong (ceiling), museums in St Louis, Buffalo, Chicago, Washington, and Indianapolis. References A10 (obit)-BEN-CHA-DAB-FIE-G&W-MAL-SMI. Sources AIW-ALA-ISH-M57-MSL-NA 74-PAF-POW-STI-TAW-TEP-WHO 08. Oil 10×20″ *Mediterranean Street* sold 1971 for $400 at auction. Charcoal on tan paper 20¾ × 14½″ *A Ride to Death Sweeping the Plain like a Whirlwind* estimated for sale 10/28/74 at $1,500 to $1,800 for auction in LA, and sold for $800. Signature example p 69 TAW.

Shirlaw was raised in NYC. At 12 he left school to work as a mapmaker in a real estate office. When he was 15 he was apprenticed for five years to a bank-note engraver. He then became a painter but was forced to return to engraving. He worked in Chicago until 1870 when he was able to go to Munich. For seven years he was the pupil of Raab, Wagner, Von Ramberg, and Lindenschmit, studying and painting. His masterpiece *Toning the Bell* was painted in Munich before being exhibited at the Philadelphia Centennial and World's Columbian Exposition. He traveled widely, taught at the ASL, made charcoal illustrations for *Century* and *Harper's Monthly,* "was a master designer, a serious and weighty painter, an influential teacher, a man of culture and intelligence, and his success was fairly commensurate with his merits." DAB.

While working as an engraver in Chicago, he spent six months sketching in the Rockies in 1869. In 1890 he was one of five special artists sent to take the census among the Indians. The report included his text on the Northern Cheyennes and the Crow agency as well as two color reproductions *The Race—Crow Indians* and *Omaha Dance.* "In these paintings, almost impressionistic in design, Shirlaw has recorded aspects on Indian life against the sweep and color of the vast Montana plains and hills." AIW. In *Century* in 1893, Shirlaw wrote and illustrated *The Rush to Death* of an Indian warrior.

SHONNARD, Eugenie Frederica. Born Yonkers, NY 1886, living Santa Fe, NM 1976. Realist Santa Fe sculptor, craftsman. Member NSS. Work in MMA, Cleveland MA, Colo Spr FAC, Brookgreen Gardens (SC), Luxembourg Mus (Paris), MNM. References A76-FIE-MAL-SMI. Sources AAT-PET-SCU-TSF. Italian obsidian 18″ high *Little Confidence* sold 9/13/72 for $90 at auction. This is not representative of price that would obtain for a mature sculpture of an Indian head. Sculpture example p 228 AAT *Pueblo Indian Woman.*

Eugenie Shonnard studied at the NY School of Applied Design for Women under Alphonse Mucha, at the ASL with James Earle Fraser, and in Paris where she received criticism from Rodin and Bourdelle. She was a frequent exhibitor in Paris 1912–23, including a one-artist exhibition in 1926.

Because there were few sculptors in New Mexico, Dr Edgar Hewett of the School of American Research invited her to Santa Fe in 1927. Her special subjects became the Pueblo Indians. In 1933 her work was exhibited at MOMA in NYC with other New Mexico artists, as it was at the NY World's Fair in 1939. She was also a painter, has carved doors, and has designed ironwork.

SHOPE, Irvin "Shorty." Born Boulder, Mont 1900, living Helena, Mont 1976. Traditional Western painter, illustrator, muralist. Member CAA from 1965. Murals in banks and public buildings. References A76-MAS. Sources COW-C71 to

74-HAR-MON-WAI 71-WNW. No current auction record. Signature example C71.

Shope was raised on his family's Circle Arrow Ranch, suffering polio at 9. He moved to Missoula at 13, after his father died. While being educated in the high school, he came under the influence of the painter Paxson. At 19 he went to work as a Montana cowboy, riding the range intermittently until he was 30. In 1924 he had taken a correspondence course in art, but Charles Russell recommended that he stay out West rather than study in NYC. In 1925–26 he exhibited locally and received some commercial assignments. In 1928 Will James got him an illustrating commission. He sold his first major oil for $350 in 1930.

Returning to college in 1931, Shope earned his degree in 1933, majoring in art and history. He moved to Helena in 1935, as a commercial artist for the state. That year he spent three months in NYC as the pupil of Harvey Dunn at the Grand Central School of Art. In 1942 Shope began easel painting on a half-time basis, and in 1946 full time, using Paxson's easel he had obtained while a student. His Blackfoot Indian paintings led to his given name, Moquea Stumik or Man-About-Size-of-Wolf-with-Heart-Big-as-Buffalo-Bull. While his work is now interpreting history, "The West is still the West, in spots, and I like it." MON.

SHRADER, Edwin Roscoe. Born Quincy, Ill 1879, died Los Angeles, Cal 1960. Illustrator for magazines and books including historical Indian subjects, landscape and figure painter, teacher. Work in Los Angeles Mus, Cal schools. References A41-FIE-MAL-SMI. Source WHO 50. No auction record. Signature example, plate *Henry Hudson* vol VIII "The Home University Bookshelf," The University Society 1927.

E Roscoe Shrader studied at the AIC and became a scholarship pupil of Howard Pyle in Wilmington. His *Henry Hudson* plate above is signed R Shrader and dated 1908, depicting the Indian presentation of handicrafts and furs. Shrader moved to California where he was known as a painter and as the director of Otis Art Institute in Los Angeles.

SHRADY, Henry Merwin. Born NYC 1871, died there 1922. Sculptor of bronzes and monuments including buffaloes and Indians. Member NSS 1902, ANA 1909, NIAL. Work, Grant Memorial in Washington and statues in Detroit, Duluth, NYC, Charlottesville, Cowboy Hall of Fame. References A22 (obit)-BEN-DAB-FIE-MAL-SMI. Sources AMA-ANT 11/52-GIL-MSL-NA 74-NSS-SCU-WHO 20. Bronze with dark patina 13½" high *Buffalo Bull* signed and dated 1899 sold 4/20/72 for $3,250 at auction. Bronze, dark patina 23" high *Elk Buffalo* signed and dated 1900 was estimated at $14,000 to $18,000 for sale 10/31/75, and sold at $24,000. Signature examples p 229 NSS and p 206 GIL. (See illustration 274.)

Son of a surgeon, H M Shrady was prevented by illness from practicing the law he studied at Columbia up to 1895. The match business he entered failed in 1900. The same year, at 29, he began sketching and painting. His first untutored painting was exhibited by the NAD and sold. The sculptor Karl Bitter observed him sketching at the zoo and offered him studio space. His small animal bronzes sold commercially and led him to be commissioned the following year, 1901, to sculpt for $50,000 an equestrian statue of Washington for the Williamsburg Bridge in NYC. Also in 1901, bronzes of a moose and a buffalo were exhibited at the Pan-American Exposition and he sculpted a panel of Indians for a monument.

In 1902 he was awarded the $250,000 commission for his life work, the Grant Memorial in Washington. Shrady spent the last 20 years of his life modeling this cavalry charge on a 252′ marble platform. When asked how he could become such a success overnight though untrained, it was said, "As the son of a noted surgeon, he easily assimilated the truth of anatomy." AMA. "It is believed that the Grant Monument commission was awarded to the unknown Shrady amid much politicking to prevent Niehaus from getting it." SCU.

SHURTLEFF, Roswell Morse. Born Rindge, NH 1838, died NYC 1915. NYC book and magazine illustrator, Eastern forest landscape painter. ANA 1881, NA 1890. Work in COR, MMA, Springfield Mus (Mass), NGA. References A15 (obit)-BEN-CHA-DAB-FIE-G&W-MAL-SMI. Sources BEY-COR-HUT-ISH-M31-NA 74-WHO 14. Oil 17×27″ *Autumn Landscape* signed and dated '86 sold 5/22/72 for $225 at auction in Los Angeles. No signature example.

Educated at Dartmouth College, Shurtleff worked in an architect's office in 1857 in New Hampshire, as a lithographer 1858–59 in Buffalo, as a wood engraver's draftsman in Boston in 1859 while studying evenings at Lowell Institute, and as a magazine illustrator in NYC 1860–61 while studying at the NAD. In the Civil War he was the first Federal officer to be wounded and taken prisoner. Released on parole, he returned to NYC to illustrate books and magazines.

While in NYC, Shurtleff made two Western illustrations for BEY, the first a full view of *Climbing Pikes Peak* in 1860 and the second *A Part of Omaha in 1867.* His studio was in Hartford 1869–75 and thereafter in NYC. He began easel paintings in 1870 with animal sub-jects, for example, *"The Wolf at the Door* with the artist just visible within and waiting outside a gaunt wolf evidently at the point of starvation or he would not call at that unpromising abode." HUT. About 1880 Shurtleff turned to forest landscapes with greater success.

SHUSTER, William Howard. Born Philadelphia, Pa 1893, died Albuquerque, NM 1969. Santa Fe modernist painter, graphic artist, illustrator, sculptor. Member Los Cinco Pintores, SIA. Work in MNM, Newark AM, ANS, BM, NY Pub Lib. References A62-FIE-MAL. Sources AAT-AIW-HAR-LOS-PIT-TSF. No current auction record but the estimated price of an oil 20×30″ showing Penitentes would be about $2,000 to $3,000 at auction in 1976. Signature example p 59 TSF. (See illustration 275.)

Will Shuster studied electrical engineering at the Drexel Inst in Philadelphia. During WWI he was injured in a gas attack. On his return he studied with J William Server in Philadelphia but was advised to go West for his health. In 1920 he moved to Santa Fe where he became the pupil of John Sloan in etching as well as in painting. His earnings were supplemented by a disability pension and by ironworking.

In 1921 Los Cinco Pintores was formed under the leadership of Bakos to provide a modernist exhibition group for Santa Fe. Shuster painted in an abstract style in 1922 but then returned to a technique closer to Sloan. He illustrated a frontier biography. He also sculpted, with an example to be found in Carlsbad Caverns National Park.

SIBELL, Muriel Vincent. See Wolle.

SICKLES, Noel Douglas. Born Chillicothe, Ohio 1910 (or 1911), living probably New Canaan, Conn 1966. Illustrator of American historical subjects including Westerns, cartoonist of "Scorchy Smith." Work in *Sat Eve Post, Life, Reader's Digest,* books. References A41-MAS. Sources ILA-IL 60, 63. No auction record. Signature example ✳324 IL 60.

Noel Sickles began as a newspaper artist, developing the syndicated adventure comic strip "Scorchy Smith" where he expanded drawings by showing full light and shade. In WWII he worked for the military in illustrating instruction manuals. After the war Sickles had abandoned his comic strip for advertising and fiction illustrating assignments. His specialty became historical subjects including Westerns.

SIMONS, George. Born Streeter, Ill 1834, died Long Beach, Cal 1917. Painter of Western subjects and portraits, photographer. Work in Council Bluffs Pub Lib (Iowa). References A18 (obit)-G&W-MAL. Source BDW. No auction record or signature example.

A pioneer settler of Council Bluffs in 1853, Simons became one of the earliest artists to work in Nebraska when he was commissioned to sketch scenes in 1854. Included were *Pawnee Indian Village on the Platte River Opposite Fremont in 1854, First Claim Cabin in Neb, The Ill-fated Handcart Expedition Leaving Florence, Neb in 1856.* His typical subjects were steamboat landings, Mormon caravans, Indians, and trading posts. One of his "most meritorious" paintings was *Kit Carson's Last Shot.* A18. Simons moved to California about 1900.

SIMPSON, Wallace. Born Moweaqua, Ill 1880, living Fort Worth, Tex 1935.

Painter of Texas ranch life, newspaper artist. No reference. Source TOB. No auction record or signature example.

Simpson was raised on a Texas Panhandle ranch along the Pease River near Childress. His early sketches were in axle grease on wagon tarpaulins before he left the cowboy life to study with Frank Reaugh. He then worked as a newspaper artist in Oklahoma City, El Paso, and on the *Dallas News* and the *Fort Worth Star-Telegram.* Simpson's studio was in Fort Worth where he specialized in depicting ranch life, particularly longhorns, paint horses, and cowboys at work or on a bucking bronco.

SIMPSON, William. Born Glasgow, Scotland 1823, died London, Eng 1899. The dean of British Special Artist-illustrators, historical painter, journalist. Member Royal Institute 1874. Work in Capetown, Edinburgh, Glasgow, Victoria and Albert, Nice museums, Peabody Mus (Harvard). References BEN-MAL. Sources AIW - AOH - FRO - HON - HUT. Pair of drawings 9¾ ×13¾" *Bengal Village* 1864 sold 3/3/70 for $605 at Christie auction. Signature example BEN.

The only formal education Simpson received was for 15 months in a Perth writing school. When he was 12 he entered an architect's office in Glasgow, and at 14 he was apprenticed to Glasgow lithographers where he made architectural sketches for reproduction. In 1851 he became a lithographic artist in London, receiving instant fame for 1855–56 plates of the Russian War. His next seven years were spent on lithographic paintings of India. In 1865 Simpson became Special Artist for ILN, reporting a royal tour of Russia in 1866, Abyssinia in 1868, and Egypt in 1869; the Franco-Prussian War in 1870, and an around the world trip in 1872 that included the marriage of the Emperor of China.

Simpson arrived in California just at

the beginning of the Modoc Indian War in April 1873. He made a topographical drawing of the Lava Beds, a series of drawings of Captain Jack's cave, and an after-the-fact sketch of *The Assassination of Gen Canby by Capt Jack*. Simpson then returned to San Francisco and a week's sketching trip to Yosemite as arranged by Bierstadt. He remained with ILN until 1885. Though self-taught in education and art, Simpson became a fluent linguist and an important correspondent.

SKEELE, Anna Katherine. Born Wellington, Ohio 1896, died Pasadena, Cal 1963. Cal painter including Indian subjects, teacher. Work in San Diego FAS, LAMA, (mural) Torrance HS (Cal). References A62 - MAL. Sources AAT - SCA-WAA. No auction record. Painting example p 148 AAT *Eagle Dance*.

A Katherine Skeele studied at the ASL, the AFA in Florence, and with Lhote in Paris. She was co-owner with her husband Frode Dann of the Pasadena SFA, where she taught through 1959. One of her listed paintings is titled *Taos Pueblo*.

SKELTON, Leslie James. Born Montreal, Can 1848, died Colo Springs, Colo 1929. Rocky Mountain landscape painter, illustrator. Work in NGC, Montreal AA, Colo Col. References A29 (obit) - BEN - FIE - MAL - SMI. Sources SHO-SPR-WHO 28. Oil 12×18″ *Rocky Mountain Landscape* signed but not dated sold 5/22/72 for $180 at auction in Los Angeles. Signature example p 19 SHO.

Skelton was raised in Montreal and educated through high school there. He studied painting in Paris about 1885, the pupil of Iwill who was a landscapist and pastelist. He moved to Colorado Springs

in the 1890s, where some years later he arranged the 1900 art exhibition at the opening of the Colorado College gallery. Beginning 1901 he exhibited his oils and pastels in Paris, London, NYC, and Montreal.

His *Sunrise on the Peak* illustrated in SHO was dated 1899. *Gathering Storm in Estes Park* was color reproduced in *Brush and Pencil* in 1903. He lent 16 paintings of Colorado scenery for reproduction on postal cards. Five million Skelton cards were sold. "Mrs Finley Shepherd some years ago (before 1924) directed that her special train should stop at Colorado Springs, in order that she might visit for half hour at Mr. Skelton's studio. Within that time she had selected several of his paintings, saying, 'I will take that one, and that, and that, and that! I don't know their prices, but please send them to me to my NY address, with bill collect.'" SPR.

SKINNER, Charlotte B (Mrs Wm Lyle Skinner). Born San Francisco, Cal 1879, living Morro Bay, Cal 1941. Cal painter and etcher. Work in Govt colln in Oregon. Reference A41-MAL. Source A41 listing of *North and Middle Sisters of the Cascades*. No auction record or signature example.

C B Skinner studied at the California School of FA and the Mark Hopkins IA, the pupil of A F Mathews and Gottardo Piazzoni.

SKIRVING, John. Active in Philadelphia 1838–41, Boston 1849, Washington 1853, Phila 1858, and Germantown 1861–65. Panoramist, architectural designer, marine painter. Reference G&W. Sources PAF-TEP. No auction record or signature example.

Skirving exhibited at the PAFA, beginning in 1838 with a marine after Bonfield and continuing until 1865 with watercolors of architectural designs. In 1849 he exhibited in Boston *Skirving's Moving Panorama: Col Frémont's Western Expedition, Pictorialized.* He used Frémont's own sketches of scenes on the overland journey to Oregon and California, in addition to published depictions of the West by others.

SLOANE, Eric. Born NYC 1910, living Cornwall Bridge, Conn 1976. Landscape painter in Taos 1925 and 1960, writer, meteorologist. NA 1968. Designer and builder Hall of Atmosphere AMNH; murals for industry. Reference A76. Source WHO 70-"Return to Taos" by Eric Sloane copyright 1960. Oil 24×39" on Masonite *Barns* signed but not dated sold 5/16/73 for $3,750 at auction, Part II the Halpert colln. Signature example ✕45 PB 5/16/73.

Sloane studied at the ASL, at Yale's School of Fine Arts in 1929, and at the NY School of Fine and Applied Art in 1935. He lectured on cloud forms and weather beginning 1940 and wrote books on the same subject beginning 1941. His series of books on Americana, illustrated with his own sketches, began in 1954.

In 1925 Sloane ran away from home in a Model T Ford, earning his way Westward as an itinerant sign painter. In Taos he guided tourists, painted signs, and learned Indian dances, in addition to painting a few scenes on board. In 1960 Sloane returned to Taos, making many sketches for his book which also contains two Western paintings in color.

SLOAN, John. Born Lock Haven, Pa 1871, died Hanover, NH 1951. Very important "Ashcan School" painter, graphic artist, illustrator, teacher, author. Not NA. Work in MMA, MNM, Mint Mus (Charlotte), Parrish AM (Southhampton), Bowdoin Col MFA, GIL, ANS, etc. References A53 (obit)-BEN-FIE-MAL-SMI. Sources AAR 3,5/74-AAT-AIC-AIW-ALA-AMA-ANT 4/55;3,6/61; 2/65,6/67-APT-ARI-ARM-CAA-CAH-CON-COR-DEP-HMA-ILA-190-INS 12/28-ISH-MAP-M31-M50-PIT-STI-TSF-WHO 50. Oil 22×27" *Gray and Brass* signed John Sloan and painted in 1907 sold 5/24/72 for $52,500 at auction (according to Sloan's diary, this painting had been rejected for NAD exhibition in 1907). As an example of a Western painting, oil 15×19½" *Road to Chimayo* signed and painted in 1926 was estimated at $15,000 to $20,000 for sale at auction but the painting did not sell. Signature example p 70 ILA. (See illustration 276.)

As a teenager Sloan worked for a dealer in old-master prints and copied all the illustrations in a dictionary. He studied at Spring Garden Inst in Philadelpia, then in 1892 at the PAFA with Anshutz and Henri whose studio was the social hub for his "black gang," Glackens, Sloan, Luks, and Shinn, the fellow artist-reporters on the *Philadelphia Press.* Sloan sketched news events on the spot, making the record a photograph now provides. Henri encouraged Sloan to paint the sketches, with spontaneity: Henri said Sloan worked so long on his paintings that his name was the past tense of slow. By 1898 Sloan was working for a NYC newspaper. By 1904 all five were in NYC. When the NAD slighted Henri in 1907, they with Davies, Lawson, and Prendergast became The Eight to hold their own exhibit. Sloan did not sell a painting. As a practicing Socialist he ranged the city, particularly Coney Island, Union Square, and the Bowery, to capture slices of life with economy and candor. He was the only member of The Eight who had not studied in Europe but he taught at the ASL 1914–26 and 1935–37. His painting philosophy is set forth in his "Gist of Art" published in 1939.

In 1919 Randall Davey persuaded Sloan to forsake Gloucester, Mass for a summer in Santa Fe. Sloan bought an adobe in 1920 for occupancy most of his remaining summers. In New Mexico, Sloan was a lion, not a radical. His work was warm "but he could never seem to take more than a visiting spectator's viewpoint when painting the Indian." TSF. "Revolutionist of an older order," his style was set. His early paintings were "all memory things," he wrote Henri, painted in the studio because New Mexico light affected his nearsightedness. His importance to Santa Fe art was in his prestige. He exhibited as a New Mexico painter from 1922 with the Taos SA to 1939 at the World's Fair.

SMALLEY, Katherine. Born Waverly, Iowa about 1865, living Colo City, Colo 1924. Colo Springs landscape painter after 1890. No reference. Source SPR. No auction record or signature example.

Miss Smalley studied at the AIC 1884–85, the pupil of Charles Corwin. She assisted in painting the cyclorama *Battle of Gettysburg,* gaining painting advice from O D Grover, the landscapist. In 1888 she moved to Denver to paint oil and pastel portraits. She settled in Colorado Springs in 1889, specializing in watercolor landscapes when portrait commissions were few. Her subjects were views in and around Colorado Springs.

SMEDLEY, William Thomas. Born West Bradford, Chester, Pa 1858, died Bronxville, NY 1920. Illustrator of Western Canada and of NYC wealthy; portrait painter. ANA 1897, NA 1905, member NIAL and SI. Work in Lib Cong (many drawings), MMA, NGA. References A20 (obit)-BEN-CHA-

DAB-FIE-MAL-SMI. Sources AOA-ILA-ISH-NA 74-POW-WHO 18. Grisaille 13×9″ *Awaiting Your Reply* sold 4/15/70 for $160 at auction. Signature example p 35 ILA.

Son of a Quaker miller, W T Smedley left school for a newspaper office at 15. He studied engraving in Philadelphia and painting at the PAFA. At 20 he went to NYC as a magazine draftsman and then to Paris to study with Laurens. He returned to a NYC studio at 22, becoming an important illustrator of social life for the magazines. His medium was pen and ink at first, changing to opaque watercolor for the later halftone engravings. A book of his drawings was published in 1899. Smedley also painted portraits that "were satisfying likenesses, skillfully and pleasingly done in academic style," but his unique contribution was to be "the illustrator and historian of the fashionable life" with "the pretty girls in wonderful toilettes." DAB.

In 1882 Smedley on commission from the publishers of "Picturesque Canada" traveled through the Canadian West for a series of illustrations. He also made sketching tours in the US before traveling around the world in 1890.

SMELLIE, Robert. Scotch landscape painter active 1858–1908. Work in State Hist Soc of Colorado. No reference. Source DCC. No current auction record or signature example.

Smellie, a romantic landscape painter, exhibited in Edinburgh, Scotland from 1858 to 1887 at the Royal Scottish Academy. He visited Denver 1888–89. DCC illustrates a painting of an 1888 political parade.

SMILLIE, George Henry. Born NYC 1840, died Bronxville, NY 1921. Eastern landscape painter who visited the

Rockies and Yosemite in 1871. ANA 1864, NA 1882. Work in MMA, COR, RI School of Design, Oakland MA, Union League Club of Phila. References A21 (obit)-BEN-CHA-DAB-FIE-G&W-MAL-SMI. Sources BAR-BOA-COR-HUT-ISH-KAH-M31-NA 74-PAF-WHO 20. Oil 17¼×26½″ *Vermont Meadows* with signature example and dated Aug '85 sold 9/28/73 for $2,000 at auction (the estimated price had been $800 to $1,000).

Son of the important engraver James Smillie and younger brother of the landscapist James David Smillie, he was educated in private schools. He was the pupil of his father and of James McDougal Hart, an important landscape painter. By the time he was 24 he was an associate member of the National Academy, a successful NY landscape painter continuing the tradition of the Hudson River School after its time had passed. He added a brightness of color and a personal gaiety. In 1881 he married the genre painter Nellie Sheldon Jacobs. They shared a studio with his brother. During his lifetime his paintings sold to the important collectors and then to the major museums.

In 1871 George Smillie "made a trip to the Rocky Mountains and the Yosemite Valley for the purpose of study and sketching." HUT. He painted Western scenes in oils and watercolors for years thereafter, for example, *Sentinel Rock, Yosemite Valley* was in the Centennial Exhibition. In *Under the Pines of the Yosemite,* "Two brown trunks rise 30 feet to the top of the picture. Indians are camping beneath, etc. The work gives us delightful associations with this romantic region." *Atlantic Monthly* 1872.

SMILLIE, James David. Born NYC 1833, died there 1909. Painter of mountain landscapes, illustrator, important engraver, writer. ANA 1868, NA 1876. Work in ACM, COR, BMFA, Oakland MA, NY Pub Lib, reproduced in "Picturesque America." References A09 (obit)-BEN-CHA-DAB-ENB-FIE-G&W-MAL-SMI. Sources AIW-ANT 7/71-BAR-BOA-COR-HUT-ISH-KAH-KW1, 2-MSL-NA 74-PAF-TEP-WHO 08. No current auction record but the estimated price of a Western landscape would be about $2,500 to $3,000 at auction in 1976. Signature example p 90 ANT 7/71.

J D Smillie was the son and pupil of the important engraver James Smillie, and the older brother of the landscape painter George H Smillie. He was educated in private schools and the U of the City of NY. After making his first engraving plate at the age of 8, he collaborated with his father until he was 31. They specialized in bank-note vignettes but also made the engravings for Emory's "Mexican Boundary Survey Report" in 1857, reproducing the Texas sketches of Schott and Weyss. "His etchings, dry points, and aquatints are his most personal contributions to the art of his day." DAB. In addition, he wrote for magazines on etching.

After 1864 he began painting, "without the benefit of schools or masters." HUT. He specialized in landscapes of the American mountain ranges, the Rockies, Sierras, Adirondacks, White, and Catskills, following the Hudson River School techniques. Smillie who traveled widely was in the West at about the same time as his brother, 1871. For vol 1 of "Picturesque America" in 1872 he both wrote and illustrated the section on *The Yosemite,* a long piece of highly professional text with 20 engravings. At the Philadelphia Centennial, he exhibited the watercolor *A Scrub-Race on the Western Prairies.* KAH illustrates *The High Sierra, California* signed by both James and George Smillie.

SMITH, Alfred Aloysius (or Trader Horn, or Alfred Aloysius Horn). Born about 1854, died 1927. No reference. Source BAR-Webster's Biographical Dictionary. No auction record or signature example.

Trader Horn traveled through Texas about 1880, teaching the "rudiments of painting" to the daughters of the rich who would "give their hearts for a picture." BAR, quoting from Smith's autobiography "Trader Horn" (1928) as edited by the English writer Mrs Ethelreda Lewis.

SMITH, Cecil A. Born Salt Lake City, Utah 1910, living Somers, Mont 1976. Montana painter of contemporary Western life, illustrator, sculptor, teacher, rancher. No reference. Sources WNW-March 1975 data from Cecil Smith. No auction record or signature example. (See illustration 277.)

Smith grew up on his family's Idaho cow ranch, the Bar Bell Land and Cattle Co that had been started by his grandfather. He attended Brigham Young U and the U of Utah, with summers spent working as an open range cowboy in the free grass years up to 1935. For his art education, Smith came to NYC to study privately with the expressionists John Carroll, Max Weber, and Kuniyoshi. By 1935 a Smith painting was included in a government collection that toured Europe while Smith had become an owner of his family's 89,000-acre rance. He was not only a working cowboy and a realistic painter, but illustrator for *Sunset Magazine,* and teacher.

In 1960 Smith began devoting himself to painting full time. His subjects are from his own experiences: "Nothing is second handed or done from scrap." In any given painting the components are identifiable, eg, in *Lonesome Land* the landscape is "Salmon River scenery" and "the little bald faced horse is Concho, one of the better horses of my string." Smith is that rare cowboy painter of real-

ism who came East to study art, not with the illustrators or at the ASL with George Bridgman but with the modernists Kenneth Hayes Miller and Kuniyoshi.

SMITH, Charles L. Born NY State about 1812, living New Orleans, La 1857. Panorama and scenic artist, decorator. Work in Republic National Bank (Dallas). Reference G&W. Source TEP. No auction record. Painting example opp p 68 TEP.

Smith was working in NYC 1840–41 as a scenic painter in the theater. He decorated the NYC auditorium with likenesses of presidents, mythological devices, and the arms of the Union.

In 1852, while he was a theatrical artist in New Orleans, Smith was brought the sketches that Lt Benton had been making along the Brazos River in Texas. The promoters were Sala and Stearns who commissioned a moving panorama of *Texas and California,* incorporating Texas history, its missions, and the battle of the Alamo. The panorama was to be 9′ high by 300′ long. The portion of the panorama that still exists shows the size to have been indeed 9′ high by 15′ per scene, and the quality of Smith's painting was superior to the general recollection of the workmanship of such "newsreels." The *Texas and California* panorama was well reviewed, "a decided hit." TEP. By 1857 Smith had completed two other panoramas, *Creation* and *Perry's Expedition to Japan.*

SMITH, Dan. Born Ivigtut, Greenland 1865, died NYC 1934. Western special artist for *Leslie's* in 1890–91, illustrator, painter, etcher. Member SI 1912. Work in NY *World, Leslie's.* References A36 (obit)-MAL. Sources AIW-CAP-ILA-POI. No current auction record but the

448

estimated price of a Western illustration would be about $900 to $1,100 at auction in 1976. Signature example p 61 CAP.

Raised in NYC, Smith went to Copenhagen at 14. There he studied at the Public Arts Institute. When he returned to the US, he studied at the PAFA. He was a member of the art staff of *Leslie's* from late 1890 to 1897. His illustrations beginning Jan 10, 1891 show the South Dakota "Indian troubles" at Wounded Knee near the Pine Ridge agency. The illustrations are "from sketches made on the spot" so Dan Smith probably was there along with fellow *Leslie's* artist J H Smith, whose credits are mingled with those of Dan Smith. Later in 1891 Dan Smith was credited for illustrations that appeared from a trip to the Southwest around Albuquerque. Western illustrations in 1892 (bear hunting), 1895 (Indians), and 1897 (Alaska) were probably drawn after photographs. From 1891 on, "these illustrations are bold drawings of Western scenes that were based on at least one, and probably several, Western trips." AIW.

After 1897 Dan Smith worked for the Hearst newspapers. He was artist-correspondent for the Spanish-American War. For more than 20 years his covers were used for the Sunday *World* magazine section. His dry-brush drawings were syndicated nationally.

SMITH, DeCost. Born Skaneateles, NY 1864, died Amenia, NY 1939. Pre-1900 painter of Indian genre, illustrator, writer. Work in AMNH and MAI. References A31-BEN-MAL-SMI. Sources AIW-ANT 3/71,3/73-HAR-ISH-KEN-POW. Oil 24×18″ *Indian with Rifle* sold in 1970 for $2,100 at auction. Signature example p 183 HAR.

DeCost Smith was raised near the Onondaga Indian Reservation and was initiated into the tribe. He studied in NYC at the McMullin School and the ASL. After seeing Indian paintings by George de Forest Brush he made his first of many Western trips in 1884. That winter was spent in Dakota Territory at Standing Rock and Fort Yates following visits to the Rosebud and Lower Brule Indian agencies. When Smith completed his studies at the Julien Academy, he was able to have an exhibition of Indian paintings at the Paris Salon.

Beginning in 1893 Smith traveled among the Indians with the artist E W Deming for a few years. Together they wrote and illustrated *Sketching Among the Sioux* for *Outing* in 1893 and *Sketching Among the Crow Indians* in 1894. They wrote *With Gun and Palette Among the Red Skins* in 1895, but the illustrations were by Remington. Smith also worked as an illustrator for the national magazines like *Century*. His autobiography "Indian Experiences" was published posthumously in 1943.

SMITH, Elmer Boyd. Born St John, NB, Can 1860, died Wilton, Conn 1943. Illustrator and writer. Work in books. References A33-FIE-MAL-SMI. Sources AHI 4/68-ILP-WHO 48-data from Jim Collins. No current auction record but the estimated price of a Western illustration would be about $1,000 to $1,200 at auction in 1976. No signature example. (See illustration 278.)

E Boyd Smith studied art in France at the Julien Academy under Boulanger and Lefebvre. After his return from France, Smith traveled through the West sketching, going by riverboat down the Ohio and Mississippi rivers. He settled in Kansas City and became the first director of the Kansas City Art Association and School of Design. By the early 1900s he moved to Connecticut where he remained the rest of his life. WHO provided a long list of books written and illustrated by him, beginning with "My

Village" in 1896, including "The Story of Pocahontas and Capt John Smith" in 1906 and "The Story of Our Country" in 1920. Smith also illustrated books written by others, for example, "The Willow Whistle" and "Land of Little Rain" showing Southwestern desert landscapes, Indians, and prospectors for Mary Austin in 1903.

SMITH, Erwin E. Born Honey Grove, Tex 1888, died Bermuda Ranch near Bonham, Tex 1947. Texas cowboy and Indian sculptor, sketch artist, photographer. No reference. Sources TOB-TXF. No auction record or signature example.

Smith studied modeling in Chicago with Lorado Taft and in Boston with Bela Pratt. He spent 25 years in ranch life, sketching cowboy and pioneer subjects and making thousands of photographs to illustrate George Patullo's Western stories. His sculpture includes *Sioux Indians* and *Head, Nez Percé Indian*. A collection of his ranch photos is in "Life on the Texas Range," 1952, text by J Evetts Haley.

SMITH, Francis Drexel. Born Chicago, Ill 1874, died Colo Springs, Colo 1956. Painter, teacher, administrator. Work in DAM, Vanderpoel colln, CSFAC, Kansas City AI. References A53-BEN-FIE-MAL. Sources NEW-SHO-SPR. No current auction record but the estimated price of a Western scene would be about $500 to $600 at auction in 1976. Signature example p 35 SHO.

F Drexel Smith studied at the AIC and the Broadmoor AA, and was in 1894 the pupil of John Vanderpoel, John F Carlson, and Everett Warner. He was a member of the first board of trustees of Broadmoor AA in 1919, having been photographed about 1913 as a member

of the "in" eating and drinking club. NEW. Smith became president of the Academy and a trustee of CSFAC. He exhibited nationally beginning 1922.

SMITH, Gean. Born NY State 1851, died Galveston, Tex 1928. Eastern painter of horses, dogs, and Western animals, illustrator. References A29 (obit)-MAL. Sources AIW-*Galveston Daily News* 1/27/24 (article) and 12/9/28 (obit), *Galveston Tribune* 12/8/28 (obit). Oil 15×30" *The Finish of the Race* sold 4/15/70 for $1,100 at auction. Photo of paintings and Smith in *News* article above. (See illustration 279.)

Smith said he was self-taught except for one lesson in the use of crayons. The lesson took one hour and cost $1 when he was 16. Smith's specialty was depicting the action and movement of animals. He said, "I never attempt to paint instantaneous action. The eye receives the impression of the result and this is what I paint. The real likeness of a horse in action is above the legs." *News*.

Smith moved from Chicago to NYC to establish his studio in 1885. He considered himself a "sports painter," and prints have been made of Smith's paintings of races. His specialty was horse portraits. In the painting *The Parade of Prize Winners* he depicted 65 horses. A painting of a champion trotter reproduced on the cover of a Waldorf menu made the menu a collector's item. *Outing* in 1893 and 1895 reproduced Smith's paintings of race horses, and "Record of the Cattle Industry" reproduced *A Stampede* in 1895. Smith retired to Galveston in 1923.

SMITH, Jack Wilkinson. Born Paterson, NJ 1873, died Monterey Park, Cal 1949.

Cal landscape painter. Member Ten Painters of LA. Work in Phoenix Munic colln. References A41-BEN-FIE-MAL. Sources NJA-SCA. No auction record or signature example.

Jack W Smith studied at the Cincinnati AA and the AIC. After working as a scene painter in Chicago, he was a commercial artist in Lexington, Ky. He won awards in California beginning 1915, having settled in Alhambra about 1906. Favorite subjects were the High Sierras, the valleys, and the shore. His sketching companion in 1927 was Clyde Forsythe. Painting titles include *The Canyon Stream, Desert Hills near Palm Springs, Planting Trout in a Sierra Lake,* and *Sunlit Rocks.*

SMITH, Jerome (or Josiah) Howard. Born Pleasant Valley, Ill 1861 (or 1860), died Vancouver, BC 1941. Special artist for *Leslie's,* cartoonist, Western painter of genre. Work in magazines and lithographs. Reference MAS. Sources AIW-CAP-CUS (J Smith). No current auction record but the estimated price of a Western illustration would be about $900 to $1,100 at auction in 1976. Signature example plate 19 CAP.

J H Smith broke Western horses on the Illinois farm where he was raised. At 18 he headed for the silver mines at Leadville. Returning to Chicago at 23, he attended art school. As a cartoonist he worked for the Chicago *Rambler.* By 1887 he was in NYC as cartoonist for *Judge.* When *Judge* merged with *Leslie's* in 1889, Smith was sent as correspondent to the Northwest. The first *Leslie's* illustration by Smith was a joint effort with Charles Russell for a full page on *Bronco Ponies and Their Uses.* Later in 1889 and 1890 there was a series of illustrations of the Northwest by Smith alone, providing a wide range of genre: horse thieves, Chinese, cattlemen, the Indian "troubles," and the ghost dance.

After 1890 Smith spent two years studying in Paris but concluded, "You can't teach an old dog new tricks." AIW. He wandered through the West as miner, cowboy, driver, and finally marrying in British Columbia where he painted Western scenes for reproduction as lithographs. One series of prints was on frontier justice.

SMITH, John Rowson. Born Boston, Mass 1810, died Philadelphia, Pa 1864. Mississippi panorama painter, scenic artist. References BEN-DAB-G&W-MAS. Sources ANT 7/43-BAR-PAF-TEP. Oil 7×9" *A Gaff-Rigged Sloop* dated 1840 sold in 1969 for $350 at auction. No signature example.

Smith was the pupil and son of John Rubens Smith, the painter and teacher, grandson of John Raphael Smith, the mezzotinter, and great-grandson of Thomas Smith of Derby, the landscape painter. Smith left his father, a controversial critic, to be apprentice to a scenic artist. He worked in the theater after 1832 in New Orleans and St Louis. This led Smith to become the first American "moving" panoramist, beginning with scenes of Boston and then of the Moscow fire. In 1839 he exhibited a Mississippi panorama that burned in Boston.

By 1844 Smith completed the repainting of his "original gigantic moving panorama of the Mississippi River extending from the Falls of St Anthony to the Gulf of Mexico depicting nearly 4,000 miles of American scenery on over four miles of canvas." At Saratoga, NY the panorama earned $20,000 in six weeks. Smith toured the country with it. In 1847 he visited Seth Eastman at Fort Snelling. In 1848 he showed the panorama to huge audiences in Europe, meanwhile painting a European panorama for America. He both "brought the old world visibly to the new and took the new world to the old." BAR. For his competition with

Banvard's similar panorama, he obtained authentication from Catlin. Little of Smith's work survives although he continued to the end of his life to paint scenery at his Carlstadt, NJ farm and in the South.

SMITH, Lillian (Lilian) W (Wilhelm). Active as pioneer Arizona illustrator, painter, teacher, designer. Work in Arizona Mus (Phoenix). Reference MAS. Source WAI 71. No current auction record or signature example.

WAI 71 includes *Navaho Healer,* an oil on board signed "L L". The data given is that the artist "designed porcelain for Goldwater's Store, Phoenix" and was "best known for her watercolors." She was the "wife of prominent Indian guide" and "cousin of Zane Grey."

MAS lists Lilian Wilhelm Smith as active in Phoenix in 1948.

SMITH, Paul Kauvar. Born Cape Girardeau, Mo 1893, living Denver, Colo 1973. Modern Colorado painter of mining towns. Work in DAM. References A73-MAS. Source DAA. No current auction record or signature example.

Paul K Smith studied commercial art in St Louis 1915–16. After WWI he studied at the St Louis SFA and Washington U. He moved to Colorado in 1921, studying at the Denver AA. Since 1923 he exhibited at the DAM where he had a one-man show in 1952.

Favorite subjects are "mining towns, decaying buildings against a mountain side." DAA. In 1958 Smith described his technique as "starting lean and finishing fat," that is, beginning with turpentine as a brush medium and ending up with a knife for pure paint.

452

SMITH, Sidney Paul. Born Salt Lake City, Utah 1904, living Denver after 1965. Utah watercolor landscapist. Work in Utah state and school collns. No reference. Source YUP. No current auction record or signature example.

Paul Smith was the pupil of Lawrence Squires and A B Wright. From 1932 to 1934 he was in NYC at the NAD, the pupil of Leon Kroll. His watercolors are described as "full-bodied," although "more reserved are his romantic Jordan River series." YUP.

Smith's wife is Ruth Wolf Smith, born Ogden, Utah 1912. Her painting is of "languorous, almost translucent figures she invents." YUP.

SMITH, William Arthur. Born Toledo, Ohio 1918, living Pineville, Pa 1976. Painter, printmaker. Member NA 1952, Nat Acad of Western Art. Work in MMA, Lib Cong, LAMA. References A76-MAL. Source PER vol 3 ⚒3. No auction record or signature example.

Smith studied at Keane's Art School in Toledo, and then at the ASL and Grand Central Art Institute in NY. Abroad he studied at the École des Beaux-Arts and Académie de la Grande Chaumière in Paris. His preferred medium is watercolor.

SMITH, William Thompson Russell. Born Glasgow, Scotland 1812, died Glenside, Pa 1896 (or 1897). Eastern panoramist, scenic artist, landscape painter, scientific illustrator. Work in BMFA, Centennial Expos. References BEN-DAB -FIE-G&W-MAL-SMI. Sources ALA-ANT 2/53,5/60,1/64,10/68,11/71, 3/72,3/73,9/74-BOA-HUT-KW1-PAF. Oil 12×16" *Old Holiday St Theatre, Baltimore* dated 1839 sold 1970 for

$3,000 at auction. Signature example p 485 ANT 10/68 *Amer Landscape.*

Russell Smith, whose father manufactured cutlery and whose mother was a doctor, was raised in Pittsburgh. Self-taught, he painted life-sized portraits and theater scenery before studying with James Reid Lambdin in Pittsburgh 1829–33. A successful scenery painter, he worked in Philadelphia, Boston, Baltimore, and Washington, took his family to Europe 1851–52 to prepare a diorama of the Holy Land, and began painting well-received landscapes. His theater scenery and drop curtains required most of his time. The large theater canvases which exceeded 50 sq ft were painted entirely by Smith to preserve his "individuality." DAB. His wife and daughter were both named Mary, and both were painters, as was his son Xanthus. When fellow Philadelphian William McIlvaine returned from the California gold fields with sketches of Panama, Mexico, and California, Russell Smith used the sketches to paint a panorama that was exhibited in Philadelphia 1850 and in Baltimore 1851.

SMITH, Xanthus Russell. Born Philadelphia, Pa 1839 (or 1838), died Edgehill (or Weldon), Pa 1929. Eastern naval, landscape, and portrait painter. Work in PAFA, Union League Club (Phila), Wanamaker colln. References A30 (obit)-BEN-DAB-G&W-MAL-SMI. Sources ANT 11/51,4/61,3/71,10/72, 2/74-BOA-PAF. Watercolor 20×14" *Chief Good Eagle* dated 1901 sold 1968 for $200 at auction. Oil 36×66" *Battle between the USS Kearsarge and CSS Alabama* dated 1869 sold 10/70 for $8,000 at auction. Signature example p 296 ANT 2/74.

Xanthus Smith was the son of the painter Russell Smith who took the family to Europe 1851–52. Xanthus Smith was educated in medicine and anatomy at the U of Pennsylvania 1856–58. He had already studied art at PAFA, the RA in London, and in Europe, receiving his first landscape commission in 1855. During the Civil War he served in the Union Navy. Thereafter he specialized in painting large views of the major naval and land battles. He also painted marines off the Maine coast and landscapes. Late in his career he turned to portraiture including Washington, Walt Whitman, Lincoln, and Indian Chief Good Eagle.

SMOKY, Lois (or Bougetah, "Of the Dawn"). Born near Anadarko, Okla 1907, living Virden, Okla 1967. Painter, one of the original "Five Kiowas." Work in GIL, MAI, McNay AI (San Antonio), and reproduced in the books of Dr Jacobson, "Kiowa Indian Art" (1929) and "American Indian Painters" (1950). No reference. Source AIP. No current auction record or signature example.

Lois Smoky had been educated in Oklahoma Indian schools. In January 1927 she joined Asah, Hokeah, Mopope, and Tsatoke to form the "Five Kiowas" at the U of Oklahoma. To accomplish this she had to overcome the Plains Indian custom that women not paint in a representational style. By the end of 1927 the pressure caused her to drop out of the program. She was replaced by Auchiah. She married and ceased painting.

SMYTH, Eugene Leslie. Born NYC 1857, died Townshend, Vt 1932. Painter. Reference MAL. Source, oil 32×48" *California Landscape* signed and dated 1893 sold 5/22/73 for $425 at auction in Los Angeles. Oil 14×22" *New England Sea Coast* sold 1972 for $140 at auction. No signature example.

SNIDOW, Gordon. Born Paris, Mo 1936, living Belen, NM 1976. Contemporary Western painter, commercial artist, lithographer, sculptor. Member CAA. Work in Montana Hist Soc, Nat Cowboy Hall of Fame, P T Cattle Co. Reference A76. Sources ACO-AHI 11/71-CAP-COW-C71 to 74-OSR-SNI-WAI 71, 72. No current auction record. Signature example on cover SNI. (See illustration 280.)

Raised in Texas and Oklahoma, Snidow graduated from high school before entering the Art Center School in Los Angeles in 1955. He settled in Albuquerque, NM as a commercial illustrator and designer in 1959. By 1963 he was exhibiting prize-winning works.

"A majority of those who paint the open range continue to draw on the subjects of Russell and Remington. Yet right before us the cowboys still live and work." SNI. Snidow "is not interested in covered wagons or Indian war parties. The cowboys in his art drive pick-ups and haul horse trailers. They use nylon ropes and smoke ready made cigarettes." OSR. "Does many sketches of the modern cowboy in different positions on location and tapes an interview at that time. Later on plays the tape as he paints the oil." WAI 71. Snidow puts real people in his paintings. While many artists blend facial characteristics, a cowboy Snidow paints in the act of branding will be easily identified as the actual man at work on the day pictured.

SNYDER, W L (or W P). Active 1870s–80s. Illustrator. No reference. Sources AIW-AOA. No auction record or signature example.

AIW lists W L Snyder as a *Harper's Weekly* artist on a staff including W A Rogers, Thomas Nast, Howard Pyle, C S Reinhart, and A B Frost. In 1873, when *Scribner's Magazine* (rather than *Harper's*) used Champney's Western illustrations, some of the reproductions are signed "W L S." AIW credits these to "W L Snyder." Page 280 of the same *Scribner's* issue bears the full signature for "W L S." It is W L Sheppard. AOA in listing *Harper's* artists for the period shows "W P S" or W P Snyder. None of the above is recorded as having been in the West except for Champney.

SOHON, Gustavus. Born Tilsit, East Prussia, Germany 1825, died Washington, DC 1903. Railway survey topographical and portrait artist in pen and pencil. Work in US Nat Mus. Reference G&W. Sources AIW-AOW-COS-KW1-POW. No auction record but the estimated price for a pencil drawing of a Flathead Indian would in 1976 be about $750 to $1,250 at auction. Signature example p 167 AOW.

Sohon emigrated to the US in 1842 to avoid compulsory military service. He worked as a bookbinder in Brooklyn for 10 years, then enlisted in the US Army. Sohon was stationed at Fort Dallas in Oregon Territory, then in 1853 was sent with supplies for Maj Isaac Stevens, the first governor of Washington Territory and in charge of the exploration of the northern railway route from the Mississippi River to Puget Sound. Sohon was assigned to Lt Mullan's party surveying the Rocky Mountain passes. He learned the Indian languages and made sketches for lithographs in the Stevens report. In 1854 Sohon made pencil portraits of the Flathead chiefs and Christian Iroquois, and in 1855 made pencil sketches of Gov Stevens negotiating treaties with Columbia Valley and Montana tribes. Sohon also drew the first panoramic view of the main chain of the Rockies and the earliest drawings of the Great Falls of the Missouri.

As a civilian Sohon returned to the Northwest to help construct the first wagon road over the Rockies. In 1862

Sohon accompanied Lt Mullan to Washington, DC to prepare the published report including 10 lithographs and giving the name Sohon pass to a mountain crossing. From 1863–65 Sohon had a photographic studio in San Francisco, and thereafter a shoe business in Washington, DC. Sohon's Indian drawings are in the National Museum (Smithsonian) —"the most authoritative pictorial series in pre-reservation days" and "ranking him among the most able artists who interpreted the plains and the Rockies." AIW.

SOLDWEDEL, Frederic. Born NYC 1886, living there 1941. Watercolor painter specializing in marine scenes, architect. References A41-FIE. Source, watercolor *California Yuccas* dated 1922. No auction record or signature example. (See illustration 281.)

Soldwedel studied in England, Italy, Greece, and France.

SOMMER, Otto (or Sommers, or A Sommers, or Otto Sommers). Landscape painter active 1860s in NJ and NY, 1870s in Europe. Work in The Los Angeles Athletic Club (as Otto Sommer), the Capitol (as Sommers), NJ Hist Soc (as Otto Sommer), Harmsen colln (as A Sommers, active 1850s, if the same artist). Reference FIE (as Sommers). Sources ANT 8/74-BOA-HAR-NJA-WHI. Oil 27¾ × 39½" *An Alpine Landscape* dated 1874 by Otto Sommers sold 11/2/73 for $1,841 at auction in London. Oil 14×20" *New England Farm* signed Otto Sommers and dated NY '67 sold 5/23/73 for $600 at auction in Los Angeles. In 1970 and 1969 auctions the listing is as Otto Sommer. Signature example p 55 WHI.

Little is known about the artist or whether more than one artist is involved. "Sommers' picture, 'Westward Ho! or, Crossing the Plains,' is a truthful transcript of Western life. The figures are not so good as the landscape, but they are life-like." BOA. In WHI, *Westward Ho!* is all figures with little landscape as it shows "tired but valiant cowhands leading short-horned cattle through the dusty plains to the West to improve the stock."

SONNICHSEN, Yngvar. Born Christiania (now Oslo), Norway 1873 (or 1875), died Seattle, Wash about 1940. Northwest landscape, portrait, and mural painter, etcher, teacher, writer. Member Puget Sound Group of NW Painters. Work in Munic Galls of Norway, Vanderpoel AA (Chicago), clubs, hall, lodge, etc. References A41 (obit)-BEN-FIE-MAL-SMI. Sources WHO 38-WNW. No current auction record or signature example.

Sonnichsen graduated from the Polytechnic School in Christiania 1894 and studied 1895–99 at the RA in Antwerp and Brussels and in Paris with Bouguereau and Constant at the Julien Academy. He exhibited in Norway 1900–4 before emigrating to Canada 1904 and moving to Seattle in 1908. Sonnichsen was known for his portraits and for landscapes of southeast Alaska. A listed title was *The Moon, Alaska.* In 1933 and 1934 he painted landscapes for Seattle public schools.

SPALDING (or Spaulding), Elizabeth (or Elisabeth). Born Erie, Pa about 1870, died Denver, Colo 1954. Colo landscape painter, charter member of Artists Club of Denver in 1893. Work in Erie Art Club (Pa), DAM, DPL, public buildings in Denver. References A41-

BEN-FIE-MAL. Sources AAT-DPL-WAA. No current auction record. Signature example p 148 AAT *New Road to the Hogback, Colo.*

Daughter of one of the first Episcopalian bishops in Colorado, Elizabeth Spalding studied at the PAFA and the ASL. In 1932 she had one-artist shows in Stockholm and Paris.

SPAMPINATO, Clemente. Born Italy 1912, living Sea Cliff, NY 1976. Sculptor in bronze and marble specializing in traditional Western subjects. Member NSS. Work in Nat Mus Sport (NYC), Rockwell Gall Western Art (Corning, NY), Delgado MA (New Orleans), Notre Dame U, Oklahoma AC (Okla City). Reference A76. Source, bronze 53″ long 61″ high *Cowboy Unhorsed* dated 1952 sold 1/27/65 for $1,100 at auction. Bronze 28″ high *At the Gate* sold 11/15/67 for $2,000 at auction. No signature example.

Spampinato studied at the AFA, the French Academy Nude, the School of Governatorate, and the Royal School of the Medal, all in Rome. His commissions include trophies, statues, and reliefs in Italy and US.

SPARKS, Arthur Watson. Born Washington, DC 1870 (or 1871), died Philadelphia, Pa 1919. Pa landscape and genre painter, teacher. References A23-BEN-FIE-MAL-SMI. Source, FIE listing of *Grand View, Ariz Canyon.* No auction record or signature example.

Sparks studied in Paris at the Julien Academy and the École des Beaux-Arts, the pupil of Laurens, Cormon, Bouguereau, Thaulow, Mucha, Ferrier, and Courtois. He was professor of painting at Carnegie Institute.

SPARKS, Will. Born St Louis, Mo 1862, living San Francisco, Cal 1941. Cal painter, muralist, illustrator, etcher, writer. Work in Bohemian Club, Palace of Legion of Honor, De Young Mem Mus, FAG (San Diego), Toledo MA. References A41-BEN-FIE-MAL-SMI. Sources AAR 11/74-BWB-work listed in A41. No current auction record. Painting example p 140 AAR 11/74.

Educated as a medical doctor, Will Sparks studied at St Louis SFA and at the Julien Academy in Paris. He arrived in California 1888, settling in San Francisco in 1891. In the 1890s he was a member of the San Francisco Bohemian Club, sharing the "hand-to-mouth existence" that had been the lot of Jules Tavernier, Amadee Joullin, Joe Strong, and Julian Rix, "a buoyant, carefree group, always high-spirited and fun-loving, and ever ready to take part in festivities and pranks." BWB. Sparks worked as editor and feature writer for the San Francisco *Evening Call* and as a teacher of anatomical drawing. By 1919 Sparks had made 36 California and Southwestern paintings. AAR. Compare the listing for William F Sparks.

SPARKS, William F. Artist for *Leslie's Weekly* in 1881. No reference. Source CAP with drawing example. No current auction record.

CAP reprints *Cattle Herders Indulging in Revolver Practice* from *Leslie's Weekly* for 1/21/81. "The railroads were beginning to edge west at this time, along with the telegraph wires." This drawing "pictured 'cattle herders' indulging in revolver practice at telegraph insulators." CAP. Compare the listing for Will Sparks.

SPAULDING, Grace. See John.

SPEED, U Grant. Born San Angelo, Tex about 1935, living Pleasant Grove, Utah 1976. Traditional Western sculptor. Member CAA 1966. Work in Nat Cowboy Hall of Fame (Okla City), Rodeo Cowboys Assn. No reference. Sources COW-C71 to 74-OSR-WAI 71,72-*Western Horseman* 1/70. No current auction record. Signature example p 60 C72.

Raised in Texas, Speed studied animal husbandry at Utah State U in Provo, intending to be a rancher. While still in college he competed as a rodeo rider until sidelined by a broken ankle. He became a school teacher in Provo. Self-taught in his spare time he also sculpted in bronze and experimented on his own for a sculpting style that would avoid copying Russell and Remington. He used his riding experiences as source for subject matter in *The End of an Acquaintance, Doubtful Outcome,* and *The Bull Rider.* Since 1970 Speed has been sculpting full time. Most of his bronzes he casts himself, including recent works that are Western portraits in bronze. "A tall soft-spoken cowboy," Speed had worked on 15 different Texas spreads before he was 22 and had served a mission for his church. C74.

SPENS, Nathaniel. Born Edinburgh, Scotland 1838, died Mountainville, Utah 1916. Utah pioneer primitive painter, sculptor, decorator. Decorations in LDS temples. No reference. Source YUP. No current auction record but the estimated price of a Utah landscape would be about $350 to $450 at auction in 1976. No signature example.

Before emigrating to the US at 24, Spens was apprenticed to a house painter. After settling in American Fork, Utah about 1865, he worked as a self-taught painter, decorator, and wood-carver. In 1890 he moved to Mountain-ville near Mt Pleasant where he was a farmer.

"Many of the paintings of Spens are copies from popular magazines, chromos, and the like. In his original work there is a good sense of color and a joyous and unself-conscious attack." YUP.

SPRAGUE, Isaac. Born Hingham, Mass 1811, died probably Grantville, Mass 1895. New England landscape painter at Fort Union, Mont 1843, illustrator. Work reproduced in "Scenery of the White Mountains." Reference G&W. Source AIW. No current auction record or signature example.

Sprague was artist-assistant to Audubon on a trip up the Missouri in 1843 to paint American quadrupeds. The boat was filled with trappers heading for their rendezvous at the headwaters. Stops for wood provided time to explore, hunt, and sketch. The Audubon party centered on Fort Union at the edge of Montana. They were in Indian country, seeking new species of fox, wolf, and antelope, hunting buffalo. AIW refers to a lost painting of Fort Union by Sprague for Alexander Culbertson, the factor, a work painted only 10 years after Catlin and Bodmer, 15 years before Wimar.

SPRUCE, Everett Franklin. Born Faulkner Cnty, Ark 1908, living Austin, Tex 1976. Modern Texas landscape and animal painter, printmaker. Work in MFA Houston, MMA, Dallas MFA, MOMA, PAFA, WMAA, etc. References A76-MAS. Sources AAT-ALA-APT-CAA-DIG 2/45-M50,57-TOB-T20-TXF-WHO 70. No current auction record but the 1950 M50 plate 9 illustrates *Goat* priced at $750 and providing signature example.

Raised in the Ozarks, Everett Spruce worked as an attendant in the Dallas Museum of Fine Arts while studying at the Dallas Art Institute 1925–29. He was also the private pupil of Olin Travis and Thomas Stell. In his early career he gained notice with a three-panel screen decorated with patterns from the "flora and fauna" of Texas. TXF. He worked as assistant and official of the Dallas Museum of Fine Arts 1931–40 and as teacher and professor at the Dallas Museum School beginning 1936. In 1940 he joined the faculty of U of Texas (Austin).

He learned to paint with "terrifying emptiness." ALA. Landscape subjects included *Twin Mountains, Water Hole No. 2,* and *Negro Shack.* His form was "angular and half-abstract," this "skillful painter who builds a half real, half fantastic world." DIG.

SPRUNGER, Elmer. Born probably Bigfork, Mont about 1915, living there 1969. Montana wildlife painter. No reference. Source MON. No auction record. Signature example centerfold MON.

Sprunger was raised near Swan Lake in northwestern Montana. His sophomore year in high school, he studied with Elizabeth Lochrie. Sprunger worked in the woods and as a shipyard draftsman in Seattle, Wash before returning to Montana in 1950 as a caretaker, carpenter, and sign painter.

He prefers hunting and fishing when he gets outdoors, so, as an artist, he limits himself to watercolor sketches and 35mm slides. The photographs are not to project on the canvas to paint but rather as a reference for accuracy. His usual subjects are elk, deer, grizzlies, and waterfowl, against the landscape of the Swan and Mission ranges or Glacier National Park. In 1969 he conceived a series of paintings on the early days of logging in northwestern Montana.

SQUIRES, C Clyde. Born Salt Lake City, Utah 1883, died Great Neck, NY 1970. Romantic illustrator for national magazines including covers for pulp Westerns. Member SI 1912. Work in *Western Romances, Life, Woman's Home Companion,* etc. References A33-MAL. Sources AAC-PUA-*Newsmagazine of Great Neck* (NY) Aug 1974. No current auction record but the estimated price of a Western illustration would be about $1,000 to $1,200 at auction in 1976. Signature example *Newsmagazine* above. (See illustration 282.)

Grandson of a pioneer Utah barber who was a friend of Brigham Young, and son of a barber-stonecutter, Squires was apprenticed to a Salt Lake City engraver. At 15 he had done layouts for the local newspapers. When he was 18 he went to NYC to study art. After a year he worked as a commercial artist drawing fashion heads in the mornings, attending the NY School of Art afternoons and evenings. He was the pupil of Henri and Kenneth Hayes Miller, and received advice from DuMond and Pyle.

In 1906 *Life* made its first acceptance of a Squires drawing. The second drawing accepted was *An Old Love Song* which *Life* issued as a premium it advertised in 26 other magazines. When Squires's first child was born, he painted his most famous work *Her Gift* which appeared in *Success* before reproductions were sold nationally, in Europe, and in Australia. As one who "always worshipped at the shrine of womankind, Clyde Squires agrees that both sexes now kneel at the shrine of the matinee idoless (the feminine of idol)." *The Western Monthly.* He painted covers for *Western Romances* and other pulp Western magazines.

SQUIRES, Henry (Harry). Born Putney, Surrey, Eng 1850, died Salt Lake City, Utah 1928. Pioneer Utah primitive landscape painter. Work in Utah St Capitol. No reference. Sources PUA-YUP. No current auction record but the estimated price of a Utah landscape would be about $400 to $500 at auction in 1976. No signature example.

Squires was brought to Salt Lake City with other Mormon converts in 1853 after crossing the plains with his parents in a covered wagon. His father John P Squires became Brigham Young's personal barber and advisor. Two of his brothers were also barbers. The third was a singer. Harry Squires was educated at the U of Deseret, graduating about 1870. A friend of the painters Lambourne and Culmer, he was self-taught as a painter. With his nephew Lawrence Squires he visited Mexican, European, and Eastern art galleries 1908–9.

SQUIRES, Lawrence. Born Salt Lake City, Utah 1887, died there 1928. Utah painter of the 1920s. Work in South Cache high school (memorial colln, Hyrum, Utah), DAM, Utah St Capitol colln, 8 Utah high schools. References A29 (obit)-MAL. Sources PUA-YUP. No current auction record but the estimated price of a Utah landscape would be about $700 to $800 at auction in 1976. Signature example p 28 YUP.

Squires's father and grandfather were barbers. He studied with Mahonri Young in 1905 while working as a barber. In 1907 he was sent to Europe as a Mormon missionary and continued on until 1910 as an art student. After returning to Utah to paint, he went to NYC in 1912 to study at the ASL, the pupil of Kenneth Hayes Miller for two years. His friends were his cousin Clyde Squires and the theatrical designer George Watson Barratt. He worked as a furniture decorator until WWI. In service, his lungs were damaged by poison gas, requiring hospitalization and cutting short his life.

In Salt Lake City with his nephew Paul Smith, he continued decorative painting on furniture. He also painted Utah landscapes. In 1924–25 he lived near Tucson, Ariz, painting "Mexican villages, Indian ruins, street scenes, the Arizona desert, cactus, hill country, churches and missions." PUA. In the 15 years he worked, it is known that he painted many oils and watercolors but he kept no record.

STAHLEY, Joseph. Born probably Rochester, NY about 1900, living probably California 1968 (living NYC 1948). Traditional Western painter, illustrator, art editor, teacher. Reference MAS. Source COW. No current auction record or signature example.

Stahley at 15 rode his horse from Rochester, NY to Chicago to study at the AIC. He also studied with Harvey Dunn, Dean Cornwell, and Nicolai Fechin. The influence toward Western painting came from Will James. Stahley worked as art editor for the publishers Houghton Mifflin, as art director for four years at a NYC ad agency, as art teacher at Rochester Institute of Technology, and for 16 years as set illustrator for motion picture companies. Stahley has said that his focus is "upon the cowboy and his horse and their resourcefulness in the big range country." COW.

STAHR, Paul. Born NYC 1883, living there 1941. Illustrator including pulp Westerns, specializing in fluorescent paint. Member SI. Work in *Life, Collier's Weekly, American Magazine, Harper's Bazaar, Woman's Home Companion.* References A41-FIE-MAL. Source AAC. No current auction record but the estimated price of a Western illustration would be about $450 to $550 at auction in 1976. No signature example.

Stahr was the pupil of John Ward and the NAD in NYC. He illustrated "The Hornet," "The Mask," and "The Scar" in addition to work for the national magazines.

STANLEY, Charles St George. Born probably England, active Colorado 1870s, and opened a studio in Georgetrator, landscape painter, writer. No reference. Source BDW. No auction record or signature example.

Stanley studied at the RA in London. He sketched in Colorado in 1867, illustrated in Leadville and painted landscapes for Colorado Central RR in the 1870s, and opened a studio in Georgetown 1878.

In 1876 he had been correspondent for *Leslie's* and *Harper's* for Gen Crook's battles with the Sioux. His Leadville studio was established in 1880. He also worked as engineer, draftsman, and writer.

STANLEY, John Mix. Born Canandaigua, NY 1814, died Detroit, Mich 1872. Important Indian painter and survey artist. Work in Smithsonian Inst, Buffalo Hist Soc, Detroit IA, MMA, Honolulu Mus. References BEN-DAB-G&W. Sources AIW-ALA-ANT 1/57, 3/59, 3/65, 4/73 - AWM - BAR - COS - DBW-DCC-DWF-GIL-HAR-HMA-150-M19-PAF-PAW-POW-SUR-TAW-TSF-WAI 71-WES-WHI. Oval oil 8×10¼" *Indian Camp* sold 10/19/72 for $12,-000. Oil 25¼×30¼" *Hunters and Traders* signed and dated 1862 sold 5/23/74 for $30,000 at auction. Signature example p 104 TAW. (See illustration 283.)

As a boy Stanley became interested in Indians around his father's tavern. He was orphaned in 1828 and apprenticed

to a coachmaker. To find a better job Stanley moved to Detroit in 1834 as a painter of houses and signs. In 1835 James Bowman, an accomplished portrait painter trained in Italy, admired a Stanley sign and took Stanley as a pupil. From 1836 to 1838 Stanley painted portraits around Chicago. In 1839 at Fort Snelling, Minn he began to devote himself to Indian portraits and scenes but could not support himself. In three years of portrait painting and taking daguerreotype likenesses in the East, he saved enough to return West. In 1842 Stanley set up a studio in Fort Gibson, Okla, painting frontiersmen and Indians. Until 1845 Stanley lived in Indian country, painting a grand Indian council at Tahlequah in 1843 and a second council of prairie Indians. By 1846 the Stanley Indian paintings were on display in Cincinnati.

Stanley left the same year to join a wagon train for Santa Fe where he became artist of the Kearny military expedition to aid in the conquest of California. The guide was Kit Carson. Kearny's official report contains lithographs from Stanley sketches. Stanley was painting Indian portraits in Oregon in 1847, and Polynesian portraits in Hawaii in 1848–49. In 1850–51 Stanley displayed his Indian Gallery in Eastern cities, and in 1852 put his collection of 150 paintings on display at the Smithsonian in order to offer it to the Government for $19,200 in return for his 10 years' work and $12,000 in expenses. Congress refused, and in 1865 the collection was destroyed by fire. Other Indian paintings by Stanley were destroyed by fire at P T Barnum's American Museum in NY.

In 1853 Stanley had become official artist for the Stevens expedition for the northern railway survey, making scores of sketches of bison, Red River white hunters, councils, and views. Stanley was dispatched to Washington with the preliminary survey report, and by 1854 he had used his field sketches to prepare a huge panorama of 42 episodes of Western scenes that required two hours for viewing. Like most of Stanley's original work, the panorama has disappeared. Stanley married in 1854. The remainder of his life was spent as a studio artist, including Indian subjects, and in arranging for chromolithography of his paintings.

STANSFIELD, John Heber. Born Mt Pleasant, Utah 1878, died there 1953. Primitive Utah landscape and portrait painter. Work in Springville AG (Utah), Utah schools. No reference. Sources PUA-YUP. No current auction record but the estimated value of a Western landscape would be $400 to $500 at auction in 1976. Signature example p 26 YUP.

Stansfield was educated in the local elementary school. Summers he herded sheep for his parents who were Utah pioneers. Self-taught as an artist, he was encouraged by Harwood and Culmer while working as a decorator and building contractor after 1905. He also taught at Snow College for 13 years.

During summer vacations he traveled. On the California coast he met and was influenced by Thomas Moran. Another summer he painted in the Canadian Rockies. Other landscape subjects were *Laguna, New Mexico* and the *Painted Desert*. "In the 1930s, Stansfield's paintings began to show a gradual change. The first indications of Stansfield's decline can be seen." YUP.

STANSON, George Curtin (or Gjura Stojana). Born Brisout near the Lower Pyrénées, France 1885, living Los Angeles, Cal 1975, with summers in Santa Fe, NM. Cal painter and sculptor including Indian subjects. Member Archaeological Inst of Amer. Work in Mus of Archaeol (Santa Fe); murals in the Biol

Mus (U Cal, La Jolla) and Golden Gate Park Mus (San Fran). References A21-BEN-FIE. Source, A21 listing of titles *On the Trail* and *After the Rain*. No auction record or signature example.

"Art and Artists of Southern California" by Moure and Smith says Stojana emigrated from Serbia in 1901, adopting the Stanson name. He worked as an artist for a San Franciso newspaper for four years, then came to Los Angeles about 1918. He was in the Pacific in 1922, settling in Los Angeles on his return in August of that year. Stanson exhibited locally. In 1928 he legally went back to his original name.

STARKEY, Mrs Jo-Anita (or Josie A). Born Gresham, Neb 1895, living Los Angeles, Cal 1962. Painter of the West, craftsman, designer. Reference A62. Source WAA. Oil on board *Wagon Train* estimated for sale 10/28/74 at $400 to $600 at auction in Los Angeles and sold for $250. Signature example *Wagon Train* above.

Mrs Starkey studied with Loren Barton, Orrin White, and Marion Wachtel. She exhibited widely in California.

STEARNS, Junius Brutus. Born Burlington (or Arlington), Vt 1810, died Brooklyn, NY 1885. Historical, genre, portrait painter. ANA 1848, NA 1849. Work in BM, NY City Hall, NY Acad of Design, Virginia Mus (Richmond, *The Life of Washington*), Butler Inst Amer Art, Tol Mus. References BEN-CHA-FIE-G&W-MAL-SMI. Sources ANT 6/65;1,5/66;1/67;8/70 (article);1/71; 6/74-BAR-BOA-JNB-PAF-STI. Oil 37×54″ *Fishing Party off Long Island* 1860 sold 4/30/69 for $6,250. Signature example p 1296 ANT 6/74. (See illustration 284.)

Stearns became a student at the National Academy of Design in NYC about 1838 when he was already accomplished enough as a painter to exhibit there and at the Apollo Association. The year he was elected NA he went to Paris and London for further study, then returned to NYC where he established his studio. He served between 1851 and 1865 as Recording Secretary of the NA. In 1867 BOA mentioned "Stearns of NY" as having won fame in portraiture. He was perhaps best known for his series of paintings depicting Washington as citizen, farmer, soldier, statesman, and Christian. ANT 8/70 reproduced a series of paintings on fishing subjects.

Many of Stearns' historical paintings included Indians. The oil 35×41" *Return to Native Grounds* dated 1868 was illustrated PB 4/20/72. ANT 6/65 on p 629 shows the 1847 painting of Mrs Dunston and nurse tomahawking sleeping Indians. ANT 1/71 on p 85 reproduces *Washington and the Indians*. PAFA lists as exhibited in 1856 *The Council of Vincennes* with Tecumseh.

STEELE, Sandra (Mrs George Steele). Born Las Vegas, Nev 1938, living Van Nuys, Cal 1968. Traditional Western painter, illustrator. Assoc member CAA. No reference. Source COW. No current auction record or signature example.

Mrs Steele, a photographer's daughter, was educated at Pierce Junior College near Los Angeles. She studied for two years with the Famous Artists School and worked for two and a half years as an animation artist at the Walt Disney Studio. Her husband is a wrangler at the Fat Jones Stables in North Hollywood.

STEFAN, Ross. Born Milwaukee, Wis 1934, living Tucson, Ariz 1976. Traditional Western painter. Work in ANS, GIL, The Ariz Bank. Reference A76. Sources ACO-AHI 12/71,3/72-EIT-HAR-WAI 71,72. Oil 22×30" *Manana Wash* signed, dated 1966, and titled on the stretcher, sold 10/27/71 for $700 at auction. Oil 24×40" *Squaw Dance* 1960 was estimated for sale 10/28/74 for $6,000 to $8,000 at auction in LA, and sold for $2,500. Signature example p 187 HAR.

Stefan was influenced to become an artist by visiting the Wisconsin studio of Dan Muller, the illustrator. Raised in Tucson where his father worked in advertising, Stefan began to paint while in his teens. At 21 he was painting full time with a studio and gallery in Tubac, Ariz. His subjects are landscapes of Southwestern deserts and mountains, as well as portraits of dwellers of the Southwest. WAI 72.

In 1972 AHI reported the retail side to the 1971 auction sale listed above: "A one-man show in New York proved far more substantial for Stefan. The show of 16 oils was a virtual sell-out opening night. Two large paintings were purchased for $1,900 and $1,200." P 44 AHI 3/72.

STEFFEN, Randy. Born Maverick Cnty, Tex about 1915, living Dublin, Tex 1974. Illustrator specializing in horses and riders including the American military and the Indian painter, sculptor, writer-historian. Fellow, The Company of Military Historians 1959. Work in Amer Quarter Horse Assn. No reference. Source, over 1,500 magazine and book illustrations. No auction record. Signature example, illustrations in "US Military Saddles, 1812–1943" by Steffen, U of Okla Press, Norman, Okla.

Steffen was educated at Stanton Prep Academy and four years at USN Academy at Annapolis. Of Sioux descent, he lived among the Sioux before working as a stuntman in Hollywood. Some sculpture titles are *Hoka Hey, The 1851*

Dragoon Troop Horse, The Defiant Young Red Cloud, The Strongheart. He has also designed Christmas cards, *Headin' for the Christmas Hay*.

Steffen's "The Horse Soldier," comprehensive study of US mounted forces from the dragoon regiments of the Continental Army in 1775 to the end of horse cavalry in 1943, contains more than 500 illustrations. Steffen spent 12 years and 11,000 miles in research.

STEIDER, Doris (Mrs C B McCampbell). Born Decatur, Ill 1924, living Albuquerque, NM 1976. New Mexico landscape painter in tempera, commercial artist. Work in W Texas Mus (Lubbock), Christmas cards, hospital murals. Reference A76. Sources 9,10/73 NMX-6/73 data from artist. No auction record. Signature example p 33 NMX.

Ms Steider studied applied design at Purdue U, graduating in 1945. After working in design and commercial art she returned for her master's degree at the U of New Mexico in 1965. "I love New Mexico colors. When people come here, they at first see only beige," she says, emphasizing that beneath the beige are the pastels that make the Southwest such a challenge for Eastern artists.

STEINEGGER, Henry. Born Switzerland about 1831, living San Francisco, Cal 1880. Lithographic artist. Work reproduced in Britton and Rey prints, ACM, Lib Cong. Reference G&W. Sources CUS-MWS W/74. No auction record. Print example p 65 MWS.

Steinegger worked in San Francisco as an employee of Britton and Rey from 1859 to 1880. In 1878 he drew the lithograph *General Custer's Death Struggle: The Battle of the Little Big Horn* for Pacific Art Company of San Francisco. It is pointed out in MWS that Steinegger copied from and combined two previous drawings. The first was William M Cary's 1876 illustration for the NY *Daily Graphic* showing a uniformed Custer erect with one foot on a dead horse, the left hand firing a pistol and the right hand swinging a saber overhead. The second was Alfred Waud's illustration for the 1876 Custer biography showing a buckskin Custer erect with the right hand firing a pistol and the left clutching a rifle. The result of Steinegger's combination was that his drawing included both Custers.

STEINKE, Bettina. Born Biddeford, Me 1913, living Santa Fe, NM 1976. Painter of Indian subjects and portraits. Member Nat Acad of Western Art, SI. Work in Nat Cowboy Hall of Fame, Fort Worth Mus, Gilcrease, Philbrook Mus (Tulsa). Reference A76. Sources HAW-PER vol 3 #3-WAA-WHO 64. No auction record. Signature example p 64 PER vol 3 #3.

Ms Steinke attended Fawcett's Art School in Newark, NJ, then Cooper Union and Phoenix Art Institute in NY. At the age of 28 she was a member of SI. In 1947 she married photographer Don Blair. As a team they traveled to Central and South America and into the Arctic, Ms Steinke sketching Indian and Eskimo subjects for future paintings. Four portraits including those of Joel McCrea and Will Rogers are in the permanent collection of the National Cowboy Hall of Fame.

STELLA, Joseph. Born Muro Lucano, Italy 1877 (or 1879, or 1880), died Astoria, NY 1946. Important Eastern modernist painter, illustrator. Work in BM, WMAA, Worcester AM, MMA, MOMA, 1913 Armory Show. References A41-BEN-FIE-MAL. Sources AAR

9/73,11/74-AAT-ALA-ARM-CAA-CAH-DEP-NEU-STI. Gouache 41×27" *Tree, Cactus, Moon* signed twice (about 1928) sold 3/14/73 for $17,000 at auction. Signature example p 145 AAT.

Stella emigrated to NYC in 1896 when he studied medicine and pharmacology. The next year he studied art at the ASL. From 1898 to 1900 and in 1902 he was the pupil of Chase at the NY School of Art. As a magazine illustrator from 1905 to 1908, he made steel mill drawings for *Survey Graphic*. In Italy and France 1909–12 the Stella "who had drawn the smoke and grime of Pittsburgh awoke to a new sense of color through friendship with Picasso, Matisse, and Modigliani, and in Rome and Florence caught a spark from the Futurist bonfire." ALA. "One of the outstanding draftsmen in the history of American art," Stella "sought to capture the quality, texture, and tempo of American life." 190.

STEPHENS, Charles H. Birthplace unknown about 1855, died Pittsburgh, Pa 1931. Philadelphia illustrator specializing in American Indian subjects. References A32 (obit)-MAL. Source p 153 IL 94 illustrating the Indian bust portrait *White Ghost*. No auction record or signature example.

Stephens was an instructor at PAFA in 1894 and a leading member of the Philadelphia Sketch Club. He "specialized in illustration of American Indians and was the owner of a collection of American Indian Art that had been exhibited at the U of Pennsylvania Museum." A32. His wife was the illustrator Alice Barber Stephens.

STEPHENS, Henry Louis. Born Philadelphia, Pa 1824, died Bayonne, NJ 1882. NYC illustrator of books and magazines, caricaturist, watercolorist. Work in *Leslie's, Harper's,* BEY. References BEN-FIE-G&W-MAS-SMI. Source BEY. No auction record or signature example.

After working in Philadelphia in the 1850s, Stephens moved to NYC about 1859 to illustrate for *Leslie's*. In 1867 five of his drawings were published in BEY. True to Stephens' reputation as a humorist, none of the drawings is straight travel reporting. The first and second are slapstick of Kansas in 1857. The fourth and fifth are the before and the after of Colorado miners in 1859. It appears that these Western drawings by Stephens were made in NYC from graphic materials available there, rather than sketched in the West.

STERNE, Maurice. Born Libau, Russia 1878 (or 1877), died Mt Kisco, NY 1957. International painter, sculptor. NA 1944, Sculptors' Guild, NIAL. Work in MMA, WMAA, MOMA, AIC, COR, BM, BMFA, Berlin, London; sculptor of monuments and murals. References A59 (obit)-BEN-FIE-MAL-SMI. Sources ALA-AMA-ANT 3/61,4/72-CAA-CON-DEP-INS 4/17-190-ISH-MCA-MSL-M50-ART 10/57 (obit)-SCU-STI-TAL-TSF-WHO 56. Oil 38×50" *Bathers* sold 12/12/69 for $2,268 at auction in London. Painting examples p LIII INS 4/17.

Sterne came to the US with his widowed mother when he was 12. He worked at odd jobs in NYC before studying at Cooper Union. In 1894 he studied anatomy under Eakins at the NAD, continuing as an art student in the US until 1904 when he won a traveling scholarship. He studied in Italy and in France, then spent 1907 in Greece, 1908–11 in Italy, then the Far East with two years in Bali until 1915 when he settled in New York.

Sterne moved to Taos in 1916 at the suggestion of Paul Burlin. He was then married to Mabel Dodge who wrote, "Sterne was released here from some inhibition that had prevented him from carrying out his deep wish to model in clay in order to arrive at directly reproducing three-dimensional impressions." TAL. He also painted gouache and charcoal sketches of Indians until 1918 when he returned to Anticoli, Italy. At the Museum of Modern Art in 1933 there was a retrospective exhibition of Sterne's works 1902–32. He was an instructor in drawing and painting at the ASL in 1953.

STEVENS, John. Born Utica NY 1819, died probably Minnesota 1879. Panoramic painter of the Sioux Massacre of 1862. Work in GIL, Minn Hist Soc. Reference G&W. Source TEP. No auction record or signature example.

A farmer who settled in Rochester, Minn in 1853, Stevens was a house and sign painter by 1858. He became a scenery painter, familiar with the broad treatment of stage sets. After the Sioux Massacre of 1862 that took place when protective federal troops were pulled out of the West for service in the Civil War, Stevens painted moving panoramas of the conflict, beginning about 1863. Like the form of "newsreel" it was, the panorama was brought up to date in 1868 with later scenes that took place after 1863 during the five years the clashes occurred. The Sioux panorama was successfully exhibited in the Midwest, with additional revisions in 1870 and 1874. These panoramas have survived in museums, which is unique.

STEVENS, Kelly Haygood. Born Mexia, Tex 1896, living Austin, Tex 1962. International painter including Indian ceremonial subjects. References A62-MAL. Source TOB. No auction record or signature example.

Kelly H Stevens was educated at the Texas School for the Deaf and at Gallaudet College in Washington, DC. He studied at the Corcoran School of Art with Brooke and Messer, at the School of Industrial Art in Trenton, NJ with McGinnis, and in Paris with the deaf painter Jean Hanan. In 1926 he traveled in Spain and in 1933 he again studied in Paris with Biloul and Morisset. Stevens taught at the NJ School for the Deaf for eight years, and then traveled in Europe.

In Texas, Stevens was known for his depictions of Indian ceremonials and dances. Blue is a dominant color for him, perhaps because of "the old Indian legend that a certain blue keeps away evil spirits." TOB.

STEVENS, Lawrence Tenney. Born Brighton, Mass 1896, probably living Tempe, Ariz 1974. Sculptor specializing in Western animals, painter, printmaker, lecturer. Member NSS. Work in BM, Will Rogers Mus (Claremore, Okla), City of Scottsdale (*Arabian Stallion*), Brookgreen Gardens (SC). References A62-BEN-MAL-SMI. Sources AHI 1/62 (article),3/72. No current auction record. Monogram example p 4 AHI 1/62.

"Steve" Stevens studied at the BMFA School and with Charles Grafly and Bela Pratt. He was awarded the Prix de Rome in 1922, permitting study at the American Academy in Rome as well as throughout the Near East until 1925. He visited Wyoming and Arizona in 1929. After WWII he moved to Tulsa, Okla and to Tempe, Ariz in 1954, "a lean, sinewy man galloping through life in Western pants and cowboy boots, his goatee quivering with laughter or indignation, his longish hair never seeming to settle on his head." AHI 1/62.

The *Rodeo Series* of sculpture shows the main rodeo events in bronze. It began with *The Cutting Horse* exhibited in 1960. His technique is to start with action sketches, then a detailed drawing to scale for the pipe-and-wire "skeleton." The clay model is built on top of the skeleton. A plaster mold is made over the clay, with parting lines established. This "waste" mold is used to make the plaster "master" that is perfected to become the positive for the bronze castings formed in wax or sand. Stevens "chases" his own bronzes and in the '60s left the bronzes with a natural surface finish rather than the usual manufactured patina.

STEVENSON, Branson Graves. Born Franklin Cnty, Ga 1901, living Great Falls, Mont 1976. Painter, printmaker, sculptor, craftsman, teacher. Work in Mont Inst Arts (Helena) C M Russell Gall (Great Falls), Mont Hist Soc (Helena), U Oregon (Eugene); murals in Great Falls. References A76-MAS. Sources BRO-MON-WNW. No auction record or signature example.

Raised in Panama where his father was Canal engineer, Stevenson studied at the Instituto Nacional de Panamá, his only art instruction. He worked as a stenographer in Colombia, then came to Montana where he was in the oil business. With his brothers he brought in one of the first Montana oil wells. In 1931 he joined Mobil, retiring in 1960 as Montana manager. In 1963 he became lecturer on art at the College of Great Falls.

Stevenson exhibited paintings and prints in Montana as early as 1936. Typical titles were *Sacajawea at Great Falls of the Missouri* and *Last Chance Gulch*. As a potter he developed glazes and decorating processes. Stevenson writes for craft periodicals and operates the "Glass Art Shop" in Great Falls.

STEVENSON, Edna Bradley. Born Hebron, Neb 1887, living Oklahoma City, Okla 1962. Okla painter in Taos 1932–34, teacher. References A62-MAS. Sources WAA-WHO 60. No auction record or signature example.

Mrs Stevenson received her certificate from the AIC in 1907, after she had studied summers at the U of Illinois 1904–6. She became head of the art department at Oklahoma City high school in 1920, then studied at Snow-Froelich School in 1921, Oklahoma City U 1929, Bisttram School in Taos 1932–34, Julien Academy in Paris 1936, Florence (Italy) 1937, and U of California at LA 1949. From 1943–58 she was Director of Art, Oklahoma City U.

STEWART, Le Conte. Born Glenwood, Utah 1891, living Kaysville, Utah 1974. Utah landscape painter, printmaker, teacher. Work in Utah and Idaho colleges and high schools, murals in LDS temples and Denver State House. References A62-BEN-FIE-MAL. Sources PUA-YUP. No current auction record. Painting example p 28 YUP.

Son of a lawyer, Stewart was educated at Ricks Academy in Idaho until about 1909. He taught school in Murray, Utah for two years before studying at the ASL, spending the summer of 1913 in Woodstock and the winter in NYC. He was the pupil of J F Carlson, DuMond, and Blumenschein. Returning to school teaching in Utah in 1914, he became an important influence on young Western artists. Except for LDS temple decorating trips such as one to Hawaii 1916–19 and Canada 1919–22, he continued as a high school and college art teacher until retirement in 1956.

"There is abstract in my work. I take great liberty with nature, moving mountains, transposing any elements to enhance the composition. This is the reconstruction of the skeleton of the scene." PUA.

STIEFFEL, Hermann. Born Wiesbaden, Germany 1826, died after 1882 (or 1886). Primitive Western landscape, fort, and Indian painter, printer, infantryman. Work in Beinecke Lib (Yale), Smithsonian Inst. Reference G&W. Sources FRO-KEN-WES. No current auction record but the estimated value of a Western drawing would be about $1,500 to $2,000 at auction in 1976. Watercolor example *Attack on Gen Marcy's Train* p 86 FRO.

Stieffel who had been a printer in NYC enlisted in the US Army in 1857. He served continuously with Company K of the 5th Infantry until discharged for disability in May 1882. His record stated, "character excellent, not married." WES.

Stieffel served in Kansas and Montana. WES shows seven watercolors from the Smithsonian collection. All are presumed to have been painted about 1879 although they show scenes as early as 1867, for example, *Sa-Tan-ti Addressing the Peace Commissioners at Council Grove, Medicine Lodge Creek, 1867.* Two of the watercolors are of Fort Harker in Kansas and two are of Fort Keough in Montana.

STIHA, Vladin. Born Belgrade, Yugoslavia about 1910, living Santa Fe, NM 1973. New Mexico painter of Pueblo Indians. Work in ANS, Tucson Fed S&L Assn. Member Nat Acad Western Art. No reference. Sources ACO-EIT-PER vol 3 ✳3-WAI 72. No auction record. Signature example p 68 PER vol 3 ✳3.

Educated in Belgrade, Stiha studied art at Vienna Academy FA in Austria and in Italy under Carlo Savierri. After exhibiting in Europe he emigrated to Argentina at the end of WWII, where he painted and exhibited until 1958. Moving again, he painted the colorful coastal life of Bahia, Brazil for 10 years.

In 1968 Stiha settled in Santa Fe

where he specialized in Pueblo Indian genre, in the tradition of Gaspard and Fechin. He concentrated on the richness and dignity of Indian life in the Southwest. Listed painting titles are *Navajo Journey* and *Children of Travois,* both oil on canvas.

STITT, Hobart (or Herbert) D. Born Hot Springs, Ark 1880, living Sudbrook, Pikesville, Md 1941. Painter of landscapes and equestrian subjects. Work in Wilmington Soc FA, Art Mus (Little Rock), Princeton U. References A41-BEN-FIE-MAL. Source p 581 ANT 10/73 *Indians in Birch Canoe* 1913 with signature example. No auction record.

Stitt studied at the St Louis Academy FA, at the PAFA with Robert Spencer and Fred Wagner, and with Howard Pyle.

STOBIE, Charles S. Born Baltimore, Md 1845, died Chicago, Ill 1931. One of the earliest Denver painters, "Mountain Charlie." Work in State Hist Soc of Colo, Stenzel colln. No reference. Sources AIW-DBW-DCC-DPL-PNW. No current auction record but the estimated price of a Western oil would be $2,500 to $3,000 at auction in 1976. Signature example p 25 PNW. (See illustration 285.)

After studying art for two years in St Andrews, Scotland, Stobie worked in an architect's office in the East until he was 20. His record of his *Crossing the Plains to Colorado in 1865* was published in *The Colorado Magazine* in 1933, without reference to his career as a painter. As a buffalo hunter and Indian scout he became an intimate of such Western personalities as William Cody, Wild Bill Hickok, and Frederic Remington. In 1866 he lived with the Ute Indians near

Grand Lake, Colo. In 1868 he served the Army as scout in the South Platte River campaign against the Cheyenne and Arapaho.

By 1868 his watercolor sketches of Ute Indians were placed at "Denver City, Colo." PNW shows a portrait of the Ute Indian Jack painted from his body after an 1877 battle near Fort Washakie. It also refers to an 1890 exhibit in Omaha with Stobie paintings: *Western Colorado* and *Land of the Utes* as well as *General George Crook, Sitting Bull, Pueblo Squaw,* and *Scalp Parade.* "Others of his paintings are known, but they are rather uncommon today." PNW.

STOCKWELL, Samuel B. Born Boston, Mass 1813, died Savannah, Ga 1854. Mississippi panorama and scenery painter. Reference G&W. Source ANT 7/43. No current auction record or signature example.

An actor's son, Stockwell worked as an actor and scenery painter at Boston's Tremont Theater in the 1830s, at Charleston in 1841, and at Mobile and New Orleans in 1843. By 1845 he was settled in St Louis as a scenery painter. Stockwell in partnership with Henry Lewis worked on a moving panorama of the Mississippi River, following the examples of John Rowson Smith and John Banvard. When the partnership dissolved, Stockwell and Lewis each exhibited separate panoramas, just before the opening of the Leon Pomarede panorama. Stockwell's work was successfully shown in St Louis, New Orleans, Charleston, the West Indies, and Boston, just as each of the competing panoramas played to large audiences. Stockwell was back in St Louis as a scenery painter in 1852–53, but died of yellow fever in Savannah the next year. Neither the Mississippi panoramas nor the apparatus that was used to "move" them exists today. None of Stockwell's paintings is known to survive.

STOJANA, Gjura (or George). See Stanson.

STONE, Willard. Born Oktaha, Okla 1916, living Locust Grove, Okla 1976. Cherokee sculptor in wood. Member Nat Acad of Western Art. Work in MNM. Reference A76. Sources MNM-PER vol 3 #3. No auction record. Signature example p 70 PER vol 3 #3.

Stone attended Bacone U in Muskogee, Okla. He was given a grant as artist-in-residence at the Gilcrease Museum in Tulsa. He works only in wood, using maple, walnut, sassafras, cherry, and red Oklahoma cedar.

STOOPS, Herbert Morton. Born Idaho 1887 (or 1888), died Mystic, Conn 1948. Illustrator of magazines and books including school texts, specializing in the Old West and military subjects. Member SI. Work in New Britain Mus (Conn). References A53 (obit)-MAL. Sources ANT 9/74,3/75-*Amer Book Collector* 2/67-SOG-ILA-ILG-IL 36-catalog Mystic AA 7/22/48 (obit). Oil 32×28″ *Sunset Trail* sold 9/13/72 for $1,500 at auction. Signature example p 20 PB 9/13/72 auction. (See illustration 286.)

Stoops was a Westerner raised on a ranch in Idaho's Rockies 60 miles from Yellowstone Park. He grew up handling horses and cattle, alongside cowboys and Indians who had seen the buffalo herds and the Plains Wars. His clergyman father sent Stoops to Utah State College. After graduation Stoops worked as artist-reporter for the *San Francisco Call* about 1910 when San Francisco was a center for important Western illustrators like Maynard Dixon. Stoops moved to Chicago to study at the AIC and work as staff artist for the *Chicago Tribune.* In

WWI, Stoops served as an artillery officer in France.

After the war Stoops settled in NYC as an illustrator specializing in Western, war, and historical scenes. His book illustrations were listed in *American Book Collector* 2/67 with advice on how to collect the 37 named books that contain Stoops' illustrations. His magazine illustrations are shown and discussed in ILA. He received the Isidor Medal for easel painting at the 1940 NA exhibition. He was doing a series of covers for *Blue Book* commemorating the birth of the then 48 states. Seventeen had been completed when he died. A physically powerful man, Stoops invoked lasting loyalties among his friends even though his welcoming bear-hug might have hurt. He was an important illustrator of the '20s, painting in the Remington tradition with Western scenes taken from his own experience. Some illustrations he signed with the pseudonyms Jeremy Cannon and Raymond Sisley.

STORELLI, Félix Marie Ferdinand. Born Turin, Italy 1778, died Paris, France 1854. French-school landscape, historical, and portrait painter. Work in European museums at Versailles, Trianon, Copenhagen, Parma. References BEN-CHA. Source HUT. Oil 20½×30″ *View of Cherokee Village Tokouo* inscribed on the reverse and dated 1819 was estimated for sale 5/11/74 at $800 to $1,000 at auction, and sold for $1,500. Painting example *Cherokee Village* shown in catalog above.

Storelli was the pupil of Palmerius and became painter and professor to the Duchesse de Berry. He exhibited at the Salon from 1806 to 1850, the father of the painter Ferdinand Michel Storelli and the grandfather of André Storelli.

The inscription on the reverse of the *Cherokee Village* painting indicates that it is after a painting made by the Duc de Montpensier in North America in 1805, titled *Souvenir de Tokouo*.

STRAHALM, Franz S (or Frank). Born Vienna, Austria 1879, died Dallas, Tex 1935. Landscape and mural painter, teacher. Work in Ney Mus (Austin), Little Rock AM; murals in Dallas and Shreveport. References A36 (obit)-MAL. Sources TOB-TXF. No auction record or signature example.

Strahalm was his father's pupil in Vienna and studied in the Hamburg Art School as well as in Italy and France. In 1909 he emigrated to Mexico City, but due to the revolution in 1911 he moved to San Antonio. He established the School in Fine Painting in 1919.

In 1926 Strahalm sketched along the Colorado and Pecos rivers. In 1927 he sketched in New Mexico including the Indian villages near Santa Fe and Taos. The same year he painted autumn scenery in West Texas. When 32 of his paintings were exhibited that November, a hotel owner bought the lot for $6,000.

STRANG, Ray C. Born Sandoval, Ill 1893, died Tucson, Ariz 1957. Traditional Western painter of cowboy genre, illustrator. Reference MAL. Sources AAC-ACO-COW-GWP. Oil 24×30″ *Breezy* estimated for sale 10/28/74 at $400 to $600 for auction in LA and sold for $600. Signature example p 77 GWP.

Strang was educated in Centralia, Ill. His studies at the AIC begun in 1915 were interrupted by service in WWI. Wounded at the Argonne, he returned to the AIC until 1920. He also studied in NYC at the ASL and the SI school. For 17 years Strang was a successful illustrator for three advertising agencies. His work appeared in advertising in the national magazines as well as in illustrations for fiction. AAC.

About 1938 Strang made a chance visit to Tucson: "I might have left with the rest of the dudes had I not realized that the Old West I wanted to paint was still the West of today." GWP. He moved to a 60-acre ranch, this "quiet, placid, kindly man," where he painted the genre scenes of the small ranchers living in the lonelier canyons, plains, and hills. Each painting has a title for the story it tells—*Slow Poke, Horse Power, Native's Return.*

STRATHEARN, Robert P (Bert). Born probably Ventura Cnty, Cal about 1875, living probably California 1968. Traditional Western painter. Work in Nat Cowboy Hall of Fame, *Western Livestock Journal* (Anaheim, Cal). No reference. Source COW. No auction record. No signature example.

Strathearn's father introduced Angus purebred cattle in Southern California. Growing up as a cowboy in the 1880s, Strathearn worked on his father's ranch. He became a successful banker in Moorpark, Cal and a credit manager. *The Los Angeles Times* and the *Express* employed him as a political cartoonist. About 1935 Strathearn began producing etchings, then paintings in oil and watercolor.

STRAYER, Paul. Born Park Ridge, Ill in 1885, living in Illinois in the 1940s. Book and magazine illustrator. Reference MAS. Source data from Allan Neville. No auction record or signature example.

Strayer studied at AIC and painted murals for Marshall Field in Chicago. He became a book illustrator, doing work for Houghton Mifflin, Doubleday, etc. He also did Western covers for the Street & Smith magazines and he illustrated Zane Grey's "Fighting Caravans" in *Country Gentleman Magazine.*

STREET, Frank. Born probably Kansas City, Mo 1893, died Englewood, NJ 1944. Illustrator for slick magazines beginning with the 1920s, including Western subjects; painter, teacher. Member SI. Work in *Sat Eve Post, Collier's, Cosmopolitan, Ladies' Home Journal.* References A47 (obit)-BEN-MAL. Sources AAC-ILA. No auction record. Signature example p 107 ILA.

Street studied at the ASL and at the Charles Chapman-Harvey Dunn School of Illustration in Leonia, NJ. As Harvey Dunn had been influenced by his relationship with his teacher Howard Pyle, so Dunn became the model for Frank Street. Dunn secured Street's first commissions and by 1924 Street was listed as living in Leonia. AAC. ILA shows a Western illustration by Street for *Collier's* in 1940.

STROBEL, Max. Active 1853 both in St Paul with Stevens and in the Rockies with Frémont. Topographic artist. Work in lithographic reproduction. Reference G&W. Source AIW. No auction record or signature example.

When Gov Stevens and John Mix Stanley arrived in St Paul in May 1853 to organize the survey for the northern railway route, Max Strobel was employed as the artist to be assistant to Stanley. A local newspaper reported, "I have seen the artist's work, as pleasing to the eye as to the mind." AIW. Because Stevens was an overly demanding leader, 25 members of the survey withdrew. Among these was Strobel, but while there he sketched the Minnesota River scenery. A view of

St Paul was reproduced in lithograph, the only Strobel artwork to survive.

By late September 1853 Strobel was with Frémont's expedition that crossed the Rockies that winter to establish the central railway route to the Pacific. The expedition's artist was S N Carvalho and the topographical engineer was F W Egloffstein. There are no existing Strobel sketches of this arduous trip, if he made any.

STROBEL, Oscar A. Born Cincinnati, Ohio 1891, died probably Scottsdale, Ariz 1967. Traditional Western painter, illustrator, printmaker. Work in Western clubs and banks, German Embassy; murals in Western hotels and bus stations. References A62-MAL. Source, oil in lot ✗480 of the 5/30/74 Morgan sale at auction; also titles credited in A41. No signature example.

Strobel studied with Duveneck, Rabes, Henri, and with Herrman in Germany. In 1932 he was at 1306 North Harper Avenue in Los Angeles. In 1941 he was listed as art instructor at Judson School in Phoenix. In 1962 he was employed as a calendar artist.

STRONG, Joseph D. Born Bridgeport, Conn 1852, died San Francisco, Cal 1900. California-school painter of cowboy genre, portrait painter. References A00 (obit)-BEN-MAL-SMI. Sources AIW-BWB-SSF. No current auction record but an oil 39½ ×20″ *The Actor* with signature example and dated Munich 1876 was estimated for sale 11/28/73 at $1,000 to $1,500 for auction in LA but did not sell.

Strong moved to San Francisco with his family when he was seven, after having lived in the Hawaiian Islands. He studied in the California School of Design that had been launched in San Francisco by Virgil Williams in 1871. Following Williams' theories that preferred the teachings at Munich rather than the more progressive Paris, Strong became the pupil there of Piloty. He won two medals at the Royal Academy of Munich before returning to San Francisco in 1877. Apart from a visit to the South Sea Islands, Strong maintained his studio in San Francisco at 7 Montgomery Avenue until his early death.

A member of the Bohemian Club, Strong was the companion of the local eccentrics like the artists Jules Tavernier, Arthur Mathews, Will Sparks, Julian Rix, and Amadee Joullin, as well as the serious painters Tom Hill, William Keith, and Charles Rollo Peters. Strong became the son-in-law of Robert Louis Stevenson who visited in 1879 and frequented Strong's studio. When Oscar Wilde lectured on "The Aesthetics Theory Applied to Home Life" in San Francisco in 1882, he was entertained at Strong's studio, earning "ample respect for his vivacity and bibacity." SSF. Mrs Strong described the artist's experiences in San Francisco before the turn of the century in "This Life I've Loved."

STUART (or Stewart), Frederick D. Born NY about 1816, living Washington, DC 1871. Survey artist, hydrographer, engraver. Illustrations in the 1844 "Narrative of the US Exploring Expedition." Reference G&W. No other source, auction record, or signature example.

Stuart was in the Pacific Northwest as part of the government expedition before 1844. He moved to Washington from NY about 1850, was listed as an engraver in 1860, was a member of another expedition in 1862, was in the Navy at the end of the Civil War, and beginning 1867 was listed as a hydrographer.

STUART (or Stewart), Gilbert Charles. Born North Kingstown (or Narragansett), RI 1755 (or 1754), died Boston, Mass 1828. Very important international portrait painter. Honorary NA 1827. Work in MMA, AIC, COR, NGA, PAFA, BMFA, etc. References BEN-CHA-DAB-ENB-FIE-G&W-MAL-SMI. Sources AAR 9/73-AIC-ALA-AMA-ANT 2,4/40;3/41;4/43;4/45;10/48; 4/49;11/51;11/52;9/53;3/54;1/59;5,8, 12/61;3/62;4,12/67;10/68;4/69;8, 10/72;3,9,11/73;5,8,11/74;3/75-ARI-BAR-BOA-COR-HUD-ISH-KW1-MSL-M15-M19-M57-NCB-NGA-NJA-PAF-STI-STU-TEP. Oil 44½ × 34½″ *Portrait of George Washington* not signed not dated sold 12/10/70 for $205,000 at auction. Signature example p 324 NCB.

Stuart's father was a Scottish millwright who emigrated to operate a snuff mill, which failed. Stuart, a poor student, sketched on fences and barns. At 13 he painted a pair of successful portraits that led to his apprenticeship at 15 to a wandering Scottish painter, Cosmo Alexander, and he accompanied him to Scotland. Alexander died in Scotland two years later and Stuart had to work his way back to Newport. Stuart painted Newport portraits between 1773 and 1775, when he sailed to London to escape the war. Because his modest technique was overshadowed by the monumental English portraits, his needs required him by 1777 to become the assistant of the American painter Benjamin West. By 1782 Stuart had his own London studio, having added his luminosity to the English decorative manner. Commissions were so numerous he limited sitters to six a day, charming them with his wit and ease of conversation. Nevertheless, the magnificence of his establishment impoverished him again, so he moved to Ireland by 1788.

In 1792 he became absorbed with the need to paint a portrait of Washington. He opened a NY studio, and was known as a glamorous and charming performer, without a rival as a painter. By 1795 he had painted the *Vaughan* portrait (right side of face) of Washington, with 39 replicas on order. In 1796 the *Lansdowne* (full length) and *Atheneum* (left side of face) versions were painted, with many replicas ordered. The portraits were more the stereotyped hero-images than likenesses. Among the large number of portraits Stuart painted in his long career was at least one Indian, *Thayandenugaa or Joseph Brant* as reproduced in *Connoisseur* June 1958. Most of Stuart's paintings were unsigned.

STUART, James Everett. Born near Dover (or New Bangor), Me 1852, died San Francisco, Cal 1941. Painter of Western landscapes with Indians. Work in Joslyn Mem (Omaha), Golden Gate Park Mus (San Fran), Southwest Mus, Crocker Gall (Sacramento), De Young Mus. References A47 (obit)-BEN-FIE-MAL-SMI. Sources ANT 11/61,9/65-HON-JNB-KEN-PNW-WHO 40. Oil 34 × 64″ *Indian Encampment on the Columbia River* signed, numbered 1898, and dated 1914, with number, title, date, and signature also on the reverse, sold 4/20/72 for $4,000 at auction. Signature example ✕61 JNB.

Stuart was educated in the public schools of San Francisco where he was brought when he was 8. He showed an aptitude for drawing at an early age. From 1868 to 1873 he studied with the portrait painter Wood in Sacramento. The next 5 years he studied at the San Francisco School of Design, the pupil of Virgil Williams, R D Yelland, Hill, and Keith. He became a minor member of the important Bohemian Club while Jules Tavernier, Julian Rix, and Joe Strong set the carefree pattern.

His early sketches were of the Sacramento and San Joaquin rivers. His first Northwest trip was 1876. In 1881 he

269. Olaf Seltzer. *Roping on the Triangle Bar*, pen and ink drawing 11 x 14″ signed (LC) O C Seltzer and dated 1933. Under the shadow of Russell. CREDIT, MONTANA HISTORICAL SOCIETY, HELENA.

270. Amos Sewell. *Seeker in a Slicker*, dry point drawing on board 10 x 8″ signed (CR) A S. Known for charcoal drawings of rural subjects. CREDIT, THE AUTHORS.

271. Jack Shadbolt. *Winter Theme No 7,* oil and lucite on canvas 42⅜ x 50¾″ signed (LR) J Shadbolt and dated 1961. Forceful and animistic and festive. CREDIT, THE NATIONAL GALLERY OF CANADA, OTTAWA.

272. J H Sharp. *Crow Indian Encampment*, oil on canvas 23¼ x 29¾" signed LR. "I didn't exactly have a right to paint Indians." CREDIT, THE ANSCHUTZ COLLECTION.

273. Louis H Sharp. *Grand Canyon*, oil on canvas 40 x 50" signed LL and dated 1924. CREDIT, THE ANSCHUTZ COLLECTION.

4. Henry Merwin Shrady. *Bull Moose*, bronze statuette
½″ high copyrighted 1900. A doctor's son assimilated
atomy. CREDIT, THE METROPOLITAN MUSEUM OF
RT, BEQUEST OF GEORGE DUPONT PRATT, 1935.

275. Will Shuster. *Blessing of the Woodmen*, oil 20 x 24″
signed UR. Los Cinco Pintores and pupil of Sloan. CREDIT,
COLLECTIONS IN THE MUSEUM OF NEW MEXICO.

John Sloan. *El Gallo (Santo Domingo Pueblo)*, oil on
vas 26 x 35″ signed LL and painted 1922. His name was
e past tense of slow.'' CREDIT, THE ANSCHUTZ COL-
TION.

277. Cecil Smith. *Lonesome Land*, oil on Masonite 20 x
29½″ signed LL. Nothing second-handed or done from
scrap. CREDIT, THE AUTHORS.

278. Elmer Boyd Smith. *The Range War*, watercolor on board 17 x 10¾″ signed (LR) E Boyd Smith. A writer and illustrator with a long list of books. CREDIT, THE AUTHORS.

279. Gean Smith. *Buffalo in Winter*, oil on canvas 26 x 2 signed LR and dated 1905. "The likeness of a horse in act is above the legs." CREDIT, THE AUTHORS.

280. Gordon Snidow. *Tommey*, drawing signed (LR) G Snidow. Tapes an interview as he sketches, to play back as he paints. CREDIT, THE ARTIST.

1. Frederic Soldwedel. *California Yuccas or Candles Christ Tree*, watercolor 14 x 10″ signed LL and dated 22. Marine painter in the desert. CREDIT, THE AUTHORS.

282. Clyde Squires. *Gun Lesson* from *Western Romances*, oil on board 15 x 11″ signed (LR) Squires and painted about 1925. "Always worshipped at the shrine of woman-kind." CREDIT, THE AUTHORS.

283. John Mix Stanley. *Group of Piegan Indians*, oil 27 x 41″ signed (LL) J M Stanley and dated 1867. Most important of the railway survey painters. CREDIT, DENVER PUBLIC LIBRARY, WESTERN HISTORY DEPARTMENT.

284. Junius Brutus Stearns. *The First Ship*, oil on canvas 37 x 54" signed (on rock) Stearns and dated 1853. Frequently used Indians in historical subjects. CREDIT, THE AUTHORS.

285. Charles Stobie. *Ute Indian*, watercolor over pencil 9 7" signed (LR) Chas Stobie and dated 1868 in Denve Mountain Charlie, the buffalo hunter and Indian scout. CRI DIT, THE AUTHORS.

286. H M Stoops. *Shoot-Out with Apaches*, oil on canvas 28 x 40" signed LR and dated 1924. Important illustrator of 1920s painting scenes from his own experiences. CREDIT, THE AUTHORS.

287. Gardner Symons. *Grand Canyon, Arizona*, oil on can vas 46 x 72". To see through the picture the work of th Master Painter. CREDIT, THE ANSCHUTZ COLLECTION.

288. Richard Tallant. *Old Indian Church, New Mexico*, oil 21¾ x 33⅝" signed (LL) Tallant and dated 1888. Painted directly from nature, all over the West. CREDIT, DENVER PUBLIC LIBRARY, WESTERN HISTORY DEPARTMENT.

289. Jules Tavernier. *Habitations Mexicaines, Las Animas, Colorado*, watercolor 4¾ x 10". The Bohemian of San Francisco Bohemians. CREDIT, DENVER PUBLIC LIBRARY, WESTERN HISTORY DEPARTMENT.

. Tom Thomson. *The Jack Pine*, oil on canvas 50¼ x 55" nted 1916-17. The leading Canadian painter of his era, an mple for the Group of Seven. CREDIT, THE NATIONAL LLERY OF CANADA, OTTAWA.

291. Jack Thurston. *The Avengers (Outlaws Three)*, tempera on board 16 x 17" signed (LR) Thurston. Specialized in motion picture illustration. CREDIT, THE AUTHORS.

293. Allen True. *St Francis of Assisi Church, Taos, NM*, oil 15½ x 20″ signed (LR) True. Native Colorado illustrator and painter of Western life. CREDIT, DENVER PUBLIC LIBRARY, WESTERN HISTORY DEPARTMENT.

292. Bruce Timeche. *Wu-pa-mau Kachina, mudheads. Let's Get Him*, watercolor 19 x 13″ signed LC and dated Hopi '64. A carver of Kachinas and ethnographic Hopi painter. CREDIT, THE AUTHORS.

294. Andy Tsinajinie. *Mounted Indian Smoking*, tempera 19 x 15″ signed (LR) Tsinajinie. "One of the most gifted of modern Navaho artists." CREDIT, THE AUTHORS.

295. Walter Ufer. *Solemn Pledge*, oil on canvas 28 x 2 painted about 1923. Handled recognizable Taos forms in anecdotal manner. CREDIT, THE AUTHORS.

296. Manuel Valencia. *Headwaters Colorado River*, oil on canvas 20 x 30″ signed (LR) M Valencia. A native of California, he spent most of his life in San Francisco. CREDIT, THE AUTHORS.

297. Jack Van Ryder. *Well of the Desert*, oil on canvas 12 x 16″ signed LL and dated 1939. Learning to read and write seemed to help him in art. CREDIT, THE AUTHORS.

298. Theodore Van Soelen. *In the Days of Grim Romance*, oil on canvas 52 x 58″ signed (LC) Van Soelen and dated 1927, If Van Soelen pictures were used on timetables, the trains would be crowded. CREDIT, THE ANSCHUTZ COLLECTION.

299. Ames Van Wart. *Indian Vase*, marble 46¾″ high. Expatriate sculptor of marble portrait busts. CREDIT, THE METROPOLITAN MUSEUM OF ART, GIFT OF THE ESTATE OF MARSHALL O ROBERTS, 1897.

300. F H Varley. *Mountains, Mist and Reflections, Kooteenay Lake*, oil on canvasboard 12 x 16″ signed (LL) Varley. Alone and penniless 1940–44, drinking heavily and painting little. CREDIT, THE NATIONAL GALLERY OF CANADA, OTTAWA.

301. Carlos Vierra. *San Juan Pueblo Mission*, oil 28 x 36″ signed LC. The earliest permanent Santa Fe artist did not understand modernists. CREDIT, COLLECTIONS IN THE MUSEUM OF NEW MEXICO.

302. Charles Von Berg. *On the Buffalo Range*, oil on canvas 37½ x 57¾″ signed (LR) Capt C L von Berg and dated 1909. Colorado scout and painter. CREDIT, DENVER PUBLIC LIBRARY, WESTERN HISTORY DEPARTMENT.

303. Harold Von Schmidt. *A Snare for the Wicked*, oil on Masonite 24 x 30″ signed (LR) V S and published 4/4/56 *Sat Eve Post*. Designated the 1960 *Pony Express* postage stamp. CREDIT, THE AUTHORS.

305. James Walker. *California Vaqueros*, oil on canvas 31 x 44″ signed (LR) J Walker and dated 1875. Painter of the Mexican War and the Civil War. CREDIT, THE ANSCHUTZ COLLECTION EX THE AUTHORS.

304. Gil Walker. *Young Cowboy and His Mount*, pen and ink drawing 5½ x 3″ signed (LC) G W. Illustrator of military and action subjects. CREDIT, THE AUTHORS.

306. Stanley King Walls. *Spanish Mission, Tucson, Ariz*, oil on board 24 x 30″ signed LC and dated 1957. English landscape painter. CREDIT, THE AUTHORS.

307. E F Ward. *The Thundering Herd*, oil on canvas 30 x 30″ signed LL and dated 1923. The painting made it on its own feet. CREDIT, THE AUTHORS.

308. Olin L Warner. *Joseph, Chief of the "Nez Percé" Indians*, bronze medallion 17½" diameter signed and dated 1889. "His statue would leap to his feet." CREDIT, THE METROPOLITAN MUSEUM OF ART, GIFT OF MR AND MRS F S WAIT, 1906.

309. H J Ware. *An Encampment with Indian Tents, Jasper, Alberta*, watercolor and gouache on blue-gray paper 6⅞ x 10¹/₁₆". British army officer on survey 1845-46. CREDIT, ROYAL ONTARIO MUSEUM, TORONTO.

310. George Smith Watchetaker. *Indian Chief*, pencil drawing 16 · 12" signed LL and dated 1959. Comanche "World's Championship Indian Dancer." CREDIT, THE AUTHORS.

311. Edwin Lord Weeks. *Seated Indian*, grisaille on canvas 11 x 9" signed LR. Painter of the African desert people. CREDIT, THE AUTHORS.

312. Dan Weggeland. *Handcart Pioneers*, signed LR. From sketches while traveling from Nebraska in 1862. CREDIT, CORPORATION OF THE PRESIDENT OF THE CHURCH OF JESUS CHRIST OF LATTER-DAY SAINTS, 1975.

313. Cady Wells. *Taos Portrait*, watercolor and ink on board 10 x 8" signed LR and painted about 1939. "Sum up weeks of looking in a few lines." CREDIT, THE AUTHORS.

314. W P Weston. *Canada's Western Ramparts*, oil on canvas 36 x 40" signed LL and painted about 1930. He "outgrouped the Group of Seven." CREDIT, THE NATIONAL GALLERY OF CANADA, OTTAWA.

315. F Ballard Williams. *Grand View, Grand Canyon of Arizona on the Santa Fe*, oil 31 x 70″ signed LL and dated 1911. Transcribes what he feels. CREDIT, THE ANSCHUTZ COLLECTION.

316. Charles Wimar. *Council Fire*, pastel 15 x 19″ signed (LL) C Wimar and dated 1860. Romantic realism by "the Indian painter." CREDIT, THE ANSCHUTZ COLLECTION.

317. Joseph Wolf. *Bison and Grizzly Bear, Rival Monarchs*, charcoal on paper 7½ x 5½″ signed (LR) J Wolf and drawn about 1869 for "School Board Reader." "The best" English animal painter. CREDIT, THE AUTHORS.

319. N C Wyeth. *Silver Queen Shot into Flight*, oil 32 x 40″ signed (LR) Wyeth and published in *Collier's* 1916. "To draw virile pictures, live virilely." CREDIT, THE ANSCHUTZ COLLECTION.

318. Stanley L Wood. *A Desperate Chance*, oil on board 10¾ x 7⅛″ signed LL and published in *Little Folks* 1921. English Special Artist-illustrator in the American West 1888. CREDIT, THE AUTHORS.

320. F C Yohn. *Custer's Last Stand*, oil on canvas 26 x 32″ signed LL and painted 1929. "A lot of composition and plenty of action." CREDIT, THE AUTHORS.

321. Harvey Young. *Westward Bound in Utah*, oil on board 19 x 29½" signed LR and titled on reverse. Creative in comfort anywhere along the tracks. CREDIT, THE AUTHORS.

322. John Young-Hunter. *End of the Santa Fe Trail*. A Renaissance hall for a studio in the sagebrush. CREDIT, MUSEUM OF NEW MEXICO.

painted Oregon landscapes. In 1886 he painted California adobes and missions before visiting Yosemite and Yellowstone. Stuart had studios in NYC where he also studied, and in Chicago, in Portland, and again in San Francisco. Through his habit of writing on the back of each painting, he is known to have made over 5,000 paintings, from Alaska to the Panama Canal and from California to Maine. The studio productions were elaborate and pretentious compared to the large oil "sketches" made in the field. His specialty was painting on aluminum. Five of these were sold for $15,000 each, but the result was not the claimed indestructibility and it is noted that "when times were bad he sold stacks of paintings for a fraction of the inscribed price of one." PNW.

STYKA, Adam. Born Kielce, Poland 1890, died probably NYC about 1970. Illustrator of Western subjects, painter of Arab genre. References BEN-MAL. No other source or signature example. Oil 13×16″ on board *Arab Women in an Oasis* sold 10/31/73 for $225 at auction in London.

Styka was the pupil of his father Jan Styka and his brother Thaddeus Styka. He studied at the École des Beaux-Arts in Paris 1908–12, then painted in North Africa such works as *The Souks at Biskra, Arab Encampment, Arab Sheiks Holding Council, Algerian Street.* His Western paintings were reproduced in color lithographs.

SULLY, Alfred. Born Philadelphia, Pa 1820, died Fort Vancouver, Wash Terr 1879. Amateur watercolorist of Western forts, soldier, Indian fighter. Work in

HON. References BEN-FIE-G&W. Sources HON-JNB-POW. No current auction record. Painting example ⚹57 JNB.

Alfred Sully was the son of Thomas Sully who was America's premier portrait painter after the death of Gilbert Stuart. Alfred was the son known as the soldier and Indian fighter, not the son who was the painter, Thomas W. Sully. He entered West Point at 16, graduating in 1841. After service in the Mexican War he sailed from NYC to Monterey, Cal where he was Quartermaster from 1848 to 1852. HON lists a small Monterey watercolor painted in 1849. He married the daughter of a distinguished Mexican-Spanish family who died before he served in the Indian campaign in Oregon. Sully also had assignments in the Dakotas and to build Fort Ridgely in Minnesota, meanwhile painting a series of watercolors in the 1850s. He fought during the Civil War, ending as a major general on an expedition against the Indians in the Northwest.

In 1870 Sully was transferred to Fort Vancouver. As post commander, he was able to devote more time to his paintings, which are of historic interest.

SUYDAM, Edward Howard. Born Vineland, NY 1885, died Charlottesville, Va 1940. Pa and Cal illustrator, painter, and printmaker. Member SI. Work in NY Pub Lib, Cal St Lib, Royal Ont Mus (Toronto). References A47 (obit)-FIE-MAL-SMI. Source 50G. No auction record. Signature example p 393 50G.

Suydam studied with Thornton Oakley at the School of Industrial Art in Philadelphia. He was an illustrator for books with locales in NYC, New Orleans, Chicago, as well as California. Books he illustrated include "Los Angeles, City of Dreams," "San Francisco, a Pageant," and "California's Missions." He also illustrated for periodicals such as *Harper's, The Forum, Country Life.*

SWANSON, Jack N. Born Duluth, Minn 1927, living Carmel Valley, Cal 1976. Traditional Western painter, sculptor. Member CAA. Work in Cowboy Hall of Fame, Read Mullan Gallery, Diamond M (Texas). Reference A76. Sources COW-C71 to 74-OSR-WAI 71. No current auction record. Signature example C71.

Raised in California, Swanson from the age of 14 worked on ranches, as a wrangler, and with standardbred horses at the race track. After service in the Navy during WWII he attended the College of Arts and Crafts in Oakland, quitting to race his quarterhorse when the teaching seemed too classically impractical. Getting back into painting was through advice from Donald Teague and John O'Shea.

Swanson operates a ranch where he raises and trains stock horses. The subjects for his paintings are the genre of his ranch, the horses and their activities.

SWEENEY, Dan. Born Sacramento, Cal 1880, died probably NYC 1958. Magazine illustrator, particularly of Western and marine subjects, of the 1930s. Work in *Collier's*. Reference MAL. Sources BWB-ILA-ILG. No auction record. Signature example p 157 ILA.

Sweeney was an artist for the *San Francisco Chronicle* and for the *Overland Monthly* whose editor grouped Sweeney with Maynard Dixon and Henry Raleigh as his beginners who had graduated to the NY magazines. BWB. Sweeney also designed theater and travel posters, becoming a world traveler in the course of his research. He was best known for his Western and marine illustrations in the form of wash drawings for *Collier's*. ILA shows an illustration for a 1940 Western story.

SWING, David Carrick. Born Cincinnati, Ohio 1864, died Phoenix, Ariz 1945. Ariz landscape painter, musician, teacher. Work in Phoenix Pub Lib, Golden Gate Int Expos (San Francisco). No reference. Source BDW. No auction record or signature example.

Swing was president of the Los Angeles Engraving Company 1905–14. He painted in Pasadena, Cal. In 1917 he moved to Arizona where he taught at Phoenix Junior College. He was known for large paintings of the Arizona desert and for murals of the Southwest in the Golden Gate International Exposition and Phoenix Masonic Temple.

SWINNERTON, James Guilford. Born Eureka, Cal 1875, died Palm Springs, Cal 1974. Desert landscape painter, illustrator, cartoonist, "the Dean of Desert Artists." Work in Gardena high school (Cal). References A41-FIE-MAS. Sources AAR 11/74-BWB-COW-GWP-HAR-POW-WAI 71,72. Oil 30¼ × 40¼" *View from Pueblo Point, Grand Canyon* signed but not dated was estimated at $4,000 to $6,000 for sale 3/4/74 at auction in Los Angeles, but did not sell. Oil 16×20" *Yuma Desert* in same sale, estimated at $1,400 to $1,800, sold for $1,600. Signature example p 74 GWP.

Swinnerton was raised in the Santa Clara valley by his grandparents, after his mother died. His grandfather had been successful in the Gold Rush. His father was a newspaper editor and judge. At 16 he enrolled in the San Francisco

Art Association Art School, the pupil of W Keith and E Carlsen. His talent for caricature led him to become newspaper cartoonist for William Randolph Hearst. His comic strip in 1892 was among the first. When he moved to NYC with Hearst, "he was making and spending large sums of money. He lived a gay, full, and fast life." GWP. His comic strips were "Little Jimmy" and "Little Tiger." At 28, however, he collapsed from tuberculosis and was sent to Colton, Cal to recuperate.

From 1903 on, Swinnerton was a painter of the desert landscape. In the beginning, the collectors rejected his paintings because the scene was not the stereotyped wasteland of the Sahara. Swinnerton persisted. As he recovered physically, he explored unfamiliar regions of New Mexico, Arizona, and southern Utah. In 1907 his Arizona subjects became favorites, including the Grand Canyon and the Indians. *Good Housekeeping* magazine printed his "Canyon Kiddies." Over the years Swinnerton has been the friend of other Western artists like Borein and Carl Eytell, and the inspiration of younger artists like McGrew, George Marks, and Bill Bender.

SYMONS, George Gardner. Born Chicago, Ill 1863 (or 1861), died Hillside, NJ 1930. Landscape painter including the Grand Canyon and the Southwestern deserts. ANA 1910, NA 1911. Work in ANS, MMA, COR, AIC, City AM (St Louis), Cincinnati Mus, etc. References A30 (obit)-BEN-FIE-MAL-SMI. Sources AMA-MSL-SCA-WHO 26. Oil 50×60″ *A Snowy Landscape* sold 2/28/72 for $1,200 at auction in LA. Painting examples AMA pp 184–85. (See illustration 287.)

Titled the "Optimist in Art," Gardner Symons was "both an Impressionist and a Realist." AMA. He studied at the AIC and then in Paris, Munich, and London. Favorite subjects for his landscapes were the Berkshires, California, and Europe, especially snow scenes. "The object of picture painting is not so much the picture painted," he said, "but rather to see through it the work of the Master Painter of them all." AMA.

"In his western scenes he shows the gorgeousness of the Grand Canyon or the sombre green of the desert." MSL. He painted entirely out-of-doors. Symons visited California in 1896 when he painted with William Wendt. Later he had a studio in Laguna Beach, Cal.

TABER, W. Active probably 1891 in San Francisco as illustrator for *The Century* magazine, photographer succeeding to Watkins' negative collection. Work in Honeyman colln. No reference. Sources CIV-HON. No auction record or signature example.

HON lists two *Century* illustrations, probably drawn from Watkins' photographs. The first was of the 1851 hanging of James Stuart in San Francisco. The second was of an 1850 view of North West Cañon on American Fork.

MAS and NJA list T Walter Taber as a NJ artist. In CIV, 18 drawings are credited to "Walton" Taber.

TAFAGA (or Tafoya), Joseph. Painter living Santa Clara Pueblo, NM in 1968. Work in MNM. No reference. Sources AIP-COW. No auction record or signature example.

TAFT, Lorado Zadoc. Born Elmwood, Ill 1860, died Chicago, Ill 1936. Important sculptor of large statuary, teacher, lecturer, writer. ANA 1909, NA 1911, NSS. Work in CSFAC; statuary at AIC, Oregon (Ill), Washington, Chicago, Denver, Urbana, etc. References A38 (obit)-BEN-DABS-ENB-FIE-MAL-SMI. Sources AIC-ALA-AMA-DCC-DEP-MSL-NA 74-NSS-POW-WHO 36-*The Nat Geog Mag* 11/37 p 544. Bronze *Standing Indian* dated 1913 sold 1/30/69 for $840 in London. Signature example p 317 NSS.

Educated at home, Taft received his MA in 1880 from the U of Illinois where his father was professor of geology. Determined to be a sculptor after having assembled broken plasters in 1874, Taft went to Paris on an allowance of $300 per year. He spent $252, remaining three years at the École des Beaux-Arts as the pupil of Dumont, Jules Thomas, and Bonnassieux. Although he could not get commissions back in Chicago in 1886, he pioneered in teaching at the AIC, introducing marble carving and group compositions. His first recognition was in 1893 at the World's Columbian Exposition. His "History of American Sculpture" was published in 1903. His "Clay Talk" lecture-demonstration was given thousands of times. His studio barn in the Chicago Midway became the Renaissance-like center of a collection of buildings housing young artists. During WWI the Government sent Taft to France to lecture the soldiers on beauty.

"A slender man, of distinguished appearance, Taft was habitually reserved and dignified, yet he was a warm and brilliant speaker with amazing generosity toward younger sculptors." DAB II. The first of his works to be cast in concrete was a statue of Blackhawk, 48′ high, on a bluff "overlooking the vast stretch of land once the hunting ground of his tribe." AMA. Near this spot Blackhawk with 40 braves had "stampeded 275 Illinois militiamen." *Nat Geog.* If Taft's work "seldom exceeded competence" in its conservative classicism (ALA), he did play an important part in the country's artistic education.

TAHOMA, Quincy. Born near Tuba City, Ariz 1921, died Santa Fe, NM 1956. Navaho painter, muralist. Work in GIL, MAI, MNM, Philbrook AC, Southwest Mus. Sources AHI 2/50,7/56-AIP-COW. No auction record but the estimated price of a watercolor 16×30″ of Navaho family riding would be about $800 to $1,000 at auction in 1976. Signature example AHI 2/50.

Tahoma in Navaho is Water Edge. He was educated at Albuquerque Indian School 1936–40 and did postgraduate work at Santa Fe Indian School where he developed his first and pastoral painting style. He worked briefly in Hollywood movie studios, then established himself as a full-time artist in Santa Fe. His subjects began as quiet and peaceful but became more intense and active, eventually stressing bloody wars and hunts.

TAIT, Agnes (Mrs William McNulty). Born NYC 1897, living Santa Fe, NM 1962. Illustrator, painter, muralist, printmaker. Work in MNM, NY Pub Lib, MMA, Lib Cong; murals in Bellevue Hosp (NY) and US PO in N Car. References A62-MAL. Sources AAT-ANT 4/69-WAA. No auction record. Painting example oil 23×46″ *To the New Lands* p 436 ANT 4/69.

A pupil of the NAD, Ms Tait was living in NYC 1931–39. By 1941 she was in Providence, RI as a portrait and mural painter.

TAIT, Arthur Fitzwilliam. Born Livesey Hall, near Liverpool, Eng 1819, died Yonkers, NY 1905. Important painter of Western, sporting, and animal subjects for Currier & Ives. ANA 1853, NA 1858. Work in COR, DAM, ACM, Phila Centennial, BM, Yale U AG, etc. References A05 (obit)-BEN-CHA-DAB-FIE-G&W-MAL-SMI. Sources AAR 3,5/74-ALA-ANT 5/45;4/67;1/49;2/50;5, 11/51;10,11/52;7/54;4/55;1/56;5,9, 12/57;10/59;7/62;2/63;3/67;3,4,10, 12/68;11/69;1,6,7/71;4,5/72;6/74; 2/75-AWM-BAR-COW-CUR-DAA-DBW-DCC-HAR-HUT-150-KW1-M19-NA 74-PAF-POW-STI-WES-WHI-WHO 03. Oil 17×27½″ *Fowl and Peacocks* signed and dated 1899 sold 4/11/73 for $16,000 at auction. Signature example p 41 SPB 5/22/73 at LA.

After attending a country school, when he was 12 Tait was employed by Agnew's, Manchester, England, art dealers. At night he studied from casts at the Royal Manchester Institute. Apart from this limited exposure and study, he was self-taught. According to HAR, Tait assisted Catlin with his *Indian Gallery* in London and Paris. To paint the wilder outdoors, Tait emigrated to NYC in 1850. He was immediately successful, with a studio on Broadway and a camp on Long Lake in the Adirondacks.

At this time the publisher N Currier had hired Ives as his bookkeeper. The firm of Currier & Ives was to produce more than 7,000 different prints, priced from five cents to three dollars. One of the finest C&I artists was Tait, beginning in 1852. Great care was used in reproduction of Tait paintings, nearly always in large folio, with the ablest hand-colorists, because Tait had the leverage of being an independent artist rather than an employee. As of 1928 the record price for a C&I print was for Tait's *The Life of a Hunter*. CUR. About 1950 Simkin claims to have seen a Tait print priced higher than the original Tait painting. Tait and Louis Maurer collaborated on the C&I series of Indians and Western life. "Neither had any knowledge of Indians. Their research was done in the Astor Library, on illustrations by Bodmer and prints by Catlin." CUR. Tait never did go "farther West than Chicago." DCC. "He was a skillful academic painter in a community which had no acquaintance with the best in art." DAB.

TALLANT, Richard H. Born Zanesville, Ohio 1853, died Estes Park, Colo 1934. Rocky Mountain landscape painter, illustrator. Work in Murray and Harmsen collns. No reference. Sources DCC-HAR. No current auction record but the estimated price of a Western landscape would be about $1,000 to $1,200 at auction in 1976. Signature example SUG 3,4/73. (See illustration 288.)

Tallant lived as a young man in the Colorado mining camps. Self-taught as an artist, he was a member of the Denver Art Club in 1886–87. The years 1889–91 were spent in Salt Lake City, but thereafter he maintained his permanent residence at Devil's Gulch near Estes Park, Colo for 31 years. He served as Justice of the Peace.

Tallant's subjects were all over the West—Mt Hood, the Tetons, the Grand Canyon, the Colorado peaks, and Pueblo scenes with Indians. His oils have been illustrations for magazines and calendars, particularly his versions of Longs Peak. "Tallant usually painted directly from nature and added the finishing touches later in his studio." DCC.

TALMAGE, Algernon M. Born Oxford, Eng 1871, died probably London, Eng 1939. English landscape painter. Member Soc of Brit Artists. Work in museums of Pittsburgh, Adelaide, Perth, Blackpool, Manchester, Buenos Aires, etc. References BEN-MAL. Source, oil 30×40″ *Indian Encampment at Dusk* estimated for sale 10/28/74 at $600 to $800 and sold for $800 at auction in Los Angeles. Oil 24½×29½″ *Beach Scene* sold 11/7/73 for $1,300 at auction in London.

Talmage exhibited in London beginning 1893, in Liverpool in 1909, and in Paris beginning 1913. He was in Western US in 1918.

TAPPAN, William Henry. Born Manchester, Mass 1821, died same 1907. Landscape sketcher, mapmaker, engraver. Work in ACM, Wis Hist Soc. References BEN-FIE-G&W-SMI. Source AIW. No current auction record. Lithograph example ⚡1700 ACM.

Tappan was the middle brother of three who were engravers in Boston. He worked in the 1840s as an engraver specializing in portraits in mezzotint, "à la manière noire." As a member of Louis Agassiz's 1848 expedition to Lake Superior, he was with a party of 17 to collect specimens for the Harvard Museum of Comparative Zoology. His role is not recorded but the 1850 report was regarded as a "model" for the future and "beautifully illustrated." DAB (Agassiz).

In 1849 Tappan traveled the overland route to Oregon. Fifty of his sketches along the way have survived. Some of them were reproduced by the State Historical Society of Wisconsin in 1931. The Tappan sketches and the sketches of Joseph G Bruff are the primary source materials for views of the route. Tappan settled in the state of Washington until returning to Manchester in 1876. He served as a legislator in Washington and Massachusetts and wrote a history of Manchester.

TAVERNIER, Jules. Born Paris, France 1844, died Honolulu 1889. Important illustrator, Cal artist. Work in GIL, Wichita AM, Bohemian Club. References BEN-MAL. Sources AIW-BAR-BWB-CAP-C&I-COS-DBW-DCC-GIL-HON-IND-JNB-KW1-SSF-TWR-POW-WHI. Oil 20×16″ *Sunday Afternoon* 1871 sold 4/10/73 for $625 at auction. Signature example p 47 TWR. (See illustration 289.)

Tavernier was the pupil of Félix Barries in Paris and was recognized as a French landscape and genre painter who exhibited in the Paris Salon from 1865 to 1870. He fought in the Franco-Prussian War, then emigrated to NY, said to have been exiled as a Communist. He immediately became an illustrator for the NY *Graphic* and for *Harper's* which in 1873 teamed him with Paul Frenzeny for a sketching tour from NYC to San Francisco that was published from 1873 to

1876. In their joint work Tavernier probably created the composition and the background while Frenzeny added the foreground detail and the copying onto the engraving block where he sometimes forgot to reverse letters. The pay was $75 a full page, $150 a double page. They were an odd pair, excitable and extravagant and yet recording the commonplace in the West with accuracy and sympathy.

The first *Harper's* sketches were the Western emigration from NYC. The artists' route was via Pittsburgh and by rail across Missouri to Kansas to the terminus in Texas, then with a cattle drive across Indian Territory to Wichita, then rail to Granada, Colo and stage to Pueblo and rail to Denver for the winter 1873–74, then Fort Laramie in Wyoming, Red Cloud Agency in Nebraska, and rail to San Francisco with an excursion to Salt Lake City.

Tavernier arrived in San Francisco in 1874, was promptly elected to the Bohemian Club, and by 1875 his studio paintings were frequently reviewed in the San Francisco press. Some of his paintings were based on his illustrations, and an Indian scene was said to have been sold in 1879 for $2,000. He became the "Bohemian of Bohemians," the boon companion of California artists Julian Rix, Joe Strong, Amadee Joullin. "He painted grand pictures in the air," it was said, "but it was not until the screws had tightened that he would put these on canvas. The sheriff was continually taking possession of his studio for nonpayment of debts, so his friends had to go through mysterious rites, give certain knocks on the door and be inspected through peep holes before they could get in." AIW. In 1884 his friends raised the money to send him to Hawaii to escape the sheriff. There Tavernier painted island landscapes but was not permitted to leave because of his debts. He died from acute alcoholism. The Bohemian Club erected a granite shaft over his grave in memory of their love.

TAYLOR, Bayard. Born Kennett Square, Pa 1825, died Germany 1878. Illustrator and travel author. Reference G&W. Sources AIW-BAR-COS-SSF-SUR. No auction record but the estimated price for a sketch of a view of San Francisco in 1849 would be about $800 to $1,000 at auction in 1976. No signature example.

Taylor was apprenticed to a printer. In 1844 he published his first volume of poems and made his first visit to Europe as a newspaper correspondent. He wandered about for two years, wrote a series of articles and a successful book, "Views A-foot." In 1849 he was sent to California by the *New York Tribune* for a series of articles on the Gold Rush. These were the basis for his book "Eldorado, or, Adventures in the Path of Empire: comprising a voyage to California, via Panama; life in San Francisco and Monterey; pictures of the gold region, and experiences of Mexican travel, with illustrations by the author. New York. London. 1850." There were eight colored lithographs from Taylor's sketches, all landscapes of the cities and the diggings.

Most of the rest of Taylor's life was in travel in Europe, Africa, and Asia. His travel sketches were exhibited at the NA. In 1853 he joined Perry's expedition to Japan. In 1862 he was secretary to the American legation in St Petersburg. In 1870 he published his scholarly metrical translation of "Faust." He became professor of German at Cornell and ambassador to Germany.

TAYLOR, James Earl. Born Cincinnati, Ohio 1839, died NYC 1901. Illustrator called "The Indian Artist," watercolorist, panoramist, writer. References A03 (obit)-BEN-G&W-MAL-SMI. Sources AIW-SOA. Oil 28×46" *House at Edge of Town* sold in 1970 for $270 at auction. Signature example p 217 SOA.

At 16 Taylor graduated from the U of

Notre Dame. At 18 he had painted a panorama of the Revolutionary War that was exhibited successfully in Western cities. When he was 21 he settled in NYC and was employed by *Leslie's* as a staff artist. He joined the Union Army in 1861, becoming war correspondent for *Leslie's* in 1863.

After the war Taylor was sent to cover the Indian Peace Commission in 1867. In June *Leslie's* published his *Branding Cattle in Texas* which is among the first of the national reports on cattle ranching. In November, illustrations appeared on the Medicine Lodge council of the Peace Commission. He continued to go West on many occasions to paint the Indians and frontier life. G&W. "The pictures he sent from the West gained for him the name of 'The Indian Artist.'" A03. In the early 1870s he was in a photo of the *Leslie's* art staff including Berghaus, Thulstrup, and Yeager. He left *Leslie's* in 1883, becoming an independent illustrator and painter. One of his 1883 sketches from the book "Battles and Leaders of the Civil War" is reproduced in SOA.

TAYLOR, Rolla S. Born Galveston, Tex 1874, living San Antonio, Tex 1941. Texas landscape painter, etcher, teacher. References A41-BEN-MAL. Sources TOB-TXF. No current auction record. Signature example opp p 32 TXF.

Son of an actor father and a painter mother who moved from Georgia after the Civil War, Rolla Taylor was raised in the then frontier town San Antonio. In his teens he studied at the Art League of San Antonio. Educated as an attorney at Cuero Institute in Cuero, Tex he abandoned law to study art with José Arpa in San Antonio, with A W Best in San Francisco, and Fred Fursman in Michigan. He also studied with Julian Onderdonk and traveled in Europe in 1929.

His encouragement brought Dawson-Watson to San Antonio.

Taylor's best-known subjects were "Texas hills and mountains and bits of dear old 'Santone.'" Typical titles were *The Old Mill,* a landmark painted during "five afternoons of careful study," and *Autumn Morning* on the San Geronimo from "two afternoons sketching." TXF.

TAYLOR, William Ladd. Born Grafton, Mass 1854, died probably Wellesley, Mass 1926. Boston illustrator including frontier life, painter, specializing in Biblical subjects. Member SI 1905. Work in *Ladies' Home Journal* and "Our Home and Country." References A27 (obit)-BEN-FIE-MAL-SMI. Sources ARM-ILA-WHO 26. No current auction record but the estimated price of a Western illustration would be about $900 to $1,000 at auction in 1976. Signature example p 39 ILA.

Taylor was educated in Worcester, Mass. He studied in a Boston art school before coming to NYC to attend the ASL. He was also the pupil of Boulanger and Lefebvre in Paris. Returning to settle in Boston, he established himself as an illustrator interested in historical subjects. His paintings were printed full-color and full-page in the *Ladies' Home Journal.* They included *The 19th Century in New England, Old Southern Days,* and illustrations from Longfellow's poems. Reprints of his pictures for framing were frequent—*Housekeeping Hearts are the Happiest* in 1904 was the most popular picture ever printed in the *Journal.* These illustrations were also reprinted in "Our Home and Country" in 1908. At the epochal 1913 Armory Show, Taylor exhibited and sold two decorative panels.

When Taylor became ill and remained in Colorado for a year, he painted his series *Pictures of the Pioneer West.*

TEAGUE, Donald (or Edwin Dawes). Born Brooklyn, NY 1897, living Carmel, Cal 1976. Western illustrator, painter of the Old West, particularly in watercolor. NA 1948 as aquarellist, member CAA, Nat Acad of Western Art. Work in Va MFA (Richmond), Frye Mus (Seattle), Air Force Acad, MCA. References A76-BEN-MAL. Sources AAC-COW-C71,72-ILA-ILG-ILP-NA 74-PER vol 3 ⚹3-POI-PWA-WAI 71-WHO 70-*Amer Artist* 6/62. No current auction record. Signature example p 109 ILA.

Teague studied at the ASL 1916–17, the pupil of Bridgman and DuMond. After service in the Navy during WWI he was the pupil of Norman Wilkinson in London. When he returned to NYC he again studied at the ASL 1919–20, the pupil of Dean Cornwell who helped Teague begin as an illustrator in 1921. Because he was a primary illustrator for *The Saturday Evening Post,* he signed *Collier's* illustrations with another name, Edwin Dawes.

In the 1920s Teague spent several summers on a Colorado ranch. When he moved to California in 1938 he specialized as a Western illustrator until *Collier's* ceased publication in 1958. "Since then, I have devoted my entire time to painting." C71. His technique is to begin with thumbnail sketches in black and white, then in color to resolve composition. Models and props are available from the nearby movie studios, so they are posed for sketching and photography. Photostats are projected and traced on watercolor paper, ready to paint. Teague has also painted *Masterpieces of the Old West* as calendar art. His work has been important to younger Western painters like Jack Swanson and Bob Meyers.

TEASDEL (or Teasdale), Mary. Born Salt Lake City, Utah 1863, died Los Angeles, Cal 1937. Utah landscape, floral, and portrait painter, teacher. Work in Carnegie Pub Lib (32 paintings in Southfield, Utah), Utah St Cap, U of Utah. References A21-MAL. Sources PUA-YUP. No current auction record but the estimated price of a Utah landscape would be $400 to $500 at auction in 1976. Signature and monogram p 20 YUP.

Daughter of a prosperous merchant, she was educated in Salt Lake City schools, graduating U of Deseret in 1886. She studied art and music. At 28 she became the pupil of Harwood. En route to Europe, she studied at the NAD in NYC in 1897, the pupil of De Forest Brush. She then spent three years studying in Paris, the pupil of Simon, Constant, and Whistler who had his studio in an old house. Whistler "tinted the walls and hung drapes. He dressed himself with immaculate care. He always wore black gloves when giving lessons and criticisms." PUA.

When she returned to Salt Lake City in 1903, she opened her own studio and was an art instructor in the schools. Painted in a bravura style, her portraits at first "brought her ridicule" while her landscapes were "still daring enough to fail of success in those early days." *Western Art*. By 1908 she was the first woman to be recognized in Utah exhibitions, as she had been the first Utah woman to be accepted in the French salons. She was painting watercolors in Los Angeles by 1931, a member of Women Painters of the West.

TEEL, Lewis Woods. Born Clarksville, Tex 1883, living El Paso, Tex 1948. Painter of the Southwestern desert in oil and of portraits in pastel, commercial artist. Reference MAL. Sources TOB-TXF. No auction record or signature example.

Son of a pioneer Texas family, Teel was raised in El Paso. He observed commercial artists in Detroit where he worked in an auto plant for two years, then set out on three years of traveling and study of paintings. When he returned to El Paso, he began sketching scenes, drawing pastel portraits, and designing magazine covers, but was advised by J H Sharp in Santa Fe that his forte was desert subjects. In 1927 he sketched in Arizona and West Texas. Teel also operated the "Desert Shop," a gallery for local artists. His son Lew Teel, Jr was an etcher.

TEICHERT, Mrs Minerva Kohlhepp. Born Ogden, Utah 1889, living Cokeville, Wyom 1974. Western muralist, painter, illustrator of historical Mormon and Western subjects, writer. Work in Wyom St Cap, Utah school and religious buildings. References A41-MAS. Sources WAN-WNW-WYA-1/31/74 letter from J A Teichert. No current auction record. Monogram example "Selected Sketches of the Mormon March" by Minerva Kohlhepp Teichert, no date or publisher shown.

Daughter of covered-wagon pioneers and raised on an isolated farm in Idaho, Mrs Teichert worked for her board to be able to attend Pocatello high school. She reached San Francisco as a nursemaid and studied at Mark Hopkins Art School. After teaching school in Idaho for a year, her savings took her to the AIC where she worked her way to graduation in 1912. She taught again in 1913, then from 1914 to 1917 attended the ASL with Henri and Bridgman on scholarship. After marrying her cowboy sweetheart as he went off to WWI, she settled into Idaho "bottoms" life as a ranch wife-painter, raising five children while writing about and painting the landscape "from Horse Island to the cataracts at American Falls, picturesque cowboys, gaudily attired bucks, dances to the Sun God and the ruins of old Fort Hall." *Relief Society Mag* 3/38.

In 1935 she turned to Latter-day Saint

subjects, *Captain Bonneville and the Trappers at Cache Valley, Saved by the Seagulls, Indians Making a Forced March by Moonlight*. During the winter of 1947 she painted a mural on the four walls of the World Room in the Manti Temple (Manti, Utah), with each wall 30 feet high and 60 feet long. "She has been a very dynamic, brilliant woman with enthusiasm and a lot of imagination." J A Teichert.

TERRY, W Eliphalet. Born Hartford, Conn 1826, died probably NYC 1896. Eastern animal and landscape painter in the West with W J Hays in 1860. Reference G&W. Sources AIW-BAW. No current auction record but the estimated price of a Western oil would be about $1,500 to $2,000 at auction in 1976. Painting example p 20 BAW.

In 1846–47 Terry studied in Rome with his cousin Luther Terry, the expatriate portrait and figure painter. Terry returned to Hartford before moving to NYC about 1851. William Jacob Hays also maintained a NYC studio and by 1852 was exhibiting at the NA and the American Art Union, as was Terry.

In the spring of 1860 Terry and Hays arrived in St Louis. On May 3 they boarded the steamer to ascend the Missouri River. Arrival at Fort Union, on the Missouri above the mouth of the Yellowstone River, was June 15. They went upriver another 80 miles to Fort Stewart in eastern Montana, their westernmost travel, remaining June 19 to July 9. Homeward bound, they docked at St. Louis July 27 along with "1,800 packages of buffalo robes, furs, peltries, etc., and a young grizzly bear." AIW. There is lengthy reporting on Hays' sketches made on the trip, but Terry is referred to as "one Terry" who "possibly may have been W E Terry, a wealthy amateur animal painter who lived for a time, at least, in Hartford." AIW. Illustrated in BAW, however, is *Indian Camp Near Yellowstone, 1860* identified as by Eliphalet Terry, with the place "Yellowstone" meaning the river at its mouth, not the region of the river's origin.

THAYER, Emma Homan (Mrs Elmer A Thayer). Born NYC 1842, died probably Denver, Colo 1908. Colo painter and illustrator who specialized in flora of Colo, writer. Reference A05. Source WHO 08. No auction record or signature example.

Mrs Thayer was educated at Rutgers College. She studied at the NAD and was one of the original members of the ASL, the pupil of Chase and Church. Her figure paintings were exhibited at the NAD. She married George A Graves at 18 and was widowed at 22. When she was 25 she remarried and in 1882 she moved to Denver.

By 1885 she had written and illustrated "Wild Flowers of Colorado." In 1887 she wrote and illustrated "Wild Flowers of the Pacific Coast."

THOMAS, Bernard P. Born Sheridan, Wyom 1918, living Boynton Beach, Fla 1975. Traditional Western painter, muralist. Sources COW-WYG-catalogs from Tucker's Art Gall. No current auction record. Signature example and portrait photo in catalogs.

Thomas was born on a ranch, "most fortunate to have worked with the cowboys of the past." When he moved into town to go to elementary school, he was a neighbor of Bill Gollings. "Just watching him in his little clobbered-up studio was all a kid needed." COW. Thomas studied at Woodbury College in Los Angeles and, after WWII, at École des Beaux-Arts in Paris on a scholarship.

Thomas has an 80-foot mural on the history of the Black Hills in a Dakota bank, and he is said to have created in Florida the largest three-dimensional mural ever painted by one artist. Thomas also paints "ranchscapes," blending into one painting the buildings, the landscape, a distant landmark, and something personal in the foreground.

THOMAS, Majorie Helen. Born Newton Center, Mass 1885, living Scottsdale, Ariz 1948. Painter and illustrator. Work in Governor's Office (Phoenix), illustration in "Old Bill Williams." References A41-FIE-MAS. Sources AIW-WAA. No auction record or signature example.

Marjorie Thomas studied at the BFMA school, the pupil of Tarbell, Benson, and Hale. She also studied with Louis Kronberg and J P Wicker. In 1924 she exhibited at the PAFA. By 1934 she was listed as living in Scottsdale. According to AIW she used a Richard Kern view as a model for her color illustration *Old Bill Williams at Cochetopa Pass* in Favour's 1936 book "Old Bill Williams."

THOMAS, Stephen Seymour. Born San Augustine, Tex 1868, died La Crescenta, Cal 1956. Pioneer Texas genre and landscape painter, international portrait painter. Chevalier, Legion of Honor 1905. Early Texas paintings Dallas MFA; later portraits widely collected including White House, MMA, Houston AM, Tex Hist Soc. References A41-BEN-FIE-MAL-SMI. Sources M57-TEP-TOB-TXF-WHO 56. Oil 10×14" *La Crescenta, Cal* sold 4/30/69 for $100 at auction. Signature example p 170 TEP.

Son of a pioneer family with the first two-story house in Texas and a grandfather who nominated Gen Houston for the Texas presidency, Seymour Thomas was a recognized artist at eight. At 16 his paintings were exhibited, reviewed in NYC, and sold at auction to finance study at the ASL 1885–88. He went on to the Julien Academy, the pupil of Lefebvre and Constant 1888–91. His genre painting *The Innocent Victim* in 1892 established his reputation so that he could spend 25 years in Paris. When he returned to NYC he remained five years before settling in California where he was active as a portrait painter.

On a visit to the US in 1897 Thomas undertook a commission for the city of Houston, an 8′×10′10″ equestrian portrait of Gen Sam Houston leading his soldiers at San Jacinto. The city did not accept the portrait because it did not "reveal the real spirit." TEP. In 1921 the portrait was finally accepted as a present from the artist who was given in appreciation a portfolio of paper currency of the Republic of Texas. TOB.

THOMASON, John William, Jr. Born Huntsville, Tex 1893, died San Diego, Cal 1944. Illustrator of the military and the West, writer. Marine Corps colonel. Reference MAL. Sources 50G-TOB-WHO 46. No auction record. Monogram example p 9 *Sat Eve Post* 10/21/39.

Son of a doctor, Thomason was educated at Southwestern U 1909–10, Sam Houston Normal Institute 1910–11, and U of Texas 1912–13. He studied at the ASL 1913–15 before enlisting in the US Marine Corps for WWI. A professional soldier, he was cited for heroism and after the war went with the Marines into Cuba and China until he became assistant to the Secretary of the Navy in 1933.

In 1925 he had been sponsored by the marine author of "What Price Glory" toward a Scribner's commission for "Fix Bayonets" which he wrote and illustrated. His early writings remained concerned with the Marines. They reflected the service attitude to the extent of set-

ting the tone for the Corps and qualifying as recruiting literature. Thomason also wrote and illustrated works on Texas including the Rangers, on Davy Crockett, and on Custer. He ascribed his style as a writer to having been compelled as a boy to read and reread the Bible.

THOMPSON, Jerome B. Born Middleboro, Mass 1814, died Glen Gardner, NJ 1886. Eastern genre, landscape and portrait painter. ANA 1851. Work reproduced in chromolithograph. References BEN-CHA-DAB-FIE-G&W-MAL-SMI. Sources AAR 11/74-ANT 10/48,1/49,11/56,5/70; 2,11/74-BOA-HUT-KAR-M19-NA 74-NJA-PAF-STI. Oil 24×20″ *Sailing in the Trough* 1859 sold 1970 for $8,250 at auction. Signature example ⨏115 M19.

Youngest child of a portrait painter who taught only the older brother to paint, Jerome Thompson was encouraged by his sister. When his enraged father smashed his work, young Thompson and his sister moved to Barnstable where he was a sign painter. Daniel Webster sat for a portrait, although the artist "had no masters and is a graduate of no schools." HUT. Another of his portraits was sketched in Nantucket in 1834, the "portrait of Abraham Quary, the last Indian of the Nantucket Tribe, age 64." ANT 1/49. This portrait was part of McKenney and Hall's "Indian Tribes of North America."

At 21 Thompson established a NYC studio, becoming known as a painter of sentimental genre. Reproduced as chromolithographs, some of his work became the most popular of the 1860s: "*The Old Oaken Bucket* is an illustration of the verses and a portrait of the early home." *New York Tribune*. "*Home, Sweet Home* is an ideal creation, and truthful to nature." *New York Turf*.

"He made many sketches in the Massachusetts Berkshires and Vermont, and in the far West." DAB. *Dakota Canyon* was dated 1880. CHA. His romantic works also included titles like *Hiawatha's Homeward Journey with Minnehaha* and *Indian Prayer* (1884). In 1852 Thompson had traveled to England to study Turner, and on his return he was noted as an avid gardener at his Mineola, LI farm. By the later stages of his life about 1865, however, he ceased exhibiting, so that the public knew his work only from the reproductions.

THOMSON, Tom. Born near Claremont, Ont, Can 1877, died Canoe Lake, Algonquin Park, Can 1917. Very important Can painter of the North Country. Work in AG Toronto, Montreal AA, NGC (5 paintings and 25 sketches), and private collns of patron and brother. References BEN-MAL. Sources CAH-CAN-CAR. No current auction record. Painting examples p 91 CAN, pp 92, 93 CAR. (See illustration 290.)

Thomson was raised in Leith near Owen Sound. In 1898 he became a machinist's apprentice, then quit to attend business school at Chatham, Ont. From 1901 to 1905 he lived in Seattle, beginning to sketch while working in photoengraving and advertising design. He moved to Toronto 1905, as a photoengraver. In 1910 he became a photoengraver for Grip Ltd, the focal point of Canadian landscape painting. In 1911 Thomson made his first North Country sketching trip, to Mississauga, establishing his practice of working as a commercial artist in winters, living in a Toronto shack, and leaving for the Northern Ontario wilderness in the spring. His first large painting *A Northern Lake* was bought by the Ontario Government in 1913. That fall he found a patron in Dr James MacCallum and received studio space from A Y Jackson. In 1914 NGC bought his *Moonlight, Early Evening*. When he drowned in 1917 he left only 20 paintings and 400 sketches.

"Tall and slim, clean-cut, dark young chap, quiet, reserved, he impressed me as full of resolution and independence." CAN. The leading Canadian painter of his era, the self-taught Thomson was an inspiration for the coming movement. He mixed Post-Impressionism, Fauvism, and Art Nouveau in a distinctively Canadian point of view that led in 1919 to the Group of Seven.

THORNTON, Mrs Mildred Valley. Born Dresden, Ontario, Can about 1900, living Vancouver, BC, Can 1941. "Recognized as a painter of Canadian Indians," portrait and landscape painter. Work in Regina club, Calgary and Vancouver hotels. No reference. Sources CAN-WNW. No current auction record or signature example.

Mrs Thornton studied at the Ontario College of Art in Toronto, the AIC, and was educated at Olivet College in Michigan. She showed at the Canadian National Exhibition in 1931 in Toronto.

THORPE, Everett Clark. Born Providence, Utah 1907, living Logan, Utah 1976. Utah portrait painter, muralist, illustrator, cartoonist, teacher. Member Nat Soc Mural Ptrs. Work in Utah colleges, Seattle AM, LA Cnty AM, U of Colorado; murals in Utah buildings. Reference A76. Source YUP. No current auction record. Painting example p 34 YUP.

Thorpe studied at the LA County AI, receiving his BS (1942) and MFA (1951) from Utah State U. He also studied at Syracuse U and at the Hans Hoffman SA. His teachers included Calvin Fletcher and LeConte Stewart in Utah, Grosz, Nordfeldt, Sepeshy, and

Zerbe. He has been professor of art at Utah State U since 1936.

Thorpe has worked as a sports illustrator for Utah newspapers beginning 1938. He has also illustrated books and magazines. A member of the National Society of Mural Painters, Thorpe has completed more than 20 murals: "Close in appearance to the work of Thomas Hart Benton, it is in many ways more satisfying than its prototype." YUP. He is said to be one of three Utah artists who could be called abstract-expressionists.

THURSTON, Jack L. Born St Catherines, Ont, Can 1919, living Westchester Cnty, NY 1975. Eastern illustrator including traditional Western subjects. Member SI. No reference. Source, March 1975 data from Jack Thurston. No auction record or signature example. (See illustration 291.)

Thurston's father was a landscape painter and semiprofessional magician. His grandfather was a captain of Great Lakes sailing ships. Thurston grew up in Niagara Falls and attended the Buffalo AI before WWII where he served Naval Intelligence as a sculptor of scale models of enemy terrain. Thurston later studied at Jepson's Fine Art School in LA and the Art Center in Hollywood.

Thurston worked as an art director in Rochester, NY, then as an illustrator. He specialized in motion picture illustration when he settled in NYC. Many of the pictures were Westerns, and Thurston also painted for book publishers. Like other good Western illustrators today, he is represented by a fine arts gallery in the West.

THWAITS (or Thwaites), no initial given (or William H). Active NYC 1854–60 and London 1880. Illustrator, landscape painter, engraver, designer. Work reproduced in "Beyond the Mississippi." References G&W-MAS. Sources AIW-BEY. No auction record. Sketch examples BEY.

Compiled 1857–67, BEY contains "more than 200 illustrations, from photographs and original sketches from the great river to the great ocean." Two simplistic illustrations are credited to "Thwaits" with no initial given. The first shows *Missouri Lead Miners,* the second the New Mexico desert. These would appear to have been drawn from existing materials such as photographs.

G&W refers to William H Thwaites in NYC 1854–60 who exhibited English and Welsh views. MAS lists W H Thwaites as an illustrator active in London 1880. The BEY-G&W-MAS references are compatible considering other spelling errors in BEY.

TIBBLES, Yosette La Flesche (Insthatheamba, Bright Eyes). Born Bellevue, Neb 1854, died Lincoln, Neb 1903. Omaha Indian painter, illustrator. No reference. Source BDW. No auction record or signature example.

Mrs Tibbles was educated in New Jersey and studied art at the U of Nebraska. She taught school and was interpreter for the Ponca Indians until she married the newspaperman Thomas H Tibbles in 1882.

TIDBALL, John Caldwell. Born Ohio Cnty, W Va 1825, died probably Montclair, NJ 1906. Railway survey artist, Civil War general, writer of military reports, army teacher. Work in Okla Hist Soc. References DAB-G&W. Sources AIW-SUR-WHO 06. No auction record or signature example.

Tidball graduated in 1848 from West Point where he undoubtedly had training in topographical drawing. As an artillery lieutenant he served against the Seminoles and in New Mexico. Then in 1853 he was named as an artist for the railway surveys to establish a route to the Pacific. There were 11 such artists, including the important John Mix Stanley, Richard Kern, Sohon, von Egloffstein, and W P Blake. Assigned to the 35th parallel expedition of Lt Whipple, Tidball and his party left Arkansas July 15, 1853. The route was across Texas, through New Mexico, across the Colorado and the Mojave desert, through the coast range, arriving March 21, 1854. Most of the illustrations in the report were by the official topographer Mollhausen. Four illustrations were from Tidball drawings, two of camp sites, the *Valley of Bill Williams' Fork* in Arizona, and *Valley of the Mohave* in California.

Tidball in 1859 served with the Harpers Ferry expedition to suppress John Brown's raid. He participated with skill and gallantry in the entire Civil War, rising from lieutenant to brigadier-general. It was Tidball who began the playing of "Taps" for military funerals, to avoid the alarm from a volley. After the war Tidball was on the West Coast, in Alaska, and acted as aide-de-camp to Sherman. He was described as "of martial appearance and austere manner" but "rich in humor and affability." DAB.

TIMECHE, Bruce. Born Shungopovi, Ariz 1923, living Phoenix, Ariz 1967. Hopi painter of portraits and ethnographic Hopi scenes, carver of Kachina dolls. Work in MAI, Mus No Ariz, Southwest Mus N Amer Indian (Marathon, Fla). No reference. Source AIP. No auction record or signature example. (See illustration 292.)

Timeche received a scholarship that enabled him to study at the Kachina School of Art, from which he graduated in 1958. He has worked on murals for the First National Bank and Desert Hills Motel in Phoenix. His genre paintings are realistic rather than symbolic. He is also "a carver of excellent Kachina dolls." AIP.

TINDALL, N. Active 1873–74. English Special Artist-illustrator. No reference. Source AOH. No auction record or signature example.

Tindall's article "An Artist in the Far West" appeared in *Graphic* in five installments in 1874. Scenes included buffalo hunting, Indians, mining, Mormons, US Cavalry, gunfighting, stagecoach travel.

TODDY, Jimmy. See Beatien Yazz.

TOFT (or Tofft, Toffts, Tufts), Peter Petersen. Born Kolding, Denmark 1825, died London, Eng 1901. Northwestern landscape painter in watercolor, illustrator. Work in Stenzel and Honeyman collns, Mont Hist Soc, illustration in *Harper's*. References BEN-MAL. Sources AIW-FRO-HON-KW1,2-PNW-TAW. No current auction record but the estimated price of a Western watercolor would be about $1,500 to $1,800 at auction in 1976. Signature example p 125 TAW.

Toft was educated and studied art in Denmark. At 16 he began his travels when he shipped on a whaler. In 1850 he arrived in California aboard the ship *Ohio*. While panning for gold in the Trinity River, he sketched his surroundings. By 1852 he was painting scenic watercolors in Oregon, Washington, and British Columbia. The last of this series was painted about 1866, the year he arrived in Fort Owen, Montana just after Christmas. Toft was the illustrator for an article on Montana that was published in *Harper's Magazine* in 1867. While living in Virginia City, Toft was invalided for most of the year by a fall from his horse. Toft also painted in Idaho.

Toft left for NYC in 1867, returning to Denmark in 1869. Some of his Western paintings were reproduced in the *Illustrated London News* in 1870. By 1871 he was in London, working as an artist and reporting on Royal Academy exhibitions through 1873 as well as exhibiting there himself through 1881. After travel to Australia where he exhibited, he returned to Copenhagen in 1890. Toft often painted replicas of his views. His practice was to include his monogram in his paintings, the letter "T" in a circle to form his initials.

TOLEDO, José Rey (Morning Star). Born Jémez Pueblo, NM 1915, living Laguna, NM 1967. Painter of the San Ildefonso movement, muralist, teacher. Work in GIL, MAI, MNM, Philbrook AC. Sources AHI 2/50,8/52-AIP. No auction record. Signature examples AHI 8/52.

Toledo also signs as Morning Star (Shobah Woonhon). His father was chief of the Jémez Arrow Society, a warrior lodge, and the first Indian owner of a modern general store in the Pueblo. Toledo was influenced toward art by his cousin Velino Shije Herrera. He attended Albuquerque Indian School, and earned his MA in art education from NMU in 1955. He has had more formal training than is usual for Indian artists but his style and subject matter remain pueblo-oriented.

He painted with the WPA 1940–41 and was an instructor at Santa Fe and Albuquerque Indian schools 1949–57.

Toledo was a successful member of the pueblo watercolor movement until the early 1960s when he became employed as a Health Education specialist.

TOMMEY, Bob. Listed in COW as a painter from Dallas known for scenes of Texas. No reference. No auction record.

The artist's undated catalog of Western bronzes describes him as self-taught and full-time as painter and sculptor of Western subjects. A Dallas resident since about 1950, Tommey also teaches and lectures. Bronze prices are $300 to $3,000, with typical titles *Bear, Longhorn Steer, Earrin' Em Down, Bushwhacked*.

TONK, Ernest. Born Evanston, Ill 1889, living Garden Grove, Cal 1968. Traditional Western painter, commercial artist, illustrator, muralist, writer. Mural in Willis Carey Hist Mus (Cashmere, Wash). No reference. Sources BAW-COW. Two gouaches 14×20″ scenes of cowboys dated 1953, 1954 sold 5/19/65 for $375 the pair at auction. Signature example p 106 COW.

When Buffalo Bill saw Tonk's drawings in Chicago in 1908, the advice was to go West while an artist could still emulate Remington and Russell. Tonk was employed in the West as cowhand, wrangler, and logger. He later operated a fruit ranch in Cashmere, Wash, painting in the winters. In the early 1920s he moved to Glendale, Cal to work as a commercial artist for the movies. As the demand for his paintings increased, he was able to paint all the time, working both in California and Washington. Tonk wrote and illustrated a "how to draw" book on horse and cattle subjects.

TORNEMAN, Axel. Active 1905 as painter of Indians. No reference. Source, graphite and pastel on brown paper 12×22″ *Scouting Party* signed with monogram and dated 1905 estimated for sale 10/28/74 at $600 to $800 at auction, as an attribution only, not as a recognized signature. No other source, auction record, or signature example.

TOSCHIK, Larry. Born Milwaukee, Wis, 1925, living Pine, Ariz 1976. Painter of Arizona birds, commercial artist, writer. Paintings of birds reproduced in *Arizona Highways,* in prints for framing, and in advertising. Member Nat Acad Western Art. Reference A76. Sources AHI 3/67, 3/70,10/71-PER vol 3 ⧣3. No auction record. Signature example p 19 AHI 10/71.

As a teenager Toschik hiked through the West to Great Falls, Mont. He worked at a variety of jobs in Montana, getting to know the Blackfoot Indians. During WWII, Toschik managed to study the art masterpieces in Italy.

After the war he was an art director. He moved to Phoenix about 1947 as a commercial artist, doing layout and design for magazines. He made drawings for *Arizona Wildlife Sportsman Magazine,* for juvenile books including one that became a Disney movie, and for wildlife manuals, one on the Arizona chaparral mule deer. In 1964 he joined the graphics department at Arizona State U and in 1967 painted for Ducks Unlimited. His series of paintings on the quail of Arizona appeared in 1971, along with an article he wrote on bird research and painting procedures.

TOUSEY, T Sanford. Active NYC at least during 1924–48 as book illustrator, art editor for publishers, author. Work in children's books on Western subjects. Reference MAS. Source AAC. No auction record or signature example.

Tousey listed himself in AAC (1924) as available for illustrations of men but not women, of men's heads but not children or "pretty girls." He worked in black and white, charcoal, or oil, but not dry brush or watercolor. MAS listed Tousey in 1948 as having been affiliated with three different book publishers.

TRAVIS, Olin Herman. Born Dallas, Tex 1888, living there 1976. Texas landscape and portrait painter, teacher. Work in Tex FA Mus (Austin), Dallas MFA, habitat backgrounds for Dallas Mus Nat Hist. References A76-BEN-FIE-MAL. Sources TOB-T20-TXF. No current auction record or signature example.

Son of a printer, Travis graduated from Metropolitan Business College and studied with R Jerome Hill in Dallas. Beginning at 21 he worked his way through the AIC for five years, the pupil of Kenyon Cox, C F Browne, and Ralph Clarkson. He then taught at the AIC and the Chicago Commercial Art School, leaving about 1913 to sketch on the Great Lakes and in the Ozarks. After he married Kathryn Hail, a former student, they established a joint studio in Chicago.

In 1923 Travis returned to Dallas with his wife, founding the Dallas AI in 1926 and a summer art colony in the Ozarks in 1927. Typical 1920s subjects are *Flickering Sunlight, West Texas Skies, Head Waters of the Concho,* at this period "reminiscent of Bruce Crane." TXF. In the 1930s he also painted Colorado landscapes. Travis was director of the Dallas AI until 1944. Mrs Travis was a still-life painter, particularly of Texas wildflowers, who had studied with George Bellows and Randall Davey.

TRIGGS, James Martin. Born Indianapolis, Ind 1924, living Larchmont, NY 1974. Illustrator of Western trompe l'oeil, Western still-life painter, writer. No reference. Source, illustration *The Colt's Single Action* in Colt's Hall of Fame. Signature example, same.

James M Triggs was educated in Glen Ellyn, Ill and Mamaroneck, NY public schools before service in WWII. He studied at Cornell U and Pratt Inst, then worked under Steven Dohanos and Coby Whitmore as a commercial artist. After adopting his trompe l'oeil style as an illustrator, he was assigned to advertising accounts. His first fiction illustrations were *Argosy* covers. In the mid-50s, Triggs specialized in writing and illustrating books and articles on aviation subjects.

In the late 1960s Triggs returned to the illustration of guns and other Western still-life subjects. His work appeared in *Guns Magazine, American Rifleman, Guns Annual, Gun Digest*, etc, as well as in advertising for Colt, Winchester, Sturm, Ruger, Smith & Wesson, etc.

TROTTER, Newbold Hough. Born Philadelphia, Pa 1827, died Atlantic City, NJ 1898. Philadelphia animal painter, particularly of the West. Work in War Dept, Penn RR, Smithsonian Inst, Valley Nat Bank (Ariz). References A98 (obit)- BEN - CHA - FIE - G&W - MAL - SMI. Sources ACO - ARC - DBW - HUT - NJA - PAF - WES. Oil 24×36¼" *The Young Bull* signed but not dated sold 11/17/72 for $600 at auction (painting listed in FIE). Signature example p 258 WES.

N H Trotter is considered to have been self-taught, working chiefly from nature in the US, although he did study at the PAFA and at The Hague in Holland with T van Starkenborg, a cattle painter. A lifelong resident of Philadelphia, he exhibited at the PAFA from 1858 as well as at the NA and the Boston Athenaeum. At the Philadelphia Centennial in 1876 he exhibited *Wounded Buffalo Pursued by Prairie Wolves*. "Trotter's *Fading Race,* a herd of buffalo speeding towards the setting sun, is poetical in conception." *Art Journal* 1877. For the War Department he painted *Indian Camp near Powder River*. Other animal titles are *Grizzly Bears on the March, Bison Fighting, Herd of Elk in Winter,* and *The Range of the Bison*.

The titles indicate time spent in the West for which dates are not available. Other titles show a trip to North Africa.

TRUE, Allen Tupper. Born Colorado Springs, Colo 1881, died Denver, Colo 1955. Western muralist, painter, illustrator, color consultant. Fellow, RSA (London). Work in Denver PL, HAR; murals in Colo St, Wyom St, and Mo St Capitols, banks, hotels, libraries, theaters. References A41-BEN-FIE-MAL-SMI. Sources SHO-SPR-WHO 50-WYA-*The Casper Tribune-Herald* 11/9/55 (obit). No current auction record but the estimated cost of an oil 20×30" showing emigrants' pastimes would be about $3,-000 to $4,000 at auction in 1976. Signature example p 39 SHO. (See illustration 293.)

True went to the U of Denver for two years, then attended the Corcoran Art School in Washington before becoming the pupil of Howard Pyle from 1902 to 1908. During this period his sketches of Western life were reproduced in *Outing*. All were Colorado scenes—*Breaking the Trail, Homesteader in the Quicksands*. He drew illustrations of the West for national magazines, *Harper's, Collier's, The Saturday Evening Post*. In 1911 he illustrated a book on Colorado—*Pioneers and Conestoga Wagon, Indians Watching Frémont's Force, Pike Leaving Two Comrades with Frozen Feet near Canon City*. He was also the pupil of Frank

Brangwyn in London and was Brangwyn's assistant for two years, helping with the decorations for the Pan-Pac Expos in 1915. True was the illustrator of the book "Song of the Indian Wars." He worked in England as well as in the West and was the subject of a one-man exhibition circulated in 29 cities. During 1924 he studied in France.

In 1935 he was government consultant on decoration and color scheme for the Boulder Dam power plant project. In 1946 he laid out the decorative color scheme for the Grand Coulee and Shasta Dam power plants. True had returned to Denver in 1917 to paint the eight murals in the Colorado State Capitol telling Western history in terms of dependence on water. His most famous design was the bucking horse for Wyoming license plates.

TSATOKE, Monroe (listed MAL as Tsa Toke). Born Saddle Mountain, Okla 1904, died Okla 1937. Painter, one of the "Five Kiowas." Work in GIL, MAI, MNM, Philbrook AC, etc. Reference MAL. Source AIP. No current auction record or signature example.

Tsatoke, or Tsa To Kee, "Hunting Horse," was the son of a Kiowa scout for Custer, grandson of a white captive. He attended Rainy Mountain Indian School. When he was as young as 11, he began to paint, entirely self-taught. He worked as a farmer. It was said of Tsatoke that as of 1926 "he could always draw pictures, but never took any art lesson until Mrs Susie Peters organized a Fine Arts Club. Mrs Willie Baze Lane also gave lessons and encouragement." In the fall of 1926 he received private instruction from Miss Mahier at the U of Oklahoma, as one of the Five Kiowas. The Kiowas supported themselves in part by giving recitals at which Tsatoke, a leading singer at Kiowa dances, was singer and drummer. His wife Martha sang a lull-

aby. In late spring 1927, Tsatoke returned to the reservation to farm for the summer. He continued his painting classes in the fall. By 1928 the Five Kiowas were an international sensation. Dr Jacobson's book on the Kiowas was published in 1929. Tsatoke was exhibiting in NYC by 1930.

When Tsatoke became ill with tuberculosis, he joined the Native American Church, painting a series of works concerning his religious experiences in the Peyote faith. These paintings were published posthumously. He was the father of the artist Lee Monette Tsatoke who also studied with Mrs Susie Peters and then became the pupil of Acee Blue Eagle.

TSCHUDI (or Tschudy), Rudolf. Born Schwanden-Glarus, Switzerland 1855, died Cincinnati, Ohio 1923. Cincinnati painter of landscapes, portraits, and still life, including historical subjects with Indians; teacher. Work in Cosmopolitan Bank (Cincinnati, 2 paintings), Evanston School (Cincinnati, 3 paintings), Glarus AM (Switzerland, 11 paintings). References A23 (obit)-BEN-FIE-MAL-SMI. Source, Oil *Indian Encampment* illustrated p 372 ANT 10/62. No current auction record.

The pupil of Ruch in Glarus, Tschudi won a medal in Cincinnati when he was 19. His historical paintings included *Surrender of Lee* and portraits of Jefferson and Lincoln.

TSINAJINIE, Andrew Van. Born Rough Rock, Ariz 1918, living Scottsdale, Ariz 1967. Important Navaho painter, illustrator. Work in AMNH, COR, GIL, MAI, MNM, U of Okla, Philbrook AC. No reference. Sources AHI 2/50,12/58-COW-LAF-MCA. Tempera on board

14×12" *Mounted Brave Drinking* signed Tsijnahjinnie estimated for sale 10/28/74 at $300 to $500 at auction in LA, but did not sell. Signature example Tsinajinie AHI 12/58 *Going to the Sing*. (See Illustration 294.)

Andy Tsinajinie has spelled his name in various ways, Tsihnahjinnie, Tsinajinnie, Tsinajininie, Tsinnaijinnie, etc. His Navaho name is Yazzie Bahe, Little Gray. In his 1950 paintings he used hogan and barn motifs above his signature. He is a musician, a member of the Navaho Salt River Band and the Navaho Tribal Band.

He has been a serious painter since 1940 and was working full time as a painter in 1967. His subject matter has varied from ceremonial scenes, war and hunting, Navaho genre, to fanciful drawings. He is known for his color phases—blue, pink, etc. He has painted fire dance scenes against a black background. In his yellow phase he used yellow as a flesh color, and in another phase, terra cotta. LAF calls "Tsinnahjinnie one of the most gifted of modern Navaho artists" who came from a most primitive part of the Navaho Reservation to Santa Fe Indian School when he was 16. He began by copying the Pueblo painters and ended by having other Indian painters copy him because of the strength of his personal style.

TUCKER, Allen. Born Brooklyn, NY 1866, died probably NYC 1939. Modern painter of portraits and landscapes including Western subjects, writer, teacher, architect. Work in BM, MMA, WMAA, Albright Gall (Buffalo), Phillips Mem Gall (Washington). References A41 (obit)-BEN-FIE-MAL-SMI. Sources AAR 11/74-ALA-ARM-190-M31-MSL. Oil 24×20" *Mountain Landscape* sold 1969 for $200 at auction. Signature example p 130 ARM.

Tucker was educated at Columbia U.

He studied art at the ASL in NY and was the pupil of J H Twachtman. He exhibited in the Paris Salon as well as in NYC and Philadelphia. His role in art history followed from his charter membership in 1911 in the Association of American Painters and Sculptors. Along with the prime movers Walt Kuhn and Arthur B Davies, the Association was responsible for the 1913 Armory Show.

The Armory Show included five paintings by Tucker. One of these was *Storm in the Rockies* dated 1912. *Western Wagon in the Rockies* an oil 24¼×20" signed and dated 1925 was sold in 1971 for $70 at auction. In 1924 Tucker had been allied with Henri, Luks, and Sloan in the functioning of the ASL. He wrote "Design and the Idea" and "There and Here."

TUCKERMAN, Lilia McCauley (Mrs Wolcott Tuckerman). Born Minneapolis, Minn 1882, living Carpinteria, Cal 1962. Cal landscape and mural painter. Work (backgrounds) in Santa Barbara MNH, mural and triptych in Cal churches. References A62-BEN-MAL. Source WAA. No auction record or signature example.

Mrs Tuckerman studied at the COR SA and was the pupil of G S Noyes, C H Woodbury, and DeWitt Parshall. She painted the backgrounds for museum animal habitats, including an elk group. She settled in California by 1919 and was listed as actively painting until 1962.

TULLIDGE, John. Born Weymouth, Eng 1836, died probably Salt Lake City, Utah 1899. Pioneer Utah landscape painter, muralist, teacher. Murals in LDS temples. No reference. Sources JUT-YUP. No current auction record but the estimated price of a major Utah landscape would be $600 to $700 at auction in 1975. Painting example p 14 YUP.

Tullidge was raised along the English seacoast. At 14 he was apprenticed as a decorative painter. He joined the LDS Church when he was 16, emigrating to Salt Lake City in 1863. Although he had little formal art training, he was considered an excellent instructor of perspective, landscape painting, and life drawing at Deseret Academy of Fine Arts beginning 1863. Tullidge worked as a scenery painter in the Salt Lake Theater. In his "attractive" landscapes, "a calm luminism pervades his work." YUP.

TURNER, Charles Yardley. Born Baltimore, Md 1850, died NYC 1918. Painter of decorative murals, literary and historical painter, teacher. ANA 1884, NA 1886. Work in MMA, MNM, Bklyn Inst Arts and Sciences, murals in Baltimore and other court houses, hotels, World's Columb Expos. References A19 (obit)-BEN - CHA - DAB - FIE - MAL - SMI. Sources ISH-M31-MSL-NA 74-WCA-WHO 18. Oil 23×12" *Woman Picking Wildflowers* 1882 sold in 1972 for $400 at auction. Signature example p 29 WCA I.

Educated in Quaker schools, Turner worked as a photographic finisher. In 1870 he graduated from the art school of the Maryland Institute which he had attended at night. He moved to NYC in 1872, working in photography while studying for six years at the NA and at the ASL of which he was a founder. From 1878 to 1881 he studied in Paris, the pupil of the muralist Laurens, the colorist Munkacsy, and the figure painter Bonnat. When he reuturned to NYC, he was an instructor at the ASL 1881–84. His oils and watercolors were an immediate success, particularly his series of paintings concerning Miles Standish.

After acting as assistant director of decoration at the Chicago World's Fair in 1893, he specialized in mural paintings. His best-known work was in the Baltimore Court House, *The Barter with the Indians* and *The Burning of the Peggy Stewart*. Turner had a Vandyke beard and well-formed features, and was an unmarried man of unusual kindliness, charm, and simplicity. DAB.

TURNER, Elmer. Born 1890, place unknown, died probably Taos, NM 1966. Taos landscape painter. Work in HAW. No reference. Source TAL. No auction record or signature example.

Turner, the husband of Ila McAfee who also painted in Taos, came to Taos in 1926. *Cottonwoods in the Canyon* is in the HAW colln. His career was ended by a physical disability.

TWACHTMAN, John Henry. Born Cincinnati, Ohio 1853, died Gloucester, Mass 1902. Important Conn impressionist landscape painter in Yellowstone Park 1895. Founding member, The Ten American Painters. Work in AIC, COR, MMA, NGA, BM, etc. References A03 (obit)-BEN-CHA-DAB-FIE-MAL-SMI. Sources AAR 9/73; 3,5/74-ALA-AMA-ANT 10/52,10/62,12/63,11/65,6/67, 5/68,4/72; 9,11/73-ARM-DEP-HUT-INS 6/25,5/28-190-ISH-M19-MSL-STI-WHO 01. Oil 24×20" *The Falls of Yellowstone Park* sold 1/27/65 for $850 at auction. Oil 18½×15¾" *Harbor Scene* estimated to sell 10/16/74 for $10,000 to $12,000 at auction but did not sell. Signature example p x INS 6/25, initials p 749 ANT 11/73.

The son of German farmer immigrants, Twachtman decorated window shades as a boy. At 15 he studied at night at Ohio Mechanics Institute, then at 18 studied with Frank Duveneck at McMicken School of Design in Cincinnati. In 1875 he went with Duveneck to the Royal Academy in Munich, the pupil of von Loefftz. He painted in Bavaria in 1876 and with Duveneck and Chase in Venice in 1877. For the next five years he painted in Cincinnati, NYC, and Europe, his style influenced by Duveneck and Munich. In 1883 Twachtman studied at the Julien Academy in Paris, with his palette lightening and his brush strokes more delicate. In 1888 he bought a farm near Greenwich, Conn. His landscapes became very personal interpretations of nature, decorative and poetic in intent. He also illustrated for *Scribner's* 1888–93.

In 1894 Twachtman was in Buffalo, painting views of Niagara. In 1895 he painted in Yellowstone park. The oil *Falls of the Yellowstone* is shown p x INS 6/25.

TYLER, Gerald Hall. Born Birmingham, Eng 1897, living Vancouver, BC, Can 1941. Canadian West Coast landscape and marine painter. No reference. Sources CAN-WNW. No current auction record or signature example.

Tyler was the pupil of W F Tyler but considered himself as mainly self-taught. He exhibited in both the Canadian East and West, and was a student of the chemistry of paint.

UFER, Walter. Born Louisville, Ky 1876, died Albuquerque, NM 1936. Important Taos painter of Indians. ANA 1920, NA 1926, Taos SA 1914. Work in AIC, ANS, LACMA, MNM, Nat Cowboy Hall Fame, GIL, COR, MMA, BM, Houston MFA. References A38 (obit)-BEN-FIE-MAL-SMI. Sources AMA-ANS-COW-DCC-EIT-HAR-HMA-ISH-M57-PIT-TAL-TSF-WAI 71-WHO 36. Oil on canvas board 30×25" *The Water Carriers* with signature example and inscribed Isleta, NM, estimated for sale 3/10/75 at $10,000 to $12,000 at auction in LA and sold for $7,500. (See illustration 295.)

Ufer, the son of a German immigrant who was a master engraver, was educated in the Kentucky public schools until 1891. He became apprenticed to a Louisville commercial lithographer in 1892, then went to the Royal Applied Art Schools in Dresden, Germany 1895–96 and the Royal Academy in Dresden 1897–98. A successful printer, he decided to utilize his realistic painting style developed in Europe by becoming a fine artist. He attended the AIC, then the J Francis Smith Art School in Chicago from 1901 to 1903 when he became a teacher and painted some portraits. He worked with Armour & Co's advertising department from 1905 until 1911. For the next two years he studied with Walter Thor in Munich. In 1913 he painted in Paris, Italy, and North Africa.

In 1914 Ufer moved to Taos. Called "energetic, outspoken, and uninhibited" (TSF) as well as "stormy, irascible, and intransigent," he painted "easily recognizable forms in an anecdotal manner," the only Taos artist who was compared to Cézanne. AMA. In 1920 he won third prize at the Carnegie International, a breakthrough in prestige for Taos and for Ufer who was getting $3,000 each for paintings. Ufer's dealer managed sales of $50,000 per year from 1921 to 1923, then persuaded Ufer to specialize in paintings of an Indian on a white horse against the background of Taos Mountain. The approach failed. Ufer broke emotionally, borrowed money, gambled, and drank. In a 1927 letter, Ufer wrote Blumenschein, "If I had money, I would be doing something more manly than paint pictures. My regret is that I cannot compete with real towering men." TSF.

ULREICH, Eduard Buk. Born Guns, Austria-Hungary 1889, living San Francisco, Cal 1962. Painter of genre, sculptor, muralist, illustrator for magazines in 1920. Murals in hotels, temples; industrial buildings, post offices. References A62-BEN-FIE-MAL. Source AAC. No current auction record or signature example.

Ulreich was the pupil of Mlle F Blumberg. He also studied at the Kansas City AI and the PAFA. In the 1920s he lived in NYC and worked as a general illustrator for books and magazines. A member of the Guild of Free Lance Artists, he included Western subjects in his illustrations. His wife "Nura" was an author and illustrator of children's books and an art instructor. Ulreich's post office murals included one in North Dakota. The murals were painted for the Federal Works Agency.

VALENCIA, Manuel. Born California 1856, died Sacramento, Cal 1935. Painter. Work in Bohemian Club (San Fran), Huntington Art Gallery (San Marino, Cal). References A36 (obit)-MAS Reference BDW. No auction record or signature example. (See illustration 296.)

Valencia spent most of his life in California painting in the San Francisco area. He painted California and Colorado landscapes and scenes of the pueblos.

VANDERHOOF (or Vanderhoff), Charles A. Birth place and date unknown, died Locust Point, NJ 1918. Eastern illustrator for *Harper's,* painter, etcher, teacher. Work in Stenzel colln. References A18 (obit)-SMI. Sources AOA-CIV-NJA-PNW. No current auction record. Signature example p 128 AOA.

Vanderhoof was a *Harper's* illustrator in 1881. AOA shows a drawing of a NYC slum. In the late 1880s he taught at Cooper Union, wrote on art, and illustrated magazines. PNW shows *Wheat Threshing in the West.* CIV indicates Vanderhoof's Civil War drawing may have been done in the 1880s.

VANDERLYN, John. Born Kingston, NY 1775, died there 1852. Important historical and portrait painter, illustrator. Member 2nd of fifteen founders, NAD, 1826. Work in MMA, COR, PAFA, Wadsworth Atheneum (Hartford), De Young Mem Mus (San Francisco). References BEN-CHA-DAB-ENB-FIE-G&W-MAL-SMI. Sources ALA-AMA-ANT 6/44,1/48,4/55,7/58,6/62;2, 7/71;11/74-ARI-BAR-BOA-BOL-COR-HUD-ISH-KW1-M15-M19-NGA-NA 74-PAF-TEP. Oil study 10×8″ *Portrait of Aaron Burr* sold in 1972 for $7,500 at auction. No signature example.

The grandson of an early Manhattan painter, Vanderlyn was educated at Kingston Academy until 16. He then moved to NYC where he worked for a print-seller while studying for three years with Archibald Robertson. His copy of a Gilbert Stuart portrait of Aaron Burr induced Burr to become Vanderlyn's patron. Burr sent Vanderlyn to study with Stuart in Philadelphia, commissioned portraits, and sponsored five years of study in Paris 1796–1801. After painting views of Niagara Falls in the wilderness in 1802, Vanderlyn returned to Europe from 1803 to 1815. In 1807 in Rome, his *Marius* received a gold medal from Napoleon. In 1812 in Paris he painted his famous nude *Ariadne.* When Vanderlyn returned to NYC in 1815, however, it was to professional tragedy. As Burr's protégé he was unpopular. Trumbull was the established artist. When Vanderlyn exhibited his panorama of Versailles, he was evicted by the city for nonpayment of debts. His panel, *The Landing of Columbus,* in the Capitol was attacked as a forgery. He died alone and penniless in a rented room.

While in Paris in 1804 Vanderlyn's first historical painting had been *The Death of Jane McCrea.* It was commissioned as an illustration for Joel Barlow's epic poem of the scalping of Jane—"and thro her face divine/Drive the descending axe"—and the neoclassical Indians in the painting became the models for countless copies in popular works by Eastern artists.

VANDERVEER, Miss M H. Active in the 1850s. Illustrator. No reference. Source BEY. No auction record. Monogram p 140 BEY.

Illustrator of *A House "Twelve by Fourteen"* in BEY, showing a land claim in 1858 in Kansas based on a house 12″×14″ instead of the required 144 square feet. There is no indication that Miss Vanderveer was in Kansas for her drawing, probably made in NYC about 1865 from existing materials such as photographs.

Compare Mary Van Der Veer born 1865 in Amsterdam, NY and living there 1941. She was listed A98 to A41-FIE as a painter, the pupil of Whistler and Chase.

VAN RYDER, Jack. Born Continental, Ariz 1898, died probably Tucson, Ariz 1968. Traditional Western painter, illustrator, etcher, writer. References A41-MAL. Sources ANT 3/65-CAP-COW-WAI 71. No current auction record but the estimated price of an oil 20×30″ showing Arizona wranglers would be about $900 to $1,200 at auction in 1976. Painting example p 342 ANT 3/65 *Apache Trail*. (See illustration 297.)

Van Ryder was an illiterate Arizona wrangler who traveled to Montana with a shipment of Mexican steers. He remained in the Northwest for years, working as a cowboy and competing in rodeos. "Eventually, he learned to read and write, and this seemed to help him in his art work, too." COW. He worked for the movies as an extra and helped paint a relief map of California. He is said to have been a pupil of Charles Russell while in Montana. His paintings nearly always tell a story of Arizona. Typical subjects are ranch life, cowboys, and Indians, particularly of the Tucson area where he became a rancher.

VAN SOELEN, Theodore. Born St Paul, Minn 1890, died Santa Fe, NM 1964. Western painter, lithographer, illustrator, muralist, writer. NA 1940. Work in PAFA, MNM, NAD, Everhart Mus (Scranton), Loomis Inst (Conn), IBM Corp. References A66 (obit)-FIE-MAL. Sources   AIW-CAP-COW-M50-PIT-

TSF-WHO 62. No current auction record but in M50, *Roundup Cook* was offered for sale at $3,500 at MMA in 1950. Signature example p 85 COW. (See illustration 298.)

Van Soelen was a student of St Paul Institute 1908–11. He studied at PAFA 1911–15, following which he began work as an artist. Because of tuberculosis he went to the Utah-Nevada mountains, then in 1916 to Albuquerque where he worked as a commercial illustrator. In 1920–21 he lived at San Ysidro's Indian trading post to gain experience with the land and its inhabitants. He had a one-man exhibition at the Cincinnati Art Museum. In 1922 Van Soelen moved to Santa Fe, then in 1926 became a permanent resident of neighboring Tesuque.

He exhibited with the New Mexico Painters society which combined the best of Taos and Santa Fe. He retained his own illustrator's style with its apparent realism. Like Thomas Moran he freely reassembled compositional elements to depict the allure of New Mexico: "If reproductions of Van Soelen pictures were used on railway time-tables, the trains to Santa Fe, Taos, etc would be far more crowded than they are at present." TSF. His specialty was ranch scenes but he also painted landscapes objectively as well as many official portraits. By the 1930s the demand for his paintings was large enough in the East to permit him to establish a second studio in Connecticut, although his affiliations remained in New Mexico. In addition he wrote for *Field & Stream*.

VAN WART, Ames. Active NYC beginning 1870, died Paris, France about 1927. Expatriate sculptor of marble portrait busts. Work in MMA. References A25-FIE-MAL. Source SCU. No auction record or signature example. (See illustration 299.)

Van Wart was the pupil of Hiram

Powers. He exhibited busts in the Paris Salons of 1904–5. His work in MMA is a marble *Indian Vase* 46¾″ high.

VARIAN, George Edmund. Born Liverpool, Eng 1865, died Brooklyn, NY 1923. Illustrator for magazines and books, painter. Work in *McClure's*. References A23 (obit)-BEN-FIE-MAL-SMI. Sources 50G-ILP-KEN 6/70-WHO 12. Two paintings, charcoal 18½×17½″ *Ceremonial Gathering* and oil on paper 23×15″ *Two Braves* sold 10/27/71 for $1,200 the pair at auction. Signature example p 63 KEN 6/70.

Varian was educated at Public School No 10 in Brooklyn. He studied at the Brooklyn Art Guild and the ASL. After working as an illustrator he was commissioned in 1902 to illustrate "The Tragedy of Pelée" for *McClure's*. He and author George Kennan and Prof Angelo Heilprin were the first to reach the crater at the top of Mount Pelée on the island of Martinique at the time of the destruction of St Pierre. They were almost killed by one of three eruptions they saw. Illustrations for "Seen in Germany" required European travel with Ray Stannard Baker. Varian exhibited at the Paris Salon in 1907.

The Varian illustration of troopers seizing Sitting Bull in 1890 is not considered historically accurate. There is no indication Varian personally witnessed the "Ghost Dance" troubles.

VARLEY, Frederick Horsman. Born Sheffield, Eng 1881, died Toronto, Ont 1969. Important Canadian portrait, figure, and landscape painter in Vancouver 1926–36, illustrator, muralist, teacher. Original member, Group of Seven 1920–33, Assoc RCA 1922. Work in NGC, U Toronto, AG Toronto, AA Montreal, U Alberta, U Brit Col; murals in Toronto church. References A70 (obit)-BEN-MAL. Sources CAH-CAN-CAR-WNW. No current auction record. Painting example frontispiece CAN. (See illustration 300.)

F Horsman Varley studied at the Sheffield School of Art in England up to 1899, then at the Antwerp Academy 1900–2. He moved to London 1904–8 as an illustrator, returning to Sheffield 1909–11. Varley went to Toronto in 1912, working with Grip Ltd, photoengravers. Grip maintained a staff of commercial artists which also included J E H MacDonald, Arthur Lismer, Frank Carmichael, Frank Johnston, and Tom Thomson. These artists became part-time landscape painters, traveling to Algonquin Park and the Canadian North Country, developing a nationalistic approach to painting. During WWI the group disbanded, with Varley for example serving as artist for the War Records Office, evoking later paintings symbolizing the futility of war.

In 1920 Tom Thomson having died in a canoeing accident, the rest of the old Grip staff joined with A Y Jackson and Lawren Harris to found the Group of Seven whose manifesto proclaimed the emergence of native Canadian art. Varley taught in Ontario 1925–26 and in Vancouver 1926–36. Of his West Coast sketches, views of the Howe Sound area were best known. Varley moved to Ottawa to teach in 1936, traveling to the Arctic in 1938 for sketches "among the most beautiful" ever produced. CAH. He was in Montreal 1940–44, "alone and penniless, drinking heavily and painting little." CAH.

VAVRA, Frank Joseph. Born St Paul, Neb 1898, died Denver, Colo 1967. Colo painter. Work in DAM and Wyom and Colo St Capitols. References A41-MAS. Sources WAN-WYA-*Denver Post* 5/2/67 (obit). No auction record or signature example. Portrait photo *Post* above.

498

Vavra grew up and attended school in Cheyenne and later worked there as a window decorator. During his convalescence from poison gas in WWI, he studied art in France with Monet. He also studied at the Denver Art Academy and was the pupil of G W Eggers, J Thompson and R A Graham. After moving from Cheyenne in 1923, he opened his first studio in Denver, painting landscapes, portraits, still life, and especially scenes of his Wyoming youth. In 1928 he bought an old building near Bailey, Colo, carving and painting it into an art object that was "the most individual studio in the Rocky Mountain region." WAN. He also taught at the U of Denver.

VEBELL, Edward T. Born probably Chicago, Ill 1921, living Westport, Conn 1974. Illustrator of action subjects including Western and military. Member SI. No reference. Source ILA. No auction record. Signature example, cover *Real West* magazine 8/72.

Vebell studied at the Professional Art School in Chicago, the Harrison Art School with E W Ball, the American Academy of Art, and the Commercial Art Institute. In WWII he was a correspondent for *Stars and Stripes* in Europe. The next two years were spent in Paris as an illustrator.

In 1947 Vebell established himself as a free-lance illustrator for the NYC market, working for *Life, True, Reader's Digest, Outdoor Life,* and *Sports Illustrated.* In addition to Western subjects, he specialized in military and sports. Vebell was also world class in the épée.

VELARDE, Publita. Born Santa Clara Pueblo, NM 1918, living Albuquerque, NM 1976. Important Pueblo woman artist, illustrator, teacher, author, lecturer. Work in DAM, GIL, MAI, MNM,

Philbrook AC, State of NM; murals in commercial buildings. Reference A76. Sources AHI 2/50-AIP-LAF-PWA 3/75. No current auction record. Painting example p 124 LAF *Turtle Dance.* Portrait photo p 5 PWA 3/75.

Ms Velarde attended mission school in Anadarko, Okla, graduating from Santa Fe Indian School in 1936, studying under Dorothy Dunn. She also studied with Tonita Pena, the "mother" of Pueblo art. In 1938 she toured the US with E T Seton, the naturalist, and became an assistant art teacher at Santa Clara Day School, building her first studio at the Pueblo. She made ethnological watercolors for Bandelier National Monument Mus where she lectured on the exhibits. Her book "Old Father, the Story Teller" was named one of the "best books of 1961."

Her early style was said to show "the poise and gentle strength" of a Pueblo woman. In 1956 she created her "earth paintings" made from crushed rock and glue on Masonite. She did not consider this to be a new trend but said she paints the beauty and dignity of the past. A winner of France's Palmes Académiques, she is one of the best-known Indian artists. PWA 3/75.

VENTRES, M P. Active Tucson, Ariz 1939–48. Painter of tempera landscape *"A" Mountain, Tucson, Ariz* shown p 154 AAT as exhibited NY World's Fair 1939. Work in DAM. References MAS. Source AAT. No auction record.

VERELST, John (or Johannes, or Jan). Born Dordrecht, Holland 1648, died London 1719. Royal court painter. Work in British Mus, GIL, Mus of Amsterdam. References BEN-MAL. Sources ANT 7/58-GIL. No current auction record but the estimated price of an Indian portrait would be about $20,000 to

$25,000 at auction in 1976. Signature example p 57 ANT 7/58.

Verelst was mentioned as in London in 1681. He was court painter for Queen Anne. Many of his portraits were reproduced as engravings. Flowers and birds were other subjects favored by Verelst.

When four Mohawk Indian chiefs were brought to London and presented to Queen Anne in 1710, it was "to publicize the need for more adequate defenses of the colony against the French. In England, these Indians were a fashionable novelty and enjoyed a sensational success." ANT. Verelst as the court painter made portraits of the visiting Indians, just as C B King did of the Plains Indians a century later in Washington. Verelst's portraits were full length with an imaginary forest scene in the background. The technique was flat and decorative, in effect like the American portrait painting of the time. The Library of Congress has the portrait *Sa Ga Yeath Qua Pieth Tow, King of the Maquas* in a mezzotint engraving by John Simon. GIL has the similar portrait *Etow Oh Koam, King of the River Nation,* mezzotint 13½×10⅛". The portraits were painted when Verelst was 62, still quite competent near the end of a successful career.

VERNER, Frederick Arthur. Born Sheridan, Ont, Can 1836, died probably Ont, Can 1928. Canadian Rockies painter of buffalo, Indians, and settlers, mainly in watercolor. Assoc member, RCA 1893; member Royal British Artists 1910. Work in ACM, NGC, Phila Centennial Expos. Reference MAL. Sources ANT 10/69-AOH-CAH-CAN. Watercolor 28×20" *Portrait of Sitting Bull* sold 10/16/69 for $4,800 at auction in London. Signature example p 90 CAH.

Son of a grammar-school principal, Verner went to England at 20 to study at Heatherly's in London and at the British Museum. He interrupted his studies to enlist for three years in the 3rd Yorkshire Regiment. In 1860 he joined the British Legion, fighting with Garibaldi for Italian liberation.

In 1862 Verner returned to Canada, becoming "one of the first, if not the very first, of our native painters to visit the West. So prolific was he that rare is the picture gallery or antique shop that cannot show one or more examples of his work." CAN. Verner spent his long life specializing in Western subjects. He visited England about 1880 "where his buffalo pictures were popular with sportsmen. The Earl of Dunraven possessed two (AOH)," along with his Bierstadt of Longs Peak and his more than 40 Bromleys. It is said that Verner enveloped his buffalo in a misty atmosphere more suited to the Scottish Highlands than to the strong contrasts of prairie shadows. CAN. A very popular Toronto painter, he moved to England about 1890.

VIERRA, Carlos. Born Moslanding near Monterey, Cal 1876, died probably Santa Fe, NM 1937. Landscape and architectural painter, muralist, photographer. Work in Harmsen colln, MNM, murals in AM of Santa Fe, Balboa Park (San Diego). Reference MAL. Sources COW-HAR-JNM-PIT-TSF. No current auction record but the estimated value of a major New Mexico landscape would be about $1,500 to $2,000 at auction in 1976. Signature example opp p 16 JNM. (See illustration 301.)

Son of a sailor, Vierra was educated in Monterey before becoming the pupil of Gittardo Piazzoni in San Francisco. When he was 25, Vierra traveled as a sailor around the Horn to NY. After two years as a marine painter in NYC, his health required moving to New Mexico.

Vierra tried living in a solitary cabin but was forced by continuing illness to go to a Santa Fe sanatorium in 1904. He opened a photographic studio in Santa Fe and painted in his spare time. He is therefore regarded as the first professional artist to have been resident in Santa Fe. Vierra studied architecture, painting a series of documentary architectural scenes of the historic Santa Fe landmarks, the Spanish-style buildings. Some of the artists arriving in Santa Fe later, like Paul Burlin in 1913, were modernists, not appreciated by Vierra any more than he accepted modern architectural forms. Vierra was also a sharpshooter and a captain in the National Guard in 1916.

VILLA, Hernando Gonzallo. Born Los Angeles, Cal 1881, died there 1952. Painter of Western subjects, illustrator, muralist, teacher. Illustrations in Cal magazines; murals in Phoenix and Los Angeles. Reference MAS. Source charcoal 39½×29½" *The Shepherd of Acoma* with signature example but not dated sold 5/23/73 for $1,100 at auction in Los Angeles. In the same sale, oil on board 23×17" *An Indian Couple* sold for $150.

Villa's parents came to Los Angeles from Baja California in 1846. He graduated from Los Angeles School of Art and Design in 1905. After a year's further study in England and Germany, Villa maintained his studio and exhibited in Los Angeles. At the Panama Pacific Exposition in 1915 in San Francisco, he won the gold medal for mural decoration. His specialty was the Old West, the Indian tribes, the Mexican vaquero, the missions, and the landscape.

He was an artist for 40 years for the Santa Fe RR. Villa created the Indian head symbolizing "The Chief," a crack train of the day. *West Coast Magazine* and *Los Angeles Town Talks* commissioned illustrations. The 5/23/73 auction sale was the remainder of the paintings in Villa's estate.

VILLIERS, Frederick. Born London, Eng 1852, died Bedhampton, Hampshire, Eng 1922. English Special Artist-correspondent. No reference. Source AOH. No auction record. Signature example p 186 AOH.

Educated in France, Villiers studied at the British Museum, the Royal College of Art, and the Royal Academy, 1869–71. He became a Special Artist for *ILN* in 1876, covering 20 campaigns up to World War I and "had seen more fighting than any soldier alive." By 1885 he had the appearance of a soldier, and Kipling used him as the hero in "The Light That Failed."

In 1889 Villiers was on his second visit to North America when he accompanied Lord Stanley, the Canadian Governor General, on a special train from Quebec to Vancouver, then the longest stretch of railroad in the world. The locomotive was wood-burning with a large pair of moose antlers over the lantern; below this, there were comfortable sightseeing seats on a railed-in platform. Villiers sketched along the right-of-way, watching a prairie fire, being received in Winnipeg mud, seeing a little white girl captive of the Blackfeet, crossing the summit of the Rockies. When Villiers repeated the rail trip in 1894, he relied on his camera rather than his pencil. These railway junkets were promotional, to boost flagging settlement of western Canada. Original works by Villiers are difficult to find. The legend under a printed illustration by Villiers might read, "Engraving after a drawing by the staff artist from a pencil sketch by Villiers."

VIOGET, Jean Jacques (or John J). Born Switzerland 1799, died San Jose, Cal 1855. Pioneer San Francisco surveyor, harborscape watercolorist. Watercolor reproduced in OCA. Reference G&W. Sources OCA-SSF. No auction record but the estimated price of an early

San Francisco watercolor would be about $1,200 to $1,500 at auction in 1976. No signature example.

After service in the French Army and apprenticeship to a naval engineer, Capt Jean Vioget appeared in the Mission settlement on San Francisco Bay in 1834. He was commissioned to square the plaza that had been a potato patch and to lay out streets that are now San Francisco's Pacific, Pine, and Stockton. After 1836 he built his own house as part of the non-Spanish settlers of the new San Francisco, with the Mission Indians dispossessed and the Spanish withdrawn.

In 1837 Vioget painted his watercolor of the harbor that was reproduced by George H Baker in 1893. Vioget also made surveys and maps for General Sutter before moving to San Jose in 1843. The early non-Spanish settlers had adopted old Mexican costumes, but by 1850 the Yankee styles were popular, except for "old Vioget." SSF. Now called "Don Juan Vioget," he had become a rich man, worth $50,000 according to "A Glance at the Wealth of the Monied Men." He was regarded as an example of the "Frenchmen" who rose to distinction. SSF.

VISCHER (or VISHER), Edward. Born Bavaria, Germany 1809, died San Francisco, Cal 1879. Pioneer lithographic artist, sketcher, author. References G&W-MAS. Sources COS-WHI. No current auction record but estimated price for a sketch would be about $500 to $750 at auction in 1976. No signature example.

At 19 Vischer went to Mexico as a business representative. He traveled South America on business, had Charles Darwin as a guest in Valparaiso, and represented the US in Acapulco. In 1842 he was imprisoned in California as a Mexican, then in 1845 sailed to Philadelphia and Europe via China. He re-turned to Mexico in 1847, and during the Gold Rush settled in San Francisco as a merchant-agent.

Vischer began sketching as a hobby, then in 1862 published a portfolio of lithographs of his sketches of the Mammoth Tree Grove. In 1864 he had his sketches photographed for better quality and continued to prefer photography over lithography. His outstanding publication was the "Pictorial of California," a set of 150 views with text, issued in 1870. Vischer also issued a set of his sketches of the Washoe Mining District including views showing camels "by the circumstance of our having travelled over that (Big Tree) route, for the sake of studying their habits," wrote Vischer, "with a little caravan of nine Bactrian camels, taken over the Sierra Nevada to Washoe in 1861."

VIVIAN, Calthea Campbell. Born Fayette, Mo about 1870, living Berkeley, Cal 1934. Cal painter, etcher, teacher. Work in Palace FA (San Francisco), Arkansas Auditorium Gallery. References A33-FIE-MAL. Sources HON-WAA. No current auction record or signature example.

Ms Vivian was the pupil of Arthur Mathews, studying at the Crocker and Hopkins Art institutes. She also studied in Paris at Lazar and Colarossi academies. She lives in California at Sacramento, Woodland, Los Angeles, San Francisco, San Jose in 1911, and Berkeley during the 1920s and early 1930s. HON lists a view of the remains of Sutter's Fort painted at the turn of the century.

VOLK, Stephen A Douglas. Born Pittsfield, Mass 1856, died Fryeburg, Maine 1935. Portrait and historical painter, illustrator, teacher. Member

SAA 1880, ANA 1898, NA 1899. Work in MMA, COR, NGA, Montclair AM, Albright Gall (Buffalo). References A36 (obit) - BEN - CHA - FIE - MAL - SMI. Sources AMA-ANT 1/65,2/67,1/70-COR-DEP-HUT-INS 5/08 (two places)-ISH-M31-MSL-NGA-NJA-NA 74-WHO 34. Oil 24×20″ *Abraham Lincoln* dated 1933 sold in 1971 for $4,500 at auction. Signature example p 35 ANT 1/70.

Douglas Volk was the son of Leonard Volk, a sculptor said to have made the only model of Lincoln from life and who made casts of Lincoln's face and hands. Douglas Volk was named after Stephen A Douglas who was both Lincoln's rival and the father's patron. While the family was living in Europe, Douglas Volk began his studies in Rome, next becoming the pupil of Gérôme in Paris 1873–78. He exhibited at the Paris Salon 1875–78 and at the Philadelphia Centennial in 1876. When Volk returned to NYC, he taught portrait painting and was commissioned in 1919 to paint portraits of WWI heroes for the NGA. His specialty was portraits of Lincoln, inspired by stories told by his father: "How I longed to have the man appear in life, if only for a moment, that I might visualize the splendid countenance." AMA. At Volk's death he was painting himself at four seated on Lincoln's lap while Volk, Sr was making a bust.

Some of Volk's historical paintings were Western, *Young Pioneer, Boy with an Arrow*. His illustrations included Indian subjects.

VON BECKH, H V A. Active 1859. Reference G&W. Source AIW. No auction record or signature example.

Von Beckh was a sketch artist with Capt J H Simpson's expedition to explore the Great Basin of Utah. In Capt Simpson's official report, the Von Breckh sketches were redrawn as watercolors by J J Young, a War Department topo-graphical draftsman. Young's watercolors are in the collection of the National Archives, but the location of Von Beckh's sketches is unknown. Young redrew sketches of artists on other expeditions of the period, eg, Mollhausen, Von Egloff-stein, and Dr Newberry. The Simpson expedition is the only mention of Von Beckh. The redrawn illustrations were incorporated in a 1947 Utah Centennial exhibition.

VON BERG, Capt Charles L. Born Schwarzwald (Black Forest), Germany 1835, died probably Colo 1918. Western landscape and genre painter, scout and hunter. Work in DPL. No reference or other source. No auction record or signature example. (See illustration 302.)

Son of the Chief Forester of Schwarzwald, Von Berg emigrated to NYC in 1854. He was employed by the Hudson's Bay Company as a fur trader at Fort Snelling, St Paul, Minn and also lived in Iowa. During the Civil War he was an army scout in the Iowa campaign against the Sioux. Later, Von Berg owned a general store and homesteaded in Iowa, was a close friend of his "look-alike" Buffalo Bill, and hunted with Gen George Cook. In 1872 he scouted in Nebraska and Colorado for Grand Duke Alexis of Russia. The rest of his life was devoted to "scouting and painting." DPL.

VON (or Van) EGLOFFSTEIN, F W (Baron). Born Prussia 1824, died London, Eng 1898. Important railway survey sketch-artist, mapmaker, inventor of a half-tone process, writer, Civil War general. Illustrations in survey reports. Reference G&W. Source AIW. No auction record or signature example.

Col John C Frémont's tragic fourth expedition in 1848 was intended to survey a winter crossing of the Colorado Rockies. Its failure with loss of life led Frémont to try again in September 1853, at his own expense with S N Carvalho as artist and Von Egloffstein as topographical engineer. When the party reached Utah in February 1854, the exhausted and frost-bitten Carvalho and Von Egloffstein dropped out, with Frémont continuing to California. At Salt Lake City, Von Egloffstein joined Lt Beckwith's official railway survey expedition for the route through northern Nevada and the Sierra Nevadas to northern California. In the printed report there are 13 illustrations by Von Egloffstein. "In none of the 12 volumes are the illustrations more specifically directed to the purpose than these." AIW.

In 1857 Von Egloffstein was topographer and Mollhausen artist on the Lt Ives expedition to explore the Colorado River. They reached the Grand Canyon April 3, 1858 and ended at Fort Defiance about May 20. Von Egloffstein returned to the east on the overland route, via Albuquerque, Santa Fe, and Fort Leavenworth. The panoramic illustrations in the Ives report are by Von Egloffstein, including what are probably the first pictorial records of the Grand Canyon. Between the Beckwith and Ives expeditions, Von Egloffstein had written a book on topographical drawing. In 1862 he enlisted as a colonel in the NY infantry and, after having been wounded, was brevetted out as a general. His military description was "eyes, blue; hair, light; height, 5 ft 7 inches." He lived in NYC 1864–73.

VON IWONSKI, Carl G. Born Hildersdorf, Silesia, Germany 1830, died Breslau, Germany 1922. Texas portrait painter including Indians, genre painter. Work in Witte Mus, Sophienburg Mus (New Braunfels), Lib Cong. Reference G&W. Sources ANT 6/48-TEP-TOB.

No current auction record but the estimated price of a major Texas genre painting would be about $8,000 to $9,000 at auction in 1976. Signature example p 126 TEP.

Von Iwonski's early education in Breslau included lessons in drawing. At 15 he was sent to Texas as an immigrant with Prince Carl of Solms-Braunfels. His family followed as soon as their estate could be sold. They settled in a blockhouse on the Guadalupe River at New Braunfels where Von Iwonski received additional art training, although he was considered self-taught. After living briefly in Horton Town about 1853, the family moved to San Antonio near the landscape painter Hermann Lungkwitz with whom Von Iwonski established a photographic gallery in 1866.

A landscape view and a group portrait were reproduced in German etchings sold in the US, but Von Iwonski's basic work was conventional portraiture in oil and pencil. For one portrait his fee was paid as diamond shirt buttons. His subjects were the well-to-do Texans, including Sam Houston and a view of his home. There are also 7×5″ oil portraits of Lipan Indians done about 1856. At the outbreak of the Civil War, Von Iwonski remained neutral, opposing slavery and secession. Two of his sketches of the surrender of the Union Army in San Antonio were printed in *Harper's Weekly* in 1861. When his father died in 1872, he and his mother returned to Germany. After studying in Berlin, he lived in Breslau "where his conversations with regard to Texas were found of particular interest." TOB. He was "a single-minded bachelor, thought by some to be a humorous individual but others recognized a quiet, reflective person." TEP.

VON LANGSDORFF, Georg Heinrich. Born Rheinhesse, Germany 1773, living Freiburg im Breisgau, Germany after

1812. Illustrator and writer of "Observations on a Journey around the World" in 1812, doctor, ethnologist. No reference. Source HON. No auction record or signature example.

Von Langsdorff was educated at Göttingen as a doctor. He accompanied Rezanov on a journey around the world 1803–7 as part of a Russian marine expedition. When the expedition reached the Russian outposts on the northern Pacific coast, the colonists were short of food. Rezanov sent a ship to San Francisco in 1806 to barter for food. Von Langsdorff sketched San Francisco from the ship, the first known view, as well as an Indian dance and Indian objects.

VON PERBANDT, Carl Adolf Rudolf Julius. Born Langendorf, East Prussia 1832, died Nahmgeist, East Prussia 1911. California landscape painter. Work in Oakland AM. No reference. Sources DCC-HAR-KAH. No auction record. Signature example p 39 KAH.

Carl von Perbandt, the younger son of Prussian landowners, studied at Düsseldorf Academy with Andreas Achenbach and Lessing. Called the "Baron," Von Perbandt brought his family to NYC about 1870. By 1877 he was painting landscapes in San Francisco. He shared a studio with Henry Raschen, the painter of Indian genre and portraits. Together they traveled among the California Indian tribes. A favorite background was old Fort Ross. Von Perbandt at times lived with the Indians. In 1893 he participated in the painting of C D Robinson's Yosemite panorama.

Von Perbandt's hobby was chess. In NYC he had been lionized by society but in San Francisco he was silent about his family connection. He returned to East Prussia in 1903.

VON SCHMIDT, Harold. Born Alameda, Cal 1893, living Westport, Conn 1976. Important illustrator of the West, painter, teacher. Member SI. Work in Cal St Cap (12 paintings of Gold Rush), Mont Hist Soc, West Point, Air Force Acad, ANS, Nat Cowboy Hall of Fame. References A62-MAL. Sources AHI 4/73-COW-CRS-CUS-HAR-ILA-ILG-IL 42,59-PAW-POW-WHO 70. No current auction record. Signature example p 204 ILA. (See illustration 303.)

Orphaned at five, Von Schmidt was raised by his grandfather, a forty-niner, and an aunt who encouraged art studies. With summers as a cowboy and lumberjack, Von Schmidt studied at the California College of Arts and Crafts 1912–13, the pupil of F H Meyers. His first cover illustration for *Sunset Magazine* was 1913. While attending the San Francisco AI 1915–18 he was an art director associated with the established Western painter Maynard Dixon. Another influence was Worth Ryder, the etcher and painter. In turn Von Schmidt was later able to act as sponsor for Will James. Von Schmidt was also active in athletics, a member of the American rugby team in the 1920 Olympics.

In 1924 Von Schmidt moved to NYC to study at the Grand Central Art School with Harvey Dunn who provided the key to dramatic emphasis in the tradition of Howard Pyle, Dunn's teacher. Von Schmidt became a leading magazine illustrator, with his work appearing mainly in *The Saturday Evening Post* for 20 years. His best-known book illustrations were for the classic "Death Comes for the Archbishop." As a teacher he was a founder of the Famous Artists School in Westport. In recognition of his accomplishments, Von Schmidt received the 1960 commission to design the postage stamp commemorating the Pony Express.

WAANO-GANO, Joe T N. Born Salt Lake City, Utah 1906, living Los Angeles, Cal 1976. Cherokee painter, illustrator, decorator, author. Fellow, Am Inst FA. Work in public buildings. Reference A76. Source AIP. Mixed media painting 23½×19½" *Sunset over a Desert Landscape* was estimated at $200 to $250 for sale 3/4/74 at auction and sold for $250. No signature example.

Waano-Gano, translated as Bow-Arrow, was educated in Salt Lake City and Los Angeles public schools, graduating 1922. The anthropologists Woodward, Hodge, and Harrington provided early guidance in art. He attended Von Schneidau School of Art 1924–28 while working as a commerical artist from 1924 to 1941. He took extension art courses and studied under Puthoff and Lukits. From 1939 to 1941 he acted in radio dramatizations of Indian legends.

In WWII he served in the US Air Force for three years, then became an airline designer of decor from 1944 to 1946. His textile designs in Indian motifs have won awards. In 1961 an auto accident affected his ability to paint, but he continues to lecture and write on the art of the American Indian.

WACHTEL, Elmer. Born Baltimore, Md 1864, died Guadalajara, Mexico 1929. Southern Cal landscape painter of the High Sierras, illustrator, craftsman. Member 10 Painters of Los Angeles. References A29 (obit)-BEN-FIE-MAL-SMI. Sources AAR 11/74-WAC. No current auction record. Signature example p 43 WAC.

Raised in Lanark, Ill, Wachtel worked as a hired farm hand. When he moved to his brother's Los Angeles ranch in 1882, he taught himself the violin and viola. By 1888 he was first violin in the Philharmonic Orchestra in Los Angeles but earned so little he also worked as a furniture-store clerk. He began still-life

sketching in his spare time, then went to study at the ASL in NYC. Quitting the ASL when he did not agree with methods, he sketched in the city streets, obtaining criticism from W M Chase. He then sailed to England and spent a year working in a London art school. On his return to Los Angeles he began to paint seriously in a studio at the rear of his parents' house. He painted "dry arroyos and tawny mountains and arid stretches of desert." WAC.

In 1904 Wachtel married the painter Marion Kavanagh. They moved to a studio on Mt Washington, then moved again close to the Sierra Madre Range. For 25 years they painted landscapes together, seldom exhibiting. Wachtel continued to write music, cutting his own player-piano rolls so he could hear them on the piano he could not play.

WACHTEL, Mrs Marion Kavanagh. Born Milwaukee, Wis 1875 (or 1876), died Pasadena, Cal 1954. Cal landscape painter. Member, 10 Painters of Los Angeles. Work in Cal St Bldg, Cedar Rapids Mus (Iowa), Vanderpoel AA (Chicago). References A53-BEN-FIE-MAL. Sources AAR 11/74-WAA-WAC. No current auction record. Signature example as monogram, frontispiece WAC.

Mrs Wachtel studied at the AIC and was the pupil of William Chase. She was painting in Chicago in 1904 and teaching at the AIC when she married Elmer Wachtel and moved to his Sichel Street studio in Los Angeles. The couple then opened a studio at Mt Washington and a few years later built a new studio in Pasadena on the rim of the Arroyo Seco, near the Sierra Madre Range. For 25 years in an auto rebuilt for painting, they sketched in California, Arizona, the High Sierras, the sea coast, and Mexico where Elmer Wachtel died. Typical titles for Mrs Wachtel were *San Gabriel Cañon,*

506

San Jacinto Cañon, and *Eucalyptus at Evening.*

After her marriage that followed a "whirlwind" courtship, Mrs Wachtel stopped painting oils in favor of watercolors. It is suggested that she knew she was a better painter than Wachtel and so avoided his medium. Her watercolors are described as characterized by broad transparent washes and as essentially decorative. AAR. After Wachtel's death, she exhibited oil paintings.

WAGONER, Harry B. Born Rochester, Ind 1889, died Phoenix, Ariz 1950. Cal landscape painter, sculptor. Member Int Soc Sculptors, Painters, and Gravers (London). References A33-MAL. Source SCA-painting *Superstition Mountain.* No auction record or signature example.

Wagoner was the pupil of Homer Pollock. After study in Paris and travel in Italy, he settled in Chicago until illness in the late 1920s caused him to spend winters in Palm Springs, Cal. He became known as the painter of the desert landscape. By 1930 he was visiting Arizona. Painting titles include *And the Desert Shall Blossom, The Apache Stronghold,* and *Entrance to Andreas Canyon.*

WAGONER, Robert. Born Marion, Ohio 1928, living Long Beach, Cal 1968. Traditional Western painter, songwriter, construction manager. No reference. Source COW. No current auction record. Signature example p 210 COW.

Wagoner studied forestry in college, served as an aviator in the Marine Corps, and was an entertainer. He wrote the song "High Country." In the 1960s he worked in the construction business while painting at night.

WALKER, Gilbert M. Born 1927 place unknown, living NYC 1966. Illustrator specializing in action subjects, particularly military and Western sketches. Work in military publications. No reference. Sources ILA-IL 59,61. No auction record. Signature example p 261 ILA. (See illustration 304.)

Gil Walker studied briefly at the ASL, the pupil of Reginald Marsh and R B Hale. He had worked as a commercial artist while still in high school. During the Korean War, Walker was an army artist, afterward remaining in Washington as a civilian doing reportorial illustrations in pen and ink. When he returned to NYC he taught art at the College of the City of NY from 1957 to 1961.

WALKER, James. Born Northamptonshire, Eng 1819, died Watsonville, Cal 1889. Painter of the Cal vaquero and of battle scenes, portraits. Work in US Capitol, US War Dept, GIL, ANS, DAM, Dentzel colln. References BEN-FIE-G&W-MAL. Sources AIW-ANS-ANT 4/53,11/60,10/61,9/65,7/66, 10/68,9/71,3/72-BAR-BOA-COW-DAA-DBW-DCC-DWF-FRO-GIL-HON-150-TAW-TEP-WHI. Oil 30×35″ *Portrait of Maj Gen Geo H Thomas* 1873 sold 11/12/71 for $1,000. Signature example p 273 GIL. (See illustration 305.)

Walker's family settled near Albany, NY when he was five. He is said to have grown up in NYC (GIL) where he presumably studied painting. After living in New Orleans, he went to Tampico, Mexico in 1841 and then to Mexico City. When the Mexican War broke out in 1846, Walker was held prisoner but escaped to volunteer as interpreter for the American Army under Gen Winfield Scott. He saw and sketched the major battles and the capture of Mexico City, remaining for the occupation as the only important American painter on the scene. In 1848 Walker returned to NYC. After a visit to South America, he established his NYC studio in 1850, finally settling down at 31 to his career as a military painter. From 1857 to 1862 Walker was in Washington, DC to paint the *Battle of Chapultepec* on commission from the Government. From 1862 to 1865 he was working on Civil War studies made during his stay in the Army. These sketches were used for the later panoramic views such as *Battle of Lookout Mountain* and *Third Day of Gettysburg.*

By the early 1870s Walker had opened his San Francisco studio. HON. During 1876 and 1877 he sketched and painted in California, particularly genre scenes of California vaqueros with great attention to details of costume and gear, thus acting as a model for the later cowboy painters of the Old West. Walker returned to NYC in 1878 en route to Europe. His final stay in California began in 1884.

WALL, Bernhardt T. Born Buffalo, NY 1872, living Sierra Madre, Cal 1953. Illustrator, etcher, historian, craftsman. Work in Brit Mus, Nat Lib (Madrid), NYHS, Huntington Lib (San Marino), many collns. References A53-MAL. Sources TOB-WHO 50-"Under Western Skies" by Wall. No current auction record. Signature examples "Under Western Skies."

Wall was educated in Buffalo public schools. He studied at Buffalo's ASL and Art Students Sketch Class, and was the pupil of J F Brown, Henry Reuterdahl, and William Auerbach-Levy. Beginning work as a lithographic artist in 1889, he became an instructor 1894–95. In the Spanish-American War he served with the 202nd NY Volunteers. From 1902–13 he was a commercial artist.

Wall visited the West 1915–16, completing the etchings issued later as "Under Western Skies." The subjects included: *Pinto Pony; Cheyenne cow-boy; Pocatello Indian; an aged Cheyenne; Preparedness* as an Indian feathering his arrow; and *Col Roosevelt at San Diego.* After 1931 Wall was an etcher of pictorial biographies, for example, 85 volumes of etchings on "Abraham Lincoln" 1931–42, 13 volumes of etchings on "Thomas Jefferson" 1933–37. Wall also lectured on "The Itch to Etch."

WALLACE, Lewis. Born Brookville, Ind 1827, died Crawfordsville, Ind 1905. Hobbyist painter and illustrator, important writer, soldier, statesman. References DAB-ENB-G&W. Sources AOA-BAR-HOR-WHO 03. No auction data or signature example.

Son of a politician, Lew Wallace was raised in Indianapolis. He ground colors for the painter Jacob Cox but was influenced against art as a livelihood. After studying law he served in the Mexican War, practiced law, and was elected to state office. In the Civil War he was promoted to general and highly praised. In 1878 his war painting *The Dead Line at Andersonville* was exhibited. The same year he was appointed governor of New Mexico. While in Santa Fe, Wallace completed his novel "Ben-Hur." His wife Susan wrote on Indian and Mexican life for the *Atlantic Monthly.* Wallace who "drew delightfully" (HOR) illustrated his wife's writings with sketches of buffalo, Indians, ranchers, sheep, quail, yucca, and Mexican and Indian genre. "All his life Wallace envied painters." BAR. "Poise and urbanity" were his apparent qualities, but he was also simple and democratic, interested in art, music, and literature. DAB.

WALLS, Stanley King. English landscape painter active in the Southwest in the 1950s. Fellow RSA. Source, 1951 painting San Xavier Mission on the Santa Cruz River south of Tucson, Ariz. (See illustration 306.)

WALTERS, Emil. Born Winnipeg, Can 1893, living Poughkeepsie, NY 1970. Landscape painter. Work in Smithsonian Inst, Mus FA (Houston), Heckscher Mus (NY), Mus of Art (Saskatoon, Can), BM, SAM, MNM etc. References A66-BEN-FIE-MAL-SMI. Sources CAE-MNM-WHO 70. No auction record or signature example.

Walters was brought to the US in 1898. He received his art training at AIC and PAFA and the Tiffany Foundation. His Western work includes *Roosevelt's Haunts* in the National Gallery of Art (Washington, DC) which showed the North Dakota country of Theodore Roosevelt's Western ranch. Later Walters specialized in Arctic and sub-Arctic subjects, especially Iceland and Greenland.

WALTON, Henry. Born probably NYC about 1804 (or 1820), died Cassopolis, Mich 1865 (or 1873). Portrait and landscape painter, lithographic artist, in California 1851–57. Work in Oakland Mus, Soc of Cal Pioneers (San Francisco), Addison Pub Lib (NY), private collections exhibited in Ithaca 1968–69. Reference G&W. Sources ANT 11/37 (cover), 6/58 (cover), 9/62 (article), 8/67, 12/68,3/70 (article). No current auction record but the estimated price of a Western landscape would be about $4,000 to $5,000 at auction in 1976. Signature example p 284 ANT 9/62.

Walton appears to have been the son of a NYC judge, probably educated in England, with training in draftsmanship. He became a book illustrator about 1830. By 1836 he was living in Ithaca,

NY painting watercolor and oil portraits but concentrating on townscapes, some drawn directly on the stone for lithography. Walton also traveled in Pennsylvania. His lithographs were "produced for virtually every Eastern printing firm in business in the 1830s." ANT 12/68. This was a "record of the folk of such towns as (Athens,) Ovid, Ithaca, Romulus, and Scipio in the days of the Greek Revival." ANT 6/58. The lithographs sold for $3.50 each but sales are said to have been so discouraging that Walton destroyed the stones. His living would have come from his portraits. Each was signed, and most were dated, with the name and age of the sitters.

In 1851 Walton joined a gold-rush party from Ithaca that landed in San Francisco in September. His drawing dated 1853 shows a gold miner in his cabin. A watercolor dated 1857 of Grass Valley, Cal, a mining village, is the only other Western painting that is known. Later in 1857, Walton settled in Michigan with his wife, Jane.

WANDESFORDE (or Wandersforde), James (or Juan, or Ivan) B (or Buckingham). Born England (or Scotland) 1817, died San Francisco, Cal after 1872. Portrait, genre, and landscape painter, book illustrator, teacher. Illustration in "The Golden Gate." References DAB (under Cornelia Fassett)-G&W. Sources BAR-POW. No auction record or signature example.

In 1852 J B Wandesforde was listed as a teacher of watercolor painting in NYC. His pupil was Cornelia Fassett. In 1858 he was living in Centerport, LI, NY. He worked in NYC until after 1860. By 1869 he was in San Francisco where he illustrated "The Golden Gate," making him one of the early American book illustrators. In 1872 he became the first president of the San Francisco Art Association.

"The technical likeness of his landscape style to that of the Hudson River School was natural enough, since England and the United States were still effectively interchanging minor landscapists." BAR. Note that WNW lists James Buckingham Wandesforde, Jr as born 8/9/11 in Seattle.

WANKER, Maude Walling (Mrs C C Wanker). Born Portland (or Oswego), Ore 1882 (or 1881), living Wecoma Beach, Ore 1962. Oregon landscape and architectural painter, teacher, mus director. Work in Ore Hist Soc, Ore St Capitol, Portland Women's Club. References A62-MAS. Sources BDW-WAA-WNW. No auction record or signature example.

Mrs Wanker was educated at the U of Oregon. She studied at the AIC and the Portland Museum AS, the pupil of Clara Stevens, Jeanne Stewart, and Eugene Steinhof. Between 1930 and 1940 Mrs Wanker painted almost 100 depictions of Oregon's "historical sites and buildings." BDW. She has taught at the Lincoln County Art Center and the Coquille Valley AA.

WAPAH NAYAH. See Richard West.

WARD, Charles Caleb. Born St John, NB, Can about 1831, died Rothesay, NB, Can 1896. Eastern genre and landscape painter. Work in MMA, H M Fuller colln. References G&W-MAL. Sources ANT 1/62,7/64,10/68. Oil 10×14¼″ *Stalking Indian* signed and dated 1889 sold 9/28/73 for $1,100 at auction. Signature examples above and p 70 ANT 7/64.

Ward's Loyalist grandfather emigrated to St John where Ward was raised. Sent to London for business education, Ward studied painting, the pupil of William Henry Hunt. In 1850–51 Ward was in NYC, exhibiting landscapes at the NA. Most of the rest of Ward's life was spent in Canada, except for 1868 to 1872 when he again had a studio in NYC and exhibited at the NA.

Few of Ward's pictures are known in the US. Most famous is *The Circus Is Coming* dated 1871 which includes a Wild West poster. *Two Boys Working the Grindstone* dated 1869 is another example of straightforward genre. *Stalking Indian* was painted when Ward would have been in Canada.

WARD, Edmund F (or E C, or Frank). Born White Plains, NY 1892, living there 1976. Magazine, book, and advertising illustrator including Western subjects, painter, muralist, teacher. Member SI, Guild of Free Lance Artists. Work in Columbia U, Rollins Col, Rockefeller Inst, City of White Plains; illustrations in *Sat Eve Post*. References A47-FIE-MAL. Sources AAC (as Frank)-GIL (as E C)-ILA-Jan 1975 data from E F Ward. No current auction record. Signature example p 250 GIL. (See illustration 307.)

Ward studied at the ASL 1910–12, the pupil of Edward Dufner, George Bridgman, and Thomas Fogarty. His influence was Harvey Dunn. Before he was 20 his illustrations were accepted for *The Saturday Evening Post*. His illustrations were somber and serious at that time, painted as large oils. Ward's best-known illustrations were for the Alexander Botts series in the *Post*. He also illustrated "Thundering Herd" by Zane Grey and "Hawkeye" by Emerson Hough. In 1924–25 he taught at the ASL. In the 1930s he painted a mural for the Federal Building in White Plains where Ward maintained his studio on Court Street.

His illustration was used for the federal postage stamp commemorating the Battle of White Plains.

Ward's painting *Enter the Law* (1924) is illustrated in GIL, credited to E C Ward. In his informational response to GIL when he was discovered to have been the painter, Ward noted he was "particularly pleased this canvas entered your collection on its own feet." Ward had not been in the West. His signatures were E F W, E W, E F Ward, and Edm F Ward.

WARD, John Quincy Adams. Born near Urbana, Ohio 1830, died NYC 1910. The "dean of Amer sculptors," in the West and NW about 1860. ANA 1862, NA 1863, NSS 1896, etc. Work in MMA, NY HS, rotunda Lib Cong, City Hall (Brooklyn), Stock Exchange, etc. References A10 (obit)-BEN-DAB-ENB-FIE-G&W-MAL-SMI. Sources ALA-AMA-ANT 1/69-BOA-HUT-KW1,2-M19-MSL-NA 74-PAF-SCU-WHO 08. Bronze 20¾" high *Portrait of a Man* (1902) sold 10/16/70 for $375 at auction. Bronze, greenish-brown patina *George Washington* 15¼" high sold 10/31/75 for $3,000 at auction. Sculpture example *Indian Hunter* ✕118 M19. Studio photo for Ward opp p 397 A10.

Son of a homesteader, Ward worked as a farmer until Henry Kirke Brown took him as a pupil in Brooklyn in 1849. After five years Brown added Ward's signature as assistant on an important commission for an equestrian Washington where Ward "spent more days inside that horse than Jonah did inside the whale." DAB. From 1857 to 1859 Ward modeled naturalistic portrait busts in Washington.

In 1857 Ward had made his first study for *Indian Hunter,* executing six small bronzes. About 1860 he conceived of using this study for a heroic group. He traveled to the West and Northwest, vis-

iting the Indians for sketches in pencil and wax. It was said that "his little models of Indian heads in red wax, taken from life in Dakotah Territory, are among the most authentic aboriginal physiognomical types extant." BOA. The large work was completed in 1864, exhibited in Paris in 1867, and purchased for Central Park in NYC by popular subscription. Thereafter, Ward's work was in constant demand. The first important American sculptor without foreign training, a strong and virile man, "Quincy Ward wasn't redheaded for nothing." DAB. A replica of *Indian Hunter* was used as the monument for his grave.

WARE, Florence Ellen. Born Salt Lake City, Utah 1891, died there 1971. Utah landscape painter, illustrator, muralist, teacher. Work in Utah AI, schools, colleges, library. References A41-MAL. Source YUP. No current auction record or signature example.

Florence Ware graduated from the U of Utah. She studied at the AIC for three years, at the California School of Arts and Crafts for one year, and with Hawthorne in Provincetown, Mass for eight months. For another two years she traveled and studied in Europe and the Near East before returning to teach at the U of Utah from 1918 to 1923. She also taught in the Extension Division for 20 years.

"Florence Ware attempts in her work a quiet portrayal of the romantic aspects of life, employing tinted color." YUP. During the 1930s she painted murals for the PWA. Her murals were of the early Salt Lake valley, *Western, Indian, Pine in the Rain,* etc. In 1932, she had been listed as living in Laguna Beach, Cal.

WARNER, Olin Levi. Born West Suffield, Conn 1844, died NYC 1896.

Conn Yankee sculptor in the NW 1889–91, medalist, designer. ANA 1888, NA 1889, NSS. Work in Centennial Expos 1876, World's Columb Expos 1893, MMA, COR, door for Lib of Cong, figures, fountains, statues, etc. References BEN-DAB-FIE-MAL-SMI. Sources ALA-AMA-ANT 12/72-ARI-BAR-COR-HUT-MSL-NA 74-SCU with signature and medal examples after p 40. No current auction record. (See illustration 308.)

Son of an itinerant Methodist minister, Olin Warner attended district school in Amsterdam, NY until he was 15 and in Brandon, Vt until he was 19. To earn money for art school he worked for six years as a telegrapher. At 25 he went to Paris, studying at the École des Beaux-Arts as the pupil of Jouffroy. After three years he returned to a NYC studio, a classic stylist out-of-step with the vogue for painterly sculpture. Forced to commercial designing, he experienced four impoverished years before gaining a portrait commission and a gallery exhibition that led him to a busy and successful career by 1876. An illustration of his *Diana* is on the cover of the "History of American Sculpture." His statue of Garrison was said to look "as if at any minute it would leap to his feet." AMA. He designed the Columbian half dollar in 1893.

Warner was in the Northwest 1889–91, executing bas-relief portrait busts of Indians taken from life. Warner died at the height of his career.

WARRE, Henry James, Sir (Captain). Born probably Durham, Eng 1819, died probably Eng 1898. English sketch artist in Oregon 1845–46 on a military survey, British army officer. Work in Amer Antiquarian Soc, PNW, Pub Archives (Ottawa); scenic watercolors reproduced

as lithographs (ACM). References G&W. Sources AOH-CAN-POW. No auction record but the estimated price of an Oregon wash drawing would be about $4,000 to $4,500 at auction in 1976. Lithograph examples ACM. (See illustration 309.)

In 1845 the British Government ordered a military survey to determine the defensibility of the Oregon region. The selection of the survey party included Lt Warre of the Royal Engineers, 14th Buckinghamshire Regiment. The party left Montreal May 5. They had already crossed the Rockies by July 31 when they began their survey at the Columbia River. They returned to Montreal the end of July 1846, at the time when a compromise treaty had been negotiated reflecting the military weakness. Warre's watercolor drawings were reproduced as 20 lithographic "Sketches in North America and the Oregon Territory" published as a folio in London in 1848. AOH illustrates *The Falls of Peloos River, Columbia River,* a competent topographical watercolor. Warre served in the Crimean and New Zealand wars, retiring as a general.

WARREN, Constance Whitney. Born NYC 1888, died Paris, France 1948. International sculptor specializing in horses and dogs. Work in MMA, statue in Okla St Capitol, monument in Texas. No reference. Sources ANT 9/44 (bronze of mounted cowboy actor William S Hart)-CWW-SCU-TOB. No current auction record or signature example.

Constance Warren began in drawing and in poster design. After she married in 1911 she settled permanently in Paris. About 1919 she concentrated on sculpture, exhibiting regularly at the Paris Salon. In 1926 she made a life-size statue of a mounted cowboy for the state capitol in Oklahoma City. From 1920 to 1927 she did 18 bronzes of cowboys on horseback.

WARREN, Melvin C. Born Los Angeles, Cal 1920, living Clifton, Texas 1975. Traditional Western painter, illustrator. Member CAA. Work in Southern Methodist U, Lyndon B Johnson Lib 15 paintings), Texas ranch collns. References A76. Sources COW-C71-OSR-PWA-WAI 72. No current auction record. Signature example C72.

Until he was 14 his family moved to different ranches in California, Arizona, New Mexico, and south and west Texas. In 1934 they settled in Seymour, Tex where he attended high school. After four years' service in the Air Force during WWII he moved to Fort Worth, graduating in 1952 from Texas Christian U with a degree in Fine Arts. He was the pupil of Samuel P Ziegler. Warren worked in commercial art, painting in his spare time.

Warren devotes full time to painting Western art. His palette emphasizes earth colors, browns, reds, and yellows. One series of paintings was on the historical cattle trails. Another was on the Texas frontier forts. "He is so critical of himself that he is able to complete only about four paintings a month." COW.

WATCHETAKER, George Smith. Born Elgin, Okla 1916, living same 1967. Comanche painter. Work in Fort Sill Mus (Okla). Source AIP. No auction record but the estimated price of a charcoal portrait *Comanche War Chief* would be about $300 to $400 at auction in 1976. No signature example. (See illustration 310.)

Watchetaker in Comanche means Hide

Away. He was educated at Haskell, graduating 1935. He has worked as a painter, decorator, and sign painter. For 1966–67 he was the holder of "World's Championship Indian Dancer."

WATSON, Dawson. See Dawson-Watson.

WAUD, Alfred R. Born Lindon, Eng 1828 (not 1818), died Marietta, Ga 1891. Important Civil War and Western illustrator for *Harper's Weekly*. Work in Lib Cong, *Harper's*, "Picturesque America," "Beyond the Mississippi." References G&W-MAS. Sources AAR 11/74-AIW-ANT 11/73,3/75-AOA-AOH-BAW - CAP - CIV - CUS - KW1,2 - MIS - POW. No current auction record but the estimated price of a Western illustration would be about $6,000 to $7,000 at auction in 1976. Signature example p 739 ANT 11/73.

A R Waud studied at the Royal Academy before coming to the US with his brother William when he was 30. He illustrated for *Harper's* 1858–82 and for Demorest's *New York Illustrated News* 1859–64. Waud was the leading *Harper's* Civil War correspondent, "a tall man, mounted on a taller horse. Blue-eyed, fair-bearded, strapping and stalwart, full of loud, cheery laughs and comic songs, armed to the teeth, yet clad in the shooting-jacket of a civilian." G A Sala, "Diary." The Library of Congress has 2,300 field sketches by Waud and his brother.

Harper's Weekly sent Waud to the South in April 1866 to report on the results of the war. Waud went directly to the frontier of the day, Cincinnati, Louisville, and Nashville, then south to Louisiana and probably into Texas. *A Drove of Texas Cattle Crossing a Stream* was published in 1867. *"Creasing" Mustangs in Texas* appeared in 1868, although Waud had returned to NYC by October 1866. A Waud sketch on railroad building illustrated "Beyond the Mississippi" in 1867, but this was probably redrawn from a photograph. It is said that "his second trip, to Nebraska Territory in 1868, produced the famous *Pilgrims of the Plains*." AOH. Illustrations by Waud of the "Northwest" were in "Picturesque America" published in 1872, along with other illustrations by such artists as Thomas Moran, Darley, and Whittredge. In 1880 and 1881 *Harper's* published a series of Waud illustrations of Dakota territory, the close of the career of "one of the most outstanding reportorial draughtsmen of the century." AOH.

WAUD, William. Born probably London, Eng before 1828, died Jersey City, NJ 1878. Illustrator for *Leslie's* and *Harper's*, architect, writer. Work in *Harper's*. Reference G&W. Sources AIW-AOA-CIV-KW2. No current auction record but the estimated price of a Western illustration would be about $700 to $800 at auction in 1976. Watercolor reproduced CIV.

William Waud studied architecture in England. About 1851 he assisted Sir Joseph Paxton in designing the London Crystal Palace. With his brother A R Waud he came to NYC about 1858. Up to 1863 his illustrations appeared in *Frank Leslie's Illustrated Newspaper*. Thereafter he worked for *Harper's*. The Library of Congress has about 2,300 Civil War field sketches by A R and William Waud. Many of the sketches were redrawn on lithographic blocks for publication.

The data does not indicate a Western trip by William Waud. The practice of staff artists would be to work from available sketches of others and from photographs such as the John Carbutt series taken along the Union Pacific right-of-way in the fall of 1866. Fifteen Waud illustrations were in the second edition of BEY, about 1869.

WAUGH, Alfred S. Born Ireland about 1810, died St Louis, Mo 1856. Western portrait painter, portrait sculptor. Reference G&W. No other source. No auction record or signature example.

Waugh studied sculpture in Dublin in 1827 and in Europe. He emigrated to Baltimore in 1833. In 1838 he sculpted in Raleigh, in 1842 in Alabama, in 1843 in Pensacola, and in 1844 in Mobile where he met the young artist John J Tisdale. In 1845 Waugh and Tisdale worked in Missouri.

In 1846 Waugh traveled to Santa Fe, NM, a trip that he covered in his autobiography "Travels in Search of an Elephant." By 1848 Waugh settled in St Louis where he established his studio, painting and sculpting portraits. He also wrote and lectured on art.

WAUGH, Sidney. Born Amherst, Mass 1904, died probably NYC 1963. International sculptor including Indian figures, teacher, writer. ANA 1936, NA 1938, NSS, NIAL. Work in sculpted groups, figures, monuments, statues, fountains, medals, in US, England, Holland, Chile, Italy, Iran, Egypt, etc. References A66 (obit)-MAL. Sources AAT-NA 74-WHO 62. No current auction record. Sculpture example p 237 AAT plaster *Primitive Science* of standing Indian.

Waugh was educated at Amherst College and MIT 1920-23. He studied in Rome 1924, in Paris with Henri Bouchard 1925–28, and Rome 1929–32. Director of the Rinehart School of Sculp-

514

ture in Baltimore, he also wrote "The Art of Glassmaking" and was an officer of the NSS, NAD, American Academy in Rome, and City Art Commission.

WEAVER, W H. Active 1867. Painter. No reference. Source, oil 14×18" *The Trail* signed and dated 1867, showing "Indian braves engaged in tracking their quarry," sold 4/20/72 for $550 at auction. No signature example.

WEBB, Vonna Owings. Born Sunshine, Colo 1876, died Manhattan Beach, Cal 1964. Mont and Cal painter of landscapes. References MAS. Source BDW. No auction record or signature example.

Daughter of the surgeon for the Northern Pacific RR, Mrs. Webb was raised in Montana. After teaching in Indiana and Montana she married in 1905, spent a few years in Chicago, and then settled in Oregon. About 1930 she moved to California where she painted marines and desert landscapes.

WEBBER, Charles T. Born Cayuga Lake, NY (or Cincinnati, Ohio) 1825, died Cincinnati, Ohio 1911. Cincinnati portrait, historical, and landscape painter, sculptor, teacher. References A09-G&W-MAL. Source AIW. No current auction record or signature example.

Webber settled in Cincinnati in 1858, after having moved to Springfield, Ohio in 1844. He was a charter member of the Cincinnati Sketch Club in 1860 and the Art Club in 1890. The McMickin School of Art and Design was organized by Webber in 1869. His best-known painting was the historical *The Underground Railroad,* in addition to *Major Daniel McCook and His Nine Sons.*

In January 1886 a party of three artists visited Santa Fe to begin a six-week tour of New Mexico. The first was Henry Worrall, a Kansas illustrator for *Harper's Weekly, Leslie's Illustrated Newspaper,* and books on Western history. The second was the younger Henry Mosler, back from France with "two commissions for Indian paintings that were to pay him $25,000 each." AIW. The third was Webber.

WEBBER, John. Born London, Eng 1750, died there 1793. English landscape painter in Pacific Northwest 1778. Member RA 1791. Work in Nat Port Gall (London), Victoria and Albert Mus, Dublin Mus, Dentzel colln. References BEN-G&W-MAL. Sources AOH-HMA-WHI. Oil 18½×24½" *Boats of the Friendly Islands* sold 3/20/73 for $4,000 at auction in London. In 1923, the watercolor *The Reapers Rest* sold for 480 fr at auction in Paris. No signature example.

Son of a Swiss sculptor, Webber was raised in Bern. He studied painting in Bern and in Paris, then returned to London in 1775 to complete his studies at the RA. He was employed as a decorative painter.

When Capt James Cook formed the party in 1776 to discover a passage from the Pacific to Europe, he engaged Webber as artist to compensate "for the inevitable imperfections of written accounts." AOH. In 1778 the expedition charted the Pacific Northwest coast as far as Bering Strait, with Webber making sketches of Washington and Oregon scenes. After Cook was killed in Hawaii in 1779 while disputing a stolen boat with natives, the expedition returned to London in 1780. Webber used his sketches for paintings to illustrate the report. He also published between 1787 and 1792 views from the trip that he engraved and colored himself. In addition, his drawing of the assassination of Capt Cook was engraved by Bartolozzi. Webber continued to exhibit in London until his death. The paintings were mainly landscapes of England, Switzerland, and Italy. John Webber's name has been variously given as Johann Weber or Wober and his birth place and date as Bern, Switzerland, 1751 or 1752.

WEEKS, Edwin Lord. Born Boston, Mass 1849, died Paris, France 1903. Genre painter specializing in Oriental subjects, illustrator for *Harper's* and *Scribner's*, writer. Chevalier, Legion of Honor 1896. Work in MMA, COR, Cercle Volney (Paris), PAFA, Phila Centennial (1876), World's Columb Expos (1893). References A05 (obit)-BEN-CHA-DAB-FIE-MAL-SMI. Sources ANT 5/67,10/69,9/70,4/74-COR-HUT-INS 1/29-ISH-M57-MSL-WHO 01. Oil 27½×35½" *The Carriage Awaits* sold 11/20/73 for $2,000 at auction in London. Signature example BEN. (See illustration 311.)

Descendant of 1656 settlers, Weeks was educated in Boston and Newton public schools. He studied in Paris at the École des Beaux-Arts, the pupil of Bonnat and Gérôme. While still a student, he painted in North Africa. The favorable response from his masters and the critics led him to specialize as an Orientalist, traveling to Palestine, Jerusalem, Damascus, and then India. His work provides "some idea of the sunlight, the color, and the strange, curiously wrought structures of the East, copying all characteristic details in their completeness," as opposed to FA Bridgman who "selects what appeals." ISH.

His illustrations for magazine articles

included paintings of American Indians. Weeks wrote books on his travels. He lived in Boston and in Paris.

WEGGELAND, Danquart Anthon. Born Christiansand, Norway 1827, died Salt Lake City, Utah 1918. Pioneer Utah portrait and landscape painter, scenery painter, muralist, teacher, "the father of Utah art." Work in Brigham Young U, Springville AM, LDS temples, Phila Centennial Expos (1876), World's Columb Expos (1893). No reference. Sources JUT-PUA-YUP. No current auction record but the estimated price of a Utah landscape would be $700 to $800 at auction in 1975. Signature example p 12 YUP. (See illustration 312.)

His father was a teacher who died in 1832. Weggeland was sent to Stavanger, Norway, when he was nine. At 16 he studied portrait painting. At 20 he was apprenticed to an interior decorator in Copenhagen, Denmark, where he entered the Royal Art Academy the next year. Homesick, he returned to Norway in 1849 to study landscape painting. In 1854 he was converted to the Mormon Church, causing him to be persecuted in Norway and in England. From 1857 to 1860 he served as a missionary, emigrating in 1861 to NYC where he studied with Daniel Huntington and G P A Healy. In 1862 he made his way to Salt Lake City, sketching while traveling from Nebraska with a wagon train of 60 ox teams.

By 1863 Weggeland with Lambourne and Ottinger was organizing the Deseret Academy of Fine Arts. He found it difficult to live as an artist: "Occasionally I could dispose of a painting or give a lesson in return for a pair of hand-knitted sox or a basket of onions or other vegetables from the garden." PUA. Weggeland was able to produce a substantial number of paintings, although his portraits were not appreciated by the pioneers who found them too elegant. His importance was enhanced as the teacher of the second generation of Utah painters, Harwood, Evans, Hafen, and Lorus Pratt.

WEINMAN, Adolph Alexander. Born Karlsruhe, Germany 1870, died probably Forest Hills, NY 1952. Sculptor including Indian subjects. NSS 1900, SAA 1903, ANA 1906, NA 1911. Work in the form of memorials, monuments, statues, plaques, pediments, friezes, doors, medals, in museums and on buildings nationally. References A52 (obit)-BEN-FIE-MAL-SMI. Sources AAT-AMA-DCC-EIT-NA 74-NSS-WHO 52. Bronze bust *Abraham Lincoln* on marble base and 10½″ high was estimated at $1,500 to $2,000 for auction 10/11/75, but did not sell. Signature example p 247 NSS, monogram plate CCVII AMA.

Brought to the US at 10, Weinman was educated in the public schools. He was soon apprenticed to Kaldenburg, a carver in wood and ivory. At 16 he studied evenings at Cooper Union. At 19 he was the pupil of Martiny, entering the ASL the next year, the pupil of Saint-Gaudens. He became the assistant to Saint-Gaudens and later Olin Warner, C H Niehaus, and D C French. Weinman was a professional sculptor beginning 1891, opening his own studio in 1904. He was consistently successful, with a lengthy list of commissions, awards, and selections to juries and professional and public committees on the arts.

Some of Weinman's sculpture was of Indians, eg, *Chief Black Bird* in the Brooklyn Institute Museum. In 1916 he designed two coins, the *Mercury* dime and the *Liberty* half-dollar, both rich in the symbolism of the day: "the American eagle, fearless in spirit and conscious of his power, perched high on a mountain crag." AMA. Weinman was considered "an earnest man, in love with his art and generous to those who go for help." AMA.

WEIR, Robert Walter. Born NYC 1803, died there 1889. Portrait, landscape, genre, and religious painter, teacher. NA 1829. Work in Rotunda of Capitol (Washington), NY City Hall, MMA, NY Hist Soc, West Point Mus, NGA. References BEN-CHA-DAB-ENB-FIE-G&W-MAL-SMI. Sources ALA-AMA-ANT 8/48 (*Red Jacket*), 11/55,11/56, 12/63,1/66,6/72,4/73 (article);4,10/74 -BAR-HUT-ISH-KAR-KW1-M31-NA 74-NJA-PAF-SOA-TEP. Oil 38¼ × 51¼″ *Hunting Dogs* sold 1/24/73 for $2,200. Oil *The Embarkation of the Pilgrims* 48×71½″ signed and dated 1857 sold 12/12/75 for $16,000 at auction. Signature example p 507 KAR.

Weir's Scotch father lost his fortune when Weir was 10. After working in a cotton factory, Weir met the painter John Wesley Jarvis and was taught by Robert Cook (or Cox) before work each day. At 18 he began painting full time and at 21 was sent to Italy by a patron. He was the pupil of Pietro Benvenuti in Florence and shared quarters with the sculptor Horatio Greenough in Rome before returning to establish a NYC studio in 1827. By 1829 he was NA. From 1834 to 1876 he taught drawing at West Point, and was remembered by Grant, Lee, Sherman, and painters like Seth Eastman and Whistler. He received $10,000 for *The Embarkation of the Pilgrims* in the Capitol, although the critics called him "an accomplished rather than an original" talent. DAB. At West Point, the influence on his work was the Italian Renaissance, and he kept alive the style of religious painting. As a landscape painter, he was among the earliest of the

Hudson River School. His 16 children included two recognized painters.

In his historical paintings Weir used Indian figures, eg, in *The Landing of Henry Hudson* (SOA). Also, *Red Jacket,* the 77-year-old Seneca chief, visited NYC in 1828 and posed in regalia for his full-length portrait by the young Weir.

WELCH, Thaddeus. Born Indiana 1844, died Santa Barbara, Cal 1919. Cal landscape painter. Work in Cal Palace of the Legion of Honor, Oakland AM, San Diego FAG. Reference MAS. Sources AIW-KAH. No current auction record. Painting examples pp 47, 49 KAH.

Thad Welch's pioneer family had crossed the plains by wagon train to an Oregon farm in 1847. In 1863 he began working for a printer in Portland, Ore. When he moved to San Francisco in 1866, it was as printer and laborer while he studied art, sketched, and painted an occasional portrait. In 1874 a woman patron sponsored study at the Royal Academy in Munich where Welch met Chase and Duveneck and commenced his long friendship with Twachtman. He studied in Paris in 1878, changing the dark Munich palette for Barbizon. In 1881 Welch returned to the US, painting in NYC and Boston including work for Prang chromolithographs. He traveled through the Southwest in 1888 and 1889, painting pueblo subjects, and was also in Australia in 1889.

In 1892 Welch again settled in California. He executed landscape commissions for Leland Stanford but was too poor to rent a studio. He lived in a cabin in Mill Valley until his paintings found favor at the Bohemian Club in San Francisco. By 1905 he was able to move to Santa Barbara with his second wife, the artist Ludmilla Pilat. Welch was a contemporary of Thomas Hill. He quoted Hill as saying Hill painted Yosemite as it ought to be rather than as it is. AIW.

WELLIVER, Les. Born North Dakota about 1920, living Kalispell, Mont 1969. Montana woodcarver of Western subjects, sculptor, painter. No reference. Source MON. No auction record. Signature example p 111 MON.

Raised on ranches near Wolf Point and Poplar, Mont, Welliver served in the U S Navy 1943–47 as aerial gunnery instructor. He worked as bartender, cook, farm hand, and roughneck.

Woodcarving is his favorite method of interpreting wildlife, Indian, or other Western scenes. He begins by sketching on paper, then selecting and roughing in an appropriate wood, usually cottonwood or juniper. A jackknife does the finish work of a carving that may take 100 hours. A "short, stocky" man with a "perpetual grin," Welliver often carves alongside a stream so that he can sit and fish while working. MON.

WELLS, Cady. Born Southbridge, Mass 1904, died Santa Fe, NM 1954. Contemporary New Mexico painter. Work in ACM, ANS, AIC, San Diego FA Gall, MNM, Fogg MA, Wadsworth Athenaeum, etc. References A59 (obit)-MAL. Sources PIT-TAL-TSF-catalog, Cady Wells Memorial Retrospective Exhibition. No current auction record but the estimated price of a gouache showing New Mexico red rocks would be about $2,500 to $3,000 at auction in 1976. Signature example p 99 TSF. (See illustration 313.)

A wealthy Harvard student, Wells had trained as a concert pianist, studied stage design, and tried a business career before coming to Taos at 28 to study painting with Dasburg. Part of the group with Ward Lockwood and Kenneth Adams, he determined on art as a career. To find his own way in expression, he went to Fogg MA in 1933 to learn art history before returning to Taos and Dasburg. By 1934 he was in a "small, secluded place hidden behind high walls" (TAL) to accomplish his meticulous small watercolors with their abstracted shapes. After exhibiting that year with the Rio Grande Painters in Santa Fe and the Heptagon Gallery in Taos, he left in 1935 for Japan to study brushwork and flower arranging.

Wells settled near Santa Fe later in 1935. He began painting in gouache about 1939, when he could "sum up weeks of looking at the mountains near Taos in a few energetic lines." TSF. Wells served in the Army 1941–45 and then turned to the Virgin Islands as a protest against the atomic energy experiments in New Mexico. After study in France in 1953, this important but little-known individualist died in New Mexico from a heart attack. Two years later MNM had a retrospective exhibition. The U of New Mexico put together a second retrospective in 1967.

WELLS, William L. Active 1890s in San Francisco, Cal. Illustrator. No reference. Source CAP. No current auction record or signature example.

Wells' Western illustrations are in "The Story of the Cowboy" by Emerson Hough. His style was similar to that of H W Hansen. CAP.

WENCK, Paul. Born Berlin, Germany 1892, living New Rochelle, NY 1941. Illustrator, painter, printmaker. Member Artists Guild, Deutscher Werkbund. Work in NYG reproduction, illustrations in "Cagliostro." References A41-MAL. Source, NYG reproduction of *Rockies from Bear Lake* (Rocky Mountain National Park). No current auction record but the estimated price of a Western landscape would be about $800 to $1,000 at auction in 1976. Signature example p 489 NYG.

Wenck is listed as the pupil of Hancke, Boese, Friederich, Herwarth, and Schaefer.

WENDT, William. Born North Germany 1865, died Laguna Beach, Cal 1946. Cal landscape painter. ANA 1912. Work in AIC, Cincinnati AM, Herron AI (Indianapolis), Mus Hist Sci & Art (LA), etc. References A47 (obit)-BEN-FIE-MAL-SMI. Sources AAR 11/74-AMA-INS 4/08-MSL-NA 74-SCA-WHO 46. Oil 14×20" *Village Scene* sold 1968 for $70 at auction. Painting examples p lxiv INS 4/08 *Verdant Hills;* opp p 65 A16 4/08 *Verdant Hills;* opp p 65 A16 *Where Nature's God Hath Wrought.*

Wendt came to Chicago in 1880 where he was educated. He was self-taught as a painter except for night courses at the AIC. He did not achieve success until he began painting in California as a visitor in 1894. He settled in Los Angeles in 1906. Named as California scenes were *Wilderness* and *Cañon Diablo.* MSL. Wendt was considered a colorist, with warm tones and brilliant effects. His wife was Julia Bracken Wendt, the sculptor, with whom he exhibited.

The outstanding name in Southern California landscape painting of his time, Wendt chose "his subject matter primarily from the rolling hills and arroyos." AAR. He traveled to Europe twice before 1906, but in 1924 was quoted as refusing to paint the Grand Canyon because it is impossible. SCA.

WEST, Benjamin. Born Springfield (now Swarthmore), Pa 1738 (or 1748), died London, Eng 1820. Important international historical, portrait, and religious painter, teacher. Charter member RA 1768, the King's historical painter 1772. Work in Yale U, Kensington Palace (London), NGA, Phila MA, NGC, Independence Hall (Phila), BMFA, PAFA, etc. References BEN-CHA-DAB-ENB-FIE-G&W-MAL-SMI. Sources AAR 3/74-AIC-ALA-AMA-ANT 2/44;2/48; 4/49;11/50;6/51;5/54;12/56;4,8/57; 1,7/58;3,12/61;6/62;2,4/67;3,5,6/68; 4/69;11/70;10 (*Penn's Treaty with the Indians* p 663),11/72;4,5,9/73;1/74-ARI-AWM-BAR-BOA-BOL-COR-ISH-KW1-MAP-M15-M19-M31-NCB-NGA-PAF-STI-TSF. Oil 40×58″ *Portrait of John Eardley* sold 11/18/71 for $86,400 in England. Oil 16×20″ *Indian Maiden* sold 1972 for $1,600 at auction. Signature example p 425 CHA.

Son of a Quaker innkeeper, West was raised near Indians who gave him his first colors. He received his initial portrait commission at 15, after painting since he was eight. He attended the College of Philadelphia in 1756, painting portraits and signs in Philadelphia and in NYC in 1759. He left for Italy in 1760, the first American to study there. During three years of critical acclaim, he modeled his style after Titian and Raphael, naming his older son after the latter. His intended "visit" to England in 1763 lasted the rest of his life. His Philadelphia sweetheart eloped across the ocean to join him. By 1766 West was a most popular English painter, a friend of King George III whose commissions consumed West's time. Among his American pupils were Peale, Stuart, Trumbull, Allston, Sully, and Morse.

West's historical paintings included Indian figures. In 1771 he painted *Penn's Treaty with the Indians* for William Penn's son Thomas. The same year, his painting *Death of General Wolfe* showed Indians in war regalia and Wolfe in military uniform in the course of West's breaking away from the practice of depicting heroes in classical togas. Early in the revolution West painted Joseph Brant, the Christian Mohawk, twice, once as an Anglican and again as a war-paint chieftain plotting with a Tory colonel.

WEST, Harold Edward. Born Honey Grove, Tex 1902, living Santa Fe, NM 1962. Southwestern painter, illustrator, printmaker. Work in MNM, NY World's Fair 1939. References A62-MAS. Source AAT. No auction record. Example of linoleum cut p 326 AAT *Just in Time*.

West illustrated "Broadside to the Sun" in 1946. He wrote and illustrated the "Cowboy Calendar" beginning 1939.

WEST, Helen. Born Melbourne, Australia 1926, living Cody, Wyom 1975. Wyom landscapes in watercolor. Sources WYG-WYW 12/71. No auction record or signature example.

Mrs West's parents moved back to the US when she was four. She lived in the East and spent her summers on Wyoming ranches. Mrs West went to high school in Billings, studied art at Montana State College, at Minneapolis AI and the AIC. She taught school in Sunlight, Wyom. Her husband is supervisor of Game District ※2.

"I paint in a realistic style as I find that it is the best way for me to relate my impressions. My paintings are derived from nature and are inspired by my surroundings. I begin them out of doors and finish them in my studio. You reach a certain degree of competence and everything sells." WYG.

WEST, Levon (pseud Ivan Dmitri). Born Centerville, SD 1900, died probably NYC 1968. International etcher and painter, photographer, writer, teacher. Work in Philadelphia MA, BMFA, MMA, NY Pub Lib, Lib Cong, "Prints of the Year" beginning 1931. References A41-MAL. Sources CAP-WHO 62. No current auction record. Signature example p 171 CAP.

Son of a minister, West was a teacher in a rural school before being educated in business at the U of Minnesota 1920–24. While in college he was an illustrator and an artist for the Great Northern Railway. He studied at the ASL in 1925, the pupil of Joseph Pennell in 1925 and 1926. Visiting Spain in 1926, he made 32 etchings there and went on to be official artist of the World Press Congress in Geneva. Lindbergh's 1927 Atlantic flight was the subject of three etchings. In 1931 West etched both the "Venice set" and five etchings of native life in Hudson Bay.

The State of Colorado made West guest artist for 1932, followed by seven etchings and 40 watercolors on American game and on Western Ranch Life. In 1935, there were watercolors of Bermuda. The same year, as "Ivan Dmitri," he began miniature photography. He went on to travel scenes in color in 1936, photographing for *The Saturday Evening Post, Rodeo, Dude Ranching,* etc. West wrote "how to" books on etching and photography.

WEST, Lowren. Born NYC 1923, living Phoenix, Ariz 1976. Modern painter including Southwestern and Indian subjects, illustrator, graphic designer. Illustrations in *New Yorker, Fortune* magazines, *Graphis.* Reference A76. Source AHI 1/74 with signature example p 39. No current auction record.

Lowren West studied painting and printmaking at the ASL, Pratt Institute, Columbia U, The New School, and the Hans Hofmann School FA. His paintings are usually in mixed media and collage to "achieve a strong tactile quality that reflects and absorbs light, while creating maximum tension between the various elements." AHI. One Lowren West subject has been Greek mythology developed in abstract terms.

West had visited Arizona several times before settling there and has begun a series of paintings on the Indians of the Southwest. Three of these are reproduced in AHI 1/74.

WEST, Walter Richard. Born near Darlington, western Okla 1912, living Lawrence, Kan 1976. Important contemporary Cheyenne painter, teacher. Outstanding Indian artist, 1964. Work in DAM, Joslyn AM, MAI, Philbrook AC, NGA, etc. Reference A76. Sources AIP-LAF-PWA 3/75. No current auction record. Signature examples pp 155, 162 LAF.

Dick West, Indian name Wapah Nahyah or Lightfooted Runner, is the son of a Cheyenne marathon runner. He graduated Haskell College in 1935, Bacone in 1938, and received his BA from Oklahoma in 1941. Olaf Nordmark provided mural instruction in 1941–42 while West was art instructor at the Phoenix AS. West then served four years in the European Theater for the US Navy, returning to the Phoenix AS in 1946. He became chairman of the Art Department at Bacone College in 1947. His work was published beginning 1941, including *National Geographic* in 1955, *Life International* in 1959, *Today* and *Saturday Review* in 1963.

West has painted both in traditional Indian-school style and in contemporary art styles such as abstract: "I do feel the Indian artist must be allowed to absorb influences outside of his own art forms and to develop them in his own manner. I see the promise of a new lane of expression that should keep the Indian's art alive and close to a more contemporary existence. Indian artists with formal art background will be going more and more in the direction of the European interpretational influence." AIP. This is the break of the modern Indian artist with the white man's early ethnological influence towards preserving the ancestral Indian craft designs when Indians first began painting on paper after 1910.

WESTON, William Percy. Born London, Eng 1879, died probably Vancouver, BC, Can 1967. Landscape painter of the Can West, teacher. Charter member, Can Group of Painters; assoc, RCA. Work in NGC, U Toronto. References A62-MAL. Sources CAH-CAN-WNW. No auction record or signature example (See illustration 314.)

W P Weston was educated at Borough Road College and studied at the Putney School of Art in London. By 1909–10 he was art instructor in Vancouver High School and Director of Art 1910–14. From 1914–46 he was art master of the Provincial Normal School. Weston was exhibiting with the Canadian Group of Painters from 1930 and the RCA from 1931. Typical titles are *Ramparts of the West, The Summit,* and *Mt Cheam.* By 1940 his work was called "decorative" and "strongly contemporary in feeling." CAN.

When Weston first arrived in Vancouver, he painted in the traditional British-school style. Under Varley's influence he began to paint the mountains in a freer manner. By 1930 it was said that he had "outgrouped the Group of Seven." CAH.

WEYGOLD, Frederick P. Born St Charles, Mo 1870, died Louisville, Ky 1941. Painter and writer of Amer Indian genre, especially of the Sioux. Reference A47 (obit). No other source, auction record, or signature example.

Weygold studied at the PAFA and in Europe.

WEYSS (or Weiss), John E. Born about 1820, died Washington, DC 1903. Western survey artist, engineer. Sketches reproduced in Emory and Wheeler surveys. Reference G&W. Sources AIW-SUR-TEP. No auction record but the estimated price of a landscape sketch would be about $450 to $550 at auction in 1976. Engraving example p 165 TEP.

The Emory survey of the Mexican boundary was carried on from 1849 to 1855. The report was published 1857–59. Volume One was topographical, illustrated by Weyss, Schott, and de Vaudricourt. It contained 76 engravings, 12 lithographs, and 20 woodcuts, mostly the work of Schott and Weyss, with lithography of Sarony, Major, and Knapp, and engravings by James Smillie, James D Smillie, and Dougal. Weyss was with the survey party its entire life, attached to the group traveling westward under Emory himself. Weyss's sketch that is best known is the view of Brownsville, Tex as engraved by James Smillie.

In the Civil War, Weyss served as a major on the staff of engineers of the Army of the Potomac. He remained "for many years connected with Western explorations and surveys under the War Department." AIW. Plates based on Weyss's drawings are included in reports as late as the Wheeler geographic survey in 1889.

WHEELER, Hughlette "Tex." Born Texas about 1900, died Christmas, Fla 1955. Western sculptor in bronze, specializing in horses and cowboys. Work in ACM, Will Rogers State Park (Santa Monica), Santa Anita Racetrack (Arcadia, Cal). No reference. Source COW. Bronze 9½" *Foal* sold 3/5/70 for $175 at auction. Sculpture example ⅸ684 ACM.

"Tex" Wheeler studied in Chicago, modeling horses and cattle. When Forsythe and Frank Tenney Johnson shared a studio in Alhambra, Wheeler and his friend J R Williams were frequent visitors, along with Charles Russell, Norman Rockwell, Ed Borein, and Dean Cornwell. After Johnson died in 1939, Wheeler used the studio to sculpt his best known work, the life-size statue of *Seabiscuit*. In 1942 he was in Santa Monica making a life-size model of Will Rogers on his favorite riding horse, Soapsuds, but the statue was never cast in bronze. His work is scarce. Wheeler also lived on the Rincon ranch in Tucson.

WHITAKER (or Monaghan), Eileen (Mrs Frederic Whitaker). Born Holyoke, Mass 1911, living La Jolla, Cal 1976. Painter in watercolor including Indian subjects. ANA 1957 as aquarellist. Work in Okla MA (Okla City), Hispanic Mus (NYC), Atlanta AM, Norfolk AM. Reference A76. Sources AHI 6/72-NA 74-WAA-W64-WHO 70. No current auction record. Signature example p 18 AHI 6/72.

Mrs Whitaker is listed A76 and WAA as Monaghan. She studied at the Massachusetts College of Art in Boston. The recipient of more than 58 awards, her work has been reproduced in books on watercolor techniques. AHI 6/72 illustrates three of her Indian watercolors, *The Weaver, Stringing Beads,* and *Navaho Procession,* all 22×29″. She is the wife of artist Frederic Whitaker.

WHITAKER, Frederic. Born Providence, RI 1891, living La Jolla, Cal 1976. Painter in watercolor including Western subjects, writer. NA 1951 as aquarellist. Work in MMA, BMFA, Hispanic Mus (NYC), Frye Mus (Seattle); watercolors reproduced as prints. References A76-MAL. Sources AHI 10/72-NA 74-WHO 70. No current auction record. Signature example p 3 AHI 10/72.

Educated in Rhode Island public schools, Whitaker studied at the RI School of Design 1907–11. He became a designer for the Gorham Co 1916–21 and for Tiffany Co in 1922. From 1922 to 1950 he was a manufacturer of religious articles such as altar vessels. In 1950 he married the watercolorist Eileen Monaghan. He is represented in more than 35 museums, has received more than 100 painting honors, has been a contributing editor for *American Artist,* and has written "how to" books on watercolor painting. His illustrated biography was published in 1972.

WHITE, Fritz. Important Western sculptor active in Denver, Colo. Member CAA. No reference. Sources C73,74-*Southwest Art* 5/74, with sculpture examples pp 65–67. No auction record. Sculpture example C74.

White began studying art at 12 and worked as a commercial artist. He started sculpting in 1962. The first bronze was *The Bugler,* followed by *Song of the Wolf, The Drover, Pawnee, Squaws Calico.* Drawing and composition are most important to a sculptor, in White's opinion, but the key is making the work come alive. He points out that a major problem of Western art is the lack of creativity due to the protected nature of the subject matter. White has spent two months on a commission in Israel, in the belief that the Israeli frontier of today most resembles the spirit of the Old West.

WHITE, George Gorgas. Born Philadelphia, Pa about 1835, died NYC 1898.

NYC book and magazine illustrator, wood engraver. Work in BEY. References A98 (obit)-BEN-G&W-MAL-SMI. Source BEY. No auction record. Initial "W" p 69 BEY.

A Quaker, White worked in Philadelphia from 1854 to 1861 as a wood engraver, the pupil of John Cassin, a lithographer of Bowen & Co after 1859. He came to NYC as a Civil War illustrator. After the war, he was a principal illustrator of BEY, along with other important Civil War artists. His 19 BEY illustrations span the period from Waukarusa, and Indian legend of 1857 in Kansas, through 1859 in Colorado and Taos, to the Panama Isthmus in 1866. Although the illustrations included gold mining, Indian attack, Mormon preaching, and Mt Hood, White undoubtedly made his fine drawings in NYC, working from materials there. "He contributed illustrations to almost all the leading magazines for over a quarter of a century." A98.

WHITE, George Harlow. Born London, Eng 1817, died probably Toronto, Can 1888. Toronto landscape painter regarded as an early interpreter of the scenes and life of Western Can. Original member RCA 1880. Work in Montreal AG. References BEN-MAL. Source CAN. No auction record or signature example.

White exhibited at the Royal Academy in London from 1839 to 1883. His first Canadian exhibition coincided in 1873 in Toronto with the first showing of the Ontario Society of Artists. Along with Lucius O'Brien, Bell-Smith, and Mower Martin, he was among the earlier painters in the Canadian West.

WHITE, John, Born probably England about 1550, died probably Ireland after

1593. English painter in watercolor, "first white man to paint in America," mapmaker, colony governor. Work in Brit Mus (70 watercolors), reproduced in 1590 in engravings by de Bry. References BEN-DAB-G&W-MAL. Sources ALA-ANT 7/58-POW (two watercolors illustrated)-LAF. No current auction record but the estimated price of a Virginia watercolor would be about $12,000 to $14,000 at auction in 1976. Engraving example p 73 LAF.

White was sent to the Virginia coast by Sir Walter Raleigh in 1585 to depict the New World to foster interest in future voyages. Having already painted scenes of Florida and Greenland, perhaps from life, White was equipped for the task of setting down the Indian genre and the flora and fauna. More than 60 of White's paintings were made in America, less than 100 years after Columbus. White "accurately drew the palisaded Indian villages, the dances; no painted detail on a warrior's leg escaped him." ALA. "For some three centuries," the paintings "conditioned all pictorial representations of the American Indians." DAB. White also made maps of the Virginia coast that influenced geographers. He returned to England with Sir Francis Drake probably later in 1585. The engraver de Bry reproduced 23 of White's paintings in his 1590 travel book published in Germany because he had been unable to obtain Le Moyne's paintings based on 1564 experiences. In the engravings "the naked redmen were given a resemblance to classical Renaissance athletes." ALA.

In 1587 White was sent back to Virginia as its second governor. His granddaughter Virginia Dare was the first English child born in America.

WHITE, Orrin Augustine. Born Hanover, Ill 1883, died Pasadena, Cal 1969. Cal landscape painter. Work in LA Mus, Ill St Mus (Springfield), Cleveland AM,

Montclair Mus (NJ). References A41-BEN-FIE-MAL-SMI. Sources SCA-WHO 50. No auction record or signature example.

Orrin A White graduated from U of Notre Dame in 1902 and from the Philadelphia School of Applied Art in 1906. During WWI he was an officer in the Engineer Corps assigned to painting camouflage. White had settled in Los Angeles by 1916. Listed titles included *Sierra Peaks, Sunset Glow,* and *Mountain Ranch.* His subjects were California and Mexico. In 1916 White held his first California exhibition in Pasadena and he built his studio there in 1924.

WHITE, Thomas Gilbert. Born Grand Haven, Mich 1877, died probably Paris, France 1939. Painter, muralist, teacher, writer. Commander, Legion of Honor. Work in Houston Mus, BM, U of Utah, U of Okla, COR, mus and gall in Paris. References A41 (obit)-FIE-MAL-SMI. Sources MSL-figures in Western murals. No current auction record or signature example.

Gilbert White was the pupil of Twachtman. He studied at the Julien Academy in Paris, under Constant and Laurens, and at the Beaux-Arts. He was also the pupil of Whistler and MacMonnies. Murals include Kentucky, Utah, and Oklahoma State Capitols, public buildings in Alabama, Connecticut, and Washington, DC, and the McAlpin Hotel, NY.

WHITE BEAR. Born 1869, active 1899. Early Hopi watercolor painter. Work in MAI, Southeast Mus of the North Amer Ind (Marathon, Fla). No reference. Sources AHI 2/50-AIP. No auction record or signature example.

White Bear's Hopi name was Kutca Honauu. In 1899 Dr J Walter Fewkes, an ethnologist, gave White Bear some watercolors "to make drawings representing the Hopi gods and to explain the symbolism of the dance rituals" of the Kachinas, the masked dancers. "The project resulted in the publication, in 1903, of about 180 Kachina drawings" in which the artist was assisted by his uncle, Homovi. AIP.

White Bear is the second known Southeast Indian artist "to make drawings on paper independent of traditional craft or ceremonial attachment." In general the Hopi drawings show "a stiffness of figure reminiscent of cave and kiva wall drawing" with "exquisite detail, finely expressed." AHI.

WHITE BEAR (or Kucha Honawah, or Fredericks, Oswald). Born Old Oraibi, Ariz 1906, living Oraibi, Ariz 1968. Hopi painter, Kachina carver, art teacher, teacher of dancing in Fred Waring Workshop. Work in MAI (72 published works), SE Mus No Am Indians; published in book and magazines. No reference. Source AHI 7/59-AIP-COW. No auction record. Signature example p 21 AHI 7/59.

White Bear, born in one of the oldest US villages, was educated in Oraibi and Phoenix Indian schools, Phoenix high school, Bacone College, and Haskell 1933–37. White Bear who had no formal art training was an art teacher for 15 years at a New Jersey YMCA where he also painted a mural. His illustrations in AHI 7/59 are of the *Home Dance* of the Hopis that takes place the end of July each year as a prayer for rain.

WHITEFIELD, Edwin. Born East Lulworth, Dorset, Eng 1816, died Dedham, Mass 1892. Topographical artist of lithographic views, the "Emigrant Agent" for Minnesota settlement, inventor, lecturer.

Work in BMFA. Reference MAS. Sources ANT 8/72 (article)-KW1 with watercolor sketch p 306-STI. No auction record.

Whitefield studied art in England after having been educated in medicine and law. He emigrated to the US about 1840, exhibiting still-life paintings by 1842. In 1845 quantities of his views of American cities and of American wildflowers appeared as lithographs. He went on to views of *Minnesota Scenery* beginning 1858, *Views of Chicago* beginning 1860, and *The Homes of our Forefathers* beginning 1879. A prolific artist, he recorded what he saw, wherever he was.

In 1856 he helped organize the Kandiyohi Town Site Company in Minnesota, making many watercolor sketches. He also established a homestead for himself, living in a log cabin with his wife, his only neighbors the Indians. Sketches of this period are not available.

WHITESIDE, Frank Reed. Born Philadelphia, Pa 1866 (or 1867), died there 1929. Landscape painter, teacher, writer, who visited Zuni Indians beginning 1890. References A29 (obit)-BEN-FIE-MAL-SMI. Sources ANT 1/71,3/73,1/75-WHO 28. No current auction record but the estimated price of a painting of Zuni genre would be about $1,500 to $2,000 at auction. in 1976. Signature example p 27 ANT 1/71.

Educated in the Philadelphia public schools, Whiteside studied at the PAFA before becoming the pupil of Laurens and Constant in Paris. He returned to Philadelphia to work as an instructor at R C high school 1890–96 and at other public and private schools including Germantown Academy in 1907. From his studio in Philadelphia and his summer home in Ogunquit, Me, Whiteside specialized in landscapes and contributed to art periodicals. "He was mysteriously shot down on the threshold of his home,

526

when he responded to a ring of the door bell." A29.

Whiteside visited and lived with the Zuni Indians at intervals from 1890 to 1920. Four of his pueblo genre paintings are shown in ANT 1/71, part of an exhibition at the Phoenix AM, "the first public exhibition since 1929 when a memorial exhibition was presented at the Philadelphia Sketch Club." ANT.

WHITTREDGE, Thomas Worthington. Born Springfield, Ohio 1820, died Summit NJ 1910. Important "Hudson River School" landscape painter in the West beginning 1866, illustrator. ANA 1860, NA 1862. Work in MMA, ACM, COR, The Century Assn (NYC), DAM, Joslyn AM (Omaha), etc; reproductions in lithographs. References A10 (obit)-BEN-CHA-DAB-FIE-G&W-MAL-SMI. Sources AAR 5,11/74-AIW-ALA-ANT 6/44;1/49;11/50;5/54;10/58;5/65; 10/69;3/70;9/71;4,9/72;1,5,10,11/73; 2,7,10/74-BAR-BOA-COR-DAA-DBW-DCC-HUT-ISH-KAR-KW2-M19-M31-MSL-NA 74-NJA-PAF-POW-STI-TAW-TSF. Oil 39×53¾" *A Scene Near Brunnen* (Switzerland) signed and dated Rome 1859 estimated at $9,000 to $12,000 sold 5/23/74 for $6,000 at auction. Signature example p 136 TAW.

Son of a farmer, Worthington Whittredge went to Cincinnati when he was 17. "After failing in several pursuits" (BOA), he worked as a house and sign painter while studying art. At 20 he learned daguerreotypes and began painting portraits in and around Cincinnati. At 23, landscape painting became his specialty. The local collectors bought his work readily. In 1849 they commissioned a series of European scenes. Whittredge studied in Düsseldorf, the pupil of Andreas Achenbach until 1854. He was the friend of Bierstadt and Leutze, and became Leutze's model for *Washington Crossing the Delaware*. Whittredge went on to Italy, returning to the NYC Studio Building on Tenth Street in 1859. His European landscapes had been sent directly to Cincinnati to pay for the trip.

"A picturesque figure, a man of fine presence and physique" (DAB), Whittredge was "tall, dark-complexioned, dignified, and very courteous." (BOA). In 1866 he accompanied Gen John Pope on a journey of inspection from Fort Leavenworth, Kan through Denver and south along the Rockies into New Mexico. The expedition returned via the Santa Fe trail. Whittredge used his field sketches for studio landscapes of the West. "The price quoted by the artist was $10,000 plus $2,000 for the frame." TAW. In 1870 he again toured the Rockies, this time with Sanford Gifford and J F Kensett, and may have made a third trip in 1877. He was in Mexico 1893 and 1896.

WIBOLTT, Aage Christian (or Jack). Born Denmark 1894, living Los Angeles, Cal 1948. Portrait and mural painter, illustrator. Work in NY World's Fair (1939), LA Jr Col, murals in LA theater. Reference A41-MAS. Source, p 163 AAT *Indian Boys with Pony,* with signature example. No current auction record.

Wiboltt studied at the Royal Academy in Copenhagen. He was listed as living at 360 North Euclid, Pasadena, in 1932.

WIDFORSS, Gunnar Mauritz. Born Stockholm, Sweden 1879, died Grand Canyon, Ariz 1934. Western landscape "painter of the national parks," illustrator. Work in NGA (collection of studies of Grand Canyon), First Nat Bank of Ariz. References A36 (obit)-DAB-MAL. Sources WAI 71,72. Oil on academy board 10×14" *Desert Landscape*

signed but not dated sold 10/27/71 for $650 at auction. Signature example "Gunnar Widforss, Painter of the Grand Canyon," 1969 Northland Press.

Son of a shopkeeper, Widforss studied to be a muralist at the Institute of Technology in Stockholm from 1896 to 1900. In search of landscape subjects, he traveled to Russia, in Europe, Africa, and from 1905 to 1908 in the US where he was not successful. He was popular in Sweden on his return; his early patrons were European royalty. He remained there until 1921 when he visited California and settled there in the course of a trip to the Orient.

In 1922 Stephen T. Mather, the director of the national parks, influenced Widforss to make the parks his specialty. Widforss illustrated the book "Songs of Yosemite" in 1923. National magazines used his paintings for covers. "The quiet Swede" toured the West, "the canyons of the Colorado and Yellowstone, Zion and Bryce canyons, the Kaibab forest, at Mesa Verde, Taos, Crater Lake and along the Monterey coast." DAB. Widforss, who was a bachelor, became a citizen because of the Grand Canyon, spending his last years in a studio on the rim, studying geological formations and painting from the different aspects in oil and watercolor. The paintings were called the "finest things of the kind that have come out of the West." NGA. When he died of a heart attack on the rim of the canyon, he was buried there. His estate was 150 landscapes. In 1969 the Museum of Northern Arizona had a retrospective exhibition.

WIEGHORST, Olaf. Born Viborg, Jutland, Denmark 1899, living El Cajon, Cal 1975. Important traditional Western painter specializing in horses, painter of horse portraits, illustrator, sculptor. Work in Cowboy Hall of Fame, ACM, Eisenhower Lib (Abilene), but mainly in private collns. No reference. Sources ACO-AHI 11/62,3/71 (article), 3/74-ANT 11/65-CAP-COW-EIT-HAR-JNB-PNW-TWR-WAI 71,72. Oil on Masonite 12×9¾" signed and with insignia but not dated, estimated at $7,000 to $8,000 and sold 9/28/73 for $7,000 at auction. Oil 24×30" *Range Ponies* 1959 estimated for sale 10/28/74 at $12,000 to $15,000 at auction in LA, and sold for $13,000. Signature and brand p 36 AHI 3/74.

Wieghorst is the son of a display artist and photo retoucher who became an engraver. Educated in Copenhagen public schools, Wieghorst was "Little Olaf—the Miniature Acrobat" from age nine until 14. AHI 3/71. Interested in horses, the American "Wild West," and painting while apprenticed in a store and on a farm, he began painting in 1916. Working as a sailor in 1918, he jumped ship in NYC where he enlisted in the US Cavalry for duty on the Mexican border. During his three years of military service as a horseshoer, he learned rodeoing and trick riding. He was mustered out in Arizona, finding work as a ranch hand on the Quarter Circle 2C Ranch whose brand is now Wieghorst's insignia. In 1923 he returned to NYC, graduating from the Police Academy in 1925. Assigned to the Police Show Team of the Mounted Division, Wieghorst began to paint in his spare time. In 1940 he found an agent for his paintings which immediately sold as calendar art and as Western illustrations. By 1942 he was receiving commissions for horse portraits and bronzes, with fees up to $500.

In 1944 Wieghorst retired from the Police Department, settling in El Cajon, Cal in 1945. By 1955 he had a waiting list of buyers. "I try to paint the little natural things, the way a horse turns his tail to the wind on cold nights, the way he flattens his ears in the rain, seasonal changes in the coat of a horse, and the psychology of his behavior. Horses have been my life." AHI. Weighorst's biography was published in 1969.

WIEST, Don. Born Wyoming about 1920, living Laramie, Wyom 1974. Modern Wyom landscape painter, teacher. No reference. Source WYG. No auction record. Painting examples p 11 *Wyoming* 2–3/58.

Wiest's childhood was spent in the "high country." He studied in Delaware, then at Colorado State College of Education at Denver U, and at the U of Wyoming. In 1958 he was associate professor of art at the U of Wyoming.

As a painter Wiest worked in what he called stylism, along the range between realism and abstraction. Stylism is treatment of the subject matter to withdraw realistic identity. "Abstraction helps me to be more positive in realism; stylization brings together that which is seen and that which is felt; realism brings to attention things which can be used in abstractions." *Wyoming*.

WIGGINS, Mrs Myra Albert. Born Salem, Ore 1869, died Seattle, Wash 1956. Northwest still-life painter, teacher, photographer. Work in Wash St Lib, Pub Lib Olympia, YWCA and YMCA Yakima, Gen Fed Women's Clubs. References A59 (obit)-BEN-MAL. Sources WAA-WNW. No auction record or signature example.

Mrs Wiggins studied with Dudley Pratt and F H Varley, at the ASL and NY SA, with William Chase, George deF Brush, W Metcalf, Twachtman, and DuMond. Her still-life paintings often included Indian artifacts. WNW lists include *American Indian Basket* in Olympia and *Indian Baskets* in Yakima.

WILCOX, Frank Nelson. Born Cleveland, Ohio 1887, living East Cleveland, Ohio 1962. Ohio painter including Indian subjects, printmaker, teacher. Work in Cleveland MA, Toledo MA, San Diego FAG, BM; dioramas in Wn Reserve Hist Soc. References A62-BEN-FIE-MAL. Source AAT. Watercolor 14½×21½" *Old Town on the Miami* sold 6/17/70 for $50 at auction. Watercolor example p 157 AAT *Desert Dusk* depicting mounted Indians.

Wilcox studied at the Cleveland SA and with H G Keller, F C Gottwald. An instructor at the Cleveland IA, he wrote and illustrated "Ohio Indian Trails."

WILD, John Caspar (or Casper). Born Zürich, Switzerland 1806 (or, about 1804), died Davenport, Iowa 1846. Landscape painter, lithographer, in Fort Snelling 1844. Work in Mercantile Lib (St Louis), Minn Hist Soc (St Paul), Davenport Pub Mus (Iowa); lithograph collns in Lib Cong and Chicago Hist Soc. Reference G&W. Sources ALA-ANT 1/46,8/48,12/49-DWF-KW1-MIS-PAF-WES. No current auction record but the estimated price of a frontier watercolor would be about $2,000 to $2,500 at auction in 1976. Signature example p 45 WES.

J C Wild spent 15 years in Paris where he studied art before emigrating to the US about 1830. He made his first American lithograph in Philadelphia in 1831. By 1835 he was in Cincinnati, active as painter and lithographer, at a time when the river cities were the frontier. Returning to Philadelphia in 1838, Wild made 20 views of the city that were released as a set of lithographs.

From 1839 to 1843 Wild lived in St Louis, employed on the *Missouri-Republican* newspaper. In 1840 he issued *Views of St Louis*. His best-known work *The Valley of the Mississippi Illustrated in a Series of Views* was published as a portfolio 1841–42. It contained 28 (or 34) lithographs of St Louis and other scenic spots along the river. Originally in black and white, the portfolio was reissued in color in a larger size. Wild was painting in Fort Snelling in 1844 before Wimar and in Davenport, Iowa in 1845. His contribution to Western painting was adding to the "documentary record the minutely detailed scenes of the Mississippi painted and lithographed from St Louis and Davenport." ALA.

WILES, Lemuel Maynard. Born Perry, Wyoming Cnty, NY 1826, died NYC 1905. Landscape and figure painter, in the West 1873–74, teacher. Work in Ingham U (NY), Pub Lib (Perry), Harmsen colln. References A05 (obit)-BEN - CHA - FIE - G&W - MAL - SMI. Sources AMA-ANT 3/56,6/67,3/71, 3/73-DCC-HUT-PAF-STI-WHO 03. No current auction record but the estimated price of a Western landscape would be about $2,500 to $3,000 at auction in 1976. Signature example p 779 ANT 6/67.

Wiles graduated from NY State Normal College in 1847, earning his master's degree from Ingham U in Le Roy, NY. Between 1848 and 1853, he studied art, first at Albany Academy, the pupil of William Hart, and then with J F Cropsey in NYC. Wiles taught drawing in Albany Academy, in the Utica public schools, for 10 years in the summers at Ingham U, at Nashville U in Tennessee, and at a summer school at Silver Lake, NY. After 1864 his studio was in NYC. ANT has had articles on the similarity of a winter scene among a Wiles, a Bonfield, and an unsigned painting of the period. He was perhaps best known as the father of the painter Irving Wiles, "his face was familiar through the double portrait by Irving Wiles of his father and mother." A05.

In 1873 Wiles visited California and Colorado by way of Panama. By 1874 he had accumulated "a large number of color studies upon which he drew for his more ambitious works." HUT. The studies provided valuable records of the old mission churches and cathedrals of the West. The later easel paintings included *Panama* in 1880, *Camp of the San Diego Indians* in 1883, and *The Bridal Veil, Yosemite.*

WILGUS, William John. Born Troy, NY 1819, died Buffalo, NY 1853. Painter of portraits including Indians. Hon member NA 1839. Work in COR, Yale; in Centennial Exhibition of NAD in 1925. References BEN-FIE-G&W-MAL. Source, portrait of an Indian chief in NA exhibition. No current auction record or signature example.

The pupil of Samuel F B Morse from 1833 to 1836, Wilgus painted in NYC until 1841. He then settled in Buffalo, NY, with trips to Georgia, Missouri, and the West Indies. Lars Sellstedt wrote Wilgus' biography.

WILKINS, James F. Born England 1808, died near Shobonier, Ill 1888. Panoramist of the overland route to the gold mines, Western genre and portrait painter, miniaturist. Work in Mo Hist Soc, St Hist Soc of Wis, Huntington Lib (Cal). Reference G&W. Source ANT 10/62 with painting example p 417 *Leaving the Old Homestead*-BDW. No auction record.

Wilkins studied at the RA before going to New Orleans 1832–43 as a portrait and miniature painter. During this period, he exhibited portraits in London. In 1844 he was in St Louis as part of the international arts settlement there at the time. In order to record the event, he joined an 1849 caravan traveling overland to the California mines and the gold rush, perhaps the first professional artist on the route. His 200 watercolor drawings were the source materials for a three-reel panorama that Wilkins painted for exhibition 1850–51 in competition with the Mississippi River panoramas of the day. The 50 surviving watercolors and Wilkins' diary were published in 1967 as "An Artist on the Overland Trail."

WILLIAMS, Frederick Ballard. Born Brooklyn, NY 1871, died probably Glen Ridge, NJ 1956. NYC landscape and figure painter who painted at the Grand Canyon. ANA 1907, NA 1909. Work in NGA, MMA, Montclair AM, Hackley AG (*Grand Canyon*), City AM (St Louis), AIC, etc. References A59 (obit)-BEN-FIE-MAL-SMI. Sources AAT-ANT 11/66,3/73-ISH-M31-MSL-NA 74-NJA-WHO 56. Oil 8×10″ *Grand Canyon* sold 3/14/68 for $250 at auction. Oil 24×16″ *Miranda* sold 1969 for $350 at auction. Signature example p 582 ANT 11/66. (See illustration 315.)

When "a lad," Williams studied at night at Cooper Union in NYC, then attended the school of John Ward Stimson, "an idealist." MSL. He also studied at the NAD and in England and France, the pupil of W H Gibson, C Y Turner, and E M Ward. "Mr Williams' landscapes are not painted out-of-doors. He transcribes what he feels rather than what he sees." MSL. As a landscapist, he is grouped with Bogert, Ranger, Dearth, and Carleton Wiggins.

WILLIAMS, James Robert. Born Halifax, Nova Scotia, Can 1888, died probably San Marino, Cal 1957. Cartoonist of "Out Our Way," traditional Western painter and sculptor. Work in newspapers as "Cowboys in the Comics." References A41-MAL. Sources AHI 9/52 (article)-COW-PER ✕1 vol 5-WHO 56. No current auction record but the estimated price of a Western drawing would be about $800 to $1,000 at auction in 1976. Signature example p 53 PER ⊁1 vol 5.

Son of an American businessman, "Jim" Williams was educated in public schools in Detroit, Mich and Conneaut, Ohio before attending Mt Union College in Alliance, Ohio. He worked as a fireman on the Pennsylvania RR, as a ranch hand in New Mexico, as a Fort Sill muleskinner with the Apaches in Oklahoma, in the US Cavalry for a three-year hitch when he did tattooing and played football, and in factories as a machinist at night so he could study art during the day.

Williams sold the cartoon panel "Out Our Way" to a newspaper syndicate in 1922. It was printed daily in more than 700 papers, the human side of "the essence of all he had observed and learned on cattle ranches." COW. The cartoons were never bitter, the gripes never mean or desperate. Other cartoons Williams also produced were "Worry Wart," "Why Mothers Get Gray," "Born Thirty Years Too Soon," and "The Willets." After living in Cleveland during the 1920s, he bought a cattle ranch near Prescott, Ariz in 1931, working the spread in the day time, doing his cartoons at night, and sculpting. The outfit was the K4, 45,000 acres "in one of the wildest spots left in the Southwest." AHI. Williams moved to the city in 1941 only after he had fallen behind on his cartoon schedule. Still rugged at 60, he was "a mild-mannered, genuinely friendly man less aware of his own importance than any national figure." AHI. One of his friends Tex Wheeler sculpted Williams on his saddlehorse "Lizard."

WILLIAMS, Virgil. Born Dixfield, Me (or Taunton, Mass) 1830, died near Mt St Helena, Cal 1886. Landscape, genre, and portrait painter, member of "California Landscape School" of the 1870s, teacher, decorator. Work in Oakland AM. References G&W-MAL. Sources ANT 5/47,6/74-BWB-KAH-PAF-SSF-TAW. Oil 14×18″ *Cabin in the Woods* signed and dated "1872 Cal" sold 4/11/73 for $1,600 at auction. Painting example p 50 KAH.

Williams studied in Paris and Rome beginning 1853, returning to Boston in 1860 to establish his studio. In 1862 he moved to San Francisco where he designed a "Pompeian-frescoed antechamber" (SSF) for the mansion of his patron R B Woodward, filling Woodward's Art Gallery with 66 pictures he had painted or collected abroad. In January 1865 when "San Francisco opened its first Art Union" (SSF), the paintings were by Williams, Charles Nahl, and Thomas Hill. Later that year Williams was back in Boston. He taught drawing at Harvard.

In 1871 Williams settled permanently in San Francisco. He started the School of Design in 1874 that "for a time shared quarters with the newly founded Bohemian Club." BWB. The school succeeded, as did some of Williams' pupils, although it was claimed that "the faculty was hopelessly tradition-bound, ignoring the work of the impressionists." BWB. As a landscape painter, Williams was the only native-born member of the San Francisco school of the 1870s, Hill, Keith, and Hahn having emigrated from Europe. Williams' wife Dona was the daughter of the portrait painter William Page. When Robert Louis Stevenson visited San Francisco in 1879, he met the local artists through his son-in-law Joe Strong. Stevenson and the Williams became friends, so that Stevenson dedicated a book to them. Paintings of California by Williams are rare although he painted many.

WILLIAMSON, John. Born near Glasgow, Scotland 1826, died Glenwood-on-the-Hudson, NY 1885. Eastern landscape painter best known for Hudson River and Catskill views. ANA 1861. References BEN-CHA-FIE-G&W-MAL-SMI. Sources ANT 8/74-BOA-DBW-HUT-NA 74-STI. Oil 24¾×37¼" *View of the Hudson River* signed with monogram and dated '59 sold 5/2/72 for $4,250 at auction. Painting example above and p 186 ANT 8/74.

Williamson was brought to Brooklyn in 1831. He was a member of the Brooklyn Art Association and began exhibiting at the NA in 1850. His paintings were of scenes in New Hampshire, the Adirondacks, Connecticut Valley, Hudson River, and Mohawk Valley. DBW lists an oil 35½×14½" *Overland Route to the Rocky Mountains* not dated and not illustrated but about 1877.

WILSON, Charles Banks. Born Springdale, Ark 1918, living Miami, Okla 1976. Painter including Indian portraits, illustrator, muralist, lithographer, teacher, writer. Work in GIL, Okla Capitol, MNM, MMA, COR, Joslyn AM (Omaha), Smithsonian Inst. Reference A76. Sources COW-GIL. No current auction record. Painting example p 14 GIL.

Wilson studied at the AIC, lithography with Francis Chapin, painting with Louis Riman and Boris Anisfeld, and watercolor with Hubert Ropp. He was head of the art department at Northeast Oklahoma A&M College (Miami) for 15 years.

His specialty was painting portraits in tempera of contemporary Oklahoma Indians, as featured in *Collier's* in 1942. In illustrating more than 28 books, he demonstrated his expertise as a historian. He also painted more than 90 watercolor illustrations for Ford Motor Co and wrote the book "Indians of Eastern Oklahoma." In the Oklahoma State Capitol, his life-size portraits of Sequoyah, Jim

Thorpe, Will Rogers, and Robert Kerr are exhibited, and murals have been commissioned for a series on the development of Oklahoma.

WILSON, Jeremiah (or Jeremy). Born in Illinois 1825 (or 1824), active Harrisburg, Pa 1863. Portrait and landscape painter in California 1850. Work in Oakland AM. Reference G&W. Source KAH. No auction record. Painting example p 51 KAH.

A census report for 1850 located Wilson on the Middle Fork of the American River, along the old Emigrant Trail that Wilson could have followed as a Forty-Niner. From 1853 to 1856 Wilson lived in Philadelphia, exhibiting at the PAFA. He was in Rome in 1859, perhaps as a student. By 1861 he was back in Philadelphia. He was living in Harrisburg in 1863, the year he painted *The High Sierra*, a 52¼×98½" panorama of the American River where he had been in 1850.

WILSON, Thomas Harrington. Active 19th century in London. English painter of genre and portraits, engraver. Work in GOD. Reference BEN. Source GOD. No current auction record. Signature example p 89 GOD.

Wilson exhibited in London from 1842 to 1886. In GOD, sketches by J Cooper, R P Leitch, and T W Wilson are reproduced from "The Northwest Passage by Land" written by Viscount Milton and Dr W B Cheadle about 1864. The book describes a trip from Chicago across Western Canada and through the mountains via Yellowhead Pass in 1862–63. The expedition followed a tradition of Western excursions by English nobility including Viscount Milton's father. The purpose of the trip was to establish a new route to the boom town at the Cariboo diggings in British Columbia. Wilson did not accompany the expedition but rather worked from materials such as photographs available in London.

WILWERDING, Walter Joseph. Born Winona, Minn 1891, living Minneapolis, Minn 1966. Wildlife painter, illustrator, teacher, writer. Work in Explorers Club Bldg (Chicago). References A66-MAL. Source WHO 66. No auction record or signature example.

Wilwerding was educated in public schools before studying at the Minneapolis SA 1910–15, the pupil of R Koehler, G Goetsch, and landscape painting with Edwin M Dawes. He painted and photographed animal life from the Everglades to the Arctic Circle. WHO 66. By 1941 his book credits included illustrations for Joaquin Miller's "True Bear Stories," "King of the Grizzlies," "Under Western Heavens," and "Indian Moons." His magazine illustrations were in *Boy's Life, Blue Book, Fauna, Western Sportsman, True West,* and *Sports Afield.* His "How To Draw" books included "Hoofed Animals" and "Textures of Animals." Wilwerding was with Art Instruction Schools of Minneapolis 1926–32 and 1941–61.

WIMAR, Charles (or Carl, or Karl Ferdinand). Born Siegburg, near Bonn, Germany 1828, died St Louis, Mo 1862 (or 1863). Important frontier painter of Plains Indians and buffaloes, portrait painter, muralist. Work in ACM, ANS, Noonday Club (St Louis), City AM (St Louis), U of Mich, Washington U, Mo Hist Soc, Peabody Mus (Harvard). References BEN-DAB-G&W-MAL. Sources AAR 9/73-AHI 3/66-AIW-ANT 2/50, 5/56,5/60,11/66,11/72-BAR-DBW-DCC-DWF-HAR-HON-150-KEN-MIS-PAF-PAW-POW-TAW-TEP-TSF-TWR-WES-WHI-WIM. Oil 33×46″ *Indians Pursued by American Dragoons* signed Charles Wimar and dated Dusseldorf 1853 estimated at $60,000 to $70,000 sold 5/23/74 for $50,000 at auction. Signature example p 67 WIM. (See illustration 316.)

Wimar began painting in oil when he was 12 in Cologne. In 1843 he emigrated to St Louis with his mother to join his stepfather who had established an inn. Near an Indian camping ground, the shy Wimar sought out Indians rather than American boys. At 18 he was apprenticed to the ornamental artist Léon Pomarede. In 1849 Pomarede joined in the "battle" of the St Louis panoramas, taking Wimar with him to make sketches up the Mississippi by steamboat to the Falls of St Anthony. After the panorama was completed, Wimar established a studio with Edward Boneau in 1851. Few paintings of this period survive.

In 1852 Wimar went to Düsseldorf Academy, the leading school of the day. For four years he was the pupil, first of Josef Fay and then of Leutze. The style was romantic realism, with a full-scale and detailed preparatory cartoon for each painting. Apart from forgeries that appeared in St Louis after the Civil War, there were only about 60 known paintings by Wimar, 17 being in Düsseldorf where he was known as "the Indian painter." His paintings of dramatic Indian scenes from history and the books of James Fenimore Cooper were sent back to St Louis for sale, one bringing as much as $300.

When Wimar returned to St Louis in 1856, his style was immediately freer and fresher. He took a six-month trip up the Missouri and Yellowstone in 1858, sketching and making some of the earliest Indian photographs. Wimar himself resembled an Indian, dressed in buckskins with straight black hair to his shoulders and high cheekbones. He made a two-month trip up river in 1859. The result was mature and authentic depiction of the Indian and buffalo in prairie life. These paintings were successful for exhibition but for financial support Wimar was required to paint portraits as well and to do decorative work. He died from tuberculosis while painting courthouse murals.

WINANS, Walter. Born St Petersburg, Russia 1852, died London, Eng 1920. Sculptor, painter, and illustrator specializing in the horse. Chevalier, Imperial Russian Order. Work in Marble Palace (St Petersburg), Hartsfeld House (London). References A20 (obit)-BEN-MAS. Sources p 300 ANT 3/69 with signature example—*Indian Fight* in the Hartsfeld House colln. Bronze, black patina, 11″ high, *A Frontiersman and His Horse* signed Walter Winans, dated Dec 31, 1890, and inscribed OP 4 sold 5/22/73 for $950 at auction.

Born in Russia of American parents, Winans was the pupil of Volkoff, Paul, Geroges, and Corboult. "A noted American sportsman" (A20), Winans was a member of Peintres et Sculpteurs du Cheval. BEN called him an artist of the English School who worked in the US.

WINGATE, Curtis. Born Dennison, Tex 1926, living probably Phoenix, Ariz 1971. Traditional Western painter in oil and watercolor, sculptor, specializing in rodeo subjects. Assoc member, CAA. Work in banks and businesses. No reference. Sources COW-WAI 71. No current auction record. Signature example p 159 COW.

As a youth Wingate did some "bronc riding" in rodeos and then served in the Marines. He was the pupil of William Schimmel for watercolors and was encouraged by Hampton and Phippen.

WINTER, George. Born Portsea, Eng 1810, died Lafayette, Ind 1876. Pioneer Indiana painter including Indian portraits and genre, portrait and landscape painter, teacher. Work in Indiana Hist Soc, Earlham Col (Richmond, Ind), St Hist Soc of Wis (Madison). References BEN-FIE-G&W-MAL-SMI. Sources ALA-ANT 3/65 pp 305, 306. No current auction record but the estimated price of an Indian painting would be about $2,500 to $3,000 at auction in 1976. No signature example.

Winter studied art briefly in London when he was 16. Emigrating to NYC in 1830, he studied for three years at the Academy of Design. Recorded by Dunlap as painting miniatures in NYC in 1834, he moved to Cincinnati in 1835 and lived in Logansport, Ind from 1836 to 1851. He then settled in Lafayette, Ind.

"The most important of Indiana's pioneer artists, Winter painted portraits of many early settlers and Indians." G&W. "The Journals and Indian Paintings of George Winter 1837–1839" was published in 1948 by the Indiana Historical Society. The "documentary record" of the West "included the rather dry fruits of George Winter's years among the redmen of the Wabash, where he painted Kick-Ke-Se-Quah and O-Shaw-Se-Quah before their fathers folded their tents and disappeared." ALA. Many of Winter's paintings have survived. ANT 3/65 reproduced *Three Potawatomie Indians* and *A Gathering of Indians near the Wabash River*. Winter's best-known pupil was John Insco Williams.

WITHROW, Eva Almond. Born Santa Clara, Cal 1858, died San Diego, Cal 1928. Genre painter of SW Indians, portrait painter. No reference. Source BDW. No auction record or signature example.

Ms Withrow specialized in celebrity

portraits in San Francisco and London. She also painted Indian subjects in the Southwest and in Southern California.

WITTMACK, Edgar Franklin. Born NYC 1894, died there 1956. Illustrator, painter. Member SI. References A59 (obit)-MAS. Sources AAC-ILG. Western oil 30×21" *The Opponents* signed and dated 1927 sold 2/24/72 for $250 at auction. Signature example p 107 ILG.

Wittmack's illustration work included Westerns for pulp magazines in the 1920s. By the '30s his work was being published on the cover of *The Saturday Evening Post*.

WOLF, Joseph. Born Moerz, near Coblenz, Prussia 1820, died Regent's Park, London 1899. "The best" English animal painter, illustrator. References BEN-MAL. Sources BRY-DNB-WOF-2/11/74 letter from Ann Datta, Brit Mus (Nat Hist). No current auction record but the estimated price of a chalk illustration 10×8" of a grizzly menacing a buffalo would be about $1,200 to $1,500 at auction in 1976. Signature example p 174 WOF *Tame and Wild*. (See illustration 317.)

Wolf was educated at Metternich, then worked on his father's farm until 16. He was called the "bird fool," because of his preoccupation with birds. He was freed to apprenticeship with lithographers in Coblenz and to lithographic work in Darmstadt. An attack of ague in 1843 prevented his working but allowed Wolf to attend Darmstadt Art School, continuing with Antwerp Academy in 1847.

Wolf emigrated to London in 1848. He was at once installed in the insect room at the British Museum, illustrating bird books. "There is hardly a book on natural history issued during Wolf's life to which he did not make some contribution, and he has been pronounced to be without exception the best all-round animal painter that ever lived. His collection of sketches numbered many thousands, and his industry was indefatigable, every spare moment being occupied in sketching. So thoroughly had he practiced draftsmanship, and so intimately did he understand his subject, that his drawings are not only extremely beautiful, but are marvels of most perfect accuracy. He was a man of particularly kindly disposition, full of intense affection for his subject. In his book illustrations, there was no straining after effect but broad clear treatment, living reproduction, and a simplicity of style that was most attractive." BRY. There is no indication that Wolf visited the US, but he was in London at the same time as Catlin.

WOLF, Pegot (or Peggy). Sculptor active Chicago 1935, Cal 1939, NYC 1948. Work in NY World's Fair 1939. References A41-MAS. Source AAT, sculpture example p 232 Mexican onyx *Indian Madonna*. No auction record.

WOLFE, Byron B. Born Parsons, Kan 1904, died near Colorado Springs, Colo 1973. Traditional Western painter, illustrator. Member CAA. Work in WYG, Whitney Gall (Cody, Wyom), Eisenhower Lib (Abilene, Kans), Mont Hist Soc (Helena), Wm Rockhill Nelson Gall (Kansas City). No reference. Sources C71 to 73-HAR. No current auction record but the estimated price of a historical Western painting would be about $1,000 to $1,200 at auction in 1976. Signature example C72.

"By" Wolfe worked on a cattle ranch

before studying art at the U of Kansas. He established his studio in Kansas City as a commercial artist specializing in Western illustrations for beer ads and newspaper reproduction. He then became art director for a local ad agency.

By 1962 Wolfe was able to paint full time, "just like retiring and doing exactly what you've always wanted to do." HAR. His studio in suburban Kansas City was filled with artifacts and gear. His illustrations have been covers for *Western*, *Western Horseman*, and *Kansas Historical Society* magazines.

WOLLE, Muriel Sibell (Muriel Vincent Sibell). Born Brooklyn, NY 1898, living Boulder, Colo 1976. Painter, illustrator, writer, teacher. Work in DAM, Springfield Mus (Mo), U Colo Mem Center (Boulder), Mont St Mus (Helena). References A76-MAL. Sources WHO 70-W64. No auction record or signature example.

Mrs Wolle graduated from the NY School of Fine & Applied Art 1920, NYU 1928, and U of Colorado 1930. She taught at the State College for Women (Tex) 1920–23, at NY School 1923–26, and at U of Colorado 1930. Her early interest was theater arts. In Colorado she began visiting ghost mining towns. By 1933 she had written and illustrated "Ghost Cities of Colorado." In 1934 she wrote "Cloud Cities of Colorado," in 1949 her popular "Stampede to Timberline," in 1953 "The Bonanza Trail," and in 1963 "Montana Pay Dirt."

WOOD, Robert. No reference. Source, oil 24×36" *Grand Teton* signed but not dated, estimated for sale 11/28/73 at $1,000 to $1,200 for auction in Los Angeles, and sold for $2,100. Signature example above as lot 122.

The biography of Porfirio Salinas places Wood with José Arpa in Texas about 1935.

WOOD, Robert E. Born Gardena, Cal 1926, living Green Lake Valley, Cal 1976. Watercolorist, teacher. Member ANA 1971, NA 1974, Nat Cowboy Acad of Western Art. Reference A76. Sources NA 74-PER vol 3 ⌗3. No auction record. Signature example p 80 PER vol 3 ⌗3.

A graduate of art from Pomona College and Claremont Graduate School, Wood specialized in watercolor. He has had more than 60 one-man exhibits, and has taught at the U of Minnesota, Otis Art Institute and Scripps College. He conducts an art school each summer in his studio in California's San Bernardino Mountains.

WOOD, Stanley. Born Bordentown, NJ 1894, living Carmel, Cal 1940. Cal painter in tempera and watercolor, lithographer. Work in BM, Mills Col Art Gall. References A41-FIE-MAL. Sources MCA-11/30/73 letter from Terry Pink Alexander, Mills Col. No auction record or signature example.

Wood was exhibiting in California in 1924. One of his works was *Old Wells Fargo Office, Columbia*.

WOOD, Stanley L. Born England about 1860, died there early 1940s. English Special Artist-illustrator, animal painter, in the American West 1888. No reference. Sources AOH-CAP-50G. No current auction record but the estimated price of an oil on board 10×14" showing cowboys spooking a town would be about $1,200 to $1,500 at auction in 1976. Signature example p 67 CAP. (See illustration 318.)

An English "special" for ILN, Wood drew *Sketches from an Indian Reservation* during an 1888 trip to South Dakota. In 1890 he made 60 illustrations for Bret Harte's "A Waif of the Plains." The illustration in CAP is *Cowboy Fireworks* for *Harper's* in 1900. It is noted as derivative of Remington's 1889 *Cowboys Coming to Town for Christmas* which in turn was preceded by Zogbaum's *Painting the Town Red.*

When Wood returned to England, it was in the role of an illustrator specializing in the American West. His sketches and paintings for *Graphic, Boy's Own Paper, Chums,* and *Little Folks* feature cowboys attacked by Indians, cowgirls in stampedes, and Indians both tame and savage. "No better horse artist ever lived than Stanley L Wood—there was more action in a Stanley Wood illustration than in the story itself." 50G.

WOODSIDE, John Archibald. Born Philadelphia, Pa 1781, died there 1852. Sign and ornamental, still-life and animal painter. Work in MMA, Ins Co of N AM (panels for fire companies), Pa Hist Soc. References BEN-FIE-G&W-MAS. Sources ANT 9/46,4/55,4/67,3/72-BAR-BOA-M15-STI. In A23, p 326 lists "Woodsides," John A. *An Indian Buffalo Hunt* 18×24″ oil sold for $60 at auction. No current auction record. Signature example p 373 BAR.

Perhaps the student of Matthew Pratt, Woodside established his Philadelphia studio in 1805. By 1810 he was a leading sign painter in his area, "with talent beyond many who paint in higher branches." M15. "He was quiet and unobtrusive in his deportment and passed his long life in the pursuit of his favorite art." *Public Ledger,* obit. Between 1817 and 1835 he

exhibited still lifes and animal paintings at the PAFA. His son Abraham was a painter and J A Jr was a wood engraver.

Woodside is best known for his ornamental painting, "the most competent artisan painter of the period. He 'finished to perfection.'" BAR. One of his signs was *The Indian Queen.* At the time, city fire companies were private, existing by subscription. To attract business, they commissioned colorful panels for the engines. Woodside specialized in such decorations, many of which featured Indian motifs. He is said to have decorated the first locomotive.

WOODVILLE, Richard Caton, Jr. Born London, Eng 1856, died St John's Wood, London, Eng 1937. English Special Artist-illustrator, military painter. Work in Russell Fnd (Mont). Reference MAL. Sources AOH-PNW. Oil 49×39″ *Ambush* sold 1971 for $816 at auction. Signature example p 224 AOH.

Caton Woodville was born after his father, an important American genre painter, had died from an overdose of morphine. AOH. He was an artist prodigy who studied at the RA in Düsseldorf 1872–75 but left after a scandal with the daughter of Jenny Lind. He completed his training at the RA in London in 1876, and the same year became a sucessful *ILN* Special Artist. He also exhibited huge historical battle paintings at the RA that brought lavish tributes and the favor of Queen Victoria although she did not approve of his many love affairs.

He began illustrating the West in 1884, but it is said that he did not visit there until his 1890 *ILN* roving assignment to depict American and Canadian outdoor life. AOH. There resulted *Bear Hunters in Montana* and *North American Indians Running Cattle* before Woodville along with Remington and J H Smith covered the 1890–91 Sioux Indian War. Like Remington, Woodville rode with the cavalry, depicting the final military defeat of the Plains Indians. For 20 years following his return to England, Woodville was the most prolific Western illustrator in Europe. However, after he had been confined to his studio because of an old war wound, his mistress died, and he shot himself.

WOODWARD, John Douglas. Born Monte Bello, Middlesex Cnty, Va 1848, died New Rochelle, NY 1924. Illustrator of travel books including the West, painter. Member SI. References A24 (obit)-BEN-MAL-SMI. Sources CIV-H72-NJA. No auction record. Signature example opp p 132 H72 *Lower Falls of Yellowstone River;* monogram example fig 36 p 133 H72 *Crystal Falls on Cascade Creek, 129 feet.*

J Douglas Woodward was the pupil of F C Welsh in Cincinnati. His illustrations for the 1872 Hayden survey report were probably drawn from photographs by party members like W H Jackson. Woodward's illustrations included the fold-out fig 14 opp p 53 *US Geological Survey En Route* and the vignette fig 13 p 53 *Camp of the US Geological Survey on Shore of Lake.*

WORES, Theodore. Born San Francisco, Cal 1860 (or 1859), died there 1939. San Fran landscape, genre, and portrait painter, illustrator, teacher. Work in LA Cnty Mus, Alaska-Yuk Expos 1909. References A33-BEN-FIE-MAL-SMI. Sources AAR 5/75-BDW-BWB. No auction record or signature example.

Wores studied in Munich, the pupil of Alex Wagner and Duveneck. In the 1890s he was part of the "buoyant, carefree group" of bohemian San Francisco artists. BWB. From 1907 to 1912 he taught at San Francisco AI. He was

known for the documentary quality of his paintings of the Southwest around Taos and Calgary Indians in Canada as well as the San Francisco Chinese. Later landscapes are of the area around Saratoga, Cal.

Wores painted in Japan in the 1880s–90s, one of the first American artists there. His California subjects included Yosemite Valley and the orchards of Santa Clara Valley.

WORLDS, Clint. Born Kernville, Cal 1922, living Orogrande, NM 1968. Traditional Western painter. No reference. Source COW. No current auction record. Signature example p 208 COW.

Worlds's family had been cattlemen in Kern County, Cal since 1870. He left home as a boy and claims to have "ridden for more outfits than any other painter." COW. Influenced as an artist by the work of Will James, he received advice from Norman Rockwell and Bill Bender. "I do not paint to entertain, I paint to enlighten." COW.

WORRALL, Henry. Born Liverpool, Eng 1825, died Topeka, Kan 1902. Pioneer Kansas field illustrator for *Harper's* and *Leslie's,* painter, caricaturist, musician. Work reproduced in magazines and Western history books. Reference G&W. Source AIW. No current auction record. Signature example ✕217 AOA.

Worrall came to Buffalo, NY with his family when he was 10. As a young man he moved to Cincinnati where, as told later by a friend, he was despondent enough to attempt suicide. He worked as a glass cutter and played, taught, and wrote music for the guitar. When he moved to Topeka in 1868, he was successful in owning a vineyard, as a musician, as a self-taught painter. As "professor" he gave "crayon and musical programmes" that sold out.

Between 1877 and 1893 Worrall's illustrations were published in *Harper's* and *Leslie's*. They were mainly scenes of Kansas genre, *The Monument at Osawatomie, The First Public Inauguration, The Colored Exodus, Departure of the Corn Train, The Opening of the Cherokee Strip*. Worrall also traveled into Colorado about 1877 and New Mexico about 1879, along the line of the Atchison, Topeka and Santa Fe RR, sketching the *Veta Pass* and *Pueblo Indians Selling Pottery*. His best-known illustration was the caricature *Drouthy Kansas* that was used to attract settlers. Worrall sketched alongside Frenzeny and Tavernier in Wichita in 1873, with Webber and Mosler in Santa Fe in 1886. Two books important in Western history were also illustrated by Worrall. "Historic Sketches of the Cattle Trade" by McCoy in 1874 contained 126 illustrations and 22 advertisements by Worrall. "Buffalo Land" by Webb in 1872 reproduced Worrall sketches as woodcuts, including scenes of buffalo hunting. "Worrall was the only Kansas artist and illustrator in the period to achieve recognition on anything approaching a national scale." AIW. His illustrations were signed variously, H Worrall, Worrall, H W, W, or monogram.

WRIGHT, Alma Brockerman. Born Salt Lake City, Utah 1875, died Le Bugue, Dordogne, France 1952. Utah portrait and landscape painter, muralist, teacher. Work in Springville AM; murals in Utah St Capitol, LDS temples in Hawaii, Canada, and Arizona. References A53-BEN-FIE-MAL. Sources PUA-YUP. No current auction record or signature example.

Wright was part of the 20th Ward group with Mahonri Young and Richards that was influenced by Ottinger. He studied at LDS College 1892–95 and at the U of Utah 1895–96, the pupil of Haag and Harwood. Wright taught at Utah colleges beginning 1896, coaching in sports such as fencing in addition to art. From 1902 to 1904 he studied in Paris at Julien Academy, Colarossi, and Beaux-Arts, the pupil of Bonnat and Laurens. Thereafter Wright taught in Utah. "He was of medium height, well built. His attractive little mustache was well trimmed and groomed. He was of serious disposition." PUA. When Wright retired in 1937 he went to France, spending WWII in a German prison camp.

WRIGHT, Henry Charles Seppings. Born probably England 1849, died Bosham, Sussex, Eng 1937. English Special Artist-illustrator, marine painter. No reference. Source AOH. No auction record. Signature example ILN 1890s.

Wright was the son of a minister. He began as a Special Artist for ILN in the 1870s, covering the discovery of the Kimberley diamond fields, the Spanish-American War in Cuba, the South African War, the Russo-Japanese War, and WWI.

ILN in 1890 ran a series of Wright sketches depicting the social life of the US, also indicating that Wright may have made an earlier trip to the US. In 1897 ILN published the sketch *Winter on the Plains of Manitoba* with cowboys rounding up cattle.

WRIGHT, Rufus. Born Cleveland, Ohio 1832, living probably San Francisco, Cal 1882. Portrait, genre, and landscape painter, lithographic artist, probably in the West in the late 1850s, teacher. Work in Chicago Hist Soc, Oakland Mus. References BEN-CHA-FIE-G&W-MAL-SMI. Sources HUT-KAH-WES-WHI. No current auction record but the estimated price of a Western genre painting would be about $3,000 to $3,500 at auction in 1976. Signature example p 52 KAH.

Wright studied at the NA and was the pupil of the portrait painter George A Baker in NYC where he was living in 1860. He also painted in Washington, DC in 1865, specializing in portraits of governmental notables of the Civil War period. From 1866 to 1872 he was teaching at the Brooklyn Academy of Design. About 1875 he began concentrating on genre paintings he exhibited at the NA: *The Inventor and the Banks, Thank You, Sir,* and *Concerned for his Sole.*

In 1859 Sarony, Major & Knapp published *City of Davenport, Iowa,* a lithograph after a drawing by Wright. This indicates a Western trip by Wright about 1857, during which period he may also have painted an 1859 Mormon panorama. The Oakland Museum has an oil *The Card Players* dated 1882 that is a genre scene of miners.

WRIGHT, Thomas Jefferson. Born probably Mount Sterling, Ky 1798, died there 1846. Texas portrait painter. Work in Tex St Archives (Austin). No reference. Sources BAR-TEP. No auction record. Painting examples pp 16, 19, 20, 22 TEP.

Son of a Welsh tailor, T Jefferson Wright received an 1822 letter of introduction from Matthew Jouett to Thomas Sully to enable Wright to study portraiture in Philadelphia. He then painted portraits in Virginia up to 1833 and came to Texas following his brother who had gained wealth in shipping. "Jeff" Wright became friendly with Sam Houston, was a major in the militia, an Indian agent, and was called Judge. He exhibited a gallery of celebrity portraits including one of George Washington and painted Texas personalities: Sam Hous-

ton, Deaf Smith the scout, Col Juan Seguin, Dr Thomas Chalkley, and Bowles the Cherokee chief.

The leading Texas painter of his day, he dressed neatly and could "swing a strong fist." TEP. When he quit as Indian agent, he defended his courage by challenging the Indian fighter Bonnell. He was also on active duty with the militia in 1842. Wright died while in Kentucky for a visit, probably from yellow fever.

WUESTE, Mrs Louise Heuser. Born Gummersbach-on-Rhine, Germany 1803, died Eagle Pass, Tex 1875. Pioneer Texas portrait painter. Work in Witte Mus (San Antonio). References G&W-MAS. Sources BAR-TEP-TOB-WAA. No current auction record. Signature example p 121 TEP.

She was the daughter of a well-to-do German merchant. Both of Mrs Wueste's sisters married prominent artists, Conrad Lessing and Adolph Schroedter, with whom she studied. She also studied in Düsseldorf, and, after her 1821 marriage to a practicing doctor, with August Sohn.

Her children emigrated to Texas under political pressure in 1852. A widow by then, she followed them to San Antonio in 1857. She took a studio at ⌗18 French Building, advertising in 1860 as portrait painter and teacher. After 1870 she moved to her son's home in Eagle Pass, a border town where she painted genre scenes of Mexicans.

WYETH, Andrew Newell. Born Chadds Ford, Pa 1917, living there 1976. Contemporary landscape, marine, and figure painter. Member NA 1945 as aquarellist, NIAL, AAAL. Work in MMA, BMFA, LA Cnty MA, AIC, Dallas MFA, Houston MFA, etc. References A76-BEN-

MAS. Sources AAR 1,3,5,11/74-ANT 1,5/67; 9/70; 7/73; 1/74-APT-ARI-CAA-COW-190-M50-M57-MCA-NA 74-POI-WHO 70. Tempera on board 17×42" *Fields in Winter* 1942 sold 5/11/66 for $34,000 at auction. Signature example ⚹88 PB 12/13/73.

Andrew Wyeth was educated privately. He was the pupil of his father, N C Wyeth, a painter and illustrator who specialized in Western subjects. Wyeth began painting professionally in 1936 and had his first one-man show in 1937 at the William Macbeth Gallery in NYC. By the early 1940s he was internationally recognized as an original talent, enthusiastically received by the critics and the public. When he was 31 he had painted masterpieces like *Christina's World*. In 1950 his *Young America* was offered for sale at $3,000. M50. When he was given the *Art in America* award in 1958 it was stated, "In a year which finds naturalism still in exile, Wyeth alone among contemporary realists continues to be warmly welcomed." His son, James Browning Wyeth, is also an artist. Andrew Wyeth has spent his summers in Maine where some of his models were of Indian descent.

WYETH, Henriette Zirngiebel (Mrs Peter Hurd). Born Wilmington, Del 1907, living San Patricio, NM 1976. Painter specializing in portraits and murals (A41). ANA 1974. Work in Roswell MA, Lubbock MA, Tex Tech U, Wilmington SFA. References A76-BEN-MAL. Sources COW-NA 74-WAA. No current auction record or signature example.

The older sister of Andrew Wyeth, Henriette Wyeth was the pupil of her father, N C Wyeth. She also studied at Normal Art School in Boston and the PAFA, the pupil of Richard Andrew, Arthur B Carles, and Henry McCarter. She married Peter Hurd while he was

studying with her father at Chadds Ford, Pa in 1929.

Hurd had been born near Roswell, NM. The Hurds returned to Roswell in the 1930s, both continuing to paint. They exhibited together in Ohio in 1967.

WYETH, Newell Convers. Born Needham, Mass 1882, died Chadds Ford, Pa 1945. Painter and illustrator of historical subjects, particularly the West, muralist, teacher. NA 1941, SI 1912. Work in ANS, murals in hotels, banks, insurance companies, schools, churches; illustrations in juvenile books. References A47 (obit)-BEN-FIE-MAL-SMI. Sources AAR 3,11/74-ACO-ALA-AMA-ANT 1, 12/64;5/66;8/67;5,6/68;3/73-COW-CUS-DEP-DIC-GIL-HAR-HMA-ILA-ILP-NA 74-WAI 71,72-WHO 44. Oil 44×33" *Train Robbery* sold 3/16/67 for $7,750 at auction. Signature example p 72 ILA. (See illustration 319.)

Wyeth studied at Mechanics Art high school, Massachusetts Normal Art School, and Eric Pape's Art School, all of Boston, and was the pupil of C W Reed. He became a member of the "Pyle school" of illustrators, studying at Chadds Ford with W H D Koerner, Stanley Arthurs, Harvey Dunn, and Frank Schoonover until Pyle's death in 1911. Arthurs inherited Pyle's studio, but Wyeth also carried on at Chadds Ford, where he, with his "huge zeal for life, emulated Pyle's approach as nearly as possible, painting much the same kind of subject matter." ILA. He completed more than 3,000 illustrations, including for example 25 books for Scribner's "Juvenile Classics," most still in print. After his outstanding success as an illustrator, he began to paint in tempera for exhibition, turning out still lifes and landscapes. WHO 44 lists his murals almost exclusively, indicating the area of his own pride. Wyeth also encouraged his children to paint, with Andrew, Henriette, and Caroline becoming professional artists, as did the two sons-in-law.

Wyeth "in his youth was able to make an extended visit to the Southwest, and he returned with a great many sketches from which he later made Western illustrations and paintings." HAR. He felt that the artist "to be able to draw virile pictures must live virilely." AMA. In fact, Wyeth's first published illustration was a bucking bronco for *The Saturday Evening Post* in 1903. His Western trips were in 1904 for *Scribner's* and in 1906 on commission for *Outing*.

WYLE, Florence. Born Trenton, Ill 1881, living Toronto, Ont, Can 1962. Can sculptor who modeled West Coast Indian subjects. Founding member, Sculptors' Soc of Can; RCA. Work in NGC, Winnipeg AG, AG Toronto; memorials, monuments, statues, fountains, tablets, figures, etc. References A62-MAL. Source CAN. No auction record or signature example.

Ms Wyle studied at the U of Illinois and the AIC. She was the artist for Canadian War Memorials in 1919 and received a medal from Queen Elizabeth in 1953. As an Eastern Canadian artist recording the West Coast, she made plaster models of Indian heads and totem poles. Her best known work was the Edith Cavell memorial at Toronto, a work both "forceful and personal." CAN.

WYTTENBACH, E (or Friedrich Salomon Moritz, or Friedrich Anton). E Wyttenbach is without reference listing, active approximately 1860 in California, sources DBW-JNB-*American Scene* vol XI no 4 "The Vaquero" reprinting an E Wyttenbach etching courtesy Cal St Lib. No current auction record. Signature example p 31 DBW.

MAS lists Friedrich Anton Wyttenbach as a German painter born Treves 1812, died same 1845. References BEN-BRY-Crocker Art Gallery (Sacramento, Cal). BRY classifies him as painter and etcher, pupil of Karl Raben and Schadow in Düsseldorf, active in Treves as an animal painter, especially in hunting scenes.

BEN lists Moritz Wyttenbach as a Swiss amateur painter of animals, born Bern 1816, died there 1889. His brother Albert was an amateur portraitist.

YAZZIE, James Wayne. Born 1943, living Sheep Springs, NM 1967. Navaho painter. Work in Amerind Fndn (Dragoon, Ariz), MAI, MNM. No reference. Sources AHI 8/68-AIP-COW. No auction record. Signature example inside back cover AHI 8/68.

Yazzie's genre work is unusual in that he depicts dramatic events such as a Navaho ceremonial dance where the actors are central but minor in the widening circles of spectators in a landscape.

YEAGER, Walter Rush. Born Philadelphia, Pa 1852, died there 1896. Illustrator for *Leslie's* in 1870s including Western trip in 1877, religious artist, designer. Work in magazines. No reference. Source AIW. No current auction record or signature example.

To depict the scenery of the West for *Frank Leslie's Illustrated Newspaper,* staff artists Ogden and Yeager accompanied the Frank Leslie party of 12 in April 1877 across the continent by rail. About 200 illustrations resulted, mostly of scenes west of Council Bluffs that appeared in *Leslie's* beginning August 1877. This was the year of the gold rush for Deadwood, the drama of booming Cheyenne, the marvels wrought by the Mormons, the "filthy" red man at train side, the silver mines of Virginia City, the Chinese in San Francisco, and the scenic wonders of California. The illustrations were generally credited to one of the artists or to both. The party traveled by Pullman car, so the artists at a brief stop would outline the sketches to be completed en route. A large number of unfinished sketches did result, and illustrations were printed for years after. Some of the illustrations were also in Mrs Leslie's book about the trip.

Walter Yeager had studied at the PAFA, joining the *Leslie's* art staff about 1874 just before Joseph Becker became head. Other staff members were Albert Berghaus, James E Taylor, and T de Thulstrup. Yeager accompanied Mrs Leslie on a trip to the Bahamas in 1879, although her favorite was Ogden. Yeager moved back to Philadelphia in 1880 to head the art department of a lithographer. By 1885 he was a free-lance artist and religious illustrator.

YELLAND, Raymond Dabb. Born London, Eng 1848, died Oakland, Cal 1900. "California school" painter of landscapes and coastal scenery, teacher. Work in HON-MCA. References A00 (obit)-BEN-CHA-FIE-MAL-SMI. Sources HON-HUT-MCA-PNW-WHO 99. No current auction record. Initials p 67 MCA.

R D Yelland was brought when he was three to New Jersey where he was educated. He was a graduate of the NAD in NYC, and was the pupil of William Page, L E Wilmarth, and for landscape J R Brevoort. For figures, he was the pupil of L O Merson in Paris. After painting for a time in Gloucester Harbor, he was in San Francisco by 1874. He began teaching with Virgil Williams at the California School of Design in 1877, remaining about 20 years. He also taught perspective at the Mark Hopkins IA and drawing at the U of California.

Yelland's works listed in CHA include *Golden Gate* 1882, *Mt Hood* 1883, *Monterey* 1884, and *Seal Rocks* 1886. "He was par excellence a teacher, a person of magnetism, much beloved." HON.

YENA, Donald. Texas painter and illustrator living in San Antonio 1971. No reference. Source COW. No current auction record or signature example.

Yena was brought to Texas at three and grew up on a farm near Castroville, the "little Alsace." Painting seriously since about 1960, his specialty is the Old West, reflected in the historic sites and buildings of Texas. He collects antique arms and costumes. When he is to paint a historic character, he dresses in the appropriate style out of his own wardrobe and poses for a photo to be used as the model. Yena has illustrated "Battles of Texas," "Six Flags of Texas," and "Antique Arms Annual" 1971.

YOHN, Frederick Coffay. Born Indianapolis, Ind 1875, died Norwalk, Conn 1933. Eastern illustrator of military and frontier subjects. Member SI 1901, Artists Guild. Work in Diamond M Foundn, Lib Cong (100 drawings), Indiana Hist Soc, Navy Dept. References A33 (obit)-BEN-DAB-FIE-MAL-SMI. Sources AIC-ALA-CUS-ILA-MSL-PER vol 5 ⚹1-WHO 32-1975 data from Albert Yohn. No auction record. Signature example p 74 ILA, p 66 PER vol 5 ⚹1 *After the Fight*. (See illustration 320.)

Son of a bookseller, F C Yohn drew newspaper portraits while still in Indianapolis high school. He studied one year at Indianapolis AS, three years at the ASL with Mowbray, and at 20 opened his NYC studio on 23rd Street. He worked for book publishers, for Scribner's which sent him to England for background material, and for a series of frontier sketches by Theodore Roosevelt. His long career included such credits as "The Trail of the Lonesome Pine," work for Jack London stories, historical scenes for insurance companies, and the record of the Mass Hist Soc. Although noted for his battle scenes painted with spirit and authenticity, demonstrating his preference for "a lot of composition and plenty of action," Yohn never witnessed a battle. His forte was accuracy of expression and racial features. Serious, reticent, a tireless worker, he spent half his time in research. DAB. While he was a leader in his generation of illustrators, he was regarded as of slenderer talent than his model, Pyle.

Yohn was a local success as an illustrator when he was 18. At 23 Scribner's sent his illustrations as part of a touring exhibition "Story of the Revolution," and Yohn was a star of the show. His style was set and his life's work established early: "The shape of Mr Yohn's head is strangely suggestive of Edgar Allan Poe but he has strength and objects to being called a genius." *The Art Interchange*, about 1900.

YOUNG, Harvey Otis (same as Harvey B). Born Lyndon (or Post Mills), Vt 1840, died Colorado Springs, Colo 1901. "Rocky Mountain school" landscape painter. Work in ANS, Penrose Pub Lib, DAM, Colo Col, COR. References A03 (obit)-BEN-G&W-MAL-SMI. Sources AIW-ANT 1/72,12/73-COW-DAA-DCC-DPL-HON-HUT-NEW-SHO-SPR-WAI 71. Oil 20½×29″ *Roundup* signed Harvey Young and dated '97 sold 10/27/71 for $1,800 at auction. Signature example p 296 NEW. (See illustration 321.)

Young whose father died in 1841 was raised by his grandfather. He was educated at St Johnsbury Academy in Vermont before employment as an ornamental painter, decorating scales. From NYC in 1959 he sailed via Panama for the California gold fields. "He combined prospecting, mining and sketching in California, Nevada, and Oregon" (AO3), working as a placer miner. In the Civil War he enlisted in the Federal Cavalry and was stationed at Walla Walla with Bret Harte, the author. Moving to San Francisco in 1866, he maintained an art studio there until he returned to NYC in 1869. After he married he sketched again in the West and made several trips to Europe, studying in Munich. In 1876 he established his studio in Paris, studying for two years at the Julien Academy, the pupil of Carolus-Duran, and exhibiting at the Salon in 1878. Young also taught. One of his Paris pupils was Comparet who had been raised in Colorado.

In 1879 Young settled in Manitou Springs, Colo. "He deserted art for a time when he made and lost a fortune in mining." AIW. Moving to Colorado Springs in 1898, Young devoted full time to painting. "General Palmer loaned his private railway car so that Young could be creative in comfort anywhere along the tracks." NEW. In his later landscapes the sky was painted with watercolor or thin gouache, the foreground with a thick gouache or oil sometimes applied with palette knife.

YOUNG, John J. Born place unknown 1830, died Washington, DC 1879. Railway survey artist of the 1850s, topographical engineer, staff artist for the War Dept, engraver. Work in ACM, railway survey reports. Reference G&W. Source AIW. No current auction record. Lithograph example ✂1433 ACM.

In 1855 Young was draftsman for the Lt Williamson railway survey to connect California's Sacramento Valley with Oregon's Columbia River. This was relatively unexplored territory. Young's views of the Cascade Range included 14 landscape scenes, one geologic scene, and 10 drawings of trees in their habitat.

In 1854 Young in his capacity as staff artist in Washington had redrawn sketches by both Campbell and Mollhausen for the report of Lt Whipple's 35th parallel survey. In 1858 Young redrew Mollhausen and Von Egloffstein sketches for the report of Lt Ives's exploration of the Colorado River. In 1859 Young painted watercolors after Dr Newberry's sketches for Capt Macomb's exploration from Santa Fe into Colorado. Watercolors after sketches by Von Beckh

were painted the same year for Capt Simpson's exploration in Utah. Young worked for the War Dept in Washington until his death.

YOUNG, Mahonri Mackintosh. Born Salt Lake City, Utah 1877, died Norwalk, Conn 1957. International sculptor, painter, etcher, teacher. ANA 1912, NA 1923, NSS, NIAL. Work in Brigham Young U (the art estate), MMA, WMAA, BM, COR, etc. References A59 (obit) - BEN - ENB -FIE - MAL - SMI. Sources AAT-AIC-ALA-AMA-ARM-50G-190-JUT-MSL-NA 74-NSS-PUA-WHO 50-YUP. Watercolor 4×11" *Red Durhams* 1935 sold 1971 for $225 at auction. This would not be indicative of the price for a Western bronze or painting. Signature example p 61 YUP.

"Hon" Young, grandson of Brigham Young, quit school to work in a bicycle shop for $2.50 weekly that he paid James T Harwood for art lessons in 1897. After raising his earnings to $5.00 weekly by newspaper drawings, he studied at the ASL in NYC from 1899 to 1900. Returning to Salt Lake City as a photoengraver, he saved enough to pay for four years in Paris 1901–5, studying at Julien Academy, Delecluse, and Colarossi, the pupil of Verlet and Laurens. In NYC in 1905, he taught at the American School of Sculpture, a proponent of the 20th-century genre modeling that was tied to the "Ash-Can school" of painting. "Young could draw ditchdiggers and prize fighters with a swift vitality like that of Daumier, and out of those drawings he created sturdy bronzes." ALA.

In 1912 the AMNH sent Young to Arizona to model life-size groups of the Hopi Indians, for ethnographic rather than artistic purposes. En route he received the commission for the 1913 Seagull Monument in Salt Lake City. His best-known work was the *This Is the*

Place monument completed 1947 at Emigration Canyon, "perpetuating in bronze and stone the heroic Mormon pioneers." PUA. On the other hand, "many of his statuettes are only a few inches in height, little bronzes a few of" which "picture Indians." AMA.

YOUNG, Phineas Howe. Born Winter Quarters (Florence), Neb 1847, died Salt Lake City, Utah 1868. Pioneer Utah landscape and portrait painter. No reference. Source YUP. No current auction record or signature example.

Son of a painter and glazier, Young studied with Dan Weggeland in Salt Lake City. Before his premature death from pneumonia, he painted Utah landscapes, figures, and a portrait of his uncle Brigham Young.

YOUNG-HUNTER, John. Born Glasgow, Scotland 1874, died probably Taos, NM 1955. Taos painter of Indians and Western landscapes, NYC painter of society portraits. Work in Tate Gall (London), Musee de Luxembourg (Paris), Walker AG (Liverpool), Wellington AM (NZ), MNM, Worcester MA, Harvard U. References A53-BEN (as Hunter)-FIE (as Hunter)-MAL-SMI. Sources HAR-TAL-TSF-WHO 57-Y/H. No current auction record but the estimated price of an oil 20×30″ showing a Taos Indian ceremonial would be about $1,500 to $2,000 at auction in 1976. Signature example Y/H. (See illustration 322.)

Young-Hunter's father Colin Hunter was a marine painter, a member of the RA. Young-Hunter was educated in England at Clifton College and studied at the RA schools and U of London, the pupil of his father, W Orchardson, Alma-Tadema, and J S Sargent. He exhibited yearly at the RA from 1900 to 1913 when he came to NYC with a letter from his friend the Duke of Argyll to help him meet Indians.

As a boy he had seen Buffalo Bill's Wild West Show in London and he retained his image of Indians. He also met Charles Russell in London in 1912. Young-Hunter's first contact in the US was at the Crow Agency in Montana where he painted and acquired gear, and his second was in Great Falls with Russell. He visited Santa Fe and Taos in 1917, becoming a full-time resident of Taos in 1942. He "built himself a Renaissance banqueting hall for a studio in the sagebrush" (TSF) where he could forego his society portraits for soft landscapes peopled with happy Indians. His Taos subjects also included Indian portraits and genre, frontier life, straight landscape, and still life. His book "Reviewing the Years" is autobiographical and also describes his painting methods. A memorial exhibition for Young-Hunter took place at the Harwood Fndn in Taos in 1956.

YVES. Active Paris about 1865. Lithographic artist. Print in ACM, GIL. No reference. Source GIL. No current auction record. Signature example p 27 GIL.

Yves signed in the plate of a colored lithograph depicting vaqueros about 1865 hunting buffaloes using the South American bolo.

ZANG, John J. Active 1883 in California. Landscape painter. Work in Wadsworth Atheneum (Hartford). No reference. Source ANT 11/48,9/73,3/74. No current auction record but the estimated price of a Western landscape would be $800 to $1,000 at auction in 1976. Signature example p 391 ANT 9/73.

ANT reprinted *Yosemite Valley, California* dated 1883 and *Winter Landscape* not dated. *Hudson from West Point* is part of the Gould collection that also consisted of works by F E Church, Cole, Eastman Johnson, and Waldo-Jewett.

ZIEGLER, Eustace Paul. Born Detroit, Mich 1881, living Seattle, Wash 1941. NW painter, muralist, printmaker, teacher. Member, Puget Sound Group of Painters. Work in Seattle AM, Jersey City AM, Palace of the Legion of Honor (San Fran); murals in Alaska and Wash hotels, schools, libs. References A41-MAL. Source WNW. No auction record or signature example.

Ziegler studied at the Detroit SFA, at Yale SFA, and with Ida Marie Perrault. Listed titles were *Alaska, Fish Pirates, Masterbuilders of the Northwest, Cabin in Snow, Mt Rainier, Boys on the Yukon.*

ZIEGLER, Samuel P. Born Lancaster, Pa 1882, died Fort Worth, Tex 1967. Painter specializing in Fort Worth landscapes, printmaker, teacher. Work in Fort Worth MA, Carnegie Lib, Tex Christian U. References A62-BEN-MAL. Sources TOB-TXF. No current auction record. Signature example opp p 144 TXF.

Son of a farmer of German descent, Ziegler worked as a hotel clerk and played the cello to pay for study at the PAFA, the pupil of Chase, Anshutz, and Breckenridge. After travel and study in Europe in 1913, he taught cello in Philadelphia while continuing to paint. In 1917 he became cello instructor at Texas Christian U, transferring to art instructor 1919.

His *The Four Gallon Hat* illustrated in TXF was painted in 1923. Landscapes were of the neighboring Hart Ranch and oil fields, as well as *Twin Mountains* at Santa Fe.

ZIMBEAUX, Frank Ignatius Seraphic (not Francis). Born Pittsburgh, Pa 1861, died Salt Lake City, Utah 1935. Romantic Utah landscape and figure painter. No reference. Source YUP. No current auction record. Self-portrait p 46 YUP.

Zimbeaux was raised in Europe, studying in Paris and London where he was influenced by the Post-Impressionist painters, along with Utah painter Henri Moser he met in Paris 1909–10. Zimbeaux moved to NYC in 1914, to Carthage (Mo), and in 1924 to Salt Lake City where he worked briefly in a photography studio. "One of Utah's great romantic figures, Zimbeaux was apt to people his landscapes with nude maidens." YUP. His son Francis Zimbeaux born 1914 continued as a romantic figure and landscape painter.

ZOGBAUM, Rufus Fairchild. Born Charleston, SC 1849, died NYC 1925. Important naval and military illustrator including army life in the American West beginning 1884, writer. Work in Adams colln, Naval War Col; murals Minn St Capitol, Fed Bldg (Cleveland), Woolworth Bldg (NYC). References A25 (obit)-BEN-DAB-FIE-MAL-SMI. Sources AIW-AOA-CAP-COW-CUS-50G-ILA-MWS Aug/73(article)-PAW-POW-TWR-WHO 12. Oil grisaille 13× 20" *Scouting Party* sold 10/27/71 for

$1,100 at auction. Gouache grisaille *Young Scout* 11×7" sold 12/12/75 for $800 at auction. Signature example p 24 TWR *Breaking Camp*.

Son of a manufacturer of musical instruments, Zogbaum grew up in NYC. He studied at the U of Heidelberg, at the ASL 1878–79, and with Bonnat 1880–82 in Paris where the works of De Neuville and Detaille influenced specialization in military subjects. For background study he visited England 1882–83 and Germany 1883. In 1884 he went to Montana for data and sketches of military life on the frontier. The result of this and later trips to Montana as well as an 1888 tour in Oklahoma was a series of illustrations for articles in *Harper's Weekly* and in books like his own "Horse, Foot, and Dragoons." Zogbaum's Western illustrations idealized army life, although they also showed cowboys at play, cattle drives, stagecoaches, and river boats. His focus was people doing things.

During the 1890s Zogbaum concentrated on naval and military subjects, becoming a painter so celebrated that his work was the subject of a Kipling poem after they had visited the naval hero Capt Robley Evans: "Zogbaum draws with a pencil/and I do things with a pen . . . Zogbaum can handle the shadows/And I can handle my style . . ." Zogbaum was a leading correspondent-illustrator of the Spanish-American War in Puerto Rico and the Caribbean as well as the Cuban coast. In 1915 he wrote a classic article "War and the Artist" for *Scribner's*.

ZORACH, Marguerite Thompson. Born Santa Rosa, Cal 1887, died Brooklyn, NY 1968. Modern Eastern painter of Sierras and Yosemite landscapes; muralist. Work in MMA, WMAA, MOMA, BM, Newark Mus. References A70 (obit)-BEN-MAL. Sources AAR 3,5/74-AAT-ALA-ARM-CAA-DEP-190-M50,

57-WAA. Watercolor 13¼×9¾" *Yosemite Valley* signed but not dated, estimated for sale 1/26/74 at $500 to $700 and sold for $800. Signature example p 53 AAR 3,4/74.

Mrs Zorach was educated in Fresno public schools. She studied in Paris and traveled in Europe 1908–11. She began in traditional art in the École de la Grande Chaumière and with Francis Auburtin, then at La Palette with John Duncan Fergusson, a post-impressionist. Returning to Fresno via the Orient, she wrote and illustrated newspaper articles. The summer of 1912 she spent in the Sierras, painting Fauve landscapes.

Later in 1912 she moved to NYC and married William Zorach. Together, as artists who had seen the changes in Paris, they were central in attempts at Cubism in America and they remained involved in modern art. In 1920 they were in Yosemite, creating a series of paintings there.

ZORACH, William. Born Eurburg, Lithuania 1887, died Bath, Me 1966. Modern sculptor, painter, writer, teacher. Member NIAL. Work in ACM, AIC, BM, BMFA, LA Cnty AM, MMA, MOMA, MNM, WMAA, etc. References A70 (obit)-BEN-FIE-MAL-SMI. Sources AAT-AIC-ALA-ANT 1/69-ARM-CAA-DEP-190-SCU-WHO 62. Watercolor 15×13" *Yosemite Valley* dated 1920 sold 5/16/73 for $1,100 at auction of Halpert colln Part II. Bronze, 44½" *Dancer* 1930 sold 10/29/70 for $8,000 at auction "as unique piece." Signature example ⚒29 PB 3/21/74.

Zorach was brought to the US at four. He studied at the Cleveland IA 1902–5, at the NAD in NYC 1908–10, and in Paris 1910–11 along with Marguerite Thompson who became his wife in 1912. The Zorachs had been influenced by Matisse's bold drawing and brilliant color. They had also observed the development of Cubism, contributing to their identification with modern painting in America. "When Zorach abandoned painting for sculpture about 1917, he chose a far more conservative means of expression than the Cubist vocabulary of his paintings." 190. By the 1930s Zorach was a leading American sculptor as his modeling was "more sentimental and less inventive, an American version of the international 'moderne.'" 190.

Zorach's *Yosemite Valley* watercolor dated 1920 was the result of a Western trip. Beginning 1929 Zorach taught sculpture at the ASL.